Economics

for the IB Diploma

Second edition

Ellie Tragakes

Cambridge University Press's mission is to advance learning, knowledge and research worldwide.

Our IB Diploma resources aim to:

- encourage learners to explore concepts, ideas and topics that have local and global significance
- help students develop a positive attitude to learning in preparation for higher education
- assist students in approaching complex questions, applying critical-thinking skills and forming reasoned answers.

CAMBRIDGE
UNIVERSITY PRESS

CAMBRIDGE
UNIVERSITY PRESS

University Printing House, Cambridge CB2 8BS, United Kingdom

Cambridge University Press is part of the University of Cambridge.

It furthers the University's mission by disseminating knowledge in the pursuit of education, learning and research at the highest international levels of excellence.

www.cambridge.org
Information on this title: www.cambridge.org/9780521186407

© Cambridge University Press 2009, 2012

First published 2009
Second edition 2012
4th printing 2013

Printed in Italy by L.E.G.O. S.p.A

A catalogue record for this publication is available from the British Library

ISBN 978-0-521-18640-7 Paperback with CD-ROM for Windows and Mac

Contents

Introduction to the student and teacher   vii
Terms and conditions of use for the CD-ROM   x

Introduction

Chapter 1 The foundations of economics
1.1 Scarcity, choice and opportunity cost   1
1.2 Economics as a social science   7
1.3 Central themes   12

Section 1 Microeconomics

Chapter 2 Competitive markets: demand and supply
2.1 Introduction to competitive markets   20
2.2 Demand   21
2.3 Supply   26
2.4 Market equilibrium: demand and supply   30
HL 2.5 Linear demand and supply functions and market equilibrium (higher level topic)   33
2.6 The role of the price mechanism and market efficiency   39

Chapter 3 Elasticities
3.1 Price elasticity of demand (*PED*)   47
3.2 Cross-price elasticity of demand (*XED*)   58
3.3 Income elasticity of demand (*YED*)   62
3.4 Price elasticity of supply (*PES*)   66

Chapter 4 Government intervention
4.1 Indirect taxes   72
HL 4.2 Indirect (excise) taxes: market outcomes, social welfare and tax incidence (higher level topic)   75
4.3 Subsidies   81
HL 4.4 Subsidies: market outcomes and social welfare (higher level topic)   84
4.5 Price controls   88

Chapter 5 Market failure
5.1 The meaning of market failure: allocative inefficiency   101
5.2 Externalities: diverging private and social benefits and costs   101
5.3 Negative externalities of production and consumption   103
5.4 Positive externalities of production and consumption   113
5.5 Lack of public goods   119
5.6 Common access resources and the threat to sustainability   121
HL 5.7 Asymmetric information (higher level topic)   132
5.8 Abuse of monopoly power (higher level topic)   135
5.9 The problem of government failure (policy failure) (supplementary material)   137

HL **Chapter 6 The theory of the firm I: Production, costs, revenues and profit (Higher level topic)**

6.1 Production in the short run: the law of diminishing returns	139
6.2 Introduction to costs of production: economic costs	144
6.3 Costs of production in the short run	145
6.4 Production and costs in the long run	151
6.5 Revenues	155
6.6 Profit	158
6.7 Goals of firms	161

HL **Chapter 7 The theory of the firm II: Market structures (Higher level topic)**

7.1 Perfect competition	168
7.2 Monopoly	181
7.3 Monopolistic competition	195
7.4 Oligopoly	201
7.5 Price discrimination	211

Section 2 Macroeconomics

Chapter 8 The level of overall economic activity

8.1 Economic activity	216
8.2 Measures of economic activity	219
HL 8.3 Calculations of GDP (higher level topic)	227
8.4 The business cycle	230

Chapter 9 Aggregate demand and aggregate supply

9.1 Aggregate demand (*AD*) and the aggregate demand curve	236
9.2 Short-run aggregate supply and short-run equilibrium in the *AD-AS* model	241
9.3 Long-run aggregate supply and long-run equilibrium in the monetarist/new classical model	248
9.4 Aggregate supply and equilibrium in the Keynesian model	250
9.5 Shifting aggregate supply curves over the long term	254
9.6 Illustrating the monetarist/new classical and Keynesian models	258
HL 9.7 The Keynesian multiplier (higher level topic)	260
9.8 Understanding aggregate demand and the multiplier in terms of the Keynesian cross model (supplementary material, recommended for higher level)	264

Chapter 10 Macroeconomic objectives I: Low unemployment, low and stable rate of inflation

10.1 Low unemployment	265
10.2 Low and stable rate of inflation	274
HL 10.3 Topics on inflation (higher level topics)	283

Chapter 11 Macroeconomic objectives II: Economic growth and equity in the distribution of income

11.1 Economic growth	293
11.2 Equity in the distribution of income	301

Chapter 12 Demand-side and supply-side policies

12.1 Introduction to demand-side policies	320
12.2 Fiscal policy	320
12.3 Monetary policy	330
12.4 Supply-side policies	338
12.5 Evaluating government policies to deal with unemployment and inflation	347

Section 3 International economics

Chapter 13 International trade
13.1 The benefits of trade   354
HL   13.2 Free trade: absolute and comparative advantage (higher level topic)   356
13.3 The World Trade Organization (WTO)   363
13.4 Restrictions on free trade: trade protection   364
13.5 Arguments for and against trade protection   375

Chapter 14 Exchange rates and the balance of payments
14.1 Freely floating exchange rates   381
14.2 Government intervention   388
HL   14.3 Calculations using exchange rates (higher level topic)   392
14.4 The balance of payments   395
14.5 The balance of payments and exchange rates   400
HL   14.6 Topics on exchange rates and the balance of payments (higher level topics)   406

Chapter 15 Economic integration and the terms of trade
15.1 Economic integration   413
HL   15.2 Terms of trade (higher level topic)   424

Section 4 Development economics

Chapter 16 Understanding economic development
16.1 Economic growth and economic development   436
16.2 Measuring economic development   449

Chapter 17 Topics in economic development
17.1 The role of domestic factors   463
17.2 The role of international trade barriers   477
17.3 Trade strategies for economic growth and development   482

Chapter 18 Foreign sources of finance and foreign debt
18.1 The meaning of foreign sources of finance   499
18.2 Foreign direct investment and multinational corporations (MNCs)   500
18.3 Foreign aid   506
18.4 Multilateral development assistance   516
18.5 The role of international debt   519

Chapter 19 Consequences of economic growth and the balance between markets and intervention
19.1 Consequences of economic growth   524
19.2 Balance between markets and intervention   531

Glossary   **540**
Index   **555**
Acknowledgements   **566**

In memory of my beloved parents

Ηβη and Κώστα

who gave me the freedom to expand my horizons

Introduction to the student and teacher

Economics is a relatively new social science that touches upon many aspects of our lives and has important effects on the well-being of all people around the world. Studying it as a social science discipline allows us to organise the way we think about the numerous economic problems faced by our own and other societies, and helps us make informed and responsible choices.

The second edition of *Economics for the IB Diploma,* written for students of Economics in the International Baccalaureate (IB) Diploma Programme, has been thoroughly revised to fully match the IB economics guide published in November 2010 (for first exams in 2013). It covers the entire IB Economics syllabus at both standard and higher levels. Each of the four parts of the book corresponds to one of the four sections of the syllabus, and the chapters within each part correspond closely to the syllabus subsections. The book supposes no prior knowledge of economics from the student. Every section and subsection begins with a simple presentation that gradually progresses to a more advanced level, enabling the student to gradually master complex topics. The book fully covers the needs of the IB economics student, in terms of both breadth and depth of coverage of all items in the syllabus.

Note to the reader about the book

New features of the book

The new edition of the book contains the following new features:

- *Learning outcomes* An important innovative feature of the new edition is that it contains each and every learning outcome of the IB economics guide. Each learning outcome appears as a bullet point enclosed in a light green box at the beginning of the section (or sub-section) of the book where it is discussed and explained. This means that you need not ever refer to the IB economics guide to ensure that you have covered every learning outcome. It also means that as you read the book you can focus your attention on the material that is indicated by the learning outcomes, this way ensuring that you have understood all the essential points.

- *Theory of knowledge connections* Another new element of the new edition is its inclusion of twenty Theory of knowledge features. Each one of these is closely connected with material covered in the text, and challenges you to think critically about economics as a social science, the nature of economic knowledge, difficulties involved in acquiring economic knowledge, why economists disagree, and the roles of values, language, ethics, beliefs and ideology in the development of economic knowledge. Each one of these features ends with questions intended to stimulate further thinking and discussions on these important theory of knowledge issues.

- *Case studies* The new edition also includes numerous 'Real world focus' features that discuss some event or aspect of the real world discussed in the text. These are followed by questions intended to focus your attention on important theoretical ideas and their relevance to real world situations.

Continuity with the first edition

The new edition also provides continuity with the first edition through inclusion of the following features:

- *Test your understanding questions* Each chapter contains a series of 'Test your understanding' questions, which appear at the end of every topic. These questions have been designed very specifically on the basis of the preceding section's learning outcomes, and can therefore help you review the section's main points. They can be used as the basis for class discussions or homework assignments. You can also use them for studying and reviewing on your own. If you can answer these questions, it means you have understood the important points of the section.

- *Standard level and higher level material* The subdivision of the book's content into two levels is clearly demarcated. A vertical bar labelled 'HL' runs down the margin of all higher level material, allowing you to easily distinguish higher level from standard level material.

- *Key points* Material that is especially important, such as important concepts, laws, definitions and conclusions, is highlighted in a box shaded light green. This helps you focus on key points of the chapter, and can facilitate reviewing.

- *Use of bullet points* There is extensive use of bullet points where there are lists of items relating to a particular topic. These will help you keep the material well organised in your mind, and can also help you review.

- *Syllabus terms and glossary* All syllabus terms are highlighted in **green bold** font at their first appearance in the book so that you can immediately recognise them. (You should note that when a syllabus term reappears in a later section of the book, it is not highlighted in green bold.) At the end of the book, there is a glossary that defines all the syllabus terms. In the glossary, terms that are part of higher level material are demarcated using the vertical 'HL' bar.

- *Supplementary material* The book includes some material that is not part of the IB Economics syllabus and that you will not be examined on. Such material is accompanied by the heading 'supplementary material' so that you can readily recognise it. It is included in the book in order to provide a more rounded view of some topics that are not bounded by the rigid IB syllabus.

Note to the reader about the CD-ROM

The CD-ROM of the second edition has been completely revamped and contains the following:

- *Chapter on 'Quantitative techniques'* This is a detailed chapter containing all the quantitative techniques you need to understand in order to excel in your IB economics course. It enables you to review everything from percentages and percentage changes to understanding the essentials of relationships between variables, and interpreting and constructing diagrams and graphs. For students taking the course at higher level, it explains everything you need to know about linear demand and supply functions, solving linear equations, and performing all necessary calculations and constructing graphs. You will also find a detailed section on how to use a graphic display calculator (GDC) as an aid to graphing. There are numerous cross-references between the book and this CD-ROM chapter; as you read the textbook, you will be referred to the relevant sections of this chapter where you can easily find important background material. This CD-ROM chapter follows the style of the book, and has numerous 'Test your understanding' questions containing exercises of the type that will appear in your exams.

- *Exam questions* This is an extensive section of the CD-ROM consisting of four parts. The first part provides background information on exams, including an explanation of assessment objectives (AOs), learning outcomes and command terms as they relate to the learning outcomes and exam questions. Each of the next three parts deals with exam papers 1, 2 and 3. You will find a very large number of exam questions for each of these papers. The questions cover each and every learning outcome in the entire economics guide, with the appropriate command terms at the appropriate level of assessment objectives.

- *Important diagrams* This section of the CD-ROM, entitled 'Important diagrams to remember' reproduces all the important diagrams of the textbook, organised according to chapter and topic within each chapter. This section enables you to do a quick review of diagrams that you should ensure you understand and can draw yourself in connection with possible questions that are likely to appear on exams.

- *Chapter on the Keynesian cross model* This chapter is an extension of Chapter 9 and is not part of required material (it is 'supplementary material'). It is concerned with the famous model attributed to John Maynard Keynes, and is recommended for students who are interested in gaining a deeper understanding of macroeconomics.
- *List of countries according to the World Bank's classification system* The World Bank classifies countries around the world according to their income levels, and this serves as a useful (though very rough and approximate) guide to classifying countries as economically more or less developed.
- *List of Nobel Prize winners* For the interested student, there is also a list of all Nobel Prize winners in Economics and a brief description of their work, beginning in 1969 when this prize was first awarded.

Note to the reader about the website

Additional materials will be provided on the IB teacher support website at ibdiploma.cambridge.org. These include:

- Markschemes for many of the exam questions in papers 1, 2 and 3 in the CD-ROM.
- Answers to all the questions in the 'Test your understanding' features of the chapter on 'Quantitative techniques' in the CD-ROM.
- Answers to the quantitative questions in the 'Test your understanding' features of the textbook.

Acknowledgements

I would like to express my sincere thanks and appreciation to DEREE – the American College of Greece for its very kind and generous support while I was writing the second edition of this book.

I am deeply grateful to Henry Tiller, former IB economics Chief Examiner, for his most detailed and insightful review of the second edition of the book, for his numerous creative suggestions for improvements that have helped make this a better book, and for his continued and enthusiastic encouragement throughout the entire writing of the second edition. There are two more people who have painstakingly read through the entire text and to who I am deeply indebted for their valuable comments and suggestions: Emilia Drogaris, a highly dedicated and committed IB economics teacher, and Andreas Markoulakis, a star student of economics at the American College of Greece. I would also like to extend my heartfelt thanks to the IB economics teachers and friends around the world who have contributed their comments and suggestions for improvements, who have alerted me to errors in the first edition, and who warmly supported me. They include Tibor Cernak, Simon Foley, Hana Abu Hijleh, Kiran Asad Javed, Jane Kerr, Pat Lasonde, James Martin, Peter Rock, Sachin Sachdeva, Vijay Peter D'Souza, Charles Wu and Kar Lun. I would like to wholeheartedly thank the students who have kindly taken the time to give me their comments and have pointed out errors. They include Duygu Alsancak, Asli Angin, Gianna Argitakos, Justin Cheng, Fritz Claessens, Thomas Fix, Philippe de Gaiffier, David Hung, Anna Bella Inglessis, Sevde Kaldiroğlu, Michael Kardamakis, Max Klose, Ayşe Kozlu, Ioannis Kremitsas, Terran Kroft, Jennifer Kuo, Amanda Lin, Geen Mak, Elif Öngüt, Naz Özal, Ilayda Özsan, Petros Rizopoulos, Peter Ng, Sing Man, Selin Selgür, Tobias Stein, Alexia Tragakes, Constantine Tragakes, Alexios Tsokos, Alkaios Tsokos, Esra Uğur, Allen Wang, Tammy Wu, Tina Wu, Lisa Xie, Gizem Yağci and Luca Ivanovic and her classmates Francesca Berruti, William Butcher, Helen Krats, Julia Laenge, Karl Renault, and Timeon Pax-McDowell. My warm thanks also go to Julia Tokatlidou, the reviewer of the first edition. Finally, I would like to thank K.A. Tsokos for his most generous and patient help especially in emergencies when my computer was acting up.

Ellie Tragakes
June 2011

Terms and conditions of use for the CD-ROM

The CD-ROM at the back of this book is provided on the following terms and conditions:

- The CD-ROM is made available for the use of current teachers and students within a purchasing institution, or for private purchasers, only. A purchase of at least one copy of the book must be made in respect of each teacher, student or private purchaser who uses the CD-ROM. The CD-ROM may be installed on individual computers or networks for use as above.

- Subject to the above, the material on the CD-ROM, in whole or in part, may not be passed in an electronic form to another party, and may not be copied (except for making one copy of the CD-ROM solely for backup or archival purposes), distributed or stored electronically. It may not be posted on a public website, and may not be altered for any reason without the permission of Cambridge University Press.

- Permission is explicitly granted for use of the materials on a data projector, interactive whiteboard or other public display in the context of classroom teaching at a purchasing institution.

- Once a teacher or student ceases to be a member of the purchasing institution all copies of the material on the CD-ROM stored on his/her personal computer must be destroyed and the CD-ROM returned to the purchasing institution.

- All material contained within the CD-ROM is protected by copyright and other intellectual property laws. You may not alter, remove or destroy any copyright notice or other material placed on or with this CD-ROM.

- The CD-ROM is supplied 'as-is' with no express guarantee as to its suitability.

Chapter 1
The foundations of economics

This chapter is an introduction to the study of economics. It is also an introduction to many topics that will be explored in depth in later chapters.

1.1 Scarcity, choice and opportunity cost

The fundamental problem of economics: scarcity and choice

The problem of scarcity

> ◆ Explain that scarcity exists because factors of production are finite and wants are infinite.

The term 'economics' is derived from the ancient Greek expression οίκον νέμειν (*oikon nemein*), which originally meant 'one who manages and administers all matters relating to a household'. Over time, this expression evolved to mean 'one who is prudent in the use of resources'. By extension, economics has come to refer to the careful management of society's scarce resources to avoid waste. Let's examine this idea more carefully.

Human beings have very many needs and wants. Some of these are satisfied by physical objects and others by non-physical activities. All the physical objects people need and want are called *goods* (food, clothing, houses, books, computers, cars, televisions, refrigerators, and so on); the non-physical activities are called *services* (education, health care, entertainment, travel, banking, insurance and many more).

The study of economics arises because people's needs and wants are unlimited, or infinite. Whereas some individuals may be satisfied with the goods and services they have or can buy, most would prefer to have more. They would like to have more and better computers, cars, educational services, transport services, housing, recreation, travel, and so on; the list is endless.

Yet it is not possible for societies and the people within them to produce or buy all the things they want. Why is this so? It is because there are not enough **resources**. Resources are the inputs used to produce goods and services wanted by people, and for this reason are also known as **factors of production**. They include things like human labour, machines and factories, and 'gifts of nature' like agricultural land and metals inside the earth. Factors of production do not exist in unlimited abundance: they are *scarce*, or limited and insufficient in relation to unlimited uses that people have for them.

Scarcity is a very important concept in economics. It arises whenever there is not enough of something in relation to the need for it. For example, we could say that food is scarce in poor countries, or we could say that clean air is scarce in a polluted city. In economics, scarcity is especially important in describing a situation of *insufficient factors of production*, because this in turn leads to insufficient goods and services. Defining scarcity, we can therefore say that:

> **Scarcity** is the situation in which available resources, or factors of production, are finite, whereas wants are infinite. There are not enough resources to produce everything that human beings need and want.

Why scarcity forces choices to be made

> ◆ Explain that as a result of scarcity, choices have to be made.

The conflict between unlimited wants and scarce resources has an important consequence. Since people cannot have everything they want, they must make *choices*. The classic example of a choice forced on society by resource scarcity is that of 'guns or butter', or more realistically the choice between producing defence goods (guns, weapons, tanks) or food: more defence goods mean less food, while more food means fewer defence goods. Societies must choose how much of each they want to have. Note that if there were no resource scarcity, a choice would not be necessary, since society could produce as much of each as was desired. But resource scarcity forces the society to make a choice between available alternatives. Economics is therefore a study of choices.

The conflict between unlimited needs and wants, and scarce resources has a second important consequence. Since resources are scarce, it is important to avoid waste in how they are used. If resources are not used effectively and are wasted, they will end up producing less; or they may end up producing goods and services that people do not really want or need. Economics must try to find how best to use scarce resources so that waste can be avoided. Defining economics, we can therefore say that:

> **Economics** is the study of choices leading to the best possible use of scarce resources in order to best satisfy unlimited human needs and wants.

As you can see from this definition of economics, economists study the world from a social perspective, with the objective of determining what is in society's best interests.

Test your understanding 1.1

1 Think of some of your most important needs and wants, and then explain whether these are satisfied by goods or by services.

2 Why is economics a study of choices?

3 Explain the relationship between scarcity and the need to avoid waste in the use of resources.

4 Explain why diamonds are far more expensive than water, even though diamonds are a luxury while water is a necessity without which we cannot live.

Three basic economic questions: resource allocation and output/income distribution

> ♦ Explain that the three basic economic questions that must be answered by any economic system are: 'What to produce?', 'How to produce?' and 'For whom to produce?'
> ♦ Explain that economics studies the ways in which resources are allocated to meet needs and wants.

Scarcity forces every economy in the world, regardless of its form of organisation, to answer three basic questions:

- **What to produce.** All economies must choose what particular goods and services and what quantities of these they wish to produce.

- **How to produce.** All economies must make choices on how to use their resources in order to produce goods and services. Goods and services can be produced by use of different combinations of factors of production (for example, relatively more human labour with fewer machines, or relatively more machines with less labour), by using different skill levels of labour, and by using different technologies.

- **For whom to produce.** All economies must make choices about how the goods and services produced are to be distributed among the population. Should everyone get an equal amount of these? Should some people get more than others? Should some goods and services (such as education and health care services) be distributed more equally?

The first two of these questions, *what to produce* and *how to produce*, are about *resource allocation*, while the third, *for whom to produce*, is about the *distribution of output and income*.

Resource allocation refers to assigning available resources, or factors of production, to specific uses chosen among many possible alternatives, and involves answering the *what to produce* and *how to produce* questions. For example, if a *what to produce* choice involves choosing a certain amount of food and a certain amount of weapons, this means a decision is made to *allocate* some resources to the production of food and some to the production of weapons. At the same time, a choice must be made about *how to produce*: which particular factors of production and in what quantities (for example, how much labour, how many machines, what types of machines, etc.) should be assigned to produce food, and which and how many to produce weapons.

If a decision is made to change the amounts of goods produced, such as more food and fewer weapons, this involves a **reallocation** of resources. Sometimes, societies produce the 'wrong' amounts of goods and services relative to what is socially desirable. For example, if too many weapons are being produced, we say there is an **overallocation** of resources in production of weapons. If too few socially desirable goods or services are being produced, such as education or health care, we say there is an **underallocation** of resources to the production of these.

An important part of economics is the study of how to allocate scarce resources, in other words how to assign resources to answer the *what to produce* and *how to produce* questions, in order to meet human needs and wants in the best possible way.

The third basic economic question, for *whom to produce*, involves the *distribution of output* and is concerned with how much output different individuals or different groups in the population receive. This question is also concerned with the **distribution of income** among individuals and groups in a population, since the amount of output people can get depends on how much of it they can buy, which in turn depends on the amount of income they have. When the distribution of income or output changes so that different social groups now receive more, or less, income and output than previously, this is referred to as **redistribution of income**.

Test your understanding 1.2

1 What are the three basic economic questions that must be addressed by any economy?

2 Explain the relationship between the three basic economic questions, and the allocation of resources and the distribution of income or output.

3 Consider the following, and identify each one as referring to output/income distribution or redistribution; or to resource allocation, reallocation, overallocation or underallocation (note that there may be more than one answer).
   (a) Evidence suggests that over the last two decades in many countries around the world the rich are getting richer and the poor are getting poorer.
   (b) In Brazil, the richest 10% of the population receive 48% of total income.

   (c) Whereas rich countries typically spend 8–12% of their income on providing health care services to their populations, many poor countries spend as little as 2–3% of income.
   (d) Many developing countries devote a large proportion of their government budget funds for education to spending on university level education, while large parts of their population remain illiterate.
   (e) If countries around the world spent less on defence, they would be in a position to expand provision of social services, including health care and education.
   (f) Pharmaceutical companies spend most of their research funds on developing medicines to treat diseases common in rich countries, while ignoring the treatment of diseases common in poor countries.

Resources as factors of production

We have seen that resources, or all inputs used to produce goods and services, are also known as factors of production.

The four factors of production

Economists group factors of production under four broad categories:

- **Land** includes all natural resources, including all agricultural and non-agricultural land, as well as everything that is under or above the land, such as minerals, oil reserves, underground water, forests, rivers and lakes. Natural resources are also called 'gifts of nature'.

- **Labour** includes the physical and mental effort that people contribute to the production of goods and services. The efforts of a teacher, a construction worker, an economist, a doctor, a taxi driver or a plumber all contribute to producing goods and services, and are all examples of labour.

- **Capital**, also known as *physical capital*, is a man-made factor of production (it is itself produced) used to produce goods and services. Examples of physical capital include machinery, tools, factories, buildings, road systems, airports, harbours, electricity generators and telephone supply lines. Physical capital is also referred to as a capital good or investment good.

- **Entrepreneurship** (management) is a special human skill possessed by some people, involving the ability to innovate by developing new ways of doing things, to take business risks and to seek new opportunities for opening and running a business. Entrepreneurship organises the other three factors of production and takes on the risks of success or failure of a business.

Other meanings of the term 'capital'

The term 'capital', in a most general sense, refers to resources that can produce a future stream of benefits. Thinking of capital along these lines, we can understand why this term has a variety of different uses, which although are seemingly unrelated, in fact all stem from this basic meaning.

- **Physical capital**, defined above, is one of the four factors of production consisting of man-made inputs that provide a stream of future benefits in the form of the ability to produce greater quantities of output: physical capital is used to produce more goods and services in the future.
- **Human capital** refers to the skills, abilities and knowledge acquired by people, as well as good levels of health, all of which make them more productive. Human capital provides a stream of future benefits because it increases the amount of output that can be produced in the future by people who embody skills, education and good health.
- **Natural capital**, also known as *environmental capital*, refers to an expanded meaning of the factor of production 'land' (defined above). It includes everything that is included in land, plus additional natural resources that occur naturally in the environment such as the air, biodiversity, soil quality, the ozone layer, and the global climate. Natural capital provides a stream of future benefits because it is necessary to humankind's ability to live, survive and produce in the future.
- **Financial capital** refers to investments in financial instruments, like stocks and bonds, or the funds (money) that are used to buy financial instruments like stocks and bonds. Financial capital also provides a stream of future benefits, which take the form of an income for the holders, or owners, of the financial instruments.

Scarcity, choice and opportunity cost: the economic perspective

- Explain that when an economic choice is made, an alternative is always foregone.

Opportunity cost

Opportunity cost is defined as the value of the next best alternative that must be given up or sacrificed in order to obtain something else.

When a consumer chooses to use her $100 to buy a pair of shoes, she is also choosing not to use this money to buy books, or CDs, or anything else; if CDs are her favourite alternative to shoes, the CDs she sacrificed (did not buy) are the opportunity cost of the shoes. When a business chooses to use its resources to produce hamburgers, it is also choosing not to produce hotdogs or pizzas, or anything else; if hotdogs are the preferred alternative, the hotdogs sacrificed (not produced) are the opportunity cost of the hamburgers. Note that if the consumer had endless amounts of money, she could buy everything she wanted and the shoes would have no opportunity cost. Similarly, if the business had endless resources, it could produce hotdogs, pizzas and a lot of other things in addition to hamburgers, and the hamburgers would have no opportunity cost. If resources were limitless, no sacrifices would be necessary, and the opportunity cost of producing anything would be zero.

The concept of **opportunity cost**, or the value of the next best alternative that must be sacrificed to obtain something else, is central to the economic perspective of the world, and results from scarcity that forces choices to be made.

1 Explain the relationship between scarcity and choice.

2 Define opportunity cost.

3 Think of three choices you have made today, and describe the opportunity cost of each one.

The production possibilities model

♦ Explain that a production possibilities curve (production possibilities frontier) model may be used to show the concepts of scarcity, choice, opportunity cost and a situation of unemployed resources and inefficiency.

The production possibilities model is a simple model of the economy illustrating some important concepts.

Introducing the production possibilities curve

Consider a simple hypothetical economy producing only two goods: microwave ovens and computers. This economy has a fixed (unchanging) quantity and quality of resources (factors of production) and a fixed technology (the method of production is unchanging). Table 1.1 shows the combinations of the two goods this economy can produce. Figure 1.1 plots the data of Table 1.1: the quantity of microwave ovens is plotted on the vertical axis, and the quantity of computers on the horizontal axis.

If all the economy's resources are used to produce microwave ovens, the economy will produce 40 microwave ovens and 0 computers, shown by point A. If all resources are used to produce computers, the economy will produce 33 computers and 0 microwave ovens; this is point E. All the points on the curve joining A and E represent other production possibilities where some of the resources are used to produce microwave ovens and the rest to produce computers. For example, at point B there would be production of 35 microwave ovens and 17 computers; at point C, 26 microwave ovens and 25 computers, and so on. The line joining

Point	Microwave ovens	Computers
A	40	0
B	35	17
C	26	25
D	15	31
E	0	33

Table 1.1 Combinations of microwave ovens and computers

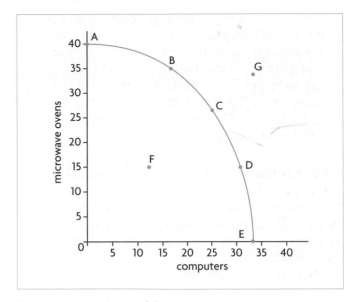

Figure 1.1 Production possibilities curve

points A and E is known as the production possibilities curve (*PPC*) or production possibilities frontier (*PPF*).

In order for the economy to produce the greatest possible output, in other words somewhere on the *PPC*, two conditions must be met:

• **All resources must be fully employed.** This means that all resources are being fully used. If there were unemployment of some resources, in which case they would be sitting unused, the economy would not be producing the maximum it can produce.

• **All resources must be used efficiently.** Specifically, there must be **productive efficiency**. The term 'efficiency' in a general sense means that resources are being used in the best possible way to avoid waste. (If they are not used in the best possible way, we say there is 'inefficiency'.) Productive efficiency means that output is produced by use of the fewest possible resources; alternatively, we can say that output is produced at the lowest possible cost. If output were not produced using the fewest possible resources, the economy would be 'wasting' some resources.

The **production possibilities curve (or frontier)** represents all combinations of the maximum amounts of two goods that can be produced by an economy, given its resources and technology, when there is full employment of resources and productive efficiency. All points on the curve known as **production possibilities**.

What would happen if either of the two conditions (full employment and productive efficiency) is not met? Very simply, the economy will not produce at a point on the *PPC*; it will be somewhere inside the *PPC*, such as at point F. At F, the economy is producing only 15 microwave ovens and 12 computers, indicating that there is either unemployment of resources, or productive inefficiency, or both. If this economy could use its resources fully and efficiently, it could, for example, move to point C and produce 26 microwave ovens and 25 computers.

However, in the real world no economy is ever likely to produce on its *PPC*.

> An economy's **actual output**, or the quantity of output actually produced, is always at a point inside the *PPC*, because in the real world all economies have some unemployment of resources and some productive inefficiency. The greater the unemployment or the productive inefficiency, the further away is the point of production from the *PPC*.

The production possibilities curve and scarcity, choice and opportunity cost

The production possibilities model is very useful for illustrating the concepts of scarcity, choice and opportunity cost:

- **The condition of scarcity does not allow the economy to produce outside its PPC.** With its fixed quantity and quality of resources and technology, the economy cannot move to any point outside the *PPC*, such as G, because it does not have enough resources (there is resource scarcity).

- **The condition of scarcity forces the economy to make a choice about what particular combination of goods it wishes to produce.** Assuming it could achieve full employment and productive efficiency, it must decide at which particular point on the *PPC* it wishes to produce.

(In the real world, the choice would involve a point inside the *PPC*.)

- **The condition of scarcity means that choices involve opportunity costs.** If the economy were at any point on the curve, it would be impossible to increase the quantity produced of one good without decreasing the quantity produced of the other good. In other words, when an economy increases its production of one good, there must necessarily be a sacrifice of some quantity of the other good; this sacrifice is the opportunity cost.

Let's consider the last point more carefully. Say the economy is at point C, producing 26 microwave ovens and 25 computers. Suppose now that consumers would like to have more computers. It is impossible to produce more computers without sacrificing production of some microwave ovens. For example, a choice to produce 31 computers (a move from C to D) involves a decrease in microwave oven production from 26 to 15 units, or a sacrifice of 11 microwave ovens. The sacrifice of 11 microwave ovens is the opportunity cost of 6 extra computers (increasing the number of computers from 25 to 31). Note that opportunity cost arises when the economy is on the *PPC* (or more realistically, somewhere close to the *PPC*). If the economy is at a point inside the curve, it can increase production of both goods with no sacrifice, hence no opportunity cost, simply by making better use of its resources: reducing unemployment or increasing productive efficiency.

The shape of the production possibilities curve

In Figure 1.2(a) the *PPC*'s shape is similar to that of Figure 1.1, while in Figure 1.2(b) it is a straight line. When the *PPC* bends outward and to the right, as in Figure 1.2(a), opportunity costs change as the economy moves from one point on the *PPC* to another. In part (a),

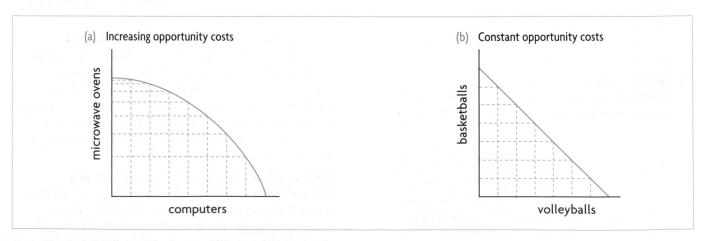

Figure 1.2 Production possibilities curve with increasing and constant opportunity costs

for each additional unit of computers that is produced, the opportunity cost, consisting of microwave ovens sacrificed, gets larger and larger as computer production increases. This happens because of specialisation of factors of production, which makes them not equally suitable for the production of different goods and services. As production switches from microwave ovens to more computers, it is necessary to give up increasingly more microwave ovens for each extra unit of computers produced, because factors of production suited to microwave oven production will be less suited to computer production. By contrast, when the *PPC* is a straight line (as in Figure 1.2(b)), opportunity costs are constant (do not change) as the economy moves from one point of the *PPC* to another. Constant opportunity costs arise when the factors of production are equally well suited to the production of both goods, such as in the case of basketballs and volleyballs, which are very similar to each other, therefore needing similarly specialised factors of production to produce them. As we can see in Figure 1.2(b), for each additional unit of volleyballs produced, the opportunity cost, or sacrifice of basketballs, does not change.

Test your understanding 1.5

1 Consider the production possibilities data in Table 1.1 and Figure 1.1. If the economy is initially at point A and moves to point B, computer production will increase by 17 units. **(a)** What is the opportunity cost of the increase in computer production? **(b)** If the economy moves from D to C, what will be the gain and what will be its opportunity cost? **(c)** If it moves from point C to B, what will be the gain and what will be its opportunity cost?

2 Use the concept of opportunity cost to explain why the following two statements have the same meaning: **(a)** productive efficiency means producing by use of the fewest possible resources, and **(b)** productive efficiency means producing at the lowest possible cost.

3 **(a)** Distinguish between output actually produced and output on the *PPC*. **(b)** Why is an economy's actual output most likely to be located somewhere inside its *PPC*?

4 Say an economy is initially at point F, producing 15 microwave ovens and 12 computers (Figure 1.1). What would be the opportunity cost of moving to a point on the production possibilities curve, such as point C, where it would be producing 26 microwave ovens and 25 computers?

1.2 Economics as a social science

The nature and method of economics

Economics as a social science

♦ Explain that economics is a social science.

The **social sciences** are academic disciplines that study human society and social relationships. They are concerned with discovering general principles describing how societies function and are organised. The social sciences include anthropology, economics, political science, psychology, sociology and others.

Economics is a *social* science because it deals with human society and behaviour, and particularly those aspects concerned with how people organise their activities and how they behave to satisfy their needs and wants. It is a social *science* because its approach to studying human society is based on the social scientific method.

The social scientific method

♦ Outline the social scientific method.

As a social science, economics tries to explain in a systematic way why economic events happen the way they do, and attempts to predict economic events likely to occur in the future. To accomplish all this, economists use the **social scientific method**. This is the same as the scientific method, which you may already be familiar with through your studies of one or more of the natural sciences (for example, biology, chemistry, and physics). It is a method of investigation used in all the social and natural sciences, allowing us to acquire knowledge of the world around us.

The social scientific (or scientific) method consists of the following steps:

Step 1: Make observations of the world around us, and select an economic question we want to answer. Let's consider an example from economics. We observe that people living in the city of Olemoo buy different amounts of oranges per week at different times in the year. We want to answer the question: why are more oranges bought in some weeks and fewer in others?

Step 2: Identify variables we think are important to answer the question. A variable is any measure that can take on different values, such as temperature, or weight, or distance. In our example the variables we choose to study are the quantity of oranges that residents of Olemoo buy each week, and the price of oranges.

Step 3: Make a hypothesis about how the variables are related to each other. A hypothesis is an educated guess, usually indicating a cause-and-effect relationship about an event. Hypotheses are often stated as: if …, then …. Our hypothesis is the following: *if* the price of oranges increases, *then* the quantity of oranges Olemooans want to buy each week will fall. Notice that this hypothesis indicates a cause-and-effect relationship, where price is the 'cause' and the quantity of oranges is the 'effect'. The hypothesis also involves a prediction, because it claims that changes in the price of oranges will lead to a particular change in the quantity of oranges Olemooans buy.

Step 4: Make assumptions. An assumption is a statement we suppose to be true for the purposes of building our hypothesis. In our example we are making two important assumptions. (a) We assume that the price of oranges is the only variable that influences the quantity of oranges Olemooans want to buy, while all other variables that could have influenced their buying choices do not play a role. (b) We assume that the residents of Olemoo

spend their money on oranges (and other things they want) so that they will get the greatest possible satisfaction from their purchases. We will examine both these assumptions later in this section.

Step 5: Test the hypothesis to see if its predictions fit with what actually happens in the real world. To do this, we compare the predictions of the hypothesis with real-world events, based on real-world observations. Here, the methods of economics differ from those of the natural sciences. Whereas in the natural sciences it is often (though not always) possible to perform experiments to test hypotheses, in economics the possibilities for experiments are very limited. Economists therefore rely on a branch of statistics called econometrics to test hypotheses. This involves collecting data on the variables in the hypothesis, and examining whether the data fit the relationships stated in the hypothesis. In our example, we must collect data on the quantity of oranges bought by Olemoo's residents during different weeks throughout the year, and compare these quantities with different orange prices at different times in the year. (Econometrics is usually studied at university level, and is not part of IB requirements.)

More on testing hypotheses and the scientific method

We have seen how hypotheses are tested using the social scientific method. If the data fit the predictions of a hypothesis, the hypothesis is accepted. However, this does not make the hypothesis necessarily 'true' or 'correct'. The only knowledge we have gained is that *according to the data used, the hypothesis is not false*. There is always a possibility that as testing methods are improved and as new and possibly more accurate data are used, a hypothesis that earlier had been accepted now is rejected as false. Therefore, no matter how many times a hypothesis is tested, we can never be sure that it is 'true'.

But by the same logic, we can never be sure that a hypothesis that is rejected is necessarily false. It is possible that our hypothesis testing, maybe because of poor data or poor testing methods, incorrectly rejected a hypothesis. Testing of the same hypothesis with different methods or data could show that the hypothesis had been wrongly rejected.

If our results from hypothesis testing are subject to so many uncertainties, how can economic knowledge about the world develop and progress? Economists and other

social and natural scientists work with hypotheses that have been tested and not falsified (not rejected). While the possibility exists that the hypotheses may be false, they use these hypotheses *on the assumption* that they are not false. As more and more testing is done, and as unfalsified hypotheses accumulate, it becomes more and more likely that they are not false (though we can never be sure). This way, it is possible to accumulate knowledge about the world, on the understanding, however, that this knowledge is tentative and provisional; in other words, it can never be proven to be correct or true.

Thinking points

- Is it possible to ever arrive at the truth of a statement about the real world based on empirical testing?

- Even assuming that testing methods could be perfected and data vastly improved, can there ever be complete certainty about our knowledge of the social (and natural) worlds?

Step 6: Compare the predictions of the hypothesis with real-world outcomes.

If the data do not fit the predictions of the hypothesis, the hypothesis is rejected, and the search for a new hypothesis could begin. In our example, this would happen if we discovered that as the price of oranges increases, the quantity of oranges Olemooans want to buy each week also increases. Clearly, this would go against our hypothesis, and we would have to reject the hypothesis as invalid. If, on the other hand, the data fit the predictions, the hypothesis is accepted. In our example, this would occur if our data show that as the price of oranges increases, Olemoo's residents buy fewer oranges. We can therefore conclude that according to the evidence, our hypothesis is a valid one.

Economists as model builders

♦ Explain the process of model building in economics.

In economics, as in other social (and natural) sciences, our efforts to gain knowledge about the world involve the formulation of hypotheses, theories, laws and models. The relationships between these ideas are explored in the Theory of knowledge feature on page 10. Here we focus on the role of models.

Everyone is familiar with the idea of a model. As children, many of us played with paper aeroplanes, which are models of real aeroplanes. In chemistry at school, we studied molecules and atoms, which are models of what matter is made of. Models are a simplified representation of something in the real world, and are used a lot by scientists and social scientists in their efforts to understand or explain real-world situations. Models represent only the important aspects of the real world being investigated, ignoring unnecessary details, thereby allowing scientists and social scientists to focus on important relationships.

Whereas sciences like biology, chemistry and physics offer the possibility to construct three-dimensional models (as with molecules and atoms), this cannot be done in the social sciences, because these are concerned with human society and social relationships. In economics, models are often illustrated by use of diagrams showing the relationships between important variables. In more advanced economics, models are illustrated by use of mathematical equations. (Note that both diagrams and mathematical equations are used to represent models in natural sciences, such as physics, as well.) To construct a model, economists select particular variables and make assumptions about how these are interrelated. Different models represent different aspects of the economic world. Some models may be better than others in their ability to explain economic phenomena.

Models are often closely related to theories, as well as to laws. A theory tries to explain *why* certain events happen and to make predictions; a law is a concise statement of an event that is supposed to have universal validity. Models are often built on the basis of well-established theories or laws, in which case they may illustrate, through diagrams or mathematical equations, the important features of the theory or law. When this happens, economists use the terms 'model' and 'theory' interchangeably, because in effect they refer to one and the same thing. For example, in Chapter 7, we will use models to illustrate the ideas contained in the theory of firm behaviour. Later, in Chapter 9, different models of the macroeconomy will be used to illustrate alternative theories of income and output determination.

However, models are not always representations of theories. In some cases, economists use models to isolate important aspects of the real world and show connections between variables but without any explanations as to *why* the variables are connected in some particular way. In such cases, models are purely descriptive; in other words, they describe a situation, without explaining anything about it. For example, the production possibilities model, which we studied on page 5, is a simple model that is very important because of its ability to *describe* scarcity, choice and opportunity cost. The model describes the basic problem of economics, which is that societies are forced to make choices that involve sacrifices because of the condition of scarcity. There is no theory involved here.

Descriptive models that are not based on a theory are in no way less important than models that illustrate a theory. Both kinds of model are very effective as tools used by economists to highlight and understand important relationships and phenomena in the economics world. In our study of economics, we will encounter a variety of economic models and will make extensive use of diagrams.

Hypotheses, theories, laws and models

We have seen that a hypothesis is an educated guess about a cause-and-effect relationship in a single event. A *theory* is a more general explanation of a set of interrelated events, usually (though not always) based on several hypotheses that have been tested successfully (in other words, they have not been rejected, based on evidence; see the Theory of knowledge feature on page 8). A theory is a generalisation about the real world that attempts to organise complex and interrelated events and present them in a systematic and coherent way to explain *why* these events happen. Based on their ability to systematically explain events, theories attempt to make predictions.

A *law*, on the other hand, is a statement that describes an event in a concise way, and is supposed to have universal validity; in other words, to be valid at all times and in all places. Laws are based on theories and are known to be valid in the sense that they have been successfully tested very many times. They are often used in practical applications and in the development of further theories because of their great predictive powers. However, laws are much simpler than theories, and do not try to explain events the way theories do.

Referring to the example of oranges (page 7), the relationship between the price of oranges and the quantity of oranges residents of Olemoo buy at each price was a hypothesis. This kind of hypothesis has been successfully tested a great many times for many different goods, and the data support the presence in the real world of such a relationship. However, this relationship is not a theory, because it only shows how two variables relate to each other, and does not explain anything about *why* buyers behave the way they do when they make decisions to buy something. To explain this relationship in a general way, economists have developed 'marginal

utility theory' and 'indifference curve analysis' based on a more complicated analysis involving more variables, assumptions and interrelationships. These theories try to answer the question *why* people behave in ways that make the observed relationship between price and quantity a valid one.

Yet, the simple relationship between the quantity of a good that people want to buy and its price, while not a theory, has the status of one of the most important *laws* of economics, called the *law of demand*. This law is a statement describing an event in a simple way. It has great predictive powers and is used as a building block for very many complex theories. We will study the law of demand in detail in Chapter 2 and we will use it repeatedly throughout this book in numerous applications, and as a building block for many theories.

In your study of economics, you will encounter many theories and some laws. Your study of both theories and laws will make great use of economic models. Models, as explained in the text, are sometimes used to illustrate theories (or laws) and sometimes to describe the connections between variables.

Thinking points

The relationships between hypotheses, theories, laws and models described here apply generally to all the sciences and social sciences based on the scientific method. Yet they may differ between disciplines in the ways they are used and interpreted. As you study economics, you may want to think about the following.

• How are theories and laws used in economics as compared with other disciplines? Do they play the same role? Are they derived in the same ways? Do they have the same meaning?

Test your understanding 1.6

1 Explain the social scientific method. What steps does it involve?

2 Why is it important to compare the predictions of a hypothesis with real-world outcomes?

3 How do models help economists in their work as social scientists?

Two assumptions in economic model-building
Ceteris paribus

♦ Explain that economists must use the *ceteris paribus* assumption when developing economic models.

When we try to understand the relationship between two or more variables in the context of a hypothesis, or economic theory or model, we must assume that everything else, other than the variables we are studying, does not change. We do this by use of the *ceteris paribus* assumption:

> **Ceteris paribus** is a Latin expression that means 'other things equal'. Another way of saying this is that all other things are assumed to be constant or unchanging.

Consider the simple relationship discussed earlier, in Step 3 of the scientific method. Our hypothesis stated that the quantity of oranges that will be bought is determined by their price. Surely, however, price cannot be the only variable that influences how many oranges Olemooans want to buy. What if the population of Olemoo increases? What if the incomes of Olemooans increase? And what if an advertising campaign proclaiming the health benefits of eating oranges influences the tastes of Olemooans? As a result of any or all of these factors, Olemooans will want to buy more oranges.

This complicates our analysis, because if all these variables change at the same time, we have no way of knowing what effect each one of them individually has on the quantity people want to buy. We want to be able to isolate the effects of each one of these variables; to test our hypothesis we specifically wanted to study the effects of the price of oranges alone. This means we have to make an assumption that all other things that could affect the relationship we are studying must be constant, or unchanging. More formally, we would say that we are examining the effect of orange prices on quantity of oranges people want to buy, *ceteris paribus*. This means simply that we are studying the relationship between prices and quantity *on the assumption* that nothing else happens that can influence this relationship. By eliminating all other possible interferences, we isolate the impact of price on quantity, so we can study it alone. (Note that this was the first assumption we made in Step 4 of our discussion of the scientific method above.)

In the real world all variables are likely to be changing at the same time. The *ceteris paribus* assumption does not say anything about what happens in the real world. It is simply a tool used by economists to construct hypotheses, models and theories, thus allowing us to isolate and study the effects of one variable at a time. We will be making extensive use of the *ceteris paribus* assumption in our study of economics. (For more information on the *ceteris paribus* assumption, see 'Quantitative techniques' chapter on the CD-ROM, page 11).

Rational economic decision-making

♦ Examine the assumption of rational economic decision-making.

Economic theories and models are based on another important assumption, that of 'rational

self-interest', or **rational economic decision-making**. This means that individuals are assumed to act in their best self-interest, trying to maximise (make as large as possible) the satisfaction they expect to receive from their economic decisions. It is assumed that consumers spend their money on purchases to maximise the satisfaction they get from buying different goods and services. (You may recall that this was the second assumption we made in Step 4 of the scientific method.) Similarly, it is assumed that firms (or producers) try to maximise the profits they make from their businesses; workers try to secure the highest possible wage when they get a job; investors in the stock market try to get the highest possible returns on their investments, and so on.

Why do we assume in economics that people act in their best self-interest? As we will discover in Chapter 2, in a market economy, the self-interested behaviour of countless economic decision-makers is also likely to be in society's best interests. This conclusion may appear strange to you, but will become clearer after you have studied the model of demand and supply and its implications in Chapter 2.

> ### Test your understanding 1.7
>
> 1 Consider the statement, 'If you increase your consumption of calories, you will put on weight.' Do you think this statement is necessarily true? Why or why not? How could you rephrase the statement to make it more accurate?
>
> 2 What does it mean to be 'rational' in economics? Do you think this is a realistic assumption?

Positive and normative concepts

♦ Distinguish between positive and normative economics.

Economists think about the economic world in two different ways: one way tries to describe and explain how things in the economy actually work, and the other deals with how things ought to work.

The first of these is based on *positive statements*, which are about something that is, was or will be. Positive statements are used in several ways:

- They may describe something (e.g. the unemployment rate is 5%; industrial output grew by 3%).
- They may be about a cause-and-effect relationship, such as in a hypothesis (e.g. if the government increases spending, unemployment will fall).

- They may be statements in a theory, model or law (e.g. a higher rate of inflation is associated with a lower unemployment rate).

The second way of thinking about the economic world, dealing with how things ought to work, is based on *normative statements*, which are about what ought to be. These are subjective statements about what should happen. Examples include the following:

- The unemployment rate should be lower.
- Health care should be available free of charge.
- Extreme poverty should be eradicated (eliminated).

Positive statements may be true or they may be false. For example, we may say that the unemployment rate is 5%; if in fact the unemployment rate is 5% this statement is true; but if the unemployment rate is actually 7%, the statement is false. Normative statements, by contrast, cannot be true or false. They can only be assessed relative to *beliefs* and *value judgements*. Consider the normative statement 'the unemployment rate should be lower'. We cannot say whether this statement is true or false, though we may agree or disagree with it, depending on our beliefs about unemployment. If we believe that the present unemployment rate is too high, then we will agree; but if we believe that the present unemployment rate is not too high, then we will disagree.

Positive statements play an important role in **positive economics** where they are used to describe economic events and to construct theories and models that try to explain these events. Positive statements are also used in stating laws. It should be stressed that the social scientific method, described above, is based on positive thinking. In their role as social *scientists*, economists use positive statements in order to describe, explain and predict.

Normative statements are important in **normative economics**, where they form the basis of economic policy-making. Economic policies are government actions that try to solve economic problems. When a government makes a policy to lower the unemployment rate, this is based on a belief that the unemployment rate is too high, and the value judgement that high unemployment is not a good thing. If a government pursues a policy to make health care available free of charge, this is based on a belief that people should not have to pay for receiving health care services.

Positive and normative economics, while distinct, often work together. To be successful, an economic policy aimed at lowering unemployment (the normative dimension) must be based on a body of economic knowledge about what causes unemployment (the positive dimension). The positive dimension provides guidance to policy-makers on how to achieve their economic goals.

Microeconomics and macroeconomics

Economics is studied on two levels. **Microeconomics** examines the behaviour of individual decision-making units in the economy. The two main groups of decision-makers we study are consumers (or households) and firms (or businesses). Microeconomics is concerned with how these decision-makers behave, how they make choices and how their interactions in markets determine prices.

Macroeconomics examines the economy as a whole, to obtain a broad or overall picture, by use of aggregates, which are wholes or collections of many individual units, such as the sum of consumer behaviours and the sum of firm behaviours, and total income and output of the entire economy, as well as total employment and the general price level.

1.3 Central themes

- Explain that the economics course will focus on several themes, which include:
  - the distinction between economic growth and economic development
  - the threat to sustainability as a result of the current patterns of resource allocation
  - the extent to which governments should intervene in the allocation of resources
  - the extent to which the goal of economic efficiency may conflict with the goal of equity.

In this section we will examine some central economic themes that will run through your study of economics. Each of the themes is beset by conflicts, or unresolved questions, over which there is disagreement among economists. There is no single 'right' or 'wrong' answer to the issues posed; answers provided by different economists depend on different perspectives. Whereas economists attempt to justify one or another perspective on the basis of economic theories or models, ultimately a decision in favour of one or another perspective may depend on the economist's personal preference for one theory over another.

The distinction between economic growth and economic development

The meaning of economic growth and economic development

All economies produce some output, which includes goods and services produced for consumers, as well as capital goods (physical capital). Over time, the quantity of output produced changes. When it increases, there is economic growth; if it decreases, there is economic contraction or *negative economic growth*.

Usually, the quantity of output produced by countries increases over long periods of time, but there are enormous differences between countries in how much output they produce and in how quickly or slowly this increases over time. Whereas countries are commonly referred to as being 'rich' or 'poor', economists try to classify them in a more precise way. The World Bank (an international financial institution that we will study in Chapter 18) divides them into 'more developed' and 'less developed' according to their income levels, which as we will discover are closely related to quantities of output produced.

Yet differences between countries in their level of economic development involve much more than just differences in incomes and quantities of output produced. Economic development refers to raising the standard of living and well-being of people. This means not only increasing incomes and output, but also reducing poverty among very poor people, redistributing income so that the differences between the very rich and very poor become smaller, reducing unemployment, and increasing provision of important goods and services such as food and shelter, sanitation, education and health care services so that they can be enjoyed by everyone in a population.

We can see from this definition that economic development is quite different from economic growth. Economic growth, or growing output, is important as a basis for economic development, because it means that more goods and services are being produced, and therefore the standards of living of people *could be potentially increased*. However, economic development may not follow automatically from economic growth. It is possible to have growth in the quantity of output produced, but this may not result in a reduction of income inequalities, poverty or unemployment, or in the provision of increased social services such as education, health care and sanitation.

Where economists disagree

While economists agree on the distinction between economic growth and economic development, and on the point that developing countries should have policies to encourage growth and development, there are disagreements over how this should be done. For example, should growth be a priority, on the assumption that some development will follow if growth occurs? Or should development objectives be a direct priority? What are the best policies that governments and international organisations can pursue to help countries achieve both economic growth and economic development? As we will see in Section 4 of this book, there are no simple answers to these questions.

Current patterns of resource allocation as a threat to sustainability

The meaning of sustainability

Economic growth and economic development in many (if not most) countries are often achieved at the expense of the natural environment and natural resources. Growth in output, or a general improvement in the standard of living of the population, very often result in increased air and water pollution, and the destruction or depletion of forests, wildlife and the ozone layer, among many other natural resources. Growing awareness of this issue has given rise to the concept of *sustainable development*, defined as 'development which meets the needs of the present without compromising the ability of future generations to meet their own needs'.[1]

Sustainable development occurs when societies grow and develop without leaving behind fewer or lower-quality resources for future generations. If we in the present use up resources at a rate that leaves fewer or lower-quality resources behind, we are satisfying our needs and wants now at the expense of people in the future, who with fewer or lower-quality resources will be less able to satisfy their own needs and wants. If we enjoy the benefits today of production and consumption by changing the global climate and by using up clean air, seas and rivers, forests and the ozone layer, we are putting future generations at a disadvantage.

Using the definition of sustainable development, we can see that **sustainability** involves using resources in ways that do not reduce their quantity or quality over time. As a rule it is used with reference to renewable resources, or those kinds of natural resources that are able to reproduce themselves (such as forests, fish and sea life, air quality, the fertility of the soil). Sustainable resource use does not mean that these kinds of natural resources should not be used at all, but rather that they should be used at a rate that gives them enough time to reproduce themselves, so that they can be maintained over time and not be destroyed or depleted.

Threats to sustainability arise from the ways that societies answer mainly the first two of the three basic economic questions. Major threats come from our current patterns of resource allocation, in other words, from the ways societies are choosing to answer the *what to produce* and the *how to produce* questions. In the *what to produce* part of resource allocation, the issue in high income societies involves consumption relying strongly on fossil fuels that pollute the environment (for example, excessive use of private cars, home heating and air conditioners). In the *how to produce* part of resource allocation, the issue involves methods of production (industrial production) that also rely on heavy use of fossil fuels. In very poor societies, inappropriate resource allocation is often caused by poverty itself, which drives very poor people to destroy their natural environment as they make an effort to survive. Examples include cutting down forests, overgrazing, soil erosion, and many more. In all these cases, there may be an unsustainable use of

resources, as fewer and lower-quality resources are left behind for future generations.

Where economists disagree

While virtually everyone today agrees on the importance of sustainability, there is vast disagreement about what this means from a practical point of view, and how this can be achieved in practice. One important reason is that the concept of sustainable resource use involves very large numbers of variables relating to scientific, environmental, economic, social and institutional conditions, that are interrelated in very complex ways, many of which are not fully understood by scientists and social scientists, are subject to numerous uncertainties and cannot even be accurately measured given the present state of scientific knowledge.

Another reason is that even if it were possible to provide answers to the technical questions, there are still very important issues of an ethical and philosophical nature that science and social science are not equipped to address. These issues are discussed in the Theory of knowledge feature in Chapter 5, page 127.

Test your understanding 1.10

1 Explain the meaning of sustainability.

2 Consider the following: 'But just as the speed and scale of China's rise as an economic power have no clear parallel in history, so its pollution problem has shattered all precedents. Environmental degradation is now so severe that pollution poses not only a major long-term burden on the Chinese public but also an acute political challenge to the ruling Communist Party.'
   (a) In your opinion, is China achieving sustainable development?
   (b) What can you conclude about China's rapid economic growth and its impacts on future generations?

The extent to which governments should intervene in the allocation of resources

The meaning of government intervention in the market

Countries around the world differ enormously in the ways they make allocation and distribution decisions. At the heart of their differences lie the methods used

---

[1] Brundtland Commission (World Commission on Environment and Development) (1987) *Our Common Future*, Oxford University Press.

to make the choices required by the *what*, *how* and *for whom to produce* questions. There are two main methods that can be used to make these choices: the *market method* and the *command method*.

In the market method, resources are owned by private individuals or groups of individuals, and it is mainly consumers and firms (or businesses) who make economic decisions by responding to prices that are determined in markets (we will see how this happens in Chapter 2). In the command method, resources (land and capital in particular) are owned by the government, which makes economic decisions by commands. In practice, commands involve legislation and regulations by the government, or in general any kind of government decision-making that affects the economy.

In the real world, there has never been an economy that is entirely a market economy or entirely a command economy. Real-world economies combine markets and commands in many different ways, and each country is unique in the ways they combine them. Economies may lean more toward the command economy (as in communist systems), or more toward the market economy (as in highly market-oriented economies). Whatever the case, in the last 30 or so years, there has been a trend around the world for economies to rely more and more on markets and less on commands. Economies that are based strongly on markets but also have some command methods are called *mixed market economies*.

In mixed market economies, the command methods of making allocation and distribution decisions are referred to as **government intervention**, because the government intervenes (or interferes) in the workings of markets. Examples of government intervention include provision of public education, public health care, public parks, road systems, national defence, flood control, minimum wage legislation, restrictions on imports, anti-monopoly legislation, tax collection, income redistribution, and many more.

Whatever the reasons for and types of government intervention in the market, government intervention changes the allocation of resources (and distribution of output and income) from what markets working on their own would have achieved.

The market economy offers important benefits that we will discover in Chapter 2. Yet it does not always produce the 'best' answers to the *what*, *how* and *for whom* questions for many reasons to be discussed in later chapters. Therefore, a market economy cannot operate effectively without some government intervention.

Where economists disagree

Whereas everyone agrees that some government intervention in markets is necessary, economists disagree widely over how much governments should intervene and how they should intervene. There are two broad schools of thought on this issue. One focuses on the positive aspects of markets, while the other focuses on the imperfections of markets.

According to the first, it is argued that in spite of imperfections, markets are able to work reasonably well on their own, and can produce outcomes that generally promote society's well-being. Markets can achieve a reasonably good allocation of resources, answering the *what to produce* and *how to produce* questions quite well. Government intervention changes this allocation of resources, and often worsens it, giving rise to resource waste. Therefore, while some minimum government intervention may be needed in certain situations, this should not be very extensive.

According to the second school of thought, markets have the potential to work well, but in the real world their imperfections may be so important that they make government intervention necessary for their correction. This means that markets, working on their own, do not do a very good job of allocating resources in society's best interests; the purpose of government intervention therefore is to help markets work better and arrive at a better pattern of resource allocation and distribution of income and output.

Test your understanding 1.11

1 Provide some more examples of command methods (government intervention) in mixed market economies.

2 What is the main source of the disagreement between those who argue there should be little government intervention in the economy and those who argue that government intervention should be more extensive?

The extent to which the goals of economic efficiency and equity might conflict

The meaning of economic efficiency and equity

Economic efficiency involves making the best use of resources and avoiding waste. It involves answering the *what* and *how to produce* questions by allocating resources in the best possible way to avoid resource waste (page 2). When economic efficiency is achieved, it means resources are allocated in a way that the economy produces the most of those goods society mostly prefers. Therefore, an important goal of government policies virtually everywhere is to increase efficiency in the economy as much as possible.

Equity refers to the idea of being fair or just. Equity is not the same as 'equality'. Equality is one possible interpretation of equity, but there are also other possible interpretations. For example, in many countries in the world, it is considered *equitable* that people with higher incomes and wealth pay higher taxes than people with lower incomes and wealth. Clearly, this notion of equity involves treating people *unequally*. (This will be discussed in the Theory of Knowledge feature on page 315.)

The idea of equity in economics often arises in connection with the distribution of income (and output), involving the *for whom to produce* question. Equity, or fairness, in the distribution of income is often interpreted as greater equality (or less inequality) in the share of income received by individuals or families in a society. The aim is not to make the distribution of income completely equal, but to ensure that people who would have little or no income in a market economy, and cannot secure enough of essential goods and services, such as food, shelter, health care, and so on, will be able to survive. Therefore, equity is also an important goal of government policies.

Where economists disagree

According to many economists, there is a trade-off between efficiency and equity (in the sense of a more equal income distribution): more income equality involves less efficiency, and vice versa. The reason they may conflict is that government intervention in markets to achieve equity (or anything else for that matter) changes the allocation of resources. What if these changes in resource allocation make the economy *less efficient*; what if they do not allow the economy to answer the *what to produce* and *how to produce* questions in the best possible way?

This idea emerged in the 1970s from a highly influential book written by a famous economist, Arthur Okun, who argued that 'the conflict between equality and economic efficiency is inescapable' (*Equity and Efficiency: The Big Trade-off, 1975*).

The following example helps explain the idea of a conflict between efficiency and equity. Imagine a pie representing society's income, distributed between the people in the economy according to how much they contribute to baking it. Some people's pieces are much larger than others; it is believed that this is unfair, and a decision is made to change how the pie is divided up so that everyone receives a fair share. A 'fair share' is interpreted to mean an 'equal share', and the pie is cut so everyone has equal size pieces. However, in the following year, when the pie is baked again, the overall size of the pie is smaller than the year before.

The shrinking of the pie means that due to income redistribution, the amount of output produced (and the income corresponding to this output) decreased. The reason behind the decrease can be found in the poorer allocation of resources, which did not allow the economy to produce the greatest possible amount of output with its resources.

Why did this happen? Arthur Okun argued that government intervention to redistribute income results in changes in work effort (people do not work as hard), in changes in savings and investment (people save and invest less) and in changes in attitudes (for example, people have less of an incentive to train and get new skills to become more productive). It follows, then, that there is a conflict between efficiency and equity (in the sense of income equality).

Other economists claim that there need not always be a conflict between equity and efficiency. According to one argument, government intervention to change income distribution could result in changes in behaviour that lead to *greater* rather than less efficiency. For example, suppose an economy has income inequalities so great that very low income people are too discouraged, or too unhealthy, or too unskilled to be able to work. Some income redistribution in their favour could increase their ability to work and make them more productive, thus *increasing both income equality and efficiency (the size of the future pie)*. Therefore, in this view there need not be an inevitable conflict between efficiency and equity, and the two may be compatible.

Test your understanding 1.12

1 Why are the goals of efficiency and equity important for any economy?

2 Can you think of any situations where inequality might be equitable?

3 What assumptions relating to human behaviour underlie the different perspectives on the relationship between equity and efficiency?

Why do economists disagree?

In examining the four themes that run through your study of economics, we have discovered four major areas where economists disagree (you will discover many more areas of disagreement as you read this book). Why do economists disagree so much? It would seem that use of the social scientific method in economics, by forcing hypotheses to undergo tests, and allowing the real-world evidence to sift through valid and invalid hypotheses, would eliminate much disagreement. Why do economists continue to disagree in spite of their use of the social scientific method? To try to answer this question, we should consider the point mentioned earlier on the difficulties of testing hypotheses due to the inability of economists to perform controlled experiments (page 8).

The social scientific method, as we have seen, involves relating evidence to educated guesses about cause-and-effect relationships between variables to see if they match. Economists face some difficulties in this effort. First, the inability to perform controlled experiments means that economists collect data about real-world events that are the result of many variables changing at the same time. To test hypotheses, economists devise complicated econometric models that try to isolate the interfering effects of numerous variables, and try to link causes with effects. Sometimes, economists have to deal with incomplete or unreliable real-world data. In some cases, they may even be faced with variables that are not measurable and have no data, in which case they must use substitute variables (called 'proxy' variables) or substitute relationships between variables. As a result of these difficulties, it is not unusual for two or more economists to be testing the same hypothesis and to come up with conflicting results.

For all these reasons, while the testing methods of economists do produce some useful results, these are sometimes not as accurate and as reliable as the results of experiments in other disciplines performed under controlled conditions. This means it may be more difficult for hypothesis testing in economics to refute (reject) invalid hypotheses. If the evidence does not reject a hypothesis, economists hold on to it and may continue to use it in their work (possibly until further testing in the future). However, this does not mean that

the hypothesis is a valid one. It may be invalid, but the evidence just has not been discriminating enough to reject it. This has important implications for economics. It means that there may be several conflicting hypotheses that economists are holding on to and working with, *not all of which are valid hypotheses*, and some of which may be false.

Moreover, economists may use these hypotheses to build theories. A theory was described in the Theory of knowledge feature on page 10 as being based on several hypotheses that have not been rejected, based on evidence. This means it is possible to have theories built on invalid hypotheses, which simply have not (yet) been shown to be invalid. But if the hypotheses on which theories are built are invalid, then surely the theories themselves are also invalid. This explains one possible reason why we sometimes see several conflicting theories being used at the same time. Maybe only one of them (or even none of them) is valid. Whatever the case, as economists usually prefer to support one theory over another, this may be an important reason why they sometimes disagree.

Thinking points

As you read this book and learn more about economics, you may want to keep the following questions in mind:

- Can you think of other possible reasons why economists often disagree?
- What other social sciences/sciences cannot test hypotheses by performing controlled experiments?
- Do you think economists disagree more or less than (or the same as) other social and natural scientists?
- Do you think the difficulties of economics are due to its being a 'young' social science that will slowly 'mature' and resolve these difficulties as econometric methods and the quality of data improve, or are they due to problems that are inherent in the nature of the subject and cannot be easily resolved?
- Do you think these difficulties seriously affect the progress and development of new economic knowledge, or can economics continue to progress in spite of these difficulties?

Assessment

Chapter 1 is an introduction to the IB Economics syllabus. There will be no examination questions based directly on the material presented here. This material will be assessed wherever it appears throughout the four sections of the IB syllabus.

Section 1
Microeconomics

Microeconomics is concerned with the behaviour of consumers, firms and resource owners, who are the most important economic decision-makers in a market economy. We will study the model of demand and supply, which forms the basis of the market economy and is one of the most important analytical tools in microeconomics. We will learn about the benefits and imperfections of free markets. We will also examine the role of governments in a variety of situations. We will see what effects governments have when they interfere in markets, as well as how they can help achieve better social outcomes when markets fail to perform well.

In addition, Section 1 will be concerned with market structures (at higher level). We will learn about different ways in which real-world industries are organised, and their advantages and disadvantages from the perspectives of consumers, firms and societies.

The tools we will develop in microeconomics are important because they provide many insights into the workings of the market economy, and into the effects of different types of government intervention. In addition, these tools are important because they form the basis of additional topics we will study in later parts of this book.

Chapter 2
Competitive markets: demand and supply

In this chapter we examine what lies at the heart of every market-based economy: the forces of demand and supply.

2.1 Introduction to competitive markets

♦ Outline the meaning of the term 'market'.

Markets

The nature of markets

A market originally was a place where people gathered to buy and sell goods. Such markets still exist today, for example cattle markets, fish markets, fruit and vegetable markets, and flea markets, involving a physical meeting place where buyers and sellers meet face to face.

The term **market** has since evolved to include any kind of arrangement where buyers and sellers of goods, services or resources are linked together to carry out an exchange.

The market may be in a specific place (such as a vegetable market), or it may involve many different places (such as the oil market). Buyers and sellers may meet (say, in a shop), or they may never meet, communicating by fax, phone, internet, classified ads, or any other method which allows them to convey information about price, quantity and quality.

A market can be local, where the buyers and sellers originate from a local area; it may be national, in which case the buyers and sellers are from anywhere within a country; or it may be international, with buyers and sellers from anywhere in the world. For example, small neighbourhood bakeries produce and sell bread and other baked goods for the local

community – this is a local market. Local takeaway restaurants also produce for the local market. The labour market, on the other hand, tends to be mostly a national market. By contrast, the world oil market includes oil producers in different countries, and buyers of oil virtually everywhere in the world, as well as wholesalers, retailers and other intermediaries involved in buying and selling oil around the world.

Goods and services are sold in product markets, while resources (factors of production) are sold in resource markets (factor markets).

Test your understanding 2.1

1 What is a market?
2 Suggest more examples of local, national and international markets.

The meaning of a competitive market

Competition is generally understood to be a process in which rivals compete in order to achieve some objective. For example, firms may compete with each other over who will sell the most output, consumers may compete over who will buy a scarce product, workers compete over who will get the best jobs with the highest salaries, countries compete over which will capture the biggest export markets, and so on. Beyond this everyday sense, competition in microeconomics occurs when there are many buyers and sellers acting independently, so that no one has the ability to influence the price at which a product is sold in the market. This should be contrasted with *market power*, also known as *monopoly power*, which refers to the control that a seller may have over the price of the product it sells.

The greater the market power, the greater is the control over price. On the other hand, the greater the degree of competition between sellers, the smaller their market power, and the weaker is their control over the price.

In this chapter we will study **competitive markets** composed of large numbers of sellers and buyers acting independently, so that no one individual seller or small group of sellers has the ability to control the price of the product sold. Instead, the price of the product is determined by the interactions of many sellers and buyers, through the forces of demand and supply.

2.2 Demand

Understanding the law of demand and the demand curve

Demand is concerned with the behaviour of buyers. Consumers (or households) are buyers of goods and services in product markets, whereas firms (or businesses) are buyers of factors of production in resource markets. In our analysis of demand and supply we will focus mainly on product markets and therefore on the behaviour of consumers as buyers (though the same general principles described here apply also to the behaviour of firms as buyers in resource markets).

Individual demand

> ◆ Explain that a demand curve represents the relationship between the price and the quantity demanded of a product, *ceteris paribus*.
> ◆ Draw a demand curve.

Consumers buy goods and services in product markets. As buyers, they are demanders of those items they wish to buy.

> The **demand** of an individual consumer indicates the various quantities of a good (or service) the consumer is *willing and able to buy* at different possible prices during a particular time period, *ceteris paribus*.

A consumer's demand for a good can be presented as a demand schedule, or a table listing quantity demanded at various prices. Table 2.1 shows a consumer's demand schedule for chocolate bars. When the price of chocolate bars is $5, the consumer is willing and able to buy two chocolate bars in a

Price of chocolate bars ($)	Quantity of chocolate bars demanded (per week)
5	2
4	4
3	6
2	8
1	10

Table 2.1   Demand schedule for a consumer

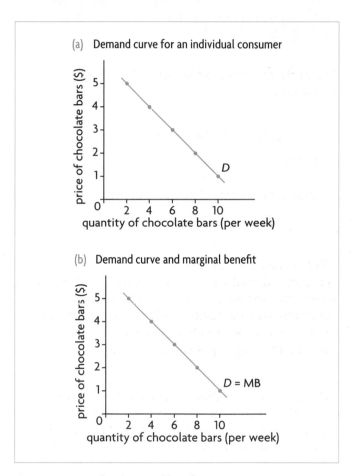

Figure 2.1   Demand and marginal benefit

week. When the price is $4, the consumer is willing and able to buy four chocolate bars in a week, and so on.

'Willing' means the consumer wants to buy the good; 'able' means that the consumer can afford to buy it. (You may want to buy a Ferrari, but can you afford it? If not, your desire to buy one will not show up as demand for Ferraris.)

Ceteris paribus means that all things other than price that can affect how much the consumer is willing and able to buy are assumed to be constant and unchanging (see Chapter 1, page 10, and 'Quantitative techniques' chapter on the CD-ROM, page 11). In fact, the consumer's demand is affected not only by price, but also by many other things, like income, tastes and prices of related goods. For the moment, we put all those other things aside and concentrate only on the relationship between the quantity of a good the consumer is willing and able to buy, and its price. Later we will also consider the effects of other influences on the consumer's demand.

The information contained in the demand schedule can be plotted as a graph, shown in Figure 2.1(a). The price of chocolate bars is plotted on the vertical axis and quantity of chocolate bars on the horizontal axis. The curve in Figure 2.1(a) is a **demand curve**. Note that even though this is a straight line, it is referred to as a 'curve'.

The demand schedule and demand curve do not tell us anything about how many chocolate bars the consumer will actually buy and what price the consumer will pay. This information will be given to us later through the interaction of demand with supply. The demand information only tells us how many chocolate bars the consumer would be prepared to buy if the price were $5, or $4, and so on.

The law of demand

♦ Explain the negative causal relationship between price and quantity demanded.

The demand curve plotted in Figure 2.1(a) illustrates a very important relationship: as the price of a good falls, the quantity of the good demanded increases. When two variables change in opposite directions, so that as one falls, the other increases, they are said to have a 'negative' (or 'indirect') relationship. This relationship is a 'causal' one, because changes in price *cause* changes in quantity demanded (for more information on causal relationships, see 'Quantitative techniques' chapter on the CD-ROM, page 11). The negative causal relationship between price and quantity demanded is known as the law of demand.

According to the **law of demand**, there is a **negative causal relationship** between the price of a good and its quantity demanded over a particular time period, *ceteris paribus:* as the price of the good increases, quantity demanded falls; as the price falls, quantity demanded increases, *ceteris paribus*.

The law of demand is most likely to be consistent with your experience. The higher the price of a good, the less of it you are probably willing and able to buy; as

the price falls, the good becomes more affordable, and you are likely to want and be able to buy more of it.

Why the demand curve slopes downward: marginal utility theory or marginal benefits

What is the economic reasoning behind the relationship in the law of demand? Consumers buy goods and services because these provide them with some benefit, or satisfaction, also known as utility. The greater the quantity of a good consumed, the greater the benefit derived. However, the extra benefit provided by each additional unit increases by smaller and smaller amounts. Imagine you buy a soft drink, which provides you with a certain amount of benefit. You are still thirsty, so you buy a second soft drink. Whereas you will enjoy this, you will most likely enjoy it less than you had enjoyed the first; the second soft drink provides you with less benefit than the first. If you buy a third, you will get even less benefit than from the second, and so on with each additional soft drink. The extra benefit that you get from each additional unit of something you buy is called the **marginal benefit** or *marginal utility* (marginal means extra or additional).

Since each successive unit of the good you consume produces less and less benefit, you will be willing to buy each extra unit only if it has a lower and lower price. It follows then that:

An explanation for the shape of the demand curve can be found in the principle of decreasing marginal benefit: since marginal benefit falls as quantity consumed increases, the consumer will be induced to buy each extra unit only if its price falls.

Therefore the demand curve in Figure 2.1(a) can also be called a marginal benefit (*MB*) curve, shown in Figure 2.1(b).

Note that different consumers have different preferences (likes and dislikes), and therefore derive different marginal benefits from consumption of a good. This is reflected in different demands (or demand curves) for different consumers.

From individual demand to market demand

♦ Describe the relationship between an individual consumer's demand and market demand.

So far we have considered the demand for a good of one individual consumer. *Market demand* shows the total quantities in the market for the good consumers are willing and able to buy at different prices (during

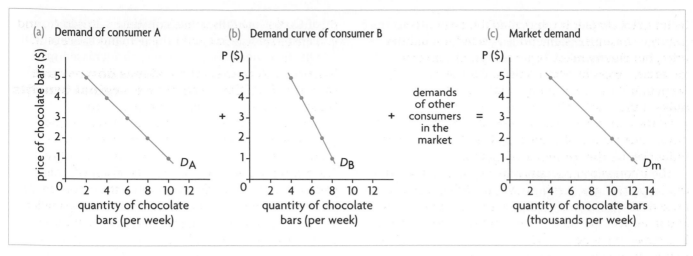

Figure 2.2 Market demand as the sum of individual demands

a particular period of time, all other things equal). Market demand is the sum of all individual demands for that good. Figure 2.2 shows how the quantity demanded by consumer A is added to the quantity demanded by consumer B, and so on until all the quantities demanded by all consumers of chocolate bars are added up. (Note that consumer A has a different demand for chocolate bars than consumer B, indicating different preferences, and therefore different marginal benefits.) For example, at the price of $4, we add the 4 bars demanded by consumer A to the 5 bars demanded by consumer B, and so on to all the quantities demanded by other consumers, to arrive at the sum of 6000 chocolate bars per week. This sum is a point on the market demand curve D_m. When we add individual demands in this way for each of the possible prices, we derive the entire market demand curve D_m, showing the total demand in the chocolate bar market.

> **Market demand** is the sum of all individual demands for a good. The market demand curve illustrates the law of demand, shown by the negative relationship between price and quantity demanded. The market demand curve is also the sum of consumers' marginal benefits.

Non-price determinants of demand and shifts of the demand curve

The non-price determinants

♦ Explain how factors including changes in income (in the cases of normal and inferior goods), preferences, prices of related goods (in the cases of substitutes and complements) and demographic changes may change demand.

The **non-price determinants of demand** are the variables other than price that can influence demand. They are the variables assumed to be unchanging by use of the *ceteris paribus* assumption when the relationship between price and quantity demanded was being examined (see 'Quantitative techniques' chapter on the CD-ROM, page 11, for a full explanation). We will now see what happens to the demand curve when these variables change.

Changes in the determinants of demand cause shifts in the demand curve: the entire demand curve moves to the right or to the left. In Figure 2.3, note that the vertical axis is labelled '*P*', standing for price, and the horizontal axis is labelled '*Q*', standing for quantity. (This is the standard labelling practice we will be following from now on.) Suppose that the original demand curve is given by D_1. If price is P_1, then the demand curve D_1 indicates that quantity Q_1

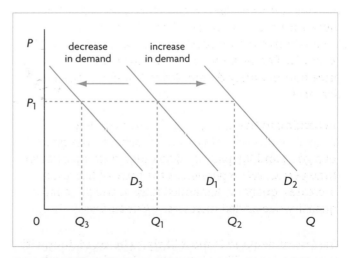

Figure 2.3 Shifts in the demand curve

will be demanded. If the demand curve shifts to the right, to D_2, at the same price P_1 a larger quantity, Q_2, will be demanded. If, on the other hand, the demand curve shifts to the left, from D_1 to D_3, then a smaller quantity, Q_3, will be demanded at the same price P_1.

> A rightward shift of the demand curve indicates that more is demanded for a given price; a leftward shift of the demand curve indicates that less is demanded for a given price. A rightward shift of the curve is called an *increase in demand*; a leftward shift is called a *decrease in demand*.

The non-price determinants of market demand include:

- **Income in the case of normal goods.** A good is a **normal good** when demand for it increases in response to an increase in consumer income (demand for the good varies directly with income). Most goods are normal goods. Therefore, an increase in income leads to a rightward shift in the demand curve, and a decrease in income leads to a leftward shift.

- **Income in the case of inferior goods.** While most goods are normal, there are some goods where the demand falls as consumer income increases; the good is then an **inferior good** (the demand for the good varies inversely with income). Examples of inferior goods are second-hand clothes, used cars and bus tickets. As income increases, consumers switch to more expensive alternatives (new clothes, new cars and cars or aeroplanes rather than travelling by bus), and so the demand for the inferior goods falls. Thus an increase in income leads to a leftward shift in the demand curve and a decrease in income produces a rightward shift.

- **Preferences and tastes.** If preferences and tastes change in favour of a product (the good becomes more popular), demand increases and the demand curve shifts to the right; if tastes change against the product (it becomes less popular), demand decreases and the demand curve shifts to the left.

- **Prices of substitute goods.** Two goods are **substitutes (substitute goods)** if they satisfy a similar need. An example of substitute goods is Coca-Cola® and Pepsi®. A fall in the price of one (say, Coca-Cola) results in a fall in the demand for the other (Pepsi). The reason is that as the price

of Coca-Cola falls, some consumers switch from Pepsi to Coca-Cola, and the demand for Pepsi falls. On the other hand, if there is an increase in the price of Coca-Cola, this will result in an increase in the demand for Pepsi as some consumers switch from Coca-Cola to Pepsi. Therefore, for any two substitute goods X and Y, a decrease in the price of X produces a leftward shift in the demand for Y, while an increase in the price of X produces a rightward shift in the demand for Y. In brief, in the case of substitute goods, the price of X and demand for Y change in the same direction (they both increase or they both decrease). Other examples of substitute goods are oranges and apples, Cadbury's and Nestlé chocolate, and milk and yoghurt.

- **Prices of complementary goods.** Two goods are **complements (complementary goods)** if they tend to be used together. An example of complementary goods is DVDs and DVD players. In this case, a fall in the price of one (say, DVD players) leads to an increase in the demand for the other (DVDs). This is because the fall in the price of DVD players results in a bigger quantity of DVD players being purchased, and the demand for DVDs increases. Therefore, for any two complementary goods X and Y, a fall in the price of X leads to a rightward shift in the demand for Y, and an increase in the price of X leads to a leftward shift in the demand for Y. In the case of complementary goods, the price of X and the demand for Y change in opposite directions (as one increases, the other decreases). More examples of complementary goods are computers and computer software, tennis shoes and tennis rackets, and table-tennis balls and table-tennis rackets. Note that most goods are not related to each other; these are called independent goods. For example, pencils and apples, cars and ice cream, telephones and books are unrelated to one another, and the change in the price of one will have little or no effect on the demand for the other.

- **Demographic (population) changes, i.e. changes in the number of buyers.** If there is an increase in the number of buyers (demanders), demand increases and therefore the market demand curve shifts to the right; if the number of buyers decreases, demand decreases and the curve shifts to the left. This follows simply from the fact that market demand is the sum of all individual demands.

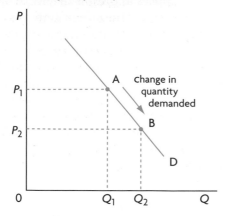

(a) A movement along the demand curve, caused by a change in price, is called a 'change in quantity demanded'

(b) A shift of a demand curve, caused by a change in a determinant of demand, is called a 'change in demand'

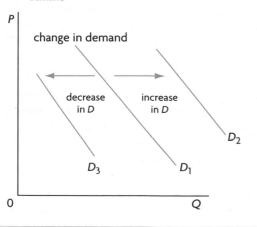

Figure 2.4 Movements along and shifts of the demand curve

Movements along a demand curve and shifts of the demand curve

+ Distinguish between movements along the demand curve and shifts of the demand curve.
+ Draw diagrams to show the difference between movements along the demand curve and shifts of the demand curve.

It is important to distinguish between movements on or along a demand curve, and shifts of a demand curve. Whenever the price of a good changes, *ceteris paribus*, it leads to a movement along the demand curve. In Figure 2.4(a), if the price falls from P_1 to P_2, the quantity of the good demanded increases from Q_1 to Q_2. A movement along the demand curve

from A to B has occurred; this is referred to as an *increase in quantity demanded*. An increase in price gives rise to a *decrease in quantity demanded*.

By contrast, any change in a non-price determinant of demand results in a shift in the entire demand curve, as shown in Figure 2.4(b); this is called a *change in demand*. For example, if there is an increase in the number of buyers, the demand curve shifts rightward from D_1 to D_2; this is called an *increase in demand*, shown in Figure 2.4(b). A decrease in the number of buyers causes a leftward shift of the demand curve from D_1 to D_3; this is called a *decrease in demand*. To summarise:

> Any change in price produces a *change in quantity demanded*, shown as a movement on the demand curve. Any change in a non-price determinant of demand leads to *a change in demand*, represented by a shift of the entire demand curve.

1 **(a)** Define 'demand'. **(b)** What is the law of demand? **(c)** Explain whether the law of demand shows a negative or positive relationship. **(d)** Show the law of demand in a diagram. **(e)** What is the relationship between individual demand and market demand? **(f)** Distinguish between a 'change in demand' and a 'change in quantity demanded' and explain the cause or causes of each. **(g)** How would you show the difference between a movement along the demand curve and a shift of the demand curve in a diagram? **(h)** What are the non-price determinants of demand?

2 Using diagrams, show the impact of each of the following on the demand curve for product A.

   (a) The number of consumers in the market for product A increases.

   (b) Consumer income increases and product A is an inferior good.

   (c) Consumer income decreases and product A is a normal good.

   (d) A news report claims that use of product A has harmful effects on health.

   (e) The price of substitute good B falls.

   (f) The price of complementary good B increases.

2.3 Supply

Understanding the law of supply and the supply curve

Supply is concerned with the behaviour of sellers, which include firms in the product markets and households in resource markets. As we are focusing on product markets, we will consider the behaviour of firms as sellers (though the same general principles also apply to sellers of factors of production in resource markets).

Individual supply

- ♦ Explain that a supply curve represents the relationship between the price and the quantity supplied of a product, *ceteris paribus*.
- ♦ Draw a supply curve.

Firms produce goods and services, and they supply them to product markets for sale. As sellers, therefore, they are suppliers of goods and services.

> The **supply** of an individual firm indicates the various quantities of a good (or service) a firm is *willing and able* to produce and supply to the market for sale at different possible prices, during a particular time period, *ceteris paribus*.

A firm's supply of a good can be presented as a supply schedule, or a table showing the various quantities of a good the firm is willing and able to produce and supply at various prices. Table 2.2 shows a firm's supply schedule for chocolate bars. The same information appears as a graph in Figure 2.5, where price is plotted on the vertical axis and quantity on the horizontal axis. The line appearing in the diagram is the **supply curve** of the firm. If the price is $4, the firm supplies 500 chocolate bars in the course of a week; if price were $3, then the firm would supply 400 chocolate bars, and so on.

As in the case of demand, where price is only one thing that determines how much is demanded, so in the case of supply, price is only one thing that influences how much the firm supplies to the market; hence the *ceteris paribus* assumption. For the moment, we will ignore other possible influences on supply and focus only on the relationship between price and quantity.

The supply schedule and the supply curve do not tell us anything about how many chocolate bars the firm will actually supply to the market nor what price the firm will receive. The supply information tells us only how many chocolate bars the firm would be prepared to produce and sell if the price were $5, or $4, and so on.

The law of supply

- ♦ Explain the positive causal relationship between price and quantity supplied.

The supply curve in Figure 2.5 illustrates an important relationship: as price increases, quantity supplied also increases. When two variables change in the same direction (as one increases, the other also increases), they are said to have a 'positive' (or 'direct') relationship. This relationship is a 'causal' one, because changes in price *cause* changes in quantity supplied (see 'Quantitative techniques' chapter on the CD-ROM, pages 10 and 12). The positive causal relationship between the two variables, price and quantity supplied, is summarised in the law of supply.

> According to the **law of supply**, there is a **positive causal relationship** between the quantity of a good supplied over a particular time period and its price, *ceteris paribus*: as the price of the good increases, the quantity of the good supplied also increases; as the price falls, the quantity supplied also falls, *ceteris paribus*.

Price of chocolate bars ($)	Quantity of chocolate bars supplied (per week)
5	600
4	500
3	400
2	300
1	200

Table 2.2   Supply schedule for a firm

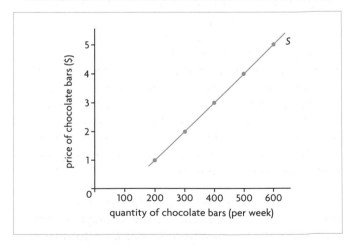

Figure 2.5   Supply curve for a firm

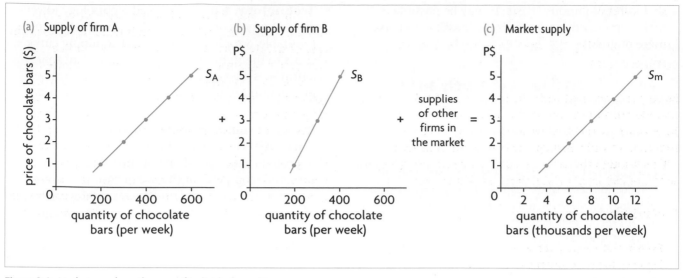

Figure 2.6 Market supply as the sum of individual supplies

Why the supply curve slopes upward

What is the economic reasoning behind the law of supply? Higher prices generally mean that the firm's profits increase, and so the firm faces an incentive to produce more output. Lower prices mean lower profitability, and the incentive facing the firm is to produce less. Therefore, there results a positive relationship between price and quantity supplied: the higher the price, the greater the quantity supplied.

From individual supply to market supply

♦ Describe the relationship between an individual producer's supply and market supply.

Market supply indicates the total quantities of a good that firms are willing and able to supply in the market at different possible prices, and is given by the sum of all individual supplies of that good. Figure 2.6 provides an example where at each price, the quantity supplied by firm A is added to the quantity supplied by firm B, and so on, until all the quantities supplied by all firms producing chocolate bars are added up. For example, at the price of $3, firm A supplies 400 bars per week and firm B supplies 300 bars. If we add these quantities together with all the quantities supplied by other firms, we obtain 8000 bars per week, which is a point on the market supply curve, S_m, corresponding to the price of $3. When the firms' supplies are added up this way for each possible price, we derive the market supply curve, S_m.

> **Market supply** is the sum of all individual firms' supplies for a good. The market supply curve illustrates the law of supply, shown by a positive relationship between price and quantity supplied.

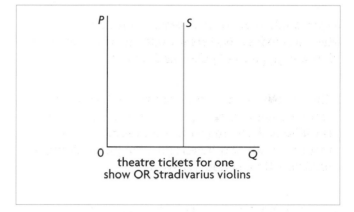

Figure 2.7 The vertical supply curve

The vertical supply curve

Under certain special circumstances, the supply curve is vertical at some particular fixed quantity, as in Figure 2.7. A vertical supply curve tells us that even as price increases, the quantity supplied cannot increase; it remains constant. The quantity supplied is independent of price. There are two reasons why this may occur:

• There is a fixed quantity of the good supplied because there is no time to produce more of it. For example, there is a fixed quantity of theatre tickets in a theatre, because there is a fixed number of seats. No matter how high the price, it is not possible to increase the number of seats in a short period of time.

• There is a fixed quantity of the good because there is no possibility of ever producing more of it. This is the case with original antiques (for example, Stradivarius violins) and original paintings and sculptures of famous artists. It may be possible to make reproductions, but it is not possible to make more originals.

Non-price determinants of supply and shifts of the supply curve

The non-price determinants

> ◆ Explain how factors including changes in costs of factors of production (land, labour, capital and entrepreneurship), technology, prices of related goods (joint/competitive supply), expectations, indirect taxes and subsidies and the number of firms in the market can change supply.

We now turn to the **non-price determinants of supply**, or the factors other than price that can influence supply. Changes in the determinants of supply cause shifts in the supply curve. A rightward shift means that for a given price, supply increases and more is supplied; a leftward shift means that for a given price, supply decreases and less is supplied. As Figure 2.8(b) shows, when supply is S_1, quantity Q_1 will be supplied at price P_1. If there is an increase in supply to S_2, at the same price P_1, then Q_2 quantity is supplied. If supply falls to S_3, then Q_3 quantity is supplied at the same price P_1.

> A rightward shift of the supply curve indicates that more is supplied for a given price; a leftward shift of the supply curve indicates that less is supplied for a given price. A rightward shift of the curve is called an *increase in supply*; a leftward shift is called a *decrease in supply*.

The non-price determinants of market supply include the following:

- **Costs of factors of production (factor or resource prices).** The firm buys various factors of production (land, labour, capital entrepreneurship) that it uses to produce its product. Prices of factors of production (such as wages, which are the price of labour) are important in determining the firm's costs of production. If a factor price rises, production costs increase, production becomes less profitable and the firm produces less; the supply curve shifts to the left. If a factor price falls, costs of production fall, production becomes more profitable and the firm produces more; the supply curve shifts to the right.

- **Technology.** A new improved technology lowers costs of production, thus making production more profitable. Supply increases and the supply curve shifts to the right. In the (less likely) event that a firm uses a less productive technology, costs of production increase and the supply curve shifts leftward.

- **Prices of related goods: competitive supply.** **Competitive supply** of two or more products refers to production of one or the other by a firm; the goods compete for the use of the same resources, and producing more of one means producing less of the other. For example, a farmer, who can grow wheat or corn, chooses to grow wheat. If the price of corn increases, the farmer may switch to corn production as this is now more profitable, resulting in a fall in wheat supply and a leftward shift of the supply curve. A fall in the price of corn results in

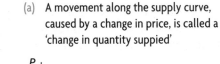

(a) A movement along the supply curve, caused by a change in price, is called a 'change in quantity supplied'

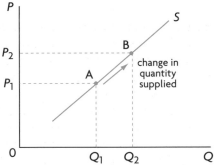

(b) A shift of the supply curve, caused by a change in a determinant of supply, is called a 'change in supply'

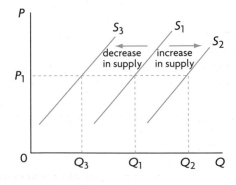

Figure 2.8 Movements along and shifts of the supply curve

an increase in wheat supply and a rightward shift of the supply curve.

- **Prices of related goods: joint supply.** *Joint supply* of two or more products refers to production of goods that are derived from a single product, so that it is not possible to produce more of one without producing more of the other. For example, butter and skimmed milk are both produced from whole milk; petrol (gasoline), diesel oil and heating oil are all produced from crude oil. This means that an increase in the price of one leads to an increase in its quantity supplied and also to an increase in supply of the other joint product(s).[1]

- **Producer (firm) expectations.** If firms expect the price of their product to rise, they may withhold some of their current supply from the market (not offer it for sale), with the expectation that they will be able to sell it at the higher price in the future; in this case, a fall in supply in the present results, and hence a leftward shift in the supply curve. If the expectation is that the price of their product will fall, they increase their supply in the present to take advantage of the current higher price, and hence there is a rightward shift in the supply curve.

- **Taxes (indirect taxes or taxes on profits).** Firms treat taxes as if they were costs of production. Therefore, the imposition of a new tax or the increase of an existing tax represents an increase in production costs, so supply will fall and the supply curve shifts to the left. The elimination of a tax or a decrease in an existing tax represents a fall in production costs; supply increases and the supply curve shifts to the right. We will study the effects of taxes in more detail in Chapter 4.

- **Subsidies.** A *subsidy* is a payment made to the firm by the government, and so has the opposite effect of a tax. (Subsidies may be given in order to increase the incomes of producers or to encourage an increase in the production of the good produced.) The introduction of a subsidy or an increase in an existing subsidy is equivalent to a fall in production costs, and gives rise to a rightward shift in the supply curve, while the elimination of a subsidy or a decrease in a subsidy leads to a leftward shift in the supply curve. We

will study the effects of subsidies in more detail in Chapter 4.

- **The number of firms.** An increase in the number of firms producing the good increases supply and gives rise to a rightward shift in the supply curve; a decrease in the number of firms decreases supply and produces a leftward shift. This follows from the fact that market supply is the sum of all individual supplies.

- **'Shocks', or sudden unpredictable events.** Sudden, unpredictable events, called 'shocks', can affect supply, such as weather conditions in the case of agricultural products, war, or natural/man-made catastrophes. For example, the Louisiana oil spill in 2010 resulted in a decrease in the supply of locally produced seafood.

Movement along a supply curve and shift of the supply curve

- Distinguish between movements along the supply curve and shifts of the supply curve.
- Construct diagrams to show the difference between movements along the supply curve and shifts of the supply curve.

Just as in the case of the demand curve, so in the case of the supply curve we distinguish between movements along the curve and shifts of the entire curve. Movements along a supply curve can occur only as a result of changes in price. In Figure 2.8(a), as price increases from P_1 to P_2, quantity supplied increases from Q_1 to Q_2. There has been a movement along the supply curve from A to B. This is called a *change in quantity supplied*. If there is a change in a non-price determinant of supply, supply will increase or decrease, and the entire curve will shift to the right or to the left, as in Figure 2.8(b). This is called a *change in supply*.

Any change in price produces a *change in quantity supplied*, shown as a movement on the supply curve. Any change in a determinant of supply (other than price) produces a *change in supply*, represented by a shift of the whole supply curve.

---

[1] This requires that the joint products are produced in more or less fixed proportions, so that it is not possible to vary the supplies of each of the joint products individually.

1 (a) Define 'supply'. (b) What is the law of supply?
   (c) Explain whether the law of supply shows
   a positive or negative relationship. (d) Show
   the law of supply in a diagram. (e) What is the
   relationship between individual supply and
   market supply? (f) Distinguish between a 'change
   in supply' and a 'change in quantity supplied'
   and explain the cause or causes of each. (g)
   How would you show the difference between a
   movement along the supply curve and a shift of
   the supply curve in a diagram? (h) What are the
   non-price determinants of supply?

2 Give some examples of goods with a vertical
   supply curve.

3 Using diagrams, show the impact of each of the
   following on the supply curve of product A.

   (a) The number of firms in the industry
       producing product A decreases.

   (b) The price of oil, a key input in the
       production of product A, increases.

   (c) Firms expect that the price of product A will
       fall in the future.

   (d) The government grants a subsidy on each
       unit of A produced.

   (e) The price of product B falls, and B is in
       competitive supply with A.

   (f) The price of product B increases, and B is in
       joint supply with A.

   (g) A new technology is adopted by firms in the
       industry producing A.

2.4 Market equilibrium: demand and supply

The market demand and market supply for chocolate
bars that we have considered separately above show the
quantities consumers and firms are *willing and able* to
buy and sell at each price, not how much they actually
buy and sell. We will now put market demand and
market supply together to find out how these interact to
determine what happens in the market for chocolate bars.

Market equilibrium

♦ Explain, using diagrams, how demand and supply interact
  to produce market equilibrium.

Excess demand (shortages) and excess supply (surpluses)

Figure 2.9 presents the same market demand and
supply curves that appeared in Figures 2.2(c) and
2.6(c). The same information appears as a demand
schedule and a supply schedule in Table 2.3.

In both Table 2.3 and Figure 2.9 we see that when
the price of chocolate bars is $3, quantity demanded is
exactly equal to quantity supplied, at 8000 chocolate
bars. Note that there is only one price where this can
occur. At a higher price, say $4, quantity supplied
(10 000 bars) is greater than quantity demanded
(6000 bars). There is *excess supply*, or a *surplus* of
4000 bars (10 000 – 6000). At the even higher price of
$5, there is a larger excess supply (surplus) of 8000 bars.

Suppose the price in this market is initially $5. At this
price, chocolate producers would be willing and able
to produce 12 000 bars, but consumers would only be
willing and able to buy 4000 bars. What will happen?
With unsold output of 8000 bars, producers will
lower their price to encourage consumers to buy more
chocolate. As the price falls, quantity supplied becomes
smaller and quantity demanded becomes bigger. As
long as there is a surplus, there will be a downward
pressure on the price. The price will keep falling until it

Price of chocolate bars ($)	Quantity of chocolate bars demanded (per week)	Quantity of chocolate bars supplied (per week)
5	4 000	12 000
4	6 000	10 000
3	8 000	8 000
2	10 000	6 000
1	12 000	4 000

Table 2.3   Market demand and supply schedules for chocolate bars

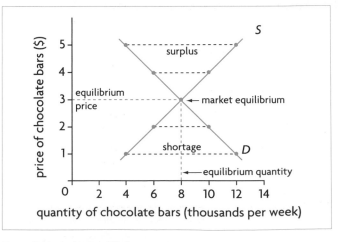

Figure 2.9   Market equilibrium

reaches the point where quantity demanded is equal to quantity supplied, and the surplus is eliminated.

At a lower price than $3, say $2, quantity demanded (10000 bars) is larger than quantity supplied (6000 bars). There is now *excess demand* or a *shortage* of 4000 bars (10000–6000). If price were even lower, at $1, the shortage would be larger, at 8000 bars. At a price of $1, producers would be willing and able to supply only 4000 bars, whereas consumers would be willing and able to buy 12000 bars. Producers will notice that the chocolate bars are quickly sold out, and so begin to raise the price. As they do so, quantity demanded begins to fall and quantity supplied begins to rise. The shortage in the chocolate market exerts an upward pressure on price. The price will keep increasing until the shortage is eliminated; this will happen when quantity supplied is exactly equal to quantity demanded.

If quantity demanded of a good is smaller than quantity supplied, the difference between the two is called a **surplus**, where there is **excess supply**; if quantity demanded of a good is larger than quantity supplied, the difference is called a **shortage**, where there is **excess demand**. The existence of a surplus or a shortage in a free market will cause the price to change so that the quantity demanded will be made equal to quantity supplied. In the event of a shortage, price will rise; in the event of a surplus, price will fall.

Market equilibrium

Equilibrium is defined as a state of balance between different forces, such that there is no tendency to change. This is an important concept in economics that we will encounter repeatedly. When quantity demanded is equal to quantity supplied, there is **market equilibrium**; the forces of supply and demand are in balance, and there is no tendency for the price to change. Market equilibrium is determined

at the point where the demand curve intersects the supply curve. The price in market equilibrium is the **equilibrium price**, and the quantity is the **equilibrium quantity**. At the equilibrium price, the quantity consumers are willing and able to buy is exactly equal to the quantity firms are willing and able to sell. This price is also known as the *market-clearing price*, or simply *market price*. In the market for chocolate bars in Figure 2.9, the equilibrium price is $3 per chocolate bar, and the equilibrium quantity is 8000 bars. At any price other than the equilibrium price, there is *market disequilibrium*. In a free market, a market disequilibrium cannot last, as demand and supply force the price to change until it reaches its equilibrium level.

When a market is in equilibrium, quantity demanded equals quantity supplied, and there is no tendency for the price to change. In a market disequilibrium, there is excess demand (shortage) or excess supply (surplus), and the forces of demand and supply cause the price to change until the market reaches equilibrium.

Changes in market equilibrium

♦ Analyse, using diagrams and with reference to excess demand or excess supply, how changes in the determinants of demand and/or supply result in a new market equilibrium.

Once a price reaches its equilibrium level, consumers and firms are satisfied and will not engage in any action to make it change. However, if there is a change in any of the non-price determinants of demand or supply, a shift in the curves results, and the market will adjust to a new equilibrium.

Changes in demand (demand curve shifts)

In Figure 2.10(a) D_1 intersects S at point a, resulting in equilibrium price and quantity P_1 and Q_1. Consider

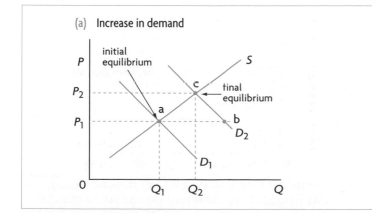
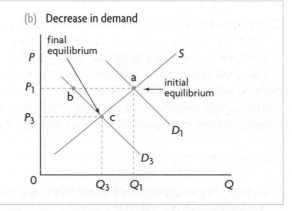

Figure 2.10 Changes in demand and the new equilibrium price and quantity

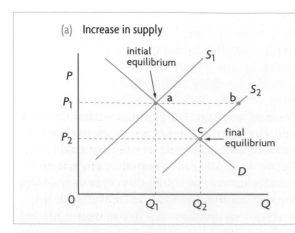

(a) Increase in supply

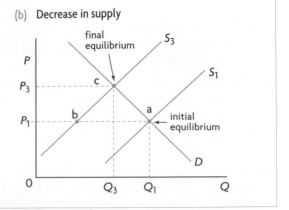

(b) Decrease in supply

Figure 2.11 Changes in supply and the new equilibrium price and quantity

a change in a determinant of demand that causes the demand curve to shift to the right from D_1 to D_2 (for example, an increase in consumer income in the case of a normal good). Given D_2, at the initial price, P_1, there is a movement to point b, which results in excess demand equal to the horizontal distance between points a and b. Point b represents a disequilibrium, where quantity demanded is larger than quantity supplied, thus exerting an upward pressure on price. The price therefore begins to increase, causing a movement up D_2 to point c, where excess demand is eliminated and a new equilibrium is reached. At c, there is a higher equilibrium price, P_2, and greater equilibrium quantity, Q_2, given by the intersection of D_2 with S.

A decrease in demand, shown in Figure 2.10(b), leads to a leftward shift in the demand curve from D_1 to D_3 (for example, due to a decrease in the number of consumers). Given D_3, at price P_1, there is a move from the initial equilibrium (point a) to point b, where quantity demanded is less than quantity supplied, and therefore a disequilibrium where there is excess supply equal to the horizontal difference between a and b. This exerts a downward pressure on price, which falls, causing a movement down D_3 to point c, where excess supply is eliminated, and a new equilibrium is reached. At c, there is a lower equilibrium price, P_3, and a lower equilibrium quantity, Q_3, given by the intersection of D_3 with S.

Changes in supply (supply curve shifts)

We now consider supply curve shifts that can arise from changes in the determinants of supply. In Figure 2.11(a), the initial equilibrium is at point a where D intersects S_1, and where equilibrium price and quantity are P_1 and Q_1. An increase in supply (say, due to an improvement in technology) shifts the supply curve to S_2. With S_2 and initial price P_1, there is a move from point a to b, where there is disequilibrium due to excess supply (by the amount equal to the horizontal distance between a and b). Therefore, price begins to

fall, and there results a movement down S_2 to point c where a new equilibrium is reached. At c, excess supply has been eliminated, and there is a lower equilibrium price, P_2, but a higher equilibrium quantity, Q_2.

A decrease in supply is shown in Figure 2.11(b) (say, due to a fall in the number of firms). With the new supply curve S_3, at the initial price P_1, there has been a move from initial equilibrium a to disequilibrium point b, where there is excess demand (equal to the distance between a and b). This causes an upward pressure on price, which begins to increase, causing a move up S_3 until a final equilibrium is reached at point c, where the excess demand has been eliminated, and there is a higher equilibrium price P_3 and lower quantity Q_3.

Test your understanding 2.4

1 In Figure 2.9, state whether there is excess supply (a surplus) or excess demand (a shortage), and how large this is if price per chocolate bar is:
(a) $5, (b) $4, (c) $3, (d) $2, and (e) $1.

2 Use a demand and supply diagram to: (a) show equilibrium price and quantity, (b) show possible disequilibrium prices and quantities, (c) relate disequilibrium prices to excess demand (shortages) and excess supply (surpluses), (d) explain the meaning of 'market equilibrium', and (e) explain the roles of demand and supply in achieving market equilibrium.

3 Use supply and demand diagrams to illustrate the following events.

(a) Freezing weather destroys the orange crop and the price of oranges rises.

(b) The mass media report on the fat content of cheese and the price of cheese falls.

(c) A new technology of production for computers is developed and the price of computers falls.

(d) The price of milk increases and the price of ice cream increases (remember that milk is an input in ice cream production).

(e) The mass media report on outbreaks of bird flu and the price of chicken falls.

4 Assuming a competitive market, use demand and supply diagrams to show in each of the following cases how the change in demand or supply for product A creates a disequilibrium consisting of excess demand or excess supply, and how the change in price eliminates the disequilibrium.

(a) Consumer income increases (A is a normal good).

(b) Consumer income falls (A is an inferior good).

(c) There is an increase in labour costs.

(d) The price of substitute good B falls.

(e) The number of firms in the industry producing product A increases.

(f) A successful advertising campaign emphasises the health benefits of product A.

Real world focus

Salmonella outbreak and the demand for eggs

A salmonella outbreak in the United States was linked to several illnesses, and resulted in the recall (withdrawal from the market) of millions of eggs. The recall led to an increase in egg prices of about 40%, resulting in a substantial drop in egg sales. At the same time, organic stores saw increases in their sales of organic eggs, as consumers chose these as a safer alternative.

Source: Adapted from 'Consumers flock to organic eggs in light of recall' in *WholeFoods Magazine*, October 2010.

Applying your skills

Using diagrams in each case, explain:

1 the effect of the egg recall on egg prices and sales

2 the effect on demand and sales of organic eggs.

2.5 Linear demand and supply functions and market equilibrium (higher level topic)

Linear demand and supply functions (equations) and market equilibrium, and their corresponding graphs are presented in 'Quantitative techniques' chapter on the CD-ROM, page 17, which reviews quantitative techniques for this course. Even if you are very strong in mathematics, you may find it helpful to read this material as it contains information on the peculiarity of demand and supply functions that reverse the axes showing the dependent and independent variables.

Linear demand functions (equations), schedules and graphs

Explaining the demand function (equation)

♦ Explain a demand function (equation) of the form $Q_d = a - bP$

The demand function appears as an equation taking the form:

$$Q_d = a - bP$$

where
Q_d = quantity demanded, and is the dependent variable (since it depends on price)
P = price, which is the independent variable
a = the Q-intercept (or the horizontal intercept)
$-b$ = the slope, calculated as $\Delta Q_d / \Delta P$.

Since the slope has a negative sign, we know that the relation between the dependent and independent variables is negative (or indirect). This ties in with what we know about the law of demand.

Once the parameters a and b are given specific values, the equation $Q_d = a - bP$ is simply a summary statement of the information that is contained in a schedule or in a graph of a demand relationship.

Plotting the demand curve from a demand function (equation)

♦ Plot a demand curve from a linear function (e.g. $Q_d = 60 - 5P$).

If we are given an equation specifying numerical values for a and b, we can make a schedule of the relationship described by the equation, and we can then use this information to plot (make a graph) of the curve.

Price of chocolate bars ($)	Quantity of chocolate bars demanded (thousands per week)
5	4
4	6
3	8
2	10
1	12
0	14

Table 2.4 Demand schedule for chocolate bars

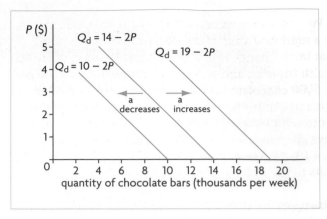

Figure 2.12 Shifts of the demand curve (changes in a in the function $Q_d = a - bP$)

Suppose we are given the demand function for chocolate bars:

$$Q_d = 14 - 2P$$

where

Q_d = quantity of chocolate bars demanded per week, in thousands (the dependent variable)

P = price of chocolate bars, in $ (the independent variable)

14 = the Q-intercept (horizontal intercept)

−2 = slope (given by $\Delta Q_d / \Delta P$).

Now simply by setting P equal to different values, we solve in each case for Q_d, thus obtaining different price–quantity combinations that make up the demand schedule. We can begin with the Q-intercept, which is the simplest to calculate: when $P = 0$, $Q_d = 14$ (thousand); this gives us the first point. We can then assume $P = 1$, in which case $Q_d = 14 - 2(1) = 12$ (thousand); this gives us a second point. Continuing with $P = 2$, $P = 3$, etc., we get a series of price–quantity combinations, shown in Table 2.4.

We can then use this information to plot the demand curve, shown in Figure 2.12. Note that this is the same demand curve that appears in Figure 2.2(c) (page 23). Care must be taken to label the axes correctly, with price in $ and quantity in thousands of chocolate bars. Using the information of the demand schedule, we can plot a series of points on the demand curve: (14,0), (12,1), (10,2), (8,3), (6,4), etc. (Remember that each point on a graph can be expressed as (h,v), where h is the value of the variable measured on the horizontal axis and v the value of the variable on the vertical axis.)

Note that since the demand curve is *linear*, we only need two points to be able to draw it. Yet it may be a good idea in practice to find more points as a check to make sure you have made no errors in your calculations; if you have three points and you cannot draw a straight line through them, you will need to recalculate your points.

Changes in the parameter a and shifts of the demand curve

* Outline why, if the 'a' term changes, there will be a shift of the demand curve.

As explained in 'Quantitative techniques' chapter on the CD-ROM, page 24, the parameter a represents the variables that are held constant under the *ceteris paribus* assumption. In this chapter, we have seen that these are all the non-price determinants of demand, which we assume to be unchanging when plotting the demand curve. Therefore, if there is a change in any determinant, it will appear as a change in the value of a, and will show up in the graph as a parallel shift of the demand curve.

Suppose there is a fall in the price of ice cream (a substitute good), which causes a decrease in the demand for chocolate bars by 4000 chocolate bars per week for any price. We already know from our earlier discussion (page 24) that this will cause a leftward shift in the demand curve. The size of this leftward shift will be 4000 chocolate bars. We can plot this simply by drawing a parallel demand curve that is 4 (thousand) units to the left of the initial one.

We now want to find the new demand function (equation) corresponding to the new demand curve. To do this we need to find the new value of the parameter a. We find this simply by taking the initial value of a = 14 (thousand) and subtracting from that the change in demand of 4 (thousand), thus obtaining:

$$14 - 4 = 10 = \text{the new value of a}$$

Therefore, the new demand function is:

$$Q_d = 10 - 2P$$

which can be seen in Figure 2.12. In the graph, note that a = 10 is the Q-intercept of the new demand curve.

We can also consider an increase in demand, shown by a rightward shift of the demand curve. Suppose that tastes change in favour of chocolate because of its health benefits, and so for any price, demand increases by 5000 chocolate bars per week, relative to the initial demand curve where a = 14. The parameter a, or the Q-intercept now increases by 5 (thousand), so that we have the new a = 14 + 5 = 19, and the new equation is $Q_d = 19 - 2P$. The demand curve shifts by 5 (thousand) units to the right, as shown in Figure 2.12.

Changes in parameter –b and the steepness of the demand curve

♦ Identify the slope of the demand curve as the slope of the demand function $Q_d = a - bP$, that is –b (the coefficient of P).
♦ Outline how a change in 'b' affects the steepness of the demand curve.

The **slope** is defined as the change in the dependent variable divided by the change in the independent variable between two points (see 'Quantitative techniques' chapter on the CD-ROM, pages 18 and 20–21). In the demand function Qd = a – bP, the slope is the coefficient of P and is therefore –b. In our demand function $Q_d = 14 - 2P$, the slope is –2.

Suppose now there is a change in the slope, so it becomes –4. The new demand curve will be written as $Q_d = 14 - 4P$. How will this change in slope affect the graph of the demand curve? We know from 'Quantitative techniques' chapter on the CD-ROM, page 27, that the *greater the absolute value of the slope, the flatter the demand curve*. Since 4>2, the new demand curve is flatter than the original demand curve. This is shown in Figure 2.13, showing our original demand curve, given by $Q_d = 14 - 2P$, and the new demand curve, given by $Q_d = 14 - 4P$. Note that the Q-intercept (or the parameter a) remains constant when the slope changes.

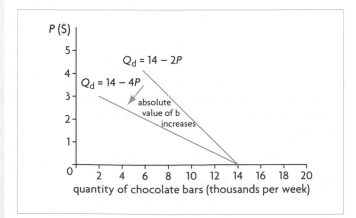

Figure 2.13 Changing the slope of the demand curve (changes in b in the function $Q_d = a - bP$)

Test your understanding 2.5

1 Given a demand function, $Q_d = a - bP$, explain what each of the variables (Q_d and P), and each of the parameters (a and –b) represent. Why is the parameter b accompanied by a negative sign?

2 Given the demand function $Q_d = 70 - 7P$, **(a)** plot the corresponding graph, **(b)** state the values of Q_d when P = 2, 5, 8 **(c)** find the vertical and horizontal intercepts using the function, and **(d)** find the intercepts on your graph and compare with your calculations (are they the same?).

3 Given the demand function $Q_d = 70 - 7P$, assume that due to an increase in income, 15 more units of Q are demanded at each price. **(a)** Show graphically how the demand curve will change. **(b)** State the new demand function. **(c)** Find the vertical (P) and horizontal (Q) intercepts of the new demand function.

4 Given the demand function $Q_d = 70 - 7P$, assume that due to a change in tastes, 20 fewer units of Q are demanded at each price. **(a)** Show graphically how the demand curve will change. **(b)** State the new demand function. **(c)** Find the vertical (P) and horizontal (Q) intercepts of the new demand function.

5 Given the demand function $Q_d = 70 - 7P$, **(a)** identify the slope. If the slope changes to –5, **(b)** show graphically how the demand curve will change, **(c)** state the new demand function, **(d)** find the vertical (P) and horizontal (Q) intercepts of the new demand function, and **(e)** outline how the change in slope has affected the steepness of the demand curve.

Linear supply functions (equations), schedules and graphs

Explaining the supply function (equation)

♦ Explain a supply function (equation) of the form $Q_s = c + dP$.

The supply function appears as an equation in the form:

$$Q_s = c + dP$$

where
Q_s = quantity supplied, and is the dependent variable (since it depends on price)
P = price, which is the independent variable
c = the Q-intercept (or the horizontal intercept)
d = the slope, calculated as $\Delta Q_s / \Delta P$

supply 35

Price of chocolate bars ($)	Quantity of chocolate bars supplied (thousands per week)
5	12
4	10
3	8
2	6
1	4
0	2

Table 2.5   Supply schedule for chocolate bars

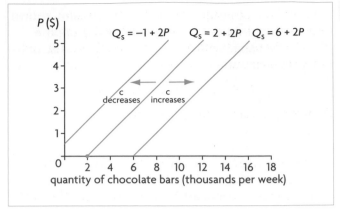

Figure 2.14 Shifts of the supply curve (changes in c in the supply function $Q_s = c + dP$)

Since the slope has a positive sign, we know that the relation between the dependent and independent variables is positive, tying in with what we know about the law of supply.

Once the parameters c and d are given specific values, the equation $Q = c + dP$ becomes a summary statement of the information in a supply schedule and graph of a supply relationship.

Plotting the supply curve from a supply function (equation)

♦ Plot a supply curve from a linear function (e.g. Qs = −30 + 20P).

If we are given a supply function specifying the numerical values of c and d, we can make a schedule of the relation described by the equation and use this information to plot a graph of the curve.

We are given the supply function:

$$Q_s = 2 + 2P$$

where

Q_s = quantity of chocolate bars supplied per week, in thousands (the dependent variable)

P = price of chocolate bars, in $ (the independent variable)

2 = the Q-intercept (horizontal intercept)

2 = slope (given by $\Delta Q_s / \Delta P$).

Setting P equal to various values, and solving for Q_s, we obtain a series of P and Q_s combinations, giving us the supply schedule. If we begin with $P = 0$, we find the Q-intercept, which is $Q_s = 2$ (thousand); then $P = 1$ gives $Q_s = 2 + 2(1) = 4$ (thousand); $P = 2$ gives $Q_s = 2 + 2(2) = 6$ (thousand), and so on. The various price–quantity combinations are shown in Table 2.5.

We then use this information to plot the supply curve, shown in Figure 2.14. Note that this is the same supply curve that appears in Figure 2.6(c) (page 27). The axes must be labelled correctly, with P in $ on the vertical axis and Q in thousands on the horizontal axis. The supply curve consists of a series of points: (2,0), (4,1), (6,2), (8,3), and so on.[2]

Since the supply curve is linear, it is only necessary to find two points, and then draw the supply curve (though it may be a good idea to find a third point to be sure that the calculations have been done correctly; you need to be sure that a straight line can be drawn through the three points).

Changes in the parameter c and shifts of the supply curve

♦ Outline why, if the 'c' term changes, there will be a shift of the supply curve.

The parameter c represents the variables that are held constant under the *ceteris paribus* assumption, known as the non-price determinants of supply (see 'Quantitative techniques' chapter on the CD-ROM, page 24). If there is a change in one of these determinants, there will be a change in the value of the parameter c, and the supply curve will therefore shift. Suppose that the number of firms producing chocolate bars increases, resulting in an increase in supply of 4000 chocolate bars per week at each price. We know the supply curve will shift to the right, and in Figure 2.14, we can see the size of this shift, which is given by the increase in supply of 4 (thousand) for all prices.

[2] The point (2,0) indicates that the quantity supplied would be 2000 chocolate bars per week at a price of $0. Yet, you may wonder, how is this possible? No firm would produce a good if it cannot sell it at a price ⸴ ⸴han zero. As explained also in 'Quantitative techniques' chapter

on the CD-ROM page 23, drawing the supply curve all the way up to the horizontal axis is a mathematical convenience. In Chapter 7, you will learn about the lowest possible price a firm is willing to accept in order to produce (see page 174 on the firm's supply curve).

To find the new supply function, we find the new value of the parameter c, by taking the initial value of c = 2 (thousand) and adding to that the change in supply of 4 (thousand), obtaining:

$$2+4 = 6 = \text{the new value of c}$$

Therefore, the new supply function is:

$$Q_s = 6+2P$$

shown in Figure 2.14. In the graph, c = 6 is the new Q-intercept of the new supply curve.

Let's consider a decrease in supply of 3000 chocolate bars at each price (say, due to the imposition of a tax) relative to the initial supply curve. There will be a parallel supply curve shift to the left by the amount of 3 (thousand). The parameter c, or the Q-intercept, decreases by 3 (thousand) so that the new value of c = $2-3 = -1$, and the new equation is $Q_s = -1+2P$. Note that the new Q-intercept is now negative (c = -1), and *this does not show up in the supply diagram*, as there is no such thing as a negative quantity. (It is not necessary to find the Q-intercept on the graph in order to be able to plot the new supply curve; we simply shift the supply curve 3 (thousand) units to the left at each price to get the new curve.) Note that here we could calculate the new P intercept (the vertical intercept) which has resulted from the shift, by setting $Q_s = 0 = -1+2P$, in which case we find $P = \frac{1}{2}$, which gives us the P intercept $(0,\frac{1}{2})$, representing the beginning of the supply curve for which Q_s has positive values. (See 'Quantitative techniques' chapter on the CD-ROM, page 22).

Changes in the parameter d and the steepness of the supply curve

* Identify the slope of the supply curve as the slope of the supply function $Q_s = c+dP$, that is d (the coefficient of P).
* Outline how a change in 'd' affects the steepness of the supply curve.

The parameter *d*, which is the coefficient of P (price), represents the slope of the supply curve. In our supply function $Q_s = 2+2P$, the slope is +2.

We now want to see how the supply curve changes if there is a change in the slope. Suppose the slope changes to +4. The new supply curve becomes $Q_s = 2+4P$. We know from our discussion of the demand curve (page 35) that *the greater the (absolute) value of the slope, the flatter the curve*. (Since d is positive in the supply function, the absolute value is not relevant.) Since 4>2, the new supply curve is flatter than in the original curve. This is illustrated in Figure 2.15, which shows the original supply curve given by $Q_s = 2+2P$ and the new supply curve given by $Q_s = 2+4P$.

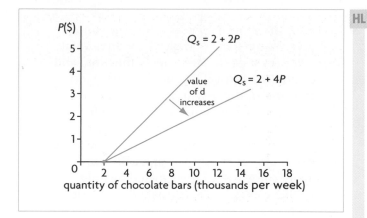

Figure 2.15 Changing the slope of the supply curve (changes in d in the function $Q_s = c+dP$)

Test your understanding 2.6

1 Given a supply function $Q_s = c+dP$, explain what each of the variables (Q_s and P), and each of the parameters (c and +d) represent. Why does the parameter d have a positive sign?

2 Given the supply function $Q_s = -20+10P$, **(a)** plot the corresponding graph, including only positive values for Q_s. **(b)** State the values of Q_s when P = 3, 4, 6. **(c)** Find the vertical and horizontal intercepts using the function; which of these does not appear in your graph? **(d)** Find the one relevant (non-negative) intercept on your graph and compare with your calculations (is it the same?).

3 Given the supply function $Q_s = -20+10P$, assume that due to a new technology, 15 more units of Q are supplied at each price. **(a)** Show graphically how the supply curve will change, including only positive values for Q_s. **(b)** State the new supply function. **(c)** Find the vertical (P) and horizontal (Q) intercepts of the new supply function; which of these does not appear on your graph?

4 Given the supply function $Q_s = -20+10P$, assume that due to a fall in the number of firms, 15 fewer units of Q are supplied at each price. **(a)** Show graphically how the supply curve changes. **(b)** State the new supply function. **(c)** Find the vertical (P) and horizontal (Q) intercepts of the new supply function; which of these does not appear on your graph?

5 Given the supply function $Q_s = -20+10P$, **(a)** identify the slope. If the slope changes

to 15, **(b)** show graphically how the supply curve changes, including only positive values for Q_s, **(c)** state the new supply function, and **(d)** find the vertical (P) and horizontal (Q) intercepts of the new supply function; which of these does not appear on your graph? **(e)** Outline how the change in slope affects the steepness of the supply curve. If the slope changes to +8, **(f)** show graphically how the supply curve will change, including only positive values for Q_s, **(g)** state the new supply function, and **(h)** outline how the change in slope affected the steepness of the supply curve.

Using linear equations to calculate and illustrate market equilibrium

You may find it helpful to read the 'Quantitative techniques' chapter on the CD-ROM page 29, for an explanation of the method used in this section to solve linear equations.

Solving simultaneous linear equations to calculate equilibrium price and quantity

♦ Calculate the equilibrium price and equilibrium quantity from linear demand and supply functions.

We will now use our demand function $Q_d = 14-2P$ and supply function $Q_s = 2+2P$ to solve for the equilibrium price and quantity. (These, of course, are the same as what we had found by examining Table 2.3 and Figure 2.9, since our functions describe the same demand and supply curves.) Putting our information together, we have:

$$Q_d = 14-2P \text{ (demand function)}$$
$$Q_s = 2+2P \text{ (supply function)}$$
$$Q_d = Q_s \text{ (at market equilibrium)}$$

where
Q_s and Q_d refer to quantities of chocolate bars in thousands and P is the price per unit in $.

Using the third equation, we can eliminate Q_s and Q_d, and solve for P:

$$14-2P = 2+2P \implies 12 = 4P \implies P = 3$$

Substituting P into the demand equation, we have:

$$Q_d = 14-2(3) \implies Q_d = 14-6 = 8$$

Therefore, the equilibrium price is $3 and the equilibrium quantity is 8, or 8000 chocolate bars.

Alternatively, substituting into the supply equation, we have:

$$Q_s = 2+2(3) \implies Q_s = 2+6 = 8$$

(which is the same as above). (Note that it is not necessary for you to do this calculation both ways, as the result is the same.)

Once you have solved for P and Q, you should check your results by substituting the values of P and Q into the equations:

$$Q_d = 14-2P \implies 8 = 14-2(3) = 8; \text{ or}$$
$$Q_s = 2+2P \implies 8 = 2+2(3) = 8$$

Therefore, the values of P and Q are correct, and we have found that at market equilibrium, $P = \$3$ and $Q = 8$, or 8000 bars, which as expected is the same as what we had found by use of the demand and supply schedules in Table 2.3 and the demand and supply diagram in Figure 2.9.

Plotting demand and supply curves from linear functions to find equilibrium price and quantity

♦ Plot demand and supply curves from linear functions, and identify the equilibrium price and equilibrium quantity.

When we are given a demand function, we can plot the demand curve using the method described on page 33, provided of course we have information on the parameters a and –b. Similarly, given a supply function, together with the values of the parameters c and d, we can plot the supply curve using the method described on page 36. Once we plot both the demand and supply curves, we can then read off the equilibrium price and quantity that result at market equilibrium; as we know from our discussion above, equilibrium price and quantity are found at the point of intersection of the demand and supply curves. In Test your understanding 2.7 you will be given exercises that will allow you to practise solving these kinds of problems.

Calculating excess demand and excess supply

♦ State the quantity of excess demand or excess supply in the above diagrams.

Once we have used demand and supply functions to graph demand and supply curves illustrating market equilibrium, it is a simple matter to calculate the quantity of excess demand (or shortage) or excess supply (or surplus) that result for prices that differ from the equilibrium price. We have already done this in our discussion of Figure 2.9 (page 30). As we know, the equilibrium price in this diagram is $3. For any price other than $3, there will be excess demand or excess supply. If quantity demanded is greater than quantity supplied, there is excess demand. If quantity supplied is greater than quantity demanded, there is excess supply.

You should review Figure 2.9 and calculate (on your own) the amount of excess supply or excess demand that arises at each price. Note that when $P = \$3$, excess demand = excess supply = 0.

Test your understanding 2.7

1 You are given a demand function $Q_d = a - bP$, where $a = 500$ and $b = 2$, and a supply function $Q_s = c + dP$, where $c = -100$ and $d = 2$. P is in $ and Q is in thousand units per week. **(a)** Calculate the equilibrium price and quantity. **(b)** Plot the demand and supply functions for the price range $P = \$50$ to $P = \$200$, and identify the equilibrium price and quantity on your graph. **(c)** When $P = \$190$, $\$170$, $\$125$, $\$85$, determine whether there is excess demand or excess supply, and calculate the amount of this in each case. **(d)** Explain how excess demand and excess supply work to restore equilibrium in the market.

2 Using the demand and supply functions of question 1, assume due to a demographic change, 300 thousand more units per week are demanded at each price, while due to a technological change, 300 thousand more units per week are supplied at each price. **(a)** State the new demand and supply functions and plot them in your graph. **(b)** Calculate the new equilibrium price and quantity. **(c)** Explain why the new equilibrium price is the same as the initial one while the new equilibrium quantity is larger.

3 **(a)** Given the demand function $Q_d = 27 - 0.7P$ and the supply function $Q_s = -5 + 0.9P$, where P is in € and Q is in million units per month, calculate the equilibrium price and quantity. **(b)** Plot the demand and supply functions, and identify the equilibrium price and quantity on your graph. **(c)** When $P = €10$, €15, €25, €30, determine whether there is excess demand or excess supply, and calculate the amount of this in each case. **(d)** Assume that the slope of the demand function falls to –0.9. State the new demand function, and **(e)** outline the effect on the steepness of the demand curve. **(f)** Assume the slope of the supply function falls to 0.7. State the new supply function, and **(g)** outline the effect on the steepness of the supply curve.

2.6 The role of the price mechanism and market efficiency

The role of the price mechanism in resource allocation

Prices determined by the forces of supply and demand in competitive markets serve some important functions that we now turn to.

Scarcity, choice and opportunity cost in resource allocation

- Explain why scarcity necessitates choices that answer the 'What to produce?' question.
- Explain why choice results in an opportunity cost.

In Chapter 1 we saw that the condition of scarcity forces societies to make choices. As the production possibilities model illustrated (Figure 1.1, page 5), assuming the economy is producing on its production possibilities curve (*PPC*), it must decide on what particular point on the *PPC* it wishes to produce. This involves a choice about *what to produce*, which is a decision on one aspect of resource allocation. It also involves a choice about which of its available resources and in what quantities, it will allocate to produce the combination of goods and services it has chosen. This is a choice on the *how to produce* question of resource allocation.

Now if a society decides to change the combination of goods it wishes to produce, in other words move from one point to another on its *PPC*, it will reallocate its resources, meaning that a new answer will be given to the *what to produce* and *how to produce* questions. Such a resource reallocation can be seen in the economy's move from point B to point C on the *PPC* of Figure 1.1. Note that this reallocation of resources involves an *opportunity cost*, since in order to produce more of one good, there must be a sacrifice of another good. In the model of Figure 1.1, an increase in computer production from 17 to 25 units in the move from point B to point C has an opportunity cost (or sacrifice) of 9 (= 35–26) microwave ovens.

> The condition of scarcity forces societies to make choices about the *what to produce* economic question, which is a resource allocation question. Choices involve an opportunity cost because of foregone (or sacrificed) alternatives that could have been chosen instead.

This brings us to an important question. How does a society make a choice about where to be on its *PPC*?

Who decides, and how is this decision carried out? In a market economy, it is simply prices in free markets, resulting from the interactions of demanders and suppliers, which make the decisions and carry them out.

Prices as signals and incentives and the allocation of resources

♦ Explain, using diagrams, that price has a signalling function and an incentive function, which result in a reallocation of resources when prices change as a result of a change in demand or supply conditions.

We have learned that when markets operate under competitive conditions, market demand and market supply, composed of numerous individual demanders and suppliers, determine equilibrium prices and quantities for goods (and services and resources). At these equilibrium positions, the buying and selling choices of all buyers and sellers are satisfied and are in balance. This market mechanism, working through prices, is known as the *invisible hand of the market*, a phrase first used by Adam Smith, the famous Scottish economist of the 18th century known as the 'Father of Economics'. The invisible hand succeeds in co-ordinating the buying and selling decisions of thousands or millions of decision-makers in an economy without any central authority. The *what to produce* question of resource allocation is answered because firms produce only those goods consumers are willing and able to buy, while consumers buy only those goods producers are willing and able to supply; and the *how to produce* question of resource allocation is answered because firms use those resources and technologies in their production process that they are willing and able to pay for.

How do prices and markets achieve the task of resource allocation?

The key to the market's ability to allocate resources can be found in the role of **prices as signals** and **prices as incentives**. As signals, prices communicate information to decision-makers. As incentives, prices motivate decision-makers to respond to the information.

We will examine the signalling and incentive functions of prices by use of the following two examples.

An example from a product market
Suppose consumers decide they would like to eat more strawberries because of their health benefits (a change in tastes); demand increases and the demand curve shifts to the right from D_1 to D_2 in Figure 2.16(a). At the initial price, P_1, this results in a shortage equal to the

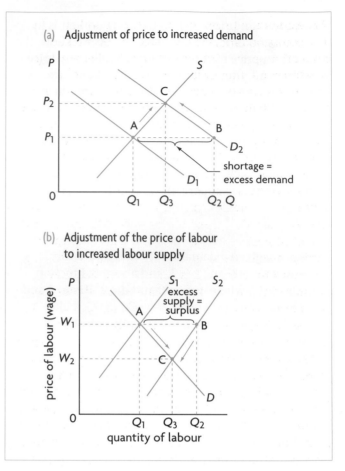

Figure 2.16 Price as a signal and incentive

difference between Q_2 and Q_1: the quantity demanded Q_2, due to the increase in demand to D_2, is larger than quantity supplied, Q_1. The price of strawberries therefore begins to rise, and will continue to rise until the shortage has disappeared. This happens at price P_2 and quantity Q_3, given by the point of intersection of the supply curve with the new demand curve, D_2.

What has happened? The new, higher price signalled or conveyed information to producers that a shortage in the strawberry market had emerged. The increase in price is also an incentive for producers to increase the quantity of strawberries supplied; at the higher price, strawberry production is more profitable, so producers move along the supply curve from point A to point C, increasing quantity supplied from Q_1 to Q_3. But the new, higher price is a signal and incentive for consumers: it signals that strawberries are now more expensive, and is an incentive for them to buy fewer strawberries. They therefore move along the new demand curve from B to C, buying fewer strawberries than at the original price P_1 (Q_3 is smaller than Q_2). The increase in the price of strawberries resulted in a *reallocation of resources*. More resources are now allocated to strawberry production. (This affects the answer to the *what to produce* question of resource allocation.)

An example from a resource market

The second example is from the labour market (a resource market). The vertical axis in Figure 2.16(b) measures the price of labour (the wage) and the horizontal axis the quantity of labour. Firms are interested in buying labour services, and their demand for labour is given by D. Owners of labour services (workers) supply their labour in the labour market, and the initial supply of labour is shown by S_1.[3]

Assume that because of immigration (foreign workers enter the country), the supply of labour increases, so the labour supply curve shifts to S_2. At the old wage, W_1, there is a surplus of labour shown by the difference between Q_2 and Q_1 of labour. The surplus causes the wage to start falling, and this falls until the surplus has disappeared. The new equilibrium wage is W_2, and the equilibrium quantity of labour Q_3, given by the intersection of D with S_2.

The falling wage has acted as a signal and an incentive. It signalled to firms that there was a surplus in the labour market, and it provided them with an incentive to hire more labour; therefore, they move along the labour demand curve from point A to point C (Q_3 is larger than Q_1). The lower wage is also a signal to workers, providing them with the incentive to move along the new supply curve, S_2, from B to C, where they offer less of their services at the lower wage (Q_3 is less than Q_2). With firms and workers responding to price signals and incentives, there occurred a reallocation of labour resources with firms now producing output with a larger quantity of labour. (This affects the answer to the *how to produce* question of resource allocation.)

Test your understanding 2.8

1 Using the production possibilities model, explain the relationship between scarcity, choice and opportunity cost.

2 What is the relationship between scarcity, choice and the *what to produce* basic economic question? How does this relate to resource allocation?

3 How do prices help answer the *how* and *what to produce* questions of resource allocation?

4 Consider the market for coffee, and suppose that the demand for coffee falls (because of a fall in the price of tea, a substitute good), leading to a new equilibrium price and quantity of coffee. Using diagrams, explain the role of price as a signal and as an incentive for consumers and for firms in reallocating resources.

5 Consider the labour market, and suppose the supply of labour falls (due to large-scale departure of workers to another country), resulting in a new equilibrium price and quantity of labour. Using diagrams, explain the role of price as a signal and as an incentive for workers (the suppliers of labour) and firms (the demanders of labour) in reallocating resources.

Real world focus

Rising prices of wheat and corn

Over the last few years, global demand for wheat has increased, driving wheat prices up. Whereas the price per bushel of wheat was $3.15 in 2006, this had climbed to about $7.00 in the summer of 2010. In the United States, there are expectations that more farmland will be planted to wheat as farmers try to take advantage of the highest wheat prices in years. Farmers are already clearing land for the fall (autumn) wheat planting.

In the meantime, a massive drought reduced the wheat crop by at least one fifth in Russia, causing a wheat shortage. Russia had been a major wheat exporter, but the Russian government said it will ban wheat exports this year.

Corn prices have also been rising, due to moisture damage in corn plants that caused corn yields (output per unit of land) to fall. There are fears that higher corn prices will lead to higher meat prices, as corn is important feed for livestock, as well as higher ethanol prices (ethanol is a biofuel sometimes made of corn).

Source: Adapted from Mark Ranzenberger, 'Price of wheat rising' in *The Morning Sun*, 30 August 2010; Dan Piller, 'Rising corn prices also affect ethanol, cattle' in *Kansas City Star*, 13 October 2010.

Applying your skills

Using diagrams in each case, explain:

1 the effect of higher demand for wheat on wheat prices

2 the signalling and incentive role of wheat prices for US wheat farmers

3 the effect of the drought in Russia on the wheat market

4 the effect of higher corn prices on meat and ethanol prices.

---

[3] The demand curve has the usual downward-sloping shape, because as the wage falls, firms are prompted to hire more labour and so the quantity of labour demanded increases. The supply curve has the usual upward-sloping shape because the higher the wage, the more willing workers will be to supply their labour in the market.

Efficiency in competitive markets

Efficiency broadly means making the best possible use of resources. We will now examine efficiency more closely and will study the role of competitive markets in achieving efficiency.

The meaning of efficiency in competitive markets

Economic efficiency is known more precisely as *allocative efficiency*, which refers to producing the combination of goods mostly wanted by society. In fact, it means more than this. Allocative efficiency is achieved when the economy allocates its resources so that no one can become better off in terms of increasing their benefit from consumption without someone else becoming worse off. In other words, the benefits from consumption are maximised for the whole of society.

If a society realises allocative efficiency, it must be the case that *productive efficiency* is also being achieved. Productive efficiency, introduced in Chapter 1 (page 5), refers to producing goods by using the fewest possible resources (producing at the lowest possible cost). As you may remember, productive efficiency is necessary for the economy to be producing on its *PPC*.

Why is it that we cannot have allocative efficiency for a society without having productive efficiency as well? The reasoning is the following. If there were productive *inefficiency*, some firms would not be using the fewest possible resources for their production. By getting rid of the inefficient firms through a reallocation of resources so that all production takes place by efficient firms, the economy would produce more output. It would then be possible to make some consumers better off without making anyone worse off. Therefore, as long as there is any productive inefficiency in the economy, it is not possible to have allocative efficiency.

While productive efficiency is necessary for achieving allocative efficiency, it is not enough. In addition, efficient producers must be producing the 'right' combination of goods that society prefers. A simple way to understand this is to consider that allocative efficiency is reached when a society produces and consumes *at its preferred point on its PPC*. Since productive efficiency is necessary to be on the *PPC*, it follows that achieving allocative efficiency means that productive efficiency is also achieved.

Since allocative efficiency refers to producing what consumers mostly want, it answers the *what to produce* question in the best possible way. Since productive efficiency means producing with the fewest possible resources, it answers the *how to produce* question

in the best possible way. As we will see below, the competitive market realises allocative (and therefore also productive) efficiency:

> The competitive market realises **allocative efficiency**, producing the combination of goods mostly wanted by society, thus answering the *what to produce* question in the best possible way. This means *productive efficiency* is also realised, involving production with the fewest possible resources, thus answering the *how to produce* question in the best possible way. These conditions are also known as *economic efficiency* or *Pareto optimality*.[4]

Introducing consumer and producer surplus

To understand how efficiency is achieved by the competitive market economy, we will study two new concepts:

* consumer surplus
* producer surplus.

Consumer surplus

* Explain the concept of consumer surplus.
* Identify consumer surplus on a demand and supply diagram.

Consumer surplus is defined as the highest price consumers are willing to pay for a good minus the price actually paid. In a competitive market, the price actually paid is determined at the market equilibrium by supply and demand. Consumer surplus is shown in Figure 2.17 as the shaded area between the demand (or marginal benefit) curve, and the equilibrium price P_e. It represents the difference between total benefits consumers receive from buying a good and the price paid to receive them.

Consumer surplus indicates that whereas many consumers were willing to pay a higher price to get the good, they actually received it for less. For example, many consumers were willing to pay price P_2 to get quantity Q_a, yet they got Q_a by paying only the lower price P_e. The difference between P_2 and P_e is consumer surplus for quantity Q_a. Similarly, many consumers were willing to pay price P_3 in order to get quantity Q_b, yet they got it by paying only P_e. Again, the difference $P_3 - P_e$ is consumer surplus for quantity Q_b. The same principle applies to all possible prices between

---

[4] This condition is named after Vilfredo Pareto, a 19th-century economist.

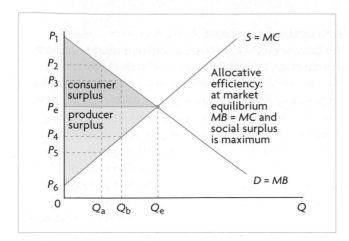

Figure 2.17 Consumer and producer surplus in a competitive market

the highest price P_1 and the equilibrium price P_e. Therefore, all the consumers who were willing to pay a higher price than P_e to get the good received some benefit over and above what they actually paid for the good. This extra benefit is called consumer surplus.

Producer surplus

♦ Explain the concept of producer surplus.
♦ Identify producer surplus on a demand and supply diagram.

Producer surplus is defined as the price received by firms for selling their good minus the lowest price that they are willing to accept to produce the good. The lowest price they are willing to accept represents the firms' cost of producing an extra unit of the good (or marginal cost), and is shown by the supply curve. (The logic behind this is very simple: the lowest price that the firm is willing to accept must be just enough to cover its cost of producing each extra unit; this cost is known as **marginal cost**, abbreviated as MC.) Producer surplus is shown as the area above the firms' supply curve and below the price received by firms, P_e, which is determined in the market. As we can see in Figure 2.17, firms that were willing to produce quantity Q_a for price P_5 actually received price P_e. The difference $P_e - P_5$ is producer surplus for quantity Q_a. Similarly, the producer surplus for quantity Q_b is given by the price P_e actually received minus P_4 that the firms were willing to accept for producing Q_b. The same principle applies to all possible prices between the lowest price P_6 and the equilibrium price P_e. Therefore, producer surplus is shown by the shaded area between the equilibrium price P_e and the supply curve.

Competitive market equilibrium: maximum social surplus and allocative efficiency

♦ Explain that the best allocation of resources from society's point of view is at competitive market equilibrium, where social (community) surplus (consumer surplus and producer surplus) is maximised (marginal benefit = marginal cost).

Competitive market equilibrium and maximum social surplus

At the point of competitive market equilibrium, the sum of consumer and producer surplus is maximum, or the greatest it can be. To see why, consider what would happen if any quantity less than Q_e were produced in Figure 2.17. If, say, Q_b is produced, the sum of consumer plus producer surplus would be smaller, as this sum would be equal to the shaded area between the demand and supply curves *only up to output Q_b*. It follows, then, that the sum of consumer plus producer surplus is maximised at the point of market equilibrium. The sum of consumer and producer surplus is known as **social surplus** (or **community surplus**).[5]

> At the point of competitive market equilibrium, social surplus, defined as the sum of consumer plus producer surplus, is maximum.

Let's now examine the importance of maximum social surplus at the point of competitive market equilibrium.

Market equilibrium and allocative efficiency

As we know, market equilibrium occurs at the point of intersection of the demand and supply curves, but depending on how we interpret the demand and supply curves, market equilibrium can be thought of differently. If we interpret the demand curve as a marginal benefit (MB) curve, and the supply curve as a marginal cost (MC) curve, then market equilibrium occurs where $MB = MC$. The equality of MB with MC tells us that the extra benefit to society of getting one more unit of the good is equal to the extra cost to society of producing one more unit of the good. When this happens, society's resources are being used to produce the 'right' quantity of the good; in other words, society has allocated the 'right' amount of resources to the production of the good, and is producing the quantity of the good that is mostly wanted by society. *This is none other than allocative efficiency*, and is shown in Figure 2.17.

---

[5] Note that the term 'surplus' is used in two senses in this chapter. In one sense it refers to 'excess supply' (see page 31) and in the other it refers to benefits received by consumers and producers. You can avoid confusing the two concepts by noting that whenever the term is used on its own, it refers to excess supply.

(To understand this, consider that if $MB > MC$, then society would be placing a greater value on the last unit of the good produced than it costs to produce it, and so more of it should be produced. If $MC > MB$, then it would be costing society more to produce the last unit of the good produced than the value society puts on it, and so less should be produced. If $MC = MB$, then just the 'right' quantity of the good is being produced.)

Putting the above points together, we can conclude that at the point of competitive market equilibrium, where $MB = MC$, and where the sum of social (consumer plus producer surplus) is maximum, the economy achieves allocative (and therefore also productive) efficiency.[6] For allocative (and productive) efficiency to be achieved for an entire economy, the condition $MB = MC$, indicating maximum social surplus, must hold in all markets.

At the point of competitive market equilibrium shown in Figure 2.17, production of a good occurs where $MB = MC$, which is also *where social surplus, or the sum of consumer plus producer surplus is maximum.* This means that markets are achieving allocative (as well as productive) efficiency, producing the quantity of goods mostly wanted by society at the lowest possible cost. Society is making the best possible use of its scarce resources.

When the competitive market realises allocative efficiency, we say that 'social welfare' is maximised. What does this mean? The term **welfare** in a general sense refers to the well-being of society. Here, it is being used in a special sense to refer to maximum social surplus, or where $MB = MC$. *Social welfare* in this context is part of a branch of economics called *welfare economics*, which examines the conditions under which competitive markets work well, meaning that they make the best possible use of scarce resources. We can therefore say that:

In competitive markets, when $MB=MC$, or when social surplus is maximum, social welfare is maximum.

A word of caution

We have seen that the competitive market succeeds in achieving allocative (and productive) efficiency, thus addressing the *what to produce* and *how to produce* questions in the best possible way, ensuring the best possible use of scarce resources. This idea suggests that there should not be government intervention in markets, as these work very well on their own. However, there are two important issues that arise, calling into question the idea that governments should not intervene.

The first is that efficiency can only arise under a number of very strict and highly unrealistic conditions that are practically never met in the real world. In the real world the market fails with respect to achieving both allocative and productive efficiency. Market failures are an important justification for government intervention (see Chapter 5).

The second is that the competitive market is unable to provide a satisfactory answer to the *for whom to produce* question, or output and income distribution, thus also inviting some government intervention. The topic of distribution and what can be done to improve outcomes will be examined in Chapter 11. It is also discussed in the Theory of knowledge feature on page 45.

These observations do not lessen the significance of the market's potential advantages; they only point out that in the real world, there is a need for government policies to counteract the failings of markets, thus allowing them to realise their potential advantages. There are important reasons why economists study the competitive market extensively, even though this is not fully achievable in practice. One is that government policies undertaken for reasons unrelated to efficiency can be assessed with respect to their efficiency consequences (see Chapter 4). Another is that it can form the basis for government policies that try to create conditions in the real world that allow actual economies to come closer to achieving economic efficiency (see Chapter 5). A third is that it provides standards for economic efficiency against which actual outcomes, which are less than perfectly efficient, can be assessed (Chapters 4 and 7).

---

[6] We can use the concept of producer surplus to explain why the achievement of allocative efficiency, where $MB = MC$, means the achievement also of productive efficiency. Suppose that firms in some markets are not producing at the lowest possible cost, i.e. they are productively inefficient. As they compete with each other to lower their costs, resources are transferred from the higher cost firms to lower cost firms. With lower costs, these firms will also have a lower minimum price they are willing to accept for selling their output, and therefore a greater producer surplus (since producer surplus is the price firms receive minus the lowest price they are willing to accept). Producer surplus will continue to increase as long as resources can be shifted out of higher cost producers and into lower cost producers, and will be maximised when all output is produced by firms producing at the lowest possible cost. Once the market produces at $MB = MC$, then it is no longer possible to increase producer surplus, and all producers are producing at the lowest possible cost.

The meaning and implications of maximum social welfare

We must be very careful when interpreting the meaning of *maximum social welfare*. The achievement of $MB = MC$, or maximum social surplus, deals with the *what to produce* and *how to produce* questions, and therefore with how a society can realise allocative efficiency.

Even if it is assumed that allocative (and productive) efficiency are achieved, in which case we have 'maximum social welfare', this tells us nothing about how output and income are, or should be, distributed. The achievement of allocative (and productive) efficiency is, in fact, consistent with any possible distribution of output or income. This means that we can have an extremely unequal distribution of output and income, where one person in society gets all the output, or a highly equal distribution where everyone gets an equal share, and both of these situations can lead to allocative (and productive) efficiency. This idea highlights the point that *when we refer to maximum social welfare, we are only talking about making the best possible use of scarce resources, while saying nothing about who gets the benefits of what the resources produce.* For any distribution of income and output, ranging from the most unequal to the most equal, it is possible to have a situation of maximum social surplus and therefore allocative efficiency.

The pursuit of efficiency, dealing with the *what to produce* and *how to produce* questions, is based on social scientific investigation, and tries to discover the most effective ways to increase efficiency in resource allocation. Many economists would argue that this is a matter of positive thinking about economics (see page 11 on the distinction between positive and normative). On the other hand, the *for whom to produce* question is a matter of normative thinking. Positive economic thinking, based on the social scientific method described in Chapter 1, is not intended to make judgements about what is fair or unfair, or equitable or inequitable. It is intended to deal with issues of things that 'are' or 'will be' under different conditions. Therefore, while it can tell us about what methods are most likely to lead to increases in efficiency, it is not intended to tell us about how income and output

should be distributed. The issue of equity (introduced on page 16) is a normative issue, because what is considered 'fair' is a matter of beliefs and value judgements about things that 'ought to be'. What share of total income, or what particular goods and services *ought* individuals to have? Is there a minimum income that people *ought* to have? If so, based on what kinds of equity principles *ought* distribution and redistribution to take place?

There are no 'right' or 'wrong' answers to these questions. The answers that are chosen are based on beliefs and value judgements about what is good for society and the people within it. According to the standard view, economists should be concerned with positive aspects of economics. Their positive thinking could tell us about the likely consequences of policies to change the distribution of income, but should not make recommendations about how the distribution of income ought to change.

Thinking points

- What is the significance of language in conveying meaning; does the expression 'maximum social welfare' accurately reflect its actual meaning? (See also the Theory of knowledge feature on page 273.)

- If economists, as social scientists, cannot make recommendations about normative issues like the distribution of income, how are these decisions made? (Think about the political process, social values, tradition and history.)

- Based on your reading about economics in the press and listening to the news, do you think that economists in the real world make a clear distinction between positive and normative ideas?

- Do you agree with the principle that economists (and social scientists generally) should only be concerned with positive thinking (social scientific investigation) and should leave normative issues (about things that ought to be) to societal decision-making?

1 Explain the meaning of allocative and productive efficiency.

2 Explain the meaning of **(a)** consumer surplus, and **(b)** producer surplus. **(c)** What is the meaning of social (or community) surplus? **(d)** What is the meaning of maximum 'social welfare'?

3 **(a)** Use a demand and supply diagram to illustrate consumer and producer surplus. **(b)** At which level of output is their sum maximum? **(c)** Explain the condition $MB = MC$, and use your diagram of part (a) to show at which level of output this condition is satisfied. **(d)** What do the conditions of maximum consumer plus producer surplus, and $MB = MC$ tell us about allocative and productive efficiency? **(e)** What do they tell us about social welfare?

4 What are some limitations of the concept of maximum social welfare?

Assessment

The Student's CD-ROM at the back of this book provides practice of examination questions based on the material you have studied in this chapter.

Standard level
- Exam practice: Paper 1, Chapter 2
  - SL/HL core topics (questions 2.1–2.14)

Higher level
- Exam practice: Paper 1, Chapter 2
  - SL/HL core topics (questions 2.1–2.14)
- Exam practice: Paper 3, Chapter 2
  - HL topics (questions 1–3)

Chapter 3
Elasticities

Elasticity is a measure of the responsiveness of a variable to changes in price or any of the variable's determinants. In this chapter we will examine four kinds of elasticities, with numerous applications to important economic problems.

3.1 Price elasticity of demand (*PED*)

Price elasticity of demand

♦ Explain the concept of price elasticity of demand, understanding that it involves responsiveness of quantity demanded to a change in price, along a given demand curve.

Understanding price elasticity of demand (*PED*)

According to the law of demand, there is a negative relationship between price and quantity demanded: the higher the price, the lower the quantity demanded, and vice versa, all other things equal. We now want to know *by how much* quantity responds to change in price.

> **Price elasticity of demand** (*PED*) is a measure of the responsiveness of the quantity of a good demanded to changes in its price. *PED* is calculated along a given demand curve. In general, if there is a large responsiveness of quantity demanded, demand is referred to as being *price elastic*; if there is a small responsiveness, demand is *price inelastic*.

The formula for *PED*

♦ Calculate PED using the following equation.

$$PED = \frac{\text{percentage change in quantity demanded}}{\text{percentage change in price}}$$

Suppose we are considering price elasticity of demand (*PED*) for good *X*. The formula used to measure its *PED* is:

$$\text{price elasticity of demand} = PED = \frac{\text{percentage change in quantity of good } X \text{ demanded}}{\text{percentage change in price of good } X}$$

If we abbreviate 'change in' by the Greek letter Δ, this formula can be rewritten as:

$$PED = \frac{\%\Delta Q_x}{\%\Delta P_x}$$

Simplifying, the above formula can be rewritten as:

$$PED = \frac{\frac{\Delta Q_x}{Q_x} \times 100}{\frac{\Delta P_x}{P_x} \times 100} = \frac{\frac{\Delta Q_x}{Q_x}}{\frac{\Delta P_x}{P_x}}$$

The sign of *PED*

♦ State that the PED value is treated as if it were positive although its mathematical value is usually negative.

Since price and quantity demanded are negatively (indirectly) related, the *PED* is a negative number. For any percentage increase in price (a positive denominator), there results a percentage decrease in quantity demanded (a negative numerator), leading to a negative *PED*. Similarly, for a percentage price decrease the result will be a percentage quantity increase, again leading to a negative *PED*. However, *the common practice is to drop the minus sign and consider PED as a positive number*. (In mathematics this is called taking the absolute value.) This is done to avoid confusion when making comparisons between different values of *PED*. Using positive numbers, we can say, for example, that a *PED* of 3 is larger than a *PED* of 2. (Had we been using the minus sign, –2 would be larger than –3.)

The use of percentages

Elasticity is measured in terms of percentages for two reasons:

- We need a measure of responsiveness that is independent of units. First, we want to be able to compare the responsiveness of quantity demanded of different goods; it makes little sense to compare units of oranges with units of computers or cars. Secondly, we want to be able to compare responsiveness across countries that have different currencies; an elasticity measured in terms of euros will not be comparable with an elasticity measured in yen or pounds. By computing changes in quantity and changes in price as percentages, we express them in common terms, thereby making it possible to compare responsiveness for different goods and across countries.

- It is meaningless to think of changes in prices or quantities in absolute terms (for example, a $15 increase in price or a 20 unit decrease in quantity) because this tells us nothing about the relative size of the change. For example, a $15 price increase means something very different for a good whose original price is $100 than for a good whose original price is $5000. In the first case there is a 15% increase, and in the second there is a 0.3% increase. Using percentages to measure price and quantity changes allows us to put responsiveness into perspective.

The same arguments apply to all other elasticities we will consider.

Calculating *PED*

◆ Calculate PED between two designated points on a demand curve using the PED equation above.

We can now use the formula above to calculate *PED*. Suppose consumers buy 6000 DVD players when the price is $255 per unit, and they buy 5000 DVD players when the price is $300.

$$PED = \frac{\frac{6000-5000}{5000}}{\frac{255-300}{300}} = \frac{\frac{1000}{5000}}{\frac{-45}{300}} = \frac{0.20}{-0.15} = -1.33 \text{ or } 1.33$$

since we drop the minus sign. Therefore *PED* for DVD players is 1.33.[1]

Test your understanding 3.1

1 (a) Explain the meaning of price elasticity of demand. (b) Why do we say it measures responsiveness of quantity *along a given demand curve*?

2 Why do we treat *PED* as if it were positive, even though it is usually negative?

3 It is observed that when the price of pizzas is $16 per pizza, 100 pizzas are sold; when the price falls to $12 per pizza, 120 pizzas are sold. Calculate price elasticity of demand.

4 A 10% increase in the price of a particular good gives rise to an 8% decrease in quantity bought. What is the price elasticity of demand?

The range of values for *PED*

◆ Explain, using diagrams and PED values, the concepts of price elastic demand, price inelastic demand, unit elastic demand, perfectly elastic demand and perfectly inelastic demand.

The value of *PED* involves a comparison of two numbers: the percentage change in quantity demanded (the numerator in the *PED* formula) and the percentage change in price (the denominator). This comparison yields several possible values and range of values for *PED*. These are illustrated in Figure 3.1 and summarised in Table 3.1.

---

[1] You may note that the value of this elasticity of demand depends on the choice of the initial price–quantity combination. In the calculation above, this was taken to be 300, 5000. If we had taken 255, 6000 as the initial price–quantity combination, we would get a *PED* value of 0.94. (You could calculate this as an exercise.) This difficulty can be overcome by use of the 'midpoint formula':

$$PED = \frac{\frac{\Delta Q_x}{\text{average } Q_x}}{\frac{\Delta P_x}{\text{average } P_x}}.$$

In the previous example,

$$PED = \frac{\frac{1000}{5500}}{\frac{45}{277.5}} = 1.12, \text{ where } 5500 = \frac{(5000+6000)}{2} \text{ and } 277.5 = \frac{(255+300)}{2}$$

i.e. we use the average of the two Q_x values and the average of the two P_x values instead of the initial Q_x and initial P_x.

- **Demand is price inelastic when *PED* < 1 (but greater than zero).** The percentage change in quantity demanded is smaller than the percentage change in price, so the value of *PED* is less than one; quantity demanded is relatively unresponsive to changes in

price, and demand is **price inelastic**. Figure 3.1(a) illustrates price inelastic demand: the percentage change in quantity demanded (a 5% decrease) is smaller than the percentage change in price (a 10% increase), therefore *PED* is less than one.

Value of *PED*	Classification	Interpretation
Frequently encountered cases		
$0 < PED < 1$ (greater than zero and less than one)	inelastic demand	quantity demanded is relatively unresponsive to price
$1 < PED < \infty$ (greater than 1 and less than infinity)	elastic demand	quantity demanded is relatively responsive to price
Special cases		
$PED = 1$	unit elastic demand	percentage change in quantity demanded equals percentage change in price
$PED = 0$	perfectly inelastic demand	quantity demanded is completely unresponsive to price
$PED = \infty$	perfectly elastic demand	quantity demanded is infinitely responsive to price

Table 3.1   Characteristics of price elasticity of demand

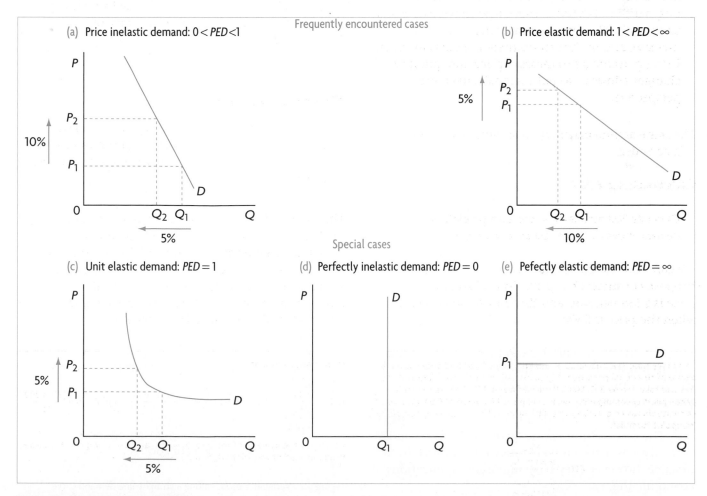

Figure 3.1   Demand curves and *PED*

- **Demand is price elastic when $PED > 1$ (but less than infinity).** The percentage change in quantity demanded is larger than the percentage change in price, so the value of PED is greater than one; quantity demanded is relatively responsive to price changes, and demand is **price elastic**. In Figure 3.1(b) the percentage change in quantity demanded (–10%) is larger than the percentage change in price (5%), therefore PED is greater than one.

In addition, there are three special cases:

- **Demand is unit elastic when $PED = 1$.** The percentage change in quantity demanded is equal to the percentage change in price, so PED is equal to one; demand is then **unit elastic**. Figure 3.1(c) shows a unit elastic demand curve, where the percentage change in quantity demanded (–5%) is equal to the percentage change in price (5%).

- **Demand is perfectly inelastic when $PED = 0$.** The percentage change in quantity demanded is zero; there is no change in quantity demanded, which remains constant at Q_1 no matter what happens to price; PED is then equal to zero and demand is **perfectly inelastic**. For example, a heroin addict's quantity of heroin demanded is unresponsive to changes in the price of heroin. Figure 3.1(d) shows that a perfectly inelastic demand curve is vertical.

- **Demand is perfectly elastic when PED = infinity.** When a change in price results in an infinitely large response in quantity demanded, demand is **perfectly elastic**. As shown in Figure 3.1(e) the perfectly elastic demand curve is horizontal. At price P_1, consumers will buy any quantity that is available. If price falls, buyers will buy all they can (an infinitely large response); if there is an increase in price, quantity demanded drops to zero. This apparently strange kind of demand will be considered in Chapter 7 (at higher level).

The numerical value of PED can therefore vary from zero to infinity. In general, the larger the value of PED, the greater the responsiveness of quantity demanded. PED for most goods and services is greater than zero and less than infinite, and other than exactly one. The cases of unit elastic, perfectly inelastic and perfectly elastic demand are rarely encountered in practice; however, they have important applications in economic theory.

Variable *PED* and the straight-line demand curve versus the slope

> ◆ Explain why PED varies along a straight line demand curve and is not represented by the slope of the demand curve.

When PED varies

Along any *downward-sloping, straight-line demand curve*, the PED varies (changes) as we move along the curve. This applies to all demand curves of the types shown in Figure 3.1 (a) and (b). It excludes unit elastic, perfectly inelastic and perfectly elastic demand curves (where $PED = 1$, $PED = 0$ and $PED =$ infinity, respectively, and does not vary). We can see in Figure 3.2 that when price is low and quantity is high, demand is inelastic; as we move up the demand curve towards higher prices and lower quantities, demand becomes more and more elastic. The figure shows the PED values along different parts of the demand curve (you will be asked to do the PED calculations as an exercise – see Test your understanding 3.2).

The reason behind the changing PED along a straight-line demand curve has to do with how PED is calculated. At high prices and low quantities, the percentage change in Q is relatively large (since the denominator of $\Delta Q/Q$ is small), while the percentage change in P is relatively small (because the denominator of $\Delta P/P$ is large). Therefore the value of PED, given by a large percentage change in Q divided by a small percentage change in P results in a large PED (elastic demand). At low prices and high quantities the opposite holds. The value of PED is

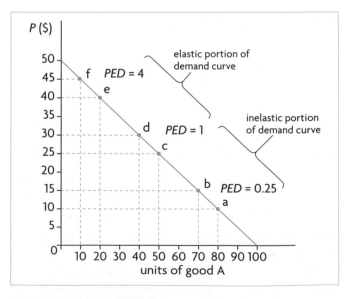

Figure 3.2 Variability of *PED* along a straight-line demand curve

given by a low percentage change in Q divided by a high percentage change in P, resulting in a low *PED* (inelastic demand).

On any downward-sloping, straight-line demand curve, demand is price-elastic at high prices and low quantities, and price-inelastic at low price and large quantities. At the midpoint of the demand curve, there is unit elastic demand.

Therefore, the terms 'elastic' and 'inelastic' should not be used to refer to an entire demand curve (with the exception of the three special cases where *PED* is constant throughout the entire demand curve). Instead, they should be used to refer to a portion of the demand curve that corresponds to a particular price or price range.

HL ### *The relationship between PED and the slope (Higher level topic)*

The varying *PED* along a straight-line demand curve should be contrasted with the *slope*, which is always constant along a straight line (see 'Quantitative techniques' chapter on the CD-ROM, page 28). In the special case of demand (and supply) functions, whose corresponding curves plot the dependent variable on the horizontal axis (in contrast to mathematical convention), the slope is defined as $\frac{\Delta Q}{\Delta P}$, or the horizontal change between two points on the curve divided by the vertical change between the same two points. A comparison of the slope with *PED* shows that the two should not be confused:

$$\text{slope of demand curve} = \frac{\Delta Q}{\Delta P}$$

$$PED = \frac{\%\Delta Q}{\%\Delta P} = \frac{\dfrac{\Delta Q}{Q}}{\dfrac{\Delta P}{P}} = \frac{\Delta Q}{\Delta P} \times \frac{P}{Q} = \text{slope} \times \frac{P}{Q}$$

In these two expressions we can see why the slope is constant, while *PED* varies along a straight-line demand curve. In a straight line, the ratio $\frac{\Delta Q}{\Delta P}$, or the slope, does not change between any pairs of points on the line. However, *PED* is defined as the slope (which is constant) times $\frac{P}{Q}$, which clearly changes as we move along the demand curve, thus accounting for the changing *PED*.

The slope of the demand curve measures the responsiveness of quantity demanded to changes in price in absolute terms, while *PED* measures the same responsiveness in percentage terms. *PED* is far

more useful as a measure of responsiveness for the reasons discussed on page 48. (See also the discussion in 'Quantitative techniques' chapter on the CD-ROM, page 28.)

PED should not be confused with the slope of a demand curve. Whereas the slope is constant for a linear (straight-line) demand curve, *PED* varies throughout its range.

Determinants of price elasticity of demand

♦ Explain the determinants of PED, including the number and closeness of substitutes, the degree of necessity, time and the proportion of income spent on the good.

We will now consider the factors that determine whether the demand for a good is elastic or inelastic.

Number and closeness of substitutes

The more substitutes a good (or service) has, the more elastic is its demand. If the price of a good with many substitutes increases, consumers can switch to other substitute products, therefore resulting in a relatively large drop (large responsiveness) in quantity demanded. For example, there are many brands of toothpaste, which are close substitutes for each other. An increase in the price of one, with the prices of others constant will lead consumers to switch to the others; hence demand for a specific toothpaste brand is price elastic. If a good or service has few or no substitutes, then an increase in price will bring forth a small drop in quantity demanded. An increase in the price of petrol (gasoline) is likely to lead to a relatively small decrease in quantity demanded, because there are no close substitutes; therefore, demand for petrol is price inelastic.

Also important is the closeness of substitutes. For example, Coca-Cola® and Pepsi® are much closer substitutes than Coca-Cola and orange juice; we say that Coca-Cola and Pepsi have greater *substitutability*. The closer two substitutes are to each other, the greater the responsiveness of quantity demanded to a change in the price of the substitute, hence the greater the *PED*, because it is easier for the consumer to switch from one product to the other.

A factor that affects the number of substitutes a good has is whether the good is defined broadly or narrowly. For example, *fruit* is a broad definition of a good if it is considered in relation to *specific fruits* such as oranges, apples, pears, and so on, which are narrowly defined. Note that a broad or narrow definition involves how goods are defined *in relation to each other*. If we had considered fruit in relation to food, *food* is the broadly defined good, and *specific foods* such as fruits, vegetables, grains, fish, and so on, are narrowly defined. (Therefore, fruit is broadly defined in relation to specific fruits, and narrowly defined in relation to food.) The point here is that the narrower the definition of a good, the more the close substitutes and the more elastic the demand (compared with the broadly defined good). The demand for apples is more elastic than the demand for fruit, because of the availability of oranges, pears or other fruits that are close substitutes for apples. The demand for fruit is more elastic than the demand for food. Similarly, a Honda has a higher price elasticity of demand than all cars considered together.

Necessities versus luxuries

Necessities are goods or services we consider to be essential or necessary in our lives; we cannot do without them. **Luxuries** are not necessary or essential. The demand for necessities is less elastic than the demand for luxuries. For example, the demand for medications tends to be very inelastic because people's health or life depend on them; therefore, quantity demanded is not very responsive to changes in price. The demand for food is also inelastic, because people cannot live without it. On the other hand, the demand for diamond rings is elastic as most people view them as luxuries. In general, the more necessary is a good, the less elastic the demand.

A special case of necessity is a consumer's addiction to a good. The greater the degree of addiction to a substance (alcohol, cigarettes, and so on), the more inelastic is the demand. A price increase will not bring forth a significant reduction in quantity demanded if one is severely addicted.

Length of time

The longer the time period in which a consumer makes a purchasing decision, the more elastic the demand. As time goes by, consumers have the opportunity to consider whether they really want the good, and to get information on the availability of alternatives to the good in question. For example, if there is an increase in the price of heating oil, consumers can do little to switch to other forms of heating in a short period of time, and therefore demand for heating oil tends to be inelastic over short periods. But as time goes by, they can switch to other heating systems, such as gas, or they can install better insulation, and demand for heating oil becomes more elastic.

Proportion of income spent on a good

The larger the proportion of one's income needed to buy a good, the more elastic the demand. An item such as a pen takes up a very small proportion of one's income, whereas summer holidays take up a much larger proportion. For the same percentage increase in the price of pens and in the price of summer holidays, the response in quantity demanded is likely to be greater in the case of summer holidays than in the case of pens.

What happens when demand is highly price inelastic?

A girl sells lemonade at a stand for 50 cents (= $0.50) a cup. On a very hot day, the lemonade becomes even more popular, and the girl realises she can raise her price a little and still sell all her lemonade. One afternoon, a diabetic boy comes along asking for lemonade with extra sugar because his blood sugar has fallen to dangerously low levels. The girl sees an opportunity and increases her price by 500%. The boy doesn't have enough money, but she tells him she will give him the lemonade right away provided he promises to run home afterward, get the money and return to pay her the full price. Having no choice, the boy agrees.

Source: Adapted from Teymour Semnani, 'Free markets don't always do the right thing regarding health care' in *The Deseret News*, 15 November 2009.

Applying your skills

1 **(a)** What can you conclude about the boy's price elasticity of demand for sweet lemonade at that particular moment? **(b)** What determinant of *PED* accounts for this?

2 What would have happened to the quantity of lemonade demanded if the other children were faced with a 500% increase in its price? Explain in terms of their price elasticity of demand for lemonade.

1 Specify the value for each of the following *PED*s and show, using diagrams, the shape of the demand curve that corresponds to each one: **(a)** perfectly elastic demand, **(b)** unit elastic demand, and **(c)** perfectly inelastic demand.

2 Provide examples of goods likely to have demand that is **(a)** elastic, and **(b)** inelastic.

3 Which price elasticity of demand values or range of values do we see most frequently in the real world?

4 Using the information in Figure 3.2, calculate *PED* between **(a)** points a and b, where price increases from $10 to $15; **(b)** points c and d, where price increases from $25 to $30; and **(c)** points e and f, where price increases from $40 to $45. **(d)** What general principle about values of the *PED* along the straight-line demand curve do your calculations show?

5 What can you say about the difference between *PED* and the slope of a straight-line demand curve?

6 Identify and explain the determinants of the price elasticity of demand.

7 State in which case demand is likely to be more elastic in each of the following pairs of goods, and why:

   (a) chocolate or Cadbury's chocolate

   (b) orange juice or water

   (c) cigarettes or sweets

   (d) a notepad or a computer

   (e) heating oil in one week or in one year

   (f) bread or caviar.

PED and the steepness of the demand curve (supplementary material)

The variety of demand curves and their *PED*s in Figure 3.1 suggest that the flatter the demand curve, the more elastic the demand (the higher the *PED*); the steeper the demand curve, the less elastic the demand (the lower the *PED)*. However, we cannot conclude whether demand is more or less elastic in different demand curves simply by comparing their steepness. The reasons for this are as follows:

• Demand curves drawn on different scales are not comparable. Figure 3.3 shows two identical demand

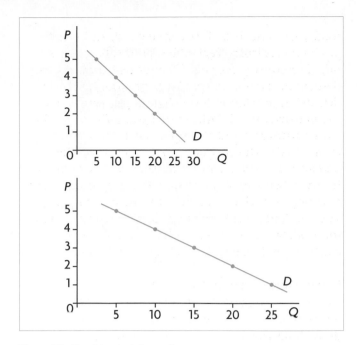

Figure 3.3 Two identical demand curves

curves with different scales on the horizontal axis. It would be incorrect to conclude that the steeper demand curve has a less elastic demand. (This applies equally to the slope, as explained in 'Quantitative techniques' chapter on the CD-ROM, page 28.)

• Even if two or more demand curves are drawn on the same diagram, so there is no problem of scale, it is still not always possible to say which curve is the more or less elastic. The reason is that *PED* is not constant along most demand curves; it varies from being highly elastic to highly inelastic.

So when is it correct to compare *PED*s of demand curves by referring to their steepness?

*PED*s can be compared by reference to the steepness of the demand curves only when the demand curves intersect at some point, that is, when the demand curves share a price and quantity combination, such as demand curves D_1 and D_2 in Figure 3.4(a). In this figure, for any price, D_1 is flatter and more elastic than D_2.

For example, if price falls from P_1 to P_2, the resulting percentage change in quantity will be larger for D_1 (increase from Q_1 to Q_3) than for D_2 (increase from Q_1 to Q_2). In general, when demand curves intersect, then for any given price, the flatter the demand curve, the

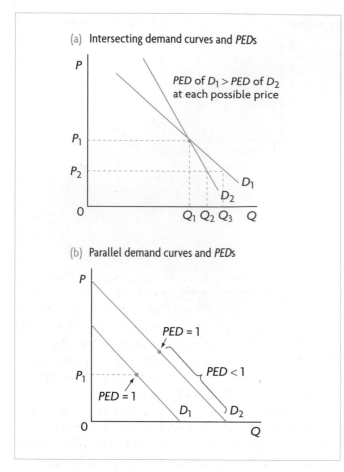

(a) Intersecting demand curves and *PEDs*

PED of D_1 > *PED* of D_2
at each possible price

(b) Parallel demand curves and *PEDs*

Figure 3.4 Demand curves and *PEDs*

PED = 1 for D_1. At this price, *PED* < 1 for D_2, as it lies in the inelastic portion of this demand curve. Therefore at P_1, *PED* corresponding to D_2 is lower than *PED* corresponding to D_1.

Applications of price elasticity of demand

Price elasticity of demand is a very important concept in economics, with numerous applications. Some of these will be considered below; others will be studied in later chapters.

PED and total revenue

♦ Examine the role of PED for firms in making decisions regarding price changes and their effect on total revenue.

PED and the effects of price changes and total revenue

Total revenue (*TR*) is the amount of money received by firms when they sell a good (or service), and is equal to the price (*P*) of the good times the quantity (*Q*) of the good sold. Therefore, $TR = P \times Q$.

We are interested in examining what will happen to the firm's total revenue (*TR*) when there is a change in the price of the good it produces and sells. We know that *P* and *Q* are negatively related to each other: an increase in *P* leads to a decrease in *Q* demanded and vice versa. What can we say about the resulting change in total revenue? Will it increase or decrease? The change will depend on price elasticity of demand of the good. We have the following three possibilities.

more elastic is the demand.[2] This generalisation holds only for comparisons between two demand curves at a particular price. It does not hold for different prices because of the variability of *PED* along the demand curve.

If demand curves do not intersect, comparing *PEDs* on the basis of steepness, even for a particular price, can be misleading. For example, the two parallel demand curves in Figure 3.4(b) do not share a price–quantity combination. It is tempting to conclude that their *PEDs* are the same at each price since they are parallel. However, this would be incorrect, because for each price, D_2 is less elastic than D_1. To see why, consider price P_1, which corresponds to the midpoint of D_1, and hence is the point at which

[2] To see why this is so, the more advanced student can consider the ratio of *PEDs* of D_1 and D_2 in Figure 3.4(a):

$$\frac{PED_1}{PED_2} = \frac{\frac{\%\Delta Q_1}{\%\Delta P}}{\frac{\%\Delta Q_2}{\%\Delta P}} .$$

where $\%\Delta Q_1$ is the percentage change in quantity for D_1, $\%\Delta Q_2$ is the percentage change in quantity for D_2, and $\%\Delta P$ is the

percentage change in price when price changes from P_1 to P_2. The $\%\Delta P$ cancels out from the numerator and denominator, and we are left with

$$\frac{PED_1}{PED_2} = \frac{\%\Delta Q_1}{\%\Delta Q_2}$$

in other words, the ratio of *PEDs* is equal to the ratio of percentage changes in quantity. This is exactly what we see in Figure 3.4(a): the flatter demand curve D_1, with the larger *PED*, has the larger percentage change in quantity.

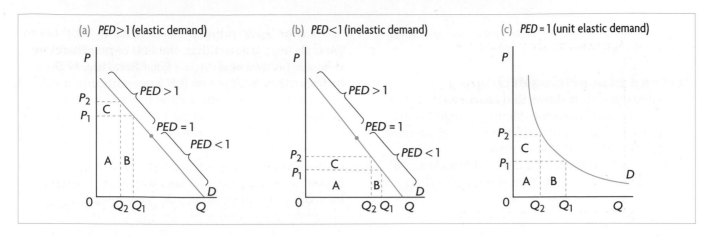

Figure 3.5 *PED* and total revenue

Demand is elastic (PED > 1)

When demand is elastic, an increase in price causes a fall in total revenue, while a decrease in price causes a rise in total revenue. To see why, consider that if demand is elastic, a 10% price increase will result in a larger than 10% decrease in quantity demanded (since *PED* > 1). The impact on total revenue of the decrease in quantity is bigger than the impact of the increase in price; therefore, total revenue falls. If there is a price decrease, a 10% price fall results in a larger than 10% increase in quantity demanded, and total revenue increases.

These results are shown in Figure 3.5(a). Since we are considering elastic demand, we examine a price change in the upper left portion of the demand curve. Total revenue is represented by the area of the rectangles obtained by multiplying price times quantity (since $TR = P \times Q$). At the initial price and quantity, P_1 and Q_1, total revenue is given by the sum of the rectangles A and B. When price increases to P_2 and quantity drops to Q_2, total revenue is given by the sum of the rectangles A and C. What happened to total revenue due to the price increase? The rectangle B was lost and the rectangle C was gained. Since the loss (B) is larger than the gain (C), total revenue fell.

We can use the same diagram to explore a price decrease when *PED* > 1, simply by assuming that the initial price and quantity are P_2 and Q_2; price then falls to P_1 while quantity increases to Q_1. The gain in *TR* is given by rectangle B, which is greater than the loss shown by rectangle C, thus total revenue increases.

> When demand is elastic, an increase in price causes a fall in total revenue, while a decrease in price causes a rise in total revenue.

Demand is inelastic (PED < 1)

When demand is inelastic, an increase in price causes an increase in total revenue, while a decrease in price causes a fall in total revenue. Since *PED* < 1, the percentage change in quantity demanded is smaller than the percentage change in price. Therefore, a 10% price increase produces a smaller than 10% decrease in quantity demanded, and total revenue rises. The effect on total revenue of the increase is larger than the effect of the decrease. If price falls, a percentage price decrease gives rise to a smaller percentage increase in quantity demanded and total revenue falls.

These results can be seen in Figure 3.5(b). We now examine the bottom right portion of the demand curve where demand is inelastic (*PED* < 1). With a price increase, total revenue gained (rectangle C) is larger than total revenue lost (rectangle B); therefore, total revenue increases. If price falls from P_2 to P_1, the gain in total revenue (rectangle B) is smaller than the loss (rectangle C) and total revenue falls.

> When demand is inelastic, an increase in price causes an increase in total revenue, while a decrease in price causes a fall in total revenue.

Demand is unit elastic (PED = 1)

When demand is unit elastic, the percentage change in quantity is equal to the percentage change in price, and total revenue remains constant. In Figure 3.5(c), as price and quantity change, the gain in total revenue is exactly matched by the loss, and total revenue remains unchanged.

> When demand is unit elastic, a change in price does not cause any change in total revenue.

These results may be summarised as follows:
Elastic *PED* (*PED* > 1): price and total revenue change in opposite directions.

Inelastic *PED* (*PED* < 1): price and total revenue change in the same direction.

Unit elastic *PED* (*PED* = 1): as price changes, total revenue remains unchanged.

PED and firm pricing decisions

The above discussion shows that businesses must take *PED* into account when considering changes in the price of their product. If a business wants to increase total revenue, it must drop its price if demand is elastic, or increase its price if demand is inelastic. If demand is unit elastic, the firm is unable to change its total revenue by changing its price.

Remember that *PED* falls as price falls along a downward-sloping straight-line demand curve. In the upper left portion, where prices are high, demand is highly elastic, and a firm can increase its total revenue by lowering price. Total revenue will continue to increase as price falls until price reaches the point on the demand curve where *PED* is unit elastic. If price falls further, total revenue will begin to fall because price is now in the inelastic range of the demand curve. *This means that total revenue is at a maximum when price is at the point where demand is unit elastic.*

A firm's total revenue should not be confused with *profit*. Profit is total revenue minus total costs. A firm interested in maximising profits may not want to maximise total revenue. As total revenue rises, it is possible that total costs may rise faster, in which case the firm's profit will be lower. Costs will be examined in Chapter 6 (at higher level).

PED in relation to primary commodities and manufactured products

◆ Explain why the PED for many primary commodities is relatively low and the PED for manufactured products is relatively high.

Why many primary commodities have a lower PED compared with the PED of manufactured products

Primary commodities are goods arising directly from the use of natural resources, or the factor of production 'land' (see Chapter 1, page 3). Primary commodities therefore include agricultural, fishing and forestry products, as well as products of extractive industries (oil, coal, minerals, and so on). Agricultural products include food, as well as other, non-edible commodities (such as cotton and rubber).

Many primary commodities have a low *PED*, which is usually lower than the *PED* of manufactured products (as well as services). Food has a highly price inelastic demand, because it is a necessity and it has no substitutes. The same applies to a variety of other primary products (such as oil and minerals). In the case of food, in developed countries the *PED* is estimated to be between 0.20 and 0.25. By contrast, the demand for manufactured products tends to be more price elastic, because these products, though they may be necessities (in some cases), they usually do have substitutes. Therefore, given a price change, quantity demanded is generally more responsive in the case of manufactured products compared with primary commodities. (Note, however, that there are exceptions. For example, medications are manufactured products, yet their demand tends to be inelastic because they are necessities and have no substitutes.)

Many primary commodities have a relatively low *PED* (price inelastic demand) because they are necessities and have no substitutes (for example, food and oil). The *PED* of manufactured products is relatively high (price elastic demand) because they usually have substitutes.

Consequences of a low PED for primary commodities

(This topic is included in learning outcomes in Chapters 15 and 17.) Low price elasticity of demand, together with fluctuations in supply over short periods of time, creates serious problems for primary commodity producers, because they result in large fluctuations in primary commodity prices, and these also affect producers' incomes. Let's see why.

Consider the diagrams in Figure 3.6. Part (a) shows relatively inelastic demand (such as for primary commodities) and part (b) shows relatively elastic demand (such as for manufactured products).[3] Both diagrams show the effects on price and quantity when there is a decrease in supply (from S_1 to S_2) and when there is an increase in supply (from S_1 to S_3). A comparison of the two diagrams reveals that shifts in the supply curve result in large price fluctuations when demand is inelastic, and much milder ones when demand is elastic. Large price fluctuations over short periods of time are referred to as *price volatility*. (Volatility means instability or high variability.)

---

[3] Note that we are assuming that the two demand curves are drawn on the same scale, and that if they were drawn in the same diagram they would intersect, therefore it is okay to compare *PEDs* (see page 53).

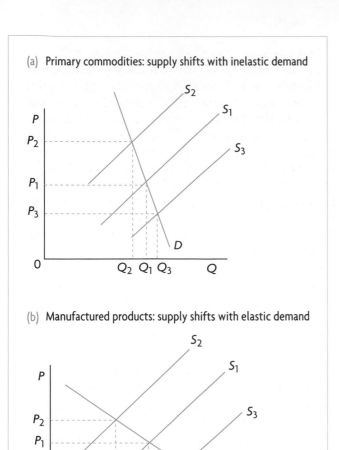

(a) Primary commodities: supply shifts with inelastic demand

(b) Manufactured products: supply shifts with elastic demand

Figure 3.6 Price fluctuations are larger for primary commodities because of low *PED*

Figure 3.6 explains why in the real world, prices of primary commodities can be highly volatile, whereas they tend to be much less so in the manufacturing and services sectors.

Two results follow from this:

- As primary commodity prices fluctuate widely, so do producers' incomes, which depend on the revenues (price × quantity) producers receive from selling their output.
- In view of the relationship between *PED* and total revenue (see page 55), a fall in the supply of a primary commodity with inelastic demand

(from S_1 to S_2 in part (a) of Figure 3.6) leads to an increase in total revenue of producers because the percentage increase in price is larger than the percentage decrease in quantity. An increase in supply leads to lower revenues (the percentage decrease in price is larger than the percentage increase in quantity).

These points lead to some unexpected conclusions. They show that a poor crop in agriculture, say due to poor weather conditions, which results in a fall in supply (S_2 in part (a) of Figure 3.6), leads to higher prices and higher total revenue for farmers. A good crop resulting in a supply increase, or S_3, leads to lower prices and lower farmers' revenues. We come, therefore, to the ironic conclusion that a poor crop may be good for farmers because it increases their revenues while a good crop may be bad for them.

If supply of agricultural products were relatively stable, the problem would be less serious as agricultural product prices would also be more stable. However, agricultural production depends on many factors beyond the farmer's control, such as drought, pests, floods, frost and other such natural disasters, as well as exceptionally good weather conditions, which occur over short periods of time. These cause frequent and large supply changes (supply curve shifts).

The problem of unstable farmer revenues is an important reason behind government intervention to support farmer incomes, which we will study in Chapter 4. The implications of unstable primary product prices for farmer revenues and the economy will be explored in Chapters 15 and 17.

PED and indirect taxes

- Examine the significance of PED for government in relation to indirect taxes.

Governments often impose taxes on specific goods. Such taxes are a type of indirect tax (to be discussed in Chapter 4). If governments are interested in increasing their tax revenues, they must consider the *PED* of the goods to be taxed. *The lower the price elasticity of demand for the taxed good, the greater the government tax revenues.*

This can be seen in Figure 3.7, showing the case of inelastic demand in part (a) and elastic demand in part (b).[4] When a tax is imposed on a good, it has the effect of shifting the supply curve upward. The reason is that for every level of output the firm is willing and able

---

[4] Here, too, as in the case of Figure 3.6, we are assuming that the two demand curves are drawn on the same scale, and that if they were drawn in the same diagram they would intersect, therefore the *PEDs* are comparable (see page 53).

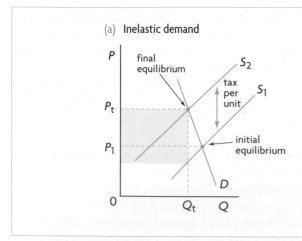

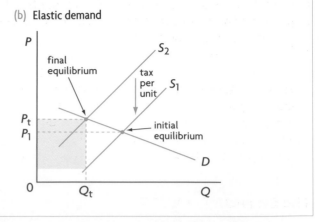

Figure 3.7 *PED*, indirect taxes and government tax revenue

to supply to the market, it must receive a price that is higher than the original price by the amount of the tax. (This is equivalent to a leftward shift of the supply curve; for an explanation see 'Quantitative techniques' chapter on the CD-ROM, page 13.) The curve shifts from S_1 to S_2 so that the vertical distance between S_1 and S_2 is equal to the amount of the tax per unit of output. The new, after-tax equilibrium occurs at price P_t and quantity Q_t, determined by the intersection of the demand curve, D, and the new supply curve, S_2. The shaded area represents the government's tax revenue, obtained by multiplying the amount of tax per unit times the number of units, or quantity Q_t. A comparison of the two figures indicates that tax revenue is larger when demand is inelastic. This result follows from the principle that when demand is inelastic ($PED < 1$), an increase in price (here due to the increase in the tax) leads to a proportionately smaller decrease in quantity demanded, and hence to an increase in total revenue (i.e. tax revenue). Indirect taxes are therefore usually imposed on goods like cigarettes and petrol (gasoline), which have a low *PED*.

Test your understanding 3.4

1 Explain and show, using diagrams, how total revenue will change if:

   (a) price increases and demand is elastic

   (b) price decreases and demand is inelastic

   (c) price increases and demand is perfectly inelastic

   (d) price increases and demand is inelastic

   (e) price decreases and demand has unit elasticity

   (f) price decreases and demand is elastic.

2 How can a firm's knowledge of price elasticity of demand for its product help it in its pricing decisions?

3 Suppose flooding destroys a substantial portion of this season's crop. Using diagrams, explain what is likely to happen to farmers' revenues, assuming the demand for the product they produce is inelastic.

4 **(a)** Why do many primary commodities have a relatively low *PED* while many manufactured products have a relatively high *PED*? **(b)** Use the concept of *PED* and diagrams to explain why agricultural product prices tend to fluctuate more (are more volatile) compared with manufactured product prices over the short term.

5 The government would like to levy indirect taxes (excise taxes) on certain goods to raise tax revenue. Using diagrams, explain how price elasticity of demand can help it decide which products it should tax.

3.2 Cross-price elasticity of demand (*XED*)

Cross-price elasticity of demand

Understanding cross-price elasticity of demand

♦ Outline the concept of cross price elasticity of demand, understanding that it involves responsiveness of demand for one good (and hence a shifting demand curve) to a change in the price of another good.

In Chapter 2, page 24, we learned that the prices of substitutes and complements of a good are among the factors that influence demand for the good and affect the position of its demand curve. We saw that changes in prices of substitutes and complements cause demand curve shifts. What we now want to ask is by how much a demand curve will shift, or what is the responsiveness of demand, given a change in the price of a substitute or complement?

> **Cross-price elasticity of demand** (*XED*) is a measure of the responsiveness of demand for one good to a change in the price of another good, and involves demand curve shifts. It provides us with information on whether demand increases or decreases, and on the size of demand curve shifts.

The formula for *XED*

◆ Calculate XED using the following equation.

$$XED = \frac{\text{percentage change in quantity demanded of good } X}{\text{percentage change in price of good } Y}$$

The formula for cross-price elasticity of demand has the same basic form as the formula for *PED*, only now we consider the relationship between the percentage change in quantity demanded of one good (*X*) and the percentage change in the price of another good (*Y*):[5]

$$\begin{array}{c}\text{cross-price}\\ \text{elasticity of} = XED = \dfrac{\text{percentage change in quantity demanded of good } X}{\text{percentage change in price of good } Y}\\ \text{demand}\end{array}$$

$$XED = \frac{\%\Delta Q_x}{\%\Delta P_y}$$

which can be rewritten as:

$$XED = \frac{\dfrac{\Delta Q_x}{Q_x} \times 100}{\dfrac{\Delta P_y}{P_y} \times 100} = \frac{\dfrac{\Delta Q_x}{Q_x}}{\dfrac{\Delta P_y}{P_y}}$$

Interpreting cross-price elasticity of demand

◆ Show that substitute goods have a positive value of XED and complementary goods have a negative value of XED.
◆ Explain that the (absolute) value of XED depends on the closeness of the relationship between two goods.

Cross-price elasticity of demand provides two kinds of information:

- the sign of *XED*: unlike *PED*, whose minus sign is ignored, cross-price elasticity of demand is either positive or negative, and the sign is very important for its interpretation
- the value of *XED:* how small or large is its absolute value (the absolute value of a number is its numerical value without its sign).

Substitutes and degree of substitutability

The meaning of a positive XED

> Cross-price elasticity of demand for two goods is positive (*XED*>0) when the demand for one good and the price of the other good change in the same direction: when the price of one increases, the demand for the other also increases. This occurs when the two goods are *substitutes* (see page 24).

For example, Coca-Cola® and Pepsi® are substitutes. Let's consider what happens to the demand for Pepsi, shown in Figure 3.8(a), as the price of Coca-Cola changes. If the

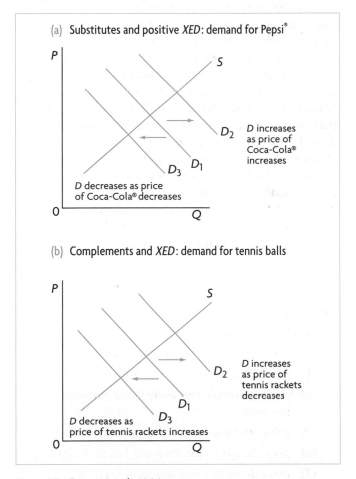

(a) Substitutes and positive *XED*: demand for Pepsi®

D increases as price of Coca-Cola® increases

D decreases as price of Coca-Cola® decreases

(b) Complements and *XED*: demand for tennis balls

D increases as price of tennis rackets decreases

D decreases as price of tennis rackets increases

Figure 3.8   Cross-price elasticities

<hr/>

[5] You may have noticed something odd: whereas *XED* is defined as responsiveness of 'demand', it is measured as a % change in 'quantity demanded'. *XED* is concerned with demand curve shifts, hence with responsiveness of 'demand'. However, when we measure *XED*, we do so by measuring changes in purchases of a good, hence in '*Q* demanded', with the understanding that this involves a shift to a new demand curve.

price of Coca-Cola increases, the quantity of Coca-Cola demanded falls, and the demand for Pepsi increases as consumers switch from Coca-Cola to Pepsi, and there results a rightward shift in the demand curve for Pepsi. If the price of Coca-Cola falls, the quantity of Coca-Cola demanded increases, and the demand for Pepsi falls as consumers now switch from Pepsi to Coca-Cola; there results a leftward shift in Pepsi's demand curve. (Note that in the case of Coca-Cola, whose own price is changing, we refer to increases or decreases in the 'quantity demanded', whereas with Pepsi we refer to increases or decreases in 'demand' because of demand curve shifts.)

In fact, the cross-price elasticity of demand for Coca-Cola® and Pepsi® has been estimated to be about +0.7.[6] This means that a 1% increase in the price of one leads to a 0.7% increase in demand for the other; or a 10% increase in the price of one leads to a 7% increase in the demand for the other. This is considered to be an example of fairly high substitutability.

> Given two pairs of substitute goods, the larger the value of cross-price elasticity of demand, the greater the substitutability between two goods, and the larger the demand curve shift in the event of a price change. For example, two substitute goods with a XED of +0.7 are stronger substitutes for each other than two goods with a XED of +0.3.

Calculating XED in the case of substitutes

Suppose the price of coffee increases from $10 per kilogram (kg) to $12 per kg and the amount of tea purchased increases from 1500 kg to 1650 kg. What is the XED?

$$XED = \frac{\dfrac{150}{1500}}{\dfrac{2}{10}} = \frac{0.1}{0.2} = +0.5$$

XED is +0.5; the positive sign tells us that coffee and tea are substitutes.

Complements and degree of complementarity

The meaning of a negative XED

> Cross-price elasticity of demand for two goods is negative ($XED < 0$) when the demand for one good and the price of the other good change in opposite directions: when the price of one good increases, the demand for the other falls. This occurs when the two goods are *complements* (see page 24).

Figure 3.8(b) shows the demand for tennis balls. If the price of tennis rackets increases, the quantity of tennis rackets demanded falls, and since tennis rackets are used together with tennis balls, the demand for tennis balls also falls; there will therefore be a leftward shift in the demand curve for tennis balls. If there is a fall in the price of tennis rackets, the quantity of tennis rackets demanded increases, and the demand for tennis balls also increases; the demand curve for tennis balls will shift to the right.

> The larger the absolute value of the negative cross-price elasticity of demand, the greater is the complementarity between two goods, and the larger is the demand curve shift in the event of a price change. Two goods with a XED of −0.8 are stronger complements than two goods with a XED of −0.5.

Calculating XED in the case of complements

Suppose the price of pencils increases from $1.00 per pencil to $1.30 and the quantity of erasers purchased falls from 1000 erasers to 800. What is the XED?

$$XED = \frac{\dfrac{-200}{1000}}{\dfrac{0.30}{1.00}} = \frac{-0.20}{0.30} = -0.67$$

XED is −0.67; the negative sign tells us that pencils and erasers are complements.

Zero XED: unrelated products

If cross-price elasticity of demand is zero ($XED = 0$) or close to zero, this means that two products are unrelated or independent of each other. For example, potatoes and telephones are unrelated to each other: a change in the price of one is unlikely to affect demand for the other.

Applications of cross-price elasticity of demand

♦ Examine the implications of XED for businesses if prices of substitutes or complements change.

There are some situations where businesses would be interested in knowing cross-price elasticities of demand for various products.

---

[6] F. Gasmi *et al.* (1992) 'Econometric analysis of collusive behavior in a soft-drink market' in *Journal of Economics & Management Strategy*, Vol. 1/2, Summer.

Substitute goods

Substitutes produced by a single business

When a business produces a line of products that are similar to each other, such as Coca-Cola® and Sprite®, both produced by Coca-Cola, it must consider the *XED* for these products when making decisions about prices. Since the two goods are substitutes, a fall in the price of Coca-Cola would be followed by a fall in the demand for Sprite. Should Coca-Cola cut the price of Coca-Cola? To make a decision it must have information about:

- *PED* for Coca-Cola, so that it can determine whether a price cut will lower or raise total revenue from Coca-Cola

- *XED* for Coca-Cola and Sprite; it is not enough to know that *XED*>0 (that the two goods are substitutes). It is also important to know the degree of substitutability between them. If the value of *XED* is positive but low (low substitutability), a percentage decrease in the price of Coca-Cola® will produce only a small percentage drop in demand for Sprite®, so that the sales of Sprite would not be seriously affected. But if the value of *XED* is positive and high, a fall in the price of Coca-Cola will produce a large drop in demand for Sprite. Increased sales of Coca-Cola would come at the expense of Sprite sales and revenues – something that the company would probably want to avoid.

Substitutes produced by rival businesses

A business is also interested in knowing the *XED* of substitutes when these are produced by rival businesses. For example, Coca-Cola would be interested in knowing the *XED* between Coca-Cola and Pepsi. A large *XED* would mean that if Coca-Cola dropped its price, Pepsi would suffer a serious drop in sales, whereas a low *XED* would mean that Pepsi would not be seriously affected. Coca-Cola would also want to know this *XED* in order to be able to predict the effect on Coca-Cola sales and revenues of any change in the price of Pepsi.

Substitutes and mergers between firms

A *merger* takes place when two firms unite to form a single firm. Businesses producing close substitutes with a high positive *XED*, might be interested in merging because that way they would eliminate the competition between them (although this is usually illegal and prevented by governments). For this reason they might want to know the size of *XED*.

Complementary goods

Knowledge of *XED* for complementary products is also useful for business pricing decisions. Products that have a low absolute value of a (negative) *XED* are weakly complementary and will not be of much interest. However, a high absolute value of a (negative) *XED* means that lowering the price of one good can result in a large increase in demand and sales for the other.

Businesses producing strongly complementary goods often collaborate. For example, sports clothing and sports equipment are highly complementary, as are charter flights and holiday hotels. A fall in the price of charter flights is likely to produce a substantial increase in holiday hotel occupancy. We find airlines frequently collaborating with hotels to take advantage of such complementarities, thus increasing sales and revenues.

It is also possible to use *XED* to estimate the impact of an indirect (excise) tax on one good on the sales of a complementary good. If two goods have a relatively high *XED*, a large tax on one could result in a significant decrease in sales of the other. For example, increases in gasoline (petrol) taxes can have a large impact on the demand for large cars.

Test your understanding 3.5

1 Explain the meaning of cross-price elasticity of demand. Why do we say it involves *a shifting demand curve*?

2 What can you conclude about the relationship of goods A and B in the following situations?
   (a) Sales of good A increase by 10% in response to a price decrease in good B of 15%.
   (b) Sales of good B decrease by 10% in response to a price decrease in good A of 15%.
   (c) Sales of good B remain unchanged in response to a price decrease in good A of 15%.

3 Suggest examples of pairs of goods that might correspond to goods A and B in parts (a), (b) and (c) of question 2.

4 If *XED* between Coca-Cola® and Pepsi® is 0.7, how will the demand for Coca-Cola change if the price of Pepsi increases by 5%? (Your answer should be in percentage terms, and should indicate whether the demand for Coca-Cola will increase or decrease.)

5 For the answer to question 4 show, using diagrams, (a) the 'change in quantity demanded', and (b) the 'change in demand' for Pepsi and Coca-Cola, respectively, that will result from the 5% increase in the price of Pepsi.

6 Suppose goods A and B have a *XED* of +0.2 and goods B and C have a *XED* of +0.8. (a) What is the relationship between the two goods in

each pair? **(b)** What can you conclude about the strength of this relationship for each pair? **(c)** Suppose the prices of A and C increase; draw a diagram showing the effect that each price increase will have on the demand for B.

7 Suppose goods D and E have a *XED* of –0.3 and goods E and F have a *XED* of –0.7. **(a)** What is the relationship between the two goods in each pair? **(b)** What can you conclude about the strength of this relationship for each pair? **(c)** Suppose the prices of D and F increase; draw a diagram showing the effect that each price increase will have on the demand for E.

8 How can knowledge of cross-price elasticities of demand help firms make pricing decisions in the case of **(a)** substitutes; **(b)** complements?

3.3 Income elasticity of demand (*YED*)

Income elasticity of demand

Understanding income elasticity of demand

♦ Outline the concept of income elasticity of demand, understanding that it involves responsiveness of demand (and hence a shifting demand curve) to a change in income.

Consumer income is another factor influencing demand for a good and the position of the demand curve.

Income elasticity of demand (*YED*) is a measure of the responsiveness of demand to changes in income, and involves demand curve shifts. It provides information on the direction of change of demand given a change in income (increase or decrease) and on the size of the change (size of demand curve shifts).

Calculating *YED*

♦ Calculate YED using the following equation.

$$YED = \frac{\text{percentage change in quantity demanded}}{\text{percentage change in income}}$$

The formula for *YED* has the same basic form as the other elasticity formulae, and shows the relationship

between the percentage change in quantity demanded of a good, *X*, and the percentage change in income, which we abbreviate as *Y*:[7]

$$\text{income elasticity of demand} = YED = \frac{\text{percentage change in quantity demanded of good } X}{\text{percentage change in income}}$$

$$YED = \frac{\%\Delta Q_x}{\%\Delta Y}$$

which can be rewritten as:

$$YED = \frac{\frac{\Delta Q_x}{Q_x} \times 100}{\frac{\Delta Y}{Y} \times 100} = \frac{\frac{\Delta Q_x}{Q_x}}{\frac{\Delta Y}{Y}}$$

Suppose your income increases from $800 per month to $1000 per month, and your purchases of clothes increase from $100 to $140 per month. What is your income elasticity of demand for clothes?

$$YED = \frac{\frac{40}{100}}{\frac{200}{800}} = \frac{0.40}{0.25} = +1.6$$

Your income elasticity demand for clothes is +1.6. We will now see how we interpret various values of income elasticity of demand.

Interpreting income elasticity of demand

Income elasticity of demand provides two kinds of information:

- the sign of *YED*: positive or negative
- the numerical value of *YED*: whether it is greater or smaller than one (assuming it is positive).

The sign of income elasticity of demand: normal or inferior goods

♦ Show that normal goods have a positive value of YED and inferior goods have a negative value of YED.

The sign of *YED* tells us whether a good is normal or inferior:

---

[7] Here, too, as with *XED*, *YED* involves the responsiveness of 'demand' to changes in income, but is measured as the % change in 'Q demanded'. (See footnote 5, page 59.)

- *YED>0* Income elasticity of demand is positive (*YED>0*) when demand and income change in the same direction (i.e. both increase or both decrease). A positive *YED* indicates that the good in question is *normal*. Most goods are normal goods (see page 24).

- *YED<0* A negative income elasticity of demand (*YED<0*) indicates that the good is *inferior*: demand for the good and income move in opposite directions (as one increases the other decreases). Examples include bus rides, second-hand clothes and used cars; as income increases, the demand for these goods falls as consumers switch to consumption of normal goods (new cars, new clothes, and so on; see page 24).

The difference between normal and inferior goods can be seen in Figure 3.9, showing a demand curve, D_1, and shifts of the curve that occur in response to increases in income. As income increases, the demand curve shifts rightward from D_1 to D_3 or D_4 when goods are normal (*YED>0*), but shifts leftward to D_2 when goods are inferior good (*YED<0*).

The numerical value of income elasticity of demand: necessities and luxuries

• Distinguish, with reference to YED, between necessity (income inelastic) goods and luxury (income elastic) goods.

Here we are making a distinction between goods that have a *YED* that is less than one (but positive) or greater than one:

- *YED<1: Necessities* If a good has a *YED* that is positive but less than one, it has **income inelastic demand**: a percentage increase in income produces a smaller percentage increase in quantity demanded. Necessities are income inelastic goods.

- *YED>1: Luxuries* If a good has an *YED* that is greater than one, it has **income elastic demand**: a percentage increase in income produces a larger percentage increase in quantity demanded. Luxuries are income elastic goods.

Necessities, such as food, clothing and housing, tend to have a *YED* that is positive but less than one; they are normal goods that are income inelastic. In the case of food, as income increases, people buy more food but the proportion of income spent on food increases more slowly than income. In developed countries,

YED for food is about 0.15 to 0.2. This means that a 1% increase in income produces a 0.15% to 0.2% increase in spending on food; or a 10% increase in income results in a 1.5% to 2% increase in spending on food. By contrast, luxuries, such as travel to other countries, private education and eating in restaurants are income elastic: as income increases, the proportion of income spent on such goods increases faster than income (the denominator in the *YED* formula is smaller than the numerator).

What is a necessity and what is a luxury depends on income levels. For people with extremely low incomes, even food and certainly clothing can be luxuries. As income increases, certain items that used to be luxuries become necessities. For example, items like Coca-Cola® and coffee for many poor people in less developed countries are luxuries, whereas for consumers in developed countries they have become necessities. Income elasticity of demand for particular items therefore varies widely depending on income levels. While *YED* for food is about 0.15–0.20 in more developed countries, it is about 0.8 in poor countries. For an increase in income of 10%, spending on food increases by only 1.5%–2% in rich countries and by 8% in poor countries.

In Figure 3.9, we see that in the case of necessities, an increase in income will produce a relatively small rightward shift in the demand curve; in the case of luxuries, the rightward shift will be larger.

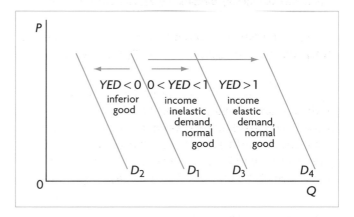

Figure 3.9 Demand curve shifts in response to increases in income for different *YED*s

Applications of income elasticity of demand

YED implications for producers and for the economy

• Examine the implications for producers and for the economy of a relatively low YED for primary products, a relatively higher YED for manufactured products and an even higher YED for services.

YED and producers: the rate of expansion of industries

Over time, as countries experience economic growth, society's income increases. Increasing income means a growing demand for goods and services. Suppose that total income in an economy grows at an average rate of about 3% per year. If goods and services have income elastic demand ($YED > 1$), this means that demand for these goods and services grows at a higher rate than 3%. Examples usually include restaurants, movies, health care and foreign travel. Other goods and services have income inelastic demand ($YED < 1$), meaning that the demand for these grows at a rate of less than 3%. Examples include food, clothing and furniture. The first group (with the elastic demand) includes goods and services produced by industries that grow and expand faster than total income in the economy, while the second group includes goods or services produced by industries growing more slowly than total income.

Income elasticity of demand and industry growth

As consumer incomes increase with economic growth, they lead to a greater amount of spending by consumers. A study was carried out in Thailand to try to find which are the sectors that stand to gain the most from increased consumer incomes and spending. The study suggests that the sectors that benefit the most from rising incomes and consumption are those with the most income elastic demand. It was found that the following sectors are likely to perform the best in Thailand: the auto sector (car sales), communication equipment (mobile phone sales), and financial services. These areas show the greatest sensitivity to changing income levels and have an income elasticity of demand greater than 2.

Source: Adapted from 'Thailand: Economic impacts of the first SP2 allotment of Bt200bn' in Thai Press Reports, 9 November 2009.

Applying your skills

1 Explain the meaning of income elastic demand.

2 Explain why goods and services with highly income elastic demand stand to gain the most from rising consumer incomes.

The higher the *YED* for a good or service, the greater the expansion of its market is likely to be in the future; the lower the *YED*, the smaller the expansion. Producers interested in producing in an expanding market may therefore want to know *YED*s of various goods and services.

In contrast to periods of economic growth, if an economy is experiencing a recession (falling output and incomes, see Chapter 8), goods and services with high *YED*s ($YED > 1$) are the hardest hit, experiencing the largest declines in sales. Products with low *YED*s ($YED < 1$) can avoid large falls in sales, while inferior goods ($YED < 0$) can even experience increases in sales.

YED and the economy

The implications of differing *YED*s for the economy follow from what happens to particular industries in the economy as income grows, discussed above.

Every economy has three sectors (or parts): the primary sector including primary products (agriculture, forestry, fishing and extractive industries), the manufacturing sector and the services sector (including entertainment, travel, banking, insurance, health care, education, and so on). With economic growth, the relative size of the three sectors usually changes over time, and these changes can be explained in terms of income elasticity of demand. Agriculture, the main part of the primary sector, produces food, which as noted above (page 63) has a *YED* that is positive but less than one (it is income inelastic). As society's income grows over time, the demand for agricultural output grows more slowly than the growth in income. Other primary products also have a low income elasticity of demand. For example, cotton and rubber have synthetic substitutes, so as income increases a relatively larger proportion of it is spent on the synthetic materials, while a relatively lower fraction goes towards cotton and rubber. By contrast, manufactured products (cars, televisions, computers, and so on) have a *YED* that is usually greater than one (income elastic), so that as society's income grows, the demand for these products grows faster than income. Many services have even higher *YED*s, so the percentage increase in the demand for these is much larger.

Therefore, over time, the share of agricultural output in total output in the economy shrinks, while the share of manufactured output grows. With continued growth, the services sector expands at the expense of both agriculture and manufacturing. In Figure 3.10, this is shown for a hypothetical growing economy in the changes of relative sector sizes from parts (a) to (b) to (c).

Economically less developed countries usually have a large primary sector due to the importance

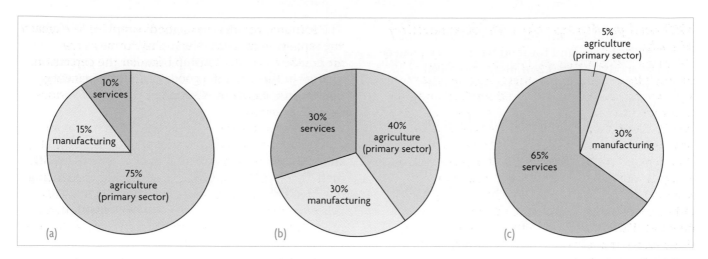

Figure 3.10 Changing relative shares (as percentage of total output) of primary, manufacturing and services sectors for a hypothetical economy as it grows

of agriculture and extractive activities, while manufacturing and services are far less important. The developed countries of today were in a similar position many decades ago. The historical experience of both more and less developed countries shows that with economic growth, the primary sector becomes less and less important, and is partly replaced by manufacturing and services. As the economy grows further, the relative importance of the primary sector continues to shrink, and manufacturing becomes increasingly replaced by services. Thus, while less developed countries are usually dominated by the primary sector, more developed countries are dominated by services. In the developed world today, among the industries experiencing the fastest growth are services, including education, health care, travel and financial services.

Note that if total output is increasing over time, a falling share for a particular sector (such as the primary sector) does not necessarily mean that primary sector output is falling; most likely it means that this sector's output is growing, but more slowly than total output. An increasing share for a sector means that its output is growing more rapidly than total output.

HL

YED *and long-term impacts on primary commodity prices (higher level topic)*

(This topic is related to learning outcomes appearing in Chapters 15 and 17.)

A low *YED* for food (agricultural products), compared with a high *YED* for manufactured products and services, has important implications for the level of prices of agricultural products relative to prices of manufactured products and services over long periods of time. We have seen that a low *YED* for food means that as income rises, a relatively smaller

proportion of income is spent on food and a relatively larger proportion on manufactured products and services, indicating that as incomes rise, demand for manufactured products and services rises more rapidly than the demand for food. The result is that the prices of these goods and services rise more rapidly than the prices of agricultural products. This has important implications for economically less developed countries, which we will study in Chapters 15 and 17.

HL

Test your understanding 3.6

1 Explain the meaning of income elasticity of demand. Why do we say it involves *a shifting demand curve*?

2 Explain the difference between normal and inferior goods and provide examples of each.

3 Your income increases from £1000 a month to £1200 a month. As a result, you increase your purchases of pizzas from 8 to 12 per month, and you decrease your purchases of cheese sandwiches from 15 to 10 per month. **(a)** Calculate your income elasticity of demand for pizzas and for cheese sandwiches. **(b)** What kind of goods are pizzas and cheese sandwiches for you? (c) Show using diagrams the effects of your increase in income on your demand for pizzas and cheese sandwiches.

4 A 15% increase in income leads to a 10% increase in demand for good A and 20% increase in demand for good B. **(a)** Explain which of the two goods is income elastic and which is income inelastic. **(b)** Which of the two goods is likely to be a necessity good and which a luxury good?

5 How can you account for the fact that income elasticity of demand for food has been estimated to be about 0.15 to 0.2 in more developed countries and about 0.8 in less developed countries?

6 What is one likely explanation behind the observed rapid growth in certain service industries, including health care, education and financial services, compared with other industries such as food (in the primary sector) and furniture (in the secondary sector)?

7 Use the concept of *YED* and a diagram to explain why agricultural product prices tend to fall relative to prices of manufactured products over the long term.

3.4 Price elasticity of supply (*PES*)

Price elasticity of supply

Understanding price elasticity of supply

♦ Explain the concept of price elasticity of supply, understanding that it involves responsiveness of quantity supplied to a change in price along a given supply curve.

Until now, we have been studying demand elasticities, all of which involve consumer responses. We now turn to examine price elasticity of supply, which concerns firm (business) responses to changes in price. According to the law of supply, there is a positive relationship between price and quantity supplied: when price increases, quantity supplied increases and vice versa. But by how much does quantity supplied change?

Price elasticity of supply (*PES*) is a measure of the responsiveness of the quantity of a good supplied to changes in its price. *PES* is calculated along a given supply curve. In general, if there is a large responsiveness of quantity supplied, supply is referred to as being *elastic*; if there is a small responsiveness, supply is *inelastic*.

Calculating *PES*

♦ Calculate PES using the following equation.

$$PES = \frac{\text{percentage change in quantity supplied}}{\text{percentage change in price}}$$

The formula for price elasticity of supply (*PES*) follows the same general form of elasticity formulae, only now we consider the relationship between the percentage change in the price of a good, *X*, and the percentage change in quantity of *X* supplied:

$$\text{price elasticity of supply} = PES = \frac{\text{percentage change in quantity of good } X \text{ supplied}}{\text{percentage change in price of good } X}$$

$$PES = \frac{\%\Delta Q_x}{\%\Delta P_x}$$

which can be rewritten as:

$$PES = \frac{\frac{\Delta Q_x}{Q_x} \times 100}{\frac{\Delta P_x}{P_x} \times 100} = \frac{\frac{\Delta Q_x}{Q_x}}{\frac{\Delta P_x}{P_x}}$$

Suppose the price of strawberries increases from €3 per kg to €3.50 per kg, and the quantity of strawberries supplied increases from 1000 to 1100 tonnes per season. Calculate *PES* for strawberries.

$$PES = \frac{\frac{100}{1000}}{\frac{0.50}{3.00}} = \frac{0.10}{0.17} = +0.59$$

Price elasticity of supply for strawberries is +0.59. We will now see how *PES* is interpreted.

Interpreting price elasticity of supply

The range of values for *PES*

♦ Explain, using diagrams and PES values, the concepts of elastic supply, inelastic supply, unit elastic supply, perfectly elastic supply and perfectly inelastic supply.

Price elasticity of supply ranges in value from zero to infinity. Because of the positive relationship between price and quantity supplied, *PES* is positive.

The value of *PES* involves a comparison of the percentage change in quantity supplied (the numerator in the formula for *PES*) with the percentage change in price (the denominator). This comparison yields the following possible values and range of values of *PES*, which are illustrated in Figure 3.11 and summarised in Table 3.2:

- **Supply is price inelastic when *PES* < 1.** The percentage change in quantity supplied is smaller than the percentage change in price, so the value of *PES* is less than one; quantity supplied is relatively unresponsive to changes in price, and supply is *price inelastic* or *inelastic*. Figure 3.11(a) shows an inelastic supply curve (*PES* < 1), where a 10% price increase leads to a 5% increase in quantity supplied. When *PES* < 1, the supply curve extends upward and to the right from the horizontal axis; its end-point cuts the horizontal axis. (Higher level students may note that this supply curve has a positive Q-intercept[8].)

- **Supply is price elastic when *PES* > 1.** The percentage change in quantity supplied is larger than the percentage change in price, so the value of the *PES* is greater than one; quantity supplied is relatively responsive to price changes, and supply is *price elastic* or *elastic*. Figure 3.11(b) shows an elastic supply curve (*PES* > 1) where the percentage increase in price (10%) is smaller than the percentage increase in quantity (15%). When *PES* > 1, the supply curve extends upward and to the right from the vertical axis; its end-point cuts the vertical axis. (Higher level students

may note that this supply curve has a negative Q-intercept.[9])

In addition, there are three special cases:

- **Supply is unit elastic when *PES* = 1.** The percentage change in quantity supplied is equal to the percentage change in price, so *PES* is equal to one; supply is *unit elastic*. In Figure 3.11(c), all three supply curves shown are unit elastic supply curves, i.e. for all three, *PES* = 1. Any supply curve that passes through the origin has a *PES* equal to unity. The reason for this is that along any straight line that passes through the origin, between any two points on the line the percentage change in the vertical axis (the price) is equal to the percentage change in the horizontal axis (the quantity). Therefore, for lines that pass through the origin, it is important not to confuse the steepness of the curve with the elasticity of the curve.

- **Supply is perfectly inelastic when *PES* = 0.** The percentage change in quantity supplied is zero; there is no change in quantity supplied no matter what happens to price; *PES* is equal to

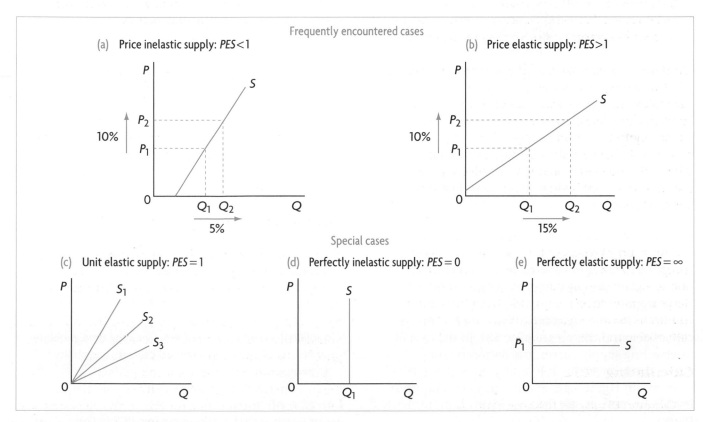

Figure 3.11 Supply curves and *PES*

---

[8] This means that in the supply function $Q_s = c + d\,P$, c > 0

[9] This means that in the supply function $Q_s = c + d\,P$, c < 0.

Value of PES	Classification	Interpretation
Frequently encountered cases		
0 < PES < 1 **(greater than zero and less than one)**	inelastic supply	quantity supplied is relatively unresponsive to price
1 < PES < ∞ **(greater than 1 and less than infinity)**	elastic supply	quantity supplied is relatively responsive to price
Special cases		
PES = 1	unit elastic supply	percentage change in quantity supplied equals percentage change in price
PES = 0	perfectly inelastic supply	quantity supplied is completely unresponsive to price
PES = ∞	perfectly elastic supply	quantity supplied is infinitely responsive to price

Table 3.2   Characteristics of price elasticity of supply

zero and supply is said to be *perfectly inelastic*. In Figure 3.11(d), the supply curve is vertical at the point of fixed quantity supplied, Q_1. This is the same as the supply curve shown in Figure 2.7 in Chapter 2, page 27). Examples of a vertical supply curve include the supply of fish at the moment when fishing boats return from sea; the season's entire harvest of fresh produce brought to market; the supply of Picasso paintings.

• **Supply is perfectly elastic when PES = ∞.** The percentage change in quantity supplied is infinite; a very small change in price leads to a very large response in quantity supplied; supply in this case is called *perfectly elastic*, and is shown in Figure 3.11(e) as a horizontal line. (We will encounter such a supply curve in Chapters 7 and 13.)

Price elasticities of supply most commonly encountered in the real world are those representing elastic or inelastic supply, with perfectly elastic, perfectly inelastic and unit elastic supply being special cases. Note that only when two supply curves intersect (when they share a price and quantity combination) is it possible to make comparisons of price elasticities of supply by reference to the steepness of the curves. (We have the same condition for making comparisons of PEDs in the case of demand curves; see page 53). In the case of intersecting supply curves, the flatter the supply curve, the more elastic it is at any given price. For example, in Figure 3.12, at any one particular price level, S_3 is more elastic than S_2, which is more elastic than S_1.

It may also be noted that PES varies along upward sloping straight-line supply curves (as in the case of PED and demand curves). A constant PES is found

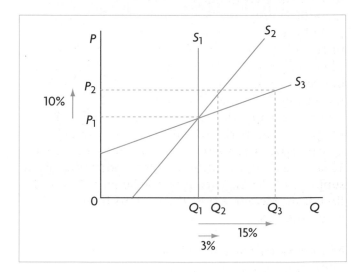

Figure 3.12 The length of time and PES

in supply curves that go through the origin (unit elasticity), as well as perfectly elastic and perfectly inelastic supply curves (constant PES at infinity and zero, respectively). Therefore, when comparing PES of two different supply curves, this should be done only at a specific price or price range.

Determinants of price elasticity of supply

♦ Explain the determinants of PES, including time, mobility of factors of production, unused capacity and ability to store stocks.

Length of time
An important factor determining PES is the amount of time firms have to adjust their inputs (resources) and the quantity supplied in response to changes in price. Over a very short time, the firm

may be unable to increase or decrease any of its inputs to change the quantity it produces. In this case, supply is highly inelastic, and may even be perfectly inelastic ($PES = 0$). In Figure 3.12, this is represented by S_1. For example, a fishing boat upon its return from a fishing trip has only so many fish to supply in the market. Even if the price of fish rises, there can be no response in quantity supplied. As the length of time that firms have increases, the responsiveness of quantity supplied to price changes begins to rise, and PES increases. In Figure 3.12, the supply curve S_2 corresponds to a time period when the fishing boat can be taken out to sea more often, and more labour can be hired to fish, so as price increases to P_2, quantity supplied increases to Q_2 (the 10% price increase from P_1 to P_2 leads to a 3% increase in quantity supplied, indicating inelastic supply, as $PES < 1$). If an even longer time period goes by, the ability of firms to respond to price changes becomes much greater. The owner of the fishing boat can now not only hire more labour but can also buy more fishing boats, thus greatly increasing the amount of fish that can be supplied. This is shown by the supply curve S_3, for which the price P_2 gives rise to the much larger quantity Q_3 (the 10% price increase from P_1 to P_2 leads to a 15% increase in quantity supplied, indicating elastic supply, as $PES > 1$). Therefore, the larger amount of time firms have to adjust their inputs increases, the larger the PES.

Mobility of factors of production

Another determinant of PES is the ease and speed with which firms can shift resources and production between different products. The more easily and quickly resources can be shifted out of one line of production and into another (where price is increasing), the greater the responsiveness of quantity supplied to changes in price, and hence the greater the PES.

Spare (unused) capacity of firms

Sometimes firms may have capacity to produce that is not being used (for example, factories or equipment may be idle for some hours each day). If this occurs, it is relatively easy for a firm to respond with increased output to a price rise. But if the firm's capacity is fully used, it will be more difficult to respond to a price rise. The greater the spare (unused) capacity, the higher is PES (the more elastic the supply); the less the spare capacity, the smaller the PES (the less elastic the supply).

Ability to store stocks

Some firms store stocks of output they produce but do not sell right away. Firms that have an ability to store stocks are likely to have a higher PES for their products than firms that cannot store stocks. Note, however, that this is something that can affect PES over relatively short periods of time, because once stocks are released in the market and sold, other factors determining PES (such as the ones noted above) come into play.

Test your understanding 3.7

1 (a) Explain the meaning of price elasticity of supply. (b) Why do we say it measures responsiveness of quantity *along a given supply curve*?

2 Specify the value or range of values for each of the following PESs, and show, using diagrams, the shape of the supply curve that corresponds to each one: (a) perfectly elastic supply, (b) unit elastic supply, and (c) perfectly inelastic supply.

3 (a) Which price elasticity of supply values or range of values do we see most frequently in the real world? (b) How would you compare these by drawing supply curves in a single diagram?

4 Explain the determinants of PES.

5 Suppose that in response to an increase in the price of good X from \$10 to \$15 per unit, the quantity of good X produced (a) does not respond at all during the first week, (b) increases from 10 000 units to 12 000 units over five months, and (c) increases from 10 000 to 18 000 units over two years. Calculate PES for each of these three time periods.

6 (a) How can you account for the difference in the size of the three elasticities of question 5? (b) Draw a supply curve that is likely to correspond to each of the three elasticities in a single diagram.

Applications of price elasticity of supply

PES in relation to primary commodities and manufactured products

♦ Explain why the PES for primary commodities is relatively low and the PES for manufactured products is relatively high.

Why many primary commodities have a lower PES compared with the PES of manufactured products

In general, primary commodities usually have a lower *PES* than manufactured products. The main reason is the time needed for quantity supplied to respond to price changes. In the case of agriculture, it takes a long time for resources to be shifted in and out of agriculture. Farmers need at least a planting season to be able to respond to higher prices. In most areas there is a limited amount of new land that can be brought into cultivation. In some regions of the world land appropriate for agriculture is shrinking due to environmental destruction (caused by overfarming that depletes the soil of minerals needed by crops). Under such conditions, what is needed is an increase in output per unit of land cultivated (crop yields), but this requires technological change in agriculture, involving new seeds or other inputs that are more productive, and takes a great deal of time. Also needed are more and better irrigation systems, although many countries face a growing water shortage. All these factors explain why a long time is needed for the quantity of an agricultural commodity to respond to increases in price.

In the case of other primary products, such as oil, natural gas and minerals, time is needed to make the necessary investments and to begin production. Because of the costs involved, firms do not respond quickly to price increases, and wait for a serious shortage (excess demand) in the commodity to arise before they take actions to increase production.

Consequences of a low PES for primary commodities

(This topic is included in learning outcomes in Chapters 15 and 17.)

Earlier, in our discussion of price elasticity of demand (*PED*), we saw that price inelastic demand for primary products is an important factor contributing to short-term price and revenue instability for producers such as farmers. Now we will see that price inelastic supply of agricultural and other primary products also contributes to price and income instability for primary product producers.

Figure 3.13 shows a fluctuating demand curve: in part (a) it interacts with inelastic supply, which is typical in the case of primary products, and in part (b) with elastic supply, which is more typical of manufactured products. Clearly, price fluctuations are substantially larger in the case of inelastic

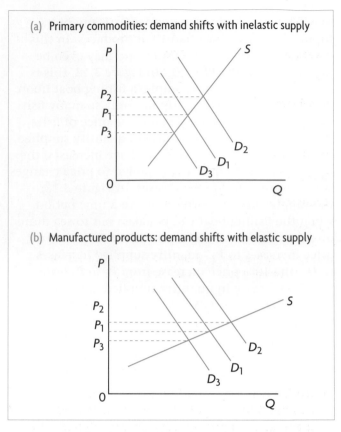

Figure 3.13 Price fluctuations are larger for primary commodities because of low *PES*

supply. Large price fluctuations mean large revenue fluctuations, or unstable revenue for producers of primary commodities. We will come back to the implications of unstable prices and revenues for producers and for the economy in Chapters 4, 15 and 17.

Short-run and long-run price elasticities of supply

It was noted above that agricultural products (as well as other primary commodities) usually have lower price elasticities of supply than manufactured products because they need more time to respond to price changes. This suggests that over longer periods of time the *PES* of agricultural products is larger.

Table 3.3 shows that this is in fact the case. The longer the time producers have to make the necessary adjustments, the greater the responsiveness of quantity supplied to price changes (see Figure 3.12).

Commodity	Short-run PES	Long-run PES
Cabbage	0.36	1.20
Carrots	0.14	1.00
Cucumbers	0.29	2.20
Onions	0.34	1.00
Green peas	0.31	4.40
Tomatoes	0.16	0.90
Cauliflower	0.14	1.10
Celery	0.14	0.95

Table 3.3   Short-run and long-run *PES* for selected agricultural commodities

Table 3.4 provides a summary of key characteristics of all the elasticities considered in this chapter.

Elasticity	Formula	Values	Description
Price elasticity of demand	$PED = \dfrac{\%\Delta Q_x}{\%\Delta P_x}$	$PED = 0$	perfectly inelastic
		$PED < 1$	price inelastic
		$PED = 1$	unit elastic
		$PED > 1$	price elastic
		$PED = \infty$	perfectly elastic
Cross-price elasticity of demand	$XED = \dfrac{\%\Delta Q_x}{\%\Delta P_y}$	$XED > 0$	substitutes
		$XED < 0$	complements
		$XED = 0$	unrelated
Income elasticity of demand	$YED = \dfrac{\%\Delta Q_x}{\%\Delta Y}$	$YED > 0$	normal good
		$YED < 0$	inferior good
		$YED > 1$	income elastic
		$YED < 1$	income inelastic
Price elasticity of supply	$PES = \dfrac{\%\Delta Q_x}{\%\Delta P_x}$	$PES = 0$	perfectly inelastic
		$PES < 1$	price inelastic
		$PES = 1$	unit elastic
		$PES > 1$	price elastic
		$PES = \infty$	perfectly elastic

Table 3.4   Elasticity concepts: a summary

Test your understanding 3.8

1 **(a)** Explain why the *PES* for many primary commodities is relatively low and for many manufactured products is relatively higher.
 (b) Use the concept of *PES* to explain why agricultural product prices are volatile over the short term.

2 Why is it important to make a distinction between short-run and long-run price elasticities of supply?

Assessment

The Student's CD-ROM at the back of this book provides practice of examination questions based on the material you have studied in this chapter.

Standard level
- Exam practice: Paper 1, Chapter 3
  - SL/HL core topics (questions 3.1–3.8)

Higher level
- Exam practice: Paper 1, Chapter 3
  - SL/HL core topics (questions 3.1–3.8)
- Exam practice: Paper 3, Chapter 3
  - HL topics (questions 4–6)

Chapter 4
Government intervention

This chapter will study three types of government intervention in markets: indirect taxes, subsidies and price controls.

4.1 Indirect taxes

Introduction to indirect taxes

The meaning of indirect taxes
Indirect taxes are imposed on spending to buy goods and services. They are paid partly by consumers, but are paid to the government by producers (firms), and for this reason are called 'indirect'. There are two types of indirect taxes:

* excise taxes, imposed on particular goods and services, such as petrol (gasoline), cigarettes and alcohol

* **taxes on spending on all (or most) goods and services**, such as general sales taxes (used in the United States) and value added taxes (used in the European Union, Canada and many other countries).

Indirect taxes differ from direct taxes, involving payment of the tax by the taxpayers directly to the government (see Chapter 11).

In this chapter, we will study excise taxes.

Indirect (excise) taxes and the allocation of resources
Taxes have the effect of changing the allocation of resources. In Chapter 2 we learned that prices act as signals and incentives, which determine the pattern of resource allocation. Since excise taxes are imposed on particular goods, they increase the price paid by consumers, causing consumers to reduce their spending on the taxed goods. Excise taxes also lower the price received by producers, causing them to produce less. Therefore, by changing price signals and incentives, excise taxes affect the allocation of resources.

The interesting question is whether excise taxes work to reduce or to increase allocative efficiency. The answer depends on the degree of allocative efficiency in the economy before the tax is imposed. If an economy

begins with an efficient allocation of resources, the excise tax creates allocative inefficiency and a welfare loss. We will see how this happens below. In an economy with an inefficient resource allocation, indirect taxes potentially have the effect of improving resource allocation, if they are designed to remove the source of allocative inefficiency. This will be studied in Chapter 5.

Why governments impose indirect (excise) taxes

♦ Explain why governments impose indirect (excise) taxes.

Governments impose excise taxes for several reasons:

* **Excise taxes are a source of government revenue.** Governments collect revenues from excise taxes. In Chapter 3 (page 57), we saw that the lower the price elasticity of demand for a good, the greater the government revenue generated. This explains why excise taxes are often imposed on goods that have a price inelastic demand (cigarettes, alcohol, petrol/gasoline).

* **Excise taxes are a method to discourage consumption of goods that are harmful for the individual.** The consumption of certain goods is considered harmful for the individual (for example, cigarette smoking, excess alcohol consumption, or gambling). Taxing these goods is likely to reduce their consumption. Taxes imposed for this purpose are referred to as 'vice taxes' or 'sin taxes'. However, the extent to which these taxes are successful in reducing consumption depends on the price elasticity of demand; if it is low, an excise tax will likely result in only a relatively small decrease in quantity demanded (see Chapter 3, page 58).

* **Excise taxes can be used to redistribute income.** Some excise taxes focus on luxury goods (expensive cars, boats, furs, jewellery, and so on). The

objective is to tax goods that can only be afforded by high-income earners. Payment of a tax on the purchase of these goods reduces after-tax income, thus narrowing differences with the incomes of lower-income earners. Hence some degree of income redistribution is achieved as income inequality is narrowed.

- **Excise taxes are a method to improve the allocation of resources (reduce allocative inefficiencies) by correcting negative externalities.** If there are market imperfections (in the form of negative externalities), preventing the achievement of allocative efficiency, excise taxes can be used to try to improve the allocation of resources. This topic will be discussed in Chapter 5.

In this chapter, we assume that the economy begins with allocative efficiency, in order to see how the introduction of indirect taxes leads to allocative inefficiency.

Indirect (excise) taxes: impacts on market outcomes and consequences for stakeholders

Distinguishing between specific and *ad valorem* taxes

♦ Distinguish between specific and *ad valorem* taxes.

Indirect, excise taxes can be:

- **specific taxes**, a fixed amount of tax per unit of the good or service sold; for example, €5 per packet of cigarettes.
- ***ad valorem* taxes**, a fixed percentage of the price of the good or service; in this case, the amount of tax increases as the price of the good or service increases.

When a tax is imposed on a good or service, it is paid to the government by the firm. This means that for every level of output the firm is willing and able to supply to the market, it must receive a price that is higher than the original price by the amount of the tax. This involves a shift of the supply curve upward by the amount of the tax. (Note that this is equivalent to a leftward shift of the supply curve, meaning that for each price, the firm is willing to supply less output; this equivalence is explained in 'Quantitative techniques' chapter on the CD-ROM page 13).

Illustrating and analysing impacts of specific and *ad valorem* taxes on market outcomes

♦ Draw diagrams to show specific and *ad valorem* taxes, and analyse their impacts on market outcomes.

Figure 4.1 shows how the supply curve shifts when a specific tax and an *ad valorem* tax is imposed. A specific tax causes a parallel upward shift, because the tax is a fixed amount for each unit of output. Therefore, in Figure 4.1(a) S_2 is parallel to S_1. With an *ad valorem* tax, shown in part (b), the new supply curve S_2 is steeper than S_1. Since the tax is calculated as a percentage of price, the amount of tax per unit increases as price increases. For example, if an *ad valorem* tax of 10% is imposed, when the price of the good is $20, the amount of tax per unit sold is $2 (= 0.1 × $20); but if the price is $30, the amount of tax per unit sold increases to $3 (= 0.10 × $30). Therefore, as the price rises, the amount of tax per unit increases.

The impacts of specific and *ad valorem* taxes on market outcomes are shown in Figure 4.2. The supply curves in both parts (a) and (b) are the same as in Figure 4.1; a demand curve has been added in each diagram. In part (a), the pre-tax equilibrium is determined by the intersection of the demand curve D and the supply curve S_1, so the price paid by consumers and received by producers is $P*$ and quantity demanded and supplied is $Q*$. If the government imposes a specific tax on the good, the supply curve shifts upwards to S_2 (= S_1 + tax). The

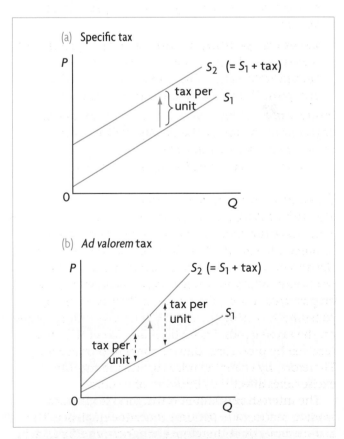

Figure 4.1 Supply curve shifts due to indirect (excise) taxes

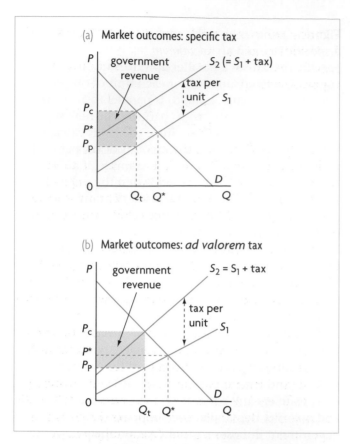

(a) Market outcomes: specific tax

(b) Market outcomes: *ad valorem* tax

Figure 4.2 Impacts of specific and *ad valorem* taxes on market outcomes

demand curve remains constant at D since demand is not affected. The new market equilibrium is determined by the demand curve D and the new supply curve S_2, so the price paid by consumers increases to P_c, and the quantity purchased falls to Q_t. The amount of tax per unit of output is shown on the vertical axis by $P_c - P_p$, or the vertical difference between the two supply curves. Whereas producers receive from consumers P_c per unit, they must pay the government $P_c - P_p$ per unit (tax per unit). Therefore, P_p is the final price received by producers after payment of the tax.

The tax is said to 'drive a wedge' between the price P_c paid by consumers and the price P_p received by producers.

The market outcomes due to the tax are the following:

- equilibrium quantity produced and consumed falls from Q^* to Q_t
- equilibrium price increases from P^* to P_c, which is the price paid by consumers
- consumer expenditure on the good is given by the price of the good per unit times the quantity of units bought; it therefore changes from $P^* \times Q^*$ to $P_c \times Q_t$

- price received by the firm falls from P^* to P_p, which is $P_p = P_c -$ tax per unit
- the firm's revenue falls from $P^* \times Q^*$ to $P_p \times Q_t$
- the government receives tax revenue, given by $(P_c - P_p) \times Q_t$, or the amount of tax per unit times the number of units sold; this is the shaded area in Figure 4.2
- there is an underallocation of resources to the production of the good: Q_t is less than the free market quantity, Q^*.

Figure 4.2(b) shows market outcomes due to the imposition of an *ad valorem* tax; these are exactly the same as in a specific tax (you can re-read the paragraphs above and relate them to Figure 4.2(b)).

Consequences of indirect excise taxes for various stakeholders

♦ Discuss the consequences of imposing an indirect tax on the stakeholders in a market, including consumers, producers and the government.

'Stakeholders' are individuals or groups of individuals who have an interest in something and are affected by it. The consequences for stakeholders are the same for both specific and *ad valorem* taxes.

Consumers
Consumers are affected in two ways: by the increase in the price of the good (from P^* to P_c, shown in Figure 4.2) and by the decrease in the quantity they buy (from Q^* to Q_t). Both these changes make them worse off, as they are now receiving less of the good and paying more for it.

Producers (firms)
Producers are affected in two ways: by the fall in the price they receive (from P^* to P_p), and by the fall in the quantity of output they sell (from Q^* to Q_t). These effects translate into a fall in their revenues, from $P^* \times Q^*$ before the tax to $P_p \times Q_t$. Firms are therefore worse off as a result of the tax.

The government
The government is the only stakeholder that gains, as it now has revenue equal to $(P_c - P_p) \times Q_t$ in Figure 4.2. This is positive for the government budget.

Workers
A lower amount of output, from Q^* to Q_t, means that fewer workers are needed to produce it; therefore, the tax may lead to some unemployment. Workers are worse off if they become unemployed.

Society as a whole

Society is worse off as a result of the tax, because there is an underallocation of resources to the production of the good ($Q_t < Q^*$).

Test your understanding 4.1

1 Explain the meaning of indirect taxes. Why are they called 'indirect'?

2 Explain some reasons why governments impose indirect (excise) taxes.

3 Why do indirect taxes affect the allocation of resources?

4 Using diagrams, (a) explain the difference between specific and *ad valorem* taxes, and (b) provide examples of each.

5 The government is considering imposing a €0.50 tax per litre of petrol (gasoline). (a) Explain whether this a specific or *ad valorem* tax. (b) Draw a diagram for the gasoline market before the imposition of the tax, showing the price paid by consumers, the price received by producers and the quantity of petrol (gasoline) that is bought/sold. (c) Draw a diagram for the petrol (gasoline) market after the imposition of the tax, showing the price paid by consumers, the price received by producers, and the quantity of petrol (gasoline) bought/sold.

6 For question (5), (a) analyse the impacts on the market of the tax on petrol (gasoline), and (b) discuss the consequences for stakeholders.

HL 4.2 Indirect (excise) taxes: market outcomes, social welfare and tax incidence (higher level topic)

Linear demand and supply functions: calculating effects of specific (excise) taxes on markets and social welfare

- Plot demand and supply curves for a product from linear functions and then illustrate and/or calculate the effects of the imposition of a specific tax on the market (on price, quantity, consumer expenditure, producer revenue, government revenue, consumer surplus and producer surplus).

HL Linear demand and supply functions and indirect (excise) taxes

Suppose we are given the following demand and supply functions:

$$Q_d = 60 - 2P$$
$$Q_s = -4 + 2P$$

where Q_d and Q_s show quantities of stimples demanded and supplied in units per day, and P is price in euros (€). Since at equilibrium $Q_d = Q_s$, we set $60 - 2P = -4 + 2P$ and solve for P, finding $P = €16$. Substituting into the demand or supply function, we find $Q = 28$, i.e. 28 units.

To plot the demand curve, we find the P and Q intercepts of the demand function. Setting $Q_d = 0$ in the demand function, we find $P = 30$. Setting $P = 0$, we find $Q_d = 60$. We can now plot the demand curve. This is shown in Figure 4.3.

To plot the supply curve, we use the supply function and set $Q_s = 0$, finding $P = 2$; this is the P intercept (0,2). To find a second point on the supply curve, we set $Q_s = 10$ (any other point will do as well) and solving for P, we have $P = 7$. We thus have a second point (10,7). We can now plot the supply curve, which is shown as S_1 in Figure 4.3. The demand curve, D, and supply curve, S_1, intersect at $P = €16$ and $Q = 28$ (28,16) confirming our solution to the demand and supply equations.

Suppose the government imposes an indirect (excise) tax on stimples of €6 per unit. This means that the supply curve will shift upward by €6 for each level of output Q.

How to graph the new supply curve, S_2

In Figure 4.3, the new supply curve, S_2 (= S_1 + tax), lies €6 above the initial supply curve, S_1. We can count €6 upward along the vertical axis from the P intercept of S_1, which is (0,2) to find the P intercept of S_2, which is (0,8) and then draw a line parallel to S_1 from this new P intercept. This is gives us the new supply curve, S_2.

How to find the new price paid by consumers, the price received by producers and the quantity bought and sold, following the imposition of the tax

After the tax is imposed, the demand curve D and the new supply curve, S_2, determine a new equilibrium price, which is P_c or the price paid by consumers, a new equilibrium quantity, Q_t, and P_p or the price received by producers ($P_p = P_c$ − tax per unit) (see also Figure 4.2). We could try to read these off the graph, however it may be difficult to do so accurately. To get accurate values, we must find the new post-tax supply function, solve for P_c and Q_t, and then use $P_p = P_c$ − tax per unit to find P_p.

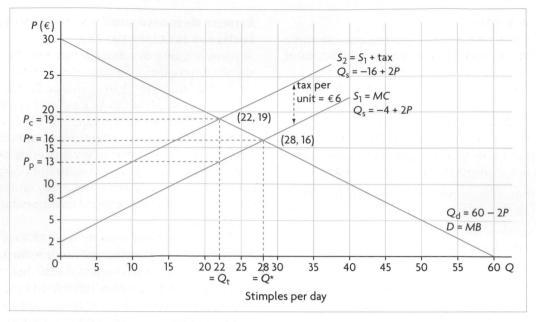

Figure 4.3 Demand and supply functions and indirect (excise) taxes

There is a very simple rule we can use to find the new supply function (see 'Quantitative techniques' chapter on the CD-ROM, page 25 for an explanation):

Given a supply function of the general form $Q_s = c + dP$, whenever there is an *upward shift* of the function by t units, where t = tax per unit, we replace P by $P - t$. The new supply function therefore becomes $Q_s = c + d(P - t)$.[1]

We can now use this rule to find the new supply function. Our initial supply function was $Q_s = -4 + 2P$. With a tax of €6 per unit, this function shifts upward by €6, so that $t = 6$. Therefore, the new supply function is

$$Q_s = -4 + 2(P - 6)$$

Simplifying:

$$Q_s = -4 + 2P - 12$$
$$Q_s = -16 + 2P,$$

which is the new supply function.

We now use our demand function and the new supply function to solve for P and Q:

$$Q_d = 60 - 2P$$
$$Q_s = -16 + 2P$$

Since at equilibrium $Q_d = Q_s$, we set $60 - 2P = -16 + 2P$ and solve for P, finding $P = €19$. Substituting into the demand or supply function, we find $Q = 22$ units.

Therefore, at the new after-tax equilibrium, the price paid by consumers is $P_c = €19$, the equilibrium quantity of stimples demanded and supplied is 22 units per day, i.e. $Q_t = 22$, and the price received by producers is $P_p = P_c -$ tax per unit $= €19 - €6 = €13$. These results are shown in Figure 4.3.

Calculating the effects of excise taxes on market outcomes and social welfare

We have found that the price paid by consumers has increased from €16 to €19, the price received by producers has fallen from €16 to €13, and the quantity produced and consumed has fallen from 28 units to 22 units.

We now want to use this price and quantity information, together with the graph in Figure 4.3, to calculate the following: consumer expenditure, producer revenue, government revenue, consumer surplus and producer surplus.

Consumer expenditure

Consumer expenditure is given by the price paid per unit of stimples times the number of stimples purchased. Therefore, before the tax, consumers spent $P^* \times Q^* = €16 \times 28$ units $= €448$ per day; after the tax was imposed, consumers spent $P_c \times Q_t = €19 \times 22$ units $= €418$ per day. Therefore consumer expenditure fell by €30 per day ($=€448 - €418$).

---

[1] You may be surprised to see that we *subtract t* from *P* when we are shifting the supply curve *upward*. The reason is that subtracting *t* from *P* actually means we are shifting the axes downward, thus actually moving the supply curve upward.

Producer revenue

Producer revenue is given by the price received per unit of stimples times the number of stimples sold. Therefore, before the tax, producer revenue was $P^* \times Q^* = €16 \times 28$ units = €448 per day, which is the same as what consumers spent; firm revenue was exactly equal to consumer expenditure. After the tax was imposed, firm revenue fell to $P_p \times Q_t = €13 \times 22$ units = €286 per day. Producer revenue fell by €162 per day (= €448 – €286). Firm revenue is now less than consumer expenditure.

Government revenue

Government revenue can be calculated in two ways:

(a) It is equal to tax per unit ($P_c - P_p$) times the number of units sold, Q_t, and is therefore €6 × 22 stimples = €132.

(b) It is also equal to the difference between consumer expenditure and producer revenue after the tax: €418 – €286 = €132.

Illustrating consumer and producer surplus

Consumer surplus and producer surplus were defined in Chapter 2, pages 42–3. In a competitive free market equilibrium, shown in Figure 4.4(a), consumer surplus appears as the shaded area above price P^* and under the demand curve up to quantity Q^*; producer surplus is the shaded area above the supply curve and under price P^* up to Q^*. At the competitive free market equilibrium, the sum of consumer and producer surplus, or social surplus, is maximum, indicating that allocative efficiency is achieved. Allocative efficiency is also indicated by $MB = MC$ (marginal benefits equal marginal costs) at the point of equilibrium. These

conditions are shown in Figure 4.4(a) (which is the same as Figure 2.17, page 42.)

What happens to social surplus after the imposition of the tax? We can see this in Figure 4.4(b). Consumer surplus becomes the shaded area under the demand curve and above P_c up to Q_t. Producer surplus becomes the shaded area above the supply curve S_1 and below P_p up to Q_t. A portion of consumer surplus became government tax revenue, and another portion was lost as triangle a. A portion of producer surplus also became government tax revenue, and another portion was lost as triangle b. Government revenue is thus the bold face rectangle.

The consumer and producer surplus that is transformed into government tax revenue comes back to society in the form of government spending from the tax revenues. Therefore, the after-tax social surplus in Figure 4.4(b) is equal to after-tax consumer and producer surplus plus government revenue. However, after-tax social surplus is less than pre-tax social surplus by the amount of triangles a + b. The areas a + b represent social surplus that is completely lost, and is called welfare loss (also known as deadweight loss).

> **Welfare loss** (deadweight loss) represents welfare benefits that are lost to society because resources are not allocated efficiently.

In this case, deadweight loss appears because the tax causes a smaller than optimum quantity to be produced: $Q_t < Q^*$. The tax has caused underproduction of the good relative to what is socially desirable, and an underallocation of resources, or allocative inefficiency.

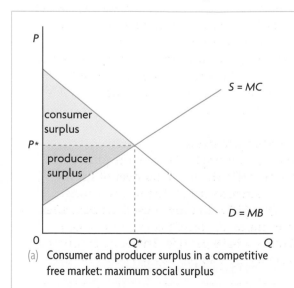

(a) Consumer and producer surplus in a competitive free market: maximum social surplus

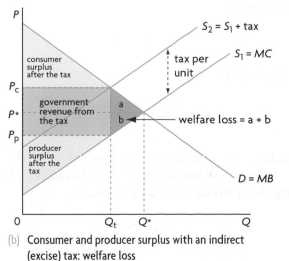

(b) Consumer and producer surplus with an indirect (excise) tax: welfare loss

Figure 4.4 Effects of indirect taxes on consumer and producer surplus

Note that at the new point of production, Q_t, $MB > MC$, meaning that the benefits consumers receive from the last unit of the good they buy are greater than the marginal cost of producing it. Consumers would be better off if more of the good were produced (for an explanation see Chapter 2, page 44).

The imposition of an indirect excise tax results in reduced consumer and producer surplus, part of which is transformed into government revenue, and part of which is a welfare (deadweight) loss. The welfare loss in this case is the result of underallocation of resources to the production of the good (underproduction). This is also indicated by $MB > MC$: too little of the good is produced and consumed relative to the social optimum.

Calculating the effects of excise taxes on consumer and producer surplus

Figure 4.5 is the same as Figure 4.4, but also shows the various values of P and Q corresponding to our demand and supply functions (the same values as in Figure 4.3). In part (a) consumer surplus is the shaded area under the demand curve and above $P^* = 16$, up to $Q^* = 28$. In part (b) it is the shaded area under the demand curve and above $P_c = 19$, up to $Q_t = 22$.

It is simple to calculate consumer surplus if we think of it as half the area of the rectangle whose one side equals the P intercept of the demand curve minus the price paid by consumers, and whose other side equals the number of units purchased:

Consumer surplus =
$$\frac{(P \text{ intercept of D curve minus } P \text{ of consumers}) \times Q \text{ purchased}}{2}$$

Therefore, consumer surplus before the tax is:

$$\frac{(30 - P^*) \times Q^*}{2} = \frac{(30 - 16) \times 28}{2} = \frac{14 \times 28}{2} = \frac{392}{2} = 196$$

Consumer surplus after the tax is:

$$\frac{(30 - P_c) \times Q_t}{2} = \frac{(30 - 19) \times 22}{2} = \frac{11 \times 22}{2} = \frac{242}{2} = 121$$

Producer surplus, in Figure 4.5(a) is the area above the supply curve S and below $P^* = 16$, up to $Q^* = 28$. In Figure 4.5(b) it is the area above the supply curve S_1 and below $P_p = 13$, up to $Q_t = 22$.

To calculate producer surplus, we can think of it as half the area of the rectangle whose one side equals the price received by producers minus the P intercept of the initial supply curve, S_1 and whose other side equals the number of units sold:

Producer surplus =
$$\frac{(P \text{ of producers minus } P \text{ intercept of } S_1 \text{ curve}) \times Q \text{ sold}}{2}$$

Therefore, producer surplus before the tax is:

$$\frac{(P^* - 2) \times Q^*}{2} = \frac{(16 - 2) \times 28}{2} = \frac{14 \times 28}{2} = \frac{392}{2} = 196$$

Producer surplus after the tax is:

$$\frac{(P_p - 2) \times Q_t}{2} = \frac{(13 - 2) \times 22}{2} = \frac{11 \times 22}{2} = \frac{242}{2} = 121$$

(You may have noticed that consumer and producer surplus are equal to each other, both before and after the tax; *this is coincidental, as they need not be equal to each other*.)

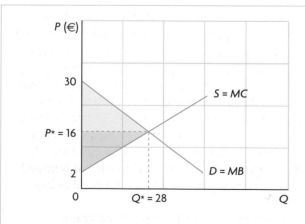

(a) Pre-tax equilibrium: maximum social surplus

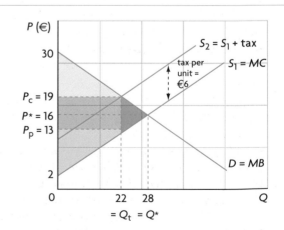

(b) Post-tax equilibrium: welfare loss

Figure 4.5 Calculating consumer and producer surplus before and after an indirect tax

The welfare loss can be found by taking the pre-tax sum of consumer and producer surplus (total social surplus), and subtracting from that the post-tax sum of benefits (post-tax consumer surplus, producer surplus and tax revenue): 196 + 196 – (121 + 121 + 132) = 18.

This is also equal to the area of the triangle:

$$\frac{(P_c - P_p)(Q^* - Q_t)}{2} = \frac{(19-13)(28-22)}{2} = \frac{6 \times 6}{2} = 18$$

Test your understanding 4.2

1 **(a)** Using a diagram showing the petrol (gasoline) market, show equilibrium price and quantity, and consumer and producer surplus that arise in a free market equilibrium. **(b)** The government decides to impose a €0.50 tax per litre of petrol (gasoline). Drawing a new diagram showing the pre-tax and after-tax equilibrium, identify the new price paid by consumers, the price received by producers, and the quantity bought and sold. **(c)** Using your diagram, illustrate consumer surplus, producer surplus, government revenue and deadweight loss at the after-tax market equilibrium. **(d)** Explain the changes in consumer surplus, producer surplus, government revenue, welfare (deadweight) loss, and allocative efficiency. **(e)** How does the relationship between marginal benefit and marginal cost at the new (after-tax) equilibrium relate to allocative efficiency (or inefficiency)?

2 In the market for good zeta, the P intercept of the demand curve is at the point (0,7), and the P intercept of the supply curve is at the point (0,1). The point of intersection of the demand curve and the supply curve at free market equilibrium is at (6,4). **(a)** Plot the demand and supply curves, and identify the equilibrium price and quantity. **(b)** Suppose that price is measured in $ and quantity of zeta in tonnes per day, and that a tax of $2 per tonne is imposed; draw the new supply function and identify the price paid by consumers, the price received by producers and the new equilibrium quantity. **(c)** Explain why the increase in price paid by consumers is smaller than the amount of tax per unit. **(d)** Using your results, calculate the change in consumer expenditure, the change in firm revenue, government revenue, the change in consumer surplus, the change in producer surplus and welfare (deadweight) loss.

(e) Identify, in your diagram, the areas that correspond to government revenue, welfare (deadweight) loss and after-tax consumer and producer surplus. **(f)** The demand function for this market is $Q_d = 14 - 2P$ and the pre-tax supply function is $Q_s = -2 + 2P$. Find the new, post-tax supply function, and using the demand function, calculate the post-tax price paid by consumers, the price received by producers and the new equilibrium quantity. Do your results match your graph?

3 A market is defined by the following equations:

$$Q_d = 10 - \frac{1}{10}P, \text{ and } Q_s = -2 + \frac{1}{10}P, \text{ where } P \text{ is in \$.}$$

(a) Find the equilibrium price and quantity mathematically, and plot the demand and supply curves. **(b)** The government imposes a tax of $20 per unit. Derive the new supply function and calculate the price paid by consumers, the price received by producers, and the new equilibrium quantity. **(c)** Calculate the change in consumer expenditure, the change in firm revenue, the change in government revenue, the change in consumer surplus, the change in producer surplus and welfare (deadweight) loss.

Tax incidence and price elasticities of demand and supply

♦ Explain, using diagrams, how the incidence of indirect taxes on consumers and firms differs, depending on the price elasticity of demand and on the price elasticity of supply.

When a good is taxed, part of the tax is paid by consumers and part by producers; therefore the tax burden is shared between the two. This is because compared to the pre-tax price, P^*, consumers pay a higher price ($P_c > P^*$) and producers receive a lower price ($P_p < P$). But how is the tax burden shared between them? The burden of a tax is referred to as **tax incidence**. The distribution of the incidence, or who has a larger burden and who has a smaller burden, depends on the price elasticity of demand and price elasticity of supply for the good being taxed.

The discussion below is based on diagrams illustrating a specific tax, however the entire analysis and all conclusions are the same in the case of an *ad valorem* tax.

Incidence of indirect taxes and price elasticity of demand

The diagrams in Figure 4.6, showing how the burden of a specific tax is shared between consumers and producers, are similar to Figure 4.2(a), only in Figure 4.6(a) demand is inelastic, whereas in part (b) it is elastic.

The full amount of tax is given by $(P_c - P_p) \times Q_t$, or the amount of tax per unit multiplied by the number of units sold; this is the entire shaded area, and is equal to the government's tax revenue. The incidence of the tax is partly on consumers and partly on producers:

tax burden (incidence) of consumers = $(P_c - P^*) \times Q_t$
tax burden (incidence) of producers = $(P^* - P_p) \times Q_t$

When demand is inelastic, as in Figure 4.6(a), most of the tax incidence is on consumers; when demand is elastic, as in Figure 4.6(b), most of the incidence is on producers.

Comparing the two diagrams, we can also see that when demand is inelastic, there is a relatively small drop in equilibrium quantity compared with when demand is elastic, i.e. the decrease from Q^* to Q_t is smaller in part (a) compared with part (b). This is what we expect, since with inelastic demand ($PED < 1$), quantity demanded is not very responsive to changes in price.

Incidence of indirect taxes and price elasticity of supply

The diagrams in Figure 4.7 are also similar to Figure 4.2(a), only now part (a) shows inelastic supply and part (b) elastic supply.

When supply is inelastic, most of the tax incidence is on producers, whereas when supply is elastic, most of the tax incidence is on consumers.

Putting *PED* and *PES* together

There is a simple rule we can use to summarise the above points:

The more elastic a schedule, the more of the tax burden that will fall on the other side.

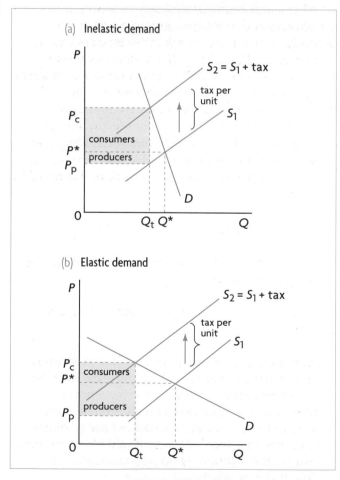

Figure 4.6 Incidence of an indirect tax with inelastic and elastic demand

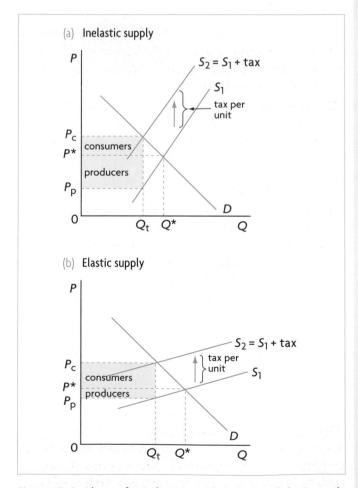

Figure 4.7 Incidence of an indirect tax with inelastic and elastic supply

Therefore, with elastic demand, producers have the higher tax incidence. With elastic supply, consumers have the higher tax incidence. If schedules are inelastic, the opposite holds, so that more of the tax burden falls on the same side. With inelastic demand, most of the tax burden is on consumers; with inelastic supply, most of the tax burden is on producers. Examining Figures 4.6 and 4.7 will enable you to confirm that these results hold.

In general, the tax burden falls proportionately more on the group whose activities are less responsive to price changes: on consumers whose purchases are not very responsive to price increases (inelastic demand), and on producers whose sales are not very responsive to price increases (inelastic supply). The low responsiveness (low price elasticities) means that as price increases due to the imposition of the tax, consumers or producers do not change their buying and selling activities substantially, and so as a result must bear a relatively larger portion of the tax burden.

Therefore, when PES>PED, the tax incidence is mainly on consumers. When PED>PES, the tax incidence is mainly on producers.

Test your understanding 4.3

1 What determines whether the incidence of an indirect tax falls mainly on consumers or mainly on producers?

2 Using diagrams, show how the incidence of an *ad valorem* tax will be shared between consumers and producers in the case of **(a)** elastic demand, and **(b)** inelastic demand. What conclusions can you draw about relative tax burdens and price elasticities of demand?

3 Using diagrams, show how the incidence of an *ad valorem* tax will be shared between consumers and producers in the case of **(a)** elastic supply, and **(b)** inelastic supply. What conclusions can you draw about relative tax burdens and price elasticities of supply?

4.3 Subsidies

Introduction to subsidies

The meaning of subsidies

A *subsidy*, in a general sense, refers to assistance by the government to individuals or groups of individuals, such as firms, consumers, industries or sectors of an economy. Subsidies may take the form of direct cash payments or other forms of assistance such as low-interest or interest-free loans (for example, to students, to low-income consumers for the purchase of goods and services such as housing, or to firms needing assistance), the provision of goods and services by the government at below-market prices; tax relief (i.e. paying lower or no taxes); and others.

In this section, we will consider only subsidies consisting of cash payments by the government to firms. Such payments are usually a fixed amount per unit of output, and are therefore *specific subsidies*.

Subsidies and the allocation of resources

Subsidies, like taxes, have the effect of changing the allocation of resources because they affect relative prices, thus changing the signals and incentives prices convey. A subsidy granted to a firm (or group of firms) has the effect of increasing the price received by producers, causing them to produce more, and lowering the price paid by consumers, causing them to buy more. Therefore, the allocation of resources changes and results in greater production and consumption than in the free market.

As with indirect taxes, we are interested in seeing whether the granting of a subsidy improves or worsens the allocation of resources. Here, too, the answer depends on the degree of allocative efficiency in the market before the subsidy. In an economy where resources are allocated efficiently, a subsidy introduces allocative inefficiency and welfare losses. This will be the topic of this section. But if the economy begins with allocative inefficiency (due to market imperfections), then a subsidy can work to improve the allocation of resources if it is designed to correct the source of the inefficiency. This will be examined in Chapter 5.

Why governments grant subsidies

♦ Explain why governments provide subsidies, and describe examples of subsidies.

There are several reasons why governments grant subsidies to firms:

• **Subsidies can be used to increase revenues (and hence incomes) of producers.** Subsidies have the effect of increasing the revenues of producers. Therefore, governments often grant subsidies to particular producers whose revenues (and therefore incomes) they would like to support. This is most commonly done for producers of agricultural products.

- **Subsidies can be used to make certain goods (necessities) affordable to low-income consumers.** Subsidies have the effect of lowering the price of the good that is paid by consumers, thus making the good more affordable. For example, a government may wish to make a food staple (such as bread or rice) more affordable to low-income earners, and can do so by granting a subsidy to producers of the good.

- **Subsidies can be used to encourage production and consumption of particular goods and services that are believed to be desirable for consumers.** A subsidy has the effect of increasing the quantity of a good produced and consumed. If a government wishes to encourage consumption of a good because it is considered to be desirable (for example, education, vaccinations), it can use a subsidy to achieve this.

- **Subsidies can be used to support the growth of particular industries in an economy.** Since subsidies have the effect of increasing the quantity of output produced, if granted to firms in a particular industry, they support the growth of that industry. For example, subsidies to the solar industry are intended to promote the growth of solar power, subsidies to ethanol production are intended to promote the production of biofuels. Other examples include chemicals, textiles, steel, fossil fuels and many more.

- **Subsidies can be used to encourage exports of particular goods.** Since subsidies lower the price paid by consumers, they are sometimes granted on goods that are exported (sold to other countries), since lower export prices increase the quantity of exports.

- **Subsidies are a method to improve the allocation of resources (reduce allocative inefficiencies) by correcting positive externalities.** It was noted above that market imperfections prevent the achievement of allocative efficiency; in some cases (such as when there are positive externalities), it may be possible to use subsidies to improve allocative efficiency (see Chapter 5).

Subsidies are a controversial topic in economics because they are very extensive and are often designed to achieve certain objectives that may not be consistent with other important objectives. For example, many countries grant subsidies to fossil fuels, which run contrary to objectives of sustainable development (see page 128), and which also contradict the objectives of other subsidies intended to support the growth of alternative energy. Fossil-fuel subsidies are known as 'perverse subsidies'. Subsidies for agriculture and exports are also highly controversial (see Chapters 13 and 17).

Subsidies: impacts on market outcomes and consequences for stakeholders

♦ Draw a diagram to show a subsidy, and analyse the impacts of a subsidy on market outcomes.

Impacts of subsidies on market outcomes
In Figure 4.8, the initial, pre-subsidy equilibrium is determined by the intersection of the demand curve D and the supply curve S_1, giving rise to equilibrium price P^* paid by consumers and received by producers, and equilibrium quantity Q^*. Now the government grants a subsidy consisting of a payment to the firm of a fixed amount for each unit of output sold. This means that for each unit of output the firm is willing and able to produce, it receives a lower price than the original by the amount of the subsidy; this produces a downward, parallel shift of the supply curve by the amount of the subsidy, to the new curve S_2 (= S_1 – subsidy). (This is equivalent to a rightward shift of the supply curve, meaning that for each price, the firm is now willing to supply more output; see 'Quantitative techniques' chapter on the CD-ROM, page 13 for an explanation.) The demand curve remains constant at D since demand is not affected. The demand curve and new supply curve S_2 determine a new equilibrium, where price is P_c (the price paid by consumers) and the quantity produced and sold increases to Q_{sb}. Since the vertical difference between the two supply curves represents the subsidy per unit of output, the firm receives price P_p, which is equal to

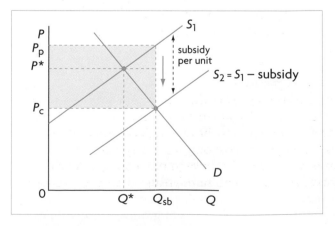

Figure 4.8 Impacts of subsidies on market outcomes

the price paid by the consumer, P_c, plus the subsidy per unit of output.

The market outcomes due to the subsidy are the following:

- equilibrium quantity produced and consumed increases from Q^* to Q_{sb}
- the equilibrium price falls from P^* to P_c; this is the price paid by consumers
- the price received by producers increases from P^* to P_p
- the amount of the subsidy is given by $(P_p - P_c) \times Q_{sb}$, or the amount of subsidy per unit multiplied by the number of units sold; this is the entire shaded area, and represents government spending to provide the subsidy
- there is an overallocation of resources to the production of the good: Q_{sb} is greater than the free market quantity, Q^*.

Consequences of subsidies for various stakeholders

♦ Discuss the consequences of providing a subsidy on the stakeholders in a market, including consumers, producers and the government.

Consumers
Consumers are affected by the fall in price of the good from P^* to P_c (Figure 4.8) and the increase in quantity purchased (from Q^* to Q_{sb}). Both these changes make them better off.

Producers
Producers are also better off, because they receive a higher price ($P_p > P^*$) and produce a larger quantity ($Q_{sb} > Q^*$), seen in Figure 4.8. The price and quantity effects translate into an increase in revenues. Before the granting of the subsidy, firms had revenues of $P^* \times Q^*$. Following the subsidy, firm revenues increase to $P_p \times Q_{sb}$.

The government
The government pays the subsidy, which is a burden on its budget. To obtain the revenues for the subsidy, the government may have to reduce expenditures elsewhere in the economy, or it may have to raise taxes, or it may have to run a budget deficit (government expenditures greater than tax revenues).

Whatever the case, the impact on the government's budget is negative.

Workers
As output expands from Q^* to Q_{sb}, firms are likely to hire more workers to produce the extra output, therefore workers who find new jobs are better off.

Society as a whole
Society as a whole is worse off because there is an overallocation of resources to the production of the good; $Q_{sb} > Q^*$. In addition, society is worse off because the higher price received by producers protects relatively inefficient ones, allowing them to continue to produce.

Foreign producers
If the subsidy is granted on exports (goods sold to other countries), it lowers price and increases the quantity of exports. While this is positive for domestic producers, it is negative for the producers of other countries who may be unable to compete with the lower price of the subsidised goods. (This topic will be discussed in Chapter 17.)

Test your understanding 4.4

1 Explain the meaning of subsidies.

2 Explain some reasons why governments grant subsidies, and provide examples.

3 Using diagrams, show how the supply curve shifts when a subsidy is granted to firms producing a particular product.

4 The government is considering granting a €0.50 subsidy per kilogram of cheese. **(a)** Draw a diagram for the cheese market before the granting of the subsidy, showing the price paid by consumers, the price received by producers and the quantity of cheese that is bought/sold. **(b)** Draw a diagram for the cheese market after the granting of the subsidy, showing the price paid by consumers, the price received by producers, and the quantity of cheese bought/sold. **(c)** Explain how your diagram for question (a) differs from your diagram for question (b).

5 Considering question 4 above, **(a)** analyse the impacts on the market of the subsidy for cheese producers, and **(b)** discuss the consequences for stakeholders.

Farm subsidies in the United States

Farmers in the United States have been receiving subsidies for certain agricultural products (corn, wheat, soybeans, cotton, rice and others) since the Great Depression of the 1930s. In 1996 a law was passed to end subsidies and create a free market in agriculture. However, the free market in agriculture never materialised. Support to farmers continues to cost tax payers about $5 billion a year. This support is justified by the common belief that the government is helping small farmers survive. Yet according to the US Department of Agriculture (the

agriculture ministry), from 1995 to 2009 the largest and wealthiest top 10% of farmers received 74% of farm subsidies. The reason is that subsidies are paid according to the amount of crop produced. Smaller farmers received very small amounts, while farmers who cultivate fruits and vegetables receive no subsidies at all.

Source: Adapted from 'Farm subsidies no illogical entitlements – next senator must push for overhaul of ag policy' in *Lexington Herald-Leader*, 11 July 2010.

Applying your skills

1 Discuss the consequences of farm subsidies for the economy and stakeholders.

2 Why do you think the government continues to grant agricultural subsidies even though they are costly and unfair?

4.4 Subsidies: market outcomes and social welfare (higher level topic)

Linear demand and supply functions: calculating effects of subsidies on markets and social welfare

♦ Plot demand and supply curves for a product from linear functions and then illustrate and/or calculate the effects of the provision of a subsidy on the market (on price, quantity, consumer expenditure, producer revenue, government expenditure, consumer surplus and producer surplus).

Linear demand and supply functions and subsidies

We will use the same method as for excise taxes (see pages 75–6) to solve for pre-subsidy and post-subsidy equilibrium price and quantity.

We are given the following demand and supply functions:

$$Q_d = 60 - 2P$$
$$Q_s = -20 + 2P$$

where Q_d and Q_s show quantities of stomfles demanded and supplied in kilograms (kg) per day,

and P is price in $. Since at equilibrium $Q_d = Q_s$, we set $60 - 2P = -20 + 2P$ and solve for P, finding $P = \$20$. Substituting into the demand or supply function, we find $Q = 20$ kg.

To plot the demand curve, we find the P and Q intercepts. Setting $Q_d = 0$ in the demand function, we find $P = 30$. Setting $P = 0$, we find $Q_d = 60$. We can now plot the demand curve D, shown in Figure 4.9.

To plot the supply curve, S_1, we use the supply function and set $Q_s = 0$, finding $P = 10$; the P intercept is therefore $(0,10)$. To find a second point we set $Q_s = 10$ (any other point will do as well), and we find $P = 15$; we thus have a second point $(10,15)$. We can now plot the supply curve, shown in Figure 4.9. The demand and supply curves intersect at $P = \$20$ and $Q = 20$ $(20,20)$, confirming our solution of the demand and supply equations.

If the government grants a subsidy on stomfles of $4 per kg, the supply curve shifts downward by $4 for each kg of output Q.

How to graph the new supply curve, S_2

The new supply curve, S_2 (= S_1 – subsidy), lies $4 below the initial supply curve, S_1. We can count $4 downward along the vertical axis from the P intercept of S_1, which is $(0,10)$ to find the P intercept of S_2, which is $(0,6)$ and then draw a line parallel to S_1 from this new P intercept. This gives us the new supply curve, S_2, appearing in Figure 4.9.

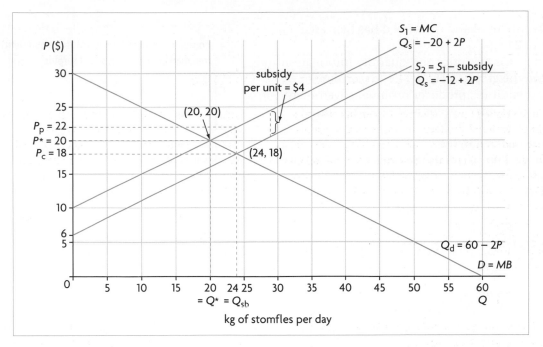

Figure 4.9 Demand and supply functions and subsidies

How to find the new price paid by consumers, the price received by producers and the quantity bought and sold, following the granting of the subsidy

After the subsidy is granted, the demand curve D and the new supply curve, S_2, determine a new equilibrium price, P_c or the price paid by consumers, and a new equilibrium quantity, Q_{sb} (see also Figure 4.8). Also, there is a price P_p received by producers, where $P_p = P_c$ + subsidy per unit = $P_c + 4$. If we try to read these off our graph in Figure 4.9, we may be inaccurate. To get accurate values we must derive the new post-subsidy supply curve, solve for P_c and Q_{sb}, and then use $P_p = P_c$ + subsidy per unit to find P_p.

There is a very simple rule we can use to find the new supply function (see 'Quantitative techniques' chapter on the CD-ROM, page 26 for an explanation):

> Given a supply function of the general form $Q_s = c + dP$, whenever there is a *downward shift* of the function by s units, where s = subsidy per unit, we replace P by $P + s$. The new supply function therefore becomes $Q_s = c + d(P + s)$.[2]

We can now use this rule to derive the new supply function. The initial supply function was $Q_s = -20 + 2P$. With a subsidy of $4 per kg, this function shifts downward by $4, so that $s = 4$. Therefore, the new supply function is:

$$Q_s = -20 + 2(P + 4)$$

Simplifying,

$$Q_s = -20 + 2P + 8$$
$$Q_s = -12 + 2P$$

which is the new supply function. We can now use the demand function and the new supply function to solve for P and Q:

$$Q_d = 60 - 2P$$
$$Q_s = -12 + 2P$$

Since at equilibrium $Q_d = Q_s$, we set $60 - 2P = -12 + 2P$ and solve for P, finding $P = \$18$. Substituting into the demand or supply function, we find $Q = 24$ kg.

Therefore, at the new equilibrium, the price paid by consumers is $P_c = \$18$, the equilibrium quantity is $Q_{sb} = 24$ kg, and the price received by producers is $P_p = P_c$ + subsidy per unit = $\$18 + \$4 = \$22$. These results are shown in Figure 4.9.

Calculating the effects of subsidies on market outcomes and welfare

We have found that the price paid by consumers has fallen from $20 to $18 per kg, the price received by producers has increased from $20 to $22 per kg, and

---

[2] Note that this is the exact opposite of what we did to find the new supply function when a tax was imposed (page 76). We now *add* s to P in order to shift the supply curve *downward*, because by doing so we are shifting the axes upward, thus actually moving the supply curve downward.

the quantity produced and consumed has increased from 20 kg to 24 kg.

We will now use this price and quantity information together with the graph in Figure 4.9 to calculate consumer expenditure, producer revenue, government expenditure, consumer surplus and producer surplus.

Consumer expenditure

Consumer expenditure equals the price paid per kg of stomfles times the number of kg purchased. Therefore, before the subsidy, consumers spent $P^* \times Q^* = \$20 \times 20$ kg $= \$400$ per day; after the subsidy, consumers spent $P_c \times Q_{sb} = \$18 \times 24$ kg $= \$432$ per day. Therefore consumer expenditure increased by \$32 per day ($= \$432 - \$400$).

Producer revenue

Producer revenue is given by the price received per kg of stomfles times the number of kg sold. Therefore, before the subsidy was granted, producer revenue was $P^* \times Q^* = \$20 \times 20$ kg $= \$400$ per day, which is exactly the same as what consumers spent; firm revenue was exactly equal to consumer expenditure. After the subsidy was granted, producer revenue increased to $P_p \times Q_{sb} = \$22 \times 24$ kg $= \$528$ per day. Producer revenue increased by \$128 per day ($= \$528 - \$400$). Note that firm revenue is now more than consumer expenditure.

Government expenditure

Government expenditure on the subsidy can be calculated in two ways:

(a) It is equal to the subsidy per kg ($P_p - P_c$) times the number of kg sold (Q_{sb}), and is therefore $\$4 \times 24$ kg $= \$96$ per day.

(b) It is also equal to the difference between producer revenue and consumer expenditure after the subsidy: $\$528 - \$432 = \$96$ per day.

Illustrating consumer and producer surplus

Figure 4.10 shows consumer and producer surplus before and after the subsidy. In (a), at the free market equilibrium before the subsidy, social (consumer plus producer) surplus is maximum and $MB = MC$, indicating the achievement of allocative efficiency. After the granting of the subsidy, both consumer surplus and producer surplus increase. In Figure 4.10(b), consumer surplus is now the area under the demand curve and above price P_c, up to output Q_{sb}. The *gain* in consumer surplus is shown by the shaded area labelled 'gain in consumer surplus'. Producer surplus becomes the area above the supply curve S_1 and below the price P_p, up to output Q_{sb}. The *gain* in

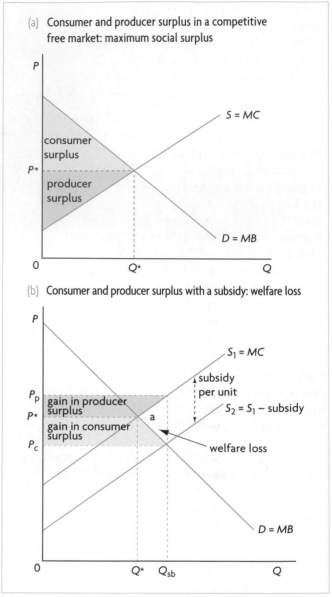

(a) Consumer and producer surplus in a competitive free market: maximum social surplus

(b) Consumer and producer surplus with a subsidy: welfare loss

Figure 4.10 Effects of subsidies on consumer and producer surplus

producer surplus is shown by the shaded area labelled 'gain in producer surplus'.

At the same time that producers and consumers gain, the government loses because of the negative effects on its budget. The subsidy is paid for by taxes that have an opportunity cost (alternative uses that are sacrificed). As we know, government expenditure to provide the subsidy is $(P_p - P_c) \times Q_{sb}$. *This is exactly equal to the gains in consumer and producer surplus plus the triangle a.* Therefore, the social losses due to government spending are greater than the gains in consumer and producer surplus by the amount a. The area a is welfare (deadweight) loss representing lost benefits for society, caused by a larger than optimum quantity produced: $Q_{sb} > Q^*$. The subsidy has caused overproduction relative to what is socially desirable, and an overallocation of resources, or allocative inefficiency.

We can also see in Figure 4.10(b) that at Q_{sb}, $MB < MC$, meaning that the benefit consumers receive from the last unit of the good they buy is less than the marginal cost of producing it. Therefore, consumers would be better off if less of the good were produced.

> The granting of a subsidy results in greater consumer and producer surplus; however, society loses due to government spending on the subsidy. Since the loss from government spending is greater than the gain in consumer and producer surplus, welfare (deadweight) loss results, reflecting allocative inefficiency, which in this case is due to overallocation of resources to the production of the good (overproduction). This is also illustrated by $MB < MC$: too much of the good is being produced and consumed relative to the social optimum.

Calculating the effects of subsidies on consumer and producer surplus

Figure 4.11 is the same as Figure 4.10, but also shows the various values of P and Q corresponding to our demand

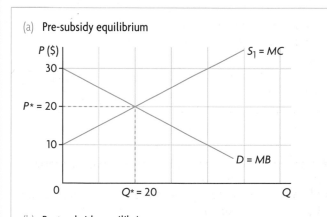

(a) Pre-subsidy equilibrium

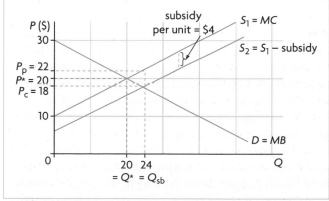

(b) Post-subsidy equilibrium

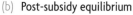

Figure 4.11 Calculating consumer and producer surplus

and supply functions (the same values as in Figure 4.9). In Figure 4.11(a) consumer surplus at the free market equilibrium (before the subsidy) is represented by the area under the demand curve and above price $P^* = 20$ up to quantity $Q^* = 20$. In part (b), after the subsidy, it is the area under the demand curve and above price $P_c = 18$ up to quantity $Q_{sb} = 24$.

We can calculate consumer surplus in the same way as with indirect taxes:

Consumer surplus =
$$\frac{(P \text{ intercept of } D \text{ curve minus } P \text{ of consumers}) \times Q \text{ purchased}}{2}$$

Therefore, consumer surplus before the subsidy is:

$$\frac{(30 - P^*) \times Q^*}{2} = \frac{(30 - 20) \times 20}{2} = \frac{10 \times 20}{2} = \frac{200}{2} = 100$$

Consumer surplus after the subsidy is:

$$\frac{(30 - P_c) \times Q_{sb}}{2} = \frac{(30 - 18) \times 24}{2} = \frac{12 \times 24}{2} = \frac{288}{2} = 144$$

Producer surplus, in Figure 4.11(a) is the area above the supply curve S_1 and below $P^* = 20$ up to $Q^* = 20$. In part (b) it is the area above the supply curve S_1 and below $P_p = 22$ up to $Q_{sb} = 24$.

Producer surplus is also calculated using the same method as with indirect taxes:

Producer surplus =
$$\frac{(P \text{ of producers minus } P \text{ intercept of } S_1 \text{ curve}) \times Q \text{ sold}}{2}$$

Therefore, producer surplus before the subsidy is:

$$\frac{(P^* - 10) \times Q^*}{2} = \frac{(20 - 10) \times 20}{2} = \frac{10 \times 20}{2} = \frac{200}{2} = 100$$

Producer surplus after the subsidy is:

$$\frac{(P_p - 10) \times Q_{sb}}{2} = \frac{(22 - 10) \times 24}{2} = \frac{12 \times 24}{2} = \frac{288}{2} = 144$$

(The equality of producer and consumer and producer surplus, before and after the subsidy, is coincidental.)

Welfare (deadweight) loss can be found by taking the pre-subsidy sum of consumer and producer surplus (total social benefits), and subtracting the post-subsidy social benefits (which are consumer surplus plus producer surplus minus government expenditure on the subsidy): $100 + 100 - (144 + 144 - 96) = 8$. It is also equal to:

$$\frac{(P_p - P_c)(Q_{sb} - Q^*)}{2} = \frac{(22 - 18)(24 - 20)}{2} = \frac{4 \times 4}{2} = 8$$

Test your understanding 4.5

1 Why does a subsidy create a welfare (deadweight) loss?

2 (a) Using a diagram showing the cheese market, show equilibrium price and quantity, and consumer and producer surplus that arise in a free market equilibrium. **(b)** The government decides to grant a £0.50 subsidy per kilogram of cheese. Drawing a new diagram showing the pre-subsidy and after-subsidy equilibrium, identify the price paid by consumers, the price received by producers and the quantity bought and sold. **(c)** Using your diagram, illustrate the increase in consumer surplus and producer surplus, government expenditure and deadweight loss at the after-subsidy market equilibrium. **(d)** Explain the changes in consumer surplus, producer surplus, government revenue, deadweight loss and allocative efficiency. **(e)** How does the relationship between marginal benefit and marginal cost at the new (after-subsidy) equilibrium relate to allocative efficiency (or inefficiency)?

3 In the market for good alpha the P intercept of the demand curve is at the point $(0,7)$, and the P intercept of the supply curve is at the point $(0,1)$. The point of intersection of the demand curve and the supply curve at free market equilibrium is at $(6,4)$. **(a)** Plot the demand and supply curves, and identify the equilibrium price and quantity. **(b)** Suppose that price is measured in £, and quantity in tonnes per day, and that a subsidy of £2 per tonne is granted. Plot the new supply curve, and find (through your graph) the price paid by consumers, the price received by producers and the new equilibrium quantity. **(c)** Using your results, calculate the change in consumer expenditure, the change in firm revenue, government expenditure, the change in consumer surplus, the change in producer surplus and deadweight loss. **(d)** The demand function for this market is $Q_d = 14 - 2P$ and the pre-subsidy supply function is $Q_s = -2 + 2P$. Find the post-subsidy supply function, and using the demand function, calculate the post-subsidy price paid by consumers, the price received by producers and the new equilibrium quantity. Do your results match your graph?

4 A market is defined by the following equations: $Q_d = 10 - \frac{1}{10}P$, and $Q_s = -2 + \frac{1}{10}P$, where P is in £. **(a)** Find the equilibrium price and quantity.

(b) The government grants a subsidy of £20 per unit. Derive the new supply function and calculate the price paid by consumers, the price received by producers and the new equilibrium quantity. **(c)** Calculate the change in consumer expenditure, the change in firm revenue, government expenditure, the change in consumer surplus, the change in producer surplus and welfare (deadweight) loss.

4.5 Price controls

Introduction to price controls

The third type of intervention we will consider involves price controls.

> **Price controls** refer to the setting of minimum or maximum prices by the government (or private organisations) so that prices are unable to adjust to their equilibrium level determined by demand and supply. Price controls result in market disequilibrium, and therefore in shortages (excess demand) or surpluses (excess supply).

Price controls differ from indirect taxes and subsidies in a fundamental way. When a tax is imposed or a subsidy granted, the market *settles at a new equilibrium*. The new equilibrium differs from the pre-tax or pre-subsidy equilibrium, but it is still a new equilibrium, because there is a balance of demand with the new supply. Price controls differ because, once they are imposed, they do not allow a new equilibrium to be established, and instead force a situation where there is *persisting market disequilibrium*.

Market disequilibrium means that the market is prevented from reaching a market-clearing price, and there emerge shortages (excess demand) or surpluses (excess supply) (see page 30). Shortages and surpluses involve a misallocation of resources and welfare losses.

In the discussion that follows, it is important to bear in mind that the term *surplus* has two different meanings. In one sense it refers to excess supply resulting when quantity supplied is greater than quantity demanded (see page 30). In the second sense it refers to the benefits that consumers or producers receive from buying or selling (see pages 42–3). This is not as confusing as it may sound, because *surplus* in the second sense is referred to as 'consumer surplus', or 'producer surplus' or 'social surplus'.

Price ceilings: setting a legal maximum price

♦ Explain why governments impose price ceilings, and describe examples of price ceilings, including food price controls and rent controls.

What is a price ceiling?

A government may in some situations set a legal maximum price for a particular good; this is called a price ceiling. It means that the price that can be legally charged by sellers of the good must not be higher than the legal maximum price. Figure 4.12 shows how this works. The equilibrium price is P_e, determined by the forces of demand and supply. The price ceiling, P_c, is set by the government at a level below the equilibrium price, leading to a shortage (excess demand), since quantity demanded, Q_d is greater than quantity supplied, Q_s. If the market were free, the forces of demand and supply would force price up to P_e. However, now this cannot happen, because the price hits the legally set price ceiling.

Note that to have an effect, the price ceiling must be *below* the equilibrium price. If it were higher than the equilibrium price, the market would achieve equilibrium, and the price ceiling would have no effect.

Impacts on market outcomes

♦ Draw a diagram to show a price ceiling, and analyse the impacts of a price ceiling on market outcomes.

By imposing a price that is below the equilibrium price, a price ceiling results in a lower quantity supplied and sold than at the equilibrium price. This is shown in Figure 4.12, where the price ceiling, P_c, corresponds to quantity Q_s that firms supply, which

is less than the equilibrium quantity Q_e that suppliers would supply at price P_e.

In addition, the price ceiling, P_c, gives rise to a larger quantity demanded than at the equilibrium price: the quantity consumers want to buy at price P_c is given by Q_d, which is greater than quantity Q_e that they would buy at price P_e.

A price ceiling does not allow the market to clear; it creates a situation of disequilibrium where there is a shortage (excess demand).

Consequences for the economy

♦ Examine the possible consequences of a price ceiling, including shortages, inefficient resource allocation, welfare impacts, underground parallel markets and non-price rationing mechanisms.

Shortages

A price ceiling, P_c, set below the equilibrium price of a good creates a shortage. At P_c, not all interested buyers who are willing and able to buy the good are able to do so because there is not enough of the good being supplied. In Figure 4.12, the shortage is equal to $Q_d - Q_s$.

Non-price rationing

The term 'rationing' refers to a method of dividing up something among possible users. In a free market, this is achieved by the price system: those who are willing and able to pay for a good will do so, and the good is rationed among users according to who buys it; this is called *price rationing*. However, once a shortage arises due to a price ceiling, the price mechanism is no longer able to achieve its rationing function. Some demanders willing and able to buy the good at P_c in Figure 4.12 will go unsatisfied. How will the quantity Q_s be distributed among all interested buyers? This can only be done through non-price rationing methods, which include the following:

* waiting in line and the first-come-first-served principle: those who come first will buy the good
* the distribution of coupons to all interested buyers, so that they can purchase a fixed amount of the good in a given time period
* favouritism: the sellers can sell the good to their preferred customers.

Underground (or parallel) markets

Underground (or parallel) markets involve buying/selling transactions that are unrecorded, and are usually illegal. In the case of price ceilings, they are a special kind of price rationing. They involve buying a good at the maximum legal price, and

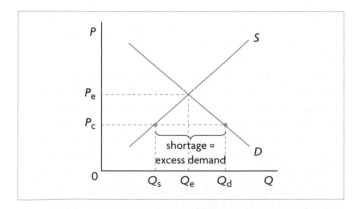

Figure 4.12 Price ceiling (maximum price) and market outcomes

then illegally reselling it at a price above the legal maximum. Underground markets can arise when there exist dissatisfied people who have not succeeded in buying the good because there was not enough of it, and are willing to pay more than the ceiling price to get it. If there were no shortage, the price of the good would be at its equilibrium price, and no one would be interested in paying a higher than equilibrium price for it. Underground markets are inequitable, and frustrate the objective sought by the price ceiling, which is to set a maximum price.

Underallocation of resources to the good and allocative inefficiency

Since a lower than equilibrium price results in a smaller quantity supplied than the amount determined at the free market equilibrium, there are too few resources allocated to the production of the good, resulting in underproduction relative to the social optimum (or 'best'). Society is worse off due to underallocation of resources and allocative inefficiency.

Negative welfare impacts

In Figure 4.13, with no price control, the market determines price P_e and quantity Q_e at equilibrium. Consumer surplus, or the area under the demand curve and above P_e, is equal to areas a + b. Producer surplus, the area under P_e and above the supply curve, is equal to areas c + d + e. Consumer plus producer surplus is maximum, and is equal to a + b + c + d + e. Also, $MB = MC$, and there is allocative efficiency.

If a price ceiling, P_c, is imposed, only the quantity Q_s is produced and consumed. Consumer surplus is now the area under the demand curve and above P_c, but only up to Q_s, since that is all that is consumed. Therefore, consumer surplus becomes a + c. Producer surplus is the area above the supply curve and below P_c, also only up to Q_s since that is all that is produced. Producer surplus therefore falls to area e. Total social surplus after the price ceiling is a + c + e. Comparing with total social surplus before the price ceiling, we see that the shaded areas b and d have been lost and represent **welfare loss** (deadweight loss), or lost social benefits due to the price ceiling. Welfare loss represents benefits that are lost to society because of resource misallocation.

We can see there is allocative inefficiency also because $MB > MC$ at the point of production, Q_s: the benefit consumers receive from the last unit of the good they buy is greater than the marginal cost of producing it. Therefore, society is not getting enough of the good, as there is an underallocation of resources to its production.

A price ceiling creates a welfare (deadweight) loss, indicating that the price ceiling introduces allocative inefficiency due to an underallocation of resources to the production of the good, seen by $Q_s < Q_e$. $MB > MC$, indicating that society is not getting enough of the good.

Consequences for various stakeholders

♦ Discuss the consequences of imposing a price ceiling on the stakeholders in a market, including consumers, producers and the government.

Consumers

Consumers partly gain and partly lose. They lose area b but gain area c from producers (see Figure 4.13). Those consumers who are able to buy the good at the lower price are better off. However, some consumers remain unsatisfied as at the ceiling price there is not enough of the good to satisfy all demanders.

Producers

Producers are worse off, because with the price ceiling they sell a smaller quantity of the good at a lower price; therefore, their revenues drop from $P_e \times Q_e$ to $P_c \times Q_s$. This is clear also from their loss of some producer surplus, area c, (which is transferred to consumers), as well as area d (welfare loss) in Figure 4.13.

Workers

The fall in output (from Q_e to Q_s) means that some workers are likely to be fired, resulting in unemployment; clearly these workers will be worse off.

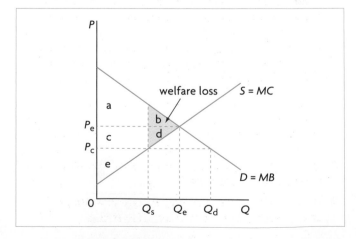

Figure 4.13 Welfare impacts of a price ceiling (maximum price)

Government

There will be no gains or losses for the government budget, yet the government may gain in political popularity among the consumers who are better off due to the price ceiling.

The examples of rent controls and food price controls

Price ceilings are for the most part set in order to make certain goods considered to be necessities more affordable to low-income earners.

Rent controls

Rent controls consist of a maximum legal rent on housing, which is below the market-determined level of rent (the price of rental housing). It is undertaken by governments in some cities around the world to make housing more affordable to low-income earners. Consequences of rent controls include:

- housing becomes more affordable to low-income earners
- a shortage of housing, as the quantity of housing demanded at the legally maximum rent is greater than the quantity available
- a smaller quantity of housing at the legally maximum rent than at the free market rent, since owners of housing supply a smaller quantity; in

Figure 4.12, at price P_c, the quantity Q_s is lower than Q_e

- long waiting lists of interested tenants waiting for their turn to secure an apartment/flat
- a market for rented units where tenants sublet their apartments at rents above the legal maximum (an underground market)
- run-down and poorly maintained rental housing because it is unprofitable for landlords to maintain or renovate their rental units since low rents result in low revenues.

Food price controls

Some governments use food price controls as a method to make food more affordable to low-income earners, especially during times when food prices are rising rapidly (for example, in the period 2008–9). The results of food price controls follow the same patterns as discussed above: lower food prices and greater affordability; food shortages as quantity demanded is greater than quantity supplied; non-price rationing methods (such as queues) to deal with the shortages; development of underground markets; falling farmer incomes due to lower revenues; more unemployment in the agricultural sector; misallocation of resources; possible greater popularity for the government among consumers who benefit.

Price controls in Vietnam

Due to high rates of inflation (a rising general price level), the Vietnamese government is considering the imposition of price controls, namely price ceilings on numerous products, including chemical fertilisers, salt, milk powder, rice, sugar, animal feeds, coal, cement, paper, textbooks and many more. If it goes ahead with these measures, the pricing rules will apply not just to domestic government-owned businesses but also private firms and foreign-owned

businesses. It is feared that Vietnam may be moving away from its freer market orientation of recent years and back toward the ways of a command economy. Foreign diplomats are warning the government that price controls will damage business confidence in the country.

Source: Adapted from The Economist Intelligence Unit, 'Vietnam economy: reform roll-back?' in ViewsWire News Analysis, 21 September 2010.

Applying your skills

1 What does it mean to move toward the ways of a 'command economy'?

2 Discuss the consequences for the economy and stakeholders that may arise if the government moves forward with the price controls.

3 Why do you think that price controls may damage business confidence?

Test your understanding 4.6

1 Using a diagram, explain why price controls lead to disequilibrium market outcomes.

2 Define a price ceiling, and providing examples, explain some reasons why governments impose them.

3 Draw a diagram illustrating a price ceiling, and analyse its effects on market outcomes (price, quantity demanded, quantity supplied, market disequilibrium) and consequences for the economy (shortages, non-price rationing, allocative inefficiency, deadweight loss).

4 (a) Explain the difference between price rationing and non-price rationing. (b) Under what circumstances does non-price rationing arise? (c) What are some forms of non-price rationing? (d) In what way are underground markets a form of price rationing?

5 (a) Draw a diagram showing producer and consumer surplus in a free market competitive equilibrium. (b) Assuming a price ceiling is imposed in this market, draw a new diagram showing the new consumer surplus, producer surplus and welfare (deadweight) loss. (c) Comparing your diagrams for parts (a) and (b), what can you conclude about consumer surplus, producer surplus and deadweight loss? (d) What is the relationship between marginal benefits and marginal costs in the new equilibrium? What does this reveal about allocative efficiency (or inefficiency)?

6 Examine the consequences of price ceilings for different stakeholders in the case of (a) rent controls, and (b) food price controls.

Calculating effects of price ceilings (higher level topic)

♦ Calculate possible effects from the price ceiling diagram, including the resulting shortage, and the change in consumer expenditure (which is equal to the change in firm revenue).

Figure 4.14 provides us with a numerical example of a price ceiling. At equilibrium, price is equal to £8 and quantity demanded and supplied is 20 000 units of the good per week. When a price ceiling is imposed at P_c = £4.50 per unit, quantity demanded becomes Q_d = 30 000 units, and quantity supplied Q_s = 10 000 units.

Shortage (excess demand)

The shortage, or excess demand, is equal to $Q_d - Q_s$, which in this case is 30 000 − 10 000 = 20 000 units per week.

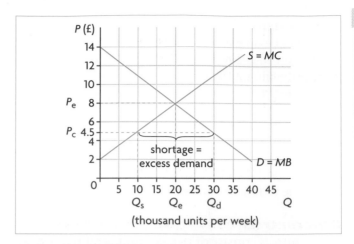

Figure 4.14 Calculating effects of price ceilings

Change in consumer expenditure

Consumer expenditure is given by the price per unit of the good times the number of units purchased. At equilibrium, prior to the price ceiling, consumers spend $P_e \times Q_e$ = £8 × 20 000 units = £160 000. After the price ceiling is imposed, consumers spend $P_c \times Q_s$ = £4.50 Q_s × 10 000 units = £45 000. The change is therefore £160 000 − £45 000 = £115 000, meaning that consumers now spend £115 000 less than at equilibrium.

Change in producer (firm) revenue

Firm revenue is the same as consumer expenditure both before and after the imposition of the price ceiling. This is because revenue is equal to price per unit times quantity of units sold, and both the price (P_c) and the quantity (Q_s) are the same for both consumers and producers. Therefore, before the price ceiling is imposed, firm revenue is £160 000, and after the price ceiling, firm revenue is reduced to £45 000. Therefore, firm revenues fall by the amount £115 000.

Test your understanding 4.7

1 In the example of the market illustrated in Figure 4.14, what would be the effect of a price ceiling set at £10?

2 Suppose a price ceiling is set at £4 per unit (Figure 4.14). Calculate (a) the shortage (excess demand), (b) the change in consumer expenditure, and (c) the change in producer revenue.

Price floors: setting a legal minimum price

What is a price floor?

A legally set **minimum price** is called a **price floor**. The price that can be legally charged by sellers of the good must not be lower than the price floor, or

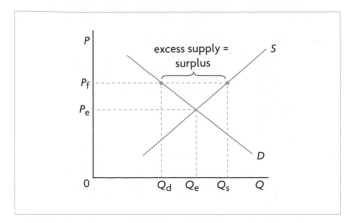

Figure 4.15 Price floor (minimum price) and market outcomes

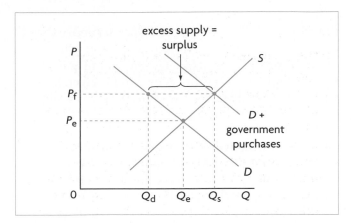

Figure 4.16 An agricultural product market with price floor and government purchases of the surplus

minimum price. In Figure 4.15, a price floor, P_f, is set above the equilibrium price, P_e. At P_e, consumers are willing and able to buy Q_d of the good, but firms are willing and able to supply Q_s of the good. Therefore, a surplus, or excess supply, equal to the difference between Q_s and Q_d, arises. If the market were free, the forces of demand and supply would force the price down to P_e. However, now this cannot happen.

Note that to have an effect, the price floor must be *above* the equilibrium price. If it were below the equilibrium price, the market would achieve equilibrium and the price floor would have no effect.

Why governments impose price floors

♦ Explain why governments impose price floors, and describe examples of price floors, including price support for agricultural products and minimum wages.

Price floors are commonly used for two reasons: (a) to provide income support for farmers by offering them prices for their products that are above market-determined prices; and (b) to protect low-skilled, low-wage workers by offering them a wage (the minimum wage) that is above the level determined in the market. Note that the first of these involves price control in product markets, while the second concerns price control in a resource market. While market outcomes are similar, each type of price control has different consequences for the economy and stakeholders. We will therefore consider each one separately.

Price floors for agricultural products

Impacts of price floors on market outcomes

♦ Draw a diagram of a price floor, and analyse the impacts of a price floor on market outcomes.

Farmers' incomes in many countries, resulting from the sale of their products in free markets, are often unstable

or too low. Some important reasons for both instability and low incomes were considered in Chapter 3. Unstable incomes arise from unstable agricultural product prices, which are due to low price elasticities of demand and low price elasticities of supply for agricultural products (see pages 56–7 and 70). Low income elasticities of demand are an important factor accounting for low farmer incomes (see page 64).

One method governments use to support farmers' incomes is to set price floors for certain agricultural products, the objective being to raise the price above their equilibrium market price; such price floors are called **price supports**. Figure 4.16 illustrates the market for an agricultural product with a price floor, P_f, set above the equilibrium price, P_e. The price floor results in a larger quantity supplied, Q_s, than the quantity supplied at market equilibrium, Q_e. In addition, the price floor, P_f, leads to a smaller quantity demanded and purchased than at the equilibrium price: the quantity consumers want to buy at P_f is Q_d, which is smaller than the quantity Q_e that they bought at price P_e.

A price floor does not allow the market to clear; it results in disequilibrium where there is a surplus (excess supply). A common practice is for the government to buy the excess supply, and this causes the demand curve for the product to shift to the right to the new demand curve 'D plus government purchases'. By buying up the excess supply, the government is able to maintain the price floor at P_f.

Consequences of agricultural price floors for the economy

♦ Examine the possible consequences of a price floor, including surpluses and government measures to dispose of the surpluses, inefficient resource allocation and welfare impacts.

Surpluses The effect of a price floor set above the equilibrium price of a good is to create a surplus (excess supply) equal to $Q_s - Q_d$, shown in Figure 4.16, since the quantity consumers demand is given by Q_d, while the quantity farmers want to supply is given by Q_s.

Government measures to dispose of surpluses
The government must make a decision about what to do with the surplus (excess supply) it purchases. One option is store it, giving rise to additional costs for storage above the costs of the purchase. Another method is to export the surplus (sell it abroad); this often requires granting a subsidy to lower the price of the good and make it competitive in world markets, since the price floor has increased the price of the good above the market price (foreign countries would not want to buy it at the high price). Clearly, subsidies involve additional costs for the government. A third option is for the government to use it as aid sent to developing countries, which often poses problems for the developing countries intended to benefit from the aid (see page 513). In general, any course chosen by the government to get rid of the surpluses is problematic.

Firm inefficiency Higher than equilibrium product prices can lead to inefficient production; inefficient firms with high costs of production do not face incentives to cut costs by using more efficient production methods, because the high price offers them protection against lower-cost competitors. This leads to inefficiency.

Overallocation of resources to the production of the good and allocative inefficiency Too many resources are allocated to the production of the good, resulting in a larger than optimum (or 'best') quantity produced. Whereas the optimum quantity is Q_e, actually Q_s is produced.

Negative welfare impacts In Figure 4.17 (which is similar to Figure 4.16), price P_e and quantity Q_e represent market equilibrium with no price floor, and where social surplus is maximum; consumer surplus is given by a + b + c and producer surplus by d + e. Also, $MB = MC$.

After a price floor, P_f, is imposed, consumer surplus becomes the area under the demand curve and above Pf, up to the quantity consumers buy, Q_d, and so falls to a. Producer surplus becomes the area above

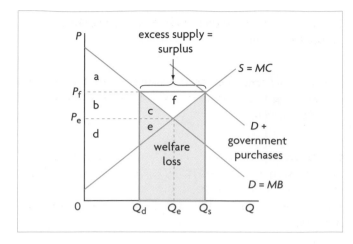

Figure 4.17 Welfare impacts of a price floor (minimum price) for agricultural products and government purchases of the surplus

the supply curve and below P_f, up to the quantity produced, Q_s, and so becomes d + e + b + c + f. This means that the sum of consumer plus producer surplus *increases* by the area f after the price floor is imposed. (This happens because producers gain the area b and c lost by consumers, and in addition gain f.)

Government spending to buy the excess supply is equal to the price paid per unit, P_f, times the surplus quantity it purchases: $P_f \times (Q_s - Q_d)$, corresponding to the rectangle outlined in bold. Since government spending is financed out of taxes with alternative uses (opportunity costs), government spending to maintain the price floor involves losses for society.

We therefore have a gain in surplus of f and a loss equal to the rectangle shown in bold. If we subtract the loss from the gain we are left with the green shaded area, which is welfare (deadweight) loss, representing loss of benefits due to allocative inefficiency caused by overallocation of resources to the production of the good. This is also shown by $MB < MC$ at the point of production, Q_s, indicating that society would be better off if less of the good were produced.

A price floor creates welfare (deadweight) loss, indicating that the price floor introduces allocative inefficiency due to an overallocation of resources to the production of the good, seen by $Q_s > Q_e$. $MB < MC$, indicating that society is getting too much of the good.

Consequences of price floors for various stakeholders

♦ Discuss the consequences of imposing a price floor on the stakeholders in a market, including consumers, producers and the government.

Consumers Consumers are worse off, as they must now pay a higher price for the good ($P_f > P_e$), while they buy a smaller quantity of it ($Q_d < Q_e$). This is clear also from their loss of some consumer surplus.

Producers Producers gain as they receive a higher price and produce a larger quantity, and since the government buys up the surplus, they increase their revenues from $P_e \times Q_e$ to $P_f \times Q_s$. Remember, this is the main rationale of agricultural price floors. Also, producers become protected against low-cost competition and do not face as strong incentives to become efficient producers; they are therefore less likely to go out of business if they are producing inefficiently (with higher costs).

Workers Workers are likely to gain as employment increases on account of greater production of the good.

Government When the government buys the excess supply, this is a burden on its budget, resulting in less government funds to spend on other desirable activities in the economy. The costs to the government are paid for out of taxes (and therefore by taxpayers). In addition, there are further costs of storing the surplus or subsidising it for export (sale to other countries).

Stakeholders in other countries The European Union, the United States and many other more developed countries rely on price floors for agricultural products to support their farmers. The surpluses are sometimes exported (sold to other countries), leading to lower world prices due to the extra supply made available in world markets. Countries that do not have price supports are forced to sell their agricultural products at low world prices. The low prices in these countries signal to local farmers that they should cut back on their production, resulting in an underallocation of resources to these products. These events often work against the interests of less

developed countries (this topic will be discussed in Chapters 13 and 17).

If excess supplies of agricultural products are used as aid to developing countries, they are sold at low (below-market) prices in local markets. Consumers of those countries gain, as they buy the good at a lower than market price, but producers lose as they have to compete with lower-priced foreign goods, and some of them may go out of business, losing their only source of income (see the Real world focus feature on page 513).

Overall, a global misallocation of resources can result, as price floors cause high-cost producers to produce more and low-cost producers to produce less than the social optimum, resulting in a waste of resources.

Test your understanding 4.8

1 Define a price floor, and providing examples, explain some reasons why governments impose them.

2 Draw a diagram illustrating a price floor that is imposed in a product market, and analyse its effects on market outcomes (price, quantity demanded, quantity supplied, market disequilibrium) and consequences for the economy (excess supply, firm inefficiency, possible illegal sales, allocative inefficiency, welfare (deadweight) loss).

3 What are some measures governments can take to dispose of surpluses that result from the imposition of a price floor in an agricultural product market? What are some problems associated with these measures?

4 Assuming a price floor is imposed in a market for an agricultural product, and that the government purchases the entire excess supply that results in order to maintain the price, **(a)** draw a diagram illustrating welfare (deadweight) loss. **(b)** What is the relationship between marginal benefits and marginal costs in the new equilibrium? What does this reveal about allocative efficiency (or inefficiency)?

5 Examine the consequences for different stakeholders of a price floor for an agricultural product whose excess supply is purchased by the government.

Calculating effects of price floors (higher level topic)

♦ Calculate possible effects from the price floor diagram, including the resulting surplus, the change in consumer expenditure, the change in producer revenue, and government expenditure to purchase the surplus.

Figure 4.18 provides a numerical example of a price floor on an agricultural product. At equilibrium, price is equal to £20 and quantity is equal to 60 000 kg per week. When a price floor is imposed at P_f = £25, quantity demanded is Q_d = 40 000 kg per week and quantity supplied is Q_s = 80 000 kg per week.

Surplus (excess supply)

The surplus, or excess supply is equal to $Q_s - Q_d$, which in this case is 80 000 – 40 000 = 40 000 kg per week.

Change in consumer expenditure

Consumer expenditure is given by the price per kg of the good times the number of kg purchased per week. At equilibrium, before the price floor, consumers spend $P_e \times Q_e$ = £20 × 60 000 kg = £1.2 million per week. After the price floor is imposed, consumers spend $P_f \times Q_s$ = £25 × 40 000 kg = £1 million per week. Therefore, consumers spend £200 000 less on the good per week.

Change in producer revenue

Before the price floor, producer revenue is the same as consumer expenditure, since revenue is equal to price per kg times quantity sold, and both the price (P_e) and the quantity (Q_e) are the same for consumers and producers. Therefore producer revenue before the price

floor is £1.2 million per week. Once the price floor is imposed and the government purchases the surplus (excess supply), firms receive revenues of $P_f \times Q_s$, and so producer revenue increases to £25 × £80 000 = £2 million per week. Therefore, the change is £800 000, or additional producer revenue of this amount per week.

Government expenditure

In order to purchase the excess supply of the agricultural product, the government spends an amount equal to the price of the good at the price floor times the number of kg purchased, or $P_f \times (Q_s - Q_d)$ = £25 × 40 000 = £1 million.

Note that government expenditure (£1 million) is equal to total producer revenue (£2 million) minus total consumer expenditure (£1 million) per week.

Test your understanding 4.9

1 In the example of the market illustrated in Figure 4.18, what would be the effect of a price floor set at £15?

2 Suppose a price floor is set at £30 per unit (Figure 4.18). Calculate **(a)** the surplus (excess supply), **(b)** the change in consumer expenditure, **(c)** the change in producer revenue, and **(d)** government expenditure needed to purchase the surplus (excess supply) and maintain the price floor.

Minimum wages

Impacts of minimum wages on market outcomes

♦ Draw a diagram of a price floor, and analyse the impacts of a price floor on market outcomes.

Many countries around the world have **minimum wage** laws that determine the minimum price of labour (the wage rate) that an employer (a firm) must pay. The objective is to guarantee an adequate income to low-income workers, who tend to be mostly unskilled. (The market-determined wages of skilled workers are usually higher than the minimum wage.) Figure 4.19 shows the market for labour. The demand for labour curve shows the quantity of labour that firms are willing and able to hire at each wage, and the supply of labour curve shows the quantity of labour that workers supply at each wage. Supply and demand determine the equilibrium 'price' of labour, which is the wage, W_e, where the quantity of labour demanded is equal to the quantity of labour supplied, Q_e.

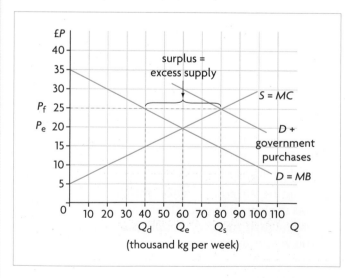

Figure 4.18 Calculating effects of a price floor on an agricultural product with government purchases of the surplus

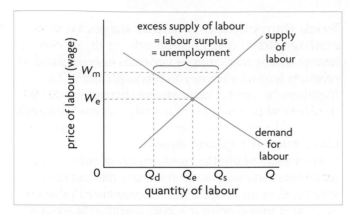

Figure 4.19 Labour market with minimum wage (price floor)

The minimum wage, W_m, lies above the equilibrium wage, W_e. Therefore, at W_m, the quantity of labour supplied, Q_s, is larger than the quantity of labour supplied when the labour market is in equilibrium (Q_e). The quantity of labour demanded, Q_d, is less than the quantity demanded at equilibrium, Q_e. There results a surplus of labour in the market equal to the difference between Q_s and Q_d. The labour market does not clear when there is a minimum wage.

Consequences of minimum wages for the economy

♦ Examine the possible consequences of a price floor, including surpluses, inefficient resource allocation and welfare impacts.[3]

Labour surplus (excess supply) and unemployment
The imposition of a minimum wage in the labour market creates a surplus of labour equal to $Q_s - Q_d$ in Figure 4.19, which is unemployment, as it corresponds to people who would like to work but are not employed. The unemployment is due partly to the decrease in quantity of labour demanded by firms (the difference between Q_e and Q_d) and partly to an increase in the quantity of labour supplied (the difference between Q_s and Q_e) which occurs because the higher wage makes work more attractive, causing a movement up the labour supply curve. This unemployment is likely to involve unskilled workers.

Illegal workers at wages below the minimum wage
Illegal employment of some workers at wages below the legal minimum may result; this often involves illegal immigrants who may be willing to supply their labour at very low wages.

Misallocation of labour resources   The minimum wage affects the allocation of *labour resources*, as it prevents the market from establishing a market-clearing price of labour. In Chapter 2, page 41, we saw how the wage acts as a signal and incentive to workers (the suppliers of labour) and firms (the demanders of labour) to determine the optimal allocation of labour resources. The imposition of a minimum wage changes these signals and incentives for unskilled labour, whose wage is affected by the price floor. Therefore, industries that rely heavily on unskilled workers are more likely to be affected, and will hire less unskilled labour.

Misallocation in product markets   Firms relying heavily on unskilled workers experience an increase in their costs of production, leading to a leftward shift in their *product* supply curve (see Chapter 2, page 28), resulting in smaller quantities of output produced. Therefore, the misallocation of labour resources leads also to misallocation in product markets.

Negative welfare impacts (supplementary material)   Figure 4.20 shows the labour market, with the market-clearing wage at W_e, and equilibrium quantity of labour demanded and supplied at Q_e. The imposition of a minimum wage, W_m, creates a labour surplus (excess labour supply), or unemployment of $Q_s - Q_d$. To examine the welfare impacts of the minimum wage, note that we are

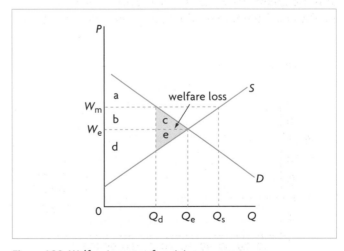

Figure 4.20 Welfare impacts of a minimum wage

---

[3] The phrase 'government measures to dispose of the surpluses' has been deleted because it does not apply to the minimum wage.

dealing with *employer surplus* (the area under the demand curve) and *worker surplus* (the area above the supply curve).

In the free market, with no minimum wage, employer surplus consists of areas a + b + c, and worker surplus consists of areas d + e, making a total social surplus of a + b + c + d + e. After the imposition of the minimum wage, employer surplus is reduced to area a, and worker surplus becomes areas d + b, so that total social surplus is a + b + d. Therefore, the minimum wage has resulted in a loss of social surplus equal to c and e, representing welfare (deadweight) loss. The deadweight loss arises because there is an underallocation of labour resources (usually unskilled labour) relative to the social optimum, since $Q_d < Q_e$.

(The reason why the welfare analysis of the minimum wage differs from that of price floors for agricultural products with government purchases of the excess supply is that the government does not 'buy' the excess labour supply that results from the minimum wage by offering the excess workers jobs.)

Consequences of minimum wages for various stakeholders

♦ Discuss the consequences of imposing a price floor on the stakeholders in a market, including consumers, producers and the government.

Firms (employers of labour)   Firms are worse off as they face higher costs of production due to the higher labour costs. This is reflected in the loss of employer surplus.

Workers (suppliers of labour)   The impacts on workers are mixed. Some gain, as they receive a higher wage than previously ($W_m > W_e$), but some lose as they lose their job. Note that the workers who lose their job are those represented by $Q_e - Q_d$. This is not the full amount of unemployment created by the minimum wage, because the minimum wage leads to *additional* unemployment of $Q_s - Q_e$, since more workers supply their labour in the market when the wage increases.

The mixed effects on workers are reflected in the gain in worker surplus of area b, and the loss of area e.

Consumers   Consumers are negatively affected, because the increase in labour costs leads to a decrease in supply of products (a leftward shift in firm supply curves) causing higher product prices and lower quantities.

Price floors and minimum wages in the real world

Economists agree that price floors for agricultural products lead to surpluses (excess supplies) and are highly inefficient for the reasons discussed above. Yet they continue to be used in many countries because of strong political pressures exerted by farmers who claim to need these for income support.

The effects of minimum wages, on the other hand, tend to be controversial, as it is uncertain whether they produce an increase in unemployment to the extent that economic theory predicts. There is agreement that if a minimum wage is set at a high level relative to the free market equilibrium wage, it is likely to create some unemployment. Yet some studies have shown that a minimum wage in some situations may have no effect or even a positive effect on *total* employment. Some firms respond to the minimum wage by maintaining the same number of workers but cutting non-wage benefits (such as paid holidays or sick leave); or they may hire fewer unskilled workers and more skilled workers. Also, it is possible that labour productivity (defined as the amount of output produced per worker) may increase due to the minimum wage, as workers feel motivated to work harder, with the result that some firms hire more unskilled labour in response to minimum wages.

While the effects of minimum wages remain controversial, there is generally strong political support for their continued use on the grounds of greater equity in income distribution.

Setting fixed prices

Sometimes prices may be fixed at a particular level, such as with ticket prices for theatres, movies and sports events, where prices are usually fixed ahead of time by the organising body (which may be private or public), and cannot increase or decrease according to supply and demand.

Figure 4.21 shows the market for tickets for a sports event. The supply curve is vertical because there is a fixed supply of tickets (due to a fixed number of seats; see page 27). The ticket price is fixed at P_{fx} by the organising body. Figure 4.21(a) illustrates an event for which there is large demand, given by D_1. If the price could respond to market forces, it would rise to P_e, but since it is fixed at P_f a shortage of tickets arises equal to the horizontal difference between points a and b. Figure 4.21(b) illustrates an event for which there is low demand, given by D_2. Here, the equilibrium price would have been P_e, however price is fixed at the higher level P_{fx}, resulting in a surplus of tickets equal to the horizontal difference between points c and d.

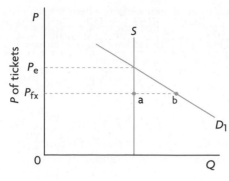

(a) Price fixing resulting in a shortage

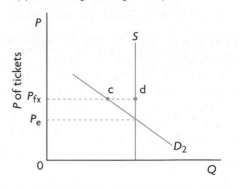

(b) Price fixing resulting in a surplus

Figure 4.21 Price fixing and surpluses and shortages

Test your understanding 4.10

1 Define a minimum wage. Why do many governments around the world impose them?

2 Draw a diagram illustrating the imposition of a minimum wage, and analyse its effects on market outcomes (the wage, quantity of labour demanded and supplied, market disequilibrium) and consequences for the economy (unemployment of labour, illegal work, resource misallocation, welfare (deadweight) loss).

3 (Optional) Assuming a minimum wage is imposed, draw diagrams to illustrate **(a)** the loss in employer surplus, (b) the gain and the loss in worker surplus, and (c) welfare (deadweight) loss. **(d)** What is the impact of the minimum wage on allocative efficiency?

4 Examine the consequences of a minimum wage for different stakeholders.

5 Using diagrams show how excess demand or excess supply of tickets results when ticket prices are set at a level that is **(a)** lower than equilibrium, or **(b)** higher than equilibrium.

Theory of knowledge

Allocative efficiency: is it really value-free?

Throughout this chapter, we have used the competitive market model, explained in Chapter 2, as the basis for making assessments about government intervention in the economy. According to this model, when there is competition in the sense of many buyers and sellers who act according to their best self-interest, and when market forces are free to determine equilibrium prices, a situation is reached where there is allocative efficiency and maximum social welfare. Scarce resources are allocated in the best possible way, producing the most of what people mostly want, and it is not possible to make anyone better off without making someone worse off, a condition called *Pareto optimality* (see page 42).

The concept of Pareto optimality emerged in the late 19th century after a period when economists were trying to make economics more scientific in its approach.

'Scientific' meant economics should get rid of any value judgements about things that 'ought to be' and base itself entirely on positive thinking (see page 11). The famous classical economists of earlier times (Adam Smith, Robert Malthus, David Ricardo, John Stuart Mill, Karl Marx and many others) openly discussed their ideas about what ought to happen in society (normative ideas) together with their positive ideas of things that 'are' or 'will be'. Yet by the late 19th century, it was believed that a true science is value-free, and economists set out to imitate the methods of the natural sciences, especially physics.

The concept of Pareto optimality, developed by Vilfredo Pareto (an Italian engineer, sociologist, economist and philosopher), was welcomed as being truly free of normative aspects. It simply stated that under certain

(continued over)

assumptions, numerous freely acting consumers and producers behaving according to their individual preferences (rational self-interest, see page 11) give rise to an outcome of maximum efficiency and maximum social welfare (defined as $MB = MC$ or maximum social surplus).

On the surface, this sounds like a value-free, positive statement. Yet in later years (and up to the present), many economists criticised it on the grounds that it is actually heavily based on normative ideas, and is therefore not value-free. The difficulty in detecting these values is that these are implicit; they are not explicit, or *openly stated* values.

Economists who question the value-free nature of Pareto optimality point out that the concept of 'welfare' is defined in relation to individual preferences of consumers and producers (decisions made on the basis of rational self-interest) that determine consumer and producer surplus. Individual preferences become the standard, or measuring stick by which economists evaluate real-world situations and government intervention in markets. As we saw in this chapter, a free competitive market is 'best'; government intervention in this market reduces welfare.

But surely there are other definitions of welfare, such as equality of opportunity, freedom from hunger and disease, human rights, fairness and many more. All these are normative concepts, but then, by the same token, welfare defined as maximum social surplus is also a normative concept, on the basis of which a judgement is made about how well or how poorly the economy works.

Some economists take these ideas further, and argue that not only Pareto optimality but the body of microeconomics on which it rests is also not value-free. The idea that societies should pursue allocative efficiency follows from *the definition of economics as the social science that tries to determine how to make the best use of scarce resources*. Yet, remember from Chapter 1, all societies must answer three basic economic questions: *what, how* and *for whom to produce*. The definition of economics covers only the first two of these and ignores the third. The reason for neglecting the *for whom to produce* question is that economists consider the first two questions to be part of positive thinking and the third a part of normative (see the Theory of knowledge feature on page 45). However, if efficiency (what and how to produce) leads to maximum welfare, where the definition of welfare is based on a value judgment, economists have gone around in a full circle and have based their so-called positive analysis on a value judgement.

In view of the above, some economists argue that the focus of government policies on efficiency, defined as Pareto optimality, diverts attention away from the problem of income distribution, and justifies government inaction in this area. What is the point of realising (or coming close to realising) Pareto optimality in the real world, if a large portion of the population is starving because they have no income?

According to Gunnar Myrdal, a Swedish economist who won the Nobel Prize in 1974, the social sciences are inevitably based on values, but these values should be made explicit:

'The only way we can strive for "objectivity" in theoretical analysis is to expose the valuations into full light, making them conscious, specific and explicit, and permit them to determine the theoretical research … there is nothing wrong, *per se*, with value-loaded concepts if they are clearly defined in terms of explicitly stated value premises.'[4]

---

[4] G. Myrdal (1970) *Objectivity in Social Research*, Gerald Duckworth.

Thinking points

- In your view, is Pareto optimality value-free, or is it implicitly based on a value judgement?

- Does language in the expression 'maximum social welfare' convey values? Is it possible to have value-free language?

- Does the inevitable use of language in the pursuit of economic knowledge complicate the job of economists as social *scientists* in pursuit of value-free knowledge?

- Do you think the natural sciences are value-free?

- Do you agree with Myrdal's claim that it may be possible to reach 'objectivity' in theoretical social science by making values explicit?

- Do you think economics is or ever can be completely value-free?

Assessment

The Student's CD-ROM at the back of this book provides practice of examination questions based on the material you have studied in this chapter.

Standard level
- Exam practice: Paper 1, Chapter 4
  - SL/HL core topics (questions 4.1–4.14)

Higher level
- Exam practice: Paper 1, Chapter 4
  - SL/HL core topics (questions 4.1–4.14)
  - HL topics (question 4.15)
- Exam practice: Paper 3, Chapter 4
  - HL topics (questions 7–12)

Chapter 5
Market failure

In this chapter we will see why the market economy fails to achieve many of its promises, and how government intervention can help markets overcome their failures.

5.1 The meaning of market failure: allocative inefficiency

♦ Analyse the concept of market failure as a failure of the market to achieve allocative efficiency, resulting in an over-allocation of resources (over-provision of a good) or an under-allocation of resources (under-provision of a good) relative to the social optimum.

The failure to achieve allocative efficiency

Our discussion so far has shown that a free, competitive market economy gives rise to a number of highly desirable outcomes. In Chapter 2 we learned that in a free competitive market, when the price of a good adjusts to make quantity demanded equal to quantity supplied, the equilibrium quantity reflects the 'best' or optimal allocation of resources to the production of that good (page 42). This condition is known as allocative efficiency, achieved when marginal benefit equals marginal cost ($MB = MC$), or when social surplus is maximum.

However, the achievement of these outcomes depends on very strict and unrealistic conditions that are practically never met in the real world. Therefore, in reality, the free market fails to achieve these highly desirable results. The study of market failure focuses on one particular failing: the free market's inability to realise allocative efficiency in a variety of circumstances.

Market failure does not necessarily lessen the market's signifcance as a mechanism that can advance the well-being of societies; instead, it suggests that for markets to realise their potential, they must be supported by appropriate government policies. Allocative efficiency is a concept used by economists to identify real-world situations that differ from the ideal of a perfect allocation of resources. Once these are identified, it is possible to design government policies aimed at reducing the extent of the inefficiencies.

Market failure refers to the failure of the market to allocate resources efficiently. Market failure results in allocative inefficiency, where too much or too little of goods or services are produced and consumed from the point of view of what is socially most desirable. Overprovision of a good means too many resources are allocated to its production (overallocation); underprovision means that too few resources are allocated to its production (underallocation).

Test your understanding 5.1

1 Using a diagram, and the concepts of consumer and producer surplus, and marginal benefits and marginal costs, explain the meaning of allocative efficiency.

2 Explain, in a general way, the meaning of market failure.

5.2 Externalities: diverging private and social benefits and costs

The meaning of externalities

♦ Describe the concepts of marginal private benefits (MPB), marginal social benefits (MSB), marginal private costs (MPC) and marginal social costs (MSC).
♦ Describe the meaning of externalities as the failure of the market to achieve a social optimum where MSB = MSC.

Understanding externalities

When a consumer buys and consumes a good, she or he derives some benefits. When a firm produces and sells a good, it incurs costs. Sometimes the benefits or costs spill over onto other consumers or producers who have nothing to do with consuming or producing the good. When this happens, there is an externality.

> An **externality** occurs when the actions of consumers or producers give rise to negative or positive side-effects on other people who are not part of these actions, and whose interests are not taken into consideration.

The other people feeling the effects of an externality are often referred to as 'third parties'. If the side-effects on third parties involve benefits, there arises a **positive externality**, also known as external (or spillover) benefit; if they involve costs, in the form of negative side-effects, there arises a **negative externality**, also known as external (or spillover) costs.

Externalities can result either from consumption activities (consumption externalities) or from production activities (production externalities).

Marginal private benefits and costs, and marginal social benefits and costs

To fully understand externalities, let's return to the demand and supply curves we studied in Chapter 2. As we know, the demand curve is also a 'marginal benefit curve' where marginal benefit is the benefit received by consumers for consuming one more unit of the good (see Figure 2.1(b), page 21). Since the benefits derived from consuming the good go to private individuals, who are the consumers buying the good, the demand curve represents marginal *private* benefits, shown as *MPB* in Figure 5.1.

The standard supply curve reflects firms' costs of production, specifically marginal costs. Marginal cost is the cost to producers of producing one more unit of the good. The supply curve therefore represents marginal *private* costs, appearing as *MPC* in Figure 5.1.

Now, if there are no externalities, so the actions of buyers and sellers do not produce side-effects on third parties, the marginal private benefit (*D*) curve and marginal private cost (*S*) curve determine an equilibrium price and quantity that reflect a **social optimum**, where there is allocative efficiency. In Figure 5.1, these are P_{opt} and Q_{opt}. A social optimum

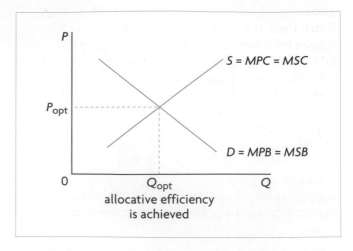

Figure 5.1   Demand, supply and allocative efficiency with no externalities

refers to a 'best' situation from the point of view of allocative efficiency.

If, however, there is an externality, additional benefits or additional costs affecting third parties arise, and the full benefits or full costs to society differ from the private ones. These involve *marginal social benefits* (*MSB*) that differ from marginal private benefits; or *marginal social costs* (*MSC*) that differ from the marginal private costs.

When this occurs, the equilibrium price and quantity determined by the intersection of the demand (*MPB*) curve and supply (*MPC*) curve is no longer a social optimum, because *allocative inefficiency* is introduced by social benefits or costs that differ from private ones.

In a diagram, social benefits appear as a marginal social benefit curve, *MSB*, representing the full benefits to society from the consumption of a good, and social costs as a marginal social cost curve, *MSC*, representing the full costs to society of producing the good. When *MSB* and *MSC* are equal to each other, there is a social optimum in which allocative efficiency is realised.

Figure 5.1 shows the case where there are no external benefits or external costs (no externalities). Therefore *D* = *MPB* = *MSB*, and *S* = *MPC* = *MSC*.

> **marginal private costs** (*MPC*) refer to costs to producers of producing one more unit of a good
>
> **marginal social costs** (*MSC*) refer to costs to society of producing one more unit of a good
>
> **marginal private benefits** (*MPB*) refer to benefits to consumers from consuming one more unit of a good
>
> **marginal social benefits** (*MSB*) refer to benefits to society from consuming one more unit of a good

Allocative efficiency is achieved when $MSC = MSB$. When there is no externality, the competitive free market leads to an outcome where $MPC = MSC = MPB = MSB$, as in Figure 5.1, indicating allocative efficiency. An externality creates a divergence between MPC and MSC or between MPB and MSB. When there is an externality, the free market leads to an outcome where $MPB = MPC$, but where MSB is not equal to MSC, indicating allocative inefficiency.[1]

We will examine four types of externalities: negative production externalities; negative consumption externalities; positive production externalities and positive consumption externalities.

These are some points to bear in mind as you read about externalities:

- All negative externalities (of production and consumption) *create external costs*. When there are external costs, $MSC > MSB$ at the point of production by the market.
- All positive externalities (of production and consumption) *create external benefits*. When there are external benefits $MSB > MSC$ at the point of production by the market.
- All production externalities (positive and negative) create *a divergence between private and social costs (MPC and MSC)*.
- All consumption externalities (positive and negative) create *a divergence between private and social benefits (MPB and MSB)*.

5.3 Negative externalities of production and consumption

- Explain, using diagrams and examples, the concepts of negative externalities of production and consumption, and the welfare loss associated with the production or consumption of a good or service.

- Explain that demerit goods are goods whose consumption creates external costs.
- Evaluate, using diagrams, the use of policy responses, including market-based policies (taxation and tradable permits) and government regulations, to the problem of negative externalities of production and consumption.

Negative production externalities (external or spillover costs)

Illustrating negative production externalities

Negative externalities of production refer to external costs created by producers. The problem of environmental pollution, created as a side-effect of production activities, is very commonly analysed as a negative production externality.

Consider a cement factory that emits smoke into the air and disposes its waste by dumping it into the ocean. There is a production externality, because over and above the firm's private costs of production, there are additional costs that spill over onto society due to the polluted air and ocean, with negative consequences for the local inhabitants, swimmers, sea life, the fishing industry and the marine ecosystem. This is shown in Figure 5.2, where the supply curve, $S = MPC$, reflects the firm's private costs of production, and the marginal social cost curve given by MSC represents the full cost to society of producing cement. For each level of output, Q, social costs of producing cement given by MSC are greater than the firm's private costs. The vertical difference between MSC and MPC represents the external costs. Since the externality involves only production (the supply curve), the demand curve represents both marginal private benefits and marginal social benefits.

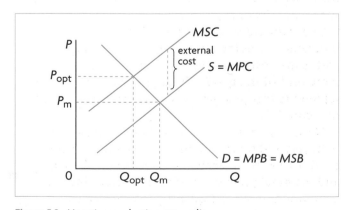

Figure 5.2 Negative production externality

---

[1] The condition $MSC = MSB$ is the same as $MC = MB$ when there are no externalities. In Chapters 2 and 4, we repeatedly referred to $MC = MB$ as the condition for allocative efficiency because we were considering markets with no market failures.

Figure 5.2 illustrates a general point that you should keep in mind whenever you examine (or draw) an externality diagram: the free market outcome is determined by the intersection of *MPB* and *MPC*, resulting in quantity Q_m and price P_m. The social optimum (or 'best') outcome is given by the intersection of *MSB* with *MSC*, which determines quantity Q_{opt} and price P_{opt}.

We can draw an important conclusion from the negative externality illustrated in Figure 5.2:

> When there is a negative production externality, the free market overallocates resources to the production of the good and too much of it is produced relative to the social optimum. This is shown by $Q_m > Q_{opt}$ and MSC > MSB at the point of production, Q_m, in Figure 5.2.

The welfare loss of negative production externalities

Welfare loss
Whenever there is an externality, there is a welfare (deadweight) loss, involving a reduction in social benefits, due to the misallocation of resources.

In Figure 5.3(a), the shaded area represents the welfare loss arising from the negative production externality. For all units of output greater than Q_{opt}, *MSC > MSB*, meaning that society would be better off if less were produced. The welfare loss is equal to the difference between *MSC* and *MSB* for the amount of output that is overproduced ($Q_m - Q_{opt}$). It is a loss of social benefits due to overproduction of the good caused by the externality. If the externality were corrected, so that the economy reaches the social optimum, the loss of benefits would disappear. It may be useful to note that the point of the welfare loss triangle always lies at the Q_{opt} quantity of output.

Welfare loss in relation to consumer and producer surplus (supplementary material)
We can use the concepts of consumer and producer surplus to understand the welfare loss due to the externality. In Figure 5.3(b), in market equilibrium, consumer surplus is equal to areas a + b + c + d, while producer surplus is equal to areas f + g + h. The value of the external cost is the difference between the *MSC* and *MPC* curves up to Q_m (the quantity produced by the market), and is therefore equal to c + d + e + g + h. The total social benefits in market equilibrium are equal to consumer surplus plus producer surplus minus the external cost:

$$(a + b + c + d) + (f + g + h) - (c + d + e + g + h)$$
$$= a + b + f - e$$

At the social optimum, or at Q_{opt} and P_{opt}, consumer surplus is equal to area a, and producer surplus is equal to area b + f. The external cost is now equal to zero. Therefore, the total social benefits are equal to consumer surplus plus producer surplus:

$$a + b + f$$

Comparing total social benefits at the market equilibrium and at the social optimum, we find that they are smaller at the market equilibrium by the area e. This is the welfare loss.

Correcting negative production externalities

Government regulations
Government regulations to deal with negative production externalities rely on the 'command' approach, where the government uses its authority to enact legislation and regulations in the public's interest (see Chapter 1, page 15, for a discussion of command decision-making).

(a) Welfare loss

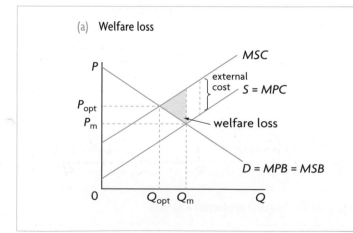

(b) Welfare loss in relation to consumer and producer surplus (supplementary material)

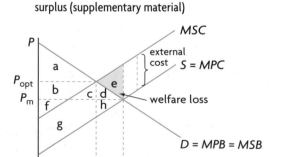

Figure 5.3 Welfare loss (deadweight loss) in a negative production externality

Regulations can be used to prevent or reduce the effects of production externalities. In the case of the polluting firm, regulations can forbid the dumping of certain toxic substances into the environment (into the rivers, oceans, and so on). More commonly, regulations do not totally ban the production of pollutants, but rather attempt to achieve one of the following:

- limit the emission of pollutants by setting a maximum level of pollutants permitted
- limit the quantity of output produced by the polluting firm
- require polluting firms to install technologies reducing the emissions.

The impact is to lower the quantity of the good produced and bring it closer to Q_{opt} in Figure 5.4 by shifting the MPC curve upward towards the MSC curve.[2] Pollutant and output restrictions achieve this by forcing the firm to produce less. Requirements to install technologies reducing emissions achieve this by imposing higher costs of production due to the purchase of the non-polluting technologies. Ideally, the higher costs of production would be equal to the value of the negative externality. The government's objective is to make the MPC curve shift upwards until it coincides with the MSC curve, in which case Q_{opt} is produced, price increases from P_m to P_{opt}, and the problem of overallocation of resources to the production of the good is corrected. If polluting firms do not comply with the regulations, they would have to pay fines.

Market-based policies

Governments can also pursue policies relying on the market to correct negative production externalities. We will consider two market-based policies: taxes and tradable permits.

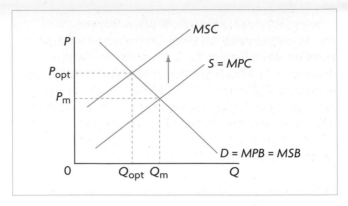

Figure 5.4 Government regulations to correct negative production externalities

Imposing a tax to correct the negative production externality The government could impose a tax on the firm per unit of output produced, or a tax per unit of pollutants emitted. In Figure 5.5(a), the tax results in an upward shift of the supply curve, from $S = MPC$ to MSC ($=MPC + tax$). The optimal (or best) tax policy is to impose a tax that is exactly equal to the external cost, so the MPC curve shifts upward until it overlaps with MSC. The new, after-tax equilibrium is given by the intersection of MSC and the demand curve, $D = MPB = MSB$, resulting in the lower, optimal quantity of the good produced, Q_{opt}, and higher, optimal price, P_{opt}.

(Bearing in mind our discussion of taxes in Chapter 4, you may note that P_{opt} is the price paid by consumers, or P_c, while the price received by producers is P_p, which is equal to P_c minus tax per unit. We can see, therefore, that the tax burden or incidence is shared between consumers and producers.)

Distinguishing between a tax on output and a tax on pollutants (emissions) Whereas both a tax per unit of output produced and a tax per unit of pollutants emitted appear to have the same result, shown in Figure 5.5(a),

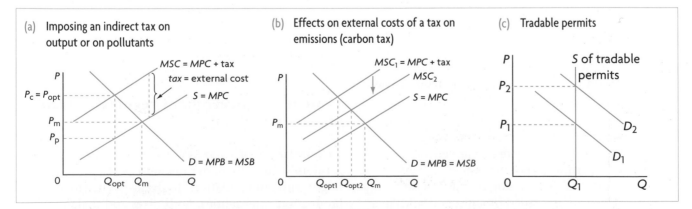

Figure 5.5 Market-based policies to correct negative production externalities

[2] See 'Quantitative techniques' chapter on the CD-ROM, page 13 for an explanation of the equivalence of upward and leftward shifts of the supply curve.

actually they work quite differently. A tax per unit of output is intended to work by directly correcting the overallocation of resources to the good, resulting in quantity Q_{opt}. A tax per unit of pollutants is intended to work by creating incentives for the firm to buy fewer polluting resources (such as fossil fuels), and to switch to less polluting technologies (alternative energy sources).

An example of a tax per unit of pollutants considered by many countries as a policy to deal with the problem of climate change is the **carbon tax**, which is a tax per unit of carbon emissions of fossil fuels. Fossil fuels do not all emit the same amounts of carbon when burned, therefore the carbon tax is calculated on the basis of how much carbon the fuel emits: *the more the carbon emitted, the higher the tax*. Following the imposition of the tax, firms must pay the higher price to buy the fossil fuel. This appears in Figure 5.5(a) as the familiar upward shift in $S = MPC$ toward MSC because of the firm's higher costs of production, but this has further consequences. Since there are other substitute energy sources with lower carbon emissions (thus taxed at a lower rate), or that do not emit carbon (if they are not fossil fuels, thus not taxed at all), the increase in the price of the high-carbon fuel creates incentives for firms to switch to other, less polluting or non-polluting energy sources.

The result is that if the firm switches to alternative, less polluting resources, Q_{opt} *in Figure 5.2 will increase, because the external costs of producing the output will become smaller.* This can be seen in Figure 5.5(b), where the MSC curve shifts from MSC_1 to MSC_2, indicating that the external costs are lower due to the use of the less polluting resources. With the fall in external costs, the optimum quantity of output increases from Q_{opt1} to Q_{opt2}. (Note that this also involves a lower tax on pollutants, shown by the smaller distance between the demand curve and MSC_2.)

> A tax on carbon (or on emissions generally) has the effect of creating incentives for producers to reduce the amount of pollution they create by purchasing less polluting resources. This reduces the size of the negative externality and increases the optimum quantity of output. A tax on the output of the polluter does not have this effect; it only reduces the amount of output produced.

Tradable permits   **Tradable permits**, also known as **cap and trade schemes**, are a relatively new policy involving permits to pollute issued to firms by a government or an international body. These permits to pollute can be traded (bought and sold) in a market. Consider a number of firms whose production pollutes the environment. The government grants each firm a particular number of permits (or rights) to

produce a particular level of pollutants over a given time period. The permits to pollute can be bought and sold among interested firms, with the price of permits being determined by supply and demand. If a firm can produce its product by emitting a lower level of pollutants than the level set by its permits, it can sell its extra permits in the market. If a firm needs to emit more pollutants than the level set by its permits, it can buy more permits in the market.

Figure 5.5(c) shows a market for tradable pollution permits. The supply of permits is perfectly inelastic (i.e. the supply curve is vertical), as it is fixed at a particular level by the government (or an international authority if several countries are participating). This fixed supply of permits is distributed to firms. The position of the demand-for-permits curve determines the equilibrium price. As an economy grows and the firms increase their output levels, the demand for permits is likely to increase, as shown by the rightward shift of the demand curve from D_1 to D_2. With supply fixed, the price of permits increases from P_1 to P_2.

Tradable permits are like taxes on emissions in that they provide incentives to producers to switch to less polluting resources for which it is not necessary to buy permits. If a firm finds a way to reduce its emissions, it can sell its permits thus adding to profits. Permits therefore are intended to reduce the quantity of pollutants emitted, thus reducing the size of the negative externality, and increasing the optimum quantity of output produced, by shifting the MSC curve downward toward MPC, as shown in Figure 5.5(b).

We will come back to both carbon taxes and tradable permits later in this chapter (page 125).

> Correction of negative production externalities involves shifting the MPC curve upward toward the MSC curve through government regulations or market-based policies. For allocative efficiency to be achieved, the quantity of the good produced and consumed must fall to Q_{opt} as price increases to P_{opt}.

Evaluating government regulations and market-based policies

Advantages of market-based policies

Economists usually prefer market-based solutions to government regulations to deal with negative production externalities. Both taxes and tradable permits have the effect of *internalising the externality*, meaning that the costs that were previously external are made internal, because they are now paid for by producers and consumers who are parties to the transaction. (Consumers also pay for external production costs, since they share with producers the burden or incidence of the tax, as we know from Chapter 4, page 74.)

In the case of taxes, taxes on emissions are superior to taxes on output. Taxes on output only provide incentives to producers to reduce the quantity of output produced with a given technology and given polluting resources, but not to reduce the amount of pollution they create or to switch to less polluting resources.

Taxes on pollutants emitted provide incentives to firms to economise on the use of polluting resources (such as fossil fuels) and use production methods that pollute less. Firms do not all face the same costs of reducing pollution; for some, the costs of reducing pollution are lower than for others, and these will be the ones most likely to cut their pollution emissions to avoid paying the tax. Firms that face the highest costs of reducing pollution will be the ones least likely to cut their pollutants, and so will pay the tax. The result is that *taxation leads to lower pollution levels at a lower overall cost*. Similarly, in the case of tradable permits, the system creates incentives for firms to cut back on their pollution if they can do so at relatively low cost. If it is a relatively low cost procedure for a firm to reduce its pollutant emissions, it will be in its interests to do so and sell excess permits. Firms that can only reduce pollution at high cost will be forced to buy additional permits. Therefore, both taxes and tradable permits are methods to reduce pollution more efficiently (at a lower cost).

We will consider the relative advantages of taxes versus tradable permits later in this chapter (page 126).

Disadvantages of market-based policies

Whereas taxes and tradable permits as methods to negative externalities are simple in theory, in practice they are faced with numerous technical difficulties.

Taxes Taxes face serious practical difficulties that involve designing a tax equal in value to the amount of the pollution. An effective tax policy requires answers to the following questions:

- **What production methods produce pollutants?** Different production methods create different pollutants. It is necessary to identify what methods produce which pollutants, which is technically very difficult.
- **Which pollutants are harmful?** It is necessary to identify the harmful pollutants, which is also

technically difficult, and there is much controversy among scientists over the extent of harm done by each type of pollutant.

- **What is the value of the harm?** It is then necessary to attach a monetary value to the harm: how much is the harm done by each pollutant worth? This raises questions that have no easy answers: who or what is harmed; how is the value of harm to be measured?

Aside from the technical difficulties, there is also a risk that even if taxes are imposed some polluting firms may not lower their pollution levels, continuing to pollute even though they pay a tax.

Tradable permits Tradable permits face all the technical limitations listed above for taxes. In addition, tradable permits require the government (or international body) to set a maximum acceptable level for each type of pollutant, called a 'cap'. This task demands having technical information on quantities of each pollutant that are acceptable from an environmental point of view, which is often not available. If the maximum level is set too high, it will not have the desired effect on cutting pollution levels. If it is set too low, the permits become very costly, causing hardship for firms that need to buy them. To date, tradable permits have been developed for just a few pollutants (CO_2, SO_2).

In addition, a method must be found to distribute permits to polluting firms in a fair way. Issues of political favouritism may come into play, as governments give preferential treatment to their 'friends' and supporters.

In practice, the most that can be hoped for is a shift of the *MPC* curve toward the *MSC* curve, as well some reduction in the size of the externality, but it is unlikely that these policies can achieve the optimal results.

Advantages of government regulations

Regulations have the advantage that they are simple compared to market-based solutions, and can be implemented more easily. The technical difficulties discussed above often make it more practical to impose regulations limiting the amounts of pollution firms can emit. In some situations, the practical difficulties in implementing market-based solutions may be so great that there is no alternative but to use regulatory methods. Moreover, regulations force polluting firms to comply and reduce pollution levels (which taxes may not always do). For these reasons, regulations are far more commonly used as a method to limit negative externalities of pollution in countries around the world.

Disadvantages of government regulations

As they do not allow the externality to be internalised, regulations create no market-based incentives, and therefore are unable to make distinctions between firms that have higher or lower costs of reducing pollution. They are also unable to provide incentives for firms to use less polluting resources, and are thus unable to lower the size of the externality. The result is that pollution is reduced at a higher overall cost. In addition, although they can be implemented more easily, they suffer from similar limitations as the market-based policies (lack of sufficient technical information on types and amounts of pollutants emitted), and so can at best be only partially effective in reducing the pollution created. Finally, there are costs of policing, and there may be problems with enforcement. Therefore, such measures can only attempt to partially correct the problem.

Test your understanding 5.3

1 **(a)** Using diagrams, show how marginal private costs and marginal social costs differ when there is a negative production externality. **(b)** How does the equilibrium quantity determined by the market differ from the quantity that is optimal from the point of view of society's preferences? **(c)** What does this tell you about the allocation of resources achieved by the market when there is a negative production externality? **(d)** Show the welfare loss created by the negative production externality in your diagram, and explain what this means.

2 Provide examples of negative production externalities.

3 For each of the examples you provided in question 2, state and explain some method(s) that could be used to correct the externality.

4 Using diagrams, show how the negative externality can be corrected by use of **(a)** taxes, and **(b)** legislation and regulations that limit the quantity of pollutants. **(c)** What are some advantages and disadvantages of each of these types of policy measures?

5 Explain how tradable pollution permits can contribute to correcting negative production externalities.

6 **(a)** What does it mean to 'internalise an externality'? How can this be achieved?

(b) Why do economists prefer market-based methods that internalise negative production externalities to command methods (such as legislation and regulations)? **(c)** What are some difficulties that governments face in designing market-based methods?

7 **(a)** In what way are taxes on emissions, and tradable permits similar with respect to their objectives? (*Hint:* think about incentives.) **(b)** How do they differ from taxes on output of the firms creating negative externalities? **(c)** What policy is preferable from the point of view of reducing the external costs of a negative environmental externality: a tax on output or a tax on emissions?

Negative consumption externalities (external or spillover costs)

Illustrating negative consumption externalities

Negative externalities of consumption refer to external costs created by consumers. For example, when consumers smoke in public places, there are external costs that spill over onto society in the form of costs to non-smokers due to passive smoking. In addition, smoking-related diseases result in higher than necessary health care costs that are an additional burden upon society. When there is a consumption externality, the marginal private benefit (demand) curve does not reflect social benefits. In Figure 5.6, the buyers of cigarettes have a demand curve, *MPB*, but when smoking, create external costs for non-smokers. These costs can be thought of as 'negative benefits', which therefore cause the *MSB* curve to lie below the *MPB* curve. The vertical difference between *MPB* and *MSB* represents the external costs. Note that since the

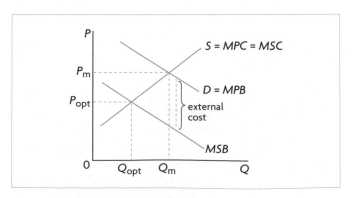

Figure 5.6 Negative consumption externality

externality involves consumption (i.e. the demand curve), the supply curve represents both marginal private costs and marginal social costs. The market determines an equilibrium quantity, Q_m, and price P_m, given by the intersection of the MPB and MPC curves, but the social optimum is Q_{opt} and P_{opt}, determined by the intersection of the MSB and MSC curves.

Other examples of negative consumption externalities include:

- heating homes and driving cars by use of fossil fuels that pollute the atmosphere
- partying with loud music until the early hours of the morning, and disturbing the neighbours.

When there is a negative consumption externality, the free market overallocates resources to the production of the good, and too much of it is produced relative to what is socially optimum. This is shown by $Q_m > Q_{opt}$ and $MSC > MSB$ at Q_m in Figure 5.6.

In general, negative externalities, whether these arise from production or consumption activities, lead to allocative inefficiency arising from an overallocation of resources to the good and to its overprovision.

The welfare loss of negative consumption externalities

Welfare loss
The welfare (deadweight) loss resulting from negative consumption externalities is the shaded area in Figure 5.7(a), and represents the reduction in benefits for society due to the overallocation of resources to the production of the good. For all units of output greater than Q_{opt}, $MSC > MSB$, indicating that too much of the good is produced. The welfare loss is equal to the difference between the MSC and MSB curves for

the amount of output that is overproduced relative to the social optimum ($Q_m - Q_{opt}$). It represents the loss of social benefits from overproduction due to the externality. If this externality were corrected, society would gain the benefits represented by the shaded area. Note that, once again, the point of the welfare loss triangle lies at the Q_{opt} quantity of output (as in the case of negative production externalities; see page 104).

Welfare loss in relation to consumer and producer surplus (supplementary material)
Figure 5.7(b) shows how the welfare loss of a negative consumption externality is related to consumer and producer surplus and the external cost. In market equilibrium, consumer surplus is equal to the areas a + b, while producer surplus is equal to the areas c + d + f. The cost of the externality is represented by a + d + e (it is the difference between the MPB and MSB curves up to Q_m). The total social benefits are therefore consumer surplus plus producer surplus minus the external cost:

$$(a + b) + (c + d + f) - (a + d + e) = b + c + f - e$$

At the social optimum, consumer surplus is equal to b + c, and producer surplus is equal to f, while external costs are zero. Therefore, the total social surplus is equal to producer plus consumer surplus:

$$b + c + f$$

Comparing the total social benefits at market equilibrium and at the social optimum, we see they are smaller at market equilibrium by the area e, which is the welfare loss.

The case of demerit goods
Demerit goods are goods that are considered to be undesirable for consumers, but which are overprovided by the market. Examples of demerit goods include cigarettes, alcohol and gambling. One important

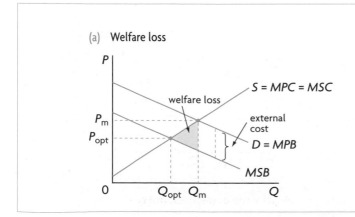

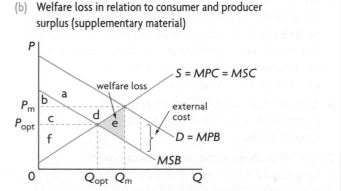

Figure 5.7 Welfare loss (deadweight loss) in a negative consumption externality

reason for overprovision is that the good may have negative consumption externalities, in which case the market overallocates resources to its production. Another reason for overprovision could be consumer ignorance about its negative effects, or indifference: consumers may not be aware of the harmful effects upon others of their actions, or they may not care.

Correcting negative consumption externalities

Government regulations

If negative consumption externalities were corrected, Q_{opt} quantity of the good would be produced, reflecting allocative efficiency. Regulations can be used to prevent or limit consumer activities that impose costs on third parties, such as legal restrictions on activities as smoking in public places. This has the effect of shifting the $D_1 = MPB$ curve towards the MSB curve in Figure 5.8(a), until D_2 overlaps with MSB. This would eliminate the externality, with production and consumption occurring at Q_{opt} and price falling to P_{opt}.

Advertising

Advertising and campaigns by the government can be used to try to persuade consumers to buy fewer goods with negative externalities, such as anti-smoking campaigns or campaigns to reduce the consumption of goods based on fossil fuel use (for example, campaigns to use public transportation to economise on petrol (gasoline) use, and to improve home insulation to reduce oil consumption for heating). The objective is to try to decrease demand for such goods, and the effects are the same as with government regulations, shown in Figure 5.8(a). The MPB curve shifts to D_2 after the campaign, where it coincides

with MSB, where Q_{opt} is produced and consumed, and the price falls from P_m to P_{opt}.

Market-based policies

Market-based policies to correct negative consumption externalities involve the imposition of indirect (excise) taxes (see Chapter 4, page 73). Indirect taxes can be imposed on the good whose consumption creates external costs (for example, cigarettes and petrol/gasoline). Note that whereas the indirect taxes discussed in Chapter 4 *introduced allocative inefficiency*, indirect taxes in the present context are intended to *lead to allocative efficiency*.

The effects of an indirect tax are shown in Figure 5.8(b). When such a tax is imposed on the good whose consumption creates the external cost, the result is a decrease in supply and an upward shift of the supply curve from MPC to MPC + tax. If the tax equals the external cost, the MPC + tax curve intersects MPB at the Q_{opt} level of output, and quantity produced and consumed drops to Q_{opt}. (The demand curve does not shift but remains at $D = MPB$.) Q_{opt} is the socially optimum quantity, and price increases from P_m to P_c. The tax therefore permits allocative efficiency to be achieved.[3]

Correction of negative consumption externalities involves either decreasing demand and shifting the MPB curve toward the MSB curve through regulations or advertising; or decreasing supply and shifting the MPC curve upward by imposing an indirect tax. Both demand decreases and supply decreases can lead to production and consumption at Q_{opt} and the achievement of allocative efficiency. The price paid by consumers falls to P_{opt} when demand decreases, and rises when supply decreases.

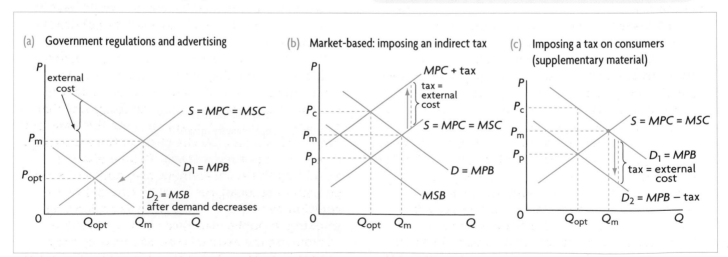

Figure 5.8 Correcting negative consumption externalities

[3] Note that the new equilibrium price, P_c, is the price paid by consumers; the price received by producers is $P_p = P_c$ minus tax per unit; see Chapter 4, page 74).

Note that the problem of overprovision of demerit goods by the market (discussed on page 109) can be addressed by all the policies discussed above to correct negative consumption externalities: regulations, advertising and indirect (excise) taxes. The objective of all these policies in the case of demerit goods is to decrease their consumption, as they are held to be undesirable.

A tax on producers or consumers? (supplementary material)

You may be wondering why the tax to correct negative consumption externalities should affect producers, shifting the supply curve upward in Figure 5.8(b), and not consumers by shifting the demand curve downward, who after all are the ones creating the externality through consumption. The reason is that *these two shifts produce identical market outcomes*.

We have seen in Figure 5.8(b) that when an indirect (excise) tax is imposed on the good causing the negative externality, the supply or *MPC* curve shifts upward. At the new equilibrium, Q_{opt} will be produced, and will be sold at the price P_c, which is the price paid by consumers, while the price received by producers is P_p.

If instead a tax per unit bought is imposed on consumers, which they pay directly to the government, this would cause a downward shift of the demand curve, as in Figure 5.8(c), from D_1 to D_2. The reason for this shift is that for each quantity consumers are willing and able to buy, the 'price' they pay includes the price of the good plus the tax per unit. This means that for each quantity, the price of the good must be lower by the amount of the tax.

The new equilibrium is determined by the intersection of the new demand curve, D_2, with the supply curve (which has not been affected), giving rise to Q_{opt}. When consumers buy Q_{opt} quantity, they pay the tax per unit plus price P_p (determined by their demand D_2), making a total price of P_c. The price P_p is the price received by producers.

Comparing Figure 5.8(b) with Figure 5.8(c), we see that the market outcomes are identical. Q_{opt} has been achieved, consumers pay price P_c, and producers receive price $P_p = P_c - $ tax. Also, the incidence is shared between consumers and producers (as we learned in Chapter 4). The only difference between the two situations is who pays the tax to the government. In practice, excise taxes on goods are paid to the government by firms, because it is administratively far easier for the government to collect taxes this way.

Evaluating market-based policies, government regulation and advertising/persuasion

As with negative production externalities, economists prefer market-based solutions to the problem of negative consumption externalities; therefore, indirect taxes are the preferred measure, as they internalise the externality. Indirect taxes create incentives for consumers to change their consumption patterns by changing relative prices; the good that is taxed becomes relatively more expensive and consumption is reduced. However, there are a number of difficulties in this approach. The first involves difficulties in measuring the value of the external costs. Take, for example, the case of passive smoking, an external cost created by smokers, or the case of petrol (gasoline) consumption, which creates external costs in the form of environmental pollution. There are many technical difficulties involved in trying to assess who and what is affected, as well as determine the value of the external costs, on the basis of which a tax can be designed.

A further difficulty is that some of the goods whose consumption leads to negative consumption externalities (for example, petrol/gasoline and cigarettes) have an inelastic demand. As you may remember from Chapter 3, page 49, when demand is inelastic, the percentage decrease in quantity demanded is smaller than the percentage increase in price (due to the tax). Therefore, it is possible that imposing taxes on such goods as petrol (gasoline) and cigarettes (both of which have an inelastic demand) works to increase government tax revenues while not significantly decreasing the quantity demanded of these goods. This could mean that in order to achieve Q_{opt}, a very high indirect tax would have to be imposed, which would very likely be politically unacceptable.

Advertising and persuasion have the advantage that they are simpler, but they too have their disadvantages. One of these involves the cost to the government of advertising campaigns, which are funded out of tax funds, meaning there are less funds available for use elsewhere in the economy (there are opportunity costs). There is also the possibility that such methods may not be effective enough in reducing the negative externality. In addition, while regulations (such as prohibiting smoking in public places) can be very effective in reducing the external costs of smoking, they cannot be used to deal with other kinds of negative consumption externalities. For example, it would be very difficult to regulate petrol (gasoline) consumption; on the other hand, imposing indirect taxes on such goods may be more effective (though subject to the limitations noted above on inelastic demand). Governments must therefore be selective in the methods they use to reduce consumption externalities, depending on the particular good that creates the external costs.

In general, given the limitations above, with all policies (regulation, advertising and taxes), it is only possible to move the economy in a direction towards correction of the externality, rather than achieving a precise allocation of resources where Q_{opt} is produced and consumed.

Test your understanding 5.4

1 **(a)** Using diagrams, show how marginal private benefits and marginal social benefits differ when there is a negative consumption externality. **(b)** How does the equilibrium quantity determined by the market differ from the quantity that is optimal from the point of view of society's preferences? **(c)** What does this tell you about the allocation of resources achieved by the market when there is a negative consumption externality? **(d)** Show the welfare loss created by the negative consumption externality in your diagram, and explain what this means.

2 Provide some examples of negative consumption externalities.

3 For each of the examples you provided in question 2, explain some methods that could be used to correct the externality.

4 Using diagrams, show how a negative consumption externality can be corrected by use of **(a)** legislation and regulations that limit the external (spillover) costs, **(b)** advertising and persuasion, and **(c)** indirect taxes. **(d)** What are some advantages and disadvantages of each of these policy measures?

5 **(a)** Explain the meaning of a demerit good, and provide examples. **(b)** How can overprovision of demerit goods be corrected?

6 How does a negative consumption externality differ from a negative production externality?

7 **(a)** What kinds of measures do economists prefer to correct negative consumption externalities? **(b)** Why might these not be very effective?

Real world focus

Could a tax on chocolate help fight obesity?

A UK doctor has suggested that chocolate should be taxed like alcohol and cigarettes if the UK is to deal with its obesity epidemic. Excessive consumption of chocolate is leading to very high rates of heart disease and diabetes. Some people eat their entire daily calorie requirement in chocolate.

A chocolate tax would make people healthier. Revenues from the chocolate tax could be used to help pay for the treatment of diseases resulting from obesity. There is a lot of negative publicity about other junk food, but an exception is made for chocolate, which has not been identified as responsible for a big part of poor health and additional health care costs that burden society.

Opponents to the tax say there is no evidence that such 'fat taxes' would work in practice. Some people point to the health benefits of eating chocolate. A Cadbury spokesperson said, 'We've known for a long time that there's good stuff in chocolate.'

Source: Adapted from Daniel Martin, 'Could a tax on chocolate help tackle obesity?' in the *Daily Mail*, 13 March 2009.

Applying your skills

Using diagrams, in each case:

1 explain what kind of externality the article is referring to

2 explain how a tax on chocolate might correct the externality

3 evaluate the desirability of a tax on chocolate.

5.4 Positive externalities of production and consumption

- Explain, using diagrams and examples, the concepts of positive externalities of production and consumption, and the welfare loss associated with production or consumption of a good or service.
- Explain that merit goods are goods whose consumption creates external benefits.
- Evaluate, using diagrams, the use of government responses, including subsidies, legislation, advertising to influence behaviour, and direct provision of goods and services.

Positive production externalities (external or spillover benefits)

Illustrating positive production externalities

Positive externalities of production refer to external benefits created by producers. If, for example, a firm engages in research and development, and succeeds in developing a new technology that spreads throughout the economy, there are external benefits because not only the firm but also society benefits from widespread adoption of the new technology. Therefore, the social costs of research and development are lower than the private costs. In Figure 5.9, the *MSC* curve lies below the *MPC* curve, and the difference between the two curves is the value of the external benefits (these can be thought of as 'negative costs'). The demand curve represents both *MPB* and *MSB* since the externality involves only production. The market gives rise to equilibrium quantity Q_m and price P_m, determined by the intersection of the *MPB* and *MPC* curves, while the social optimum is given by Q_{opt} and P_{opt}, determined by the intersection of the *MSB* with *MSC* curves. Since $Q_m < Q_{opt}$, the market underallocates resources to research and development activities that lead to new technologies, and not enough of them are undertaken.

When there is a positive production externality, the free market underallocates resources to the production of the good: too few resources are allocated to its production, and too little of it is produced. This is shown by $Q_m < Q_{opt}$ and $MSB > MSC$ at Q_m in Figure 5.9.

More examples of positive production externalities include:

- Firms train workers who later switch jobs and work elsewhere; external benefits are created as the new employers and society benefit from the trained workers.
- A pharmaceutical company develops a new medication that benefits not only its users but also those around them from the improved quality of life and increased life expectancy.

The welfare loss of positive production externalities

Welfare loss
The underallocation of resources to the production of a good with a positive production externality leads to a welfare loss, shown in Figure 5.10(a) as the shaded area. This loss is equal to the difference between the *MSB* and *MSC* curves for the amount of output that is underproduced relative to the social optimum $(Q_{opt} - Q_m)$. It involves external benefits for society that are lost because not enough of the good is produced. If the externality were corrected, society would gain the benefits represented by the shaded area. Note that the point of the welfare loss triangle lies at the Q_{opt} quantity of output.

Welfare loss in relation to consumer and producer surplus (supplementary material)
Figure 5.10(b) shows the welfare loss in relation to consumer and producer surplus and the externality. At market equilibrium, consumer surplus is area a, producer surplus is area b + e, and the external benefits are c + f (the difference between the *MPC* and *MSC* curves up to the point of production by the market, Q_m). The total benefits are therefore consumer surplus plus producer surplus plus external benefits:

$$a + (b + e) + (c + f) = a + b + e + c + f$$

At the social optimum, consumer surplus is a + b + c + d, producer surplus is e + f + g, and external benefits are zero, making a total of:

$$(a + b + c + d) + (e + f + g) = a + b + c + d + e + f + g$$

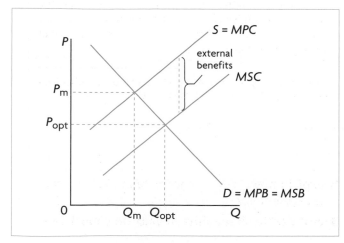

Figure 5.9 Positive production externality

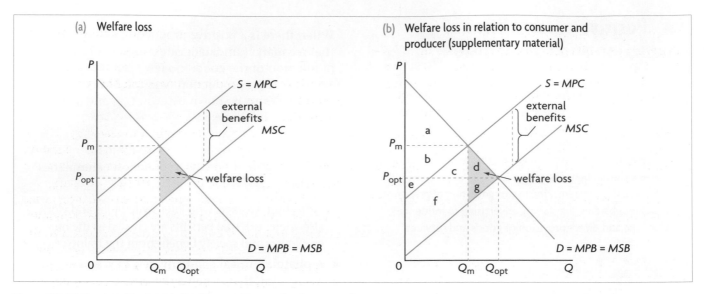

Figure 5.10 Welfare loss (deadweight loss) in a positive production externality

Comparing total benefits at market equilibrium and at the social optimum, we find that at the social optimum there are additional benefits of the amount d + g, corresponding to the shaded area in the figure. This is the amount of welfare that is lost at market equilibrium due to underallocation of resources arising from the positive production externality.

Correcting positive production externalities

Direct government provision
A solution often pursued by governments involves direct government provision of the good or service creating the positive production externality. For example, governments often engage in research and development (R&D) for new technology, for medicine and pharmaceuticals, and many other areas. The

government can also directly provide training for workers. Governments pay for such activities with government funds, raised through taxes. Figure 5.11(a) shows that when the government intervenes by providing goods and services itself, this has the effect of shifting the supply curve (= MPC curve) downward (or to the right), toward the MSC curve so that the optimum quantity of the good, Q_{opt}, will be produced, with price falling from P_m to P_{opt}.

Subsidies
We studied subsidies and their effects in Chapter 4, where we saw how their introduction into a perfect market (with no market failures) creates allocative inefficiency. Now, we will see how subsidies can correct allocative inefficiency by correcting a market failure.

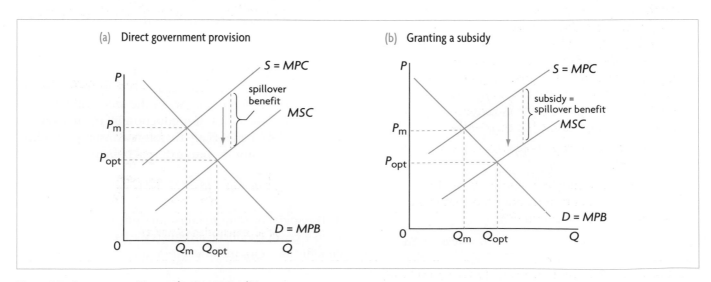

Figure 5.11 Correcting positive production externalities

If the government provides a subsidy to a firm per unit of the good produced that is equal to the external benefit, then the marginal private cost (MPC = supply) curve shifts downward (or rightward[4]) until it coincides with the MSC curve, as shown in Figure 5.11(b). The result is to increase quantity produced to Q_{opt} and to lower the price from P_m to P_{opt}. The problem of underallocation of resources and underprovision of the good is corrected, and allocative efficiency is achieved.

You may note that direct government provision and subsidies have the same market outcomes.

Correction of positive production externalities involves shifting the MPC curve downward toward the MSC curve through direct government provision or by subsidies. For allocative efficiency to be achieved, the quantity produced and consumed must increase to Q_{opt} as price falls to P_{opt}.

Evaluating policies to correct positive production externalities

This topic will be discussed together with policies to correct positive consumption externalities below (see page 118) because of similarities of the policies involved.

Test your understanding 5.5

1 **(a)** Using diagrams, show how marginal private costs and marginal social costs differ when there is a positive production externality. **(b)** How does the equilibrium quantity determined by the market differ from the quantity that is optimal from the point of view of society's preferences? **(c)** What does this tell you about the allocation of resources achieved by the market when there is a positive production externality? **(d)** Show the welfare loss created by the positive production externality in your diagram, and explain what this means.

2 Provide some examples of positive production externalities.

3 For each of the examples you provided in question 2, explain some methods that can be used to correct the externality.

Positive consumption externalities (external or spillover benefits)

Illustrating positive consumption externalities

When there is a **positive externality of consumption**, external benefits are created by consumers. For example, the consumption of education benefits the person who receives the education, but in addition gives rise to external benefits, involving social benefits from a more productive workforce, lower unemployment, higher rate of growth, more economic development, lower crime rate, and so on. Similarly, the consumption of health care services benefits not only the person receiving the services but also society and the economy, because a healthier population is more productive, enjoys a higher standard of living and may have a higher rate of economic growth. In Figure 5.12, we see that the marginal social benefit (MSB) curve lies above the marginal private benefit (MPB) curve, and the difference between the two consists of the external benefits to society. The socially optimum quantity, Q_{opt}, is given by the point where $MSB = MSC$, and the quantity produced by the market is given by the point where $MPB = MPC$. Since $Q_{opt} > Q_m$, the market underallocates resources to education, and too little of it is produced.

When there is a positive consumption externality, the free market underallocates resources to the production of the good, and too little of it is produced relative to the social optimum. This is shown by $Q_m < Q_{opt}$ and $MSB > MSC$ at Q_m in Figure 5.12.

In general, positive externalities (external benefits), whether these arise from production or consumption activities, lead to an underallocation of resources to the good in question, and therefore to its underprovision.

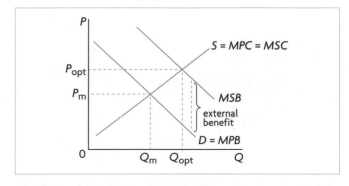

Figure 5.12 Positive consumption externality

[4] See 'Quantitative techniques' CD-ROM, page 13 for an explanation of the equivalence of downward and rightward shifts of the supply curve.

The welfare loss of positive consumption externalities

Welfare loss

The welfare loss arising from a positive consumption externality is the shaded area in Figure 5.13(a), and is the difference between the *MSB* and *MSC* curves for the amount of output that is underproduced relative to the social optimum ($Q_{opt} - Q_m$). It represents the loss of social benefits due to underproduction of the good. If this externality were corrected, society would gain the benefits represented by the shaded area. Once again, we see that the point of the welfare loss triangle lies at the Q_{opt} quantity of output.[5]

Welfare loss in relation to consumer and producer surplus (supplementary material)

In Figure 5.13(b) we see how the welfare loss arises in relation to consumer and producer surplus and the external benefits. In market equilibrium, consumer surplus is equal to areas b + d, producer surplus is area g, and the external benefits are a + e (or the difference between *MSB* and *MPB* up to production at Q_m by the market). The total social benefits in market equilibrium are equal to consumer surplus plus producer surplus plus the external benefits:

$$(b + d) + g + (a + e) = b + d + g + a + e = a + b + d + e + g$$

At the social optimum, consumer surplus is given by a + b + c, producer surplus is d + e + f + g, and the external benefits are zero. Therefore the total social benefits are:

$$(a + b + c) + (d + e + f + g) = a + b + c + d + e + f + g$$

Comparing the total social benefits at market equilibrium with those at the social optimum, we find that at the social optimum they are greater by the amount c + f. This is the welfare loss that arises when production occurs at market equilibrium as a result of an underallocation of resources due to the positive consumption externality.

The case of merit goods

Merit goods are goods that are held to be desirable for consumers, but which are underprovided by the market. (Note that the term 'good' in the expression 'merit good' applies to both goods and services.) Reasons for underprovision include:

- **The good may have positive externalities.** In this case too little is provided by the market. Examples of merit goods include education (for the reasons noted above in the discussion of externalities); immunisation programmes (which benefit not only those who have received them but also the broader population by wiping out a disease).

- **Low levels of income and poverty.** Some consumers may want certain goods or services but cannot afford to buy them. Remember demand shows the quantities of a good or service that

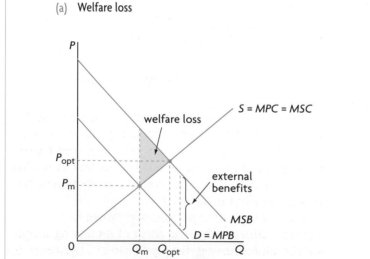
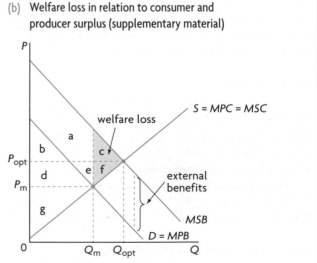

Figure 5.13 Welfare loss (deadweight loss) in a positive consumption externality

---

[5] You may have noticed that in the case of negative externalities of production and consumption, where $Q_{opt} < Q_m$, the welfare loss triangle always points leftward. By contrast, in the case of positive externalities of production and consumption, where $Q_{opt} > Q_m$, the welfare loss triangle always points rightward

consumers are willing and able to buy at different prices. If they have low incomes, they may be willing but not able to buy something, in which case their desire does not show up in the market, and market demand (the sum of all individual demands) is too low. Examples include health care services, medicines, education and recreational facilities, which people on low incomes often cannot afford to buy in the market.

- **Consumer ignorance.** Consumers may be better off if they consume certain goods and services but they may be ignorant of the benefits, and so do not demand them. For example, preventive health care (such as immunisation, annual health check-ups) can prevent serious diseases, but lack of knowledge about the benefits may lead consumers to demand too little of these services.

Note that more than one factor may be at work simultaneously; for example, the underprovision of health care services can result from all three reasons listed above.

Correcting positive consumption externalities

Legislation

Legislation can be used to promote greater consumption of goods with positive externalities. For example, many countries have legislation that makes education compulsory up to a certain age (note that education is a merit good). In this case, demand for education increases, and the demand curve $D_1 = MPB$ shifts to the right (or upward), as in Figure 5.14(a). Ideally, it will shift until it reaches the MSB curve, where $D_2 = MSB$, and Q_{opt} is produced and consumed.

Advertising

Governments can use advertising to try to persuade consumers to buy more goods with positive externalities. For example, they can try to encourage the use of sports facilities for improved health. The objective is to increase demand for such services, and the effect is the same as with legislation, shown in Figure 5.14(a): D_1 shifts to $D_2 = MSB$ and Q_{opt} is produced and consumed, while price increases to P_{opt}.

Direct government provision

Governments are frequently involved in the direct provision of goods and services with positive consumption externalities. The most important examples include government (public) provision of education and health care in virtually all countries in the world. Education and health care are merit goods

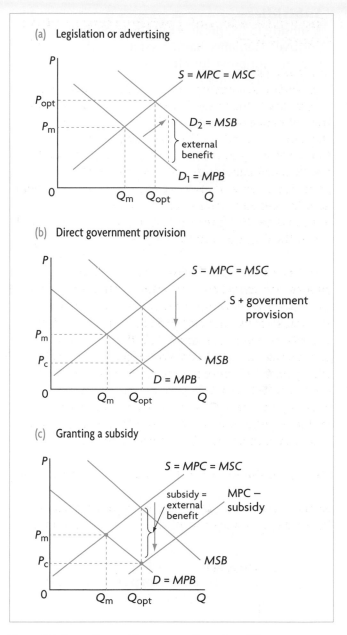

Figure 5.14 Correcting positive consumption externalities

with external benefits so large and important that it is widely believed that they must not be left to private sector provision alone. In most countries where there is government provision of health care and education, there is also private sector provision of these services (though to varying degrees).

Direct government provision is shown in Figure 5.14(b), and has the effect of increasing supply and therefore shifting the supply curve S rightward (or downward) to S + government provision. To achieve the social optimum Q_{opt}, the new supply curve must intersect MPB at the level of output Q_{opt}, as seen in the figure. At the new equilibrium, price falls to P_c, Q_{opt} is produced and allocative efficiency is achieved. (However, note that P_c is not P_{opt}; it lies below P_{opt}.)

Subsidies

A subsidy to the producer of the good with the positive externality has the same effects as direct government provision. It results in increasing supply and shifting the supply curve rightward (or downward), as shown in Figure 5.14(c) (which is the same as Figure 5.14(b)). If the subsidy is equal to the external benefit, the new supply curve is $MPC -$ subsidy, and it intersects MPB at the Q_{opt} level of output. Again, price falls from P_m to P_c, Q_{opt} is produced and allocative efficiency is achieved.

Correction of positive consumption externalities involves either increasing demand and shifting the MPB curve towards the MSB curve through legislation or advertising; or increasing supply and shifting the MPC curve downward by direct government provision or by granting a subsidy. Both demand increases and supply increases can lead to production and consumption at Q_{opt} and the achievement of allocative efficiency. The price paid by consumers increases when demand increases, and falls when supply increases.

Note that the problem of underprovision of merit goods by the market (defined above, see page 116) can be addressed by all the methods noted above: legislation, advertising, direct government provision and granting of subsidies. All are intended to increase the amount of the good produced and consumed, as increased consumption of such goods is held to be desirable for society.

Evaluating policies to correct positive production and consumption externalities

Both direct government provision and subsidies are widely used as methods to deal with positive consumption externalities, and to a lesser extent also with positive production externalities. Both methods are very effective in increasing the quantity of the good produced and consumed, and both have the added advantage of lowering the price of the good to consumers (though P_{opt} is not achieved).

There are, however, difficulties involved in achieving the optimum results (where $MSC = MSB$). First, both direct government provision and granting of subsidies involve the use of government funds that rely on tax revenues. Governments generally have very many possible alternative uses for these funds, each of which has an opportunity cost. As it is not possible for the government to directly provide or subsidise all goods and services with positive externalities, choices must be made on (a) which goods should be supported, and (b) by how much they should be supported. Ideally,

choices should be made on the basis of economic criteria, which would specify the amount of social benefits expected in relation to the cost of providing them, the objective being to maximise the benefits for each good and service to be provided or subsidised for a given cost. However, in practice it is very difficult to measure the size of the external benefits, and therefore to calculate precisely which goods and services should be supported and the level of support they should receive. In addition, both direct provision and subsidies are often highly political in nature, as different groups compete with each other over who will receive the most benefits. Governments are often susceptible to political pressures and sometimes make choices based on political rather than economic criteria.

Therefore, in the real world it is very unlikely that governments are able to shift the MPC or MPB curves by the amount necessary to correct the positive externalities. The most that can be hoped is that the policies in question will be a step in the right direction.

Legislation and advertising are subject to similar limitations concerning calculating the size of external benefits. Only sometimes can they be effective, and then can only help shift the MPB curve in the right direction, rather than achieve a demand increase that will bring the economy to the Q_{opt} level of output. For example, they can have very positive effects in certain cases (such as legislation requiring schooling up to a minimum age or advertising on the importance of good nutrition), but in other cases are ineffective (for example, they cannot on their own increase consumption of health care services and education to the optimum level). Moreover, they have the further effect of raising the price of the good to consumers, which may make the good unaffordable for some consumer groups. Therefore, legislation and advertising sometimes can be used more effectively if they are implemented together with direct provision and subsidies. A good example is education, where compulsory schooling up to a certain age (legislation) goes together with direct government provision.

Test your understanding 5.6

1 **(a)** Using diagrams, show how marginal private benefits and marginal social benefits differ when there is a positive consumption externality.
(b) How does the equilibrium quantity determined by the market differ from the quantity that is optimal from the point of view of society's preferences? **(c)** What does

this tell you about the allocation of resources achieved by the market when there is a positive consumption externality? **(d)** Show the welfare loss created by the positive consumption externality in your diagram, and explain what this means.

2 Provide some examples of positive consumption externalities.

3 For each of the examples you provided in question 2, explain some methods that could be used to correct the externality.

4 How does a positive consumption externality differ from a positive production externality?

5 **(a)** Explain the meaning of a merit good, and provide examples. **(b)** How can underprovision of merit goods be corrected?

6 What policy options are available to governments wishing to correct a positive consumption externality?

7 Discuss advantages and disadvantages of the policy measures that governments can use to correct positive externalities of production and consumption.

5.5 Lack of public goods

Market failure and public goods

Public goods versus private goods: rivalry and excludability

◆ Using the concepts of rivalry and excludability, and providing examples, distinguish between public goods (non-rivalrous and non-excludable) and private goods (rivalrous and excludable).

To understand what public goods are, it is useful to consider the definition of private goods. A **private good** has two characteristics:

- It is **rivalrous**: its consumption by one person reduces its availability for someone else; for example, your computer, textbook, pencils and clothes are rivalrous, because when you buy them, another person cannot buy the same ones; most goods are rivalrous.

- It is **excludable**: it is possible to exclude people from using the good; exclusion is usually achieved by charging a price for the good; if someone is unwilling or unable to pay the price, he or she will not have the benefit of using it; most goods are excludable.

Since most goods are rivalrous and excludable, it follows that most goods are private goods.

A **public good** has the following two characteristics:

It is **non-rivalrous**; its consumption by one person does not reduce consumption by someone else.

It is **non-excludable**; it is not possible to exclude someone from using the good.

Goods that are non-rivalrous and non-excludable are also known as *pure public goods*. For example, a lighthouse is non-rivalrous, because its use by one person does not make it less available for use by others. Also, it is non-excludable, because there is no way to exclude anyone from using it. Other examples of public goods include the police force, national defence, flood control, non-toll roads, fire protection, basic research, anti-poverty programmes and many others.

Public goods and the free rider problem

◆ Explain, with reference to the free rider problem, how the lack of public goods indicates market failure.

How do public goods relate to market failure? In the case of excludable goods, it is possible to prevent people from buying and using a good simply by charging a price for it; those who do not pay the price do not buy it and do not get to use it. Therefore, private firms have an incentive to provide excludable goods because they can charge a price for them, and therefore can cover their costs. Non-excludable goods differ: if a non-excludable good were to be produced by a private firm, people could not be prevented from using it even though they would not pay for it. Yet no profit-maximising firm would be willing to produce a good it cannot sell at some price. As a result, the market fails to produce goods that are non-excludable, giving rise to resource misallocation, as no resources are allocated to the production of public goods.

Public goods illustrate the **free rider problem**, occurring when people can enjoy the use of a good without paying for it. The free rider problem arises from non-excludability: people cannot be excluded from using the good. Public goods are a type of market failure because due to the free rider problem, private firms do not produce these goods: the market fails to allocate resources to their production.

Quasi-public goods (public goods that are not 'pure')

Some goods do not fit neatly into the category of private goods or public goods. They can be considered to be 'impure' public goods, also known as 'quasi-public goods'. These goods are:

- non-rivalrous (like public goods), and
- excludable (like private goods).

Examples include public museums that charge an entrance fee and toll roads. All these are excludable because consumers must pay to use them. Since the price system can be made to work here to exclude potential users, they could be provided by private firms. However, they all have very large positive externalities, thus justifying direct government provision.

Correcting the market's failure to provide public goods

Implications of direct government provision

♦ Discuss the implications of the direct provision of public goods by the government.

We have seen that the market fails to allocate resources to the production of public goods. This means the government must step in to ensure that public goods are produced at socially desirable levels. Thus public goods are directly provided by the government, are financed out of tax revenues and are made available to the public free of charge (or nearly free of charge).

Government provision of public goods raises some issues of choice about (a) which public goods should be provided, and (b) in what quantities they should be provided. These issues are similar to what was noted above in connection with direct government provision and subsidies for goods with positive externalities (page 118). Limited government funds force choices on what public goods to produce, and each choice has an opportunity cost in terms of other goods and services that are foregone (or sacrificed). Here, too, the government must use economic criteria to decide which public goods will provide the greatest social benefits for a given amount of money to be spent on providing the goods. However, in the case of public goods, governments face a major additional difficulty in calculating expected benefits. With private goods that are provided or subsidised by the government, it is possible to make estimates of expected benefits by using the market price of the good. (Remember the market price of a good reflects the benefits consumers receive and so reveals its value to consumers.) Therefore, the government can use the market price of private goods with positive externalities to estimate benefits and their value to consumers, but with public goods there is no such possibility as they are not produced by the market (private firms) and have no price.

This means the government must try to estimate the demand (or 'price') of public goods through such means as votes or surveys of people who are asked how much a good would be worth to them. This information is used in *cost–benefit analysis*, which compares the estimated benefits to society of a particular good with its costs. If the total benefits expected to arise from a public good are greater than the total costs of providing it, then the good should be provided. If benefits are less than costs, then the good should not be provided. Assuming that cost–benefit analysis indicates a public good should be provided, the decision on how much of it to provide is made by comparing marginal benefits with marginal costs: the public good should be provided up to the point where $MB = MC$.

Whereas the costs of providing a public good are relatively easy to estimate, there are clear difficulties in estimating benefits. A major difficulty arising with surveys is that people who really want something are likely to exaggerate its value. Therefore, cost–benefit analysis is a very rough and approximate method used to make choices about public goods.

Test your understanding 5.7

1 **(a)** Explain the meaning of rivalry and excludability. **(b)** How do these concepts relate to the distinction between public goods and private goods?

2 Provide some examples of public goods, and explain how they relate to the concepts of rivalry and excludability.

3 **(a)** What are quasi-public goods? **(b)** How can they be defined in terms of rivalry and excludability?

4 Use the concept of resource allocation and the free rider problem to explain how public goods are a type of market failure.

5 **(a)** How do governments respond to the lack of public goods? **(b)** What are the implications of direct government provision?

5.6 Common access resources and the threat to sustainability

Common access resources and environmental sustainability

Common access resources and market failure

The meaning of common access resources

♦ Describe, using examples, common access resources.

Environmental problems can be studied by examining a special category of resources known as common access resources. **Common access resources** are resources that are not owned by anyone, do not have a price and are available for anyone to use without payment. Examples include clean air, lakes, rivers, fish in the open seas, wildlife, hunting grounds, forests, biodiversity, the fertility of the soil that occurs in nature, open grazing land, the ozone layer, the stable global climate, and many more.

Why common access resources are a type of market failure

♦ Explain that lack of a pricing mechanism for common access resources means that these goods may be overused/depleted/degraded as a result of activities of producers and consumers who do not pay for the resources they use, and that this poses a threat to sustainability.

Common access resources differ from any other kind of resource or good, because they possess a special combination of characteristics: they are rivalrous and non-excludable (page 119).

A good is *rivalrous* when its use by some people reduces availability for others. Most goods, including common access resources, are rivalrous. If we use up clean air, there is less left over for use by others; when we catch fish in the open sea, there are fewer fish left over for others to catch; if we destroy the stability of the global climate, it will not be available for use by future generations.

A good is *non-excludable* when it is not possible to exclude anyone from using it. Most goods and resources are excludable, because they have a price. However, open access resources differ because *they have no price and anyone can use them without payment;* therefore they are non-excludable.

(Common access resources are like private goods in that they are rivalrous, and they are like public goods in that they are non-excludable.)

The rivalry and non-excludability characteristics of common access resources pose serious threats to the environment. Rivalry means that consumption by some reduces availability for others. Non-excludability means that consumers and producers use them abundantly and often overuse them *because they have no price.*

There is no end to examples of overuse of common access. When factories, homes or cars use fossil fuels that emit pollutants into the atmosphere or into oceans, rivers and lakes, they 'overuse' a portion of these natural resources without paying for them. Some of these activities result in ozone depletion, with harmful effects on life from the sun's radiation; they 'overuse' part of the ozone layer. They also give rise to global warming, with possibly devastating effects on agriculture, health and ecosystems; this involves 'overusing' the benefits provided by a stable global climate. When fish are overfished, the fishing industry uses up an excessive amount of the global stock of fish and possibly disrupts the marine ecosystem. Similarly, when forests are cleared to create land for use in agriculture or for the sale of timber by the lumber industry, there are huge consequences in terms of loss of biodiversity and threats to wildlife and the ozone layer. Land is being overgrazed because of excessive grazing; arable land is lost because of soil erosion and salinisation; wildlife is endangered because of the destruction of natural habitats due to the encroachment of settlers and agriculture. *In all these cases, common access resources are used without payment, leading to serious environmental degradation and depletion.*

Sustainability and common access resources

♦ Describe sustainability.

The meaning of sustainability

Sustainability refers to the ability of something to be maintained or preserved over time. It can be explained in terms of the joint preservation of the environment and the economy: for the environment it refers to environmental preservation (lack of destruction); for the economy it refers to the preservation of humankind's ability to provide goods and services to satisfy needs and wants into the future.

The problem of sustainability arises because of conflicts between environmental and economic goals. Economic goals involve efforts to increase the quantities of output produced and consumed;

focusing on economic goals while disregarding the environment may result in its irreversible destruction. Environmental goals involve the preservation of the environment; but focusing on environmental goals while disregarding the economy may result in humankind's inability to satisfy needs and wants.

The important question, then, is how to strike a balance between environmental and economic goals, so that both can be satisfied into the future. The answer to this question is provided by the concept of *sustainable development* (introduced briefly in Chapter 1, page 14), defined as 'development that meets the needs of the present without compromising the ability of future generations to meet their own needs'.[6] This means that societies should pursue economic growth *that does not deplete or degrade natural resources*, so that future generations will not have fewer or lower-quality natural resources to satisfy their own needs.

> Sustainability refers to maintaining the ability of the environment and the economy to continue to produce and satisfy needs and wants into the future; sustainability depends crucially on preservation of the environment over time.

The maximum sustainable yield of common access resources (supplementary material)

A simple example shown in Figure 5.15(a) illustrates the meaning of sustainable resource use. Fish in the open seas are a common access resource that anyone has access to without payment. The horizontal axis measures the number of fishing boats, and the vertical axis measures the quantity of fish caught in tonnes. The first, second and third boats each catch 4 tonnes; therefore, in this range of 'constant average yield' (yield refers to the amount of output), the three boats together catch 12 tonnes, or 4 tonnes each on average.

When a fourth boat goes out to sea, it brings back only 3 tonnes of fish; this translates into a smaller quantity of fish caught by each boat on average. The four boats together have caught 15 tonnes, or an average of 3.75 tonnes (= $\frac{15}{4}$) instead of 4 tonnes.

When the fifth boat is added, the five boats catch 17 tonnes, and the average catch falls further to 3.4 tonnes (= $\frac{17}{5}$). With the sixth boat, the total is only 19 tonnes or 3.2 tonnes for each boat on average. This is the range of 'decreasing average yield', meaning that each boat that goes out brings back a smaller amount of fish than the previous one.

What happens if a seventh boat goes out? The total amount of fish caught by the seven boats together (17 tonnes) is *less* than what was caught by 6 boats (18 tonnes). As the graph indicates, in this range of 'absolutely decreasing yield', as more and more boats go fishing, the total amount of fish they bring back becomes less and less.

This example illustrates that the fish were plentiful for the first three boats, but with the addition of the fourth, fishing became more difficult because it began to put pressure on the supply of fish in the ocean.

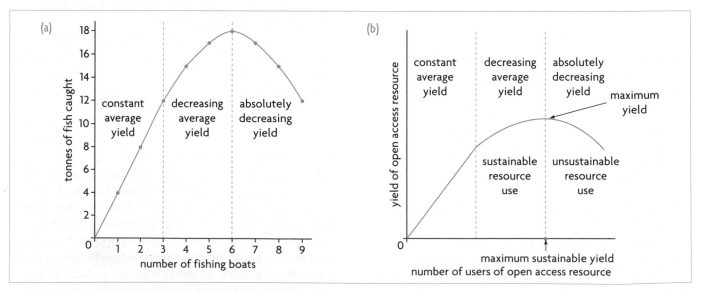

Figure 5.15 Illustrating sustainable and unsustainable resource use

---

[6] Brundtland Commission (World Commission on Environment and Development) (1987) *Our Common Future*, Oxford University Press.

As the supply of fish was more and more depleted, it became increasingly difficult to catch fish, so the average quantity of fish brought back fell with the addition of each boat. Finally, with the addition of the seventh boat, the fish supply was *overused*; the fish population was no longer able to reproduce itself, and therefore the quantity of fish in the ocean began to drop.

Figure 5.15(b) shows that the point of maximum yield of a common access resource is the resource's *maximum sustainable yield*. *This is the maximum use that can be made of the resource that is also sustainable, in that the resource can reproduce itself.* All points to the left of the maximum sustainable yield indicate sustainable levels of use; points to the right indicate unsustainable use, meaning that the resource is being depleted or degraded. The further to the right, the greater the resource depletion or degradation. In the real world, many open access resources are used unsustainably, i.e. to the right of their maximum sustainable yield.

Note that while it is an easy matter to discuss the maximum sustainable yield of a resource in theoretical terms as we have done here, it is very difficult in practice to determine what this actually is for any resource.

> Sustainable resource use means that resources are used at a rate that allows them to reproduce themselves, so that they do not become degraded or depleted.

Distinguishing between the 'pollution of affluence' and the 'pollution of poverty'

We often think of environmental degradation as the by-product of production and consumption activities resulting from increasing quantities of output produced and consumed (economic growth). This type of environmental damage has been termed 'pollution of affluence' and arises mainly from industrial production and high-income consumption patterns that involve the heavy use of fossil fuels (such as oil), using up open access resources like clean air, rivers, lakes, and so on, and leading to climate change.

However, there is another type of very important environmental damage, which occurs mainly in developing countries, and which arises from production and consumption activities that are due to poverty. This second type of environmental damage has been termed 'pollution of poverty', and is due to economic activities pursued by very poor people in an effort to survive.

High-income production and consumption based on fossil fuels as a threat to sustainability

In section 5.3 we studied negative production and consumption externalities, which show how societies are worse off when production or consumption activities give rise to external costs. The concept of negative externalities can be used to illustrate the problem of overuse of common access resources and its effects on sustainability. The overuse of common access resources and their depletion/degradation are the external costs of industrial production and high-income consumption activities, both based on use of fossil fuels. In the negative production externality of Figure 5.2 (page 103), the difference between the *MPC* and *MSC* curves can be interpreted as the social cost arising from the cement factory's overuse of clean air, water, sea life and ozone layer on account of its dependence on fossil fuels; it can also be interpreted as the cost to society of causing global warming (destroying the stability of the global climate). The burning of fossil fuels creates external costs in terms of overuse of common access resources.

If it were possible to make the cement factory pay for the overuse of these resources, the producer would not necessarily stop its polluting activities entirely, and would not stop *using* common access resources. However, it would stop *overusing* them, thus leading to a sustainable use of common access resources.

Figure 5.2 can be used to illustrate the overuse of any common access resource as a negative production externality. For example, if the *MPC* curve represents the private costs of a fishing firm that fishes in the open seas, the external costs could be depletion of the stock of fish, and environmental damage due to disruption of the marine ecosystem, or the common access resources that the fishing firm has overused but not paid for.

Overuse of common access resources can also be seen to result from negative consumption externalities, shown in Figure 5.6 (page 108). Take the demand for heating oil, represented by the demand curve *MPB*. The overuse of clean air (the common access resource) is the external cost that causes the marginal social benefit curve (*MSB*) to lie below the *MPB* curve.

Poverty as a threat to sustainability

According to the Brundtland Report, which coined the term 'sustainable development' (page 14), poverty is the most important cause of environmental destruction, due to the overexploitation by poor people of their scarce environmental resources. Poor people lack modern agricultural inputs, and being too poor to buy inputs that preserve the soil's fertility, they deplete the soil's natural minerals, making soils less productive. Poor people usually have higher birth rates and higher population growth, creating pressures for them to open up new lands for agriculture. With suitable agricultural land becoming increasingly scarce, they cut down forests (deforestation) in search of new farmland, they move to fragile lands in mountains and hills, causing soil erosion, and they overgraze animals on pasture lands, depleting the nutrients there as well. Lacking modern energy sources, they also cut down forests to obtain firewood. Poor people have limited abilities to borrow to finance the purchase of inputs, and this works against their ability to make improvements in sanitation, irrigation, improved agricultural inputs and land improvements, which would reverse or reduce these types of environmental degradation (see Chapter 17).

The production and consumption activities of very poor people that endanger the environment and sustainability can also be interpreted as negative externalities involving overuse of common access resources. In Figure 5.2, the *MPC* curve may be a

farmer's private costs of farming, with the difference between the *MPC* and *MSC* curves representing overuse of forests that have been cleared for agriculture, or the overuse of soil leading to depletion of nutrients.

> The threat to sustainability lies in the *increased scale of economic activities around the world*, which may be due to economic growth based on the use of fossil fuels; or it may be due to the increasing numbers of very poor people who engage in environmentally destructive activities in an effort to survive.

Whereas the pollution of poverty occurs mainly in developing countries, this is not to say that developing countries are not guilty of creating some 'pollution of affluence'. Increasingly, the pollution of affluence arises also in developing countries that grow by engaging in industrial production and consumption activities without regard for the environment.

A note on renewable and non-renewable resources, and sustainability

Non-renewable resources are those resources that do not last indefinitely, because they have a finite supply (they need tens of thousands or millions of years to reproduce themselves). Examples include metals, minerals and fossil fuels, such as oil, natural gas and coal. Many of these resources, with the exception of fossil fuels, do not get destroyed through their use, and so through effective recycling could be made to last indefinitely. By contrast, fossil fuels are destroyed when used, and moreover have devastating effects on the earth's atmosphere, the global climate and the ozone layer.

Renewable resources are those resources that can last indefinitely if they are managed properly (not overused), because they are reproduced over relatively short periods of time by natural processes. Examples include forests, wildlife, fish, biomass, water resources, geothermal power, soil fertility and biodiversity. The idea of sustainable resource use applies mainly to *renewable resources*, because given appropriate management, these resources can be made to last forever. On the other hand, through mismanagement or overuse, these resources become depleted and degraded, indicating unsustainability.

The idea of sustainable resource use does not apply to non-renewable resources like fossil fuels. If resources are non-renewable, they could be used sustainably only if they were not used at all. On the other hand, as we have seen, the idea of sustainability is relevant to fossil fuels when referring to the negative externalities that are created by their use.

1 Discuss the impacts of production and consumption activities on the environment, making a distinction between the roles played by growth based on fossil fuels and by poverty.

2 Using diagrams, show what kinds of market failures are particularly relevant to analysing environmental problems.

Government responses to threats to sustainability

♦ Evaluate, using diagrams, possible government responses to threats to sustainability, including legislation, carbon taxes, cap and trade schemes, and funding for clean technologies.

This section should be studied in connection with the material presented on pages 106–8 (on negative production externalities) and 111–12 (on negative consumption externalities).

Legislation

Legislation (laws and regulations) intended to limit threats to sustainability typically involve emissions standards, quotas, licences, permits or outright restrictions. Examples include:

- restrictions on emissions from cars
- requirements for cars to use catalytic converters to reduce air pollution
- restrictions on emissions from factories and industrial production
- requirements for steel mills and electricity generating plants to install smokestack scrubbers to reduce emissions
- banning the use of harmful substances (e.g. asbestos)
- restrictions regarding hunting seasons and hunting areas
- issuing licences or permits for particular activities (such as hunting)
- prohibiting construction (such as housing) or industry or agriculture in protected areas
- restrictions on the quantity of logging
- restrictions in the form of quotas for fishing (maximum permissible quantity of fish that can be caught) or in the form of the size of shipping fleets,

or total bans for specific areas or specific times of the year

- establishment of protected areas for the protection of biodiversity and endangered ecosystems.

Regulations and restrictions have the advantage that they are simple to put into effect and oversee. In most of the examples above, they can be quite effective, such as in the case of restricting car emissions, banning the use of harmful substances, restrictions on hunting, logging and fishing, and establishment of protected areas. In the case of emissions of industrial production, they avoid the technical difficulties that arise in the use of market-based solutions and force polluters to cut emissions (see page 107).

However, they also face limitations. In the case of emissions of pollutants, they do not offer incentives to reduce emissions, to increase energy efficiency and to switch to alternative fuels; and they cannot distinguish between high- and low-cost polluters, which would limit the overall cost of reducing pollution (for more information, see page 108). They also involve costs of monitoring and supervision to detect possible violations.

Overall, the effectiveness of legislation must be assessed in relation to the particular use for which it is intended, as it can be more effective in some situations than in others.

Carbon taxes versus cap and trade schemes

Perhaps the single most pressing and complex threat to the global ecosystem is global warming, caused by emissions of greenhouse gases, the most important of which is carbon dioxide. When we speak of the contribution of greenhouse gases to global warming, we refer to those gases emitted by manmade processes, and specifically by the burning of fossil fuels (oil, coal and natural gas). Whereas it is known with a reasonable degree of certainty that manmade greenhouse gases cause global warming, there is tremendous uncertainty in calculating the precise contribution of each of these to increases in global temperatures.

Two measures under discussion in the global community that can be taken to deal with the problem of carbon dioxide emissions are carbon taxes and cap and trade schemes.

Carbon taxes

The *carbon tax*, introduced on page 106, is a method to reduce emissions of carbon dioxide, emitted when fossil fuels are burned. The carbon tax aims at taxing the use of fossil fuels in accordance with the amount of carbon each one emits. Therefore, *fuels that emit more carbon are taxed at a higher rate than those emitting less carbon.*

Since the tax varies with carbon emissions, fossil fuel users face the incentive to switch to fuels that emit less carbon, or even no carbon (non-fossil fuel energy sources). Figure 5.5(b) (page 105) shows how the external costs become smaller as a result of using less polluting fuels, and how as a result the optimum quantity of the good produced increases.

Some countries have introduced carbon taxes (for example, Denmark, Finland, France, Ireland, Netherlands, Poland, Sweden), as well as some states in Canada and the United States, while in others the carbon tax is hotly debated together with cap and trade schemes.

Cap and trade schemes

Cap and trade schemes refer to *tradable permits*, discussed on page 106 and illustrated in Figure 5.5(c). Such schemes impose a cap (a maximum amount) on the total amount of carbon dioxide that can be released by producers into the atmosphere. Permits to release carbon dioxide are distributed to producers, and the permits can be bought and sold in a market. Cap and trade schemes may be set up within a country; or within a group of countries such as the European Union Emissions Trading System (EU ETS; see page 130); or globally, such as the Kyoto Protocol (see page 129).

Evaluating carbon taxes and cap and trade schemes

As market-based methods to reduce emissions, both carbon taxes and cap and trade schemes provide incentives to firms to switch to less polluting forms of energy. However, they differ in how they attempt to do this. Carbon taxes fix the price of the pollutant in the form of a tax on carbon and allow the quantity of carbon emitted to vary, depending on how firms respond to the tax; cap and trade schemes fix the quantity of the permissible pollutant, and allow its price to vary, depending on supply and demand.

Most economists prefer carbon taxes to cap and trade schemes for a variety of reasons:

- **Carbon taxes make energy prices more predictable.** Fossil fuel prices in global markets fluctuate according to demand and supply. Under cap and trade schemes, the price of fossil fuels might fluctuate even more due to fluctuations in the price of carbon. By contrast, since carbon taxes fix the price of carbon emissions, the price of fossil fuels is likely to be relatively more predictable. Price predictability is important for businesses that need to plan their costs ahead of time.
- **Carbon taxes are easier to design and implement.** Cap and trade schemes are difficult to

design and implement as they involve complicated decisions such as setting the cap at the right level and distributing the permits among all interested users. Carbon taxes may be simpler to design and use.

- **Carbon taxes can be applied to all users of fossil fuels.** Cap and trade scheme proposals often target one particular industry, or small group of industries. Carbon taxes can be applied to all users of fossil fuels, including all producers and consumers.
- **Carbon taxes do not offer opportunities for manipulation by governments and interest groups.** Politicians often prefer cap and trade schemes to carbon taxes, and it is believed that this may be because it is easy to manipulate the distribution of permits for the benefit of preferred groups and supporters, without affecting the impacts on the environment (because of the cap). Carbon taxes do not allow for such manipulation.
- **Carbon taxes do not require as much monitoring for enforcement.** Cap and trade schemes require monitoring of emissions, otherwise firms may try to cheat by emitting more pollutants than they are permitted. Carbon taxes are easier to monitor as they only involve payment of a tax depending on the type and quantity of fossil fuels purchased.
- **Cap and trade schemes face strong political pressures to set the cap too high.** If the cap on pollutants is set too high, it would have a very limited or no impact on reducing carbon emissions.
- **Carbon taxes are less likely to be used to restrict competition between firms.** A possible disadvantage of tradable permits over taxes is that some firms could buy up more tradable permits than they actually need, thus driving up their price, in an effort to keep new firms from entering the market (as a result restricting competition).

There are also some arguments against carbon taxes and in favour of cap and trade schemes:

- **Carbon taxes may be too low.** Governments may be unwilling to set carbon taxes high enough for these to provide the necessary incentives for users to switch to less polluting energy sources.
- **Carbon taxes cannot target a particular level of carbon reduction.** Since carbon taxes cannot fix (or cap) the permissible level of carbon emissions, they lead to uncertain carbon-reducing outcomes. Cap and trade schemes work by fixing the total amount of the permissible carbon emissions.
- **Carbon taxes are regressive.** A regressive tax is one where the tax as a fraction of income is higher for low-income earners than it is for

higher-income earners, and go against the principle of equity (see Chapter 11, pages 313–4). A carbon tax on a firm is an indirect tax whose burden (incidence) falls on both producers and consumers (see page 74). Therefore, consumers would also be affected, and lower-income consumers would be affected proportionately more than higher-income consumers.

- **Carbon taxes must be adjusted for inflation.** During periods of inflation (a rising price level), the market will automatically result in rising prices of tradable permits according to supply and demand, which is an advantage. In the case of carbon taxes, an upward adjustment would have to be decided on by the government (or international body), which could be politically and administratively more difficult.

Theory of knowledge

The ethical dimensions of sustainability and preserving the global climate

In Chapter 1, page 14, we saw that solutions to the problem of sustainability face major technical difficulties due to uncertainties and incomplete knowledge of social and natural scientists regarding the complex relationships between environmental, economic, social and institutional variables. These kinds of technical difficulties are also responsible for the uncertainties surrounding both regulatory and market-based economic policies to address environmental externalities discussed in the present chapter.

Over and above the technical difficulties, the problem of sustainability faces major ethical issues of fairness and justice, relating to intergenerational equity (running from generation to generation), as well as equity across nations and social groups within nations of the present generation.

In the area of climate change alone, important issues include (a) how will the burden of having to make sacrifices in the present be distributed among countries; (b) how will the impacts of climate change be evaluated; and (c) how will intergenerational equity be accounted for?[7]

To determine the distribution of sacrifices, a possible ethical principle that can be used is 'the polluter pays' principle, according to which the sacrifice is distributed according to how much each country contributes to climate change. In one variant of this principle, it would be necessary to take into account cumulative (historical) contributions to greenhouse gas emissions. This would place an extra burden on the developed countries of today, which over time, have contributed far more to emissions than developing countries. As a counterargument, opponents refer to 'excusable ignorance', meaning it should not be necessary to pay for past emissions if these were made without knowledge of their effects on the global climate. According to a different ethical principle, the past would be ignored and future emissions rights would be distributed to all countries on a *per capita* basis.

On the second issue, concerning evaluation of impacts of climate change, one approach involves welfare analysis. This has given rise to disagreements about how to calculate welfare and add it up across individuals in the present as well as in the future. Another approach focuses on human rights as the basis for evaluating impacts, such as the rights to food, water and shelter, which may be threatened by climate change.

Intergenerational equity, the third issue, is closely related to the evaluation of impacts of climate change, as these must account for impacts not only on the present generation but future generations as well.

These kinds of questions clearly belong to the normative realm of thought. Given the technical difficulties as well, it is no wonder that there are broad disagreements over sustainability, and no easy solutions appear on the horizon.

---

[7] The World Bank (2009) *World Development Report 2010: Development and Climate Change.*

Thinking points

- What do you think should be the role of science and social science in providing answers to these kinds of questions?

- To what extent do you think market forces can be relied upon, if at all, to deal with problems of environmental sustainability?

- Market economies are based upon human behaviour motivated by rational self-interest (see page 11). To what extent do you think this self-interest is the root cause of the environmental problems that beset the human race today? (See also the Theory of knowledge feature on page 131.)

- Given that, historically, economically more developed countries have been mainly responsible for today's environmental problems, do you agree with the view that economically less developed countries should simply ignore calls for them to limit their growth rates to prevent further global warming?

Funding for clean technologies

The need for clean technologies

Clean technologies aim toward a more responsible and productive use of natural resources, which also reduce negative environmental impacts. They include wind power, solar energy, biofuels, geothermal energy, nuclear power, energy storage (such as the development of fuel cells), fuel efficiency (less waste in use of energy), recycling and many more.

Many of these technologies are already available to reduce carbon emissions, including using more efficient use of fossil fuels (avoiding waste in their use), and the use of low- or no-emission power-generation methods, such as wind power and solar power. However, the very large potentials of these two approaches are nowhere close to being realised, mainly because there are not enough appropriate policies in place that would promote their greater use. These policies include the kinds of regulatory and market-based policies that we have discussed above. In addition, they involve a more rational use of subsidies (to be discussed below).

But even if these already existing technologies were more widely used, it is believed that they are nowhere close to enough to bring carbon emissions to acceptable levels. This means there is an urgent need for the development of new technologies that can be adopted by countries around the world on a large scale to prevent unacceptable increases in global temperatures.

Funding for clean technologies

It is very important that both private firms and governments be involved in activities leading to innovation and development of low-emissions technologies and environmentally friendly sources of energy. Yet funding for these activities is barely sufficient. According to the World Bank's *World Development Report 2010*:

> '... today's global efforts to innovate and diffuse climate-smart technologies fall far short of what is required for significant mitigation and adaptation in the coming decades. Investment in research, development, demonstration and deployment (RDD&D) is lacking ...
>
> Neither public nor private funding of energy-related research is remotely close to the amounts needed for transitioning to a climate-smart world. In absolute terms, global government energy RD&D [research, development and demonstration] budgets have declined since the early 1980s, falling by almost half from 1980 to 2007 ...'[8]

Within governments, the priority attached to innovation in energy has been steadily falling over the years. Government spending on energy RD&D as a percentage of government spending on total RD&D fell from over 20% in 1980 to less than 4% in 2007. Private sector spending on energy RD&D, estimated at $40 billion to $60 billion a year, is far greater than public sector (government) spending of about $7 billion a year (2007 figures). However, even within the private sector, spending on energy RD&D is not a high priority, as it represents a mere 0.5% of revenue, compared with 8% of revenue spent on RD&D in the electronics industry and 15% of revenue in the pharmaceutical sector.[9]

Because of the far greater resources at their disposal, developed countries have been playing a leading role in climate-smart technology development. Some developing countries have begun to play a more active role, in 2007 contributing 23% of new investments in energy efficiency and renewable energy compared to 13% in 2004. However, most of these investments were concentrated in three countries only, Brazil, China and India.[10]

Funding for clean technologies clearly has opportunity costs. However, given its urgency governments should make a greater effort to allocate resources to technological innovations in this area, and should also make efforts to promote private sector funding and participation.

Eliminating environmentally harmful subsidies

Subsidies encourage the production and consumption of the subsidised good (see page 81). When environmentally damaging production activities are subsidised, they result in greater production, leading to greater environmental damage. Subsidies to industrial forestry encourage commercial logging, resulting in destruction of forests. Subsidies to production of fossil fuel energy result in a greater amount of fossil fuel production. Consumption subsidies are commonly imposed on fossil fuel energy, agricultural inputs (such as fertilisers and pesticides) and water. Both production and consumption subsidies are often

---

[8] The World Bank (2009) *World Development Report 2010*, pp. 288 and 292.
[9] The World Bank (2009) *World Development Report 2010*.

[10] The World Bank (2009) *World Development Report 2010*.

the result of 'policy failures', involving the pursuit of a policy for one purpose that creates problems in another area (environmental destruction). Subsidies should therefore be studied for their environmental impacts, and changed or eliminated accordingly.

In the case of fossil fuels, subsidies are often granted to promote the industrial sector by keeping costs down, to promote international competitiveness of industrial products (make them less expensive in international markets through lower costs of production), to support domestic fuel production to ensure adequate domestic supply and to reduce reliance on foreign energy sources (for countries that are fossil fuel producers) and to keep fuel prices down for consumers. The effects of subsidies on fossil fuels are entirely inconsistent with the pursuit of sustainable development.

Figure 5.16 makes an interesting comparison between spending by governments around the world on subsidies to energy and petroleum products, and spending by governments on energy research and development. (These subsidies are concentrated mainly in developing countries, as developed countries have for the most part eliminated energy and petroleum subsidies.) Figure 5.16 shows how governments around the world massively underfund technological innovation in the area of energy.

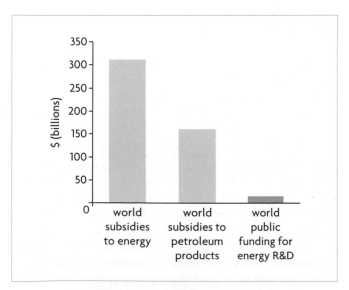

Figure 5.16 World government spending on energy and petroleum subsidies and on energy research and development

Source: **The World Bank (2009)** *World Development Report 2010: Development and Climate Change*, p. 293.

The role of international co-operation

♦ Explain, using examples, that government responses to threats to sustainability are limited by the global nature of the problems and the lack of ownership of common access resources, and that effective responses require international co-operation.

Policies are made mainly by national governments. However, the overuse of common access resources often has international repercussions, in which case co-operation among governments is crucially important as a method of controlling and preventing negative consequences on certain resources, such as the global climate and the ozone layer. In addition, co-operation among governments is very important for the development and diffusion of new technologies intended to deal with global environmental issues. Co-operation between governments may be global or regional.

For example, the ozone layer has suffered ozone depletion, leading to reduced protection against the sun's ultraviolet radiation. This resulted from human activities involving the production of nitrogen oxides and chlorofluorocarbons (CFCs). The ozone layer is an open access resource. No one owns it, and no one can claim damages for its destruction. The responsibility for its destruction lies with polluting activities within virtually every country, and the consequences of its destruction are felt globally. The same considerations apply to the global climate.

One of most successful examples of international collaboration for the environment is the Montreal Protocol, signed in 1987 and coming into effect in 1989, intended to phase out substances that have caused depletion of the ozone layer. By 2009, all member states of the United Nations had ratified the agreement, and significant progress has been made in the area of phasing out ozone-depleting substances.

Another major (but less successful) international collaborative agreement for the environment is the Kyoto Protocol of 1997–2012. Its objective was to make signatory countries commit themselves to reduce emissions of carbon dioxide and other greenhouse gases over a period of 15 years to slow down the problem of global warming and climate change. It also contained provisions for the development of a market of tradable emissions permits, according to which each participating country was to be assigned certain pollution permits which it would be able to trade (buy and sell) with other countries. However, the Kyoto Protocol came under a lot of criticism and has not been implemented in full. Many environmental specialists argued that even if it were implemented, the agreed reductions in emissions were too small to have sufficient impact on the problem of global warming. While there have been numerous discussions on a successor agreement to the Kyoto Protocol, nothing concrete has emerged as of summer 2011.

A more successful example of a regional collaborative arrangement is the European Union's cap and trade scheme for carbon, known as the European Union Emissions Trading System (EU ETS), which was initiated in January 2005. The scheme covers the sectors of power and heat generation, oil refineries, metals, pulp and paper, and energy intensive industry. In this system, one permit, or EU Allowance (EUA) permits the holder to release one tonne of carbon dioxide. Each emitter of carbon is allocated EUAs, which are traded in a rapidly growing carbon market.

Test your understanding 5.10

1 Explain some advantages and disadvantages of each of the following policy measures to deal with threats to sustainability: **(a)** legislation, **(b)** carbon taxes, and **(c)** cap and trade schemes.

2 What are some key issues surrounding the debate between carbon taxes versus cap and trade schemes?

3 **(a)** Explain the significance of funding for clean technologies to deal with threats to sustainability. **(b)** What might be some reasons for the underfunding of technological innovations in the development of clean technologies?

4 Using examples, explain under what circumstances international co-operation among governments is essential for the preservation of the environment.

Real world focus

Business leaders in Australia debate carbon taxes versus cap and trade schemes

The head of BHP Billiton (a very large resources company in Australia) suggested that a tax on carbon be imposed in Australia ahead of a global agreement. He argued that this should be done in order to anticipate a global price that would result from an international agreement to limit carbon emissions.

Other business leaders disagreed. They argued that taking action before an international agreement is arrived at would damage Australia's economy and result in a loss of its international competitiveness. Also, some noted that a carbon tax would not have a major impact on carbon emissions. According to one argument, the price elasticity of demand for petrol (gasoline) is low; while a tax may have a short-term effect, people soon get used to the higher price and they go on using what they were using before the tax. Therefore, a cap and trade scheme would be more effective in cutting emissions, though this should only be adopted after a global agreement is reached, since not only a carbon tax but also a cap and trade scheme would negatively affect Australia's competitiveness.

Source: Adapted from Andrew Burrell and Matt Chambers, 'Business leaders condemn Klopper's carbon price call' in *The Australian*, 17 September 2010.

Applying your skills

1 Using a diagram, explain why a carbon tax and a cap and trade scheme would affect Australia's international competitiveness.

2 Using diagrams, explain how **(a)** a carbon tax, and **(b)** a cap and trade scheme can help cut carbon emissions.

3 Evaluate the view of some Australian business leaders that a cap and trade scheme is a better policy than a carbon tax to lower carbon emissions.

Economic thinking on sustainability and Elinor Ostrom, winner of the 2009 Nobel Prize in Economics

In our study of sustainability, we have seen that in economists' way of thinking, environmental destruction is analysed in terms of negative externalities. Even common access resources can be analysed and understood in terms of negative externalities: their overuse is simply the *external cost of* people's ordinary transactions that do not take account of consequences on the environment. In other words, the destruction of the environment is something that is thought of as being *outside the normal sphere of events*.

An important reason for thinking this way about the environment is that microeconomic theory is based on the idealised and fictional world of perfect markets with no failures, driven by economic decision-makers who make choices according to their best self-interest, responding to prices as signals and incentives, all of which leads to maximum social welfare.

Economists' understanding of externalities as the divergence between private and social costs and private and social benefits is based on just this assumption of narrow self-interest: consumers and firms consume and produce taking only their own private interests into account, ignoring possible external costs that their actions give rise to. External costs arise *because consumers and producers are assumed to behave in ways that ignore the interests of society at large*. In fact, the problem of overuse of common access resources arises because *there are no markets and no prices*. Therefore, from this point of view, it is inevitable that self-interested people will overuse resources they do not have to pay for.

The two main categories of measures to deal with environmental externalities we discussed, government regulations and market-based policies, are both based on this assumption about self-interested behaviour. Regulations use the command approach to force producers and consumers to reduce the external costs of their self-interested actions, and market-based policies create price incentives that try to bring the self-interested behaviour of economic decision-makers in line with society's best interests.

Yet all this raises some interesting questions. Does it make sense to view environmental destruction purely as the by-product of people's indifference toward the environment because they are self-interested beings? Are there situations when people do not display the narrow self-interested behaviour assumed by standard economic

theory? If so, what are the implications, and what would be the appropriate policy responses?

These are the kinds of questions posed by Elinor Ostrom, an American political scientist who became the first woman to receive the Nobel Prize in Economics (2009) for her work on the management of common access resources. In one of her major works, Ostrom writes that her central question

'is how a group of principals who are in an interdependent situation can organise and govern themselves to obtain continuing joint benefits when all face temptations to free-ride, shirk, or otherwise act opportunistically.'[11]

Ostrom spent decades studying how communities organise themselves to manage open access resources such as fish stocks, woods, lakes, pastures and groundwater basins. She discovered that communities often develop complex mechanisms on how to make decisions and how to enforce rules, resulting in outcomes that differ widely from those predicted by standard economic theory. In an interview in 2010, she said:

'If you are in a fishery or have a pasture and you know your family's long-term benefit is that you don't destroy it, and if you can talk with the other people who use that resource, then you may well figure out rules that fit that local setting and organise to enforce them. But if the community doesn't have a good way of communicating with each other or the costs of self-organisation are too high, they won't organise, and there will be failures.'[12]

Ostrom and her colleagues have performed hundreds of experiments, which show that when people are users of a common access resource, they are often able to find solutions on how to manage it sustainably, without overusing and destroying it, *provided they have good methods of communication between them*.[13] They make rules about how each user should behave and contribute to the management of the resource, and rules of enforcement and sanctions against those who violate the rules. Many studies by Ostrom and other scholars of real-life situations involving the management of common access resources, confirm the results of these experiments.

(If you decide to read further about Ostrom's work, you will find that she uses the term 'common pool resources'; other scholars use 'common property resources'. Both these terms mean common access resources that are governed by a set of rules.)

(continued over)

Ostrom's findings do not run entirely counter to the conclusions of standard economic theory, since lack of good methods of communication between people do result in the failures we studied in this chapter. However, her findings depart from standard economic theory in a very important respect: she has found that *these failures are not inevitable*, because rational economic behaviour does not always mean acting in one's own best self-interest; it often means acting in what is in the *group's best interests*. This kind of action arises as a result of institutions that permit communication between the resource users, leading to binding agreements, with monitoring and enforcement rules that ensure sustainable resource use.

Ostrom's conclusions focus on the point that people often behave *co-operatively rather than competitively*, and this has very important policy implications. Sometimes, the best method of preserving common access resources is by allowing the resource users themselves to manage them, rather than through centralised government interference. When the conditions for co-operative solutions are present, the government's role should be to promote institutions that enable the users to manage the resource, such as a court system for resolving disputes and institutions that provide scientific knowledge for resource management. Often, this involves recognising that local co-operative institutions may be superior to institutions that are imposed on people from above or from outside.

One requirement for sustainable resource management is that there must be boundaries of an area (such as a pasture, a wood or a lake, and so on) corresponding to the area that the resource users are managing. This raises the question whether Ostrom's approach is suitable for dealing with global problems such as the oceans and climate change. She herself notes the following:

'I really despair over the oceans … It's so tempting to go along the coast and scoop up all the fish you can and then move on. With very big boats you can do that. I think we could move toward solving that problem, but right now there are not many instrumentalities for doing that.

Regarding global climate change, I'm more hopeful. There are local public benefits that people can receive at the same time they're generating benefits for the global environment. Take health and transportation as an example. If more people would walk or bicycle to work and use their car only when they have to go some distance, then their health would be better, their personal pocketbook would be better, and the atmosphere would be better. Of course, if it's just a few people it won't matter, but if more and more people feel "This is the kind of life I should be living" that can substantially help the global problem. Similarly, if we invest in re-doing the insulation of a lot of buildings, we can save money as well as help the global environment. Yes, we want some global action but boy, if we just sit around and wait for that? Come on!'

---

[11] Elinor Ostrom (1990) *Governing the Commons: The Evolution of Institutions for Collective Action,* Cambridge University Press.

[12] Interview with Elinor Ostrom, by Fran Korten, Yesmagazine. org, 27 February 2010.

[13] The experiments are carried out at the Workshop in Political Theory and Policy Analysis at Indiana University where Ostrom is a professor.

Thinking points

- How realistic do you think is the assumption that economic decision-makers are motivated by rational self-interest in making economic decisions?

- Many economists argue that even if rational self-interest is not a realistic assumption, it does not matter as long as the predictions of a theory fit with what happens in the real world (see also the Theory of knowledge feature on page 166). What does Ostrom's work tell us about this perspective?

- If people sometimes behave co-operatively rather than competitively, what are the implications for the idea that environmental destruction is caused by externalities?

- Ostrom suggests that many people would change their behaviour if they understood that certain choices would be in their own best interests as well as in society's best interests (for example, biking rather than using a car). But many people may not know about such joint personal and social benefits. What can be done about this?

HL 5.7 Asymmetric information (higher level topic)

- Explain, using examples, that market failure may occur when one party in an economic transaction (either the buyer or the seller) possesses more information than the other party.
- Evaluate possible government responses, including legislation, regulation and provision of information.

The competitive market mechanism presupposes that all firms and all consumers have complete information regarding products, prices, resources and methods of production. However, the real world is full of examples where firms, consumers and resource owners are in situations where information is missing. **Asymmetric information** refers to situations where buyers and sellers do not have equal access to information, and usually results in an underallocation of resources to the production of goods or services.

Examples where information is available to sellers but not to buyers

Sellers often have information about the quality of a good or service that they do not make available to consumers. Sellers of used cars have information about the car's quality that they are unlikely to reveal to potential buyers if the car has a defect. In a free and unregulated market, sellers of food could sell products that are unsafe for human consumption, possibly leading to illness and even death. Sellers of medicines could sell unsafe medications that could be ineffective or dangerous to human health. Individuals claiming to be doctors, some of whom have little or no training, could practise medicine and even surgery, resulting in huge costs in terms of human health and safety.

In a free unregulated market, the result is usually to underallocate resources to the production of the good or service. Consumers are likely to be aware of possible dangers to themselves, and will be cautious about buying the good or service, resulting in a lower demand and less production. However, if consumers are unaware of possible hidden dangers, such as with unsafe food or toys, there could result an overallocation of resources to the production of these goods and services.

Possible government responses

Regulation

According to one method, governments can pass laws and regulations that ensure quality standards and safety features that must be maintained by producers and sellers of goods and services, such as food, medications, private schools, toys, buildings and all types of construction.

These methods are not without their difficulties, however. Legislation and regulation are time-consuming, bureaucratic procedures, which sometimes work to slow down economic activities. It takes a long time, for example, to test new medications and certify their safety, and is a very costly process. Also, regulatory and quality control activities have very large opportunity costs. Just in the case of food safety control, which involves not only food and beverage products but also hygiene in restaurants, there are a huge number of products and service providers involved, who require regulation and monitoring from the level of the farm (regarding the kinds and amounts of chemical inputs) to the moment the food reaches the table.

Provision of information

Governments may also respond by directly supplying information to consumers, or by forcing producers to provide information, thus protecting consumers in their purchasing decisions. This may include information about the quality of medical care by different providers, about communicable diseases, crime rates by neighbourhoods, health hazards related to different activities, products or substances, nutritional labelling on foods, and so on. In some countries, particularly in Europe, governments provide fee schedules for services (such as legal, medical, architectural) to ensure that consumers receive a particular quality of services for a particular range of prices.

When the government is the provider of information, there are difficulties involving the collection and dissemination of all the necessary information to consumers, the accuracy of the information, as well as opportunity costs in providing the information. When a private seller/producer is the provider of the information, there are serious questions whether information regarding all hazards in products or substances and materials used in products, or all information regarding the quality of services (whether legal, medical, financial, and so on) is accurate and complete.

Another problem is that it is sometimes not possible to eliminate an information asymmetry between sellers and buyers, because no matter what regulations and information are provided, there is still some room for the seller to hide some information from the buyer. In the areas of health care and law, doctors and lawyers have specialised, technical information about their clients that the clients themselves do not possess. Doctors and lawyers often use this information for their own private gain by selectively revealing information to their clients that causes them to demand more services than are necessary. This practice leads to what is known as 'supplier-induced demand', or demand that is induced (created) by the supplier, which would not have appeared if the client had equal access to information.

Licensure

In the case of doctors, most countries around the world have laws requiring doctors to be licensed, and a licence can only be obtained upon proof of adequate medical competence. Licensing is similarly required for many other professions in many countries, from teachers and lawyers to plumbers and electricians.

Some economists criticise licensing, because it may work to limit the supply of people in a profession, raising the price of their services and increasing their incomes at the expense of consumers who must pay higher prices.

Examples where information is available to buyers but not to sellers

Asymmetric information, where the buyer has information not available to the seller, often arises in the area of insurance services, where the buyer of insurance has more information than the seller. Another example occurs in the labour market.

The problem of moral hazard and possible responses

Explaining moral hazard
Moral hazard refers to situations where one party takes risks, but does not face the full costs of these risks. It usually arises when the buyer of insurance changes his or her behaviour after obtaining insurance, so that the outcome works against the interests of the seller of insurance. For example, buyers of car theft insurance may be less careful about protecting their car against theft, because they will be reimbursed if someone steals their car. Some buyers of medical malpractice insurance (doctors) may be less careful about avoiding malpractice, because of the knowledge that malpractice costs will be covered by the insurer. Unemployment insurance may lead some people to be less hesitant about becoming unemployed, in the knowledge that their insurance will provide them with some income.

In all these cases, the buyers of insurance have information about their future intentions that is not available to the sellers of insurance. In a free, unregulated market, the result of moral hazard is to underallocate resources to the production of insurance services, as sellers of insurance try to protect themselves against higher costs due to the risky behaviour of the buyers of insurance.

Many economists have argued that the financial crisis that began in 2008 was partly a case of moral hazard. It is possible that many financial institutions would be more careful about making risky loans and engaging in other highly risky financial transactions if they did not believe that the government would support them in the event of difficulties. (Note that this is not a matter of taking out an insurance policy in the strict sense of the term, but it is a sort of 'insurance' nonetheless in that the government provides a kind of assurance of protection in the event that financial institutions face difficulties due to poor loan repayments.)

The term 'moral hazard' does not refer to unethical or immoral behaviour. It is simply a historical remnant of a very old insurance term that originally meant 'subjective'.

Evaluating responses to moral hazard
Problems of moral hazard in insurance are usually dealt with by the provider of insurance. This is often done by making the buyer of insurance pay for part of the cost of damages (these payments are known as 'out-of-pocket payments'). This is intended to make

the insurance buyer face the consequences of risky behaviour, thus leading to less risky behaviour.

A problem with out-of-pocket payments is that it has different effects depending on the income level of insurance buyers. Private insurance companies usually offer a range of policies from which buyers can choose, where the lower the cost of the insurance, the higher the out-of-pocket payments. Lower-income earners usually choose low-cost policies with high out-of-pocket payment because these are more affordable, while higher-income earners choose the opposite. This means that lower-income earners are more likely to change their risky behaviour because they are offered less insurance protection, while higher-income earners are less likely to change their risky behaviour.

In the financial area, moral hazard is dealt with through government regulation of financial institutions, intended to oversee and prevent highly risky behaviour. This raises a whole set of issues regarding the types and degrees of government regulations that are required if these are to be effective.

The problem of adverse selection and possible responses

Explaining adverse selection
Adverse selection arises when buyers of insurance have more information about themselves than the sellers of insurance. It arises most often in the area of health insurance. Buyers of health insurance know more about the state of their health than sellers of insurance, and those with health problems are unlikely to tell the full truth to the insurance company. In a free unregulated market, adverse selection results in an underallocation of resources to health insurance services, as the insurance company reduces the supply of insurance to protect itself against having to provide insurance coverage to very high risks, or people who are more likely to become ill. Adverse selection also leads to high insurance costs for insurance buyers.

Evaluating possible responses to adverse selection
Private insurance companies usually protect themselves against adverse selection by offering a range of policies where the lower the cost of the insurance, the higher the out-of-pocket payments. This offers people choice, so that those who believe they have a low risk of getting sick can buy a low-cost policy with higher out-of-pocket payments, while higher-cost policies with lower out-of-pocket payments can be selected by people who believe they have high levels of health risk.

However in practice, it does not work out this way. One reason is that lower-income earners choose low-cost policies with high out-of-pocket payments because these are more affordable (as in the case of moral hazard), *regardless of the state of their health*. From the perspective of equity or fairness (see page 16), this is undesirable because it discriminates against those on low incomes. Another reason is that in trying to protect themselves against high risks, insurance companies usually refuse to insure people above a certain age, as elderly people generally have a higher chance of becoming ill. The result is that those who mostly need health insurance coverage, poor people who cannot afford to buy health care in the private market, and elderly people who are more likely to become ill, are left with little or no insurance coverage.

To deal with this problem, government responses may take the form of direct provision of health care services at low or zero prices to an entire population, financed by tax revenues, thus ensuring that the entire population has health insurance coverage (as in countries with a National Health Service); alternatively, they make take the form of social health insurance, which may cover a country's entire population (as in many European countries), or which selectively covers only certain vulnerable groups of the population (as in the United States).

A potential problem with government-funded or social health care systems involves difficulties in controlling costs of providing health care and growing burdens on the government or social health insurance budgets.

The problem of safety in the workplace and possible responses

Safety in the workplace

Employers, or buyers of labour resources, are generally interested in providing some workplace safety, because a very unsafe working environment disrupts production. However, it is possible that the level of safety chosen by some employers is not sufficient from the perspective of workers. Some employers may find it in their interests to hide information from potential employees regarding unsafe working conditions, with negative consequences for the safety of the workers they employ. This represents market failure due to asymmetric information in the labour market.

Evaluating possible responses to safety in the workplace

Governments can provide information to workers about safety conditions in various firms, or they may require employers to provide information to prospective workers about hazards and safety conditions, or they may set minimum safety standards

in the workplace that all employers must abide by. The most commonly used approach is the third, involving government-set safety standards.

While this has the effect of improving safety conditions for workers, it is difficult for the government to cover all possible safety and hazard eventualities, given the very different working environments of different industries and types of work. The provision of information might be more effective, though it is difficult to provide information on all types and levels of dangers in the workplace. Labour unions, for example, often provide this kind of information to their members, but they usually cover only some particular trades and professions in particular industries.

Test your understanding 5.11

1   What kinds of information problems give rise to market failure?

2   **(a)** Provide some examples of information asymmetries where information is available to sellers but not to buyers. **(b)** Explain how governments can intervene to correct these information asymmetries. **(c)** What are some advantages and disadvantages of these types of government intervention?

3   **(a)** Provide some examples of information asymmetries where information is available to buyers but not to sellers. **(b)** Explain how governments can intervene to correct these information asymmetries. **(c)** What are some advantages and disadvantages of these types of government intervention?

5.8   Abuse of monopoly power (higher level topic)

♦   Explain how monopoly power can create a welfare loss and is therefore a type of market failure.
♦   Discuss possible government responses, including legislation, regulation, nationalisation and trade liberalisation.

The meaning of monopoly power

Monopoly and *monopoly power* will be discussed in detail in Chapter 7. Monopoly is a type of market structure where there is a single firm dominating the market for a product, and where high barriers to entry (factors making it difficult for other firms to enter the industry) ensure that the monopoly position of the single seller can be preserved. **Monopoly power**, also known as **market power**, refers to the ability of a firm or a group of firms to control the price of the product they sell. Monopoly power can be exercised not only by monopolies, but also by firms in oligopolies, where there are a few large sellers.

Monopoly power is considered to be socially undesirable because it leads to:

- a welfare loss, as social surplus is less than maximum (see Figure 7.15, page 190)
- allocative inefficiency: $MB > MC$ and therefore there is an underallocation of resources to the good (see Figures 7.15 and 7.16, page 190)
- productive inefficiency: production does not take place at the lowest possible cost (see Figure 7.16, page 190)
- lower output and a higher price of the industry than the output and price of a more competitive market (see Figure 7.14, page 189).

We will examine all these issues in Chapter 7.

Possible government responses

Below is a summary of some of the more important government responses. All these (with the exception of nationalisation) will be discussed in later chapters (for each policy, you are referred to the relevant chapter).

Legislation

Legislation in the form of anti-monopoly laws can be used to prevent the development of substantial monopoly power or the exercise of monopoly power. For example, legislation is often used to prevent collusion (agreement to fix prices) among oligopolistic firms and to encourage competition between them, to break up monopolies or near-monopolies that have been found to engage in monopolistic practices into smaller units that will behave more competitively, to prevent mergers between firms that would result in too much monopoly power, and in general to encourage competitive behaviour in the economy. (See Chapter 7, page 192.)

Regulation

Governments usually regulate monopolies that are 'natural monopolies'. A natural monopoly is a single firm that can produce enough output to satisfy the entire market at a lower cost of production than two or more firms (examples include utilities such as gas, water and electricity, as well as postal services and others). Because of the natural monopoly's low costs of

production, it may not be in society's interests to break it up into two or more smaller firms. Yet the natural monopoly is likely to engage in the usual practices resulting in the undesirable social effects noted above. Therefore, governments around the world often regulate natural monopolies, forcing outcomes that are more favourable to consumers: prices can be set at lower levels and quantities produced at higher levels than the unregulated monopolist. (See Chapter 7, page 193.)

Nationalisation

Nationalisation refers to a transfer in ownership of a firm away from the private sector and toward government ownership. A nationalised firm is a government-owned firm. Government ownership of a monopoly is sometimes pursued as an alternative to government regulation of privately owned natural monopolies. It is a method that historically has been preferred in most European countries, as well as many other countries around the world, but not in the United States, which has tended to prefer regulation of natural monopolies. The objectives of government ownership are similar to the objectives of government regulation of natural monopolies: to ensure that prices are lower and output greater than would result from an unregulated monopoly.

Since the 1980s, there has been a trend in many countries around the world to privatise government-owned firms. Privatisation is the opposite of nationalisation, as it involves a transfer of ownership away from the public and toward the private sector. Within the European Union, where a number of natural monopolies had been under government ownership, prices of a number of services, such as telephone and electricity services, were substantially higher compared to the United States where similar services were regulated but not under government ownership. The reason was that the higher costs of the producers were passed on to consumers in the form of higher prices. Within the European Union, many formerly nationalised industries have been privatised.

In addition, many economically less developed countries that historically had many firms under government ownership have also been privatising some of these. (See Chapter 12, page 340 on privatisation.)

Trade liberalisation

Trade liberalisation involves the removal by the government of barriers to international trade, or the buying and selling of goods and services between different countries. If a firm within the domestic economy exercises substantial monopoly power, this means that it faces limited competition from competitor firms. Trade liberalisation has the effect of increasing imports (goods purchased from other countries), and therefore increasing the competition faced by the domestic firm. As a result of increasing competition, the monopoly power of the domestic firm (or firms) is reduced. (See Chapter 17 for more details.)

Test your understanding 5.12

1 **(a)** Why is abuse of monopoly power socially undesirable? **(b)** What impacts does this kind of market failure have on the allocation of resources and on welfare?

2 Identify some policies that governments can pursue to reduce monopoly power.

Table 5.1 lists the various kinds of market failures considered in sections 5.3–5.8, and shows what impact the free, unregulated market will have on the allocation of resources to the production of the good or service.

Type of market failure	The market's impact on resource allocation
Negative production externality	Overallocates resources
Negative consumption externality	Overallocates resources
Positive production externality	Underallocates resources
Positive consumption externality	Underallocates resources
Merit goods	Underallocates resources
Demerit goods	Overallocates resources
Public goods	Underallocates resources (or allocates no resources)
Overuse of common access resources	Overallocates resources
Asymmetric information	Underallocates resources (usually)
Monopoly power	Underallocates resources

Table 5.1 Market failures and their impacts on resource allocation

5.9 The problem of government failure (policy failure) (supplementary material)

We have learned that government intervention in markets is essential to ensure that markets work effectively and that failures are corrected. Yet government intervention does not always improve the operation of markets. We have already seen examples of government intervention in markets that has the effect of worsening the allocation of resources (indirect taxes, subsidies and price controls; see Chapter 4). Economists generally do not look upon price controls favourably, because these intensify problems of resource misallocation. Yet they are often used because governments are driven by various objectives, not all of which involve improving the functioning of the economy. Another example involves the use of 'perverse subsidies', such as subsidies for fossil fuels, with the effect of encouraging fossil fuel production and consumption, contributing to environmental pollution, and reducing incentives for the development of alternative, non-polluting, energy sources (page 128).

Government failure, also known as policy failure, occurs when government intervention in markets results in less efficient outcomes than those that would have arisen without the intervention. It occurs for the following reasons:

- Governments respond to political pressures created by the influence of powerful interest groups and the sometimes narrow interests of their supporters. This is certainly the case in the use of price supports to support farmers' incomes in many developed countries.

- Governments do not always have all necessary information to formulate appropriate policies.

- Intervention in markets is complex, and may often lead to unintended consequences. For example, a policy intended to correct a problem in one area may lead to the unintended creation of a problem in another part of the economy.

- Government policies have a certain inertia that is sometimes difficult to change. Once particular laws, rules and regulations have been established, they cannot be changed easily because of inflexibility of the political process.

Assessment

The Student's CD-ROM at the back of this book provides practice of examination questions based on the material you have studied in this chapter.

Standard level

- Exam practice: Paper 1, Chapter 5
  - SL/HL core topics (questions 5.1–5.20)

Higher level

- Exam practice: Paper 1, Chapter 5
  - SL/HL core topics (questions 5.1–5.20)
  - HL topics (questions 5.21 and 5.22)

Chapter 6
The theory of the firm I: Production, costs, revenues and profit

Higher level topic

This chapter and the next are concerned with the behaviour of firms. Much of firm behaviour depends on the type of market structure within which the firm operates, which will be studied in Chapter 7. The present chapter introduces the fundamental concepts necessary to analysing firm behaviour: production, costs, revenues and profit.

HL 6.1 Production in the short run: the law of diminishing returns

All firms use inputs (or resources, or factors of production) to produce output. The quantities of inputs needed to produce output is determined by a technical relationship explaining why firms behave the way they do. This technical relationship depends on a distinction between the short run and the long run.

The short run and the long run

♦ Distinguish between the short run and long run in the context of production.

The difference between the short and long run is the following:

- The **short run** is a time period during which at least one input is fixed and cannot be changed by the firm. For example, if a firm wants to increase output, it can hire more labour and increase materials, tools and equipment, but it cannot quickly change the size of its buildings, factories and heavy machinery. As long as these inputs are fixed, the firm is operating in the short run.

- The **long run** is a time period when all inputs can be changed. Using the example above, in this time period the firm can build new buildings and factories and buy more heavy machinery; it can change all of its inputs. In the long run the firm has no fixed inputs; we say all inputs are *variable*.

Note that the short run and the long run do not correspond to any particular length of time. Some industries may require months to change their fixed inputs while others may require years.

Total product, marginal product and average product

♦ Define total product, average product and marginal product, and construct diagrams to show their relationship.

Understanding and illustrating total, marginal and average product curves

In this section, we will study the relationship between inputs and output in the short run. Since we are studying the short run, we know the firm has both fixed and variable inputs. For simplicity, let's consider a hypothetical firm that uses only two inputs, land and labour, where land is the fixed input and labour is the variable input; we can think of this firm as a simple farm. The only way the farm can increase the quantity of its output in the short run is by increasing the quantity of labour it uses. We can now distinguish between:

- **Total product** (*TP*) is the total quantity of output produced by a firm.

- **Marginal product** (MP) is the extra or additional output resulting from one additional unit of the variable input, labour; it tells us by how much output increases as labour increases by one worker. Marginal product is given by:

$$MP = \frac{\Delta TP}{\Delta\, units\ of\ labour}$$

- **Average product** (*AP*) is the total quantity of output per unit of variable input, or labour; this tells us how much output each unit of labour (each worker) produces on average. Average product is given by:

$$AP = \frac{TP}{units\ of\ labour}$$

Table 6.1 shows an example of the total product that results as the number of units of labour working on the fixed land (the farm) increases. Once we are given the information in columns 1 and 2, we can easily calculate marginal and average product. To find marginal product, we take an increase in *TP* and divide it by the increase in the units of labour. For example, the marginal product of the third worker is

$$\frac{(9-5)}{(3-2)} = \frac{4}{1} = 4$$

the marginal product of the sixth worker is

$$\frac{(21-18)}{(6-5)} = \frac{3}{1} = 3$$

To find average product, we take the total product and divide it by the units of labour that produce that amount of product. For example, the average product of the third worker is

$$\frac{9}{3} = 3;\ \text{of the sixth worker it is}\ \frac{21}{6} = 3.5$$

The total, marginal and average products of Table 6.1 are drawn in Figure 6.1. Part (a) plots the total product data of column 2 of the table, while part (b) plots the marginal and average product data of columns 3 and 4. The vertical axis in both figures measures units of output, and the horizontal axis measures units of the variable input (labour). Note that the scale of variable input units on the horizontal axis is identical in both parts, so the *MP* and *AP* curves in part (b) correspond to the *TP* curve in part (a). Both (a) and (b) are divided into three parts:

- **Increasing marginal product.** When labour units are between 0 and 4, the marginal product of labour is increasing, as we see in part (b): the addition to total product made by each unit of

(1) Units of variable input (labour)	(2) Total product (units of output) = TP	(3) Marginal product (units of output) = MP $MP = \frac{\Delta TP}{\Delta\, units\ of\ labour}$	(4) Average product (units of output) = AP $AP = \frac{TP}{units\ of\ labour}$
0	0	–	–
1	2	2	2
2	5	3	2.5
3	9	4	3
4	14	5	3.5
5	18	4	3.6
6	21	3	3.5
7	23	2	3.3
8	24	1	3
9	24	0	2.7
10	23	–1	2.3
11	21	–2	1.9

Table 6.1   Total, marginal and average products

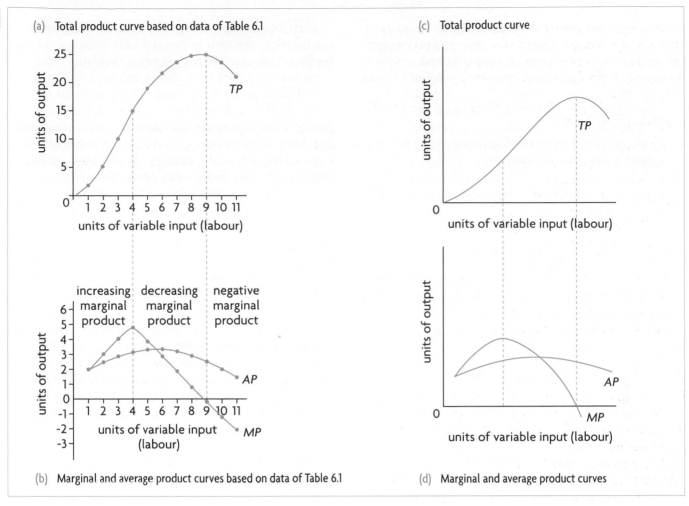

(a) Total product curve based on data of Table 6.1

(b) Marginal and average product curves based on data of Table 6.1

(c) Total product curve

(d) Marginal and average product curves

Figure 6.1 Total, marginal and average products

labour gets bigger and bigger. When 4 workers are employed, marginal product, equal to five units of output, is maximum.

- **Decreasing marginal product.** When labour units are between 4 and 9, the marginal product of labour is decreasing (and positive, or greater than zero), as we see in part (b). Here, the addition to total product made by successive units of labour becomes smaller and smaller.

- **Negative marginal product.** At 8 and 9 units of labour, total product is maximum, as we see in part (a), and the ninth unit of labour adds zero units of output; the marginal product of the ninth unit of labour is zero, shown in part (b). Beyond 9 units of labour, total product begins to fall and corresponds to the negative marginal product of

the tenth and eleventh workers that we see in part (b).[1]

The relationship between the marginal and average product curves

Average product also rises at first and then falls (see Figure 6.1(b)). Note the relationship between the average and marginal product curves: when the marginal product curve lies above the average product curve ($MP > AP$), average product is increasing; and when the marginal product curve lies below the average product curve ($MP < AP$), average product is decreasing. *This means the marginal product curve always intersects the average product curve when this is at its maximum.* The reason lies in the mathematical relationship between the average and marginal values of any variable.

[1] The mathematically inclined student will note that the marginal product, measuring the change in total product arising from an additional unit of labour, is the slope of the total product curve. (The slope is here interpreted in the mathematically correct way, referring to the change in the vertical axis divided by the change in the horizontal axis; see 'Quantitative techniques' chapter on the CD-ROM, page 19.)

Therefore, with increasing marginal product, MP increases (Figure 6.1(b)) because the slope of the TP curve is increasing (Figure 6.1(a)). With decreasing marginal product, MP falls because the slope of the TP curve decreases. When 9 units of labour are employed, the slope of the TP curve is 0 (i.e. the marginal product of the ninth worker is zero) and beyond that the MP, or the slope of the TP curve, becomes negative.

Consider a simple example involving test scores. Say you have an average of 80 in your tests and you would like to increase your average. If your next text score (the 'marginal' score) is greater than your average of 80, your average will increase. If your next test score is lower than your average of 80, then your average will fall. This relationship between average and marginal test scores is exactly the same as the relationship between average and marginal products.

Generalised product curves

Figures 6.1 (c) and (d) show the total, marginal and average product curves that result in the general case when a variable input is added to a fixed input. These curves show the technical relationship between inputs and output that we need to understand to study firm behaviour in the short run. We turn to this relationship next.

Law of diminishing returns

♦ Explain the law of diminishing returns.

In the short run, the technical relationship between inputs and output is provided by the law of diminishing returns.

According to the **law of diminishing returns** (also known as the *law of diminishing marginal product*), as more and more units of a variable input (such as labour) are added to one or more fixed inputs (such as land), the marginal product of the variable input at first increases, but there comes a point when it begins to decrease. This relationship presupposes that that the fixed input(s) remain fixed, and that the technology of production is also fixed.

The law of diminishing returns is reflected in the data of Table 6.1 and the curves of Figure 6.1. When there are zero workers on the land, there is no output at all; it is equal to zero. When one worker is hired, there will be some output and so total product is two units. Marginal product is also equal to two units. But one worker alone on the farm must do all the ploughing, planting, harvesting, and so on, and so output is quite low. When a second worker is hired, the two workers share the work, and total product increases to five units, indicating that the output produced by the two together is more than double the output of the first working alone. The additional (or marginal) product due to the second worker (three units) is greater than that of the first (two units). This process is repeated with the addition of the third and fourth workers, and marginal product increases with the addition of each one.

With four workers, marginal product is the greatest it can be; when the fifth worker is added, marginal product begins to fall, and falls continuously thereafter. This is the point at which diminishing returns begin. Why does this happen? On the farm, it happens because of overcrowding: each additional worker has less and less land to work with, and so produces less and less output. Eventually, the conditions on the farm become so crowded that the ninth worker adds zero extra output; with the addition of the tenth worker the marginal product is negative and total product begins to fall.

More generally, marginal product will begin to fall at some point not just on a farm with a fixed piece of land, but whenever more and more units of a variable input are added to a fixed input (provided the technology of production is unchanging). For example, in the case of a factory where more and more workers are hired, each worker will have fewer and fewer machines and equipment to work with, and so will add less and less output.

Imagine what would happen if diminishing returns did not exist. Using our farm example, it would be possible for food production to increase indefinitely just by continuously adding variable inputs to a fixed piece of land – a clear impossibility!

Real world focus

David Ricardo and the end of agricultural output growth

David Ricardo, a famous English economist of the 19th century, believed that agricultural output would eventually stop growing, because as more and more labour and capital inputs were added to land that was fixed in quantity, the additional output of labour and capital would become smaller and smaller until it would no longer be possible for total output to increase further.

Applying your skills

1 Explain the law that describes the process Ricardo was referring to.

2 Do you think Ricardo's fears were justified?

3 How can you explain the growth of agricultural output in the real world in spite of a fixed quantity of land?

Calculating total, average and marginal product

♦ Calculate total, average and marginal product from a set of data and/or diagrams.

If we are given data on the total product of a firm, it is a simple matter to calculate average and marginal product; we simply apply the formulae shown on page 140. If we are given data on average product, we can find total product by using $TP = AP \times$ units of variable input; and from TP we then calculate marginal product as well. If we are given marginal product, we find total product by adding up the successive marginal products of each additional unit of labour. The example in Table 6.2 shows the calculations made to find total product from marginal product.

To calculate TP, AP or MP from a diagram, we simply read off the information appearing in the graph, and apply exactly the same principles as in Table 6.2 to calculate the variable or variables we are interested in.

Units of labour (variable input)	1	2	3	4	5
Marginal product (*MP*)	20	25	20	15	10
Total product (*TP*)	20	45 (= 25 + 20)	65 (= 20 + 25 + 20)	80 (= 15 + 20 + 25 + 20)	90 (= 10 + 15 + 20 + 25 + 20)

Table 6.2   Calculating total product

Test your understanding 6.1

1 Distinguish between the short run and the long run in relation to production.

2 Define **(a)** total product, **(b)** marginal product, and **(c)** average product.

3 Why does marginal product reach a point when it begins to decrease?

4 What happens to average product when $MP > AP$? When $MP < AP$?

5 Copy the following table, then fill in the missing figures to show production in the short run.

Units of variable input (labour)	Total product	Marginal product	Average product
0	0		
1	10		
2	22		
3	35		
4	46		
5	54		
6	59		
7	61		
8	60		

6 Using the information in question 5:

(a) Plot the total product, marginal product and average product curves.

(b) Define the law demonstrated by the pattern shown by the marginal product and average product figures and curves.

(c) Why does this law only hold in the short run?

(d) With how many units of the variable input do we see the beginning of diminishing returns (diminishing marginal product)? Show this in your diagram.

(e) With how many units of the variable input do we see the beginning of negative returns? Show this in your diagram.

(f) Explain the relationship between the average product and marginal product curves.

7 Copy the following table, then fill in the missing figures to show production in the short run.

Units of variable input (labour)	Total product	Marginal product	Average product
0		−	
1		3	
2		5	
3		4	
4		3	
5		2	
6		0	
7		−1	
8		−3	

8 Using the data in question 7, **(a)** plot the total product, marginal product and average product curves. **(b)** With how many units of the variable input do we see the beginning of diminishing returns (diminishing marginal product)? Show this in your diagram. **(c)** With how many units of the variable input do we see the beginning of negative returns? Show this in your diagram.

9 Copy the following table, then fill in the missing figures to show production in the short run.

Units of variable input (labour)	Total product	Marginal product	Average product
0			–
1			4.00
2			5.00
3			4.33
4			3.75
5			3.20
6			2.50

6.2 Introduction to costs of production: economic costs

Costs of production as opportunity costs

◆ Explain the meaning of economic costs as the opportunity cost of all resources employed by the firm (including entrepreneurship).

When firms use resources to produce, they incur **costs of production**, which include money payments to buy resources plus anything else given up by a firm for the use of resources. The resources include land, labour, capital and entrepreneurship (see Chapter 1, page 3). Because of scarcity, the use of any resource by a firm involves a sacrifice of the best alterative use of that resource, which is an opportunity cost. Therefore all production costs are opportunity costs, and are known as economic costs.

In economics, because of the condition of scarcity, economic costs, which include all costs of production, are opportunity costs of all resources used in production.

Explicit, implicit costs and economic costs

◆ Distinguish between explicit costs and implicit costs as the two components of economic costs.

We can distinguish between two kinds of economic costs (opportunity costs), depending on who owns the resources used by the firm. Resources are either owned by the firm itself, or are owned by outsiders to the firm from whom the firm buys them.

Explicit costs
When the firm uses resources it does not own, it buys them from outsiders and makes payments of money to the resource suppliers. For example, a firm hires labour and pays a wage; it purchases materials and pays the price to the seller; it uses electricity and pays the electricity supplier, and so on.

Payments made by a firm to outsiders to acquire resources for use in production are **explicit costs**.

The opportunity cost of using resources not owned by the firm is equal to the amount paid to acquire them; these payments could have been made to buy something else instead, which is now being sacrificed.

Implicit costs
The firm may own some of the resources that it uses for its production, such as, for example, an office building. In this case, the firm does not make a money payment to acquire the resource. There is still a cost involved in the use of the self-owned resource, which is the sacrifice of income that would have been earned if the resource had been employed in its best alternative use.

The sacrificed income arising from the use of self-owned resources by a firm is an **implicit cost**.

In the case of the office building owned and used by the firm, the opportunity cost is the rental income that could have been earned if the building were rented out. The hours of work a firm owner puts into his or her own business have an opportunity cost equal to what the firm owner could have earned if s/he had worked elsewhere. The entrepreneurial abilities the firm owner puts into the business (risk-taking, innovative, organisational and managerial abilities) entail a further opportunity cost equal to what these abilities could have earned elsewhere.

Economic costs

Adding together explicit and implicit costs, we get the firm's economic costs.

> **Economic costs** are the sum of explicit and implicit costs, or total opportunity costs incurred by a firm for its use of resources, whether purchased or self-owned. When economists refer to 'costs' they mean 'economic costs'.

Suppose you had a job with a salary of £60 000 a year, which you decided to quit to open your own business. You estimate that your entrepreneurial talent you are putting into your business is worth £45 000 a year. You set up your office in a spare room of your house that you used to rent out for £4000 a year. Further, you borrow £30 000, for which you are paying interest of £2000 a year, and use the borrowed amount to buy supplies and materials. You also hire an assistant whom you pay £18 000 a year. Your explicit, implicit and economic costs are:

Implicit costs
£60 000 (opportunity cost of your foregone salary)
+£45 000 (opportunity cost of your entrepreneurial talent)
+£ 4000 (opportunity cost of foregone rental income from your spare room)
£109 000

Explicit costs
£ 2000 (interest on your loan)
+£30 000 (purchase of supplies and materials)
+£18 000 (assistant's salary)
£50 000

Economic costs (= total opportunity costs)
£109 000 (implicit costs)
+£ 50 000 (accounting costs)
£159 000

> ### Test your understanding 6.2
>
> 1 Explain **(a)** explicit costs, and **(b)** implicit costs. Provide examples of each.
> 2 Why do both explicit costs and implicit costs represent opportunity costs to the firm?
> 3 Why are economic costs greater than explicit costs?
> 4 Explain the meaning of economic cost, using the concepts of explicit, implicit and opportunity costs.

6.3 Costs of production in the short run

Short-run costs

We can put together the concepts we learned above to study costs of production in the short run.

Fixed, variable and total costs in the short run and long run

> • Explain the distinction between the short run and the long run, with reference to fixed costs and variable costs.

The distinction between fixed inputs and variable inputs discussed on page 139 in connection with the short and long run leads us to a distinction between fixed and variable costs:

- **Fixed costs** *arise from the use of fixed inputs.* Fixed costs are costs that do not change as output changes. Examples of fixed costs include rental payments, property taxes, insurance premiums and interest on loans. They do not increase if the firm produces more output, and do not decrease if it produces less. Even if there is zero output, these payments still have to be made in the short run. Fixed costs arise only in the short run, as in the long run there are no fixed inputs.
- **Variable costs** *arise from the use of variable inputs.* These are costs that vary (change) as output increases or decreases, therefore they are 'variable'. An example is the wage cost of labour. To produce more output, the firm hires more labour, and has

increased wage costs. The more variable inputs a firm uses, the greater the variable costs.

- **Total costs** **are the sum of fixed and variable costs.**

In the short run, a firm's total costs are the sum of fixed and variable costs. In the long run there are no fixed costs, therefore a firm's total costs are equal to its variable costs.

Total, average and marginal costs

♦ Distinguish between total costs, marginal costs and average costs.

Average costs

Average costs are costs per unit of output, or total cost divided by the number of units of output. They tell us how much each unit of output produced costs on average. From our definitions above, we have three total costs, each one corresponding to an average cost:

Total costs	Average costs
total fixed costs (*TFC*)	**average fixed costs** (*AFC*)
total variable costs (*TVC*)	**average variable costs** (*AVC*)
total costs (*TC*)	**average total costs** (*ATC*)

To calculate average costs, we simply divide each of the totals by the units of output (*Q*) that the firm produces:

$$AFC = \frac{TFC}{Q} \qquad AVC = \frac{TVC}{Q} \qquad ATC = \frac{TC}{Q}$$

It was noted above that total cost is the sum of fixed costs plus variable costs:

$$TC = TFC + TVC$$

Similarly, average total costs are the sum of average fixed costs plus average variable costs:

$$ATC = AFC + AVC$$

Marginal costs

Marginal cost (*MC*) *is the extra or additional cost of producing one more unit of output*. It tells us by how much total costs increase if there is an increase in output by one unit. It is calculated by considering the change in total cost (*TC*) resulting from a change in output. In addition, it can be calculated by considering the change in total variable cost (*TVC*) that results from a change in output. The reason why the two

are equivalent is that fixed costs are constant (do not change) as output increases or decreases. Marginal cost is given by:

$$MC = \frac{\Delta TC}{\Delta Q} = \frac{\Delta TVC}{\Delta Q}$$

where the Greek letter Δ stands for 'change in'.

Test your understanding 6.3

1 Define **(a)** fixed costs, **(b)** variable costs, and **(c)** total costs, and explain how they are related to the distinction between the short run and the long run.

2 Which of the following are fixed and which are variable costs:

   (a) insurance premiums on the value of the property owned by a business

   (b) interest payments on a loan taken out by a business

   (c) wage payments to the workers that are hired by a business

   (d) payments for the purchase of seeds and fertiliser by a farmer.

3 **(a)** Define the three kinds of average costs, and explain how they are derived from the three kinds of total cost. **(b)** How are the three kinds of average costs related to each other?

4 Define marginal cost, and explain how it is related to total cost and total variable cost.

Costs curves and product curves

♦ Draw diagrams illustrating the relationship between marginal costs and average costs, and explain the connection with production in the short run.

Drawing the short-run cost curves

In this section, we will draw diagrams of a firm's total, average and marginal costs. Let's continue with our example of the data in Table 6.1 (page 140), and assume that the farm incurs fixed costs of €200 per week (for rent for the land), and that the cost of labour is €100 per worker (per unit of labour) per week. We now have all the information we need to calculate the firm's short-run production costs, which appear in Table 6.3:

- Columns 1 and 2 contain the same data on total product and corresponding labour input that appear in Table 6.1.

146 Section 1: Microeconomics

(1) Total product = TP or Q (units)	(2) Labour (units of labour)	(3) Total fixed cost = TFC (€)	(4) Total variable cost = TVC (€)	(5) Total cost = TC TC = TFC+TVC (€)	(6) Average fixed cost = AFC $AFC = \dfrac{TFC}{Q}$ (€)	(7) Average variable cost = AVC $AVC = \dfrac{TVC}{Q}$ (€)	(8) Average total cost = ATC $ATC = \dfrac{TC}{Q}$ or $ATC =$ AFC+AVC (€)	(9) Marginal cost = MC $MC = \dfrac{\Delta TC}{\Delta Q}$ $MC = \dfrac{\Delta TVC}{\Delta Q}$ (€)
0	0	200	0	200	–	–	–	–
2	1	200	100	300	100	50	150	50
5	2	200	200	400	40	40	80	33.3
9	3	200	300	500	22.2	33.3	55.5	25
14	4	200	400	600	14.3	28.6	42.9	20
18	5	200	500	700	11.1	27.8	38.9	25
21	6	200	600	800	9.5	28.6	38.1	33.3
23	7	200	700	900	8.7	30.4	39.1	50
24	8	200	800	1000	8.3	33.3	41.6	100

Table 6.3   Total, average and marginal costs

- Column 3 shows the farm's total fixed cost (TFC) of €200; this payment has to be made even when total product is zero.
- Column 4 shows the farm's total variable cost, which is the number of workers (from column 2) times €100 per worker.
- Column 5 calculates total cost, which is the sum of total fixed cost (column 3) plus total variable cost (column 4).
- Column 6 shows average fixed cost, obtained by dividing total fixed cost (column 3) by the number of units of output (column 1).
- Column 7 calculates average variable cost, obtained by dividing total variable cost (column 4) by the number of units of output (column 1).
- Column 8 shows average total cost, obtained by dividing total cost (column 5) by the number of units of output (column 1): alternatively, average total cost is the sum of AFC plus AVC.
- Column 9 shows marginal cost, obtained by dividing the change in total cost (from column 5) by the change in the number of units of output (from column 1); for example, when total cost increases from €200 to €300, so that $\Delta TC = 100$, TP increases from 0 to 2 units of output, so that $\Delta Q = 2$. Dividing 100 by 2, we obtain $MC = 50$. Marginal cost can also be calculated as the change in total variable cost divided by the change in total product, because

$\Delta TVC = \Delta TC$. (You can confirm this by comparing the figures in column 4 with those in column 5.)

All the cost information of Table 6.3 is shown graphically in Figure 6.2 (a) and (b). (Parts (c) and (d) show cost curves in the general case for a firm in the short run.) Both parts (a) and (b) measure costs on the vertical axis, and units of output on the horizontal axis. Part (a) illustrates the three total cost curves (TFC, TVC, TC), and part (b) the three average cost curves (AFC, AVC, ATC) and the marginal cost (MC) curve.

In part (a):

- The TFC curve is parallel to the horizontal axis, as it represents a fixed amount of costs that do not change as output changes.
- The TVC curve shows that TVC increases as output increases. However, it does not increase at a constant rate; *this is due to the law of diminishing marginal returns*.
- The TC curve is the vertical sum of TFC and TVC, and so the vertical difference between TC and TVC is equal to TFC.

In part (b):

- The AFC curve indicates that AFC falls continuously as output increases, because it represents the amount of fixed costs (TFC) divided by an ever growing quantity of output.

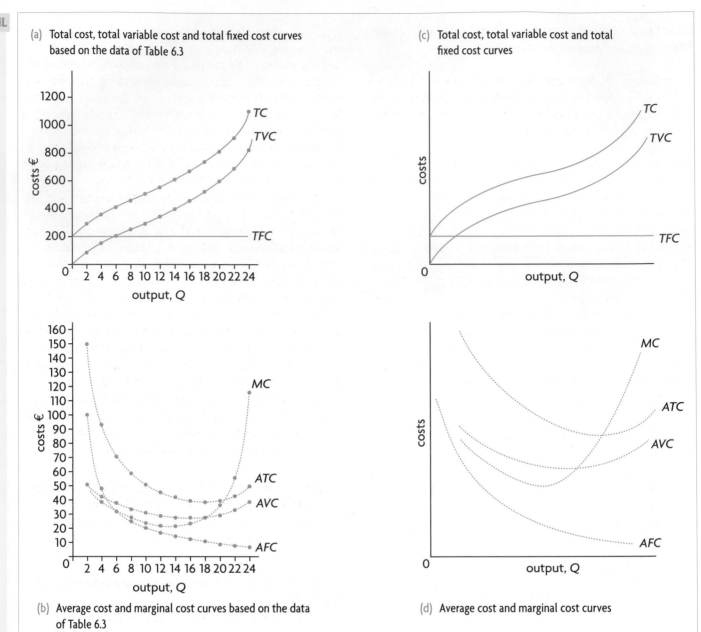

(a) Total cost, total variable cost and total fixed cost curves based on the data of Table 6.3

(b) Average cost and marginal cost curves based on the data of Table 6.3

(c) Total cost, total variable cost and total fixed cost curves

(d) Average cost and marginal cost curves

Figure 6.2 Total, average and marginal cost curves

- The three remaining curves, *AVC*, *ATC* and *MC*, though they are different from each other, all follow the same general pattern: at first they fall, they reach a minimum, and then they begin to rise.[2]

- The *ATC* curve is the vertical sum of *AFC* and *AVC*, and so the vertical difference between the *ATC* and the *AVC* curves at any level of output is equal to *AFC*.

- *The MC curve intersects both the AVC and ATC curves at their minimum points.* The reason is the same as in the case of marginal and average products, discussed on page 141 above (recall the example of

test scores, which applies equally well here). When marginal cost is below average variable cost ($MC < AVC$), average variable cost is falling; when marginal cost is above average variable cost ($MC > AVC$), then average variable cost is rising. The same applies to the relationship between marginal cost and average total cost: when $MC < ATC$, *ATC* is falling, and when $MC > ATC$, *ATC* is rising.

The U-shapes of the *AVC*, *ATC* and *MC* curves are due to the law of diminishing returns. We will discover why in the next section.

---

[2] The mathematically inclined student may note that marginal cost (*MC*) represents the slope of the total cost (*TC*) curve. (Again, as with MP and TP (page 141), the slope is interpreted in the mathematically correct way; see footnote 1.)

Relating the cost and product curves: the law of diminishing returns

♦ Explain the relationship between the product curves (average product and marginal product) and the cost curves (average variable cost and marginal cost), with reference to the law of diminishing returns.

The law of diminishing marginal returns is very important in determining the shape of the cost curves. Figure 6.3 shows that the product curves (*MP* and *AP*) are mirror images of the cost curves (*MC* and *AVC*). The *MC* curve mirrors the *MP* curve, and the *AVC* curve mirrors the *AP* curve. (Note the labelling of the axes of the product and cost curves, which are different from each other.) How can we explain this interesting pattern?

Remember that at low levels of output, the marginal product of labour increases, meaning that the extra output produced by each additional unit of labour rises. When this happens, the additional cost of one more unit of output, or marginal cost, falls.

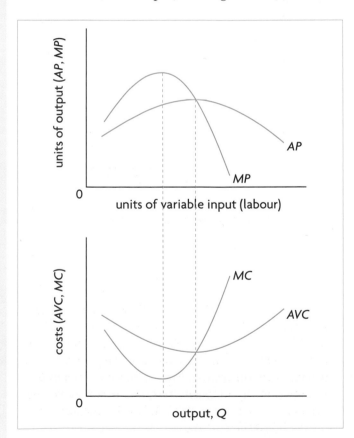

Figure 6.3 Product curves and cost curves are mirror images due to the law of diminishing returns

Decreasing marginal product, on the other hand, means that the additional output of each unit of labour is falling, and so the additional cost of each extra unit of output (marginal cost) must be increasing. In Table 6.1 we saw that maximum marginal product occurs when four units of labour are hired; this is also when marginal cost is minimum (see Table 6.3). In other words, *when the additional output produced by an extra worker is the most it can be, then the extra labour cost of producing an additional unit of output is the least it can be.*

The explanation for the shape of the average variable cost curve can also be found in the law of diminishing returns. When average product is increasing, this means that each additional unit of output can be produced with fewer and fewer units of labour; therefore, the labour cost of each unit of output (average variable cost) falls. But when average product is falling, additional units of output require more and more units of labour, and so the labour cost of each unit of output, or average variable cost, begins to increase.[3] Note from Table 6.1 that when five units of labour are hired, average product is maximum; this is the point of production where average variable cost is minimum (see Table 6.3). This happens because when workers on average produce the most they can produce, the labour cost of producing each unit of output is the lowest it can be.

> The U-shape of the *AVC*, *ATC* and *MC* curves is due to the law of diminishing returns. This law also explains why the *AVC* and *MC* curves are mirror images of the *AP* and *MP* curves.

Shifts in the cost curves (supplementary material)

The cost curves shift in response to two factors: changes in resource prices, or changes in technology. If resource prices increase, an increase in costs of production results. Which particular curves are affected depends on whether the price increases involve fixed or variable costs. If there is an increase in a fixed cost of production, this affects *TFC* and *TC*, as well as *AFC* and *ATC*, all of which shift upward. Variable costs and marginal cost remain unaffected. This is shown in Figure 6.4(a), where we see *AFC* and *ATC* curves shifting upward to the dotted lines, while *AVC* and *MC* remain unchanged. If, on the other hand, there is an increase in variable costs (say, because of an increase in wages), *TVC* and *TC*, as well as *AVC*, *ATC* and *MC*, will increase. This can be seen in Figure 6.4(b), where *AVC*, *ATC* and

[3] Another way to see this numerically is to consider the average product figures in Table 6.1. We know that each unit of labour costs €100, i.e. €100 = cost per unit of labour. If we divide 100 by average product, we have:

$$\frac{\text{cost per unit of labour}}{\text{output per unit of labour}} = \text{variable cost per unit of output,}$$

which is average variable cost. When the units of labour are few, AVC is high; as the labour units increase AVC falls, and after reaching a minimum, AVC begins to rise, thus resulting in the U-shaped curve.

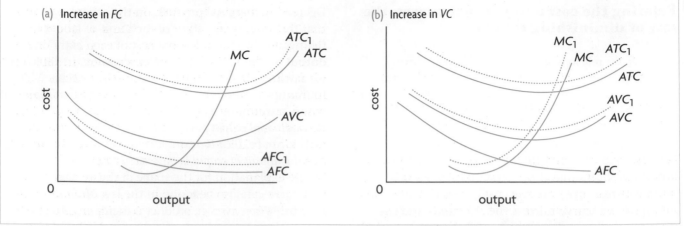

Figure 6.4 Shifts in the cost curves

MC have shifted upward to the dotted lines. If resource prices fall, leading to decreases in costs of production, the corresponding curves shift downward.

Changes in technology also impact upon costs of production because they increase the amount of output that can be produced by a given level of inputs. An improved technology would therefore shift the product curves of Figure 6.1 (*TP*, *AP* and *MP*) upwards, and this would correspond to a downward shift in the cost curves.

Calculating costs

♦ Calculate total fixed costs, total variable costs, total costs, average fixed costs, average variable costs, average total costs and marginal costs from a set of data and/or diagrams.

To calculate costs, it is only necessary to remember and understand the relationships between the various cost concepts we have studied above: $TC = TFC + TVC$; dividing through by Q we obtain average costs, where $ATC = AFC + AVC$. Finally, marginal cost is $\Delta TC/\Delta Q$, or $\Delta TVC/\Delta Q$. You will have several opportunities to calculate costs both in this chapter and the next.

To calculate costs from a diagram, we simply read off the information appearing in the graph, and apply the same principles as above to calculate the cost variable or variables we are interested in.

Test your understanding 6.4

1 For question 5 of Test your understanding 6.1, suppose that the price of labour is $2000 a month per worker and fixed costs are $1500 a month. Calculate *TFC*, *TVC*, *TC*, *AFC*, *AVC*, *ATC* and *MC* up to the point of maximum total product (61 units of output).

2 Using the data of question 1, **(a)** plot *TFC*, *TVC* and *TC*, and **(b)** in a different diagram plot *AFC*, *AVC*, *ATC* and *MC*.

3 Why does the average fixed cost curve decline continuously throughout its range?

4 What accounts for the U-shape of the average variable cost curve and the average total cost curve?

5 In your diagram for question 2(a), explain what is represented by (a) the vertical distance between the *TC* and *TFC* curves, and (b) the vertical distance between the *TC* and *TVC* curves.

6 In your diagram for question 2(b), explain what is represented by **(a)** the vertical distance between *ATC* and *AFC*, and **(b)** the vertical distance between *ATC* and *AVC*.

7 How does the law of diminishing marginal product affect the shape of the marginal cost curve?

8 Why does marginal cost intersect both average variable cost and average total cost at their minimum points?

9 Draw two diagrams showing the relationships between the *AP* and *MP* curves, and the *AVC* and *MC* curves. How are the product curves related to the cost curves? What accounts for this relationship?

10 (Optional) Using diagrams, show how **(a)** a fall in insurance premiums, and **(b)** a fall in wage rates would affect the positions of the *AFC*, *AVC*, *ATC* and *MC* curves of a firm.

6.4 Production and costs in the long run

Production in the long run: returns to scale

• Distinguish between increasing returns to scale, decreasing returns to scale and constant returns to scale.

Let's examine the long-run relationship between inputs and output. An important point to bear in mind is that in the long run, there are no fixed inputs. All inputs are variable. We are interested in seeing what happens to output when the firm changes *all of its inputs*. There are three possibilities, explained using the example in Table 6.4:

Constant returns to scale

Suppose a firm doubles all of its inputs. In Table 6.4, both land and labour double in quantity. With constant returns to scale, output also doubles. **Constant returns to scale** *means that output increases in the same proportion as all inputs: given a percentage change in all inputs, output increases by the same percentage.*

Increasing returns to scale

If a firm doubles all inputs and there are increasing returns to scale, output more than doubles. In the example, as land and labour double in quantity, the quantity of output increases from 100 to 250 units, which is more than double. **Increasing returns to scale** *means that output increases more than in proportion to the increase in all inputs: given a percentage increase in all inputs, output increases by a larger percentage.*

Decreasing returns to scale

If a firm doubles all its inputs and there are decreasing returns to scale, there results a less than double increase in output. In the example, land and labour have doubled in quantity, but output has increased only from 100 to 150 units. **Decreasing returns to scale** *means that output increases less than in proportion to the increase in all inputs: given a percentage increase in all inputs, output increases by a smaller percentage.*

It seems logical to think that if a firm doubles all its inputs, then output should also double; there should be constant returns to scale. Why does it happen that output can sometimes increase more than or less than in proportion to the increase in inputs? We will discover the answer when we consider costs of production in the long run below. For now, it is important that you do not confuse decreasing returns to scale, discussed here, with diminishing returns (page 142). Diminishing returns occur only in the short run, because they show *what happens to output as a variable input is added to a fixed input.* Decreasing returns to scale can occur only in the long run, showing *what happens to output when all inputs are variable.*

Costs of production in the long run

Long-run average total cost curve in relation to short-run average total cost curves

• Outline the relationship between short-run average costs and long-run average costs.

Remember that in the long run there are no fixed inputs and therefore no fixed costs; all inputs are variable. When a firm varies inputs that were fixed in the short run, it changes its size or scale.

It is convenient to think of the long run as the *firm's planning horizon.* If a firm wants to expand production, it must think in terms of increasing its fixed inputs, otherwise its production will run into diminishing returns. As the firm plans its future activities in the long run, it can select any size or scale of operation depending on the quantity of output it is aiming for. The particular size it selects will be the one that minimises costs for that level of output.

Let's consider our farmer who produces with two inputs, land and labour. The farmer wants to expand production and considers the long-run options. Suppose, too, that there are only four possible

Land (1st input)	Labour (2nd input)	Output with constant returns to scale	Output with increasing returns to scale	Output with decreasing returns to scale
1 acre	5 workers	100 units of output	100 units of output	100 units of output
2 acres	10 workers	200 units of output	250 units of output	150 units of output

Table 6.4   Constant, increasing and decreasing returns to scale

farm sizes. Each one is represented by a different short-run average total cost curve (*SRATC*), shown in Figure 6.5(a).

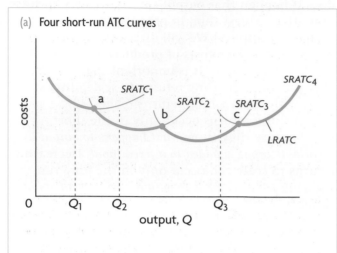

(a) Four short-run ATC curves

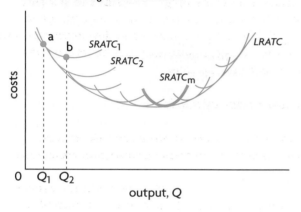

(b) Long-run average total cost curve in relation to short-run average total cost curves

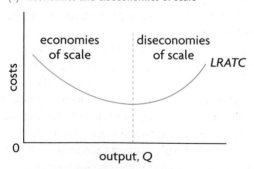

(c) Economies and diseconomies of scale

Figure 6.5 The long-run average total cost curve

Initially, the farmer produces output Q_1 on $SRATC_1$, but then decides to increase production. Which *SRATC* should the farmer select? The answer depends on how much output the farmer wants to produce, and which *SRATC* will minimise cost for that level of output. In the short run, it is possible to increase output to Q_2, without changing farm size, by remaining on $SRATC_1$. Yet a larger farm size, corresponding to $SRATC_2$, can produce output Q_2 at a lower average cost. In the short run, it is possible to produce at the lowest possible cost on $SRATC_1$ only up to point a; beyond this the farmer should consider increasing farm size (going into the long run) and moving onto $SRATC_2$. Once the farmer is on $SRATC_2$, output can increase at the lowest possible cost until point b is reached, where the farmer once again should consider increasing farm size (going into the long run again) and switching to $SRATC_3$. We can see then that points like a, b and c represent output levels at which the farmer should increase the farm size in order to continue to minimise average costs as output increases. It follows that *the farmer's planning horizon is made up of the bold-face portions of the short-run average cost curves in Figure 6.5(a),* connecting all possible points of intersection between *SRATC* curves.

In practice, it is likely that there will not only be four possible firm sizes as in our example, but many more, shown in Figure 6.5(b). In this case, the long-run average total curve is the curve that just touches (i.e. is tangent to) each of the short-run cost curves. **Long run average total costs** represent the lowest possible average cost, or cost per unit of output, for every level of output, when all resources are variable. When the firm plans its activities over the long run, it can choose where on the long-run curve it wishes to be; it will then end up on the *SRATC* curve at the point where this just touches the long-run curve (i.e. the point of tangency between the two).[4]

> The **long-run average total cost curve** (*LRATC*) is defined as a curve that shows the lowest possible average cost that can be attained by a firm for any level of output when all of the firm's inputs are variable. It is a curve that just touches (is tangent to) each of many short-run average total cost curves. It is also known as a planning curve.

---

[4] While a decision to produce a particular level of output in the long run involves selection of the firm scale that minimises costs for that level of output, the firm will not necessarily be operating at the lowest possible cost on the *SRATC* curve of its choice. In Figure 6.5(b), say a firm wants to produce output Q_1; it will then choose to be on $SRATC_1$ at point a, which is the point where $SRATC_1$ just touches the long-run curve, corresponding to output level Q_1. But the point of minimum average cost on $SRATC_1$ is point b, representing output Q_2, not point a. Therefore, minimum average cost in the short run is not necessarily the same as minimum average cost

in the long run. When the long-run curve is downward sloping, there will always be a larger firm size that can achieve lower average costs than the short-run minimum (i.e. $SRATC_2$ achieves lower average costs than point b on $SRATC_1$); and when the long-run curve is upward sloping, there will always be a smaller firm size that can achieve lower average costs than the short-run minimum. There is only one *SRATC* curve whose minimum coincides with the long-run minimum, and that is $SRATC_m$, shown in bold in Figure 6.5(b).

The shape of the *LRATC* curve: economies and diseconomies of scale

♦ Explain, using a diagram, the reason for the shape of the long-run average total cost curve.

As we can see in Figure 6.5 (b) and (c), the long-run average total cost curve (*LRATC*) has a U-shape.

The reasons for the U-shape of the long-run average total cost (*LRATC*) curve have nothing whatever to do with diminishing returns, which are a feature only of short-run production and costs. The U-shape of the *LRATC* curve can be found in economies and diseconomies of scale, in turn related to increasing and decreasing returns to scale.

Economies of scale

♦ Describe factors giving rise to economies of scale, including specialisation, efficiency, marketing and indivisibilities.

Economies of scale are decreases in the average costs of production over the long run as a firm increases all its inputs. Economies of scale explain the downward-sloping portion of the *LRATC* curve: as output increases, and a firm increases all inputs, average cost, or cost per unit of output, falls.

Falling average costs as output increases mean the firm is experiencing *increasing returns to scale* (page 151). To see this, consider that if input prices are constant and inputs double, this means that costs also double (since costs of inputs = price of inputs x quantity of inputs), but when there are increasing returns to scale, as inputs double, output will more than double. This means that costs per unit of output (or average costs) must be falling.[5]

There are several reasons why this can occur:

- **Specialisation of labour.** As the scale of production increases, more workers must be employed, allowing for greater labour **specialisation**. Each worker specialises in performing tasks that make use of skills, interests and talents, thus increasing efficiency and allowing output to be produced at a lower average cost.

- **Specialisation of management.** Larger scales of production allow for more managers to be employed, each of whom can be specialised in a particular area (such as production, sales, finance, and so on), again resulting in greater efficiency and lower average cost.

- **Efficiency of capital equipment.** Large machines are sometimes more efficient than smaller ones; for example, a large power generator is more efficient than a small one (it can produce more output per unit of inputs). However, a small firm with a small volume of output cannot make effective use of large machines, and so is forced to use smaller, less efficient ones.

- **Indivisibilities of capital equipment.** Some machines are only available in large sizes that require large volumes of output in order to be used effectively. They cannot be divided up into smaller pieces of equipment.

- **Indivisibilities of efficient processes.** Some production processes, such as mass production assembly lines, require large volumes of output in order to be used efficiently. Even if all inputs are used in proportionately smaller quantities, it may not be possible to achieve the same degree of efficiency.

- **Spreading of certain costs, such as marketing, over larger volumes of output.** Costs of certain activities such as marketing and advertising, design, research and development result in lower average costs if they can be spread over large volumes of output.

Diseconomies of scale

♦ Describe factors giving rise to diseconomies of scale, including problems of co-ordination and communication.

Diseconomies of scale are increases in the average costs of production as a firm increases its output by increasing all its inputs. Diseconomies of scale are responsible for the upward-sloping part of the *LRATC* curve: as a firm increases its scale of production, costs per unit of output increase.

Increasing average costs as output increases mean that the firm is experiencing decreasing returns to scale (page 151). If input prices are constant, and inputs double, costs also double (again, costs of inputs = price of inputs x quantity of inputs), but when inputs double, the increase in output will be less than double when there are decreasing returns to scale. This means that costs per unit of output (or average costs) must be increasing.

Reasons for diseconomies of scale can include the following:

- **Co-ordination and monitoring difficulties.** As a firm grows larger and larger, there may come a point where its management runs into difficulties

---

[5] It may be noted that economies of scale actually have a broader meaning than increasing returns to scale. The reason is that in returns to scale, input proportions are fixed, whereas in economies of scale it is possible to have varying input proportions.

of co-ordination, organisation, co-operation and monitoring. The result involves growing inefficiencies causing average costs to increase as the firm expands.

- **Communication difficulties.** A larger firm size may lead to difficulties in communication between various component parts of the firm, again resulting in inefficiencies and higher average costs.
- **Poor worker motivation.** If workers begin to lose their motivation, to feel bored and to care little about their work, they become less efficient, with the result that costs per unit of output start to increase.

Constant returns to scale

Constant returns to scale may appear in some long-run average total cost curves as in Figure 6.6(a), where there is a horizontal segment of the curve between the

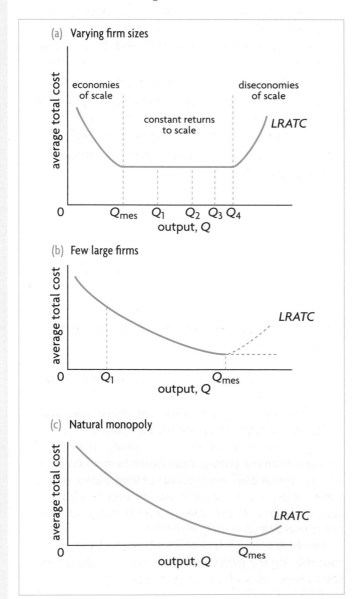

Figure 6.6 Minimum efficient scale and the structure of industries

downward-sloping and the upward-sloping portions. Constant returns to scale involve constant long-run average costs over a certain range of output. In this range, as output increases (with all inputs increasing), average costs do not change, i.e. the firm does not encounter economies or diseconomies of scale.

Firms are generally eager to take advantage of economies of scale, and try to avoid diseconomies of scale. Empirical studies agree that firms can achieve substantial economies of scale by increasing their size, but there is some debate over whether firms experience diseconomies. *Some studies suggest that after exhausting economies of scale, many firms exhibit constant returns to scale, and do not run into diseconomies of scale even as size becomes very large.*

Real world focus

Economies of scale in the tourism industry

Travelplanet.pl and Invia are two Polish online tourism companies that are planning to merge. A merger takes place when two (or more) companies join together and form a single company. The aim of the merger is to obtain economies of scale through their co-operative interactions. The merger will result in the biggest online tourism company in Central Eastern Europe.

Source: Adapted from 'Travelplanet.pl closer to merging with Invia' in *Polish News Bulletin*, 1 April 2010.

Applying your skills

1 Using a diagram, show how a merger of two companies can result in economies of scale.

2 Explain the possible sources of economies of scale arising from the merger.

The minimum efficient scale and the structure of industries (supplementary material)

There is a point on the long-run average total cost curve that represents the lowest level of output at which the lowest long-run total average costs are achieved, called the *minimum efficient scale (MES)*. In Figure 6.6 this is represented by Q_{mes}. The minimum efficient scale is the level of output at which economies of scale are exhausted; beyond that level of output average costs will either be constant or they will begin to increase. When there are constant returns to scale, the minimum efficient scale can be achieved by firms of varying sizes, producing any output ranging from Q_{mes} to Q_4 in Figure 6.6(a).

The importance of the concept of minimum efficient scale lies in the information it can reveal about the structure of industries, such as whether it is likely that an industry will consist of many firms, some of which are smaller and some larger, as opposed to a small number of large firms, or at the extreme a single very large firm providing for the entire market. Each of these possibilities is illustrated in Figure 6.6.

The *LRATC* curve in Figure 6.6(a) indicates that the firm reaches the minimum efficient scale at a low level of output, shown as Q_{mes}, and then begins to experience constant returns to scale. If this level of output, Q_{mes}, is a small fraction of the total market, then there are likely to be many firms of varying sizes in the industry; examples include clothing and shoe manufacturing, other light manufacturing such as furniture and wood products, food processing, retailing and banking. These tend to be industries that fall under the market structure of monopolistic competition (see Chapter 7, page 195).

Figure 6.6(b) shows the *LRATC* curve of a firm that experiences economies of scale over a very large range of output. It is only at the very large level of output of Q_{mes} that the minimum efficient scale is achieved, at which point the firm runs into either diseconomies of scale or constant returns to scale (shown by the dotted lines). Here, Q_{mes} represents a large fraction of the market. This means that there can only be a small number of large firms in this industry. If smaller firms tried to enter this industry, they would have difficulty competing with the larger firms because of their higher average costs. (Compare the average total costs of a firm producing output Q_1 with the average costs of a firm producing at Q_{mes}.) Examples of such industries include car and refrigerator manufacturers, heavy industries such as aluminium and steel, and pharmaceutical industries. These tend to be industries that fall under the market structure of oligopoly (see Chapter 7, page 201).

In Figure 6.6(c), the minimum efficient scale occurs at a level of output, Q_{mes}, so large that if the firm expands to that point where it exhausts all economies of scale, it will be supplying the entire market. Such a firm is called a natural monopoly (see Chapter 7, page 187).

(It may be noted that the U-shaped long-run average total cost curve does not cover firms under perfect competition (see page 168). This is because firms under perfect competition do not experience economies and diseconomies of scale, as we will see in Chapter 7.)

> **Test your understanding 6.5**
>
> 1 Using a numerical example, distinguish between increasing, constant and decreasing returns to scale.
>
> 2 **(a)** Define the long-run average total cost (*LRATC*) curve. **(b)** Why do you think this curve is also referred to as a 'planning curve'? **(c)** How is the *LRATC* curve related to short-run average cost curves?
>
> 3 Describe some factors that can cause **(a)** economies of scale, and **(b)** diseconomies of scale.
>
> 4 **(a)** Using a diagram, show the relationship between economies and diseconomies of scale and the shape of the *LRATC*. **(b)** What do constant returns to scale signify?
>
> 5 What is the relationship between **(a)** increasing returns to scale and economies of scale, and **(b)** decreasing returns to scale and diseconomies of scale?
>
> 6 If, as many economists suggest, a firm is unlikely to run into diseconomies of scale after achieving all possible economies of scale, what would its long-run average total cost curve look like?
>
> 7 (Optional) Explain the concept of minimum efficient scale.

6.5 Revenues

Total revenue, marginal revenue and average revenue

Distinguishing between total, marginal and average revenue

♦ Distinguish between total revenue, average revenue and marginal revenue.
♦ Illustrate, using diagrams, the relationship between total revenue, average revenue and marginal revenue.

Revenues are the payments firms receive when they sell the goods and services they produce over a given time period. We make a distinction between three fundamental revenue concepts: total, marginal and average revenue.

The firm's **total revenue** (*TR*) is obtained by multiplying the price at which a good is sold (*P*) by the number of units of the good sold (*Q*):

$$TR = P \times Q$$

The firm's **marginal revenue** (MR) is the additional revenue arising from the sale of an additional unit of output:[6]

$$MR = \frac{\Delta TR}{\Delta Q}$$

The firm's **average revenue** (AR) is revenue per unit of output sold:

$$AR = \frac{TR}{Q}$$

Note that *AR is always equal to P*, or the price of the product. The reason is that since $AR = \dfrac{TR}{Q}$, it follows that $TR = AR \times Q$, but since $TR = P \times Q$, this means that $AR = P$.

Whereas the *definitions* of revenues given above apply to all firms, the *analysis* of revenues is not the same for all firms, because this depends on whether or not the firm has any control over the price at which it sells its product. In Chapter 2, page 20, it was noted that firms under highly competitive conditions have no ability to influence price. Firms operating under less competitive conditions do have varying degrees of control over price, depending on their degree of market power (see page 20 for a review of these concepts). We will study these differences under the topics of market structures in Chapter 7. For now, we will make a distinction between situations where:

- the firm has no control over price, and price is constant as output varies
- the firm has some degree of control over price, and price varies with output.

Revenue curves where the firm has no control over price

Table 6.5 shows how we calculate total, marginal and average revenue from information on the price and quantity of the good in situations where a firm has no control over price. Columns 3, 4 and 5 are calculated from the information in columns 1 and 2, using the definitions of total, marginal and average revenue given above. Note that *the price at which the good is sold does not change*; this occurs only under perfect competition, where the firm has no control over the price at which it sells its product. Figure 6.7 plots the data of Table 6.5. We will examine these revenue curves, their meaning and implications in detail in Chapter 7, page 169.

(1) Units of output (Q)	(2) Product price (P) (€)	(3) Total revenue TR = P×Q (€)	(4) Marginal revenue $MR = \dfrac{\Delta TR}{\Delta Q}$ (€)	(5) Average revenue $MR = \dfrac{TR}{Q}$ (€)
0	10	-	-	-
1	10	10	10	10
2	10	20	10	10
3	10	30	10	10
4	10	40	10	10
5	10	50	10	10
6	10	60	10	10
7	10	70	10	10

Table 6.5 Calculating total, marginal and average revenue when price is constant (the firm has no control over price)

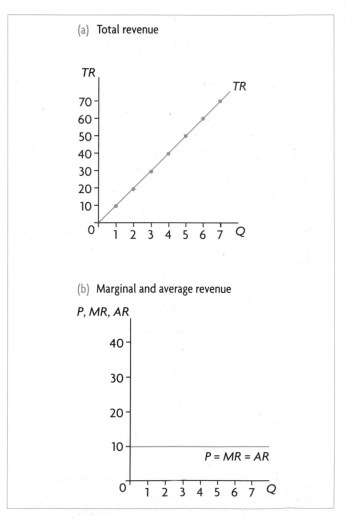

Figure 6.7 Total, marginal and average revenue curves when price is constant (the firm has no control over price)

---

[6] The mathematically inclined student will note that MR is the slope of the TR curve (where slope is interpreted in the mathematically correct way; see footnotes 1 and 2).

(1) Units of output (Q)	(2) Product price (P) (€)	(3) Total revenue (TR = Q×P) (€)	(4) Marginal revenue $MR = \dfrac{\Delta TR}{\Delta Q}$ (€)	(5) Average revenue $AR = \dfrac{TR}{Q}$ (€)
0	–	–	–	–
1	12	12	12	12
2	11	22	10	11
3	10	30	8	10
4	9	36	6	9
5	8	40	4	8
6	7	42	2	7
7	6	42	0	6
8	5	40	−2	5
9	4	36	−4	4
10	3	30	−6	3

Table 6.6 Calculating total, marginal and average revenue when price varies (the firm has some control over price)

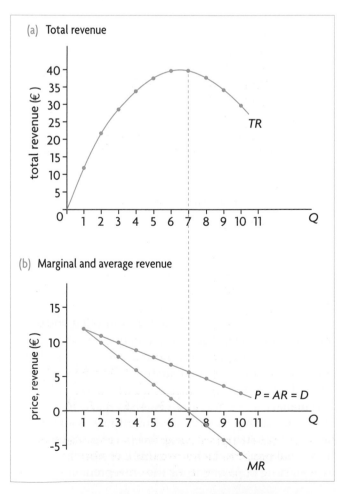

Figure 6.8 Total, marginal and average revenue curves when price varies (the firm has some control over price)

Revenue curves where the firm has some control over price

Table 6.6 shows how we calculate total, marginal and revenue from price and quantity information in the case where the firm has some control over price. The method of calculation is exactly the same as in the competitive case above, where columns 3–5 are calculated using the information of the first two columns. The difference is in the price data, appearing in column 2, showing that *the price at which the good is sold changes as the quantity of output changes*. This occurs under all market models that we will study in Chapter 7 other than perfect competition. Figure 6.8 plots the data of Table 6.6. These revenue curves, their meaning and implications will be examined in detail in Chapter 7, page 184.

Calculating revenues

♦ Calculate total revenue, average revenue and marginal revenue from a set of data and/or diagrams.

To calculate revenues, it is only necessary to remember and understand the relationships between the various revenue concepts, beginning with the idea that $TR = P \times Q$. If you are given data on P and Q, you can find TR, and from there you can calculate $AR = \dfrac{TR}{Q}$ and $MR = \dfrac{\Delta TR}{\Delta Q}$. You can also work backwards to find TR and MR if you know AR and Q, or to find TR and AR if you know MR and Q. Remember also that $AR = P$ in all cases, so that if you know AR, you also know the price of the product.

To calculate revenues from a diagram, we simply read off the information appearing in the graph, and apply exactly the same principles as above to calculate the revenue variable or variables we are interested in.

Test your understanding 6.6

1 Define **(a)** total revenue, **(b)** marginal revenue, and **(c)** average revenue.

2 Given the following price and quantity data for a product, calculate total revenue, marginal revenue and average revenue.

Price ($)	5	5	5	5	5
Quantity (thousand units)	0	1	2	3	4

3 Plot the data for total, marginal and average revenue you calculated in question 2.

4 Given the following price and quantity data for a product, calculate total revenue, marginal revenue and average revenue.

Price ($)	8	7	6	5	4	3	2
Quantity (thousand units)	2	3	4	5	6	7	8

5 Plot the data for total, marginal and average revenue you calculated in question 4.

6 **(a)** Explain why the shapes of the curves for total, marginal and average revenue you graphed for question 3 differ from those of question 5. **(b)** What can you conclude about how price changes (or does not change) for each unit of output sold in questions 3 and 5? **(c)** What is the relationship between price and average revenue?

7 Given the following data, calculate total revenue and marginal revenue for each level of output. What is the price at each level of output?

Quantity (thousand units)	1	2	3	4	5	6
Average revenue €	20	18	16	14	12	10

8 Given the following data, calculate total revenue and average revenue for each level of output. What is the price at each level of output?

Quantity (thousand units)	1	2	3	4	5	6
Marginal revenue (£)	14	12	10	8	6	4

6.6 Profit

Distinguishing between economic and normal profit

Economic profit

♦ Describe economic profit as the case where total revenue exceeds economic cost.[7]

In a general sense, profit equals total revenue minus total costs. The precise meaning of the term 'profit' in this expression depends on the meaning of 'costs'. Earlier in

this chapter (page 144) we made a distinction between explicit costs, implicit costs and economic costs or total opportunity costs (the sum of explicit plus implicit costs). In economics, economic profit is defined as:

economic profit = total revenue − economic costs
= total revenue − the sum of explicit costs + implicit costs

In economics, even when we use the term 'profit' on its own, we mean 'economic profit', indicating that we have taken all costs (explicit plus implicit) into consideration.

Normal profit

♦ Describe normal profit as the amount of revenue needed to cover the costs of employing self-owned resources (implicit costs, including entrepreneurship) or the amount of revenue needed to just keep the firm in business.

When economic profit is equal to zero, and total revenue is equal to total economic costs, the firm is said to be making normal profit.

Normal profit can be defined as the minimum amount of revenue that the firm must receive so that it will keep the business running (as opposed to shutting down). It can also be defined as the amount of revenue that covers all implicit costs (including the payment for entrepreneurship, which is itself an implicit cost). This presupposes that total revenues are just enough to cover both explicit and implicit costs. Therefore, a firm earns normal profit when total revenue = economic costs, and economic profit = zero. This is called the break-even point of the firm.

These apparently different definitions are in fact consistent: the minimum amount of revenue the firm must receive to make it worthwhile to stay in business and keep all its resources employed in the firm is equal to the revenue that covers the firm's implicit costs, after revenues have also covered explicit costs.

It should be stressed that normal profit also includes the payment for entrepreneurship. Entrepreneurship, you will remember, includes the talents to organise and manage a business and take risks (page 4). Entrepreneurship receives a payment just as all other factors of production do, and this payment is included in normal profit. In fact, if we think of normal profit as consisting of payment for the entrepreneur's

---

[7] 'Economic profit' in this learning outcome actually refers to *positive* economic profit as opposed to *negative* economic profit (i.e. a loss).

entrepreneurial and risk-taking functions, as well as the opportunity costs of employing self-owned resources, we can see that normal profit is not 'profit' in the customary sense, but is actually a cost of production.

Why a firm continues to operate even when earning zero economic profit

- Explain why a firm will continue to operate even when it earns zero economic profit.

It was noted above that the firm earns normal profit when economic profit is zero, meaning that total revenue is just equal to total economic costs. It follows that when we say a firm is 'earning normal profit', the firm is earning just the necessary revenues to cover payment for entrepreneurship (a cost) and all other implicit costs of self-owned resources, after revenues have also covered explicit costs. Therefore, when a firm is earning normal profit, it has covered all its opportunity costs, and will continue to operate.

Positive and negative economic profit

- Explain that economic profit is profit over and above normal profit, and that the firm earns normal profit when economic profit is zero.[8]
- Explain the meaning of loss as negative economic profit arising when total revenue is less than total cost.

Economic profit can be positive, zero or negative. Positive economic profit is also known as **supernormal profit**, or **abnormal profit**, because it involves profit over and above normal profit. If economic profit is zero, the firm is earning normal profit. And if economic profit is negative, the firm is making a loss. To summarise:

> Economic profit can be positive, zero or negative.
>
> Positive economic profit: $TR >$ economic cost; the firm earns supernormal profit (or abnormal profit).
>
> Zero economic profit: $TR =$ economic cost; the firm earns normal profit.
>
> Negative economic profit: $TR <$ economic cost; the firm makes a **loss**.

We can see these relationships in Figure 6.9. In Figure 6.9(a) the firm's total revenue is £180 000. Implicit costs = £109 000, explicit costs = £50 000, and the sum is economic costs of £159 000. Economic profit is therefore £21 000 (= £180 000 − £159 000).

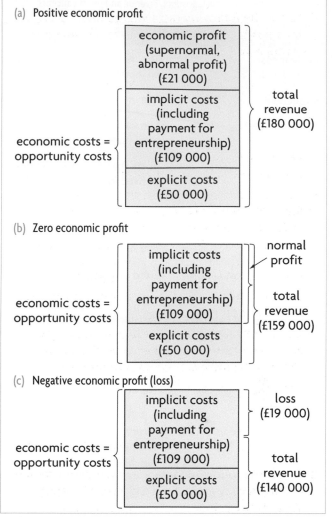

Figure 6.9 Illustrating economic profit (positive and negative) and normal profit

Figure 6.9(b) shows a firm making zero economic profit. The firm's total revenue has fallen to £159 000, which is equal to its economic costs; therefore, the firm is earning normal profit. The firm in this situation will not shut down even though it is earning zero economic profit, because it is earning normal profit; its revenue is enough to cover all opportunity costs (including entrepreneurship).

In Figure 6.9(c) the firm is earning negative economic profit (loss). Total revenue has fallen to £140 000, of which £50 000 is used to cover explicit costs, and there are £90 000 left over to go toward covering implicit costs. However, this is not enough, as implicit costs are £109 000. Therefore, the firm is making an economic loss of £19 000, and will shut down (go out of business) as soon as it is able to do so (we will see how in Chapter 7).

Table 6.7 summarises the cost, product, revenue and profit concepts we have studied.

---

[8] Profit over and above normal profit is *positive* economic profit, since negative economic profit refers to loss. See also footnote 7.

Table 6.7   Summary of cost, product, revenue and profit concepts

Cost concepts	Definition	Equation
Explicit cost	The monetary payment made by a firm to an outsider to acquire an input.	
Implicit cost	The income sacrificed by a firm that uses a resource it owns.	
Economic cost	The sum of explicit and implicit costs, also equal to the firm's total opportunity costs.	
Total fixed cost (TFC)	Costs that do not change as output changes; arise from the use of fixed inputs.	
Total variable cost (TVC)	Costs that vary (change) as output changes; arise from the use of variable inputs.	
Total cost (TC)	The sum of fixed and variable costs.	$TC = TFC + TVC$
Average fixed cost (AFC)	Fixed cost per unit of output.	$AFC = \dfrac{TFC}{Q}$
Average variable cost (AVC)	Variable cost per unit of output.	$AVC = \dfrac{TVC}{Q}$
Average total cost (ATC)	Total cost per unit of output.	$ATC = AFC + AVC$
Marginal cost (MC)	The change in cost arising from one additional unit of output.	$MC = \dfrac{\Delta TC}{\Delta Q} = \dfrac{\Delta TVC}{\Delta Q}$
Long-run average total cost (LRATC) curve	A curve showing the lowest possible average cost that can be attained for any level of output when all of the firm's inputs are variable.	
Product concepts		
Total product (TP or Q)	The total amount of product (output) produced by a firm.	
Marginal product (MP)	The additional product produced by one additional unit of variable input.	$MP = \dfrac{\Delta TP}{\Delta \text{ units of variable input}}$
Average product (AP)	Product per unit of variable input.	$AP = \dfrac{TP}{\text{units of variable input}}$
Revenue concepts		
Total revenue	The total earnings of a firm from the sale of its output.	$TR = P \times Q$
Marginal revenue	The additional revenue of a firm arising from the sale of an additional unit of output.	$MR = \dfrac{\Delta TR}{\Delta Q}$
Average revenue	Revenue per unit of output.	$AR = \dfrac{TR}{Q}$
Profit concepts		
Economic profit	Total revenue minus economic costs (or total opportunity costs, or the sum of explicit plus implicit costs).	
Normal profit	The minimum amount of revenue required by a firm so that it will be induced to keep running, which is that part of revenue that covers implicit costs, including entrepreneurship (after all explicit costs have been covered).	

1 Define economic profit and normal profit, and explain the difference between them.

2 Why do you think positive economic profit is also called 'supernormal' profit or 'abnormal' profit?

3 What is the relationship between earning normal profit and the break-even point of a firm?

4 Explain why economic profit can be positive, zero or negative.

5 A firm earns zero economic profit, and yet it does not shut down. Explain why.

6 A firm had implicit costs of $35 000 per year and explicit costs of $75 000 per year, which remained constant for each year between 2009 and 2011. In 2009 its total revenues were $150 000, in 2010 they were $110 000, and in 2011 they were $95 000. **(a)** In which year did the firm earn normal profit? **(b)** In which year did the firm consider shutting down? Why? **(c)** In which year did the firm earn supernormal profit? How much supernormal profit did it earn? **(d)** How much economic profit did it make each year (remember, economic profit may be positive, zero or negative). **(e)** What was the break-even point of the firm?

6.7 Goals of firms

Profit maximisation

- Explain the goal of profit maximisation where the difference between total revenue and total cost is maximised or where marginal revenue equals marginal cost.
- Calculate different profit levels from a set of data and/or diagrams.

Standard economic theory of the firm assumes that firm behaviour is guided by the firm's goal to maximise profit. **Profit maximisation** involves determining the level of output that the firm should produce to make profit as large as possible.

Yet firms do not always make a profit; in some cases their total revenue is not sufficient to cover all costs, in which case they make a loss. If a firm is making a loss, it may eventually go out of business,

but until it decides to shut down, it will be interested in producing the quantity of output that will make its loss as small as possible. Therefore, the theory of the firm is also concerned with how much output a loss-making firm should produce in order to minimise its loss.

There are two approaches to analysing profit maximisation (or loss minimisation): one involves use of the total revenue and total cost concepts, and the other involves use of marginal revenues and costs. Both these approaches yield the same results for the profit-maximising (or loss-minimising) level of output, though the second approach is more relevant to analysing market structures (as we will see in Chapter 7).

Profit maximisation based on the total revenue and cost approach

This approach is based on the simple principle that

$$\text{profit} = \text{total revenue } (TR) - \text{total cost } (TC)$$

where profit refers to economic profit and TC is the firm's *economic or opportunity costs* (explicit plus implicit costs).

> The firm's profit-maximisation rule is to produce the level of output where $TR - TC$ (= economic profit) is as large as possible.

The amount of profit made by the firm is equal to the numerical difference between TR and TC. If this difference is positive, the firm is making a profit (supernormal profit); if it is negative, the firm is making a loss; if it is zero, the firm is earning normal profit.

Calculating different profit levels

We can see how economic profit is calculated based on the total revenue and total cost approach using the information in Figure 6.9. In part (a), $TR > TC$, and the firm makes an economic profit of £21 000 (= $TR - TC$). In part (b), $TR = TC$, therefore the firm is making zero economic profit, though it is earning normal profit which allows it to stay in business. In part (c), $TR < TC$, and so the firm is making a loss of £19 000 (= $TR - TC = -£19 000$), and will eventually go out of business.

Figure 6.10 puts together TR and TC curves we have already studied. It shows the total revenue curve of a firm with no ability to influence price (as in Figure 6.7), and a total cost curve (as in Figure 6.2(c)). In part (a), we look at levels of output where TR lies above TC, and find the Q where the difference

(a) Profit-maximising firm produces at Q_2 and makes economic profit: $TR - TC = c - d$

(b) Profit-maximising firm produces at Q_2 and makes zero economic profit: $TR - TC = 0$ (it earns normal profit)

(c) The loss-minimising firm produces at Q_2 (if it produces) and makes a loss = $TC - TR = a - b$ (negative economic profit since $TR < TC$)

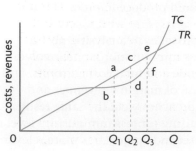

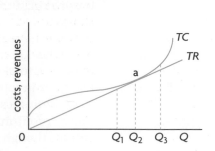

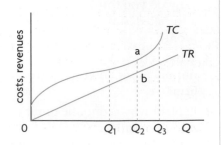

Figure 6.10 Profit maximisation using the total revenue and total cost approach when the firm has no control over price

between TR and TC is largest. This occurs at Q_2, where profit is the vertical distance between points c and d. (You can see that profit levels a–b and e–f are smaller). In part (b), the firm produces at Q_2 where $TR = TC$, indicating zero economic profit (the firm earns normal profit). At all other levels of output, $TC > TR$. In part (c) there is no Q where $TR > TC$, therefore we look for the Q where the difference between TC and TR is smallest. This is at Q_2, where the firm makes a loss (negative economic profit) of a–b.

Figure 6.11 illustrates the case of a firm that does have control over price, showing its total revenue curve (as in Figure 6.8(a)), together with a total cost curve (as in Figure 6.2(c)). The method of finding the firm's maximum profit is exactly the same as above. We look for the level of output where the

difference between total revenue and total cost is largest. Part (a) shows the case of a profit-making firm; profit is maximised at output level $Q_{\pi max}$. At points a and b where the TC curve intersects the TR curve, economic profit is zero (the firm would be earning normal profit). In part (b) there is no level of output where $TR > TC$; therefore, this firm can only make a loss. Loss is minimum at output level Q_{lmin}.

In the event that you are asked to find the profit-maximising level of output and the amount of profit (or loss) made by a firm based on data on total costs and revenues, you must first calculate the amount of profit (or loss) that results at each level of output (using the profit = $TR - TC$ principle), and then determine which profit level is largest or which

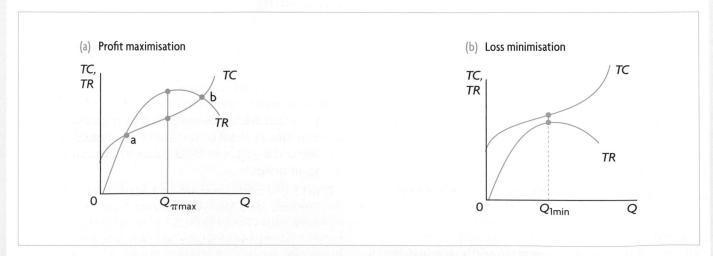

Figure 6.11 Profit maximisation using the total revenue and total cost approach when the firm has control over price

loss level is smallest. The corresponding output will be the profit-maximising or loss-minimising one. You will be given the opportunity to perform such calculations in Test your understanding 6.8.

Profit maximisation based on the marginal revenue and cost approach

Profit maximisation using this approach is based on a comparison of marginal revenue (MR) with marginal cost (MC) to determine the profit-maximising level of output.

> The firm's profit-maximisation rule is to choose to produce the level of output where $MC = MR$. The same rule is used by the firm that is interested in minimising its loss.

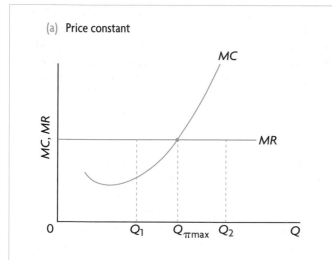

(a) Price constant

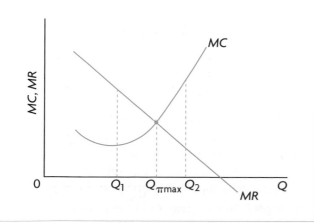

(b) Price varies with output

Figure 6.12 Profit maximisation using the marginal revenue and marginal cost approach

In Figure 6.12, both parts (a) and (b) show the standard MC curve that we studied earlier (page 148). There are two kinds of marginal revenue curves, depending on whether or not the firm has control over the price of its output (pages 156–7). Part (a) shows the MR curve of the firm with no control over price. Part (b) shows the MR curve of the firm with some control over price. Both parts (a) and (b) illustrate the identical principle about profit maximisation.

According to the profit-maximising rule, $MC = MR$, the point of intersection between the MC and MR curves determines the profit-maximising level of output; this is $Q_\pi$max in Figure 6.12 (a) and (b). Why is this so? Consider a firm producing output Q_1 in both parts (a) and (b), where $MR > MC$. If this firm increases its output by one unit, the additional revenue it would receive (MR) will be greater than its additional cost (MC). It is therefore in the firm's interests to increase its level of output until it reaches $Q_{\pi max}$ where $MR = MC$. If it continues to increase output beyond $Q_{\pi max}$, say to Q_2, where $MR < MC$, the additional revenue it would receive for an extra unit of output is less than the additional cost, and so it should cut back on its Q. There is only one point where the firm can do nothing to improve its position, and that is $Q_{\pi max}$, where $MR = MC$, and profit is the greatest it can be.

When we are given data for MC and MR (and no information on total costs and total revenues), all we can do is find the profit-maximising level of output (where $MC = MR$), but we cannot find the amount of profit (or loss) unless we have more information. We will see how this is done in Chapter 7. You will be given the opportunity to find the profit-maximising level of output using the $MC = MR$ rule in the exercises below.

Test your understanding 6.8

1 **(a)** What are the two approaches to profit maximisation by firms? **(b)** What is the profit-maximising rule of firms in each of the two approaches?

2 **(a)** Say a firm is producing a level of output Q where $MC > MR$. What should it do to increase its profit (or reduce its loss)? **(b)** If it is producing Q where $MC < MR$, what should it do?

3 Assume that a firm that has no control over its price sells its output at $5 per unit. **(a)** Given the following data, use the total revenue and total cost approach to determine the level of output at which the firm will maximise profit. **(b)** How much profit will it make? **(c)** Graph *TR* and *TC* and find the profit-maximising *Q* and profit on your graph; do they match your calculations? **(d)** Calculate the amount of profit (or loss) when $Q = 3$, $Q = 6$, $Q = 10$ and find these on your graph. Do your results match?

Units of output (Q)	1	2	3	4	5	6	7	8	9	10
Total cost ($)	15	18	20	21	23	26	30	35	41	48

4 Given the data in question 3, **(a)** determine the level of output at which the firm will maximise profit using the marginal revenue (*MR*) and marginal cost (*MC*) approach. (*Hint:* you must use the information in the question to find *MR* and *MC*.) **(b)** Graph the resulting *MR* and *MC* curves. **(c)** Did you find the same profit-maximising level of output as in question 3?*

5 Suppose that a firm with some control over price faces the costs and prices per unit of output shown in the table below. **(a)** Use the total revenue and total cost approach to determine the level of output at which the firm will maximise profit. **(b)** How much profit will it make? **(c)** Graph *TR* and *TC* and find the profit-maximising *Q* and profit on your graph; do they match your calculations? **(d)** Calculate the amount of profit (or loss) when $Q = 2$, $Q = 3$, $Q = 8$ and find these on your graph. Do your results match your calculations?

Units of output (Q)	1	2	3	4	5	6	7	8
Total cost ($)	15	18	20	21	23	26	30	35
Price ($)	10	9	8	7	6	5	4	3

6 Given the data in question 5, **(a)** determine the level of output at which the firm will maximise profit using the marginal revenue (*MR*) and marginal cost (*MC*) approach. (*Hint:* you must use the information in the question to find *MR* and *MC*.) **(b)** Graph the resulting *MR* and *MC* curves. **(c)** Did you find the same profit-maximising level of output as in question 5?*

---

* When using the *TR* and *TC* approach your results give two profit-maximising levels of output, whereas the *MR* and *MC* approach gives only one. This is because the *MR* and *MC* approach is actually more precise than the *TR* and *TC* approach. It is good idea to use the larger of the two values of output that you get by using the *TR* and *TC* approach.

Additional goals of firms

♦ Describe alternative goals of firms, including revenue maximisation, growth maximisation, satisficing and corporate social responsibility.

Over the years, economists have developed many theories about firm behaviour. The following is a brief survey of some of the more important ones.

Revenue maximisation

In one theory of firm behaviour, it is argued that the separation of firm management from firm ownership, which increasingly dominates business organisation, has meant that firms' objectives have changed. Whereas profit maximisation may be the dominant motive of the traditional owner-managed firm, firm managers who are hired by the owners to perform management tasks may be more interested in increasing sales and maximising the revenues that arise from larger quantities sold. This goal of firms is referred to as **revenue maximisation**.[9] Increasing sales and maximising revenues may be more useful to a firm than profit maximisation for the following reasons:

- Sales can be identified and measured more easily over the short run than profits, and increased sales targets can be used to motivate employees.

- Rewards for managers and employees are often linked to increased sales rather than increased profits.

- It is often assumed that revenue from more sales will increase more rapidly than costs; if this is the case, profit ($= TR - TC$) will also increase.

- Increased sales give rise to a feeling of success, whereas declining sales create a feeling of failure.

Growth maximisation

In other approaches it is assumed that firms may be interested in maximising their growth rather than their profits.[10] **Growth maximisation** can be attractive for the following reasons:

- A growing firm can achieve economies of scale and lower its average costs.

- As a firm grows it can diversify into production of different products and markets and reduce its dependence on a single product or market.

- A larger firm has greater market power and increased ability to influence prices.

---

[9] The revenue-maximisation goal of firms was described by W. J. Baumol in 1959.

[10] This is based on the work of R. Marris and others.

- A larger firm reduces its risks because it may be less affected in an economic downturn and is less likely to be taken over (bought) by another firm.
- The objective of growth maximisation reconciles the interests of both owners and managers, because both groups have much to gain from a growing firm (other maximisation objectives pit firm owners against firm managers; for example, profit maximisation is favoured by owners while revenue maximisation is favoured by managers).

Managerial utility maximisation

In this view, when firm management is separated from firm ownership, managers develop their own objectives that revolve around the maximisation of their own utility (satisfaction).[11] Managerial utility can be derived from increased salaries, larger fringe benefits (such as company cars and expense accounts), employment of more staff that gives rise to a feeling of importance, and investments in the managers' favourite projects. The result of all these activities may be to cut into profits and make these lower than they would otherwise be.

Satisficing

All of the above objectives assume that the firm tries to maximise some variable, whether it is profit, revenue, growth or managerial utility. H. Simon, a Nobel Prize-winning economist, has argued that the large modern enterprise cannot be looked upon as a single entity with a single maximising objective; instead it is composed of many separate groups within the firm, each with its own objectives which may overlap or may conflict. This multiplicity of objectives does not allow the firm to pursue any kind of maximising behaviour. Firms therefore try to establish processes through which they can make compromises and reconcile conflicts to arrive at agreements, the result of which is the pursuit of many objectives that are placed in a hierarchy. This behaviour was termed **satisficing** by Simon, referring to the idea that firms try to achieve satisfactory rather than optimal or 'best' results.

Ethical and environmental concerns: corporate social responsibility

The self-interested behaviour of firms often leads to negative consequences for society. Many of these were examined in Chapter 5 under the topic of market failure and negative production externalities. It is often the case that the well-being of firms is not consistent with the welfare of society. A prime example is the self-interested firm that pollutes the environment. In addition, firms can engage in actions that most

consumers would consider to be ethically unacceptable, such as the practice in many developing countries of employing children who are extremely poorly paid and forced to work long hours, or employing labour that is forced to work under unhealthy or dangerous conditions. These situations may arise in countries where there is widespread poverty, and government legislation protecting the rights of children and workers is either non-existent or poorly enforced.

However, many firms are increasingly recognising that the pursuit of self-interest need not necessarily conflict with ethical and environmentally responsible behaviour. A negative image of the firm held by workers and customers (buyers of the product) can cut deeply into the firm's revenues and profits by lowering worker productivity and the firm's sales. Further, socially irresponsible firm behaviour may lead to government regulation of the firm intended to minimise the negative consequences of the firm's actions for society, whereas socially responsible behaviour could instead result in avoidance of government regulation. Therefore, firms face strong incentives to display **corporate social responsibility** by engaging in socially beneficial activities. These can take many forms, including:

- avoidance of polluting activities
- engaging in environmentally sound practices
- support for human rights, such as avoiding exploitation of child labour and labour in general in less developed countries, or avoiding investments in countries with politically oppressive regimes
- art and athletics sponsorships
- donations to charities.

Many of these practices are the result of increased consumer awareness of social and environmental issues, growing consumer concern over ethical and environmental aspects of business practices, and even consumer activism that results in boycotts of offending firms. One indication of the influence and concern of consumers is the rapidly growing interest in investments in companies (through stock markets) that meet certain social, ethical and ecological criteria.

Economists used to think that ethical and environmentally responsible behaviour of firms would reduce their profits. This was based on considering only the cost aspect of profits; for example, firms using cheap child labour face lower costs, and hence will make higher profits than firms avoiding such practices. Yet profits depend not only on costs, but also on revenues. If consumers avoid buying the products

---

[11] This is based on the work of O. E. Williamson in 1963.

of offending firms, revenues will decline and profits will go down in spite of the lower costs. The same arguments also apply to firms that may be pursuing some strategy other than profit maximisation, such as revenue maximisation.

A number of studies have attempted to measure the effects of socially responsible behaviour on the profits of firms. Does ethical and environmentally responsible behaviour lower or increase firms' profits? The results of these studies have been inconclusive.

The behaviour of firms themselves, however, suggests that they often do not want to risk consumer displeasure.

Test your understanding 6.9

Discuss some possible goals of firms other than profit maximisation that may influence their behaviour.

Theory of knowledge

How realistic is profit maximisation as the firm's main goal?

Standard economic theory assumes that profit maximisation is the most important goal of firms. As we will see in the next chapter, the theory of the firm is based very heavily on the assumption of profit maximisation. Yet this assumption is criticised for several reasons:

- The use of marginal concepts (*MR* and *MC*) in the theory is unrealistic; firms cannot easily identify marginal revenues and marginal costs, and do not even try to do so; therefore, this theory does not accurately describe methods actually used by firms to determine price and output.

- The model is based on the assumption that firms have perfect information at their disposal, whereas in fact the information on which they base their decisions is highly fragmentary and uncertain; firms do not know what demand curves they face for their products and they do not know how competitor firms will behave in response to their actions.

- Short run profit maximisation may be unrealistic; firms may not try to maximise profits in the short run, as they might prefer lower profits in the short run in exchange for larger profits over the long run.

- The factors determining demand and supply for products and resources are continuously changing, with demand and supply curves continuously shifting, so that any profit-maximising decisions regarding prices and output made today under current conditions may be irrelevant by the time the output is produced and ready for sale in the market.

- There is real-world evidence suggesting that firm behaviour may be motivated by a variety of objectives other than profit maximisation, which were discussed on pages 164–6.

Milton Friedman, an American Nobel Prize-winning economist, argued in a famous book[12] that it does not matter if the assumptions of a theory are unrealistic, as long as the theory has predictive powers. In fact, good theories are often based on unrealistic assumptions that do not accurately describe the real world, because the role of assumptions is to portray only the important aspects of a process that is modelled or theorised about, ignoring the irrelevant details.

Paul Samuelson, another American Nobel Prize-winning economist, fundamentally disagreed. Samuelson argued that the predictions of a theory can only be as empirically valid as the theory itself, and as the assumptions on which the theory rests. If the assumptions are unrealistic or invalid, then the theory and its predictions will similarly be invalid; it is not possible to have a theory with predictive powers if its assumptions are unrealistic. If the predictions of a theory are empirically valid, so is the theory and its assumptions. Logically, then, it is not possible to separate the predictions of a theory from the assumptions of the theory; they all stand or fall together.

[12] Milton Friedman (1953) 'The Methodology of Positive Economics' in Essays in Positive Economics, University of Chicago Press.

Thinking points

- Remember that a theory tries to explain real-world events. Does it matter if a theory is based on unrealistic assumptions?

- As you read through Chapter 7, you may want to keep these issues in mind, as we will encounter further unrealistic assumptions in some market models discussed in that chapter (see also the Theory of knowledge feature on page 211).

⊙ Assessment

The Student's CD-ROM at the back of this book provides practice of examination questions based on the material you have studied in this chapter.

Higher level
- Exam practice: Paper 1, Chapter 6
  - HL topics (questions 6.1–6.8)

- Exam practice: Paper 3, Chapter 6
  - HL topics (questions 13–15)

Chapter 7
The theory of the firm II: Market structures

Higher level topic

This chapter continues our study of firm behaviour. We will use the general principles outlined in Chapter 6 to study how firms behave within the market structure in which they operate.

HL Introduction to market structures

A firm (or business) is an organisation that employs factors of production to produce and sell a good or service. A group of one or more firms producing identical or similar products is called an *industry*. For example, the car industry consists of firms that are car manufacturers (Ford, Honda, Mercedes, etc.); the shoe industry consists of firms that are shoe manufacturers; and so on. There are many kinds of industries with various characteristics, which economists analyse by use of models called market structures. A **market structure** describes the characteristics of market organisation that influence the behaviour of firms within an industry. There are four market structures identified by economists:

- perfect competition
- monopoly
- monopolistic competition
- oligopoly.

7.1 Perfect competition
Assumptions of the model

- Describe, using examples, the assumed characteristics of perfect competition: a large number of firms; a homogeneous product; freedom of entry and exit; perfect information; perfect resource mobility.

The model of **perfect competition** is based on the following assumptions: HL

- **There is a large number of firms**. The large number means that each firm's output is small in relation to the size of the market. Also, it means that firms act independently of each other and the actions of each one do not affect the actions of the others.

- **All firms produce identical, or homogeneous products.** The products produced by the firms in each industry are identical, and are referred to as *homogeneous*. It is not possible to distinguish the product of one producer from that of another.

- **There is free entry and exit.** Any firm that wishes to enter an industry can do so freely as there is nothing to prevent it from doing so; similarly, it can also leave the industry freely. In other words, there are no barriers to entry into and exit from the industry.

- **There is perfect (complete) information.** Perfect information means that all firms and all consumers have complete information regarding products, prices, resources and methods of production. This ensures that no firm has access to information not available to others that would allow it to produce at a lower cost compared to its competitors. Also, it ensures that all consumers are aware of the market-determined price, and would therefore not be willing to pay a higher price for the product.

- **There is perfect resource mobility.** Resources bought by the firms for production are completely mobile. This means that they can easily and without any cost be transferred from one firm to another, or from one industry to another.

Although these assumptions are rarely if ever fully met in the real world, some industries are described more accurately by the model of perfect competition than by any other: some agricultural commodities (wheat, corn, livestock), other commodities (silver and gold), and the foreign exchange market (where currencies are bought and sold). In spite of its limited applicability to real-world industries, this model is studied because it offers important insights into the workings of the market, studied in Chapter 2. Also, as we will learn in this chapter, it serves as a standard used by economists to assess the degree of efficiency achieved in the other market structures.

Demand and revenue curves

♦ Explain, using a diagram, the shape of the perfectly competitive firm's average revenue and marginal revenue curves, indicating that the assumptions of perfect competition imply that each firm is a price taker.
♦ Explain, using a diagram, that the perfectly competitive firm's average revenue and marginal revenue curves are derived from market equilibrium for the industry.

The demand curve (average revenue curve) facing the firm

Consider a market or industry (these terms are used interchangeably) for a product produced under perfect competition. Figure 7.1(a) shows standard market demand and supply curves for this product, which determine the equilibrium price, P_e. Figure 7.1(b) shows the demand curve for the product *as it appears to the individual firm*. It is perfectly elastic, appearing as a horizontal line at P_e determined in the market. A perfectly elastic demand curve has a price elasticity of demand (*PED*) equal to infinity throughout its range (see Chapter 3, page 49). What does this mean for the firm?

The individual firm, being small, can do nothing to influence this price; it must accept P_e and sell whatever output will maximise profit. The firm is therefore a **price-taker**. If the firm raises its price above P_e, it will not sell any output because buyers will buy the product elsewhere at the lower price P_e. On the other hand, since it can sell all it wants at price P_e, it would have nothing to gain and something to lose (some revenue) if it dropped its price below P_e. Therefore, the firm sells all its output at P_e.

> The demand curve for a good facing the perfectly competitive firm is perfectly elastic (horizontal) at the price determined in the market for that good. This means the firm is a price-taker, as it accepts the price determined in the market.

The firm's revenue curves

The firm we are considering is the one studied in Chapter 6, page 156, when we introduced revenue data and curves for the firm that is *unable to control price*. Let's consider once again the example used in Table 6.5 and Figure 6.7 (page 156). Assume that a perfectly competitive firm sells a good at €10 per unit. We can now calculate the firm's total revenue, marginal revenue and average revenue, and see what happens to these as output increases. The data are shown again in Table 7.1. Column 3 shows total revenue, calculated by multiplying units of output in column 1 by price shown in column 2. Column 4 calculates marginal revenue, by taking the change in total revenue and dividing it by the change in output. Column 5 shows average revenue, obtained by dividing total revenue by quantity of output. The data in the table reveal an interesting pattern:

> No matter how much output the perfectly competitive firm sells, $P = MR = AR$ and these are constant at the level of the horizontal demand curve. This follows from the fact that price is constant regardless of the level of output sold.

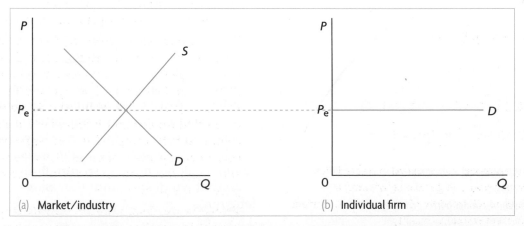

(a) Market/industry (b) Individual firm

Figure 7.1 Market (industry) demand and supply determine demand faced by the perfectly competitive firm

(1) Units of output (Q)	(2) Product price (P) (€)	(3) Total revenue $TR = P \times Q$ (€)	(4) Marginal revenue $MR = \dfrac{\Delta TR}{\Delta Q}$ (€)	(5) Average revenue $MR = \dfrac{TR}{Q}$ (€)
0	10	–	–	–
1	10	10	10	10
2	10	20	10	10
3	10	30	10	10
4	10	40	10	10
5	10	50	10	10
6	10	60	10	10
7	10	70	10	10

Table 7.1   Total, marginal and average revenue when price is constant

This result holds only for firms operating under perfect competition, because these are the only firms that have no control over price and are forced to sell all their output at the single price determined in the market.

The data of Table 7.1 are plotted in Figure 7.2, where we see in part (a) that total revenue increases

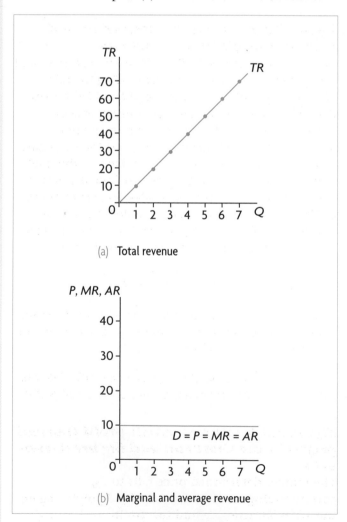

(a)   Total revenue

(b)   Marginal and average revenue

Figure 7.2   Revenue curves under perfect competition

at a constant rate, i.e. it is a straight line. Part (b) shows that since price is constant at €10, $P = MR = AR$, and they all coincide with the horizontal demand curve.

Test your understanding 7.1

1 What are the assumptions defining the perfectly competitive market model?

2 **(a)** Explain why the perfectly competitive firm is a price-taker. **(b)** What would happen if this firm tried to raise its price above the market price? **(c)** What would happen if it lowered its price below the market price?

3 How is the demand curve facing the perfectly competitive firm related to the industry/market equilibrium?

4 **(a)** Using a diagram, explain the relationship between the firm's average revenue (AR) and marginal revenue (MR) in perfect competition. **(b)** How are they related to product price? **(c)** How are they related to the demand curve facing the firm? **(d)** How are they related to the principle that each firm is a price-taker?

Profit maximisation in the short run

♦ Explain, using diagrams, that it is possible for a perfectly competitive firm to make economic profit (supernormal profit), normal profit or negative economic profit in the short run based on the marginal cost and marginal revenue profit maximisation rule.

♦ Distinguish between the short-run shut-down price and the break-even price.

♦ Explain, using a diagram, when a loss-making firm would shut down in the short run.

Remember, the short run is the period when the firm has at least one fixed input. You should bear in mind that this means the number of firms in the industry is also fixed. To enter or leave an industry, a firm must be able to vary *all its inputs*. Since this cannot be done in the short run, firms cannot enter or leave the industry (until they move into the long run).

When a firm wants to maximise profit in the short run, what must it do? Since it is a price-taker, it cannot influence its selling price. It can only make a choice on how much quantity of output it should produce. We will see how the firm does this using the marginal revenue and marginal cost rule (introduced in Chapter 6, page 163).

Short-run profit maximisation based on the marginal revenue and marginal cost rule

The analysis consists of three steps:

(i) Compare marginal revenue with marginal cost to determine profit-maximising (or loss-minimising) level of output. As we know from Chapter 6, a firm interested in maximising profit (or minimising loss) produces output where $MR = MC$. This can be seen in Figure 6.12(a), page 163, where $Q_{\pi max}$ was shown to be the profit-maximising level of output.

(ii) Compare average revenue (or price) and average total cost to determine the amount of profit (or loss) per unit of output. A comparison of average revenue (which is equal to price) with average cost shows the amount of profit (or loss) per unit of output. We know profit = $TR - TC$. If we divide this throughout by output, Q, we get an expression for profit per unit of output, in other words, in terms of averages:

$$\frac{profit}{Q} = \frac{TR}{Q} - \frac{TC}{Q}$$

Alternatively,

$$\frac{profit}{Q} = AR - ATC$$

(since $AR = \frac{TR}{Q}$, and $ATC = \frac{TC}{Q}$).

Moreover, since $P = AR$ (shown in Table 7.1 and Figure 7.2(b)), it follows that

$$\frac{profit}{Q} = P - ATC$$

This is the key to calculating the size of the firm's profit or loss per unit of output.

(iii) Find total profit (or total loss). To do this, we multiply $\frac{profit}{Q}$ by Q (or $\frac{loss}{Q}$ by Q).

At the profit-maximising level of output Q:

- If $P > ATC$, the firm makes supernormal profit (positive economic profit).

- If $P = ATC$, the firm breaks even, making zero economic profit, though it is earning normal profit.

- If $P < ATC$, the firm makes a loss (negative economic profit).

Making economic profit, breaking even and shutting down in the short run

Using the above three-step approach, we will examine the behaviour of the perfectly competitive firm in the short run, making use of the diagrams in Figure 7.3. Each of these diagrams contains identical cost curves (AVC, ATC and MC; note that MC always intersects AVC and ATC at their minimum points). What differs between the diagrams is the position of the perfectly elastic demand curve, showing different possible prices that the firm, being a price-taker, must accept.

Figure 7.3(a): profit maximisation and economic profit in the short run

When market price is P_1, $P_1 = MR_1 = AR_1 = D_1$ represent the demand curve facing the firm. Using the rule $MR = MC$, the intersection of the MR and MC curves determines the firm's profit-maximising level of output, Q_1 (simply draw a line from the point of intersection to the horizontal axis). We then compare P_1 with ATC along this same vertical line at the level of output Q_1. Since $P_1 > ATC$, we conclude the firm is making profit per unit equal to $P_1 - ATC$, represented by the vertical distance between points a and b. To find total profit, we multiply profit per unit times the total number of units produced; this is given by

$$profit = \frac{profit}{Q} \times Q$$

and is represented by the shaded area in the diagram. Note that all profit measures in our discussion refer to economic profit (supernormal profit).

When $P > ATC$ at the level of output where $MC = MR$, the firm earns positive economic profit (supernormal profit).

Figure 7.3(b): zero economic profit (normal profit) in the short run and the break-even price

The market-determined price falls to P_2, corresponding to demand curve D_2. Applying again the $MR = MC$ rule, we find the profit-maximising level of output Q_2. Comparing P_2 with ATC at output Q_2, we see they are equal to each other;

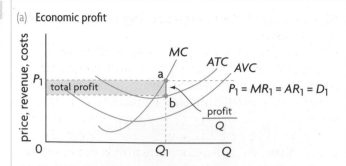

(a) Economic profit

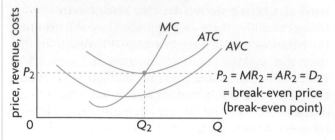

(b) Zero economic profit (normal profit)

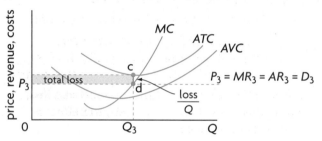

(c) Economic loss: the firm continues to produce

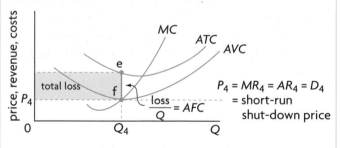

(d) Loss in the short run and the shut-down price

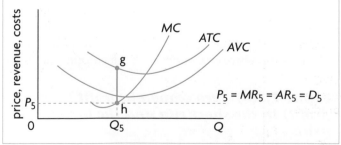

(e) The loss-making firm that will not produce

Figure 7.3 Short-run equilibrium positions of the perfectly competitive firm

therefore, profit per unit is $P_2 - ATC = 0$. Therefore, economic profit is zero and the firm is earning normal profit. When economic profit is zero, price equals minimum ATC: this is a **break-even price**, meaning that at this price the firm breaks even, so that its total revenues are equal to its total economic costs (implicit plus explicit).[1]

> The price P = minimum ATC is the firm's *break-even price*. At this price the firm is breaking even: it is making zero economic profit, but is earning normal profit.

Figure 7.3(c): loss minimisation in the short run

If the market price falls below minimum ATC, such as P_3, corresponding to demand curve D_3, the firm does not earn enough revenue to cover all its costs. Using the $MC = MR$ rule, we see that the profit-maximising or loss-minimising level of output is Q_3, at which $P_3 < ATC$, indicating the firm is making a negative profit, or loss. Therefore, Q_3 is the firm's loss-minimising output. $ATC - P_3$, or the difference between points c and d, represents the firm's loss per unit of output, or $\dfrac{\text{loss}}{Q}$.

If we multiply this vertical distance by Q_3, we get the firm's total loss, given by the shaded area.

What should this firm do? Should it continue producing at a loss or should it stop producing and shut down? To answer this question, we must remember that the firm is in the short run. This means if it stops producing, it will have zero revenue and zero variable costs (it will have fired all its workers, and will not be purchasing any other variable inputs), but *since it will still have some fixed inputs it will have some fixed costs* (such as interest payments on loans, insurance payments and rental payments). The fixed costs are costs that must be paid even though the firm has zero output. Therefore, with zero revenues and zero variable costs, the firm that does not produce in the short run will have a loss equal to its fixed costs.

Remember, the firm's objective is to make its loss as small as possible. What if by producing some output the firm can receive enough revenue to cover all its variable costs plus a portion of its fixed costs? If the firm can do this, it will be better off producing, because then its loss will be smaller than its fixed costs. This answers the loss-making firm's question: it is better to produce rather than

---

[1] The break-even price is any price at which the firm breaks even, i.e. makes zero economic profit. A price that is equal to minimum ATC is just one possible break-even price. This particular break-even price is of special significance because it corresponds to the perfectly competitive firm's profit-maximising level of output.

shut down, as long as the loss it makes by producing is less than its total fixed cost. In terms of our per unit analysis, the firm should produce as long as the loss per unit incurred by producing is less than its average fixed cost (*AFC*).

This is illustrated in part (c). The vertical difference between *ATC* and *AVC* is equal to *AFC* (since *AFC*+*AVC* = *ATC*). Therefore, loss per unit, given by *ATC*–P_3 at output level Q_3 (the distance between c and d), is smaller than *AFC*. Therefore, this firm should not shut down in the short run; it should produce its loss-minimising output.

> When *ATC*>*P*>*AVC* at the level of output where *MC* = *MR*, the firm is making a loss but should continue producing because its loss is smaller than its fixed cost. Graphically, this occurs when the demand curve lies below minimum *ATC* and above minimum *AVC*.

Figure 7.3(d): loss in the short run and the short-run shut-down price

The price *P* = minimum *AVC* is called the **shut-down price**, and is P_4 in part (d), corresponding to demand curve D_4. At this price, the firm's loss per unit of output is exactly equal to *AFC*, or *ATC* – *AVC* (the vertical difference between points e and f). At the shut-down price, the firm is indifferent between producing Q_4, determined by *MC* = *MR*, and not producing at all, because either way it will have a loss equal to fixed costs.

> The price *P* = minimum AVC is the firm's *shut-down price* in the short run. At this price, the firm's total loss is equal to its total fixed cost.

Figure 7.3(e): the loss-making firm that will not produce

If the price falls below the shut-down price, or below minimum *AVC*, the firm should shut down (stop producing). As part (e) shows, if the firm were to produce, it would produce Q_5 units of output, where *MC* = *MR*. But at Q_5 the loss per unit is equal to the distance between points g and h, which is greater than *AFC*. Therefore, the firm is better off not producing at all, and its loss will equal its fixed costs.

> When price falls below the shut-down price, so that *P*<minimum *AVC*, the firm should shut down in the short run, and will make a loss equal to its fixed costs.

The firm's short-run decisions on how much to produce and whether or not it should produce are summarised in Figure 7.4. The cost curves, prices and demand curves are the same as those in Figure 7.3 (a)–(e).

> In perfect competition in the short run:
> - When *P*>*ATC*, the firm makes economic profit.
> - When *P* = minimum ATC, the firm makes zero economic profit but earns normal profit; this P is a break-even price of the firm (at the break-even point).
> - When *ATC*>*P*>*AVC*, the firm produces at a loss, but its loss is less than fixed costs; therefore, it continues to produce.
> - When *P* = minimum *AVC*, the firm's loss = fixed costs; this *P* is the firm's short-run shut-down price.
> - When *P*<*AVC*, i.e. when price falls below the shut-down price, the firm shuts down (stops producing); its loss will then be equal to its fixed costs.

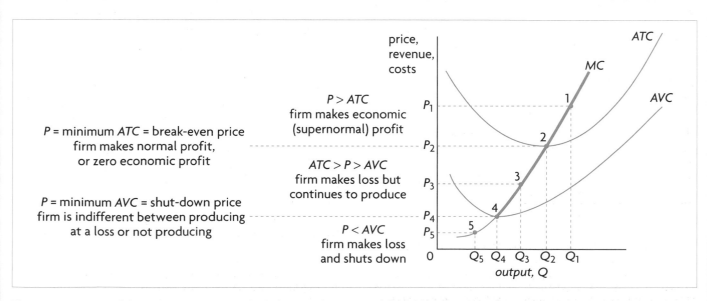

Figure 7.4 Summary of the perfectly competitive firm's short-run decisions, and the firm's short-run supply curve

- **There are significant barriers to entry.** The monopolist owes its dominance in the market and the absence of competitor firms partly to the inability of other firms to enter the industry. Anything that prevents other firms from entering the industry is called a **barrier to entry**.

Monopoly lies at the opposite extreme of market structures to perfect competition. As a single seller, the monopolist faces no competition from other firms and it has substantial market power (the ability to control price). Yet a pure monopoly is quite rare in the real world. Like perfect competition, it is studied because of the insights it offers into the ability of firms to exercise market power, also known as monopoly power. Monopoly power arises whenever a firm faces a demand curve that is downward-sloping. As we will see throughout the rest of this chapter, firms in all market structures except perfect competition face a downward-sloping demand curve, and therefore have varying degrees of monopoly power, or the ability to influence the price at which they sell their output.

Barriers to entry

* Describe, using examples, barriers to entry, including economies of scale, branding and legal barriers.

There are several kinds of barriers to entry. These are described below.

Economies of scale
Economies of scale result in the downward-sloping portion of a firm's long-run average total cost curve (*LRATC*), permitting lower average costs to be achieved as the firm increases its size (see page 153). A barrier to entry exists when economies of scale are extensive and the *LRATC* curve declines over a very large range of output. In Figure 7.8 the average total costs of a large firm on $SRATC_1$ are substantially lower than the average costs faced by a smaller firm on $SRATC_2$. The large firm can charge a lower price than the smaller firm, and can force the smaller firm into a situation where it will not be able to cover its costs. Therefore, if new firms try to enter the industry on a small scale they will be unable to compete with the larger one.

On the other hand, a new firm attempting to enter the market on a very large scale so as to be able to take advantage of economies of scale would encounter huge start-up costs, and would be unlikely to take the risk involved. Economies of scale form a significant barrier to entry in the case not only of monopolies but also of oligopolies (see page 201).

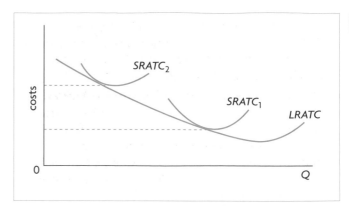

Figure 7.8 Economies of scale as a barrier to entry

Branding
Branding involves the creation by a firm of a unique image and name of a product. It works through advertising campaigns that try to influence consumer tastes in favour of the product, attempting to establish consumer loyalty. If branding of a product is successful, many consumers will be convinced of the product's superiority, and will be unwilling to switch to substitute products, even though these may be qualitatively very similar. Branding may work as a barrier to entry by making it difficult for new firms to enter a market that is dominated by a successful brand. Note that branding need not lead to a monopoly (it is a method used by firms in monopolistic competition and oligopoly, as we will discover below), but it does have the effect of limiting the number of new competitor firms that enter a market. Examples of branding include brand-name items (such as NIKE®, Adidas®, CocaCola®, etc.)

Legal barriers
Legal barriers include the following:

- **Patents** are rights given by the government to a firm that has developed a new product or invention to be its sole producer for a specified period of time. For that period, the firm producing the patented product has a monopoly on the product. Examples include patents on new pharmaceutical products, Polaroid and instant cameras, Intel and microprocessor chips used by IBM computers.

- **Licences** are granted by governments for particular professions or particular industries. Licences may be required, for example, to operate radio or television stations, or to enter a particular profession (such as medicine, dentistry, architecture, law and others). Such licences do not usually result in a monopoly, but they do have the impact of limiting competition.

- **Copyrights** guarantee that an author (or an author's appointed person) has the sole rights to print, publish and sell copyrighted works.
- **Public franchises** are granted by the government to a firm which is to produce or supply a particular good or service.
- **Tariffs, quotas and other trade restrictions** limit the quantities of a good that can be imported into a country, thus reducing competition.

Not all of these legal barriers lead to monopoly, but they all have the effect of limiting competition, thus contributing to the creation of some degree of monopoly power.

Control of essential resources

Monopolies can arise from ownership or control of an essential resource. A classic example of an international monopoly is DeBeers, the South African diamond firm, that mines roughly 50% of the world's diamonds and purchases about 80% of diamonds sold on open markets. Whereas it is not the sole diamond supplier, its large market share allows it to have a significant control over the price of diamonds. On a national level, an example is Alcoa (the Aluminum Company of America), which, following the expiration of patents in 1909, was able to maintain its monopoly position on the production of aluminium within the United States until the Second World War, because of its control of almost all the bauxite resources within the country. On a local level, professional sports leagues create a local monopoly by signing long-term contracts with the best players and securing exclusive use of sports stadiums. A local monopoly is a single producer/supplier within a particular geographical area. Local monopolies appear more commonly than national or international ones. For example, a local grocery store in a residential area

located some distance from any other stores may be a local monopoly.

Aggressive tactics

If a monopolist is confronted with the possibility of a new entrant into the industry, it can create entry barriers by cutting its price, advertising aggressively, threatening a takeover of the potential entrant, or any other behaviour that can dissuade a new firm from entering the market.

Demand and revenue curves under monopoly

- Explain that the average revenue curve for a monopolist is the market demand curve, which will be downward sloping.
- Explain, using a diagram, the relationship between demand, average revenue and marginal revenue in a monopoly.

The demand curve facing the monopolist

Since the pure monopolist is the entire industry, the demand curve it faces is the industry or market demand curve, which is downward-sloping. This is the most important difference between the monopolist and the perfectly competitive firm, which faces perfectly elastic demand at the price level determined in the market.

The two demand curves shown in Figure 7.9 indicate that the perfectly competitive firm is a price-taker with zero market power, while the monopolist is a *price-maker* with a significant degree of market power.

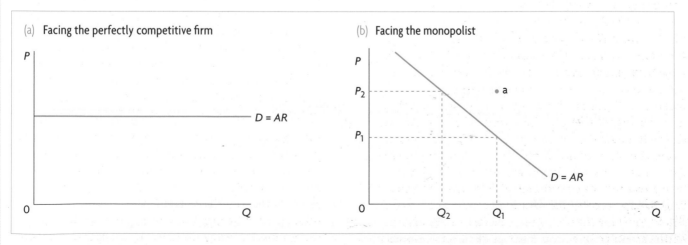

Figure 7.9 Demand curves

All firms under market structures other than perfect competition are to varying degrees price-makers, as they all face downward-sloping demand curves. Of these, the monopolist has the greatest degree of market power, or the ability to influence price, because it is the sole or dominant firm in the industry.

However, whereas the monopolist has a large control over price, this control is limited by the position of the market demand curve. Given the demand curve in Figure 7.9(b), when it chooses how much output to produce, say Q_1, it simultaneously determines the price at which the good can be sold, or P_1. It could not possibly sell output Q_1 at a price such as P_2, since the price–quantity combination P_2 and Q_1 is at a point a lying off the demand curve. The monopolist can sell its output at price P_2 if it wants to, but will only be able to sell quantity Q_2 at that price. In other words, the monopolist cannot make independent decisions on both price and quantity; it can only choose price–quantity combinations that are on the market demand curve.

The monopolist's revenue curves

In perfect competition where the firm is a price-taker, the market-determined price is constant for all output, leading to the perfectly elastic (horizontal) demand curve. But when a firm faces a downward-sloping demand curve, price is no longer constant for all output: more output can only be sold at a lower price. Let's consider once again the example used in Table 6.6 and Figure 6.8 in Chapter 6 (page 157), when we introduced revenue data and curves for the firm that has some ability to control price. Table 7.2 provides the same data for a monopolist's total, marginal and average revenues, and the diagrams in Figure 7.10 plot these data.

Looking at Table 7.2 and Figure 7.10, we may note the following:

- As price (P) falls, output (Q) increases because of the downward-sloping demand curve). Total revenue (TR), obtained by $Q \times P$, at first increases, reaches a maximum at six and seven units of output, and then begins to fall.

- Marginal revenue, showing the change in total revenue resulting from a change in output, falls continuously; MR is equal to zero when total revenue is at its maximum (at seven units of output), and becomes negative when total revenue falls.[2]

- Average revenue (column 5 of Table 7.2) is equal to price (see column 2):

(1) Units of output (Q)	(2) Product price (P) (€)	(3) Total revenue (TR = P×Q) (€)	(4) Marginal revenue $MR = \dfrac{\Delta TR}{\Delta Q}$ (€)	(5) Average revenue $AR = \dfrac{TR}{Q}$ (€)
0	–	–	–	–
1	12	12	12	12
2	11	22	10	11
3	10	30	8	10
4	9	36	6	9
5	8	40	4	8
6	7	42	2	7
7	6	42	0	6
8	5	40	−2	5
9	4	36	−4	4
10	3	30	−6	3

Table 7.2   Total, marginal and average revenue when price varies with output

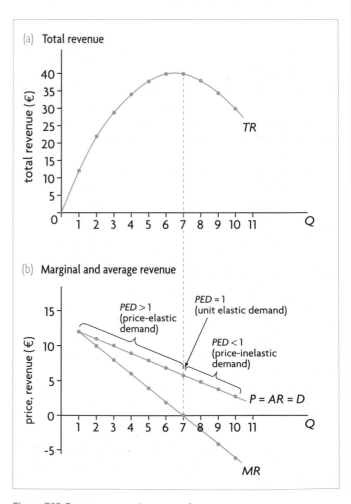

Figure 7.10 Revenue curves in monopoly

[2] Marginal revenue represents the slope of the total revenue curve (just as marginal cost is the slope of the total cost curve).

Since $TR = P \times Q$, and $AR = \dfrac{TR}{Q}$, it follows that P *is equal to AR.*

- *The AR and P curves represent the demand curve facing the firm.*

- *The MR curve lies below the demand curve.* The reason is that, unlike in perfect competition, where $MR = P$, here the firm must lower its price in order to sell more output. The lower price is charged not only for the last unit of output but all the previous units of output sold. Marginal revenue, or the extra revenue from selling an additional unit of output, is therefore equal to the amount of the price of the last unit sold minus what is lost by selling all the other units of output at the now lower price.[3]

The monopolist's output and price elasticity of demand

◆ Explain why a monopolist will never choose to operate on the inelastic portion of its average revenue curve.

In Table 7.2 and Figure 7.10, in the range of output where total revenue is increasing and marginal revenue is positive, the demand curve facing the firm (represented by $P = AR$) is price elastic ($PED > 1$); in the range of output where total revenue is falling and marginal revenue is therefore negative, the demand curve is price inelastic ($PED < 1$). (The reason can be found in Chapter 3, page 50, where we discussed the changing PED along a straight-line demand curve.) Figure 7.10 shows the relationship between PED and total revenue. When demand is elastic, price and total revenue change in opposite directions: in part (b) as price falls from €12 to €6 along the elastic portion of the demand curve, we see total revenue increasing in part (a). When demand is inelastic, price and total revenue change in the same direction: as price falls beyond €6 (along the inelastic portion of the demand curve in part (b), we see total revenue falling in part (a). Total revenue is maximum, and $MR = 0$ where $PED = 1$.

These observations have important implications for the level of output produced by the monopolist.

The monopolist will not produce any output in the inelastic portion of its demand curve (which is also its average revenue curve).

In Figure 7.10(b), the monopolist will not produce any output greater than seven units, which is where TR is maximum and $MR = 0$. If it did, its total revenue would fall and marginal revenue would be negative.

Test your understanding 7.6

1 What are the assumptions defining the market model of monopoly?

2 Using a diagram, explain how economies of scale can result in a monopolistic market structure by posing barriers to entry.

3 How can branding and legal factors provide barriers to entry into an industry? Provide some examples.

4 **(a)** Compare and contrast the demand curve facing the perfectly competitive firm and that facing the monopolist. **(b)** What is the relationship between market power and the differences between the two demand curves? **(c)** Why is one firm a price-taker and the other a price-maker?

5 **(a)** Explain the relationship between the monopolist's average revenue (AR) and marginal revenue (MR). **(b)** How are they related to product price? **(c)** How are they related to the demand curve facing the firm?

6 Explain why the average revenue curve is the demand curve facing the monopolist. Why is this curve downward-sloping?

7 Why will the monopolist avoid producing in the inelastic portion of its demand curve? Use diagrams to support your answer.

8 What is the maximum level of output that a monopolist would consider producing? What would the monopolist be maximising at this level of output? Use a diagram to support your answer.

Profit maximisation by the monopolist

◆ Explain, using a diagram, the short- and long-run equilibrium output and pricing decision of a profit-maximising (loss-minimising) monopolist, identifying the firm's economic profit (or losses).

◆ Explain the role of barriers to entry in permitting the firm to earn economic profit.

---

[3] To understand this, consider the following numerical example. Say output increases from 3 to 4 units. Marginal revenue will be the result of a gain and a loss. The gain is €9, obtained from selling the fourth unit of output at the price of €9. The loss is equal to €1 for each of the initial 3 units of output that previously were selling for €10 and must now sell for €9, equal to €3. Marginal revenue is equal to the gain minus the loss, or $9 - 3 = 6$.

Profit maximisation based on the marginal revenue and cost approach

The monopolist interested in maximising profit (or minimising loss) follows the same three-step approach used by the perfectly competitive firm:

(i) The monopolist determines the profit-maximising (or loss-minimising) level output using the $MC = MR$ rule.

(ii) For that level of output, it determines profit per unit or loss per unit by using

$$\frac{\text{profit}}{Q} = P - ATC$$

If $P > ATC$, the monopolist is making a profit; if $P = ATC$ it is earning normal profit (zero economic profit); if $P < ATC$ it is making a loss.

(iii) The firm multiplies $\frac{\text{profit}}{Q}$ by Q to determine total profit, or $\frac{\text{loss}}{Q}$ by Q to determine total loss.

Figure 7.11 (a) and (b) show the standard ATC and MC curves (derived in Chapter 6, page 148). On these cost curves, the monopolist's demand and marginal revenue curves are added. Consider first part (a).

- We first find where $MR = MC$, which determines the profit-maximising level of output, $Q_{\pi max}$.

- At $Q_{\pi max}$, we draw a vertical line upward to the AR (or demand) curve (point a) and from there extend a horizontal line leftward to the vertical axis; this will determine the price, P_e, at which the monopolist sells output $Q_{\pi max}$.

- For output $Q_{\pi max}$, we find profit per unit $\left(\frac{\text{profit}}{Q}\right)$, given by $P - ATC$; this is the vertical distance between the average revenue (demand) and ATC curves, or between points a and b.

- To find total profit, we multiply profit per unit times the total number of units produced, which is

$$\text{profit} = \frac{\text{profit}}{Q} \times Q$$

and is represented by the shaded area.

The monopolist need not always make profits; it may make losses if price cannot cover ATC. This is shown in Figure 7.11(b), where the monopolist is minimising loss. At the level of output Q_{lmin}, determined by $MR = MC$, the monopolist's loss is minimised. The price that will be charged is given by P_e, found by extending a line upward to the demand curve at output level Q_{lmin}. Loss per unit of output $\left(\frac{\text{loss}}{Q}\right)$ is given by $ATC - P$ (the distance c–d), and total loss is given by the shaded area, found by multiplying loss per unit of output by the total number of units produced.

Just as in perfect competition, the loss-making monopolist continues to produce in the short run as long as its losses are smaller than its fixed costs ($P > \text{minimum } AVC$). In the long run (when all resources are variable), the loss-making monopolist is likely to shut down or move its resources to another more profitable industry. However, the distinction between the short run and the long run is not as important in monopoly as it is in perfect competition. In perfect competition, the distinction between the short and long runs is of crucial importance because as firms enter and exit an industry in the long run, economic (supernormal) profits and losses disappear, and firms are left with normal profits in their long-run equilibrium. This is not possible in monopoly, due to the presence of barriers to entry.

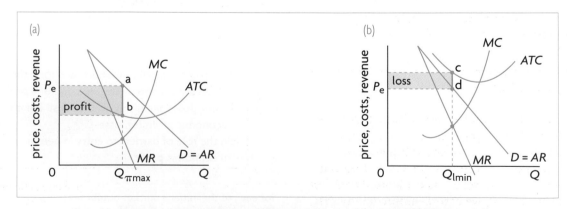

Figure 7.11 Profit maximisation and loss minimisation in monopoly: marginal revenue and cost approach

Under monopoly, high barriers to entry prevent potential competitor firms from entering a profit-making industry, and the monopolist can therefore continue making economic (supernormal) profits indefinitely in the long run.

Revenue maximisation by the monopolist

Comparing revenue-maximisation with profit maximisation

♦ Explain, using a diagram, the output and pricing decision of a revenue-maximising monopoly firm.
♦ Compare and contrast, using a diagram, the equilibrium positions of a profit-maximising monopoly firm and a revenue-maximising monopoly firm.

In Chapter 6, page 164, we saw that according to an alternative theory, firms try to maximise revenue rather than profit. How does the output and price of such a firm compare with those of the profit maximiser?

The answer to this question can be seen in Figure 7.10. In part (a), total revenue (TR) is maximum when seven units of output are produced. This corresponds to the point where marginal revenue (MR) is equal to zero in part (b). Therefore, the revenue-maximising monopolist produces that level of output where $MR = 0$.

Comparing the profit-maximising firm with the revenue-maximising firm shows that the revenue maximiser produces a larger quantity of output and sells it at a lower price than the profit maximiser. This can be seen in Figure 7.12. The profit maximiser equates MC with MR, and produces quantity Q_π which it sells at price P_π. The revenue maximiser produces quantity Q_r which it sells at price P_r.

Calculating the revenue-maximising level of output

♦ Calculate from a set of data and/or diagrams the revenue-maximising level of output.

Bearing in mind that revenue maximisation involves choosing the level of output where $MR = 0$, it is a simple matter to find the corresponding level of output. In a diagram, it is simply the level of output where the MR curve intersects the horizontal axis. For example, in Figure 7.10, we can see immediately that the level of output where revenue is maximised is where $Q = 7$ units of output.

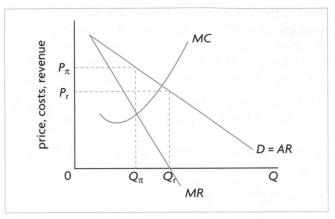

Figure 7.12 Comparison of profit maximisation and revenue maximisation by the monopolist

When given data, we similarly find the revenue-maximising level of output by finding the quantity that corresponds to $MR = 0$. Therefore, in Table 7.2, we see that the quantity of output where revenue is maximised is 7, which corresponds to $MR = 0$.

Natural monopoly

♦ With reference to economies of scale, and using examples, explain the meaning of the term 'natural monopoly'.
♦ Draw a diagram illustrating a natural monopoly.

A *natural monopoly* is a firm that has economies of scale so large that it is possible for the single firm alone to supply the entire market at a lower average cost than two or more firms. A natural monopoly is illustrated in Figure 7.13.

If the market demand for a product is within the range of falling $LRATC$, this means that a single large firm can produce for the entire market at a lower average total cost than two or more smaller firms. When this occurs, the firm is called a **natural monopoly**.

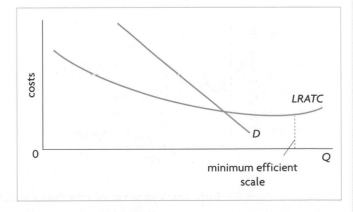

Figure 7.13 Natural monopoly

There are two factors at work making for a natural monopoly: costs and market demand. In Figure 7.13, at the point where market demand, *D*, intersects the *LRATC* curve, *LRATC* is still declining, meaning that economies of scale have not yet been fully exhausted and the minimum efficient scale occurs at a higher level of output. (The minimum efficient scale is the lowest level of output at which lowest average total costs are achieved; see page 154.) As output increases, average costs fall, and keep on falling even beyond the point where the entire market demand for the product is satisfied. A market like this cannot support more than one firm. In fact, natural monopoly acts as a strong barrier to entry of new firms into the industry because potential entrants realise that it would be extremely difficult to attain the low costs of the already existing firm. Examples of natural monopolies include water, gas and electricity distribution, cable television, fire protection and postal services. The falling average costs over a very large range of output often occur because of very large capital costs (such as laying pipes for water distribution, or laying cables for electricity distribution, or putting a satellite into orbit).

A natural monopoly may stop being 'natural' if changing technologies create conditions that allow new competitor firms to enter the industry and begin production at a relatively low cost. Once this happens and technological changes result in lower costs for firms, it may no longer be the case that a single firm exhausts economies of scale. This has happened in recent years with technological change in telecommunications, forcing telephone companies that previously were natural companies to compete with new entrants into the market.

Test your understanding 7.7

1 Do the profit-maximising rules used by the monopolist differ from those used by the perfectly competitive firm?

2 How does the profit-making monopolist determine **(a)** the price at which output will be sold, and **(b)** whether the firm is earning economic (supernormal) profit, normal profit, or incurring a loss? **(c)** Is there any difference in the method used by the perfectly competitive firm and the monopolist to determine profits or losses?

3 Using diagrams, show the case where a monopolist **(a)** earns economic profit (show profit per unit and total profit), (b) earns normal profit, and (c) incurs losses (show loss per unit and total loss).

4 **(a)** What is the difference, if any, between the short-run and long-run equilibrium of a monopolist? **(b)** Why can a monopolist continue to earn economic profits in the long run?

5 The data in the table below show the demand curve and costs (*ATC* and *MC*) facing a monopolist. **(a)** Calculate the monopolist's total revenue and marginal revenue for each level of output. **(b)** What is this monopolist's profit-maximising level of output? **(c)** At what price will this level of output be sold? **(d)** Find the monopolist's profit per unit and total profit. **(e)** Plot the demand curve, marginal revenue curve, average total cost curve and marginal cost curve, and confirm your results for parts (b)–(d).

Units of output	Price ($)	Average total cost ($)	Marginal cost ($)
1	10	14.0	4.0
2	9	8.5	3.0
3	8	6.3	2.0
4	7	5.0	1.0
5	6	4.4	2.0
6	5	4.2	3.0
7	4	4.1	4.0
8	3	4.3	5.0

6 **(a)** Using diagrams illustrating total revenue and marginal revenue of a monopolist, show the revenue-maximising level of output. **(b)** Using the data of question 5, find the level of output (*Q*) and price (*P*) of a revenue-maximizing monopolist. **(c)** How do these results compare with the *P* and *Q* of the profit-maximizing monopolist?

7 Can a perfectly competitive firm maximise revenue? Why or why not?

8 (a) What is the relevance of economies of scale to natural monopoly? **(b)** Using a diagram and examples, explain what a natural monopoly is. **(c)** Why is a natural monopoly a strong barrier to entry into an industry? **(d)** Why do you think governments often do not break up natural monopolies in order to increase competition?

Monopoly market outcomes and efficiency

Higher price and lower output by the monopolist compared to the industry in perfect competition

A comparison of monopoly with perfect competition at the level of the industry reveals that price is higher and quantity of output produced lower in monopoly. Figure 7.14 shows the long-run equilibrium positions of a perfectly competitive industry, composed of many small firms, and of a monopoly, which is the entire industry. Part (a) for the perfectly competitive industry shows equilibrium price and quantity to be P_{pc} and Q_{pc}. Point a, where the industry demand and supply curves intersect, appears also in part (b), showing what would happen to price and quantity if the perfectly competitive industry were organised as a monopoly. The MC curve of part (a), or the competitive industry's supply curve becomes the monopolist's marginal cost curve.[4] The demand curve remains unchanged, but the monopolist's marginal revenue (MR_m) curve lies below D. When the

profit-maximising monopolist applies the $MR = MC$, the result is output Q_m and price P_m.

Since $Q_m < Q_{pc}$, the industry under monopoly produces a smaller quantity of output than the industry under perfect competition. And since $P_m > P_{pc}$, the monopolist sells output at a higher price than the perfectly competitive industry. Higher prices and lower output go against consumers' interests.

Allocative and productive inefficiency

♦ Explain, using diagrams, why the profit-maximising choices of a monopoly firm lead to allocative inefficiency (welfare loss) and productive inefficiency.

Allocative inefficiency: loss of consumer and producer surplus

The higher price and lower output of the monopolist have important implications for consumer and producer surplus. Whereas the perfectly competitive industry achieves allocative efficiency shown by $MB = MC$ and maximum social surplus, monopoly does not. This can be seen in Figure 7.15, which is the same as Figure 7.14, only consumer and producer surplus have been drawn in. In part (a), area A represents consumer surplus, while area B is producer surplus, with A + B showing maximum social surplus. Part (b) shows the inefficiencies that result in monopoly.

• Area C, consumer surplus in monopoly, is smaller than area A in perfect competition. Part of A was

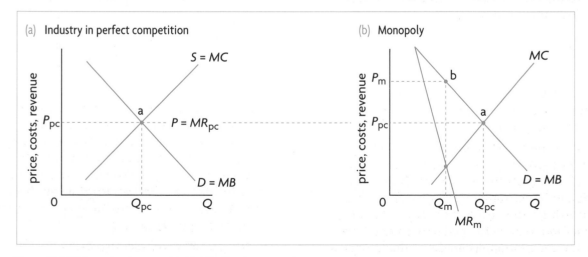

Figure 7.14 Higher price, lower output by the firm in monopoly

[4] However, note that the monopolist's MC curve is not its supply curve. In fact, the monopolist does not have a supply curve, because there is no single relationship between price and quantity supplied in monopoly. The reason is that the $MC = MR$

rule for the monopolist may result in different prices for the same quantity, depending on demand conditions for the monopolist's product.

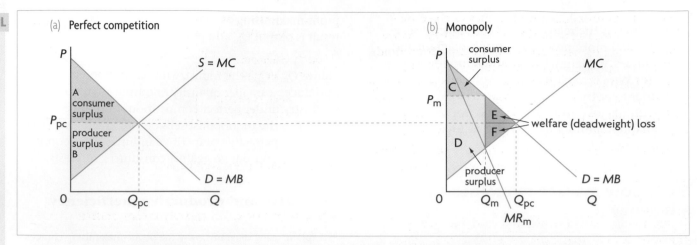

Figure 7.15 Consumer and producer surplus and welfare (deadweight) loss in monopoly compared with perfect competition

converted into producer surplus because of the higher monopoly price (P_m rather than P_{pc}), and another part of A was lost as triangle E because of the lower monopoly quantity (Q_m rather than Q_{pc}). Area E represents a welfare (deadweight) loss.

- Area D, producer surplus in monopoly, shows that producer surplus has increased by taking away a portion of consumer surplus (due to the monopolist's higher price), and it has also decreased by losing area F (due to the monopolist's lower quantity). Area F is also a welfare (deadweight) loss.

- E+F represents loss of social benefits (consumer and producer surplus) due to monopoly's higher price and lower quantity.

Note that the presence of welfare (deadweight) loss means that MC and MB are no longer equal. At

the point of monopoly production, Q_m, $MB > MC$, meaning that there is an underallocation of resources to the good, and consumers are not getting as much of it as they would have liked.

The presence of welfare (deadweight) loss in monopoly indicates there is allocative inefficiency, shown also by $MB > MC$ at Q_m, indicating too little of the good is produced. Also, the monopolist gains at the expense of consumers as a portion of consumer surplus is converted into producer surplus.

Allocative inefficiency: P > MC

Figure 7.16 shows the long-run equilibrium position of the firm in perfect competition and monopoly.

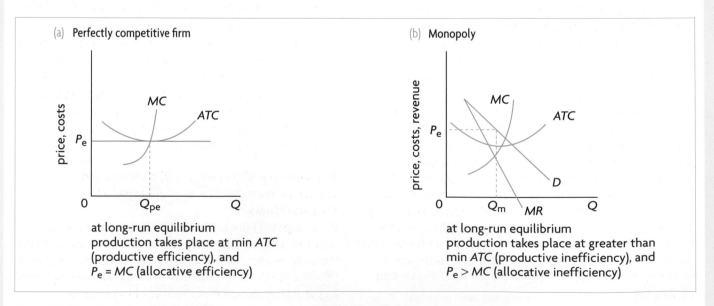

Figure 7.16 Allocative and productive inefficiency in perfect competition and monopoly

The condition for allocative efficiency is given by $P = MC$ at the profit-maximising level of output. As we know from our earlier discussion, this condition holds for the firm in perfect competition (page 179). In Figure 7.16(b) we can see that at the profit-maximising level of output Q_m, the monopolist's price, P_e, is higher than marginal cost. This is hardly surprising, since $P > MC$ is the same as $MB > MC$ (since $P = MB$), which we saw in Figure 7.15(b). Therefore, we conclude once again that the monopolist does not achieve allocative efficiency.

> In monopoly the underallocation of resources to the good is indicated also by $P > MC$ at the profit-maximising level of output.

Productive inefficiency: production at higher than minimum ATC

The condition for productive efficiency is that production takes place at minimum ATC (as explained on page 179). Figure 7.16 indicates that whereas the perfectly competitive firm is productively efficient, the monopolist is not. The output produced by the monopolist, Q_m, is not at the point of minimum ATC. At Q_m, the monopolist's average total costs (ATC) are higher than minimum ATC; therefore, there is productive inefficiency.

> The monopolist produces at higher than minimum average total cost, and there is therefore productive inefficiency.

Lack of competition in monopoly may lead to higher costs (X-inefficiency)

Whereas in perfect competition firms are under constant pressure to produce with the lowest possible costs to survive, in monopoly the lack of competition can make the monopolist less concerned about keeping costs low. Higher costs could arise due to poor management, a poorly motivated workforce, lack of innovation and use of new technologies. This is known as *X-inefficiency*, defined as producing at a *higher than necessary ATC*. This is a separate issue from the lack of productive efficiency noted above. Lack of productive efficiency means that while the firm does not produce at the point of minimum ATC, it does produce at some point on the ATC curve. X-inefficiency indicates that the firms' costs are higher than ATC, shown in Figure 7.17.

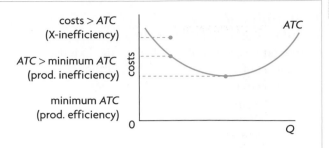

Figure 7.17 X-inefficiency in monopoly

Why a monopoly may be desirable

> ♦ Explain why, despite inefficiencies, a monopoly may be considered desirable for a variety of reasons, including the ability to finance research and development (R&D) from economic profits, the need to innovate to maintain economic profit, and the possibility of economies of scale.

Product development and technological innovation

A number of factors suggest that monopolies have good reasons to pursue innovation:

- Their economic profits provide them with the ability to finance large research and development (R&D) projects.
- Protection from competition due to high barriers to entry may favour innovation and product development, by offering firms the opportunity to enjoy the profits arising from their innovative activities (new inventions, new products, new technologies, etc.). This, after all, is the rationale of awarding firms patent protection for a period of time.
- Firms may use product development and technological innovation as a means of maintaining their economic profits over the long term, by creating barriers to entry for new potential rivals. If a firm can develop a new product that potential rivals are unable to produce, the rivals may be less likely to try to enter the industry and compete with the innovating monopolist.

Possibility of greater efficiency and lower prices due to technological innovations

If monopolies pursue R&D that leads to technological innovations, they may adopt production processes and new technologies that can make them more efficient (i.e. able to produce at a lower cost), and some of these lower costs could be passed to consumers in the form of lower prices.

Economies of scale

Economies of scale lead to falling average costs over a large range of output and firm scale. Extensive economies of scale are a major argument in favour of large firms that can achieve lower costs as they grow in size.

When a monopoly can achieve substantial economies of scale, it is even possible that its lower costs will permit price and output levels that approach those of a perfectly competitive industry. Perfectly competitive firms, because of their small size, are unable to achieve economies of scale. This is shown in Figure 7.18, where Q_m and P_m are the output and price of the standard monopolist, and Q_{pc} and P_{pc} are the output and price of the perfectly competitive industry. Suppose the monopolist succeeds in achieving significant economies of scale, so its costs fall, and its MC curve shifts downward to MC_{es}. The intersection of MC_{es} with the monopolist's MR curve determines the profit-maximising level of output, Q_{pc}, which is identical to that of the perfectly competitive industry. Moreover, the monopolist sells output Q_{pc} at price P_{pc}, which is the price of the perfectly competitive industry. Note that if the MC_{es} curve were even lower, then the monopolist would produce a larger quantity of output and sell it at a lower price than the perfectly competitive industry.

Consumers can therefore gain from economies of scale because lower costs of production translate into lower prices, as well as increased quantity of output. Society as a whole also gains because lower costs of production mean increased efficiency in the use of resources. A perfectly competitive firm, due to its very small size, cannot capture economies of scale.

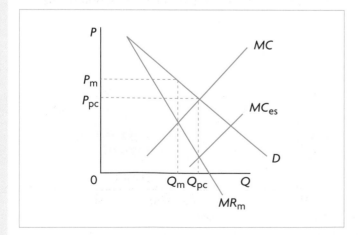

Figure 7.18 Economies of scale leading to lower price and greater quantity by the monopolist than in perfect competition

Test your understanding 7.8

1 Using a diagram, compare and contrast the price and output outcomes of a perfectly competitive industry and an industry organised as a monopoly.

2 Using diagrams, compare and contrast social welfare achieved by a perfectly competitive industry and a monopolistic industry. What is the meaning of $MB > MC$ at the monopolist's equilibrium level of output?

3 Using diagrams, show whether or not the monopolist achieves **(a)** productive efficiency, and **(b)** allocative efficiency, and compare with the firm in perfect competition.

4 Why do you think monopoly as a market structure, and monopoly power generally, come under heavy criticism and are held to be against society's best interests?

5 What are some factors that may make monopoly a desirable market structure?

Legislation and regulation to reduce monopoly power: an evaluation

♦ Evaluate the role of legislation and regulation in reducing monopoly power.

Whereas monopoly may offer some potential benefits to society, there is general agreement that its disadvantages outweigh its advantages. Therefore, most countries around the world do not encourage monopoly. If there are natural monopolies, these are usually owned or regulated by the government, so that they will not be permitted to engage in behaviour that goes against society's interests.

The term *monopoly power*, which refers to the ability of a firm to set prices, applies not only to monopoly, but also to oligopoly. Oligopolistic firms sometimes act together (or 'collude'), usually illegally, to acquire greater monopoly power. If they are successful, they end up acting as if they were a monopoly. Therefore, legislation to reduce monopoly power applies not only to monopolies but also to firms that try to behave like monopolies.

Legislation to reduce monopoly power

Legislation to reduce monopoly power may take the following forms.

Legislation to protect competition

Most countries have laws that try to promote competition by preventing *collusion* between oligopolistic firms (agreements to collaborate, often to fix prices) for the purpose of restricting competition between them, as well as preventing anti-competitive behaviour by a single firm that dominates a market. The objective is to try to prevent monopolistic behaviour by one or a group of firms, and therefore achieve a greater degree of allocative efficiency. A well-known example of a single firm accused of anti-competitive behaviour is Microsoft, found guilty of restricting consumer choice and preventing competitor firms from selling operating systems, thus maintaining its operating systems monopoly. Firms that are found guilty of anticompetitive behaviour are usually asked to pay fines (as in the case of Microsoft), or may be broken up into smaller firms.

There are some difficulties that arise in connection with competition policies:

- There may be difficulties in interpreting the legislation in connection with the behaviour of the offending firms. Different people may have different views on what actions involve anti-competitive behaviour. The laws themselves may be vague, allowing much room for different interpretations.

- Laws in a particular country may be enforced to varying degrees, with some governments enforcing them more strictly than others, depending on their priorities or their political and ideological views. Some governments may accept the principle that government intervention in the market in the form of strict enforcement of competition policies is necessary to protect consumers against monopolistic practices and to achieve allocative efficiency. Other governments may accept the principle that government intervention in the market is not necessary to achieve consumer protection and allocative efficiency, because over long periods of time, the market and competitive forces on their own accomplish these functions. There is no 'right' or 'wrong' answer to this issue, as it depends on normative ideas about the economy (see page 11).

- If firms collude (agree to collaborate, such as by fixing prices), it is difficult to discover evidence of the collusion and to prove it, as collusion occurs secretly, since it is illegal.

Legislation in the case of mergers

A merger is an agreement between two or more firms to join together and become a single firm. Mergers may occur for a number of reasons, such as an interest in capturing economies of scale (a single larger firm may be able to produce at lower average costs), or an interest in firm growth (the firms would like to become larger), or interest in acquiring monopoly

power, which is made possible by the larger size of the new, larger firm.

Mergers are an issue in competition policy because of the possibility that the single firm created from the merging of smaller firms may be very large and have too much monopoly power. Legislation usually involves limits on the size of the combined firms.

Difficulties with merger policies include questions and uncertainties about what firms should be allowed to merge and what firms should not, related to issues of interpreting the legislation as well as ideological differences among different governments on the desirability or not of a high degree of monopoly power (as in the case of competition policies).

Regulation of natural monopoly

If there is a natural monopoly (explained on page 187), it is not in society's interests to break it up into smaller firms, as this would result in higher average costs and would be inefficient. Therefore, governments usually regulate natural monopolies, to ensure more socially desirable price and quantity outcomes. Figure 7.19 shows a natural monopoly; the demand curve intersects the ATC curve before ATC reaches its minimum, indicating that economies of scale have not been full exhausted. Using the $MC = MR$ rule, we find the unregulated monopoly produces Q_m output and sells it at price P_m, with economic profit per unit given by $a-b$. The government can step in to regulate this monopoly in two ways: through marginal cost pricing or average cost pricing.

Marginal cost pricing

The 'best' or optimal policy is force the monopoly to charge a price equal to marginal cost, since with $P = MC$, the monopolist would achieve allocative efficiency. This is called *marginal cost pricing*, and is shown in Figure 7.19, where the intersection of the

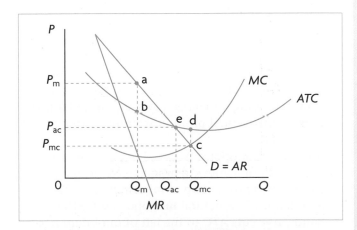

Figure 7.19 Comparing regulated with unregulated natural monopoly: marginal cost pricing (mc) and average cost pricing (ac)

demand (or *AR*) and *MC* curves give rise to price P_{mc} and to quantity Q_{mc}. You can see that Q_{mc} is larger than Q_m produced by the unregulated firm, and P_{mc} is lower than P_m charged by the unregulated firm. Marginal cost pricing forces an efficient allocation of resources, and quantity of the good produced increases to the socially desirable level.

However, marginal cost pricing leads to losses for the natural monopolist. The reason is that P_{mc} lies below the *ATC* curve at the point of production, so price is too low to allow the firm to cover its average costs (loss per unit is given by d – c). As long as the demand curve cuts the *ATC* curve to the left of minimum *ATC*, as in a natural monopoly, it is not possible for the *MC* curve to cut the demand curve at a point above *ATC*. This means that marginal cost pricing will always lead to losses for the natural monopoly. (This need not occur in the standard monopoly diagrams representing a monopoly that is not a natural monopoly.)

Therefore, although marginal cost pricing leads to an efficient solution, it is impractical, as the losses forced on the monopolist would make it go out of business (shut down) in the long run.

Average cost pricing

To avoid creating losses for the natural monopolist, governments can force the firm to charge a price equal to its average total costs (*P = ATC*). This is called *average cost pricing*. This price is determined by the intersection of the demand curve with the *ATC* curve, occurring at point e in Figure 7.19, and giving rise to price P_{ac} and quantity Q_{ac}. Average cost pricing results in a higher price than marginal cost pricing ($P_{ac} > P_{mc}$) and a lower quantity ($Q_{ac} < Q_{mc}$), indicating that it is not as efficient as marginal cost pricing. However, it is far superior to the price–quantity combination achieved by the market for the unregulated monopoly, as you can see by comparing P_{ac} with P_m, and Q_{ac} with Q_m.

Average cost pricing is also known as *fair return pricing*, because the monopolist is forced to earn normal profit. You can see this by noting that when *P = ATC*, the price is just enough to cover the firm's costs of production (explicit plus implicit costs). Therefore, the firm is no longer making a loss, and is no longer making a supernormal profit; it is simply earning normal profit.

When the monopolist is forced to produce where *P = ATC*, it is not achieving productive efficiency, which involves production at minimum *ATC*. This cannot happen in a natural monopoly, since the demand curve cuts *ATC* to the left of minimum *ATC*.

Although neither allocative nor productive efficiency are achieved through average cost pricing,

this policy offers two very important advantages: (a) the monopolist makes normal profit and is not in danger of having to shut down; and (b) it is more efficient than the market solution.

Yet, average cost pricing also has disadvantages. A monopolist in a free, unregulated market faces incentives to keep its average costs low, in order to maximise profits. If through regulation it is guaranteed a price equal to its average costs, it loses this incentive. Even if average costs go up due to inefficiency, it will still receive a price covering its costs.

Another possible disadvantage is that the regulated monopoly may continue to survive as a monopoly, even though it may stop being a natural monopoly (if technological improvements change cost conditions, such as in telecommunications). Continued regulation provides protection to the firm from new competitors that would have been able to produce more efficiently.

Test your understanding 7.9

1 **(a)** What are the objectives of government legislation to reduce monopoly power in the areas of competition and mergers? **(b)** What are some problems encountered in efforts to apply these laws?

2 Using a diagram, explain the advantages and disadvantages of **(a)** marginal cost pricing, and **(b)** average cost pricing, as methods used by government to regulate natural monopolies.

Advantages and disadvantages of monopoly compared with perfect competition

♦ Draw diagrams and use them to compare and contrast a monopoly market with a perfectly competitive market, with reference to factors including efficiency, price and output, research and development (R&D) and economies of scale.

This section summarises points that have been discussed above.

Price and output

Figure 7.14 showed why the monopolist produces a smaller quantity of output and sells it at a higher price than a perfectly competitive industry.

Efficiency

The monopolist's failure to achieve allocative efficiency was shown in Figure 7.15 (in terms of loss of social surplus and the appearance of welfare loss) and in Figure 7.16 in terms of $P > MC$. Both diagrams also show that $MB > MC$, all of which are indications that the monopolist underallocates resources to the production of a good, and that consumers would be better off if more of the good were produced.

In addition, Figure 7.16 shows the monopolist's failure to achieve productive efficiency, because production takes place at higher than minimum ATC.

Finally, the absence of competition faced by the monopolist may lead to X-inefficiency (Figure 7.17).

On the other hand, there is a possibility that innovations in the area of new technology development may lower their costs of production, thus leading to increased efficiencies.

Perfectly competitive firms achieve both allocative and productive efficiency in long-run equilibrium (and allocative efficiency in short-run equilibrium). Also, they are less likely to display X-inefficiency because they are under continuous pressure to lower their costs due to the presence of many competitor firms.

Research and development (R&D)

Firms in perfect competition are unlikely to engage in R&D for several reasons. They have no economic profits in long-run equilibrium with which they can finance R&D. They sell homogeneous products and therefore are not interested in product development that would differentiate their products (make them different from other firms in the industry). They are unable to create barriers to entry as they are too small and so have no incentive to engage in R&D.

Monopolies, on the other hand, have economic profits they can maintain over the long run because of their monopoly position, and this gives them the financial resources they need to pursue R&D. They also have incentives to engage in new product development and innovations because of patent protection that maintains their monopoly power, and the possibilities that new innovations may create barriers to entry that will contribute to the maintenance of their monopoly power.

However, the opposite may also occur. High barriers to entry, shielding monopolies from competition, could make them less likely to innovate than smaller firms (such as in monopolistic competition; see below), which are constantly under pressure to innovate in order to maintain or increase their share of sales in the market.

Economies of scale

Firms in perfect competition have no possibility of achieving economies of scale because of their small size. Monopolies, because of their size, are very well

placed to take advantage of economies of scale, and may use these to create a barrier to entry of new firms (Figure 7.8). On the other hand, economies of scale offer advantages in the form of lower average costs and lower prices as well as greater quantities for consumers, and could possibly approach those achieved in perfect competition (Figure 7.18).

> **Test your understanding 7.10**
>
> Using diagrams, compare and contrast the market structures of perfect competition and monopoly, emphasising the advantages and disadvantages of each.

7.3 Monopolistic competition

Assumptions of the model

♦ Describe, using examples, the assumed characteristics of a monopolistic competition: a large number of firms; differentiated products; absence of barriers to entry and exit.

The model of **monopolistic competition** is based on the following assumptions:

- **There is a large number of firms.** This is similar to perfect competition, where the large firm number ensures that each firm has a small share of the market, and that each firm acts independently of the others.

- **There are no barriers to entry and exit.** This assumption is also similar to perfect competition in that there are no significant barriers to entry of new firms into the industry.

- **There is product differentiation.** Unlike in perfect competition, where firms in each industry produce an identical product, in monopolistic competition each firm produces a product that is different from any other. Product differentiation can be achieved by:
  - *physical differences* – products may differ in size, shape, materials, texture, taste, packaging, etc. (think, for example, of the variety of clothes, shoes, books, processed foods, furniture)
  - *quality differences* – products can differ in quality
  - *location* – some firms attempt to differentiate their product by locating themselves in areas that allow easy access for customers, such as

hotels near airports and convenience stores in residential areas

○ *services* – some firms offer specific services to make their products more attractive, such as home delivery, product demonstrations, free support, warranties and purchase terms

○ *product image* – some firms attempt to create a favourable image by use of celebrity advertising or endorsements, by brand names, or attractive packaging.

Examples of monopolistically competitive industries include book publishing, clothing, shoes, processed foods of all kinds, jewellery, furniture, textiles, drycleaners, petrol (gas) stations, restaurants.

Product differentiation and the demand and revenue curves

Elements of competition and monopoly

♦ Explain that product differentiation leads to a small degree of monopoly power and therefore to a negatively sloping demand curve for the product.

As the term 'monopolistic competition' suggests, this market structure combines elements of both competition and monopoly. It resembles perfect competition because there are many firms in the industry and there is freedom of entry and exit. It is like monopoly because of product differentiation. Each firm in an industry is a 'mini-monopoly' in the specific version of the good that it produces. For example, Adidas is a monopoly in Adidas® shoes, NIKE is a monopoly in NIKE® shoes, and Puma is a monopoly in Puma® shoes. This means that each of these producers faces a downward-sloping demand curve for its product. However, because each

of these products is at the same time a substitute for the other, this demand curve is relatively elastic, i.e. it is more elastic than in monopoly, but less elastic than in perfect competition, as shown in Figure 7.20.

In perfect competition, if a firm raises its price, it loses all its sales to its competitors (Figure 7.20(a)). In monopoly, if a firm raises its price, it loses some but not all sales, as it is the sole producer of the good and consumers have no alternative product they can buy (Figure 7.20(b)). In monopolistic competition (Figure 7.20(c)), if a firm raises its price, it will lose more sales than the monopolist, because consumers now do have substitutes they can switch to; but it will lose fewer sales than the perfectly competitive firm because of product differentiation – the available substitutes are not perfect substitutes, as they are in perfect competition.

This has important implications: it means that if consumers can be convinced that the product they are purchasing (for example, Puma® shoes) is superior to the available substitutes (Adidas® and NIKE® shoes), then Puma has succeeded in establishing a mini-monopoly for its product. Therefore if the price of Puma shoes increases, only some, and not all, buyers of Puma shoes will switch to other brands. Those who believe that Puma shoes are superior will continue to buy them, in spite of the higher price.

The roles of price and non-price competition

♦ Distinguish between price competition and non-price competition.
♦ Describe examples of non-price competition, including advertising, packaging, product development and quality of service.

Price competition occurs when a firm lowers its price to attract customers away from rival firms, thus

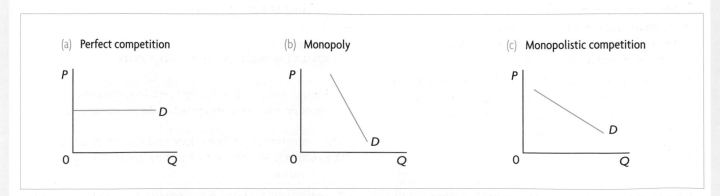

Figure 7.20 Demand curves facing the firm under three market structures

increasing sales at the expense of other firms. **Non-price competition** occurs when firms use methods other than price reductions to attract customers from rivals. The most common forms of non-price competition are product differentiation (including all the features noted above, such as physical and quality differences, packaging, services provision, location, etc.), advertising and branding (creating brand names for products). Monopolistically competitive firms engage heavily in product differentiation through R&D in product development (research that leads to new and/or better products), as well as in advertising and branding. Firms that can attract customers by use of these methods increase their monopoly power and their ability to control the price of their product. They can charge a higher price without risking loss of buyers to rival firms. In general, the more differentiated the product is from its substitutes and the more successful the advertising and branding as methods of convincing consumers about the superiority of a product, the less elastic will be the demand curve facing the firm,[5] the greater the monopoly power (the ability to control price), and the larger the firm's potential to increase short-run economic profits.

Monopolistically competitive firms compete with each other on the basis of both price and non-price competition. The more successful they are in increasing their sales and market share through non-price competition, the less they need to rely on price competition. By contrast, firms that are less able to achieve consumer loyalty for their product, and whose product is less differentiated from substitutes, may have to rely more on price competition to increase their sales and market share.

Test your understanding 7.11

1 What are the assumptions defining the market model of monopolistic competition?

2 List some examples of monopolistically competitive firms in your neighbourhood.

3 In what ways is a monopolistically competitive firm like a firm in perfect competition; in what ways is it like a monopoly?

4 **(a)** What do firms in monopolistic competition try to achieve through product differentiation, advertising and branding? **(b)** How do these activities relate to the demand and revenue curves facing the firm?

5 What is **(a)** price competition, and **(b)** non-price competition? **(c)** How do monopolistically competitive firms compete with each other? **(d)** Provide examples of non-price competition.

6 Why do you think we never see price competition and non-price competition in **(a)** perfectly competitive firms, and **(b)** monopolies?

Profit maximisation

Economic (supernormal) profit or loss in the short run

◆ Explain, using a diagram, the short-run equilibrium output and pricing decisions of a profit-maximising (loss-minimising) firm in monopolistic competition, identifying the firm's economic profit (or loss).

The short-run equilibrium position of the individual firm in monopolistic competition is identical to that of the monopolist, the only difference being in the price elasticity of demand of the demand curve facing the firm, as the demand curve is more elastic and flatter in monopolistic competition than in monopoly. In the short run, the firm can make either supernormal profit (i.e. positive economic profit), normal profit or losses (negative economic profit). Each of these possibilities is shown in Figure 7.21. The firm applies the $MR = MC$ rule to find the profit-maximising or loss-minimising level of output (Q_e), and then for that level of output compares price (given by the demand curve) with ATC to determine profit per unit or loss per unit.

In part (a) of Figure 7.21 the firm earns supernormal profits, since $P > ATC$ at Q_e; in part (b) the firm's economic profit is exactly zero since $P = ATC$ at Q_e, and therefore the firm is earning normal profit; and in part (c), the firm is making losses because $P < ATC$ at Q_e. Total profit or total loss is found by multiplying

$$\frac{\text{profit}}{Q} \text{ by } Q \text{ or } \frac{\text{Loss}}{Q} \text{ by } Q.$$

Normal profit in the long run

◆ Explain, using diagrams, why in the long run a firm in monopolistic competition will make normal profit.

The assumption of free entry and exit of firms in the industry is very important in determining the

---

[5] Advertising and branding work by making the demand curve shift to the right and making it rotate so it becomes steeper.

These two changes mean that demand increases and it becomes less elastic.

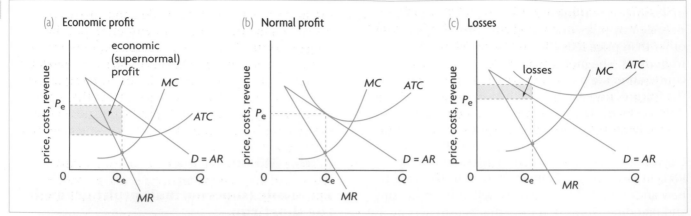

Figure 7.21 Short-run equilibrium positions of the firm in monopolistic competition

long-run equilibrium of the firm (just as in perfect competition).

> In monopolistic competition, in the long run, profit-making industries attract new entrants; in loss-making industries, some firms shut down and exit the industry. The process of entry and exit of firms in the long run ensures that economic profit or loss is zero and all firms earn normal profit.

The profitable industry

Figure 7.21(a) shows the short-run equilibrium of a firm making economic (supernormal) profit. In the long run, when firms can adjust their sizes by changing their fixed inputs, economic profit draws new entrants into the industry. As new firms enter, they attract customers away from the existing firms. The impact on existing firms is to shift the demand curve they face to the left. Firms will continue to enter, and the demand curve facing them will keep shifting leftward, until it reaches the point where it is tangent to (it just touches) the ATC curve. Here, the firms in the industry earn normal profits (economic profit falls to zero), and entry of new firms into the industry stops.

Figure 7.22 shows the long-run equilibrium of the monopolistically competitive firm. At the level of output where $MR = MC$, $P = ATC$; therefore, economic profit is zero and each firm is earning normal profit. (This figure is the same as Figure 7.21(b), where it happens that a firm is earning normal profit in the short run.)

The unprofitable industry

Figure 7.21(c) shows the short-run equilibrium of a loss-making firm. The presence of losses will make some firms shut down completely and leave the industry in the long run. As they do so, their

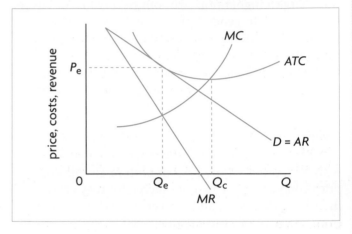

Figure 7.22 Long-run equilibrium of the firm in monopolistic competition

customers switch their purchases to the remaining firms, which experience an increase in demand for their product. This appears as a rightward shift of the demand curve facing them, and this process continues until losses disappear and firms are earning normal profit. This occurs when the demand curve is tangent to (just touches) the ATC curve, so that at the level of output where $MR = MC$, $P = ATC$, and economic profit is zero. Once again, the long-run equilibrium is that shown in Figure 7.22, where the firm is earning normal profit (zero economic profit).

Criticisms of the model

- This model suggests that firms make decisions only on quantity of output and price, whereas, as we have seen, a major aspect of their decisions in fact involves non-price competition (product development, advertising and branding). Profit-maximisation decisions are therefore more complex than the model indicates.

- In the real world, entry into the industry may not be as free as the model suggests, and this is another factor leading to some monopoly power.
- Another difficulty is that in view of product differentiation, it is not possible to derive an industry demand curve, as each product is different from the others. Therefore, we can only examine monopolistic competition at the level of the firm.

Efficiency in monopolistic competition

♦ Explain, using a diagram, why neither allocative efficiency nor productive efficiency are achieved by monopolistically competitive firms.

Allocative and productive inefficiency

Allocative efficiency is given by the condition $P = MC$, and productive efficiency by the condition that production takes place at minimum ATC.

Figure 7.22, showing the long-run equilibrium of the firm in monopolistic competition, indicates that neither allocative nor productive efficiency is achieved.

Comparing price with marginal cost along the vertical line at the equilibrium level of output, Q_e, we can see that price is higher than MC, indicating that there is an underallocation of resources to the production of the good: society would have liked to have more units of the good produced. Also, production occurs at greater than minimum average total cost, and therefore average cost is higher than what is optimal from society's point of view.

Productive inefficiency, product differentiation and excess capacity

A firm's capacity output is that output where ATC is minimum; this is the output level at which the firm's capacity is fully used. In Figure 7.22, capacity output is Q_c, yet by the profit-maximising rule $MR = MC$ the firm produces output Q_e which is smaller than Q_c. The difference between capacity output and profit-maximising output is called excess capacity; this is the amount of output that is lost when firms underuse their resources and produce an amount of output that does not minimise ATC. If all firms produced at the point of minimum ATC, the same quantity of total (industry) output could have been produced by fewer firms, and the costs to society would have been lower. Excess capacity results from

the firm's downward-sloping demand curve. (Only if the demand curve were horizontal could it be tangent to the ATC curve at its minimum point, as in perfect competition.) Excess capacity is therefore the result of product differentiation, leading to the downward-sloping demand curve. Note that excess capacity is closely related to productive inefficiency: they are both the result of production at greater than minimum ATC.

There are numerous examples of excess capacity: restaurants with empty tables, petrol (gas) stations with no one at the pump, retail outlets of all kinds with few customers, hotels with empty rooms.

Yet product differentiation leads to greater product variety. Because consumers enjoy product variety, it is often argued that monopolistic competition may not be as inefficient as appears at first sight, and that excess capacity may be the 'price' consumers pay for having greater product variety.

Comparison of monopolistic competition with other market structures

♦ Compare and contrast, using diagrams, monopolistic competition with perfect competition, and monopolistic competition with monopoly, with reference to factors including short run, long run, market power, allocative and productive efficiency, number of producers, economies of scale, ease of entry and exit, size of firms and product differentiation.

Below is a summary of the important differences between the market models.

Monopolistic competition and perfect competition

- **Number of firms.** Perfect and monopolistic competition are similar in that they have a large number of firms.
- **Free and entry and exit.** In both market models there is free entry and exit of firms.
- **Normal profit in the long run, supernormal profit or loss in the short run.** Firms in both perfect and monopolistic competition earn zero economic profit (normal profit) in the long run. Further, firms in both market models can earn economic (supernormal) profit or make losses in the short run. The profits and losses disappear in the long run because in both models there is free entry and exit of firms, which ensures entry into profitable industries and exit from unprofitable ones.

- **Market power and the demand curve.** Firms in perfect competition have no market power; they are unable to influence price, since they are price-takers, as reflected in the perfectly elastic (horizontal) demand curve they face. Firms in monopolistic competition, however, do have some market power (ability to influence price), and this is reflected in their downward-sloping demand curve.

- **Productive and allocative efficiency.** Whereas the perfectly competitive firm achieves both productive and allocative efficiency in long-run equilibrium, the monopolistically competitive firm achieves neither. Fewer than optimal resources are allocated to the production of the good, and average cost is not minimum at the point of production, with the result that consumers pay a higher price for the good than in perfect competition.

- **Excess capacity.** Since the firm under perfect competition produces the level of output where *ATC* is minimum, it is making full use of its plant and has no excess capacity. The firm under monopolistic competition produces a lower level of output than that where *ATC* is minimum, and therefore has excess capacity.

- **Product variety.** Whereas all firms in perfect competition produce the identical product, under monopolistic competition firms go to great lengths to differentiate their products. From the consumer's perspective, product variety is usually an advantage; perfect competition cannot offer this advantage. It is often argued that production at higher than minimum ATC due to excess capacity in monopolistic competition is the 'price' consumers pay for greater product variety compared with perfect competition where average costs are lower but variety is nonexistent.

- **Economies of scale.** Firms in perfect competition cannot achieve economies of scale because they are very small. Firms in monopolistic competition may have some small room for achieving economies of scale but only to a relatively small degree as these firms also tend to be relatively small.

Monopolistic competition and monopoly

- **Number of producers.** Monopolistic competition is similar to perfect competition in that there is a large number of firms, whereas in monopoly there is a single firm, or else the industry is dominated by one large firm.

- **Size of firms.** In monopolistic competition firms are usually small, whereas in monopoly the fact that there is a single or dominant firm suggests a very large size.

- **Barriers to entry.** Monopolistic competition is characterised by free entry and exit, whereas in monopoly there are high barriers to entry.

- **Normal and economic profits.** Whereas the firm under monopolistic competition earns normal profit in the long run, the monopoly can earn economic (supernormal) profits due to high barriers to entry that prevent new entrants from entering the industry.

- **Competition and prices.** Free entry and exit under monopolistic competition drive economic profits down to zero in the long run, and allow prices to be lower for the consumer than is possible under monopoly, where barriers to entry allow the firm to maintain profits over the long run.

- **Market power.** Both a monopoly and firms in monopolistic competition have market power (the ability to set price), and therefore both face downward-sloping demand curves. However, a monopoly is likely to have more market power because there are no substitutes for the good produced by the monopolist (the availability of substitutes means that consumers can switch to substitute goods, thus reducing the firm's market power).

- **Allocative and productive efficiency.** Both these market structures face downward-sloping demand curves, and therefore both have *MR* curves that lie below the demand curve. This means that at the profit-maximising level of output (found by $MR = MC$), $P > MC$ for both (i.e. no allocative efficiency). Also, *ATC* is higher than minimum *ATC* at the point of production for both (i.e. no productive efficiency).

- **Competition and costs.** Competition between firms in monopolistic competition puts a downward pressure on costs as firms compete with each other. These competitive pressures may force less efficient firms to leave the industry. The absence of competition in monopoly does not exert such a downward pressure on costs.

- **Economies of scale.** Some small economies of scale may be achieved by the firm under monopolistic competition, but the potential for this is much greater under monopoly, which can be to the benefit of the consumer through lower prices.

- **Research and development.** The economic profits that monopolies can earn over the long run puts them in a better position than monopolistically competitive firms with respect to financing R&D. However, the pressures of competition faced by monopolistically competitive firms may induce them to pursue R&D for product development in order to maintain/increase their sales.

1 Use diagrams to explain how a firm in monopolistic competition can **(a)** earn positive economic (supernormal) profit (show profit per unit and total profit), **(b)** earn normal profit, and **(c)** incur losses (show loss per unit and total loss).

2 What is the role of free entry and exit of firms in monopolistic competition in the adjustment from short-run to long-run equilibrium?

3 **(a)** Using a diagram, show the firm's long-run equilibrium position in monopolistic competition. **(b)** Comment on whether the firm achieves economic profit or normal profit in long-run equilibrium.

4 Does the firm in monopolistic competition achieve allocative and productive efficiency?

5 Explain what is meant by the idea that excess capacity is the 'price' of product variety.

6 Evaluate monopolistic competition in comparison with **(a)** perfect competition, and **(b)** monopoly.

7.4 Oligopoly

Assumptions of oligopoly

♦ Describe, using examples, the assumed characteristics of an oligopoly: the dominance of the industry by a small number of firms; the importance of interdependence; differentiated or homogeneous products; high barriers to entry.

Oligopoly is more complex than the other market models. Therefore, there are several models of oligopolistic behaviour, which share the following characteristics:

- **There is a small number of large firms.** The term 'oligopoly' derives from the Greek word ολιγοπώλιο meaning 'few sellers'. Oligopolistic industries are dominated by a small number of large firms, though in any one industry the firms are likely to vary in size.

- **There are high barriers to entry.** All the barriers to entry discussed under monopoly are relevant to oligopoly. They include economies of scale, making it very difficult for new firms starting on a small scale to compete due to very high

costs (for example, the aircraft and car industries); legal barriers such as patents (the pharmaceutical industry); control of natural resources (such as oil, copper, silver); aggressive tactics such as advertising or threats of takeovers of potential new firms. An additional barrier to entry in oligopoly involves high start-up costs (the costs of starting a new firm) associated with developing a new or differentiated product. Many established oligopolies spend enormous sums on product differentiation and advertising, making it difficult for new firms to match such expenditures.

- **Products produced by oligopolistic firms may be differentiated or homogeneous (undifferentiated).** Differentiated products include pharmaceuticals, cars, aircraft, breakfast cereals, cigarettes, refrigerators and freezers, cameras, tyres, bicycles, motorcycles, soaps, detergents. Homogeneous products are fewer; examples include oil, steel, aluminium, copper, cement.

- **There is mutual interdependence.** Firms in perfect and monopolistic competition, due to their large numbers in an industry, behave independently of each other, so when they make decisions such as how much to produce they do not take the possible actions of other firms into consideration. By contrast, the small number of firms in oligopolistic industries makes the firms mutually interdependent; decisions taken by one firm affect other firms in the industry, so they depend on each other. If any one firm changes its behaviour, this can have a major impact on the demand curve facing the other firms. Therefore, firms are keenly aware of the actions of their rivals.

Strategic behaviour and conflicting incentives

♦ Explain why interdependence is responsible for the dilemma faced by oligopolistic firms—whether to compete or to collude.

Mutual interdependence has important implications for the behaviour of oligopolistic firms:

- **Strategic behaviour.** Strategic behaviour is based on plans of action that take into account rivals' possible courses of action. It is similar to playing a card game, or chess, where individual players' actions are based on the expected actions and reactions of their rival(s). Strategic behaviour of oligopolistic firms is the result of their mutual interdependence. For example, a firm plans a course of action X assuming its rivals will follow one policy, and it plans course of action Y assuming its rivals follow a different policy. Under oligopoly, firms planning their strategies make great efforts to guess the actions and reactions of their rivals in order to formulate their own strategy.

- **Conflicting incentives.** Firms in oligopoly face incentives that conflict, or clash with each other:

  ○ *Incentive to collude* – the term **collusion** refers to an agreement between firms to limit competition between them, usually by fixing price and therefore lowering quantity produced. By colluding to limit competition, they reduce uncertainties resulting from not knowing how rivals will behave, and maximise profits for the industry as a whole.

  ○ *Incentive to compete* – at the same time, each firm faces an incentive to compete with its rivals in the hope that it will capture a portion of its rivals' market shares and profits, thereby increasing profits at the expense of other firms.

Clearly, firms in an industry cannot both collude and compete; they must do one or the other.

Explaining oligopolistic behaviour by use of game theory

♦ Explain how game theory (the simple prisoner's dilemma) can illustrate strategic interdependence and the options available to oligopolies.

The characteristics of mutual interdependence, strategic behaviour, and conflicting incentives are illustrated very effectively by **game theory**, a mathematical technique analysing the behavior of decision-makers who are dependent on each other, and who use strategic behaviour as they try to anticipate the behaviour of their rivals. Game theory has become an important tool in microeconomics, and is based heavily on the work of American mathematician and economist John F. Nash (the subject of the 2001 film, *A Beautiful Mind*), who together with John Harsanyi and Reinhard Selten, received the 1994 Nobel Prize in Economics.

The game we will use here illustrates the **prisoner's dilemma**, showing how two rational decision-makers, who use strategic behaviour to maximise profits by trying to guess the rival's behaviour, may end up being collectively worse off. The final position that results from the game is called a *Nash equilibrium*.

Suppose there are two oligopolistic firms in the space travel industry: Intergalactic Space Travel (IST) and Universal Space Line (USL). Each firm must decide on a pricing strategy, i.e. what price to charge consumers for its space travel services, and can choose either a high-price or a low-price strategy. Each firm is interested in making its own profit as large as possible, but its profit will depend on the particular combination of pricing strategies that the two firms choose.

Figure 7.23 shows four possible combinations of pricing strategies and their corresponding profit outcomes (called 'payoffs') for the two firms. This figure represents a 'payoff matrix'. For example, if both IST and USL choose the high-price strategy, in box 4, each will have profit of 40 million Zelninks (abbreviated as Zs). Box 3 shows the profit outcomes of differing price strategies; USL with a low-price strategy makes 70 million Zs, and IST with a high-price strategy makes 10 million Zs. The reason why the low-price firm makes much higher profits is that by charging a low price it captures a large portion of sales from its rival.

Suppose the two firms begin in box 1, where they are competing with each other on the basis of price (price competition) and therefore have a low price, leading to a low profit of 20 million Zs each. Realising that they will both be better off if they enter into a collusive agreement and charge a high price, they collaborate and agree to adopt a high-price strategy, thus entering box 4 where each one earns profits of 40 million Zs.

Now each firm faces a dilemma. Let's look at the dilemma from IST's point of view (though USL is thinking along the same lines). IST realises that by

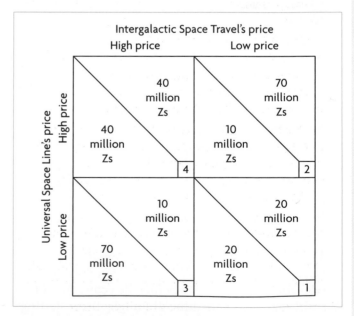

Figure 7.23 Game theory: the prisoner's dilemma

sticking to the agreement, it will continue to earn 40 million Zs, along with USL. On the other hand, IST also realises that by secretly breaking the agreement, and charging a lower price, it can earn the much higher profit of 70 million Zs, while USL earns only 10 million Zs. In addition, IST realises that USL might break the agreement, in which case IST will find itself making only 10 million Zs (worse than even when it was in competition with USL, making 20 million Zs).

What should IST do? As it tries to 'outguess' USL, it is likely to cut its price to beat USL to the higher profits, but since USL is thinking along exactly the same lines, they are both likely to adopt the low-price strategy, in which case they will end up in box 1 where they both have low prices and low profits. This is the Nash equilibrium, in which both firms become worse off.

> The Nash equilibrium shows that there is sometimes a conflict between the pursuit of individual self-interest and the collective firm interest. This conflict is the prisoner's dilemma. Although the firms could be better off by cooperating, each firm, trying to make itself better off, ends up making both itself and its rival worse off.

This game illustrates many real-world aspects of oligopolistic firms, which:

- are mutually interdependent – what happens to the profits of one firm depends on the strategies adopted by other firms; this is known as **strategic interdependence**

- display strategic behaviour – they plan their actions based on guesses about what their competitors are likely to do

- face conflicting incentives – they face the incentive to collude (agree to fix prices and move to box 4 where they both earn high profits); and they face incentives to compete, or in this case to 'cheat' on the agreement, by lowering their price

- become worse off as a result of price competition (trying to capture sales from their rivals by cutting prices) – since the rivals are likely to match the price cuts, all firms end up with lower prices and lower profits (box1); this is called a **price war**

- have a strong interest in avoiding price wars, because they realise that everyone will become worse off through price cutting – this creates a strong incentive for them to compete on the basis of factors other than price (non-price competition).

We will examine these aspects of oligopolistic behaviour in more detail below.

The concentration ratio

◆ Explain how a concentration ratio may be used to identify an oligopoly.

As oligopolies involve a small number of large firms that dominate an industry, it is important to know how 'concentrated' the industry's output is among the industry's largest firms, as this information may provide clues on whether oligopolies have too much monopoly power. A **concentration ratio** provides an indication of the percentage of output produced by the largest firms in an industry. There is no fixed number of firms for which a concentration is calculated. For example, we could say that the 3-firm concentration ratio of industry X is 78%, which means that the three largest firms of industry X produce 78% of the industry's total output; or the 4-firm concentration ratio of industry Y is 45%, which means that the four largest firms in industry Y produce 45% of the industry's total output. Table 7.3 provides some examples of concentration ratios in the United States. We can see there are wide variations from industry to industry, with the most concentrated industry of those appearing in the table being transportation equipment and the least concentrated being furniture.

Concentration ratios are used to provide an indication of the degree of competition in an industry. They suggest that the higher the concentration ratio, the lower the degree of competition, while a low concentration ratio would indicate a greater degree of competition.

In general, an industry is considered to be oligopolistic if the four largest firms control 40% of output. (This is an arbitrary cut-off point, as there is nothing special about a concentration ratio of 40%.)

Industry	4-firm	8-firm
Food	35.0%	46.7%
Chemicals	44.8%	58.7%
Transportation equipment	64.3%	77.7%
Furniture	18.8%	26.5%
Textile mill products	32.0%	44.9%

Table 7.3   Selected concentration ratios in domestic US manufacturing

Source: http://www.swarthmore.edu/SocSci/Economics/fpryor1/Concentration_ratios.pdf

Concentration ratios have several weaknesses that limit their usefulness as a measure of the degree of competition:

- Whereas concentration ratios reflect concentration in a national market, they do not reflect competition from abroad. An industry may have a high concentration ratio, but if there are imports from other countries, this is not accounted for, giving the impression of greater concentration and less competition than there actually is.

- Concentration ratios provide no indication of the importance of firms in the global market; there may be some competition in a domestic market, but the firms may have a very strong, or dominant position in the global market.

- Concentration ratios do not account for competition from other industries, which may be important in the case of substitute goods, such as in the case of different metals. Whereas there may be a high concentration ratio in the aluminium industry, for example, this would be lower if considered together with copper, with which aluminium competes.

- Concentration ratios do not distinguish between different possible sizes of the largest firms. For example, a three-firm concentration ratio of 90% could consist of three firms with 30% of the market each, or of three firms, one of which has 60% of the market and the other two have 15% each. Another measure of concentration, the Herfindahl index, takes account of this problem. It takes the square of each percentage share and sums them, thus attaching a larger weight to firms with a large size, offering a better indication of the degree of market power in an industry.[6] Yet with the exception of accounting for firm size, the Herfindahl index is subject to the same limitations as the concentration ratios above.

Test your understanding 7.13

1 Identify the main assumptions of the oligopolistic market structure.

2 **(a)** What are the conflicting incentives faced by oligopolistic firms? **(b)** How do they relate to the interdependence of the firms? **(c)** What kind of behaviour does interdependence make such firms engage in (that tends to resemble a card game)?

---

3 **(a)** Referring to the conflicting incentives faced by oligopolistic firms, explain why the payoff matrix shown below illustrates the 'prisoner's dilemma' confronting the players of this game. **(b)** Explain the possible profit outcomes of the two firms. **(c)** How are these outcomes related to the firms' interdependence?

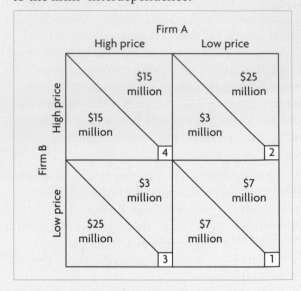

4 **(a)** Explain the meaning of 'concentration ratio' and provide examples (they may be hypothetical). **(b)** What is the purpose of calculating concentration ratios? **(c)** What are some shortcomings of concentration ratios?

Collusive oligopoly

- Explain the term 'collusion', give examples, and state that it is usually (in most countries) illegal.

Collusion in oligopoly refers to an agreement between firms to limit competition, increase monopoly power and increase profits. The most common form of collusion involves price-fixing agreements such as by holding prices constant at some level, raising prices by some fixed amount, fixing price differences between different products, adopting a formula for calculating prices, and others. (See the discussion below on cartels for more examples of collusion).

Collusion is illegal in most countries, because it works to limit competition. Collusion may be formal,

---

[6] In the first case the Herfindahl index is $30^2 + 30^2 + 30^2 = 3 \times 900 = 2700$. In the second case it is $60^2 + 15^2 + 15^2 = 3600 + 225 + 225 = 4050$. The higher index of the second case indicates the very high degree of market power of the single firm with the 60% market share.

usually taking the form of a cartel, or it may be informal, such as price leadership.

Open/formal collusion: cartels

♦ Explain the term 'cartel'.
♦ Explain that the primary goal of a cartel is to limit competition between member firms and to maximise joint profits as if the firms were collectively a monopoly.

A **cartel** is a formal agreement between firms in an industry to take actions to limit competition in order to increase profits it therefore involves **formal collusion** (or **open collusion**). The agreement may involve limiting and fixing the quantity to be produced by each, which results in an increase in price; fixing the price at which output can be sold; setting restrictions on non-price competition (such as advertising); dividing the market according to geographical or other factors; or agreeing to set up barriers to entry. Whatever the case, the objective is to limit competition, increase the monopoly power of the firms, and increase profits.

Suppose the firms of an industry decide to form a cartel by fixing price. Figure 7.24 illustrates how the cartel maximises profit. Note that this figure is identical to Figure 7.11(a) (page 186), which illustrates profit maximisation for a monopolist.

> The key objective of a cartel is to limit competition between the member firms and attempt to maximise joint profits. Cartel members collectively behave like a monopoly.

In Figure 7.24 the demand curve and marginal revenue curve shown are for the industry as a whole. The MC curve is the sum of all the MC curves of all the firms in the cartel. The cartel equates MR with MC to find the cartel's profit-maximising level of output, $Q_{\pi max}$, and then determines price P_e (given by the demand curve). It is then a question of dividing up industry output $Q_{\pi max}$ between all the firms, or deciding how much of the total quantity will be produced by each firm. One way this can be done is to agree on what share of the market each firm will have based on historical market shares. Another way is that firms may agree to compete with each other for market shares using non-price competition (product differentiation and advertising).

The best-known example of a cartel is OPEC (Organization of the Petroleum Exporting Countries), composed of a group of 13 oil-producing countries. OPEC periodically tries to raise the world price of oil by cutting back on its total output. Each member country is assigned an output level (quota) that it is permitted to produce. The restricted quantity of oil results in a higher price.

Firms participating in a cartel have much to gain in terms of monopoly power and increased profits. However, cartels are illegal in most countries, as they restrict competition and are therefore held to be against consumers' and society's best interests.

Obstacles to forming and maintaining cartels

♦ Analyse the conditions that make cartel structures difficult to maintain.
♦ Explain the incentive of cartel members to cheat.

The following factors make it difficult for a cartel to be established and maintained:

* **The incentive to cheat.** Every firm in a cartel faces an incentive to cheat on the agreement, by offering to secretly lower the price for some buyers, or else offer other concessions. A firm that cheats can increase its market share and its profit at the expense of other firms, but if many firms cheat, or if cheating is discovered by other firms in the cartel, then the cartel is in danger of collapsing.

* **Cost differences between firms.** Ideally, each firm would like to have a share of output allowing it to equate its MC with MR, as this will maximise profit for each individual firm as well as for the cartel as a whole. However, this is extremely difficult in practice, since each firm faces different costs and cost curves. Since the price agreed upon by the cartel is common to all the firms, firms with higher average costs have lower profits, while lower-cost firms enjoy higher profits. Cost differences between firms lead

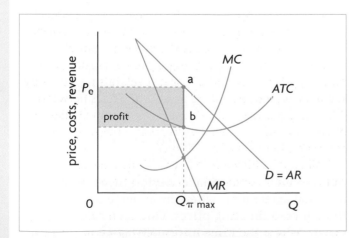

Figure 7.24 Profit maximisation by a price-fixing cartel

to difficulties in agreeing on a common price and on how to allocate the output among the firms.

- **Firms face different demand curves.** Firms are likely to face different demand curves partly because they have different market shares and partly because of product differentiation. The more differentiated the product, the greater the differences between demand curves. Differences in demand curves mean difficulties in reaching agreement on a common price.

- **Number of firms.** The larger the number of firms, the more difficult it is to arrive at an agreement regarding price and the allocation of output, as the greater number of differing views make agreement and compromise more difficult to achieve.

- **The possibility of a price war.** A possible outcome of one or more firms cheating on the cartel agreement is a price war where one firm's price cut is matched by retaliatory price cuts by other firms. The result of a price war is to make all the firms of an industry collectively worse off due to lower prices and lower profits (as we saw in the game theory example).

- **Recessions.** During recessions (periods of low or falling incomes and low levels of economic activity) sales fall and profits are reduced; at such times firms have a stronger incentive to lower prices and cheat on the agreement, endangering the survival of the cartel.

- **Potential entry into the industry.** If a cartel is successful, it will make large economic profits, encouraging entry of new firms into the industry. If there are new entrants, increased industry supply will drive price down cutting into the cartel's profits. The cartel's long-run survival therefore depends on high barriers to entry that block potential new entrants.

- **The industry lacks a dominant firm.** The presence of a dominant firm facilitates reaching agreement, as this firm can assume a leadership position in the negotiations leading to the agreement. For example, in the case of OPEC, the dominant member of the cartel is Saudi Arabia, which is also the largest producer of oil among all the members. The lack of a dominant firm makes agreement among the cartel members more difficult to reach.

Tacit/informal collusion: price leadership and other approaches

- Describe the term 'tacit collusion', including reference to price leadership by a dominant firm.

The difficulties involved in establishing and maintaining cartels as well as their illegality

sometimes make firms turn towards informal types of collusion. **Tacit collusion** (or **informal collusion**) refers to co-operation that is implicit or understood between the co-operating firms, without a formal agreement. The objectives of tacit collusion are also to co-ordinate prices, avoid competitive price-cutting, limit competition, reduce uncertainties and increase profits. Also, tacit collusion attempts to bypass the obstacles created by the illegality of formal collusion (cartels).

One type of informal collusion is **price leadership**, where a dominant firm in the industry (which may be the largest, or the one with lowest costs) sets a price and also initiates any price changes. The remaining firms in the industry become price-takers, accepting the price that has been established by the leader. The implicit agreement (as there is no formal agreement) binds the firms as far as price goes, but they are free to engage in non-price competition. A characteristic of price leadership arrangements is that price changes tend to be infrequent, and are undertaken by the leader only when major demand or cost changes occur. Examples of industries that have at different times followed the price leadership model include US Steel, Kellogg's (breakfast cereals) and R. J. Reynolds (cigarettes).

Obstacles to sustained price leadership are similar to the obstacles faced by cartels:

- Cost differences between firms, particularly in cases where there is significant product differentiation, make it difficult for firms to follow a leader.

- Whereas some firms may follow the leader, others may not, in which case the leader risks losing sales and market share if it initiates a price increase that is not followed.

- Firms still face the incentive to cheat by lowering their price (below that of the leader) to capture market share and increase profits; a breakdown in price leadership can result in a price war among firms.

- High industry profits can attract new firms that will cut into market shares and profits of established firms and endanger the price leadership arrangement.

- Price leadership, depending on where and how it is practised, may or may not be legal.

Another type of informal collusion involves informal agreements where firms agree to use a rule for co-ordinating prices. One such rule is *limit pricing*, where the firms informally agree to set a price that is lower than the profit-maximising price, thus earning less than the highest possible profits and so discouraging new firms from entering the industry. With limit pricing, firms may end up sacrificing some profit in order to avoid attracting new firms into the industry.

Test your understanding 7.14

1 **(a)** What is collusion? **(b)** What do firms in oligopoly try to achieve through collusion?

2 **(a)** What is a cartel and how is it related to collusive oligopoly? **(b)** What are the objectives of a cartel? **(c)** Using a diagram, show how a cartel resembles a monopoly. **(d)** Why do you think cartels are illegal in most countries?

3 Why do cartel members face incentives to cheat?

4 What are the obstacles to forming and maintaining cartels?

5 **(a)** What is the meaning of tacit collusion? **(b)** Explain price leadership as one type of tacit collusion.

Non-collusive oligopoly: the kinked demand curve

* Explain that the behaviour of firms in a non-collusive oligopoly is strategic in order to take account of possible actions by rivals.
* Explain, using a diagram, the existence of price rigidities, with reference to the kinked demand curve.

In the real world, prices of oligopolistic industries tend to be rigid or 'sticky'; once a particular price is reached, it tends to be relatively stable (it sticks) over long periods of time. Moreover, in situations when prices do change, they tend to change together for all the firms in an industry. While price rigidities can be easily explained by collusive oligopoly, they also appear in situations of **non-collusive oligopoly**, where oligopolistic firms do not agree, whether formally or informally, to fix prices or collaborate in some way.

The **kinked demand curve** is a model that has been developed to explain price rigidities of oligopolistic firms that do not collude, and is illustrated in Figure 7.25. In this model, firms do not make formal or informal agreements with each other on how to fix or co-ordinate prices. Instead, their pricing behaviour is strategic, and is strongly influenced by their expectations of how rival firms

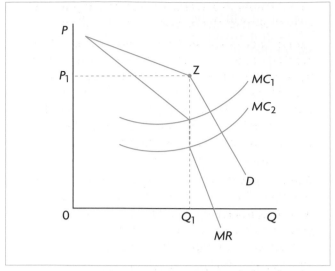

Figure 7.25 The kinked demand curve

will react if they undertake a price change. These expectations are reflected in the kinked (i.e. not straight) demand curve facing each firm, as shown in the figure. Note that corresponding to the kinked demand curve is a broken marginal revenue curve; the break in *MR* occurs exactly at the point of the kink in the demand curve, and is a reflection of the abrupt drop in marginal revenue at the point where the demand curve suddenly bends.

Imagine three firms, A, B, and C, each producing output Q_1 and selling it at price P_1; this price–quantity combination is point Z at the kink of the demand curve. We want to see why the firms perceive the demand curve facing them as having this peculiar shape.

Say that firm A considers a price change, but before changing (increasing or decreasing) its price, it tries to predict how firms B and C will react, and what will be the consequences of their reaction. Firm A's reasoning is as follows:

* If I raise my price, what will B and C do? They are unlikely to increase their price, because if they continue to sell at P_1, many of my customers will leave me and start buying from B and C. Therefore, B's and C's market share will increase, and mine will fall. I should therefore not increase my price. My demand curve is relatively *elastic above* P_1, because for any price increase I will face a relatively large decrease in sales and revenues, and my profits may fall (though not all my customers will leave me because of my differentiated product).

* If I drop my price, what will B and C do? They are likely to drop their price as well, because if they do not, I will capture a large portion of their

sales, and I will be better off at their expense. But if they drop their price, I will capture only a small part of their market shares. My demand curve is relatively *inelastic below P1*, because for any price decrease I will have only a small increase in sales and revenues, and my profits may fall. I should therefore not drop my price.

- I should therefore not change my price, and should continue selling at P_1.

This line of reasoning is the same for all three firms, A, B and C.

This simple model illustrates three important points:

- **Firms that do not collude are forced to take into account the actions of their rivals in making pricing decisions.** Otherwise they risk lowering their revenues and profits, which in turn could lead to price instability. The kinked demand curve model illustrates the interdependence of oligopolistic firms.

- **Even though the firms do not collude, there is still price stability.** Firms are reluctant to change their price because of the likely actions of their rivals, which could result in lower profits for the firm initiating price changes.

- **Firms do not compete with each other on the basis of price.** They do not try to increase their sales by attracting customers through lower prices. A lower price not only invites price cuts by rivals, with resulting lower profits for all the firms, but also risks setting off a price war if some firms overreact with price cutting.

Figure 7.25 also shows that the non-colluding firms' price and output decision is consistent with a whole range of different costs. MC_1 is the upper limit and MC_2 is the lower limit of marginal costs that are consistent with producing output Q_1 and selling this at price P_1, by use of the $MC = MR$ profit-maximising rule. This is the result of the broken portion of the MR curve.

In the kinked demand curve model, each firm perceives the demand curve it faces to be elastic for prices above P_1 and inelastic for prices below P_1. If one firm raises its price above P_1, the others will not follow; if it lowers its price below P_1, the others will match the price decrease. In either case, the firm will be worse off. Therefore, no firm takes the initiative to change its price, and they all remain 'stuck' at point Z for long periods of time.

However, the model is subject to limitations:

- It cannot explain how the firms arrived at point Z, the point of the kink in the demand curve.

- It is inappropriate as an explanation of oligopolistic pricing behaviour during periods of inflation, when prices increase, and during recession, when prices often drop, to the point that at times they can set off price wars.

Test your understanding 7.15

1 How does non-collusive oligopoly differ from collusive oligopoly?

2 **(a)** Show the kinked demand curve model using a diagram. **(b)** How can you account for the shape of the kinked demand curve (use the elasticity concept in your answer). **(c)** What does this model try to explain? **(d)** Why is the behaviour of firms described by this model strategic?

The role of non-price competition in oligopoly

- Explain why non-price competition is common in oligopolistic markets, with reference to the risk of price wars.
- Describe, using examples, types of non-price competition.

Unlike firms in monopolistic competition that compete on the basis of both price and non-price competition, oligopolistic firms go to great lengths to avoid price competition. An important reason is that they are very careful not to trigger a price war, where one firm's price cut is matched by a retaliatory price cut by another firm. As our discussion of game theory showed, a price war makes all the firms of an industry collectively worse off due to lower prices and lower profits. A price war may even lead to prices lower than average costs, leading to losses for the firms. Firms in oligopoly are better off co-ordinating their pricing behaviour where they can, and when they do not collude they still avoid competitive price-cutting.

However, oligopolistic firms usually do engage in intense non-price competition, involving efforts by firms to increase market share by methods other than price, which typically include product development, advertising and branding (see page 197).

Rising beer prices

Big beer companies, Anheuser-Busch Inbev and Miller Coors are raising prices at the same time, during a recession and while demand for beer is falling. Both groups usually adjust the price of a six-pack each year to reflect changes in costs of production, but their ability to do so at a time when customers are hurting reflects the market power that has come with increased concentration: the two groups now control 80% of the beer market.

There has been a huge increase in the degree of concentration in the beer industry: the number of American brewers fell by more than 90% between 1947 and 1995. More recently, South African Breweries bought Miller, and

later SABMiller began a joint venture with Molson Coors. After buying Miller, South African Breweries tried to take a market share from Bud only to find Bud cutting its prices. A price war followed as other beer companies were forced to follow the price cuts. This was a good outcome for consumers – 'the summer of 2005 was a beer drinker's dream'.

All this has changed. With prices rising as demand is falling, the case almost begs for an investigation into anti-competitive behaviour.

Source: Adapted from Aliza Rosenbaum, Rob Cox and Pierre Briancon, 'Rising beer prices hint at oligopoly' in *The New York Times*, 27 August 2009.

Applying your skills

1 What is the implication of the statement that beer prices are rising during a recession and while demand is falling?

2 What might be a consequence of the rising degree of concentration in the beer industry?

3 What are some possible explanations for the beer industry's ability to raise the price of beer even though demand for beer is weak?

4 Explain the meaning of 'price war' and the statement that 'the summer of 2005 was a beer drinker's dream'.

Non-price competition is very important in oligopoly for the following reasons:

- Oligopolistic firms often have considerable financial resources (due to large profits) that they can devote to both R&D and advertising and branding. Whereas monopolistically competitive firms also engage in non-price competition, their resources for these purposes are generally not as large.

- The development of new products provides firms with a competitive edge; they increase their monopoly power, demand for the firm's product becomes less elastic, and successful products give rise to opportunities for substantially increased sales and profits.

- Product differentiation can increase a firm's profit position without creating risks for immediate retaliation by rivals. It takes time and resources for rival firms to develop new competitive products. It would be very difficult to engage in a 'new product war' as opposed to a price war, in which price

cuts can be very quickly matched or exceeded by rival firms.

Test your understanding 7.16

1 Provide examples of non-price competition, and explain why it is important to firms in oligopoly.

2 **(a)** Why do oligopolistic firms avoid price competition? **(b)** What is a price war, and why do oligopolistic firms avoid it?

Evaluating oligopoly (supplementary material)

Criticisms of oligopoly

To the extent that oligopolistic firms succeed in avoiding price competition, they achieve a considerable degree of monopoly power, and therefore face the same criticisms as monopoly:

- Neither productive nor allocative efficiency is achieved.

- Higher prices are charged and lower quantities of output are produced than under competitive conditions.
- There may be higher production costs due to lack of price competition (X-inefficiency).

In addition, there is a further argument against oligopoly:

- Whereas many countries have anti-monopoly legislation that protects against the abuse of monopoly power, the difficulties of detecting and proving collusion among oligopolistic firms means that such firms may actually behave like monopolies by colluding and yet may get away with it.

Benefits of oligopoly

The benefits of oligopoly are also similar to the benefits of monopoly:

- Economies of scale can be achieved due to the large size of oligopolistic firms, leading to lower production costs to the benefit of society and the consumer (through lower prices).
- Product development and technological innovations can be pursued due to the large economic (supernormal) profits from which research funds can be drawn. This benefit of oligopoly is more important than in the case of monopoly, since non-price competition forces firms to be innovative in order to increase their market share and profits.
- Technological innovations that improve efficiency and lower costs of production may be passed to consumers in the form of lower prices.

Over and above the benefits of oligopoly that are similar to monopoly, oligopoly also offers the following advantage:

- Product development leads to increased product variety, thus providing consumers with greater choice (monopoly does not offer product differentiation and variety).

Advantages and disadvantages of advertising

Oligopolies engage heavily in advertising as part of non-price competition. The only other market structure where advertising figures prominently is monopolistic competition, where firms also engage in non-price competition. Firms in perfect competition obviously do not advertise, as they produce a

homogeneous product, whereas in monopoly there is no need for advertising as the monopolist is the sole producer.

Economists disagree on the efficiency aspects of advertising. The following arguments suggest that advertising can increase efficiency:

- Advertising provides consumers with information about alternative products; it makes it easier for consumers to search for the product that is best suited to their needs, and therefore reduces time and effort wasted on searching for alternative products.
- Advertising by rival firms increases competition between them, and therefore contributes to decreasing their monopoly power.
- Advertising facilitates introduction of new products by providing information to consumers; in this way, competition (non-price) increases between firms.
- By facilitating the introduction of new products, advertising can help lower barriers to entry of new firms into an industry.
- By facilitating the introduction of new products, advertising can also provide firms with an extra incentive to engage in research and development for the development of new products.

The following arguments suggest that advertising contributes to lowering efficiency:

- Huge sums spent on advertising by large oligopolistic firms can create barriers to the entry of new firms that cannot match such expenditures.
- Advertising increases costs of production and means higher prices for consumers.
- Successful advertising increases a firm's monopoly power.
- Consumers may become confused and misled about product quality, and may pay higher prices for inferior products.
- Advertising may create needs that consumers would not otherwise have, resulting in a waste of resources as consumers buy goods and services they would not have wanted if they were not influenced by advertising.

Some of the points noted above contradict each other. It is possible that different circumstances give rise to different (positive or negative) results.

Perfect competition and the real world

The model of perfect competition is the basis of an idealised free-market economy, where price is the rationing system that supplies answers to the *what* and *how to produce* questions.[7] The market and the price mechanism are the means by which allocative and productive efficiency are achieved, thus avoiding waste of resources.

Many economists have strongly criticised preoccupation with the perfectly competitive model. They note that the real world is dominated by large oligopolistic firms and monopolistically competitive firms, and the model of perfect competition bears no relationship to either of these. Trying to test the perfectly competitive model would be meaningless given the real-world context of firm behaviour. The very concept of 'competition' has vastly different meanings, with competition in perfect competition being anonymous and equivalent to complete absence of market power (no ability to influence price), and competition in the other two market models involving efforts to capture market shares from rival firms, either through price cuts or through product differentiation and advertising (non-price competition). These real-world types of competition are completely irrelevant for the perfectly competitive firm that can neither gain anything by lowering its price nor can it differentiate and advertise its product.

In addition, many economists question the notion of equilibrium (an idea borrowed from physics), and point out that equilibrium for the firm makes sense only under conditions of complete certainty and perfect knowledge.

As there is no such thing in the real world, there can be no equilibrium.

On the other hand, defenders of the perfectly competitive market model argue that this can be used as a 'parable' that can approximate (or describe very roughly) the outcomes of real-world firm behaviour, regardless of whether these firms are oligopolistic or monopolistically competitive. They also argue that in spite of its lack of realism, this model serves as a tool for assessing real-world situations that depart from the ideals of allocative and productive efficiency, thus helping governments prescribe policy measures to deal with issues in the industrial sector.

---

[7] It also answers the *for whom to produce* question on income distribution. However, the answer provided is generally highly unsatisfactory, and for this reason becomes a normative issue about how governments should intervene in markets to change market-determined income distribution (see Chapter 11).

Thinking points

- How useful do you think is the model of perfect competition?
- Do you think it matters that it is based on highly unrealistic assumptions (see also the Theory of knowledge feature on page 166)?
- Do you think economists should focus more on developing and using more realistic market models, based on monopolistic competition and oligopoly?

7.5 Price discrimination

Definition and conditions for price discrimination

The single-price firm versus the price-discriminating firm

- Describe price discrimination as the practice of charging different prices to different consumer groups for the same product, where the price difference is not justified by differences in cost.

So far in our study of firm behaviour we have assumed that firms under all market structures charge a single price for all units of output they sell. This applies not only to firms under perfect competition (where price is constant for all units of output), but also to firms under monopoly, oligopoly and monopolistic competition. In monopoly, for example, we have seen that while price varies according to quantity of output sold, once the firm decides what quantity of output to produce, all the units of output are sold at the same price. In Figure 7.9(b) (page 183), if the firm chooses to produce Q_1 units of output, all of it will be sold at the single price P_1. If it had chosen Q_2 units of output, all of it would be sold at the single price P_2. Firms that sell all their output at the same price do not practise price discrimination.

Yet firms often find that they can increase their profits by selling their product at different prices. **Price discrimination** is the practice of charging a different price for the same product to different consumers when the price difference is not justified by differences in costs of production. (If price differences are due to differences in a firm's costs of production, then they do not qualify as 'price discrimination'.)

Conditions for price discrimination

♦ Explain that price discrimination may only take place if all of the following conditions exist: the firm must possess some degree of market power; there must be groups of consumers with differing price elasticities of demand for the product; the firm must be able to separate groups to ensure that no resale of the product occurs.

For a firm to be able to practise price discrimination, the conditions outlined below must hold.

The price-discriminating firm must have some market power

The price-discriminating firm must have some degree of market power, or some ability to control price; in other words, it must face a downward-sloping demand curve. Price discrimination can therefore occur in all market structures except perfect competition.

Natural monopolies (such as electricity, gas and water companies), having a significant degree of market power, practise price discrimination whenever they can. For example, electricity companies often charge lower prices at night than during the day for consumption of electricity. Water companies often charge different prices according to the quantity of water consumed. Oligopolistic firms also often practise price discrimination; for example, airlines as a rule charge higher fares during peak travel seasons such as during summer months. Similarly, firms in monopolistic competition also price discriminate: cinemas (movie theatres) may charge different prices to children or older people, or different prices according to viewing time; restaurants often offer discounts (lower prices) for particular groups of customers or on particular days.

On the other hand, the perfectly competitive firm can sell any amount of output at the single price determined in the market; if it increases price to

some customers, it will lose them to different sellers; and it would have no reason to lower price for some customers since it can sell its entire output at the market price. Therefore, the perfectly competitive firm has no possibility of charging different prices for the same good.

Separation of consumers into groups to avoid the possibility of resale

Consumers must be separated from each other on the basis of some characteristic, such as time, geography, age, gender, technology, income or other factors. Firms differentiate their prices on the basis of these characteristics. For example, cinemas (movie theatres) and hotels often charge lower prices to older people and children (consumer separation by age); telephone companies sometimes offer lower rates for evening or weekend calls (consumer separation by time); publishers often charge different prices for the same books in different countries (consumer separation by geography). The price-discriminating firm must ensure that it is not possible (or at least is very difficult and costly) for any consumer to buy at the low price and resell at the higher price. If resale were possible or easy, consumers would avoid purchasing from the higher price firm, and would try to buy the product from other consumers who had bought at the lower price. In some cases, resale is impossible due to the nature of the product, especially where services are involved, such as in the case of medical services, legal services and education.

Different price elasticities of demand

Consumers must have different price elasticities of demand (*PED*s) for the good. This is because consumers with a relatively low *PED* will be willing to pay a higher price for a good than consumers with a relatively higher *PED*. This will become clearer in the discussion that follows.

Third-degree price discrimination

♦ Draw a diagram to illustrate how a firm maximises profit in third-degree price discrimination, explaining why the higher price is set in the market with the relatively more inelastic demand.

Third-degree price discrimination[8] is based on the principle that different consumer groups have different price elasticities of demand for a product. This is the most common type of price discrimination, occurring

---

[8] First-degree price discrimination involves discrimination among individual consumers; second-degree price discrimination involves discrimination between quantities of a good purchased. Both these are beyond the scope of the IB syllabus.

when consumers are separated into different groups (or markets), hence is also known as 'discrimination among consumer groups'. The firm charges higher prices to consumers with a lower *PED*, and lower prices to those with a higher *PED*. Examples include:

- cinemas (movie theatres), museums, hotels, transport companies and others often charge lower prices for children and older people than to the rest of consumers
- airlines charge higher prices for business travellers than for leisure travellers
- airlines charge higher prices the closer the booking date is to the date of travel
- restaurants and theatres may offer special discounts (i.e. lower prices) on week nights
- hotels offer discounts (i.e. lower prices) for winter or mid-week stays
- telephone companies often charge lower rates in the evenings and at weekends
- hairdressers may charge higher prices for women
- drycleaners may charge higher prices for women's clothes
- bars may offer lower prices for a short period immediately after working hours (5 or 6 p.m.).

The condition that makes this kind of price discrimination profitable for a firm is that each consumer group must have a different *PED*. For example, business travellers' demand for airline tickets is relatively inelastic (low *PED*), and therefore airline tickets are often more expensive if there is no stay-over on a Saturday night (on the assumption that business travellers are usually unwilling to stay overnight on a Saturday). Children and elderly people have a more elastic demand (higher *PED*) for movies, transport

services and other products and are therefore charged lower prices. The demand for telephone services by businesses is less elastic during the day on weekdays, and therefore higher prices are charged during those hours. The demand for hotels in winter and on weekdays, as well as the demand for restaurant meals on weekdays, are more elastic than during holidays and on weekends, and therefore lower prices are charged during these times. Similarly, the demand for drinks in bars is more elastic in the early hours of the evening and therefore here, too, lower prices are charged.

The firm's profit-maximising strategy in third-degree price discrimination is illustrated in Figure 7.26. Assume there are two consumer groups (or two markets) for product X, distinguished from each other on the basis of differing *PED*s. Part (a) shows the consumer group of market 1 to have a relatively inelastic demand (low *PED*), while part (b) shows the consumer group of market 2 to have a relatively elastic demand (high *PED*). The two marginal revenue curves are added horizontally, leading to the total market marginal revenue curve in part (c), which also shows the firm's marginal cost curve.

To maximise profit, the firm equates market *MR* with *MC*, thus finding the profit-maximising level of output Q_3. Output Q_3 must now be divided between the two markets. The firm does this by equating its *MC* of the total market with the *MR* of each individual market: $MC = MR = MR_1 = MR_2$. This determines output level Q_1 in market 1, sold at price P_1 (given by the demand curve D_1), and output level Q_2 in market 2, sold at price P_2 (given by the demand curve D_2). (Note that $Q_1 + Q_2 = Q_3$.) Figure 7.26 shows that the firm will charge:

- a higher price (P_1) for the consumer group with relatively inelastic demand

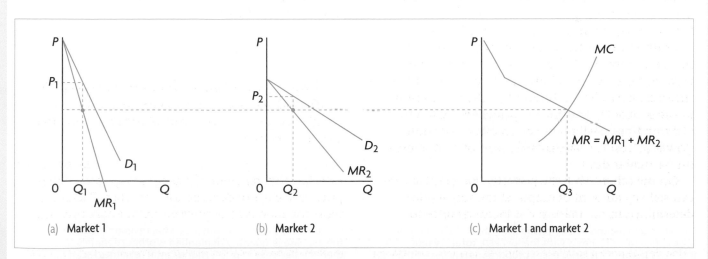

(a) Market 1   (b) Market 2   (c) Market 1 and market 2

Figure 7.26 Third-degree price discrimination

• a lower price (P_2) for the consumer group with relatively elastic demand.

Third-degree price discrimination results in higher revenues and profits for firms.[9] If profits did not increase, firms would not practise price discrimination.

Effects of price discrimination (supplementary material)

Apart from the effects on revenues and profits, the results of third-degree price discrimination are very complex and ambiguous, as they depend on a variety of factors, making it difficult to draw general conclusions.

• There is a possibility of increased monopoly power. A firm that uses aggressive tactics to increase its monopoly power can use price discrimination to charge high prices in one market and low prices in another market with the intention of driving out rival firms that may be unable to compete with the low price. If it succeeds, it increases its monopoly power.

• Total output may increase or decrease. If it increases, it does not reach the socially optimum level (allocative efficiency is not achieved).

• If output increases, then under certain conditions allocative efficiency will also improve; if output falls, then allocative efficiency will worsen.

• Prices will be lower for some groups and higher for other groups, compared to the single price charged by the single-price firm. Therefore, some consumer groups can benefit if a product that was previously not affordable now comes within their reach (for example, students, pensioners, leisure travellers who plan far ahead of time, mid-week restaurant goers, and many others). On the other hand, those groups who have to pay higher prices will clearly lose, and for some of them, the product will become unaffordable.

• Consumer surplus increases for some groups (those that gain from the price fall) and it decreases for other groups (those that lose from the price increase).

• What happens to overall consumer surplus depends on what happens to output. If output falls, consumer surplus falls; if output increases, consumer surplus may either increase or decrease, depending on the particular situation.

Test your understanding 7.17

1 (a) Explain the meaning of price discrimination. (b) What conditions must hold for price discrimination to take place? (c) Why do firms practise price discrimination?

2 Why is it impossible for a perfectly competitive firm to practise price discrimination?

3 (a) Provide examples of third-degree price discrimination. (b) How does this depend on the price elasticity of demand of different consumer groups that are charged different prices?

4 Using a diagram, show how a firm maximises profit in third-degree price discrimination.

Assessment

The Student's CD-ROM at the back of this book provides practice of examination questions based on the material you have studied in this chapter.

Higher level
• Exam practice: Paper 1, Chapter 7
  ○ HL topics (questions 7.1–7.19)

• Exam practice: Paper 3, Chapter 7
  ○ HL topics (questions 16–17)

---

[9] You can understand this by considering that when the firm raises price for consumers with the low *PED*, total revenue increases because the price rise is proportionally larger than the decrease in quantity demanded. When the firm lowers price for consumers with the high *PED*, total revenue increases because the increase in quantity demanded is proportionally larger than the decrease in price. Higher total revenues mean higher economic profits.

Section 2
Macroeconomics

Macroeconomics studies the economy as a whole. In contrast to microeconomics, where we examine specific product and resource markets and the behaviour of individual decision-making units such as consumers, firms and resource owners, we now focus on the larger picture of the economy, composed of collections of many consumers, firms, resource owners and markets. Instead of individual product prices, we study the general price level of the economy; instead of demand for individual products, we examine total demand for goods and services; and instead of individual firm and industry supply, we examine the total output produced in the economy. Further, we study total employment, total investment, total exports and imports and more such totals or wholes, which in macroeconomics are called *aggregates*.

The study of macroeconomics arises because there are some important economic objectives that cannot be understood and analysed at the level of microeconomics. The most important **macroeconomic objectives** involve how to achieve:

- full employment
- a stable or gently rising price level
- economic growth
- an equitable distribution of income
- external balance (balance of trade and avoidance of balance of payments problems).

The first four objectives are the subject of Section 2 of this book, which is on macroeconomics, where we will also study different kinds of policies governments can pursue as they try to achieve them. External balance is discussed in Section 3, which deals with the international economy.

Chapter 8
The level of overall economic activity

In this chapter we will discover how economists measure an economy's total output and income, as well as growth in output and income.

8.1 Economic activity

The circular flow of income model

The model in a closed economy with no government

- Describe, using a diagram, the circular flow of income between households and firms in a closed economy with no government.
- Identify the four factors of production and their respective payments (rent, wages, interest and profit) and explain that these constitute the income flow in the model.
- Outline that the income flow is numerically equivalent to the expenditure flow and the value of output flow.

The **circular flow of income model** illustrates a number of concepts and relationships that will help us understand the macroeconomy. In its simplest version, shown in Figure 8.1, the model illustrates a **closed economy**, meaning it has no links with other countries (it is 'closed' to international trade), and is also a model of an economy with no government

It is assumed that the only decision-makers are households (or consumers) and firms (or businesses); both are shown in square boxes. Households and firms are linked together through two markets: product markets and resource markets, shown in diamonds.

Households are owners of the four factors of production: land, labour, capital and entrepreneurship (see Chapter 1, page 3, for a review of the factors of production). Firms buy the factors of production in resource markets and use them to produce goods and services. They then sell the goods and services

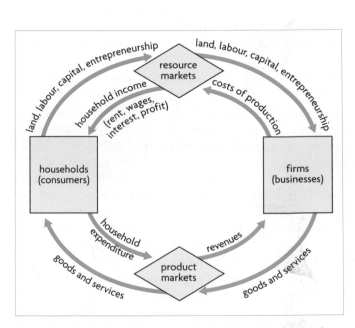

Figure 8.1 Circular flow of income model in a closed economy with no government

to consumers in product markets. We therefore see a flow in the clockwise direction of factors of production from households to firms, and of goods and services from firms to households.

In the counterclockwise direction, there is a flow of *money* used as payment in sales and purchases. When households sell their factors of production to firms, they receive payments taking the form of **rent** (for land), **wages** (for labour), **interest** (for capital) and **profit** (for entrepreneurship). These payments are the *income of households*. The payments that households make to buy goods and services are *household expenditures* (or consumer spending). The payments that firms make to buy factors of production represent their *costs of* *production*, and the payments they receive by selling goods and services are their *revenues*. All payment flows, known as *money flows*, are shown in Figure 8.1

This model demonstrates an important principle: the **income flow** from firms to households is equal to the **expenditure flow** from households to firms. In other words, the household incomes coming from the sale of all the factors of production equals the expenditures by households on goods and services. This is the **circular flow of income**.

In addition, these two flows must be equal to the value of goods and services, or the value of total output produced by the firms, known as the **value of output flow**. The reasoning of this is as follows: if each good and service is multiplied by its respective price, we obtain the value of each good and service, and adding them all up we arrive at the value of total output. This value is the same as consumer expenditure, since spending by consumers is equal to each item they buy multiplied by its price. Therefore:

> The circular flow of income shows that in any given time period (say a year), the value of output produced in an economy is equal to the total income generated in producing that output, which is equal to the expenditures made to purchase that output.

Adding leakages and injections

♦ Describe, using a diagram, the circular flow of income in an open economy with government and financial markets, referring to leakages/withdrawals (saving, taxes and import expenditure) and injections (investment, government expenditure and export revenue).

The real-world economy is more complicated than this simple model suggests. We arrive at a closer picture of the real world by adding **injections** and **leakages** (also known as **withdrawals**) to the money flow of Figure 8.1. To understand what these are, consider a pipe with water flowing through it, as in Figure 8.2. As water flows through the pipe, some leaks out (the leakages), while new supplies of water are injected in (the injections). It is the same with the flows of money in the circular flow model.

Leakages and injections are paired together so that what leaks out of the flow can come back in as an injection. The most important pairs are the following:

leakages	injections
saving	investment
taxes	government spending
imports	exports

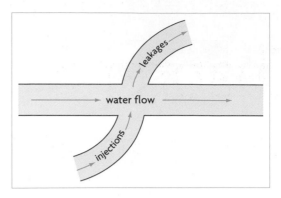

Figure 8.2 Leakages and injections

Saving and investment

Saving is the part of consumer income that is not spent but is saved. Investment is spending by firms for the production of capital goods, which is one of the four factors of production (physical capital, see Chapter 1, page 4). This is why capital goods are also known as investment goods. How are saving and investment linked together as leakages and injections?

When households save part of their income, this represents a leakage from the circular flow of income because it is income that is not spent to buy goods and services. Households place their savings in financial markets (bank accounts, purchases of stocks and bonds, etc.). Firms obtain funds from financial markets (through borrowing, issuing stocks and bonds, etc.) to finance investment, or the production of capital goods. These funds therefore flow back into the expenditure flow as injections. This process is shown in Figure 8.3, which, in addition to the money flows of Figure 8.1, shows the three leakage/injection pairs above. (For simplicity, this figure contains only money flows.) Leakages appear in the left-hand side of the figure, and injections on the right. We can see that saving leaks out of the flow of consumer expenditures, and after passing through financial markets is injected back into the expenditure flow as investment.

Taxes and government spending

Taxes and government spending are connected to each other through the government. Households pay taxes to the government; this is a leakage because it is income that is not spent to buy goods and services. The government uses the tax funds to finance government expenditures (on education, health, defence, etc.) and this spending is an injection back into the expenditure flow.

Imports and exports

Imports are goods and services produced in other countries and purchased by domestic buyers. Exports are goods and services produced domestically and purchased by foreigners. When an economy has

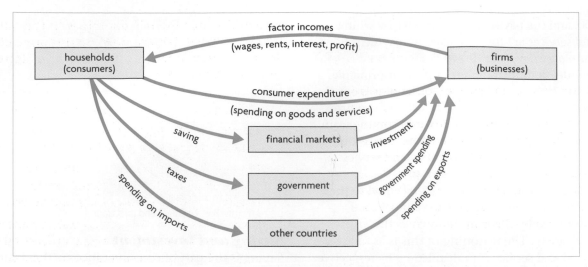

Figure 8.3 Circular flow of income model with leakages and injections

international trade through imports and exports, it is known as an **open economy**. Imports and exports are linked together through 'other countries'. Imports are a leakage because they represent household spending that leaks out as payments to the other countries that produced the goods and services. Exports are an injection because they are spending by foreigners who buy goods and services produced by the domestic firms.

The size of the circular flow in relation to the size of leakages and injections

♦ Explain how the size of the circular flow will change depending on the relative size of injections and leakages.

In the real world, leakages and injections are unlikely to be equal, and this has important consequences for the size of the circular flow. If a leakage is greater than an injection, then the size of the circular flow becomes smaller. Suppose saving (a leakage) is larger than investment (an injection). This means that part of the household income that leaks as saving into financial markets does not come back into the flow as investment. The result is that fewer goods and services are purchased, firms cut back on their output, they buy fewer factors of production, unemployment increases (since firms buy a smaller quantity of labour) and household income is reduced.

If a leakage is smaller than an injection, the size of the circular flow becomes larger. Suppose spending on exports is greater than spending on imports; then the expenditure flow increases since the injection is larger than the leakage. Foreigners demand more goods and services, firms begin to produce more by purchasing more factors of production, unemployment falls (as firms buy a larger quantity of labour), and household income increases. To summarise:

Leakages from the circular flow of income (saving, taxes and imports) are matched by injections into the circular flow of income (investment, government spending and exports), though these need not be equal to each other. If injections are smaller than leakages, the income flow becomes smaller; if injections are larger than leakages the income flow becomes larger.

8.2 Measures of economic activity

Understanding measures of economic activity

Introduction to measures of economic activity

Measurement of economic activity involves measuring an economy's national income or the value of output, and is referred to as 'national income accounting'. The output of an economy is referred to as 'aggregate output', which means total output. Knowing national income and the value of aggregate output is very useful because this allows us to:

- assess an economy's performance over time (are income and output increasing over time; are they decreasing?)
- make comparisons of income and output performance with other economies
- establish a basis for making policies that will meet economic objectives.

You may have noticed that we often refer to the 'value' of output. Why speak in terms of values, and not in terms of quantities, as we did in microeconomics? The answer is that in macroeconomics we must find a way to add up quantities of output of hundreds of thousands of different goods and services. Yet how can we add up quantities of computers, apples, cars and theatre tickets? What unit of measurement can we use? To get around this difficulty, we measure output in money terms, or the value of goods and services. The 'value' of a good is simply its quantity multiplied by its price. Sometimes 'value' may not be explicitly mentioned. For example, one may speak of 'the level of aggregate output' or simply 'aggregate output'. Whatever is the case, in macroeconomics output is always in value terms.

How economic activity is measured

♦ Examine the output approach, the income approach and the expenditure approach when measuring national income.

The circular flow of income model showed that the value of aggregate output produced is equal to the total income generated in producing that output, which is equal to the expenditures made to purchase that output. For this reason, the term **national income**, or the total income of an economy, is sometimes used interchangeably with the value of *aggregate output*. We will now use this principle to see how national income or the value of aggregate output is measured.

There are three ways to measure the value of aggregate output, suggested by the circular flow of income model, all giving rise to the same result:

- the **expenditure approach** adds up all spending to buy final goods and services produced within a country over a time period
- the **income approach** adds up all income earned by the factors of production that produce all goods and services within a country over a time period
- the **output approach** calculates the value of all final goods and services produced in a country over a time period.

The expenditure approach

The expenditure approach measures the total amount of spending to buy final goods and services in a country (usually within a year). The term 'final' refers to goods and services ready for final use, and can be contrasted with intermediate goods and services, or those purchased as inputs for the production of final goods. When we measure the value of aggregate output, we include only purchases of final goods and services. (For example, food items like meat and vegetables are intermediate goods for a restaurant that uses them to prepare a meal, and the meal is the final good. If in measuring expenditures we included spending on the food items plus spending on the meal, this would involve double counting and the value of aggregate output would be exaggerated. On the other hand, meat and vegetables bought by a household for consumption count as final goods, since they are not used as inputs for the production of another good or service.)

Total spending is broken down into four components:

- **Consumption** spending, abbreviated as *C*, includes all purchases by households on final goods and services in a year (except housing, which is classified under investment).[1]
- **Investment** spending, abbreviated as *I*, includes:
  - spending by firms on capital goods (i.e. buildings, machinery, equipment, etc.)

---

[1] Spending by consumers is classified as spending on (i) consumer durable goods (with an expected life of more than three years, such as cars, refrigerators, washing machines, televisions, etc.), (ii) consumer non- durable goods (with an expected life of less than three years, such as food, clothing and medicines), and (iii) services (entertainment, banking, health care, education, etc.).

○ spending on new construction (housing and other buildings).[2]

- **Government spending, abbreviated as _G_,** refers to spending by governments within a country (national, regional, local). It includes purchases by the government of factors of production, including labour services. It also includes investment by government, which is referred to as 'public investment' (usually on capital goods including roads, airports, power generators, building schools and hospitals, etc.).

- **Net exports (exports minus imports), abbreviated as _X – M_,** refers to the value of all exports (abbreviated as _X_) minus the value of all imports (abbreviated as _M_). Exports are goods and services produced within the country and so must be included in the measurement of aggregate output. Imports, however, involve domestic spending on goods and services that have been produced in other countries, and so must be subtracted from expenditures measuring domestic output.

If we add together the four components of spending, we obtain a measure of aggregate output known as gross domestic product (GDP):

$$C + I + G + (X - M) = \text{GDP}$$

> **Gross domestic product** or GDP is defined as the market value of all final goods and services produced in a country over a time period (usually a year). It includes spending by the four components, $C + I + G + (X - M)$. It is one of the most commonly used measures of the value of aggregate output.

Some clarifications concerning investment

Investment refers to spending by firms or the government on capital goods and on construction. There is a common misconception that investment is undertaken only by firms. This is incorrect, because as we have seen in the discussion above, investment is also undertaken by governments (public investments).

One reason for this misconception is that firms are major decision-makers whose contribution to GDP is in the form of investment.

Another issue is that for the purposes of measurement of aggregate output, investment in 'capital' includes only spending on physical capital. It does not include spending on human capital and often it does not include spending on natural capital (see Chapter 1, page 4 for these distinctions). This can be confusing, because economists often refer to 'investments in human capital' and 'investments in natural capital', and yet these 'investments' do not appear as investments in measures of aggregate output. Many economists argue that national income accounting methods should be changed to include these types of investments as well.

Note that measures of aggregate output also do not include financial capital (see page 4), but this is justifiable as financial capital does not represent value of goods and services produced.

The income approach

The income approach adds up all income earned by the factors of production within a country over a time period (usually a year): wages earned by labour, rent earned by land, interest earned by capital, and profits earned by entrepreneurship. When all factor incomes are added up, the result is national income. Whereas national income is often used as a measure of the level of economic activity, it is not the same as GDP. To calculate GDP using the income approach, it is necessary to make some adjustments to national income.[3]

The output approach

The output approach measures the value of each good and service produced in the economy over a particular time period (usually a year) and then sums them up to obtain the total value of output produced. It includes the value of all final goods and services, in order to avoid the double counting that would arise from including the values of intermediate goods and services.[4]

---

[2] Investment spending includes one more item: changes in inventories. Inventories refer to output produced by firms that remains unsold. Businesses as a rule keep inventories to help them meet unexpected increases in the demand for their product. Since inventories are output, it means that they must be counted as part of the aggregate output that is being measured. However, since they are output that has not been sold, they cannot be counted under consumption expenditure; they are therefore counted under investment.

[3] A detailed consideration of these adjustments is beyond the scope of this book. For the interested student, they will be mentioned briefly here. If we add depreciation and indirect taxes to national income, we obtain a measure of aggregate output called gross national income (GNI). The difference between GNI and GDP will be considered later in this chapter. Depreciation refers to the wearing out of capital goods, and will also be considered later. The reason we add depreciation and indirect taxes to national income in order to obtain GNI (and GDP) is that the value of output measured by the expenditure approach includes both these items.

By contrast, national income, measuring only the incomes of the factors of production, does not include either of the two.

[4] The method used to obtain the value of only final goods and services is to count only the value added in each step of the production process. For example, say the production of a good goes through the following steps. Firm A sells raw materials for $700 to firm B. Firm B uses the raw materials and produces an intermediate good that it sells to firm C for $1100. Firm C uses this intermediate good to produce a final good that it sells for $1700. How much value has been added in this process? Firm A added $700 of value. Firm B added $400 of value (= $1100 – $700), and firm C added $600 of value (= $1700 – $1100). When we add these up we obtain: $700 + $400 + $600 = $1700. Note that the sum of the values that were added in each step of the production process is exactly equal to the value of the final product. If we had added up the values of the two intermediate products and the final product, we would have: $700 + $1100 + $1700 = $3500, which greatly exaggerates the value of the product due to double counting. By counting only values added in each step of the production process, the problem of double counting is avoided.

The output approach calculates the value of output by economic sector, such as agriculture, manufacturing, transport, banking, etc. The value of output of each sector is then added up to obtain the total value of output for the entire economy. This approach provides us with the opportunity to study the performance of each individual sector and to make comparisons of performance across sectors.

The three approaches give rise to the same result, after allowance is made for statistical differences that arise in the course of measuring the different variables involved.

Test your understanding 8.2

1 Why are the terms 'national income' and 'aggregate output' often used interchangeably?

2 Why is it useful to know the value of aggregate output?

3 Explain why **(a)** we measure aggregate output in value terms, and **(b)** we count only the value of final goods and services when measuring the value of output.

4 What are the four expenditure components of GDP? Explain each of these.

5 **(a)** Explain three ways that GDP can be measured. **(b)** Why do they give rise to the same result?

Distinctions relating to measures of the value of output

Distinction between GDP and GNI/GNP

♦ Distinguish between GDP and GNP/GNI as measures of economic activity.

On page 217, we learned that the value of output produced in an economy is equal to the total income generated in producing that output. However, in the real world, this equality does not always hold. Sometimes the output of an economy is produced by factors of production that belong to foreigners. Consider the case where a United States multinational firm in India remits (sends back) its profits to the United States. The output of the multinational is produced in India, but the profit income is received by residents in the United States. Does the profit income count as Indian or US income and output? Consider also a Russian worker who lives and works in Spain, and sends a large part of her income to her family in Russia. Her output is produced in Spain, but the income she sends home is Russian income; should this income count as Russia's or Spain's income and output?

The concepts 'domestic' and 'national' are used to distinguish between measures of aggregate output and income that deal with this issue. The term 'domestic' in 'gross domestic product' means that output has been produced by factors of production within the country, regardless of who owns them (residents or foreigners). The term 'national' is used in another measure of aggregate output known as **gross national income** (GNI) (formerly known as **gross national product** (GNP)). The term 'national' in GNI means that the income it measures is the income of the country's residents, regardless where this income comes from.

In the example above, the profit income remitted to the United States is included in Indian GDP because it is created by production taking place in India, but it is part of United States GNI because it is income received by United States' residents. For the Russian worker in Spain, the value of her output is included in Spain's GDP, but her income sent to Russia is part of Russia's GNI.

GDP is the total value of all final goods and services produced within a country over a time period (usually a year), regardless of who owns the factors of production. GNI (or GNP) is the total income received by the residents of a country, equal to the value of all final goods and services produced by the factors of production supplied by the country's residents regardless where the factors are located.

We will discuss GDP and GNI further on page 227 (at higher level) and in Chapter 16. It may interest you to turn to Table 16.4 (page 453) to see some international comparisons.

Distinction between nominal values and real values

♦ Distinguish between the nominal value of GDP and GNP/GNI and the real value of GDP and GNP/GNI.

Earlier we noted that in macroeconomics we measure output in value terms, and we defined 'value' to be the quantity of a good multiplied by its price. **Nominal value** is money value, or value measured in terms of prices that prevail at the time of measurement. For example, if a pair of shoes costs £100, this is its nominal value. If you buy this pair of shoes, £100 is your nominal expenditure on these shoes. If your monthly income is £2000, this is your nominal income. Therefore, when we calculate the value of aggregate output, or expenditure, or income, in money terms, we speak of nominal GDP, nominal expenditure, nominal income, etc.

Yet prices change over time, and this poses a measurement problem. Let's say that nominal GDP increases in a year. This increase may be due to changes in the quantities of output produced, or changes in the prices of goods and services, or a combination of both. We have no way of knowing what part of the increase is due to changes in output and what part to changes in prices. Yet we are interested in knowing how much the *quantity* of goods and services has increased. We must therefore find a measure of GDP that is not influenced by price changes.

To eliminate the influence of changing prices on the value of output, we must calculate real values. **Real value** is a measure of value that takes into account changes in prices over time. Meaningful comparisons over time in the value of output, or expenditures, or income, or any variable that is measured in money terms, require the use of real values. For example, when we make comparisons of GDP in a country over time, we must be sure to use real GDP values, as these have eliminated the influence of price changes, and give us an indication of how actual output produced has changed.

> **Nominal GDP** or GNI is measured in terms of current prices (prices at the time of measurement), which does not account for changes in prices. **Real GDP** or real GNI are measures of economic activity that have eliminated the influence of changes in prices. When a variable is being compared over time, it is important to use real values.

Distinction between total and *per capita*

> ♦ Distinguish between total GDP and GNP/GNI and *per capita* GDP and GNP/GNI.

Per capita means per person or per head. A *per capita* measure takes the total value (of output, income, expenditure, etc.) and divides this by the total population of a country. Therefore *per capita* GDP of a country is total GDP of that country divided by its population.

The distinction between total and *per capita* measures is very important for two reasons:

- **Differing population sizes across countries.** Let's say there are two countries that have identical total GDPs of £10 billion. Country A has a population of 1 million people and country B has a population of 2 million people. If we divide total GDP by population we get GDP *per capita* of £10 000 for country A and £5000 for country B. Whereas both countries have identical GDPs, country B's *per capita* GDP is only half that of country A, because of differing population sizes.

- **Population growth.** Changes in the size of GDP *per capita* over time depend very much on the relationship between growth in total GDP and growth in population. In general, if total GDP increases faster than the population, then GDP *per capita* increases. But if the country's population increases faster than total GDP, then GDP *per capita* falls.

> Total measures of the value of output and income (such as GDP and GNI), provide a summary statement of the overall size of an economy. *Per capita* figures are useful as a summary measure of the standard of living in a country, because they provide an indication of how much of total output in the economy corresponds to each person in the population on average.

Distinction between gross and net (supplementary material)

You may be wondering what the term 'gross' in 'gross domestic product' and 'gross national income' refers to. It is related to spending to produce capital. You may remember from Chapter 1 that physical capital, a produced factor of production, consists of buildings, equipment and machinery. All of these have a finite life; in other words, they do not last forever. Within any given year, some of the capital goods in an economy become worn out and are thrown away. This capital that gets worn out is called *depreciation*.

Each year, the worn out capital goods must be replaced. This means that in any year, of the total new production of capital goods, a part goes to replace capital goods that have been thrown out and the rest are new additions of capital goods.

Investment, as we know, refers to spending by businesses on capital goods. Total investment is known as *gross investment*, and is divided into two parts:

- the part that goes toward replacing thrown-out capital goods (depreciation)
- the part that consists of new additions of capital goods, known as *net investment*.

To put it more simply:

gross investment = depreciation + net investment

total investment = worn-out + additions of
                       capital goods new capital

In the expression for gross domestic product, $GDP = C+I+G+(X-M)$, I refers to gross (or total) investment. This is because GDP measures an economy's total output, and therefore includes total spending on capital goods, including replacements of depreciated capital and new additions to capital goods.

In an alternative way of measuring aggregate output, net investment is used to arrive at *net domestic product* (NDP):

$$NDP = C + In + G + X - M$$

where In = net investment. Therefore NDP = GDP – depreciation.

Test your understanding 8.3

1 **(a)** Define GDP and GNI, and explain how they differ. **(b)** Think of some examples of countries where (i) GNI is likely to be larger than GDP, and (ii) GDP is likely to be larger than GNI.

2 Why do price changes over time pose a problem when we want to make comparisons of GDP (or any measure of output or income) over time?

3 Explain the difference between nominal GDP and real GDP (or nominal and real GNI).

4 Why is it important to use real values when making comparisons over time?

5 You read in the newspaper that government spending on education in your country increased by 7% last year. What information do you need to be able to make sense of this figure?

6 Explain the difference between a total GDP (or GNI) and *per capita* GDP (or GNI).

7 Why is it sometimes important to make a distinction between total measures and *per capita* measures of income and output?

Evaluating national income statistics

♦ Evaluate the use of national income statistics, including their use for making comparisons over time, their use for making comparisons between countries and their use for making conclusions about standards of living.

When real *per capita* GDP or real *per capita* GNI of a country increases over time, we might expect that the population of this country achieves a higher standard of living. Alternatively, if GDP *per capita* or GNI *per capita* in one country is higher than in another country, we might expect that the first country enjoys a higher standard of living. But would these conclusions be valid?

The answer is that we cannot be sure. There are two reasons why this is so. One is that **national income statistics** (or statistical data used to measure national income and output and other measures of economic performance) do not accurately measure the 'true' value of output produced in an economy. The other is that standards of living are closely related to a variety of factors that GDP and GNI are unable to account for. As a result, *per capita* figures of both GDP and GNI may be misleading when used to make comparisons over time or comparisons between countries, and when used as the basis for standard of living conclusions.

Why national income statistics (GDP/GNI) do not accurately measure the 'true' value of output

The limitations listed below show why measures of aggregate output and income are unable to reflect the 'true' value of these variables. Many of them have potential solutions, and if they were systematically pursued, they would go some way to reduce the inaccuracies of the GDP and GNP measures.

- **GDP and GNI do not include non-marketed output.** GDP measures the value of goods and services that are traded in the marketplace and that generate incomes for the factors of production. Yet some output of goods and services is not sold in the market and does not generate any income; this is called 'non-marketed output'. An example is one's own work on repairing and improving one's home; if the home repairs were carried out by hired workers, GDP would be greater by the amount of their wages. In less developed countries households are often quite self-sufficient, with a substantial portion of production, such as agricultural production, taking place for a household's own use and consumption, and never reaching the marketplace. Non-marketed output therefore is likely to be far greater in less developed countries compared to more developed ones. Many countries attempt to arrive at an estimate of non-marketed output, and by adding this to figures on marketed output arrive at a closer approximation of 'true' GDP/GNI.

- **GDP and GNI do not include output sold in underground (parallel) markets.** Here we have the case where goods are traded in markets and do generate incomes, but they go unrecorded and therefore are not included in GDP/GNI. An 'underground market' (also known as a 'parallel' or an 'informal market') exists whenever a buying/selling

Calculating real GDP using a price index (deflator)

Understanding the difference between nominal and real GDP

The distinction between nominal and real values was discussed on page 221. We will now use a numerical example to show how *real GDP* can be calculated from nominal GDP. This is normally done by statistical services in each country and our example here is for illustration purposes only (you will not have to perform such calculations).

Table 8.2 assumes a simple economy producing three items (burgers, haircuts and tractors). Part (a) shows their quantities and prices for three years and the corresponding nominal GDP. In 2001, 37 burgers selling at £3 each made the total value of burgers £111; 15 haircuts at £18 each had a value of £270; and 10 tractors at £50 each made the total value of tractors £500. Adding up the three total values, we find nominal GDP of £881 in 2001. The nominal GDP figures for 2002 and 2003 are calculated in the same way.

Part (b) of Table 8.2 shows that to find real GDP, it is only necessary to find the value of quantities

produced in 2001, 2002 and 2003 using *the same prices of a single year*, called a *base year*. Any year can be used as the base year. In the table the base year is 2001. To calculate real GDP, we simply multiply the quantities of output produced each year by 2001 prices.

For example, in 2002, the 40 burgers are valued at the 2001 burger price of £3; the 17 haircuts are valued at the 2001 price of £18, and the 11 tractors are valued at the 2001 price of £50. Adding up the resulting values of the three items in column 7, we get a measure of real GDP of £976 in 2001 prices. Similarly, for 2003, the three quantities are also valued at the 2001 prices. Therefore, *real GDP is a measure of output valued at constant (unchanging) prices*.

Examining the changes in real GDP that occurred between 2001 and 2003, we find that real GDP increased from 2001 to 2002 (from £881 to £976), but decreased between 2002 and 2003, falling from £976 to £941. Note that real GDP fell in 2002–03 even as nominal GDP increased over the same period; price increases caused nominal GDP to rise, while falling quantities meant that real GDP was falling.

(a) Calculating nominal GDP

(1) Goods and services	(2) 2001 Q	(3) 2001 P	(4) 2001 value $(Q \times P)$	(5) 2002 Q	(6) 2002 P	(7) 2002 value $(Q \times P)$	(8) 2003 Q	(9) 2003 P	(10) 2003 value $(Q \times P)$
Burgers	37	£3	£111	40	£4	£160	39	£5	£195
Haircuts	15	£18	£270	17	£20	£340	18	£21	£378
Tractors	10	£50	£500	11	£60	£660	10	£65	£650
Nominal GDP			£881			£1160			£1223

(b) Calculating real GDP

(1) Goods and services	(2) 2001 Q	(3) 2001 P	(4) 2001 output in 2001 P $(Q \times P)$	(5) 2002 Q	(6) 2001 P	(7) 2002 output in 2001 P $(Q \times P)$	(8) 2003 Q	(9) 2001 P	(10) 2003 output in 2001 P $(Q \times P)$
Burgers	37	£3	£111	40	£3	£120	39	£3	£117
Haircuts	15	£18	£270	17	£18	£306	18	£18	£324
Tractors	10	£50	£500	11	£50	£550	10	£50	£500
Real GDP			£881			£976			£941

Table 8.2 Nominal and real GDP in a hypothetical economy

(Note that in the base year, 2001, nominal GDP is equal to real GDP; this is always so for the base year since real GDP is valued at base year prices.)

> Nominal GDP measures the value of current output valued at current prices, while real GDP measures the value of current output valued at constant (base year) prices.

When we refer to real GDP figures, we must also refer to the specific base year used for the computation. In the example above, we say 'in 2003 real GDP at 2001 prices was £941'. The figure of £941 is otherwise meaningless, because if we had used a different base year, we would have arrived at a completely different figure for 2003 real GDP. It is also meaningless to compare real GDP figures calculated on the basis of different base years.

Understanding how the GDP deflator is derived

In the real world, the above method of converting nominal values into real values is extremely lengthy and complicated, as there are hundreds of thousands of products whose values must be measured. However, this is not a problem because economists use short-cut methods that take the form of price indices. A price index is a measure of average prices in one period relative to average prices in a base year. A price index commonly used to convert nominal GDP to real GDP is a **price deflator** known as the **GDP deflator**:

$$GDP\ deflator = \frac{nominal\ GDP}{real\ GDP} \times 100$$

Statistical services derive the GDP deflator by using the values of nominal and real GDP they have already calculated (by the method in Table 8.2):

$$GDP\ deflator\ in\ 2001 = \frac{881}{881} \times 100 = 100.0$$

$$GDP\ deflator\ in\ 2002 = \frac{1160}{976} \times 100 = 118.8$$

$$GDP\ deflator\ in\ 2003 = \frac{1223}{941} \times 100 = 130.0$$

These results are summarised in Table 8.3.
Note that the GDP deflator is 100.0 for 2001. *The index number for the base year is always equal to 100, for all indices.* This follows from the equality of nominal and real GDP in 2001, as we had selected 2001 to be the base year.

Year	Nominal GDP	Real GDP	GDP deflator
2001	£881	£881	100.0
2002	£1160	£976	118.8
2003	£1223	£941	130.0

Table 8.3   Nominal and real GDP

Using the GDP deflator to calculate real GDP

* Calculate real GDP, using a price deflator.

Statistical services in each country regularly publish GDP deflators (and other price indices; indices is the plural of index). Using this information, it is a simple matter for economists to calculate real GDP from nominal GDP:

$$real\ GDP = \frac{nominal\ GDP}{price\ deflator} \times 100$$

For example, suppose we are given the following values of nominal GDP: £7 850 billion in 2001; £9 237 billion in 2002; and £10 732 billion in 2003. We are also given the GDP deflator in Table 8.3, and are asked to calculate real GDP:

$$real\ GDP\ in\ 2001 = \frac{7850}{100.0} \times 100 = £7\,850\ billion$$

$$real\ GDP\ in\ 2002 = \frac{9237}{118.8} \times 100 = £7\,775\ billion$$

$$real\ GDP\ in\ 2003 = \frac{10,732}{130.0} \times 100 = £8\,255\ billion$$

Note that an increasing GDP deflator indicates rising prices on average, while a decreasing GDP deflator indicates falling prices on average. Suppose we have the following price index representing the GDP deflator:

2004	2005	2006	2007	2008
95.7	97.7	100.0	105.9	102.4

We can see that whereas prices on average increased in the period 2004–7, in 2008 *they fell*. We can also see that the base year is 2006. Note that it is possible for some years to have a price index that is less than 100.0, which means simply that in those years, the average price level was lower than in the base year.

Test your understanding 8.6

1 Calculate nominal GDP, given the following information from the national accounts of Flatland for the year 2007 (all figures are in billion Ftl, the national currency). Consumer spending = 125; government spending = 46; investment spending = 35; exports of goods and services = 12; imports of goods and services = 17.

2 Now suppose that profits of foreign multinational corporations in Flatland and incomes of foreign workers in Flatland that were sent home in 2007 were Ftl 3.7 billion. The profits of Flatland's multinational corporations abroad and income of Flatland workers abroad that were sent back to Flatland were Ftl 4.5 billion. What was Flatland's GNI in 2007?

3 You read in one source of information that real GDP in a hypothetical country in 2001 was $243 billion; in another source of information you read that real GDP in 2002 was $277 billion. What information do you need to be sure that the two figures can be compared with each other?

4 You are given the following information on an imaginary country called Lakeland.

Year	2006	2007	2008	2009	2010
Nominal GDP (billion Lkl)	19.9	20.7	21.9	22.6	22.3
GDP deflator	98.5	100.0	102.3	107.6	103.7

(a) Which year is the base year? (b) Calculate real GDP for each of the five years in the table. (c) For which year is real GDP the same as nominal GDP? Why? (d) In 2008 – 9, nominal GDP increased, but real GDP fell (check that this is what your calculation shows). Explain how this could have happened. (e) In 2009–10, nominal GDP fell, but real GDP increased (check that this is what your calculation shows). Explain how this could have happened.

8.4 The business cycle

Introduction to economic growth

Calculating economic growth

Economic growth, introduced in Chapter 1, page 13, refers to increases in the quantity of output produced over a period of time (typically a year), and is usually expressed as:

- a percentage change in real GDP (or real GNI) over a specified period of time, or
- a percentage change in real GDP *per capita* (or real GNI *per capita*) over a specified period of time.

For example, if real GDP in a hypothetical country was $50 billion in 2004 and increased to $51 billion in 2005, its rate of growth over this period would be given by $\frac{51-50}{50} \times 100\% = 2\%$ in the period 2004–5.
However, the percentage change representing growth is not always a positive value; if real GDP has fallen it will be negative. Suppose that real GDP in a hypothetical country was $60 billion in 2006 and $57 billion in 2007; we can calculate its rate of growth to have been −5% in 2006–7. The negative rate of growth indicates that real GDP fell during this period. (You may wish to review the 'Quantitative techniques' chapter on the CD-ROM, page 1, explaining percentage changes and calculations of economic growth.)

Distinguishing between a decrease in GDP and a decrease in GDP growth

♦ Distinguish between a decrease in GDP and a decrease in GDP growth.

It is very important to distinguish between a decrease in GDP, and a decrease in GDP growth. A decrease in GDP involves a fall in the value of output produced, such as from $60 billion in 2006 to $57 billion in 2007, which as we saw above gives rise to a *negative rate of growth* of −5%. A decrease in GDP growth, by contrast, involves *falling rates of growth*, though the rates of growth may be *positive*. The difference between the two is shown in Table 8.4. In

Year	Real GDP ($ billion)	Real GDP growth
2007	210.0	–
2008	215.5	2.6% (increasing GDP)
2009	219.5	1.9% (increasing GDP, falling GDP growth)
2010	223.1	1.6% (increasing GDP, falling GDP growth)
2011	217.0	−2.7% (decreasing GDP, negative GDP growth)

Table 8.4 The difference between a decrease in GDP and decrease in GDP growth

2009 and 2010, this economy experienced falling rates of growth; note that the rates of growth are positive but lower relative to the growth rate of the previous year. In 2011, the economy experienced a decrease in GDP, reflected in a negative rate of growth.

Understanding the business cycle

The cyclical pattern and phases of the business cycle

• Explain, using a business cycle diagram, that economies typically tend to go through a cyclical pattern characterised by the phases of the business cycle.

Whereas real output in most countries around the world grows over long periods of time, output growth virtually everywhere in the world is uneven and irregular. In some years (or months) real output may grow rapidly, in other years (or months) more slowly, and in still others it may even fall, indicating negative growth.

Fluctuations in the growth of real output, consisting of alternating periods of expansion (increasing real output) and contraction (decreasing real output), are called **business cycles**, or *economic fluctuations*.

A business cycle is shown in Figure 8.4, which plots real GDP on the vertical axis, against time on the horizontal axis. GDP is measured in real terms, so that the vertical axis measures changes in the volume of output produced after the influence of price-level changes has been eliminated.

Each cycle consists of the following phases:

• **Expansion.** An expansion occurs when there is positive growth in real GDP, shown by those parts of the curve in Figure 8.4 that slope upward.

During periods of real GDP growth, employment of resources increases, and the general price level of the economy (which is an average over all prices) usually begins to rise more rapidly (this is known as inflation, to be discussed in Chapter 10, page 274).

• **Peak.** A peak represents the cycle's maximum real GDP, and marks the end of the expansion. When the economy reaches a peak, unemployment of resources has fallen substantially, and the general price level may be rising quite rapidly; the economy is likely to be experiencing inflation.

• **Contraction.** Following the peak, the economy begins to experience falling real GDP (negative growth), shown by the downward-sloping parts of the curve. If the contraction lasts six months (two quarters) or more, it is termed a **recession**, characterised by falling real GDP and growing unemployment of resources. Increases in the price level may slow down a lot, and it is even possible that prices in some sectors may begin to fall.

• **Trough.** A trough represents the cycle's minimum level of GDP, or the end of the contraction. There may now be widespread unemployment. A trough is followed by a new period of expansion (also known as a recovery), marking the beginning of a new cycle.

The term 'business cycle' suggests a phenomenon that is regular and predictable, whereas business cycles are in fact both irregular, as they do not occur at regular time intervals, and unpredictable. For these reasons, many economists prefer to call them 'short-term economic fluctuations'.

While each cycle typically lasts several years, it is not possible to generalise, as there is wide variation in duration (how long the cycle lasts), as well as in intensity (how strong the expansion is and how deep

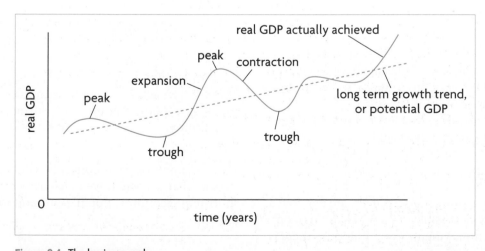

Figure 8.4 The business cycle

the contraction or recession is). Expansions usually last longer than contractions. These are the reasons why the curve in Figure 8.4 has an irregular shape.

Short-term fluctuations and the long-term growth trend

♦ Explain the long-term growth trend in the business cycle diagram as the potential output of the economy.

The long-term growth trend and potential output

Figure 8.4 shows a straight line going through the cyclical line; this represents average growth over long periods of time (many years), and is known as the long-term growth trend. The long-term growth trend shows how output grows over time when cyclical fluctuations are ironed out. As you can see in the figure, real GDP actually achieved fluctuates around potential GDP (it fluctuates around the long-term growth trend).

The output represented by the long-term growth trend is known as potential output or potential GDP. To understand the meaning of potential output, we must examine the relationship between real GDP and unemployment.

How unemployment relates to actual and potential output

When real GDP fluctuates, it does so together with other macroeconomic variables. One of the most important of these is the level of unemployment of labour, or how many people in the workforce are out of work. When real GDP grows in the expansion phase, unemployment falls; in the contraction phase when real GDP falls, unemployment increases. You can easily see why: in an expansion, real GDP increases because firms increase the quantity of output they produce; to do this, they hire more labour (and other resources) and unemployment falls. In a contraction, real GDP falls because firms cut back on production; as they lay off workers, unemployment increases.

For every economy, there is a level of real GDP at which the economy experiences 'full employment'. This is known as the full employment level of output, or full employment level of real GDP. The term 'full employment' does not mean that all resources, including all labour resources, are employed to the greatest extent possible. Whenever the economy produces its 'full employment level of output', there is

still some unemployment, known as the 'natural rate of unemployment'.

(We will examine the reasons why unemployment never falls to zero in Chapter 10. For example, at any time, there are some people who are in between jobs, some who are moving from one geographical area to another, some people who are training or retraining to be able to get a new or better job, and some people who are temporarily out of work. Therefore, there are always some people who are unemployed.)

Coming back to potential output, we can now say that this is the level of output produced when there is 'full employment', meaning that unemployment is equal to the natural rate of unemployment. It follows then that along the long-term growth trend, unemployment is equal to the natural rate of unemployment. But when actual GDP is greater than potential GDP, unemployment is lower than the natural rate; when actual GDP is less than potential GDP, unemployment is greater than the natural rate.

Cyclical fluctuations, potential output and output gaps

Figure 8.5 introduces another concept related to the business cycle. When actual GDP lies above potential GDP (as at point d), or below potential GDP (as at point e), there results a *GDP gap*, also known as an *output gap*. The output gap is simply actual GDP minus potential GDP, and may be positive or negative. When actual GDP is equal to potential GDP (as at points a, b, c) the output gap is equal to zero.

Figure 8.5 shows that actual GDP fluctuates around full employment GDP, also known as potential GDP. When the economy's actual GDP is at points such as a, b and c, actual GDP is equal to potential GDP, and the economy is achieving full employment, where unemployment is equal to the natural rate of unemployment. When the economy's actual GDP is greater than potential GDP, such as at point d, there is an output gap, and unemployment falls to less than the natural rate. When actual GDP is less than potential GDP, such as at point e, there is an output gap where unemployment is greater than the natural rate.

The usefulness of these concepts will become apparent in later chapters when we make use of them to analyse short-term economic fluctuations and long-term growth.

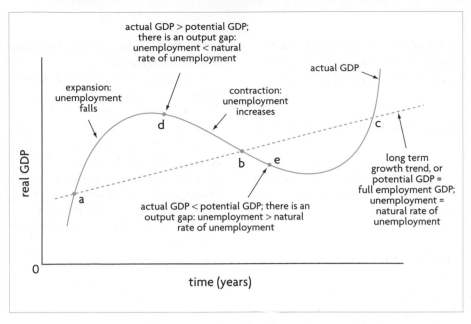

Figure 8.5 Illustrating actual output, potential output and unemployment in the business cycle

Potential output: worrying about what cannot be observed

The International Monetary Fund (IMF)* notes that everyone thinks about potential output at a time of recession. 'What would be merely a curiosity during better times – after all, potential output is a highly abstract concept …– has become a particular worry in the context of the global economic crisis.' The worry in Europe is that a deep and long-lasting recession may affect potential output and make the economic recovery more difficult.

A problem is that there are disagreements over how to measure potential output. Yet it is important to know what this is, because estimates of the difference between actual output and potential output, or the output gap, provide policy-makers with guidance on what policies are appropriate to help bring the economy out of the recession. A small output gap has very different policy implications from a larger output gap. Therefore, the first step for policy-makers 'is to ask economists to do their best to correctly estimate potential output in the aftermath of the crisis. The more that is known about what is happening to potential output, the less reason there is about getting it wrong.'

* The IMF is an international financial institution which we will study in Chapter 18.

Source: Adapted from Ajai Chopra, 'Potential output: worrying about what cannot be observed' in *iMFdirect*, 13 August 2009.

Applying your skills

1 Define potential output, and show it in a business cycle diagram in relation to actual output.

2 Using the same diagram, identify the output gap that arises when an economy is in recession. (Can you see why knowing the size of potential output helps estimate the size of the output gap?)

Why we study the business cycle

Why do we study the business cycle? Economic growth over long periods of time, represented by an upward-sloping potential output line, is a highly desirable objective. Growth in real output provides opportunities to achieve higher incomes and higher standards of living.

However, large cyclical fluctuations over short periods of time are not desirable. In the upward phases of the business cycle, the economy often experiences a rapidly rising price level (inflation), which is not good for the economy. In the downward phases, the economy experiences falling incomes and growing unemployment, causing hardship for many people and frustrating the objective of economic growth. We will study the effects of inflation and unemployment in Chapter 10.

In an ideal world, every economy would experience economic growth over long periods of time, with continuous low levels of unemployment and a stable or gently rising price level (low inflation). Rapid economic growth, full employment, and price stability are among the key macroeconomic objectives of economies. Figure 8.6 illustrates these objectives in terms of the business cycle.

Using the business cycle, we can understand macroeconomic objectives to include the following:

- Reducing the intensity of expansions and contractions: this is aimed at making output gaps as small as possible (the dotted line in Figure 8.6(a)), by flattening the cyclical curve. This would lessen the problems of rising price levels in expansions and unemployment in contractions.

- Increasing the steepness of the line representing potential output (the dotted line in Figure 8.6(b)), by achieving more rapid economic growth over long periods of time.

In the next chapter we will develop analytical tools to help us understand the causes of the business cycle, and in Chapter 12 we will study government policies intended to achieve full employment, price stability and economic growth.

Test your understanding 8.7

1 Using numerical examples, distinguish between a decrease in GDP and a decrease in GDP growth.

2 Using the business cycle diagram, distinguish between short-term fluctuations and the long-term growth trend.

3 Using a diagram, (a) identify the phases of the business cycle, (b) explain how they relate to unemployment, and (c) explain the difference between actual and potential output.

4 How does the 'natural rate of unemployment' relate to the 'full employment level of output' and to 'potential output'?

5 What would you conclude about an economy whose business cycle showed (a) a horizontal potential GDP line, and (b) a downward-sloping potential GDP line?

6 (a) What are three key macroeconomic objectives of economies? (b) Use a business cycle diagram to illustrate what it means to achieve these objectives.

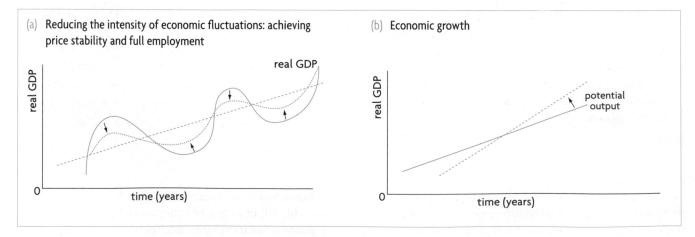

Figure 8.6 Illustrating three macroeconomic objectives

The business cycle, actual output and potential output: using variables that cannot be observed

We have seen in our discussion of the business cycle (see Figure 8.5) that economists are concerned with two representations of output growth: growth of actual output and growth of potential output. Growth of actual output is straightforward to measure and show graphically; it consists of real GDP (or GNI) calculated for each year, and plotted on the vertical axis against time measured on the horizontal axis. When such data are plotted for any country over long periods of time, a cyclical pattern is likely to emerge (though an irregular one, for reasons explained in the text, page 231), known as the business cycle, or short-term economic fluctuations. Therefore, the empirical evidence supports the existence of a business cycle.

The case of potential output is different. Potential output is defined as full employment output, where unemployment is equal to the natural rate of unemployment , and its growth is identified with the long-term growth trend. However, for any particular economy, for any particular year, no one really knows what potential output is; nor does anyone know what the natural rate of unemployment is. Economists do not have any variable called 'potential output' or 'natural rate of unemployment' that they can observe in the real world and measure. Of course, economists make efforts to estimate the value of potential output (and the natural rate of unemployment), and to estimate how potential output changes over time (see Chapter 11). This then raises the question, does potential output actually *exist*, in the way that actual output can be said to exist, or is it a mythical idea that economists have created to help with their analysis of the macro economy?

It is not possible to provide a definite answer to this question; since potential output cannot be observed or measured, we cannot know if it exists. However, when theorising, there is nothing wrong with assuming the existence of something that cannot be directly observed; in other words, something whose existence is not supported by direct evidence. (Note that this is very different from making unrealistic assumptions, which conflict with the real world.) Physicists do this sometimes, with success. For example, to explain an event at the sub-atomic level (within atoms) it was necessary to presume the existence of a particle, though there was no direct evidence that such a particle actually existed. This fictional particle was named a neutrino, and 20 years later the neutrino was experimentally detected.

Sometimes, the unobserved variable may be supported by indirect evidence. For example, say we cannot observe X, but if X exists, then it is likely that Y exists; if we can observe and measure Y, then we can infer some characteristics about X. In the case of the neutrino, its existence was inferred from indirect evidence. (Note, however, that inference is not a full-proof method to arrive at conclusions about something, and may lead to wrong conclusions. For example, it may be true that if X exists, then Y also exists; but this does not necessarily mean that if Y exists, then X exists. To understand why, suppose that X = it is raining, and Y = it is cloudy. If X is true (it is raining), then Y is true (it is cloudy). But if Y is true (it is cloudy), X (it is raining) is not necessarily true.)

Some economists argue that the existence of potential output is supported by indirect evidence, which may be helpful in making estimates about its size. Estimates of potential output can be very useful to economists concerned with economic policy. For an example, see the Real world focus feature on page 233.

Thinking points

- Can you think of other variables used by economists that are not directly observable or measurable?

- Do you think the inability to observe some variables makes the social scientific method less 'scientific'?

- What kinds of difficulties might be created for policy-makers who use the concept of 'potential output' to determine appropriate policies for the economy?

💿 Assessment

The Student's CD-ROM at the back of this book provides practice of examination questions based on the material you have studied in this chapter.

Standard level
- Exam practice: Paper 1, Chapter 8
  - ○ SL/HL core topics (questions 8.1–8.8)

Higher level
- Exam practice: Paper 1, Chapter 8
  - ○ SL/HL core topics (questions 8.1–8.8)
- Exam practice: Paper 3, Chapter 8
  - ○ HL topics (question 18)

Chapter 9
Aggregate demand and aggregate supply

In this chapter we will develop the aggregate demand–aggregate supply (*AD-AS*) model of the macroeconomy, an important analytical tool for studying output fluctuations, changes in the price level and unemployment, and economic growth.

9.1 Aggregate demand (*AD*) and the aggregate demand curve

Explaining aggregate demand and the aggregate demand curve

The meaning of aggregate demand and the aggregate demand curve

♦ Describe consumption, investment, government spending and net exports as the components of aggregate demand.
♦ Construct an aggregate demand curve.

Aggregate demand is the total quantity of aggregate output, or real GDP, that all buyers in an economy want to buy at different possible price levels, *ceteris paribus*. The *aggregate demand (AD) curve* shows the relationship between the aggregate output buyers want to buy, or real GDP demanded, and the economy's price level, *ceteris paribus*. Figure 9.1(a) presents an aggregate demand curve. The horizontal axis measures aggregate output, or real GDP, and the vertical axis measures the general price level in the economy, which is an average over the prices of all goods and services.

Aggregate demand is not just the demand of all consumers, as one might think from the study of microeconomics. It consists of all the components of aggregate expenditure that we studied in Chapter 8, page 219:

• the demand of consumers (*C*)
• the demand of businesses (firms) (*I*)

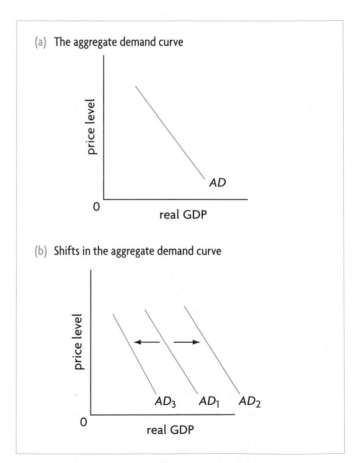

Figure 9.1 The aggregate demand (AD) curve

• the demand of government (*G*)
• the demand of foreigners for exports (*X*) minus the demand for imports (*M*) (*X*−*M* or net exports).

Aggregate demand is the total amount of real output (real GDP) that consumers, firms, the government and foreigners want to buy at each possible price level, over a particular time period. The **aggregate demand (AD) curve** shows the relationship between the total amount of real output demanded by the four components and the economy's price level over a particular time period. It is downward-sloping, indicating a negative relationship between the price level and aggregate output demanded.[1]

The negative (downward) slope of the aggregate demand curve

♦ Explain why the *AD* curve has a negative slope.

The reasons behind the downward slope of the aggregate demand are very different from demand in a single market in microeconomics. They include the following:

- **The wealth effect.** Changes in the price level affect the real value of people's wealth. (Wealth is not the same as income; wealth is the value of assets that people own, including their houses, stocks and bonds, their jewellery, works of art, and so on.) If the price level increases, the real value of wealth falls. People feel worse off and cut back on their spending on goods and services. Therefore, as the price level increases, less output is demanded, leading to an upward movement along the *AD* curve. If there is a fall in the price level, the real value of wealth increases, people feel better off and increase their spending, thus more output is demanded, causing a downward movement along the *AD* curve.

- **The interest rate effect.** Changes in the price level affect rates of interest, which in turn affect aggregate demand. If there is an increase in the price level, consumers and firms need more money to carry out their purchases and transactions. This leads to an increase in the demand for money, which in turn leads to an increase in rates of interest.[2] As interest rates rise, the cost of borrowing increases leading to a decrease in consumer purchases financed by borrowing, as well as in

investment spending by firms that must borrow to finance their expenditures. Therefore, increases in the price level lead to a fall in quantity of output demanded, or an upward movement along the *AD* curve. A fall in the price level leads to a rise in quantity of output demanded, or a downward movement along the *AD* curve.

- **The international trade effect.** If the domestic price level increases while price levels in other countries remain the same, exports become more expensive to foreign buyers who will now demand a smaller quantity of these. At the same time, goods produced in other countries become relatively cheaper, so domestic buyers increase their purchases (imports) from foreign countries. Therefore, a rising price level produces a fall in exports and a rise in imports so that net exports, $X-M$, fall. Falling net exports represent a fall in quantity of output demanded or an upward movement along the *AD* curve. A fall in the domestic price level relative to other countries leads to a larger amount of exports demanded and lower amount of imports demanded, so that net exports, $X-M$, rise. Therefore, there is a downward movement along the *AD* curve.

How aggregate demand differs from microeconomic demand

♦ Distinguish between the microeconomic concept of demand for a product and the macroeconomic concept of aggregate demand.

In microeconomics, demand for a product reflects the willingness and ability of *consumers* to buy a *single product* at different possible prices of that product, over a particular time period (*ceteris paribus*). In macroeconomics, aggregate demand reflects the willingness and ability of *all possible buyers* (consumers, businesses, government and foreigners) to buy the economy's *aggregate output*, or total real GDP, at different possible price levels, over a time period (*ceteris paribus*).

The differences between the two can also be seen in the very different explanations of their negative (downward) slopes. In microeconomics, the demand curve is downward-sloping because of the diminishing marginal benefits that consumers derive as they

---

[1] You may have noticed something odd about the definition of aggregate demand. In Chapter 8, page 220 we defined GDP to be equal to spending by the four components: $C+I+G+(X-M)$. Now we are saying that aggregate demand is also equal to $C+I+G+(X-M)$. Yet aggregate demand is not the same as GDP. The explanation for this apparent oddity can be found in the section in the CD-ROM 'Understanding aggregate demand and the multiplier in terms of the Keynesian cross model', included as supplementary material.

[2] Interest rates can be thought of as the 'price' of money services. Using standard microeconomic analysis, we can see that as the demand for money increases, while the supply is constant, the interest rate rises. If, on the other hand, the demand for money falls, while the supply of money is constant, the interest rate falls. We will examine interest rates in Chapter 12.

consume more and more of a product (see page 22). As marginal benefits fall with increasing purchases, consumers will be induced to buy an extra unit of a product only if its price falls. In macroeconomics, the downward slope of the aggregate demand curve is due to the wealth effect, the interest rate effect and the international trade effect, discussed above. The idea of diminishing marginal benefits does not come into play.

We can see the difference between the two concepts also by considering that the variable plotted on the horizontal axis in each case is different in a fundamental way. In microeconomics, the horizontal axis measures *quantity of a single good*. This quantity has nothing whatever to do with consumers' incomes. In macroeconomics, the horizontal axis measures the quantity of total output, or real GDP of an economy, but real GDP, as we know from the circular flow model (Figure 8.1, page 216), also represents the *total income* of an economy. This creates a special relationship between aggregate demand and aggregate output or income, which we will discover when we study the multiplier effect on page 260 (at higher level).

The determinants of aggregate demand (shifts in the *AD* curve)

The meaning of aggregate demand curve shifts

The aggregate demand curve can shift to the right or to the left. It is important to distinguish between movements along the aggregate demand curve, caused by changes in the price level, discussed above, and shifts of the aggregate demand curve, caused by the **determinents of aggregate demand**, to which we turn next. (This is analogous to shifts of and movements along the demand curve in microeconomics.) Aggregate demand curve shifts are shown in Figure 9.1(b).

A rightward shift from AD_1 to AD_2 means that aggregate demand increases: for any price level, a larger amount of real GDP is demanded. A leftward shift from AD_1 to AD_3 means that aggregate demand decreases: for any price level, a smaller amount of real GDP is demanded.

Since aggregate demand is composed of consumer spending (*C*), investment spending (*I*), government spending (*G*), and net export spending (*X*−*M*), changes in aggregate demand and therefore shifts in the aggregate demand curve can be caused by any factor that produces a change in one of these four components. You may find it useful to review the meaning of the four components in Chapter 8, page 219.

The determinants of aggregate demand, or the factors that can shift the aggregate demand curve are grouped below under each of the components of aggregate demand.

Causes of changes in consumption spending

♦ Explain how the *AD* curve can be shifted by changes in consumption due to factors including changes in consumer confidence, interest rates, wealth, personal income taxes (and hence disposable income) and level of household indebtedness.

- **Changes in consumer confidence.** Consumer confidence is a measure of how optimistic consumers are about their future income and the future of the economy. If consumers expect their incomes to increase, or if they are optimistic about the future of the economy, they are likely to spend more on buying goods and services, and the *AD* curve shifts to the right. Low consumer confidence indicates expectations of falling incomes and worsening economic conditions, due to fears of cuts in wages or unemployment, causing decreases in spending, appearing as a leftward shift of the *AD* curve. Governments around the world regularly measure consumer confidence (through surveys based on questionnaires of consumers) to try to predict the level of consumer spending.

- **Changes in interest rates.** Some consumer spending is financed by borrowing, and so is influenced by interest rate changes. An increase in interest rates makes borrowing more expensive, resulting in lower consumer spending, and therefore a leftward shift in the *AD* curve. A fall in interest rates makes borrowing less expensive, and results in more consumer spending and a rightward shift in the *AD* curve. Interest rates can change as a result of a type of government policy called 'monetary policy' (see Chapter 12).

- **Changes in wealth.** Wealth was explained above (page 237). An increase in consumer wealth (for example, an increase in stock market values, or an increase in the value of homes) makes people feel wealthier; therefore, they spend more and the *AD* curve shifts to the right. A decrease in wealth lowers aggregate demand; the *AD* curve shifts to the left.

- **Changes in personal income taxes.** If the government increases **personal income taxes** (taxes paid by households on their incomes), then consumer **disposable income**, which is the income left over after personal income taxes have been paid, falls; therefore, spending drops, and the *AD* curve shifts to the left. If personal income taxes are lowered, the result is higher disposable income and a rightward shift in the *AD* curve. Changes in taxes are the result of a type of government policy called 'fiscal policy' (see Chapter 12).

- **Changes in the level of household indebtedness.** 'Indebtedness' refers to how much money people owe from taking out loans in the past. If consumers have a high level of debt (due to past use of credit cards or taking out loans to finance consumption), then they are under pressure to make high monthly payments to pay back their loans plus interest, and so are likely to cut back on their present expenditures. Therefore, a high level of indebtedness lowers consumption spending and shifts the *AD* curve to the left. A low level of indebtedness increases consumption spending and shifts the *AD* curve to the right.

Causes of changes in investment spending

♦ Explain how the *AD* curve can be shifted by changes in investment due to factors including interest rates, business confidence, technology, business taxes and the level of corporate indebtedness.

- **Changes in business confidence.** Business confidence refers to how optimistic firms are about their future sales and economic activity. If businesses are optimistic, they spend more on investment, and the *AD* curve shifts to the right. Business pessimism, on the other hand, results in a leftward shift in the *AD* curve.
- **Changes in interest rates.** Increases in interest rates raise the cost of borrowing, and force businesses to reduce investment spending financed by borrowing, and therefore the *AD* curve shifts to the left. Decreases in interest rates mean businesses can now finance their investment spending by borrowing at a lower cost, and the *AD* curve shifts to the right. As noted above, interest rates change as a result of monetary policy (see Chapter 12).
- **Changes (improvements) in technology.** Improvements in technology stimulate investment spending, thus causing increases in aggregate demand and a rightward shift in the *AD* curve.
- **Changes in business taxes.** If the government increases taxes on profits of businesses (as part of its fiscal policy; see Chapter 12), firms' after-tax profits fall; therefore, investment spending decreases and

the *AD* curve shifts to the left. Decreases in taxes on profits result in increased aggregate demand and a rightward *AD* curve shift.

- **The level of corporate indebtedness.** As in the case of consumer indebtedness, if businesses have high levels of debt due to having borrowed a lot in the past, they will be less inclined to make investments and the *AD* curve shifts to the left. A low level of corporate indebtedness, on the other hand, leads to more investment and a rightward shift in the *AD* curve. (A 'corporation' is a business that is legally separate from its owners.)
- **Legal/institutional changes.** Sometimes, the legal and institutional environment in which businesses operate has an important impact on investment spending. This is often the case in many developing and transition economies where laws and institutions do not favour small businesses. For example, small businesses often do not have access to credit, meaning they cannot borrow easily to finance investments. Many developing and transition economies do not have the necessary laws that secure property rights (the legal rights to ownership). In such situations, increasing access to credit (the ability to borrow) and securing property rights would result in increases in investment spending, shifting the *AD* curve to the right.

Causes of changes in government spending

♦ Explain how the *AD* curve can be shifted by changes in government spending due to factors including political and economic priorities.

- **Changes in political priorities.** Governments have many expenditures, arising from provision of merit goods and public goods, spending on subsidies and pensions, payments of wages and salaries to its employees, purchases of goods for its own use, and so on. It may decide to increase or decrease its expenditures in response to changes in its priorities. Increased government spending shifts the *AD* curve to the right, and decreased government spending shifts it to the left.
- **Changes in economic priorities: deliberate efforts to influence aggregate demand.** The government can use its own spending as part of a deliberate attempt to influence aggregate demand. The effects of such changes in government spending on aggregate demand are exactly the same as above. This is another aspect of fiscal policy (to be discussed in Chapter 12).

Causes of changes in export spending minus import spending

♦ Explain how the *AD* curve can be shifted by changes in net exports due to factors including the income of trading partners, exchange rates, and changes in the level of protectionism.

- **Changes in national income abroad.** Consider aggregate demand in country A, which has trade links with country B. If country B's national income increases, it will import more goods and services from country A, so that country A's exports will increase. Therefore the *AD* curve in country A shifts to the right. If, on the other hand, country B's national income falls, it will buy less from country A, and country A's *AD* curve shifts to the left.

- **Changes in exchange rates.** An exchange rate is the price of one country's currency in terms of another country's currency. Consider again country A, and assume that the price of its currency increases, becoming more expensive relative to the currency of country B. Country B now finds country A's output more expensive, and so it imports less from country A; therefore, country A's exports fall, and its *AD* curve shifts to the left. At the same time, country A now finds country B's output cheaper, and so it increases its imports from country B. Therefore, the increase in price of country A's currency has two effects: a fall in its exports and an increase in imports so that net exports, $X - M$, fall, and the *AD* curve shifts to the left. In the opposite situation, where the price of country A's currency decreases, an increase in exports and a decrease in imports will result, so that $X - M$ increases, and country A's *AD* curve shifts to the right. (This will become clearer after we study exchange rates in Chapter 14.)

- **Changes in the level of trade protection.** 'Trade protection' refers to restrictions to free international trade often imposed by governments (see Chapter 13). Suppose country A trades freely with country B (with no trade restrictions). However country B's government decides to impose restrictions on imports from country A. Country A's exports will fall, and its *AD* curve will shift to the left. On the other hand, in country B, lower imports mean that the value of $X - M$ increases, and its *AD* curve shifts to the right.

Table 9.1 summarises the factors that can cause movements along or shifts of the aggregate demand curve.

Movements along the aggregate demand curve are caused by:
Changes in the price level, leading to:
• the wealth effect
• the interest rate effect
• the international trade effect

Shifts in the aggregate demand curve are caused by:
Changes in consumer spending, arising from:
• changes in consumer confidence
• changes in interest rates (monetary policy)
• changes in wealth
• changes in personal income taxes (fiscal policy)
• changes in the level of household indebtedness
Changes in investment spending, arising from:
• changes in business confidence
• changes in interest rates (monetary policy)
• changes (improvement) in technology
• changes in business taxes (fiscal policy)
• changes in the level of corporate indebtedness
• legal/institutional changes
Changes in government spending, arising from:
• changes in political priorities
• changes in economic priorities: deliberate efforts to influence aggregate demand (fiscal policy)
Changes in foreigners' spending, arising from:
• changes in national income abroad
• changes in exchange rates
• changes in the level of trade protection

Table 9.1   Distinguishing between movements along and shifts of the aggregate demand curve

Shifts in the *AD* curve and national income

It is important to note that income is not included among the factors that can shift the *AD* curve. The reason is that *changes in national income cannot initiate any AD curve shifts*. This follows from the point noted earlier (page 238), that real GDP, measured on the horizontal axis, also represents national income. It is not possible for any variable measured on either of the two axes to cause a shift of a curve (for an explanation, see the 'Quantitative techniques' chapter on the CD-ROM, page 14).[3] This point will become clearer when we discuss the multiplier effect (page 260).

---

[3] Note that this does not contradict the ability of changes in disposable (or after-tax) income due to changes in taxes to affect aggregate demand (pages 238–39). This is because changes in taxes and disposable income do not affect national income, as they simply involve a transfer of income from households to the government. National income remains unchanged.

A clarification

In connection with our discussion of the negative slope of the *AD* curve, you should take care not to confuse the wealth effect, resulting from a change in the price level (causing a movement along the *AD* curve), with changes in wealth which cause shifts in the aggregate demand curve. The first case refers to a change in *the real value of wealth that has resulted from a change in the price level*. The second case refers to changes in real wealth *that have come about without any change in the price level*. The same must be said about the difference between the interest rate effect that results from a change in the price level (and produces movements along the *AD* curve), and changes in interest rates that occur without any change in the price level, hence causing shifts of the *AD* curve.

Test your understanding 9.1

1 **(a)** Define aggregate demand and explain each of its four components. **(b)** Show aggregate demand diagrammatically, and define the relationship it represents.

2 Why is the aggregate demand curve negatively sloped?

3 Define 'demand' and 'aggregate demand', and explain why the two are different.

4 Using diagrams, distinguish between a movement along the *AD* curve and a shift of the *AD* curve, and provide examples of the causes of each. What are the four components of spending that cause shifts of the aggregate demand curve?

5 Using diagrams, show the impact of each of the following on the aggregate demand curve; explain what happens to aggregate demand in each case; and identify the component(s) of aggregate expenditure involved.

   (a) Consumer confidence improves as consumers become optimistic about future economic conditions.

   (b) The government decides to increase taxes on firms' profits.

   (c) Firms become fearful that a recession is about to begin.

   (d) The government decides to increase its spending on health care services.

   (e) There is a decline in the real estate market (average house prices fall).

   (f) The central bank (a government organisation) decides to increase interest rates.

   (g) There is an increase in the level of indebtedness of consumers and firms.

   (h) Real incomes in countries that purchase a large share of country A's exports fall; examine the impact on aggregate demand in country A.

   (i) The government lowers personal income taxes (taxes on income of households).

   (j) New legislation makes property rights more secure.

   (k) There is an appreciation (an increase) in the value of the euro relative to the US dollar; examine the impact on aggregate demand in eurozone countries (countries that use the euro).

   (l) There is an appreciation (an increase) in the value of the euro relative to the US dollar; examine the impact on aggregate demand in the United States.

   (m) A non-governmental organisation (NGO) introduces a programme providing credit to small farmers, making it easier for small farmers to borrow to finance the building of irrigation projects.

9.2 Short-run aggregate supply and short-run equilibrium in the *AD-AS* model[4]

Whereas aggregate demand and the aggregate demand curve are straightforward and uncontroversial, aggregate supply is a hotly debated topic among economists. Most of the disagreements focus on the shape of the aggregate supply curve. We will study three aggregate supply curves in this chapter.

Short-run aggregate supply

The short run and long run in macroeconomics

The short run and the long run in macroeconomics differ from the corresponding distinction in microeconomics. The *short run in macroeconomics* is the period of time when prices of resources are roughly constant or inflexible (they do not change much in response to supply and demand). This applies especially to wages, or

---

[4] The order of learning outcomes in the IB syllabus under the headings 'Aggregate supply (*AS*)' and 'Equilibrium' has been changed in order to facilitate presentation of the material.

the price of labour. The *long run in macroeconomics* is the period of time when the prices of all resources, including the price of labour (wages), are flexible and change along with changes in the price level.

Wages, or the price of labour resources, are of special interest because they account for the largest part of firms' costs of production, and therefore strongly affect the quantity of output supplied by firms. Wages do not change very much over relatively short periods of time. The price of labour (wages) is often rigid (unchanging), because:

- labour contracts fix wage rates for certain periods of time, perhaps a year or two or more
- minimum wage legislation fixes the lowest legally permissible wage
- workers and labour unions resist wage cuts
- wage cuts have negative effects on worker morale, causing firms to avoid them.

The distinction between the short run and the long run in macroeconomics does not affect aggregate demand, but is very important for aggregate supply, to which we turn next.

Defining aggregate supply and the short-run aggregate supply curve

♦ Describe the term 'aggregate supply'.

We begin by defining aggregate supply and the short-run aggregate supply curve.

Aggregate supply is the total quantity of goods and services produced in an economy (real GDP) over a particular time period at different price levels.

The **short-run aggregate supply curve** (*SRAS*) shows the relationship between the price level and the quantity of real output (real GDP) produced by firms when resource prices (especially wages) do not change.

Figure 9.2(a) illustrates a short-run aggregate supply curve, indicating that there is a positive (or direct) relationship between the price level and real GDP supplied: a higher price level is associated with a greater quantity of real GDP, and a lower price level with a lower quantity of real GDP.

Why the *SRAS* curve is upward-sloping

♦ Explain, using a diagram, why the short-run aggregate supply curve (*SRAS* curve) is upward sloping.

The explanation for the positive relationship between the price level and real output (real GDP) is based on firm profitability: when there is an increase in the price level, this means that output prices have increased; but with unchanging resource prices (since the economy is in the short run), firms' profits increase. As production becomes more profitable, firms increase the quantity of output produced, resulting in the positive relationship between the price level and the quantity of real GDP supplied.

Similarly, a falling price level means falling output prices; with constant resource prices, firm profitability falls, and output decreases. Again, we have the positive relationship between the price level and the quantity of real GDP supplied.

Changes in short-run aggregate supply (shifts in the *SRAS* curve)

♦ Explain, using a diagram, how the *AS* curve in the short run (*SRAS*) can shift due to factors including changes in resource prices, changes in business taxes and subsidies and supply shocks.

A change in the price level leads to a movement on the *SRAS* curve. A number of factors (other than the price level) cause shifts of the *SRAS* curve, illustrated in Figure 9.2(b). This distinction is analogous to what we

(a) The upward-sloping *SRAS* curve

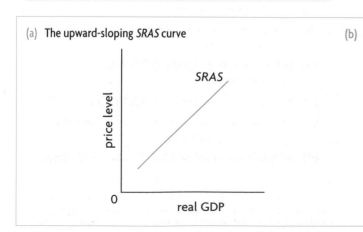

(b) Shifts in the *SRAS* curve

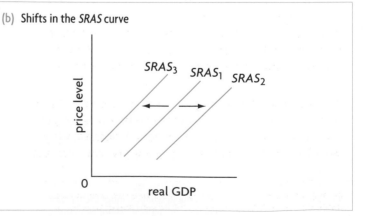

Figure 9.2 The short-run aggregate supply curve (*SRAS*)

learned in Chapter 2 in connection with shifts of end movements along the supply curve for a specific good.

A rightward shift from $SRAS_1$ to $SRAS_2$ means that short-run aggregate supply increases: for any particular price level, firms produce a larger quantity of real GDP. A leftward shift from $SRAS_1$ to $SRAS_3$ means that aggregate supply decreases: for any particular price level, firms produce a smaller quantity of real GDP.

Important factors that cause $SRAS$ curve shifts involve changes in firms' costs of production, changes in taxes and subsidies, and sudden events called 'supply shocks':

- **Changes in wages.** Wages can change for a number of reasons, such as, for example, changes in minimum wage legislation, or changes brought about by labour union bargaining with employers. If wages increase, with the price level constant, firms' costs of production rise, resulting in a leftward shift in the $SRAS$ curve, such as from $SRAS_1$ to $SRAS_3$ in Figure 9.2(b). If wages decrease, with the price level constant, firms' costs drop, giving rise to a rightward shift in the $SRAS$ curve, such as from $SRAS_1$ to $SRAS_2$.

- **Changes in non-labour resource prices.** Changes in the price of non-labour resources, such as the price of oil, equipment, capital goods, land inputs, and so on affect the $SRAS$ curve in the same way as changes in wages. An increase in the price of a resource shifts the $SRAS$ curve to the left; a decrease shifts it to the right.

- **Changes in business taxes.** Business taxes are taxes on firms' profits, and are treated by firms like costs of production. Therefore, higher taxes on profits are like increases in production costs and so shift the $SRAS$ curve to the left. Lower taxes on profits are like lower production costs and shift the $SRAS$ curve to the right.[5]

- **Changes in subsidies offered to businesses.** Subsidies have the opposite effect to taxes, as they involve money transferred from the government to firms. If they increase, the $SRAS$ curve shifts to the right; if they decrease, the $SRAS$ curve shifts to the left.

- **Supply shocks.** Supply shocks are events that have a sudden and strong impact on short-run aggregate supply (see also Chapter 2, page 29). Some supply shocks directly affect aggregate supply. For example, a war or violent conflict can result in destruction of physical capital and disruption of the economy, leading to lower output produced and a leftward shift in the $SRAS$ curve. Unfavourable weather conditions can cause a fall in agricultural output, also shifting the $SRAS$ curve to the left. Beneficial supply shocks such as unusually good weather conditions with a positive effect on agricultural output lead to an increase in aggregate supply and a rightward shift in the $SRAS$ curve. Supply shocks sometimes work by producing sudden changes in firms' costs of production. For example, a sudden increase in the price of a major input (such as oil) increases firms' costs.

Over short periods of time, the **$SRAS$** curve shifts to the left or to the right mainly as a result of factors that influence firms' costs of production (such as changes in wages, changes in non-labour resource prices and changes in business taxes or subsidies), as well as supply shocks.

Test your understanding 9.2

1 **(a)** Define aggregate supply. **(b)** Explain why the short-run aggregate supply curve is upward-sloping.

2 **(a)** Distinguish between the short run and the long run in macroeconomics. **(b)** What are some of the factors that cause wages to be inflexible (not change very easily and rapidly)?

3 **(a)** Show the short-run aggregate supply ($SRAS$) curve in a diagram, and explain what relationship it represents. **(b)** What factors can cause a movement along the $SRAS$ curve? **(c)** What factors cause shifts in the $SRAS$ curve?

4 Using diagrams, show the impact of each of the following on the $SRAS$ curve; explain what happens to $SRAS$ in each case.

  (a) The price of oil (an important input in production) increases.

  (b) Below-zero temperatures destroy agricultural output.

  (c) The government lowers taxes on firms' profits.

  (d) The government eliminates subsidies on agricultural products.

  (e) There is an increase in the minimum wage.

---

[5] You may remember that in Chapters 4 and 5 when we studied taxes and subsidies we shifted the supply curve upward and downward. A downward shift is equivalent to a rightward shift, and an upward shift is equivalent to a leftward shift. These same relationships apply to *aggregate* supply as well. See 'Quantitative techniques' chapter on the CD-ROM, page 13 for an explanation.

Short-run equilibrium in the *AD-AS* model

Illustrating short-run equilibrium

♦ Explain, using a diagram, the determination of short-run equilibrium, using the *SRAS* curve.

We will now put the aggregate demand curve and the short-run aggregate supply curve together, to determine short-run macroeconomic equilibrium.

In the *AD-AS* model, the **equilibrium level of output** (or **real GDP**) occurs where aggregate demand intersects aggregate supply. In the short run, equilibrium is given by the point of intersection of the *AD* and *SRAS* curves, and determines the price level, the level of real GDP and the level of employment.

This is shown in Figure 9.3 where Pl_e is the equilibrium price level and Y_e is the equilibrium level of real GDP. As we know, the level of real GDP is closely related to how much unemployment there is in the economy. As real GDP increases, firms hire more labour and unemployment falls; as real GDP decreases, firms need fewer labour resources, and unemployment rises. Therefore, the equilibrium level of real GDP also determines how much unemployment there is in the economy.

At any price level and real GDP other than Pl_e and Y_e, the economy is in disequilibrium. At price level Pl_1, there is an excess amount of real GDP supplied, putting a downward pressure on the price level,

which falls until it reaches Pl_e. At a price level lower than Pl_e, such as Pl_2, there is an excess amount of real GDP demanded, putting an upward pressure on the price level, which moves upward until it settles at Pl_e. At Pl_e, the amount of real GDP demanded is equal to the amount supplied, and there is short-run equilibrium.

Three short-run equilibrium positions: recessionary (deflationary) gaps, inflationary gaps and short-run full employment equilibrium

There are three possible kinds of short-run macroeconomic equilibrium positions for the economy, shown in Figure 9.4. All are defined in relation to the economy's potential GDP, or the full employment level of real output (GDP), where unemployment is equal to the natural rate of unemployment (see page 232). Potential output appears as Y_p in Figure 9.4 a–c, where a vertical line drawn at Y_p represents the level of real GDP at which there is 'full employment'. The three kinds of equilibria are:

- **Figure 9.4(a): recessionary (deflationary) gap.** In part (a), equilibrium real GDP, Y_e, lies to the left of potential GDP, Y_p. When real GDP is less than potential GDP, the economy is experiencing a recessionary gap (also known as a deflationary gap), and unemployment is greater than the natural rate of unemployment. Why does this happen? The recessionary gap has been created because at the price level Pl_e, the amount of real GDP that the four components of aggregate demand want to buy is less than the economy's potential GDP. *There is not enough total demand in the economy* to make it worthwhile for firms to produce potential GDP. This also means that firms require less labour for their production; therefore, unemployment is greater than the natural rate of unemployment.

- **Figure 9.4(b): inflationary gap.** In part (b), equilibrium real GDP, Y_e, lies to the right of potential GDP, Y_p. When real GDP is larger than potential GDP, the economy is experiencing an inflationary gap, and unemployment is less than the natural rate of unemployment. An inflationary gap arises because with aggregate demand *AD*, the quantity of real GDP that the four components want to buy at the price level (Pl_e) is greater than the economy's potential output. *There is too much*

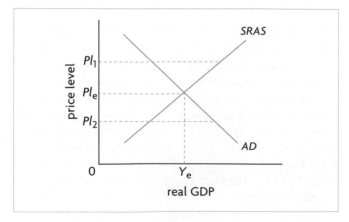

Figure 9.3 Short-run macroeconomic equilibrium

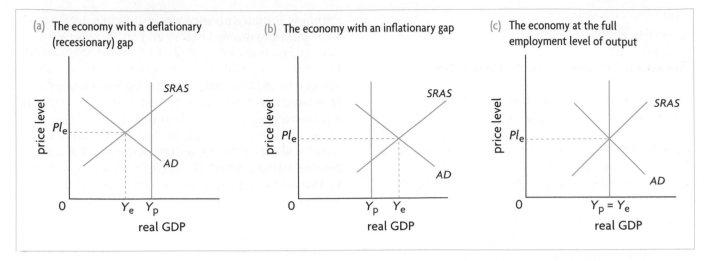

(a) The economy with a deflationary (recessionary) gap

(b) The economy with an inflationary gap

(c) The economy at the full employment level of output

Figure 9.4   Three short-run equilibrium states of the economy

total demand in the economy, and firms respond by producing a greater quantity of real GDP than potential GDP. To produce more output, firms' labour needs increase, and unemployment falls to become less than the natural rate of unemployment.

- **Figure 9.4(c): full employment level of real GDP.** In part (c), equilibrium real GDP is equal to potential GDP. When the economy is producing its potential GDP, unemployment is equal to the natural rate of unemployment and there is no recessionary or inflationary gap.

Recessionary (deflationary) and inflationary gaps represent short-run equilibrium positions of the economy. A **recessionary (deflationary) gap** is a situation where real GDP is less than potential GDP (and unemployment is greater than the natural rate of unemployment) due to insufficient aggregate demand. An **inflationary gap** is a situation where real GDP is greater than potential GDP (and unemployment is smaller than the natural rate of unemployment) due to excess aggregate demand. When the economy is at its full employment equilibrium level of GDP, the *AD* curve intersects the *SRAS* curve at the level of potential GDP, and there is no deflationary or inflationary gap. This is the economy's **full employment level of output**.

You can see that the three short-run equilibrium states of the economy correspond to the phases of the business cycle that we studied in Chapter 8: Y_e of

Figure 9.4(a) corresponds to a point like e in Figure 8.5 (page 233), where the economy is experiencing recession, unemployment is greater than the natural rate and actual GDP is less than potential GDP. Y_e of Figure 9.4(b) corresponds to a point like d in Figure 8.5, where unemployment is lower than the natural rate and actual GDP is greater than potential GDP. Finally, Y_p of Figure 9.4(c) corresponds to points like a, b, and c in Figure 8.5, where the economy is producing actual GDP equal to potential GDP, with unemployment at its natural rate. Therefore, recessionary and inflationary gaps are two types of output gaps.

Impacts of changes in short-run equilibrium

- Examine, using diagrams, the impacts of changes in short-run equilibrium.

The short-run equilibrium of an economy changes whenever there is a change in aggregate demand or short-run aggregate supply. Suppose there occurs an increase in aggregate demand, due to any of the factors discussed earlier (such as an increase in national income abroad, or an increase in investment spending). In Figure 9.5(a), the *AD* curve shifts from AD_1 to AD_2, resulting in an increase in the price level from Pl_1 to Pl_2, and an increase in real GDP, from Y_1 to Y_2. These changes also lead to a fall in unemployment.

If there is a decrease in aggregate demand (due, for example, to pessimism among firms or

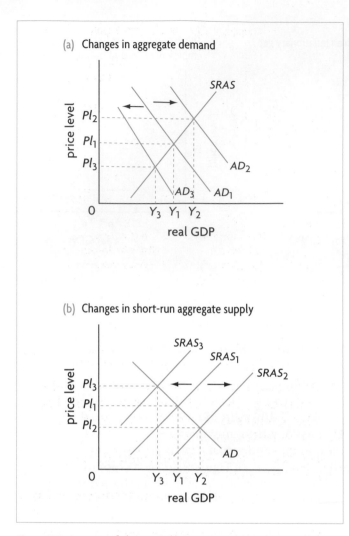

(a)   Changes in aggregate demand

(b)   Changes in short-run aggregate supply

Figure 9.5 Impacts of changes in short-run macroeconomic equilibrium

a fall in net exports), the *AD* curve shifts from AD_1 to AD_3; the price level and real GDP fall from Pl_1 to Pl_3 and from Y_1 to Y_3, while unemployment increases.

Figure 9.5(b) shows shifts in the *SRAS* curve. A rightward shift from $SRAS_1$ to $SRAS_2$ (for example, because of a technological improvement or lower business taxes), result in a lower price level, Pl_2, a higher level of real GDP, Y_2, and lower unemployment. On the other hand, a leftward shift from $SRAS_1$ to $SRAS_3$ (say, because of an increase in business taxes or an increase in the price of a

resource) produce an increase in the price level to Pl_3, a fall in real output to Y_3 and an increase in unemployment.

Shifts in *AD* or *SRAS* as possible causes of the business cycle

It is now a simple matter to consider the possible causes of the business cycle studied in Chapter 8. In Figure 9.6(a) and (b), the economy is initially at full employment equilibrium, producing potential output *Yp* (for the moment ignore the 'LRAS' label of the vertical line, which will be explained below). In part (a), a fall in aggregate demand, shifting the *AD* curve leftward from AD_1 to AD_2 causes a recessionary gap. If the economy experiences an increase in aggregate demand, appearing as a rightward shift in the *AD* curve from AD_1 to AD_3, this causes an inflationary gap.

Shifts in the *SRAS* curve can also contribute to economic fluctuations.[6] In Figure 9.6(b), starting again from full employment equilibrium, a fall in *SRAS*, shifting $SRAS_1$ to $SRAS_2$, leads to an economic contraction, with real GDP falling to Y_2 and unemployment increasing. Note, however, that this contraction differs from the recessionary gap resulting from the fall in aggregate demand: the fall in aggregate supply leads to *an increase in the price level, along with a decrease in real GDP*. This special set of circumstances is especially undesirable for an economy, as it involves the appearance of two problems: recession (with unemployment) and a rising price level. This is known as *stagflation* (combining 'stagnation' with 'inflation'), a term coined in the 1970s. At the time, stagflation was caused largely by increases in oil prices due to the actions of OPEC (Organization of the Petroleum Exporting Countries), which cut back its production of oil, giving rise to increases in the price of oil, a major input in production.

An increase in *SRAS*, shifting $SRAS_1$ to $SRAS_3$ leads to an economic expansion as real GDP increases to Y_3 and unemployment falls. This expansion results in a falling price level, in contrast to the rising price level following an increase in aggregate demand.

Most economists believe that changes in aggregate demand are more important than changes in aggregate supply as causes of the business cycle.

---

[6] It may be noted that changes in aggregate supply can cause contractions and expansions; however, these are not called deflationary (recessionary) or inflationary gaps. The reason is that deflationary and inflationary gaps are defined in terms of the level of actual aggregate demand relative to

the aggregate demand that is required to bring about full employment equilibrium. A deflationary gap is therefore caused by insufficient aggregate demand, and an inflationary gap by too much aggregate demand.

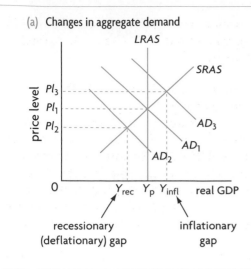

(a) Changes in aggregate demand

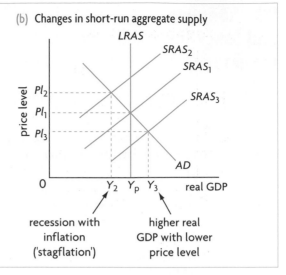

(b) Changes in short-run aggregate supply

Figure 9.6 Possible causes of the business cycle

The Greek economy still shrinking

The Greek economy is expected to contract by 4.8% in 2010. The contraction is mainly due to decreases in consumer and private investment spending, as net exports are showing an improvement. The forecast for 2011 is that the economy will contract a further 3.6%, partly due to drastic cuts in government spending, together with increases in indirect taxes and corporate (business) taxes. Consumer and business confidence are very low. Consumer spending will continue to decrease as unemployment rises and real wages fall. Investment spending is also forecast to fall further.

Source: Economist Intelligence Unit, ViewsWire News Analysis, 15 November 2010.

Applying your skills

1 How do low consumer and business confidence influence aggregate demand?

2 Using a short-run *AD-AS* diagram, show the effects on aggregate demand of **(a)** falling consumer, investment and government spending, **(b)** improved net exports, and **(c)** increased indirect taxes and business taxes.

3 Using information in the extract, state two reasons explaining the falls in **(a)** consumer spending, and **(b)** investment spending.

4 Using an *AD-AS* diagram, explain what kind of output gap the Greek economy is experiencing.

1 Using diagrams, show the effects of each of the following on short-run equilibrium, explaining what happens to the equilibrium price level, output and unemployment.

   (a) The price of oil (an important input in production) increases.

   (b) Firms are pessimistic about the future of the economy.

   (c) Below-zero temperatures destroy agricultural output.

   (d) The government lowers taxes on firms' profits.

   (e) There is a large rise in stock market prices.

   (f) The government eliminates subsidies on agricultural products.

   (g) A war destroys a portion of an economy's physical capital.

2 **(a)** Using diagrams and the short-run *AD-AS* model, show the three short-run equilibrium states of the economy and illustrate (i) a recessionary gap, (ii) an inflationary gap, and (iii) full employment equilibrium. **(b)** How are the three equilibrium states related to the phases of the business cycle?

3 Assuming the economy is in a position of full employment equilibrium, explain how the events in question I can contribute to short-run economic fluctuations.

9.3 Long-run aggregate supply and long-run equilibrium in the monetarist/new classical model

The monetarist/new classical model

Defining the long-run aggregate supply curve and long-run macroeconomic equilibrium

- Explain, using a diagram, that the monetarist/new classical model of the long-run aggregate supply curve (*LRAS*) is vertical at the level of potential output (full employment output) because aggregate supply in the long run is independent of the price level.
- Explain, using a diagram, the determination of long-run equilibrium, indicating that long-run equilibrium occurs at the full employment level of output.

This section examines the theoretical perspective of **monetarist/new classical** economists, which builds on the work of the classical economists of the 19th century. Both the monetarist/new classical and classical perspectives are based on the following key principles: the importance of the price mechanism in co-ordinating economic activities; the concept of competitive market equilibrium; and thinking about the economy as a harmonious system that automatically tends towards full employment. While economists generally accept these principles in the study of microeconomics, there is major disagreement over their relevance to the study of economics at the macro level.[7]

The meaning of aggregate supply in the monetarist/new classical (and all other) perspectives is the same as that defined on page 242. What differs is how economists interpret *the shape of the aggregate supply curve*.

The monetarist/new classical approach to aggregate supply rests crucially on the distinction made earlier between the macroeconomic short run and long run. It examines what happens to aggregate supply when the economy moves into the long run, when all resource prices including wages change to match changes in the price level. The long-run supply relationship between the price level and aggregate output is referred to as **long-run aggregate supply (LRAS)**, shown graphically as the ***LRAS* curve**. The *LRAS* curve is vertical at potential GDP, or the full employment level of real GDP, Y_p, as shown in Figure 9.7. A vertical *LRAS* curve means that in the long run a change in the price level does not result in any change in the quantity of real GDP produced.

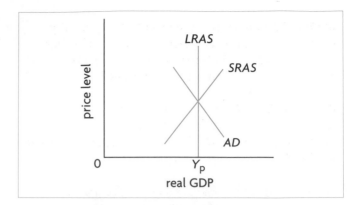

Figure 9.7 The *LRAS* curve and long-run equilibrium in the monetarist/new classical model

The economy is in long-run equilibrium when the *AD* curve and the *SRAS* curve intersect at any point on the *LRAS* curve, seen in Figure 9.7. Note that the economy's long-run equilibrium is the same as the short-run equilibrium where the intersection of *AD* with *SRAS* occurs at the economy's potential GDP, as in Figure 9.4(c).

Since the *LRAS* curve is vertical at potential GDP, it follows that the vertical line at Y_p appearing in Figure 9.6 (as well as in Figure 9.4) is the *LRAS* curve. In these figures, you can see the short-run equilibria in relation to the economy's long-run equilibrium.

According to the monetarist/new classical perspective, the long-run aggregate supply (**LRAS**) curve is vertical at the full employment level of output, or potential GDP, indicating that in the long run the economy produces potential GDP, which is independent of the price level.

Why the *LRAS* curve is vertical

There is a very simple explanation for the vertical shape of the *LRAS* curve. Since wages (and other resource prices) are now changing to match output price changes, firms' costs of production remain constant even as the price level changes. Therefore, as the price level increases or decreases, *with constant real costs, firms' profits are also constant, and firms no longer have any incentive to increase or decrease their output levels.*

For example, say the price level increases. In the short run, with wages (and other input prices) constant, firms' profits increase, and firms therefore increase the quantity of output produced by moving upward along an upward-sloping *SRAS* curve. However, in the long run, wages (and other resource prices) also increase by the same amount. In effect, nothing has changed from the firms' point of view, and so they have no reason to increase the quantity of output they

---

[7] Very briefly, monetarism (attributed mainly to Nobel Prize-winning economist Milton Friedman) emphasises the role of money, claiming that changes in the money supply have major effects on output in the short run and on the price level in the long run. New classical economists (associated partly with another Nobel Prize-winning economist, Robert Lucas, as well as others) emphasises the important of individuals' 'rational expectations' of inflation and government policy actions.

produce. Similarly, any price level decrease is fully matched by the same decrease in wages (and other resource prices), so that firms have no incentive to decrease the quantity of output produced.

Why the *LRAS* curve is situated at the level of potential GDP (or why inflationary and deflationary gaps cannot persist in the long run)

♦ Explain why, in the monetarist/new classical approach, while there may be short-term fluctuations in output, the economy will always return to the full employment level of output in the long run.

In our discussion above, we saw that recessionary and inflationary gaps are two possible short-run equilibrium positions of the economy where the equilibrium level of real GDP differs from potential GDP. If the *LRAS* curve is vertical at potential GDP, it follows that recessionary and inflationary gaps are only short-run phenomena that cannot persist in the long run. As soon as the economy moves into the long run, the recessionary and inflationary gaps disappear, and the economy achieves full employment equilibrium.

To see how this occurs, consider Figure 9.8(a), where an economy is initially in long-run equilibrium at point a producing potential output, Y_p. A fall in aggregate demand from AD_1 to AD_2 causes the economy to move in the short run from point a to point b, where there arises a recessionary gap; at b, real GDP has fallen to Y_{rec} and the price level has fallen from Pl_1 to Pl_2. However, the economy cannot remain there in the long run. In the long run, the fall in the price level is matched by a fall in wages (and falls in other resource prices), so the *SRAS* curve shifts to the right from $SRAS_1$ to $SRAS_2$ until the economy is back on the *LRAS* curve, at point c. *The assumption of wage and price flexibility in the long run has allowed the economy to automatically come back to its long-run equilibrium level of output.* The recessionary gap is eliminated, and the only thing that changes due to the fall in aggregate demand is the fall in the price level (from Pl_1 to Pl_3).[8]

In Figure 9.8(b) we see what happens if there is an increase in aggregate demand. Beginning from long-run equilibrium at point a, aggregate demand shifts from AD_2 to AD_1; in the short run the economy moves to point b, real GDP increases to Y_{infl} where there is an inflationary gap, and the price level increases from Pl_1 to Pl_2. However, the economy cannot remain at point b in the long run, because once wages (and other resource prices) increase to match the increase in the price level, *SRAS* shifts from $SRAS_2$ to $SRAS_1$, and the economy arrives at point c, which is once again on the *LRAS* curve. In the long run, the inflationary gap is eliminated and the only thing that changes after the increase in aggregate demand is the increase in the price level (to Pl_3).[9]

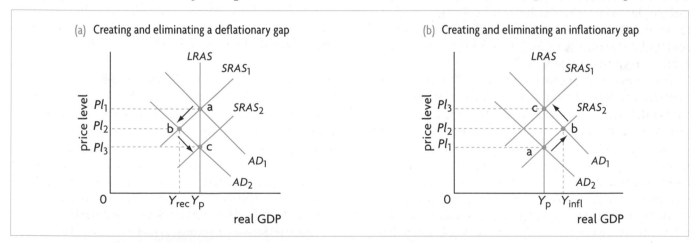

(a) Creating and eliminating a deflationary gap

(b) Creating and eliminating an inflationary gap

Figure 9.8 Returning to long-run full employment equilibrium in the monetarist/new classical model

[8] You may be wondering why wages will fall in the long run, thereby causing the shift in the *SRAS* curve that makes the economy move back to full employment equilibrium. The reason involves adjustments that take place in the labour market. As we know from our earlier discussion, if there is a recessionary gap, aggregate demand is weak and there is unemployment of labour that is greater than the natural rate of unemployment. This means that there is a surplus of labour in the labour market; in other words, the quantity of labour supplied is greater than the quantity of labour demanded. This creates pressures on wages to fall, so as to bring about a balance between the quantity of labour demanded by firms and the quantity supplied by workers. Therefore, wages fall in the long run, in order to eliminate the labour surplus, and when there is

no longer any surplus labour, the economy reverts to long-run equilibrium through the shift in the *SRAS* curve.

[9] When there is an inflationary gap, unemployment falls below the natural rate, and there is a shortage of labour in the labour market. Firms have a strong demand for labour (as well as other resources) and workers would like to negotiate higher wages because the price level has increased. In the long run, the wage is free to change in response to the forces of supply and demand, and moves upward to the point where quantity of labour demanded is brought into balance with quantity of labour supplied. When this occurs, the economy returns to long-run equilibrium through the shift in the *SRAS* curve.

In the monetarist/new classical perspective, recessionary (deflationary) and inflationary gaps are eliminated in the long run. This ensures that in the long run the *LRAS* curve is vertical at the level of potential GDP. The economy has a built-in tendency towards full employment equilibrium.

Impacts of changes in long-run equilibrium (or why in the long run aggregate demand influences only the price level)

♦ Explain, using diagrams, the impacts of changes in the long-run equilibrium.

A change in long-run equilibrium occurs when the *SRAS* and *AD* curves intersect at a different point on the *LRAS* curve. This can be seen in Figure 9.8, where a change in long-run equilibrium is indicated by a move from point a to c (in both parts (a) and (b)). The change from one equilibrium to another is shown more clearly in Figure 9.9 (which ignores the short-run changes). We thus see that for a given *LRAS* curve, a change in long-run equilibrium means that *only the price level changes*, leaving the equilibrium level of real GDP unchanged at potential output, Y_p.

This illustrates another important principle of the monetarist/new classical view: changes in aggregate demand can have an influence on real GDP only in the short run; in the long run, they only result in changing the price level, having no impact on real GDP, as this remains constant at the level of potential output and the *LRAS* curve (see also Figure 9.13(a), page 254).

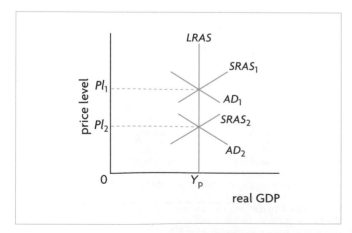

Figure 9.9 Changes in long-run equilibrium in the monetarist/new classical *AD-AS* model

In the monetarist/new classical perspective, changes in aggregate demand can influence real GDP only in the short run; in the long run, the only impact of a change in aggregate demand is to change the economy's price level. Increases in aggregate demand in the long run are therefore inflationary (cause inflation).

Test your understanding 9.4

1 **(a)** Define and use a diagram to show the long-run aggregate supply (*LRAS*) curve. **(b)** What can we say about the level of unemployment in the economy that occurs at the level of real GDP where the *LRAS* curve is situated? **(c)** What does the vertical shape of the *LRAS* curve tell us about the relationship between the price level and real GDP in the long run?

2 **(a)** Define and use a diagram to show long-run equilibrium in the *AD-AS* model (show the relationship between the *LRAS*, *SRAS* and *AD* curves). **(b)** What can we say about the level of unemployment at long-run equilibrium?

3 Draw two diagrams, illustrating recessionary and inflationary gaps in relation to the *LRAS* curve.

4 Can inflationary or deflationary gaps (short-term fluctuations) persist in the long run according to the monetarist/new classical perspective? Explain.

5 Why do monetarist/new classical economists argue that in the long run aggregate demand can only affect the price level? Use a diagram to illustrate your answer.

6 Use a diagram to explain changes in long-run equilibrium and their impacts on the price level and real GDP.

9.4 Aggregate supply and equilibrium in the Keynesian model

This section presents the theoretical model of Keynesian economists. Keynesian economists base their ideas on the work of John Maynard Keynes, one of the most famous economists of the 20th century, whose work in the first half of the century came to form the basis of modern macroeconomics. Keynes questioned the classical and monetarist/new classical economists' view of the economic system as a harmonious system that automatically tends towards full employment, and showed that it is possible for economies to remain in a position of short-run equilibrium for long periods of time.

Getting stuck in the short run

Wage and price downward inflexibility

The $LRAS$ curve in the monetarist/new classical model depends on the idea that all resource prices and product prices are fully flexible and respond to the forces of supply and demand. However, what if resource prices cannot fall, even over long periods of time? Keynesian economists argue that there is an asymmetry between wage changes in the upward and downward directions. Under conditions of an economic expansion and strong aggregate demand (rightward shifts in the AD curve causing an inflationary gap), with unemployment lower than the natural rate and a rising price level, wages quickly begin to move upward. Yet in a recessionary gap, where aggregate demand is weak and the economy is in recession with unemployment greater than the natural rate, wages do not fall easily, even over long periods of time, because of a variety of factors (such as labour contracts, minimum wage legislation; worker and union resistance to wage cuts; see page 242).

Keynesian economists also argue that not only wages but also product prices do not fall easily, even if an economy is in a recessionary gap. The reasoning is that in a recession, if wages will not go down, firms will avoid lowering their prices because that would reduce their profits. Furthermore, large oligopolistic firms may fear price wars; if one firm lowers its price, then others may lower theirs more aggressively in an effort to capture market shares, and then all the firms will be worse off. Such factors, it is argued, make prices unlikely to fall even in a recession.

The inability of the economy to move into the long run

If wages and prices do not fall easily, this means the economy may get stuck in the short run, and cannot move into the long run. Consider Figure 9.10(a), which is similar to Figure 9.8(a). Beginning at point a where an economy is producing potential output Y_p, aggregate demand falls so the AD curve shifts from AD_1 to AD_2. The monetarist/new classical model predicts that the economy will move to point b in the short run, where there is a recessionary gap and the price level falls from Pl_1 to Pl_2; in the long run it will move to point c, where there is an even lower price level, Pl_3, and the economy is once again producing potential output Y_p.

However, if the price level cannot fall from Pl_1, where it was initially, the economy will move to point d on the new, lower, aggregate demand curve, AD_2. Even if the price level succeeds in falling to Pl_2, so the economy moves to point b, the economy may get stuck there if wages do not fall (remember that wages must fall for the $SRAS$ curve to shift to $SRAS_2$ on the $LRAS$ curve). It follows that if the price level cannot fall, or if wages cannot fall, the economy gets stuck in the short run, and is unable to move into the long run where it eliminates the recessionary gap.

This argument suggests that the $SRAS$ curve has the shape shown in Figure 9.10(b). The horizontal part of the curve is based on the Keynesian idea that wages and prices do not move downward. Point d in Figure 9.10(a) corresponds to point d in Figure 9.10(b). The economy is in a recessionary gap and may stay there indefinitely unless the government intervenes with specific policies.

In the Keynesian model, inflexible wages and prices mean that the economy cannot move into the long run. Inflexible wages and prices are shown graphically by a horizontal section of the Keynesian aggregate supply (AS) curve.

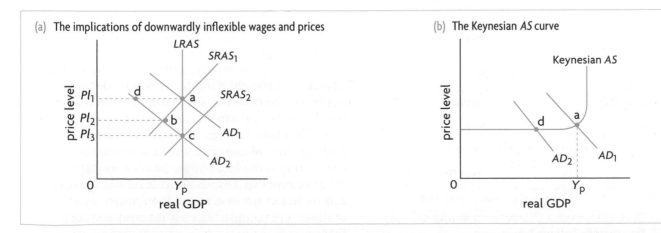

(a) The implications of downwardly inflexible wages and prices

(b) The Keynesian AS curve

Figure 9.10 Keynesian analysis

Keynesians would not suggest that wages and prices can never fall. They would agree that if a recession or depression (which is a very severe recession) continues for a long enough time (perhaps years), wages and prices would eventually begin to fall. In the meantime a long-lasting recession would be very costly in terms of unemployment, low incomes and lost output. Therefore, it would be necessary for the government to intervene with active policies to help the economy come out of the recession.

The shape of the Keynesian aggregate supply curve

♦ Explain, using a diagram, that the Keynesian model of the aggregate supply curve has three sections because of 'wage/price' downward inflexibility and different levels of spare capacity in the economy.

Figure 9.11 shows that the **Keynesian aggregate supply curve** has three sections. In section I, real GDP is low, and the price level remains constant as real GDP increases. In this range of real GDP, there is a lot of unemployment of resources and **spare capacity**. Spare capacity refers to physical capital (machines, equipment, etc.) that firms have available but do not use. Firms can easily increase their output by employing the unemployed capital and other unemployed resources, without having to bid up wages and other resource prices. In section II, real GDP increases are accompanied by increases in the price level. The reason is that as output increases, so does employment of resources, and eventually bottlenecks in resource supplies begin to appear as there is no longer spare capacity in the economy. Wages and other resource prices begin to rise, which means that costs of production increase. The only way that firms will be induced to increase their output is if they can sell it at higher prices.

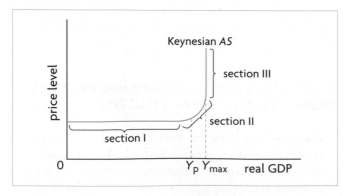

Figure 9.11 The Keynesian aggregate supply curve

Therefore, growing output leads to an increasing price level.

At output level Y_p, the economy has reached its full employment level of real GDP. This is also its potential output level, and unemployment has fallen to the point where it is now equal to the natural rate of unemployment. However, as we know, the natural rate of unemployment is not maximum employment, as unemployment can fall further, which is what happens when real GDP continues to increase beyond Y_p. Real GDP can continue to increase until it reaches section III.

In section III, the *AS* curve becomes vertical at Y_{max}, indicating that real GDP reaches a level beyond which it cannot increase anymore; at this point, the price level rises very rapidly. Real GDP can no longer increase because firms are using the maximum amount of labour and all other resources in the economy. Since real GDP cannot increase further, any efforts on the part of firms to increase their output only result in greater increases in the price level.

The three equilibrium states of the economy in the Keynesian model

♦ Explain, using the Keynesian *AD-AS* diagram, that the economy may be in equilibrium at any level of real output where *AD* intersects *AS*.

♦ Explain, using a diagram, that if the economy is in equilibrium at a level of real output below the full employment level of output, then there is a deflationary (recessionary) gap.

♦ Explain, using a diagram, that if *AD* increases in the vertical section of the *AS* curve, then there is an inflationary gap.

Macroeconomic equilibrium in the Keynesian model is determined by the point where the *AD* curve intersects the Keynesian *AS* curve. This can occur at any level of real GDP. There are three equilibrium states of the economy, shown in Figure 9.12.

Figure 9.12(a) shows the *AD* curve intersecting the *AS* curve in its horizontal section, determining Y_e, which is less than Y_p (potential GDP), indicating a recessionary (deflationary) gap with unemployment greater than the natural rate. Aggregate demand is too weak to induce firms to produce at Y_p. In part (b), the economy is producing at Y_e, which is greater than Y_p, and is experiencing an inflationary gap. There is strong aggregate demand, unemployment has fallen below its natural rate, and as the economy approaches its maximum capacity, the price level has increased. Part (c) shows the case where the economy has achieved full employment equilibrium, or potential output, at Y_p.

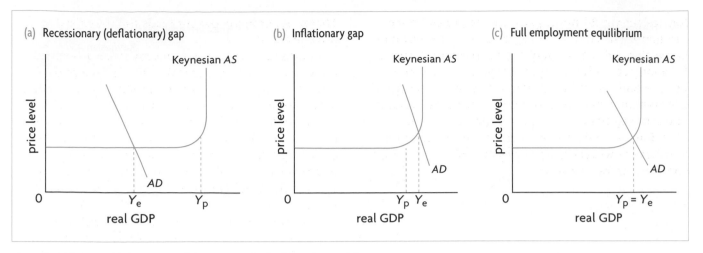

Figure 9.12 Three equilibrium states of the economy in the Keynesian model

These three equilibrium states of the economy can be related to the business cycle (see page 233): Y_e in Figure 9.12(a) corresponds to a point like e in Figure 8.5, where there is a recessionary gap; Y_e of Figure 9.12(b) corresponds to a point like d in Figure 8.5, where there is an inflationary gap; and Y_p of Figure 9.12(c) corresponds to points like a, b and c in Figure 8.5, where the economy's actual output is equal to its potential output.

It should be noted that 'potential output' and 'natural unemployment', which we have used to illustrate the three kinds of equilibrium, are actually *monetarist* concepts. On the other hand, inflationary and deflationary (recessionary) gaps are *Keynesian* concepts. As our analysis shows, the two models can usefully borrow concepts from each other in order to show how different real-world situations can be understood and interpreted differently depending on the theoretical approach used.

Some key features of the Keynesian model

Recessionary gaps can persist over long periods of time

♦ Discuss why, in contrast to the monetarist/new classical model, the economy can remain stuck in a deflationary (recessionary) gap in the Keynesian model.

One of the most important ideas arising from the Keynesian interpretation of the *AD–AS* model is that recessionary gaps can persist over long periods of time. According to Keynes, this happens partly because of the inability of wages and prices to fall. In addition, the problem is caused by insufficient aggregate demand. Whenever aggregate demand intersects the horizontal section of the Keynesian

AS curve, the economy is in a recessionary gap because aggregate demand is too low, and its four components are unable to buy enough output to make it worthwhile for firms to produce potential GDP. Therefore, equilibrium GDP is lower than potential GDP. In Figure 9.12(a), the equilibrium level of real GDP settles at Y_e, and can remain there indefinitely. This has important implications for economic policy. It means that the government must intervene in the economy with specific measures to help it come out of the recessionary gap.

Keynesian analysis is therefore essentially a short-run analysis. This does not mean that Keynesian economists do not consider what happens over long periods of time; it means only that they do not accept the idea that the economy can move into what monetarist/new classical economists define as the long run (where there is full resource and product price flexibility). Therefore, in the Keynesian perspective the economy does not automatically tend towards full employment equilibrium.

In the Keynesian model, an economy can remain for long periods of time in an equilibrium where there is less than full employment (i.e. a recessionary/deflationary gap), caused by insufficient aggregate demand.

Increases in aggregate demand need not cause increases in the price level

♦ Discuss why, in contrast to the monetarist/new classical model, increases in aggregate demand in the Keynesian *AD-AS* model need not be inflationary, unless the economy is operating close to, or at the level of full employment.

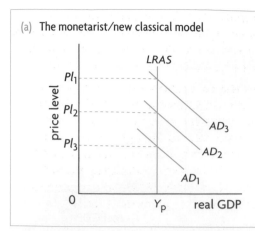

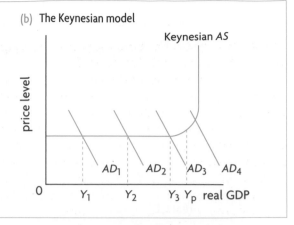

(a) The monetarist/new classical model

(b) The Keynesian model

Figure 9.13 Effects of increases in aggregate demand on real GDP and the price level

Another important idea arising from the Keynesian model is that increases in aggregate demand need not always cause increases in the price level. In the monetarist/new classical model, increases in aggregate demand always result in price-level increases. In the short run, as *AD* shifts to the right causing a movement along an upward-sloping *SRAS* curve, an increase in real GDP and an increase in the price level result (see Figure 9.5(a)). In the long run, increases in aggregate demand give rise only to increases in the price level, leaving real GDP unaffected, as in Figure 9.13(a). In the Keynesian model, when the economy is in the horizontal part of the *AS* curve, increases in aggregate demand lead to increases in real GDP without affecting the price level. This can be seen in Figure 9.13(b). It is only when the Keynesian *AS* curve begins to slope upward, when it is close to the full employment level of output, that further increases in aggregate demand begin to result in changes in the price level as well.

1 Define aggregate supply. Does the meaning of this concept change in the context of the *SRAS*, *LRAS* or Keynesian *AS* curves?

2 **(a)** Explain what it means for the shape of the aggregate supply curve if wages and prices are inflexible in the downward direction. **(b)** Can the economy move into the long run? **(c)** What does the horizontal section of the *AS* curve tell us about spare capacity in the economy?

3 **(a)** Use a diagram to show the Keynesian *AS* curve. **(b)** What does the flat section of this curve indicate about the relationship between the price level and real GDP? **(c)** What does the upward-sloping section indicate about this relationship? **(d)** What does the vertical section indicate?

4 Using the Keynesian model and diagrams, show the three short-run equilibrium states of the economy, noting recessionary (deflationary) and inflationary gaps and their relationship to the full employment equilibrium position of the economy (potential output).

5 Using diagrams illustrating the Keynesian model, show and explain what happens to the equilibrium level of real GDP and the price level if aggregate demand shifts within **(a)** the horizontal section of the Keynesian *AS* curve, **(b)** the upward-sloping section of the Keynesian *AS* curve, and **(c)** the vertical section of the Keynesian *AS* curve.

6 Why can an economy remain in an equilibrium position where there is less than full employment (a recessionary gap) for long periods of time in the Keynesian model?

7 **(a)** Using the Keynesian model, explain when increases in aggregate demand can be expected to lead to increases in the price level (inflation) and when they are unlikely to do so. **(b)** How does the Keynesian model differ from the monetarist/new classical model in its prediction of inflation following an increase in aggregate demand?

9.5 Shifting aggregate supply curves over the long term

♦ Explain, using the two models above, how factors leading to changes in the quantity and/or quality of factors of production (including improvements in efficiency, new technology, reductions in unemployment, and institutional changes) can shift the aggregate supply curve over the long term.

Changes in aggregate supply over the long term

Economic growth and aggregate supply curve shifts in *AD-AS* models

So far, we have considered the *LRAS* and Keynesian *AS* curves in fixed, unchanging positions. Yet over time, these curves can shift to the right or to the left. Each of these two curves represents a particular level of potential output, which is the total quantity of goods and services produced by an economy when there is 'full employment' of its resources. Therefore, both curves shift to the right or to the left in response to factors that change potential output.

An increase in potential output signifies economic growth over the long term; a decrease signifies negative growth (or a fall in real output). Increases in potential output, shifting aggregate supply curves and long term economic growth are illustrated in Figure 9.14.

Factors that change aggregate supply (shift *AS* curves) over the long term

The most important factors that cause increases in potential output and rightward shifts in the *LRAS* and Keynesian *AS* curves are the following:

- **Increases in quantities of the factors of production.** If the quantity of a factor of production increases, the *LRAS* curve and Keynesian *AS* curve shift to the right. For example, an increase in the quantity of physical capital, or the quantity of land (such as when there is a discovery of new oil reserves) means that the economy is capable of producing more real GDP. (If the quantity of factors of production decreases, the *LRAS* and *AS* curves shift to the left.)

- **Improvements in the quality of factors of production (resources).** Improvements in resource quality shift the *LRAS* and *AS* curves to the right. For example, greater levels of education, skills or health

lead to an improvement in the quality of labour resources. More highly skilled and educated workers or healthier workers can produce more output than the same number of unskilled or less healthy workers.

- **Improvements in technology.** An improved technology of production means that the factors of production using it can produce more output, and the *AS* curves shift to the right. For example, workers who work with improved machines and equipment that have been produced as a result of technological innovations will be able to produce more output in the same amount of time.

- **Increases in efficiency.** When an economy increases its efficiency in production, it makes better use of its scarce resources, and can as a result produce a greater quantity of output. Therefore, potential output increases, and the *AS* curves shift to the right. (Decreases in efficiency would shift the *LRAS* and *AS* curves to the left.)

- **Institutional changes.** This point is related to efficiency in resource use because changes in institutions can sometimes have important effects on how efficiently scarce resources are used, and therefore on the quantity of output produced. For example, the degree of private ownership as opposed to public ownership of resources, the degree of competition in the economy, the degree and quality of government regulation of private sector activities, and the amount of bureaucracy can each affect the quantity of output produced (see Chapter 12, page 340 for a further discussion).

- **Reductions in the natural rate of unemployment.** The natural rate of unemployment is the unemployment that is 'normal' or 'natural' for an economy when it is producing its 'full employment' level of output. It includes unemployed people who are in between

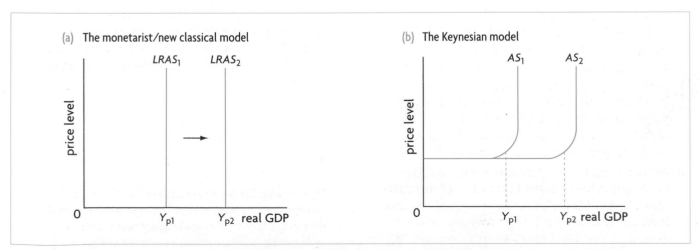

Figure 9.14 Increasing potential output, shifts in aggregate supply curves and long-term economic growth

jobs, who are retraining in order to become more employable, and others. The natural rate of unemployment differs from country to country and it can change over time. If it decreases, the economy is making better use of its resources, and can therefore produce a larger quantity of output. Therefore, potential output increases, and the *AS* curves shift to the right. (An increase in the natural rate of unemployment would result in a leftward shift in the *LRAS* and Keynesian *AS* curves.)

We will return to these topics in Chapters 10 and 11.

Long-term growth versus short-term economic fluctuations

All the factors listed above, affecting the positions of the *LRAS* and Keynesian *AS* curves, usually need an extended period of time to make their influence felt on the economy, and for this reason are referred to as influencing *long-term growth*. Figure 9.15 illustrates how macroeconomic equilibrium changes over the long term when potential output is increasing.

Over long periods of time, most economies experience positive economic growth. This can be seen in the business cycle diagram that we studied in Chapter 8 (Figure 8.4, page 231), showing an upward-sloping, long-term growth trend, indicating that the economy's real GDP is growing over time. The long-term growth trend, you may remember, was referred to as *potential output*; this is none other than the real GDP level at which the *LRAS* curve is situated, and the potential output we see in the Keynesian model. Therefore, it follows that:

> Long-term growth in the business cycle diagram, showing increases in potential output corresponds to rightward shifting *LRAS* or Keynesian *AS* curves.

Yet economic growth also occurs over short periods of time. Using the business cycle diagram again (page 231), we see that in an expansion there is growth of real GDP, though this is usually followed by a contraction, involving negative growth or declining real GDP.

Short-term economic growth in the monetarist/ new classical model is shown in Figure 9.5 (page 246). It can be caused by increases in aggregate demand, illustrated in part (a) by the rightward shift of the *AD* curve from AD_1 to AD_2, resulting in a real GDP increase from Y_1 to Y_2. It can also be caused by increases in short-run aggregate supply, seen in part (b) as the rightward shift of the *SRAS* curve from $SRAS_1$ to $SRAS_2$, also causing real GDP to increase from Y_1 to Y_2. Note that *short-term economic growth does not involve an increase in potential output*, and therefore there is no rightward shift of the *LRAS* curve.

In the Keynesian model, short-term economic growth can be seen in Figure 9.13(b), where successive increases in aggregate demand from AD_1 to AD_2 and AD_3 result in growth of real GDP from Y_1 to Y_2 and Y_3. Note that here, too, *short-term economic growth does not involve an increase in potential output*, and hence no rightward shift of the *AS* curve. (In this model, only increases in aggregate demand cause short-term economic growth).

In the real world, it is very difficult to examine economic activity and arrive at accurate conclusions about what part of growth is due to short-term fluctuations and what part to growth in potential output caused by the factors listed above. However, economists continuously make efforts to measure potential output and its growth, as having estimates of these can help governments formulate appropriate policies to guide the macroeconomy in the desired directions (see the Theory of knowledge feature on page 235 and the Real world focus feature on page 233).

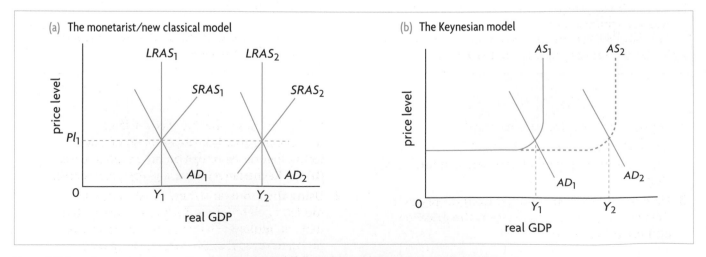

Figure 9.15 Long-term economic growth: achieving potential (full employment) output in a growing economy

The relationship between the *SRAS* and *LRAS* curves in the monetarist/new classical model

If an economy is experiencing long-term economic growth, its *LRAS* curve will be shifting rightward, indicating increases in potential output. Yet over long periods of time, its *SRAS* curve will be shifting rightward as well, as we saw in Figure 9.15. Any factor that shifts the *LRAS* curve must, over the long term, also shift the *SRAS* curve.

Are there any factors that can shift the *SRAS* curve without shifting the *LRAS* curve? There are certain events with only a temporary effect on aggregate supply, and these can shift the *SRAS* curve for a short while, leaving the *LRAS* curve unchanged. Consider, for example, bad weather conditions that cause a drop in agricultural output. The *SRAS* curve shifts to the left for that season, but then moves back to the original position when the weather changes back to normal patterns; the *LRAS* curve remains unaffected. Changes in firms' costs of production, such as changes in wages, or changes in the prices of other key inputs (such as oil), may similarly affect only the *SRAS* curve. This applies to temporary changes that do not have a lasting impact on real GDP produced.

As an economy grows over time, it is likely that aggregate demand also increases; this is why we see *AD* shifting to the right in figure 9.15(a) and (b). The reason is that many of the factors that cause the *LRAS* (and *SRAS*) curves to shift also cause the *AD* curve to shift. For example, increases in the quantity of physical capital, affecting *AS*, result from private and public investments, also shifting *AD*. We will return to this topic in Chapter 12.

Real world focus

Stagflation

In the summer of 2008, the world economy was facing rising oil and food prices due to decreases in global supply. Economist Jeffrey Sachs wrote:

'Three decades ago, in a bleak stretch of the 1970s, an economic phenomenon emerged that was as ugly as its name: stagflation. It was the sound of the world hitting a wall, a combination of no growth and inflation. It created an existential crisis for the global economy, leading many to argue that the world had reached its limits of growth and prosperity. That day of reckoning was postponed, but now, after a 30-year [interruption], at least a mild bout of stagflation has returned, and matters could get worse. We are back to the future, with the question we asked 30 years ago: How can we combine [solid] economic growth with tight global supplies of such critical commodities as energy, food, and water? It's worth comparing the earlier episode of stagflation with our current [troubles] to help us find our way. In fact, this time the resource constraints will prove even harder to overcome than in the last round, since the world economy is much larger and the constraints are much tighter than before …

Fortunately, there is a better way forward than we took after 1974. We need to adopt coherent national and global technology policies to address critical needs in energy, food, water and climate change … There is certainly no shortage of ideas, merely a lack of [government] commitment to support their timely development, demonstration, and diffusion. Solar power, for example, has the potential to meet the world's energy needs many times over …

Yet it will be the new technologies, deployed quickly and on a global scale, that offer the real keys to energy and food security, and the chances for sustained economic [growth and] development globally. In the years ahead, technological development, with both public and private funding, must become a core part of our national economic and security arsenal.'

Source: Jeffrey D. Sachs, 'Stagflation is back. Here's how to beat it' in *Fortune*, Vol. 157/12, 9 June 2008.

Applying your skills

1 Explain the meaning of stagflation.

2 Using the short-run *AD-AS* model, explain how decreases in supply of oil and food can lead to stagflation.

3 How do decreases in *AS* differ from decreases in *AD* with respect to the effects on the price level and unemployment?

4 Using diagrams, show the effects of large-scale public and private investments in new technology development on **(a)** the *LRAS* curve, **(b)** the Keynesian *AS* curve, and **(c)** the *AD* curve.

5 Using the monetarist/new classical *AD-AS* model, explain Jeffrey Sachs's argument that new technology development can solve the problem of stagflation over the long term.

1 Illustrate diagrammatically the impacts on an economy's *LRAS* and the Keynesian *AS* curve of the following:

(a) There is a widespread introduction of a new technology that increases labour productivity.

(b) The government provides training programmes for workers to retrain and improve their skills.

(c) A developing country receives large amounts of foreign aid, which allows it to purchase a large quantity of capital goods.

(d) An extensive nationwide public health campaign undertaken by the government improves levels of health of the population.

(e) The government introduces anti-monopoly legislation, reducing the monopoly power of firms and increasing the economy's productive efficiency.

2 (a) Using diagrams and the concept of potential output, explain the relationship between the *LRAS* and Keynesian *AS* curves and long-term economic growth. (b) Can you think of some factors that can affect the *SRAS* curve but not the *LRAS* curve?

3 (a) Using diagrams, explain the difference between long-term economic growth and short-term economic growth due to economic fluctuations. (b) Describe the causes of each. (c) How does potential output change/not change in each case?

9.6 Illustrating the monetarist/new classical and Keynesian models

Figure 9.16 shows how the monetarist/new classical and Keynesian models relate to each other. Point a in both parts determines full employment equilibrium output, or potential GDP. Note that the *LRAS* curve in part (a) is not the same as the vertical section of the Keynesian *AS* curve, as the latter vertical section represents the maximum possible output that the economy can produce if it uses all its resources.

Point b in both parts represents a recessionary (deflationary) gap, which occurs due to low aggregate demand, given by AD_2 in parts (a) and (b). Point c in

both parts represents an inflationary gap, which arises due to strong aggregate demand, given by AD_3.

Finally, economic growth is illustrated in both parts by the rightward pointing arrows. In part (a) it is represented by a rightward shift of the *LRAS* curve; in part (b) by a rightward shift of the Keynesian *AS* curve.

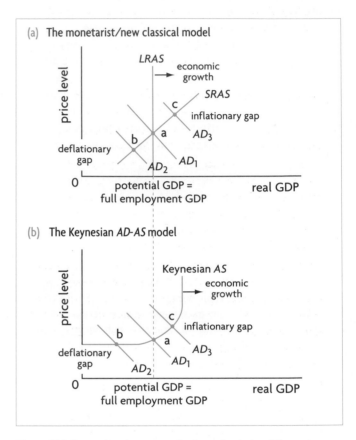

Figure 9.16 Comparing the monetarist/new classical and Keynesian models

1 Explain why use of the *LRAS* curve to account for economic growth leads to the policy implication that governments should focus on policies that try to influence the supply side of the economy.

2 Explain why use of the Keynesian three-section aggregate supply curve leads to the policy implication that governments should focus on the policies that try to influence the demand side of the economy.

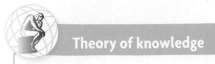

Conflicting economic perspectives and the role of economists' political beliefs and ideology

The two perspectives we have studied in this chapter, the monetarist/new classical and Keynesian, are based on very different ways of viewing the economic world. The differences between the two are not just of theoretical interest; they have important implications for the real world, because each perspective provides very different policy recommendations to deal with macroeconomic problems.

The monetarist/new classical perspective

In the monetarist/new classical perspective, the economy is seen as a stable system that automatically tends towards long-run equilibrium where there is full employment at the natural rate of unemployment. This argument has important implications for the short-term fluctuations of the business cycle and long-term economic growth. Since short-term fluctuations (recessionary and inflationary gaps) correct themselves automatically, there is no need for the government to do anything to correct them. Instead, the government must ensure that markets work as competitively as possible, so that all resource and product prices are able to rise or fall as required to allow the economy to settle at its point of long-run equilibrium, at the level of potential GDP.

In fact, continues the argument, if governments do intervene with policies intended to correct short-term fluctuations, they may achieve the opposite of the intended results. Rather than reduce the size of fluctuations, they may make them bigger. Many monetarist/new classical economists believe that the departures of actual GDP from potential GDP that occur in real-world business cycles are as large as they are because of government intervention in the economy.

When it comes to promoting economic growth, aggregate demand cannot affect real GDP over the long run. If aggregate demand increases, it will only result in increasing price levels and inflation. Governments should therefore concentrate on policies that affect the supply side of the economy, which attempt to shift the *LRAS* curve to the right, with the objective of increasing real GDP without causing inflation.

The Keynesian perspective

In the Keynesian perspective, the economy is an unstable system because of repeating short-term fluctuations that cannot automatically correct themselves. Such fluctuations arise mainly due to changes in aggregate demand caused by spontaneous actions of firms and consumers. Keynes himself considered business cycle fluctuations to be caused mainly by changes in investment spending caused by changes in firms' expectations about the future. Optimism about the future increases investment spending, causing a rightward shift in the *AD* curve; pessimism decreases investment spending, leading to a leftward shift. Keynes referred to alternating waves of optimism and pessimism as 'animal spirits'.

In the Keynesian view, when there is a recessionary gap, there are many factors preventing the operation of market forces, and so wages and product prices do not fall easily even over long periods of time. This means the economy can remain in a less than full employment equilibrium (recessionary gap) for long periods. Therefore, there is an important role for government policy to play to restore full employment and raise real GDP to the level of potential GDP. Governments should focus on policies that increase aggregate demand when there is a recessionary gap, and decrease aggregate demand when there is an inflationary gap. Policies to influence aggregate demand are particularly important when aggregate demand is low.

Why does the debate persist?

Most economists today are unlikely to be purely 'monetarist'/'new classical' or purely 'Keynesian'. After decades of debate, many would argue that elements of both perspectives have some merit, and that policies attempting to influence both aggregate supply and aggregate demand are important in achieving the goals of reducing short-term fluctuations while promoting economic growth. Even so, most economists are still likely to side more with one perspective or the other. Why has the disagreement not been resolved after all these years? According to Mark Blaug, a prominent UK economist, there has been:

'... an unending series of efforts to produce a decisive empirical test of the Keynesian and monetarist view of the causes of economic fluctuations. A detached observer might be forgiven for thinking that this discussion has proved nothing but that empirical evidence is apparently incapable of making any economist change his mind ... But a closer look at the literature reveals ... a growing appreciation of the limitations of all the current statistical tests of the relative effectiveness of [government] policies ... At the same time, it must be admitted that the persistence of this controversy, despite all the moves and countermoves in both camps, can only be explained in terms of certain deep-seated "hard core"

(continued over)

disagreements about the self-adjusting capacity of the private sector in mixed economies and, hence, the extent to which [government] policy is in fact stabilizing or destabilizing … Once again, the debate between Keynesians and monetarists shows that economists (like all other scientists) will characteristically defend the core of their beliefs from the threat of observed anomalies…'[10]

Blaug is suggesting that the controversy persists because economists have different beliefs. What kind of beliefs could these be? On a general level, they must be beliefs about the superiority of one perspective over the other. However, this begs the question, where did these beliefs come from, and how can they be justified? Certainly not by the scientific method, based on empirical testing, since as Blaug clearly tells us, it has not been possible for an empirical test to falsify one or the other perspective based on the effectiveness of their policy recommendations. Therefore, very likely, these are beliefs that come from outside the realm of social scientific thinking, which may be political and ideological beliefs stemming from personal values.

Most economists do not deny the role of values and ideology in economics. Nobel Prize-winning economist, Robert Solow, writes the following:

'Social scientists, like everyone else, have class interests, ideological commitments, and values of all kinds. But all social science research, unlike research on the strength of materials or the structure of the haemoglobin molecule, lies very close to the content of those ideologies, interests, and values. Whether the social scientist wills it or knows it, perhaps even if he fights it, his choice of research problem, the questions he asks, the questions he doesn't ask, his analytical framework, the very words he uses, are all likely to be, in some measure, a reflection of his interests, ideologies and values.'[11]

---

[10] Mark Blaug (1980) *The Methodology of Economics*, Cambridge University Press, pp. 217 and 221.

[11] Robert M. Solow (1996) 'Science and ideology in economics' in D. M. Hausman, *The Philosophy of Economics*, Cambridge University Press.

Thinking points

- Do you agree with Solow that it is very likely that personal value judgements influence economists' choices between alternative theories (the choice of 'analytical framework') and more generally their work as social scientists?

- Is the effective use of the scientific method influenced by economists' personal beliefs and ideologies?

- Do the social sciences, and economics in particular, differ from the natural sciences by having political beliefs and ideologies influence thinking?

- What kind of political beliefs and ideologies do you think are likely to be linked with (a) the monetarist/new classical perspective, and (b) the Keynesian perspective?

HL

9.7 The Keynesian multiplier (higher level topic)

The nature and importance of the multiplier

Introducing the multiplier

Suppose there is an increase in one of the components of aggregate demand, due to a change in C, or I, or G, or $X-M$ expenditures. This will produce an increase in aggregate demand, and an increase in real GDP. Yet the final increase in real GDP will most likely be greater than the initial increase in expenditures. The reason for this can be found in the **Keynesian multiplier**, defined as the change in real GDP divided by the initial change in expenditure:

$$\text{multiplier} = \frac{\text{change in real GDP}}{\text{initial change in expenditure}}$$

so that

$$\text{initial change in expenditure} \times \text{multiplier} = \text{change in real GDP}$$

HL

As a rule, the multiplier >1; therefore, the change in real GDP is likely to be greater than the initial change in expenditure.

The multiplier is attributed to John Maynard Keynes, and for this reason is often referred to as the 'Keynesian multiplier'. It is an important concept because it shows that whenever there is a change in a component of AD, there is likely to be a multiplied effect on real GDP. This is important for policy-makers who often try to influence the level of aggregate demand in order to affect the level of real GDP and unemployment.

Understanding the multiplier in terms of leakages and injections

- Explain, with reference to the concepts of leakages (withdrawals) and injections, the nature and importance of the Keynesian multiplier.
- Calculate the multiplier using either of the following formulae:

$$\frac{1}{(1-\text{MPC})}$$

$$\frac{1}{(\text{MPS}+\text{MPT}+\text{MPM})}$$

Why does a change in expenditure produce a larger change in total aggregate demand and real GDP? The explanation is that the initial change in expenditure produces a chain reaction of further expenditures, with the effect of increasing *AD* and real GDP to a value greater than the initial expenditure.

Assume an initial increase in investment spending of $8 million (due to business optimism or any other factor affecting investment spending). This spending of $8 million results in an increase in real GDP of $8 million. However, the story does not end there, because the $8 million increase in real GDP produces a further chain of spending, called *induced spending* (it is induced, or caused by the change in real GDP). The $8 million increase in investment spending is used by businesses to pay for materials, equipment, labour, etc., and all this spending translates into income for owners of the factors of production, who then use it to increase their consumption spending. As consumption spending increases, it results in a further increase in real GDP and incomes, which produce more consumption spending, and this process continues to increase real GDP beyond the amount of the initial investment of $8 million.

To calculate the value of the multiplier, we must look at consumer spending more carefully. We know from the circular flow model that a portion of income flows out of the expenditure flow in the form of leakages: consumers save part of their income, they pay taxes to the government, and they buy imported goods and services. The remaining part of income is spent on buying domestic goods and services, called consumption expenditures. This introduces us to a new concept, the **marginal propensity to consume**, abbreviated as *MPC*, defined as the fraction of additional income that households spend on consumption of domestically produced goods and services. For example, if the *MPC* is $\frac{3}{4}$, this means that given an increase in national income of $10 million, $\frac{3}{4}$ of this, or $7.5 million is consumption expenditure, and the remaining $\frac{1}{4}$ of income, or $2.5 million, leaks out in the form of saving, taxes and spending on imports.

Corresponding to the marginal propensity to consume (*MPC*) is the **marginal propensity to save** (*MPS*, or fraction of additional income saved), the **marginal propensity to tax** (*MPT*, or fraction of additional income taxed), and the **marginal propensity to import** (*MPM*, or fraction of additional income spent on imported goods and services). Note that the *MPC*+*MPS*+*MPT*+*MPM*=1. To see why, imagine that national income increases by $1. It follows that the fractions of the $1 that will be consumed, saved, spent on taxes and spent on imports will add up to $1.

Assuming, as in Table 9.2 that the *MPC* = $\frac{3}{4}$, we can determine the value of the multiplier. The initial increase in investment spending of $8 million results

Initial increase in investment expenditure of $8 million:	Change in income (real GDP) ($ million)	Induced change in consumption expenditure ($ million)
1st round	8	$\frac{3}{4} \times 8 = 6$
2nd round	6	$\frac{3}{4} \times 6 = 4.5$
3rd round	4.5	$\frac{3}{4} \times 4.5 = 3.38$
4th round	3.38	$\frac{3}{4} \times 3.38 = 2.5$
(process continues an infinite number of times)		
Total	32	$\frac{3}{4} \times 32 = 24$

Table 9.2   Determining the value of the multiplier with the MPC = $\frac{3}{4}$

in an equivalent increase in income (or real GDP) of $8 million. Since the *MPC* = $\frac{3}{4}$, this results in $6 million of consumption expenditure ($\frac{3}{4} \times$$8 million = $6 million). In the second round of income changes, the induced consumption expenditure of $6 million leads to an equivalent increase in income of $6 million, which when multiplied by the *MPC* produces new induced consumption spending of $4.5 million. This process continues, with induced consumption spending and changes in income getting smaller and smaller until finally they drop to zero. Adding up all changes in income we arrive at a total increase of $32 million. This is the amount by which real GDP has increased. This increase is equal to the initial change in investment spending of $8 million plus the total increase in induced consumption spending of $24 million.

It thus follows that in this example, the value of the multiplier is:

$$\text{multiplier} = \frac{\text{change in real GDP}}{\text{initial change in expenditure}}$$

$$= \frac{\$32 \text{ billion}}{\$8 \text{ billion}} = 4$$

Alternatively, we can say that

$$4 \times \$8 \text{ million} = \$32 \text{ million}$$

It is clear from the table that the value of the multiplier of 4 depends on the induced changes in consumption, which depend on the value of the *MPC*, assumed here to be $\frac{3}{4}$. The relationship between the multiplier and the *MPC* is:

$$\text{multiplier} = \frac{1}{1 - MPC}$$

If the *MPC* = $\frac{3}{4}$:

$$\text{multiplier} = \frac{1}{1 - \frac{3}{4}} = 4$$

Chapter 9 **Aggregate demand and aggregate supply**   261

Therefore, if we know the value of the *MPC*, we can calculate the value of the multiplier.

Now we know from above that

$$MPC + MPS + MPT + MPM = 1$$

Rearranging this expression, we can write:

$$1 - MPC = MPS + MPT + MPM$$

We can therefore rewrite the multiplier as:

$$\text{multiplier} = \frac{1}{1-MPC} = \frac{1}{MPS+MPT+MPM}$$

The value of the multiplier is given by $\frac{1}{1-MPC}$, which is equivalent to $\frac{1}{MPS+MPT+MPM}$. Therefore, if we know the value of the *MPC*, we can calculate the value of the multiplier. Alternatively, if we know the value of the *MPS*, *MPT* and *MPM*, we can calculate the value of the multiplier.

Based on these expressions, we can arrive at the following conclusions: *the larger the MPC, the smaller the value of the denominator of the first fraction, and so the greater is the multiplier*. Therefore, the greater the proportion of income spent on consumption, the greater the multiplier. Alternatively, we can see from the second fraction that *the smaller the leakages from the spending stream, the greater the multiplier*. Therefore the smaller the saving, or the level of taxes, or the volume of imports, the larger will be the size of the multiplier.

Whereas we calculated the multiplier based on an increase in investment spending, the same result would be obtained given an initial increase in any injection into the income flow, whether it is I, G, or X − M (as well changes in C that have not been caused by changes in income).

Everything that has been said about the multiplier in relation to increases in expenditure applies equally to decreases in expenditures. Therefore, in the example above, if we had looked at a decrease in investment expenditure of $8 million, and an *MPC* of $\frac{3}{4}$, there would result a decrease in GDP of $32 million (= $8 million×4).

Calculating the multiplier and its effects on real GDP

♦ Use the multiplier to calculate the effect on GDP of a change in an injection of investment, government spending or exports.[12]

Suppose a country with a real GDP of £135 billion and an MPC of $\frac{4}{5}$ experiences an increase in exports of £2 billion. What is the change in real GDP, and the final value of real GDP?

To answer this question, we must first find the multiplier, which is

$$\frac{1}{1-MPC} = \frac{1}{1-\frac{4}{5}} = \frac{1}{\frac{1}{5}} = 5$$

Therefore, there will be an increase in real GDP of

£2 billion×multiplier = £2 billion×5 = £10 billion

Therefore, the final value of real GDP will be

£135 billion + £10 billion = £145 billion

If there had been a *decrease* in exports of £2 billion, there would result a £10 billion *decrease* in real GDP, thus making the final value of real GDP = £135 billion − £10 billion = £125 billion.

The multiplier, aggregate demand and real GDP

How the multiplier relates to aggregate demand

♦ Draw a Keynesian *AD-AS* diagram to show the impact of the multiplier.

Using the example of an $8 million increase in investment spending, we can see its effects on aggregate demand in Figure 9.17. The total aggregate

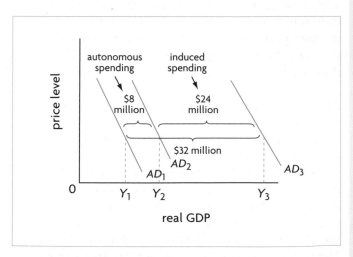

Figure 9.17 Aggregate demand, real GDP and the multiplier in the Keynesian model

---

[12] The IB syllabus refers to changes in injections of *I*, *G*, or *X − M* as causes of multiplied effects on GDP. However, the same applies to *C* as long as changes in *C* are *autonomous*, that is, have not been caused by changes in income. The factors listed in Table 9.1 (page 240) with respect to *C* all produce autonomous changes in *C*, and therefore give rise to the multiplier effect.

demand shift is divided into two parts. The first part is the $8 million increase in investment spending, and is called *autonomous spending*, meaning it has not been caused by a change in income. The second part is the effects on aggregate demand of the multiplier, which is $24 million of *induced spending*, meaning spending caused by changes in income. The total effect on aggregate demand is the sum of autonomous plus induced spending, and is $32 million. This is equivalent to taking the initial change in autonomous investment spending and multiplying it by the multiplier: $8 million × 4 = $32 million.

All the factors listed in Table 9.1 under 'Shifts in the aggregate demand curve' (page 240) can cause a change in spending resulting in a multiplier effect. All these factors involve changes in autonomous spending, because all are unrelated to income. (It is important to remember the point on page 240 that the factors listed in Table 9.1 are non-income factors.) This means that *the multiplier effect can only be initiated by a change in spending that is not caused by a change in income.*

We are now in a position to understand why this is so. Consider the AD-AS model in Figure 9.12 (page 253). Each diagram shows an economy that is *in equilibrium*. This equilibrium determines a particular level of national income or real GDP. Since the economy is in equilibrium, *it is impossible for national income (or real GDP) to change unless something acts upon it from outside the system.* This 'something' must be unrelated to income, and can be any of the factors listed in Table 9.1, all of which are autonomous.

In our example, the outside change was autonomous investment spending of $8 million. This outside factor caused a change in income, and only then was it possible for the change in income to cause changes in consumption and aggregate demand; these are the induced changes shown in Figure 9.17 as the shift from AD_2 to AD_3.

The effect of the multiplier in relation to the price level

In order for the multiplier to have the greatest possible effect on real GDP, it is necessary that the price level is constant. We can see why in Figure 9.18, which shows the Keynesian AD-AS model with three equal AD curve shifts: from AD_1 to AD_2, then to AD_3, and finally to AD_4. Each of the shifts is the sum of autonomous spending plus induced spending due to the multiplier. The horizontal distance between each AD curve is identical. However, each shift occurs in a different section of the AS curve. The shift from AD_1 to AD_2 is in the horizontal part where the price level is constant, and *the increase in real GDP from Y_1 to Y_2 is exactly*

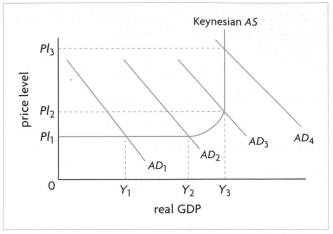

Figure 9.18 How the effect of the multiplier changes depending on the price level

equal to the increase in aggregate demand. Here we have the full multiplier effect. The shift from AD_2 to AD_3 occurs in the upward-sloping part of the AS curve, and whereas it is identical in size to the first AD shift, the increase in real GDP, from Y_2 to Y_3, is smaller, because part of the multiplier effect is absorbed by the increase in the price level. The shift from AD_3 to AD_4 occurs in the vertical part of the AS curve, and results in no change at all in real GDP. The increasing price level has absorbed the entire multiplier effect, which in this portion of the AS curve is zero.

In the monetarist/new classical model, increases in aggregate demand always (both in the short run and in the long run) lead to increases in the price level, and for this reason in this model it is never possible for real GDP to increase by the full amount of the increase in AD.

The multiplier is based on Keynesian thinking, which emphasises the point that when an economy is in a recessionary gap (in the horizontal section of the AS curve), unemployed resources and spare capacity allow aggregate demand to increase without putting an upward pressure on the price level. In this situation, any autonomous increase in spending leads to a substantially larger increase in real GDP.

Therefore, when we use the multiplier to calculate the effects on real GDP of a change in autonomous spending, *we are presupposing a constant price level.*

> The full effect of the multiplier can be experienced only when the price level is constant. If the price level is increasing, the greater the price level increase, the smaller is the size of the multiplier effect.

HL 9.8 Understanding aggregate demand and the multiplier in terms of the Keynesian cross model (supplementary material, recommended for Higher level)

The Keynesian cross model is a useful model to study in order to get a better understanding of aggregate demand and its relationship to aggregate output (real GDP). It is also useful to illustrate and explain the concept of the multiplier. To learn more about this topic, you can read the relevant section in the CD-ROM – 'Supplementary material for Chapter 9'.

Test your understanding 9.8

1 **(a)** Define the multiplier. **(b)** Why are changes in real GDP likely to be larger than the initial change in spending by a component of aggregate demand? **(c)** Why is the multiplier important?

2 **(a)** Define the marginal propensity to consume (MPC). **(b)** Why is the MPC important in determining the size of the multiplier? **(c)** What role do leakages play in determining the size of the multiplier?

3 Calculate the multiplier when the MPC is **(a)** $\frac{4}{5}$, **(b)** $\frac{3}{4}$, **(c)** $\frac{2}{3}$, and **(d)** $\frac{1}{2}$.

4 Based on your answers to question 3, what can you conclude about the relationship between the size of the MPC and the size of the multiplier?

5 Calculate the value of the multiplier when **(a)** the $MPS = MPT = MPM = 0.1$, and **(b)** the $MPS = 0.13$, $MPT = 0.12$, and the $MPM = 0.15$.

6 Based on your answers to question 5, what can you conclude about the relationship between the size of $MPS+MPT+MPM$ and the size of the multiplier? Explain the reasoning behind this relationship.

7 In a country with a real GDP of $50 billion and an $MPC = \frac{2}{3}$, find the change in real GDP and the final value of real GDP (assuming a constant price level) for each of the following: **(a)** an increase in net exports (exports minus imports) of $2 billion, **(b)** a fall in investment spending of $3 billion, **(c)** an increase in government spending of $7 billion, and **(d)** a decrease in consumption spending of $1.5 billion.

8 Answer all the parts of question 7 assuming that the $MPS+MPT+MPM = \frac{1}{4}$.

9 Using a diagram showing the Keynesian AD-AS model, show the effects of the multiplier when **(a)** the price level is constant, and **(b)** the price level is increasing. **(c)** Why is it not possible to show the full multiplier effect using the monetarist/new classical model?

Assessment

The Student's CD-ROM at the back of this book provides practice of examination questions based on the material you have studied in this chapter.

Standard level
• Exam practice: Paper 1, Chapter 9
  ○ SL/HL core topics (questions 9.1–9.15)

Higher level
• Exam practice: Paper 1, Chapter 9
  ○ SL/HL core topics (questions 9.1–9.15)
• Exam practice: Paper 3, Chapter 9
  ○ HL topics (question 19)

264 Section 2: Macroeconomics

Chapter 10
Macroeconomic objectives I: Low unemployment, low and stable rate of inflation

This chapter is concerned with two important macroeconomic objectives: low unemployment and low and stable rate of inflation.

10.1 Low unemployment

Unemployment and its measurement

Defining unemployment

♦ Define the term 'unemployment'.

Unemployment, in a general sense, refers to idle, or not fully used resources. When economists use the terms 'unemployment' (or 'employment') on their own, they usually refer to unemployment or employment of labour. If they want to refer to another factor of production, they refer to it explicitly, such as 'unemployment of capital resources', or more generally, 'unemployment of resources'.

Our discussion in this chapter will focus on the economy's labour resources. Unemployment is defined as follows:

> **Unemployment** refers to people of working age who are actively looking for a job but who are not employed.

A closely related term is **underemployment**, referring to people of working age with part-time jobs when they would rather work full time, or with jobs that do not make full use of their skills and education. Examples include people who work fewer hours per week than they would like, or trained individuals,

such as engineers, economists, or computer analysts, who work as taxi drivers, or waiters or waitresses, or anything else unrelated to their profession, when they would rather have a job in their profession.

Both unemployment and underemployment mean that an economy is wasting scarce resources by not using them fully. In the case of unemployment this is obvious. With underemployment, working at a job other than in one's profession also involves resource 'waste', because some resources that were used for training and education are wasted when people are forced to work at a job that does not make use of their skills.

Calculating unemployment: the unemployment rate

♦ Explain how the unemployment rate is calculated.

The *labour force* is defined as the number of people who are employed (working) plus the number of people of working age who are unemployed (not working but seeking work). The labour force is actually a fraction of the total population of a country, because it excludes children, retired persons, adult students, all people who cannot work because of illness or disability, as well as all people who do not want to work.

Unemployment can be measured as a number or percentage:

- As a number, unemployment is the total number of unemployed persons in the economy, i.e. all persons of working age who are actively seeking work but are not employed.
- As a percentage, unemployment is called the *unemployment rate*, defined as

$$\text{unemployment rate} = \frac{\text{number of unemployed}}{\text{labour force}} \times 100$$

For example, if the unemployment rate in an economy is 6%, this means that six out of every 100 people in the labour force are unemployed.

Underemployment can similarly be measured as a number or as a percentage. If the underemployment rate is 15%, this means that 15 out of every 100 people in the labour force are underemployed.

Difficulties in measuring unemployment

♦ Explain the difficulties in measuring unemployment, including the existence of hidden unemployment, the existence of underemployment, and the fact that it is an average and therefore ignores regional, ethnic, age and gender disparities.

The unemployment rate is one of the most widely reported measures of economic activity, used extensively as an indicator of economic performance. Yet it is actually difficult to obtain an accurate measurement of unemployment.

Official statistics often underestimate true unemployment because of **hidden unemployment**, arising from the following:

- Unemployment figures include unemployed persons who are actively looking for work. This excludes 'discouraged workers', or unemployed workers who gave up looking for a job because, after trying unsuccessfully to find work for some time, they became discouraged and stopped searching. These people in effect drop out of the labour force.
- Unemployment figures do not make a distinction between full-time and part-time employment, and count people with part-time jobs as having full-time jobs though in fact they are underemployed.
- Unemployment figures make no distinction on the type of work done. If a highly trained person works as a waiter, this counts as full employment.
- Unemployment figures do not include people on retraining programmes who previously lost their jobs, as well as people who retire early although they would rather be working.

In addition, official statistics may overestimate true unemployment, because:

- unemployment figures do not include people working in the underground economy (or informal economy). This is the portion of the economy that is unregistered, legally unregulated and not reported to tax authorities. Some people may be officially registered as unemployed, yet they may be working in an unreported (underground) activity.

A further disadvantage of the national unemployment rate (calculated for an entire nation) is that it is an average over the entire population, and therefore does not account for differences in unemployment that often arise among different *population groups* in a society. Within a national population, unemployment may differ by:

- region – regions with declining industries may have higher unemployment rates than other regions
- gender – women sometimes face higher unemployment rates than men
- ethnic groups – some ethnic groups may be disadvantaged due to discrimination, or due to lower levels of education and training
- age – youth unemployment (usually referring to persons under the age of 25) often face higher unemployment rates than older population groups, often due to lower skill levels; people who are ageing also sometimes face higher unemployment rates as employers may be less willing to employ them
- occupation and educational attainment – people who are relatively less skilled may have higher unemployment rates than more skilled workers (though in some countries higher unemployment rates may be found among highly educated groups).

Calculating the unemployment rate (higher level topic)

♦ Calculate the unemployment rate from a set of data.

To calculate the unemployment rate, we use the definition of unemployment together with the formula for the unemployment rate given above. Suppose there is a population of 35.5 million people, of whom 17.3 million are in the labour force, 1.5 million work part time though they would rather work full time, 0.5 million are discouraged workers, and 1.4 million are looking for work but cannot find any. What is the unemployment rate?

The unemployment rate is $\frac{1.4}{17.3} \times 100 = 8.1\%$, which is the number looking for work but unable to find any divided by the size of the labour force, times 100. Note that we ignore the size of the total population (it is irrelevant), as well as the number of people who are working part-time (they are considered to be employed) and the number of discouraged workers (they are not considered to be unemployed or part of the labour force).

Consequences of unemployment

Unemployment of labour is one of the most important economic concerns to countries around the world, as it affects many aspects of economic and social life. Reduction of unemployment is a key objective of governments everywhere, as its presence has major economic and social consequences.

Economic consequences

♦ Discuss possible economic consequences of unemployment, including a loss of GDP, loss of tax revenue, increased cost of unemployment benefits, loss of income for individuals, and greater disparities in the distribution of income.

Unemployment has the following economic consequences:

- **A loss of real output (real GDP).** Since fewer people work than are available to work, the amount of output produced is less than the level the economy is capable of producing. This is why unemployment means that an economy finds itself somewhere inside its production possibility curve (*PPC*; see Chapter 1, page 5), producing a lower level of output than it is capable of producing.

- **A loss of income for unemployed workers.** People who are unemployed do not have an income from work. Even if they receive unemployment benefits, they are likely to be worse off financially than if they had been working.

- **A loss of tax revenue for the government.** Since unemployed people do not have income from work, they do not pay income taxes; this results in less tax revenue for the government.

- **Costs to the government of unemployment benefits.** If the government pays unemployment benefits to unemployed workers, the greater the unemployment, the larger the unemployment benefits that must be paid, and the less tax revenue left over to pay for important government-provided goods and services such as public goods and merit goods.

- **Costs to the government of dealing with social problems resulting from unemployment.** The social problems that arise from unemployment (noted below) often require government funds to be appropriately dealt with.

- **More unequal distribution of income.** Some people (the unemployed) become poorer while others (the employed) are able to maintain their income levels. Since certain population groups (ethnic groups, regional groups, etc. discussed above) may be more hard hit by unemployment than others, the effects of increasing income inequalities and resulting poverty tend to be concentrated among population groups who are more disadvantaged to begin with. If unemployment is high or tends to persist over long periods of time, this may lead to increased social tensions and social unrest.

- **Unemployed people may have difficulties finding work in the future.** When people remain out of work for long periods, they may not find work easily at a later time in the future. This can happen because the unemployed workers may partly lose their skills due to not working for a long time, or because in the meantime new skills may be required that workers have not been able to keep up with, or because firms have found ways to manage with fewer workers. This process is known as *hysteresis* (from the Greek word υστέρηση meaning 'delay' or 'lagging behind something', in this case the lagging behind of employment). Hysteresis suggests that high unemployment rates in the present may mean continued high unemployment rates in the future, even when economic conditions become more favourable.

Personal and social consequences

♦ Discuss possible personal and social consequences of unemployment, including increased crime rates, increased stress levels, increased indebtedness, homelessness and family breakdown.

Unemployment has the following personal and social consequences:

- **Personal problems.** Being unemployed and unable to secure a job involves a loss of income, increased indebtedness as people must borrow to survive, as well as loss of self-esteem. All these factors cause great psychological stress, sometimes resulting in lower levels of health, family tensions, family breakdown and even suicide.

- **Greater social problems.** High rates of unemployment, particularly when they are unequally distributed for the reasons noted earlier, can lead to serious social problems, including increased crime and violence, drug use and homelessness.

Test your understanding 10.1

1 Define unemployment and explain how it differs from underemployment.

2 How do we measure the unemployment rate?

3 Explain why unemployment figures are not usually accurate.

4 Identify some of the economic and social consequences of unemployment.

HL

5 (**higher level**) In an economy with a labour force of 27.3 million people and 3.1 million unemployed people, what is the unemployment rate?

Types and causes of unemployment

- Describe, using examples, the meaning of frictional, structural, seasonal and cyclical (demand-deficient) unemployment.
- Distinguish between the causes of frictional, structural, seasonal and cyclical (demand-deficient) unemployment.

We will examine four types of unemployment: structural, frictional, seasonal and cyclical.

In Chapters 8 and 9, we saw that an economy producing real GDP equal to potential GDP has 'full employment', meaning that there is some unemployment equal to the natural rate of unemployment. In fact, the first three types of unemployment we will consider (structural, frictional and seasonal) make up the natural rate of unemployment.

Structural unemployment

- Explain, using a diagram, that structural unemployment is caused by changes in the demand for particular labour skills, changes in the geographical location of industries, and labour market rigidities.

Structural unemployment occurs as a result of changes in demand for particular types of labour skills, changes in the geographical location of industries and therefore jobs, and labour market rigidities.

Changes in demand for particular labour skills

The demand for particular types of labour skills changes over time. This may be the result of technological change, which often leads to a need for new types of skills, while the demand for other skills falls. For example, computer technology, the introduction of automated teller machines (ATMs), and electrical relays and digital switching technology greatly reduced the need for typists, bank tellers and telephone operators, while increasing the need for workers with computer literacy and computer programming and other skills. In addition, changes in demand for labour skills may occur because of changes in the structure of the economy, leading to some growing industries and some declining industries. Workers who lose their jobs in declining industries may not have the necessary skills to work in growing industries, and become structurally unemployed. For example, as the agricultural sector declines in relative importance and the manufacturing and services sectors grow, agricultural workers may lose their jobs. Workers lacking the necessary skills to work in industry or services may become structurally unemployed. (This type of structural change was explained in terms of income elasticity of demand (*YED*); see Chapter 3, page 64.)

These kinds of changes lead to *mismatches* between labour skills demanded by employers and labour skills supplied by workers. Such mismatches cause structural unemployment.

Changes in the geographical location of jobs

When a large firm or even an industry moves its physical location from one region to another, there is a resulting fall in demand for labour in one region and an increase in the region where it relocates. (The same problem could arise if a large firm or industry closes down.) If people cannot move to economically expanding regions, they may become structurally unemployed. Sometimes firms relocate to foreign countries, increasing the overall structural unemployment within a country. Once again, the result will be a *mismatch* between labour demanded and labour supplied within a geographical region (or country).

Using a diagram to show structural unemployment arising from mismatches between labour demand and labour supply

Structural unemployment arising from mismatches between labour demand and supply can be shown indirectly in a *product* supply and demand diagram.[1] Figure 10.1(a) shows how falling demand for a product (a shift from D_1 to D_2) results in a smaller quantity supplied (fall to Q_2 from Q_1). Such falling demand could be for a product produced in a declining industry, or one that was produced in a local industry that has relocated elsewhere (for example, demand for textiles produced in Naoussa; see the Real world focus feature on page 270). The smaller quantity supplied means firms require less labour to produce the particular product; therefore, workers who lack skills to find a job in another industry, or workers who cannot relocate to another area become structurally unemployed.

Labour market rigidities

Labour market rigidities are factors preventing the forces of supply and demand from operating in the labour market. They include:

- **minimum wage legislation**, which leads to higher than equilibrium wages and causes unemployment
- **labour union activities and wage bargaining with employers**, resulting in higher than equilibrium wages also causing unemployment
- **employment protection laws**, which make it costly for firms to fire workers (because they must pay compensation), thus making firms more cautious about hiring
- **generous unemployment benefits**, which increase the attractiveness of remaining unemployed and reduce the incentives to work.

Although economists do not always agree on the effects of these factors on unemployment, many argue that they are responsible for higher unemployment rates in countries with strong labour protection systems (such as in Europe) compared to countries with weaker labour protection systems (such as the United States).

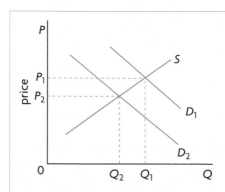

(a) Fall in demand for a product produced in a declining industry, or produced in a local industry that relocates, causes a fall in Q produced; employers fire workers with inappropriate skills or local workers no longer needed due to relocation

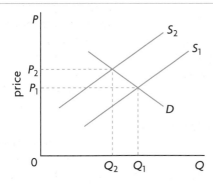

(b) Labour market rigidities lead to an increase in costs of production (supply shifts to the left), causing a fall in Q produced; employers hire fewer workers

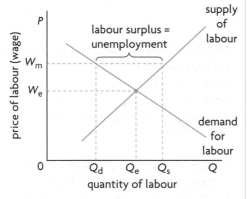

(c) Minimum wage legislation and labour union activities lead to higher than equilibrium wages and lower quantity of labour demanded

Figure 10.1 Structural unemployment

---

[1] Use of a labour market diagram to show mismatches between labour demand and labour supply would lead to misleading conclusions. Although changes in labour skills demanded and changes in geographical location of industries could be shown by a leftward shift in the demand for labour curve, the problem is that this predicts a fall in the equilibrium wage (the price of labour), which would solve the problem of unemployment. However, the problem of structural unemployment caused by the mismatches discussed above is not so simple. If there are no jobs, or if employers do not want to hire workers with the 'wrong' skills, structurally unemployed people cannot be employed no matter what happens to wages. Some economists make use of a different type of labour market diagram, which shows two labour supply curves: one for the labour force, and another representing the willingness of workers to take on jobs at different wage levels; the horizontal difference between the two supply curves at the market clearing wage represents natural unemployment (of which structural is the most important). This diagram presents natural (hence structural) unemployment as being wholly voluntary; jobs exist, but workers choose not to take them because they do not want them. This is a highly inaccurate representation of structural unemployment, which is that people want to work but cannot find jobs.

Using diagrams to show structural unemployment arising from labour market rigidities

Unemployment arising from minimum wage legislation, labour union activities and employment protection laws can be shown indirectly, through a product supply and demand diagram, as in Figure 10.1(b). Higher than equilibrium wages and employment protection lead to higher costs of production for firms, causing the firm supply curve to shift to the left, leading to a smaller quantity of output produced (Q_2 instead of Q_1). Firms therefore hire a smaller quantity of labour, and this contributes to structural unemployment of this type.

Unemployment arising from minimum wages and labour union activities leading to higher than equilibrium wages, can also be shown in a labour market diagram, as in Figure 10.1(c) (which is the same as Figure 4.19, page 97). The higher than equilibrium wage, W_f, results in unemployment of labour equal to $Q_s - Q_d$

Structural unemployment (of all types) is a serious type of unemployment because it tends to be long term. A certain amount of structural unemployment is unavoidable in any dynamic, growing economy, and is therefore considered to be part of 'natural unemployment'. However, this does not mean that it cannot be lowered. There are many policies governments can pursue to reduce it, including measures encouraging workers to retrain and obtain new skills, and to relocate (move) to areas with greater employment opportunities; providing incentives to firms to hire structurally unemployed workers; and measures to reduce labour market rigidities. These policies will be discussed in Chapter 12.

Frictional unemployment

Frictional unemployment occurs when workers are between jobs. Workers may leave their job because they have been fired, or because their employer went out of business, or because they are in search of a better job, or they may be waiting to start a new job. Frictional unemployment tends to be short term, and does not involve a lack of skills that are in demand. It is therefore less serious than structural unemployment.

A certain amount of frictional unemployment is inevitable in any growing, changing economy, where some industries expand while others contract, some firms grow faster than others, and workers seek to advance their income and professional positions. An important cause of frictional unemployment is incomplete information between employers and workers regarding job vacancies and required qualifications. Imagine 100 job vacancies and 100 job applicants who have exactly the right job

The textile industry in Naoussa

Naoussa is a city in northern Greece with a centuries-old textiles industry, based on highly labour-intensive production methods. When the markets of neighbouring transition economies opened up in the 1990s, Greek firms found it profitable to relocate to countries including Albania, Bulgaria, FYROM [the Former Yugoslav Republic of Macedonia], and Romania, on account of their far lower labour costs. The Greek government introduced legislation intended to lower labour costs (easier firing rules, extension of over-time work), yet Greek firms used some of these provisions to reduce their local workforce and move abroad.

In 2005, the removal of trade barriers on imports of Chinese textiles (according to WTO rules; see page 488) led to a huge increase in Chinese textiles in the Greek market, forcing many Greek textile firms to close down as they were unable to compete with the lower-cost Chinese imports.

Naoussa was one of the areas most strongly affected. The combination of firm relocations and firm closures led to the loss of tens of thousands of jobs. In 2005, unemployment in Naoussa was estimated to have reached a record 35–40%.

Source: Adapted from Mary Lembessi, 'Clothing exports dealt a blow' in *Kathimerini*, 23 September 2005; European industrial relations observatory on-line, 'Measure adopted in support of redundant textiles workers', 2 October 2006.

Applying your skills

1 What kind of unemployment was Nasoussa experiencing by 2005?

2 Use a demand and supply diagram to explain how this type of unemployment came about.

3 **(a)** Use a demand and supply diagram to show the effects of legislation intending to lower labour costs in the textile industry. **(b)** Why do you think this legislation was ineffective in keeping Greek firms from relocating?

qualifications. Because of incomplete information, it takes time for the right applicants to get matched up with the right jobs. Therefore, frictional unemployment is part of natural unemployment.

Measures to deal with frictional unemployment aim at reducing the time that a worker spends in between jobs and improving information flows between workers and employers. We will consider these measures in Chapter 12.

Seasonal unemployment

Seasonal unemployment occurs when the demand for labour in certain industries changes on a seasonal basis because of variations in needs. Farm workers experience seasonal unemployment because they are hired during peak harvesting seasons and laid off for the rest of the year. The same applies to lifeguards and gardeners, who are mostly in demand during summer months, people working in the tourist industry, which varies from season to season, shop assistants, who are in greater demand during peak selling months, and many others.

Some seasonal unemployment is unavoidable in any economy, as there will always be some industries with seasonal variations in labour demand. Therefore, seasonal unemployment is also part of natural unemployment. Measures to deal with seasonal unemployment are similar to those for lowering frictional unemployment.

Structural, frictional and seasonal unemployment: the natural rate of unemployment

Since 'full employment' means there is unemployment equal to the natural rate, what we really mean is that when an economy has full employment, it has unemployment equal to the sum of structural, frictional and seasonal unemployment.

Moreover, since the natural rate of unemployment is unemployment when the economy is producing potential output, *a fall in the natural rate of unemployment is reflected by an increase in potential output,* appearing as a rightward shift of the *LRAS* curve and the Keynesian *AS* curve (as discussed on page 255). We can now see that such *AS* shifts can occur due to a reduction

in structural, frictional or seasonal unemployment. (However, note that an increase in potential output does not necessarily mean that structural, fictional or seasonal unemployment have fallen, as potential output may increase for a variety of reasons; see page 255 and page 300 for a summary of these).

Cyclical (demand-deficient) unemployment

♦ Explain, using a diagram, that cyclical unemployment is caused by a fall in aggregate demand.

We have seen what types of unemployment exist when an economy is producing at its potential or full employment level of output. What about unemployment arising when the economy produces less than its potential output? Unemployment now consists of additional unemployment, over and above the natural rate, which is known as cyclical unemployment.

Cyclical unemployment, as the term suggests, occurs during the downturns of the business cycle, when the economy is in a recessionary gap. The downturn is seen as arising from declining or low aggregate demand (*AD*), and so is also known as **demand-deficient unemployment**. As real GDP falls due to a fall in *AD*, unemployment increases because firms lay off workers. In the upturn of the business cycle, as real GDP increases, the recessionary gap becomes smaller and cyclical unemployment falls. When the economy produces real GDP at the level of potential output, there is no longer any cyclical unemployment.

Although cyclical unemployment is a Keynesian concept, it can be illustrated by use of both the monetarist/new classical and Keynesian versions of the *AD-AS* model, shown in Figure 10.2. In both parts, the economy is initially producing potential output Y_p,

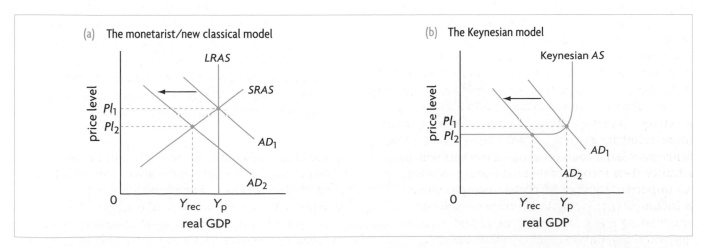

Figure 10.2 Cyclical unemployment

with zero cyclical unemployment. A fall in aggregate demand, causing AD_1 to shift to AD_2, creates a recessionary gap as real output falls to Y_{rec}. At Y_{rec}, the new unemployment created is cyclical unemployment.

Since cyclical unemployment arises from a deficiency of aggregate demand, measures to reduce this unemployment involve the use of government policies to increase aggregate demand, and eliminate the recessionary gap. We will study these policies in Chapter 12.

The four types of unemployment in relation to the *AD-AS* model

The four types of unemployment are shown in relation to the *AD-AS* model in Figure 10.3. (For simplicity, the monetarist/new classical model is shown.) At output Y_p, real GDP is equal to potential or full employment GDP, where there is unemployment equal to the natural rate, or the sum of structural, frictional and seasonal unemployment, and cyclical unemployment is equal to zero.

If GDP falls to any level less than Y_p, there is a recessionary gap, and unemployment increases so that in addition to structural plus frictional plus seasonal unemployment there is also cyclical (demand-deficient) unemployment. If GDP increases to any level greater than Y_p, there is an inflationary gap, and unemployment falls below the natural rate of unemployment. This means that some workers who were structurally, frictionally or seasonally

unemployed now find jobs. However, these jobs tend to be of a short duration, because the economy does not usually remain in an inflationary gap indefinitely. The government is likely to step in with policies (that we will study in Chapter 12) to bring the economy back to output level Y_p, where unemployment will once again reach the natural rate.

Whereas it is a simple matter to distinguish between the four types of unemployment on a theoretical level, in the real world it can be very difficult to identify and distinguish between the different types of unemployment. The labour market is in a continuous state of change, with some workers quitting their jobs, others being fired, with some unemployed workers waiting for an appropriate job and others retraining for a new job, with some firms expanding, others contracting, and with some people newly entering the labour force and others leaving. The uncertainties surrounding the causes of unemployment mean that it is not always an easy matter for governments to devise appropriate policies to lower it.

Evaluating government policies to address the different types of unemployment

♦ Evaluate government policies to deal with the different types of unemployment.

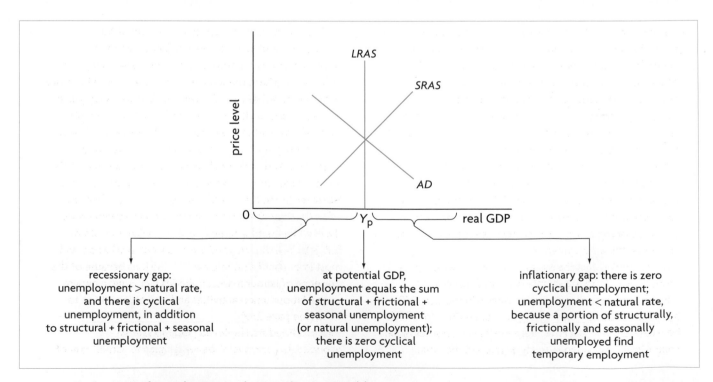

Figure 10.3 The four types of unemployment in relation to the *AD-AS* model

Government policies to deal with the different types of unemployment have only been touched upon briefly, and will be explored in greater depth and evaluated in Chapter 12. What you must bear in mind for now and later when you are reading Chapter 12 is that different types of unemployment require different policies. The most important difference is between cyclical (demand-deficient) unemployment, with potential solutions in the aggregate demand side of the macroeconomy, and the natural rate of unemployment (of which structural unemployment is the most serious) with potential solutions in the aggregate supply side of the macroeconomy.

Test your understanding 10.2

1 Does full employment mean the absence of unemployment? Explain.

2 Describe, using examples, the meaning and causes of structural, frictional and seasonal unemployment.

3 Use diagrams to show structural unemployment arising from **(a)** a change in demand for labour skills, **(b)** a change in the geographical location of industries, and **(c)** higher than equilibrium wages.

4 Explain how the sum of structural, frictional and seasonal unemployment relates to the concepts of 'full employment' and potential output in the context of the *AD-AS* model.

5 Using monetarist/new classical and Keynesian *AD-AS* diagrams, how would you illustrate **(a)** a lower rate of structural unemployment, and **(b)** a lower rate of natural unemployment?

6 Using a diagram, explain cyclical (demand-deficient) unemployment and the circumstances under which it arises.

7 What are the different kinds of unemployment an economy is likely to be experiencing when it is in **(a)** a recessionary gap, **(b)** an inflationary gap, and **(c)** when it is producing real GDP equal to potential GDP?

Theory of knowledge

What is 'natural' about the natural rate of unemployment?

We have defined the natural rate of unemployment to be the sum of structural, frictional and seasonal unemployment, or more simply all unemployment other than that caused by the business cycle. To call this unemployment 'natural' appears strange; it suggests there is something normal, usual or standard about these types of unemployment. Yet, what can be 'natural' about particular types of unemployment?

It is also strange that natural unemployment corresponds to 'full employment'. Even though, as we know, it is never possible to have full employment in the sense of zero unemployment, why should the presence of structural, frictional and seasonal unemployment be known as 'full employment'?

We can understand the reasons behind the use of these terms if we put the natural rate concept in historical perspective. This concept was developed in the late 1960s by Milton Friedman, the founder of 'monetarism', for which he received the Nobel Prize. (Edmund Phelps, another Nobel Prize winner, also independently developed this concept.)

The natural rate concept is a reflection of the monetarist model, which views the economy as a stable system that automatically tends toward long-run equilibrium where there are no recessionary or inflationary gaps (see page 249). In this view, the forces of supply and demand work to allocate resources efficiently, and the most efficient allocation that is possible is reached when the economy is at long-run equilibrium. If the labour market worked completely perfectly according to supply and demand, unemployment would in fact drop to zero. However, in the real world this does not occur, *because of institutions that lead to labour market imperfections*: there will always be some people who cannot instantly find jobs due to lack of information, but in addition, and most importantly, people cannot find jobs because of the presence of labour market rigidities including minimum wages, labour union activities and lack of incentives to work (see page 269).

In fact, Friedman believed (and monetarist economists continue to believe) that the natural rate of

(continued over)

unemployment is caused only by labour market rigidities. In the long run, labour market rigidities can explain *all types of unemployment*, including frictional, seasonal and all of structural unemployment discussed above (cyclical unemployment, you may remember, is zero when the economy is at long-run equilibrium). If people become unemployed because industries change or move, in the long run in a free competitive market they would all respond to market incentives and they would all find jobs.

Therefore, in this view, in the long run, all unemployment arises *naturally* from an imperfectly working labour market. Since the labour market institutions that lead to this natural unemployment are considered as given (fixed) in any economy, it is 'reasonable' to consider that the economy has *full employment* when all workers are employed *except those who are unemployed due to the labour market imperfections.*

It is worth quoting Nobel Prize-winning economist Robert Solow once again:

'Whether the social scientist wills it or knows it, perhaps even if he fights it, his choice of research problem, the questions he asks, the questions he doesn't ask, *his analytical framework, the very words he uses,* are all likely to be, in some measure, a reflection of his interests, ideologies and values.'[2] (emphasis added)

Friedman was an enthusiastic believer in the powers of the free market to solve the major economic problems, and he strongly opposed government intervention. His political convictions and values undoubtedly influenced his theoretical orientations, as well as his choice of words. His ideas had an important impact on policy-making, especially during the 1970s and 1980s, and his influence can still be felt to the present day. He was highly influential in the development of supply-side policies (see Chapter 12).

Some economists criticise his natural rate concept (as all his other ideas), especially since the 1990s. James K. Galbraith, a Keynesian economist (and son of the famous economist John Kenneth Galbraith), wrote the following:

'Alas, the location of the natural rate is not actually observed. Worse, the damn thing will not sit still. It is not only invisible, it moves! … [Economists] obsessively estimate and re-estimate the location of the natural rate, in order to guide their policy judgements. Sadly, they have never yet been able to predict its location …'[3]

In addition to being difficult to estimate, the natural rate of unemployment is also imprecise as to its meaning. In this text, we follow the practice of most textbooks in using the term "natural rate of unemployment" to refer to the sum of structural, frictional and seasonal unemployment. This is a convenient way to make a distinction between cyclical and all other types of unemployment. This does not presuppose that it is easy or even possible to actually measure any type of unemployment individually. As noted in the text, in the real world it is very difficult to distinguish between the different kinds of unemployment.

We end with a question. Why do economists bother to measure the 'natural rate of unemployment' and why is this so important? We will return to this question in the Theory of Knowledge feature on page 290 (at higher level).

---

[2] Robert M. Solow (1996) 'Science and ideology in economics' in D. M. Hausman, *The Philosophy of Economics*, Cambridge University Press.
[3] James K. Galbraith (1996) 'The surrender of economic policy' in *The American Prospect*, March–April.

Thinking points

- Do the terms 'natural' rate of unemployment and 'full employment' have a normative aspect? What do they suggest in terms of government policy action (or inaction) to reduce the rate of unemployment?

- Can the use of language to reflect an underlying political ideology interfere with the use of the scientific method?

- Do you agree with Friedman (and other economists) that all non-cyclical unemployment can be explained in terms of labour market institutions that create rigidities in the labour market?

10.2 Low and stable rate of inflation

Inflation and deflation

Inflation, disinflation and deflation

- Distinguish between inflation, disinflation and deflation.

Inflation is defined as a sustained increase in the general price level. When we speak of the 'general price level' we refer to an average of prices of goods and services in the entire economy, not to the price of any one particular good or service. 'Sustained' means that the general price level must increase to a new level and not fall back again to its previous lower level. Further, an increase in the general price level does not necessarily mean that prices of all goods and services are increasing; prices of some goods and services may be constant or even falling, while others are increasing. The presence of inflation indicates that prices of goods and services are increasing *on average.*

Deflation is defined as a sustained decrease in the general price level. As in the case of inflation, deflation refers to an average of prices; it is likely to be uneven, with some prices constant or even increasing.

Inflation is far more common than deflation; in fact, since the 1930s (the period of the Great Depression), most economies around the world have been experiencing a rising price level, or inflation.

Students sometimes confuse the difference between changes in the price level and changes in the rate of inflation. In our discussions of the *AD-AS* model, we have frequently seen increases in the price level; these indicate inflation. A change in the rate of inflation, by contrast, refers to a change in how fast the price level is rising. If the price level increases by 5% in one year and then increases by 7% the next year, this represents *an increase in the rate of inflation*. If the price level increases by 10% in one year and by 7% the next year, this represents *a decrease in the rate of inflation*, and is called **disinflation**. Disinflation therefore occurs when inflation occurs at a lower rate.

You must also be careful not to confuse a fall in the rate of inflation, or disinflation, with a fall in the price level, or deflation. A fall in the rate of inflation, such as from 10% to 7%, means that the price level is increasing at a lower rate, hence is disinflation. A fall in the price level indicates that deflation is occurring.

Measuring inflation and deflation

The consumer price index

♦ Explain that inflation and deflation are typically measured by calculating a consumer price index (CPI), which measures the change in prices of a basket of goods and services consumed by the average household.

Measures of inflation (and deflation) are obtained by use of price indices (*indices* is the plural of *index*). A price index is a measure of average prices in one period relative to average prices in a reference period called a base period. One of the most commonly used price indices to measure inflation is the consumer price index (CPI).

The consumer price index (CPI) is a measure of the cost of living, or the cost of goods and services purchased by the typical household in an economy. It is constructed by a statistical service in each country, which creates a hypothetical 'basket' containing thousands of goods and services that are consumed by the typical household in the course of a year. The

value of this basket is calculated for a particular year (called a base year); this is done by multiplying price times quantity for each good and service in the basket, and adding up to obtain the total value of the basket. The value of *the same basket* of goods and services is then calculated for subsequent years. The result is a series of numbers that show the value of the *same basket* of goods and services for different years. The CPI is then constructed to show how the value of the basket changes from year to year by comparing its value with the base year.

Once the consumer price index is constructed, inflation and deflation can be expressed as a percentage change of the index from one year to the other, which is simply a measure of *the percentage change in the value of the basket from one year to another*. Since the value of the basket changes from one period to another because of changes in the prices of the goods in the basket, these percentage changes reflect changes in the average price level. A rising price index indicates inflation; a falling price index indicates deflation. CPIs and rates of change in the price level are also calculated on a monthly basis and a quarterly basis. (Section 10.3, page 283, shows how a consumer price index is constructed and used to calculate the rate of inflation or deflation.)

The **consumer price index** (CPI) is a measure of the cost of living for the typical household, and compares the value of a basket of goods and services in one year with the value of the same basket in a base year. Inflation (and deflation) are measured as a percentage change in the value of the basket from one year to another. A positive percentage change indicates inflation. A negative percentage change indicates deflation.

Problems with the consumer price index (CPI)

♦ Explain that different income earners may experience a different rate of inflation when their pattern of consumption is not accurately reflected by the CPI.
♦ Explain that inflation figures may not accurately reflect changes in consumption patterns and the quality of the products purchased.

The CPI, we have seen, is based on a *fixed basket of goods and services* defined for a particular year, meant to reflect purchases of consumer goods and services by the typical household. The use of such a basket leads to some problems:

- **Different rates of inflation for different income earners.** The rate of inflation calculated by use of the CPI reflects the change in average prices of goods and services included in the basket. However, different consumers have different consumption patterns depending on their income levels, and these may differ from what is included in the basket. This means they face different rates of inflation than what is calculated on the basis of the CPI basket.

- **Different rates of inflation depending on regional or cultural factors.** Exactly the same idea as above applies to consumer groups whose purchases differ from the typical household's consumption patterns, because of variations in tastes due to cultural and regional factors.

- **Changes in consumption patterns due to consumer substitutions when relative prices change.** Each good and service included in the basket is weighted (multiplied by the number of units of the good or service purchased by the typical household over a year). However, as some goods and services become cheaper or more expensive over time, consumers make substitutions, buying more units of the cheaper goods and less of the more expensive ones. This results in changing weights (number of units consumed by the typical household), but because the weights in the basket are fixed, the changes in consumption patterns cannot be accounted for in the CPI. Therefore, the CPI gives a misleading impression of the degree of inflation, usually overstating it.

- **Changes in consumption patterns due to increasing use of discount stores and sales.** In many countries, consumers increasingly make use of discount stores and sales, thus buying some goods and services at lower prices than those used in CPI calculations. This is another reason why the CPI tends to overstate inflation.

- **Changes in consumption patterns due to introduction of new products.** In this case, too, a fixed basket of goods and services cannot account for new products introduced into the market, as well as older products that become less popular or are withdrawn (consider for example the replacement of videotapes by DVDs).

- **Changes in product quality.** This is another problem related to the use of a fixed basket of goods and services. The CPI cannot account for quality changes over time.

- **International comparisons.** The CPIs of different countries differ from each other with respect to the types of goods and services included in the basket, the weights used and methods of calculation. This limits the comparability of CPIs and inflation rates from country to country. To address this problem, the European Union (EU) has devised a Harmonised Index of Consumer Prices (HICP). The HICP determines consistent and compatible rules that must be followed by EU countries in order to calculate CPIs that are consistent with each other.[4]

- **Comparability over time.** Virtually all countries around the world periodically revise their CPI baskets and change the base year (usually about every ten years) to try to deal with many of the problems noted above. In many countries the weights of goods and services are changed as often as every year. This means that whereas price index numbers are comparable over short periods of time, over longer periods comparability is lessened because of cumulative changes in the basket of goods and services.

The core rate of inflation

- Explain that economists measure a core/underlying rate of inflation to eliminate the effect of sudden swings in the prices of food and oil, for example.

There are certain goods, notably food and energy products (such as oil) that have highly volatile prices (meaning they fluctuate widely over short periods of time). Reasons for price volatility include wide swings in supply or demand, causing large and abrupt price changes. When such goods are included in the CPI, they may give rise to misleading impressions regarding the rate of inflation. To deal with this problem, economists measure a **core rate of inflation**, which usually is done by constructing a CPI that does not include food and energy products with highly volatile prices.

---

[4] These rules include how products are classified, what products are to be included and excluded from the index, how new products will be entered into the index, how quality changes will be accounted for, how and when the basket is to be revised, and how the index is to be calculated. However, the HICP does not determine a uniform basket for all countries (this is done in recognition of the point noted above that different regions/countries have different consumption patterns due to diverse tastes, cultural factors and income levels). The HICP succeeds to a large extent in resolving the comparability problem, and whereas it is not intended to replace national CPIs, it is used in all cases where comparisons across countries need to be made. The HICP is calculated by all European Union countries plus Iceland and Norway. The first base year to be used was 1996, and the index began being calculated from January 1997.

The producer price index (PPI)

♦ Explain that a producer price index measuring changes in the prices of factors of production may be useful in predicting future inflation.

The **producer price index** (PPI) is actually several indices of prices received by producers of goods at various stages in the production process. For example, there is a PPI for inputs, a PPI for intermediate goods and a PPI for final goods (at the wholesale level, not retail). PPIs measure price level changes from the point of view of producers rather than consumers. Price level changes measured by PPIs are considered to be predictors of changes in the consumer price index (CPI) and hence predictors of the rate of inflation, because they measure price changes at an earlier stage in the production process. For example, if prices of inputs or intermediate prices are rising, it is likely that the prices of the final products paid by consumers will also rise at a later date. Also, if wholesale prices are rising, that also indicates that the higher prices will eventually be passed on to consumers.[5]

Test your understanding 10.3

1 **(a)** Distinguish between inflation, deflation and disinflation, and provide numerical examples illustrating each of these. **(b)** Explain, using examples, the difference between an increase in the price level and an increase in the rate of inflation.

2 **(a)** Describe the meaning of the consumer price index (CPI) and explain the purpose for which it is constructed. **(b)** Why does the CPI fail to present an accurate picture of the rate of inflation for all consumer groups?

3 **(a)** Distinguish between the consumer price index (CPI) and the producer price index (PPI). **(b)** Why can the PPI be useful for predicting changes in the CPI?

4 Describe the meaning of a core rate of inflation and how this is calculated.

Rate of inflation slows in Thailand

The consumer price index in Thailand rose by 3% in April from the year before, compared to 3.7% in February and 4.1% in January. The core inflation rate, which excludes food and energy costs, increased by 0.5% year-on-year. The producer price index, based on 506 products, showed a much higher increase, of 8.5%. This reflected increases in agricultural, mining and industrial costs.

The falling rate of inflation reflects consumer caution in spending, which is due to political trouble. It is believed that the current inflation has cost-push causes, arising from higher oil and other input prices, rather than demand-pull causes, stemming from greater demand.

Source: 'April Consumer Price Index rises 3% year-on-year' in *Thai Press Reports*, 5 May 2010.

Applying your skills

1 Explain the meaning and use of the **(a)** consumer price index (CPI), **(b)** producer price index (PPI), and **(c)** core inflation rate.

2 Explain whether the slowdown in Thailand's rate of inflation represents deflation or disinflation.

3 What does Thailand's PPI predict about its future CPI?

4 **(a)** Using diagrams, explain the difference between cost-push and demand-pull inflation. **(b)** Why is it believed that current inflation in Thailand is due to cost-push rather than demand-pull factors? (See pages 280–1.)

Consequences of inflation

Inflation, and especially a high rate of inflation, poses problems for an economy, because it affects particular population groups especially strongly, as well as the economy as a whole.

The relationship between inflation, purchasing power and nominal and real income

To understand why problems can arise, let's consider the relationship between inflation and purchasing power,

---

[5] Wholesale prices are prices received by producers and manufacturers, to be contrasted with retail prices, or the final prices paid by consumers.

and nominal and real income (these concepts were introduced in Chapter 8, page 221). Purchasing power refers to the quantity of goods and services that can be bought with money. Imagine you have £60 to spend on shirts. You can think of this as your 'nominal income'. When the price is £20 per shirt, you can buy three shirts. If the price increases to £30 per shirt, you can only buy two shirts. Your money, or your nominal income of £60 has not changed, yet the purchasing power of the £60, or what this money can buy, has fallen due to the increase in price. 'Real income' is the same as 'purchasing power'; it refers to what your money can buy: it decreases as prices rise, and increases as prices fall.

Changes in real income, money income and the general price level are related to each other in the following way:

% change in real income (or purchasing power) =
% change in nominal income – % change in the price
level (or the rate of inflation)

These relationships illustrate some important points. Inflation leads to a fall in real income, or purchasing power, only if nominal income is constant, or if nominal income increases more slowly than the price level. Say there is a 5% increase in the price level, which is a 5% rate of inflation. How will your real income be affected? If your nominal income also increases by 5%, your real income, or purchasing power, remains unchanged. Therefore, for you, inflation is not a problem. If, however, your nominal income remains constant or increases by less than 5%, your real income falls, and you will be worse off since the purchasing power of your income is reduced.

Consequences of inflation

♦ Discuss the possible consequences of a high inflation rate, including greater uncertainty, redistributive effects, less saving, and the damage to export competitiveness.

Redistribution effects

Inflation redistributes income away from certain groups in the economy and towards other groups. Redistribution arises in situations where certain groups lose some purchasing power and become worse off, while other groups gain purchasing power and become better off. Groups who lose from inflation include:

- **People who receive fixed incomes or wages.** When individuals receive an income or wage that is fixed or constant, as the general price level increases they become worse off. This occurs when:
  - workers have wage contracts fixing their wages over a period of time
  - pensioners receive fixed pensions
  - landlords receive fixed rental income
  - individuals receive fixed welfare payments.

- **People who receive incomes or wages that increase less rapidly than the rate of inflation.** When individuals' incomes do not keep up with a rising price level (do not increase as fast as the price level), a fall in their real incomes results and they therefore become worse off. These groups may include all those noted above plus any other kind of income receiver whose income is not increasing as rapidly as the price level.

- **Holders of cash.** As the price level increases, the real value or purchasing power of any cash held falls.

- **Savers.** People who save money may become worse off as a result of inflation. In order to maintain the real value of their savings, savers must receive a rate of interest that is at least equal to the rate of inflation. Suppose you deposit $1000 in a bank account that pays you no interest. If there is inflation, the real value of your savings will fall. However, you may be able to protect the purchasing power of your savings. Say the rate of inflation is 5% per year. If you receive interest on your deposit at the rate of 5% per year, what you will lose through inflation will be exactly matched by what you gain through interest income. In this case, the real value (or purchasing power) of your savings remains unaffected. In general, savers who receive a rate of interest on their savings lower than the rate of inflation suffer a fall in the real value (or purchasing power) of their savings.

- **Lenders (creditors).** People (or financial institutions such as banks) who lend money may be worse off due to inflation. Assume you lend your friend €100 for one year (and you do not charge interest). If in the course of the year there is an increase in the price level (inflation), the real value of the €100 you will get back from your friend at the end of the year will have fallen. If you charged your friend a rate of interest equal to the rate of inflation, then the real value of your loan to your friend will be exactly maintained. In general, lending at a lower interest rate than the rate of inflation makes the lender (creditor) worse off at the end of the loan period.

Groups who gain from inflation include:

- **Borrowers (debtors).** In the example above, your friend who borrowed €100 from you benefits since the €100 paid back after one year is worth less than one year ago. If you had charged interest, your friend (the borrower) would benefit as long as the rate of interest is lower than the rate of inflation. In general, borrowing at a lower interest rate than the rate of inflation makes the borrower (debtor) better off at the end of the loan period.

- **Payers of fixed incomes or wages.** As long as nominal wages, pensions, rents, welfare payments, etc., are fixed while there is inflation, the payers (whether they are firms, the government, payers of rent, etc.) benefit as the real value of their payments falls due to inflation.

- **Payers of incomes or wages that increase less rapidly than the rate of inflation.** As long as incomes of any kind increase less rapidly than the rate of inflation, the payers of these incomes benefit due to the falling real value of their payments.

Uncertainty

Inability to accurately predict what inflation will be in the future means that people cannot predict future changes in purchasing power (of income, wealth, loans and anything else that is measured in terms of money). This causes uncertainty among economic decision-makers. Firms, in particular, become more cautious about making future plans under uncertainty about future price levels, because they are unable to make accurate forecasts of costs and revenues, as these depend on the future prices of their inputs and their products. Their uncertainty leads them to make fewer investments, which in turn may lead to lower economic growth.

Menu costs

Menu costs are costs incurred by firms when they have to print new menus (in restaurants), catalogues, advertisements, price labels, etc., due to changes in prices. The higher the rate of inflation, the more often firms have to change their prices and therefore, the higher the menu costs.

Money illusion

Money illusion refers to the idea that some people feel better off when their nominal income increases, even though the price level may increase at the same rate and possibly even faster. When this occurs, people are under the illusion that they are better off whereas in fact they are not: their real income or purchasing power has not changed at all, and may even have decreased. If money illusion is widespread, it has negative consequences because it leads consumers to make wrong spending decisions.

International (export) competitiveness

When the price level in a country increases more rapidly than the price level in other countries with which it trades, its exports become more expensive to foreign buyers, while imports become cheaper to domestic buyers. The country's international competitiveness, or its ability to compete with foreign countries, is reduced. The result is that the quantity of exports falls, and the quantity of imports increases. This in turn may create difficulties for the country's balance of payments. (This will be explained in Chapter 14.)

Consequences of hyperinflation (supplementary material)

Hyperinflation consists of very high rates of inflation. It is defined as occurring when the price level increases by more than 50% per month, though it can reach thousands or even millions of percentage points per year. One of the most dramatic hyperinflations in history occurred in Germany after the First World War, when the price level in 1924 was more than 100 trillion times higher than in 1914. In more recent years, many hyperinflations have been concentrated in Latin America from the mid-1980s to early 1990s, and in eastern European and former Soviet Union countries in the early 1990s following the collapse of the Soviet Union. Peak annual rates of inflation came to about 7500% in Peru in 1990; 3080% in Argentina in 1989; 2950% in Brazil in 1990; 1735% in Russia in 1992; 4735% in Ukraine in 1995; and 1060% in Bulgaria in 1997. One of the most serious cases of hyperinflation occurred in Zimbabwe, where the rate of inflation went from over 1000% in 2006, to 12 000% in 2007, and to over 11 million % (on an annual basis) in the summer of 2008.

Hyperinflation results from very significant increases in the supply of money, which impact directly on the price level. Hyperinflations occur when governments resort to printing money, thereby increasing its supply.

Hyperinflation has serious negative consequences, over and above those discussed above, because money loses its value very rapidly. Consumers increase their spending to benefit from the current lower prices, thereby feeding aggregate demand (which causes demand-pull inflation; see page 280). Workers demand higher nominal wages to maintain the real value of their current and future incomes, thereby feeding cost-push inflation (see page 281). Therefore, an *inflationary spiral* is created (a process where inflation sets in motion a series of events that worsen the inflation).

Serious hyperinflations result in a massive disruption of economic activity: businesses stop investing in productive activities and invest instead in assets that are believed to maintain their value as prices rise (gold, real estate or jewels); firms also withhold goods from sale in the market so that they can sell them later at higher prices; lenders (creditors) suffer massive losses as the real value of debts falls dramatically. At the extreme, money loses its value altogether and people resort to barter (the direct exchange of goods or services, eliminating the need for money), which in itself makes production and exchange extremely difficult. Serious hyperinflations can also lead to political and social unrest.

What is an appropriate rate of inflation?

Most governments prefer a *low and stable rate of inflation*, not a zero rate of inflation. Why is a zero rate of inflation, meaning a constant price level, not the preferred objective? The reason is that a zero rate of inflation comes dangerously close to deflation, which as we will see below (page 282) can cause serious problems for an economy.

There is no one particular rate of inflation that is ideal, but many governments would like to see this in the range of about 2–3% per year. Less than 2% might be considered as coming close to deflation; more than 4% is seen as being too high.

Test your understanding 10.4

1 Using a numerical example, explain the relationship between inflation and purchasing power.

2 Explain what happens to your real income (your purchasing power) in each of the following situations: **(a)** your nominal income increases by 5% and the rate of inflation is 8%, **(b)** your nominal income falls by 10%, and the rate of inflation is 3%, and **(c)** your nominal income increases by 7% and the rate of inflation is 7%.

3 **(a)** Inflation results in redistribution of purchasing power. Explain who is likely to gain and who is likely to lose from the redistribution effects of inflation. **(b)** What are some other negative consequences of inflation (other than redistribution)?

Types and causes of inflation

We will examine two causes of inflation: demand-pull inflation and cost-push inflation.

Demand-pull inflation

• Explain, using a diagram, that demand-pull inflation is caused by changes in the determinants of *AD*, resulting in an increase in *AD*.

Demand-pull inflation is caused by increases in aggregate demand, in turn brought about by changes in any of the determinants of aggregate demand (see Chapter 9, page 238). Assume the economy is initially at full employment equilibrium, producing potential GDP, shown as Y_p in

Figure 10.4 parts (a) and (b). The economy experiences an increase in aggregate demand appearing as a rightward shift of the *AD* curve from AD_1 to AD_2 in both diagrams. The impact on the economy is to increase the price level from Pl_1 to Pl_2, and to increase the equilibrium level of real GDP from Y_p to Y_{infl}. The increase in the price level from Pl_1 to Pl_2 due to the increase in aggregate demand is known as demand-pull inflation.

Note that demand-pull inflation is associated with an inflationary gap: real GDP is greater than full employment GDP, and unemployment falls to a level below the natural rate of unemployment. The demand for labour is so large that some workers who are structurally, frictionally or seasonally unemployed temporarily find jobs.

> **Demand-pull inflation** involves an excess of *aggregate demand* over *aggregate supply* at the full employment level of output, and is caused by an increase in aggregate demand. It is shown in the AD-AS model as a rightward shift in the AD curve.

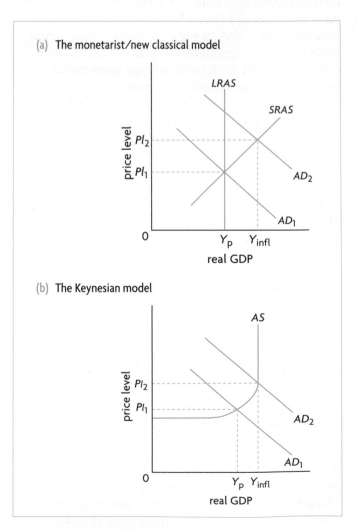

Figure 10.4 Demand-pull inflation

Cost-push inflation

♦ Explain, using a diagram, that cost-push inflation is caused by an increase in the costs of factors of production, resulting in a decrease in *SRAS*.

Cost-push inflation is caused by increases in costs of production or supply-side shocks. Assume the economy is initially at the full employment level of output, Y_p in Figure 10.5, and suppose there is an increase in costs of production. The *SRAS* curve shifts from $SRAS_1$ to $SRAS_2$, leading to an increase in the price level from Pl_1 to Pl_2, and a fall in the equilibrium level of real GDP from Y_p to Y_{rec}. The increase in the price level due to the fall in *SRAS* is known as cost-push inflation.

Cost-push inflation is analysed only by means of the monetarist/new classical *AD-AS* model. The Keynesian model is not equipped to deal with short-term fluctuations of aggregate supply. Keynes was concerned with showing the importance of *aggregate demand* in causing short-term fluctuations. The output level Y_{rec}, though indicating a recession, is not called a recessionary/deflationary gap, because output gaps (whether recessionary or inflationary) can only be caused by too little or too much aggregate demand (see page 246, footnote 6).

In Chapter 9, we saw that a decrease in *SRAS* poses a special set of problems because it leads to both inflation and a fall in real GDP (with more unemployment) (see page 246 as well as the Real World Focus feature on page 257). The presence of both inflation and unemployment is called *stagflation*, a combination of the words 'stagnation' and 'inflation'. This should be contrasted with an increase in aggregate demand leading to demand-pull inflation,

which results in a higher price level but an *increase* in real GDP (with less unemployment). Cost-push inflation is more difficult to deal with effectively, as we will discover in Chapter 12.

Cost-push inflation is caused by a fall in aggregate supply, in turn resulting from increases in wages or prices of other inputs, shown in the *AD-AS* model as leftward shifts of the *AS* curve.

Evaluating government policies to address the different types of inflation

♦ Evaluate government policies to deal with the different types of inflation.

Government policies to deal with the different types of inflation will be studied and evaluated in Chapter 12. As in the case of different types of unemployment, each of which has its own set of appropriate policies, so in the case of inflation, demand-pull and cost-push inflation must be addressed by the use of different kinds of policies. We will evaluate the various policies to deal with inflation in Chapter 12.

Test your understanding 10.5

1 Using appropriate diagrams, explain the difference between demand-pull and cost-push inflation.

2 Why is cost-push inflation potentially more serious than demand-pull inflation?

3 Using diagrams, show the effects on the price level of the following events, and explain whether it is cost-push or demand-pull inflation:

   (a) Real GDP in foreign countries that trade with your country increases, leading to increased demand for your country's exports.

   (b) Businesses are optimistic that a recession is about to end, and so increase investment spending.

   (c) An increase in housing prices makes consumers increase their consumption expenditures.

   (d) A sudden increase in the price of oil, a key input in production, occurs.

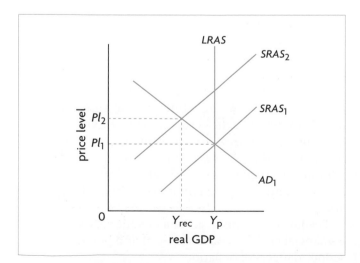

Figure 10.5 Cost-push inflation

Consequences and causes of deflation

Why deflation occurs rarely in the real world

Deflation is not a common phenomenon. Whereas it is often the case that the price of a particular good or service may fall over time, it is rare to see the general price level of an economy falling. There are several factors that account for this:

- **Wages of workers do not ordinarily fall.** This means it is difficult for firms to lower the prices of their products, as this would cut into their profits, especially since wages represent a large proportion of firms' costs of production. There are several reasons why wages do not fall easily (labour contracts, minimum wage legislation, worker and union resistance to wage cuts, ideas of fairness, fears of negative impacts on workers' morale, etc.).

- **Large oligopolistic firms may fear price wars.** If one firm lowers its price, then others may lower theirs more aggressively in an effort to capture market shares, and then all the firms will be worse off. Therefore, firms avoid cutting their prices.

- **Firms want to avoid incurring menu costs resulting from price changes**, particularly if they believe that the lower prices will prevail only for short periods of time. Therefore, they avoid lowering their prices.

Whereas deflation occurs rarely, it has appeared periodically, for example in Britain and the United States in the late 19th century, in the United States during the depression of the 1930s (1933–7), and in Japan from 1999 to 2006. In 2003 and again in 2008, there were serious concerns in Europe and the United States that deflation might occur. Deflation is generally feared more than inflation, because it may pose potentially serious problems for an economy. The negative consequences of deflation are discussed below.

Consequences of deflation

- ♦ Discuss the possible consequences of deflation, including high levels of cyclical unemployment and bankruptcies.

Redistribution effects
The redistribution effects of deflation are the opposite of those of inflation: with a falling price level, individuals on fixed incomes, holders of cash, savers and lenders (creditors) all gain as the real value of their income or holdings increases. By contrast, borrowers (debtors) and payers of individuals with fixed incomes lose with a falling price level, as they must pay out sums that have an increasing real value.

Uncertainty
Deflation, like inflation, creates uncertainty for firms, which are unable to forecast their costs and revenues due to declining price levels.

Menu costs
Menu costs (the costs to firms of printing new menus, catalogues, advertisements, price labels, etc.) are similar in the case of deflation as in the case of inflation, as both simply involve changes in prices.

Risk of a deflationary spiral with high and increasing cyclical unemployment
A deflationary spiral involves a process where deflation sets into motion a series of events that worsen the deflation. Deflation discourages spending by consumers, because they postpone making purchases as they expect that prices will continue to fall. Deflation also discourages borrowing by both consumers and firms, for the reason noted above: the real value of debt increases as the price level falls. The result is that consumer and business spending falls, causing aggregate demand to fall. If the economy is already in recession, this will become deeper with falling *AD*, unemployment increases further, incomes and prices fall further, deflationary pressures increase further, spending and borrowing decrease further, and so on in a downward spiral.

Risk of bankruptcies and a financial crisis
As we saw above, deflation results in an increase in the real value of debt. If the economy is in recession, and incomes are falling while the real value of debt is increasing, the result will most likely be bankruptcies of firms and consumers who are unable to pay back their debts. If such bankruptcies become widespread, banks and financial institutions will be affected, and a large risk of a major financial crisis arises.

The last two items, risks of a deflationary spiral and a financial crisis, reveal the special and potentially serious dangers of deflation.

Causes of deflation

From an analytical point of view, we can make a distinction between two causes of deflation: decreases in aggregate demand, held to lead to a 'bad' kind of deflation, and increases in aggregate supply, held to lead to 'good' deflation.

To see how 'bad' deflation could arise, suppose the economy is at a point of long run equilibrium as in Figure 10.2(a) (page 271), and assume there is a decrease in aggregate demand (for example, due to business pessimism) so that the AD curve shifts from AD_1 to AD_2. Whereas the AD-AS model predicts a drop in the price level, or deflation, this is unlikely to occur over a short period of time for the reasons discussed above, accounting for the highly infrequent occurrence of deflation.[6] However if low aggregate demand persists over a long period, the price level falls to P_2. This is 'bad' deflation because it is associated with recession, falling incomes and output, and cyclical unemployment. These are the circumstances that characterised the deflation of the Great Depression during the 1930s, and more recently in Japan.

'Good' deflation, on the other hand, can be shown in a diagram to be caused by a rightward shift of the $LRAS$ curve, with the AD curve constant (or also shifting to the right but by less than the LRAS shift), so that the new point of equilibrium occurs at a lower price level. This is held to be 'good' deflation because it is associated with economic expansion, rising incomes and output, increasing employment and economic growth. Some economists argue that it was under such circumstances that the deflation of Britain and the United States in the late 19th century occurred.

The fear in 2003 that deflation might occur possibly involved both kinds of deflation. It was held that the downward pressure on prices was due partly to advances in information technology (causing an increase in aggregate supply) and partly to falls in aggregate demand.

However, it must be stressed that while it may be possible to make an analytical distinction between 'good' and 'bad' deflation, no deflation is ever *good*. An important reason is that as we have seen above, deflation discourages spending because it reduces borrowing due to increases in the real value of debt, and also because consumers postpone purchases in the expectation that prices will fall. These factors cause aggregate demand to fall regardless of the causes of deflation. For these reasons, deflation is generally feared and is considered by economists to be a greater threat than inflation.

10.3 Topics on inflation (higher level topics) HL

Constructing a weighted price index and calculating the rate of inflation

How to construct a weighted price index

♦ Construct a weighted price index, using a set of data provided.

It is suggested that you review the explanation of the consumer price index (CPI, page 275) before reading this section.

We will construct a consumer price index (CPI) for a simple economy where consumers typically consume three goods and services: burgers, DVDs and haircuts, shown in column 1 of Table 10.1. Column 2 gives us the quantities of each that the typical household buys in a year; these are the *weights*. Note that a **weighted price index** is a price index that 'weights' the various goods and services according to their relative importance in consumer spending.[7] To construct a CPI, we follow these steps:

1 Decide which of the years will be the base year; we choose 2009.

---

[6] The infrequent occurrence of deflation will be explained by the 'ratchet effect', to be discussed in Chapter 12, page 324.

[7] In the real world, the weights used to construct the CPI are based on the proportion of consumer spending on each good or service on average, rather than on the quantity of each good or service consumed.

(1) Good and services	(2) Quantity (number of units) in basket (weights)	(3) Prices of basket goods and services in base year (2009)	(4) Value of basket goods and services in base year (2009)	(5) Prices of basket goods and services in 2010	(6) Value of basket goods and services in 2010	(7) Prices of basket goods and services in 2011	(8) Value of basket goods and services in 2011
Burgers	37	$3	$111	$4	$148	$5	$185
DVDs	25	$15	$375	$14	$350	$16	$400
Haircuts	15	$18	$270	$20	$300	$21	$315
Total value of basket			$756		$798		$900

Table 10.1   Constructing a hypothetical price index

2 Use the price of each good and service in the base year (2009), to calculate its base year value (multiply quantity in column 2 by 2009 prices in column 3); these values appear in column 4.

3 Add up all values in column 4 to get the total value of the basket in the base year; this is $756, appearing at the bottom of column 4.

4 Use the price of each good and service in 2010 to calculate its 2010 value (multiply the number of units in the basket (column 2) by 2010 prices (column 5)); then do the same using 2011 prices (column 7); the resulting values appear in column 6 for 2010 and column 8 for 2011.

5 Add up the values in column 6 to obtain the total value of the basket in 2010; this is $798 appearing at the bottom of column 6; do the same to find the value of the basket in 2011, which is $900, appearing at the bottom of column 8.

We now have all the information we need to construct our price index for 2009, 2010 and 2011. Note that:

$$\text{price index for a specific year}$$
$$= \frac{\text{value of basket in a specific year}}{\text{value of same basket in base year}} \times 100$$

Therefore, the price index numbers for 2009, 2010 and 2011 are:

$$\text{price index for 2009} = \frac{756}{756} \times 100 = 1.00 \times 100 = 100.0$$

$$\text{price index for 2010} = \frac{798}{756} \times 100 = 1.055 \times 100 = 105.5$$

$$\text{price index for 2011} = \frac{900}{756} \times 100 = 1.190 \times 100 = 119.0$$

Note that the price index for the base year is always equal to 100.

To construct a weighted price index, (i) find the value of the basket in current prices for each year; (ii) use the formula above to find the price index number for each year.

In the real world, calculations of price indices are complicated as they involve collecting price data on thousands of goods and services and carrying out all necessary computations. This is done by specialised statistical services in every country.

Using a weighted price index (the CPI) to calculate the rate of inflation

♦ Calculate the inflation rate from a set of data.

Using the price index constructed above, we can calculate the rate of inflation (the percentage change in the price level). The percentage change in a variable A is calculated by the following:

$$\% \text{ change in } A = \frac{\text{final value of } A - \text{initial value of } A}{\text{initial value of } A} \times 100$$

(See 'Quantitative techniques' chapter on the CD-ROM page 2 for more information.)

To calculate the percentage change in the price level from 2009 to 2010, we have

% change in price level from 2009 to 2010

$$= \frac{105.5 - 100.0}{100.0} \times 100 = 5.5\%$$

In fact, we did not need to do this calculation: we can simply read the inflation rate from the price index, since $105.5 - 100.0 = 5.5\%$.

When the price level is presented as a price index, the rate of inflation is equal to the index number of any year minus the index number of the base year (which is always 100).

Therefore, it follows that the rate of inflation in the period 2009–11 is 119.0 – 100.0 = 19.0%. However, it is only possible to read off the rate of inflation from a price index in this simple way in those cases involving a percentage change in the price level *relative to the base year*, whose price index number is equal to 100.[8] In other cases, we must use the formula above to calculate the rate of inflation. For example, to find the rate of inflation in 2010–11:

% change in price level in 2010–11

$$= \frac{119.0 - 105.5}{105.5} \times 100 = 12.8\%$$

Note that a price index with increasing values over time (such as the example above) indicates inflation. Decreasing values over time indicate deflation. Also, note that the first year in a price index need not be the base year. For example, suppose we have the following price index:

2000	2001	2002	2003	2004
97.5	100.0	107.3	109.7	107.8

The base year is 2001, for which the price index is 100. This price index indicates that inflation has occurred in 2000–1, 2001–2, and 2002–3, but *deflation* has occurred in 2003–4.

Calculating real income

In Chapter 8, we learned how to calculate real GDP from nominal GDP using the GDP deflator (page 228). We can now use the CPI to calculate real income (of consumers, pensioners, or other social groups):

$$\text{real income} = \frac{\text{nominal income}}{\text{CPI}} \times 100$$

Clearly, if nominal income increases by the same percentage as the price level (measured by the CPI), real income remains unchanged. The CPI is, in fact, very useful for calculating adjustments that must be made to nominal income (of wage-earners, pensioners, etc.) in order for these groups to maintain a constant or increasing real income. This is discussed further below (as supplementary material).

A word of caution

Since the CPI compares price levels based on goods and services in a specific basket, it only makes sense to calculate inflation rates from a price index constructed by use of the same basket. Further, it is not possible to make comparisons of price levels (i.e. calculate rates of inflation) across years by use of price indices that have a different base year, even if the basket of goods and services is the same. Therefore, for comparisons of index numbers to be meaningful, the index numbers must be calculated using the same base year, and for the same basket of goods and services.

Calculating the rate of inflation using the GDP deflator

In Chapter 8, we learned that the GDP deflator measures the average level of prices of all goods and services included in GDP.

The rate of inflation based on the GDP deflator is calculated in the same way as with the consumer price index. In our example (page 229) the average price level of goods and services included in GDP increased by 18.8% in 2001–2 (= 118.8 – 100.0), and by 30.0% in 2001–3 (= 130.0 – 100.0). The rate of increase in the period 2002–3 is:

% change in price level in 2002–3

$$= \frac{130.0 - 118.8}{118.8} \times 100 = 9.4\%$$

Comparing the CPI with the GDP deflator (supplementary material)

Rates of inflation derived from the consumer price index and from the GDP deflator follow the same general pattern, and tend to move in the same direction (both moving upward or downward), but they are not the same. The two price indices are based on prices of a different set of goods and services, and they also differ in how they measure price changes.

The consumer price index is based on *a fixed basket of goods and services, valued at prices that change over time*. The GDP deflator is based on *actual output produced that changes over time, valued at fixed, base year prices*. It follows, then, that the GDP deflator does not face the problems of the CPI resulting from the CPI's use of a fixed basket (see

---

[8] Note that we can only use this rule for years *after* the base year and not before. For example, if the CPI is 92 in 2007 and 100 in 2008, we cannot say there is an 8% increase in the price level in the period 2007–08.

To convince yourself, do the calculation. You will find that the rate of inflation is 8.7%.

page 275), and as a result is a more accurate measure of changes in the overall price level, or rate of inflation.

Yet of the two measures, the CPI is the one used by governments and the private sector to estimate adjustments to nominal incomes needed to maintain their real value (such as workers' nominal wages, pensions, welfare payments, etc.). Also, central banks use the CPI as a guide to monetary policy (discussed in Chapter 12).

There are two main reasons why the CPI is preferred:

- **The GDP deflator includes irrelevant goods from the consumer's perspective and excludes imports.** The CPI measures price changes of goods and services bought by typical households, including those produced domestically as well as imports. The GDP deflator measures prices of all goods and services included in GDP (everything produced domestically), and therefore includes prices of exports, capital goods and goods purchased by the government, all of which are of no interest to consumer groups interested in keeping track of their real incomes (such as wage earners and pensioners). Also, the GDP deflator excludes prices of imports, which can be of great interest to consumers who buy imported goods (such as imported oil for home heating and car fuel purposes). Summing up, the CPI reflects changes in the cost of living for consumers; the GDP deflator reflects changes in average prices for the economy as a whole.

- **The GDP deflator does not allow goods and services to be weighted in accordance with their relative importance in the typical household's budget.** The use of a fixed basket of goods and services, to which particular weights are attached, offers an important advantage: it allows for the measurement of average price changes faced by the typical household. The weights attached to particular goods and services in the base year basket are in accordance with their relative importance in the typical household's budget. For example, the weights attached to food in the basket may be completely different from the relative importance (or weight) of food products in GDP. For the consumer, what matters is the relative importance of household spending on food, not the relative importance of food products in GDP.

Test your understanding 10.7

1 Consider the following price index for the period 1997–2001:

1997	97
1998	95
1999	100
2000	105
2001	107

(a) Which is the base year? (b) What was the rate of inflation in the periods 1999–2000, and 1999–2001? (c) What was the rate of inflation in 1998–99, and 2000–1? (d) In what period of time does this index indicate that deflation occurred? (e) Did disinflation occur at any time? Explain.

2 Why do you think it is important to use 'weights' for the goods and services consumed by the typical household?

3 Using the data below, (a) construct a consumer price index using 2009 as the base year. (b) Identify the weights you are using. (c) Calculate the rates of inflation/deflation for the years 2008–9, 2009–10, 2010–11. (d) Identify the years when inflation/deflation/disinflation occurred, and explain your conclusions. (e) Construct a new price index using 2010 as the base year. (f) Calculate the rates of inflation/ deflation for the same three-year periods as in question (c). (g) Compare the rates of inflation/ deflation you found using the two price indices (they should be the same!). (h) Would it make sense to compare an index number from the first price index with an index number from the second price index? Explain your answer.

Good/ service	Quantity in basket	Price per unit in 2008 (£)	Price per unit in 2009 (£)	Price per unit in 2010 (£)	Price per unit in 2011 (£)
Pizzas	25	7	6	7	6
DVDs	9	15	17	18	18
Bus rides	47	2	4	4	3

4 (Optional) Why is the CPI preferred by governments and consumers as a measure of the rate of inflation, even though the GDP deflator is a more accurate measure of the rate of inflation?

286 Section 2: Macroeconomics

Possible relationships between unemployment and inflation

The Phillips curve

♦ Discuss, using a short-run Phillips curve diagram, the view that there is a possible trade-off between the unemployment rate and the inflation rate in the short run.

The **Phillips curve** is concerned with the relationship between unemployment and inflation. In the late 1950s, the New Zealand economist A.W. Phillips published a study showing that there appeared to be a long-term negative relationship between the unemployment rate and the rate of change in nominal (money) wages; this relationship was later extended by economists to apply to the relationship between unemployment and inflation. The relationship showed that the lower the rate of inflation, the higher the unemployment rate; and the higher the rate of inflation, the lower the unemployment rate. This relationship is shown in Figure 10.6(a), where the unemployment rate is measured along the horizontal axis, and the rate of inflation along the vertical axis. (Note that the vertical axis does not measure the price level, as in the AD-AS model.)

The Phillips curve suggests that if there is a constant negative relationship between the two variables, then every economy faces a trade-off between inflation and unemployment: it can choose between a relatively low rate of inflation and a higher unemployment rate, such as point a on the curve, or a higher rate of inflation and a lower unemployment rate, such as point d. Whereas,

ideally, it would be preferable for any economy to have low inflation and low unemployment, such as point e, this is not possible according to the theory of the Phillips curve, as the only achievable points are those on (or close to) the curve.

The reasoning behind the shape of the curve can be illustrated by use of the AD-AS model, shown in Figure 10.6(b). Assume a fixed, upward-sloping SRAS curve, and imagine a succession of aggregate demand increases (which could be caused by any of the factors we are familiar with from Chapter 9 (Table 9.1, page 240). As aggregate demand shifts from AD_1 to AD_2, the price level rises from Pl_1 to Pl_2, the level of real GDP increases from Y_1 to Y_2, and the level of unemployment correspondingly falls. The same process is repeated as aggregate demand increases from AD_2 to AD_3, and then to AD_4, and so on. With every increase in aggregate demand, we have an increase in the price level and a fall in unemployment. It follows, then, that we can simply think of each point on the Phillips curve (such as a, b, c or d) as corresponding to the point of intersection of SRAS with a different AD curve (a, b, c or d). The 'choice' of where to be on the Phillips curve in part (a) thus corresponds to a 'choice' of AD curve in part (b) of the figure.[9]

The breakdown in the relationship: stagflation

♦ Explain, using a diagram, that the short-run Phillips curve may shift outwards, resulting in stagflation (caused by a decrease in SRAS due to factors including supply shocks).

(a) The shape of the Phillips curve

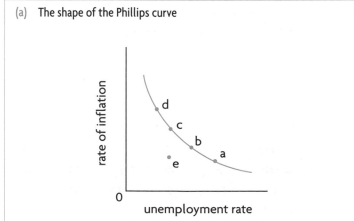

(b) The reasoning behind the Phillips curve in terms of the AD-AS model

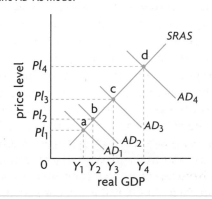

Figure 10.6 The Phillips curve

[9] The correspondence between Figure 10.6 (a) and (b) is not entirely accurate. The vertical axis of part (a) measures the rate of inflation, or the percentage increase in the price level. The vertical axis of part (b) measures the price level, which is very different from the rate of inflation. There can be increases in the price level with no increase in the rate of inflation and even with a decrease in the rate of inflation (or disinflation; for example, the rate of inflation increases by 5% in 2000 and by 3% in 2001). The succession of AD curves in part (b), leading to increasingly larger rises in the price level, has been drawn with this point in mind, even though it is still not accurate.

During the 1960s, many economists came to believe that the Phillips curve did offer the possibility of choice between inflation and unemployment. At that time aggregate supply was relatively stable, and major changes in economic activity were caused by swings in aggregate demand. Most economists at the time were very strongly influenced by Keynesian thinking, believing that demand-side policies (see Chapter 12) were very important in influencing the level of economic activity and real GDP. The Phillips curve appeared to offer governments the possibility of using demand-side policies to choose between various alternatives. High aggregate demand would lead to low unemployment and higher inflation, while low aggregate demand would lead to higher unemployment and lower inflation.

Events of the 1970s and 1980s upset this line of thinking, and the stable relationship between inflation and unemployment that was suggested by the Phillips curve appeared to break down. Whereas it had been supposed that aggregate supply could remain stable over long periods of time, a number of aggregate supply shocks led to a period of **stagflation**, a term coined at the time to refer to the new phenomenon of stagnation (or recession) with unemployment and inflation simultaneously. The most important of the supply shocks involved the oil price increases brought on by the actions of OPEC (Organization of the Petroleum Exporting Countries), which restricted the global supply of oil). Another supply shock involved food price increases resulting from worldwide crop failures (restricting the global supply of food).

The impacts of these events on the Phillips curve and on the *SRAS* curve are shown in Figures 10.7(a) and (b). In part(b), we see that as the supply shocks cause the *SRAS* curve to shift leftward from $SRAS_1$ to $SRAS_2$ and then to $SRAS_3$, the result is higher price levels (from Pl_1 to Pl_2 and Pl_3) and lower levels of

GDP (from Y_1 to Y_2 and Y_3), signifying increases in unemployment. In other words, decreases in *SRAS* (with *AD* constant) result in higher price levels and higher unemployment. This phenomenon is inconsistent with the logic of the Phillips curve, and was interpreted to involve *outward shifts in the Phillips curve*, which until then was thought to be stable and constant. The outward Phillips curve shifts appear in part(a), indicating that higher rates of inflation are associated with higher rates of unemployment; the moves from point a to b and c in part (a) correspond to points a, b and c in part (b).

The long-run Phillips curve and the natural rate of unemployment

♦ Discuss, using a diagram, the view that there is a long-run Phillips curve that is vertical at the natural rate of unemployment and therefore there is no trade-off between the unemployment rate and the inflation rate in the long run.

♦ Explain that the natural rate of unemployment is the rate of unemployment that exists when the economy is producing at the full employment level of output.

In the late 1970s, the Nobel Prize-winning, monetarist economist Milton Friedman attacked the idea of a stable negative relationship between inflation and unemployment, and argued that there is only a temporary trade-off between inflation and unemployment, not a permanent one. Friedman made a distinction between a short-run Phillips curve and a long-run Phillips curve.

The short-run Phillips curve is what we have considered above in Figure 10.6(a), which we can see once again in Figure 10.8(a), represented by $SRPC_1$ and $SRPC_2$. According to Milton Friedman, in the long run,

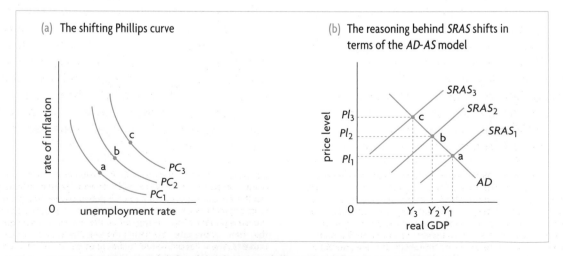

Figure 10.7 Stagflation: outward shifts of the short-run Phillips curve due to decreasing *SRAS*

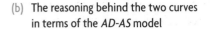

HL

(a) The shape of the *LRPC* and *SRPC*

(b) The reasoning behind the two curves
in terms of the *AD-AS* model

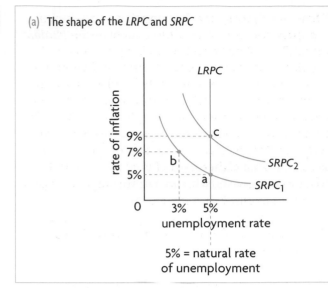

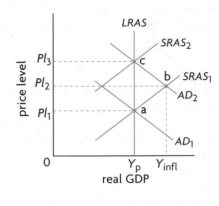

Figure 10.8 The short-run and long-run Phillips curves

this negative relationship no longer holds. Instead, the long-run Phillips curve is vertical at the level of 'full employment', or where unemployment equals the **natural rate of emploment**. (In fact, the 'natural rate of unemployment' is a concept first introduced by Milton Friedman.) The long-run Phillips curve is *LRPC* in Figure 10.8(a).

Why is the long-run Phillips curve vertical at the economy's natural rate of unemployment? The answer is quite simple: it is so for the same reasons that the *LRAS* curve is vertical at the level of real GDP corresponding to the natural rate of unemployment (see pages 248–9). Consider Figure 10.8, and suppose the economy is initially at point a in both parts. (Note that Figure 10.8(b) is the same as Figure 9.8(b), page 249.) In part (b), point a indicates that the economy is at a point of long-run equilibrium on AD_1, $SRAS_1$ and the *LRAS* curve, with real GDP equal to potential GDP shown by Y_p. At Y_p, unemployment is equal to the natural rate of unemployment, which we assume to be 5%. In part (a), point a indicates that the economy is on a short-run Phillips curve, $SRPC_1$, where it is experiencing a rate of inflation of 5% and unemployment of 5%, or the natural rate of unemployment.

Suppose there occurs an increase in aggregate demand, so that the *AD* curve in part (b) shifts from AD_1 to AD_2. In the short run the economy moves to point b on the $SRAS_1$ curve, corresponding to a

higher price level, Pl_2, increased real GDP, Y_{infl}, and lower unemployment (unemployment falls below the natural rate). This corresponds to point b on the $SRPC_1$ in part (a), where there is a higher inflation rate of 7% and lower unemployment at 3%.

The economy moved to point b in the short run, because in the short run wages are constant; with the price level increasing, firm profitability increases, output increases and unemployment falls. But in the long run, point b cannot be a point of equilibrium, because, as we know from Chapter 9, wages will rise to meet the increases in the price level, causing the *SRAS* curve to shift leftward from $SRAS_1$ to $SRAS_2$, where it intersects AD_2 at a point on the *LRAS* curve, or point c. Point c in part (b) is associated with a higher price level Pl_3, but real GDP has fallen back to Y_p, and the rate of unemployment has returned to the natural rate. In part (a), these changes mean the economy has moved to point c, where the short-run Phillips curve has shifted to the right to $SRPC_2$ (remember, when the *SRAS* curve shifts leftward with a constant *AD* curve, the *SRPC* curve shifts rightward, as we saw in Figure 10.7). At point c, there is a higher rate of inflation, now standing at 9%, and unemployment has climbed back up to 5%, or the natural rate. The vertical line connecting a and c is the long-run Phillips curve (*LRPC*), situated at the natural rate of unemployment.[10]

---

[10] This same argument is often made in terms of actual and expected rates of inflation. Let's assume that when the economy is initially at point a, nominal wages are set on the expectation that the rate of inflation will be 5%, and therefore nominal wages have been agreed with employers to increase by 5% so as to maintain a constant real wage. Let's say that the increase in aggregate demand, however, in actual fact gives rise to an inflation rate of 7%. Real wages decline as a result, firm profitability increases, real GDP increases as the economy moves upward along $SRAS_1$, and unemployment falls below the natural rate to 3%. Thus we have the movement from point

a to point b on $SRAS_1$ and on $SRPC_1$. In the long run, the economy moves to point c because nominal wages adjust to actual rates of inflation, with the result that real wages increase to their previous level, firm profitability falls to its original level, real GDP falls to Yp, and unemployment climbs back to the natural rate of 5%. The only difference from the initial equilibrium is that there is now a higher rate of inflation, of 9%. In the long run, when the actual rate of inflation is equal to the expected rate of inflation, nominal wages increase in line with the actual rate of inflation, real wages remain constant, and the trade-off between inflation and unemployment disappears.

According to the short-run Phillips curve in Figure 10.6(a), there is a negative relationship between the rate of inflation and the unemployment rate, suggesting that in the short run policy-makers can choose between the competing alternatives of low inflation or low unemployment by using policies that affect aggregate demand. The long-run Phillips curve is vertical at the natural rate of unemployment, indicating that unemployment is independent of the rate of inflation, and that policy-makers do not have a choice between the two competing alternatives. In the long run, the only impact of an increase in aggregate demand is to increase the rate of inflation, while the level of real output and unemployment remain unchanged at the natural rate of unemployment.

Since the natural rate of unemployment occurs at long run equilibrium, it is also known as *equilibrium unemployment*.

The short-run Phillips curve is a tool preferred by Keynesian economists, who see in this the possibility of using policies that focus on influencing aggregate demand to make choices about the rate of inflation and the rate of unemployment (and therefore the level of real GDP). By contrast, the long-run Phillips curve is an analytical tool preferred by monetarist/new classical economists, who are highly skeptical about the effectiveness of demand-side policies, and who use it to show that expansionary demand-side policies are more likely to result in inflation than to influence unemployment and real GDP. These economists prefer policies that focus on influencing aggregate supply. We will come back to these issues in Chapter 12.

Theory of knowledge

Choosing between low unemployment and low inflation: the role of politics and ideology in economic policy

We return to the question posed at the end of the Theory of knowledge feature on page 274: what is so important about measuring the natural rate of unemployment? In addition, how may the choice of policy goals be affected by the general political mood and ideology of societies and their governments?

Based on the Phillips curve analysis, we can easily answer the first question. If the actual rate of unemployment is above the natural rate, policy-makers can use demand-side policies to increase aggregate demand, without fearing inflation. If, however actual unemployment is at or below the natural rate, any increase in aggregate demand only temporarily lowers unemployment, as this will go back to the natural rate once wages have adjusted, only at a higher price level (see Figure 10.8). In the long run, the increase in aggregate demand only creates inflation. Therefore, knowing the natural rate is important as a guide to policy-makers.

However, if the natural rate changes often, and cannot even be accurately estimated (see page 274), there may be serious doubts about how reliable it is as the basis for guiding policy. Yet, since the 1970s, Friedman's thinking has been highly influential in creating a policy approach in many countries that focuses on keeping inflation low, even if unemployment is high. The argument is that *since demand-side policies to change aggregate demand cannot lower unemployment anyway, policy should focus on keeping inflation low.*

Many economists disagree with this perspective. According to Nobel Prize-winning economist Joseph Stiglitz:

'Policies that focus exclusively on inflation are misguided ... As a practical matter, ... the relationship between unemployment and inflation is highly unstable. It is virtually impossible to discern the relationship from the data except in a few isolated periods.

[Policy-makers] face considerable uncertainty about the level of the [natural rate of unemployment]. Thus, they still face a trade-off between pushing unemployment too low, and setting off an episode of inflation, and not pushing hard enough resulting in an unnecessary waste of resources.

How one views these risks depends on the costs of undoing mistakes ... The weight of the evidence indicates that the cost of undoing the mistake of pushing unemployment down too far is itself very low... In this view, [policy-makers] should aggressively pursue low unemployment, until it is shown that inflation is rising.

By contrast, inflation "hawks"[11] argue that inflation must be attacked [preventively]... [T]his stance is a matter of religion, not economic science. There is simply little or no empirical evidence that inflation, at the low to moderate rates that have prevailed in recent decades, has any significant harmful real effects on output, employment, growth or the distribution of income. Nor is there evidence that inflation, should it increase slightly, cannot be reversed at a relatively minor cost ...

(continued over)

The view [that nothing can be done about unemployment] belongs to a school of modern macroeconomics that assumes ... perfectly competitive markets... Because markets [in this view] are always efficient, there is no need for government intervention. More [dangerously], many supporters of this view, when confronted with the reality of unemployment, argue that it arises only because of government-imposed rigidities and trade unions. In their "ideal" world without either, there would, they claim, be no unemployment.'[12]

The idea that control of inflation is more important than keeping unemployment low is politically conservative, and is often embraced by people who believe in the superiority of free markets over government intervention to solve economic problems. Less conservative economists and workers who have only their job to rely on as a source of income, tend to prefer low unemployment over low inflation (provided of course that inflation is moderate and does not get out of hand). They also tend to favour some intervention in markets aiming to keep unemployment low.

The natural rate concept, favouring low inflation over low unemployment, became attractive to policy-makers for two reasons. One was that because of stagflation, it forced economists to question the Keynesian use of demand-side policies to deal with economic fluctuations. The second, and very important reason, was that since the late 1970s, there occurred a shift in the general political mood *away*

from government intervention and toward the market (particularly in the United States and United Kingdom); the natural rate concept with its strong free-market orientation, offered itself as an appealing theoretical approach to policy-making. Its free-market recommendations, including abolishing or reducing minimum wages and reducing labour union power, were attractive to policy-makers who opposed intervention in markets. Therefore the natural rate concept was conveniently adopted as a guide to policy, placing a greater emphasis on controlling inflation rather than reducing unemployment.

---

[11] Inflation hawks are policy-makers who believe that inflation has highly negative effects and should be controlled.
[12] Joseph Stiglitz (2006) *The Phelps Factor*, Project Syndicate.

Thinking points

- What does Stiglitz mean when he says the perspective of inflation hawks 'is a matter of religion, not economic science'?
- On the basis of what knowledge criteria have societies made a consistent choice over many years to make a priority of low inflation over low unemployment?
- Why do many economists consider the policy choice between low inflation and low unemployment to be a battle between conservative and non-conservative economists?

Test your understanding 10.8

1 Using the concept of the short-run Phillips curve, explain why many economists during the 1960s considered that policy-makers had a choice between low inflation and high unemployment, or high inflation and low unemployment.

2 (a) What events of the 1970s and 1980s made economists believe that the short-run relationship between inflation and unemployment was unstable (not fixed and permanent)? (b) Explain, using a diagram(s) and the concept of stagflation, the relationship between shifts in the *SRAS* curve and the position of the short-run Phillips curve.

3 (a) Using one or more diagrams, show how the long-run Phillips curve differs from

the short-run Phillips curve. (b) What does the long-run Phillips curve tell us about the relationship between the rate of inflation and the rate of unemployment in the long run?

4 (a) What is the relationship between the long-run Phillips curve and the natural rate of unemployment? (b) What is the relationship between the long-run Phillips curve and the full employment level of output?

5 According to the theory of the Phillips curve, what will happen to the rate of inflation, the rate of unemployment and real GDP if policy-makers attempt to increase aggregate demand in order to increase the level of real GDP (a) in the short run, and (b) in the long run?

$1457 in 2010 and $1410 in 2011. By how much did real GDP *per capita* grow in 2009–10 and in 2010–11?

$$2009\text{–}10 \text{ change in real GDP } per\ capita = \frac{1457 - 1402}{1402} \times 100$$

$$= \frac{55}{1402} \times 100 = 3.9\%$$

$$2009\text{–}11 \text{ change in real GDP } per\ capita = \frac{1410 - 1457}{1457} \times 100$$

$$= \frac{-47}{1457} \times 100 = -3.2\%$$

Note that in the second period, economic growth was negative.

Relating growth in real GDP to growth in real GDP per capita

Suppose real GDP is growing in a hypothetical economy, so it has a positive growth rate. Does this mean it also has positive *per capita* GDP growth? The answer depends on how fast the population is growing. If real GDP is growing faster than the population, then the amount of real GDP that corresponds to each person on average increases, resulting in positive growth in real GDP *per capita*. If, on the other hand, the population is growing faster than real GDP, then the amount of GDP per person on average decreases, and the growth rate of real GDP *per capita* is negative.

If we know the percentage change in real GDP and the percentage change in the population, we can find the percentage change in real GDP *per capita* in a very simple way:

% change in real GDP *per capita* = % change in real GDP – % change in population

For example, if real GDP grew by 2% in a year, and the population grew by 1.5%, then real GDP *per capita* growth was 0.5%. If, however, the population grew by 2.5%, then the % change in real GDP *per capita* was –0.5%, indicating that output per person fell.

The significance of economic growth

Economic growth rates achieved by countries around the world vary widely. While some countries experience rapid growth, others grow much more slowly, while others contract for a period of time. This can be seen in Table 11.1, showing average annual growth rates of real GDP *per capita* for several countries for the period 1990–2007. At the bottom of the table, we see that the world growth rate over the same period was 1.6% per year on average.

	Average annual growth (%) 1990–2007
China	8.9
Vietnam	6.0
Ireland	5.8
India	4.5
Botswana	4.3
Greece	2.7
United Kingdom	2.4
United States	2.0
Argentina	1.5
Japan	1.0
Switzerland	0.8
Kenya	0.0
Paraguay	−0.3
Moldova	−1.3
Burundi	−2.7
World	**1.6**

Table 11.1   Real GDP *per capita* percentage growth

Source: Data from United Nations Development Programme, *Human Development Report 2009*, (available at http://hdr.undp.org/en/reports/).

Differing growth rates have enormous implications for a country's economic performance over long periods of time. Let's consider what would happen to *per capita* GDPs of three hypothetical economies that grow at different rates over a period of 17 years (as in the table). Imagine that each economy starts out in the year 2000 with a GDP *per capita* of $1000. The first one grows for 17 years at the high annual rate of 8.9%; the second country grows at the world average rate of 1.6%; and the third country contracts at the rate of –2.7% (negative growth). The results are presented in Table 11.2.

The country that grows at 8.9% per year for 17 years succeeds in more than quadrupling its GDP *per capita*. The country that grows at the world average rate of 1.6% per year for 17 years only adds $310 to its GDP *per capita*. In contrast, the country that contracts at 2.7% per year for 17 years loses one-third of its *per capita* GDP.

2000 GDP *per capita*	Annual growth rate	2017 GDP *per capita*
$1000	8.9%	$4261
$1000	1.6%	$1310
$1000	−2.7%	$634

Table 11.2   Growth of real GDP *per capita* in hypothetical economies

The enormous cumulative impact that rates of growth have on levels of real GDP *per capita* explains why governments around the world focus strongly on policies intended to increase their growth.

Test your understanding 11.1

1 Describe the meaning of economic growth.

2 When we calculate economic growth, should we use nominal or real values of GDP? Why?

3 What is the advantage of calculating growth of real GDP in *per capita* terms rather than growth of real GDP?

4 **(higher level)** Suppose an economy had real GDP *per capita* of €1579 in 2007, €1611 in 2008 and €1597 in 2009. Find the rate of economic growth **(a)** in 2007–8, and **(b)** in 2008–9. **(c)** When did the economy experience negative growth?

5 **(higher level)** How is it possible that a country can have positive real GDP growth and yet have negative real GDP *per capita* growth?

6 **(higher level)** Suppose that an economy's real GDP grew by 2.2% in 2007, and its population grew by 1.5% during the same year. By how much did its real GDP *per capita* grow?

The production possibilities model and the causes of economic growth

Explaining economic growth in terms of the production possibilities model

Increases in actual output

♦ Describe, using a production possibilities curve (*PPC*) diagram, economic growth as an increase in actual output caused by factors including a reduction in unemployment and increases in productive efficiency, leading to a movement of a point inside the *PPC* to a point closer to the *PPC*.

What are the causes of growth? We can find the answer to this question in the production possibilities model studied in Chapter 1 (page 5). Remember that the production possibilities curve (*PPC*) shows combinations of maximum output that can be produced by an economy with fixed resources and technology, *provided there is full or maximum*

employment of resources and productive efficiency. Maximum employment in this model does not mean 'full employment' as in *AD-AS* models; it means that all resources are employed to the fullest extent and there is no unemployment.

In Chapter 1, page 6, we learned that any economy is most likely to be actually situated at some point inside its *PPC*, as it is very difficult ever to achieve full productive efficiency and maximum employment of all resources. The further away an economy is situated from its *PPC*, the greater is resource unemployment and productive inefficiency. Therefore, by reducing unemployment and increasing productive efficiency, a country moves closer to its *PPC* and increases the actual quantity of output produced. Therefore, *reductions in unemployment and increases in productive efficiency are two factors that can cause growth of actual output*. In Figure 11.1(a), the movement from point A to point B illustrates growth of actual output.

Increases in production possibilities

♦ Describe, using a *PPC* diagram, economic growth as an increase in production possibilities caused by factors including increases in the quantity and quality of resources, leading to outward *PPC* shifts.

Reduction of unemployment and inefficiencies can only result in a limited amount of economic growth. As the economy moves closer to its *PPC*, the ability to achieve more growth is exhausted, and more growth can only occur if there is an increase in production possibilities, illustrated by an outward shift of the *PPC*. An outward shift of the *PPC* means the economy can produce more of both goods (X and Y), shown in Figure 11.1(b) by the shifts from PPC_1 to PPC_2 to PPC_3. In this figure, the increases in production possibilities are accompanied by outward movements of the economy's points of actual production, from A to B to C.

The factors that lead to outward shifts of the *PPC*, or increases in production possibilities are:

• increases in the quantity of resources (factors of production) in the economy

• improvements in the quality of resources (for example, through more educated labour, or improved physical capital through technological change).

As its production possibilities increase, an economy must make efforts to keep unemployment at low levels and reduce inefficiencies to ensure that its actual

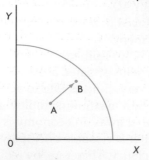

(a) Economic growth as an increase in actual output caused by reductions in unemployment and productive inefficiency

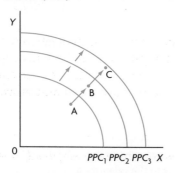

(b) Economic growth as an increase in production possibilities caused by increases in resource quantities or improvements in resource quality

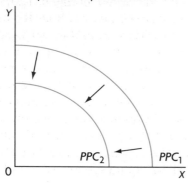

(c) Decrease in production possibilities

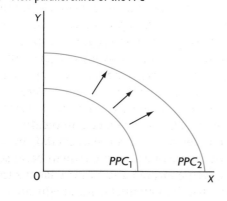

(d) Non-parallel shifts of the PPC

Figure 11.1 Using the production possibilities model to illustrate economic growth

output continues to grow along with production possibilities, as in Figure 11.1(b). For example, an increase in the size of the labour force will do little to increase actual output produced if much of this labour remains unemployed (in this case the economy could remain stuck at point A even as PPC_1 shifts to PPC_2). Similarly, the discovery of major oil reserves may do little to expand actual output if these reserves remain unexploited, or if their exploitation is undertaken inefficiently.

The *PPC* can also shift inward, indicating a decrease in production possibilities, or that less of the two goods can be produced, as shown in Figure 11.1(c). This results from a decrease in the quantity of resources or deterioration in resource quality.

An outward or inward shift need not be parallel; this is illustrated in Figure 11.1(d). For example, a technological change favouring the production of one good (X) increases the production of that good proportionately more. Similarly, an influx of unskilled workers into a country results in a larger proportionate increase in the production of goods using relatively more unskilled labour.

Investment, capital and productivity

The roles of physical, human and natural capital in economic growth

♦ Explain the importance of investment for economic growth, referring to investment in physical capital, human capital and natural capital.

To understand why increases in resource quantities and improvements in resource quality cause increases in production possibilities, we will use the expanded meaning of *capital*, introduced in Chapter 1 (page 4). 'Capital' generally refers to resources that can produce a future stream of benefits. This future stream of benefits arises from investment, or spending undertaken to create that stream of benefits.

The three factors of production: land, or natural resources; labour, or human resources; and physical capital, can be interpreted as a type of 'capital':

- **Physical capital,** also referred to as 'capital goods' is the standard type of capital; as we know from Chapter 8 (page 219) it results from investments, or spending to produce machines, equipment, roads, etc.
- **Human capital** refers to the skills, abilities, knowledge and levels of health of workers. Human capital results from investments, or spending on education, training, provision of health care

services, clean water supplies, good nutrition, and generally anything that affects levels of education and health.

- **Natural capital** includes everything that traditionally falls within 'land', or 'natural resources'. It includes everything under the land (mineral deposits, metals, oil, natural gas, etc.) plus everything on the land (rivers, lakes, oceans, forests, soils, etc.), plus a country's overall natural environment and ecosystem (air, wildlife, biodiversity, climate, ozone layer, and so on). Whereas 'land' and 'natural capital' include the same things, there is an important difference in how the two terms are interpreted. 'Land' is assumed to be given by nature and does not change. 'Natural capital' does change, because it can be destroyed (by cutting down forests, polluting the air and water, depleting fish). It can also be improved (by planting more forests, improving soil quality). Maintaining natural capital and improving its quality depend on investments that aim to preserve and improve natural resource quantity and quality.

By expanding the meaning of 'capital', we have extended the meaning of 'investment' to apply to all three factors of production listed above:

Factor of production	Type of capital
physical capital	is related to investments in physical capital
labour = human resources	is related to investments in human capital
land = natural resources	is related to investments in natural capital

Investments can be undertaken by the private sector (firms or private individuals) or by the public sector (the government). There are a number of situations where government investments are necessary, particularly when there are market failures (externalities and the need to provide merit goods and public goods). Whatever the case, *investment is crucial to building capital of any type*.

We will now see how investments in the three types of capital lead to economic growth.

Physical capital, technology and economic growth

An increase in the *quantity of physical capital* involves an increase in the number of machines, tools, equipment, road systems, ports, etc. available in an economy.

An improvement in the *quality of physical capital* depends on technological advances, which lead to new and better machines, tools and equipment. Technological advances are usually incorporated into new capital goods; for example, a new computer that is faster and more powerful incorporates within it the new technology that makes it faster and more powerful. When a technological advance is incorporated into a capital good, it is referred to as being *embodied* in the new capital.

Therefore, 'improved capital goods' are capital goods that embody a new technology. Use of capital goods embodying new technologies leads to a larger quantity of output produced; for example, the use of a more powerful computer allows a worker to produce more output.

> Increases in the quantity and improvements in the quality of physical capital, arising from investments in physical capital and new technology, are among the most important sources of economic growth over long periods of time.

Human resources, human capital, and economic growth

The quantity of labour can sometimes be an important source of economic growth; for example, the influx of foreign workers into Germany in the 1960s and 1970s played an important role in promoting its growth. However, many countries (especially less developed ones) sometimes face high levels of unemployment and underemployment. Therefore, increases in the quantity of labour may not always be a source of growth.

Far more important than increases in the quantity of labour is improvement in the quality of labour, determined by skills, abilities, knowledge and levels of health of the workforce. Improved labour quality is the result of investments in human capital, including spending on education, building schools, providing meals for schoolchildren and providing vocational training; as well as spending to provide medical services, immunisation, and ensuring access by the overall population to health care services, together with the provision of sanitation and clean water supplies, and keeping the environment unpolluted.

Higher levels of skills, knowledge and health, resulting from investments in human capital, are a very important source of economic growth because a highly skilled, well-educated and healthy labour force is more productive than an unskilled, uneducated and unhealthy one: a skilled and healthy worker can produce more output than a worker who is unskilled or unhealthy.

Increased quantities of labour are unlikely to be a source of economic growth over long periods, but improvements in the quality of labour, arising from investments in human capital, are among the most important sources of growth.

Natural resources, natural capital and economic growth

When thinking about the contribution of natural resources (natural capital) to economic growth, it is useful to make a distinction between two kinds of natural capital: marketable commodities (commodities that are bought and sold) such as timber, minerals, metals, natural gas, coal and oil; and ecological resources such as soil quality, rivers, clean air, biodiversity, the ozone layer (and, more generally, common access resources).

The role of marketable commodities *Marketable commodities can contribute to growth but are not essential.* For example, the United States benefited enormously from its large tracts of good quality agricultural land, oil reserves and mineral deposits. Yet the evidence suggests that countries do not need to be rich in marketable commodity-type natural resources to achieve high rates of growth. There are many economies, such as Israel, Japan, Hong Kong, Singapore, South Korea, Switzerland, Taiwan and others, that have achieved high rates of growth over long periods and have attained high levels of GDP *per capita*, in spite of producing few if any marketable commodities.

The role of ecological goods and common access resources *Ecological goods and common access resources are crucially important to long-term growth.* Long-term economic growth depends critically on the ability of countries to maintain, and if possible improve, environmental quality, and therefore natural capital that includes common access resources. The reasons can be found in the concept of sustainability, discussed in Chapter 5, page 121, where we saw that environmental destruction on a large (unsustainable) scale means leaving behind fewer and lower quality resources for future generations. Environmental destruction can have direct effects on the amount of output produced; for example, a farmer working with poorer quality soils produces less output; fisheries in fish-depleted seas have a smaller catch. Despite this, it can also have important indirect effects; for example, workers whose health is affected by environmental pollution become less productive, and this involves depletion of human capital together with depletion of natural capital.

Analysed in terms of the production possibilities model, these effects involve an inward shift of the *PPC*

due to fewer and lower quality environmental and human resources (natural and human capital) and therefore lower (or even negative) economic growth in the future, seen in Figure 11.1(c) (page 296). Therefore, continued economic growth in the future requires investments in the present in natural capital for environmental preservation.

Marketable commodity-type natural resources can contribute to economic growth, but are not an essential source of growth. However, maintaining the quantity and quality of ecological resources through investments in natural capital is critically important for continued economic growth over long periods.

The central importance of productivity as a source of economic growth

♦ Explain the importance of improved productivity for economic growth.

The contributions of resource quantities and quality to economic growth can be summarised in the concept of **productivity**, referring to the quantity of output produced for each hour of work of the working population. For an economy as a whole, productivity can be measured as real GDP divided by the total number of hours worked.

An improvement in productivity means that workers become more productive: the quantity of output produced in an hour of work increases. Improvements in productivity lead to economic growth, because each hour of work now produces more output.

What are the factors that cause improvements in productivity? They are exactly the factors making the most important contributions to long-term economic growth discussed above.

Improvements in productivity arise from factors that make labour more productive, so that each hour of work produces more output. These factors include:

- increases in quantity and improvements in quality of physical capital (through investments in physical capital and technological change)

- improvements in the quality of labour (through investments in human capital)

- improvements in (or at least maintenance of) the quantity and quality of ecological resources (through investments in natural capital).

In the production possibilities model, productivity improvements result in outward shifts of the *PPC*.

Consumption versus investment: present choices and future growth possibilities (supplementary material)

The *PPC* model is a useful tool for illustrating how choices made by an economy in the present affect the position of its *PPC* in the future. Consider two countries, Flatland and Mountainland, with identical resources and technologies in the present, and therefore identical *PPC*s; these are shown as PPC_p in Figure 11.2 for both countries. Each country must make a choice in the present concerning what quantity of consumer goods to produce and what quantity of capital goods to produce (this may be physical, human or natural capital), that is, each must choose where it wants to be on its PPC_p.

Consumer goods are goods that satisfy immediate consumer needs and wants; they represent *consumption* in the present (for example, food, clothing, books, DVD players, cars and so on). The production of capital goods, on the other hand, depends on *investment*, which is made possible through saving (recall the circular flow model, Chapter 8, page 216). Investment therefore involves a sacrifice of some present consumption. The consumption sacrificed today is the opportunity cost of building capital.

Flatland chooses to produce relatively more consumer goods in the present (point *X*), while Mountainland chooses to produce relatively more capital goods (point *Y*). (For simplicity, we are assuming that each country can produce *on* its *PPC*.) What are the future consequences of each country's present choice? PPC_f, showing the future *PPC* for both countries, indicates that Mountainland expects to experience a larger *PPC* shift. Why is this so? Mountainland expects a larger shift because it produces more or improved capital goods, thus increasing its future production possibilities more

than Flatland. Mountainland therefore expects *greater possibilities for economic growth* in the future. This illustrates an important principle.

> In order to have long-term economic growth, it is necessary to sacrifice some consumption in the present in order to make investments that will result in the formation of new capital for use in the future.

Remember that investment is financed by saving, which is that portion of income that is not consumed. Many countries, particularly low-income developing ones, have incomes so low that most of this goes toward consumption, leaving little for saving and investment. If these countries had to rely only on their own resources, it would be very difficult for them to achieve economic growth. What can these countries do? They have two options. One is to borrow from abroad, either from other countries or from international financial institutions, and use the borrowed funds to finance investments that will help them grow. The other option is to accept foreign investments, which involve investments by foreigners in the domestic economy. We will discuss both these options in Chapter 18.

Economic growth and the *LRAS* curve

♦ Describe, using an *LRAS* diagram, economic growth as an increase in potential output caused by factors including increases in the quantity and quality of resources, leading to a rightward shift of the *LRAS* curve.

Economic growth in the context of the *PPC* model is very closely related to economic growth in *AD-AS* models. In Chapter 9, page 255, we learned about the factors that cause long-term economic growth in

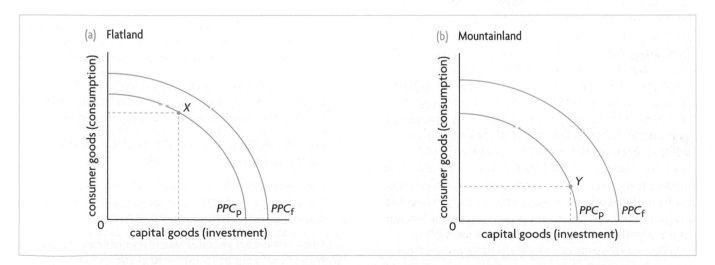

Figure 11.2 Present choices and future growth

the *AD-AS* model, showing up as shifts in the *LRAS* curve (as well as the Keynesian *AS* curve), indicating increases in potential output. These factors are summarised in Table 11.3, which also shows how they relate to the production possibilities model. We see that improved efficiency and reduced unemployment, causing points of production to move closer to a *fixed PPC*, can cause the *LRAS* curve to shift to the right (though only natural unemployment is included[1]). Also, the *LRAS* curve can shift to the right as a result of institutional changes, which are not included in the *PPC* model.[2]

AD-AS model	Factors causing growth	Production possibilities model
rightward *LRAS* shifts (increases in potential output)	increased resource quantity improved resource quality technological change	outward *PPC* shifts (increases in production possibilities)
	improved efficiency only natural ← reduced unemployment → all types	movement of production point closer to *PPC*
	institutional changes	not included

Table 11.3   Factors that cause economic growth

Real world focus

Long-term economic growth in the euro zone

According to the president of the European Central Bank, the euro zone countries* face a falling rate of growth in potential output. Whereas it is estimated that this is about 2.1%, according to forecasts it could fall to 1.25% by 2040 if reforms are not carried out. This growth rate is also lower than that of many industrialised countries.

One reason given for a low and falling growth rate in potential output is a slowdown in productivity growth, which fell from an average annual rate of 2.4% in the 1980s and early 1990s to 1.3% in the period 1996–2005. The labour force is lagging behind in the use of information and communications technology, and unemployment is high.

To increase potential output growth, it is necessary to tackle the problem of high unemployment through labour market reforms, including removing disincentives to work and increasing wage flexibility. In addition, there is a need for greater competition in product markets, as well as a reduction in bureaucratic procedures. Whereas it takes 47 days to open up a new business in Spain and 38 in Greece, it only takes 5 days in the United States. Also, it is important to implement policies that promote innovation and technological change.

---

*Euro zone countries are the countries of the European Union (EU) that have adopted the euro.
Source: Adapted from AFX Asia Focus, 'Trichet says euro zone potential growth rate mediocre', 16 October 2006.

Applying your skills

1   What type of unemployment do you think is being referred to in the extract, and what are its causes? (See Chapter 10, page 268.)

2   Use diagrams to explain the effects of a reduction in this type of unemployment on **(a)** the *LRAS* curve, and **(b)** the *PPC* model (use Table 11.3 as a guideline).

3   Using diagrams, explain how improvements in productivity impact on economic growth, in **(a)** the *AD-AS* model, and **(b)** the *PPC* model.

4   According to the extract, what factors are causes of low productivity and low potential output growth?

---

[1] This excludes cyclical unemployment, as reductions in this do not affect the position of the *LRAS* curve. See page 271 for an explanation.
[2] It is not surprising that there are some differences between the two models, as each has been constructed to illustrate different principles. The *LRAS* curve is intended to show that potential output is independent of the price level. The production possibilities model does not deal with the price level, and is better suited to illustrate the principles of resource scarcity and opportunity costs of economic choices.

1 Using diagram(s), explain the difference between an increase in actual output and an increase in production possibilities.

2 Use the production possibilities model and diagrams to show how the following can result in economic growth (positive or negative), distinguishing between *PPC* shifts and movements of a point closer to or further from a given *PPC*:

   (a) a discovery of new oil reserves

   (b) a fall in natural unemployment

   (c) an increase in cyclical unemployment

   (d) an improvement in levels of health of the population

   (e) an improvement in productive efficiency

   (f) the widespread use of a new technology

   (g) a violent conflict destroys a portion of a country's factories, machines and road system

   (h) large cuts in government spending on education and health care lower levels of education and health in a population

   (i) an increase in the quantity of capital goods

   (j) an improvement in the level of education and skills of workers

   (k) industrial pollution destroys the environment.

3 Using diagrams, explain the effects that each of the items **(a)–(k)** in question 2 will have on a country's *LRAS* curve

4 Explain the relationship between investment and capital, and relate it to physical, human and natural capital.

5 Referring to land, labour and physical capital, and the concept of capital as applied to each of these resources, explain how each one can contribute to economic growth.

6 **(a)** Define productivity. **(b)** Explain why improved productivity is important for economic growth. **(c)** What are the most important factors that result in productivity improvements? **(d)** Show productivity growth using *PPC* and *LRAS* diagrams.

7 (Optional) Using a diagram, explain why economic growth has an opportunity cost in terms of consumption in the present.

Possible consequences of economic growth

♦ Discuss the possible consequences of economic growth, including the possible impacts on living standards, unemployment, inflation, the distribution of income, the current account of the balance of payments, and sustainability.

Economic growth has many possible consequences as it affects numerous aspects of an economy. Some of the consequences are positive while others may be negative. Whether these will be positive or negative often depends on the particular circumstances that an economy finds itself in.

To examine the possible consequences of growth, we must first learn more about the macroeconomy, the international economy, as well as development economics. We will therefore return to this topic in Chapter 19, page 524, after having studied the necessary background material.

11.2 Equity in the distribution of income

Equity and the distribution of income

Equity and equality in the distribution of income

♦ Explain the difference between equity in the distribution of income and equality in the distribution of income.

The distinction between equity and equality was introduced in Chapter 1 (page 16). *Equity* is the condition of being fair or just, while *equality* is the state of being equal with respect to something. Equality with respect to income would mean that each member of a society receives exactly the same income. This may or may not be equitable, depending on how equity is interpreted. If it is believed that income distribution is equitable or fair if it is distributed equally, then equity in income distribution means income equality. However, if it is believed that it is equitable or fair for people's income to be in proportion to their work effort (a different equity principle), this would give rise to income inequality, since not everyone's work effort is the same.

total population in the economy, also in cumulative percentages (therefore this, too, runs from 0 to 100%). ('Cumulative' means that 20 represents the poorest 20% of the population, 40 represents the poorest 40%, and so on.) The diagonal line in the diagram represents perfect equality in income distribution, as it shows that if income were perfectly equally distributed, 20% of the population would received 20% of income, 40% would receive 40% of income, and so on. The Lorenz curve plots the *actual relationship* between percentages of the population and the shares of income they receive.

Figure 11.3 plots two Lorenz curves, one for Bolivia, and one for Belarus (based on the data in Table 11.4). In the case of Bolivia, the poorest 20% of the population receives 2.7% of income; this is shown by point a. Point b on Bolivia's curve is obtained by adding the 2.7% of income of the poorest quintile to the 6.5% of income received by the second quintile, giving 9.2%, or the cumulative income of the bottom 40% of the population. Similarly, point c is obtained by adding the percentages of income received by the bottom three quintiles, giving 20.2% of income, and finally to find point d we add the incomes of the bottom four quintiles, getting 38.8% of income for 80% of the population. When these points are joined together starting from 0 and going up to 100% of the population, we obtain Bolivia's Lorenz curve. Points e, f, g and h on Belarus' curve are calculated and plotted in exactly the same way.

Note that to plot a Lorenz curve, we could use income distribution figures that divide the population into ten deciles (or tenths), or any other convenient subdivision.

In general, the closer a Lorenz curve is to the diagonal representing perfect income equality, the greater is the equality in income distribution. As we can see in Figure 11.3, Belarus clearly has greater income equality than Bolivia.

The Gini coefficient

♦ Explain how the Gini coefficient is derived and interpreted.

The Gini coefficient, named after Corrado Gini, an Italian statistician, is a summary measure of the information contained in the Lorenz curve of an economy. It is defined as

$$\text{Gini coefficient} = \frac{\text{area between diagonal and Lorenz curve}}{\text{entire area under diagonal}}$$

The Gini coefficient has a value between 0 and 1. If there were perfect income equality, the coefficient would be zero, since the numerator of the ratio would be zero. The larger the Gini coefficient, and the closer it is to 1, the greater is the income inequality, since the further away is the Lorenz curve from the diagonal. (A perfectly unequal income distribution would be where a single household receives all the income of the economy, and the numerator would be equal to the entire area under the diagonal, making the Gini coefficient equal to 1.)

The last column in Table 11.4 shows Gini coefficients that correspond to each of the income distributions. Belarus' Gini coefficient is 0.28, while Bolivia's is 0.58, indicating Belarus' relatively more equal income distribution.

Table 11.5 lists the Gini coefficients of some economically more developed countries.

The **Gini coefficient** is a summary measure of income inequality, and in a Lorenz diagram is the ratio of the area between the diagonal and the Lorenz curve, to the total area under the diagonal. It has a value between 0 and 1; the closer the value is to 0, the greater the income equality; the closer the value is to 1, the greater the income inequality.

Using Lorenz curves to illustrate income redistribution

Later in this chapter, we will consider methods governments can use to redistribute income, to make the distribution of income more equal. Graphically, this appears as a shift of a country's Lorenz curve closer to the diagonal line, and is reflected in a lower Gini coefficient. Figure 11.4 shows how a Lorenz curve shifts towards the diagonal after the government pursues policies to redistribute income to increase the degree of income equality in the economy.

Country	Gini coefficient
United States	0.41
United Kingdom	0.36
Australia	0.35
Greece	0.34
Canada	0.33
Netherlands	0.31
Germany	0.28
Norway	0.26
Denmark	0.25

Table 11.5 Gini coefficient of selected economically more developed countries

Source: United Nations Development Programme, *Human Development Report 2009.*

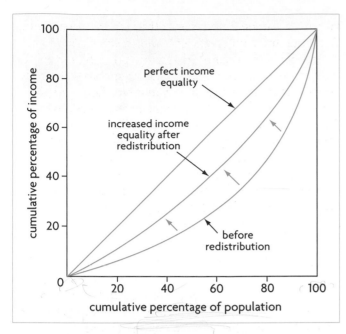

Figure 11.4   Lorenz curves and income redistribution

Test your understanding 11.4

1 What is the meaning of deciles and quintiles, and how do we use them to measure income distribution?

2 Using the data in Table 11.4, explain which country has a more equal income distribution, **(a)** Philippines or Vietnam, or **(b)** Ghana or Pakistan.

3 **(a)** Define the Gini coefficient. **(b)** How do we derive it from a Lorenz curve diagram? **(c)** What is its possible range of values? **(d)** How do we interpret its possible values with regard to income equality/inequality?

4 **(a)** Choose any two countries from Table 11.4 and draw their Lorenz curves in a single diagram. **(b)** Explain how you use your Lorenz curve to determine which country has a more equal distribution of income. **(c)** How can you use the corresponding Gini coefficients to compare the income distributions of the two countries?

5 Using the data in Table 11.5, explain whether the United Kingdom or Norway has a more equal distribution of income.

6 **(a)** How does redistribution of income change the position of a country's Lorenz curve? **(b)** How would redistribution be reflected in a Gini coefficient? (Make sure you distinguish between redistribution that increases or decreases income equality.)

Poverty

Absolute and relative poverty

♦ Distinguish between absolute poverty and relative poverty.

Poverty refers to an inability to satisfy minimal consumption needs. Beyond this general definition, there are different perspectives on how best to define poverty. In one view, poverty refers to the inability of people to satisfy their basic needs in an absolute sense that is constant and unchanging. In another, poverty is a relative concept that varies across societies and changes over time. These two perspectives are reflected in two definitions of poverty: absolute poverty and relative poverty.

Absolute poverty

Measures of **absolute poverty** begin by defining a minimum income level called a 'poverty line'. According to the OECD, a poverty line is: 'An income level that is considered minimally sufficient to sustain a family in terms of food, housing, clothing, medical needs and so on.'[3] Most countries have a national poverty line, determined by government authorities as an appropriate amount of income required to satisfy minimum needs. In addition, there are internationally determined poverty lines such as two defined by the World Bank, commonly used for developing countries:

- living on less than $1.25 a day, defined as *extreme poverty*
- living on less than $2 a day, defined as *moderate poverty.*

Once a poverty line has been determined, the amount of poverty is found by taking the percentage of a population (or the number of individuals) whose income falls below the poverty line.

Data on extreme and moderate poverty in developing countries, based on a very extensive study by the World Bank, appear in Table 11.6. The study estimates that there are nearly 1.4 billion people in the world living in extreme poverty (using the $1.25 a day poverty line), and that there are 2.6 billion people living in moderate poverty (less than $2 a day), representing nearly half the total population of developing countries.

Columns 4 and 5 in the table indicate that significant progress was made in reducing the percentage of people in extreme poverty, which fell from about 42% in 1990 to 25% in 2005. Columns 1 and 2 show that a significant

---

[3] OECD, Glossary of Statistical Terms, Poverty Line.

Region	Extreme poverty: millions of people living on less than $1.25 a day			Extreme poverty: % of population living on less than $1.25 a day		Moderate poverty: % of population living on less than $2.00 a day	
	(1) 1990	(2) 2005	(3) % change	(4) 1990	(5) 2005	(6) 1990	(7) 2005
East Asia and Pacific	873.4	316.2	−63.8	54.7	16.8	79.8	38.7
(of which China)	(683.2)	(207.7)	(−69.6)	(60.2)	(15.9)	(84.6)	(36.3)
Eastern Europe and Central Asia	9.1	17.3	90.1	2.0	3.7	6.9	8.9
Latin America and Caribbean	42.9	46.1	−7.5	9.8	8.4	19.7	16.6
Middle East and North Africa	9.7	11.0	13.4	4.3	3.6	19.7	16.9
South Asia	579.2	595.6	2.8	51.7	40.3	82.7	73.9
(of which India)	(435.5)	(455.8)	(4.7)	(51.3)	(41.6)	(82.6)	(75.6)
Sub-Saharan Africa	299.1	390.6	30.6	57.9	51.2	76.2	73.0
Total	1,813.4	1,376.7	−24.1	41.6	25.2	63.2	47.0

Table 11.6   Absolute poverty: extreme and moderate poverty

Source: Data from Shaohua Chen and Martin Ravallion (2008) 'The developing world is poorer than we thought, but no less successful in the fight against poverty', World Bank, Development Research Group, Policy Research Working Paper 4703.

decrease in terms of absolute numbers has also occurred. However, progress has been highly uneven across geographical regions. The greatest declines in extreme poverty occurred in the East Asia and Pacific region. A region of concern is Sub-Saharan Africa, where half of the total population lives in extreme poverty (column 5), and nearly three-quarters in moderate poverty (column 7). The country with the largest number of extremely poor people is India, with 42% of its total population living on less than $1.25 a day.

In addition to the World Bank's poverty lines, many developing countries also have national poverty lines. In higher income developing countries, these are often set at a higher income level than those of the World Bank, so that a larger percentage of people are considered poor by national standards. However, in lower income countries, these are usually set at a lower income level, so that a smaller percentage of people are considered poor. This is not surprising, since the World Bank's definitions of extreme and moderate poverty are arbitrary, being too low for higher income countries and too high for lower income ones.[4]

More developed countries use national poverty lines to determine absolute poverty. For example, in the United States the poverty rate was 13.2% in 2007, compared to 22.4% in 1959 when poverty first began to be measured, and 11.1% in 1973, which was the lowest rate ever recorded.[5]

Relative poverty

Relative poverty is a concept that compares the income of individuals or households in a society with median[6] incomes. It is closely related to how equally or unequally society's income is distributed among its total population. If income were equally distributed, there would be no relative poverty, since no one would be poor relative to someone else. In general, the more unequal the distribution of income, the greater is the degree of relative poverty.

The idea behind relative poverty is that poverty is much more than being unable to afford a minimum of basic goods and services. Even though people may be able to buy basic necessities, they are still poor if they cannot afford goods and services and a lifestyle that are typical in a society. The measurement of what is 'typical' is based on a standard determined by the median income level. If people's incomes fall far below this median level, they are considered poor.

---

[4] For information on specific country estimates of poverty rates, see United Nations Development Programme, Human Development Reports.
[5] Erik Eckholm, 'Last year's poverty rate was highest in 12 years' in the *New York Times*, 10 September 2009; A. M. Sharp, C. A. Register and P. W. Grimes (2006) *Economics of Social Issues*, McGraw-Hill Irwin.

[6] The 'median' is the number that is in the middle of a series of numbers. Therefore, the median income is that income that lies in the middle of all income levels, so that half of income levels are greater and half are lower. Note that the median is different from the average, or mean.

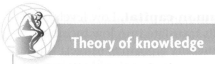
Absolute and relative poverty

The concepts of absolute and relative poverty have different implications for the meaning of poverty. The concept of absolute poverty, based on an absolute poverty line that does not change over time (except for adjustments for inflation), suggests that with economic growth everyone will eventually rise above the poverty line. Therefore, many countries that experience long-term growth have been seeing falling absolute poverty rates. The relative poverty line, by contrast, changes constantly over time as incomes grow, and the poor are those who cannot keep up with rising average/median incomes. Relative poverty has actually been *increasing* in many countries over recent decades, due to increasing income inequalities (see Chapter 17).

The following famous passage, written by Adam Smith (the 'Father of Economics') in the 18th century in his classic book, *The Wealth of Nations*, offers an explanation of the difference between the two meanings of poverty, by referring to the meaning he attaches to 'necessaries':

> 'By necessaries I understand, not only the commodities which are indispensably necessary for the support of life, but whatever the custom of the country renders it indecent for creditable people, even of the lowest order, to be without. A linen shirt, for example, is, strictly speaking, not a necessary of life. The Greeks and Romans lived, I suppose, very comfortably, though they had no linen. But in the present times, through the greater part of Europe, a creditable day-labourer would be ashamed to appear in public without a linen shirt, the want of which would be supposed to denote that disgraceful degree of poverty, which, it is presumed, nobody can well fall into without extreme bad conduct … Under necessaries therefore, I comprehend, not only those things which nature, but those things which established rules of decency have rendered necessary to the lowest rank of people.'[7]

According to Adam Smith, a person who has the basic necessities of life required for physical survival but does not have a linen shirt is relatively poor, but not absolutely poor. One who does not even have the basic necessities of life is absolutely poor (and, of course, also relatively poor).

As noted in the text, measures of poverty are important because they form the basis for anti-poverty programmes such as transfer payments. Different countries use different measures for this purpose. For example, in the United States the official poverty measure used to determine eligibility for government assistance is an absolute one; in the European Union, the official poverty measure is a relative one (though both calculate absolute and relative poverty rates).

---

[7] Adam Smith (1937) *An Inquiry into the Nature and Causes of the Wealth of Nations*, New York, Modern Library, pp. 821–2 (Book V, Chapter II, Part II, Article 4th).

Thinking points

- Does society have a moral obligation to help the poor?
- Adam Smith identifies 'necessaries' to be 'those things which established rules of decency have rendered necessary'. Would he define poverty in the absolute or in the relative sense?
- What kinds of criteria are important for making a choice between absolute and relative poverty as the basis for anti-poverty programmes (social scientific, ethical, or other)?
- A society's choice between an absolute or relative poverty measure as the basis for policy rests on some principle of equity. What do you think might be an equity principle for the US use of absolute poverty and for the EU use of relative poverty? How do the equity principles differ from each other?

Measurement of relative poverty involves specifying a particular percentage of median income below which there is poverty. Often this is taken to be 50%. For example, say the median annual family income in an economy is $20 000. Taking 50% of this, we have $10 000. Any family whose annual income falls below $10 000 is considered poor (in relative terms). Table 11.7 presents data on relative poverty in some economically more developed countries.

Whereas the discussion above has been in terms of *national* poverty rates, it is very important to note that poverty rates differ widely among social groups in a society. In general, older people, children, single-parent households, women, and racial and ethnic groups that suffer discrimination, face higher poverty rates than national averages. This applies to most countries in the world, both more and less developed.

The role of cash transfers

Cash transfers are used in many countries around the world, both economically more and less developed, as a method to redistribute income and reduce income inequalities. In more developed countries, they are used to maintain income during difficult times, such as during unemployment, sickness or disability. In New Zealand, they amount to 13% of household disposable income; in Sweden they amount to more than 32%.

Some economically less developed countries, like Brazil and Mexico, use conditional cash transfers, meaning that these are granted to poor households on condition that they meet certain requirements, usually linked with children's education and health care. More than 30 countries offer conditional cash transfer programmes. However, it has been found that such programmes cannot succeed on their own, as it is also important to ensure availability and quality of necessary education and health services. In addition, conditional transfers are administratively more demanding, requiring greater co-ordination of different agencies and monitoring of compliance.

Governments and international organisations are discovering the important contributions to income redistribution of unconditional cash transfers. There is evidence that unconditional cash transfers may be more appropriate for securing poor people's access to food and other basic necessities, especially in Africa where basic services are often in short supply. A project in Malawi showed that such cash transfers led to increased school enrolment, improved nutrition, and increased expenditures on basic necessities.

Source: Adapted from United Nations Human Development Programme, *Human Development Report 2010*.

Applying your skills

1 Explain how cash transfers can help redistribute income.

2 Using a Lorenz curve diagram, show how the Lorenz curve of a country would change following an increase in cash transfers toward poor households. How would the Gini coefficient change?

3 Explain why unconditional cash transfers may in certain situations be more effective than conditional transfers. How does this relate to the provision of merit goods by the government?

Subsidised provision or direct provision of merit goods

♦ Explain that governments undertake expenditures to provide directly, or to subsidise, a variety of socially desirable goods and services (including health care services, education, and infrastructure that includes sanitation and clean water supplies), thereby making them available to those on low incomes.

Merit goods are goods that are beneficial for consumers, often with positive consumption externalities, that are underprovided by the market and underconsumed (see page 116). From the point of view of income redistribution, the issue here concerns low consumer incomes and poverty. If income distribution were left entirely to the market, two of the most important merit goods that would be underconsumed due to low incomes and poverty would be education and health care. Education and health care are so important that they are often viewed as fundamental human rights.

This means that it is not enough for governments just to provide education and health care (to supplement the insufficient quantities provided by the market). Governments must also ensure that these are affordable for very low income groups. This can be accomplished when governments offer education and health care services that are free (or nearly free) of charge to consumers, and is called 'subsidised provision' of the goods and services, because the government offers them to consumers at a price (often zero) that is far below the cost of producing them. Governments may also provide subsidies to private providers to increase supply (see page 117). In addition, education and health care can be made more affordable through transfer payments (see the Real world focus feature above).

Other merit goods that may require subsidised or direct provision by the government, and that are especially important in developing countries that concentrate large groups of people on very low incomes, include **infrastructure**, which includes numerous kinds of physical capital, such as clean water supplies, sanitation and sewerage. Subsidisation or direct provision by the government makes these more affordable to poor people. (Infrastructure will be discussed in more detail in Chapter 17.)

Whatever the merit good, the government uses tax revenues to provide the good in larger quantities than the market would have provided, and additionally to make it available at very low (or zero) prices. The provision of subsidised merit goods offers some redistribution by making certain goods available to people on low incomes who would not otherwise be able to afford them.

Government intervention in markets

Governments often intervene in markets in ways that change the distribution of income. We studied some examples in Chapter 4, such as:

- minimum wage legislation – by setting a legal minimum wage, the government raises the lowest permissible wage above the equilibrium market level, thereby raising the wages of low-income (and usually unskilled) workers
- food price ceilings – by setting maximum prices for certain food products (prices below the market-determined equilibrium price), governments can make food more affordable for low-income groups
- price floors for farmers – by setting legal minimum prices for certain agricultural products (often involving government purchases of the resulting surpluses), governments raise their prices above the equilibrium market price in order to support farmers' incomes.

Taxation

Taxation makes redistribution possible through transfer payments and subsidised provision of merit goods since these are paid for out of tax revenues. However, over and above this important role, taxation is itself an important instrument for redistribution, because it can lower income inequalities by taking more taxes from the rich than from the poor. This is the topic of the next section.

Test your understanding 11.6

1 What are transfer payments?

2 Using examples, explain how transfer payments, subsidised or direct government production of merit goods, and government intervention in markets contribute to income redistribution.

The role of taxation in promoting equity (income redistribution)

Taxes are the most important source of government revenues, and provide the funds for many purposes, such as public goods, transfer payments and merit goods, correcting externalities, providing subsidies, changing the allocation of resources, changing the distribution of income, and many more. We are now interested in seeing how taxes can be used to achieve greater equity in the distribution of income, interpreted as greater equality.

Direct and indirect taxes

♦ Distinguish between direct and indirect taxes, providing examples of each, and explain that direct taxes may be used as a mechanism to redistribute income.

There are two very broad categories of taxes: direct taxes and indirect taxes.

Direct taxes

Direct taxes are taxes paid directly to the government tax authorities by the taxpayer. The most important kinds of direct taxes include the following:

- **Personal income taxes.** This is the most important source of government tax revenues in many countries (especially more developed countries), and involves taxes paid by households or individuals in households. They are paid on all forms of income, including wages, rental income, interest income and dividends (which are income from ownership of shares in a company, and are therefore income from profits).
- **Corporate income taxes.** Corporations are businesses (firms) that have formed a legal body called a 'corporation' that is legally separate from its owners. Corporate income taxes are taxes on the profits of corporations.
- **Wealth taxes.** These are taxes on the ownership of assets. The two most common wealth taxes are *property taxes*, based on the value of property owned, and *inheritance taxes*, based on the value of property inherited.

The revenue collected from all of the above forms of taxation is paid into the government's budget, and is used to finance a broad variety of government expenditures. In contrast to these, there is an additional form of direct taxation:

Calculations using marginal and average tax rates (higher level topic)

♦ Calculate the marginal rate of tax and the average rate of tax from a set of data.

Average tax rates

An **average tax rate** is defined as tax paid divided by total income, expressed as a percentage. All the tax rates appearing in Table 11.8 are average tax rates.

An average tax rate can be calculated for any type of tax. For example, suppose a family with an annual income of €50 000 spends €40 000 on goods and services, which includes an *indirect* tax (a value added tax or sales tax) of 18%. Therefore 18% of the €40 000 represents payments on the indirect tax. This family must pay a total amount of €40 000 × 0.18 = €7200 on indirect taxes. As a percentage of income, this amount of tax represents $\frac{€7200}{€50 000} = 0.144$, or 14.4% of income.

Therefore, the average indirect tax rate for this family is 14.4%. (You may wish to review the 'Quantatitive techniques' chapter on the CD-ROM, page 1, on the use of percentages.)

Suppose we have information on a family's average income tax rate and its average indirect tax rate, and we would like to find its total average tax rate, i.e. all taxes paid, direct plus indirect, as a percentage of income. To calculate this, we add the two average tax rates to find the sum. If, in the example above, the same family has an average income tax rate of 22.7%, what is its total average tax rate? It is 22.7% + 14.4% = 37.1%. This means that 37.1% of the total income of €50 000 is paid as taxes, including both direct and indirect.

Marginal tax rates

A **marginal tax rate** is defined as the tax rate paid on additional income. In the real world, income taxes in a progressive tax system are calculated using successive layers of income, and applying a different tax rate to each layer. The layers of income are called tax brackets, and the corresponding tax rates are called 'marginal tax rates'. A numerical example will help you understand this. Column 1 of Table 11.10 shows tax brackets (the layers of income) in a hypothetical economy, and column 2 gives us the marginal tax rate that applies to each bracket.

Suppose we want to calculate the amount of income tax paid on an annual income of $59 000. The total tax paid will be 0 for the first $10 000 of this income; 9% on income between $10 001 and $25 000; 22% on

income between $25 001 and $55 000; and finally 40% on income between $55 001 and $59 000. We calculate the total tax paid as follows.

$$(0 \times \$10\,000) + (0.09 \times \$15\,000) + (0.22 \times \$30\,000)$$
$$+ (0.40 \times \$4000)$$
$$= 0 + \$1350 + \$6600 + \$1600 = \$9550$$

What is the average tax rate for the income of $59 000? It is total tax paid divided by income expressed as a percentage, or $\frac{\$9550}{\$59\,000} = 0.162$, or 16.2%.

Using the information in Table 11.10, let's now calculate the income tax paid on income of $175 000.

$$(0 \times \$10\,000) + (0.09 \times \$15\,000) + (0.22 \times \$30\,000$$
$$+ (0.40 \times \$60\,000) + (0.55 \times \$60\,000)$$
$$= 0 + \$1350 + \$6600 + \$24\,000 + \$33\,000$$
$$= \$64\,950 = \text{income tax paid}$$

The average tax rate on income of $175 000 is 37.1%

i.e. $\frac{\$64\,950}{\$175\,000} = 0.371$, or 37.1%

Comparing the average tax rate for income of $59 000 (16.2%) with the average tax rate of income of $175 000 (37.1%), we see that the higher income has a higher average tax rate, just as expected since this is a progressive tax system.

(1) Annual income ($)	(2) Marginal tax rate (%)
0–10 000	0
10 001–25 000	9
25 001–55 000	22
55 001–115 000	40
115 001 or more	55

Table 11.10   Calculating marginal and average tax rates

Test your understanding 11.8

The following questions are based on the data in Table 11.10.

1 Calculate the amount of income tax paid by families with annual income levels of **(a)** $6500 **(b)** $15 700 **(c)** $31 000 **(d)** $47 000, and **(e)** $120 000.

2 For each of the items in question 1, **(a)** calculate each family's average income tax rate. **(b)** What happens to the average tax rate as income increases? Why? **(c)** What is each family's marginal tax rate?

3 Suppose that the family with income of $31 000 has spending of $25 000 on goods and services, of which 20% is an indirect tax.
   (a) What is the amount of indirect tax paid?
   (b) Calculate the amount of indirect tax paid as a percentage of income (the average indirect tax rate).

4 For the family with income of $31 000, calculate its average tax rate, including both direct and indirect taxes (the average income tax rate plus the average indirect tax rate).

Equity in income distribution versus efficiency: an evaluation

♦ Evaluate government policies to promote equity (taxation, government expenditure and transfer payments) in terms of their potential positive or negative effects on efficiency in the allocation of resources.

The issue of a possible trade-off between equity and efficiency was introduced in Chapter 1, page 15 (you may find it helpful to refer to this). While most economists and others would agree that a certain amount of income redistribution is necessary in any society, there are intense disagreements over how much is appropriate and how this should be best achieved to avoid possible negative consequences on efficiency.

Taxes and allocative efficiency

Taxes affect the allocation of resources and make it different from what would have been achieved in a free market economy (with no government intervention). When taxes are used to correct market failures, they are intended to move the economy towards a more efficient allocation of resources (see Chapter 5). However, of the very large variety of taxes levied by governments, most are not implemented with the intention of correcting market failures. Many economists argue that a variety of taxes worsen the allocation of resources, causing allocative inefficiency. The reason is that taxes change the after-tax relative prices of goods and services and factors of production. Since resource allocation in the market system is guided by prices that act as signals and incentives, and since prices in the absence of market failures give rise to the 'best' allocation of resources, it follows that some taxes cause allocative inefficiency.

Income taxes, equity and efficiency in resource markets

A relatively high degree of equality in income distribution cannot be achieved without a highly progressive tax system, which would involve taxing significant amounts of income away from high-income earners. According to a perspective we will study in Chapter 12 ('supply-side economics'), high income taxes act as a disincentive to work as well as to save, particularly among high-income earners who would be taxed more heavily. Income taxes reduce after-tax income, and as a result reduce the quantity of labour offered in the market, and also reduce savings. Lower savings has a negative effect on investment, and therefore on the production of new capital goods. Therefore, in this perspective high income taxes affect the price mechanism in the resource markets of labour and capital, causing allocative inefficiency. Lower quantities of labour and capital in turn translate into lower rates of growth for the economy.

(Higher level students may note that the argument is usually made in terms of the disincentive effects of high *marginal* tax rates.)

Indirect taxes, equity and efficiency in product markets

General expenditure taxes/sales taxes are commonly used around the world on the grounds that when a tax is levied *on all goods and services at the same percentage*, then there is no change in relative prices, and therefore no impact on resource allocation, because the signals and incentives that prices convey remain the same. Therefore, general expenditure taxes are consistent with the goal of allocative efficiency. However, these taxes are regressive (see page 313), thus leading to a more *unequal* distribution of income.

In practice, as we have seen, different VAT rates or sales taxes are sometimes applied to different categories of goods and services, while some goods and services are exempted from taxes altogether, the objective being to exclude certain necessities from taxation and make them more affordable to low-income earners. Such exemptions are consistent with the principle of increasing equity in the distribution of income. However, at the same time the allocation of resources is affected because of relative price changes in product markets.

In the case of excise taxes (indirect taxes imposed on specific goods, discussed in Chapters 4 and 5), the outcome again affects the allocation of resources by changing relative prices and hence the signals and incentives they convey. Excise taxes intended a period of successive deficits. An important advantage of doing so is that interest payments on past loans are reduced. Since interest payments are a type of current expenditure (as noted above), reducing these frees up some funds that can be used for more desirable current expenditures (such as provision of merit goods) or for capital expenditures. Also, if there is a budget deficit, the reduction in interest payments allows the size of the deficit to be reduced.

Test your understanding 12.1

1 Outline the objectives of fiscal policy.

2 Explain **(a)** the sources of government revenues, and **(b)** the types of government expenditures.

3 What is the difference between 'government budget deficit' and 'government debt'?

4 Explain the meaning of public debt in relation to budget surpluses and deficits.

5 Explain the difference between a budget deficit, budget surplus and balanced budget.

The role of fiscal policy

Fiscal policy and aggregate demand

♦ Explain how changes in the level of government expenditure and/or taxes can influence the level of aggregate demand in an economy.

Fiscal policy refers to manipulations by the government of its own expenditures and taxes to influence the level of aggregate demand. (Since this is purposeful policy, it is 'discretionary'.) The components of aggregate demand are consumption (C), investment (I), government spending (G), and net exports ($X-M$). Fiscal policy can affect three of these four components (see Table 9.1, page 240):

• The level of the government's own spending, G, can be changed.

• The level of consumption spending, C, can be influenced if the government changes taxes on consumers (personal income taxes), changing their level of disposable income, which is the income of consumers after income taxes have been paid.

• The level of investment spending, I, can also be influenced if the government changes taxes on business profits.

Expansionary fiscal policy

♦ Describe the mechanism through which expansionary fiscal policy can help an economy close a deflationary (recessionary) gap.

♦ Construct a diagram to show the potential effects of expansionary fiscal policy, outlining the importance of the shape of the aggregate supply curve.

Suppose the economy is experiencing a recessionary (deflationary) gap caused by insufficient aggregate demand. This is shown in Figure 12.1 (a) and (b), where the aggregate demand curve AD_1 intersects both the $SRAS$ curve and the Keynesian AS curve at a level of real GDP, Y_{rec}, that is below the full employment (potential output) level, Y_p. Part (a) is based on the monetarist/new classical model, while part (b) is based on the Keynesian model. The effects of fiscal policy can be illustrated equally well by both. The government's objective is to try to shift AD_1 to AD_2,

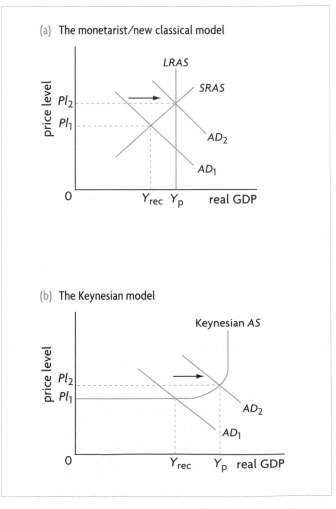

Figure 12.1 Effects of expansionary policy: eliminating a recessionary (deflationary) gap

where the economy will achieve full employment or potential output, Y_p, thereby closing the recessionary gap. Fiscal policy undertaken to eliminate a recessionary gap is called **expansionary fiscal policy**, because it works to expand aggregate demand and the level of economic activity. Expansionary fiscal policy may consist of:

- increasing government spending
- decreasing personal income taxes
- decreasing business taxes, or
- a combination of increasing spending and decreasing taxes.

An increase in government spending impacts directly on aggregate demand, which increases. If the government decreases taxes, aggregate demand is affected in a two-step process. If personal income taxes are cut, the result is a rise in disposable income, which is then likely to lead to an increase in consumption spending, causing the AD curve to shift to the right. If business taxes are cut, after-tax business profits increase, which in turn is likely to lead to higher investment spending and therefore higher AD. In all three cases, AD is intended to shift to the right from AD_1 to AD_2, allowing the economy to achieve full employment or potential output Y_p.

Finally, the government may decide to pursue a policy of increasing government spending and lowering taxes simultaneously. How can it increase its own spending while keeping taxes constant or decreasing them? It can do so by borrowing to finance the excess of spending over tax revenues. If initially it has a balanced budget, an increase in G while taxes remain constant or fall creates a budget deficit. If it already has a budget deficit at the outset, the deficit will become larger. If it has a budget surplus at the outset, then the surplus either will become smaller, or it will shrink until it eventually turns into a deficit.

Both the new classical and the Keynesian models predict that an increase in AD increases real GDP. However, the size of the increase in real GDP will not be the same in the two cases. The increase in real GDP will be smaller in the monetarist/new classical model than in the Keynesian one, because of the upward-sloping $SRAS$ curve. The effects differ also in the case of the price level. In the monetarist new/classical model, the increase in AD always results in a rise in the price level because of the upward-sloping $SRAS$ curve. In the Keynesian model, the increase in AD may result in no increase in the price level at all if the AD shift occurs entirely within the horizontal section of the AS curve. If the AD shift reaches into the upward-sloping part of the Keynesian AS curve, as shown in

Figure 12.1(b), there will be only a very small increase in the price level.

Contractionary fiscal policy

- Describe the mechanism through which contractionary fiscal policy can help an economy close an inflationary gap.
- Construct a diagram to show the potential effects of contractionary fiscal policy, outlining the importance of the shape of the aggregate supply curve.

Suppose the economy is experiencing an inflationary gap caused by excessive aggregate demand, shown in Figure 12.2 (a) and (b): the aggregate demand curve AD_1 intersects the $SRAS$ curve and the Keynesian AS curve at a level of real GDP, Y_{infl}, that is greater than the full employment or potential output level, Y_p. The government's objective now is to attempt to shift AD_1 to AD_2, so that AD_2 intersects aggregate supply at the full employment level of output, Y_p, thereby closing the inflationary gap. Fiscal policy undertaken to close an inflationary gap is called **contractionary fiscal policy**, because it works to contract aggregate demand and the level of economic activity. Contractionary fiscal policy consists of:

- decreasing government spending
- increasing personal income taxes
- increasing business taxes, or
- a combination of decreasing spending and increasing taxes.

A decrease in government spending has a direct influence on the aggregate demand curve, causing it to shift to the left. An increase in personal income taxes or business taxes is intended to affect aggregate demand in a two-step process. As personal income taxes increase, after-tax income falls, causing consumption spending and aggregate demand to fall. As taxes on profits increase, after-tax profits fall, leading businesses to spend less on investment and causing aggregate demand to fall. In all three cases, the aggregate demand curve is meant to shift to the left.

The government can also pursue a combination of decreases in government spending with increases in personal income and business taxes. Depending on the initial conditions that prevail in the government's budget, such a combination of policies would lead to the creation of a budget surplus, or the shrinkage of a budget deficit, or turning a budget deficit into a surplus.

Note that the effects of a fall in aggregate demand *may* be different depending on the model considered. If AD falls in the downward-sloping part of the

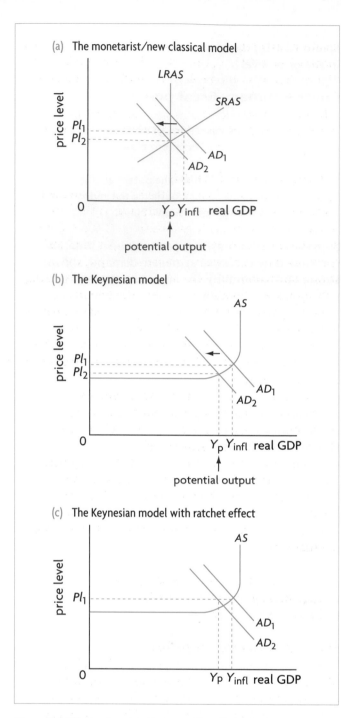

(a) The monetarist/new classical model

(b) The Keynesian model

(c) The Keynesian model with ratchet effect

Figure 12.2 Effects of contractionary policy: eliminating an inflationary gap

AS curve in the Keynesian model (as in part b), the effects on the price level and real GDP are similar in the two models, because the slope of the two curves is similar. However, if *AD* were to decrease into the horizontal part of the *AS* curve, the fall in real GDP will be larger, and the drop in the price level smaller (or none at all) compared with the monetarist/new classical model. (The argument is analogous to that noted above in connection with expansionary policy.)

The Keynesian model with the ratchet effect

We know that a feature of the Keynesian model is that the price level can easily increase with strong aggregate demand, but does not easily fall even as aggregate demand decreases. Therefore, the decrease in the price level shown in Figure 12.2(b) does not make sense. To take this into account, many economists refer to the 'ratchet effect', shown in Figure 12.2(c).[2] According to the ratchet effect, the price level moves up when there is an increase in *AD*, and then remains at the same level until there is a further increase in *AD*. In Figure 12.2(c), the change from AD_1 to AD_2 causes real GDP to fall to Y_p, but the price level remains constant at pl_1. This is a more realistic representation of what usually happens in the real world. (You may note that the decrease in *AD* required to bring real GDP to Y_p from Y_{infl} is smaller with the ratchet effect than without.)

> Fiscal policy involves manipulations by the government of its own expenditures and taxes to influence the *G*, *C*, or *I* components of aggregate demand. Expansionary fiscal policy can be used when there is a recessionary gap, and aims to shift the *AD* curve to the right leading to equilibrium at the full employment level of real GDP (potential GDP). Contractionary fiscal policy can be used when there is an inflationary gap, and aims to shift the *AD* curve to the left leading to equilibrium at the full employment level of real GDP (potential GDP).

Test your understanding 12.2

2 **(a)** What are the objectives of fiscal policy? **(b)** Distinguish between expansionary and contractionary fiscal policy. **(c)** What are the components of aggregate demand that fiscal policy can influence?

3 Using diagrams, show how the government can use fiscal policy when there is **(a)** a recessionary gap, and **(b)** an inflationary gap.

4 Using the monetarist/new classical model, explain how the following policies can impact on real GDP, the price level and unemployment:
   (a) The government lowers income taxes.
   (b) The government decreases its spending on defence.
   (c) The government increases taxes on business profits.
   (d) The government increases its spending on the country's road and highway system.

---

[2] A ratchet is a simple machine that allows for something to move only in one direction.

5 (a) Answer parts (a)–(d) in question 4 above using the Keynesian *AD-AS* model. **(b)** Explain how the predictions of the two models differ. **(c)** Note when the ratchet effect comes into play. **(d)** How does the ratchet effect affect your answers concerning changes in the price level?

The role of automatic stabilisers

♦ Explain how factors including the progressive tax system and unemployment benefits, which are influenced by the level of economic activity and national income, automatically help stabilise short-term fluctuations.

Automatic stabilisers

Automatic stabilisers are factors that automatically, without any action by government authorities, work toward stabilising the economy by reducing the short-term fluctuations of the business cycle. (Since they are automatic, they represent 'non-discretionary' policy; see page 320.) There are two important stabilisers: progressive income taxes and unemployment benefits.

Progressive income taxes

In the upswing of the business cycle, as real GDP and incomes rise, government tax revenues automatically increase, causing after-tax (disposable) income to be lower than it would otherwise be. The downward pressure on disposable incomes acts to dampen aggregate demand, and this tends to counteract the economic expansion, or make it smaller than it would otherwise be.

In a recession, the opposite occurs. With real GDP and incomes falling, government tax revenues automatically decline, causing after-tax (disposable) income to be higher than it would otherwise be, exerting an upward pressure on aggregate demand, which reduces the severity of the recession.

This pattern of events works with both proportional and progressive income taxes (see page 312 for a review of these concepts). However, the stabilising effects of income taxes are greater with progressive taxation. The reason is that with progressive taxation, the average tax rate increases as income/real GDP increases. Therefore, in an upswing, with higher real GDP, government tax revenues are relatively higher and disposable income relatively lower compared to what they would have been with proportional

taxation. In a recession, progressive taxes mean that as income/real GDP fall, disposable income is relatively higher than it would be with proportional taxation.

The more progressive an income tax system, the greater the stabilising effect on economic activity.

Unemployment benefits

In a recession, as real GDP falls and unemployment increases, unemployment benefits rise as they are offered to more unemployed workers. If there were no unemployment benefits, unemployed workers' spending would fall quite dramatically, putting a strong downward pressure on consumption spending and aggregate demand. However, the presence of unemployment benefits means that as workers become unemployed, their consumption will be maintained to some extent as their benefits partially replace their lost income, thus lessening the downward pressure on aggregate demand.

In an expansion, unemployment benefits are reduced as unemployment falls; therefore, consumption increases less than it would in the absence of unemployment benefits.

It is important to bear in mind that a progressive tax system and unemployment benefits cannot by themselves stabilise the economy and eliminate inflationary and recessionary gaps on their own. They can only help reduce the severity of economic fluctuations.

The multiplier and fiscal policy (supplementary material) (higher level topic)

HL

Discretionary fiscal policy

The effects of fiscal policy depend on the value of the multiplier (see Chapter 9, page 260). If the government increases *G* as part of an expansionary policy, the multiplier effect should lead to a larger increase *in real GDP*. How much larger depends on the multiplier, which in turn depends on the size of the marginal propensity to consume, *MPC*. The larger the *MPC*, the larger the size of the multiplier, and the greater is the expansionary impact of the government's increase in spending.

Since $MPC + MPS + MPT + MPM = 1$, a large *MPC* necessarily means that the leakages are small, and therefore the government's injection of spending will have a relatively large impact on real GDP. If, however, there is a high marginal propensity to import (*MPM*), then the *MPC* is correspondingly lower, and the value of the multiplier is also lower, reducing the impact on aggregate demand of the government's injection of spending. A large fraction of the additional income made possible by the government's increase in spending leaks out of the economy in the form of spending to buy imports, thereby reducing the impact in the domestic economy of the government's increase in spending.

An expansionary fiscal policy involving tax cuts is different from the above, though its impacts also depend on the size of the multiplier. Whereas an increase in G enters into the spending stream in its entirety, a cut in income taxes causes consumption to increase, but by less than the amount of the tax cut, because a tax cut is shared between an increase in consumption and an increase in leakages.

A simple calculation illustrates the difference.

Suppose that the MPC is $\frac{3}{4}$; this means that the multiplier = 4, since

$$\frac{1}{1-MPC} = \frac{1}{1-\frac{3}{4}} = \frac{1}{\frac{1}{4}} = 4$$

Suppose too that government spending increases by $1. It follows that aggregate demand increases by $1 \times 4 = \$4$. Now suppose that, instead, there is a tax cut of $1. With the $MPC = \frac{3}{4}$, this leads to an increase in consumption of $0.75 and an increase in leakages of $0.25. The impact of the tax cut on aggregate demand is calculated in the usual way: we multiply the initial increase in consumption of $0.75 by the multiplier of 4, and we have $0.75 \times 4 = \$3$. Therefore, aggregate demand increased by $3 due to the cut in taxes, whereas it increases by $4 from an increase in government spending.

> The effectiveness of fiscal policy is affected by the size of the multiplier: the larger the multiplier, the stronger the impact of fiscal policy on real GDP. Also, an increase in government spending has a larger impact on aggregate demand than an equivalent decrease in taxes.

Non-discretionary fiscal policy: automatic stabilisers

You may be wondering how automatic stabilisers actually work in terms of how they affect aggregate demand and real GDP. Automatic stabilisers work by

reducing the value of the multiplier, because they lower the size of the MPC. A smaller multiplier means smaller induced changes in consumption spending that arise from an initial change in a component of aggregate demand, and therefore a smaller change in real GDP.

Remember that the multiplier is

$$\frac{1}{1 - MPC} = \frac{1}{MPS + MPT + MPI}$$

where MPT is the marginal propensity to tax, defined as the fraction of additional income taxed. The more progressive the income taxes, the larger the MPT, the smaller the MPC, and therefore the smaller the multiplier. For example, given an increase in a component of AD (such as an autonomous change in investment[3]), the induced change in real GDP due to the multiplier will be *smaller*, the more progressive the income taxes.

Unemployment benefits also stabilise the economy by reducing the value of the multiplier through a lower MPC. To see how this happens, suppose the $MPC = \frac{3}{4}$, indicating a multiplier of 4. If there occurs a $1 fall in autonomous investment spending, it leads initially to a $1 fall in income (creating a recessionary gap). If there are no unemployment benefits, the $1 fall in income will initially result in a $0.75 fall in consumption spending. Suppose then that unemployment benefits are introduced, partially replacing lost income and supporting consumption, so that the $1 fall in income leads initially to a $0.50 fall in consumption spending. This means that the MPC (defined as the fraction of additional income consumed) falls from $\frac{3}{4}$ to $\frac{1}{2}$. The multiplier has therefore fallen from 4 to 2. A smaller multiplier indicates that the induced changes in real GDP will be smaller.

Fiscal policy and long-term economic growth: the impact on potential output

> ♦ Explain that fiscal policy can be used to promote long-term economic growth (increases in potential output) indirectly by creating an economic environment that is favourable to private investment, and directly through government spending on physical capital goods and human capital formation, as well as provision of incentives for firms to invest.

---

[3] The meaning of autonomous changes was explained in Chapter 9, page 262. In the context of the multiplier, they refer to changes that have not been caused by changes in income.

Fiscal policy focuses mainly on short-term stabilisation. However, it can also contribute to long-term growth of potential GDP. It can do so indirectly, by providing a stable macroeconomic environment, and directly, by leading to aggregate expenditures that result in growth of potential GDP.

Indirect effects on potential output

Consumers and firms need a stable economic environment to be able to plan and carry out their economic activities. Firms, in particular, must make plans in many areas, including what capital goods to invest in, and whether, how and in what areas to pursue research and development (R&D) and technological innovations. Investment is the key to the formation of new capital goods, and R&D is the driving force of technological changes, both of which are very important factors in increasing production possibilities and increasing potential GDP (shifting the LRAS curve to the right in the monetarist/new classical context). To be in a position to plan over long periods of time, firms need economic stability, consisting of avoidance of sharp economic upturns (inflation) and downturns (recession and unemployment). Fiscal policy aiming at economic stabilisation is therefore important in creating the macroeconomic environment that encourages activities impacting on long-term economic growth.

Direct effects on potential output

In addition, fiscal policies can impact directly on the growth of potential GDP:

- They can allocate a portion of government spending to the development of physical capital goods, such as infrastructure (roads and transport systems, telecommunications, harbours, airports, etc.), as well as on R&D, which improves technology, and therefore improves the quality of capital goods, and improves the productivity of labour.

- They can allocate a portion of government spending to the development of human capital, such as training and education programmes that increase the quality of the labour force and improve the productivity of labour.

- They can provide incentives to encourage investment by firms through lower business taxes (as well as other measures to be considered later), thereby contributing to new capital formation and R&D that promotes technological innovations.

All these factors work to increase potential output, thus supporting long-term economic growth. These effects can be seen in Figure 9.15 (page 256). Suppose an economy is initially in equilibrium producing real output Y_1, and the government pursues a variety of demand-side fiscal policies, including increases in government expenditures on infrastructure, R&D and training and education, thereby increasing the quantity of capital goods, and improving the level of technology and the quality of labour force. These policies produce increases in aggregate demand over the short term, so that AD shifts from AD_1 to AD_2. However, these policies also impact on aggregate supply, because of the increase in the quantity of capital goods, the improvements in the quality of labour, etc., so that the LRAS and SRAS curves (part (a)) and the Keynesian AS curve (part (b)) also shift to the right. The demand-side policies initiate a sequence of events that result not only in an increase in aggregate demand but also in growth in potential output over the long term.

> Demand-side policies have not only demand-side but also supply-side effects, and can therefore affect long-term economic growth by increasing potential output. Their contribution to economic growth includes creating a stable economic environment, as well private investment spending and government spending, in turn leading to increases in potential output (through new capital formation, increased R&D and technological improvements, and improvements in the quality of the labour force).

Evaluating fiscal policy

> ◆ Evaluate the effectiveness of fiscal policy through consideration of factors including the ability to target sectors of the economy, the direct impact on aggregate demand, the effectiveness of promoting economic activity in a recession, time lags, political constraints, crowding out, and the inability to deal with supply-side causes of instability.

The discussion above focuses on the potential positive effects of fiscal policies. However, the complexities of the real world present some difficulties that often prevent these policies from achieving the desired and expected impacts. We will now consider strengths and weaknesses of fiscal policies.

Strengths of fiscal policy

- **Pulling an economy out of a deep recession.** Until the Great Depression of the 1930s, classical economists believed that short-term economic fluctuations were self-correcting: in a recession, wage and price flexibility would correct the problem and the economy would eventually return to full employment equilibrium. (This is very similar to the thinking of monetarist/new classical economists; see Chapter 9.) Yet the experience of the Great Depression, which involved low levels of output and incomes and high unemployment over a long period of time, showed that market forces acting alone were unable to pull the economy out of the deep recession. In the now classic work, *The General Theory of Employment, Interest and Money* (1936), John Maynard Keynes (the originator of 'Keynesian economics') argued that wages and prices were inflexible in the downward direction even in the face of steep recession, and that low aggregate demand could keep the economy stuck in a recessionary gap indefinitely. This can occur when the *AD* curve intersects the Keynesian aggregate supply (*AS*) curve at a point on its horizontal section, where real GDP is less than full employment GDP. The strength of fiscal policy is to pull an economy out of a deep recession. In the global recession that began in autumn 2008, fears of a major global recession made governments around the world turn to expansionary fiscal policy, in the form of increased government spending and tax cuts, in order to stimulate low aggregate demand.

- **Dealing with rapid and escalating inflation.** Inflationary pressures arising when there is an inflationary gap can sometimes get out of hand, resulting in rapid increases in the price level. Contractionary fiscal policy may then be used effectively to help bring the problem under control.

- **Ability to target sectors of the economy.** Fiscal policy can target specific sectors by making changes in the composition of government spending depending on government priorities. For example, it may focus on changing the amount of spending on:
  - education and particular levels within education
  - health care, focusing if necessary on particular social groups that may be in greater need
  - infrastructure and particular types of infrastructure (airports, roads, hospitals, etc.) as well as the locations of infrastructure, focusing if necessary on economically depressed regions that could benefit more from increased physical capital

  - other merit goods
  - a variety of public goods (police force, public parks, etc.)
  - and so on with the various types of government spending.

- **Direct impact of government spending on aggregate demand.** Changes in government spending impact directly on aggregate demand, and this can be helpful to policy-makers who want to be reasonably certain that changes in spending are likely to change aggregate demand in the desired direction. Changes in taxes are less direct, as they work by changing consumer disposable income and firm after-tax profits, and this poses some uncertainties about their effects on aggregate demand. (For example, in a recession if consumers are insecure about the future, tax cuts may lead to greater saving rather than greater spending; see below).

- **Ability to affect potential output.** Fiscal policy can affect potential output and long-term economic growth indirectly (by creating a stable macroeconomic environment) and directly through investments in human capital and physical capital (infrastructure) and through offering incentives to firms to invest.

Weaknesses of fiscal policy

- **Problems of time lags.** Fiscal policy is subject to a number of delays in timing called time lags. There is a lag until:
  - the problem (recessionary or inflationary gap) is recognised by the government authorities and economists
  - the appropriate policy to deal with the problem is decided upon by the government
  - the policy takes effect in the economy.

  Some months may pass in the case of each of these, and by the time the policy action has taken effect the problem may have become less or more severe, so that the policy action is no longer the most appropriate one.

- **Political constraints.** Government spending and taxation face numerous pressures that are unrelated to fiscal policy. Spending for social services (merit goods such as health care and education) and public goods is undertaken for its own sake and cannot easily be cut if a contractionary policy is required. On the other hand, tax increases are politically unpopular and may be avoided by the government even though they might be necessary. Tax decreases could also be inappropriately enacted because they are politically popular. The upshot is that political factors may sometimes lead to unsuitable fiscal policies.

- **Crowding out.** If the government pursues an expansionary fiscal policy involving spending increases without an increase in revenues, it is forced to borrow; this is called *deficit spending*. Government borrowing involves an increase in the demand for money, and leads to an increase in the rate of interest (we will see how on page 331 below). A higher interest rate in turn can lead to lower investment spending by private firms, or a 'crowding out' of private investment. This means that the government's expansionary fiscal policy is weakened, since a greater G (government spending) is counteracted by a lower I (investment spending). Crowding out is illustrated in Figure 12.3. In part (a) there is a rightward shift from AD_1 to AD_2 due to the increase in G, and a leftward shift from AD_2 to AD_3 due to the fall in I. This shows partial crowding out, where the fall in investment spending is smaller than the increase in government spending. Part (b) shows complete crowding out, where the fall in I is equal to the increase in G. Crowding out is controversial. Some economists, mainly in the Keynesian tradition, believe that in a recession, the stimulus provided to the economy by the government's increased spending may raise output and employment, improve business expectations about their future sales, and increase investment spending in spite of the increase in the interest rate. In this case, the government's deficit spending is less likely to crowd out private investment. Other economists, mainly in the monetarist/new classical tradition, believe that investment spending will be crowded out in the event of deficit financing even in a recession.

- **Inability to deal with supply-side causes of instability.** If instability is caused by supply-side factors, leading to stagflation, where there is falling real GDP and inflation simultaneously (see page 281), fiscal policy is unable to deal with it effectively. Inflation requires a contractionary policy, while the recession requires an expansionary policy. A contractionary policy could address the problem of inflation, but would make the recession worse; an expansionary policy could help get the economy out of recession, but would worsen the problem of inflation.

- **In a recession, tax cuts may not be very effective in increasing aggregate demand.** Tax cuts are less effective in a recession than increases in government spending because part of the increase in after-tax income is saved. If the proportion of income saved rises due to pessimism about the future, the impacts of tax cuts on aggregate demand are even weaker. Increases in government spending are more powerful because they work in their entirety to increase aggregate demand.

- **Inability to 'fine tune' the economy.** Whereas fiscal policy can lead the economy in a general direction of larger or smaller aggregate demand, it cannot 'fine tune' the economy; it cannot be used to reach a precise target with respect to the level of output, employment and the price level. If fiscal policy were successful, it would be possible to use it to keep the economy's real GDP at or very close to its potential output level. However, experience has shown that this cannot be done, as there are many factors affecting aggregate demand simultaneously that the government cannot control.

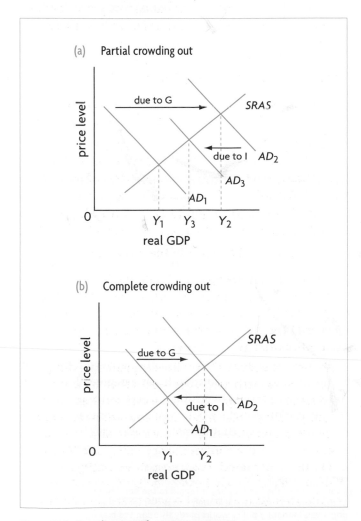

Figure 12.3 Crowding out of private investment

1 Explain the meaning of automatic stabilisers.

2 How do **(a)** unemployment benefits, and **(b)** a progressive tax system work to stabilise the downward movements of aggregate demand?

3 How do **(a)** unemployment benefits, and **(b)** a progressive tax system work to stabilise the upward movements of aggregate demand?

4 Using a diagram, explain how demand-side policies **(a)** have supply-side effects, and **(b)** can impact on long-term economic growth.

5 Explain some strengths and weaknesses of fiscal policy.

6 Why do decisions on whether or not to use fiscal policy measures depend on more than just economic considerations?

7 Using a diagram, explain crowding out.

12.3 Monetary policy

The role of central banks and interest rate determination

The role of central banks

♦ Describe the role of central banks as regulators of commercial banks and bankers to governments.

♦ Explain that central banks are usually made responsible for interest rates and exchange rates in order to achieve macroeconomic objectives.

Monetary policy is carried out by the central bank of each country. The central bank must be distinguished from commercial banks. **Commercial banks** are financial institutions (which may be private or public[4]) whose main functions are to hold deposits for their customers (consumers and firms), to make loans to their customers, to transfer funds by cheque (check) and electronically from one bank to another, and to buy government bonds.[5]

The **central bank** is usually a government financial institution with a number of important responsibilities:

• **Banker to the government.** The central bank acts as a banker to the government in ways that are similar to how commercial banks act as bankers to their customers. It holds the government's cash (as deposits), it receives payments for the government and makes payments for the government (the government writes cheques (checks) paid from an account in the central bank). It also manages the government's borrowing by selling bonds to commercial banks[6] and the public, and acts as an adviser to the government on financial and banking matters.

• **Banker to commercial banks.** The central bank also acts as a banker to commercial banks by holding deposits for them and can also make loans to them in times of need. (The central bank does not act as a banker to consumers and firms.)

• **Regulator of commercial banks.** The central bank regulates and supervises commercial banks, making sure they operate with appropriate levels of cash and according to rules that ensure the safety of the financial system. This is a very important function, because the funds that commercial banks use to make loans are the savings and other deposits that consumers and firms deposit with commercial banks.

• **Conduct monetary policy.** The central bank is responsible for monetary policy, based on changes in the supply of money or the rate of interest. The central bank is also usually responsible for the determination of exchange rates (the price of the domestic currency in terms of foreign currencies) because of the close relationship between interest rates and exchange rates (see Chapter 14).

Every country has a central bank. In the countries of the European Union that have formed the European Monetary Union (the countries that have adopted the euro, also known as 'euro zone' countries), the national central banks maintain many of their functions, noted above, but the responsibility for monetary policy has been transferred to a single organisation, the European Central Bank.

Central bank independence (supplementary material)

Although the central bank is usually a government institution, in many countries it has a degree of independence from government interference in the pursuit of monetary policy. A key advantage of independence is that monetary policy can be

---

[4] In developed countries, commercial banks tend to be mostly private. In less developed countries, many commercial banks are public. There is a general trend around the world for commercial banks to be privatised (they are sold by the public sector to the private sector).

[5] The buying and selling of bonds from and to the central bank is a central feature of monetary policy, explained on page 332, as supplementary material. Bonds, it should be noted, are simply debt. When the

government or a private firm borrows to finance a deficit, it issues a certificate (a bond) that promises to pay interest at various intervals until a certain date when the money is repaid to the bond holder. The holder of the bond is therefore the lender, and the issuer of the bond is the borrower. Monetary policy works partly through the buying and selling of *pre-existing* government bonds.

[6] See footnote 5.

conducted with a view to what is considered to be in the best longer-term interests of the economy, without interference from political pressures (such as encouraging economic activity just before an election). There is a general trend around the world for governments to make central banks increasingly independent, though there are broad differences over how 'independence' is interpreted. For example, in the United States the Federal Reserve (the US central bank) can decide on the goals of monetary policy and on the ways that these goals should be achieved. In many other countries, including the United Kingdom and the euro zone countries, the respective central banks, which are the Bank of England and the European Central Bank, are given the goals by the UK government and the European Parliament, and can only determine independently the best ways to achieve these given goals.

Determination of the rate of interest

♦ Explain, using a demand and supply of money diagram, how equilibrium interest rates are determined, outlining the role of the central bank in influencing the supply of money.

The money market and the rate of interest

Monetary policy impacts indirectly on aggregate demand through the rate of interest. To understand how monetary policy works, we must first consider how the rate of interest is determined.

When we borrow money, we must make a payment for the loan in addition to repaying the principal (the amount of the loan); this payment for a loan is interest. Interest is usually expressed as a percentage of the principal to be paid per year; this percentage is called the rate of interest. For example, let's say you borrow $1000 for one year at the rate of interest of 10% per year; at the end of the year you must pay back the principal of $1000, plus $100 of interest (calculated as 10% of $1000).

In the real world there are many different rates of interest, depending on a number of factors, such as the level of risk of a loan (the greater the risk, the higher the interest rate); the length of the period of time over which the loan must be paid, known as 'maturity' (the longer the time period, the higher the interest rate); the size of the loan (the larger the loan, the lower the interest rate); the degree of monopoly power of the lender (the greater the monopoly power, the higher the

interest rate), and others. However, when economists analyse the rate of interest in the context of economic models (as we are doing here), they simplify the analysis by adopting the common practice of referring to 'the rate of interest' as if there were only one.

We can understand how the rate of interest is determined very simply as an application of the familiar concepts of supply and demand in a special market, the money market, shown in Figure 12.4(a). **Money** is defined as anything that is acceptable as payment for goods and services; more precisely, money consists of currency (coins and paper money) and cheque (checking) accounts. The money market is a market where the demand for money and the supply of money determine the equilibrium rate of interest. The horizontal axis measures the quantity of money in the economy, and the vertical axis measures the rate of interest.

The rate of interest can be thought of as the 'price' of money services. The demand for money, D_m, shows the relationship between the rate of interest and the quantity of money demanded, and has the familiar downward-sloping shape of a demand curve. As the rate of interest falls, the quantity of money demanded by the public (consumers, firms, the government) increases.[7]

The **supply of money** is fixed at a level that is decided upon by the central bank. It appears in Figure 12.4(a) as a vertical line, S_m, because it does not depend on the rate of interest. The point of intersection between D_m and S_m determines the equilibrium rate of interest, i, illustrated in Figure 12.4(a).

If the central bank changes the money supply, the S_m curve shifts, thus determining a new rate of interest. This is shown in Figure 12.4(b). Suppose initially the money supply is at S_{m1}; with demand for money D_m, the equilibrium rate of interest is i_1. If the central bank increases the money supply, S_{m1} shifts to S_{m2}, and the equilibrium rate of interest falls to i_2. If the central bank decreases the money supply, S_{m1} shifts to S_{m3}, and the equilibrium rate of interest rises to i_3.

An increase in the supply of money leads to a fall in the rate of interest; a decrease in the supply of money leads to an increase in the rate of interest.

(Using the money market diagram in Figure 12.4(a), you can see that an increase in the demand for money due to increased government borrowing (D_m shifts to

---

[7] To understand why the demand for money is downward-sloping, we must look more closely into what 'money' is. Money provides important services because it allows consumers, firms and the government to carry out all their buying and selling exchanges, or their spending. In addition, money can be used as a form of saving when it is used to buy bonds (see footnote 5.) Since bonds pay interest, this means that the rate of interest is very important in determining how much of their income people want to hold as money, and how much of it they want to hold in the form of bonds. (Using the money market diagram in Figure 12.4(a) you can see that an increase in the demand

for money due to increased government borrowing (D_m shifts right) leads to a higher interest rate, which lies behind crowding out; see page 329.) When people hold money, they sacrifice the interest they could have received if they had bought bonds; in other words, interest is the opportunity cost of holding money. The higher the interest rate, the greater the opportunity cost, in terms of sacrificed interest, and therefore the lower the quantity of money demanded. As the interest rates falls, the opportunity cost of holding money decreases, and therefore the quantity of money demanded rises. This is the explanation behind the downward-sloping demand for money curve.

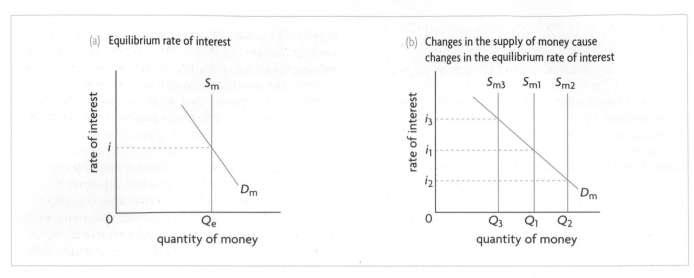

Figure 12.4 The money market and determination of the rate of interest

the right) leads to a higher interest rate. This is what may cause 'crowding out'; see page 329.)

Controlling the money supply or the rate of interest?

In practice, when the central bank conducts monetary policy, it can focus on controlling either the money supply or the rate of interest. Of course, making a decision on one automatically determines the other. Central banks in many countries used to try to control the money supply. However, growing difficulties in effectively doing this led central banks in many countries to abandon the focus on the money supply and to control instead the interest rate. The central bank decides upon a target interest rate it wants to achieve, and then takes steps to adjust the money supply so that the actual equilibrium interest rate will become equal to the target interest rate.

To see how this works, suppose the Bank of Riverland (Riverland's central bank) decides to increase the interest rate from i_1 to i_3 in Figure 12.4(b). To do so, it takes measures to reduce the supply of money until the interest rate increases to i_3. If the actual, market interest rate deviates from the target rate, it will continue to adjust the money supply in order to achieve the target rate. You can see, then, that central banks do not actually set or fix interest rates, but rather allow these to be determined by the market.

Therefore, if you hear in the news that the Bank of Riverland increased the interest rate from 3.25% to 3.50%, you would understand that 3.50% is the new target interest rate that the Bank of Riverland is trying to achieve by reducing the money supply.

In the real world there are many interest rates (as explained above), so what interest rate do central banks target? This varies from country to country, depending on the nature of the monetary system. In the United Kingdom, the central bank targets the 'base rate', which is the interest rate at which the Bank of England (the central bank) lends to commercial banks. In the United States, the Federal Reserve (the central bank) targets the 'federal funds rate', which is the rate used by commercial banks to borrow and lend from and to each other over a 24-hour period. The European Central Bank (of the euro zone countries) targets the 'minimum refinancing rate', which is the interest rate paid by commercial banks when they borrow from their respective national central bank to refinance their accounts.

How the central bank changes the money supply (supplementary material)

The most important instrument used by central banks to influence the supply of money is called 'open market operations'.

When commercial banks receive deposits from their customers, they do not keep all this cash within their vaults. The funds they must legally keep are called required reserves, which are a legally determined fraction of total deposits, called the required reserve ratio. The rest are called excess reserves and can be lent out by banks. Suppose you deposit £1000 into your bank, and the required reserve ratio is 20%. The bank must keep £200 of required reserves in its vaults, and can lend out the remaining £800 of excess reserves. Suppose individual A borrows the £800 and buys a computer from individual B, who then deposits this amount in her bank. This bank must keep 20% of £800 or £160 (= 0.20×£800), and can lend out the remaining amount, which is £640 (= £800−£160). This process continues an infinite number of times, and in the end the amount of new loans that have been created will be £4000. (This amount is the result of a process where the amount of initial excess reserves of £800 are multiplied by a 'monetary multiplier', equal to $\frac{1}{\text{required reserve ratio}}$, which in this case is $\frac{1}{0.20} = 5$.)

This simple example shows that when banks make loans, they are actually *creating new money*. It also shows that *the more excess reserves commercial banks have, the more loans they can make, and the more new money is created*. This is the principle on which the central bank's open market operations work.

Suppose a central bank wishes to lower the interest rate, and must therefore increase the money supply. It will use open market operations to *buy* government bonds from commercial banks. The payments for the bonds received by the commercial banks increase their excess reserves, which they can use to make more loans, and therefore the money supply increases. If the central bank wants to raise the interest rate, it *sells* bonds to commercial banks; as the banks must pay the central bank for these, their excess reserves and therefore their lending ability are reduced, and the money supply is lowered.

Test your understanding 12.4

1 Explain the functions of central banks and their role with respect to achieving macroeconomic objectives.

2 **(a)** Explain the importance of the money supply in determining the rate of interest. **(b)** What is the government authority that is responsible for changing the supply of money and carrying out monetary policy?

3 **(a)** Using a diagram, explain how equilibrium interest rates are determined. **(b)** What would a central bank do if it wanted (i) to lower interest rates, and (ii) to increase interest rates?

The role of monetary policy

Changes in interest rates and aggregate demand

* Explain how changes in interest rates can influence the level of aggregate demand in an economy.

The point of changing the money supply so as to change interest rates is ultimately to influence aggregate demand. Changes in interest rates affect two of the four components of aggregate demand:

investment, I, and consumption, C (see Table 9.1, page 240). Since some consumer spending is paid for out of borrowing, a change in interest rates is intended to affect the amount of consumer spending (C). Similarly, changes in interest rates affect the amount of borrowing by businesses to finance their investment expenditures (I).

An increase in interest rates is intended to lower consumer and business borrowing and hence spending (lower C and I), and therefore shift AD to the left. A decrease in interest rates is intended to increase consumer and business borrowing and hence spending (higher C and I), and therefore shift AD to the right.

Expansionary (easy) monetary policy

* Describe the mechanism through which easy (expansionary) monetary policy can help an economy close a deflationary (recessionary) gap.
* Construct a diagram to show the potential effects of easy (expansionary) monetary policy, outlining the importance of the shape of the aggregate supply curve.

Consider the case where the economy is experiencing a recessionary gap due to insufficient aggregate demand, as in Figure 12.1 (a) and (b). The central bank decides to increase the money supply, causing a rightward shift in the supply of money curve from S_{m1} to S_{m2} as shown in Figure 12.4(b). With the demand for money constant, the interest rate falls from i_1 to i_2.

The drop in the rate of interest means a lower cost of borrowing; therefore, consumers and firms are likely to borrow more and spend more, so that consumption spending (C) and investment spending (I) increase. The effect is to increase aggregate demand and cause a rightward shift of the AD curve. This is shown in Figure 12.1 (a) and (b), where the recessionary gap has been closed through the shift from AD_1 to AD_2.

Note that, just like with fiscal policy, the effects of the AD increase are different depending on the shape of the AS curves. In the monetarist/new classical model, there is a smaller increase in real GDP and a larger increase in the price level compared to the Keynesian model.

An increase in the money supply by the central bank is referred to as an **easy monetary policy**. It is also an **expansionary monetary policy**, since the objective is to expand aggregate demand and the level of economic activity.

Contractionary (tight) monetary policy

♦ Describe the mechanism through which tight (contractionary) monetary policy can help an economy close an inflationary gap.

♦ Construct a diagram to show the potential effects of tight (contractionary) monetary policy, outlining the importance of the shape of the aggregate supply curve.

Suppose now that the economy is experiencing an inflationary gap caused by excess aggregate demand, as in Figure 12.2 (a), (b) and (c). The central bank reduces the money supply; this appears in Figure 12.4(b) as a leftward shift of the S_m curve, from S_{m1} to S_{m3}. With the demand for money constant, the result is a higher rate of interest, i_3, or a higher cost of borrowing, and therefore reduced borrowing by consumers and firms. The effect of lower investment spending (I) and lower consumer spending (C) is to decrease aggregate demand. This is shown in all parts of Figure 12.2, where the inflationary gap has been closed through the shift from AD_1 to AD_2.

As in the case of fiscal policy, if AD falls within the upward-sloping part of the AS curve in the Keynesian model, the effects on the price level and real GDP are similar to those in the monetarist/new classical model, as shown in parts (a) and (b). But if AD were to decrease into the horizontal part of the AS curve, there would be a larger fall in real GDP and a smaller fall in the price level in the Keynesian model. Note also the ratchet effect, shown in Figure 12.2(c), which takes into account the unlikelihood of the price level in the Keynesian model as AD decreases (see page 324).

A decrease in the money supply by the central bank is referred to as a **tight monetary policy**, or **contractionary monetary policy**, as the objective is to contract aggregate demand and therefore the economy.

Monetary policy is carried out by the central bank, which aims at changing interest rates to influence the I and C components of aggregate demand. In a recessionary gap, the central bank may pursue an expansionary (easy monetary) policy through lower interest rates to encourage I and C spending, the objective being to shift the AD curve to the right leading to equilibrium at the full employment level of real GDP (potential GDP). In an inflationary gap, the central bank can pursue a contractionary (tight monetary) policy through higher interest rates aimed at discouraging I and C spending, causing the AD curve to shift to the left leading to equilibrium at the full employment level of real GDP (potential GDP).

The effects of both types of policy have been illustrated by use of the same diagrams (Figures 12.1 and 12.2). Yet this simple diagrammatical analysis hides important differences between the two types of policy, related to the different channels that affect spending of the various AD components. These differences are summarised in Table 12.1, which provides an outline of fiscal and monetary policy measures, their effects on spending and their impacts on aggregate demand.

Expansionary policy (in recession)

Type of policy	Measures	Effects
Fiscal policy	increase government spending	increase AD
	lower personal income taxes → increase consumption spending	increase AD
	lower business taxes → increase investment spending	increase AD
Monetary policy	increase supply of money → lower interest rate →	
	(i) increase consumption spending	increase AD
	(ii) increase investment spending	increase AD

Contractionary policy (in inflation)

Type of policy	Measures	Effects
Fiscal policy	decrease government spending	decrease AD
	raise personal income taxes → decrease consumption spending	decrease AD
	raise business taxes → decrease investment spending	decrease AD
Monetary policy	decrease supply of money → raise interest rate →	
	(i) decrease consumption spending	decrease AD
	(ii) decrease investment spending	decrease AD

Table 12.1 Demand-side policies to correct recessionary and inflationary gaps

1 **(a)** What are the objectives of monetary policy? **(b)** Distinguish between expansionary and contractionary monetary policy. **(c)** Why do you think expansionary monetary policy is also called an 'easy monetary policy' **(d)** Why is contractionary monetary policy also known as a 'tight monetary policy'? **(e)** What are the components of aggregate demand that monetary policy can influence? **(f)** What is the role of the rate of interest in monetary policy?

2 Using diagrams, show how the government can use monetary policy when there is **(a)** a recessionary gap, and **(b)** an inflationary gap.

3 Using the monetarist/new classical model, explain the impact on real GDP, the price level and unemployment, of the following policies of a country's central bank: **(a)** a fall in the rate of interest **(b)** an increase in the rate of interest.

4 **(a)** Answer parts (a) and (b) in question 3 above using the Keynesian *AD-AS* model. **(b)** Explain how the predictions of the two models differ. **(c)** Note when the ratchet effect comes into play. **(d)** How does the ratchet effect affect your answers concerning changes in the price level?

Monetary policy and inflation targeting

◆ Explain that central banks of certain countries, rather than focusing on the maintenance of both full employment and a low rate of inflation, are guided in their monetary policy by the objective to achieve an explicit or implicit inflation rate target.

In the discussion above, we have seen how monetary policy may be used as a stabilisation tool, focusing on the goals of full employment and a low and stable rate of inflation. However, in recent years more and more central banks around the world are trying a kind of monetary policy that aims at maintaining a particular targeted rate of inflation (for example, Australia, Brazil, Canada, Chile, Finland, Israel, Mexico, New Zealand, Norway, Sweden, Switzerland, the United Kingdom, the European Union and many others).

The International Monetary Fund (IMF) defines **inflation targeting** as:

'... the public announcement of medium-term numerical targets for inflation with an institutional commitment by the monetary authority to achieve these targets. Additional key features include increased communication with the public and the markets about the plans and objectives of monetary policymakers and increased accountability of the central bank for attaining its inflation objectives.'[8]

Many countries pursuing inflation targeting usually have targets of between 1.5% and 2.5%, with one percentage point above and below as a 'tolerance' margin. While the central bank is committed to pursuing the inflation target, it is free to determine what policy tools it will use to achieve it. The inflation target is set in terms of the consumer price index (CPI), which also takes into account the prices of imported goods (included in the CPI basket). However, inflation targeting is usually based on forecasts or predictions of *future* inflation based on the CPI (see Chapter 10, page 275 for a discussion of the CPI).

To achieve an inflation target, central banks use monetary policy, described above. If predicted inflation is higher than the target, they use contractionary policy to increase interest rates and lower aggregate demand, thus lowering the rate of inflation. If predicted inflation is lower than the target, they use expansionary policy to lower interest rates and increase aggregate demand.

Advantages of inflation targeting

● **A lower rate of inflation.** Particularly in countries that have experienced persistent high rates of inflation, inflation targeting can be a method to reduce it.

● **A more stable rate of inflation.** This refers to reduced fluctuations in the rate of inflation, likely to be achieved when a target rate is pursued.

● **Improved ability of economic decision-makers (firms, consumers) to anticipate the future rate of inflation.** Public knowledge about the central bank's objectives on inflation reduces uncertainty and facilitate economic decision-making about the future (such as investment decisions).

● **Greater co-ordination between monetary and fiscal policy.** Knowledge about inflation

---

[8] The IMF is an international financial institution that we will study in Chapter 18. IMF, 'De Facto Classification of Exchange Rate Regimes and

Monetary Policy Frameworks', 31 April 2008 (http://www.imf.org/external/np/mfd/er/2008/eng/0408.htm).

targets allows the government to plan its fiscal policy to complement the central bank's monetary policy.

- **Greater central bank transparency and accountability.** The central bank becomes more open about its activities and more accountable to the government and the public. If it fails to bring inflation close to the target, it must provide an explanation.

Disadvantages of inflation targeting

- **Reduced ability of the central bank to pursue other macroeconomic objectives.** If the central bank focuses only or mainly on inflation at a particular target rate, it is unable to use monetary policy to pursue other goals, such as for example, the full employment level of real GDP or exchange rate stability.

- **Reduced ability of the central bank to respond to supply-side shocks.** In the event of a supply-side shock, such as a sudden increase in oil prices, leading to cost-push inflation and stagflation, the central bank may need flexibility to pursue an expansionary policy to bring the economy out of recession, and this may mean a higher rate of inflation than the target.

- **Reduced ability of the central bank to deal with unexpected events, such as financial crises.** A financial crisis may also require an expansionary monetary policy, which might also lead to inflation higher than the target.

- **Finding an appropriate inflation target.** An inflation target that is too high or too low can lead to problems. If it is too low, it may lead to higher unemployment; if it is too high, it could lead to the problems resulting from high inflation.

- **Difficulties of implementation.** Inflation targeting is based heavily on forecasts of future inflation and economic activity, and forecasts are often highly unreliable.

Evaluating monetary policy

- Evaluate the effectiveness of monetary policy through consideration of factors including the independence of the central bank, the ability to adjust interest rates incrementally, the ability to implement changes in interest rates relatively quickly, time lags, limited effectiveness in increasing aggregate demand if the economy is in deep recession and conflict among government economic objectives.

Like fiscal policy, monetary policy is intended to achieve particular objectives, but does not always work as expected.

Strengths of monetary policy

Some of the strengths of monetary policy are that it is not subject to some of the weaknesses of fiscal policy:

- **Relatively quick implementation.** Monetary policy can be implemented more quickly than fiscal policy because it does not have to go through the political process, which is very cumbersome and time consuming (though, as we will see below, monetary policy is also subject to some time lags).

- **Central bank independence.** This was discussed above (page 330) as an advantage because independence from the government means the central bank can take decisions that are in the best longer term interests of the economy, and therefore exercises greater freedom in pursuing policies that may be politically unpopular (such as higher interest rates making borrowing more costly).

- **No political constraints.** Even if a central bank is not independent of the government, monetary policy is still not subject to the same kinds of political pressures as fiscal policy, since it does not involve making changes in the government budget, whether in terms of government spending that would affect merit and public goods provision, or government revenues (taxes).

- **No crowding out.** Monetary policy does not lead to crowding out, which may result from higher interest rates due to an expansionary fiscal policy (based on deficit financing). The monetary policy counterpart to an expansionary fiscal policy is an easy monetary policy, which leads to lower (not higher) interest rates.

- **Ability to adjust interest rates incrementally (in small steps).** Interest rates can be adjusted in very small steps, making monetary policy better suited to 'fine tuning' of the economy in comparison with fiscal policy. However, it should be stressed that it is also subject to limitations, and that there is in fact no policy tool that economists can use to fully 'fine tune' an economy.

Weaknesses of monetary policy

- **Time lags.** Unlike fiscal policy, monetary policy can be implemented and changed according to perceived needs relatively quickly, because it does not depend on the political process. However, like fiscal policy, it remains subject to time lags (delays), including a lag until the problem is recognised, and a lag until the policy takes effect. Changes in interest rates can take several months to have an impact on aggregate demand, real output and the price level. By then, economic conditions may have changed so that the policy undertaken is no longer appropriate.

- **Possible ineffectiveness in recession.** Whereas monetary policy can work effectively when it restricts the money supply to fight inflation, it is less certain to be as effective in a deep recession.

Expansionary monetary policy is intended to increase aggregate demand by encouraging investment and consumption spending through lower interest rates. This process presupposes that banks will be willing to increase their lending to firms and consumers, and that firms and consumers will be willing to increase their borrowing and their spending. However, in a severe recession, banks may be unwilling to increase their lending, because they may fear that the borrowers might be unable to repay

US fiscal policy and recession: two views

In February 2009, the Obama administration in the United States approved a fiscal stimulus package of $787 billion to support the US economy that was in recession. This had the effect of increasing the budget deficit. In spite of the fiscal measure, unemployment grew to over 10%. In the meantime, due to expansionary monetary policy, interest rates had fallen to nearly zero.

A Keynesian view on appropriate fiscal policy

The recession was deeper than originally estimated; therefore, a new fiscal stimulus package is required to supplement the first one. Recession involves low aggregate demand, and the government must step in by increasing its own spending. Through the multiplier, this works to increase spending in the economy by a multiplied amount, thus directly increasing *AD* and real GDP. Without the initial expansionary fiscal policy, the recession would have been deeper and longer, and unemployment much higher. The government's budget deficit increased, but this is unavoidable in recession, because of automatic stabilisers that work to lower taxes and increase government spending on unemployment benefits.

A monetarist/new classical view on appropriate fiscal policy

The government should not have implemented the first fiscal stimulus package at all. It could have focused on reducing the budget deficit; this would improve business confidence, which would increase investment, and therefore economic growth. Otherwise, it could have implemented tax cuts,

which are preferable to increased government spending, because deficit spending leads to higher interest rates that crowd out private investment spending. This reduces the expansionary effect of government spending. The increase of unemployment to over 10% suggests that the stimulus package did not work as expected.

A Keynesian response

The idea of reducing the budget deficit in a recession does not make sense. A household that spends more than its income can cut back on its spending, but if a government does that, the effect will be to reduce output and incomes, and increase unemployment, possibly making it even more difficult for the government to pay back its debts in the future. It is very unlikely that higher interest rates will crowd out investment in a recession when interest rates are already very low. Also, tax cuts have a smaller effect on increasing *AD*, because part of the tax cut is lost as increased saving; and if consumer confidence is very low, consumers may not spend their higher after-tax incomes and save most of it.

A monetarist/new classical response

Increased government spending adds to big government, which is inefficient, and acts as a drag on the economy. The focus should be on stimulating the economy without increasing the size of the government. Tax cuts offer this expansionary stimulus and at the same time create incentives for people to work more, thus possibly leading to lower unemployment.

Applying your skills

1 Explain the meaning of **(a)** the multiplier, **(b)** automatic stabilisers, **(c)** deficit spending, and **(d)** crowding out.

2 What assumptions about the macroeconomy are made by **(a)** Keynesian economists, and **(b)** monetarist/new classical economists, which lead them to differing conclusions about appropriate fiscal policy?

the loans. If firms and consumers are pessimistic about future economic conditions, they may avoid taking out new loans, and may even reduce their investment and consumer spending, in which case aggregate demand will not increase (it may even decrease), and monetary policy will be unable to pull the economy out of recession. This is not something that happens often; however, it appears to have occurred during the Great Depression of the 1930s, in Japan in the late 1990s and early 2000s, and in the global recession that began in the autumn of 2008.

- **Conflict between government objectives.** Manipulation of interest rates affects not only variables in the domestic economy (consumption and investment spending, inflation, unemployment) but also variables in the foreign sector of the economy, such as exchange rates. The pursuit of domestic objectives may conflict with the pursuit of objectives in the foreign sector (see Chapter 14).

- **Inability to deal with stagflation**. Monetary policy is a *demand-side policy*, and is therefore unable to deal effectively with supply-side causes of instability, just like fiscal policy (see page 329 for a full discussion).

Test your understanding 12.6

1 Explain why both fiscal and monetary policies are not very well suited to dealing with instabilities caused by decreases in *SRAS*.

2 **(a)** What is inflation targeting? **(b)** Explain some of the strengths and weaknesses of this type of monetary policy.

3 Explain some strengths and weaknesses of monetary policy.

12.4 Supply-side policies

Objectives of supply-side policies

♦ Explain that supply-side policies aim at positively affecting the production side of an economy by improving the institutional framework and the capacity to produce (that is, by changing the quantity and/or quality of factors of production).

♦ State that supply-side policies may be market-based or interventionist, and that in either case they aim to shift the *LRAS* curve to the right, achieving growth in potential output.

Supply-side policies focus on the production and supply side of the economy, and specifically on

factors aimed at shifting the long-run aggregate supply (*LRAS*) or Keynesian *AS* curves to the right, to increase potential output and achieve long-term economic growth (see Figure 9.14, page 255). They do not attempt to stabilise the economy by reducing the severity of the business cycle. Instead, they focus on increasing the quantity and quality of factors of production, as well as on institutional changes intended to improve the productive capacity of the economy.

There are two major categories of supply-side policies: **interventionist** and **market-based**. Interventionist policies rely on government intervention to achieve growth in potential output, and are usually favoured by economists influenced by Keynesian economic thinking. Market-based policies emphasise the importance of well-functioning competitive markets in achieving growth in potential output, and are usually favoured by monetarist/new classical economists.

Interventionist supply-side policies

Interventionist supply-side policies presuppose that the free market economy cannot by itself achieve the desired results in terms of increasing potential output, and argue that government intervention in specific areas is required. Earlier in this chapter we discussed some of the measures involved under the heading 'Fiscal policy and long-term economic growth' (page 326). Here we will see that these policies form part of interventionist supply-side policies.

Investment in human capital: education and health services

♦ Investment in human capital: Explain how investment in education and training will raise the levels of human capital and have a short-term impact on aggregate demand, but more importantly will increase *LRAS*.

Investment in human capital can take the following important forms:

- **Training and education.** More and better training and education lead to an improvement in the quality of labour resources, increasing the productivity of labour, which is one of the key causes of economic growth (see page 297). Education, you may also remember, has numerous positive externalities, thereby justifying government intervention. Public training and education programmes can assist workers to become more employable, thus reducing the natural rate of unemployment. Specific measures include setting up retraining programmes for structurally unemployed workers to obtain skills in greater demand; assisting young people to pursue training and education through grants or low interest loans; direct government hiring and provision of on-the-job training; providing grants to firms that offer on-the-job training; offering subsidies to firms that hire structurally unemployed workers; assisting workers to relocate to geographical areas where there is a greater demand for labour through grants and subsidies (such as provision of low-cost housing); providing information on job availability in various geographical areas; establishing government projects in the depressed areas that result in new employment creation.

- **Improved health care services and access to these.** When workers (and the general population) have access to good quality health care services, they become healthier and more productive. Improved health care services and access to these by the working population is therefore another factor leading to improvements in the quality of labour resources, increasing the economy's potential output. Health care also has many positive externalities, justifying government intervention. (See Chapter 17, page 463, for a full discussion of the positive externalities of education and health.)

Investments in human capital result in an increase in aggregate demand over the short term, and over the longer term lead to increases in potential output, by shifting the *LRAS* or Keynesian *AS* curves to the right.

Investment in new technology

> ◆ Investment in new technology: Explain how policies that encourage research and development will have a short-term impact on aggregate demand, but more importantly will result in new technologies and will increase *LRAS*.

Research and development (R&D) is the fundamental activity behind the development of new technologies, resulting in new or improved capital goods (physical capital), which is another important cause of increases in potential output and economic growth (see page 297). R&D also has positive externalities, thereby justifying government intervention (see page 113).

Governments in many countries around the world are therefore heavily involved in R&D. In addition, governments often provide incentives to private sector firms to engage in R&D activities; these usually take the form of tax incentives, as well as the granting of patents for the protection of inventions.

Government spending in support of new technology development leads to increases in aggregate demand over the short term and increases in potential output over the longer term shifting the *LRAS* or Keynesian *AS* curves to the right.

Investment in infrastructure

> ◆ Investment in infrastructure: Explain how increased and improved infrastructure will have a short-term impact on aggregate demand, but more importantly will increase *LRAS*.

Infrastructure is a type of physical capital, and therefore results from investment; it includes power, telecommunications, roads, dams, urban transport, ports airports, irrigation systems, etc. Many types of infrastructure qualify as merit goods or public goods, thereby justifying government intervention. More and better infrastructure increases efficiencies in production as it lowers costs. Good road, railway and other transport systems, for example, save time and effort spent in transporting goods and services, allowing more output to be transported and costs to be lowered. The availability of effective telecommunications permits faster and easier communications, enabling economic activities to be carried out more efficiently. More and better infrastructure improves labour productivity. Investments in infrastructure therefore work to increase aggregate demand over the short term, but they also contribute to increases in potential output and *AS* increases over the longer term.

Industrial policies

> ◆ Industrial policies: Explain that targeting specific industries through policies including tax cuts, tax allowances and subsidised lending promotes growth in key areas of the economy and will have a short-term impact on aggregate demand but, more importantly, will increase *LRAS*.

Industrial policies are government policies designed to support the growth of the industrial sector of an economy. All policies considered above, government investments in human capital, new technologies and infrastructure are industrial policies. Further measures that fall under industrial policy include the following:

- **Support for small and medium-sized enterprises or firms (SMEs).** Governments can provide support to small and medium-sized firms, which may take the form of tax exemptions, grants, low-interest loans and business guidance. This provides support for the private sector, promoting efficiency, more capital formation, more employment possibilities and therefore increases aggregate demand as well as potential output.
- **Support for 'infant industries'.** 'Infant industries' are newly emerging industries in developing countries, which sometimes receive

government support in the form of grants, subsidies, tax exemptions, and tariffs or other forms of protection against exports (we will study these in Chapter 14). This also provides support for growth of the private sector and increases in aggregate demand and growth in potential output.

Market-based supply-side policies

In the early 1980s, some highly influential monetarist/new classical economists in the United Kingdom and the United States began to emphasise the view that growth in real GDP depends on the supply side of the economy. This view was adopted by the government headed by Margaret Thatcher in the United Kingdom, and by the government under Ronald Reagan in the United States. Since then, many governments throughout the world have pursued policies influenced by market-based supply-side thinking. In this view, the economy's real GDP tends automatically towards long-run full employment equilibrium and potential GDP (see page 249). The focus of government policies should therefore be less on stabilisation, and more on creating conditions that allow market forces to work well.

This perspective suggests that an economy pursuing supply-side policies will be able to achieve rapid growth, price stability and full employment all at the same time. These advantages are seen to arise because as the economy tends towards full employment equilibrium, it automatically eliminates recessionary and inflationary gaps, thus eliminating the problem of unemployment in recessionary gaps, and the problem of inflation in inflationary gaps. This can be seen in Figure 9.15(a) (page 256). If increases in aggregate supply match increases in aggregate demand so that the *LRAS* and *SRAS* curves shift by the same amount as the *AD* curve, there need not be any price level increases.

Market-based supply-side policies can be grouped under three headings:

1 Encouraging competition
2 Labour market reforms
3 Incentive-related policies.

Encouraging competition

♦ Policies to encourage competition: Explain how factors including deregulation, privatisation, trade liberalisation and anti-monopoly regulation are used to encourage competition.

Greater competition among firms forces them to reduce costs, contributing to greater efficiency in production and improving the allocation of resources, with the possible added benefit of improving the quality of goods and services. These benefits amount to releasing resources that were being used unproductively and putting them to use in more productive activities, thus allowing potential output to increase and the *LRAS* curve to shift to the right.

- **Privatisation.** Privatisation, involving a transfer of ownership of a firm from the public to the private sector, can increase efficiency due to improved management and operation of the privatised firm. This is based on the argument that government enterprises are often inefficient as they have bureaucratic procedures, high administrative costs and unproductive workers, because they do not face incentives to lower costs and maximise profits. The private sector may therefore be more efficient than the public sector.

- **Deregulation.** Deregulation involves the elimination or reduction of government regulation of private sector activities, and is based on the argument that government regulation stifles competition and increases inefficiency. There are two main types of regulation (and deregulation): economic and social. 'Economic regulation' involves government control of prices, output, and other activities of firms, offering them protection *against competition*. In the last two to three decades, many countries have moved toward removal of government regulations, and hence economic deregulation. A main form of deregulation has been to allow new, private firms to enter into monopolistic or oligopolistic industries, thus forcing existing firms to face competition. The objective has been to increase efficiency, lower costs and improve quality. Industries affected include transport, airlines, television broadcasting, telecommunications, natural gas, electricity, financial services and others. 'Social regulation' involves protecting consumers against undesirable effects of private sector activities (many of these involve negative externalities) in numerous areas, including food, pharmaceutical and other product safety, worker protection against injuries, and pollution control. In contrast to economic regulation, social regulation is being strengthened in many countries in the interests of public safety. Some economists, however, argue that social regulation is excessive, giving rise to costly and inefficient bureaucratic procedures, paperwork and unnecessary government interference, and should therefore be reduced.

- **Private financing of public sector projects.** Historically, public sector projects (such as building roads, harbours, airports, schools, hospitals and other infrastructure) have been financed out of the government budget (tax revenues). In more recent years, a number of countries have introduced private financing of public projects, called *private financing initiatives*, where a private firm builds, finances and operates public services. The capital and services are owned by the private company, and the government buys the services from the private firm. Such initiatives increase competition, because private sector firms compete with each other to be selected by the government to take on the project; the government selects the private firm that offers to build and run the service at the lowest cost and provide the best quality.

- **Contracting out to the private sector (outsourcing).** Here, public services are provided by private firms based on a contractual agreement between the government and the private service provider. Examples include information technology, human resources management and accounting services. These result in increased competition as private firms compete with each other to get contracts with the government, thereby resulting in improved efficiency, lower costs of production and improved quality.

- **Restricting monopoly power.** Increased competition can result from restricting monopoly power of firms by enforcing anti-monopoly legislation, by breaking up large firms that have been found to engage in monopolistic practices into smaller units that will behave more competitively, and by preventing mergers between firms that might result in too much monopoly power. Greater scope for the forces of supply and demand may result in increased efficiency, lower costs and improved quality.

- **Trade liberalisation.** International trade between countries has become freer in recent decades due to reductions in trade barriers. This topic will become clearer after you read Chapter 14, where you will discover that according to economic theory, free or freer trade increases competition between firms both domestically and globally, resulting in greater efficiency in production and an improved allocation of resources. We will study trade liberalisation in detail in Chapter 17.

Labour market reforms

- Labour market reforms: Explain how factors including reducing the power of labour unions, reducing unemployment benefits and abolishing minimum wages are used to make the labour market more flexible (more responsive to supply and demand).

Labour market reforms are sometimes referred to as 'increasing **labour market flexibility**', or reducing labour market 'rigidities'. These reforms are intended to make labour markets more competitive, to make wages respond to the forces of supply and demand, to lower labour costs and increase employment by lowering the natural rate of unemployment (labour market rigidities were discussed in Chapter 10 as one cause of structural unemployment, which is the most important part of natural unemployment; see page 269). Lower costs of production can lead to increased profits, and this in turn may result in greater investment by firms, increased R&D, increased capital goods production, and therefore increases in potential output (economic growth).

- **Abolishing minimum wage legislation.** Elimination or reduction of the legal minimum it is argued, reduces unemployment by allowing the equilibrium wage to fall. The benefits of increased wage flexibility (in the downward direction) would include lower unemployment, since firms can hire more labour at the lower wage; greater firm profits, as wage costs would be lowered; more investment and economic growth.

- **Weakening the power of labour (trade) unions.** Unionised labour frequently succeeds in securing high wage increases; if labour unions are weakened, wages will be more responsive to the forces of supply and demand, and will therefore be more likely to fall in the event that there is unemployment. This would also lead to increased wage flexibility with the same benefits as in the case of abolishing minimum wage legislation.

- **Reducing unemployment benefits.** Unemployment benefits are payments to workers who have lost their jobs, and are meant to provide some income to the unemployed during the period of time they are searching for a new job. It is argued that unemployment benefits have the unintended effect of reducing the incentive to search for a new job, causing some unemployed workers to remain unemployed for longer periods than necessary. Therefore, reducing unemployment benefits is expected to lower unemployment, as it would encourage the unemployed to look for work. This could work to reduce the natural rate of unemployment.

- **Reducing job security.** Many countries have laws that protect workers against being fired, making it costly for firms to fire workers because of high levels of compensation that must be paid to the worker being laid off. It is argued that reducing workers' job security by making it easier and less costly for firms to let go workers has the effect of increasing employment, because firms are more likely to hire new workers if they know they can fire them easily and without cost if they are no longer needed. In addition, reducing job security would decrease firms' labour costs because of the lower costs of firing, and would therefore increase profits, investment and economic growth.

Incentive-related policies

♦ Incentive-related policies: Explain how factors including personal income tax cuts are used to increase the incentive to work, and how cuts in business tax and capital gains tax are used to increase the incentive to invest.

Incentive-related policies involve cutting various types of taxes, which are expected to change the incentives faced by taxpayers, whether firms or consumers.

- **Lowering personal income taxes.** As we know, the government can change personal income taxes as part of fiscal policy, thereby changing the level of aggregate demand. Supply-side economists argue that changes in personal income taxes have an even greater impact on aggregate supply. Cuts in personal income taxes lead to higher after-tax incomes, creating an incentive for people to provide more work: this can happen through an increase in the number of hours worked per week; an increase in the number of people interested in finding work (who were formerly not interested in working); an increase in the number of years worked, as people may decide to retire later; a decrease in unemployment as unemployed workers choose to shorten the duration of their unemployment. All these factors may work to shift the *LRAS* curve to the right, increasing potential output.

- **Lowering taxes on capital gains and interest income.** In many countries, people must pay taxes on 'capital gains', which are profits from financial investments (such as stocks and bonds) or from buying and selling real estate. In addition, they may have to pay taxes on income from interest on savings deposits. If the taxes they must pay on these sources of income are reduced, they may be more motivated to save, thus increasing the amount of savings available for investment. More investment means a greater production of capital goods and an increase in potential output.

- **Lowering business taxes.** Lower taxes on business profits can work to increase aggregate demand by increasing investment spending. Supply-side economists argue that cutting taxes on firms' profits is a supply-side measure because increases in the level of after-tax profits mean that firms have greater financial resources for investment and for

pursuing technological innovations through more R&D. Both these effects give rise to greater potential output.

Evaluating supply-side policies

♦ Evaluate the effectiveness of supply-side policies through consideration of factors including time lags, the ability to create employment, the ability to reduce inflationary pressure, the impact on economic growth, the impact on the government budget, the effect on equity, and the effect on the environment.

We turn to an evaluation of the effectiveness of supply-side policies by considering several factors.

Time lags

Most supply-side policies, both interventionist and market-based, work after significant time lags, making their effects on *the supply side* of the economy (aggregate supply) over the longer term. This is because the activities set into motion (increased competition, labour market reforms, changing incentives, investments, new human and physical capital, R&D, and so on), need time to materialise and affect potential output. However, interventionist policies also have an effect on aggregate demand over the short term. Therefore, in a recession, such policies could have the added advantage that they can help close a recessionary gap. Yet, if an economy is experiencing inflation, they could contribute to destabilising the economy by adding to inflationary pressures.

Impact on economic growth

Increases in potential output

You may recall from Chapter 9 and Chapter 10 that long-term economic growth is caused by investments in various forms of capital and new technologies, resulting in increased productivity of labour. In addition, economic growth is encouraged by the development of institutions involving incentives and the promotion of the market system and the freer working of supply and demand, allowing the private sector to work well. We have seen how a variety of supply-side policies seek to achieve these outcomes. Economists generally agree that supply-side policies play a very important role in increasing potential output.

Arguments favouring interventionist policies

However, economists disagree on whether interventionist or market-based polices are more effective in increasing potential output. Supporters of interventionist policies argue in terms of the major advantages of targeted government support in areas such as investment, R&D, training and education, provision of credit on favourable terms (low interest rates, long repayment periods), and so on; they argue that the market is unlikely to provide them as needed. Moreover, industrial policies allow the government to support particular industries that are held to offer the greatest possibilities for growth in the future. They point to the experiences of a group of Asian countries (the 'Asian Tigers'; see Chapter 17, page 484), which achieved very high rates of growth by use of highly interventionist policies focusing on investments in human capital and industrial policies. They also point

to the questionable growth performance of many developing countries that adopted market-based supply-side policies in the 1980s (see Chapter 17, pages 485–86).

Arguments favouring market-based policies

Supporters of market-based policies argue that government interference in the market may lead to inefficiencies and resource misallocation, whereas reliance on the market can achieve long-term growth while avoiding these disadvantages. A major argument against government intervention and industrial policies involves the idea of government failure (see page 137), according to which government interference may result in less efficient outcomes because of the influence of political pressures, lack of necessary information and unintended and unwanted consequences of government actions. It is argued that governments may lack the ability to choose the right industries to support, and incorrect choices will lead to a poor allocation of resources.

In addition, supporters of market-based policies note that interventionist policies rely heavily on government spending, and use resources that might have better alternative uses elsewhere (opportunity costs). Governments require substantial amounts of tax revenues to be able to provide the support services, which means high taxes and a large government sector. High taxes act as disincentives to work, and a large government sector promotes inefficiencies.

The debate over incentive-related policies

Tax cuts (incentive-related policies) are among the more controversial market-based policies, because of their questionable effects on work, saving and growth of potential output. Tax cuts, as we know, have both demand-side and supply-side effects. Some economists question the strength of the supply-side effects, believing these to be small compared to the impact on aggregate demand. For example, increases in disposable income due to cuts in personal income taxes may result in the decision to work less if people prefer to use their extra (after-tax) income to increase their time for leisure. Also, workers may decide to use their higher after-tax income to consume more rather than save, in which case the tax cuts may not significantly affect saving and investment. In the United States, for example, whereas there have been a series of tax cuts, savings are at their lowest point in the past 80 years. In countries where tax cuts were implemented as supply-side policies (such as in the United Kingdom and the United States), economists disagree on whether or not these have worked to increase potential output. The reason is that whatever growth has occurred has been the result of both demand-side and supply-side effects of demand-side and supply-side policies, and it is very difficult to detect which particular policy has been responsible for each particular effect.

Ability to create employment (reduce unemployment)

One of the objectives of supply-side policies, we have seen, is to create employment. This does not refer to a reduction of cyclical unemployment, arising from business cycle fluctuations and requiring demand-side policies for its correction. It refers to a reduction of the natural rate of unemployment (structural, frictional, seasonal).

Interventionist policies involving investments in education and training can make a direct impact on a reduction of unemployment by:

- enabling workers to acquire the skills, training and retraining necessary to meet the needs of employers (structural unemployment)
- providing assistance to workers to relocate (structural unemployment)
- providing information that reduces unemployment when workers are between jobs (frictional unemployment) or between seasons (seasonal unemployment).

In addition, a focus on education and training of the general population can contribute to employment creation because better-educated and trained people are more employable.

Market-based policies involving labour market reforms may also contribute to reducing the natural rate of unemployment by focusing on making the labour market more responsive to supply and demand (lower wages and production costs, easier hiring and firing, etc.).[9]

Market-based policies that focus on encouraging competition, on the other hand, may well *increase* unemployment, at least over the short term. In the case of privatisation, as privatised firms try to make their operations more efficient, they often try to cut costs by firing workers. Contracting out to the private sector leads to government job losses, and job losses for the country as a whole if projects are contracted out to firms in other lower cost

countries, as is sometimes the case. In addition, economic deregulation has frequently led to increased unemployment, due to increased competitive pressures that cause firms to fire workers in order to lower their costs. It is possible that increased unemployment on account of these policies may be short term, and may be reversed over the longer term as the economy begins to benefit from the broader effects of supply-side policies.

Ability to reduce inflationary pressure

Supply-side policies, whether interventionist or market-based, are likely to reduce inflationary pressures over the longer term. The reason is that these policies are intended to increase potential output, shifting the *LRAS* curve to the right. As an economy grows, if increases in aggregate demand are matched by increases in aggregate supply, there will be little or no upward pressure on the price level. This can be seen in Figure 9.15 (page 256).

The ability of supply-side policies to reduce inflationary pressures can also be understood in terms of the focus on keeping firms' costs of production down through increases in efficiency (due to increased competition) and lower wage costs (due to increased labour market flexibility).

Impact on the government budget

Interventionist policies and incentive-related market-based policies have negative effects on the government budget, though for entirely different reasons. Interventionist policies are heavily based on government spending, and therefore are a burden on the budget. Incentive-related policies involve tax cuts, and therefore reduced government revenues. Both these policies can create a budget deficit (or can increase the size of the deficit if there was one to begin with).

Effects on equity

In keeping with our earlier discussion on equity (Chapter 11), this is interpreted to mean greater income equality. Supply-side policies have mixed effects on equity.

Interventionist policies that focus on investments in human capital that are broadly distributed throughout the population are likely to have positive effects on equity over the longer term. The reason is that educated, skilled and healthy

---

[9] It should be noted, however, that there is some question over whether reducing minimum wages will actually result in increased employment. Some economists argue that paying workers a higher than equilibrium wage encourages them to work harder, increasing their productivity (the output produced per worker). Increased labour productivity causes firms to increase their demand for labour, which has the impact of increasing employment and justifying the higher wages. If this argument is correct, there would be little benefit for firms if governments cut the minimum wage.

workers are more likely to be employed and be an active and productive part of society, with the result that income is likely to be relatively more equally distributed. In addition, interventionist policies that lower the natural rate of unemployment reduce inequality by providing incomes to previously unemployed workers.

Market-based policies tend to have negative effects on equity. Greater competition may have a negative effect if it results in some unemployment, which involves a loss of income. Labour market reforms involve changes in legislation and institutions that provide protection for workers with very low incomes and with income uncertainties (minimum wage legislation, protection against being fired, unemployment benefits). Reducing protection results in lower incomes for some workers and increased job insecurity, and contributes to increasing income inequalities. Minimum wage legislation, for example, is intended to protect unskilled workers on very low incomes. Unemployment benefits and job security are especially important to people on very low incomes who have nothing to fall back on if they are left unemployed.[10]

In the case of incentive-related policies, tax cuts intended to create incentives to work, save and invest may also worsen income distribution. The argument that high taxes create disincentives to work and save applies mainly to higher income groups who face higher average tax rates; therefore, to reverse this problem, tax cuts must be designed to affect the after-tax incomes of higher income groups. Yet this would make the tax system less progressive, thus reducing the redistributive effects of personal income taxes and making income distribution less equal (see page 314). In addition, since it is the wealthy who enjoy capital gains and earn most of the interest income and business profits, tax cuts in these areas will affect wealthy people by increasing their after-tax incomes more than they will affect lower income groups of the population.

Another point concerns the prices of products sold by privatised firms. If private firms have a degree of market power, they are likely to raise their prices over what the government used to charge (as well as restrict the quantity of output produced), with the result that their products become less affordable. This may have damaging consequences for lower income groups, particularly if the privatised firms provide necessities or merit goods, such as utilities, including power, water supplies, sewage systems, etc. Subsidised provision of merit goods is a mechanism used to redistribute income in favour of greater income equality (see page 310), and this is reduced if prices increase due to privatisation. Similar considerations apply to private financing of public sector projects, which sometimes results in higher prices than when the government is the provider. (This is a particularly pronounced problem in many less developed countries, where privatisation of services has made these unaffordable for very poor people.)

Effects on the environment

It is possible that market-based policies to increase competition (privatisation, dergulation) may have negative effects on the environment because of the increased scope for activities leading to negative externalities affecting the environment. On the other hand, the government could limit these by taking the appropriate measures to correct or reduce the external costs of private sector activities.

Concluding comments

It is unlikely that any policy can yield positive results without some negative consequences. Most economists believe that interventionist and market-based policies should complement each other, and the particular mix of policies that should be used will likely be different according to each country's particular economic and social conditions.

Test your understanding 12.8

1 Explain advantages and disadvantages of interventionist supply-side policies, including **(a)** investment in human capital, **(b)** investment in human capital, **(c)** investment in infrastructure, and **(d)** industrial policies.

2 Explain advantages and disadvantages of market-based supply-side policies, including **(a)** policies to encourage competition, **(b)** labour market reforms, and **(c)** incentive-related policies.

---

[10] It should also be remembered that unemployment benefits can play an important role in a recession. As firms cut back on output and unemployment increases, unemployed workers suffer a loss of income, which puts a downward pressure on consumer spending. If unemployment benefits are high, they compensate for the loss of income of the unemployed, thus helping maintain the level of consumption spending (see page 325). In the autumn of 2008, when it was apparent that the United States was in recession, some economists called for increases in unemployment benefits.

'Flexicurity' in Denmark

The people of Denmark appear to have achieved a combination of things that many economists would consider impossible. The Danish economy has been one of the best performing in the world; GNI *per capita* in ($PPP) ranks eighth in the world; the poverty rate is the third lowest in the world; the unemployment rate is the lowest in the European Union; it has the second most equal distribution of income in the world; and according to the 'World Map of Happiness', the Danes are the happiest people in the world; all this while also paying the highest taxes in the world.

Government officials from Europe and the United States have been travelling to Denmark to discover the secret of its success, which lies partly in the unique practice of 'flexicurity', derived from 'flexibility' and 'security'.

The flexibility part of 'flexicurity' is based on Denmark's highly flexible labour market. Workers can be easily fired with little prior notice, meaning they can also be easily hired (because there is little or no cost involved in firing). There is a very large turnover in the labour market, with 30% of the labour force switching jobs each year. Most of these switches are not due to lay-offs, but moving on to better jobs. Though this gives rise to a high rate of frictional unemployment, Denmark has achieved the lowest unemployment rate in the European Union.

The security part of 'flexicurity' is based on Denmark's extensive social protection system. Once a worker is fired, s/he is entitled to very generous unemployment benefits, amounting to 90% of the wage. However, unemployment benefits are extended for only four years over a lifetime of work. This provides workers with the incentive to find a new job soon after they have been laid off.*

One condition of receiving unemployment benefits is that workers must be available to take on a job that is offered to them through government job centres after 12 months of unemployment. In addition, the government provides free education and training to unemployed workers to help them easily find new jobs. Most workers belong to labour unions that work very closely with businesses to discover what skills and education employers require. This helps reduce the level of structural unemployment in the economy. Denmark has a highly skilled and educated labour force.

The security part of 'flexicurity' is also based on public provision of free education from kindergarten through university, free health care and hospitals, retirement pensions at 87% of workers' income, housing subsidies for low-income earners, and numerous other social benefits.

An additional possible explanation for Denmark's economic success is its strongly market-oriented economy, based on free trade, competition, and limited government ownership or intervention in business. It is also considered to be the country with the least amount of bureaucracy and the shortest amount of start-up time for new firms in the European Union.

Denmark also has the highest income tax rates in the world, with incomes taxed at nearly 50% on average. Personal income taxes are strongly progressive, and this contributes to the high degree of income equality. Also, it has a very high value added tax (an indirect tax), at 24%. High taxes are necessary to pay for the very generous unemployment benefits, free education and health care, and other merit goods provided by the government. On the other hand, business taxes are comparable with most other European countries.

*At the time of writing, there was some discussion about reducing this to two years, on account of difficulties created by the global financial crisis.

Source: Jeffrey Stinson, 'Denmark a unique mix of welfare, economic growth' in *USA Today*, 8 March 2007; 'Flexicurity model turning heads' in *The Copenhagen Post*, 14 February 2007.

Applying your skills

1 What policies in Denmark are useful for maintaining low rates of **(a)** frictional unemployment, and **(b)** structural unemployment?

2 How does a highly progressive tax system contribute to greater equality in income distribution? (See Chapter 11, page 313.)

3 It is often argued that highly flexible labour markets lead to greater income inequality (page 344). What policies does Denmark use to ensure this does not occur?

4 Denmark has combined high economic growth rates together with the highest taxes in the world. What does this suggest about possible disincentive effects of very high taxes?

5 Denmark's unemployment benefits are among the most generous in the world, yet it has very low unemployment rates. What policies are used to avoid possible disincentive effects of unemployment benefits toward work?

6 What does the Danish experience of high economic growth rates together with one of the most equal income distributions in the world suggest about the possible conflict between equity (in the sense of income equality) and efficiency?

7 Denmark has a unique mixture of interventionist and market-oriented supply-side policies that appear to contribute to its success. Explain what these are.

12.5 Evaluating government policies to deal with unemployment and inflation

Having studied demand-side and supply-side policies, we are in a position to evaluate policies to deal with inflation and unemployment (see Chapter 10, pages 272 and 281).

Unemployment policies

> ♦ Evaluate government policies to deal with the different types of unemployment.

Different types of unemployment (explained in Chapter 9) require different kinds of policies for their solution. The main distinction is between cyclical (demand-deficient) unemployment and natural unemployment.

Cyclical unemployment

Since cyclical unemployment is caused by low or falling aggregate demand, measures to correct it involve expansionary demand-side policies, or fiscal and monetary policies. The intended effects of such policies are shown in Figure 12.1 (a) and (b), where the economy is initially in a recessionary gap producing output Y_{rec}. Efforts by the government or central bank to shift AD from AD_1 to AD_2 are intended to increase real GDP Y_p representing potential output. As AD shifts to the right, the recessionary gap shrinks, and cyclical unemployment falls until it is eliminated at Y_p.

The strengths and weaknesses of demand-side policies in bringing an economy out of recession apply equally to their ability to deal with cyclical unemployment (see pages 327 and 336). In summary form, they include the following.

Strengths of fiscal policy

- Pulling an economy out of deep recession, which is likely also to involve a high rate of cyclical unemployment.
- Direct impact of government spending on aggregate demand.

Weaknesses of fiscal policy

- Time lags.
- Political constraints.
- Crowding out.
- Tax cuts not as effective as government spending.
- Inability to fine-tune the economy.

The influence of automatic stabilisers

In a recession, the presence of progressive income taxes and/or unemployment benefits make the recession less severe, and therefore cyclical unemployment not as high as it would have been if these stabilisers were not present.

Strengths of monetary policy

- Quick implementation and incremental adjustment of interest rates.
- Central bank independence and no political constraints.
- No crowding out.

Weaknesses of monetary policy

- Time lags.
- Possible ineffectiveness in a deep recession.
- Conflict among government objectives. A recession and cyclical unemployment require lower interest rates, but this may lower the exchange rate (depreciation), which may result in imported inflation (this will be explained in Chapter 14).

An evaluation should also consider the relative merits of fiscal versus monetary policies. For example, unless the economy is facing a deep recession, it is likely that most economists would prefer monetary policy to deal with recession and cyclical unemployment, because of its relative advantages over fiscal policy.

Note that supply-side policies cannot be used to deal with cyclical unemployment.

Natural unemployment

Structural unemployment is the most serious part of natural unemployment, and most economic policies intended to lower the natural rate of unemployment focus on this.

Natural unemployment can be addressed mainly by supply-side policies. Of demand-side policies, monetary policy is ineffective in dealing with it. Fiscal policy, as a *stabilisation tool*, is also ineffective. To see why, suppose that an economy is producing at the level of potential output, with unemployment equal to the natural rate. If aggregate demand is increased through fiscal or monetary policy, the natural rate of unemployment will fall temporarily; however, this will cause inflation (you can see this by using either the monetarist/new classical or Keynesian models). Policy-makers would therefore reduce aggregate demand to lower the rate of inflation and unemployment falls once again to its natural rate.

However, fiscal policy can have important effects on natural unemployment because of its *supply-side effects*. These kinds of fiscal policy measures are included within interventionist supply-side policies.

This section summarises the relevant points made earlier in the evaluation of supply-side policies.

Interventionist supply-side measures

Measures to reduce structural unemployment include setting up retraining programmes; support for re-training through grants and low interest loans; direct government hiring and provision of on-the-job training; grants to firms offering on-the-job training; subsidies to firms hiring structurally unemployed workers; grants and subsidies to assist relocation; information on job availability in various geographical areas; government projects in the depressed areas for employment creation.

Measures to reduce frictional unemployment aim at improving information flows between employers and job seekers, reducing the time a worker spends searching for a job. Improved information can result from the establishment of job centres, employment agencies and other methods of facilitating information exchanges such as job websites.

Measures to reduce seasonal unemployment include provision of information to workers on jobs available during off-peak seasons in other industries.

The advantages of such policies are that they have a direct positive impact on employment creation, without contributing to increased income inequalities and loss of job security. Disadvantages include the negative impacts on the government budget and opportunity costs of government spending.

Market-based supply-side measures

Market-based measures to deal with unemployment include labour market reforms that increase labour market flexibility. As we know, reducing the minimum wage could potentially reduce unemployment by lowering wages of unskilled workers; weaker labour unions reduce the upward pressure on wages making it easier for firms to hire because of lower costs; reducing job security makes it easier for firms to hire because they can more easily fire; and reduction of unemployment benefits increase workers' incentives to find work.

These measures are aimed at structural, frictional and seasonal unemployment. The advantages of these policies are that they can reduce the natural rate of unemployment without negative effects on the government budget. The major disadvantages are

that they contribute to income inequality and loss of protection for low-income workers.

Inflation policies

> ♦ Evaluate government policies to deal with the different types of inflation.

It is important to bear in mind the distinction between demand-pull and cost-push inflation (explained on pages 280–81), as this determines the types of policies appropriate to deal with each one.

Demand-pull inflation

Demand-pull inflation is caused by increases in aggregate demand that create an inflationary gap. Therefore, appropriate policies to deal with it are contractionary demand-side policies, or fiscal and monetary policies that attempt to bring about a decrease in aggregate demand, so that AD_2 shifts toward AD_1 in Figure 12.2 (a) and (b) to bring the economy back to potential output Y_p.

The strengths and weaknesses of demand-side policies in bringing an economy out of an inflationary gap apply equally to their ability to deal with demand-pull inflation (see pages 327 and 336). In summary form, they include the following.

Strengths of fiscal policy

- Dealing with rapid and escalating inflation.
- Direct impact of government spending on aggregate demand.

Weaknesses of fiscal policy

- Time lags.
- Political constraints.
- Inability to fine-tune the economy.

Strengths of monetary policy

- Quick implementation and incremental adjustment of interest rates.
- Central bank independence and no political constraints.

Weaknesses of monetary policy

- Time lags.
- Conflict among government objectives. Inflation requires higher interest rates, but this may increase the exchange rate (appreciation), which

will make imports cheaper and exports more expensive to foreigners. If the country has a trade deficit (more imports than exports), a currency appreciation may work to increase the size of the trade deficit, which is not desirable (see Chapter 14).

An evaluation should also consider the relative merits of fiscal versus monetary policies. Most economists would prefer monetary policy to deal with an inflationary gap, because of its relative advantages over fiscal policy.

Note that supply-side policies cannot be used to deal with demand-pull inflation over short periods of time, because demand-pull inflation has causes lying on the demand-side, and supply-side policies work with a long time lag. However, over long periods, supply-side policies do have the tendency to reduce inflationary pressures that might have demand-side causes, because they shift the *LRAS* or Keynesian *AS* curves to the right.

Cost-push inflation

Cost-push inflation is caused by an increase in costs of production or supply-side shocks, causing a leftward shift in the *SRAS* curve, and results not only in a higher price level but also a fall in real output and a rise in unemployment. When this occurs, demand-side policies are not appropriate, because whereas the problem of inflation requires a decrease in aggregate demand, the problem of unemployment requires an increase in aggregate demand.

There are no general solutions to the problem of cost-push inflation. Sometimes, governments committed to a low rate of inflation use contractionary monetary policy (raising interest rates) to lower aggregate demand. However, this comes at the cost of more recession and therefore increased cyclical unemployment.

Other than this, policies that can be pursued depend very much on the specific cause of the increase in costs. For example, if cost-push inflation is due to increases in wages, the appropriate solution may lie in supply-side policies that attempt to stop or reverse the wage increases. These could involve labour market measures such as lowering the minimum wage, or reducing the power of labour unions so that these are unable to negotiate high wage increases with employers.

If the increase in costs is due to an increase in the price of an imported input, then the solution is less obvious. An imported cause of cost-push inflation around the world over the past 40 years has involved increases in the price of oil, an input that is heavily used as energy in most lines of production in both industry and agriculture. There are no easy solutions to this type of cost-push inflation. Since the early 1970s, when the price of oil began to increase, many countries have attempted to address the problem through efforts to develop alternative forms of energy, as well as by encouraging users to economise on the use of products that depend on oil as an input. Note that these are not supply-side or demand-side policies, but rather focus on reducing the *demand for oil*, so as to lower its price. If the price of oil falls, there results a rightward shift of the *SRAS* curve due to lower costs of production. However, this is a policy that takes a long time to take effect.

Another type of cost-push inflation may arise if firms with substantial monopoly power (such as oligopolies) increase their profits by increasing the prices they charge to consumers. In this case, policies pursued may be to break up the monopoly power of firms, and encourage competition (market-based supply-side policies).

Another type of cost-push inflation may occur if a country's currency falls in value, resulting in an increase in the prices it has to pay for imported goods (this will be explained in Chapter 14). Firms that are heavy users of imported inputs and raw materials experience an increase in their costs of production and cost-push inflation will result. One possible solution to this problem is to implement policies that aim to reduce dependence on imports ('expenditure switching' policies). However these policies come with their own problems, which we will discover in Chapter 14.

Inflation targeting

Inflation targeting, you may remember from page 335, is a special type of *monetary policy* that tries to keep inflation at a targeted rate. Inflation targeting does not make a distinction between cost-push and demand-pull inflation. It targets an inflation rate regardless of its causes. The advantages and disadvantages of inflation targeting were discussed on pages 335–36. Briefly, this policy has been quite successful at maintaining low and stable rates of inflation,. However, this may come at the cost of losing the ability to pursue other important objectives, such as low unemployment, or being able to respond to supply-side shocks. For example, if is an oil price shock causing cost-push inflation and stagflation, commitment to maintaining the low, target rate of inflation may mean accepting a deeper and more long-lasting recession together with a higher rate of cyclical unemployment.

Paradigm shifts in macroeconomics

Thomas Kuhn was a physicist who became very well known for his work in the philosophy of science through his famous book, *The Structure of Scientific Revolutions*. Kuhn argued that science (and by extension, social science), does not grow and progress in a continuous way through a gradual build-up of knowledge, but rather progresses through abrupt 'scientific revolutions', known as paradigm shifts. The word *paradigm* comes from the Greek word παραδειγμα (*paradeigma*), which means pattern, or example, or representation. Kuhn used it to refer to a thought pattern that defines a scientific discipline at a particular time. According to Kuhn, a paradigm is not just a theory, but a whole world view that goes along with a theory or set of theories, which is shared by the members of the scientific community. A paradigm shift occurs when there is change in the paradigm of a discipline. A paradigm shift does not occur easily, as there is resistance to the shift by adherents to the paradigm being challenged.

Some economists argue that there occurred two major paradigm shifts in macroeconomics in the 20th century, and that there may be a third one occurring as a result of the global financial crisis that began in 2008.

From classical economics to Keynesian economics

In the early 20th century, economists were guided in their macroeconomic policies by the principles of 'classical economics', which were based strongly on the microeconomic theory of supply and demand. Classical economists believed in the ability of the market and the price mechanism to solve all the major economic problems and allocate resources in the most efficient way. These principles, which are still accepted for the microeconomy, were then believed to apply to the macroeconomy as well. Major disruptions to the macroeconomy, affecting output and employment, were thought to be caused by factors external to the market system (such as wars, droughts or taxes), and were believed to be short-run phenomena that would be solved by the market, without interference by the government.

However, the Great Depression of the 1930s, which caused very large declines in output and large increases in unemployment, and which persisted for years, forced economists to question the ability of the market system to automatically generate the aggregate demand that was needed to get the economy out of the depression.

In 1936, John Maynard Keynes published his famous book, *The General Theory of Employment, Interest and Money*, in which he explained that the rigidity of wages and prices would not allow the market system to correct a recession (or depression) and bring the economy back to full employment. Soon after, with the outbreak of the Second World War in 1939, massive increases in government military expenditures showed economists the powerful effects of aggregate demand increases on employment and output.

The lessons of this experience brought forth a 'revolution' in economic thinking, or a paradigm shift, involving abandonment of the classical paradigm and a shift to the Keynesian one. In contrast to the classical world view, in which well-functioning markets meant there was not much for governments to do, in the Keynesian world view, markets were not self-correcting, and required active demand management (fiscal and monetary policies) to deal with economic fluctuations; government intervention in markets was indispensable for the proper functioning of the macroeconomy. By the end of the 1960s, many economists believed they had discovered in government intervention and demand management the secret to sustained economic growth, with low inflation and low unemployment.

From Keynesian economics to monetarist/new classical economics

In the early 1970s, this state of affairs was disrupted by the appearance of stagflation, or the simultaneous increase in inflation and unemployment, caused by falling aggregate supply (due to oil price and food price shocks). Economists realised that demand-side policies were not as effective as they were previously thought to be, since what was needed was expansionary policy for high unemployment and contractionary policy for inflation.

The decade of the 1970s saw high inflation and low output growth. This brought forth a new 'revolution' in economic thinking, or paradigm shift, involving the ideas of Milton Friedman, the founder of monetarism, which appeared to address the problem of stagflation, and also fitted in well with a political and ideological turn toward a market orientation that was occurring at the time as a reaction to the idea of big government (see the Theory of knowledge feature on page 290). The world view of monetarist economists was similar to that of the classical economists, based on a belief in the ability of markets to lead to efficient outcomes and address the problems of the macroeconomy, again implying that the role of government should be small. Though demand management continued to be used, the new world view paved the way for the supply-side policies that dominated the 1980s and 1990s, which focused on trying to make the market system work more effectively.

The global financial crisis and a new paradigm shift?

The global financial crisis that began in 2008 revealed the weaknesses of excessive deregulation of the financial sector, and the failure of markets to work as well as had been supposed. In addition to the enormous sums of money spent by governments to save banks and other financial institutions from failing, there have also been numerous calls for increased regulation and oversight of financial activities on both national and global fronts. This raises the question whether another paradigm shift, involving greater government intervention and less reliance on the market may be imminent. Nobel Prize-winning economist, Joesph Stiglitz, writes:

'The blame game continues over who is responsible for the worst recession since the Great Depression . . . But the economics profession bears more than a little [responsibility]. It provided the models that gave comfort to regulators that markets could be self-regulated, that they were efficient and self-correcting . . . Today, not only is our economy in a shambles but so too is the economic paradigm that predominated in the years before the crisis . . .

Fortunately, while much of the mainstream focused on these flawed models, numerous researchers were engaged in developing alternative approaches. Economic theory had already shown that many of the central conclusions of the standard model were not [reliable] . . .

Changing paradigms is not easy. Too many have invested too much in the wrong models. Like the Ptolemaic attempts to preserve earth-centric views of the universe, there will be heroic efforts to add complexities and refinements to the standard paradigm. The resulting models will be an improvement and policies based on them may do better, but they too are likely to fail. Nothing less than a paradigm shift will do.

But a new paradigm, I believe, is within our grasp: the intellectual building blocks are there . . .'[11]

Joseph Stiglitz and another Nobel Prize-winning economist, George Akerlof, note:

'The economic and financial crisis has been a telling moment for the economics profession, for it has put many long-standing ideas to the test. If science is defined by its ability to forecast the future, the failure of much of the economics profession to see the crisis coming should be a cause of great concern . . .

Just as the crisis has reinvigorated thinking about the need for regulation, so it has given new impetus to the exploration of alternative strands of thought that would provide better insights into how our complex economic system functions . . .

Fortunately, while some economists were pushing the idea of self-regulating, fully efficient markets that always remain at full employment, other economists and social scientists have been exploring a variety of different approaches . . .

Much of the most exciting work in economics now under way extends the boundary of economics to include work by psychologists, political scientists, and sociologists. We have much to learn, too, from economic history.'[12]

---

[11] Joseph Stiglitz, 'Needed: a new economic paradigm' in the *Financial Times*, 19 August 2010.
[12] George Akerlof and Joseph E. Stiglitz, 'Let a hundred theories bloom' in *Project Syndicate*, 26 October 2009.

Thinking points

- Can you detect a pattern in the balance between markets and government intervention that has been occurring in the shift from one paradigm to another?
- Can you think of any paradigm shifts that may have occurred in another social science or science you are studying?
- Based on the paradigm shifts described above, what has happened in the economy in each case to bring forth a paradigm shift?
- What kind of events do you think are likely to lead to paradigm shifts in other social sciences and in the natural sciences? Do they differ from those in economics?
- Why do you think paradigm shifts do not happen easily? Why do they occur infrequently?

1 **(a)** What policies would you recommend to deal with cyclical (demand-deficient) unemployment? What policies would you not recommend? Explain the advantages and disadvantages of your policy recommendations. **(b)** Answer part (a) for the case of structural, frictional and seasonal unemployment.

2 **(a)** What policies would you recommend to deal with demand-pull inflation? What policies would you not recommend? **(b)** Explain the advantages and disadvantages of your policy recommendations.

3 **(a)** What policies would you recommend to deal with cost-push inflation? What policies would you not recommend? **(b)** Explain the advantages and disadvantages of your policy recommendations.

Assessment

The Student's CD-ROM at the back of this book provides practice of examination questions based on the material you have studied in this chapter.

Standard level
- Exam practice: Paper 1, Chapter 12
  - SL/HL core topics (questions 12.1–12.23)

Higher level
- Exam practice: Paper 1, Chapter 12
  - SL/HL core topics (questions 12.1–12.23)
  - HL topics (questions 12.24 and 12.25)

Section 3
International economics

In our study of economics so far, we have been examining 'closed' economies, or economies that are closed to economic relations with other countries. In the real world, countries have many kinds of economic links with other countries. These links involve flows of goods, services and resources, as well as flows of payments and money across countries for many purposes. Section 3 is concerned with these international economic links. We will study international trade theory, where we will learn why countries trade with each other, and what are the benefits of trade. We will also examine international trade policy, where we will discover the reasons why many countries use policies that restrict the flows of international trade, as well as the consequences of trade restrictions.

International economics is also concerned with flows of payments from one country to another. We will see how countries measure the flows of money they receive from other countries and that they send out to other countries, and we will study the problems that can arise in the event of imbalances between these flows, as well as policies to correct such imbalances. We will learn that there are very strong interconnections between events in the domestic economy and the international economy. These interconnections mean that very often a country cannot pursue economic policies to correct a domestic economic problem without also taking into account the effects on its economic relations with other countries.

International economics is built on many of the economic principles of microeconomics as well as of macroeconomics. We will therefore be referring extensively to topics that we covered in Sections 1 and 2. While building on micro and macro principles, international economics also goes beyond these and develops new theories and tools, because economic relations between countries are in some ways different from economic relations within countries.

Chapter 13
International trade

In this chapter we examine questions on the flow of goods and services from country to country: why do countries trade; do they always benefit from trade; what can they do to increase the well-being of their populations through trade?

13.1 The benefits of trade

♦ Explain that gains from trade include lower prices for consumers, greater choice for consumers, the ability of producers to benefit from economies of scale, the ability to acquire needed resources, a more efficient allocation of resources, increased competition, and a source of foreign exchange.

What is trade?

International trade involves the buying and selling of goods and services across international boundaries. International trade has taken place since ancient times, by Egyptians, Greeks, Romans and Phoenicians, and later by all major powers throughout history up to the present. However, it has never been so important to the economies of virtually all countries in the world as it is today. Countries sell goods and services produced domestically to buyers abroad; these are called *exports*; and they buy goods and services from other countries for domestic use; these are *imports*. In recent decades, the value of exports and imports as a share of GDP has been increasing in most countries around the world. As a result, international trade has come to play a major role in economic activities and economic performance of countries everywhere.

The gains from trade

Countries trade with each other because they derive a number of important benefits or 'gains from trade'.

Benefits of trade

Increases in domestic production and consumption as a result of specialisation

Many of the benefits of trade arise from **specialisation**. Specialisation occurs when an individual, firm or country concentrates production on one or a few goods and services. Here, we are referring to specialisation by a country in the production of a range of goods or services it can produce efficiently (at a low cost). A country that does not trade must itself produce all the goods and services consumed, and therefore cannot specialise. However, if it uses its resources to specialise in the production of those goods and services it can produce more efficiently (with lower costs of production), it can produce more of these, and trade some of them for other goods produced more efficiently in other countries. This way it is able to produce a greater quantity of output because it does not 'waste' its scarce resources on producing goods and services at a relatively high cost. It can also increase its consumption of goods and services, because by exporting part of its larger domestic output in exchange for other output produced more cheaply elsewhere, it can acquire a larger overall quantity of goods and services. This, in summary form, is the theory of comparative advantage, which we will study in more detail later at higher level.

The possibility of increased production and consumption through specialisation is made possible because countries can take advantage of differences in quantities and quality of factors of production, as well as levels of technology, which altogether are called **factor endowments**. Depending on their factor endowments, different countries are more efficient in the production of certain goods and services than others. For example, Greece is a mountainous country with a large coastline. It is therefore better suited to producing shipping services, and less well suited to agricultural production. Switzerland, being a landlocked country, is not well suited to shipping, but has developed technologies that have made it well suited to the production of high quality watches and clocks.

Economies of scale in production
Economies of scale were studied at higher level in Chapter 6, page 153. They involve the ability of firms to decrease average costs of production (cost per unit of output) by becoming larger and increasing the quantity of output produced. When a firm lowers its average costs, it becomes more efficient, and can sell its output at a lower price. In the absence of trade, the amount of output any firm can produce is limited by the size of the domestic market. If the domestic market is small (if the country is small), the firm is unable to grow and take advantage of economies of scale. The possibility of trade and exports to other countries involves an expansion in the size of the market, allowing firms to produce more output, achieve economies of scale and enjoy the benefits of lower costs, which include lower prices and therefore greater export competitiveness, or the ability to compete better in foreign markets.

Greater choice for consumers
The goods and services each country can produce differ widely with respect to their variety and their quality. By trading with each other, countries can import a larger variety of goods and services, possibly of higher quality, than the ones they can produce themselves. This increases choice for consumers.

Increased competition and greater efficiency in production
When countries trade with each other, domestic firms become exposed to competition from products produced by firms in other countries. They are therefore forced to become more efficient; in other words, they must try to produce at the lowest possible cost. If they do not become more efficient, they will have to sell their output at higher prices to cover their higher costs; consumers will prefer the lower-priced imported products, and higher cost firms may go out of business. Therefore, increased competition leads to greater efficiency.

Lower prices for consumers
Increased competition and efficiency among firms leads to lower prices for consumers. In addition, as imports consist of goods that are produced more efficiently in other countries, this is an additional factor leading to lower prices for consumers.

Acquiring needed resources
Countries may need for their domestic production a number of natural resources or capital goods that are not available domestically. For example, oil is a resource that virtually all countries depend on, yet most are forced to rely on imported oil because they do not produce it themselves. The same may apply to a variety of other resources such as timber, minerals and semi-finished products used as inputs, as well as capital goods (machinery and equipment) used in production. Trade allows countries to import inputs they need for domestic production.

Free trade and a more efficient allocation of resources
If trade is free, meaning that there is no government intervention imposing restrictions on trade, it can lead to a more efficient allocation of resources. (This will be studied later in this chapter.)

Source of foreign exchange
When countries sell goods and services to other countries, they acquire **foreign exchange** (or foreign currencies), which allows them to make payments to other countries for the goods and services they import, or make other payments abroad. (We will learn about foreign exchange in Chapter 14.)

Trade makes possible the flow of new ideas and technology
As goods and services flow from one country to another, they enable new ideas and new technologies and skills to be transferred from one country to another.

Trade makes countries interdependent, reducing the possibility of hostilities and violence
Strong international trade links between countries can form the basis for economic relationships that reduce the possibility of war or other hostilities. For example, one of the reasons behind the establishment of the European Economic Community in 1957 (the EEC, the precursor of the European Union) was to eliminate the possibility of future wars between France and Germany. The strong economic interdependence created by trade (and other) links between these countries makes the possibility of war between them inconceivable today.

Trade as an 'engine for growth'
Increased specialisation, economies of scale, greater efficiencies in production, acquisition of needed resources, increased competition, technological advances and expanding markets, all made possible by international trade, contribute to increases in

Now suppose that Coffenia and Robotia agree to trade with each other at the 'price' ratio of 1:1; in other words, 1 unit of coffee trades for 1 robot.[1] They agree to trade (exchange) 3 units of coffee for 3 robots (Coffenia exports 3 units of coffee which Robotia imports, and Robotia exports 3 robots which Coffenia imports). The results are shown in columns 7 and 8 of Table 13.1, where Coffenia consumes 5 units of coffee (= 8−3 units of exports) and 3 robots (which it imports), and Robotia consumes 3 units of coffee (which it imports) and 3 robots (= 6−3 of exports).

Figure 13.1(c) shows that as a result of trade, Coffenia consumes at point G and Robotia at point H. Whereas *both countries are producing on their PPC*, due to trade they can consume at a point outside their PPC!

How can this be explained? Both countries become better off *because specialisation according to absolute advantage leads to a 'global' reallocation of resources where production takes place by the most efficient (low-cost) producers*.

The theory of comparative advantage

The meaning of comparative advantage
The theory of absolute advantage can explain only a small part of gains from specialisation and trade. A much more powerful argument explaining how countries can benefit from trade was provided by a well-known economist of the 19th century, David Ricardo, in his famous theory of comparative advantage. Ricardo was able to show that countries can gain from specialisation and trade even if one country has the absolute advantage in both goods. In order for this surprising result to hold, it is only

necessary that countries have *different opportunity costs* for their goods, so that the production of one good is relatively cheaper in one country than in another, even if it is not absolutely cheaper. **Comparative advantage** refers to the situation where one country has a lower opportunity cost (relative cost) in the production of a good than another country.

Using data to draw comparative advantage diagrams

◆ Draw a diagram to illustrate comparative advantage from a set of data.

Consider a simple world economy of two countries, Cottonia and Microchippia, producing cotton and microchips. Table 13.2 shows the quantities of each good that one worker can produce in one day if only one or the other good is produced. Cottonia can produce either 20 units of cotton (and 0 units of microchips) or it can produce 10 units of microchips (and 0 cotton). Microchippia can produce either 25 units of cotton (and 0 units of microchips) or 50 units of microchips (and 0 units of cotton). We can see that Microchippia has an absolute advantage in the production of *both cotton and microchips*, because with the same resources (one worker in one day) it can produce more of both goods than Cottonia.

Figure 13.2 plots the *PPCs* of each of the two countries based on the data of Table 13.2 (assuming straight-line *PPCs*). Microchippia's absolute advantage in the *production* of both goods is apparent from the fact that *its PPC lies entirely above the PPC of Cottonia.*

	Production possibilities when each country produces only cotton or only microchips		Opportunity cost of cotton	Opportunity cost of microchips
	(1) Cotton	(2) Microchips	(3)	(4)
Cottonia	20 or	10	$\dfrac{10 \text{ units of microchips}}{20 \text{ units of cotton}} = \dfrac{1}{2}$	$\dfrac{20 \text{ units of cotton}}{10 \text{ units of microchips}} = 2$
Microchippia	25 or	50	$\dfrac{50 \text{ units of microchips}}{25 \text{ units of cotton}} = 2$	$\dfrac{25 \text{ units of cotton}}{50 \text{ units of microchips}} = \dfrac{1}{2}$

Table 13.2   Comparative advantage

[1] We are using the price ratio of 1:1 for convenience only; many other price ratios would have been equally suitable.

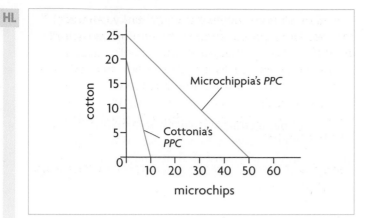

Figure 13.2   Comparative advantage

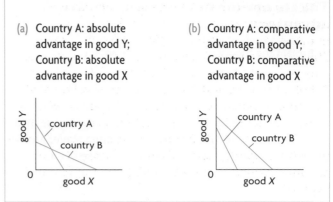

Figure 13.3   Absolute and comparative advantage

Determining which country has a comparative advantage in which good

♦ Draw a diagram to show comparative advantage.

When comparing the *PPC*s of two countries, we can see immediately whether one country has the absolute advantage in one or both of the goods. If the *PPC*s intersect, as in Figure 13.1, this means that each country has an absolute advantage in one of the two goods (for example, Coffenia in coffee and Robotia in robots). If the *PPC*s do not intersect, as in Figure 13.2(a), this means that the country with the *PPC* lying fully above the second *PPC* has an absolute advantage in the production of both goods (in our example this is Microchippia).

If two *PPC*s do not intersect, as in Figure 13.2, how can we determine comparative advantages? Very simply, *the country that has the flatter* PPC *has a comparative advantage in the good measured on the horizontal axis*. It follows that the country with the steeper *PPC* has a comparative advantage in the good measured along the vertical axis. In Figure 13.2, Microchippia's *PPC* is flatter than Cottonia's *PPC*; therefore, Microchippia has a comparative advantage in microchips, which are measured along the horizontal axis. Cottonia, with the steeper *PPC*, has the comparative advantage in cotton.

These points are summarised in Figure 13.3.

Calculating opportunity costs from a set of data

♦ Calculate opportunity costs from a set of data in order to identify comparative advantage.

We will now calculate opportunity costs to identify comparative advantage. Opportunity cost, as you may

remember (see page 4), is defined as the next best alternative that must be sacrificed in order to obtain something else.

Columns 3 and 4 in Table 13.2 calculate the opportunity costs of the two goods in each country. (Since we are using straight-line *PPC*s, this means that opportunity costs are constant throughout the *PPC*; see page 6 for an explanation). The opportunity cost of cotton is the quantity of microchips that must be sacrificed to produce an extra unit of cotton, while the opportunity cost of microchips is the amount of cotton that must be sacrificed per unit of microchips gained. To calculate the opportunity cost of cotton we divide the maximum number of microchips that can be produced by the maximum amount of cotton in the same country, thus finding microchips sacrificed per unit of cotton gained; we do a similar calculation to find the opportunity cost of microchips.

The results show that Microchippia has a lower opportunity cost in producing microchips, but Cottonia has a lower opportunity cost in producing cotton. Though Cottonia has a *higher absolute cost* in producing cotton, it has a *lower relative cost*, meaning that if Cottonia wants to produce more cotton, it needs to sacrifice a smaller quantity of microchips than does Microchippia. Therefore, Cottonia has a comparative advantage in cotton production, while Microchippia has comparative advantage in microchips.

This ties in with our conclusions above based on the *PPC*s of Cottonia and Microchippia. In fact, it is possible to calculate opportunity costs directly from Figure 13.2, using exactly the same method as above.

A country has a comparative advantage in the production of the good that has a lower opportunity cost (lower relative cost).

The theory (or law) of comparative advantage

♦ Explain the theory of comparative advantage.

The theory of comparative advantage is so important that it is often referred to as the *law of comparative advantage*, which states that if countries specialise and trade according to their comparative advantage, global production and consumption will increase because of an improvement in the global allocation of resources. Therefore, Cottonia should specialise in the production of cotton and Microchippia should specialise in the production of microchips; Cottonia should export cotton and import microchips and Microchippia should export microchips and import cotton. This will make both countries better off and an improvement in the 'global' allocation of resources will result.

In fact, it can be shown that with trade, both countries will consume at a point outside their *PPC*s. In Figure 13.4(a), Cottonia produces at point A of its *PPC* where it specialises entirely in cotton; in Figure 13.4(b), Microchippia produces at point C where it specialises entirely in microchips. They then decide to trade cotton and microchips at the price ratio of 1 : 1, so that 1 unit of cotton trades for 1 unit of microchips, and they agree to exchange (trade) 10 units of microchips for 10 units of cotton. Thus with trade, Cottonia finds itself consuming 10 units of cotton (= 20 − 10 units of exports) and 10 units of microchips (which it imports), or at point B which lies outside its *PPC*. Microchippia finds itself consuming 40 units of Microchips (= 50 − 10 units of exports) and 10 units of cotton (which it imports), or point D, which also lies outside

its *PPC*. Therefore, whereas under autarky (no trade) they would be producing and consuming on their *PPC*, as a result of specialisation and trade both countries succeed in increasing their consumption to a greater level than what is possible under autarky.

> A country has a comparative advantage in the production of a good when this can be produced at a lower opportunity cost than its trading partner. According to the **theory (or law) of comparative advantage**, as long as opportunity costs in two (or more) countries differ, it is possible for all countries to gain from specialisation and trade according to their comparative advantage. The global allocation of resources improves, resulting in greater global output and greater global consumption, allowing countries to consume outside their *PPC*.

The case of parallel PPCs

What if the *PPC*s of two countries are parallel to each other, as in Figure 13.5? Here, country A has an absolute advantage in the production of both good Y and good X. The fact that the two *PPC*s are parallel means that the two countries face identical opportunity costs for the two goods.[2] If opportunity costs are identical, there is no country in which one good is relatively cheaper; therefore, there is no country that has a comparative advantage in the production of one or the other good. Under these circumstances (which do not occur very often in the real world), there are no possibilities for countries to gain from specialisation and trade, and there is therefore no point in these countries specialising and trading with each other.

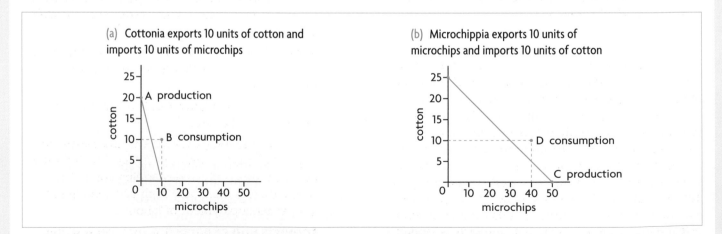

(a) Cottonia exports 10 units of cotton and imports 10 units of microchips

(b) Microchippia exports 10 units of microchips and imports 10 units of cotton

Figure 13.4 The gains from specialisation and trade based on comparative advantage: both countries consume outside their *PPC*

---

[2] This follows from the point that two parallel lines have identical slopes, and since the slope is the opportunity cost of the good measured on the horizontal axis, it follows that opportunity costs are identical.

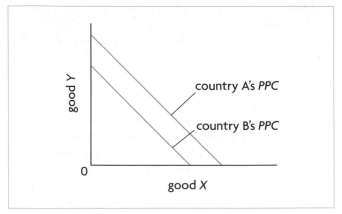

Figure 13.5 Identical opportunity costs: no gains from trade

Absolute advantage as a special case of comparative advantage

As we have seen, according to the theory of comparative advantage, countries gain from specialisation and trade as long as they have different relative costs of production, i.e. different opportunity costs for their goods, regardless of whether or not one country has an absolute advantage in the production of all the goods. This means that the theory of absolute advantage is simply a special case that is included in the theory of comparative advantage. Considering the case of Coffenia and Robotia, the fact that Coffenia has an absolute advantage in coffee and Robotia in robots does not affect the conclusions of the theory of comparative advantage.

The sources of comparative advantage

* Describe the sources of comparative advantage, including the differences between countries in factor endowments and the levels of technology.

The sources of comparative advantage were noted earlier in our discussion of the first benefit of trade (page 354), where we saw that countries can increase production and consumption of goods through specialisation and trade because of differences in factor endowments, meaning differences in quantities and quality of factors of production, and in levels of technology. For example, a worker who is highly educated and skilled will likely be able to produce a greater quantity of output per day than one who is less educated and less skilled. Similarly, a worker working with technologically advanced machines is also likely to be able to produce more output than one working with simpler machinery. A country with a temperate climate will find it more costly

to produce crops such as coffee or cocoa, which are better suited to tropical climates. Mountainous countries are less well suited to agriculture than countries with fertile plains.

The real-world relevance of the theory of comparative advantage

* Discuss the real-world relevance and limitations of the theory of comparative advantage, considering factors including the assumptions on which it rests, and the costs and benefits of specialisation (a full discussion must take into account arguments in favour and against free trade and protection—see below).

The theory of comparative advantage forms the basis of trade policies in many countries. Its key conclusion, that free trade increases global production and consumption, leading to an improved global allocation of resources, forms the justification of the major policy trend since the early 1990s around the world toward *trade liberalisation*, involving the freeing up of trade through the gradual removal of trade restrictions. However, in spite of its potentials, the theory of comparative advantage is strongly criticised:

* **The theory of comparative advantage depends on many unrealistic assumptions:**
  * **Factors of production are immobile and fixed.** In other words, they do not move from one country to another and do not change. Yet in the real world, factors of production, particularly labour and capital, can and often do move. Moreover, there are likely to be changes in quality, such as when labour acquires more skills and education.
  * **Technology is fixed.** This is highly unrealistic since new technologies are continuously being introduced.
  * **There is perfect competition.** In reality this is rarely if ever the case.
  * **There is full employment of all resources** (countries produce on their *PPC*s). This is hardly ever met, especially in developing countries, where there is often very high unemployment and underemployment of labour.
  * **Imports and exports balance each other.** In the real world, this is rarely the case, and in the event that there are serious trade imbalances, particularly a trade deficit where imports are much larger than exports, serious payments

problems may arise; in other words, problems of how to pay for all the extra imports.

- **There is free trade,** meaning that governments do not intervene in markets, and trade flows (imports and exports) are determined entirely by market forces. In reality, there is strong government intervention in markets that influences quantities of imports and exports.

- **It is unrealistic to ignore transportation costs.** In the real world, there are costs of transportation for imports and exports that change relative prices and may limit the benefits of specialisation.

- **Specialisation according to comparative advantage may not allow necessary structural changes to occur in an economy.** As an economy grows and develops, major changes in its structure usually occur, with the agricultural sector becoming less important, and manufacturing and services becoming more important (see Figure 3.10, page 65). These changes are especially important for developing countries, and indicate that comparative advantage changes over time in response to such structural changes. Moreover, comparative advantage changes because of changes in the quantities and quality of factors of production and technology (as noted above). For example, an agricultural economy may have a comparative advantage in agricultural products, but as it becomes more industrialised, its comparative advantage may change in favour of manufactured products. If countries specialise according to their comparative advantage, they would have to go on producing and exporting according to that same advantage, and this would not permit the necessary structural changes to take place in the economy. This is an important issue for developing countries that we will return to later in this chapter and in Chapter 17.

- **Trade on the basis of comparative advantage may lead to excessive specialisation.** If a country has a comparative advantage in only one or a few products, specialisation according to comparative advantage may lead to too much specialisation, which may make countries vulnerable if they become too dependent on factors beyond their control. For example, if there is a fall in exports due to a global recession, or a fall in export prices due to declining demand for the goods over long periods

of time, the result will be falling revenues from exports, falling incomes and economic decline. Further, primary products (including agricultural products) are subject to strong price fluctuations, which lead to unstable export revenues, also with negative impacts on the economy. The theoretical explanation behind long-term declining prices and short-term fluctuating prices of agricultural products and other primary commodities was provided in Chapter 3 in terms of elasticities (price elasticity of demand, price elasticity of supply and income elasticity of demand). These are issues that are especially relevant to developing countries that are dependent on exports of just a few primary products (see Chapters 15 and 17).

Test your understanding 13.2

1 Explain the difference between **(a)** the terms 'absolute advantage' and 'comparative advantage', and **(b)** the theory of absolute advantage and the theory of comparative advantage. **(c)** Which of the two theories is a more powerful explanation of the benefits from trade. Why?

2 **(a)** Draw a diagram showing Oceanland's absolute advantage in shipping services and Flatland's absolute advantage in agricultural products. **(b)** Using *PPC* diagrams, explain how Oceanland and Flatland can gain from specialisation and trade. **(c)** Show possible points of production and consumption in your diagrams for each of the two countries after specialisation and trade.

3 Lakeland has an absolute advantage over Mountainland in the production of both fish and computers, but Lakeland has a comparative advantage in fish production. **(a)** Draw a diagram showing the absolute and comparative advantages of the two countries. **(b)** Explain how Lakeland and Mountainland can gain from specialisation and trade. **(c)** Show possible points of production and consumption in your diagrams for each of the two countries after specialisation and trade.

4 **(a)** Using the data in Table 13.1, calculate the opportunity cost of coffee and robots in Coffenia and Robotia. **(b)** Use your results of differing opportunity costs to explain why the theory of absolute advantage is a special case of the theory of comparative advantage.

HL

5 Answer these questions based on the following diagrams:

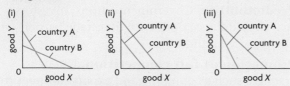

(i)

country A

country B

good Y

0   good X

(ii)

country A

country B

good Y

0   good X

(iii)

country A

country B

good Y

0   good X

(a) In diagram (i), which of the two countries has the absolute advantage in the production of which goods?

(b) In diagram (ii), can either country benefit from specialisation and trade? Why or why not?

(c) In diagram (iii), does either country have an absolute advantage in the production of either good?

(d) In diagram (iii), can either country benefit from specialisation and trade? Why or why not? If they can benefit, what good should each one specialise in?

6 According to the theory of comparative advantage, under what circumstances is it not worthwhile for countries to specialise and trade?

7 For each case below, **(a)** calculate opportunity costs for country A and country B, and determine the good in which each country has a comparative advantage (if any). **(b)** Draw *PPC* diagrams indicating comparative advantage. **(c)** Indicate which good each country should specialise in, and which it should export and import.

Production possibilities for country A and country B

	Country A	Country B
good X	8	2
good Y	2	4
good X	8	2
good Y	6	4
good X	1	4
good Y	2	2
good X	6	3
good Y	3	1
good X	1	2
good Y	2	4

8 **(a)** What are some of the unrealistic assumptions on which the theory of comparative advantage rests? **(b)** What are some of the problems that countries may run into if they specialise and trade according to their comparative advantage?

13.3 The World Trade Organization (WTO)

♦ Describe the objectives and functions of the WTO.

History

During the Great Depression of the 1930s, when countries around the world were suffering major declines in output and very high rates of unemployment, they resorted to tariffs and other restrictions to limit imports and protect domestic production and employment. As each country raised its tariffs, it provoked retaliatory tariff increases from its trading partners, resulting in 'tariff wars' that greatly reduced the volume of international trade without positive effects on output and employment. In 1947, 29 countries formed an agreement known as the General Agreement on Tariffs and Trade (GATT), intended to gradually liberalise (free up) international trade and prevent further outbreaks of tariff wars. Up to that time, all countries had been free to impose any type of trade protection measures on imports from other countries.

The GATT was based on the following principles:

- Non-discrimination – equal, non-discriminatory treatment for all member countries. This means that a country's trade policy cannot discriminate between its trading partners (for example, it cannot impose a higher tariff on imports from one country and a lower one on imports from another country). Exception was made for bilateral and regional trading blocs (see Chapter 15).

- Elimination of non-tariff trade barriers – gradual elimination of non-tariff barriers. Exceptions were made for agricultural products and countries with balance of payments difficulties.

- Consultations to resolve trade disputes – GATT provided a forum for discussions to resolve disagreements between countries.

The members of GATT would periodically conduct 'rounds' of negotiations in which they tried to achieve the above objectives. They conducted eight rounds in total, the last one being the 'Uruguay Round' (because it was launched in Punte del Este in Uruguay), which lasted from 1986 to 1994. In 1994, by which time the member countries had increased to 124, an agreement was reached to replace the GATT by a new international trade body. This body was established in January 1995, and was called the **World Trade Organization (WTO)**.

WTO functions and objectives

Today, the WTO provides the institutional and legal framework for the trading system that exists between member nations worldwide. As of July 2011, it had 153 members, which account for over 97% of global trade. In addition, there were 31 'Observer' countries, which must apply for full membership within five years of having Observer status.

The WTO describes itself as an organisation for liberalising trade, which operates a system of trade rules and provides a forum for trade negotiations and settling trade disputes. It has the following functions:[3]

- **It administers WTO trade agreements.** The WTO helps in the implementation and administration of international trade agreements.
- **It provides a forum for trade negotiations.** The WTO provides a forum for members to discuss their trade problems and negotiate trade agreements on how to liberalise trade. This is one of the most important WTO functions.
- **It handles trade disputes.** When WTO members disagree on trade issues, the WTO makes decisions to resolve the differences on the basis of the legal foundations of the trade agreements.
- **It monitors national trade policies.** The WTO carries out periodic reviews of its members' national trade policies. Members are required to notify the WTO of any changes in trade policy. The WTO also examines new trading bloc arrangements (trading blocs are explained in Chapter 15).
- **It provides technical assistance and training for developing countries.** The assistance provided to developing countries concerns trade-related issues arising from WTO trade agreements.
- **It facilitates co-operation with other international organisations.** The WTO co-operates with other international organisations (such as the World Bank and International Monetary Fund discussed in Chapter 18), in order to facilitate co-ordination of global polices.

The trading system promoted by the WTO is based on the following principles:

- **Non-discrimination.** The WTO continues the GATT's emphasis on equal, non-discriminatory treatment for all member countries (excepting trading blocs).

- **Free trade.** Trade barriers should be lowered through negotiations.
- **Predictability.** Governments, firms, investors, etc., should have confidence that trade barriers will not be raised arbitrarily.
- **Promotion of fair competition.** Unfair practices such as dumping and export subsidies (to be explained below) are discouraged.
- **Development and economic reform should be encouraged.** Developing countries should be offered flexibility with respect to lowering their trade barriers, more time to adjust to change and special privileges.

The role of the WTO in the global trading system will be evaluated in Chapter 17 (page 488).

Test your understanding 13.3

1 What is the World Trade Organization (WTO)?
2 What are the main objectives and functions of the WTO?

13.4 Restrictions on free trade: trade protection

♦ Evaluate the effect of different types of trade protection.

In this section, we will consider a variety of methods used by governments to restrict international trade flows, known as **trade protection**.[4] As we consider each type of trade protection, we will also evaluate it with respect to its effects on stakeholders and resource allocation.

Defining trade protection

Free trade versus protection

Free trade refers to the absence of government intervention of any kind in international trade, so that trade takes place without any restrictions (barriers) between individuals or firms in different countries. Free trade, according to the theory of comparative advantage, would lead to an efficient global allocation of resources, and maximisation

---

[3] World Trade Organization, 'Understanding the WTO: What is the World Trade Organization?' (http://www.wto.org/english/thewto_e/whatis_e/tif_e/fact1_e.htm).

[4] Note that what used to be called 'protectionism' by the IB is now referred to as 'trade protection'. This is part of a more general effort on the part of the IB to avoid words that end in 'ism', because of the frequent association of such words with doctrines and dogma.

of global output, with all countries sharing in the benefits of trade.

   Trade protection involves government intervention in international trade through the imposition of trade restrictions (barriers) to prevent the free entry of imports into a country or to protect the domestic economy from foreign competition.

   The topic of free trade versus trade protection is highly controversial and has occupied economists for over 300 years. In recent decades it has become one of the most important international policy issues. In this section we will study and evaluate a range of trade protection measures, and will consider a variety of arguments against and in favour of trade protection.

Using diagrams to illustrate international trade

Imagine a country called Tradenia that produces bindles. Figure 13.6(a) shows the familiar equilibrium price and quantity of bindles determined in Tradenia's domestic market under autarky (no international trade). When Tradenia decides to open its economy to international trade, the question arises, should bindles be imported or exported? The answer depends on the domestic price of bindles when there is no trade, compared with the price of bindles in the international bindle market. The international bindle market involves many individuals or firms in countries around the world that buy and sell bindles, and the world bindle price is determined by world demand and world supply. Whether Tradenia will import or export bindles depends on whether its domestic bindle price is higher or lower than the world price.

Suppose (for simplicity) that the Tradenian market for bindles is relatively small compared to the overall size of the world bindle market, so that its buying and selling activities do not have the ability to influence the world price. This means that the world supply curve facing Tradenia is perfectly elastic, appearing as a horizontal line at the world price of bindles. A perfectly elastic supply curve means Tradenia can buy or sell any quantity of bindles it wishes at the world price. This is shown in Figure 13.6(b), showing the world price, P_w, to be higher than Tradenia's domestic price, P_d. Once Tradenia opens its economy to international trade, it accepts the world price P_w, and the domestic price, P_d will no longer be relevant. At the higher price P_w, the quantity of bindles supplied, Q_s, is larger than the quantity of bindles demanded, Q_d. This excess quantity supplied, which is $Q_s - Q_d$, is available to be sold to buyers abroad, or exported. It follows then that *under free trade, when the world price is higher than the domestic price, the good in question is exported.*

   In Figure 13.6(c), the world price of bindles, P_w, is lower than the domestic price, P_d. Accepting the world price P_w, where the quantity of bindles demanded, Q_d, is larger than quantity of bindles supplied, Q_s, Tradenia now has an excess quantity demanded, $Q_d - Q_s$, which is the quantity of bindles to be purchased from abroad, or imported. *Under free trade, when the world price is lower than the domestic price, the good in question is imported.*

   Higher level students may note that Figure 13.6 (b) and (c) are illustrations of the principle of comparative advantage. In part (b), the lower domestic price compared to the world price indicates that the country has a comparative advantage in the production of the good, can produce it more efficiently (at a lower cost)

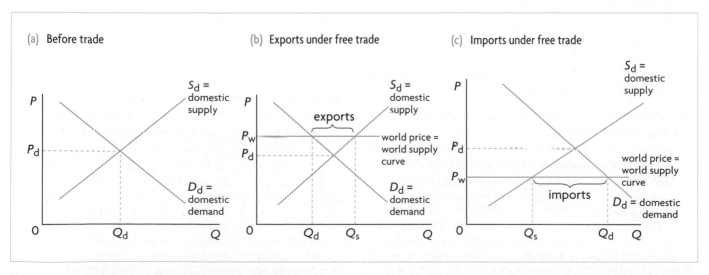

Figure 13.6   Using diagrams to illustrate international trade

than other countries, and can therefore sell it at a lower price. When it opens the economy to international trade, it accepts the higher world price, it increases its domestic production of the good and exports part of it to other, less efficient countries. In part (c), the higher domestic price compared to other countries indicates that the country has a comparative disadvantage: it is less efficient than other countries, therefore charges a higher price domestically. When it opens itself to trade, it accepts the lower world price, and the excess demand is satisfied by imports produced in other countries more efficiently.

Most types of trade protection policies involve restrictions on imports, that is, cases where the country in question has a comparative disadvantage in the production of the good, and is therefore an importer. We will therefore examine cases where the world price of a good is lower than the domestic price.

Tariffs

Tariffs and their effects

♦ Explain, using a tariff diagram, the effects of imposing a tariff on imported goods on different stakeholders, including domestic producers, foreign producers, consumers and the government.

Tariffs, also known as 'customs duties', are taxes on imported goods, and are the most common form of trade restriction. Tariffs may serve two purposes. One is to protect a domestic industry from foreign competition (a protective tariff), and the other is to raise revenue for the government (a revenue tariff). Whatever the tariff's purpose, the effects on the economy are the same.

The effects of a tariff are illustrated in Figure 13.7. Part (a) shows that under free trade, the country accepts the world price P_w, at which it produces quantity Q_1 (given the intersection of S_d with the world supply curve), demands quantity Q_4 (given by the intersection of D_d, with the world supply curve), and imports $Q_4 - Q_1$. Suppose a tariff is imposed on the imported good. As a result, the price of the imported good rises, to $P_w + t$, causing the domestic price of the good to rise above the world price by the amount of the tariff, to $P_w + t$.

Let's now examine the effects of the tariff:

- **Increase in quantity supplied, decrease in quantity demanded and decrease in imports.** At $P_w + t$, domestic quantity supplied increases from Q_1 to Q_2, domestic quantity demanded falls from Q_4 to Q_3, and the quantity of imports falls to $Q_3 - Q_2$.

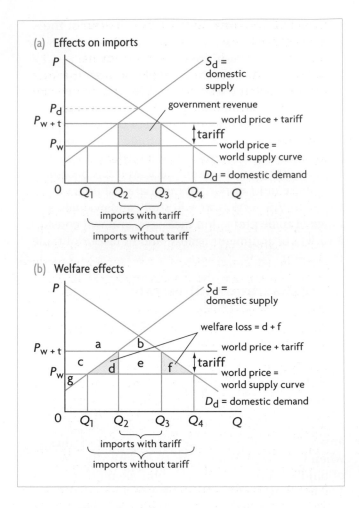

Figure 13.7 Effects of a tariff

- **Domestic consumers are worse off.** Consumers lose from the tariff, because they must pay a higher price, $P_w + t$; and they can only buy a smaller quantity, Q_3 (rather than Q_4).

- **Domestic producers are better off.** Domestic producers gain from the tariff, because they receive a higher price, $P_w + t$, and they sell a larger quantity, Q_2 (rather than Q_1).

- **Domestic employment increases.** Since domestic producers sell a larger quantity, this has the effect of increasing employment in the domestic economy.

- **The government gains tariff revenues.** The amount of revenue that the government receives from the tariff is shown by the shaded area in Figure 13.7(a), determined by multiplying the amount of tariff (per unit of the good) times the quantity of imports. Since the tariff is paid by consumers (who pay the price $P_w + t$), the government's tariff revenue represents income that is transferred from consumers to the government.

- **Domestic income distribution worsens.** There is a negative impact on income distribution, because the tariff is a type of regressive tax (see Chapter 11, page 313), which burdens people on lower incomes proportionately more than people on higher incomes; as income increases, the proportion of income paid as tax falls. Therefore, tariffs worsen income distribution.

- **Increased inefficiency in production.** The increase in domestic output represents an increase in production by relatively inefficient domestic producers, resulting in a waste of scarce resources (inefficiency). Remember, the reason why the domestic price before trade is higher than the world price is that domestic producers are not as efficient as foreigners who produce and export the same good; while foreigners have a comparative advantage in the production of the good, domestic producers have a comparative disadvantage. The tariff therefore causes an increase in production by relatively inefficient producers.

- **Foreign producers are worse off.** The producers of the exporting countries are worse off, because whereas they receive the world price, P_w, for their exports, they export a smaller quantity, since the quantity of imports in the importing country is reduced. The exporting countries therefore lose export revenues due to the fall in the quantity of exports.

- **A global misallocation of resources results.** The decrease in consumption, and the shift of production away from more efficient foreign producers and towards more inefficient domestic producers, indicate that there is an increase in the misallocation of resources both domestically and globally.

The effects of tariffs on consumer and producer surplus

Figure 13.7(b) shows the effects of the tariff on consumer and producer surplus. Part (b) is identical to part (a), except that it labels the areas in the triangles and rectangles. Consumer surplus is the area under the demand curve and above the price paid by consumers. Before the imposition of the tariff it includes the areas a+b+c+d+e+f, representing the area under the demand curve and above the world price P_w. Producer surplus before the tariff is the area g below the price producers receive and above the supply curve. Therefore, social (consumer plus producer) surplus is a+b+c+d + e+f+g.

After the tariff is imposed, consumer surplus drops to a+b, indicating that consumers are worse off, and producer surplus becomes c+g, having increased by the amount of c, indicating that producers are better off. Also, the government gains the revenue equal to e. Therefore, social surplus after the tariff is a+ b+c + e+g.

To find the effect of the tariff on social surplus, we can subtract surplus after the tariff from surplus before the tariff to find the difference:

$$(a+b+c+d+e+f+g) - (a+b+c+e+g) = d+f =$$
welfare (deadweight) loss

appearing as the shaded areas in the diagram. It results from a misallocation of resources caused by increased production by inefficient producers (area d) and decreased consumption of consumers (area f).

Calculating the effects of tariffs from diagrams (higher level topic)

HL

* Calculate from diagrams the effects of imposing a tariff on imported goods on different stakeholders, including domestic producers, foreign producers, consumers and the government.

The tariff diagram in Figure 13.8 is similar to Figure 13.7, only we are given numerical data for prices and quantities of a good measured in millions of units. We would like to calculate the following information.

Tariff per unit
The tariff per unit is the world price+tariff minus the world price, or $9-$7 = $2 per unit.

Quantity of imports
Imports before the tariff are 2.8 million-1 million = 1.8 million units. Imports after the tariff are

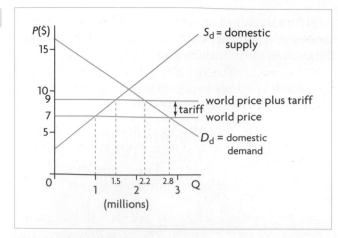

Figure 13.8 Calculating the effects of a tariff

2.2 million–1.5 million = 0.7 million units. Therefore, imports fall by 1.8 million–0.7 million = 1.1 million units.

Domestic consumers

The price paid by consumers increases from $7 to $9, or by $2 per unit. The quantity purchased by consumers falls from 2.8 million units to 2.2 million units, or by 0.6 million units. Consumer expenditure before the tariff is $7×2.8 million = $19.6 million, and after the tariff it is $9×2.2 million = $19.8 million. Therefore, consumer expenditure increases. Note however, that *this need not happen*. It is possible for consumer expenditure to fall, if the quantity effect on expenditure is larger than the price effect. Consumers are worse off regardless, because they must pay a higher price for a smaller quantity.

Domestic producers

The price received by producers increases from $7 to $9, or by $2 per unit. The quantity produced also increases from 1 million to 1.5 million units, or by 0.5 million units. Therefore, producer revenue increases from $7×1 million units = $7 million before the tariff to $9×1.5 million units = $13.5 million after the tariff, or by $6.5 million (= $13.5 million–$7 million). Producers are better off.

Government revenue

Government revenue from the tariff increases from zero to an amount equal to the tariff per unit ($2) times the quantity of imports *after* the tariff has been imposed (0.7 million units). It is therefore $2 × 0.7 million = $1.4 million. The government budget therefore gains.

Foreign producers

Exports of foreign producers to the country that imposes the tariff fall by an amount equal to the fall in the country's imports, calculated above to be 1.1 million units. Export revenues of the foreign producers fall by an amount equal to the fall in the

quantity of exports (1.1 million units) times the world price ($7), which is $7.7 million (= $7×1.1 million). Therefore, foreign producers are worse off.

Test your understanding 13.5

1 Under free trade, the price of computers in Lakeland was $300 per unit; domestic computer production was 100 000 units per year and imports stood at 250 000 units per year. Following the imposition by the government of a $50 per unit tariff on computers, domestic production increased to 200 000 units and imports fell to 70 000 units. Calculate **(a)** the new price paid by consumers, **(b)** the new price received by domestic producers, **(c)** computer sales before the tariff, and **(d)** computer sales after the tariff.

2 Using your answer to question 1, calculate the **(a)** change in consumer expenditure, **(b)** change in domestic producer revenue, **(c)** change in the government's budget, **(d)** change in foreign producers' quantity of computer exports to Lakeland, and **(e)** change in foreign producers' export revenues from computer exports to Lakeland. (You may find it useful to use a tariff diagram to do your calculations. The diagram does not have to be drawn to scale.)

Import quotas

Import quotas and their effects

♦ Explain, using a diagram, the effects of setting a quota on foreign producers on different stakeholders, including domestic producers, foreign producers, consumers and the government.

An **import quota** (or more simply, **quota**) is a legal limit to the quantity of a good that can be imported over a particular time period (typically a year). The effects of quotas are similar to the effects of tariffs, except that they usually do not create revenue for the government. We can see the effects of an import quota in Figure 13.9(a). Suppose initially the economy is importing under free trade; quantity Q_1 is supplied by domestic producers, quantity Q_4 is demanded, and the excess of quantity demanded over quantity supplied, $Q_4 - Q_1$, represents imports. The government then decides to impose a quota on imports, limiting the quantity that can be legally imported to $Q_3 - Q_2$. This restriction in effect shifts the supply curve to the right by the amount of the quota. In Figure 13.9(a), the new, after-quota supply curve is shown by S_{dq} and represents domestic supply plus the quantity specified by the quota.[5] The new equilibrium domestic price is determined by the intersection of the domestic demand curve with S_{dq}, and is P_q.

When the government sets a quota, it issues a limited number of quota licences determining the legal limit on the quantity of imports. These licence holders gain quota revenues (also known as 'quota rents') because whereas they buy the good at the world price P_w, they sell it to consumers at the higher domestic price P_q. Usually, the government gives the licences to governments of exporting countries, which then distribute them to their own producers or exporters, who buy at the price P_w and sell at P_q. As a result, the exporters (or producers) of exporting countries receive the quota revenues.[6] Because of this, foreign governments/producers prefer having quotas rather than tariffs imposed upon their exports.

With the exception of who gets the quota revenue, the effects of an import quota are the same as in the case of a tariff:

- **Increase in quantity supplied, decrease in quantity demanded and decrease in imports.** Domestic production increases to Q_2, domestic quantity demanded falls to Q_3, and the quantity of imports falls to Q_3-Q_2.

- **Domestic consumers are worse off.** As in the case of a tariff, consumers lose from the quota, because they must pay a higher price, P_q, and they can only buy a smaller quantity, Q_3 (rather than Q_4).

- **Domestic producers are better off.** As in the case of a tariff, domestic producers gain from the quota, as they receive a higher price, P_q, and they sell a larger quantity, Q_2 (rather than Q_1).

- **Domestic employment increases.** As in the case of a tariff, domestic employment increases since producers increase the quantity of output they produce.

- **The government neither gains nor loses.** Since the government gives the import licences to foreign governments, the government budget is not affected.

- **Domestic income distribution worsens.** Quotas do not involve a tax in the same way that tariffs do; however, they do result in a higher price, and the difference P_q-P_w, or the increase in price, has the same effect as the tariff in that it is regressive. In other words, the amount P_q-P_w represents a higher fraction of income when income is low, and decreases as a fraction of income as income rises. Therefore, quotas have the effect of worsening the distribution of income in the same way that tariffs do.

- **Increased inefficiency in production.** As in the case of tariffs, an increase in production by relatively inefficient domestic producers results.

- **The exporting countries may be worse off or better off.** As in the case of a tariff, the producers of the exporting countries export a smaller quantity. There is, therefore, a loss of export revenues due to the fall in the quantity of exports. However, since the exporting countries receive the import licences, they gain the quota revenues. Therefore, whether

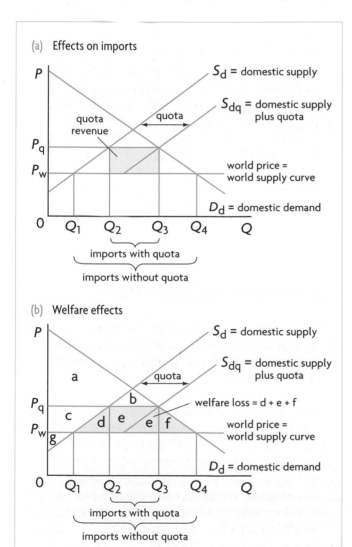

(a) Effects on imports

(b) Welfare effects

Figure 13.9   Effects of a quota

they will be worse off or better off depends on which is larger: the loss of export revenues or the gain of quota revenues.

- **A global misallocation of resources results.** The decrease in consumption, and the shift of production away from more efficient foreign producers and towards more inefficient domestic producers indicates that there is an increase in the misallocation of resources globally.

The effects of quotas on consumer and producer surplus

The effects of quotas on consumer and producer surplus are shown in Figure 13.9(b). They are the same as the effects of tariffs, with the exception of quota revenues. Before the quota, consumer surplus is the area a+ b + c+d+e+f, and producer surplus is area g. After the quota, consumers have surplus equal to area a+ b, and producers have surplus equal to g+c. Areas d and f have been lost as welfare (deadweight) loss, due to inefficiencies in production (area d) and reduced consumption (area f). Note that up to this point, welfare loss is identical to that arising from tarriffs (see Figure 13.7). In addition, area e, which represents quota revenue, is transferred abroad to exporting countries. Therefore, the total surplus lost due to the quota is d+e+f. As a result, quotas result in greater welfare losses for the domestic economy than tariffs.

Test your understanding 13.6

1 Draw a diagram showing the effects of a quota on **(a)** the domestic price of the protected good, **(b)** quantity produced domestically, **(c)** quantity consumed by domestic consumers, **(d)** quantity of imports, and **(e)** quota revenue.

2 Using your diagram of question 1, and assuming the government gives quota licences to exporting firms, discuss the effects of a quota on **(a)** domestic consumers, **(b)** domestic producers, **(c)** domestic employment, **(d)** foreign producers (*Hint:* take into account loss of export revenues and gain of quota revenue), **(e)** the government, **(f)** efficiency in production, and **(g)** the global allocation of resources.

3 **(a)** What is the main difference between the effects of a tariff and a quota? **(b)** Explain why foreign producers under certain circumstances may prefer quotas to tariffs.

4 Evaluate the effects of a quota taking into account various stakeholders, the domestic economy, the economies of exporters, and the global economy.

Real world focus

US sugar quotas

Americans consume nearly 10 million metric tonnes of sugar per year, of which about 77% is produced domestically and the remaining 23% is imported. Sugar imports are limited by import quotas, which result in a domestic price of sugar of $0.38 per pound compared to the world price of $0.22 per pound (in 2009). The imports come from about 40 countries, each of which is issued a quota licence that specifies how much sugar they can export to the United States.

The sugar quotas are supported by sugar farmers, though they run against the interests of US consumers who must pay the higher price, as well as confectioners who use sugar as an input in production. An increase in import quotas of 300 000 metric tonnes may be approved for 2010, far less than the 1 million tonne increase wanted by sugar users, which was blocked by sugar farmers.

Many studies have confirmed that sugar quotas deprive millions of more efficient farmers in developing countries of export markets and export revenues.

Source: Carolyn Cui and Bill Tomson, 'USDA says it may relax sugar quotas' in *Wall Street Journal*, 14 April 2010; Mark J. Perry, 'Sugar tariffs cost Americans $2.5 billion in 2009', Carpe Diem (http://mjperry.blogspot.com/2010/01/sugar-tariffs-cost-americans-25-billion.html), 30 January 2010.

Applying your skills

1 Explain why US sugar farmers try to block increases in sugar quotas.

2 Using a diagram, explain impacts of sugar quotas on various stakeholders.

3 Evaluate the use of sugar import quotas.

Calculating the effects of quotas from diagrams (higher level topic)

♦ Calculate from diagrams the effects of setting a quota on foreign producers on different stakeholders, including domestic producers, foreign producers, consumers and the government.

The quota diagram in Figure 13.10 is similar to Figure 13.9, only we are given numerical data for prices and quantities of a good measured in millions of units. We would like to calculate the following information.

Import quota

The import quota can be read off as 16 million – 11 million = 5 million units, i.e. this is the permissible number of units that can enter the country per time period (such as a year).

The price after the quota is imposed

The price paid by consumers and received by *domestic* producers increases from €10 to €14.

Quantity of imports

Imports fall from 15 million units (=20–5) before the quota to 5 million units (=16–11) after the quota (this is the number of units permitted by the quota), i.e. imports fall by 10 million units.

Domestic consumers

The price paid by consumers increases from to €10 to €14, or by €4 per unit. The quantity purchased by consumers falls from 20 million units to 16 million units,

or by 4 million units. Consumer expenditure before the quota is €10×20 million = €200 million, and after the quota it is €14×16 million = €224 million. Therefore, consumer expenditure increases by $24 million. Note, however, that as in the case of tariffs, *this need not happen*. Consumers in any case will be worse off because they must pay a higher price for a smaller quantity.

Domestic producers

The price received by producers also increases from €10 to €14, or by €4 per unit. The quantity produced increases from 5 million to 11 million units, or by 6 million units. Therefore producer revenue increases from €10×5 million units = €50 million before the quota to €14×11 million units = €154 million after the quota, or by €104 million (= €154 million–€50 million). Producers are better off.

The government

The government budget is not affected.

Foreign producers

Exports of foreign producers to the country imposing the quota fall by an amount equal to the fall in the country's imports, calculated above to be 10 million units. Export revenues of the foreign producers fall by an amount equal to the fall in the quantity of exports (10 million units) times the world price (€10), which is €100 million (= €10×10 million). However, since the foreign producers receive the quota revenue (by receiving the quota licences), they gain €20 million (equal to the increase in price per unit due to the quota, or €4, times the number of units allowed by the quota, or 5 million). Therefore, their losses are €80 million (= €100 million–€20 million). (It is also possible in some situations for the gain from quota revenue to be greater than the loss of export revenues, so that foreign producers could be better off with the quota than without it.)

Test your understanding 13.7

1 Under free trade, the price of mobile phones in Riverland is €100 per unit; domestic sales are 700 000 units per year, of which 500 000 units are imported. Following the imposition of an import quota of 200 000 units per year, domestic sales fall to 500 000 units per year, and the price increases to €120 per unit. Find the quantity of mobile phones produced domestically **(a)** before the quota, and **(b)** after the quota. **(c)** What is the quantity of imports after the quota?

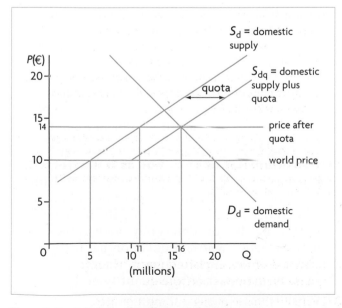

Figure 13.10 Calculating the effects of an import quota

2 Using your results in question 1, calculate the **(a)** change in consumer expenditure, **(b)** change in producer revenue, **(c)** quota revenue, **(d)** change in foreign producers' quantity of exports, and **(e)** change in foreign producers' export revenues. (You may find it useful to use a quota diagram to do your calculations; it does not have to be drawn to scale.)

3 Assuming that quota revenues are gained by foreign producers, explain **(a)** the effect on the government's budget, and **(b)** the total gains/ losses of foreign producers', taking into account both export revenues and quota revenues.

Subsidies

♦ Explain, using a diagram, the effects of giving a subsidy to domestic producers on different stakeholders, including domestic producers, foreign producers, consumers and the government.

Subsidies were discussed in Chapter 4, page 81, where we saw that a subsidy is a payment by the government to a firm for each unit of output produced. In the context of trade protection there are two kinds of subsidies. One is intended to protect domestic firms that compete with imports, called a 'production subsidy', and the other is a subsidy intended to protect domestic firms that export, called an 'export subsidy'. We are mainly concerned with production subsidies.

Production subsidies and their effects

Subsidies that reduce the quantity of imports

In the context of trade protection, *production subsidies* are payments per unit of output granted by the government to domestic firms that compete with imports. In Figure 13.11(a), under free trade, the country would produce quantity Q_1 of the good, quantity demanded would be Q_2, and excess demand of $Q_2 - Q_1$ would be satisfied by imports. Now suppose the government grants a subsidy to domestic firms producing the good per unit of output produced. We know from Chapter 4 (page 82) that the subsidy causes the domestic supply curve to shift downward by the amount of

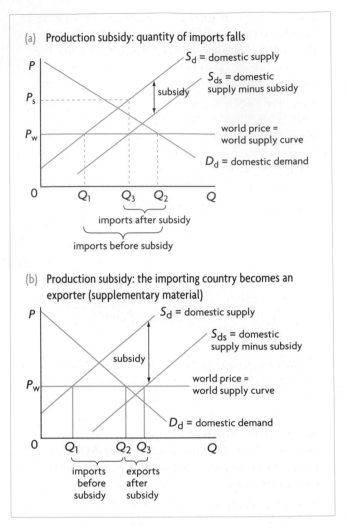

Figure 13.11 Production subsidies

the per unit subsidy, to S_{ds}. The good continues to sell at the world price, P_w. The effects of the production subsidy are the following:

- **Increase in quantity supplied, decrease in imports.** The domestic firms supply the larger quantity Q_3, determined by the intersection of the after-subsidy supply curve S_{ds}, with the world price line. As a result, the quantity of imports falls from $Q_2 - Q_1$ to $Q_2 - Q_3$.

- **Consumption of the good is not affected.** Consumption of the good both before and after the subsidy is at Q_2 units of output, and the price stays the same, at P_w. Following the imposition of the subsidy, consumers buy more of the domestic good whose production has increased, and less of the imported good. Therefore, there is no impact on the quantity of the good consumed.

- **Domestic producers are better off.** As a result of the subsidy, domestic producers receive the price P_s (= P_w plus the subsidy per unit), and domestic production expands from Q_1 to Q_3. Therefore, producers benefit.

- **Negative effect on the government budget.** This is negatively affected as the government must spend tax revenues on the subsidy. The amount spent on the subsidy is $P_s - P_w$ (the subsidy per unit) times Q_3, or the quantity produced domestically.

- **Taxpayers are worse off.** Taxpayers lose as a portion of tax revenues is spent on production subsidies that have the effect of increasing production of inefficient producers. The amount lost is what is spent on the subsidy out of the government budget (see above). These funds could have been spent elsewhere with benefits for taxpayers (such as spending on merit goods).

- **Domestic employment increases.** The increase in domestic production from Q_1 to Q_3 causes domestic employment to increase.

- **Increased inefficiency in production.** As in the case of tariffs and quotas, production of domestic inefficient producers increases, while the production of more efficient foreign producers falls.

- **The exporting countries are worse off.** Foreign producers exporting the good are worse off because they can export less of the good, and export revenues of these countries fall.

- **A global misallocation of resources results.** The shift of production from efficient to inefficient producers involves an increase in the global misallocation of resources, negatively affecting economies.

Why economists prefer subsidies to tariffs or quotas

The effects of production subsidies are not as harmful as those of tariffs and quotas, because while they encourage inefficient production (like tariffs and quotas), they do not have negative effects on consumption, which remains the same before and after the subsidies. For this reason, economists argue that if a country must use some form of protection, subsidies are preferable to tariffs or quotas.

Subsidies that result in exports of the protected good (supplementary material)

If the production subsidy is large enough, the country may actually become an exporter of the good, even though it has a comparative disadvantage in its production. This is shown in Figure 13.11(b). Before the subsidy, domestic production is at Q_1, consumption is at Q_2, and imports are $Q_2 - Q_1$. The subsidy shifts the domestic supply curve from S_d to S_{ds}, and the new quantity of domestic production is determined by the point of intersection of the after-subsidy supply curve, S_{ds}, with P_w, at Q_3. Q_3 is larger than Q_2, meaning that domestic production is greater than that needed to satisfy domestic quantity demanded, or Q_2. The extra quantity produced, given by $Q_3 - Q_2$, represents the amount of the good that is exported.

The effects of the subsidy in this case are the same as when the subsidy reduces imports, except that it is likely that with the higher cost country now becoming an exporter of a good in which it has a comparative disadvantage, an even greater domestic and global misallocation of resources may result.

Test your understanding 13.8

1 Draw a diagram showing the effects of a production subsidy on **(a)** the domestic price of the subsidised good, **(b)** quantity produced domestically, **(c)** quantity consumed by domestic consumers, and **(d)** quantity of imports.

2 Using your diagram of question 1, discuss the effects of a production subsidy on **(a)** domestic consumers, **(b)** domestic producers, **(c)** domestic employment, **(d)** foreign producers, **(e)** the government, **(f)** efficiency in production, and **(g)** the global allocation of resources.

3 Evaluate the effects of production subsidies, taking into account various stakeholders, the domestic economy, the economies of exporters and the global economy.

4 Why do economists prefer production subsidies to tariffs and quotas?

EU and US cotton subsidies

In a period of nine years, the European Union and United States have spent $32 billion on subsidies for their cotton farmers. Whereas the market price for cotton is $1.50 per pound, the EU pays its farmers $2.51 per pound. The World Bank estimates that if these subsidies were eliminated, cotton prices in West Africa would increase by 12.9%, amounting to $250 billion per year. This amount is lost each year by West African cotton farmers, who are forced to sell a smaller quantity at a lower price due to EU and US oversupply of cotton. Oxfam estimates that removal of the subsidies would add $46–$114 per year to each household, where annual income *per capita* is about $200.

Source: Catherine Boyle, 'Fair deal call for growers of cotton in West Africa' in *The Times*, 15 November 2010.

Applying your skills

1 Using a diagram, explain the effects of cotton subsidies on various stakeholders.

2 Explain how West African farmers are disadvantaged by cotton subsidies.

3 Evaluate the use of cotton subsidies.

HL

Calculating the effects of production subsidies from diagrams (higher level topic)

* Calculate from diagrams the effects of giving a subsidy to domestic producers on different stakeholders, including domestic producers, foreign producers, consumers and the government.

The subsidy diagram in Figure 13.12 is similar to Figure 13.11, only we are given numerical data for prices and quantities of a good measured in millions of units. We want to calculate the following information.

Subsidy per unit
The subsidy per unit is the vertical difference between the two supply curves, or £7 − £5 = £2 per unit.

Quantity of imports
Imports before the subsidy are 9 million units (= 16 million − 7 million). Imports after the subsidy are 4 million units (= 16 million − 12 million). Therefore, imports fall by 5 million units (= 9 million − 4 million).

Domestic consumers
Consumers are not affected. They pay the same price, £5, and they buy the same quantity, 16 million units before and after the subsidy. The only difference is that now less of the quantity consumed is imported and more is produced domestically.

Domestic producers
The price received by producers increases from £5 to £7, or by £2 per unit, which is the subsidy per unit.

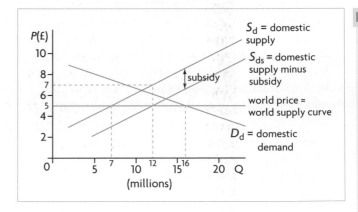

HL

Figure 13.12 Calculating the effects of production subsidies

The quantity produced also increases from 7 million to 12 million units, or by 5 million units. Therefore, producer revenue increases from £5×7 million units = £35 million before the subsidy to £7×12 million units = £84 million after the subsidy, or by £49 million (= £84 million − £35 million). Producers are better off.

Government expenditure and taxpayers
Government expenditure on the subsidy increases from zero to an amount equal to the subsidy per unit (£2) times the quantity produced domestically *after* the subsidy has been granted (12 million units). It is therefore £2×12 million = £24 million. The government budget therefore loses. Taxpayers are worse off by the equivalent amount, as their tax funds are spent on subsiding inefficient producers with no benefits to themselves.

Foreign producers

Exports of foreign producers to the country granting the subsidy fall by an amount equal to the fall in the country's imports, calculated above to be 5 million units. Export revenues of the foreign producers fall by an amount equal to the fall in the quantity of exports (5 million units) times the world price (£5), which is £25 million (= £5×£5 million). Therefore, foreign producers are worse off.

Test your understanding 13.9

1 Under free trade, the price of televisions in Forestland was £200 per unit; domestic television production was 300 000 units and domestic television sales were 900 000 units. Following the imposition of a £50 per unit subsidy on televisions, domestic production increased to 550 000 units. State/calculate the **(a)** post-subsidy price paid by consumers, **(b)** post-subsidy price received by domestic producers, **(c)** pre-subsidy quantity of imports, **(d)** post-subsidy quantity of imports, and **(e)** post-subsidy television sales.

2 Using your results in question 6, state/calculate the **(a)** change in consumer expenditures, **(b)** change in producer revenue, **(c)** change in the government's budget, **(d)** change in foreign producers' quantity of exports, and **(e)** change in foreign producers' export revenues. (You may find it useful to use a subsidy diagram to do your calculations. This does not have to be drawn to scale.)

A note on export subsidies

Export subsidies are similar to production subsidies in that they involve a payment by the government per unit of the subsidised good, except that the subsidy is paid for each unit of the good that is exported. They have the effects of increasing the domestic quantity produced, reducing the quantity consumed, and increasing the quantity of exports, and lead to domestic and global resource misallocation. According to international trade agreements (under the World Trade Organization, see page 363), export subsidies have been declared to be illegal. Yet countries around the world continue to use them.

Administrative barriers

♦ Describe administrative barriers that may be used as a means of protection.

In addition to the above trade restrictions, governments may impose a variety of additional obstacles to imports, which can be termed **administrative barriers**.

Whenever a good is imported from another country, it must go through a number of customs procedures involving inspections, valuation (determining the value of the good), and others. In an effort to impose obstacles to imports and reduce their quantity, countries may increase the amount of red-tape checks and procedures, making them very time-consuming and difficult. In addition, importing countries can impose requirements that imported goods must be packaged in particular ways. Since exporters do not always fulfil the requirements, the quantity of imports is reduced.

Further, many countries impose requirements that imported goods must fulfill particular technical standards, which involve health, safety and environmental conditions. In many cases, these standards automatically eliminate a range of imports. In other cases, certain products must undergo testing and inspection procedures that are so costly and time-consuming that once again the effect is to reduce the quantity of imports.

In some cases, the imposition of such standards is justified by governments' concern for the health and safety of the domestic population, as well as possible negative environmental effects of imported goods. However, it is generally believed that the excessive use of these kinds of measures by governments is a disguised attempt to limit imports, and therefore is a kind of trade protection.

Test your understanding 13.10

Why are health, safety and environmental standards applied to imported goods and administrative import procedures considered to be a type of trade protection?

13.5 Arguments for and against trade protection

Arguments against trade protection

♦ Discuss the arguments against trade protection, including a misallocation of resources, the danger of retaliation and 'trade wars', the potential for corruption, increased costs of production due to lack of competition, higher prices for domestic consumers, increased costs of imported factors of production and reduced export competitiveness.

Economists are often critical of trade protection because it worsens the allocation of resources and imposes a variety of costs on the domestic and the global economy. We have seen in some detail who

Impact on:	Tariffs	Quotas	Production subsidies	Administrative barriers
Consumers	−	−	×	−
Producers	+	+	+	+
Employment (workers)	+	+	+	+
Government	+	×	−	×
Taxpayers	×	×	−	×
Income distribution	−	−	×	×
Efficiency in production	−	−	−	−
Society as a whole	−	−	−	−
Foreign producers	−	−	−	−
Global resource allocation	−	−	−	−

Table 13.3 Summary of trade barrier effects

Key: + denotes a gain; − denotes a loss; x denotes no impact.

gains and who loses from the imposition of a variety of protectionist measures in international trade. Table 13.3 provides a summary of the effects.

Based on the information in Table 13.3, we may note the following:

- **Producers and workers (through the increase in domestic employment) are the only groups that gain from all types of trade protection.** This is hardly surprising, since trade protection policies are usually undertaken with a view to protecting domestic production and domestic employment.

- **However, the gain of producers has a cost in terms of higher costs of production and reduced efficiency.** These result from all types of trade protection. In fact, long-term reliance on protection against foreign competition eliminates incentives for firms to lower costs and operate efficiently.

- **Consumers lose in most cases.** This is due to higher prices of protected goods and lower quantities of goods available in the market (the only exception is subsidies, where the quantity consumed and price paid by consumers remain unaffected). The losses experienced by consumers as a rule are greater than the benefits to producers, confirmed by many studies that measure the effects of trade restrictions.

- **Income distribution in most cases worsens.** The exceptions are subsidies and administrative barriers, where the price paid by consumers does not change.

- **Foreign producers are worse off in all cases.**

- **Society as a whole and global resource allocation lose under all forms of trade protection.** This is not surprising, since the theory of comparative advantage shows how free trade can achieve the greatest amount of production and consumption through the achievement of allocative efficiency on a global scale. Protection worsens domestic and global resource allocation.

There are some additional points worth mentioning:

- **Trade protection may have negative effects on a country's export competitiveness.** Some domestically produced goods that are protected may be used as inputs in the production of other goods that are exported. For example, if a fertiliser industry is protected from fertiliser imports, the domestic price of fertiliser will be higher than the world price; farmers buying the fertiliser face higher costs of production, causing the final agricultural products to sell at a higher price. This results in lower competitiveness in export markets.

- **Trade protection may give rise to trade wars.** As one country imposes barriers on imports, other countries may retaliate by imposing their own barriers. This can produce chain reactions with countries becoming more and more protectionist, with serious negative effects on global output and resource allocation.

- **Trade protection creates a potential for corruption.** For example, restrictions on imports may pave the way for bribes and illegal smuggling of goods into a country, or may result in tariff and other revenues going into the pockets of bureaucrats rather than the government budget.

Arguments for trade protection

♦ Discuss the arguments in favour of trade protection, including the protection of domestic jobs, national security, protection of infant industries, the maintenance of health, safety and environmental standards, anti-dumping and unfair competition, a means of overcoming a balance of payments deficit and a source of government revenue.

We have explored a variety of measures that governments use to create barriers to international trade. These barriers create some winners and some losers, but in all cases result in inefficiency in production and a global misallocation of resources. Why, then, do governments around the world continue to use trade protection policies? We will consider a number of arguments used in defence of protection measures, and we will evaluate the extent to which these arguments can be justified. There are three groups of arguments: those that are qualified, questionable, and incorrect.

Qualified arguments

Qualified arguments are those that can be justified under particular conditions. Their validity may depend on non-economic considerations, or on the expectation that longer-term economic benefits of trade protection are greater than short-term economic costs.

Infant industry argument

An **infant industry** is a new domestic industry that has not had time to establish itself and achieve efficiencies in production, and may therefore be unable to compete with more 'mature' competitor firms from abroad. Mature foreign firms, operating with lower costs of production, are able to sell at lower prices; domestic firms, being unable to compete, are unable to grow and may be forced to shut down. This argument rests on the principle of economies of scale, according to which a firm achieves lower average costs as it grows in size and produces more output (see page 355). Therefore, to achieve economies of scale (lower average costs), a new firm with high costs of production that has not yet grown in size may need protection from imports until it grows to a size where protection is no longer needed.

This argument was first used in 1791 by Alexander Hamilton, the first US Secretary of the Treasury, to introduce tariffs to protect US industry and promote economic growth. Today, it is used mainly for developing countries trying to expand their production into new areas and industries. Economists consider it to be one of the strongest arguments in favour of trade protection with a theoretical justification. It is justified on the grounds that a country may have a comparative advantage in the production of a particular *industrial* good, but cannot specialise in it unless it first receives some protection. This argument is therefore consistent with the theory of comparative advantage. There is, however, an important condition attached to this argument: the protection offered to infant industries must only be temporary; over a longer period, once the industry matures, the protection must be eliminated and the industry must compete in global markets under conditions of free trade.

In spite of its strong theoretical justification, there are some dangers in the infant industry argument. One is that it may be difficult for governments to know which particular industries have the potential to become low-cost producers (achieve economies of scale), presenting difficulties in the selection of industries to protect. Another is that once the selection is made, industries protected from competition may not have a strong incentive to become efficient. A third is that governments may continue to protect an industry long after it has matured and is no longer an infant.

Strategic trade policy

Strategic trade policy is a new argument in favour of trade protection that appeared in the 1980s. It is closely related to the infant industry argument, except that it applies to developed countries as well. This argument calls for protection of high technology industries to help them achieve economies of scale and create a comparative advantage. It is argued that certain industries, such as computers, telecommunications and semiconductors, are very important to the future growth of an economy, and must therefore receive protection until they grow to a size large enough to achieve the necessary economies of scale. Supporters of strategic trade policies point to Japan's success in semiconductors, which it is claimed was achieved through government protection. Protection in this case involves not just barriers to trade but also a variety of interventionist supply-side measures including tax advantages, low-interest loans and government financing of research and development (industrial policies; see page 339). Strategic arguments are used by the United States and the European Union to justify government protection of high technology industries. This kind of protection has given rise to disagreements in current discussions on trade rules (under the World Trade Organization, see page 363).

There are some problems associated with the strategic trade policy argument. There are difficulties in identifying the industries that will achieve economies of scale and should be protected. There are also difficulties in selecting appropriate protective policies. Further, it is likely that all or most developed countries will try to use such policies for the same industries at the same time, which contradicts the idea of trying to create 'comparative advantage'. Finally, there is a danger that governments will continue to protect these industries long after protection is no longer necessary.

National security
According to this argument, certain industries are essential for national defence (such as aircraft, weapons, chemicals, certain minerals), and should be protected so that a country can produce them itself. In times of war or a national emergency, a country should not have to depend on imports for its defence. Moreover, there may be dangers in having 'unfriendly' nations specialise in weapons production.

While there is some merit to this argument, a problem is that it can be used by industries that have an indirect use in defence (such as the steel industry) to try to acquire protection against foreign competition. The national defence argument is a non-economic one, and so decisions should be made on political and military, not economic, grounds. Yet it is sometimes difficult to draw the line between what is essential for national defence and what is not. In the United States, goods like candles, gloves, umbrellas, plastics and others receive protection on the grounds that they are needed for national defence.

Health, safety and environmental standards
Many countries maintain health, safety and environmental standards that all imported products must meet before they are allowed to enter. Each country sets its own standards, and governments are justifiably concerned that imported goods may fall short of these. However, there is a concern that these standards may sometimes be used as a form of 'hidden' protection to keep certain goods out if they are competing with domestically produced goods (see page 375).

Efforts of a developing country to diversify
Diversification means change involving greater variety; economic diversification refers to increasing the variety of goods and services produced, and is the opposite of specialisation. Specialisation forms the basis of the theory of comparative advantage. Yet, in the case of some countries, specialisation according to comparative advantage may not be appropriate, and countries may be better off diversifying their production and exports. This often applies to developing countries that are very highly specialised in producing and exporting one or a few primary commodities (for example, Cuba in sugar, Ecuador in bananas, Ethiopia in coffee).

There are several important arguments in favour of diversification of production and exports in developing countries, and these will be discussed in Chapter 17. To be able to diversify, countries may have to use trade protection policies to keep out imports of goods they would like to produce themselves. For example, if a country would like to diversify into production of computers, it will have to impose barriers on imports of computers; alternatively, the government could provide subsidies to domestic computer producers.

This argument applies only to developing countries. Moreover, it is based on the expectation that the long-term economic benefits of diversification, involving more economic growth and development, will be greater than the short-term costs in terms of inefficiencies caused by protection. However, there may be a risk involved in that governments may not know which products or industries are the most appropriate to select for protection that will allow for successful diversification.

Questionable arguments
Questionable arguments have limited validity, though they may not be entirely incorrect, and perhaps may have some value under very special circumstances in offering short-term, temporary solutions to problems.

Tariffs as a source of government revenue
One use of tariffs is to collect government revenue, a very common practice in the early stages of development of currently more developed countries. In the United States, for example, tariff revenues accounted for 56% of federal (central) government revenues in 1880; by 1900 these were 41%, and by 2000 they had fallen to less than 1%. Today, the use of tariffs for revenue purposes is more frequent in developing countries, where tariff revenues can sometimes account for as much as half or more of all government revenues. The reason for strong reliance on tariffs for revenues is related to the ease with which imports can be taxed, since they are goods

that must pass through borders where they can be monitored.[7]

However, tariffs have certain disadvantages, as they are a regressive type of tax, and so have negative impacts on income distribution; in addition, they also have negative effects on allocative efficiency. The convenience of relying on tariff revenues may also work as an excuse for governments to delay tax system reform. Therefore, reliance on tariffs as a source of government revenues should be a temporary measure to be gradually phased out as countries grow and develop.

Means to overcome balance of payments deficit

A balance of payments deficit occurs when the outflow of money from a country is greater than the inflow, and usually happens when there is an excess of imports over exports (see Chapter 14). If imports are greater than exports, it would seem that a way to correct the problem would be to impose barriers to the entry of imports into the country, limiting imports and therefore the need to make payments abroad. However, decreased imports would come at the expense of falling exports in exporting countries, and there is a risk of retaliation (see page 376). Trade protection could be used as a short-term emergency measure if there is a serious balance of payments deficit. Over the longer term there are other, more effective ways to deal with this problem.

Anti-dumping

Dumping refers to the practice of selling a good in international markets at a price that is below the cost of producing it (usually by providing export subsidies, see page 375). Dumping is considered to be an unfair trade practice, and is illegal according to international agreements. Nonetheless, it is a practice that continues to be used. According to the **anti-dumping** argument in favour of trade protection, if a country suspects that a trading partner is practising dumping, it should have the right to impose tariffs or quotas in order to limit imports of the subsidised, or dumped good.

The main problem with this argument is that because of difficulties involved in proving that dumping is being practised, many governments often use it as an excuse to offer protection to their domestic producers when this protection is not necessary or justifiable.

Protection of domestic jobs

According to this argument, restrictions on imports are needed to protect domestic employment. Import restrictions cause consumers to shift consumption away from imports and towards goods produced domestically. As domestic production increases, unemployment falls, since firms need to hire more labour in order to increase their supply of goods.

The problem with this argument is that if unemployment in the domestic economy falls due to import restrictions, this means that unemployment increases in the countries that are forced to export less. The foreign countries that are hurt may retaliate by imposing import restrictions of their own. If the government's objective is to increase employment in the economy, fiscal, monetary or supply-side policies may be more appropriate. If, on the other hand, the government wants to increase employment in a particular industry, a subsidy is likely to be more appropriate than import restrictions (tariffs and quotas), because subsidies have fewer negative effects (see page 373).

Incorrect arguments

Incorrect arguments offer no justification for protection, and are based on incorrect economic reasoning.

Wage protection argument

According to this argument, some foreign countries can produce at lower costs because of low wages ('cheap labour'). It follows that imports from those countries will sell at lower prices, domestic firms will be unable to compete, and protection then becomes necessary to restrict imports from low-wage countries.

This argument is very popular, and has been used repeatedly by developed countries to restrict imports from low-wage developing countries. However, it is based on incorrect economic reasoning. A low-wage country very likely has a comparative advantage in producing goods that make heavy use of its labour resources, precisely because these are cheaper. This is the basis of specialisation and trade according to comparative advantage. Therefore, the low-wage countries should specialise in the production of goods that make a lot of use of their cheap labour, and developed countries with more expensive labour should not impose import restrictions on these goods.

---

[7] By contrast, income taxes, which currently make up the largest share of government revenues in developed countries, are more difficult to levy and collect in economically less developed countries, partly because large shares of the population survive on very low incomes, partly because a very large proportion of the population are self-employed and working in the informal sector where taxes are not collected, and partly because of poor enforcement of tax collection and high tax evasion rates.

Is there a moral aspect in the economic argument in favour of free trade?

Perhaps the strongest economic argument in favour of free trade is that it leads to greater efficiencies in production and an improved allocation of resources. If the different types of trade protection discussed in this chapter were removed, there would be efficiency improvements. Yet everyone recognises that these efficiency gains involve both winners and losers: those who gain from trade protection lose from the removal of trade protection; and the losers from trade protection become the gainers after its removal.

In view of the fact that there are both gainers and losers, is it possible to argue in favour of free trade on a purely social scientific basis, without moral judgements? Welfare analysis shows that the gains to society are greater than the losses from a removal of trade barriers, but even so, there is still a moral judgement involved in the statement 'It's okay to sacrifice the well-being of some people for the sake of gains in the well-being of a larger number of people.' Economists (and others) recognise this point.

How then to get around this problem, so as to be able to recommend free trade on a scientific basis? Economists found the solution in what is known as the Hicks/Kaldor criterion[8], according to which if the winners can afford to compensate the losers and still be better off, then the removal of trade barriers and the switch to free trade is *scientifically justified*.

In practice, this could mean that the government taxes the gainers and then somehow pays the losers for their losses. However, in the real world this practically never happens. When it never happens, economists, for their part, can argue that they have done their job as economists, and from there on it is the governments' responsibility to pursue the right policies.

However, if economists recommend, and governments adopt free trade policies, *in full knowledge that there will not be any compensation of the losers*, is the recommendation still free of moral judgements? Or is it based on the same moral judgement as that noted above, that 'It's okay to sacrifice the well-being of some people for the sake of gains in the well-being of a larger number of people.'

We will return to the topic of free trade in the Theory of knowledge feature on page 494.

---

[8] This work is based on the work of British economist John Hicks and Hungarian-born economist Nicholas Kaldor. Hicks and Kaldor were among the more influential economists of the 20th century.

Thinking points

- Do you agree that there is a moral judgement in the economic argument in favour of free trade?

- If there is a moral judgement, does it matter that it is generally 'covered up' and ignored in discussions of free trade?

- Do economists have a moral responsibility toward societies when making policy recommendations, or can they make recommendations in the belief that they are functioning purely as social scientists?

Test your understanding 13.11

1 Using examples of barriers to trade, discuss some arguments against trade protection.

2 **(a)** Explain the infant industry argument.
(b) What is its theoretical justification? **(c)** What are some potential problems it may give rise to?

3 **(a)** Identify some qualified arguments in favour of trade protection. **(b)** Under what special circumstances are they considered to be valid?
(c) What problems can they give rise to?

4 **(a)** Identify some questionable arguments in favour of trade protection. **(b)** Why they are considered to be questionable?

5 **(a)** What is one incorrect argument in favour of trade protection? **(b)** Explain why it is inconsistent with economic reasoning.

Assessment

The Student's CD-ROM at the back of this book provides practice of examination questions based on the material you have studied in this chapter.

Standard level
- Exam practice: Paper 2, Chapter 13
  - SL/HL core topics (Text/data 1 and 2, questions A.1–A.5)

Higher level
- Exam practice: Paper 2, Chapter 13
  - SL/HL core topics (Text/data 1 and 2, questions A.1–A.5)
- Exam practice: Paper 3, Chapter 13
  - HL topics (questions 23–26)

Chapter 14
Exchange rates and the balance of payments

This chapter examines the monetary or financial side of international links between countries. We will look at the balance of payments, exchange rates, and how countries deal with a variety of problems that arise in the context of international monetary flows.

14.1 Freely floating exchange rates

Introducing exchange rates

Demand and supply of foreign exchange

At any moment in time, there is a continuous flow of money in and out of every country in the world. This happens because the residents of each country, whether individuals, or groups of individuals, or firms, or the government, have *transactions* (or dealings of any kind involving money) with the residents of other countries. International transactions involve the use of different national currencies, known as *foreign exchange*. These national currencies are traded for each other in the foreign exchange market, where individuals, firms, banks, other financial institutions and governments buy and sell currencies. The foreign exchange market is not a centralised meeting place, but involves any location where one currency can be exchanged for another, and any individual or organisation that engages in the exchange of one currency for another.

Suppose you are a resident of Russia traveling to Denmark. You will want to exchange some of your roubles for Danish kroner. To do this, you 'sell' your roubles and 'buy' Danish kroner in the foreign exchange market. The reason you must do so is that the residents of any country usually prefer to be paid in the currency of that country. Likewise, residents of European Monetary Union countries (the countries of the European Union that have adopted the euro, also known as 'euro zone' countries) want to be paid in euros, residents of Chile want to be paid in Chilean pesos, and residents of Malaysia want to receive payments in ringgits (which is the Malaysian dollar).

The foreign exchange market, like any market, is made up of demand and supply of currencies. As a traveller from Russia, when you change your roubles into Danish kroner, you *demand* Danish kroner, and you *supply* roubles in the foreign exchange market.

In another example, suppose residents in the United Kingdom and Japan want to trade with each other. When Japanese residents import from the United Kingdom, they must buy British pounds with which to pay UK exporters; they therefore *demand* British pounds in the foreign exchange market. To receive the pounds, they sell or *supply* yen in the foreign exchange market. When UK residents import from Japan, they *demand* yen, and *supply* pounds in the foreign exchange market to receive the yen. This simple two-country example illustrates the equivalence between the demand for a foreign currency and the supply of a domestic currency. The demand for pounds is equivalent to a supply of yen, and the demand for yen is equivalent to a supply of pounds. There is a similar equivalence in the real world, where there are many different currencies: the demand for yen is equivalent to the supplies of all other currencies offered (or sold) in the foreign exchange market to buy yen. Similarly, the demand for pounds is equivalent to the supply of all other currencies offered to buy pounds.

> The demand for foreign currencies generates a supply of domestic currency; and demand for the domestic currency generates a supply of foreign currencies. In a simple two-currency example using pounds and yen, it follows that:
>
> **demand for pounds ⇔ supply of yen**
> **demand for yen ⇔ supply of pounds**

Exchange rates

If national currencies can be exchanged for each other, there must be some mechanism of establishing the 'value' of each currency. This is done through the **exchange rate**, which relates the value of one currency to another. Consider a hypothetical exchange rate between the US dollar and the euro:

- number of US dollars per euro: 1.5 dollars = 1 euro
- number of euros per dollar: 0.67 euro = 1 dollar

The first expression gives the 'value' or 'price' of 1 euro in terms of dollars, showing how many dollars must be given up to buy 1 euro, as well as how many dollars can be obtained if one euro is given up. The second gives the 'value' or 'price' of 1 dollar in terms of euros, showing how many euros must be given up to buy 1 dollar, as well as how many euros can be obtained in exchange for one dollar. The two expressions are equivalent. They have to be, since the value of each currency is expressed in terms of the other. (See page 392 on how to calculate one expression from the other.)

To understand how exchange rates are determined, we will consider two 'pure' exchange rate systems: the floating (or flexible) exchange rate system, and the fixed exchange rate system. We will also study the actual system in use today, known as a managed float, or managed exchange rate system, which lies in between the two 'pure' systems, though it is closer to the system of floating exchange rates.

Determination of freely floating exchange rates

- Explain that the value of an exchange rate in a floating system is determined by the demand for, and supply of, a currency.
- Draw a diagram to show determination of exchange rates in a floating exchange rate system.

The equilibrium exchange rate

In a freely floating exchange rate system (or flexible exchange rate system), exchange rates are determined by market forces, or the forces of demand and supply. There is no government intervention in the foreign exchange market to influence the value of currencies.

Consider a highly simplified world with two currencies, the US dollar and the euro. In a freely floating system, the 'price' of the dollar and the 'price' of the euro are each determined in the same way that

prices are determined in any free market. However, as we know from our discussion above, the 'price' of one currency is always expressed in terms of another currency, as there is no independent unit we can use to express the value of currencies. (In a market for computers or cars or shoes or any good, service or resource, price is measured in terms of units of money, which serves as a unit of measurement of value. In the case of currencies, there is no independent unit to measure value; therefore, value is measured in terms of another currency.)

Figure 14.1(a) shows the market for dollars. The horizontal axis measures the quantity of dollars, and the vertical axis measures the price of dollars in terms of euros. The demand curve represents the demand for dollars, and the supply curve represents the supply of dollars.

The demand for dollars, shown by a familiar downward-sloping curve, comes from euro zone residents who need dollars to carry out transactions in the United States: euro zone importers buying goods from the US, euro zone investors who want to invest in the US, consumers going on holiday to the US, etc.

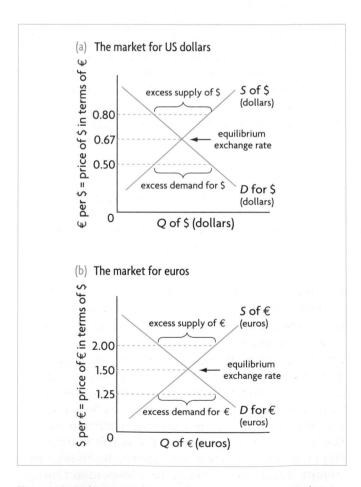

Figure 14.1 Exchange rate determination in a freely floating exchange rate system

The downward slope of the curve indicates that as the price of dollars in terms of euros increases, euro zone residents buy fewer dollars. For example, if 0.80 euro are needed to buy 1 dollar, euro zone residents buy fewer dollars than if 0.5 euro is needed to buy 1 dollar.

The supply of dollars, shown by a familiar upward-sloping curve, comes from US residents who would like to give up dollars to buy euros: US residents who would like to import goods from euro zone countries, or who want to take a holiday in a euro zone country, or who plan to invest in a euro zone country, etc. To see why the supply-of-dollars curve is upward-sloping, consider that if the price of dollars is 0.5 euros per dollar, US residents need to supply 1 dollar to buy 0.5 euro worth of euro zone goods; if the price of dollars increases to 0.8 euro per dollar, then by giving up 1 dollar, US residents can buy 0.8 euro worth of euro zone goods. As the price of dollars goes up, euro zone goods become cheaper, and so more dollars are supplied. Therefore, as the price of dollars in terms of euros increases, the quantity of dollars supplied increases.

The intersection of the demand and supply curves determines the equilibrium 'price' of the dollar in terms of the euro; this 'price' is the equilibrium exchange rate, which is 0.67 euro per dollar. If the exchange rate were higher, say at 0.8 euro per dollar, there would be an excess supply of dollars. At any lower exchange rate, such as 0.5 euro per dollar, there would be an excess demand for dollars.

> In a **freely floating exchange rate system**, the forces of demand and supply cause the exchange rate to settle at the point where the quantity of a currency demanded equals quantity supplied. This is the equilibrium exchange rate.

Figure 14.1(b) shows the market for euros. Since the demand for dollars is equivalent to the supply of euros, and the supply of dollars is equivalent to the demand for euros, it follows that when we determine the 'price' of dollars, we also determine the 'price' of euros. The demand curve, showing demand for euros by US residents who want to buy euros to import, travel, invest, etc. in euro zone countries, is a reflection of the supply-of-dollars curve in part (a). The supply curve, showing the supply of euros from euro zone residents who want to buy dollars to import, travel, invest, etc. in the US, is a reflection of the demand-for-dollars curve in part (a). The intersection of the demand-for-euros and supply-of-

euros curves determines the equilibrium exchange rate, or the 'price' of the euro in terms of the dollar, which is 1 euro = 1.5 dollars. At any higher price of the euro there would be an excess supply of euros; at any lower price there would be an excess demand for euros.

The two equilibrium exchange rates in Figure 14.1 are equivalent to each other. At any other exchange rate, the markets are in disequilibrium. When the price of dollars in terms of euros is 0.80, there is an excess supply of dollars that corresponds to an excess demand for euros. When the price of dollars in terms of euros is 0.50, the excess demand for dollars reflects an excess supply of euros.

Once an exchange rate settles at its equilibrium value, it will remain there until there is a change in demand or supply of the currency, expressed as a shift in the currency demand or supply curve.

Exchange rate changes: appreciation and depreciation

> ◆ Distinguish between a depreciation of the currency and an appreciation of the currency.
> ◆ Draw diagrams to show changes in the demand for, and supply of, a currency.

We will examine exchange rate changes using the dollar–euro example, as above. The value of the dollar increases if there is (a) an increase in the demand for dollars, causing the demand-for-dollars curve to shift to the right, or if there is (b) a decrease in the supply of dollars, causing the supply-of-dollars curve to shift to the left. These shifts are illustrated in Figure 14.2. An increase in the value of a currency in a floating exchange rate system is called an **appreciation** of the currency.

The value of the dollar decreases if there is (a) a decrease in the demand for dollars, causing a leftward shift in the demand-for-dollars curve, or if there is (b) an increase in the supply of dollars, causing a rightward shift in the supply-of-dollars curve. A fall in the value of a currency in a floating exchange rate system is called a **depreciation** of the currency.

In Figure 14.2, assume that the market for dollars and euros is initially in equilibrium. Suppose that, because of a change in consumer tastes, euro zone consumers want to import more goods from the United States. This leads to an increase in the demand for dollars, and an increase in the supply of euros that are given up to buy the dollars. In part (a), the

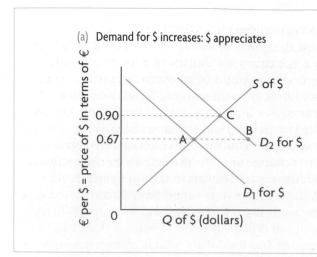

(a) Demand for $ increases: $ appreciates

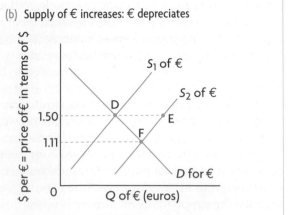

(b) Supply of € increases: € depreciates

Figure 14.2 Exchange rate changes in a freely floating exchange rate system

demand-for-dollars curve shifts to the right, from D_1 to D_2, leading to a new, higher equilibrium exchange rate of 0.90 euro = 1 dollar. The price of the dollar in terms of euros has increased, and *the dollar has appreciated*, or increased in value relative to the euro. At the same time, in part (b), the increase in the supply of euros appears as a shift to the right in the supply-of-euros curve, from S_1 to S_2, resulting in a new, lower equilibrium exchange rate of 1.11 dollar = 1 euro. The price of the euro in terms of the dollar has fallen, so *the euro has depreciated*, or decreased in value relative to the dollar. The new exchange rates of 1 dollar = 0.90 euro, and 1 euro = 1.11 dollar, are equivalent: $\dfrac{1 \text{ dollar}}{0.90 \text{ euro}} = \dfrac{1.11 \text{ dollar}}{1 \text{ euro}}$. Therefore, an appreciation of one currency involves a depreciation of the other currency.

If the US had wanted to import more from euro zone countries, the results would be the opposite of the above (see Test your understanding 14.1, question 5, which asks you to illustrate the exchange rate changes as an exercise).

The same general principles apply to the international system consisting of many national currencies. When one currency appreciates it does so against all others in a floating exchange rate system, meaning that all others depreciate relative to it. When a currency depreciates, all other currencies appreciate relative to it.

> In a floating exchange rate system, appreciation (increase in value) and depreciation (decrease in value) of a currency occur as a result of changes in demand or supply for a currency.

Test your understanding 14.1

1 Why are exchange rates measured in terms of the quantity of another currency?

2 How are exchange rates determined in a floating exchange rate system?

3 Explain whether each of the following affects the demand or supply of the US dollar:
   (a) An investor from the United States invests in the stock market of Brazil.
   (b) A Peruvian importer buys goods from the United States.
   (c) A US resident travels to China as a tourist.
   (d) The United States contributes to foreign aid in Africa.

4 Define appreciation and depreciation of a currency.

5 Suppose the United States would like to increase its imports from euro zone countries. Using diagrams, show the effects on (a) the value of the US dollar, and (b) the euro. (c) Which currency will appreciate and which will depreciate?

Causes of changes in exchange rates

♦ Describe the factors that lead to changes in currency demand and supply, including foreign demand for a country's exports, domestic demand for imports, relative interest rates, relative inflation rates, investment from overseas in a country's firms (foreign direct investment and portfolio investment) and speculation.

In the real world, there are numerous ongoing changes in demand and supply of currencies, causing exchange rates of most currencies around the world to fluctuate on a daily or even hourly basis. We will now consider factors that cause these changes to determine how they impact on equilibrium exchange rates.

Foreign demand for a country's exports

Changes in foreign demand for a country's exports affect its exchange rate. If there is an increase in foreigners' demand for Swiss watches, the demand for Swiss francs increases, the demand-for-francs curve shifts to the right, and the franc appreciates. A decrease in the foreign demand for a country's exports causes its currency to depreciate.

As demand for a country's exports increases, its currency appreciates, *ceteris paribus*.

Domestic demand for imports

Changes in a country's demand for imports affect its exchange rate. If consumers in the United States import more foreign-made cars, US importers must buy foreign currencies, and to do so they supply (sell) US dollars in the foreign exchange market. As the supply of dollars increases, the supply-of-dollar curve shifts to the right, and the dollar depreciates. If the US demand for foreign cars falls, there is a leftward shift in the supply-of-dollars curve, and the dollar appreciates.

As a country's imports increase, its currency depreciates, *ceteris paribus*.

Relative interest rate changes

Financial capital (defined in Chapter 1, page 4) refers to funds that are used to make financial investments, or investments that receive a return based partly on the rate of interest. The higher the rate of interest in a country, the more attractive the financial investments in that country. For example, if interest rates in the United Kingdom increase relative to interest rates in other countries, financial investments become more attractive in the United Kingdom, financial capital flows to the United Kingdom, demand for British pounds increases, the demand-for-pounds curve shifts to the right, and the pound appreciates. Similarly, if interest rates in the United Kingdom fall relative to interest rates in other countries, financial capital flows out of the United Kingdom, the supply of pounds increases (as investors demand other currencies), the supply-of-pounds curve shifts to the right, and the pound depreciates.

A country's interest rates and the value of its currency change in the same direction, *ceteris paribus*.

Relative rates of inflation

If Sweden experiences a higher rate of inflation than other countries, demand for its exports falls as other countries now find them too expensive; at the same time, imports from other countries with lower inflation rates increase as Swedes find them cheaper. The fall in Swedish exports causes demand for Swedish currency, the kronor, to decrease, while the increase in imports causes supply of Swedish kronor to increase. There is therefore a leftward shift in demand and a rightward shift in supply, and both these factors cause the Swedish kronor to depreciate.

Higher inflation in a country relative to other countries leads to currency depreciation, *ceteris paribus*.

Investment from abroad

There are two types of investment by foreigners: foreign direct investment (investment by multinational corporations; see Chapter 18) and financial investments, discussed above in connection with interest rates. Both types of investment have the same impact on interest rates, because they affect the demand for a country's currency. If foreigners want to invest in China, they must buy Chinese yuan, and the demand-for-yuan curve shifts to the right, appreciating the yuan. If foreigners wanted to sell their investments in China, there would be a sale of yuan as foreigners buy other currencies for use elsewhere, depreciating the yuan.

An increase in foreign investment from abroad (of any type) results in currency appreciation, *ceteris paribus*.

Changes in income

If income levels in India increase relative to other countries, Indian residents demand more imports from other countries, the supply of the Indian rupee increases as Indian residents exchange it for other currencies with which to buy the imports, the supply-of-rupees curve shifts to the right, and the rupee depreciates.

A country's level of income relative to other countries and the value of its currency change in opposite directions, *ceteris paribus*.

Speculation

Currency **speculation** involves buying and selling currencies in order to make a profit from changes in exchange rates. Buying and selling is based on expectations of future exchange rate changes. If currency speculators expect a country's currency to appreciate, they buy it in the hope of selling it later after its appreciation, thereby making a profit. However, as they buy the currency they may cause it to appreciate; there is therefore a self-fulfilling prophecy at work. If speculators believe a currency will depreciate, they sell it (they can then buy it back at a lower exchange rate), but in the process of selling they cause its value to fall. Speculators can therefore cause exchange rate changes through their actions of buying and selling.

A widespread expectation that a currency will appreciate leads to currency buying that contributes to bringing about the appreciation. Expectation that a currency will depreciate leads to selling that contributes to bringing about the depreciation.

Use of foreign currency reserves

Every central bank holds reserves of foreign currencies that they sometimes buy or sell in order to influence the value of the domestic currency (see page 398). If the central bank buys a foreign currency, it must supply (sell) the domestic currency in the foreign exchange market, the supply curve shifts to the right, and the currency depreciates. If the central bank sells a foreign currency, it demands (buys) the domestic currency, the demand curve shifts to the right, and the currency appreciates.

Test your understanding 14.2

1 Identify factors that cause changes in exchange rates.

2 For each of the following events, draw an exchange rate diagram and show how a shifting currency demand or supply curve causes an appreciation or depreciation of the currency:

(a) An increase in interest rates in the United States relative to the rest of the world; show the impact on the US dollar and on the British pound.

(b) An increase in the rate of inflation in Thailand relative to its trading partners; show the impact on the baht (Thailand's currency) and on the ringgit (Malaysia's currency; Malaysia is a trading partner of Thailand).

(c) Currency speculators believe that the euro will appreciate; show the impact on the euro.

(d) Japan is in recession, and incomes are falling; show the impact on the Japanese yen.

(e) China experiences an increase in tourism; show the impact on the Chinese yuan.

(f) Fashion favours Indian textiles; show the impact on the Indian rupee.

Evaluating effects of exchange rate changes

♦ Evaluate the possible economic consequences of a change in the value of a currency, including the effects on a country's inflation rate, employment, economic growth and current account balance.

When a currency appreciates, a unit of it can buy more of other currencies; therefore, it can buy more foreign goods. As a result, foreign goods, or imports, become cheaper. At the same time, more of other currencies are needed to buy the appreciated currency, so that foreigners can buy fewer of the domestic goods; therefore, domestic goods, or exports, become more expensive to foreigners.

When a currency depreciates, the opposite happens. It loses its value relative to other currencies, so imports become more expensive while exports become cheaper to foreigners. The depreciated currency can therefore buy fewer foreign goods, or imports, while foreigners can buy more domestic goods, or exports.

These effects of exchange rate changes have some important consequences that we now turn to.

Effects on the rate of inflation

Exchange rate changes can affect inflation in two ways.

Cost-push inflation

A currency depreciation, as we have seen, makes imports more expensive. If domestic producers are heavily dependent on imported factors of production, their costs of production increase, resulting in a leftward shift of the *SRAS* curve, resulting in cost-push inflation (see page 281). The more inelastic the demand for the imported input (such as the demand for oil), the greater is the cost-push inflation.

A currency appreciation, by making imports less expensive, results in lowering inflationary pressures in the economy.

Demand-pull inflation

Exchange rate changes affect aggregate demand by influencing net exports ($X-M$). A currency depreciation, by making exports cheaper and imports more expensive, works to increase the quantity of exports and lower the quantity of imports, thus increasing net exports ($X-M$). An increase in net exports results in a rightward shift of the aggregate demand curve. Using the Keynesian *AD-AS* model, we can see that whether or not this will cause demand-pull inflation depends on where the economy is in the business cycle. If it is in recession, an increase in *AD* will not cause demand-pull inflation. However, if the economy is producing at or close to potential output, the result will be inflationary pressures due to excess aggregate demand (see page 254).

A currency appreciation will work to reduce demand-pull inflationary pressures in an economy due to a decrease in net exports ($X-M$).

Effects on employment

We have seen that a currency depreciation increases net exports and therefore aggregate demand. This causes a fall in cyclical unemployment if the economy is in a recessionary gap (see pages 245 and 253). If the economy is at or close to potential GDP, the increase in aggregate demand may cause a *temporary* decrease in natural unemployment; however, this will come with strong demand-pull inflationary pressures.

A currency appreciation, by reducing net exports and aggregate demand, will create a recessionary gap and therefore lead to cyclical unemployment if the economy begins at or close to potential output, or will lead to an increase in cyclical unemployment if it is already in a recessionary gap.

Effects on economic growth

The effects of exchange rate changes on economic growth work directly through net exports and aggregate demand, discussed above, but they may also have effects on aggregate supply.

A currency depreciation increases net exports, increasing aggregate demand, thus causing an increase in real GDP produced. Increases in aggregate demand, you may remember, cause increases in real output. However, the increases in exports caused by the lower value of the domestic currency may be short-term benefits because of the inflationary impacts of depreciation (both cost-push and demand-pull inflation).

Also, if the growth of export industries leads to increased investment spending in the domestic economy (production of capital goods), there may be effects on aggregate supply, causing increases in potential output (rightward shifts in the *LRAS* or Keynesian *AS* curves).

A currency appreciation, by directly reducing net exports is likely to have a dampening effect on the growth of real GDP. However, under certain circumstances it may have a positive indirect effect on GDP growth. Since a currency appreciation makes imports cheaper, there may result increased imports of factors of production that can be used to increase private or government investment spending and therefore impact positively on potential output.

Effects on the current account balance

The current account balance will be studied in Section 14.4. For now we can say that it consists mainly of the 'balance' of exports and imports of goods and services (the value of exports minus the value of imports). For reasons we will discover later in this chapter, major differences between the value of exports and the value of imports are considered undesirable, especially if they persist over long periods.

As we know, depreciation is likely to cause imports to fall and exports to increase. If a country has an excess of imports over exports to begin with (a trade 'deficit'), its trade deficit is likely to become smaller after a period of time. If it has an excess of exports over imports to begin with (a trade 'surplus'), its trade surplus is likely to become larger. An appreciation, by contrast, will cause imports to increase and exports to fall, thus having the opposite effects on the current account balance. These points will become clearer to you after you have studied the rest of this chapter. Higher level students will study this topic further under the Marshall-Lerner condition, page 409.

Effects on foreign debt

A depreciation, by lowering the value of the domestic currency, causes the value of foreign debt to increase. Suppose Mountainland owes foreigners $1000, and initially has an exchange rate of Mnl 1.5 = $1 (Mnl is Mountainland's national currency); its foreign debt is therefore Mnl 1500. If the Mnl depreciates, so that now Mnl 2 = $1, Mountainland's foreign debt of $1000 becomes Mnl 2000. This is a problem faced by many developing countries, which find themselves having a larger debt burden if their currency depreciates. On the other hand, a currency appreciation causes the value of foreign debt to fall.

Test your understanding 14.3

Explain the possible effects of exchange rate changes on a country's **(a)** inflation rate, **(b)** employment, **(c)** economic growth, **(d)** current account balance, and **(e)** foreign debt.

14.2 Government intervention

Fixed exchange rates

Understanding a fixed exchange rate system

♦ Describe a fixed exchange rate system involving commitment to a single fixed rate.

In a **fixed exchange rate system**, exchange rates are fixed by the central bank of each country, and are not permitted to change in response to changes in currency supply and demand. Maintaining the value of a currency at its fixed rate requires constant intervention by the central bank or government of each country. This intervention takes the form of buying and selling currencies by the central bank (explained on page 386 above), as well as making other adjustments in the domestic economy. The objective of all these policies is to shift the demand or supply curves for the currency, to eliminate disequilibrium in the foreign exchange market.

To see how this works, consider a country called Bopland whose national currency is the bople. The market for boples is shown in Figure 14.3(a). The central bank of Bopland has fixed the bople–US dollar exchange rate at 2 US dollars = 1 bople. Initially there is equilibrium in the bople market, at point A. Suppose there occurs a leftward shift in the demand for boples (because, for example, of a fall in demand for Bopland's exports), so the demand-for-boples curve shifts from D_1 to D_2. At the fixed exchange rate of 2 dollars = 1 bople, there is an excess supply of boples (the distance A–B). Under a floating exchange rate, the exchange rate would fall to 1.50 dollars per bople (point C), eliminating the excess supply; but if the fixed exchange rate of 2 dollars per bople is to be maintained, the central bank or government must intervene.

Intervention to maintain fixed exchange rates

♦ Explain, using a diagram, how a fixed exchange rate is maintained.

Using official reserves to maintain the exchange rate

In the example above, there is an excess supply of boples, and so the central bank of Bopland intervenes to buy the excess boples by selling some of its foreign currency reserves. This shifts the demand for boples

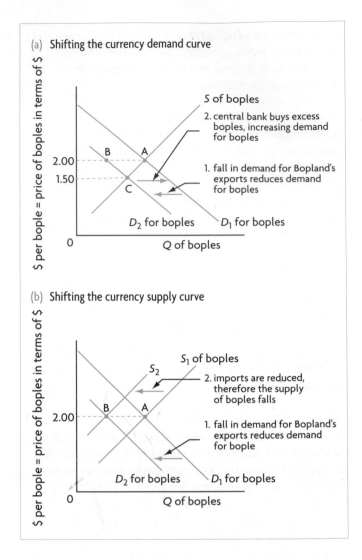

Figure 14.3   Fixed exchange rates: maintaining the value of the bople at 1 bople = $2.00

curve back to D_1, and the fixed exchange rate of 2.00 dollars = 1 bople is maintained.

If there had been an excess demand for boples, the central bank would sell some boples by buying dollars.

However, if Bopland faces an excess supply of boples and a downward pressure on the bople's value over a long time, its central bank will eventually run out of foreign currency reserves, and will be unable to go on buying excess boples. At that point, the government must use additional methods to maintain the fixed exchange rate.

The need for additional measures to maintain a fixed exchange rate arises primarily when there is an excess supply of the domestic currency over a long time. In the opposite situation, where there is an upward pressure on the currency due to excess demand, the central bank can keep on selling the domestic currency and buying foreign exchange, thus maintaining the exchange rate.

Measures to deal with a downward pressure on a currency's value include:

Increases in interest rates

The government can increase interest rates, which attract financial investments from other countries (see page 385). This leads to a higher demand for the domestic currency, shifting the demand for boples back to D_1 in Figure 14.3(a). However, increases in interest rates involve contractionary monetary policy, which may lead to a recession in the domestic economy.

Borrowing from abroad

If the country borrows from abroad, its loans will come in the form of foreign exchange, which when converted into boples will cause an increase in the demand for boples and hence a rightward shift in the demand curve toward D_1. However, extensive borrowing from abroad comes with a number of costs (see page 521 in Chapter 18).

Efforts to limit imports

The government could use policies to limit imports, because this reduces the supply of the domestic currency (since it reduces the demand for foreign exchange needed to buy the imports), and causes a leftward shift in the currency supply curve. In Figure 14.3(b), this appears as a shift from S_1 to S_2, with the exchange rate remaining fixed at \$2.00 = 1 bople (point B, given by the intersection of D_2 with S_2). To limit imports, governments can use (a) contractionary fiscal and monetary policies, which lower aggregate demand, lower incomes, and therefore result in fewer imports, or (b) trade protection trade policies, which work to directly lower the quantity of imports that can enter the country. However, contractionary policies may lead to recession, while trade protection comes with numerous disadvantages, including the possibility of retaliation by trading partners, which would result in lower exports.

Imposing exchange controls

Exchange controls are restrictions imposed by the government on the quantity of foreign exchange that can be bought by domestic residents of a country. This restricts the outflows of funds from the country, whether for the purchase of imports, or for investments abroad, or for foreign travel, or anything at all that would involve a supply of the domestic currency (due to a demand for foreign exchange). However, exchange controls have the effect of causing serious resource misallocation (see page 495 in Chapter 17).

Whereas in a floating exchange rate system the 'price' of a currency adjusts to changes in supply and demand, in a fixed exchange rate system the currency supply and demand are made to adjust to the fixed exchange rate, through central bank and government intervention.

Changing the fixed exchange rate: devaluation and revaluation

♦ Distinguish between a devaluation of a currency and a revaluation of a currency.

If a country experiences serious difficulties in maintaining the fixed exchange rate, a different fixed rate can be set. If the currency has a higher value than can be maintained through intervention, the government may change the fixed rate to a new, lower value; this is called **devaluation** of the currency. If, on the other hand, the currency has a lower value than can be maintained by intervention, the government may set a new higher value; this is called **revaluation** of the currency.

As an example of devaluation suppose 2 US dollars exchange for 1 British pound; the dollar devalues and, at the new fixed rate, 3 dollars exchange for 1 pound. Before the devaluation, 2 dollars were needed to buy 1 pound; now 3 dollars are needed, because the dollar has lost some of its value. This is equivalent to a revaluation of the pound relative to the dollar (the pound increases in value).

Like depreciation, devaluation results in cheaper exports to foreigners and more expensive imports for domestic residents, thus giving rise to more exports and fewer imports. Like appreciation, revaluation leads to more expensive exports to foreigners and cheaper imports for domestic residents, and therefore fewer exports and more imports.

Historically, a system of fixed exchange rates was in place until 1973. In the period 1879–1934, the fixed rate system was known as the 'gold standard', as countries fixed their exchange rates relative to the value of gold. In the period 1944–73, the fixed rate system came to be known as the Bretton Woods system, which no longer tied currencies to gold, and permitted periodic devaluations or revaluations. Under this system, when any country revalued/devalued its currency, it did so not against just one other currency but against all other currencies simultaneously, since all currencies were fixed against each other. This is analogous to the appreciation and depreciation that take place under flexible exchange rates.

1 Describe a fixed exchange rate system.

2 **(a)** Using a diagram, explain some methods that central banks and governments can use to maintain a fixed exchange rate. **(b)** Why do each of these lead to problems?

3 **(a)** Distinguish between devaluation and revaluation. **(b)** When is each of these undertaken by a government?

4 Distinguish between **(a)** depreciation and devaluation, and **(b)** appreciation and revaluation.

5 Why is it easier to maintain a fixed exchange rate when there are upward pressures on the value of a currency than when there are downward pressures?

Managed exchange rates (managed float)

Understanding managed exchange rates

♦ Explain how a managed exchange rate operates, with reference to the fact that there is a periodic government intervention to influence the value of an exchange rate.

In between the two extremes of fixed exchange rates and floating exchange rates is the system of **managed exchange rates**, or the managed float. Combining elements of both, though closer to floating exchange rates, this is the current system, in use since 1973. Exchange rates are for the most part free to float to their market levels (i.e. their equilibrium levels) over long periods of time; however, central banks periodically intervene to stabilise them over the short term.

The objective of central bank intervention is to prevent large and abrupt fluctuations in exchange rates that could arise if currencies were left entirely to free market forces. Large and abrupt exchange rate changes disrupt the orderly flow of international trade and create uncertainties that undermine investment and economic activity. In a managed float, the currency is supposed to move towards its long-term equilibrium position determined by the market. Central banks intervene so that this adjustment can occur in a smooth and orderly way, without major and abrupt fluctuations that may destabilise the economy.

Intervention mainly takes the form of buying and selling of currencies by the central bank, influencing currency demand and supply. In addition, central banks may change interest rates, which also impact upon exchange rates. Very infrequently (mainly in the event of a severe disequilibrium where there is a strong downward pressure on the value of a currency), governments may have to resort to contractionary macroeconomic policies or trade protection measures (as in the case of fixed exchange rates).

Pegging exchange rates

A number of developing countries peg (i.e. fix) their currencies to the US dollar, and float together with it, while a few transition economies peg their currencies to the euro. The way this works in practice is that the pegged currency is allowed to fluctuate only within a narrow range above and below a target exchange rate relative to the dollar or the euro, so that if the actual exchange rate hits the upper or lower limit of the range, the central bank intervenes to keep it within the limits.

To see how this works, suppose Bopland decides to peg the bople to the US dollar, as shown in Figure 14.4. The target exchange rate chosen is 2 US dollars = 1 bople; the bople is allowed to fluctuate up to a maximum of 2.10 dollars = 1 bople, and a minimum of 1.90 dollars = 1 bople. Suppose that market forces cause the exchange rate to drop to 1.90 dollars = 1 bople due to a fall in the demand for boples from D_1 to D_2. At that point the Bank of Bopland (the central bank) will intervene by buying boples (and selling dollars), so that the demand-for-boples curve will stop shifting leftward and the bople stops falling. If the bople increases in value and hits the maximum of 2.10 dollars = 1 bople because of an increase in the

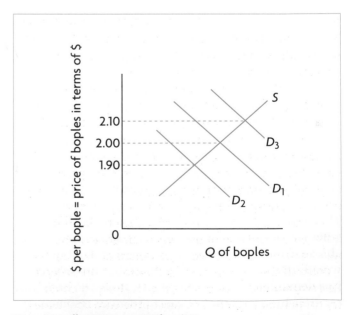

Figure 14.4 Illustrating a pegged currency

demand for boples from D_1 to D_3, the central bank will intervene by selling boples (and buying dollars) to prevent a further rise in the value of the bople.

A pegged currency combines fixed and managed exchange rates, because the pegged currencies are fixed within the specified range of the US dollar (or the euro), and they float in relation to all other currencies, together with the dollar (or the euro). The main reason for pegging currencies is that this stabilises the exchange rate of the pegged currency in relation to the currency to which it is pegged, preventing abrupt or strong fluctuations. Developing countries that peg their currencies to the US dollar experience exchange rate stability relative to the dollar as well as relative to each other, and this facilitates trade flows with the United States as well as between the countries with pegged currencies.

> Under the managed float, exchange rates are determined mainly through market forces, but with periodic intervention by central banks aiming to smooth out abrupt fluctuations. Intervention takes mainly the form of the buying and selling of official reserves. Some developing and transition economies peg their currencies to the US dollar or euro; pegged currencies are fixed in relation to the dollar or euro, and float in relation to all other currencies.

Consequences of overvalued and undervalued currencies

♦ Examine the possible consequences of overvalued and undervalued currencies.

An **overvalued currency** is one that has a value that is too high relative to its equilibrium free market value. Its exchange rate has been set at a higher level than the equilibrium market exchange rate. An **undervalued currency** is one whose value is too low relative to its equilibrium free market value; its exchange rate is low relative to the one the market would have determined.

Overvalued and undervalued currencies cannot come about in a freely floating exchange rate system, where exchange rates are determined purely by demand and supply. However, they can and do often occur in fixed and managed exchange rate systems.

We can use Figure 14.1(a) (page 382) to illustrate both overvalued and undervalued currencies. The market determines a price of US dollars at 0.67 euro = 1 dollar. If the US central bank (known as the Federal Reserve) wanted to overvalue the US dollar, it could try to maintain a price in terms of the euro above the equilibrium, such as at 0.80 euro = 1 dollar. In the case

of an undervaluation, the central bank would select a price of the dollar in terms of the euro below the equilibrium price, such as at 0.50 euro = 1 dollar. The overvaluation or undervaluation of the currency can be achieved by central bank and government interventions that maintain the exchange rate at the selected level (or range of levels, as when a currency is pegged).

There are a number of advantages that may arise from overvaluation and undervaluation of currencies, though these generally come with costs.

Overvalued currencies

Most developing countries have at one time or other had overvalued exchange rates. If an exchange rate is overvalued, imports become cheaper. The main reason for overvaluing their exchange rates is that many developing countries have wanted cheap imports of capital goods, raw materials and other inputs for use in manufacturing industries, to speed up industrialisation.

However, overvalued exchange rates come with many disadvantages. One of the most important of these is that exports become more expensive, thus negatively affecting domestic exporters. Increased imports and reduced exports lead to a worsening current account balance (referred to above, page 387, and explained below, page 397), resulting in payments difficulties. In addition, by increasing imports, overvalued exchange rates can disadvantage domestic producers who have to compete with artificially low-price imports, with negative consequences for domestic employment and resource allocation. Overvaluation has often resulted in the need for countries to devalue or depreciate their currencies to correct the overvaluation.

Undervalued currencies

When a currency is undervalued, exports become less expensive to foreign buyers, while imports become more expensive domestically. Some developing countries have used undervaluation as a method to expand their export industries, expand their economies and therefore also increase their employment levels. Achieving these objectives by means of an undervalued currency is considered to involve the creation of an unfair competitive advantage compared to other countries that do not undervalue their currencies, and which suffer the consequences of increased imports and lower exports. Currency undervaluation is therefore considered to be a kind of 'cheating'. In the context of a managed float, undervalued currencies are sometimes referred to as a 'dirty float'. Correction of the undervalued currency would involve revaluation or appreciation of the currency.

Comparing and contrasting fixed and floating exchange rate systems

♦ Compare and contrast a fixed exchange rate system with a floating exchange rate system, with reference to factors including the degree of certainty for stakeholders, ease of adjustment, the role of international reserves in the form of foreign currencies and flexibility offered to policy makers.

This topic will be discussed on page 402, below, after we have covered the necessary material on the balance of payments.

Test your understanding 14.5

1 (a) In what ways is the managed float an exchange rate system that lies between fixed and floating exchange rate systems? **(b)** Why is it closer to floating exchange rates?

2 What are the reasons for government intervention in a managed float?

3 What does it mean to peg a currency in the context of the managed float system?

4 (a) Distinguish between overvalued and undervalued exchange rates. **(b)** What are the reasons for overvaluing or undervaluing a currency? **(c)** What are the disadvantages of each?

5 (a) Why can overvalued and undervalued exchange rates not arise in a freely floating exchange rates system? **(b)** Why are undervalued currencies sometimes referred to as a 'dirty float'?

HL 14.3 Calculations using exchange rates (higher level topic)

Calculating the value of a currency in terms of another

♦ Calculate the value of one currency in terms of another currency.

Example 1   A hypothetical exchange rate of 1.5 US dollars = 1 euro gives us the price of one euro in terms of dollars. If we want to find the price of one dollar in terms of euros, we divide the unit currency (euro) by the other currency (dollars).

Therefore:

$$1 \text{ dollar} = \frac{1}{1.5} \text{ euro} = 0.67 \text{ euro}$$

The expressions 1.5 dollars = 1 euro, and 0.67 euro = 1 dollar are equivalent.

Example 2   The exchange rate 0.37 Russian rouble = 1 Japanese yen gives the price of 1 yen in terms of roubles. Find the price of 1 rouble in terms of yen.

$$1 \text{ rouble} = \frac{1}{0.37} \text{ yen} = 2.70 \text{ yen}$$

The expressions 0.37 rouble = 1 yen, and 2.70 yen = 1 rouble are equivalent.

In the real world, exchange rates are usually expressed to many decimal places. For example, we may find that 1 rouble = 2.70135 yen. Even a very small change in an exchange rate can amount to large differences in the total values being traded if large quantities of money are involved.

Calculating prices in different currencies

♦ Using exchange rates, calculate the price of a good in different currencies.

Suppose an importer in the United Kingdom imports wine from France (which is a euro zone country). The exchange rate between British pounds (£) and euros (€) is £1.22 = €1. The importer wants to import 1000 bottles at the price of €5 per bottle. Since the importer will supply £ to make the payment in €, she is interested in finding the cost in £.

In terms of euros, the cost is 1000×€5 = €5000. To find this amount in pounds, we simply multiply it by 1.22 (since €1 = £1.22), and we find 1.22×5000 = £6100.

Calculating changes in the value of a currency from a set of exchange rate data

♦ Calculate the changes in the value of a currency from a set of data.

Interpreting exchange rate data

Suppose you are given a set of data on exchange rate changes over time, shown in Table 14.1.

The data show the value of 1 bople (the currency of a country called Bopland) in terms of US dollars ($). Has the bople appreciated or depreciated in the period from January to December 2010? In January, 1 bople was worth $1.22, while in December it was worth $1.69. The value of the bople increased, in other words the bople appreciated relative to the dollar. However,

January 2010	1.22	July 2010	1.40
February 2010	1.25	August 2010	1.37
March 2010	1.33	September 2010	1.45
April 2010	1.39	October 2010	1.58
May 2010	1.47	November 2010	1.63
June 2010	1.43	December 2010	1.69

Table 14.1   US$ per 1 bople; average monthly exchange rates

it did not appreciate every month. In June, July and August it depreciated (or lost some value) compared to the previous month.

Calculating percentage changes in the value of a currency

What was the percentage change in the value of the bople between January and December 2010? (For a review of percentage changes, see 'Quantatitive techniques' chapter on the CD-ROM, page 1.)

% change in the bople (January–December) =

$$\frac{1.69-1.22}{1.22}\times100 = \frac{0.47}{1.22}\times100 = 38.52\%$$

Therefore, the bople appreciated by 38.52% relative to the dollar during 2010.

The bople appreciation relative to the dollar corresponds to a dollar depreciation relative to the bople. To find the percentage change in the value of the dollar for this period, we must first find the 'price' of the dollar in terms of boples. In January, $1.22 = 1 bople; therefore,

$$\$1 = \frac{1}{1.22 \text{ bople}} = 0.82 \text{ bople}$$

In December, $1.69 = 1 bople; therefore,

$$\$1 = \frac{1}{1.69 \text{ bople}} = 0.59 \text{ bople}$$

We can now use this information to find the percentage change in the dollar:

% change in the $ (January–December) =

$$\frac{0.59-0.82}{0.82}\times100 = \frac{-0.23}{0.82}\times100 = -28.05\%$$

The negative percentage change indicates a fall in the value of the dollar; therefore, the dollar depreciated by 28.05% relative to the bople in 2010.

[1] The reason for this is that percentage changes are calculated relative to an initial value. Since the initial values are different for the two currencies, their percentage changes are also different.

This exercise indicates that although an appreciation of currency X relative to currency Y is equivalent to a depreciation of currency Y relative to currency X, the percentage changes *are not the same* (with one being positive and the other negative).[1]

Currency demand and supply functions

Calculating the exchange rate from linear functions

♦ Calculate the exchange rate for linear demand and supply functions.

The exchange rate is the 'price' of a currency (measured in terms of another currency). Therefore, if we are given linear currency demand and supply functions of the form $Q_d = a-bP$ and $Q_s = c+dP$, the problem of calculating the exchange rate, or 'price' of the currency, is identical to what we did when we found the price of standard goods in Chapter 2 (see also 'Quantatitive techniques' chapter on the CD-ROM, page 29 for a review).

We will examine the market for boples, on the assumption that Bopland has adopted a freely floating exchange rate system, so the bople exchange rate is determined by supply and demand. The 'price' of the bople is the exchange rate in terms of dollars.

We are given the following demand and supply functions: $Q_d = 8-2P$, and $Q_s = 2+2P$, where Q_d and Q_s are in millions of boples per day, and P is the value of the bople in terms of dollars. We therefore have the following equations:

$$Q_d = 8-2P \text{ (bople demand function)}$$
$$Q_s = 2+2P \text{ (bople supply function)}$$
$$Q_d = Q_s \text{ (at equilibrium)}$$

Using the third equation, we can eliminate Q_s and Q_d, and solve for P:

$$8-2P = 2+2P \;\Rightarrow\; 6=4P \;\Rightarrow\; P=\$1.5 \text{ per bople}$$

Since P is the value of the bople in terms of $, we have found that the equilibrium exchange rate is 1 bople = $1.50.

If we want to also find the equilibrium quantity of boples bought and sold per day, we substitute the 'price' P into the demand equation:

$$Q_d = 8-2P \;\Rightarrow\; Q_d = 8-2(1.5) \;\Rightarrow\; Q_d = 8-3 = 5$$

Therefore, the equilibrium quantity is 5 million boples bought and sold per day.

Alternatively, substituting into the supply equation, we have:

$$Q_s = 2 + 2P \implies Q_s = 2 + 2(1.5) \implies Q_s = 2 + 3 = 5$$

(which is the same as above).

(Note that it is not necessary for you to do this calculation both ways, as the result is the same.)

Plotting currency demand and supply curves from linear functions

♦ Plot demand and supply curves for a currency from linear functions and identify the equilibrium exchange rate.

Given currency demand and supply functions such as the above, it is a simple matter to plot the corresponding demand and supply curves, using the method described in the 'Quantitative techniques' on the CD-ROM, page 29, and applied in Chapter 2. Once we plot both the demand and supply curves, we can read off the equilibrium price (and quantity) that result at market equilibrium.

Figure 14.5 plots the currency demand and supply functions given above. The vertical axis measures dollars per bople (or the price of one bople in terms of dollars), and the horizontal axis measures the quantity of boples traded per day in millions of boples. The equilibrium 'price' of boples is $1.50 per bople, where 5 million boples are demanded and supplied. At any higher exchange rate, such as $1.70, there would be an excess demand for boples, and in a freely floating exchange rate system the bople would appreciate. At any lower exchange rate, such as $1.30 boples, there would be an excess supply of boples, resulting in a bople depreciation.

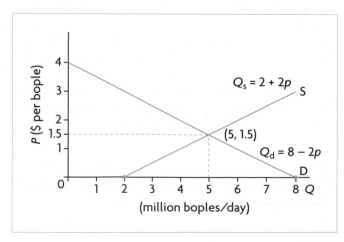

Figure 14.5 Plotting currency demand and supply curves from linear functions

Test your understanding 14.6

1 (a) 1 Canadian dollar = 0.99 US dollar. What is the value of 1 US dollar in terms of Canadian dollars? (b) 1 Indian rupee = 1.84 Japanese yen. Calculate the 'price' of 1 Japanese yen in terms of Indian rupees. (c) 1 Japanese yen = 1.34 Sri Lankan rupee. What is the value of 1 Sri Lankan rupee in terms of Japanese yen? (d) 1 British pound = 1.62 Canadian dollars. Find the value of 1 Canadian dollar in terms of British pounds.

2 The price of item X in India is 50 Indian rupees. Using the exchange rates in question 1, find its price in (a) Japanese yen, and (b) Sri Lankan rupees. (c) Importers in Japan and Sri Lanka want to import 1000 units of item X. What is their cost in yen and Sri Lankan rupees, respectively?

3 The price of item Y in Canada is 75 Canadian dollars. Using the exchange rates in question 1, find its price in (a) US dollars, and (b) British pounds. (c) What is the cost of 5000 units of item Y in US dollars and pounds?

4 On 1 June 2010, 1 British pound was worth US $1.46; on 1 November, 1 British pound was worth US $1.60. (a) Which currency appreciated and which depreciated? (b) Calculate the percentage appreciation of the appreciating currency. (c) Calculate the percentage depreciation of the depreciating currency.

5 (a) Using the table below, determine which currency appreciated, and which depreciated from 1–30 September. (b) Calculate the percentage appreciation of the appreciating currency. (c) Calculate the percentage depreciation of the depreciating currency.

Euros to 1 US$ (value of 1 US dollar per euro)

1 Sept. 2010	1.2800
8 Sept 2010	1.2697
16 Sept 2010	1.2989
23 Sept 2010	1.3364
30 Sept 2010	1.3611

6 (a) In the equations $Q_d = 7 - 3P$ and $Q_s = -5 + 3P$, Q_d and Q_s refer to quantity of $ demanded and supplied in millions per day, and P is the value of the $ in terms of €. Assuming a freely floating exchange rate system, calculate the equilibrium exchange rate for the $ in terms of €. (b) Plot the demand and supply curves, and determine the equilibrium exchange rate on your graph. Does it match your calculations?

14.4 The balance of payments

Introducing the balance of payments

The role of the balance of payments

♦ Outline the role of the balance of payments.
♦ Distinguish between debit items and credit items in the balance of payments.

Innumerable transactions between residents of different countries involve activities like importing and exporting, travel, investments in stocks and bonds, investments by multinational corporations, buying property, sending or receiving gifts, and in general, anything that gives rise to a flow of money across international boundaries. All these transactions are recorded in the balance of payments:

> The **balance of payments** of a country is a record (usually for a year) of all transactions between the residents of the country and the residents of all other countries. Its role is to show all payments received from other countries, called **credits**, and all payments made to other countries, called **debits**. In the course of a year, all inflows of payments (credits) must exactly equal the outflows of payments (debits); the sum of all credits is equal to the sum of all debits.

Why do countries record all their foreign transactions; why do they keep records of all possible inflows and outflows of money? No attempt is ever made to record all money flows within countries. The reason is that when money flows into or out of a country, it involves the exchange of different national currencies. These currency exchanges are an important part of understanding the balance of payments.

Relating the demand and supply of a currency to the balance of payments

We will consider the balance of payments accounts of Bopland, whose national currency is the bople. All the inflows of money from abroad into Bopland, or all credits, can only be made if foreigners buy boples; therefore, credits represent a foreign demand for boples, corresponding to a foreign supply of all other currencies given up to buy boples. Outflows of money from Bopland to other countries, or debits, represent a Boplander supply of boples, corresponding to Boplander demand for foreign currencies.

> In the balance of payments accounts of a country, all credits (inflows of money into the country) create a foreign demand for the country's currency; and all debits (outflows of money from the country) create a supply of the domestic currency.

The structure of the balance of payments[2]

Table 14.2 shows Bopland's balance of payments for the year 2010. The balance of payments consists of three accounts: the current account, the capital account and the financial account. Each of the items in the three accounts is accompanied by a plus or minus sign: the plus sign denotes credits (money inflows) and the minus sign denotes debits (money outflows).

The current account

♦ Explain the four components of the current account, specifically the balance of trade in goods, the balance of trade in services, income and current transfers.
♦ Distinguish between a current account deficit and a current account surplus.

Balance of trade in goods
Items 1 and 2 in Table 14.2 show the value of exports and the value of imports of goods respectively. Exports of goods are the sale of goods to other countries, for which payment is received in boples; therefore, exports are a credit and have a plus sign. Imports of goods are the purchase of goods from other countries, for which payment is made in foreign currencies (generating a supply of boples); imports are therefore a debit and have a minus sign. The **balance of trade in goods** is calculated by subtracting imports from exports, or what is the same thing, adding items 1 and 2 (note that we must take into account the minus sign), so the balance of trade in goods is $40 - 65 = -25$ billion boples, indicating a negative balance of trade in goods, or a *deficit* in this balance.

> A **deficit** in an account occurs whenever a balance has a negative value, meaning that debits are larger than credits (there is an excess of debits).

---

[2] The structure presented here is based on what appears in the appendix of the IB's Economics Guide, First examinations 2013.

Balance of trade in services

Items 3 and 4 are analogous to items 1 and 2, only they involve the value of exports and value of imports of services. Services include a variety of activities, such as insurance, tourism, transportation and consulting. When foreigners visit Bopland as tourists, Bopland is exporting tourism services; similarly, when foreigners buy insurance from Boplander companies, this represents exports of insurance services. When Boplanders visit other countries as tourists, or buy insurance from other countries, they are importing tourism and insurance services. Table 14.2 shows that Bopland's exports of services are larger than its imports of services, and so the **balance of trade in services** (items 3+4), is +10 billion boples. Bopland therefore has a *surplus* in its balance of trade in services.

Current account	
1. Exports of goods	+40
2. Imports of goods	−65
Balance of trade in goods (items 1+2)	**−25**
3. Exports of services	+25
4. Imports of services	−15
Balance of trade in services (items 3+4)	**+10**
Balance of trade in goods and services (items 1+2+3+4)	**−15**
5. Income (inflows minus outflows)	−6
6. Current transfers (secondary income) (inflows minus outflows)	+1
Balance on current account (items 1+2+3+4+ 5+6)	**−20**
Capital account	
7. Capital transfers (inflows minus outflows)	+0.7
8. Transactions in non-produced, non-financial assets (inflows minus outflows)	+0.3
Balance on capital account (items 7+8)	**+1**
Financial account	
9. Direct investment (inflows minus outflows)	+23
10. Portfolio investment (inflows minus outflows)	−4
11. Reserve assets (official reserves)	+1
Balance on financial account (items 9+10+11)	**+20**
12. Errors and omissions	−1
Balance (sum of all items from 1 to 12)	0

Table 14.2 Balance of payments of Bopland, 2010 (in billions of boples)

A **surplus** in an account occurs whenever a balance has a positive value, meaning that credits are larger than debits (there is an excess of credits).

Balance of trade in goods and services

The next line states 'Balance of trade in goods and services', which is the sum of all the items 1–4. This is often referred to as the 'trade balance' or 'balance of trade' for short, and includes the value of all exports minus the value of all imports. (You may note that this corresponds to what we refer to as the 'net exports' component of GDP, abbreviated as $X-M$.) Bopland has a negative trade balance (−15 billion boples).

Income

Item 5, or **income**, refers to all inflows into Bopland of rents, interest and profits from abroad, minus all outflows of rents, interest and profits. Boplanders may earn income abroad, such as if they own rental property abroad that earns rental income, or have bank accounts abroad that earn interest, or if they own stocks in another country that earn dividend income, or if they own a subsidiary of a multinational corporation that earns profits. Whatever income flows into Bopland from abroad is a credit, while whatever income flows out of Bopland is a debit. In Bopland, income outflows are greater than income inflows, leading to a value of −6 billion boples for income.

Current transfers

Item 6, or **current transfers**, refers inflows into Bopland due to transfers from abroad like gifts, remittances (money sent home by Boplanders living abroad), foreign aid and pensions, minus outflows of such transfers to other countries. This item is positive (+1 billion boples), indicating that credits are greater than debits, as Bopland receives more transfers from abroad than it makes to other countries.

Balance on current account

When we add up all the items in the current account (items 1–6), we get the **balance on current account**. Bopland has a *deficit* on its current account of −20 billion boples; the debits (outflows) are larger than the credits (inflows) by this amount.

From the point of view of demand and supply of boples, *the deficit on this account means there is an excess supply of the currency in the foreign exchange market*: the quantity of boples supplied (debits created by Boplanders) is larger than the quantity of boples demanded (credits created by foreigners). (The quantity of boples demanded to make the credits possible is equal to the sum of all the credits, or +40+25 + 1 = +66 billion boples; whereas the quantity of boples supplied to make the debits possible is equal to the sum of all the debits, or −65 − 15 − 6 = −86. Adding the credits to the debits we have +66 − 86 = −20 billion boples, which is excess supply of boples, or the deficit on the current account.)

In general, the trade balance (meaning the balance of trade in goods and services) is the most important part of the current account in most countries. Therefore, a deficit on the current account is usually due to an excess of imports of goods over exports, whereas a surplus on the current account is usually due to an excess of exports of goods over imports.

> The current account of the balance of payments is the sum of: (1) the balance of trade in goods; (ii) the balance of trade in services; (iii) income inflows minus outflows; and (iv) current transfer inflows minus outflows. The most important part of the current account in most countries is the balance of trade in goods and services (i+ii).

The capital account

> ◆ Explain the two components of the capital account, specifically capital transfers and transactions in non-produced, non-financial assets.

The capital account consists of two items. In item 7, **capital transfers**, include inflows minus outflows for such things as debt forgiveness (when debt is cancelled), non-life insurance claims and investment grants (money given as a gift by governments to finance physical capital).

Item 8, transactions in **non-produced, non-financial assets**, consist mainly of the purchase or use of natural resources that have not been produced (land, mineral rights, forestry rights, water, fishing rights, airspace and electromagnetic spectrum). It includes all inflows of funds into Bopland (credits) minus outflows of funds from Bopland (debits) due to such transactions.

The sum of items 7 and 8 gives the **balance on capital account**, in which Bopland has a surplus of +1 billion boples, meaning that the credits (payment inflows) are more than the debits (payment outflows). The quantity of boples demanded is larger than the quantity of boples supplied. Therefore, *a surplus on an account indicates there is an excess demand of the currency in the foreign exchange market*.

In general, the capital account is relatively unimportant in terms of size compared to the other two accounts.

> The **capital account** of the balance of payments of a country is composed of inflows minus outflows of funds for capital transfers and transactions in non-produced, non-financial assets. The capital account is relatively small compared to the current account and financial account.

The financial account

> ◆ Explain the three main components of the financial account, specifically, direct investment, portfolio investment and reserve assets.

The financial account consists of three items.

Direct investment
Item 9 deals with **direct investment** (better known as 'foreign direct investment', to be studied in Chapter 18). This includes investments in physical capital, such as in buildings and factories, usually undertaken by multinational corporations. The figure for this item includes inflows due to direct investment by foreigners in Bopland (credits) minus outflows due to Boplander investment abroad (debits). Bopland accepted more direct investments by foreigners than it made in other countries, by the amount of 23 billion boples.

Portfolio investment
Item 10, **portfolio investment**, shows financial investments (such as stocks and bonds). In Bopland, inflows (credits) for the purchase of stocks and bonds were less than outflows (debits) for the same purpose (−4 billion boples).

Inflows of funds into Bopland due to borrowing by the Boplander government from foreign lenders (foreign government debt, to be discussed in Chapter 18) appear as credits under portfolio investment. Similarly, Boplander loans to foreign governments lead to an outflow of funds from Bopland appearing as debits under portfolio investment.[3]

(You may note the distinction between inflows or outflows of funds due to the purchase of assets, and inflows or outflows of funds due to income generated by the purchase of assets. If a multinational

---

[3] The reason is that when a government borrows it issues bonds that are purchased by the lenders (see page 330, footnote 5). From the point of view of the lenders to Bopland, the purchase of Boplander government

bonds by foreigners represents financial investments in Bopland. Similarly, Boplander lending to other countries represents financial investments abroad.

corporation decides to invest in Bopland by purchasing physical capital, the result is an inflow of funds into Bopland, appearing as a credit in Bopland's *financial* account. If the owners of the multinational corporation decide to take their profits out of Bopland and back to the home country, there is an outflow of funds from Bopland, appearing as a debit in Bopland's *current* account.)

Reserve assets

Item 11, **reserve assets** (or official reserves), refers to foreign currency reserves that the central bank can buy or sell to influence the value of the country's currency (see page 386). Suppose the Central Bank of Bopland holds reserves of US dollars. If it sells dollars, it does so by buying boples. This is an inflow of boples, appearing as a credit in the financial account. Table 14.2 shows the Central Bank to have bought 1 billion boples, appearing with a plus sign (a credit). (If the central bank had sold boples by buying dollars, this would be an outflow of boples and would appear as a debit in the financial account.)

> The **financial account** of the balance of payments consists of inflows minus outflows of funds for (i) direct investment, (ii) portfolio investment, and (iii) reserve assets.

Balance on financial account

The **balance on financial account**, given by the sum of items 9, 10 and 11, shows a surplus of 20 billion boples (the credits are more than the debits). Therefore, there is an excess demand of 20 billion boples in the foreign exchange market for this account.

Errors and omissions

In the real world, it is extremely difficult (if at all possible) to record every single transaction between a country and all other countries, and some of these go unrecorded. However, since the sum of all credits must equal the sum of all debits (to be explained below), it is necessary for actual accounts to include an item creating this equality. This is the role of **errors and omissions**. If the sum of credits is larger than the sum of debits, then this includes a debit item to create the equality. If the sum of debits is larger, then the statistical discrepancy consists of a credit. This is simply a statistical 'trick' that does not affect our analysis of the balance of payments. In the case of Bopland, net errors and omissions are −1 billion boples (a debit), making the sum of debits equal to the sum of credits.

A clarification concerning the capital account and the financial account

We will pause a moment to clarify some confusing terminology. Economists often use the term 'capital account' to refer to both the capital and financial accounts that appear in Table 14.2. However, since 1997, countries around the world are increasingly using the classification system shown in Table 14.2 in their balance of payments. Therefore, if you come across the expression 'capital account' in your general reading, you should be aware that reference is being made to what is actually the 'financial account', together with the relatively unimportant 'capital account'.

The relationships between the accounts

The meaning of 'balance' in the balance of payments

> ◆ Explain that the current account balance is equal to the sum of the capital account and financial account balances.

In the balance of payments, the sum of all the items is always zero. This is another way of saying that the sum of all credits always balances with the sum of all debits.

However, there is more to the idea of *balance* in the balance of payments. As you can see in Bopland's case, the deficit in the current account of −20 billion boples is exactly matched by the surplus in the combined capital and financial accounts (together with errors and omissions): +1+20−1 = +20 billion boples. In other words, the excess supply of boples in the current account, which is in deficit, is exactly matched by an excess demand for boples in the remaining two accounts (plus errors and omissions) which altogether are in surplus.

> The current account balance is matched by the sum of the capital account balance and the financial account balance (plus errors and omissions). A current account deficit is matched by a surplus in the other three items combined. A current account surplus is matched by a deficit in the other three items combined. More simply,
>
> current account+(capital account+financial account+errors and omissions) = 0
>
> therefore,
>
> current account = −(capital account+financial account+errors and omissions)

We turn now to an explanation of this point.

Why the current account and financial account are interdependent

• Examine how the current account and the financial account are interdependent.

When a country trades with other countries, its imports of goods and services are unlikely to be equal to its exports. If imports are greater than exports, it has a deficit in its trade balance, and since this is the most important component of the current account, it is also likely to have a current account deficit. Using the production possibilities model, we can see this in Figure 14.6(a). The country's *PPC* defines the maximum it can produce, but the country is attaining a point outside its *PPC*, such as point C, because it is importing more than it is exporting.[4]

If there is a current account deficit, there must be a financial account surplus (the capital account being very small), which provides it with the foreign exchange it needs to pay for the excess of imports over exports. The surplus on the financial account may arise from investments in physical or financial capital by foreigners, including loans from foreigners. It follows, then, that a deficit in the current account is matched by a surplus in the financial account (along with the unimportant capital account).

If the economy's exports of goods and services are greater than its imports, it has a surplus in its current account, meaning it is buying from foreigners less than what it sells to them. While it is producing somewhere on the *PPC*, it is consuming less, so the output available for domestic consumption is at a point inside its *PPC*, such as D in Figure 14.6(b). The difference between what it consumes and what it produces is the excess of exports over imports.

When there is a surplus on the current account, the country is accumulating foreign exchange (as it earns more foreign exchange from exports than it pays out to buy imports), which it can use to buy assets abroad (direct or portfolio investments, including loans to other countries). It follows, then, that a surplus in the current account is matched by a deficit in the financial account.[5]

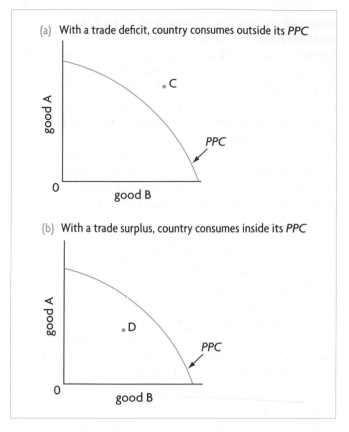

Figure 14.6 Using a *PPC* to illustrate a trade deficit and a trade surplus

In fact, most economists believe that the surplus or deficit of a financial account of a country *is the result* of what is happening in the current account. If there is a deficit in the current account, the financial account is a reflection of the need to finance that deficit; if there is a surplus in the current account, the financial account reflects investments in foreign countries undertaken to dispose of the extra foreign exchange.

A current account deficit means a country consumes more than it produces; and it pays for extra output consumed through a financial account surplus. A current account surplus means a country consumes less than it produces, and part of the income generated from the sale of extra output produced corresponds to a financial account deficit.

---

[4] Higher level students should note that achieving a point outside the *PPC* by means of a trade deficit is very different from achieving such a point by specialisation and trade according to comparative (or absolute) advantage (see pages 357 and 360). The theory of comparative advantage presupposes that imports and exports balance each other, so there is no trade deficit or trade surplus: a point outside the *PPC* is achieved because of an increase in allocative efficiency, and is beneficial for the trading partners. By contrast, being outside the *PPC* by means of a trade deficit may have positive or negative consequences

for the economy, depending on a number of factors. See page 406 for a full explanation.
[5] More realistically, in terms of the three accounts in Table 14.2, the spending of foreign exchange that is over and above receipts of foreign exchange in the current account, leading to a deficit in this account must be somehow paid for, and that can only happen through a surplus in the financial and capital accounts. If, on the other hand, spending is less than receipts in the current account, there will be foreign exchange left over to be used for investments and lending abroad.

The meaning of 'imbalance' in the balance of payments

Since the balance of payments must always balance, why do we often hear the expressions 'balance of payments deficit' or 'balance of payments surplus'? A balance of payments deficit means there is a deficit in the combined current, capital and financial accounts (plus errors and omissions), *excluding central bank intervention*. A balance of payments surplus means there is a surplus in the combined three accounts (plus errors and omissions), *excluding central bank intervention*. Bopland, for example, has a balance of payments deficit:

current account deficit (–20 billion)+capital account surplus (+1 billion)+financial account surplus excluding the central bank purchase of 1 billion (+19 billion)+errors and omissions (–1 billion) = –1 billion = balance of payments deficit

The reason for central bank intervention can be found in just this deficit. By buying up excess boples of 1 billion, the central bank creates a balance in the balance of payments.

Such imbalances (deficits or surpluses) occur in virtually all countries all the time, but a 'balance' is always created in the sense that debits are made to equal credits. There are many ways to do this, which involve either reliance on market forces or on government intervention. We will now see how this is accomplished.

Test your understanding 14.7

1 Define the balance of payments. What is its role?

2 **(a)** Define debits and credits, relating to the demand for or supply of a currency in the foreign exchange market. **(b)** Provide some examples of money flows into and out of the country where you live, and explain whether these are credits, or debits.

3 Explain, providing examples, **(a)** the four components of the current account, **(b)** the two components of the capital account, and **(c)** the three components of the financial account.

4 What is the role of the item 'errors and omissions' in the balance of payments?

5 **(a)** What is the meaning of a 'deficit' and a 'surplus' on an account? Explain in terms of debits and credits. **(b)** Explain the meaning of a deficit or surplus in the current account. **(c)** What items in the balance of payments are most likely responsible for a deficit or surplus?

6 Explain why **(a)** a trade surplus means that a country is consuming less than it is producing, and **(b)** a trade deficit means that a country is consuming more than it is producing.

7 Explain the relationship between the current account, capital account, financial account and errors and omissions

8 **(a)** What do we mean when we say that the balance of payments always balances? **(b)** If the balance of payments always balances, how can there be a 'balance of payments surplus' or a 'balance of payments deficit'?

9 Explain why current account deficits are likely to be roughly matched by financial account surpluses, and current account surpluses to be roughly matched by financial account deficits.

14.5   The balance of payments and exchange rates

Relating current account deficits and surpluses to exchange rates

How are current account deficits or surpluses always made to match capital plus financial account surpluses or deficits? (Alternatively, what is essentially the same thing, why do the balance of payments always balance?) The answer depends on the kind of exchange rate system in force, freely floating, managed, or fixed.

Balancing deficits with surpluses under freely floating exchange rates

♦ Explain why a deficit in the current account of the balance of payments may result in downward pressure on the exchange rate of the currency.

♦ Explain why a surplus in the current account of the balance of payments may result in upward pressure on the exchange rate of the currency.

Under freely floating exchange rates, there is no government or central bank intervention, and the market determines the equilibrium exchange rate (see page 382). (In Table 14.2, there would be no buying or selling of currencies by the central bank, and the entry for item 11 on reserve assets would be zero.)

In Figure 14.2(a) (page 384), at the initial equilibrium exchange rate of 0.67 euro = 1 US dollar, the quantity

---

of dollars demanded is equal to the quantity of dollars supplied. In equilibrium, the sum of credits is equal to the sum of debits in the US balance of payments. Similarly, in Figure 14.2(b), at the (identical) exchange rate of 1.5 dollars = 1 euro, the quantity of euros demanded is equal to the quantity of euros supplied, so the sum of credits is equal to the sum of debits for the euro zone countries as well. In both cases, *there is a balance in the balance of payments.*

If the euro zone countries' demand for imports from the United States increases, in Figure 14.2(a) the demand for dollars increases and the demand curve shifts to the right from D_1 to D_2. At the initial equilibrium exchange rate of rate 0.67 euro = 1 dollar, there is an excess demand for dollars equal to the horizontal distance between A and B. The United States now has a *surplus on its current account*, and since nothing has changed in the remaining accounts, it has *excess credits in its balance of payments*. An imbalance has therefore been created.

Part (b) shows that the increased demand for imports from the United States has caused the supply of euros to increase, and the supply curve shifts to the right from S_1 to S_2. At the initial equilibrium exchange rate of 1.5 dollars = 1 euro, there is an excess supply of euros equal to the horizontal distance between D and E. The euro zone countries have a *current account deficit*, corresponding to *excess debits in their balance of payments*. The current account surplus in the United States corresponds to a current account deficit in the euro zone countries.

We know that under freely floating exchange rates, market forces cause the exchange rate to change: the dollar appreciates to 0.90 euro = 1 dollar, which is equivalent to the depreciation of the euro to 1.11 euro = 1 dollar. In the United States the dollar appreciation causes imports to increase and exports to decrease until the current account surplus is eliminated. In the euro zone countries the euro depreciation causes imports to fall and exports to increase until the current account deficit is eliminated.[6] This leads to an important conclusion:

Under freely floating exchange rates, when there is a deficit in the current account, market forces create a downward pressure on the currency exchange rate. When there is a surplus in the current account, market forces create an upward pressure on the currency exchange rate. As a result, exchange rate changes automatically eliminate current account deficits and surpluses, and create a balance in the balance of payments.

Balancing deficits with surpluses through government intervention

Managed exchange rates (managed float)
The managed float is close to freely floating exchange rates, only it includes periodic interventions by the central bank to influence exchange rate changes (see page 390). The most common intervention involves buying and selling of reserve currencies, as with the Central Bank of Bopland's intervention. As we saw above (page 400), Bopland has a deficit in its balance of payments, meaning there are excess debits due to an excess supply of boples. In a freely floating system, the central bank would not have intervened, and *the bople would have depreciated*. However, the Central Bank of Bopland sold dollars and bought 1 billion boples, creating a credit of that amount, therefore offsetting the deficit of –1 billion boples. *The result was to avoid depreciation and maintain the bople's exchange rate.* An alternative would have been for the central bank to create a smaller credit (say 0.5 billion boples), in which case the bople would have depreciated, but less than under a freely floating system.

In a managed exchange rate system, the balance of payments is made to balance by a combination of central bank buying and selling of currencies and market forces.

Fixed exchange rates
Suppose now that Bopland has a fixed exchange rate. If excess debits persist year after year, the Central Bank of Bopland can keep selling dollars and buying boples, creating the necessary credits to match the

---

[6] To see how this happens, consider the following chain of events. Given the initial change in the demand for dollars, the appreciation of the dollar makes US exports more expensive and imports from euro zone countries cheaper; while the depreciation of the euro makes euro zone exports cheaper and imports from the US more expensive. More expensive US exports are in effect more expensive imports from the United States for euro zone countries, and this has the effect of lowering the quantity of dollars demanded by euro zone countries, meaning a move from B to C in part (a) in Figure 14.2, as well as lowering the quantity of euros supplied by euro zone countries, meaning a move from E to F in part (b). At the same time, cheaper euro zone exports in effect are cheaper US imports from euro zone countries, which increase the quantity of euros demanded by the US, or a move from D to F in part (b) and increase the quantity of dollars supplied by US importers, or the move from A to C in part (a). As a result, US imports (debits) and euro zone exports (credits) increase, while US imports (credits) and euro zone exports (credits) decrease. Both current account imbalances are eliminated.

excess debits, thus maintaining the fixed exchange rate. But at some point, the Bank of Bopland will run out of dollars to sell. The government or central bank must therefore find ways to increase credits or decrease debits to maintain a balance. To increase credits, the central bank can increase interest rates, thus attracting foreign financial investments, or the government can borrow from abroad; both actions increase credits in the financial account. The government could limit imports (through contractionary fiscal and monetary policies or trade protection), or it could impose exchange controls; both these actions decrease the debits.

These measures are exactly the same as those needed to maintain the fixed exchange rate, studied on page 388. It follows that:

> In a fixed exchange rate system, the balance of payments is made to balance by policies that keep the exchange rate fixed.

You can see, then, that the idea of *balance* in the balance of payments is very closely connected to exchange rates. The reason is that *everything that is recorded in the balance of payments creates a demand for or supply of a domestic currency*. Since the value of the domestic currency is determined by currency supply and demand (in all exchange rate systems), it follows that *balance in the balance of payments means there is a balance between the demand for and supply of a currency*.

Comparing and contrasting exchange rate systems

> ♦ Compare and contrast a fixed exchange rate system with a floating exchange rate system, with reference to factors including the degree of certainty for stakeholders, ease of adjustment, the role of international reserves in the form of foreign currencies and flexibility offered to policy makers.

Now that we have studied the balance of payments and learned about the connection between the balance of payments and exchange rates, we are in a position to evaluate exchange rate systems.

Degree of certainty for stakeholders

Fixed exchange rates
Under fixed exchange rates, there is a high degree of certainty for firms, consumers and the government because they know what exchange rates will be in the future. This certainty makes it easier for businesses to plan future investments domestically and abroad, sales of their products to other countries (exports), costs of imported inputs, and other activities because they do not have to take into account possible exchange rate changes that would change relative prices from country to country. Consumers can better plan travel abroad, purchases of imported goods and services and financial investments in other countries. Governments can similarly plan activities involving foreign transactions (purchases of imported goods and services, payments of interest and capital on foreign loans, etc.).

For the same reasons, fixed exchange rates favour international trade. The absence of exchanges rate changes makes it possible to calculate accurately the prices of goods and services in different countries.

In addition, speculation is limited. Fixed exchange rates remove a cause of currency instability due to speculation. (An exception occurs when people believe that a country may devalue or revalue its currency, in which case there is room for speculation.)

Floating exchange rates
Floating exchange rates cause uncertainty as stakeholders cannot be sure what the value of currencies will be in the future. This may have negative effects on trade and investment flows due to inability to plan accurately for the future.

In addition, large and abrupt exchange rate changes can cause serious problems for countries that depend heavily on exports. Occasionally, these can result in financial crises, due to very large current account deficits (which may sometimes require intervention by the International Monetary Fund, through loans that help finance the deficits, such as for example in Mexico, Thailand and Russia in the 1990s (see page 496).

Further, currency speculation under floating exchange rates can be destabilising. If speculators expect a currency to depreciate due to large current account deficits, they can sell the currency in anticipation of its depreciation, and as a result cause it to depreciate more than it otherwise would.

The role of foreign currency reserves

Fixed exchange rates
Central bank intervention to maintain a fixed exchange rate (see page 388) requires sufficient supplies of reserves of foreign currencies. If there is a current account deficit, reserve currencies can be sold to buy the domestic currency, thus creating credits in the financial account to offset the excess debits in the current account. Problems can arise if central banks do not have enough reserves to carry out the necessary interventions.

Floating exchange rates

Under floating exchange rates there is no need for central banks to hold foreign currency reserves since there is no need for intervention in foreign exchange markets. The balance of payments balances entirely through market forces (see page 401).

Ease of adjustment

Fixed exchange rates

Under fixed exchange rates, there are no easy methods to correct imbalances in the balance of payments. External shocks (such as a sudden increase in oil prices leading to current account deficits for oil importers) cannot be handled quickly and easily. Large or persistent current account deficits require large quantities of foreign currency reserves or access to foreign borrowing. If these are not readily available, the country must resort to contractionary policies, trade protection or exchange controls, all with serious negative repercussions (see below). If current account deficits persist, the country may have to devalue its currency.

Floating exchange rates

One of the most important advantages of flexible exchange rates is their ability to adjust automatically to excess demand or supply of the domestic currency, thus automatically bringing about a balance in the balance of payments. A current account deficit is eliminated through currency depreciation; a surplus is eliminated by currency appreciation.

As a result, there is easy adjustment to external shocks. *A sudden increase in oil prices leading to a current account deficit is met by a fall in the value of the currency.* This mechanism allows the economy to be shielded against the effects of negative external developments.

Flexibility offered to policy-makers

Fixed exchange rates

Fixed exchange rates do not offer flexibility to policy-makers. The need to maintain the exchange rate at a fixed level forces the government and central bank to pursue a range of policies that come with certain disadvantages, particularly in the case where the currency is under pressure to lose its value. These policies were considered on page 389, where we saw that:

- interest rates increases attract financial investments but have contractionary effects in the domestic economy
- borrowing from abroad also increases inflows of funds, but extensive borrowing may lead to high

levels of debt resulting in a range of problems (see Chapter 18)

- contractionary fiscal and monetary policies to limit imports may create a recession and unemployment in the domestic economy
- trade protection to limit imports results in increased inefficiency in production, increased domestic and global misallocation of resources and may result in retaliation
- exchange controls limit currency outflows but result in major resource misallocation.

Floating exchange rates

Floating exchange rates offer greater flexibility to policy-makers. Domestic economic policy does not need to respond to balance of payments problems, and can be carried out in accordance with domestic priorities. For example, if there is a current account deficit, there is no need to pursue contractionary fiscal and monetary policies (which would create a recession). The government can pursue expansionary fiscal and monetary policies, and the current account deficit will automatically be corrected through currency depreciation.

However, while domestic policy retains its independence under floating exchange rates, it may still have some undesirable or unintended effects in the foreign sector of an economy. For more information on this see point, see page 405.

Evaluating the managed float (managed exchange rates)

The managed float, currently in use today, came about spontaneously following the collapse of the system of fixed exchange rates in 1973. Supporters of the managed float argue that it is superior to fixed exchange rates because it offers flexibility to pursue policies according to the needs of the domestic economy. Its flexibility further allows economies to adjust more easily to shocks (such as abrupt increases in the price of oil). Also, they claim it is superior to fully flexible exchange rates because it offers governments the opportunity to prevent very sudden and large exchange rate fluctuations, and it also works to make currency speculation more difficult because speculators do not know if and when a central bank will intervene in a currency market to change the value of a currency.

On the other hand, critics of the managed float argue it cannot do enough to prevent large currency fluctuations, which are especially damaging to economies highly dependent on exports. They argue that sharp drops in exchange rates played a major role in bringing about the severe financial crisis experienced by some Asian countries in the late 1990s (see page 496). Also, the managed float does not appear to be successful in eliminating large trade imbalances, as the experience of the United States indicates. Further it offers countries the opportunity to 'cheat' by undervaluing their currencies and gaining an unfair competitive advantage (the 'dirty float'; see page 391).

Few economists today would suggest returning to a fixed exchange rate system. However, some economists emphasise the need for increased international collaboration that would exercise some oversight over the management of exchange rates (as well as other macroeconomic policy issues).

China and the global economy

Countries that greatly overspend relative to what they produce, such as the United States, have large trade deficits, while those that greatly underspend (or oversave) relative to what they produce, like China, have large trade surpluses. For many years, China has been using export revenues to buy assets in the United States, thus providing it with part of the foreign financing necessary for its excess of imports over exports.

The United States, faced with a huge and growing trade deficit, is demanding that China should increase its spending on imports. Attention focuses on China's role in the global economy because for years it has followed a highly export-oriented growth policy, leading to large trade surpluses. The United States accuses it of having benefited from an undervalued renminbi (RMB*). With the global economy in recession, China is asked to contribute to stepping up growth in the global economy by increasing its imports from other countries. The United States wants it to revalue its currency and take measures in the domestic economy to encourage consumers to spend more. It is expected this will reduce the US trade deficit with China.

The Chinese government is aware of the role that increased consumer spending could play, and is taking measures to encourage more spending. However, it does not want to revalue the currency. There are fears that this could result in closure of export firms and widespread unemployment, possibly even leading to social unrest. In addition, it is unclear whether even a large revaluation of the RMB would help reduce the US trade deficit with China. In

the three years before the RMB was pegged to the US dollar (in 2008), it had appreciated by more than 20% relative to the dollar, and yet still the US trade deficit with China had increased.

US Nobel Prize-winning economist, Jospeh Stiglitz, agrees with the Chinese perspective. He notes that the global recession, by weakening global demand for Chinese exports, has negatively affected Chinese manufacturers. If the RMB rises in value, many of them will go bankrupt and serious social problems could result. He also argues that even if China (along with India and other Asian countries) were to increase their demand for imports, this would not be enough to rescue the US and the global economy, because they would not make a large enough impact.

If global demand for goods and services remains weak, there is a danger that global growth will also remain weak. With many countries in recession and unemployment very high, weak growth makes trade protection policies look attractive. This raises the danger of trade wars and currency wars that could lead the world into a serious global recession once again.

---

* Elsewhere the term 'yuan' has been used for the Chinese currency. The yuan and renminbi (RMB) refer to the same currency and are used interchangeably.

Source: Peter Ford, 'Why some economists see a looming US-China trade war' in *Christian Science Monitor*, 17 September 2010; Asia Pulse, 'Stiglitz says Yuan appreciation would hurt Chinese jobs' in *Asia Pulse*, 18 October 2010.

Applying your skills

1 Use *PPC* diagrams to explain the meaning of the statement that countries that overspend relative to what they produce have trade deficits and countries that underspend (oversave) relative to what they produce have trade surpluses.

2 Making use of the component parts of the balance of payments accounts, explain how China uses export revenues to buy US assets that help the US finance more imports.

3 (a) Explain how an undervalued currency encourages exports and discourages imports.
(b) How does revaluation change this?
(c) Why could many Chinese manufacturers go bankrupt if the RMB is revalued?

4 Why do weak growth and unemployment make trade protection policies look attractive?

5 How can trade wars and currency wars lead to a global recession?

1 Using Bopland as an example, and its national currency, the bople, use exchange rate diagrams to show why **(a)** a deficit in the current account is likely to result in a downward pressure on the value of the currency, and **(b)** a surplus in the current account is likely to result in an upward pressure on the value of the currency.

2 Using the example of Bopland, explain how its balance of payments deficit could be corrected in the three exchange rate systems (floating, managed, fixed).

3 Compare and contrast floating and fixed exchange rate systems, referring to degree of certainty, ease of adjustment, international reserves and flexibility in policy-making.

Fiscal and monetary policy and conflicting objectives in an open economy (supplementary material)

When an economy is open to international trade and financial flows, in addition to the goals of price stability, full employment and economic growth, it has the further goals of achieving a reasonable balance of trade and avoiding sharp fluctuations in its exchange rate. However, economies may be unable to achieve all these objectives at the same time. Governments often find that by pursuing a policy to correct one problem, they may create a problem elsewhere.

Fiscal policy
An expansionary fiscal policy financed by government borrowing may lead to higher interest rates, which may crowd out private investment, weakening the expansionary effect of increased government spending (see page 329). In an open economy, a higher interest rate has the additional effect of appreciating the currency, which in turn lowers exports and increases imports (net exports, $X-M$, fall), which also weakens the expansionary effects of the increase in government spending.

Monetary policy

Expansionary monetary policy and the trade balance
Expansionary monetary policy intended to increase aggregate demand (in a recession) lowers interest rates, but also depreciates the currency, increasing exports and decreasing imports (a rise in net exports, $X-M$). An increase in net exports strengthens the expansionary effects of lower interest rates, but also affects the trade balance. If the economy has a trade deficit, an increase in $X-M$ makes it shrink, but if there is a trade surplus, an increase in $X-M$ makes it grow larger. Therefore, *expansionary monetary policy improves a trade deficit and worsens a trade surplus.*

Contractionary monetary policy and the trade balance
Contractionary monetary policy, which may be used to fight inflation, involves higher interest rates intended to lower aggregate demand, but also results in currency appreciation, and therefore falling exports and increasing imports (net exports, $X-M$ fall). While a fall in net exports strengthens the contractionary effects of tight money policy, it also affects the trade balance. If there is a trade deficit, the fall in net exports makes this grow bigger; if there is a trade surplus, the fall in net exports makes it shrink. Therefore, *contractionary monetary policy worsens a trade deficit but improves a trade surplus.*

Preventing currency speculation and recession
If an economy is concerned that speculators may 'attack' its currency (sell it because of the expectation that it will fall), it may raise interest rates to make the currency more attractive. However, this may create a recession, or, if the economy is already in recession, make the recession worse.

Cost-push inflation (due to higher import prices) and recession
If an economy is experiencing cost-push inflation due to increased import prices, higher interest rates appreciate the currency, and lower import prices, thus helping correct the problem of cost-push inflation. However, higher interest rates may create a recession or make an already existing recession worse. Remember, cost-push inflation has the effect of shifting the *SRAS* curve to the left, so the economy already has a tendency to go into recession; this will be worsened by the higher interest rates.

These potential problems do not contradict the point made earlier (page 403) that policy-making under freely floating exchange rates is flexible. Under fixed exchange rates, fiscal and monetary policies must respond to balance of payments needs. Under floating exchange rates, fiscal and monetary policy can be undertaken in response to domestic needs; however, policies sometimes have unintended and undesirable consequences in the foreign sector.

14.6 Topics on exchange rates and the balance of payments (higher level topics)

Calculating elements of the balance of payments

♦ Calculate elements of the balance of payments from a set of data.

Given the components of the balance of payments and their relationships (pages 395–98), we can calculate various elements in the balance of payments. You are given some exercises in Test your understanding 14.9.

Test your understanding 14.9

Answer the questions below based on the table showing the balance of payments accounts of Lakeland (2010, billion Lkl).

Current account	
Exports of goods	+310
Imports of goods	−525
Balance of trade in goods	
Exports of services	+52
Imports of services	−71
Balance of trade in services	
Balance of trade in goods and services	
Income	+25
Current transfers	+73
Balance on current account	
Capital account	
Capital transfers	−3
Transactions in non-produced, non-financial assets	+7
Balance on capital account	
Financial account	
Direct investment	+107
Portfolio investment	+29
Reserve assets	−7
Balance on financial account	
Errors and omissions	
Balance	

1 Copy out the table, then fill in the blanks. Check your results by using the relation: current account = capital account +financial account+errors and omissions.

2 Which of the three accounts are in surplus and which in deficit? Explain your answer using the concept debits = credits.

3 Use a *PPC* diagram to show how much Lakeland is consuming in relation to how much it is producing.

4 Is Lakeland experiencing a balance of payments deficit or a balance of payments surplus?

5 Is it possible that the value of the Lkl is determined in a freely floating exchange rate system? Explain your answer.

Consequences of persistent current account deficits

♦ Discuss the implications of a persistent current account deficit, referring to factors including foreign ownership of domestic assets, exchange rates, interest rates, indebtedness, potential output, international credit ratings and demand management.

Most countries in the world have current account deficits. Moreover, most balance of payments problems usually arise in connection with current account deficits, mainly due to an excess of imports over exports over long periods of time. Current account deficits for short periods of time, or current account deficits that alternate with current account surpluses, do not generally pose problems.

As the central bank does not have endless amounts of foreign currency reserves to pay for a current account deficit, it must do so either through loans (borrowing from abroad) or by selling some of its physical or financial assets; all these methods result in inflows of foreign exchange. Yet both borrowing and sales of assets may pose problems if pursued for a long time.

Persistent current account deficits financed by loans

Many developing countries since the 1970s and transition economies since the 1990s have found themselves in the situation where current account deficits over many years are paid for by financial account surpluses created by borrowing from the rest of the world. While these countries can enjoy increased levels of consumption over what they produce (see Figure 14.6(a), page 399), there are several possible problems that may arise:

- **Possible need for higher interest rates to attract foreign financial investments, leading to recession.** If a country has difficulty getting loans, it may have to increase its interest rates to attract financial investments. However, higher interest rates discourage domestic investment and consumption spending, possibly creating a recession in the economy.

- **High indebtedness.** If a country borrows over long periods of time, it runs the risk of accumulating so much debt that it may be unable to pay it back; this is called a risk of default. Risks of default, along with actual default, come with many problems, such as significant currency depreciation, difficulties of getting more loans and painful demand-side policies (see below and Chapter 18).

- **Depreciating exchange rate.** A current account deficit puts a downward pressure on the exchange rate. Large depreciations can lead to imported inflation. If there is a risk of default, the downward pressure on the currency is much stronger because people do not want to hold currencies whose value is expected to fall further, and the currency becomes vulnerable to speculative attacks.

- **Poor international credit ratings.** International agencies rank countries according to how 'credit-worthy' they are, meaning how likely they are to repay their loans in full and on time. Countries with large and persistent current account deficits have low credit ratings, making it more difficult to get more loans in the future (no one wants to lend to a country that may be unable to pay back its loans). Under such circumstances, a country may have to raise its interest rates very high to attract foreign financial capital, and this can create a serious recession or make an existing recession deeper.

- **Painful demand management policies.** Countries with serious current account deficits must often pursue contractionary and other policies. We will consider these policies on page 408.

- **Cost of paying interest on loans.** The interest payments that must be made on loans use up national income of the country that could have been spent elsewhere in the domestic economy, such as for the purposes of investment, or consumption, or provision of merit and public goods.

- **Fewer imports of needed capital goods.** Interest payments on loans also use up scarce foreign exchange earnings (from exports) that could have been used on imports of capital goods or other inputs for production; the country may therefore not be in a position to secure all needed imports for its production.

- **Possibility of lower economic growth.** If loans accumulate over long periods of time, the cumulative impacts of the above may mean lower economic growth, as resources are used up on interest payments and loan repayments.

- **Lower standard of living in the future.** In order to be able to pay back the loans in the future, the local population will at some point have to consume less than they produce, giving rise to a decline in their standard of living. The reason is that paying back their debts requires a financial account deficit, corresponding to a current account surplus. (This is similar to one's personal finances: if you spend more than you earn by borrowing, in the future when you pay back your debts you will have to spend less than you earn. See also Figure 14.6(b), page 399.)

However, these problems *need not necessarily arise*. Borrowing can lead to economic growth, and if *per capita* output and income increase, it becomes possible to have increased consumption of goods and services even as loans are being paid back. Important requirements for this to happen are:

- the current account deficit remains relatively small and does not get out of hand by excessive borrowing

- borrowed funds are used to finance imports of capital goods and other inputs needed in production (instead of consumer goods imports)

- some production is geared towards export industries so that exports increase, making increased export earnings possible (to help pay back loans and interest, and finance more capital goods imports).

Economic growth under the above conditions is the rationale for lending to developing countries as well as to transition economies. However, as we will see in Chapter 18, things have not always worked out this way for developing countries.

Persistent current account deficits financed by the sale of domestic assets

Persistent current account deficits can also be financed by a financial account surplus created by sales of domestic assets to foreigners (such as purchases of land, factories, buildings, stocks, bonds, etc.). Some developed countries are in this category, the best-known being the United States (which is the largest debtor nation in the world[7]). Such countries do not incur debts that must be paid back; therefore, the problems that may arise are only partly similar to the case of financing by borrowing:

- **Higher interest rates to attract foreign financial investments, leading to recession.** Long-term current account deficits may lead to a need for higher interest rates to induce foreign financial investors to make financial investments in the domestic economy, thus creating recessionary effects.

- **High indebtedness.** As in the case of borrowing, continued sales of domestic assets result in the accumulation of high levels of 'debt' (meaning foreign ownership of domestic assets), which it may be difficult to regain (i.e. to have ownership come back to the domestic economy).

- **Depreciating exchange rate.** For the same reasons as with borrowing, a persistent current account deficit puts a downward pressure on the exchange rate.

- **Poor international credit ratings and a loss of confidence in the currency and economy.** The ability of a country to go on indefinitely financing its current account deficit by selling off its assets depends very much on the confidence that foreign investors have in the domestic economy and currency. If there is a belief that the currency may depreciate substantially, or that the economy will not perform well in the future, they may be unwilling to continue to invest in the country, or they may even try to sell their assets in the country, in which case the country will be unable to finance its current account deficit. This is likely to result in a significant and rapid depreciation of the domestic currency.

- **Painful demand management policies.** As in the case of borrowing, it may become necessary to pursue contractionary and other policies in an effort to reduce the size of these (see below).

- **Lower standard of living in the future.** Countries that sell off their assets do not have to pay back loans; however, they are selling off a portion of their domestic property. In this case, they will have to consume less than the amount they produce in the future if they want to regain possession of their domestic assets.

Here, too, these problems need not necessarily arise, if the country achieves economic growth that allows it to secure increases in *per capita* output and income large enough to allow increasing consumption levels together with a current account surplus and a financial account deficit (involving the purchase from foreigners of domestic assets).

Evaluating methods to correct persistent current account deficits

- ♦ Explain the methods that a government can use to correct a persistent current account deficit, including expenditure switching policies, expenditure reducing policies and supply-side policies, to increase competitiveness.
- ♦ Evaluate the effectiveness of the policies to correct a persistent current account deficit.

Expenditure-reducing policies (reductions in aggregate demand)

Contractionary fiscal and monetary policies reduce aggregate demand and therefore output and incomes, in turn leading to lower demand for imports. In addition, reduced aggregate demand is likely to give rise to a lower rate of inflation, which may make domestic goods more competitive, thus increasing exports. The combination of fewer imports and more exports may work to reduce the size of the current account deficit. These policies are known as **expenditure-reducing policies**, because they try to influence the levels of imports and exports by reducing domestic expenditures through lower aggregate demand.

This approach comes with disadvantages, as it may create a recession in the domestic economy. Moreover, there is also a risk that higher interest rates (contractionary monetary policy) leads to currency appreciation, which may discourage exports and encourage imports, thus partly cancelling out the beneficial effects of expenditure-reducing policies on imports and exports.

Expenditure-switching policies

Trade protection

Countries with a long-term current account deficit could resort to increased trade protection, creating or increasing barriers to trade (see Chapter 13). These are known as **expenditure-switching policies**,

---

[7] A 'debtor' nation is one that has either accumulated large debts to other countries, or that has sold large quantities of domestic assets to foreigners. In both cases, this is done to pay for current account deficits, arising from an excess of imports over exports.

because they are intended to switch consumption away from imported goods and towards domestically produced goods. These policies can reduce the current account deficit by directly restricting imports. However, they have a number of negative effects, such as higher domestic prices of protected goods, lower domestic consumption, inefficiency and a domestic and global misallocation of resources. There also arises a danger that countries against which the protective barriers are imposed may retaliate with their own barriers, creating a spiral of protectionist policies that can have serious consequences on global trade and global growth.

Depreciation

The currency of a country with a persistent current account deficit is likely to face a strong downward pressure on its value. The government may allow the currency to depreciate, in which case it encourages exports (which become cheaper to foreigners) and discourages imports (which become more expensive to domestic buyers). This is another type of expenditure-switching policy, because it, too, switches consumption away from imports and towards domestically produced goods. However, this policy too may have negative effects on the domestic economy. Higher import prices due to the lower value of the currency often result in higher domestic inflation. If the imported goods include capital goods and other production inputs, firms experience higher costs of production, which may be passed on to consumers in the form of higher prices. This is a type of cost-push inflation, and by shifting the *SRAS* curve to the left, may have recessionary effects.

Depreciation and managed changes in exchange rates

The central bank may wish to encourage currency depreciation to maintain an undervalued currency in the hope of giving a stronger push to its exports, as well as greater discouragement to its imports. Undervaluation is sometimes used as a method to expand export industries, expand the economy and increase employment (see page 391). However, this creates an unfair competitive advantage and is sometimes referred to as a 'dirty float'. A dirty float risks retaliation by other countries that may wish to cancel out the competitive advantage of the dirty floater. In addition, an undervalued currency may create inflationary pressures in the economy due to the higher import prices arising from currency depreciation.

Supply-side policies to increase competitiveness

Market-oriented supply-side policies are intended to lower costs of production for firms, and by shifting the *SRAS* and *LRAS* curves to the right can result in lower rates of inflation (see Chapter 12). Several policies, such as increasing competition, reducing the power of labour unions, reducing or eliminating the minimum wage, cutting business taxes, deregulation, and others, could have the effect of making firms more competitive in global markets. Over a long period of time, lower rates of inflation may increase exports, thereby addressing the current account deficit.

Countries can also use interventionist supply-side policies, such as support for training, education, research and development and industrial policies, to promote industries that produce for export.

A disadvantage of supply-side policies is that they generally take a long time to make their effects felt. (For further evaluation of these policies see Chapter 12.)

Marshall–Lerner condition and J-curve

Marshall–Lerner condition

♦ State the Marshall–Lerner condition and apply it to explain the effects of depreciation/devaluation.

When a country's currency devalues or depreciates, its imports become more expensive domestically and exports become less expensive to foreigners. This suggests that the quantity of imports decreases and the quantity of exports increases. The question of interest is whether a devaluation or depreciation reduces the size of a trade deficit (and therefore a current account deficit). The Marshall–Lerner condition is a condition that, if satisfied, allows devaluation or depreciation to lead to an improvement in a country's balance of trade (and therefore in its current account).

The Marshall–Lerner condition involves the devaluing/depreciating country's price elasticity of demand for imports (PED_m) and foreigners' price elasticity of demand for the country's exports (PED_x). Elasticities are important because what matters is not changes in the *quantities* of imports and exports, but rather changes in the *values* of imports and exports.

If *PED* for imports is less than 1, a percentage increase in the price of imports (due to the devaluation/depreciation) leads to a smaller percentage decrease in quantity of imports demanded, so that the value of imports increases, producing a negative effect on the trade balance; if there is a trade deficit, this will tend to become larger. On the other hand, if *PED* for imports is greater than 1, the value of imports will fall, producing a positive effect on the trade balance. In general, the larger the *PED* for imports, the greater the scope for improvements in a trade deficit.

The *PED* for exports is also important. The larger the *PED* for exports, the larger the increase in quantity of exports that results following a devaluation/depreciation, and the larger the positive effect on the trade balance.

Yet it is not necessary for both PED_x and PED_m to be larger than one for a devaluation or depreciation to result in a smaller trade deficit. According to the Marshall–Lerner condition, it is only necessary that *their sum* be larger than one.

> **The Marshall–Lerner condition states the following:**
>
> • If the sum of the *PED*s for imports and exports is greater than 1, i.e. $PED_m + PED_x > 1$, devaluation/depreciation will improve the trade balance (will make a trade deficit smaller).
>
> • If the sum of the two *PED*s is less than 1, devaluation/depreciation will worsen the trade balance (will make a trade deficit bigger).
>
> • If the sum of the two *PED*s is equal to 1, devaluation/depreciation will leave the trade balance unchanged.

The greater the price elasticities of demand for imports and for exports, the greater the scope for improvements in the trade balance. With low *PED*s, it would be necessary to have large devaluations/depreciations to obtain significant trade balance improvements. The higher the *PED*s, the smaller the devaluation or depreciation needed to obtain trade balance improvements.

Understanding the Marshall–Lerner condition in more detail (supplementary material)

The Marshall–Lerner condition leads to the surprising conclusion that devaluation or depreciation can improve the balance of trade (hence the current account) even if $PED_m < 1$ and $PED_x < 1$, as long as the sum of the two elasticities is greater than one.

The explanation for this result lies in the fact that devaluation or depreciation leads to a change in the price of exports only when this price is expressed in terms of foreign (appreciating) currencies; by contrast, *the price of exports remains the same in terms of the domestic currency*. (To see why this is so, consider an export good X produced in Riverland that sells for Rvl 2 per unit. Riverland exports good X to the United States at the

exchange rate US\$1= Rvl 2, so that US residents can buy 1 unit of X for \$1. Suppose then that the Rvl depreciates relative to the dollar and the new exchange rate is \$1= Rvl 4. US residents can now buy 2 units of X for \$1, meaning that the price of X fell to \$0.50 per unit. In Riverland, however, the price of X is still Rvl 2 per unit.)

Given a depreciation, the quantity of exports will always increase in view of the fall in price in terms of foreign currencies. However, since the price of the good remains the same in terms of the domestic currency, the result will be an increase in export revenues (in terms of the domestic currency), regardless of the size of the *PED* for exports. Now if $PED_m > 1$, there is a fall in import expenditures. Therefore, together with the increase in export revenues there follows an improvement in the trade balance. On the other hand, if $PED_m < 1$, there is an increase in import expenditures. In order to have an improvement in the trade balance, the increase in export revenues must be larger than the increase in import expenditures. This occurs when $PED_m + PED_x > 1$, or when the Marshall–Lerner condition holds.

J-curve effect

> ♦ Explain the J-curve effect, with reference to the Marshall–Lerner condition.

A devaluing/depreciating country may see a worsening trade balance in the period immediately following the devaluation or depreciation of its currency; later, the trade deficit will begin to shrink, and the trade balance will begin to improve, provided the Marshall–Lerner condition holds. This is known as the **J-curve effect**, shown in a graph that plots the balance of trade (the value of exports minus imports) on the vertical axis and time on the horizontal axis, shown in Figure 14.7. As both parts indicate, all values greater than zero on the vertical axis illustrate a trade surplus, and all values less than zero illustrate a trade deficit. When the trade balance is equal to zero (at the origin), then exports are equal to imports. It follows that as the values increase along the vertical axis, a trade deficit becomes smaller until it reaches $(X - M) = 0$, and above that becomes a trade surplus.

In part (a), the country initially has a value of exports equal to the value of imports (no trade deficit or surplus); following the devaluation/depreciation a trade deficit arises, which later becomes a trade surplus. In part (b), the country initially has a trade deficit, which becomes larger immediately following the devaluation/depreciation, and which then improves, eventually becoming a surplus. This is called a J-curve because of its shape.

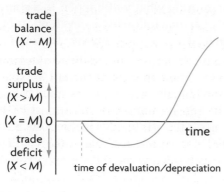

(a) Value of exports is equal to value of imports at time of devaluation/depreciation

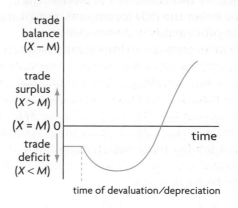

(b) Trade deficit at time of devaluation/depreciation

Figure 14.7 J-curve effect

The explanation behind the shape of the J-curve can be traced directly to the Marshall–Lerner condition. In the period immediately following a currency devaluation/depreciation, price elasticities of demand for imports and exports are very low, and the Marshall–Lerner condition is not satisfied: $PED_m + PED_x < 1$. Therefore, the trade balance deteriorates. As time passes, $PEDs$ for imports and exports increase, and if there comes a point when $PED_m + PED_x > 1$, then the trade balance begins to improve.

The reason for initial very low $PEDs$ for imports and exports lies in time lags (time delays) between devaluation/depreciation and its effects on quantities of exports and imports demanded. Devaluation/depreciation involves changes in relative prices: imports become more expensive in the domestic economy and exports become cheaper to foreigners. However, consumers and producers need time to adjust to the price changes. Although imports have become more expensive to domestic consumers and producers, they are still purchased for a variety of reasons, such as the time needed for buyers to become aware of the price changes, or prior commitments, or the time needed to place new orders, or particular preferences of buyers that need time to change. In the meantime, the price of exports has fallen for foreigners; however, they too have prior commitments, particular preferences and so on, and therefore the quantity demanded increases only slowly. With $PED_m + PED_x < 1$ initially, the trade balance deteriorates, resulting in the downward-sloping portion of the J-curve.

As time passes, consumers and producers adjust to the changes in prices, $PEDs$ of both imports and exports increase, quantity of imports demanded falls and quantity of exports demanded increases and the balance of trade begins to improve (the upward-sloping portion of the J-curve).

Empirical evidence supports the existence of a J-curve. According to studies estimating $PEDs$ for imports and exports in developed countries, it was found that over short periods of time (less than six months) most manufactured goods have $PEDs$ that are too low to satisfy the Marshall–Lerner condition; the sum of $PEDs$ for imports and exports is less than 1, indicating the downward-sloping part of the J-curve (a worsening trade balance). In a period of more than six months and less than a year, the $PEDs$ for most products have increased to the point that the Marshall–Lerner condition is satisfied, so that the sum of the two $PEDs$ is greater than 1, leading to an improving trade balance.

Consequences of persistent current account surpluses

♦ Discuss the possible consequences of a rising current account surplus, including lower domestic consumption and investment, as well as the appreciation of the domestic currency and reduced export competitiveness.

Countries with a current account surplus are net purchasers of assets abroad or net lenders to other countries (thus having financial account deficits). Persistent current account surpluses may lead to the following problems:

• **Low domestic consumption.** Large and persistent current account surpluses mean lower consumption levels and lower standards of living for the population relative to where a country has a current account deficit or a balanced current account where credits equal debits (see Figure 14.6(b)).

- **Insufficient domestic investment.** The financial account deficit means that funds are leaving the country, resulting in a risk of insufficient domestic investment, limiting economic growth prospects.

- **Appreciation of the domestic currency.** A current account surplus puts an upward pressure on the value of a currency (see page 401), which can lead to lower exports and higher imports (reduced net exports), which may have a dampening effect on the domestic economy (through lower aggregate demand).

- **Reduced export competitiveness.** As the domestic currency appreciates, exports become more expensive to foreigners, and this makes it more difficult for domestic firms to compete with firms abroad.

Test your understanding 14.10

1 How is it possible that a country with no balance of payments deficit or surplus may still experience balance of payments problems over the long term?

2 Discuss some problems faced by countries that have a persistent current account deficit and a financial account surplus.

3 Discuss some problems faced by economies that have a persistent current account surplus and a financial account deficit.

4 Distinguish between expenditure-reducing and expenditure-switching policies.

5 **(a)** What are some policies that countries can use to limit imports so as to reduce a current account deficit? **(b)** What are some possible disadvantages of these policies?

6 **(a)** What are some policies that countries can use to increase exports so as to reduce a current account deficit? **(b)** What are some possible disadvantages of these policies?

7 Why are the price elasticities of demand (*PED*s) for imports and exports important in determining what will happen to a country's trade balance following a devaluation or depreciation of the domestic currency?

8 Suppose a country has a deficit in its balance of trade, and devalues its currency. Explain what will likely happen to its trade balance if **(a)** its *PED* for imports is 0.2 and its *PED* for exports is 0.5, **(b)** its *PED* for imports is 0.7 and its *PED* for exports is 0.3, and **(c)** its *PED* for imports is 0.8 and its *PED* for exports is 0.6.

9 **(a)** State the Marshall–Lerner condition. **(b)** Draw a diagram illustrating the J-curve effect. **(c)** Explain the shape of the J-curve in relation to the Marshall–Lerner condition.

Assessment

The Student's CD-ROM at the back of this book provides practice of examination questions based on the material you have studied in this chapter.

Standard level
- Exam practice: Paper 2, Chapter 14
  - SL/HL core topics (Text/data 3–8, questions A.6–A.20)

Higher level
- Exam practice: Paper 2, Chapter 14
  - SL/HL core topics (Text/data 3–8, questions A.6–A.20)
- Exam practice: Paper 3, Chapter 14
  - HL topics (questions 27–29)

Chapter 15
Economic integration and the terms of trade

This chapter examines two topics: economic integration and the terms of trade.

15.1 Economic integration

Economic integration refers to economic co-operation between countries and co-ordination of their economic policies, leading to increased economic links between them. It occurs because of numerous benefits that may be derived by the co-operating countries. There are various degrees of integration, depending on the type of agreement made between the co-operating countries, and the degree to which barriers between them are removed.

Preferential trade agreements

The meaning of preferential trade agreements

♦ Explain that preferential trade agreements give preferential access to certain products from certain countries by reducing or eliminating tariffs, or by other agreements relating to trade.

A **preferential trade agreement** (PTA) is an agreement between two or more countries to lower trade barriers between each other on particular products. Trade barriers may remain on the rest of the products, and on imports from non-member countries. The result is that a member of the agreement has easier access to the markets of other members for the selected products than countries that are not members.

PTAs sometimes involve co-operation between members on other issues, such as labour standards, environmental issues, or intellectual property. They

can take several forms, including free trade areas, customs unions or common markets, and they may be bilateral (involving two countries) or regional (involving several countries). We will discuss all of these below.[1]

Bilateral, regional and multilateral (WTO) trade agreements

♦ Distinguish between bilateral and multilateral (WTO) trade agreements.

A **bilateral trade agreement** is an agreement between two countries, whereas a **multilateral trade agreement** involves an agreement between many countries. Another distinction involves **regional trade agreements**, which as the term suggests involves agreements between a group of countries that are within a geographical region. The main objective of bilateral, regional and multilateral trade agreements is to promote *trade liberalisation*, which is free (or freer) trade by reducing or eliminating trade barriers between members.

The trade agreements reached under the World Trade Organization (WTO; see page 363) are *multilateral*, because they include WTO member countries around the world (153 in 2011) and because they require all member countries to reduce trade barriers at the same time. One of the fundamental principles of the WTO is *non-discrimination*, meaning that a country cannot discriminate between any WTO members (see page 364). This means it cannot impose higher barriers on imports from one country and lower ones on

---

[1] 'Preferential trade agreement' is sometimes used in another sense to refer to the weakest form of economic integration, coming *before* the formation of bilateral or regional trading blocs. This type of PTA is not of interest to us because it is not allowed by WTO rules.

imports from another country. *This is a fundamental principle for the development of free trade globally.* However, the WTO makes an exception for bilateral and regional trade agreements, even though all preferential trade agreements involve discrimination against non-member countries.

Comparing and contrasting trading blocs

♦ Distinguish between a free trade area, a customs union and a common market.

♦ Compare and contrast the different types of trading blocs.

A **trading bloc** is a group of countries that have agreed to reduce tariff and other barriers to trade for the purpose of encouraging free or freer trade and co-operation between them. Beginning with the lowest degree of economic integration, we can distinguish between the following trading blocs.

Free trade area

A **free trade area** (FTA) consists of a group of countries that agree to gradually eliminate trade barriers between themselves, and is the most common type of trading bloc. Each member country retains the right to pursue its own trade policy towards other non-member countries (i.e. to impose its own trade barriers). In trade relations between members, there may be free trade in some products, and some protection in other products.

Examples of free trade areas are NAFTA (North American Free Trade Agreement), including Canada, Mexico and the United States, ASEAN (Association of Southeast Asian Nations) and SAARC (South Asian Association for Regional Cooperation).

One problem that arises in free trade areas is that a product may be imported into the FTA by the country that has the lowest external trade barriers, and then sold to countries within the FTA that have higher external trade barriers. This problem arises because each country has its own individual barriers toward non-members. It creates difficulties for those countries with higher barriers because they may end up importing more of the good than they would like. To deal with this problem, FTAs make complicated 'rules of origin' for imports, designed to prevent goods from entering countries with lower external barriers.

Customs union

A **customs union** consists of a group of countries that fulfils the requirements of a free trade area (elimination of trade barriers between members) and in addition adopts a common policy towards all non-member countries. Each country in a customs union is no longer free to determine its own trade policy towards non-member countries, but must adopt the policy agreed upon by the customs union. Also, the member countries of the customs union act as a group in all trade negotiations and agreements with non-members. A customs union therefore involves a higher degree of economic integration than a free trade area.

Examples of customs unions include CEFTA (Central European Free Trade Agreement), SACU (South African Customs Union), PARTA (Pacific Regional Trade Agreement), and others.

Customs unions have the advantage over FTAs in that they avoid having to create complicated 'rules of origin' for imports, since they all have the same common external barriers, usually a common external tariff. However, customs unions must co-ordinate their policies toward non-members. This gives rise to the possibility of disagreements, as they may not all agree on what are appropriate levels of tariff and other barriers for non-members.

Common market

A **common market** is an even higher degree of economic integration, in which countries that have formed a customs union proceed further to eliminate any remaining barriers to trade between them. They continue to have a common external policy (as in a customs union), and in addition, they agree to eliminate all restrictions on movements of any factors of production within the common market. The factors of production of importance are labour and capital, which in a common market are free to cross all borders and move, travel and find employment freely within all member countries.

The best-known common market is the European Economic Community (EEC, the precursor of the present European Union), formed in 1957. Another example is the Caribbean Community (CARICOM) Single Market and Economy (CSME).

A common market offers major advantages to its members compared to FTAs and customs unions. Members enjoy free trade and all its advantages (lower prices, greater consumer choice, etc.). Workers are free to move and work in any member country without restrictions, and capital can also flow from country to country without restrictions. This results in a better use of factors of production. For example, there may be high unemployment in one country, and a high demand for labour in another country. This encourages unemployed workers to seek work in the country facing labour shortages. Similarly, if the profitability of investing is greater in one country than in another, capital gravitates to the more profitable country, making better use of capital resources. Factor mobility across countries improves the allocation of resources.

However, the development of a common market requires even greater policy co-ordination among members than in a customs union, and requires the willingness of member governments to give up some of their policy-making authority to an organisation with powers over all the member governments. Both these requirements can be difficult to accomplish, and need a long time for all countries to make the necessary policy changes to achieve co-ordination. For this reason there are far fewer common markets in the world than free trade areas and customs unions.

Increased competition and other possible advantages of trading blocs

♦ Explain that economic integration will increase competition among producers within the trading bloc.

Economic integration over the long term can be expected to bring about many of the benefits of free trade (see page 354), including the following.

Increased competition
The removal of trade barriers results in increased competition among producers in member countries. With low or no barriers, imports increase, forcing domestic producers to compete with lower cost producers from other countries. Trade barriers, on the other hand, protect inefficient domestic producers. Increased competition offers major advantages in terms of production by more efficient producers, lower prices for consumers and improved allocation of resources.

Expansion into larger markets
This is an obvious benefit arising from the ability of firms to sell beyond their national boundaries, increasing their exports and leading to greater economic growth.

Economies of scale (higher level topic)

♦ Explain that different forms of economic integration allow member countries to gain from economies of scale.

This follows from the above point. In a small market a firm cannot take advantage of economies of scale since a firm cannot grow large enough so that its

long-run average costs begin to fall substantially. When an economy opens itself up to free trade with other countries, its exports are likely to increase (assuming it is a relatively efficient producer), and as the size of the market expands, the firm can achieve lower costs of production on average (economies of scale), lower prices for consumers and greater export competitiveness. Economies of scale are one of the major benefits of free trade.

Lower prices for consumers and greater consumer choice
The elimination of trade barriers (along with increased competition and economies of scale) results in lower prices for consumers. In addition, increased imports mean a greater of variety of goods from which consumers can choose.

Increased investment
Enlarged markets often give rise to increased investment by firms that want to take advantage of the larger market size. This investment may be internal, that is, by firms originating from a country within the trading bloc, or external, originating from a country outside the bloc (by multinational corporations). A major incentive for outsider firms to invest within the bloc is that they escape the tariff or other protection imposed by the trading bloc on imports from outside. Therefore, an incentive faced by countries forming trading blocs is to attract investments by multinational corporations.

Better use of factors of production: improved resource allocation
If a trading bloc develops into a common market, which involves free movement of factors of production, this also results in better use of these within the bloc. As discussed above, unemployed workers in one country may seek a job elsewhere where there are more employment opportunities. Capital can also move freely in search of greater profits.

Improved efficiency in production and greater economic growth
The elimination of trade barriers, leading to a better utilisation of resources and improved efficiency in production, allow for more rapid economic growth.

Political advantages
Greater economic integration is likely to result in a reduced likelihood of hostilities between countries whose economies become more interdependent through increased trade, investment, labour and financial flows.

Possible disadvantages of trading blocs

Trading blocs may not be the best way to achieve trade liberalisation

Many economists believe that while the establishment of trading blocs with free trade between members may be an improvement over trade protection, trading blocs are inferior to the WTO's multilateral approach of reducing trade barriers towards all countries. Trading blocs involve an increasing amount of discrimination, violating the WTO's non-discrimination principle (see page 413 above).

Trading blocs may create obstacles to the achievement of free trade on a global scale

Some economists believe that the break-up of the world trading system into many blocs can create trade conflicts between different blocs that may slow down the process of global trade liberalisation. Trading blocs may enjoy free trade and all its benefits *within the bloc*, but trade barriers on non-members may result in limiting rather than increasing trade *on a global scale*. This would lead to a worse global allocation of resources, lower global output, a weakened role for the WTO, and a risk of breaking up the global economy into many regional trading blocs.

Unequal distribution of gains and possible losses

Countries forming a trading bloc are unlikely to gain equally from the operation of the trading bloc, and this creates the potential for conflicts between the members and makes it difficult to reach agreements. It is also possible for some countries to gain while others become worse off in some respects. The same applies to gains and losses *within* the member countries, as some stakeholders are likely to gain while others lose. These are issues we will come back to in Chapter 17 when we evaluate preferential trade agreements as a trade strategy to achieve economic growth and development (page 490).

Test your understanding 15.1

1   **(a)** What are preferential trade agreements? **(b)** What is the difference between bilateral, regional and multilateral trade agreements?

2   **(a)** Why do trading blocs violate the WTO's principle of non-discrimination? **(b)** Why do you think the WTO permits the formation of trading blocs?

3   **(a)** Define a free trade area, customs union, and common market, and explain the differences between them. **(b)** How do these illustrate an increasing degree of economic integration?

4   **(a)** Explain the role of competition in trading blocs. Why is increased competition an advantage? **(b)** Identify further advantages and disadvantages of trading blocs.

5   Why do you think countries that want to form a trading bloc usually start by forming a free trade area, gradually moving towards a customs union, and eventually towards a common market?

Trade creation and trade diversion (higher level topic)   HL

♦   Explain the concepts of trade creation and trade diversion in a customs union.[2]

The benefits of trading blocs discussed above are long-term (or 'dynamic') benefits. In addition, there are short-term (or 'static') benefits, as well as possible costs, which are measured in the concepts of trade creation and trade diversion. Any type of trading bloc can lead to trade creation, or trade diversion, or both, depending on the particular country and the particular product.

Trade creation

When a trading bloc is established, patterns of trade between countries change, since trade between the members is encouraged through the lowering of trade barriers, while trade with non-members is discouraged through the maintenance of trade barriers. **Trade creation** refers to the situation where higher cost products (imported or domestically produced) are replaced by lower cost imports after the formation of a trading bloc.

Consider an example. Suppose Cottonia and Microchippia both produce cotton. Cottonia has a comparative advantage in cotton; it has a lower cotton price, and therefore Microchippia imports cotton from Cottonia. Initially, Microchippia imposes tariffs on its cotton imports, this way protecting its own cotton producers. Then Cottonia and Microchippia form a bilateral trade agreement, and tariffs on

---

[2] The IB syllabus refers specifically to trade creation and trade diversion as arising in customs unions. However, they can arise in any type of trading bloc.

cotton are abolished. Microchippia's cotton imports increase (corresponding to an increase in Cottonia's cotton exports), and its domestic production of cotton decreases. This is a case of *trade creation*, because higher cost domestic cotton production in Microchippia is partly replaced by lower cost imports of cotton.

Note that since trade creation involves the removal of tariffs, its benefits include getting rid of the disadvantages that come with imposing tariffs (see pages 366–67). The decrease in Microchippia's domestic production of cotton leads to greater efficiency in production, and together with the increase in consumption made possible by more imports, there is greater allocative efficiency.

Trade diversion

Trade diversion refers to the situation where lower cost imports are replaced by higher cost imports from a member after the formation of the trading bloc.

Suppose Cottonia, Robotia and Microchippia all produce cotton. Cottonia is the lowest cost producer of the three, followed by Robotia, and then by Microchippia, which is the highest cost producer. Initially, Microchippia imposes a tariff on all imports of cotton, regardless of country of origin. Since Cottonia is the lowest cost producer, Microchippia imports from Cottonia and not from Robotia (Cottonia's cotton price plus the tariff is lower than Robotia's price plus the tariff). Microchippia then decides to form a trading bloc with Robotia. It therefore eliminates the tariff on cotton from Robotia, and maintains the tariff on cotton from Cottonia. The result is that it now becomes cheaper for Microchippia to import cotton from Robotia rather than Cottonia. Microchippia's imports have shifted from a lower cost producer, Cottonia, to a higher cost producer, Robotia; this is therefore a case of *trade diversion*.[3]

The possibility of trade diversion resulting from a trading bloc is an additional argument *against* trading blocs, and *in favour* of multilateral (WTO) trade liberalisation. The reason is that trade diversion cannot occur with multilateral reduction or elimination of trade barriers. Trade diversion occurs when an importing country is forced to import from a higher cost producer within a trading bloc, whereas before it joined the trading bloc it was importing from a lower cost producer elsewhere. If all countries reduce their barriers at the same time, it

is not possible for lower cost imports to be replaced by higher cost imports; the importing country will simply import from lower cost producers who sell at lower prices.

Trade creation has the effect of increasing social welfare, while trade diversion reduces it. Therefore, whereas a trading bloc creates free trade for the members, it may or may not improve the allocation of resources. Resource allocation will improve only if trade creation effects are larger than trade diversion effects. Yet, you should remember that trade creation and trade diversion refer to short-term (static) benefits and costs of trading blocs, in contrast to long-term (dynamic) benefits discussed in the previous section. It is generally believed that the long-term benefits for the members of trading blocs are more important than the short-term effects. According to some studies, the long-term effects may be five or six times more important than the short-term ones. Therefore, even if a trading bloc leads to trade diversion over the short term, it is possible that the long-term positive effects will more than compensate countries for possible short-term losses.

> ### Test your understanding 15.2
>
> 1 Explain the difference between trade creation and trade diversion.
>
> 2 Why is it not possible for trade diversion to occur in the context of multilateral (as opposed to bilateral or regional) trade agreements?
>
> 3 Distinguish between short-term (static) and long-term (dynamic) benefits of trade.

Monetary union

> ♦ Explain that a monetary union is a common market with a common currency and a common central bank.

The meaning of monetary union and the example of European Monetary Union (EMU)

Monetary union involves a far greater degree of integration than a common market, and occurs when the member countries of a common market adopt a common currency and a common central bank responsible for monetary policy. A monetary union has been formed by a number of the countries of the

---

[3] A full analysis of trade diversion is actually a little more complicated, because trade diversion comes with some benefits. However, this discussion is beyond the scope of this book.

South American nations form Unasur

On 23 May 2008, the presidents of 12 South American nations signed a treaty establishing the Union of South American Nations, known as Unasur, modelled on the European Union. The formation of Unasur was part of South America's process of continuing economic integration. It joined together two existing trading blocs: Mercosur, a customs union including Argentina, Brazil, Paraguay, Uruguay and Venezuela, and the Andean Community, another customs union consisting of Bolivia, Colombia, Ecuador and Peru. Unasur has also been joined by Chile, Guyana and Suriname, and includes all the nations of South America.

The elimination of trade barriers needed to form a free trade area between all member nations is to take place gradually. In addition, there are plans for the development of a regional defence council intended to resolve inter-regional disputes, as well for a common defence policy for regional security.

The aim is eventually to achieve monetary union through the establishment of a single central bank and adoption of a single currency. This is expected to occur gradually as some countries are economically weaker than others, with significant differences in levels of GDP per capita and macroeconomic performance. In addition, there are important political differences between members that must be addressed and resolved.

Unasur foresees close co-operation between member countries in the areas of energy and infrastructure improvements, including transport (roads and ports) and communication, allowing closer trade and business links between member countries. Economic integration will be facilitated by the building of the Interoceanic Highway linking countries of the Pacific Coast, especially Chile and Peru, with Brazil and Argentina, and highways through the continent providing better connections of inland countries (Bolivia and Paraguay) to ports.

In 2007, seven of the founding countries established the South American Bank in Buenos Aires, intended to finance economic development projects for the improvement of competitiveness and the promotion of scientific and technological capabilities.

(higher level) It has been pointed out that in the early years after the formation of Mercosur (see above), trade between the members tripled at the same time that trade with non-members declined. A World Bank study indicated that increased trade between the member countries may have resulted in more trade diversion than in trade creation. The study concluded that trading blocs could potentially have negative effects on both member and non-member countries because trading blocs could prevent member countries from specialising and exporting according to their comparative advantage. The question is whether Unasur may also have trade diverting effects.

On the other hand, the same World Bank study also noted that the study did not take into account possible benefits from political co-operation and dynamic, or longer term, benefits from trade.

The countries of South America attach great importance to the principle of increasing economic integration from which they expect important benefits. Regional integration has reinforced political stability and economic growth. Integration is expected to increase the size of markets, diversify exports and permit achievement of economies of scale, creating increased efficiencies in production, new employment opportunities and attracting foreign direct investment.

Trade between member countries has been increasing, as have cross-border investments and business collaborations. Member countries are becoming less dependent on traditional markets for exports (the United States and the European Union). They are successfully diversifying their exports, and have become less vulnerable to external shocks. All Unasur members are democracies, and for the most part are performing well economically. These factors provide them with confidence and optimism that Unasur will succeed. With a combined population of 382 million people and GDP of US$2.3 trillion, Unasur is expected to become a strong economic power with a presence in global economic and political affairs. Moreover, Argentina and Brazil, which historically have seen each other as rivals vying for control over natural resources and power, are increasingly co-operating on a number of projects, suggesting that co-operation and integration can help nations overcome their differences.

Source: 'South America nations found union', BBC News, 23 May 2008 (http://news.bbc.co.uk/1/hi/world/americas/7417896.stm); 'South America eyes common currency', Forbes.com (http://www.forbes.com/feeds/afx/2008/05/26/afx5047714.html) ©Thomson Financial News, 26 May 2008; Cali Zimmerman, 'Unasur uniting South America' in *NuWire Investor*, 30 May 2008 (http://www.nuwireinvestor.com/articles/unasur-uniting-south-america-51659.aspx); Alexander J. Yeats, 'Does Mercosur's trade performance raise concerns about the effects of regional trade arrangements?', World Bank, International Economics Department, February 1997.

Applying your skills

1 How does Unasur represent economic integration?

2 Explain what Unasur member countries hope to gain from integration.

3 **(higher level)** Suppose one Unasur country (country A) has an absolute advantage over another Unasur country (country B) in the production of all goods. Using a diagram, explain under what conditions it may still be possible for both countries to gain by trading with each other.

4 **(higher level) (a)** Explain how trade diversion might not permit countries to specialise according to their comparative advantage.
(b) Is this necessarily a bad thing?

European Union, known as the 'euro zone countries'. There are many other trading blocs around the world that have plans to form a monetary union in the future.

Following years of preparation for monetary union, 11 countries of the European Union adopted a single currency, the euro, in 1999. These countries were Austria, Belgium, Finland, France, Germany, Ireland, Italy, Luxembourg, the Netherlands, Portugal and Spain. They were joined by Greece in 2001, Slovenia in 2007, Cyprus and Malta in 2008, Slovakia in 2009 and Estonia in 2011. The countries that have adopted the euro are members of the European Monetary Union (EMU). On 1 January 1999, the new currency, the euro, came into being and the currencies of the participating countries were irrevocably locked together through fixed and absolutely unchangeable exchange rates. Euro notes and coins were introduced on 1 January 2002 and for the period of one year they co-existed with national currencies. On 1 January 2003, the national currencies of the participating countries were abandoned and the euro became the sole currency of the euro zone countries.

The creation of the European Monetary Union was one of the most significant economic events in the post-Second World War period, as it was the first time ever that such a large group of countries gave up their national currencies to adopt a single common currency. As part of their preparation for membership, the countries had to agree to a number of conditions known as 'convergence requirements', including limiting their rate of inflation, limiting their budget deficit to 3% of GDP, and limiting their government debt to 60% of GDP. Moreover, in adopting the common currency, they gave up a significant part of their economic sovereignty to a supranational body, the European Central Bank, which assumed the responsibility for monetary policy for all the member countries. Following the adoption of the euro, the member countries gave up control of their money supply and their ability to carry out their own monetary policy, transferring these powers from each of their national central banks to a single institution, the European Central Bank.

Monetary union, or the formation of a single currency, can be partly thought of as a system of 'fixed' exchange rates among the participating currencies, but one in which there is no possibility of changing the value of one currency in relation to another (no possibility of revaluing or devaluing). From this perspective, some of the advantages and disadvantages of monetary union are similar to the advantages and disadvantages of fixed versus flexible exchange rates (see page 402). In addition, monetary union has a further very significant characteristic: the creation of a single currency, overseen and controlled by a single central bank. This characteristic offers further potential benefits, as well as possible costs.

Possible advantages and disadvantages of monetary union

♦ Discuss the possible advantages and disadvantages of a monetary union for its members.

Advantages

- **A single currency eliminates exchange rate risk and uncertainty.** Exchange rate fluctuations create risks and uncertainties for traders and investors, who do not know what the future exchange rates will be. A single currency eliminates the risks and uncertainties, with benefits for importers and exporters, consumers and investors, thereby encouraging trade and investments across boundaries. This contributes to achieving a more efficient allocation of resources.

- **A single currency eliminates transaction costs.** Whenever there is a conversion of one currency into another, banks (or others) charge a fee for the conversion; this is a type of transaction cost. A single currency eliminates these transaction costs, resulting in significant savings that have the effect of encouraging trade, investments and international financial flows of all kinds. It has been estimated that the savings from the elimination of transaction costs of currency conversions within the euro zone countries amounts to about 1% of the combined GDPs of the countries involved.

- **A single currency encourages price transparency.** Price transparency refers to the ability of consumers and firms to compare prices in all the countries that have adopted a common currency without having to make exchange rate calculations and conversions. This makes it easier for all economic decision-makers to see price differences quickly and accurately across countries, and has the effect of promoting competition and efficiency.

- **A single currency promotes a higher level of inward investment.** Inward investment refers to investments from outsiders towards the member countries with a common currency, and these can be expected to rise because of the absence of currency risk within an expanded market, resulting in greater economic growth.

- **Low rates of inflation give rise to low interest rates, more investment and increased output.** A single currency under the control of a

Therefore, for countries in the EMU that needed to reduce their deficits and debts, the only available domestic policy tools that could support growth were supply-side measures intended to increase international competitiveness.

These, however, need a long time to take effect. Another problem is that supply-side measures by themselves are not enough to solve the debt problem. Highly indebted governments must also try to deal directly with deficits and debt by cutting government expenditures and increasing taxes. This is the very opposite of what is required for growth, since these policies are actually contractionary: *they work to lower GDP rather than increase it.*

Why doesn't Greece leave the EMU?

An obvious course of action would be for Greece to leave the EMU, return to its national currency (the drachma), and regain its ability to conduct independent monetary and exchange rate policies. However, this option would not be seriously considered by Greece or any other euro zone country, except as a last resort. If one country were to leave the euro zone due to debt problems, this could lead to a chain of events with potentially disastrous consequences: it could shatter the confidence of investors in the ability of euro zone countries to pay back their debts, leading to sales of euro assets, a drastic fall in the value of the euro, inability of governments to borrow, a series of defaults in countries within the EMU, possibly extending to other indebted countries outside the euro zone (such as the United Kingdom), and a massive global financial crisis with a very deep global recession.

The importance of co-operation between euro zone countries

In a situation like this, an EMU-wide policy of mutual assistance and co-operation would have been very useful. The European Central Bank could have considered lower interest rates to help the countries in great need of some stimulus. The European Investment Bank could have considered investments that would counteract the effects of budget cuts and tax increases. A 'solidarity fund' could have been established to offer low-interest loans for investments in countries needing to encourage their growth. In fact, had there been an EMU-wide fiscal authority the problem might have been avoided altogether, or at least might have been far less severe. Prominent economists, including Joseph Stiglitz, Paul Krugman (both Nobel Prize winners) and Martin Feldstein, have compared the euro zone to the United States, explaining that the reason why the United States works well as a currency area is that there is a centralised fiscal policy. As Paul Krugman writes:

'Consider the often-made comparison between Greece and the state of California. Both are in deep fiscal trouble, both have a history of fiscal irresponsibility. . .

But California's fiscal woes just don't matter as much, even to its own residents, as those of Greece. Why? Because much of the money spent in California comes from Washington, not Sacramento. State funding may be slashed, but Medicare reimbursements, Social Security checks, and payments to defence contractors will keep on coming.

What this means, among other things, is that California's budget woes won't keep the state from sharing in a broader US economic recovery. Greece's budget cuts, on the other hand, will have a strong depressing effect on an already depressed economy.'[5]

In early 2010, the euro zone countries, under the leadership of Germany, failed to present a united front in the face of a member country's debt problems. According to Gustav A. Horn, Director of Germany's Macroeconomic Policy Institute, 'the EU should have explained credibly and clearly that it would take a shared common responsibility of an equal member of the common internal market'.[6] Instead, as the EU hesitated and delayed taking action, financial markets reacted by demanding ever-increasing and prohibitively high interest rates in order to lend to Greece, making it impossible for Greece to borrow from private investors. As a result, Greece was forced to borrow from the EU and the International Monetary Fund (IMF, to be discussed in Chapter 18). In Horn's words,

'As a result of the active assistance of the German government, what has happened is exactly the thing that was supposed to be avoided, and what could have been avoided – namely that Greece has indeed been forced to ask for financial help from other European countries.'[7]

The EU/IMF loans were made on condition that Greece pursues highly contractionary policies, involving very harsh cuts in government spending and huge tax increases. Because of its large debt, Greece would in any case have had to pursue contractionary policies, as explained above. However, with the lack of an independent monetary and exchange rate policy, the budget cuts and tax increases had to be far greater. Since the Greek economy was already in recession, this had the effect of making the recession much deeper, at a high human cost in terms of unemployment, reduced social benefits and increasing poverty.
According to Joseph Stiglitz:

'. . . one hoped the Greek tragedy would convince policymakers that the euro cannot succeed without greater cooperation (including fiscal assistance). But Germany (and its Constitutional Court), partly following popular opinion, opposed giving Greece the help that it needs.

To many, both in and outside of Greece, this stance was peculiar: billions had been spent saving big banks, but evidently saving a country of 11 million people was taboo. It was not even clear that the help Greece needed should be labeled a bailout: while the funds given to financial institutions like AIG[8] were unlikely to be recouped, a loan to Greece at a reasonable interest rate would probably be repaid.'[9]

The growing seriousness of the European sovereign debt crisis

By the spring of 2011, it was becoming increasingly apparent that the 'bailout' for Greece by the EU and IMF was based

(continued over)

on a serious shortcoming: negative growth rates experienced by the Greek economy due to the severe recession made it much more difficult for Greece to make its debt repayments. Higher taxes and lower government spending led to lower incomes and lower tax revenues, and therefore an increased need to continue to borrow to make debt repayments. Greece was getting caught in an unsustainable debt situation, or 'debt trap', where a country must keep taking out more and more new loans to pay the old ones, thus increasing rather than reducing the level of its debt (see page 521 in Chapter 18).

In the meantime, the European debt crisis was spreading to other countries. In November 2010, Ireland requested financial assistance from the EU and IMF due to the accumulation of government debt arising from efforts to rescue its failing banks. This was followed by a similar request in May 2011 by Portugal, that was also facing mounting debt problems due to an excess of government spending over tax revenues. By the summer of 2011, there were major fears that Spain and Italy might also be requiring bailouts.

In July 2011, euro zone leaders and the European Central Bank, recognising the seriousness of the situation, worked out a deal including a new bailout package for Greece, a partial write-off of Greek debt (debt reduction), measures supporting economic growth, and lower interest rates and longer repayment periods for government borrowing for Greece, Ireland and Portugal.

The crisis reveals the flawed nature of the EMU

Financial markets reacted positively to the measures, as these restored some confidence in the euro zone's willingness to collectively deal with the debt problem. However, many economists argued that such measures would only postpone the debt problem rather than solve it. When the euro was established, it was believed that this would lead to greater economic *convergence* among euro zone countries. However, what can be seen is greater *divergence*, which ironically is partly due to the euro itself. Some euro zone countries (Germany, Finland and Austria) have increased their export competitiveness, accumulating large trade surpluses, while others (Greece, Portugal, Spain, the Netherlands) have lost competitiveness, and therefore have trade deficits. Germany's very large trade surpluses (80% of Germany's export revenues come from euro zone countries) owe their existence partly to an 'undervalued'

currency. If the euro did not exist, its national currency would appreciate, it would lose part of its strong competitive advantage, and its growth performance would be weakened. At the same time, weaker euro zone countries' currencies would depreciate, giving them the competitive advantage they strongly need to support their economies.

As the German Finance Minister has admitted, Germany became so prosperous 'because it has more advantages from European integration than any other country'.[10]

Since exchange rate adjustments are not possible within the euro zone, there is an urgent need for another adjustment mechanism for EMU to work. Many economists argue that the present EMU institutions must be supplemented by an EMU-wide fiscal authority, with powers to tax, spend and invest, transfer funds and monitor member countries. This would allow depressed areas to receive the necessary funds and investments to boost their growth. Yet there is tremendous opposition to this within the EMU countries themselves. Some of the countries that are by far the strongest opponents to close cooperation and fiscal policy coordination are the same ones that have gained the most from European integration.

Over the longer term, it appears unlikely that the EMU can work without fiscal mechanisms of coordination, mutual support and surveillance, which would also allow its members to share both the benefits and costs of EMU membership more equally.

Source: Paul Krugman, A Money Too Far' in the *International Herald Tribune*, 6 May 2010; Paul Krugman, 'Learning from Greece' in the *New York Times*, 8 April 2010; Joseph Stiglitz, 'Reform the euro or bin it' in the *Guardian*, 5 May 2010; Joseph Stiglitz, 'A principled Europe would not leave Greece to bleed' in the *Guardian*, 25 January 2010; Martin Feldstein, 'For a solution to the euro crisis, look to the States' in the *Washington Post*, 18 May 2010; 'Acropolis now', *The Economist*, 29 April 2010.

---

[4] Paul Krugman, 'Learning from Greece' in the *New York Times*, 8 April 2010.
[5] Paul Krugman, 'A money too far' in the *International Herald Tribune*, 6 May 2010.
[6] Gustav A. Horn, "How Germany made the Greek debt crisis worse", Speigelonline International, 27 April 2010.
[7] ibid
[8] AIG (American Internation Group) is the largest insruance company in the world. It was rescued from bankruptcy in 2008 through a bailout by the US government that cost US taxpayers $182 billion.
[9] Joseph Stiglitz, 'Reform the euro or bin it' in the *Guardian*, 5 May 2010.
[10] Quoted in 'Forget Greece: Europe's real problem is Germany' in the *Washington Post*, 21 May 2010.

Applying your skills

1 What is the difference between a government *deficit* and government *debt*?

2 **(a)** Explain how economic growth helps countries lower their debt-to-GDP ratio.
(b) Using an *AD-AS* diagram, explain why contractionary policies make it more difficult to lower the debt-to-GDP ratio.

3 Explain why a common currency can be interpreted as being 'undervalued' for countries

with trade surpluses and 'overvalued' for countries with trade deficits.

4 Explain how Greece's experience illustrates the disadvantages of monetary union.

5 What conditions of optimum currency areas must the euro zone countries address to improve the EMU and ensure its continued existence?

15.2 Terms of trade (higher level topic)

Understanding the terms of trade

Explaining the terms of trade

> ♦ Explain the meaning of the terms of trade.

The **terms of trade** is a concept that relates the prices that a country receives for its exports to the prices it pays for its imports, and can be defined as

$$\text{terms of trade} = \frac{\text{average price of exports}}{\text{average price of imports}} \times 100$$

Note that prices of exports and imports are both measured in terms of the domestic currency (alternatively, in terms of a foreign currency; in other words, both are measured in terms of the *same currency*).

Although the terms of trade measure prices of exports relative to prices of imports, it is also a measure of the amount of imports that can be bought per unit of exports. An increase in the price of exports, with the price of imports constant, means more imports can be bought with the same quantity of exports. On the other hand, an increase in the price of imports, with the price of exports constant, means fewer imports can be bought with the same quantity of exports. This will be explained below.

Distinguishing between an improvement and a deterioration in the terms of trade

> ♦ Distinguish between an improvement and a deterioration in the terms of trade.

Suppose Robotia exports robots and imports coffee. Initially, Robotia receives $10 per robot exported and pays $1 per unit of coffee imported. It therefore imports 10 units of coffee by exporting 1 robot. If the terms of trade change, so the price of robots increases to $15 per robot (the price of coffee remaining constant), Robotia imports 15 units of coffee for one robot. Robotia gets more imports for the same amount of exports. This is an **improvement in the terms of trade**, which is an increase in the value of the ratio of average export prices to average import prices. It involves a fall in the opportunity cost of imports.

If the price of coffee goes up to $2 per unit (with the price of exports constant), Robotia imports

only 5 units of coffee for one robot. Robotia now gets fewer imports for the same amount of exports. This is a **deterioration in the terms of trade**, and involves a decrease in the value of the ratio of average export prices to average import prices. It involves an increase in the opportunity cost of imports.

An improvement in the terms of trade can arise from either an increase in the price of exports or a fall in the price of imports. Similarly, a deterioration can arise from either a fall in the price of exports or an increase in the price of imports.

Measuring and calculating the terms of trade

> ♦ Explain how the terms of trade are measured.
> ♦ Calculate the terms of trade using the equation:
>
> $$\frac{\text{index of average export prices}}{\text{index of average import prices}} \times 100$$

Export prices and import prices are measured by a weighted price index constructed for each, using a base year (see page 283 on weighted price indices). Both price indices must be computed using the same base year for the ratio to have any meaning. To calculate the terms of trade, the price index for exports is divided by the price index for imports, and the result is multiplied by 100:

$$\text{terms of trade} = \frac{\text{index of average export prices}}{\text{index of average import prices}} \times 100$$

The value of the terms of trade is always 100 for the base year (100 divided by 100 and multiplied by 100).

For example if the base year is 2000, the terms of trade for the year 2000 is 100. Suppose that in 2002 the index of export prices is 103 and the index of import prices is 105. The terms of trade in 2002 are:

$$\text{terms of trade in 2002} = \frac{103}{105} \times 100 = 98.1$$

The terms of trade have deteriorated in the period 2000–02: average export prices have fallen relative to average import prices; we can also say that import prices have increased relative to export prices (the two expressions are equivalent).

Suppose in 2004 the index of export prices was 115 and index of import prices was 104. The terms of trade for 2004 are:

$$\text{terms of trade in 2004} = \frac{115}{104} \times 100 = 110.6$$

This indicates that the terms of trade improved in 2000–04 (as well as in the period 2002–04). Average export prices have increased relative to average import prices.

> An increase in the ratio of the index of average export prices to the index of average import prices shows an improvement in the terms of trade. A decrease in that ratio shows a deterioration in the terms of trade.

Test your understanding 15.4

1 Define (a) the terms of trade, (b) an improvement in the terms of trade, and (c) a deterioration in the terms of trade. (d) Explain how the terms of trade are measured.

2 Explain why (a) a terms of trade improvement means a country can buy more imports per unit of exports, and (b) a terms of trade deterioration means a country can buy fewer imports per unit of exports.

3 If the base year is 2003, what can you conclude about the terms of trade of a country if (a) in 2004, the terms of trade is measured to be 105.0, and (b) in 2005, it is 97.0?

4 The table below shows indices of average export and import prices for Riverland. (a) Which is the base year? (b) Calculate the terms of trade for each year shown. (c) Explain in which years there was a terms of trade improvement or deterioration relative to the base year. (d) Explain in which years there was a terms of trade improvement or deterioration relative to the previous year.

	2007	2008	2009	2010
Index of average export prices	100.0	103.2	109.8	110.5
Index of average import prices	100.0	104.7	105.3	107.5

Causes of changes in the terms of trade

Since the terms of trade are defined to be the average of export prices divided by the average of import prices, they are affected by any factors that give rise to changes in relative prices of internationally traded goods (exports and imports), as well as changes in exchange rates. In general, if the world price of a product increases, countries that export it experience an improvement in their terms of trade, whereas importing countries experience deterioration; if the world price falls, exporters experience deterioration and importers face an improvement. Clearly, changes in prices of internationally traded goods have a different (and opposite) impact on countries depending on whether they are exporters or importers of the goods.

Causes of changes in the short term

> ♦ Explain that the terms of trade may change in the short term due to changes in demand conditions for exports and imports, changes in global supply of key inputs (such as oil), changes in relative inflation rates and changes in relative exchange rates.

Changes in global demand

Increases in the global demand for a product cause its price to increase; decreases in global demand cause its price to fall. Some changes in demand may occur over relatively short periods of time for a variety of reasons. Changes in consumer tastes, for example in favour of textiles made of cotton, give rise to an increase in the global demand for cotton, and therefore an increase in its global price. This is expected to result in a terms of trade improvement for cotton exporters, and deterioration for cotton importers. Changing needs of producers for products used as inputs in production can also result in changing global demand over short periods of time. An example is the increased demand for cereals by farmers in developing countries who use these as animal feed in a growing livestock industry, leading to increases in the global price of cereals; this leads to a terms of trade improvement for cereal exporters and deterioration for cereal importers.

Changes in global supply

Prices of internationally traded products also change in response to changes in supply, which can occur over short periods of time due to a number of factors. For example, restrictions in the availability of an important input in production, such as oil, can have major impacts on supply over very short periods of time, causing its price to increase. Oil price increases give rise to terms of trade improvements for oil-exporting countries and deterioration for oil-importing countries. An increase in oil (or other input) supply has the opposite results.

In agriculture, weather conditions such as drought or flooding, pests, animal diseases, etc., affect the supply of agricultural products. Increases in supply lower global prices, causing a deterioration in the terms of trade of exporting countries and an improvement for importing countries. Decreases in global supply raise global prices, working in favour of the terms of trade of exporting countries and against importing countries.

Changes in the domestic rate of inflation relative to other countries

Price level changes in a country, relative to other countries, have immediate effects on its terms of trade. A higher rate of domestic inflation means the country's export prices increase relative to its import prices, resulting in an improvement in its terms of trade; at the same time this corresponds to a deterioration in the terms of trade of countries that import goods from the high inflation country.

Changes in domestic inflation may occur due to demand-pull factors (such as excess demand in the domestic economy), as well as cost-push factors (due to increases in costs of production, such as rapid increases in wages).

Changes in exchange rates

Exchange rates fluctuate continuously over short periods of time, and affect prices of both exports and imports, thus impacting on the terms of trade. If a currency depreciates/devalues, prices of imports increase in terms of the domestic currency. Note, however, that the prices of exports remain unchanged *in terms of the domestic currency* (export prices fall for foreigners). Since both the numerator and denominator of the terms of trade are measured in terms of the *domestic* currency, it follows that the depreciating country experiences a deterioration in its terms of trade, only on account of the increase in import prices. In the case of appreciation/revaluation, import prices fall, while export prices remain unchanged *in terms of the domestic currency*. Therefore, appreciation leads to an improvement in the terms of trade, on account of the fall in import prices. (For an explanation of this point, see Chapter 14, page 410.)

Causes of changes in the long term

♦ Explain that the terms of trade may change in the long term due to changes in world income levels, changes in productivity within the country and technological developments.

Growth in incomes, affecting global demand

Economic growth and increases in incomes are an important long-term cause of changing demand patterns, which affect terms of trade. As incomes increase, the demand for goods and services increases.

However, the effects on relative prices and terms of trade are different depending on the income elasticity of demand (*YED*) for particular products. *YED*, showing the responsiveness of demand to a change in income, is low for food and other primary products (usually less than 1), and higher for manufactured products and services (usually above 1). It follows that over long periods of time, as incomes increase, the prices of food and other primary products rise less rapidly than the prices of manufactured goods and of services. This means that countries that export mainly manufactured goods or that import primary products have been experiencing improving term of trade over many years, whereas countries that export mainly primary products and import manufactured products have been facing deteriorating terms of trade over long periods of time. We will come back to this issue on page 432 (see also page 65).

Changes in productivity

Productivity (output per unit of hour worked; see page 298) tends to increase over long periods of time, and is an important factor influencing domestic supply. Productivity may increase because of technological advances, improved management that increases efficiency, or more highly educated or skilled workers. Increases in productivity lower costs of production, shifting the supply curve to the right, and leading to lower product prices. If productivity increases occur in industries producing goods for export, the terms of trade will likely deteriorate as export prices fall relative to import prices.

Technological advances

Technological advances have a similar effect on the terms of trade as increases in productivity (they are often causes of productivity improvements), and are one of the more important factors influencing supply over the long term. A technological advance causes a rightward shift of the supply curve in industries using the new technology, leading to a lower price. There are numerous examples of technological change in recent decades, such as telecommunications, transport, agriculture, information technology, and many more, resulting in falling prices and changing terms of trade for exporters and importers.

Trade protection

A small country that uses trade protection to restrict imports or expand exports cannot affect world import and export prices, and faces a perfectly elastic world supply curve (see page 365). However, if a country has a large share in the world market for an import or export good, it may be able to affect the level of world prices. For example, it is likely that the United States, having a large share of the world's automobile imports, could lower world demand for automobiles, and therefore lower the prices of automobile exports of other countries, by restricting its imports through trade protection. This would result in an improvement in the terms of trade for the United States. On the other hand, subsidies granted by large producers of a good may result in an increase in global supply and hence a fall in its price. There is substantial evidence that subsidies granted by the United States and the European Union on their agricultural products have the effect of increasing global supply and depressing world prices. Exporters of the same products (usually in developing countries) therefore face deterioration in their terms of trade as the price of their export goods falls.

Test your understanding 15.5

1 Explain why an increase in the price of a product results in a terms of trade improvement for country X and deterioration for country Y depending on whether the countries are exporters or importers of the good.

2 Identify the likely impacts on the terms of trade of country X in the following situations:

(a) There is a fall in global demand for country X's main exports.

(b) There is an increase in incomes of a country X's main trading partners, influencing the demand for country X's exports of manufactured products (with a *YED* > 1).

(c) Drought reduces the global supply of wheat, and country X is a wheat exporter.

(d) OPEC restricts the supply oil, and country X is an oil importer.

(e) There is an increase in labour productivity in country X, affecting country X's export industries.

(f) Expansionary fiscal policy in country X leads to an increase in aggregate demand causing an increase in the rate of inflation relative to other countries.

(g) The European Union and the United States decide to eliminate subsidies on agricultural products, which country X produces for export.

Consequences of changes in the terms of trade

The terms of trade and global output and income redistribution

♦ Explain how changes in the terms of trade in the long term may result in a global redistribution of income.

Lasting, or long-term improvements in the terms of trade redistribute global output and income towards the country experiencing the improvement. This follows from the principle that *a country can purchase a larger quantity of imports with the same quantity of exports*. It means that by giving up the same amount of output to other countries in the form of exports, the country acquires more and more output produced elsewhere in the form of imports. The gain of extra output produced elsewhere corresponds to lost output for countries experiencing long-term deteriorating terms of trade. These countries suffer a transfer of output and income away from the domestic economy, because *they are forced to export increasing quantities of exports in order to maintain a particular quantity of imports*. Therefore, the result is a global redistribution of output and income.

The country with improving terms of trade has greater opportunities for growth, because it can increase its imports of capital goods or other important inputs for production, and it can also enjoy improved standards of living because of the possibility of importing more consumer goods. The country with deteriorating terms of trade has fewer possibilities to acquire needed imports for production, and faces prospects for lower growth as well as smaller lower standard of living improvements. Many developing countries find themselves in this situation (see page 433 below).

The terms of trade and effects on the current account

♦ Examine the effects of changes in the terms of trade on a country's current account, using the concepts of price elasticity of demand for exports and imports.

How the terms of trade and the current account are related

One reason why countries are interested in changes in their terms of trade is that these affect their balance of trade. Since the balance of trade is the most important component of a country's current account in its balance of payments, changes in the terms of trade affect the current account.

The balance of trade measures the value of export goods and services minus the value of import goods and services (see page 396). We can also say that the balance of trade measures export revenues minus import expenditures. Values of exports and imports are determined by export and import quantities times their respective prices. Since the terms of trade involve export and import prices, it follows that changes in the terms of trade cause changes in the balance of trade.

A change in the terms of trade leads to an improvement in the balance of trade (a smaller trade deficit or a larger trade surplus) if it causes an increase in the value of exports or a decrease in the value of imports.[11]

Will an improvement in the terms of trade always lead to an improvement in the balance of trade? The answer is no, not always. The reason is that the effects of terms of trade changes depend not only on changes in the prices of exports and imports, but *also on quantity changes*, because the balance of trade depends on the *values* of exports and imports (price times quantity). What happens to the values of exports and imports in turn depends on the *cause of the change in the terms of trade*. As we will see, if the cause lies in *changes in demand*, then the terms of trade and balance of trade change in the same direction. However, if the cause lies in *changes in supply*, then the terms of trade and balance of trade change in the same direction only under certain conditions.

In the discussion that follows, we are making the assumption that a change in the price of a single commodity leads to changes in a country's terms of trade. This is a realistic assumption for countries whose exports are dominated by a single (or few) commodities, but is less realistic for countries that have diversified exports. (See page 431 for a more detailed discussion of this point.)

Changes in global demand

In Figure 15.1(a), the demand curve represents the global demand for an internationally traded good, and the supply curve represents the global supply of that good. Let's suppose that this internationally traded good is wheat. If there is an increase in global wheat demand, the demand curve shifts from D_1 to D_2, the quantity of wheat traded globally increases from Q_1 to Q_2, and the price of wheat rises from P_1 to P_2. Suppose Flatland is a producer and exporter of wheat. In view of the higher global price, Flatland experiences an improvement in its terms of trade, and also exports a larger quantity of wheat. Since both the price and quantity of wheat exported increase, Flatland's export revenues also increase. Therefore, *when there is an increase in global demand for a good, the improved terms of trade lead to an improvement in the balance of trade* (smaller trade deficit or larger surplus). By contrast, a global fall in demand for wheat, shown by the leftward shift from D_1 to D_3, results in a lower equilibrium price and quantity; the terms of trade deteriorate, export revenues fall and the balance of trade worsens.

Suppose Mountainland is a wheat importer. As demand for wheat increases, a higher wheat price means a deterioration in the terms of trade, and with a greater quantity of imports, the balance of trade worsens. In the opposite case of a fall in price due to a fall in demand, the terms of trade improve and the trade balance also improves as the quantity of imports falls.

When the terms of trade change due to a *change in the global demand* for a good, the terms of trade and the balance of trade change in the same direction: either they both improve or they both deteriorate. This applies to both exporting and importing countries.

Changes in global supply: the role of PED for exports and imports

The role of PED   When the terms of trade of a country change because of changes in supply, the effects on the trade balance may be different from those above. The reason can be seen in Figure 15.1(b), again showing the global demand and global supply of an internationally traded good. Here, shifts in the global supply curve lead to new equilibrium prices, occurring *along the given demand curve*, so that quantity demanded and price change *in opposite directions* because of the law of demand. This means we cannot examine effects on the trade balance without going into the price elasticity of demand (*PED*) for exports and imports.

---

[11] If a country has a surplus in its balance of trade, an increase in the value of exports or a decrease in the value of imports leads to a larger surplus, which may not necessarily be an improvement in the trade balance, especially if this surplus is very large to begin with. However, historically and to the present, a trade deficit has been commonly referred to as an 'unfavourable trade balance' and a surplus as a 'favourable trade balance'. Therefore by extension a decrease in a deficit or an increase in a surplus is an 'improvement in the trade balance'. This practice originated in the Mercantilist period of the 16th–18th centuries, when it was believed that a country's economic strength is based on achieving and maintaining a trade surplus. In today's world, most countries have deficits in their balance of trade; therefore, a balance of trade improvement usually refers to a reduction in the trade deficit.

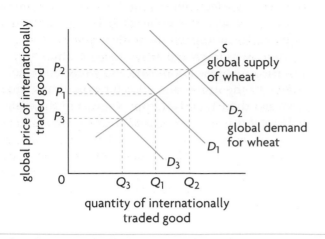

(a) Changes in global demand: terms of trade and balance of trade change in same direction

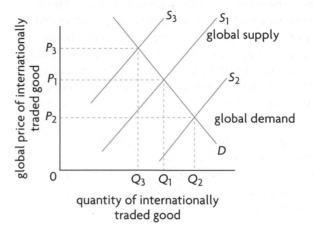

(b) Changes in global supply: effects of terms of trade changes on the balance of trade depend on *PEDs* for exports and imports

Figure 15.1 Changes in global demand or supply: terms of trade impacts on the balance of trade

The price elasticity of demand for exports (PED_x) is the responsiveness of quantity of exports demanded to a change in the price of exports:

$$PED_x =$$

$$\frac{\text{percentage change in quantity of exports demanded}}{\text{percentage change in price of exports}}$$

The price elasticity of demand for imports (PED_m) is the responsiveness of quantity of imports demanded to a change in the average price of imports:

$$PED_m =$$

$$\frac{\text{percentage change in quantity of imports demanded}}{\text{percentage change in price of imports}}$$

The case of inelastic demand Let's consider the international market for wheat, and suppose that due to exceptionally good weather conditions in a number of countries, an increase in the global supply of wheat occurs, causing the supply curve in Figure 15.1(b) to shift to the right from S_1 to S_2. Wheat, being an agricultural commodity, has a relatively inelastic demand ($PED<1$).

Suppose that Flatland is a wheat exporter. It faces a lower export price of wheat, and therefore deteriorating terms of trade, and a larger quantity of wheat exports. Since Flatland is a wheat exporter, we must consider the *PED for exports* to determine the impact of its terms of trade change on its balance of trade. Since $PED_x<1$, the increase in the quantity of its wheat exports is proportionately smaller than the fall in the export price, leading to a fall in the value of wheat exports.

Therefore, *Flatland's deterioration in its terms of trade causes a deterioration in its balance of trade* (a larger trade deficit or smaller trade surplus).

Suppose that Mountainland is a wheat importer. It faces a lower import price, and therefore improving terms of trade, and a larger quantity of wheat imports. Since Mountainland is a wheat importer, its *PED for imports* is relevant to analysing the effects of the terms of trade change on its trade balance. Since $PED_m<1$, the increase in the quantity of wheat imports is proportionately smaller than the fall in the import price, leading to a fall in the value of wheat imports. Therefore, *Mountainland's improvement in its terms of trade leads to an improvement in its balance of trade* (a smaller trade deficit or larger trade surplus).

We can see that the results for Mountainland, the wheat importer, are the exact opposite of the results for Flatland, the wheat exporter. This is just as we expect, for as noted above, changes in prices of internationally traded goods have a different (and opposite) impact on countries depending on whether they are exporters or importers of the goods.

What if there had been a decrease in the global supply of wheat? The analysis of effects on exporters' and importers' terms of trade and balance of trade will be left for you to do as an exercise (see Test your understanding 15.6 on page 430).

The case of elastic demand Now suppose that Figure 15.1(b) represents the international market for computers, and that due to major productivity increases, the global supply of computers increases from S_1 to S_2, leading to a fall in price. Let's assume that the demand for computers is relatively elastic, so that $PED>1$.

Flatland, a computer exporting country, faces deteriorating terms of trade in view of the price decline. Since its $PED_x > 1$, the increase in the quantity of its computer exports is proportionately larger than the decrease in price, so *Flatland's deteriorating terms of trade result in an improvement in its trade balance* (smaller trade deficit or larger surplus). In fact, many manufactured goods exports tend to have a price elastic demand ($PED_x > 1$), and so a fall in price due to technological advances or increases in productivity tend not to be a problem and lead to improvements in the balance of trade of exporting countries. This is a good example of a case where deteriorating terms of trade work in favour of exporting countries.

Mountainland, a computer importing country, faces an improvement in its terms of trade due to the fall in the global price of computers. However, since its $PED_m > 1$, the increase in the quantity of its computer imports is proportionately larger than the decrease in price, so that *Mountainland's improving terms of trade result in a deterioration in its trade balance* (larger trade deficit or smaller trade surplus).

Once again, we see that the results for the computer importing country are the exact opposite of the computer exporting country, just as we would expect.

What if there had been a decrease in the global supply of computers, involving a leftward shift in the global supply from S_1 to S_3? This too will be left for you to analyse as an exercise (see Test your understanding 15.6 below).

All the above seemingly confusing results can be understood and remembered easily using the following rule:

Given a *change in global supply* that causes a change in a country's terms of trade, when $PED_x < 1$ or when $PED_m < 1$ (inelastic demand), the terms of trade and balance of trade move in the same direction (both improve or both deteriorate). When $PEDx > 1$ or $PED_m > 1$ (elastic demand), the terms of trade and balance of trade move in *opposite directions*: an improvement in the terms of trade causes a deterioration in the trade balance, while a deterioration in the terms of trade causes an improvement in the trade balance. These results apply to both exporting and importing countries.

Changes in exchange rates

Changes in exchange rates involve depreciation or appreciation of currencies under floating and managed exchange rate systems. Depreciation leads to deteriorating terms of trade (see page 426 above). The effect on the trade balance is analysed in terms of the Marshall–Lerner condition, according to which if $PED_x + PED_m > 1$, depreciation leads to an improvement in the trade balance. If this condition does not hold, a currency depreciation leads to a worsening trade balance (see page 409).

Currency appreciation leads to improving terms of trade. The effects on the trade balance can be considered as the Marshall–Lerner condition in reverse. An appreciation leads to a worsening trade balance if the sum of the PEDs for exports and imports is greater than 1, and an improvement in the trade balance if this sum is less than 1.

Changes in the rate of inflation

We have seen above (page 426) that changes in the domestic rate of inflation relative to that of other countries also cause changes in the terms of trade. However, it is extremely complicated to analyse the effects of such terms of trade changes on the balance of trade for several reasons. One is that in a flexible (or managed) exchange rate system a change in the rate of inflation is likely to lead to changes in the exchange rate (see page 385), which in turn have their own effects on the terms of trade and balance of trade (as discussed above). In addition, an increase in the rate of inflation may lead to government or central bank policies to deal with this, which in turn set in motion a series of events with their own effects on the terms of trade and balance of trade. Therefore, in the absence of further information on all these factors, it is not possible to make generalisations about the effects of changes in the rate of inflation on the terms of trade and balance of trade.

Test your understanding 15.6

1 Explain how changes in the terms of trade can result in a global redistribution of output and income.

2 What is the relationship between the terms of trade and the balance of trade?

3 **(a)** Explain, using a diagram, how an increase in the demand for a country's exports is likely to affect its terms of trade and its balance of trade. **(b)** Do *PED*s for exports and imports come into play?

4 Under what circumstances are *PED*s for imports and exports **(a)** important, or **(b)** irrelevant, in determining the effects of terms of trade changes on the balance of trade?

5 Under what conditions can a technological advance in an export industry lead to an improvement in a country's trade balance, even though its terms of trade may deteriorate?

6 Suppose that due to poor weather conditions there is a fall in the global supply of wheat exports. Using a diagram like that in Figure 15.1(b), explain the effects on the terms of trade and balance of trade of **(a)** wheat exporters, and **(b)** wheat importers. **(c)** How are the effects on importers and exporters related to each other?

7 Suppose that the formation of a global computer-producing cartel restricts the global supply of computer exports. Using a diagram like that in Figure 15.1(b), explain the effects on the terms of trade and balance of trade of **(a)** computer exporters, and **(b)** computer importers. **(c)** How are the effects on importers and exporters related to each other?

8 **(a)** Explain the relationship between exchange rate changes and a country's terms of trade. **(b)** Under what conditions can exchange rate changes be expected to lead to an improvement in a country's trade balance and current account?

Impacts of short-term fluctuations and long-term deterioration in the terms of trade in economically less developed countries

♦ Explain the impacts of short-term fluctuations and long-term deterioration in the terms of trade of economically less developed countries that specialise in primary commodities, using the concepts of price elasticity of demand and supply for primary products and income elasticity of demand.

Changes in the terms of trade tend to be more important for developing countries, and particularly those developing countries that specialise in the production of a few commodities for export. Developed countries usually produce a larger variety of goods and services for export. The same applies to a number of 'middle income' developing countries (according to the World Bank's classification) that have made headway with industrialisation, and have diversified their production for export. In these countries, it is unlikely that all or most of their export goods will face a similar change in terms of trade at the same time. Therefore, whatever changes do occur are likely to 'cancel out' to some extent.

On the other hand, countries that specialise and export just a few commodities (mostly developing countries) find themselves in a far more vulnerable position, due to short-term fluctuations or long-term deterioration in terms of trade.

Short-term fluctuations

Short-term fluctuations in the terms of trade are often related to 'commodity booms', or sudden large increases in commodity prices, followed by abrupt declines. When countries export (or import) the commodities in question, fluctuations in commodity prices translate into fluctuations in countries' terms of trade. A major commodity boom occurred in the decade of the 2000s.

Commodity price fluctuations are the result of abrupt changes in global demand or supply of commodities. Such changes have strong effects on commodity prices because commodities have a low price elasticity of demand ($PED < 1$) and low price elasticity of supply ($PES < 1$). These topics were studied in Chapter 3, which you should review in connection with the present topic.

In Figure 3.6 (page 57), we saw that supply curve shifts lead to much larger price fluctuations in the case of primary (including agricultural) products that have low PEDs compared to manufactured products. Also, Figure 3.13 (page 70) showed how demand curve shifts cause larger price fluctuations for products with a low PES compared with those of products with a high PES. We also examined the reasons why primary commodities tend to have a low PED and a low PES (pages 56 and 70).

Because the exports of many less developed countries tend to be based heavily on commodities, the terms of trade of these countries are far more affected by commodity price fluctuations. Yet short-term fluctuations in the terms of trade come with a number of negative effects:

- Fluctuations in the terms of trade create uncertainties and can be highly destabilising. In the private sector they have negative effects on investment and consumption. Producers and consumers are unable to plan; producers are unable to determine the future profitability of investments.
- Changing relative prices affect the signalling function of prices and result in poor resource allocation outcomes and inefficiency.
- Windfall gains from higher export prices are often spent on increased imports of consumer goods rather than on investments in domestic manufacturing or imports of needed capital goods.
- Windfall gains also increase domestic income inequalities through short-term transfers of income towards those who gain from higher prices and away from those who lose from lower prices; only to redistribute income once again a short time later when prices fall again.
- Windfall gains may further increase social tensions due to infighting over who will capture the most gains.

- Terms of trade fluctuations affect the banking system through a large growth of bank deposits in times of rising prices and large withdrawals in times of falling prices.

- Terms of trade fluctuations also affect the government, particularly when commodity production is under public ownership, and can be highly destabilising in view of wild fluctuations in revenues, translating into unstable government spending and inappropriate fiscal policies. Whereas governments must ensure that increased revenues are spent in ways that will support growth and development (such as through increased provision of merit goods including education, health care and infrastructure), they are often tempted to spend it on such items as increased public sector wages, or on investments that depend strongly on imports that cannot be maintained following drops in revenues that come with commodity price declines.

- Perhaps most importantly, rapid and large improvements in the terms of trade when export prices increase do not favour policies that promote diversification of production and exports. Whereas countries should use the increased revenues and resources made possible by higher commodity prices to diversify their production and reduce the economy's dependence on a small number of export commodities, the increases in export revenues actually work to reinforce the dependence of the economy on just those few commodities that provide the windfall gains (see Chapter 17, page 493).

All in all, terms of trade fluctuations are difficult for both the private sector and governments to manage, and over the longer term may work to lower the rate of growth of an economy, as well as to make it more difficult to achieve economic development.

Long-term deterioration

A large body of empirical research indicates that developing countries that specialise in the export of non-oil commodities have been experiencing deteriorating terms of trade over long periods of time. (Oil exporters have been experiencing improving terms of trade.) According to one study, in the period 1900–86, relative prices of all non-fuel primary commodities fell by 0.6% a year.[12] More recently, in the period 1980–2000, the prices of key agricultural commodities fell on average by roughly 50%. In the

case of certain products, including tropical beverages, sugar and cotton, the fall was even greater.[13]

Factors behind the long-term deterioration in the terms of trade include the following.

Low income elasticity of demand for primary products   An important explanation behind deteriorating terms of trade for primary products lies in the low income elasticity of demand (*YED*) for these compared to the higher *YED* for manufactured products and services. Food has a relatively low income elasticity of demand (see page 64). In addition, certain non-food primary products (such as rubber and cotton) face competition from synthetic materials that can be substituted in place of the primary products, also leading to a low *YED* for these products.

With a low *YED*, as income increases, a relatively lower fraction of the increase is spent on primary products and a relatively higher fraction on manufactured products (and services), so demand for primary products grows relatively slowly compared to demand for manufactured products. These changes in demand produce a tendency for prices of primary products, exported mainly by developing countries, to fall relative to prices of manufactured products, exported mainly by developed countries. (This does not mean prices of primary products fall in absolute terms, but that they rise more slowly compared to manufactured goods prices.)

Technological advances in agriculture   In the case of many primary products, slow growth in demand over decades (due to low *YED*s) has been accompanied by large increases in supply resulting from technological progress, further depressing prices. This can be seen in Figure 15.2, where a relatively small increase in demand is accompanied by a relatively larger increase in supply due to technological change, resulting in a fall in price.

Protection of agriculture in developed countries   Many developed countries (such as the United States and members of the European Union) face the same problem of low income elasticity of demand for agricultural products within their own borders. As demand for agricultural products grows less rapidly than the demand for other goods and services, there is a downward pressure on agricultural product prices, lowering farmers' incomes. Farmers exert pressure on governments to protect the domestic market, and governments respond by imposing tariffs and other barriers on imports of agricultural commodities, as well as by granting subsidies. Because

---

[12] Enzo R. Grilli and Maw Cheng Yang (1988) 'Primary commodity prices, manufactured goods prices, and the terms of trade of developing countries: What the long run shows' in *World Bank Economic Review*, 2.1: 1–44.

[13] Food and Agriculture Organization (FAO) (2002), 'Dependence on single agricultural commodity exports in developing countries: magnitude and trends'.

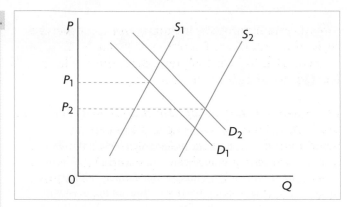

Figure 15.2 Long-term declines in primary product prices due to low growth in demand (due to low *YED*s) and high growth in supply (due to technological advances)

of the very large size of the United States and the European Union, protection against imports has major effects by lowering the world demand for imports of protected agricultural products, while subsidies increase world supply. Lower demand and increased supply work to depress world agricultural product prices (see also page 427).

Oligopolistic market structures in more developed countries   The exports of developed countries, consisting mainly of manufactured goods, are often produced by oligopolistic firms with a substantial degree of monopoly power and the ability to influence prices. Less developed countries produce more primary commodities that tend to be more competitively organised, lacking in any significant power to influence prices. Therefore, there is a tendency for prices of manufactured exports to increase relative to prices of primary good exports, leading to a deterioration in the terms of trade of developing countries, as they face both relatively lower export prices (or primary goods) and higher import prices (of manufactured goods).

Effects of deteriorating terms of trade
Deteriorating terms of trade have the following effects on the economies of developing countries:

- A transfer of income away from countries experiencing deterioration in their terms of trade, and towards those whose terms of trade are improving occurs (see page 427 above).

- Countries must keep increasing their exports to maintain a constant level of imports; there is a continuously increasing opportunity cost of imports.

- Opportunities for importing badly needed capital goods and other inputs for production become increasingly limited in view of the increasing opportunity cost of imports.

- Scarce domestic resources (with the exception of labour, which is abundant) must be transferred to production for export, making diversification of the economy more difficult to achieve.

- Falling export earnings mean increasing balance of trade deficits and balance of payments problems (see page 406 on the effects of persistent current account deficits).

- The inability to pay for the excess of imports over exports (the growing trade deficits) forces countries to resort to borrowing (credits in the financial account) to obtain the necessary foreign exchange.

- Increasing levels of debt mean that countries accumulate future obligations in terms of making interest payments and repaying their debts, with further costs to the economy (see page 521 in Chapter 18).

- Falling export earnings mean falling rural incomes and increasing poverty.

- Falling output and incomes mean less government revenue with which the government can make necessary investments in infrastructure and provide badly needed merit goods.

- Growth and development prospects are damaged.

- Countries may become trapped in poverty cycles (see page 444 in Chapter 16).

Many of the countries with very high dependence on one or a few commodity exports are among the poorest in the world, often deeply indebted, locked in poverty, and with very poor prospects for future growth and development.

Test your understanding 15.7

1 Explain why changes in the terms of trade tend to be more important for developing countries that specialise in the production and export of a few commodities.

2 Why are price elasticity of demand and price elasticity of supply important in causing large price fluctuations in primary commodity prices that give rise to short-term fluctuations in the terms of trade?

3 Explain some of the consequences of short-term fluctuations in the terms of trade for countries that are commodity exporters.

4 **(a)** What is the role of income elasticity of demand in the long-term deterioration in the terms of trade in some developing countries?
(b) What other factors might be responsible for this long-term deterioration?

5 Explain some possible effects on the economy of a country experiencing a long-term deterioration in its terms of trade.

Coffee and deteriorating terms of trade

The Food and Agriculture Organization (FAO) of the United Nations describes the consequences of the decline in coffee prices that occurred until the early 2000s, as an example of the broader consequences of price declines in commodity markets generally. It argues that the coffee crisis alone during the 1990s destroyed the livelihood of more than 20 million households. Whereas at the end of the 1980s coffee exporters received $12 billion for their exports, in 2003 they received a mere $5.5 billion, at the same time as the quantity of coffee they were exporting had increased. Whereas low world prices reduced costs and increased profit margins for coffee roasters of developed countries, a farmer in Tanzania received less than 1 cent for every $1 worth of high quality Arabica coffee sold in a coffee house in the United States. In Ethiopia, where coffee provides more than 60% of foreign exchange earnings and 10% of government revenue, and where one quarter of the population is directly or indirectly involved with coffee production and marketing, the volume of exports increased by more than two-thirds in the period 1995–2003 while export earnings fell dramatically. In Nicaragua, extreme poverty increased by 5% among coffee farmers, although it declined for other parts of the population not involved with coffee. James Wolfensohn, former president of the World Bank, remarked in 2003 that the reduction of coffee prices and also other commodities is undermining the economic sustainability of countries and millions of families in Latin America, Africa and Asia.[14]

Source: Food and Agriculture Organization (FAO) (2002) 'Dependence on single agricultural commodity exports in developing countries: magnitude and trends'.

[14] *El Pais*, 19 May 2003.

Applying your skills

1 Using examples from the text, explain the meaning of deteriorating terms of trade using the idea that a country can buy fewer imports per unit of exports.

2 Explain the impacts of deteriorating terms of trade on the economies of developing countries.

Assessment

The Student's CD-ROM at the back of this book provides practice of examination questions based on the material you have studied in this chapter.

Standard level
- Exam practice: Paper 2, Chapter 15
  - SL/HL core topics (Text/data 9–11, questions A.21–A.26)

Higher level
- Exam practice: Paper 2, Chapter 15
  - SL/HL core topics (Text/data 9–11, questions A.21–A.26)
  - HL topics (Text/data 12, questions A.27–A.30)
- Exam practice: Paper 3, Chapter 15
  - HL topics (question 30)

Section 4
Development economics

Section 4 is concerned with economically less developed countries. We have already touched upon many economic issues bearing upon economic development. In this section we will bring these together and expand upon them. We will examine the meaning of economic development and how this is measured, the sources of economic growth and development as well as the goals of development. We will also explore a number of factors that act as barriers to as well as facilitators of growth and development, and a variety of policies that developing countries can pursue to promote their growth and development.

Section 4 brings together many concepts and tools we studied in earlier chapters. Development economics is a special area of economics that draws on and applies the principles of economics (micro and macro as well as international economics) to the problems of economically less developed countries. However, it is much more than a simple application of these principles. The important questions we want to answer, such as what makes countries grow and develop, what prevents them from growing and developing, and what are the best ways to pursue growth and development objectives, cannot always be answered by use of economic principles alone. In addition, as we will discover, economic development depends very much on institutional factors, as well as on value judgements about what is considered to be good for development. Because of the special circumstances that developing economies find themselves in, it is often necessary to devise new ways of thinking about their economic problems, in order to understand and explain the nature of these problems, as well as to determine how they can best be addressed.

Chapter 16
Understanding economic development

This chapter examines the relationship between economic growth and economic development. In addition, it identifies characteristics that many economically less developed countries share in common. The focus of the last part of the chapter is on how we measure economic development, and the difficulties that measurement methods give rise to.

16.1 Economic growth and economic development

Distinguishing between economic growth and economic development

Economic growth versus economic development

♦ Distinguish between economic growth and economic development.

Economic growth refers to increases in output and incomes over time, often measured on a *per capita* basis. *Economic development* refers to a process that leads to improved standards of living for a population as a whole (see Chapter 1, page 13, for an introduction to the difference between the two concepts). Increasing levels of output and incomes resulting from economic growth mean that societies can better satisfy the needs and wants of their populations and secure improvements in their standards of living. However, while economic growth can make improved levels of living possible, it does not by itself guarantee that this will occur. Persisting poverty and the failure of many countries to secure long-lasting improvements in the well-being of their populations, even if they have achieved respectable rates of growth over extended periods of time, have shown that economic development is a highly complex and sometimes elusive process.

The multidimensional nature of economic development

♦ Explain the multidimensional nature of economic development in terms of reducing widespread poverty, raising living standards, reducing income inequalities and increasing employment opportunities.

The evolving meaning of economic development

The meaning of economic development has changed over the years. In the 1950s and 1960s, economists thought that economic growth and economic development were practically one and the same. A famous development economist, Charles P. Kindleberger, wrote in 1965, 'Growth and development are often used synonymously in economic discussion, and this is entirely appropriate'.[1] It was believed that economic growth over long periods would automatically provide economic and social benefits for the entire population. Larger quantities of goods and services, including health care and education, and employment opportunities and social change would eventually be spread out over most people in an economy. This was termed the 'trickle-down theory': benefits of growth would eventually trickle down to everyone.

By the late 1960s and early 1970s, it was becoming clear that many less developed countries were not performing according to expectations. The GNI *per capita* gap between rich countries and poor countries had more than doubled on average in the period

---

[1] Charles P. Kindleberger (1965) *Economic Development*, McGraw-Hill.

1950–75.[2] While some less developed countries were growing rapidly (especially some oil-rich countries), others were experiencing very low or even negative growth rates (especially in Africa). The number of people living in extreme poverty (defined then as living on less than US$1 per day) was increasing rather than decreasing. It was apparent that the benefits of economic growth were not 'trickling down' to the poorest members of society.

Economists began to understand that since economic growth, where it did occur, did not always work to eliminate widespread poverty and improve standards of living, what was needed was an approach that would directly deal with the problems of developing countries, and specifically the problem of persisting poverty. In a new view, less developed countries should combine the older focus on economic growth with new ideas on redistribution of income and wealth, and improved access of the poor to basic goods and services.

The many dimensions of economic development

By the 1970s, economic development came to be understood as a process with many dimensions, and it is this view that still holds today.

Economic development can be defined as a process where increases in real *per capita* output and incomes are accompanied by improvements in standards of living of the population and reductions in poverty, increased access to goods and services that satisfy basic needs (including food, shelter, health care, education, sanitation and others), increasing employment opportunities and reduction of unemployment, and reductions of serious inequalities in incomes and wealth.

Human development

Thinking about development has progressed further in more recent years, building on an even broader interpretation of development that was provided by Denis Goulet as early as 1971. Goulet defined three core values of development: life sustenance, self-esteem and freedom:[3]

- **Life sustenance** refers to access to basic services (merit goods) such as education and health care

services, as well as satisfaction of basic needs like food, clothing and shelter.

- **Self-esteem** involves the feeling of self-respect; development is desirable because it provides individuals with dignity, honour and independence. Self-esteem is related to the absence of exploitation and dominance associated with poverty and dependence.

- **Freedom** involves freedom from want, ignorance and squalor; it is freedom to make choices that are not available to people who are subjected to conditions of poverty.

The economist Amartya Sen, who won the Nobel Prize in Economics in 1998 for his work on poverty and economic development, takes Goulet's ideas further, and sees improvements in human well-being as arising from a process of expanding freedoms:

'Development can be seen . . . as a process of expanding the real freedoms that people enjoy. Focusing on human freedom contrasts with narrower views of development, such as identifying development with the growth of gross national product, or with the rise in personal incomes, or with industrialisation, or with technological advance, or with social modernisation. Growth of GNP or of individual incomes can, of course, be very important as *means* to expanding the freedoms enjoyed by the members of the society. But freedoms depend also on other determinants, such as social and economic arrangements (for example, facilities for education and health care), as well as political and civil rights (for example, the liberty to participate in public discussion and scrutiny) . . .'[4]

Sen's approach has been crystallised in the concept of *human development*, introduced in the first Human Development Report of the United Nations Development Programme (UNDP) in 1990.[5]

Human development is a process of expanding human freedoms: the freedom to satisfy hunger; to be adequately fed; to be free of preventable illnesses; to have adequate clothing and shelter; to have access to clean water and sanitation; to be able to read, write and receive an appropriate education; to be knowledgeable; to be able to find work; to enjoy legal protection; to participate in social and political life; and, in general, to have the freedom to develop one's potential and lead a full and productive life.

---

[2] David Morawetz (1977) *Twenty-Five Years of Economic Development: 1950–1975,* World Bank.

[3] D. Goulet (1971) *The Cruel Choice: A New Concept on the Theory of Development*, Atheneum.

[4] Amartya Sen (2001) *Development as Freedom*, Oxford University Press. Emphasis in the original.

[5] The United Nations Development Programme (UNDP) is an agency of the United Nations designed to promote development in economically less developed countries and reduce poverty. The UNDP's Human Development Reports are compiled annually and provide statistical and other information on numerous issues relating to human development in less developed countries around the world.

Based on the concept of human development, the UNDP makes a distinction between *income poverty* and *human poverty*. Income poverty occurs when income falls below a nationally or internationally determined poverty line (see Chapter 11, page 305). Human poverty involves deprivations and the lack of opportunities that allow individuals 'to lead a long, healthy, creative life and to enjoy a decent standard of living, freedom, dignity, self-esteem and the respect of others'.[6]

To understand the distinction between the two, consider a villager whose income increases, so that now he or she is able to purchase more goods and services. If there are no schools or health care services in the area, or if the village is infested with malaria, the higher income will be of little use in securing a higher standard of living. Income poverty is reduced through higher income, but human poverty cannot be lowered without measures to provide a broad range of social services to the entire population. On the other hand, if people on low incomes have access to education, health services, improved sanitation, improved water supplies, etc., human poverty can be reduced even while income poverty remains.

Sources of economic growth in economically less developed countries

♦ Explain that the most important sources of economic growth in economically less developed countries include increases in quantities of physical capital and human capital, the development and use of new technologies that are appropriate to the conditions of the economically less developed countries, and institutional changes.

The sources of economic growth are the same everywhere (see pages 295–99), but in less developed countries there are certain sources of growth that are especially important.

Increases in the quantity of physical capital

Physical capital is an important source of growth because it makes possible increases in labour productivity (output per unit of labour input). It is especially important in developing countries, which tend to have relatively limited amounts of capital in relation to their large supplies of labour. This means that labour productivity tends to be low relative to what we find in economically more developed countries.

Increases in the quantity of human capital

Human capital is also a very important source of growth because of its contribution to increasing the productivity of labour. In developing countries it acquires a special significance because there are large portions of populations in many countries that have relatively low levels of educational attainment, and also low levels of health. This means that there is a huge scope for increasing the amount of human capital, and this can make a very significant difference to productivity, employment opportunities, output growth and development prospects. The importance of human capital will be discussed further in Chapter 17.

Development and use of new appropriate technologies

New technology contributes to improving the *quality* of physical capital. While new technology in general contributes to economic growth, in developing countries it is especially important to consider the *appropriateness* of new technologies to local conditions. There are many technologies developed and used in economically advanced countries that are not well-suited to the conditions of less developed ones. More developed and less developed often differ from each other not only with respect to economic factors, and also climatic, ecological and geographical conditions, and this sometimes means that countries require technologies that are well-suited to their particular local conditions. We will discuss this further in Chapter 17.

Institutional changes

The World Bank defines institutions as 'the rules, organizations and social norms that facilitate co-ordination of human action'.[7] There are many economic, legal and social institutions that influence economic growth. In many economically less developed countries, there is a need to develop institutions relating to property rights (laws and regulations that define rights to ownership, use and transfer of property); a well-functioning legal system that provides effective enforcement of laws, contracts and mechanisms for settling conflicts; an efficient, fair and transparent tax system; banking and credit institutions that provide effective links between savers and investors, and broad access by the population (including the poor) to credit; institutions that protect against corruption; and more. Many developing countries are making great efforts to build strong market economies, yet a market system cannot function well without well-developed institutions such as these.

---

[6] United Nations Development Programme, *Human Development Report 1997* (available at http://hdr.undp.org/en/reports/).

[7] The World Bank (2003) *World Development Report, 2003: Sustainable Development in a Dynamic World: Transforming Institutions, Growth and Quality of Life*, Oxford University Press.

The questionable role of commodity-type natural resources in economic growth

In Chapter 11, we learned that commodity-type natural resources can contribute to economic growth, but are not essential for growth (page 298). In fact, it has been observed that since the 1960s resource-poor developing countries have been growing faster than resource-rich countries. This surprising trend has been termed the 'curse of natural resources' because it suggests that resource-rich countries might have been better off if they did not have these natural resources. Examples of countries that have experienced low and sometimes negative rates of growth in spite of their abundant supplies of natural resources include Russia (rich in oil, natural gas, metals and timber), Nigeria, Mexico and Venezuela (rich in oil), Congo and Sierra Leone (rich in mineral deposits), South Africa (rich in oil and mineral deposits), and others.

The reasons behind the better performance of resource-poor countries can be found in their earlier diversification into manufacturing and their earlier industrialisation. Their inability to rely on the production and export of commodities made them turn early on toward labour-intensive manufacturing (making good use of their large labour supplies), together with investments in human capital and appropriate technologies. Resource-rich countries, on the other hand, became heavily dependent on production and export of primary commodities, which often led to short-term volatility of export revenues, long-term deteriorating terms of trade, poor fiscal performance (government spending that gets out of control), the need to resort to external borrowing and hence the accumulation of large debts, and balance of payments difficulties. Also, the presence of precious natural resources sometimes became a source of conflict because of increasing income inequalities, as well as between contending groups that would like to gain control over them. (We will come back to these topics in Chapter 17.)

Relating economic growth to economic development

♦ Explain the relationship between economic growth and economic development, noting that some limited economic development is possible in the absence of economic growth, but that over the long term economic growth is usually necessary for economic development (however, it should be understood that under certain circumstances economic growth may not lead to economic development).

Economic growth can occur without economic development. It was this experience for many countries in the 1950s and 1960s that gave rise to a rethinking and redefining of economic development. Can economic development occur without economic growth?

Some economic development is possible in the absence of rapid growth, if appropriate policies are followed to provide access to basic social services for the poor. The production possibilities model we studied in Chapters 1 and 11 shows how this can occur. In Figure 16.1, an economy produces some combination of industrial goods (measured on the vertical axis) and merit goods (measured on the horizontal axis). The merit goods include education, health care services, sanitation, and clean water supplies, made available to people on low incomes, who would not otherwise have access to them. (For simplicity it is assumed that actual output is at some point on the production possibilities curve (PPC)). An economy that does not experience growth can still achieve some economic development, by reallocating its resources such that it cuts back on industrial production and increases merit goods production; this would entail a movement along PPC_1 from point A to a point like B.

Over long periods of time, the possibilities for improving the population's well-being by moving along the same PPC will be exhausted, and further improvements will depend on outward PPC shifts, such as from PPC_1 to PPC_2 in Figure 16.1. Such outward shifts, representing economic growth as an increase in production possibilities (see page 295), are therefore necessary for economic development to be maintained. Growing output *per capita* translates into higher incomes and an improved ability to provide the goods and services needed by the population.

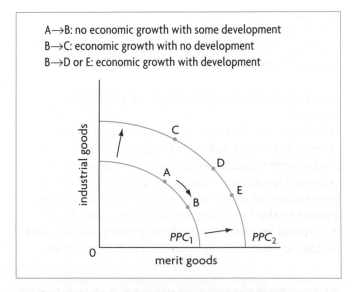

Figure 16.1 Economic growth and economic development

However, economic growth *does not guarantee that economic development will occur*. If an economy moves from point A to point C, for example, there is little if any increase in merit good provision. We will return to this point in Chapter 19.

Distinguishing between economically more developed and less developed countries

The World Bank[8] divides countries into four groups according to their level of GNI (GNP) *per capita*. These groups (based on 2008 GNI *per capita*) are:

- **Economically less developed countries:**
  - low income, with GNI per capita of US$975 or less
  - lower middle income, with GNI per capita of $976–$3855
  - upper middle income, with GNI per capita of $3856–$11905.
- **Economically more developed countries:**
  - high income, with GNI *per capita* of $11906 or more.

The 'World Bank country classification' chapter on the CD-ROM lists all the countries in these country groups. The first three groups (low, lower middle and upper middle income) comprise the **economically less developed countries**, while the high income economies are the **economically more developed countries**.

The less developed countries include most of the countries of Africa, Asia, Latin America and the Middle East, and parts of eastern Europe and the former Soviet Union. High income, or more developed economies, include the countries of North America, western Europe, Australia, Japan and New Zealand, as well as some eastern European and some oil-producing countries in the Middle East.

However, it must be stressed that *classifying countries by level of GNI (or any other output or income measure) does not accurately represent their level of development*. The World Bank points out that 'Classification by income does not necessarily reflect development status'. We will see in this chapter that a country's level of development varies widely depending upon what characteristic is used to measure development; whereas one country may be quite developed with respect to one characteristic, it may be less so with respect to another.

Further, it is important to note that classifying countries as developing or developed based on *per capita* GNI levels hides the lack of uniformity *within* countries. The United States, for example, one of the economically most advanced countries in the world, has pockets of poverty, with lack of access to basic services such as health care, low educational attainment, high unemployment and low income levels. Similarly, most less developed countries have pockets of great wealth concentrated in the hands of a small proportion of the population, with good access to health care, high levels of education, lower birth rates and higher life expectancy.

Common characteristics of developing countries

We will now consider some important characteristics that tend to be shared by developing countries. It is important to note that these *do not apply uniformly to all developing countries*. Different countries can be considered as more or less developed with respect to different characteristics, and we cannot arrive at

---

[8] The World Bank is an international financial institution that lends to developing countries to assist them in their development efforts; see page 516.

conclusions about levels of development without looking at each characteristic for each country individually.

Low levels of GDP/GNI *per capita*

This can be seen in Table 16.1 for selected countries, as well as in the 'World Bank country classification' chapter in the CD-ROM, which classifies countries as economically more or less developed according to GNI levels. By definition, according to the World Bank, economically less developed countries are those with GNI *per capita* levels below a certain level. However, as the CD-ROM table clearly indicates, within the three groups of economically less developed countries, there are huge differences in income levels.

High levels of poverty

We learned about poverty in Chapter 11. All countries in the world have poverty. However, almost all of extreme poverty (living on less than $1.25 per day) and most of moderate poverty (living on less than $2.00 per day) are concentrated in less developed countries. Yet as Table 11.6 (page 306) indicates, there are huge differences between countries in amounts of poverty, both in terms of absolute numbers and in terms of the proportion of a country's population that is poor. It is suggested that you refer also to pages 308–9 on the causes and consequences of poverty, as much of this material is relevant to poverty in developing countries.

Relatively large agricultural sector

In Chapter 3 (page 64) we learned that economically less developed economies have large agricultural sectors (and large primary sectors generally). Relatively low income elasticities of demand for agricultural products play a role in reducing the relative size of the agriculture sector as countries grow and develop, while agriculture increasingly becomes replaced by industry and services. The developed countries of today were in the same situation decades ago. Table 16.1 lists several countries in order of declining GNI *per capita* (in US$ PPP (purchasing power parity), and shows the contribution of agriculture to GDP. The lower the level of *per capita* GNI, the larger the contribution of the agricultural sector.

Large urban informal sector

A *formal sector* refers to the part of an economy that is registered and legally regulated; an *informal sector* by definition lies outside the formal economy, and refers

Country	GNI per capita (US$ PPP)	Agriculture, value added (% of GDP)
United States	46 730	1
United Kingdom	37 360	1
Greece	28 440	3
Portugal	22 870	2
Russia	18 390	5
Brazil	10 260	7
China	6770	10
India	3260	17
Vietnam	2850	22
Kyrgyzstan	2200	29
Kenya	1570	28
Uganda	1190	34

Table 16.1   GNI *per capita* (US$ PPP) and contribution of agriculture to GDP, 2009

Source: The World Bank, World Development Indicators (http://data.worldbank.org/indicator).

to economic activities that are unregistered and legally unregulated.

Informal sectors exist everywhere in the world, but are much more important in developing countries. The term **urban informal sector** was introduced in the early 1970s by the International Labour Organization (ILO)[9] to refer to the unregistered urban sector in developing countries, and the vast range of activities of a large and growing share of the urban population as a way of survival.

This range of activities includes everything from barbers, cobblers, carpenters, tricycle and pedicab drivers, garbage collectors and small shop owners and street vendors (selling an enormous variety of foods and snacks as well as clothing, detergents, soaps and almost every conceivable household item), to working in restaurants, hotels and sweatshops (manufacturing enterprises where workers are paid very low wages and work long hours under unhealthy conditions), in construction, in domestic household work, or in offices as temporary help.

The term 'informal sector' has a far broader and different meaning in developing countries compared with developed ones. In developing countries, it has to do with work that can make all the difference between physical survival and starvation for individuals and

---

[9] The International Labour Organization is an agency of the United Nations concerned with global labour issues.

their family. As the ILO stresses, informal sector activities in developing countries are not undertaken to avoid payment of taxes or bypass labour or other legislation as in developed countries. In developed countries, the informal sector includes unregistered work resulting in tax evasion, as well as corruption, crime, etc., which are illegal. These activities are not included in the ILO's definition of the informal sector in developing countries.

The informal sector is responsible for a large and rising share of urban employment. In developing countries, *one-half to three-quarters of total non-agricultural employment is in the informal sector*. Moreover, employment in the informal sector is growing more rapidly than employment in the formal sector, especially during times of economic recession. As firms in the formal sector cut back on employment, all those who lose their jobs are forced to seek work in the informal sector.

The large size and growth of the urban informal sector is due to several factors. One has to do with policy failures of the 1950s, 1960s and beyond, that focused on industrialisation and completely neglected the agricultural sector. If rural incomes and rural employment possibilities had increased, the massive departure of the rural poor towards urban areas might have been avoided. Secondly, it is related to rapid population growth (see below). Thirdly, cities still attract people from rural areas who are poor, landless and destitute, looking for work that will enable them to make a better living or simply to survive. However, employment opportunities in the urban formal sector are limited, and the formal sector demands skills that rural migrants lack.

The informal sector poses many problems: no worker protection; workers are vulnerable to exploitation; environmental dangers and health hazards in slums with no basic services like water sanitation and sewerage; no access to credit for workers; limited possibilities for education and training, and many more.

Even so, it is also seen as an opportunity for increased employment opportunities in countries that cannot create enough formal sector jobs. To take advantage of these opportunities, governments must adopt policies to assist the informal sector, such as access to credit to allow businesses to be set up or expanded; training and education for activities important in the informal sector; provision of necessary infrastructure (water, sanitation, etc.); and

improved access to health services and education. Such measures would promote the creation of new jobs and improved standards of living for informal sector workers.

High birth rates and population growth

The problem of high birth rates
Developing countries usually have higher birth rates, and this contributes to higher population growth rates. This can be seen in columns 5 and 6 in Table 16.2, which show that while the number of births per woman are falling everywhere, they tend to be higher in developing countries compared to developed ones. Higher birth rates correspond to higher population growth rates, shown in columns 7 and 8.

Columns 1 and 2 show total population figures. In 2010, nearly 85% of the world's population was living in developing countries (column 3), and due to higher birth rates in these countries the share of their population is expected to increase (column 4).

Column 9 shows the 'dependency ratio'; this refers to the percentage of economically dependent people, or people who must be supported by the working population. It includes children and elderly people, or those who cannot work to support themselves. In developed countries (OECD[10]), nearly half of the population (49.7%) is dependent on the working population. The table shows that most of the developing country groups have higher dependency ratios, the most striking group being sub-Saharan Africa, where nearly 85% of the population is dependent. Very high dependency ratios are the result of high population growth rates, resulting in a large proportion of children in the population.[11] A high dependency ratio means that the income of a family must be stretched to cover the needs of more family members. When the family income is low to begin with, as in most households in many developing countries, the income per person that results is often barely enough to cover basic needs.

The challenges of population growth
As of 2010, the world's population was approximately 6.9 billion, of which only 15.3% were living in more developed countries. It is expected that by 2030 the world's population will be 8.3 billion, and that this will stabilise before the end of the

---

[10] Organisation for Economic Co-operation and Development (OECD), an organisation consisting of 33 mostly economically more developed countries.

[11] By contrast, developed countries tend to have relatively more elderly people in their dependent populations. This is the result of relatively low population growth rates.

Country group	(1) Total population (millions) 2010	(2) Total population (millions) 2030*	(3) Developed or developing as % of world 2010	(4) Developed or developing as % of world 2030*	(5) Total fertility rate (births per woman) 1990–95	(6) Total fertility rate (births per woman) 2010–15*	(7) Average annual growth 1990–95	(8) Average annual growth 2010–15*	(9) Dependency ratio (per 100 people aged 15–64) 2010
Developed	**1056.0**	**1,129.6**	**15.3**	**13.6**					
OECD**	1026.3	1,093.3			1.7	1.6	0.7	0.4	49.7
Non-OECD	29.7	36.3			2.2	1.9	2.5	1.2	39.6
Developing	**5843.4**	**7169.0**	**84.7**	**86.4**					
Arab States	348.2	477.9			4.7	2.6	2.4	1.9	61.9
East Asia and the Pacific	1,974.3	2,204.3			2.3	2.8	1.3	0.8	42.5
Europe and Central Asia	410.3	416.4			2.1	1.6	0.3	0.2	43.5
Latin America and the Caribbean	582.7	683.6			3.0	2.2	1.7	1.0	53.2
South Asia	1,719.1	2,158.2			4.1	2.5	2.1	1.4	56.8
Sub-Saharan Africa	808.8	1,228.6			6.1	3.6	2.8	2.4	84.8
World	**6899.4**	**8298.6**	**100.0**	**100.0**					

Table 16.2   Demographic indicators by country group

* forecast

** OECD = Organisation for Economic Co-operation and Development, including a group of 33 mostly developed countries.

Source: United Nations Development Programme, *Human Development Report 2010.*

present century at about 9–10 billion (not shown in the table). However, due to higher birth rates in developing countries, most of the increase of 2–3 billion people over the current size of the population will be in developing countries. This places an enormous burden on the developing world in terms of abilities to absorb the growing numbers of people by creating employment opportunities, avoiding pressures on the environment, improving quality of health services, education, infrastructure and other services, and improving standards of living of the poor.

While there is no birth rate or population growth rate that is considered to be the 'right' one for any country, it is believed that high birth and population growth rates may slow down economic growth and development because:

- rapid population growth requires an even more rapid output and income growth in

order for *per capita* income and output to increase

- high population growth entails a high dependency burden, yet the more the dependent members of a family, the less income there is per person; very often a large family size pushes the family into poverty

- there are negative consequences for mothers whose health is adversely affected by frequent and numerous childbirths

- rapid population growth contributes to environmental degradation, which is borne more heavily by the poor (see page 124).

Low levels of health and education

Developing countries tend to have low levels of health as well as education. These two topics will be discussed on pages 454–57, when we study indicators of development, and will examine data on health and education indicators (Tables 16.6 and 16.7).

Low levels of productivity

Low levels of health and education, as well as a scarcity of capital goods and appropriate technology, translate into low levels of productivity of labour in developing countries, or lower levels of output produced per hour of work. As we know from Chapter 11, improvements in labour productivity are a key source of economic growth, and this in turn is made possible by increases in the quantities of physical capital, improvements in the quality of capital through the increased use of appropriate technology, and increases in human capital (investments in education and health).

Dual economies

A **dual economy** (or dualism) arises when there are two different and opposing sets of circumstances that exist simultaneously. Examples include:

- wealthy, highly educated people and poor, illiterate people
- a formal and informal urban sector
- a high-productivity industrial sector and a low-productivity traditional sector
- a low-productivity agricultural sector and a high-productivity, urban industrial sector
- a 'modern' commercial agricultural sector and a 'traditional'subsistence agricultural sector.

Various kinds of dualism often characterise less developed countries. One of the challenges of economic development is to eliminate every aspect of dualism and develop less polarised and more uniform economic and social structures.

The poverty cycle (trap)

♦ Explain that in some countries there may be communities caught in a poverty trap (poverty cycle) where poor communities are unable to invest in physical, human and natural capital due to low or no savings; poverty is therefore transmitted from generation to generation, and there is a need for intervention to break out of the cycle.

Poverty is caused by many factors, but one of the key causes of poverty in some situations can be poverty itself. When conditions of poverty feed on themselves and create more poverty, they give rise to the poverty cycle, also known as the poverty trap.

Understanding the poverty cycle

People who are very poor spend their entire incomes just on bare essentials (food and other essential items), and often even this is not enough for survival. The physical capital they have is very low, whether this is farm tools, roads, water supplies or sanitation systems. Their human capital is very low: they have little if any education, low levels of skills and poor levels of health. Their natural capital often becomes depleted as they destroy their natural environment in an effort to survive (depletion of minerals in the soils, cutting of forests, overfishing of lakes, rives and oceans, etc.). To come out of their state of poverty, they need more capital: physical, human and natural. The new capital can only be created by saving, which would enable them to make the necessary investments to increase their capital, but since all their income is spent on necessities, there is nothing left over to save; therefore, they cannot make investments in the capital they need. As a result, they are trapped in a situation where their poverty leads to more poverty, in a cycle. The poverty cycle is illustrated in Figure 16.2.

A **poverty cycle (poverty trap)** arises when low incomes result in low (or zero) savings, permitting only low (or zero) investments in physical, human and natural capital, and therefore low productivity of labour and of land. This gives rise to low, if any, growth in income (sometimes growth may be negative), and hence low incomes once again. A poverty cycle may occur in a family, a community, a part of an economy, or in an economy as a whole. An important feature of the poverty cycle is that poverty is transmitted from generation to generation.

How poverty is transmitted across generations

There are a number of ways that poverty is transmitted across generations:

- People who earn very low incomes usually have very low productivity because of their low skill levels or poor levels of health, as well as low levels of physical capital (such as agricultural equipment, irrigation, clean water supplies, sanitation).
- They often cannot afford to send their children to school, either because the children work to supplement the family income, or because the parents cannot afford transport costs to school or the school fees.

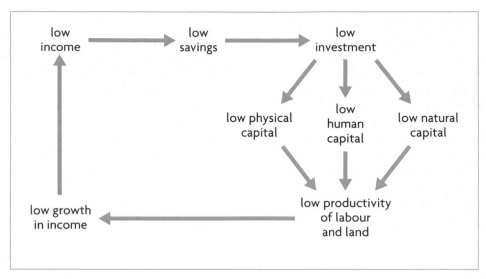

Figure 16.2 The poverty cycle (poverty trap)

They also cannot afford the necessary medical care for themselves or for their children, and sometimes cannot provide enough food for the family, leading to malnourished and physically disadvantaged children.

They often have large families, whether because they see children as a source of additional income (if the children work), or as a source of security in old age, or because they do not have access to family planning services. Large families increase the level of poverty, as the income of the parents must be stretched to cover the needs of more people.

In all these cases, the children are penalised for life, as they grow into adulthood lacking skills, often unable to realise their full health potential, and condemned to low productivity and low incomes.

Moreover, poor people who are unable to buy or invest in modern agricultural inputs (fertilisers, irrigation facilities, improved seeds) because their incomes are too low are forced to overuse their land, thus depleting the soil of essential nutrients, with the result that their children will be forced to work on soils of poorer quality that have lower yields (lower output per unit of land). Once again, poverty is transmitted to the next generation. Similar conclusions hold for any aspect of environmental degradation caused by the survival needs of poor people.

Since poor people cannot make investments because they do not have enough savings, it would help if they could borrow to finance the necessary investments in human, physical and natural capital, all of which would raise their productivity and increase their incomes. However, banks do not usually lend to poor people, who lack the necessary collateral. Therefore, the poor remain without access to the credit that could help raise them out of their poverty, and poverty is carried into the next generation.

Breaking out of the poverty cycle

Poor people and poor communities trapped in a poverty cycle cannot emerge from this on their own. They require the intervention of the government, which must undertake investments in human capital (health services, education, nutrition), physical capital in the form of infrastructure (sanitation, water supplies, roads, power supplies and irrigation), and natural capital (conservation and regulation of the environment to preserve environmental quality). Further, the government must take the necessary steps to ensure that poor people can participate in private sector activities, such as ensuring access to credit so that the poor can borrow to finance private investments. However, the public investments needed to break out of the poverty trap depend on the availability of government revenues. What if the country is so poor and overall savings so low that the government does not have the revenues required to undertake the necessary investments? Then an entire country is trapped in a poverty cycle. There are many countries in sub-Saharan Africa that are trapped in this way.

When an entire nation is trapped in a poverty cycle, it cannot make the necessary public investments on its own. Escape from the poverty cycle is then only possible if resources are provided through foreign aid. The role of foreign aid will be discussed in Chapter 18.

diverted to military or police activities. The 1984–85 famine in Ethiopia resulting in over 1 million deaths (with another 7 million people severely affected) was caused as much by political instability, internal war and violence as by drought. According to the World Bank, the most important cause of famine in developing countries is not poverty or low agricultural output, but military conflict.

There is a close relationship between political instability and levels of income: in general, low levels of income *per capita* are associated with higher levels of political instability. The causality (cause and effect) runs in both directions: political instability is a cause of low incomes because it gives rise to low economic growth for the reasons listed above; and low incomes are a cause of political instability because they lead to widespread dissatisfaction and frustration with economic conditions for which the government is held responsible, and therefore to politically destabilising activities.

International development goals

Millennium Development Goals

♦ Outline the current status of international development goals, including the Millennium Development Goals.

In September 2000, the United Nations hosted the largest meeting of world leaders ever to take place in history, at which 147 heads of state and government and 189 countries adopted the Millennium Declaration, a global statement of commitment to eliminating extreme poverty, hunger, disease and environmental damage, through development strategies based on the needs of the poor, human rights and sustainable development. What differentiates the Millennium Declaration from statements of earlier years is that it establishes specific goals known as the Millennium Development goals, as well as targets to be achieved within a period of 15 years, and specifies indicators to be used to monitor countries' progress towards achieving the goals and targets. The eight goals, 18 targets and some of the 48 indicators of the Declaration are listed in Table 16.3 on pages 450–51. (Indicators will be explained on page 449.)

As the table shows, there is one or more target corresponding to each goal, while there are several indicators that have been specified to monitor and measure the progress made in each country with respect to each target. For example, the second target of goal 1, to halve in the 25 years to 2015 the proportion of people suffering from hunger, is measured by two indicators: the proportion of underweight children under five years of age, and the proportion of the population whose dietary energy consumption is below the minimum.[14]

The Millennium Development Goals (with their corresponding targets and indicators) are very important tools used by international organisations and national governments in their fight against poverty and efforts to achieve economic development. They are used systematically to monitor and measure progress (or setbacks) that are achieved in each country with respect to each of the goals.

Test your understanding 16.2

1 (a) Explain some common characteristics of economically less developed countries.
(b) Explain why it is dangerous to generalise about how these characteristics apply to different countries (for examples, see Tables 16.6 and 16.7).

2 Use the concept of income elasticity of demand (page 47) to explain why the relative size of the agricultural sector shrinks as income increases.

3 In what ways does the informal sector in less developed countries differ from that of developed countries?

4 How can high birth rates work against economic growth and development?

5 (a) Using a diagram, explain the poverty cycle. (b) How is the poverty cycle transmitted from generation to generation? (c) Why is government intervention necessary to break out of this cycle?

6 Identify some of the factors causing diversity among less developed countries.

7 Use an AD-AS diagram to show how political instability works against economic growth.

8 (a) Explain the meaning of the Millennium Development Goals. (b) Using an example from Table 16.3, explain how goals are related to targets and indicators.

---

[14] The United Nations Development Programme's Human Development Reports, as well as indicators and other information, can be accessed through the UNDP's website (www.undp.org; http://hdr.undp.org/en/reports/; or http://hdr.undp.org/en/statistics/).

16.2 Measuring economic development

The complexities of measuring economic development

Economic development, being a complex and multidimensional process, is not accurately reflected in any single measure. Economists therefore consider individual economic attributes or characteristics that distinguish countries according to their level of economic or human development.

Individual attributes and characteristics are measured by use of *indicators*. An indicator is a measurable variable that indicates the state or level of something being measured. For example, GDP *per capita* is an indicator of the level of output per person. The number of years of life expectancy is an indicator of a population's state of health. The proportion of a population that can read and write (literacy) is an indicator of the level of education. All these are attributes of economic or human development.

The data comprising economic or human development indicators (such as GDP, or life expectancy, or literacy) are compiled by statistical services in every country over a period of years and are made available to international organisations such as the World Bank and United Nations agencies. Indicators are extremely useful for:

- monitoring how a country changes (develops) over time with respect to the attribute measured by the indicator
- making comparisons between countries with respect to the attribute
- assessing how well a country is performing with respect to particular goals or targets of development (for example, an increase in the literacy rate indicates an improvement in educational level)
- devising appropriate policy measures to deal with specific problems.

In addition to individual attributes and their indicators, economists also use *composite indicators*. A composite indicator is a summary measure of several dimensions or goals of development. We will consider both individual and composite indicators of development.

Individual and composite indictors, used in combination with *per capita* GDP (or GNI) statistics, though enormously useful as measures of different aspects of development, are also subject to limitations:

- Each indicator measures only one aspect of development. Since development is a multidimensional process, it is often necessary to combine the use of many indicators to obtain an overall picture of a country's level of development.
- Indicators are based on statistical information, and this poses a distinct set of problems:
  - Some countries have a limited capacity for collection of statistical data.
  - Data are not fully available in many countries.
  - Definitions of variables and methods used by statistical services vary from country to country, despite efforts by international organisations (such as the World Bank and United Nations agencies) to achieve standardisation.

These statistical problems mean that the indicators cannot always be precise and should be used as rough guides of trends over time or differences between countries, rather than as very precise measures.

Single indicators

There are many hundreds of indicators used as measures of different characteristics of an economy and of dimensions of development. We will consider some examples below.

Comparing and contrasting GDP *per capita* and GNI *per capita*

- Distinguish between GDP *per capita* figures and GNI *per capita* figures.
- Compare and contrast the GDP *per capita* figures and the GNI *per capita* figures for economically more developed countries and economically less developed countries.

GDP is an indicator of the value of output produced within a country, and GNI is an indicator of the income (or value of output) received by the residents of a country, usually within a year (see page 221). *Per capita* means that these values are calculated on a per person basis.

For some countries the difference in the sizes of GDP *per capita* and GNI *per capita* is not very large. This happens when inflows of income into a country are roughly balanced by income outflows, or if most of the production in a country is by factors of production owned by its residents. Otherwise, the difference can be quite significant. The factors of production that mainly account for differences are labour and capital.

When a country has many workers from other countries (labour) who send part of their wages back home, or foreign corporations (capital) that send their

Table 16.3   Millennium goals, targets and indicators

Goals	Targets	Indicators
1 Eradicate extreme poverty and hunger.	1 Halve, between 1990 and 2015, the proportion of people whose income is less than $1 a day.	1 Proportion of population below $1 (1993 PPP) per day. 2 Poverty gap ratio (the poverty gap is the amount of income required to raise everyone's income to at least $1 a day). 3 Share of poorest quintile (i.e. the poorest fifth) in total income.
	2 Halve, between 1990 and 2015, the proportion of people who suffer from hunger.	4 Prevalence of underweight children under five years of age. 5 Proportion of population below minimum level of dietary energy consumption.
2 Achieve universal primary education.	3 Ensure that by 2015 children everywhere will be able to complete primary schooling.	6 Net enrolment ratio in primary education. 7 Proportion of pupils starting grade 1 who reach grade 5. 8 Literacy rate, 15–24 years old.
3 Promote gender equality and empower women.	4 Eliminate gender disparity in primary and secondary education, preferably by 2005, and in all levels of education no later than 2015.	9 Ratio of girls to boys in primary, secondary and tertiary education. 10 Ratio of literate women to men, 15–14 years old. 11 Share of women in wage employment in the non-agricultural sector. 12 Proportion of seats held by women in national parliament.
4 Reduce child mortality.	5 Reduce by two-thirds, between 1990 and 2015, the under-five mortality rate.	13 Mortality rate of children under five. 14 Infant mortality rate. 15 Proportion of one-year-old children immunised against measles.
5 Improve maternal health.	6 Reduce by three-quarters, between 1990 and 2015, the maternal mortality ratio.	16 Maternal mortality ratio. 17 Proportion of births attended by skilled health personnel.
6 Combat HIV/AIDS, malaria and other diseases.	7 Have halted by 2015 and begun to reverse the spread of HIV/AIDS.	18 HIV prevalence among pregnant women. 19 Condom use rate or the contraceptive prevalence rate. 20 Ratio of school attendance of orphans to school attendance of non-orphans aged 10–14 years.
	8 Have halted by 2015 and begun to reverse the incidence of malaria and other major diseases.	21 Prevalence and death rates associated with malaria. 22 Proportion of population in malaria-risk areas using effective malaria prevention and treatment measures. 23 Prevalence and death rates associated with tuberculosis. 24 Proportion of tuberculosis cases detected and cured under internationally recommended TB control strategy.

(continued over)

Goals	Targets	Indicators
7 Ensure environmental sustainability.	9 Integrate the principles of sustainable development into country policies and programmes and reverse the loss of environmental resources.	25 Proportion of land area covered by forest. 26 Ratio of area protected to maintain biological diversity to surface area. 27 Energy use (kg oil equivalent) per $1000 GDP (PPP). 28 Carbon dioxide emissions *per capita* and consumption of ozone-depleting CFCs. 29 Proportion of population using solid fuels.
	10 Halve, by 2015, the proportion of people without sustainable access to safe drinking water and sanitation.	30 Proportion of population with sustainable access to an improved water source, urban and rural. 31 Proportion of population with access to improved sanitation, urban and rural.
	11 By 2020, to have achieved a significant improvement in the lives of at least 100 million slum dwellers.	32 Proportion of households with access to secure tenure.
8 Develop a global partnership for development.	12 Develop further an open, rule-based, predictable, non-discriminatory trading and financial system. 13 Address the special needs of the least developed countries. 14 Address the special needs of landlocked developing countries and small island developing states. 15 Deal comprehensively with the debt problems of developing countries through national and international measures in order to make debt sustainable in the long term.	For targets 12–15: 12 indicators including measures of development assistance, developed country imports from developing countries, tariffs imposed by developed countries on developing country agricultural exports, debt relief, debt service and others.
	16 In co-operation with developing countries, develop and implement strategies for decent and productive work for youth.	45 Unemployment rate of young people aged 15–24 years, male and female and total.
	17 In co-operation with pharmaceutical companies, provide access to affordable essential drugs on a sustainable basis.	46 Proportion of population with access to affordable essential drugs on a sustainable basis.
	18 In co-operation with the private sector, make available the benefits of new technologies, especially information and communications.	47 Telephone lines and cellular subscribers per 100 population. 48 Personal computers in use per 100 population and Internet users per 100 population.

Source: Data from United Nations Development Programme (www.undp.org).

Country	(1) GDP *per capita* (converted into US$ by use of exchange rates)	(2) GDP *per capita* (converted into US$ PPP)
Burundi	115	346*
Bangladesh	431	1241
Chad	658	1544*
Lesotho	798	1541
Pakistan	879	2496
India	1046	2753
Philippines	1639	3406
Indonesia	1918	3712
China	2432	5383
Colombia	4014	7764
Kazakhstan	6772	10 863
Russia	9079	14 690
Chile	9878	13 880
Hungary	13 766	18 755
Korea (Republic of)	20 014	24 801
Greece	27 955	28 517
New Zealand	32 086	27 336
Japan	34 313	33 632
Australia	39 066	34 923
Canada	40 329	35 812
United Kingdom	45 442	35 130
United States	45 592	45 592
Switzerland	56 207	40 658
Ireland	59 324	44 613

Table 16.5   GDP *per capita* using exchange rates and purchasing power parities, 2007

* According to the CIA Factbook.

Source: Data from United Nations Development Programme, *Human Development Report 2009* (available at http://hdr.undp.org/en/reports/)

Table 16.5, showing GDP *per capita* calculated both by use of standard exchange rates (column 1) and by use of purchasing power parities (column 2), reveals an interesting pattern: for the poorer countries starting at the top of the table, GDP figures based on PPPs are higher than those based on exchange rates; for the wealthier countries at the bottom of the table, GDP figures based on PPPs are lower than those based on exchange rates.

The reason for this is that prices of goods and services on average tend to be lower in countries with low *per capita* GDPs, and higher in countries with high *per capita* GDPs. To understand what this means, consider two countries that produce an identical quantity of output, but that have different prices for this output. When the value of output is calculated in terms of US$ using exchange rates, it appears lower in the lower price country than in the higher price country, even though the quantity of output is the same. This is exactly what happens in the real world. In column 1, the output of lower price countries at the top end of the table appears lower than the equivalent output of higher price countries at the bottom end. Column 2, using PPPs to convert GDP *per capita*, eliminates the impact on GDP of differing price levels, and as a result, the differences in *per capita* GDP between countries shrink enormously. Comparing Ireland with Burundi, we see that Ireland's GDP *per capita* based on exchange rates is 516 times greater than Burundi's; based on purchasing power parities, it is 129 times greater than Burundi's. The second comparison is a much better indicator of the differences in output produced in Burundi and Ireland.

In the case of the United States, the two figures are identical, since it is the purchasing power of the US$ within the United States that is used as the basis for the PPP conversions.

Everything that has been said here about comparisons of GDP *per capita* across countries applies equally to GNI *per capita* (or any other output or income measure).

Comparisons of GDP *per capita* (or GNI *per capita*) across countries require measures of *per capita* output or income based on conversions of national currencies into US$ by use of purchasing power parities (PPPs), to eliminate the influence of price differences on the value of output or income.

Purchasing power parity exchange rates are computed and published on a regular basis by several international bodies, including the Organisation for European Co-operation and Development (OECD), European Union, the World Bank and United Nations agencies.

Comparing and contrasting health indicators

◆ Compare and contrast two health indicators for economically more developed countries and economically less developed countries.

Health indicators measure characteristics of populations related to health. Three commonly used health indicators are life expectancy at birth, infant mortality and maternal mortality. Data for all three, together with GNI per capita (US$PPP), for selected countries are provided in Table 16.6. (We are using GNI *per capita* as this is a better indicator of living standards, and we are using values in US$ PPP to eliminate the influence of price-level differences across countries.)

Life expectancy at birth refers to the number of years one can expect to live, calculated as the average number of years of life in a population. It is one of the most commonly used indicators of development. *Infant mortality* refers to the number of infant deaths from the time of birth until the age of one, per 1000 live births. This is indicator 14 corresponding to goal 4 of the Millennium Development Goals (see page 450). *Maternal mortality* refers to the number of women who die per year as a result of pregnancy-related causes, per 100 000 live births. This is indicator 16 corresponding to goal 5 in the Millennium Development Goals.

Table 16.6 shows that higher levels of GDP *per capita* (US$ PPP) tend to be linked with higher life expectancies, and lower infant and maternal mortalities. This is what we would expect, since higher income countries have more resources to provide the necessary services and appropriate living conditions for their populations. However, there are very wide departures from this broad pattern, suggesting that *income per capita is not the only factor that determines health outcomes in a country.*

Among more developed countries, the United States stands out for its lower life expectancy and higher infant and maternal mortalities compared to other more developed countries.

Among less developed countries, we find some very surprising health outcomes. For example, Sri Lanka, with GNI *per capita* less than one-third of Russia's, surpasses Russia in life expectancy by six years. Moldova and Sri Lanka stand out for their low infant mortality compared to many countries with much higher incomes *per capita*. Moldova, especially, is striking for its very low maternal mortality. The table is full of such examples.

How is it possible that some countries have managed to achieve far better health outcomes than others with similar or even lower incomes *per capita*? The answer is that for any given level of income *per capita*, life expectancy is *higher*, and infant mortality and maternal mortality are *lower*, when there are:

- adequate public health services (such as immunisation, provision of health information and education), and prevention of communicable diseases (such as malaria, tuberculosis, HIV/AIDS)

- adequate health care services with broad access by the entire population
- a healthy environment, including safe drinking water, sewerage and sanitation, and low levels of pollution
- an adequate diet and avoidance of malnutrition
- a high level of education of the entire population
- absence of serious income inequalities and poverty.

Therefore, health outcomes depend a lot on how well countries achieve these objectives. For example:

- Health outcomes in the United States may be due to inequalities in income and education resulting in pockets of poverty, connected to poor housing and living conditions, poor nutrition and health, and insufficient access to medical care (due to lack of medical coverage). Such factors result in worse health outcomes among low-income groups, which lowers the average over the entire American population.
- Health outcomes in countries like Moldova and Sri Lanka (and many others) are due to government policies placing a high priority on public health and the provision of health care services for low-income groups, as well as on education.
- Health outcomes in sub-Saharan African countries are due to a very large extent to the disastrous impacts of HIV/AIDS, as well as problems with sanitation, safe drinking water, lack of education and information, poor public health and health care services, and premature deaths due to diseases that are both preventable and treatable (such as malaria).

The discussion of health indicators illustrates that:

- GNI *per capita* (or any other income or output measure) is an insufficient indicator of health outcomes.
- Limited resources, due to low GNI *per capita*, are not always the most important cause of poor health outcomes. Most (if not all) countries, both more and less developed, can do more with their available resources to meet economic development goals. They can reallocate resources towards provision of more social services and merit goods, improving the institutions through which these services are delivered, as well as reducing poverty.
- Some development issues apply not only to developing, but to developed countries as well, because of the presence of poverty in wealthy societies that make people on low incomes subject to similar deprivations as poor people in developing economies.

Country	GNI *per capita* (US$ PPP) 2008	Adult literacy rate (% of people aged 15 and above (2007 or 2008)	Primary school enrolment**** (% of children of official school age) (2007 or 2008)	Secondary school enrolment**** (% of children of official school age) (2007–8)
High-income countries				
Norway	58 810	100	98.4	96.6
United States	47 094	99**	91.5	88.2
Australia	38 692	99**	97.0	87.5
United Kingdom	35 087	99**	97.2	91.3
Finland	33 870	100*	96.3	96.8
Portugal	22 105	94.6	98.9	87.9
Middle- and low-income countries				
Uruguay	13 808	98.2	97.5	67.7
Chile	13 561	98.6	94.4	85.3
Turkey	13 359	88.7	93.9	71.2
Brazil	10 607	90.0	92.6	77.0
Azerbaijan	8747	99.5	96.0	98.3
Egypt	5470	66.4***	93.6	–
Swaziland	5132	86.5	82.8	28.6
Georgia	4902	99.7	98.7	80.8
Sri Lanka	4886	90.8	99.7	–
Morocco	4628	56.4	89.5	–
Bolivia	4357	90.7	97.4	69.9
Indonesia	3957	92.0***	94.8	69.7
Mongolia	3619	97.3	88.7	82.0
India	3337	62.8***	89.8	–
Moldova	3149	98.3	83.3	79.1
Pakistan	2678	54.7	66.1	32.5
Kyrgyzstan	2291	99.3	83.5	80.5
Cameroon	2197	75.9	88.3	–
Nigeria	2156	60.1	61.4	25.8
Tajikistan	2020	99.7	97.3	82.5
Cambodia	1868	77.0	88.6	34.1
Bangladesh	1587	55.0	88.0	41.5
Zambia	1359	70.7	95.2	49.0
Gambia, The	1358	45.3	68.7	41.8
Uganda	1224	74.6	97.1	19.2
Burundi	402	65.9	99.4	–

Table 16.7   Education indicators in relation to GNI *per capita* (US$ PPP)

* 2000 data

** 2003 data

*** 2006 data

**** Net enrolment ratios, defined as enrolled children of official school age as percentage of the population of the corresponding school age

Source: Adult literacy rates for Norway, United States, Canada, Australia, United Kingdom, Finland from CIA Factbooks; all other data from The World Bank, World Development Indicators; United Nations Development Programme, *Human Development Report 2010.*

the relative position of a variable in a list. This will become clearer below.

The Human Development Index

♦ Explain the measures that make up the Human Development Index (HDI).
♦ Compare and contrast the HDI figures for economically more developed countries and economically less developed countries.
♦ Explain why a country's GDP/GNI *per capita* global ranking may be lower, or higher, than its HDI global ranking.

The Human Development Index (HDI), the best-known and most widely used index of the UNDP, is a summary measure of human development. The HDI measures average achievement in three dimensions: a long and healthy life, access to knowledge and a decent standard of living. As of 2010, these three dimensions are measured by the following indicators:[15]

• a long and healthy life is measured by life expectancy at birth (see page 456 above)
• access to knowledge is measured by mean years of schooling and expected years of schooling
• a decent standard of living is measured by GNI *per capita* (US$ PPP).

Each dimension is expressed as a value between 0 and 1, with 0 being the lowest possible value for the dimension, and 1 being the highest.

The composite index is the average over the three dimensions. Each country receives an HDI value from 0 to 1, and the countries are ranked according to their HDI values.

HDI ranks and HDIs (i.e. HDI values) for selected countries, together with their corresponding GNI *per capita* (in US$ PPP), appear in Table 16.8, where countries are listed in order of declining HDIs. Countries have been selected to show how it is possible to achieve similar levels of human development with very different levels of GNI *per capita*.

For example, Norway and Australia have similar HDIs, indicating that they have attained approximately the same level of human development, yet Australia has accomplished this with a lower GNI *per capita*. The same can be said for Singapore and the Czech Republic, Kuwait and Latvia, etc. The most striking pair of countries is Tajikistan and South Africa. Tajikistan's GNI *per capita* is roughly one-fifth of South

Country	HDI rank 2010	Human Development Index (HDI) 2010	GNI *per capita* (US$ PPP) 2008
Norway	1	0.938	58 810
Australia	2	0.937	38 692
Singapore	27	0.846	48 893
Czech Republic	28	0.846	32 678
Kuwait	47	0.771	55 719
Latvia	48	0.769	12 944
Albania	64	0.719	7,976
Russian Federation	65	0.719	10 845
Brazil	73	0.699	10 607
Georgia	74	0.698	4,902
Moldova	99	0.623	3,149
Egypt	101	0.620	5,889
South Africa	110	0.597	9,812
Tajikistan	112	0.580	2,020
Malawi	153	0.385	911
Sudan	154	0.379	2,051

Table 16.8   Human Development Index and GNI *per capita* (US$ PPP) for selected countries

Source: United Nations Development Programme, *Human Development Report 2010* (http://hdr.undp.org/en/reports/).

Africa's, and yet their HDIs are very close. We can conclude that *Tajikistan, with about one-fifth the income per person of South Africa, has slightly surpassed South Africa's level of human development.*

Comparisons between HDIs and GNI *per capita* confirm the points made earlier (page 455):

• GNI (or GDP) *per capita* used alone can be a poor measure of the different dimensions of development.

• Many countries, even with their given levels of GNI *per capita*, are capable of making significant improvements in the well-being of their populations by making different choices regarding the resources allocated to health, education and other services or merit goods.

• Economic and human development issues apply not only to developing countries, but to developed countries as well.

---

[15] As of 2010, the UNDP changed some of the indicators used to measure human development. In the dimension of education, 'mean years of schooling' has replaced literacy, and 'expected years of schooling' has replaced gross enrolment. In the dimension of standard of living, GNI per

capita (US$ PPP) has replaced GDP per capita (US$ PPP), as GNI per capita is a better indicator of income received by residents of a country on average, than GDP per capita. It should be noted that the UNDP has also made changes in its other human development indicators, briefly noted below.

The HDI is very useful as a tool for governments wishing to devise policies focusing on economic and human development, and *it is far superior to single indicators as a measure of development.* However, the HDI, too, has its shortcomings. This is because economic and human development are much broader concepts with more dimensions than are reflected in the HDI. The HDI does not provide us with information about income distribution, malnutrition, demographic trends, unemployment, gender inequalities, political participation, etc.

Other composite indicators (supplementary material)

Inequality-adjusted Human Development Index

The Inequality-adjusted Human Development Index (IHDI) measures human development in the same three dimensions as the HDI adjusted for inequality in each dimension. The IHDI attempts to measure losses in human development that arise from inequality.

Gender Inequality Index

The Gender Inequality Index (GII) measures inequalities between the genders in three dimensions: reproductive health, empowerment and in the labour market. It measures the loss in human development of women due to inequalities in these areas.

Multidimensional Poverty Index

The Multidimensional Poverty Index (MPI) measures multiple deprivations in the areas of health, education and standard of living. It is a measure of human poverty, to be contrasted with income poverty, occurring when income falls below a nationally or internationally determined level (see page 438 for an explanation of this distinction).

Test your understanding 16.3

1 **(a)** Explain why it is easier to measure economic growth than to measure economic development. **(b)** What are some of the difficulties involved in measuring economic development? **(c)** How do economists measure economic development?

2 What is the difference between individual and composite indicators? Provide some examples of each.

3 **(a)** Explain the difference between GDP *per capita* and GNI *per capita*. **(b)** What factors account for differences between the two measures? **(c)** Explain which of the two is likely to be a better indicator of a country's standard of living, and the level of output produced per person.

4 **(a)** What are purchasing power parities? **(b)** Why are they important for making valid comparisons of GDP or GNI across countries?

5 **(a)** Using Table 16.6, explain some differences in health outcomes between more and less developed countries. **(b)** Provide examples of countries that have achieved good health outcomes relative to their level of income. **(c)** Provide examples of countries that could likely achieve better outcomes, even with their given level of income. **(d)** Use a *PPC* diagram to illustrate your answers.

6 Answer all the parts of question 5 using Table 16.7, referring to education outcomes.

7 **(a)** What are composite indicators? **(b)** Explain the three dimensions of development measured by the Human Development (HDI). **(c)** What are the advantages of using the Human Development Index over GDP or GNI *per capita* as a measure of economic and human development?

8 **(a)** How do the HDI rank and HDI value differ between more and less developed countries? **(b)** What does it mean if a country's GNI *per capita* rank is (i) higher than its HDI rank, and (ii) lower than its HDI rank?

9 Use examples of individual or composite indicators (you may use the tables in the text) to illustrate the following points:

(a) GNI *per capita* is sometimes a poor indicator of levels of economic and human development.

(b) Many countries around the world can do more to promote the well-being of their populations through a reallocation of resources, even in the absence of economic growth.

(c) Some economic development issues apply to more developed countries as well as less developed countries.

(d) Countries may be more developed with respect to some indicators and less developed with respect to other indicators.

The World Bank's development diamond

The World Bank has developed an alternative method, the 'development diamond', to make cross country comparisons involving more than one development indicator. A development diamond, shown in both parts of Figure 16.3, is a polygon illustrating development in four dimensions, each represented by an indicator measured in one of the four corners of the polygon (i.e. on one of the four axes shown). The shaded polygon is a 'reference diamond', representing the average value of indicators for a country's specific income group (low, lower middle, upper middle, high income; see page 440 for an explanation of the World Bank's income categories). The black lines (solid and broken) show a particular country's indicators in relation to the reference diamond. *A point outside the reference diamond shows that a country is performing better than the group's average, while a point inside the reference diamond shows below-average performance.* By plotting indicators for more than one country, it is possible to compare the performance of two countries with each other.

Figure 16.3(a) shows the reference diamond for the income group of 'lower middle income countries', and the development diamonds for India and Tajikistan, both of which belong to that income group. The broken line, representing India's diamond, shows that India has a higher GNI per capita ($ PPP) than the average of its income group, and has below-average performance in access to improved sanitation, maternal mortality, and prevalence of child malnutrition. The solid line, showing Tajikistan's diamond, indicates that Tajikistan's GNI per capita ($ PPP) is slightly lower than the average of its income group, but Tajikistan has higher than average performance in the other three indicators. It is also possible to compare India and Tajikistan with each other.

In Figure 16.3(b), the reference diamond represents averages for countries in the 'low income' group. The two countries shown in relation to the reference diamond were selected because their GNI *per capita* ($ PPP) figures (not shown in the diamonds) are very close to each other; both are somewhat above the average of their income group. In addition, the two countries have very close human development ranks and indices; these appear in Table 16.9.

Figure 16.3(b) shows that Bangladesh has performed better than Ghana and better than the average for its income group in reducing child (under-five) mortality; it has also performed better than Ghana in providing access to improved sanitation, though it is lagging a little behind the average of its income group. Ghana, on the other hand, has performed better than Bangladesh and better than the average for its income group in reducing child malnutrition, and has also performed better than Bangladesh in achieving adult literacy; it is doing slightly better than its income group with respect to this goal.

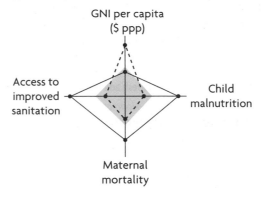

(a) Development diamonds for India and Tajikistan

- - - India

—— Tajikistan

Shaded polygon is the average for lower middle income countries

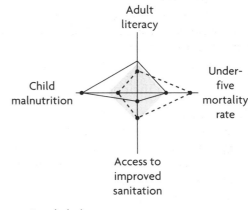

(b) Development diamonds for Bangladesh and Ghana

- - - Bangladesh

—— Ghana

Shaded polygon is the average for low income countries

Figure 16.3 Development diamonds[16]

Source: The World Bank, *World Development Report, 2010.*

[16] In the case of several variables appearing in the diagrams (child malnutrition, maternal mortality and under-five mortality), the lower the value, the better off is the country. The values of such variables for the reference diamond have been calculated by taking the average value for the income group and dividing by the value of the variable for the country.

(continued over)

substitute for other, complementary government policies needed to combat poverty. The alleviation of poverty cannot be achieved by reliance on micro-credit schemes alone. Instead such schemes should complement other anti-poverty policies that are the responsibility of the public sector. For example, government has a role to play in the provision of merit goods, including education, health care services and infrastructure. Poor people should not have to borrow to be able to pay for health care and education, and no amount of borrowing by poor people will produce the needed investments in infrastructure (sanitation, clean water supplies, transport, etc.). Similarly, government must provide protection for people who are disabled, physically or mentally ill, displaced (due to war or other conflict) or in other vulnerable groups, as these people are not appropriate clients for micro-credit.

- **Micro-credit schemes contribute to the growth of the informal sector.** The micro-enterprises that are created through micro-credit operate for the most part in the informal sector, which is unregulated by the government, where workers have no social protection, and where exploitative conditions often prevail (see page 441). Micro-credit encourages the growth of this controversial sector.

- **Some extremely poor and highly unskilled people may be harmed by micro-credit.** The poorest of the poor usually lack skills of all kinds, including skills necessary to begin a micro-enterprise; for example, same basic literacy and numeracy skills increase the likelihood that the micro-enterprise will do well. In such cases, micro-credit is less likely to result in the establishment of a successful micro-enterprise, and may end up burdening some extremely poor people with payments on loans that have not produced a stable source of income. In view of this risk, some micro-credit schemes try to integrate credit with the provision of education so that borrowers will acquire the skills required to use their loans effectively, as well as health care and other community development programmes.

- **Interest rates in micro-credit schemes are too high.** Interest rates in micro-credit schemes tend to be higher than market rates of interest on commercial bank loans (although they are much lower than in informal credit markets, such as moneylenders). The costs of providing very many, very small loans are higher than the costs of providing fewer large loans. High interest rates are necessary if MFIs are to be able to cover the costs of providing micro-credit. Some economists argue that the high interest rates should be subsidised to make repayment easier for very poor people. Yet donor funds are neither sufficient, nor reliable enough, to be able to cover interest rate subsidies and at the same time allow micro-credit schemes to keep on growing. A compromise would involve creating programmes that offer subsidised interest rates only for the poorest borrowers.

Micro-credit schemes alone, in the absence of other anti-poverty measures (including provision of education, health care and infrastructure), will not solve the problem of poverty and enable the poor to escape the poverty cycle. However, they are one very important measure among others that can help poor people participate in the process of growth and development.

> ### Test your understanding 17.2
>
> 1 Explain the importance of access to credit in economic growth and development.
>
> 2 **(a)** Define micro-credit schemes, and discuss their objectives. **(b)** What are some advantages and disadvantages of micro-credit?
>
> 3 Use an *AD-AS* diagram to show the effects of an increase in credit leading to an increase in consumption and investment spending.

The empowerment of women

- d. The empowerment of women

The problem of gender inequalities

Many development countries face serious gender inequalities, or inequalities between women and men, and girls and boys. These relate to control of resources and access to opportunities, and are the result of discrimination against girls and women, with profound consequences for growth and development.[8]

---

[8] There are many factors explaining this attitude towards women and girls. For example, whereas boys are often looked upon as a source of income and old-age security for the parents, girls in many societies are an economic burden, as they must receive a dowry in marriage only to move away and join the husband's household and family. Therefore, when family resources are scarce, boys are often given priority over girls. Moreover, in patriarchal societies, men exercise control and authority over women and the family, women's role is in the home, with participation in the labour market occurring not by choice but by necessity (if the husband's income is not enough to support the family).

Gender inequalities result in serious deprivations and limited access of women and girls to social, economic and political opportunities compared with men and boys. Eliminating the deprivations and creating conditions of equality of opportunities is called **empowerment**. The empowerment of women is very important in economic development, because not only does it improve the well-being of girls and women affected, but it also gives rise to major external benefits that spill over into other areas influencing growth and development.

Consequences of gender inequality: deprivations faced by women and girls

Gender inequalities in health: the problem of 'missing women'

Women and girls face higher mortality (death) rates in many developing countries compared with men and boys. These result in lower numbers of women in a population. Whereas the ratio of women to men in France, the United Kingdom and the United States is greater than 1.05, in some less developed countries it is much lower: 0.95 in Egypt, 0.94 in Bangladesh, China and West Asia, 0.93 in India and 0.90 in Pakistan. (A ratio of women to men of 1.05 means that there are 105 women for every 100 men. The main reason for this is biological: women have higher survival rates than men. A ratio of 0.90 means that there are 90 women for every 100 men.) Based on these figures, it is easy to calculate how many more women these countries should have had if they had had the same ratio of women to men as in developed countries. The shortfall in the number of women is known as the problem of 'missing women', i.e. they are 'missing' due to unnecessary deaths. It is estimated that there are more than 50 million women missing in China alone, and many more than 100 million missing in Asia and North Africa.[9]

The main reason behind the phenomenon of 'missing women' lies in the neglect of girls during infancy and childhood with respect to their health and nutrition. When incomes are low and necessities like food and health care are scarce, boys are more likely to receive adequate amounts of food and the health care they require. Deprivations in necessary nutrition and health care make girls more likely to die than boys.

Gender inequalities in education and training

As in the case of nutrition and health care, girls do not always have the same opportunities as boys to receive an education, particularly in low-income families where resources are insufficient to educate all children equally. Moreover, cultural factors further dictate that a girl's education is not as important as a boy's, since girls are often not intended to seek work in the labour market on reaching adulthood. In some societies, educated girls are less marriageable.

Table 17.1 provides data on three indicators showing gender inequalities in education: adult literacy, school life expectancy (number of years of schooling expected) and ratio of girls to boys at primary and secondary levels. With the exception of the Philippines, in all the countries shown, adult female literacy is lower than adult male literacy. The data on school life expectancy, as well as the ratio of girls to boys in school, indicate that in some countries girls receive fewer years of schooling than boys. In general, countries where girls tend to be most disadvantaged with respect to education tend to be more concentrated in the Middle East and Africa.

There are also exceptions. In the Philippines, Mexico and Iran, there are more girls than boys in school at the primary and secondary levels; in Iran, girls are also expected to stay in school longer than boys. Moreover, the data show that over time, the gender disparities in literacy will diminish: the girls who are in school today will become part of the literate population in the future. Yet in spite of improvements, in many countries gender equality in education will not be realised in the foreseeable future.

Gender inequalities in the labour market

Lower levels of education and skills place women at a great disadvantage relative to men, as they do not have qualifications to take on jobs requiring skills. Even if a woman has the same level of skills as a man, discrimination prevents her from securing a high-level job. Women are more likely to work in the informal sector, which means that, apart from receiving lower incomes, they cannot receive the benefits offered to workers in the formal sector (job security, legal protection of workers' rights, pensions, etc.) and are subject to the exploitation that often accompanies work in an unregulated labour market. Further, women are far more likely than men to have unpaid responsibilities (child-rearing, household chores, and subsistence farming, i.e. cultivating food for the family, not for sale in the market, which is usually performed by women).

---

[9] Amartya Sen (1999) *Development as Freedom*, Oxford University Press.

Country	Female adult literacy (% of adult women who are literate)	Male adult literacy (% of adult men who are literate)	School life expectancy (years) girls	School life expectancy (years) boys	Ratio of girls to boys in primary and secondary education
Philippines	92.7	92.5	12	12	102
Mexico	85.3	86.9	14	14	102
Indonesia	86.8	94.0	13	13	98
Peru	89.4	96.4	14	13	99
Turkey	79.6	95.3	11	12	93
Iran	70.4	83.5	15	13	116
Nigeria	60.6	75.7	8	10	85
Malawi	49.8	76.1	9	9	99
India	47.8	73.4	10	11	92
Morocco	39.6	65.7	9	11	88
Pakistan	36.0	63.0	6	8	80
Senegal	29.2	51.1	7	8	96
Benin	23.3	47.9	6	10	73
Niger	15.1	42.9	4	5	74

Table 17.1   Gender inequalities in education

Source: The World Bank, World Development Indicators; CIA World Factbooks, 2010 (most recent data available).

Gender inequalities in inheritance rights and property rights

In many less developed countries inheritance rights and property rights are passed mainly to men. Whereas many countries have passed laws ensuring equality between the sexes in inheritance rights, these laws are often not enforced. The same countries usually also restrict the rights of women to own property. Land is overwhelmingly owned by men, even in societies where agricultural work is mainly the responsibility of women.

Gender inequalities in access to credit

Women face serious restrictions in obtaining credit. Over and above the problem of discrimination, lack of property rights means that women have little if anything they can use as collateral. Moreover, their low earning power makes them far less attractive candidates to receive credit from the point of view of credit institutions (banks).

Gender inequalities in income, wealth and poverty

A number of factors combine to ensure that women's incomes are on average substantially lower than men's: lower levels of education and skills, discrimination against women in the labour market so that women are paid less for the same work, and the preponderance of women's work in the informal sector. Moreover, lack of inheritance and property rights of women ensure that most wealth (such as land and other assets) is concentrated in the hands of men.

These factors contribute to making women among the poorest parts of the population in many developing countries. Poverty among women is particularly pronounced when women are heads of households (i.e. there is no man in the household earning an income); because of their very low earning potential, female-headed households are located in the poorest regions, with limited or no access to sanitation, clean water, health services, etc.

Positive externalities (external benefits) of women's empowerment

For many years, economic development and poverty alleviation efforts made no distinctions between the sexes with regard to their possible implications for growth and development. Since the 1980s and 1990s, development economists have realised that women's empowerment has enormous effects on growth and development, extending beyond the women themselves. These external benefits can be thought of as consumption externalities of women's health and education, analysed as standard health and education externalities.

The most important external benefits include the following:

- **Improvements in child health and nutrition and lower child mortality.** Increased education of women has major positive effects on the health of children, because improved knowledge about health, health services, basic hygiene and nutrition improve childrens' levels of health and reduce child mortality. Increased education of men leads to a smaller improvement in children's health. Also, increases in women's income levels have a greater positive effect on their children's health than increases in men's incomes.[10]

- **Improvements in educational attainment of children.** Mothers have a major influence over the education of their children, and studies show that the more educated the mother, the more educated the children. As in the case of health, increases in men's education have a smaller impact on their children's education. Further, increases in women's incomes also have a greater impact on their children's education than increases in the incomes of men.

- **Quality of human resources.** The impacts of increased education and incomes of women on levels of health and education of their children have enormous cumulative effects on the quality of human resources in a country that extend over many years, with the potential to affect profoundly the course of economic growth and development, as well as human development. Development policies that focus on improving the education of women also have a major potential to help poor families and communities break out of the poverty cycle in which they may be trapped.

- **Lower fertility (lower birth rates).** Increased education of women, more and better work outside the home, and higher incomes lead to having fewer children, because of later marriage and greater reproductive choice, and therefore lower population growth, with all its related benefits (see page 442).

The Nobel Prize-winning Indian economist Amartya Sen views women as 'active agents of change'. Sen writes that the role of women 'is one of the more neglected areas of development studies, and one that is most urgently in need of correction.' Nothing today in the political economy of development is as important 'as an adequate recognition of political, economic and social participation and leadership of women.'[11] Reflecting this idea, the UNDP has developed a composite indicator, the Gender Inequality Index (GII), measuring gender differences in various dimensions (see Chapter 16, page 460).

Income distribution

♦ e. Income distribution

Income distribution and economic growth

Economists have been debating the relationship between economic growth and income distribution over many decades. They used to believe that in the early years of growth, high income inequality is necessary. One reason given was that government spending to alleviate poverty and improve income distribution (such as through spending on merit goods) would take scarce resources away from investments in industrial production, thus reducing growth. Another argument was based on the belief that the rich save more than the poor, resulting in more investment, more physical capital and hence more growth. Therefore, with a more equal income distribution, savings would drop, investments would be lower, and growth would be reduced.

Today, economists argue that the opposite is the case: highly unequal distributions of income are actually *a barrier to growth and development. Not only is high income inequality not necessary, but greater equality in income distribution may lead to more rapid growth and more development.* The reasons are as follows:

- High income inequality may lead to lower overall savings because the groups with the highest savings rates are the middle classes and not the most wealthy. Higher income groups often buy expensive luxury goods to display their income and wealth,

---

[10] One explanation is that women, who tend to be more concerned about their children's well-being, have limited, if any, control over how the husband's income is spent; men, on the other hand, are more likely to spend increases in their income on activities outside the home, including purchases reflecting social status.

[11] Amartya Sen (1999) *Development as Freedom*, Oxford University Press, p. 203. We first encountered Amartya Sen in Chapter 7, Section 7.2, in connection with his contribution to the concept of 'human development'.

resulting in reduced savings. Also, savings of higher income groups often leave the country as financial investments abroad, thus reducing resources available for domestic investments.

- Government spending on merit goods (education, health care, sanitation, etc.) can improve income distribution by increasing the income-earning potential of the poor, but also leads to greater economic growth and development by increasing human capital.

- Highly unequal income distributions mean that the poor are unable to obtain credit, as they have no collateral, meaning fewer investments for people on lower incomes, leading to lower growth and development. Also, opportunities to pay for education and health care through borrowing are reduced, leading to lower human capital and lower growth and development.

- An improved income distribution increases the demand for locally produced goods and services,

thus encouraging local production and promoting local employment and investment. With high income inequalities, these potential benefits are lost.

- The concentration of income and wealth in a few hands results in significant political control and the ability of powerful groups to influence government policies for their own benefit, even though these policies may go against growth and development objectives favouring the interests of the whole population.

- A more equal distribution of income leads to greater political stability; highly unequal distributions can lead to social dissatisfaction, unrest and political instability, resulting in lower growth.

Note that the first three factors listed above are related to the topic of equity versus efficiency (see page 15), and provide examples where greater equity is linked with greater efficiency in the allocation of resources, leading to greater economic growth.

Indigenous peoples and inequality in human development

Important inequalities working against growth and development involve not only income inequalities but also inequalities in human development. The UNDP's *Human Development Report 2010* notes the following about human development inequalities among indigenous groups:

'An estimated 300 million indigenous peoples from more than 5000 groups live in more than 70 countries. Some two-thirds reside in China. Indigenous peoples often face structural disadvantages and have worse human development outcomes in key respects. For example, recent Mexican government analyses show that while extreme ... poverty is 10.5 percent nationally, it exceeds 39 percent among indigenous Mexicans.

When the Human Development Index (HDI) is calculated for aboriginal and non-aboriginal people in Australia, Canada, New Zealand and the United States, there is a constant gap of 5–18 percent. Indigenous peoples in these countries have lower life expectancy, poorer education outcomes and

smaller incomes. In India 92 percent of people of Scheduled Tribes live in rural areas, 47 percent of them in poverty. In Chhattisgarh, with a sizable share of Scheduled Tribes, the statewide literacy rate is 64 percent – but that of tribal peoples is only 22 percent.

Some evidence suggests that a schooling gap between indigenous and nonindigenous peoples remains. In China, India and Lao PDR geography, climate and discrimination based on ethnicity make it difficult to deliver basic infrastructure to remote areas, where many indigenous peoples and ethnic minorities live.

Work in Latin America and the Caribbean exploring access to land and discrimination shows that a focus on broad-based growth can benefit indigenous peoples but is unlikely to be enough to close the gap. More targeted strategies are needed, as proposed by indigenous peoples and as informed by their views and priorities.'

Source: United Nations Development Programme, *Human Development Report 2010*.

Applying your skills

Based on information in the extract, explain why human development inequalities are a global problem, affecting economically more developed as well as economically less developed countries.

For example, the Asian economies that have grown very rapidly, known as the 'Asian Tigers' (Taiwan, South Korea, Singapore, Malaysia, and others; see page 484) have more equal income distributions than countries in Latin America and Africa, which have been growing far less rapidly. The Asian Tigers placed a very strong emphasis on the development of human capital, with positive effects on the equality of income distribution and very successful growth and development outcomes.

Infrastructure

The importance of infrastructure

Infrastructure includes public utilities (including power, telecommunications, piped water supplies, sanitation and sewerage, etc.), roads, dam and canal works for irrigation and drainage, urban transport, ports and airports.

Infrastructure is a type of physical capital, and therefore results from investments. It plays a major role in most economies, representing about 20% of total investments in developing countries. The availability of infrastructure, and broad access to the services it offers make major contributions to economic growth, economic development and poverty alleviation.

Infrastructure provision in developing countries (as well as in developed ones) is mostly a government responsibility. Government's role is the result of a long historical process justified by infrastructure's great political, economic and strategic importance, concerns about monopoly power if it were in private hands, and interest in providing essential services to the overall population of a country. Note that many types of infrastructure qualify as public goods or as merit goods, i.e. goods with positive externalities in consumption.

Infrastructure and economic growth and development

Infrastructure increases productivity and lowers costs of production. Good road and railway systems save time and effort in transporting goods and services, thereby allowing more output to be transported and production costs to be lowered. The availability of effective telecommunications permits faster and easier communications, enabling economic activities to be carried out more efficiently. Irrigation contributes to higher yields (output per unit of land) and expansion of agricultural output.

The availability of infrastructure also facilitates modernisation and diversification of the economy. The growth of electronic communication and data exchange has contributed to more efficient practices and expansion of manufacturing, financial services and government economic activities. The availability of power (electricity) allows for increases in worker productivity through the introduction of simple electrically powered machines and equipment. Safe water sources, sanitation and sewerage permit countries to diversify into the production of processed foods. The quantity and quality of infrastructure are important for a country's international competitiveness, because they determine shipping costs. Lack of transport infrastructure increases costs of transporting goods, thereby damaging the country's ability to compete in international markets. The availability of good quality infrastructure also attracts foreign direct investment.

Infrastructure provides services that are essential for maintaining a basic standard of living. Safe water supplies, sanitation and sewerage systems have major effects on levels of health of a population, contributing to the reduction of avoidable illnesses and premature deaths.

Transport services also affect health and education by bringing people in remote rural areas closer to educational and health facilities. Transport increases employment opportunities by allowing the movement of people across longer distances, thus increasing incomes and contributing to the alleviation of poverty. It also facilitates access to markets, reducing the time and costs of transporting goods. The availability of transport can be crucially important to integrating people in remote and isolated rural areas into the market economy.

Availability of water supplies, along with infrastructure supplying energy (electricity and gas), have major impacts on gender equity. When these services are not available, women and girls are forced to spend a large proportion of their time carrying water and fuel-wood; in some African countries these activities take as much as two-thirds of women's household time. The availability of piped water supplies, and electricity and gas, by freeing time, increases school enrolment among girls. In the case of women, the availability of these services leads to increased employment outside the home, and reduced fertility (fewer children in the family) and hence reduced poverty.

In addition, the availability of safe energy sources (electricity and gas) results in less indoor air pollution (arising from the burning of polluting fuels for cooking and light), with strong positive effects on the health of women and children, who spend more time indoors. The introduction of irrigation over large areas, by increasing yields (output per unit of land) similarly increases incomes and contributes to raising people out of poverty. Construction and maintenance of infrastructure contributes to creating employment opportunities for the people who work to construct and maintain the facilities, thus also increasing incomes. The employment-creating effects are especially strong in the case of labour-intensive methods used to build roads.

Yet most developing countries perform poorly in infrastructure development and provision. For example, of the 6.1 billion of people in the world today, 1.1 billion do not have access to a clean water supply; 2.6 billion lack adequate sanitation; 3 billion have no access to modern energy sources for cooking and heating; more than 1 billion in rural areas lack access to reliable transportation; and nearly half of the world's population have no access to a telephone.[12] The reasons for this poor performance can be summarised under the following headings:

- **Problems of financing.** Governments charge users for their consumption of infrastructure services (for example, charges for connection to piped water and sewerage, water use, telephone charges, etc.). However, in developing countries, as part of government social policy intended to make services affordable, the prices charged for infrastructure services have been kept below cost, resulting in insufficient revenue for the state enterprises providing infrastructure.

- **Inadequate maintenance and poor quality.** Lack of revenues means that infrastructure facilities are often poorly maintained, resulting in low quality and unreliable services.

- **Limited access by the poor.** Lack of revenue also means constraints in quantity of infrastructure facilities that can be constructed, so that in many countries it has not been possible to provide services for the entire population. It is generally the poor who tend to suffer disproportionately from lack of access, both in rural areas and in urban slums.

- **Misallocation of resources.** The infrastructure provided is sometimes inappropriate given the needs of the population and the country's level of economic development; investments may be made in infrastructure facilities that remain underused because there is not enough demand for their services (such as power, telecommunications, ports), while other services (such as more roads, or better maintenance and improvements in service quality) are neglected.

- **Neglect of the environment.** Infrastructure can have numerous negative environmental effects, including the failure to adequately control unnecessary emissions, wasteful consumption of water in poorly designed or poorly maintained irrigation facilities, building roads and dams in ecologically vulnerable areas, and others.

Test your understanding 17.3

1 What are some of the more important areas of gender inequalities?

2 **(a)** What are some external benefits of women's empowerment? **(b)** Use an externality diagram to show how positive consumption externalities of education and health care for women are a type of market failure. **(c)** What can government do to correct this market failure?

3 **(a)** Explain some ways that infrastructure contributes to growth and development. **(b)** Use *PPC* and *AD-AS* diagrams to show the effects of investment in infrastructure on economic growth. **(c)** Use an externality diagram to show how positive consumption externalities in infrastructure are a type of market failure.

---

[12] The World Bank, 'FAQs: Infrastructure', 2007 (www.worldbank.org).

UN resolution recognises water as a right

On 28 July 2010, the United Nations General Assembly passed a resolution recognising access to clean water and sanitation as a fundamental human right. The resolution states that 'the right to safe and clean drinking water and sanitation [is] a human right that is essential for the full enjoyment of life and all human rights'. It urges governments and international organisations to support efforts to provide safe, clean, accessible and affordable drinking water and sanitation to all.

Lack of access to clean water and sanitation is one of the most important barriers to economic development and the achievement of decent living standards. According to *The Economist*:

'If water has the capacity to enhance life, its absence has the capacity to make it miserable …

Some of its most pernicious influences, though, never make the headlines. This is how they might read: "Over 1.2 billion people have to defecate in the open." "The largest single cause of child deaths is diarrhoea or disease related to it." "Nearly 1

billion people have no access to piped drinking water or safe taps or wells." Each of these statements is linked to water.'

At the turn of the century there were 500 million people living in countries that are chronically short of water; this is expected to rise to 4 billion people by 2050. Water is being increasingly converted into a commodity, which is priced and sold. This weakens the idea of access to water as a human right.

The Millennium Development Goals (MDGs; see page 448) are committed to halving the number of people without access to safe drinking water and sanitation by 2015. Efforts must be accelerated if this goal is to be achieved.

The UN resolution was therefore welcomed as a historic step in this process by supporters of water rights.

Source: 'Enough water is not enough: it must also be clean' in *The Economist*, 22 May 2010; Centre for Economic and Social Rights, 'UN resolution recognizes water as a right', 2 August 2010.

Applying your skills

1 Do you agree that access to water should be considered as a fundamental and universal human right? Why?

2 Explain different possible ways that access to clean water can contribute to economic development.

17.2 The role of international trade barriers

♦ With reference to specific examples, explain how the following factors are barriers to development for economically less developed countries.

International trade has been termed the 'engine for growth' for the currently high income countries, whose growth and development during the 19th and early 20th centuries was based on expanding international export markets that in turn promoted the development of manufacturing industries. International trade and export expansion has similarly worked as a powerful driving force of growth and development in a number of highly successful developing countries, such as China, Korea, Malaysia, Singapore, Taiwan, and others. However, for many more countries, international trade has not given rise to the expected benefits.

To be considered successful as an 'engine for growth' as well as an 'engine for development', international trade must help achieve the following objectives:

- increased rates of economic growth based on production of goods exported to foreign markets
- increased incomes through improved employment opportunities, particularly for poor people to help raise them out of poverty
- increased export earnings that can be used to finance imports of key inputs, including appropriate capital goods and technology to be used in production
- diversification of domestic production and exports, including the progressive development of manufacturing and services.

We turn now to consider the factors that often prevent international trade from achieving the above objectives.

Over-specialisation on a narrow range of products: missing out on the benefits of diversification

♦ a. Over-specialisation on a narrow range of products

Developing countries, especially the lower income ones, tend to specialise in the production and export of only a

Tariff escalation as a barrier to economic growth and development

The following passage appeared in one of the Human Development Reports of the United Nations Development Programme.

'Tariff escalation is one of the more pernicious forms of perverse graduation. Developed countries typically apply low tariffs to raw commodities but rapidly rising rates to intermediate or final products. In Japan tariffs on processed food products are 7 times higher than on first-stage products; in Canada they are 12 times higher. In the European Union tariffs rise from 0 to 9% on cocoa paste and to 30% on the final product.

This tariff structure prevents developing countries from adding value to their exports. Tariff escalation is designed to transfer value from producers in poor countries to agricultural processors and retailers in rich ones – and it works. It helps explain why 90% of the world's cocoa beans are grown in developing countries, while only 44% of cocoa liquor and 29% of cocoa powder exports originate in those countries. Escalating tariffs help to confine countries like Cote d'Ivoire and Ghana to the export of unprocessed cocoa beans, locking them into a volatile, low value-added raw cocoa market. Meanwhile, Germany is the world's largest exporter of processed cocoa, and European companies capture the bulk of the final value of Africa's cocoa production.'

Source: United Nations Development Programme, *Human Development Report 2005*, p. 127.

Applying your skills

1 What is tariff escalation?

2 Explain how tariff escalation works against the interests of developing countries that are trying to diversify their production and exports.

Agricultural trade and rich country subsidies

Agricultural support by rich countries is one of the most problematic issues in international trade. Agriculture is one of the most protected sectors of developed countries, justified on the grounds that farmers earn low incomes and must therefore be assisted. Yet the evidence indicates that most of the benefits of protection are actually enjoyed by very large farmers.[14] This protection has major negative consequences for many developing country primary product exports and for poverty alleviation.

Most developed countries have some form of support system for their farmers, of which the two best known are the European Union's Common Agricultural Policy (CAP) and the United States' farm policy. Both farm protection systems involve a mix of price floors and subsidies (see Chapter 4).

European Union Common Agricultural Policy (CAP)

The European Union's Common Agricultural Policy (CAP) sets a price floor (minimum price) for each product that is protected under the price support system. This minimum price is called an *intervention price*. The resulting surplus of the product is purchased at the intervention price by the European Union (EU) authorities, and is either stored or exported. Since the intervention price is higher than the world market price, the product can only be exported through the payment of export subsidies covering the difference between the two prices. Export subsidies are therefore another characteristic of this support system. Also, the CAP provides production subsidies on other agricultural products.

United States farm policy

As in the EU, agriculture in the United States is protected through a mix of price supports and

---

[14] It is not surprising that the largest farmers get most of the benefits of protection, since subsidies are paid out on the basis of the size of the farm, as well as on the basis of historical production, or quantity produced over a period of years.

production and export subsidies, although they are designed differently. The US price support system (which covers a number of products including some that are very important to developing countries) consists of a *target price* that the farmer is guaranteed for the product. When the target price is greater than the market price, the consumer pays the market price and the farmer receives a subsidy covering the difference between the two prices. In addition, farmers receive subsidies (independently of price), and many products also enjoy export subsidies to ensure their competitiveness in international markets.

Negative consequences of developed country farm support in developing countries

Over and above the negative consequences of protection in the domestic economy (high consumer prices, protection of inefficient producers, costs to taxpayers of protection, etc. – see page 376), there are a number of negative consequences for the global economy and developing countries:

- **Global misallocation of resources.** Higher prices received by developed country farmers due to price supports, as well as production subsidies, result in an overallocation of resources to the production of protected goods in the developed countries, and therefore excess production and surpluses. However, export subsidies artificially lower the international price of the goods, making it more difficult for farmers in developing countries to compete. Very low prices force some farmers in developing countries to abandon or reduce cultivation of the product, resulting in an underallocation of resources to the product. Therefore, too much of the protected good is produced in the developed countries (overallocation of resources) and too little in developing countries (underallocation of resources).

- **Global inefficiency.** Developing countries can often produce certain agricultural products at a far lower cost than developed countries, yet because of protection, the more inefficient developed country producers continue to produce, capturing global market shares from the more efficient developing country producers. For example, the United States is the world's largest exporter of cotton, which receives price supports and subsidies worth billions of dollars annually, yet it also has among the

highest costs of cotton production in the world (more than double the costs in Brazil and several African countries that directly compete with the United States).[15]

- **Lower export earnings for developing countries.** Developing countries that specialise in exporting products receiving protection in developed countries suffer due to lower exports, as well as lower prices (due to the rich-country subsidies), and therefore have lower export earnings; this can contribute to balance of payments difficulties and increased debt burdens.

- **Increased poverty among affected farmers.** Low exports and low prices received by developing country farmers and the inability to compete with the farmers of developed countries means lower incomes, lower investment possibilities for farmers, lower employment opportunities for farm workers, and increased poverty. Some displaced farmers are forced to migrate to the cities, where they find work in the informal sector while contributing to the growth of urban slums.

The irrationality of developed country farm support in relation to developing country needs is illustrated by the following: in the early 2000s, *developed countries were spending just over $1 billion a year on aid to developing country agriculture, and they were also spending just under $1 billion a day in supporting their own farmers.*[16]

Other non-tariff barriers: the 'new trade protection'

There is some concern that certain non-tariff barriers have begun to increase in recent years, the most important of which involve technical regulations, standards and requirements, testing and certification, labelling and packaging requirements; customs and administrative procedures; and sanitary measures including food safety and quality standards. Because these kinds of non-tariff barriers have been rising rapidly in recent years, they are referred to as the 'new trade protection'. Non-tariff barriers cover the entire range of products exported by developing countries. Whereas the need for minimum safety and quality standards is not in question, there are concerns that some of these controls are being used as a hidden way to limit quantities of imports. (See page 375 on administrative barriers.)

---

[15] Congressional Research Service, 'Cotton production and support in the United States', Report for Congress, 24 June 2004.

[16] United Nations Development Programme, *Human Development Report 2005*.

Long-term changes in the terms of trade (higher level topic)

♦ With reference to specific examples, explain how the following factor is a barrier to development for economically less developed countries.

  a. Long-term changes in the terms of trade

This topic was fully explained in Chapter 15 in connection with long-term deteriorating terms of trade (page 432). You should bear in mind that this is one of the major international trade barriers to economic growth and development.

Test your understanding 17.4

1 What must international trade succeed in doing in order to be considered to be 'an engine for growth and development'?

2 Explain why too much specialisation on primary commodity exports may have negative effects on developing countries' efforts to grow and develop.

3 Explain the benefits of diversification of production and exports. How can countries gain from diversifying into higher value-added production?

4 Explain the possible negative effects of short-term volatility of commodity prices.

5 What are some factors making it difficult for developing countries to access foreign markets for their exports?

6 What are some negative effects of **(a)** tariff escalation, and **(b)** developed country farm support?

 7 **(higher level) (a)** Explain how deterioration of a country's terms of trade can act as a barrier to growth and development. **(b)** How do arguments in favour of diversification run counter to the theory of comparative advantage?

17.3 Trade strategies for economic growth and development

♦ With reference to specific examples, evaluate each of the following as a means of achieving economic growth and economic development.

International trade strategies are very important to economic growth and development. In developing countries they have formed the basis of growth and development strategies, and it *is hardly possible to consider one without also considering the other*.

Import substitution

♦ a. Import substitution

Import substitution, also known as *import-substituting industrialisation*, refers to a growth and trade strategy where a country begins to manufacture simple consumer goods for the domestic market to promote its domestic industry (for example, shoes, textiles, beverages, electrical appliances, etc.). Import substitution depends on protective measures (tariffs, quotas, etc.) preventing the entry of imports that compete with domestic producers.

The rationale of import substitution

Many Latin American countries had adopted these policies from the 1930s onward. By the 1950s and 1960s, most developing countries around the world, including in Africa and Asia, were pursuing industrialisation based on import substitution. Import substitution was attractive for the following reasons:

- **Independence seen as an opportunity to modernise.** In the 1950s, many countries, especially in Africa, were newly independent states. During the colonial period, their economies had been forced to specialise in the production of primary commodities for export, and were viewed as markets for the manufactured goods produced in the developed world. These countries saw their independence as an opportunity to modernise their economies by shutting out manufactured imports from developed countries, which they would begin producing themselves.

- **Historical experience of developed countries.** Most currently developed countries had used some import-substituting policies in the initial phases of their industrialisation.

- **Export pessimism.** During the 1950s and 1960s, developing countries were pessimistic over the idea of depending on exports as the basis of growth. Many of them specialised in primary commodities, were faced with declining export prices and were fearful of a long-term deterioration in their terms of trade.

- **Avoiding balance of payments problems.** It was expected that savings on the use of foreign exchange to buy imports would arise, since these would be reduced.

- **Infant industry argument.** The theoretical justification for import substitution was provided by the infant industry argument that recommended the use of trade barriers to protect 'infant' domestic firms against competition from imports (see page 377).

Import-substitution policies and consequences

Import substitution policies had the following common characteristics and consequences:

- **High levels of protection of domestic firms, inefficiency and resource misallocation.** Protection took mainly the form of tariffs, quotas and import licences. High levels of protection and the resulting lack of competition resulted in high costs and inefficiency in private sector and public sector industries, as well as a misallocation of resources. Consumers also had to pay high prices for consumer goods.

- **Overvalued exchange rates.** Many developing countries overvalued their exchange rates by fixing them at a higher level than the free market level, reducing the price of imports and increasing the price of exports (see page 391). The objective was to allow firms to import capital inputs more cheaply; however, it had two negative effects:
  - Cheap capital imports led to capital-intensive production methods (inappropriate technologies), unemployment and growth of the urban informal sector (see pages 441 and 465).
  - It made agricultural exports more expensive, worsening rural poverty.

- **Too much government intervention in the economy.** Most import-substituting countries relied heavily on industrial policies (interventionist supply-side policies; see page 339), in which the government played a very important role (protective trade barriers, overvalued exchange rates, subsidised credit, tax allowances, production subsidies, wage subsidies, price controls, etc.), as well as extensive public ownership of firms and industries (fertilisers, steel, petrochemicals, cement, banking and financial services, infrastructure, and many others). The result was to encourage serious misallocation of resources and inefficiencies in production.

- **Neglect of agriculture.** Agriculture was neglected, and due to the failure to make investments in the agricultural sector, there was an increased need for food imports.

- **Deterioration in the balance of payments and debt position.** The balance of payments deteriorated because of:
  - increasing imports of capital equipment for domestic firms as inputs in production
  - an increased need for food imports due to the inability of the agricultural sector to provide enough food
  - an outward flow of financial capital due to profit repatriation of foreign multinational corporations (profits taken to the home country), and by domestic wealthy groups seeking high returns for their financial investments.

- **Encouragement of capital-intensive production methods.** Policy-makers encouraged capital-intensive technologies, as it was believed that this would promote more rapid growth. No effort was made to increase access to credit or provide other support for small entrepreneurs who were more likely to use labour-intensive techniques.

- **Negative impacts on employment and income distribution.** Capital-intensive technologies and the neglect of small producers in agricultural and in the urban sectors worsened the problem of unemployment and contributed to the development and growth of the urban informal sector. Many countries also saw a worsening of income distribution and increasing poverty.

- **Limited possibilities for growth over the longer term.** Whereas many countries did achieve increased rates of growth in the early periods of import-substituting policies, there came a point when it was no longer possible to grow through import substitution. This was due to serious inefficiencies (high costs) of production. Many firms enjoying protection never 'grew up' to become efficient, lowcost producers, firms that should have closed down were kept going, while others that should have been set up or expanded were not.

- **Greater likelihood of corruption.** Strong government intervention opened up possibilities for corruption such as the payment of bribes to government officials to secure particular policies (for example, more tariff protection).

Many of the problems of import substitution were becoming obvious during the 1960s. A few countries such as Egypt and India reacted by increasing protective barriers for capital goods imports to solve balance of payments problems. Some other countries began to move towards a different approach, that of export promotion, for example, Brazil, Israel, Mexico, Singapore, South Korea and Taiwan, as well as southern European countries. By the 1970s and 1980s, there was general agreement among economists that import substitution had not lived up to expectations.

Export promotion

♦ b. Export promotion

Export promotion refers to a growth and trade strategy where a country attempts to achieve economic growth by expanding its exports. Like import substitution, export promotion was based on strong government intervention, justified by the idea that this is necessary to help countries develop a strong manufacturing sector oriented towards exports.

The experience of export promotion

Export-promotion strategies evolved gradually as an extension of import substitution. In many cases, the industries that became the strongest exporters were the ones that had earlier received strong import-substituting protection. (In these cases, import substitution was successful as a temporary industrialisation strategy that was transformed to an export orientation of protected infant industries that 'matured'.)

The economies that first turned to export promotion included China, Hong Kong, Indonesia, Japan, Malaysia, Singapore, South Korea, Taiwan and Thailand. These form part of a group called the *newly industrialising economies (NIEs)*; they are known as the Asian Tigers. While each economy was unique in the blend of policies, some typical policies included the following:

- **State ownership and control of financial institutions (banking and insurance).** This was done to provide subsidised credit to the industries being promoted, such as for example subsidised interest rates and other favourable borrowing terms.
- **Targeting of industries for export.** Industries that were selected for support were those that used increasingly higher skill levels and technological levels, aiming for higher value-added production activities.
- **Industrial policies to support export industries.** Industrial policies included investment grants, production subsidies to export industries, exemptions from tariffs of imported inputs needed for export industries, tax exemptions, export subsidies, and foreign exchange licences, special benefits granted to multinational corporations that were export oriented.

- **Some protection of domestic industries.** Protection of some domestic industries continued, but only selectively (selective import substitution).
- **Requirements imposed on multinational corporations.** Specific requirements were imposed on multinational corporations in an effort to maximise the benefits of foreign direct investments, such as the promotion of research and development (R&D), transfer of desired and targeted technologies into the domestic economy, training of domestic workers, and the use of local inputs where possible.
- **Large public investments in key areas.** Governments spent heavily on education and skills, R&D, and expansion and modernisation of the transport and communications infrastructure.
- **Provision of incentives for private sector R&D for high technology products.** Governments provided strong incentives to private sector firms to engage in R&D in high technology areas, the objective being to encourage the development of domestic skill levels and technological developments appropriate to local conditions.

These policies resulted in immensely successful export performance and the achievement of very high economic growth rates. Since the 1950s, the newly industrialising economies have been the fastest growing economies in the developing world. In addition, they succeeded in making significant improvements in their levels of economic and human development.

Factors behind the success of export promotion over import substitution

Why were the NIEs, or the Asian Tigers, so successful? The following factors have been singled out:

- **Expansion into foreign markets.** Domestic production can grow beyond the domestic market, and can take advantage of economies of scale.
- **Benefits of diversification.** Industrial policies began with support for simple, labour-intensive goods (for example, textiles and clothing), and later supported diversification into higher value-added manufacturing based on increasing skill and technology levels (see pages 478 and 493).
- **Major investments in human capital.** Governments made heavy investments in education, training and skills.
- **Appropriate technologies.** Governments supported R&D for the development of appropriate technologies, as well as the transfer from abroad of technologies appropriate to local conditions (see page 465).

- **Increased employment.** There were increased employment opportunities resulting from the use of labour-intensive technologies.
- **Export earnings avoided balance of payments problems.** The result was significant increases in exports and export earnings, which avoided balance of payments difficulties.

Trade liberalisation

◆ c. Trade liberalisation

The Washington Consensus

The spectacular successes in export growth of the Asian Tigers (NIEs) made a sharp contrast to the performance of the majority of developing countries. In the early 1980s, many of these were showing poor export and growth performance, and were also highly indebted. This was the time when monetarist/new classical economists were introducing their supply-side ideas, emphasising the importance of limited government intervention and the competitive free market.

As a trade and growth strategy, limited government intervention meant **trade liberalisation** (the elimination of trade barriers to achieve free trade) and a free market approach in the domestic economy. The free trade and free market approach to growth and development came to be known as the *Washington Consensus*, because it was shared by the World Bank, the International Monetary Fund, the United States Congress, and a number of US agencies (all of which are based in Washington, DC). The main policies recommended by the Washington Consensus included:

- trade liberalisation (lowering and eliminating tariff and other barriers to trade)
- interest rate liberalisation (freeing up of interest rates)
- moving toward freely floating exchange rates
- privatisation
- deregulation
- lifting restrictions to foreign direct investments (by multinational corporations)
- limiting borrowing by the government (keeping budget deficits under control)

- maintaining some government spending for health, education and infrastructure.

Most of these measures involved freeing up markets and cutting back on the role of government. They were based on the idea that reliance on market forces and free trade improves efficiency and the domestic and global allocation of resources, and increases economic growth.

Since the 1980s, many developing countries have increasingly adopted liberalising policies by following the policy prescriptions listed above. Examples include Argentina, Brazil, China, Chile, India, Kenya, Sri Lanka, Tanzania, Turkey, the countries of East Asia, and many more. However, these countries did not completely abandon their interventionist policies, but instead began a gradual reduction of government intervention in the market, with some countries liberalising more, or more rapidly, than others.

The effects of economic and trade liberalisation

By the 1990s there was evidence that liberalisation of trade and the economy was not bringing about the expected benefits. The following conclusions on the effects of liberalisation can be reached.

Limited benefits for export growth and diversification

Many countries found themselves losing their export shares in world markets (an export share is the proportion of a country's exports in relation to global exports). The losses were the greatest in Africa. The UNDP notes that if, by the early 2000s, Africa had still had its 1980 share of world exports, its exports would be greater by US$119 billion (in constant $ in terms of the year 2000); this is equivalent to about five times the amount of aid provided by donors in 2002.[17]

Whereas some countries increased their exports, on the whole liberalisation policies did not succeed in helping developing countries diversify their production into increased manufacturing for export. In 2000, just five developing countries were responsible for two-thirds of developing country low technology manufactured exports, while only six developing countries were responsible for more than four-fifths of developing country medium and high technology manufactured exports.[18] In most Latin American and African countries, growth

---

[17] United Nations Development Programme, *Human Development Report 2002* (available at http://hdr.undp.org/en/reports/).

[18] United Nations Development Programme, *Human Development Report 2005* (available at http://hdr.undp.org/en/reports/). The five countries in

the first group are China (32%), Taiwan (11%), South Korea (10%), Mexico (8%) and India (6%). The six countries in the second group are South Korea (16%), China (14%), Mexico (14%), Singapore (14%), Taiwan (14%) and Malaysia (9%).

of manufacturing exports was slow to moderate, and there was no significant change indicating diversification of production into manufacturing. In some Latin American countries there resulted *a decline* in the relative share of manufacturing. In general, the countries that tended to fare best were those that had already developed significant export sectors (the East Asian countries).[19]

Partly, these negative effects of liberalisation were due to the trade protection policies used by developed countries on developing country exports, including protection of agriculture and tariff escalation (see page 479). In addition, they were due to the growing reliance on free market policies. Remember, the great successes of the East Asian countries were based on industrial policies involving strong government intervention. With less government support, many developing countries were not able to perform well.

Limited effects on economic growth

There is no evidence indicating that economic and trade liberalisation encouraged economic growth. According to well-known development economists, 'There is little evidence that open trade policies – in the form of lower tariff and non-tariff barriers to trading – are significantly associated with economic growth.'[20] Furthermore, 'Perhaps the most comprehensive assessment of the links between economic growth and trade liberalisation undertaken to date concluded that there is no clear link between them. This means that the projected benefits are merely hypothetical.'[21]

According to the United Nations Development Programme:

'One of the prevailing myths of globalization is that increased trade has been the catalyst for a new era of convergence. The argument suggests that expanded trade is narrowing the income gap between rich and poor countries, with the developing world benefiting from access to new technologies and new markets. Like most myths, this one combines elements of truth with a large amount of exaggeration. Some countries are catching up, albeit from a low base. However, successful integration is the exception rather than the rule, and trade drives global inequality as well as prosperity. For the majority of countries the globalization story is one of divergence and marginalization.'[22]

Increasing income inequalities and poverty within developing countries

There is clear evidence that economic and trade liberalisation have resulted in greater income inequalities and poverty. A World Bank study notes that trade liberalisation leads to lower income growth among the poorest 40% of the population, but higher income growth for the higher income groups. In other words, it helps the rich get richer and the poor get poorer.[23]

The reason is that economic and trade liberalisation creates both 'winners' and 'losers'. When new export markets are opened up, those who find employment in the production of export goods will be better off; people who find jobs in a growing formal sector (if it is growing) will also gain; people with some education and skills may also gain as they are better able to exploit new opportunities in the more competitive environment made possible by liberalisation. However, there will also be those who will become worse off as a result of the changes introduced by liberalisation and free (or freer) trade. They include:

- less educated or illiterate people, who are unable to compete in the new environment
- poor people who lack collateral, and who cannot get credit to open or expand a business to take advantage of new opportunities
- people who live in remote geographical areas with no transport links to markets
- people who have nothing to export, and no possibilities of producing for export
- people in agriculture who switch to producing commodities for export, making themselves more vulnerable to wide fluctuations (volatility) in cash-crop prices
- people who lose their jobs as public employees due to cutbacks in the size of the public sector (in Zimbabwe, people in this category are referred to as the 'new poor')
- people who may become unemployed due to privatisation of public enterprises, which fire workers to lower costs
- people affected by cuts in government spending on merit goods, forced by a greater reliance on market forces

[19] S. M. Shafaeddin (2005) 'Trade liberalisation and economic reform in developing countries: structural change or de-industrialization?', Discussion Paper, UN Conference on Trade and Development (UNCTAD), (available at www.unctad.org).
[20] F. Rodriguez and D. Rodrik (1999) 'Trade policy and economic growth: a skeptic's guide to the cross-national evidence', Discussion Paper, National Bureau of Economic Research.

[21] L. Alan Winters (2000) 'Trade liberalisation and poverty', Paper, Centre for Economic Policy Research, London, and Centre for Economic Performance, London School of Economics.
[22] United Nations Development Programme, *Human Development Report 2005.*
[23] M. Lundberg and L. Squire (1999) *Inequality and Growth: Lessons for Policy,* The World Bank.

- people affected by lower levels of social protection caused by supply-side policies (such as lower minimum wages, lower protection against being fired, etc.; see page 341)
- people who are forced from the formal into the informal sector, where wages are lower and social protection is non-existent, due to removal of trade protection leading to the closure of formal sector firms that can no longer compete (in Zambia, for example, formal employment fell by 15% in the decade of the 1990s[24]).

International trade theory recognises that free trade is likely to give rise to both winners and losers. However, it argues that since the overall gains will be greater than the overall losses, the gainers can compensate the losers, with the result that no one need be worse off. Yet, in the real world, such compensation rarely (if ever) takes place.

The free market approach of the Washington Consensus was questioned even by some individuals within the World Bank itself. Joseph Stiglitz, as Chief Economist of the World Bank, wrote the following on the Washington Consensus in 1998:

'The neoliberal model[25] accords the government a minimal role, essentially one of ensuring macroeconomic stability, with an emphasis on price stability, while getting out of the way to allow trade liberalisation, privatization, and getting the prices right. Many of these policies are necessary for markets to work well and contribute to economic success, but they are far from sufficient. Some aspects of the neoliberal model might not even be necessary conditions for strong growth, and if undertaken without accompanying measures . . . they may not bring many gains and could even lead to setbacks. Some countries have closely followed the dictates of the neoliberal model, but have not seen especially strong economic performance. Other countries have ignored many of the dictates . . . and have experienced among the highest rates of sustained growth the world has ever seen.'[26]

The New Development Consensus: trade liberalisation with government intervention

Since the late 1990s, supporters and critics of the Washington Consensus have been moving towards a new consensus (the New Development Consensus), led by Joseph Stiglitz. In the new view, trade liberalisation continues to be important, but in developing countries there should also be some government intervention to help create the conditions needed for markets to work without resulting in the negative effects described above. The following are some of the ideas in this view:[27]

- Governments must support education, health services and infrastructure development, as well as research and development (R&D) and transfer of technology for both industry and agriculture.
- Avoidance of large budget deficits is important, but if contractionary fiscal policy is needed, it should not affect spending on education, health and infrastructure.
- Governments must pay attention to the effects of policies on income distribution, and must pursue policies that promote income equality and alleviation of poverty.
- Governments must provide a proper regulatory framework for markets to work effectively; for example, there should be effective regulation for competition (otherwise privatisations may lead to the development of private monopolies).
- Efforts must be made to promote market-supporting institutions as these are a prerequisite for successful market-based economic development (property rights, an effective tax systems, effective banking and credit system, etc.).
- Developed countries must assist economic development by increasing foreign aid and providing increased access to their markets for developing country exports.
- Developing countries should receive special treatment by international trade agreements under the World Trade Organization regarding removal of rich country trade protection measures (for example, in agriculture).

The New Development Consensus sees an important role for governments in developing countries because of their special circumstances. Markets and free trade are important, but these cannot promote growth and development without human capital (health and education), technology development, infrastructure, effective institutions, industrial policies and a trading system that encourages developing country exports. Therefore, *government intervention is important to help create the conditions needed for markets and free trade to work well.*

---

[24] Winters (2000) 'Trade liberalisation and poverty'.
[25] By the term 'neoliberal model', Stiglitz is referring to the free market approach of the Washington Consensus.
[26] Joseph E. Stiglitz (1998) 'Knowledge for development: economic science, economic policy, and economic advice', Annual World Bank Conference on Development Economics, Washington, DC, April 1998.

[27] Joseph E. Stiglitz (1998) 'More instruments and broader goals: moving towards the Post-Washington Consensus', Annual Lecture, World Institute for Development Economics Research, Helsinki, 1998; and 'Towards a new paradigm for fevelopment strategies and processes', Prebisch Lecture, UNCTAD, Geneva, 1998.

1 **(a)** Define import substitution and explain why it has an inward orientation. **(b)** What were some factors that led most developing countries to adopt import substitution as an industrialisation strategy in the 1950s? **(c)** Discuss some of the key policies that were associated with import-substituting strategies. **(d)** Evaluate the effectiveness of these strategies with respect to their impacts on economic performance and economic growth and development.

2 **(a)** Define export promotion and explain why it has an outward orientation. **(b)** What were some of the countries that adopted an export orientation during the 1960s, and what prompted them to do so? **(c)** Discuss some of the key policies that were associated with export promotion. **(d)** Evaluate the effectiveness of these policies with respect to economic performance, export growth and economic growth and development.

3 **(a)** Define trade liberalisation, referring to its objectives. **(b)** What were the main ideas behind the Washington Consensus? **(c)** Explain the connections between the market-based supply-side policies discussed in Chapter 12 and the Washington Consensus.

4 **(a)** Explain the effects of liberalising policies on export growth, diversification, economic growth and income distribution. **(b)** What is the role of government intervention according to the New Development Consensus on liberalisation? **(c)** How do the recommendations of the New Development Consensus fit with the policies pursued by the Asian Tigers that succeeded in achieving high rates of growth and broad-based development?

The role of the World Trade Organization (WTO)

♦ d. The role of the WTO

The objectives and functions of the WTO were described in Chapter 13. We will now evaluate its role in economic growth and development.

Potential benefits

The WTO claims to offer ten benefits to the global trading system:[28]

1 'The system helps to keep the peace.' By encouraging the smooth flow of trade and helping to resolve trade disputes, the WTO helps promote peace between countries.

2 'The system allows disputes to be handled constructively.' Greater liberalisation means there is greater room for disputes. The WTO helps countries settle their disputes in a constructive way.

3 'A system based on rules rather than power makes life easier for all.' Decisions are made by consensus, agreements are ratified by governments, and all countries, including the rich and the poor, have the right to challenge each other through the WTO.

4 'Freer trade cuts the cost of living.' Trade protection raises prices; lower trade barriers made possible by the WTO result in lower prices.

5 'It gives consumers more choice, and a broader range of qualities to choose from.' More international trade made possible by lower trade barriers increases the range of goods and services available to consumers.

6 'Trade raises income.' Lower trade barriers increase international trade, which leads to higher incomes.

7 'Trade stimulates economic growth, and that can be good for employment.' Trade leads to increased growth, and this may mean more employment (though some jobs are lost).

8 'The basic principles make the system economically more efficient, and they cut costs.' Trade allows countries to specialise and use resources more efficiently.

9 'The system shields governments from narrow interests.' Governments can view trade policy in a more balanced way, defend themselves against narrow interests, and better represent the broader interest.

10 'The system encourages good government.' Whereas trade protection may provide opportunities for corruption and bad governance, trade liberalisation means more discipline for the government and improved governance.

Many of these benefits are among the benefits of free trade (1, 4, 5, 6, 7 and 8), while the rest are the potential benefits of an effective system of trading rules (2, 3, 4 and 10). All are benefits arising from a well-functioning global trading system. Yet the WTO is one of the most controversial organisations in the world, rousing passionate feelings among both

---

[28] This information is taken from the WTO website, www.wto.org.

supporters and critics. To understand the controversy, let's take a step backwards and begin with a look at the GATT's 'Uruguay Round', concluded in 1994.

Evaluating the Uruguay Round

The Uruguay Round resulted in the most comprehensive and far-reaching trade negotiations in history. It succeeded in reducing tariffs for thousands of products, with tariffs dropping by 33% on average, and the share of goods with no tariffs increasing from 20–22% to 40–45%. It provided new rules for promotion of trade in services; protection of intellectual property (patents, new technologies, books, databases, etc.); gradual elimination of quotas in textiles and clothing; and restrictions on agricultural subsidies (subsidies granted by developed country governments to protect their farmers).

While not all the agreements were put into effect as planned, supporters argued that the Uruguay Round was a major success in furthering the cause of free trade and a trading system that supports growth and possibilities for improved standards of living everywhere.

Critics argued that the agreements were ineffective in providing countries with equal opportunities to share in the benefits of increased trade, noting that the new trade rules supported developed country interests far more than those of developing countries.

Developed countries received greater tariff reductions than developing ones

Whereas developed country exports enjoyed tariff reductions of 45% on average, developing country exports received tariff reductions of 20–25%. As a result of the Uruguay Round agreements, developing countries face tariffs on their exports that are 10% higher than the world average, and the least developed (poorest) countries face tariffs that are 30% higher.

Tariffs on textiles remained much higher for developing country exports

The agreements eliminated quotas on developing country textile exports and also reduced tariffs on textiles, but following the reductions, tariffs on developing country textiles exports were three times greater than the average tariffs on developed country textile exports. This is of special importance to developing countries because textiles are a low technology industry that can make heavy use of the abundant supplies of labour in developing countries, and for these reasons textiles usually make up a large share of output in countries that are just beginning to industrialise.

Tariff escalation does not permit developing countries to diversify their production and exports

Tariff escalation (the practice of developed countries to impose lower tariffs on imports of raw materials and increasing tariffs on semi-processed and processed products) works to discourage developing countries from diversifying into food processing or other manufacturing activities (see page 479). The Uruguay Round did not address the problem of tariff escalation.

Developed countries make increasing use of non-tariff barriers against developing country exports

Developed countries have been making increasing use of non-tariff barriers to protect their domestic markets against imports from developing countries (anti-dumping measures and administrative, safety, health and environmental standards). The agreements tried to reduce the scope of non-tariff barriers, but they kept much flexibility in how the rules can be interpreted, allowing room for such measures to continue to be used.

Agricultural subsidies of developed countries were not reduced

Whereas the Uruguay Round provided for reductions in agricultural subsidies, these were not implemented because of resistance in developed countries, and while there have been many discussions there has been no move to enforce reductions.

Protection of intellectual property increases costs of acquiring new technology by developing countries

One of the areas of the Uruguay Round's agreements was that there would be increased protection of intellectual property. This is an area of interest mainly to developed countries, because that is where most of the new 'intellectual property' is generated. Developing countries need to have greater access to new ideas and technologies, and yet the protection created by the agreements makes it more difficult and costly for them to be able to acquire these.

Multinational corporations no longer have to buy supplies locally

Multinational corporations (MNCs) are firms based in one country that produce in other countries as well (see Chapter 18). One of the benefits that MNCs may provide to developing countries is that if they purchase supplies locally, they generate increased demand for locally produced goods and services, and therefore increased local employment. One of the provisions of the Uruguay Round agreements was that MNCs are not obliged to buy materials locally. This provision is in the interests of MNCs (most of which have their base in developed countries), but it deprives developing countries of important potential benefits.

The 1997 Human Development Report of the United Nations Development Programme (UNDP) summarises the impacts of the Uruguay Round:

> 'Poor countries often lose out because the rules of the game are biased against them, particularly those relating to international trade. The Uruguay Round made little difference. Although developing countries have three-quarters of the world's people, they will get only a quarter to a third of the income gains generated and most of that will go to a few powerful exporters in Asia and Latin America.'[29]

Another study has estimated that of welfare gains (measured in US dollars) attributed to the Uruguay Round, 74% have gone to developed countries and 26% to developing ones.[30]

The Doha Development Round: inability to reach agreement

In 1999, the WTO initiated a 'Millennium Round' of negotiations in Seattle. However, the talks broke down before any agreement was reached, while in the meantime tens of thousands of people gathered to demonstrate against globalisation. In 2001, a new attempt was made to begin negotiations under the 'Doha Development Round' (launched in Doha, Qatar). The mood at the time was very much influenced by the Millennium Declaration in which 189 countries had committed themselves to reducing extreme poverty in developing countries by pursuing the Millennium Development Goals (see page 450), as well as other poverty alleviation initiatives inspired by the turn of the millennium. The Doha Round intended to address development and poverty issues, and for this reason was termed a 'Development' Round.

However, not long after the Doha Round was launched, it became apparent that developed country interests were dominating the negotiations. Conflicts between developing and developed countries, as well as serious disagreements between the United States, the European Union and Japan, repeatedly brought the meetings to a deadlock. Whereas the Doha Round was to end in 2004, the agreement was postponed, and at the end of July 2008, it collapsed. Later it was once again revived, but as of 2011 there were no signs that an agreement was about to be reached.

Unresolved issues between developed and developing countries include the unwillingness of developed countries to eliminate their subsidies on agricultural products; the remaining high tariff protection against developing country exports; continuing use of tariff escalation by developed countries, as well as growing use of anti-dumping and administrative, health, etc., standards as 'hidden' protection. Further important unresolved issues include environmental issues, labour issues, intellectual property rights, and more.

Test your understanding 17.6

1 What are the objectives of the World Trade Organization?

2 What are some positive contributions of the World Trade Organization (and the GATT on which it is based) to the global trading system?

3 Identify some of the criticisms that are levelled against the World Trade Organization.

Bilateral and regional preferential trade agreements

♦ e. Bilateral and regional preferential trade agreements

In Chapter 15 we learned that bilateral and regional preferential trade agreements are an alternative path to trade liberalisation than the multilateral approach of the WTO.

The growth of preferential trade agreements

In the last few years, there has been a very large increase in the number of bilateral and regional trade agreements around the world. The number of trade agreements reported to the WTO grew from 20 in 1990 to 159 in 2007, and was in the several hundreds by 2010. One reason for this growth is that many countries are becoming frustrated with what

---

[29] United Nations Development Programme, *Human Development Report 1997* (available at http://hdr.undp.org/en/reports/), p. 85.

[30] D. K. Brown, A. V. Deardorff and R. Stern (2002) 'Computational analysis of multilateral trade liberalisation in the Uruguay Round', Discussion Paper 489, School of Public Affairs, University of Michigan.

they believe is the slow progress made by the WTO. Another is that developing countries see in trading blocs the possibilities of enjoying the benefits of free trade, bypassing the obstacles created by rich country trade protection, and at the same time maintaining some of the benefits of trade protection (toward non-members).

Chapter 15 offered an evaluation of trading blocs in terms of their advantages and disadvantages as a method to achieve free trade. (You should refer to this discussion as it is closely related to our present topic; see pages 415–16.) We will now evaluate trading blocs as a strategy to achieve growth and development. To do so, we must make the distinction between regional and bilateral trade agreements.

Regional free trade agreements (FTAs): potential benefits for growth and development

Economists generally agree that free trade agreements have the greatest potential to help developing countries achieve growth and development when they involve:

- *regional* agreements
- geographical closeness
- a similar level of development and technological capabilities
- similar market sizes
- a shared commitment to co-operation.

These conditions allow countries to achieve the benefits of integration listed on page 415. Regional groupings allow countries to expand their markets (and achieve economies of scale) and to diversify production and exports. Larger markets increase domestic and foreign direct investment. When countries are at a similar level of development and have similar technological capabilities as well as similar market sizes, the new competition created by increased imports is more 'fair' and easier to deal with (it does not involve 'unfair' competitive advantages of foreign firms caused by lower costs due to use of more advanced technologies, greater managerial know-how, larger size due to larger home markets, etc.).

If there is a shared commitment to co-operation, there are several policies that can be pursued jointly by members so they can further benefit from their integration. They can invest in transport infrastructure needed for trade, as well as in energy and water supplies needed for growth and development. They can collaborate on research and development (R&D)

projects and new technology development that would be mutually beneficial. They can work together on environmental issues of common interest.

All these factors greatly increase the likelihood that integration will lead to increased growth and more development.

While it is difficult for all the conditions listed above to be met in practice, it is not surprising that we usually find neighbouring countries forming regional blocs such as in Latin America (MERCOSUR), southeast Asia (ASEAN), eastern and southern Africa (COMESA), central Africa (CEMAC), Central America (CAIS), etc.

Bilateral free trade agreements (FTAs): risks for growth and development

Most of the several hundred trade agreements in existence are bilateral, and most bilateral agreements are between developing and developed countries that are *not* usually in the same geographical region (though there are exceptions). The developed countries mainly involved are first the United States, which has made agreements with a number of developing countries, followed by the European Union (which though consisting of many countries acts as a unit) that also has agreements with developing countries and transition economies, and thirdly Japan, with agreements mainly in the Asia-Pacific region.

A bilateral agreement has the potential to provide a developing country with access to the market of the developed country, and the prospect of gaining such access (not available to other countries) is the reason why developing countries enter into such agreements. However, this potential comes with some serious risks:

- The developing country must make equal and matching (or 'reciprocal') cuts in tariff and other barriers, which are often much greater than those required by WTO agreements. This puts even efficient developing country firms at a competitive disadvantage because they are forced to compete with lower cost developed country firms (which are larger, with greater technological, managerial and marketing capabilities). The result may be to destroy even efficient local firms.
- When many developing countries form FTAs with the same developed country in order to gain market access, the advantage they each hope to gain individually is lost, as they must now all compete with each other for the developed country market. In addition, their exports may be unable to compete with the lower cost domestically produced goods in

Free trade between the European Union (EU) and African, Caribbean and Pacific (ACP) countries

Rich countries, led by the European Union and the United States, are threatening to undermine the system of free trade promoted by the World Trade Organization, by establishing bilateral preferential trade and investment agreements with developing countries. Jagdish Bhagwati, an Indian economist who is one of the most prominent international trade specialists, refers to the very numerous bilateral relationships of the newly emerging global trading system as a 'spaghetti bowl', and as the 'plague' of special relationships.

In 2000, the European Union (EU) and 79 African, Caribbean and Pacific nations (ACP) signed the Cotonou Agreement (in Cotonou, Benin). The agreement, which came into effect in 2003, has the stated aim of reducing poverty and promoting the integration of ACP nations into the global economy. This is to be done through bilateral 'Economic Partnership Agreements' (EPAs) between the European Union and each individual ACP nation. Many of the ACP nations are among the poorest in the world.

Since 2007–8, EPAs came under increasing criticism from numerous sources, including ACP governments, international trade experts, local organisations of farmers and businesses, United Nations agencies and the World Bank. The critics argue that whereas the Cotonou Agreement was intended to benefit the ACP countries, the EPAs that are being negotiated and signed will work against the interests of these countries, and will endanger their economic growth and development prospects.

It is noted that the EU is using bilateral agreements to gain access to ACP markets that it would not have been able to achieve though the World Trade Organization (WTO), where developing countries can join together and present their interests as one, thereby gaining a more favourable treatment. The bilateral nature of EPAs is a major threat to the multilateralism of the WTO. EPAs also weaken the ability of developing countries to negotiate favourable agreements with the WTO, and they divide developing countries by creating different interests. EPAs lead to significant trade diversion as countries are forced to reduce their imports from lower cost, more efficient producers, and they increase the costs of trade as each agreement has its own rules and bureaucratic procedures.

The EU has forced many ACP countries to sign EPAs, by threatening to eliminate their access to EU markets if they did not do so. The countries that have been forced into signing the EPAs are generally very poor, and highly dependent on a very small number of commodities for export. Many of these depend on EU markets for more than 40% of their exports. Loss of access to EU markets would mean the loss of hundreds of thousands of jobs, destroying their economies.

In the area of trade, whereas the Doha Round of the WTO negotiations had proposed that least developed countries be exempted from tariff cuts, all of the ACP countries must cut their tariffs on 80–98% of their trade with the EU over a 15-year period, with no sector excluded. According to many experts, these tariff cuts are more than what is required by the current WTO rules.

Trade liberalisation of the past 10–20 years has been disastrous for many ACP countries. Instead of increasing competitiveness of local producers, market liberalisation often destroyed them. In Senegal, for example, one-third of manufacturing jobs disappeared. The World Bank has acknowledged that its advice on opening up to free trade was 'too optimistic'.

ACP countries' export earnings are very low, because they export agricultural products in their 'raw', unprocessed form. Whereas they should process and manufacture more, adding value to their production, they have been unable to do so because of tariffs imposed by the EU (and other developed countries) on their processed exports (tariff escalation).

The EU has not committed itself to eliminating the protection it offers to its own farmers through subsidies. However, it has agreed to offer tariff-free and quota-free access for almost all ACP products. This should eliminate the problem of tariff escalation. However, there are fears that ACP exports will be unable to compete in European markets, because of higher costs of production, and if they do succeed, and large quantities begin to enter EU markets, the EU has ensured that it can use safeguards that will limit the entry of such goods. At the same time, whereas 12–20% of ACP imports are exempted from having to cut tariffs, these do not include manufacturing or high value-added products.

Critics therefore argue that the new trading rules with the EU lock ACP countries into existing patterns of trade, making it difficult for them to lower their dependence on commodities and develop their manufacturing.

Source: 'Partnership or power play?' Oxfam International, April 2008; 'Signing the future away', Oxfam International, March 2007.

Applying your skills

1 Why does Jagdish Bhagwati liken bilateral trade agreements to a 'spaghetti bowl'?

2 Compare and contrast bilateral trade agreements with multilateral and regional trade agreements as a means for poor countries to grow and develop.

the developed country. Thus, increases in exports may be limited.

- Increased imports and only slightly increasing exports may result in trade deficits, balance of payments problems and increasing foreign debt. They may also result in greater unemployment, worsening income distribution and increased poverty.

- Bilateral negotiations put developing countries at a disadvantage due to weaker bargaining power compared to the multilateral negotiations of the WTO where they can join together and present their interests as one, thereby gaining a more favourable treatment. For example, bilateral negotiations cannot achieve a reduction in developed country agricultural subsidies, which is of crucial interest to developing countries.

- The developing country must agree to other requirements not usually in its best interests (such as freer rules on foreign direct investment, stricter rules on intellectual property rights).

- Bilateral agreements divide developing countries by creating different interests. Also, bilateral trade agreements weaken regional trade agreements when a member country makes a bilateral agreement with a third country.

According to the United Nations Conference on Trade and Development (UNCTAD),[31] developing countries are better off pursuing regional trade agreements. The trend toward bilateral trade agreements:

'threatens the viability of existing regional cooperation arrangements among developing countries, and, most importantly, the options available to these countries for pursuing their national development strategies.

FTAs can result in some export gains, and possibly increased FDI (foreign direct investment) flows, but the size and durability of these benefits is highly uncertain, as are the net gains for trade and output growth. This is because the FTA will most likely lead to an increase in imports, with implications for the trade balance and, in some cases, the external debt position. Moreover, if future … FTAs are modeled on those that have been negotiated so far, it is likely that they will considerably reduce or fully remove policy options and instruments available to a developing country to pursue its development objectives.'[32]

In the words of Joseph Stiglitz, '… a series of such agreements may leave many developing countries worse off than they would be even with another unfair multilateral agreement' (reference is being made to the Uruguay Round of the WTO).[33]

Diversification

♦ f. Diversification

Diversification involves a reallocation of resources into new activities that broaden the range of goods or services produced. It was introduced on page 478, where we saw that a major disadvantage of over-specialisation involves losing the benefits of diversification. We learned that diversification by adding value to locally produced goods provides the benefits of more varied production, increased employment, establishing more firms, and using higher skill and technology levels.

It is hardly possible to overemphasise the importance of diversification as a strategy for growth and development. It permits countries to achieve the following important objectives:

- **Sustained increases in exports.** It is not enough to increase exports over a short period of time, only to suffer a decline again; the increase must be one that can be maintained over long periods. This can only be achieved through diversification into markets for which there is a sustained increase in global demand, a condition which commodity exports do not satisfy. The UNDP notes that success in world trade depends increasingly on entry into higher value-added markets for manufactured goods.[34]

- **Development of technological capabilities and skills.** Diversification encourages technological and skill developments; it provides incentives to acquire new technologies and higher training, education and skill levels, which are very important for economic growth and development. This was one factor behind the spectacular success of the Asian Tigers discussed above (see page 484).

- **Reduced vulnerability to short-term price volatility and long-term price declines.** Diversification protects countries against losses from

---

[31] UNCTAD is a United Nations organisation concerned with international trade issues in developing countries.
[32] UNCTAD, *Trade and Development Report, 2007* (available at http://www.unctad.org/en/docs/tdr2007_en.pdf).

[33] J. E. Stiglitz and A. Charlton (2005) *Fair Trade For All*, Oxford University Press.
[34] United Nations Development Programme, *Human Development Report 2005* (available at http://hdr.undp.org/en/reports/).

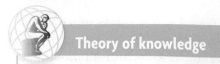

Moral issues of trade liberalisation in developing countries

In the Theory of knowledge feature on page 380, we considered the moral judgement that is implied in the recommendation that countries adopt free trade. In this section, our topic is broader and perhaps more serious, and involves the moral implications of the trade (and economic) liberalisation policies recommended for developing countries (and sometimes forced upon them; see page 485) by developed ones.

The issues involved here are numerous, but can be divided into two broad categories: trade protection policies of more developed countries that prevent developing country access to their markets (agricultural protection of farmers, high tariff barriers, tariff escalation) and the trade liberalisation policies of the Washington Consensus, the WTO and bilateral trade agreements.

Nobel Prize-winning economist Joseph Stiglitz, referring to the free market approach to international trade that since the 1990s has dominated development policies, writes the following about moral and ethical issues in relations between developed and developing countries:

'Economists have long bought into the importance of self-interest not only in explaining behavior, but also in yielding efficient outcomes. But economists have also long been aware of the limitations of these perspectives. Not only does the self-interest/market paradigm often fail to generate efficient outcomes, but even when it does, these outcomes may not [be consistent with] with notions of social justice …

Ethics in the relationship between developed and less developed countries dictates that the developed countries treat the less developed countries fairly, aware of their disadvantaged economic position, and acknowledging that taking advantage of one's own economic power inevitably will hurt the poor within developing countries. [There are] several instances where, in global economic relationships, this precept has been grossly violated: an international trade agenda set to advance the interests of the more developed countries, at least partially at the expense of the less developed — so much so that on average the world's poorest region was actually worse off at the end of the last round of trade negotiations;[35] and an international environmental agreement that provided that those rich countries who today are polluting more be entitled to continue polluting more into the future.'[36]

---

[35] This is a reference to Sub-Saharan Africa.
[36] Joseph Stigltiz, 'Ethics, economics advice and economic policy 'Initiative for Policy Dialogue, 24 October 2005.
[37] Joseph Stiglitz (2005) 'Ethics, economics advice and economic policy'.

Thinking points

- Do developed country societies have a moral obligation to help developing ones (especially the poorer ones)?

- Consider the following question posed by Joseph Stiglitz. 'At one level, it is natural for a country to pursue its own interests. But … at what point does this pursuit of a country's own interest (or, as is more frequently the case, special interests within one's country) at the expense of the poor, become a moral issue?'[37]

- Are developed countries morally justified in promoting bilateral free trade agreements with developing countries when they refuse to give up protection of their farmers?

- How fair are the trade rules of the WTO?

- Do the organisations of the Washington Consensus bear any moral responsibility toward developing countries for mistaken policies that in some cases were damaging to the poor of those countries (such as countries in Sub-Saharan Africa)?

---

fluctuating export prices and deteriorating terms of trade (see pages 431 and 479).

- **Use of domestic primary commodities.** Countries that already produce primary products are in a special position to use these as the basis for their diversification into manufacturing, as the domestic availability of the necessary raw materials can work to stimulate industry. This is called 'vertical diversification', and involves increased processing of raw materials. A number of developing countries provided a major boost to their growth and development through this type of diversification (for example, Malaysia, Thailand, Indonesia, China, Chile and Mauritius).

1 Compare and contrast the roles of the WTO and regional and bilateral trade agreements as methods to advance the growth and development prospects of developing countries.

2 Discuss the potential advantages and disadvantages of **(a)** bilateral trade agreements, and **(b)** regional trade agreements as a strategy to promote growth and development in developing countries.

3 Explain how diversification can help a developing country grow and develop.

Capital liberalisation

Whereas there is no learning outcome on capital liberalisation in this section of the IB syllabus, Section 4.8 of the syllabus refers to 'liberalised capital flows' as one type of market-oriented policy that should be evaluated for its strengths and weaknesses. It is therefore discussed in this chapter.

The meaning of capital liberalisation

Capital liberalisation refers to the free movement of financial capital in and out of a country. It occurs through the elimination of *exchange controls* (see Chapter 14, page 389), which are government restrictions on the quantity of foreign exchange that can be bought by domestic residents of a country, thus limiting the outflows of funds. A country that has exchange controls has a *non-convertible currency*; the domestic currency cannot be freely exchanged for (or 'converted into') foreign currencies. Non-convertibility of a currency may apply to current account or financial account transactions.

A fully *convertible currency*, by contrast, is one that can be freely exchanged for other foreign currencies. Capital liberalisation therefore involves the elimination of exchange controls, making a currency fully convertible.

Non-convertibility for current account transactions

The practice of non-convertibility for current account transactions (mainly foreign trade) was common in earlier decades, when tight government control of foreign exchange was justified on the grounds that governments must be able to influence international trade to pursue particular objectives, such as promotion of key industries and sectors, often in connection with import-substituting policies. The domestic currency could be exchanged for foreign currencies only for specific imports and exports.

Today, most countries have convertible currencies for current account transactions. The benefits of currency convertibility for current account transactions are based on the idea that international trade should take place in competitive markets, where prices determined in free markets act as signals and convey all necessary information regarding the quantities and qualities of internationally traded goods and services, promoting global efficiency in trade. Non-convertibility for international trade purposes restricts the amount of foreign exchange that can be bought and sold and prevents the functioning of the market mechanism: it impedes international trade flows in accordance with the forces of supply and demand, it encourages inefficient resource allocation, it encourages inefficiency in production, and it prevents economic activities from taking place in accordance with the preferences of consumers and producers. Clearly, convertibility for current account transactions offers major advantages, and for this reason has been adopted in most countries in the world.

Non-convertibility for financial account transactions

The most common form of non-convertibility today involves financial account transactions. This does not mean that there is no convertibility for financial account flows; rather it means that there is government control over what flows are permissible. Exceptions are made for debt service payments, for funds to be used in inward foreign direct investments (when a foreign multinational corporation wants to invest in the local economy), and other kinds of financial capital flows, such as for inward flows due to borrowing from abroad or for financial investments by foreigners.

Many developing countries still maintain non-convertibility for financial account flows for the following reasons:

- To avoid *capital flight*, which is the large-scale transfer of funds to another country, usually undertaken when residents or businesses of a country are fearful that their wealth or income are threatened (due to the possibility of confiscation, or sudden increases in taxation, or high rates of inflation, serious balance of payments problems and the possibility of devaluation/depreciation, political instability, and so on). Capital flight can be a serious problem because it involves a loss of financial capital that could have been invested domestically. Also, as it consists of the sale of the domestic currency (to buy the foreign exchange that leaves the country), it exerts a downward pressure on the value of the currency. If there are restrictions on currency convertibility, financial capital cannot leave the country.

- To avoid currency speculation, which involves buying and selling of foreign exchange in the expectation of making short-term profits (see Chapter 14, page 385). Currency speculation can lead to exchange rate instability with negative consequences for investment and economic growth; this is avoided when the currency is non-convertible for capital flows.

- To assist in conducting a monetary policy independently of exchange rate considerations. Consider an economy in recession, where the government would like to pursue an expansionary monetary policy (i.e. lower interest rates) to stimulate economic activity. If the currency is fully convertible, lower interest rates will result in financial capital outflows, currency depreciation and possibly balance of payments difficulties. If the currency is non-convertible for financial capital flows, the lower interest rate will not lead to a capital outflow, there will be no depreciation, and the country can pursue its pro-growth policy without worrying about consequences in the foreign sector.

On the other hand, full convertibility offers advantages by permitting or encouraging:

- access by domestic residents to foreign capital markets, and offering opportunities to diversify their financial investments

- access by domestic residents to more varied and cheaper sources of finance for investment and trade

- foreign direct investment

- inflows of financial capital as foreigners make domestic financial investments in the knowledge that they can sell their assets and take their financial capital out of the country if they so wish

- competition between financial institutions, resulting in greater efficiency and lower costs

- an efficient global allocation of savings, since savers are free to make financial investments anywhere in the world where they can obtain the highest returns, with positive impacts on global rates of growth.

Full convertibility also prevents the development of a black or informal market for buying and selling foreign exchange. Due to all of the above factors, it contributes to greater economic growth.

Conditions that should be met before adopting full currency convertibility

In order for a country to fully liberalise its currency, it must first create an economic and political environment that will minimise the risks of full convertibility. It must be reasonably certain that capital flight, currency speculation and exchange rate volatility are unlikely to occur, and that there is no need for it to isolate its domestic monetary policy from its external sector. Developing countries must therefore have:

- a stable political system and economic policy orientation, inspiring confidence in the economy

- sound fiscal and monetary policies that encourage confidence

- sound macroeconomic policies that work to avoid wide exchange rate fluctuations and large balance of payments deficits

- strong financial institutions that operate under prudent government regulation so as to avoid excessive risks

- a market orientation of the economy, with a well-functioning price system that facilitates a more efficient allocation of resources and financial capital that inspires confidence in the market mechanism.

Some of these conditions have not yet been fully met in many developing countries; this explains the continued use of non-convertible currencies for capital flows.

Currency convertibility and financial crises

The severe financial and economic crisis experienced by several East Asian countries in the late 1990s (South Korea, Thailand, Indonesia) provides evidence of the risks of undertaking full capital liberalisation prior to meeting all of the above conditions. These economies, which on the whole had been reasonably successful with respect to their growth and development performance, had extended convertibility of their currencies from the current to the financial account (under severe pressure to do so by the International Monetary Fund). In 1997, an imminent recession, together with declining confidence in the economy and the financial system, triggered speculative attacks on their currencies, resulting in massive capital flight, and significant downward pressures on the values of the currencies. The International Monetary Fund stepped in with loans and imposed higher interest rates (a tight monetary policy) on the grounds that these would stop the capital flight and help support the currencies, however the downward pressure on the currencies continued because confidence was so low. At the same time, high interest rates created massive contractions in economic activity (negative growth), with devastating effects on the lives of millions of people (huge increases in unemployment, poverty, hunger and malnutrition).

At that time, a number of well-known economists argued that non-convertibility for capital flows should be re-imposed, so that interest rates could be lowered to ease the recession without the risk of continuing capital flight. It was argued that had the currencies been non-convertible for capital flows from the beginning, the financial crisis might well have been avoided. In the words of Nobel Prize-winning economist Joseph Stiglitz, 'I believe that capital account liberalization was *the single most important factor leading to the crisis*' (emphasis in original).[38] (Note that Stiglitz uses the term '*capital account*' to refer to what is actually the '*financial account*'; see Chapter 14, page 398.)

Currency convertibility for the financial account, therefore, offers benefits that come with major risks; only when developing countries have created economic and political environments that minimise the risks can they fully liberalise their financial capital flows.

Test your understanding 17.8

1 Explain the meaning of capital liberalisation.

2 What are the potential advantages and risks of full capital liberalisation?

3 What conditions must be met before a country can safely liberalise its capital flows?

Real world focus

Can developing countries imitate the trade and growth strategies of the Asian Tigers?

Why were the Asian Tigers able to grow and develop successfully using export promotion, while countries that opened up to international trade in later years were less successful? The answer to this question has two parts.

The first part of the answer is that the Asian Tigers faced lower trade barriers on their exports of manufactured and processed goods to developed countries than developing countries faced in later years. Some tariff and non-tariff barriers in rich countries on manufactured and processed goods exports from developing countries were increased during the 1980s, after the successful entry of East Asian exports into developed country markets. This increased protection was undertaken to protect developed country domestic producers against low-cost competing goods, and to protect their workers against losing their jobs due to the entry of low-cost imports.

Some of these trade barriers have since been reduced as a result of the Uruguay Round of the World Trade Organization (WTO) agreements; however, barriers still remain at high levels. The difficulties of the Doha Round to reach agreement were in large measure due to inability to agree on further reductions of trade barriers to developing country exports (see page 490).

The second part of the answer to the question is that countries that opened up to international trade in the 1980s did not follow the strategy of the Asian Tigers. The Asian Tigers' export promotion was based on strong government intervention, whereas countries that turned to more open international trade in the 1980s did so on the basis of market-based policies. The successes of the Asian Tigers owed a lot to government intervention in the form of industrial policies. These encouraged the development of manufacturing and higher value-added production through support of education and training, research and development (R&D) and the adoption of appropriate technologies making heavy use of abundant labour supplies, support to industries targeted for exports, etc. By contrast, those developing countries that opened up to international trade in the context of market-based policies could not rely on this type of government support for their export industries.

Therefore, developing countries that opened up to trade during the 1980s did not fare as well as the Asian Tigers, partly because they faced high trade barriers on their exports, and partly because their growth and development strategy was market-led, thus not permitting much government support for export industries.

In view of the above, what can developing countries do at present? We can conclude with the following general comments:

- **A trade strategy that is open to international trade is superior to import substitution.** A strategy encouraging exports offers far greater potential for economic growth and development. The reasons for this can be found both in the arguments outlining the benefits of trade, as well as in the disappointing experiences of countries that pursued import-substitution strategies.

- **There are significant advantages in a strategy open to trade based on diversification of exports into manufacturing and higher value-added activities.** By diversifying production into manufacturing, processing and higher value-added activities for both domestic consumption and export, developing countries avoid the disadvantages of excessive specialisation in primary goods

(continued over)

---

[38] Joseph E. Stiglitz (2002) *Globalization and its Discontents*, Penguin.

production and export, and also benefit from opportunities to increase employment, and skill and technology levels.

- **Developed country trade protection is a major obstacle to a successful trade strategy in developing countries.** Trade protection by developed countries prevents developing countries from capturing the benefits of international trade, since trade protection limits their access to large and growing developed country markets.

- **Trade liberalisation among countries that are at different stages of economic development may be dangerous for the relatively less developed countries.** Experience shows that trade liberalisation among partners who are highly unequal can lead to de-industrialisation (loss of industry) due to the inability to compete, increased poverty, greater unemployment and a larger informal sector. The benefits of trade liberalisation in such instances are captured mainly by the economically stronger trading partners.

- **A possible way out of these problems may be through the formation of regional trading blocs as the basis of an outward orientation of developing countries.** In view of barriers to trade imposed by developed countries, and the dangers of trade liberalisation among economically unequal partners, many economists suggest that developing countries should form regional trading blocs. Increased integration through more trade between countries within geographical groupings could allow them to enjoy the benefits of increased exports, while avoiding some of the risks and obstacles created by rich country protection. Trade liberalisation is far more likelty to be mutually beneficial to trading partners when it takes place among countries that are at a similar level of economic development.[39] Developing countries should be aware that bilateral trading agreements with rich countries pose major risks to their growth and development efforts, and that they are likely to be better off liberalising their trade through multilateral agreements of the WTO rather then through bilateral trade agreements.

- **International trade as a growth and development strategy is likely to be more successful when accompanied by industrial policies.** It is likely that market-based policies are not as effective as industrial policies as the basis for a trade strategy. Many developing countries, especially the poorer ones, do not have the necessary institutions that support the development of infrastructure, human capital (health and education), technology development, etc. These ideas are reflected in the New Development Consensus. In certain cases, an outward orientation focused on increasing exports may also include some selective import-substituting policies, involving protection of certain industries on the basis of the infant industry argument, one of the strategies of the Asian Tigers.

- **Developing countries should be cautious about adopting full capital liberalisation on financial account transactions.** Full currency convertibility should be adopted when countries have the economic and political conditions that minimise the risks of full convertibility.

---

[39] Note, however, that while regional trading blocs may offer major potential advantages to the members of the bloc, there may result greater inefficiency and resource misallocation on a global scale (see Chapter 15, page 416).

Applying your skills

1 Why is it more difficult for developing countries today to imitate the trade and growth strategies of the Asian Tigers?

2 What trade and growth strategies open to developing countries today are likely to be more successful?

Assessment

The Student's CD-ROM at the back of this book provides practice of examination questions based on the material you have studied in this chapter.

Standard level
- Exam practice: Paper 2, Chapter 17
  - SL/HL core topics (Text/data 14–20, questions B.2–B.13)

Higher level
- Exam practice: Paper 2, Chapter 17
  - SL/HL core topics (Text/data 14–20, questions B.2–B.13)

Chapter 18
Foreign sources of finance and foreign debt

In this chapter we will study foreign direct investment (FDI), foreign aid, multilateral assistance, and the debt problem of developing countries.

18.1   The meaning of foreign sources of finance

The topics we will study in this chapter are all related to foreign sources of finance. Foreign sources of finance refer to funds that flow into a country from abroad, other than payments received for exports of goods and services. These inward flows are recorded as credits in the balance of payments, because they involve inflows of foreign exchange, and therefore work to balance out debits.

Figure 18.1 shows the main foreign sources of finance (in the top row) in relation to the topics we will study in this chapter, which appear in bold-face boxes. In developing countries, these inflows of funds are often used to pay for trade deficits, though they have other functions as well.[1]

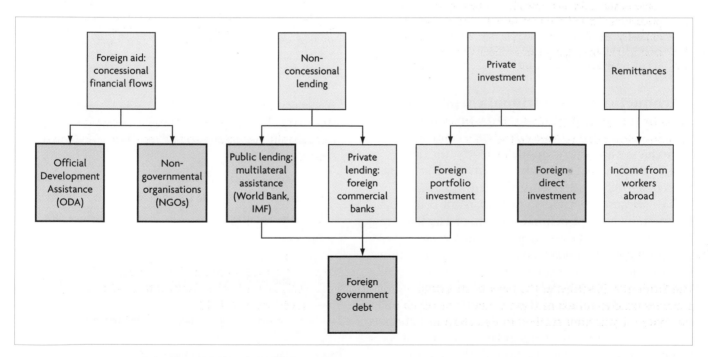

Figure 18.1 Main sources of foreign finance in developing countries

[1] Remittances, involving income from workers abroad, were briefly discussed in Chapter 16, page 452, and foreign portfolio investment was mentioned in Chapter 14, page 385. Private lending by foreign commercial banks will be discussed in the present chapter in the history of the government debt problem, page 520.

In general, the functions of foreign sources of finance are the following:

- **Helping countries acquire foreign exchange.** Foreign sources of finance create credits in the balance of payments. Therefore, if there is a deficit in the current account, which is likely to be due to a trade deficit, these inflows lead to a supply of foreign exchange (credits) used to pay for this deficit.[2]

- **Adding to insufficient domestic savings.** Developing countries, because of their relatively low incomes, often have a low amount of savings, leading to low levels of investment. Foreign sources of finance can be used in addition to domestic savings to help countries increase investments in numerous areas that support growth and development.

- **Adding to technical skills, management skills and technology.** Developing countries often have low levels of skills and technology. Some foreign sources of finance can help countries develop their skills and technology levels, which are a big push in favour of growth and development.

18.2 Foreign direct investment and multinational corporations (MNCs)

The nature of foreign direct investment and multinational corporations

♦ Describe the nature of foreign direct investment (FDI) and multinational corporations (MNCs).

Introducing multinational corporations

Foreign direct investment (FDI) is investment by firms based in one country (the home country) in productive activities in another country (the host country). A firm that undertakes foreign direct investment is referred to as a **multinational corporation (MNC)**, because it operates in more than one country. A 'corporation' is a type of firm composed of a legal entity that is separate from the individuals who own it.

Multinational corporations run business operations in both the home country and in other (host) countries. Historically, MNCs have been active since about the middle of the 19th century. Their importance grew in the 1950s when US multinationals stepped up their investments in Europe as part of European postwar reconstruction. In the last two to

three decades their growth has been explosive. For the greater part of the 20th century, foreign direct investment originated in developed countries and was also directed mainly towards developed countries. Since the 1980s, developing countries have been receiving an increasing share of total foreign direct investment inflows, approaching half of total annual FDI inflows (see Table 18.1 below).

Multinational corporations have their headquarters mostly in developed countries, dominated by the European Union, Japan and the United States. However, developing and transition countries are rapidly increasing their share in global foreign direct investments. While in 1990 only 10% of total MNCs had headquarters in developing countries, in 2009 this share had risen to more than 25%.[3] Whereas most multinational corporations are privately owned, there are also a few state-owned firms that are expanding abroad, particularly from developing countries.

The scope and growth of multinational corporations

The world of multinational corporations is vast and growing very rapidly. In the early 1990s, there were an estimated 37000 multinational corporations globally; by 2009, they had increased to 82000 and employed 80 million people in their foreign affiliates alone. The production of their foreign affiliates (i.e. excluding production in home countries) amounted to 11% of

Host region	% of world	% of developing countries
World	100.0	
Economically more developed countries	54.2	
Economically less developed countries	45.8	100.0
Latin America and Caribbean	11.2	24.4
North Africa and Middle East	8.3	18.1
Sub-Saharan Africa	3.9	8.4
East Asia	14.8	32.4
(of which, China)	(9.1)	(19.9)
South and South East Asia and Oceania	7.7	16.7

Table 18.1 Geographical distribution of foreign direct investment inflows, 2009

Source: UNCTAD, World Investment Report 2010.

---

[2] It might be thought that foreign sources of finance are recorded in the balance of payments as credits in the financial account, but this is not always the case. For example, grants and concessional financial flows, as well as remittances are entered under 'current transfers' in the current account.

[3] United Nations Conference on Trade and Development (UNCTAD), *World Investment Report 2010.*

global GDP and the value of their exports was 33% of global exports.[4]

The larger of the multinational corporations are enormous in size. In 2008, the top ten non-financial multinational corporations (ranked by size of foreign assets) had total assets of US$3 trillion, and total sales of $2.3 trillion.[5] In 2008, the value of sales of the top ten MNCs was about three times the total GDP of all the countries of Sub-Saharan Africa combined, and the value of their total assets was nearly four times Sub-Saharan African GDP. Further, their total assets were about the same as the GDP of China, and two and a half times the GDP of India.[6]

Yet foreign direct investment remains a small share of total private investment in developing countries; total investment by local firms tends to be far greater than total investment by multinational corporations. This raises an interesting question. If foreign direct investment forms only a small share of total private investment in developing countries, why is it the subject of heated discussions and controversy? The answer is that foreign direct investment is qualitatively very different from local investment. It differs because of the very large size of MNCs, their significant economic and political power, and their superior technical and managerial expertise, know-how and technologies.

Foreign direct investment is by far the most important source of foreign finance flows to developing countries. However, for many low-income developing countries that are almost completely bypassed by MNCs, foreign aid is the main source of foreign finance.

Why MNCs expand into economically less developed countries

♦ Explain the reasons why MNCs expand into economically less developed countries.

Multinational corporations expand into developing countries (as elsewhere) in the hope of securing higher profits. Developing countries offer possibilities for MNCs to:

• **increase sales and revenues.** Some developing countries have large or rapidly growing markets (for example, China, India and countries in Latin America), which offer the potential for large increases in sales and revenues. If the firm is located within the country, it can more easily capture a market share, as well as speed up delivery of products and save on transportation costs.

• **bypass trade barriers.** Producing in countries with trade barriers allows MNCs to bypass these and secure access to local markets.

• **lower costs of production.** Labour costs as a rule take up a large proportion of total production costs, and developing countries generally have lower labour costs than in developed countries. This is a key reason for example, why the United States has multinational corporations operating in Mexico.

• **use locally produced raw materials.** If an MNC needs raw materials in the form of natural resources for its production, it is far less costly to obtain them locally than to import them, on account of transportation costs.

• **further their activities in natural resource extraction.** Some MNCs specialise in the extraction of natural resources (oil, aluminium, bauxite, etc.). Many developing countries are very rich in natural resources (for example in Africa), and therefore it is natural for MNCs to want to locate in such resource-rich countries.

Developing country characteristics that attract multinational corporations

♦ Describe the characteristics of economically less developed countries that attract FDI, including low cost factor inputs, a regulatory framework that favours profit repatriation and favourable tax rules.

Geographical distribution of foreign direct investment

Table 18.1 shows the distribution of global foreign direct investment inflows between developed and developing countries, as well as between geographical regions. In 2009, the share of developing country inflows was over 46% of global inflows.

Foreign direct investment in developing countries is not evenly distributed throughout geographical regions, as Table 18.1 indicates. In 2009, East Asia (mainly China) and Latin America and the Caribbean had the largest shares of FDI inflows, while Sub-Saharan Africa was lagging far behind. However,

---

[4] UNCTAD, *World Investment Report 2010*.
[5] UNCTAD, *World Investment Report 2009*. The top ten non-financial firms (ranked by foreign assets) and their respective home countries were General Electric (United States), Vodafone Group (United Kingdom), Royal Dutch/Shell Group (Netherlands/United Kingdom), British Petroleum (United Kingdom), ExxonMobil (United States), Toyota Motor Corporation (Japan), Total (France), EDF (France), Ford Motor Company (United States), E.ON AG (Germany).
[6] Calculated from data in UNCTAD, *World Investment Report 2010*, and United Nations Development Programme, *Human Development Report 2010*.

though small, Sub-Saharan Africa's share is growing rapidly, as it was only 2% of the world total in 2005.

Four developing countries alone, Brazil, Russia, India and China, received 19% of world FDI inflows, corresponding to 40% of developing country inflows. These countries are known as 'BRIC' (from the first letter of each country); they are similar in that they have very large and rapidly growing domestic markets, liberalised economies and a great wealth of natural resources. By contrast, many of the poorest countries in the world receive negligible amounts of foreign direct investment.

Attractive characteristics of developing countries

The above pattern suggests that multinational corporations are highly selective in their choice of hosts, preferring to invest in countries that display certain characteristics. Aside from seeking host countries that provide low-cost labour and natural resources, they are attracted to countries offering an economic and political environment that is most likely to ensure profitability and safety. The most important of these characteristics include the following:

- political stability and political institutions that ensure a stable political environment

- a stable macroeconomic environment (low inflation, stable currency, acceptable levels of foreign debt, absence of major balance of payments problems)

- an institutional environment that favours foreign direct investment, such as

  - freedom to repatriate profits (i.e. send profits to the home country)

  - freedom to engage in foreign exchange transactions (no exchange controls, thus can import possible needed inputs without restrictions; see page 495)

  - favourable tax rules (to ensure low tax payments)

  - lack of restrictions regarding foreign ownership

  - well-established property rights

  - rules that minimise the risk of nationalisation (a takeover of private property by the state)

- a liberalised (free market) economy with limited government intervention (including privatisation of state-owned enterprises)

- liberal (free market) trade policy with an emphasis on exports

- large markets

- rapid economic growth and expectations of continued rapid growth

- well-functioning infrastructure, including transportation and communications, that will facilitate imports and exports

- a well-educated labour force.

The characteristics required of host countries are those that provide MNCs with the freedom to pursue their economic interests with the least amount of government interference, in a safe economic and political environment that minimises uncertainties and potential risks of losses on their investments. Recipients of the largest amounts of foreign direct investment are countries that best satisfy these conditions, and are mostly concentrated in the middle-income groups (upper middle and lower middle) of developing countries.

In view of the requirements of MNCs, it is easy to see that the rapid growth of foreign direct investment around the world in the past two to three decades has been driven by the liberalisation of the global economy and the domestic economies of many countries. Since the 1980s, as developing countries turned more and more toward the market as the basis for policy, so MNCs have found it profitable to establish affiliates in hospitable foreign countries that accommodate their needs.

Advantages and disadvantages of FDI for economically less developed countries

> ♦ Evaluate the impact of foreign direct investment (FDI) for economically less developed countries.

Multinational corporations are profit-seeking entities; they are not organisations concerned with the growth and development problems of developing countries. Why then do developing countries view them as a mechanism that can help accelerate growth and development?

Potential advantages of MNCs for host developing countries

- **MNCs can supplement insufficient foreign exchange earnings.** Investment funds flowing into a country from abroad appear as credits in the financial account, and can help offset a current account deficit. As the activities of multinational corporations are usually export oriented, the country's exports are expected to increase, resulting in increased export earnings and positive effects on the country's balance of payments position.

- **MNCs can supplement and improve upon local technical skills, management skills and technology.** When multinational corporations set up affiliates in developing countries, they bring with them technical and managerial expertise, as well as new production technologies, which can be learned and adopted by the local labour force (workers and managers) and local businesses. This involves technological improvements as well as improvements in human capital (the acquisition of new skills and knowledge by the local labour force), and is considered to be one of the important advantages of foreign direct investment for developing countries.

- **MNCs can supplement insufficient domestic savings and increase investment and new capital formation.** The inflows of FDI funds into a country can supplement insufficient domestic savings, increasing the amount of investment.

- **MNCs can lead to greater tax revenues in the host country.** If multinational corporations are taxed by the government of the host country, this will contribute to increased tax revenues.

- **MNCs can help promote local industry.** When MNCs buy locally produced goods and services as inputs into their production, they promote the development of local industries. This may lead to the growth of existing local firms, or the establishment of new local firms to provide inputs to the MNC.

- **MNCs can increase local employment and help lower unemployment in the host country.** By establishing productive facilities (investing) in the host country, MNCs can increase employment by hiring local workers. In addition, the promotion of local industry also contributes to increasing domestic employment.

- **MNCs can lead to higher economic growth in the host country.** Increased levels of investment, improved technology and increases in human capital as well as the promotion of local industry and greater tax revenues, can lead to higher economic growth in the host country with increased possibilities for pursuing development objectives.

Potential disadvantages of MNCs for host developing countries

We will now consider the point of view that the benefits listed above may not come about. In addition, we will consider some possible negative effects of MNCs on growth and development.

Why the benefits listed above might not come about

- **MNCs may not always supplement insufficient foreign exchange earnings.** MNCs usually do bring foreign exchange into the host country. However, MNCs also engage in activities that result in foreign exchange outflows. These outflows may occur because of repatriation of profits (profits sent back to the host country); or because MNCs import raw materials and other inputs for use in production; or because they finance their activities by borrowing from the parent corporation in the home country, in which case they must repay the loan plus pay interest. The result is that the net inflows of foreign exchange (inflows minus outflows) may be small.

- **MNCs may not improve on local technical skills, management skills and technology.** Critics argue that MNCs' influence on the development of local skills may be very small, as in practice the links between MNC activities and the local economy are often limited, in which case local workers do not have the opportunity to learn from the MNC. Also, MNCs often hire personnel from the home country, thus limiting learning opportunities for the local labour force.

- **MNCs may not lead to greater tax revenues in the host country.** While MNCs are taxed by host country governments, they enjoy many tax privileges and benefits, often lowering the amount of tax paid. Tax benefits are offered as an incentive to attract MNCs into the host country. Another reason why MNCs pay less tax involves the practice of *transfer pricing*, which allows MNCs to lower their stated profits. Transfer pricing works in the following way. Many MNCs buy and sell inputs and intermediate products from their various affiliates in other countries. By claiming to local tax authorities that the prices they have paid for the purchase of inputs from their affiliates abroad is higher than the actual price paid, their profits appear lower than true profits. Since the amount of tax paid is a percentage of profit, lower-stated profits mean lower taxes (sometimes significantly lower). It is estimated that lost tax revenues due to transfer pricing are in the billions of dollars each year.

- **MNCs may not help promote local industry.** The operation of MNCs sometimes forces local competing firms to go out of business, or alternatively does not permit new local firms to establish themselves in industries that are directly competitive with the MNC.

- **MNCs may not help lower unemployment in the host country.** If, as noted above, MNCs prevent the development of local industry, then their job-creating impact will be limited. In addition, some MNCs may sometimes import into the host country capital-intensive technologies that are inappropriate to local conditions given large labour supplies, thus contributing to unemployment and underemployment, and the growth of the urban informal sector. (However, some MNCs engage in labour-intensive activities that make extensive use of cheap local labour).

Further possible negative effects of MNCs

- **MNCs and environmental degradation.** MNCs often pursue activities that cause serious environmental degradation. They prefer to invest in countries that impose few environmental restrictions, and they have been known to engage in activities that have caused tremendous environmental damage.[7] Moreover, MNCs are responsible for the production of the bulk of industrial pollutants (such as chlorofluorocarbons, a main cause of ozone depletion, as well as pesticides, plastics, petroleum, industrial chemicals, and many others). It has been estimated that about 80% of greenhouse gas emissions are caused by substances produced by MNCs.

- **MNCs promote inappropriate consumption patterns in developing countries.** Critics charge that MNCs, through advertising, create new consumption needs and promote inappropriate consumption patterns. This charge applies to the role of MNCs in developed countries as well, but what makes it more powerful in the case of developing countries is that populations plagued by hunger, malnutrition, disease and lack of basic services can less afford to spend their small incomes on unnecessary goods while their basic needs remain unsatisfied. Examples include consumption of soft drinks, sweets, fast foods, white bread, expensive brand name goods, and many others.

- **MNCs may use government resources to build infrastructure needed by MNCs rather than for poverty alleviation.** MNCs sometimes require infrastructure (road systems, ports, telecommunications, etc.) which the developing country must make available if it is to become attractive as a host country. To build these types of infrastructure, it may have to shift some of its scarce resources away from needed merit goods (clean water, sanitation, schools and health care services) and toward infrastructure for MNCs.

- **MNCs may use their economic and political power to bring about policies that may work against economic development.** The very large size of many MNCs gives them exceptional economic and political power that they can use to influence host governments to pursue policies that are in their own interests but against economic development. For example, MNCs are interested in investing in countries that have weak labour protection laws, because little or no labour protection results in lower costs of production; and they are interested in investing in countries with weak environmental regulations, as this allows them to avoid costs associated with environmental protection. When the interests of MNCs and those of developing countries conflict, developing country governments find themselves in a weak bargaining position because if they do not give in to MNC demands, they will lose the investment to another developing country that is more willing to compromise. For example, in Thailand and Peru, MNCs threatened to relocate to other countries if environmental regulations were enforced. In Peru, a mining company pressured the government not to undertake health tests for children living close to the mining operations.

- **Competition between developing countries to host MNCs and the 'race to the bottom'.** Many developing countries compete with each other over which will create better conditions to attract MNCs. Yet MNC demands may conflict with what is in a country's best interests. This has been termed 'the race to the bottom', because the desire to host MNCs may involve sacrifices of needed development, lowering government tax revenues, and use of local resources for infrastructure instead of merit good provision. Additional sacrifices may involve too much economic and trade liberalisation.

Test your understanding 18.1

1. **(a)** Describe foreign direct investment (FDI) and multinational corporations (MNCs). **(b)** Explain why MNCs have an interest in expanding into developing countries. **(c)** In view of their relatively small share in total private investment in developing countries, why are MNCs a highly controversial topic?

2. **(a)** What characteristics of developing countries do MNCs look for when deciding where to invest? **(b)** How can you account for the fact that low-income countries receive negligible amounts of foreign direct investment? **(c)** What factors account for the massive growth in foreign direct investment in developing countries in recent years?

3. Explain some advantages and some disadvantages of MNCs in developing countries.

4. Why have some observers referred to the competition between developing countries to attract MNCs as the 'race to the bottom'?

---

[7] One of the greatest disasters caused by MNCs involved an explosion in a Union Carbide plant in India in 1984 that killed more than 20000 people and left more than 100000 with serious and permanent health problems. While destruction on such a scale is unusual, there are numerous well-documented cases of MNCs undertaking environmentally unsustainable activities.

MNCs, pollution, and social responsibility

Oil MNCs in Nigeria

The Niger delta (in Nigeria), with 606 oil fields, has been termed the 'pollution capital of the world'. It is estimated that more oil is spilled in the delta each year than was lost in the Gulf of Mexico from the leak in BP's Deepwater Horizon rig in the spring of 2010. Local people can hardly believe the measures taken in the United States to protect the Louisiana shoreline from the effects of the spill. The head of Friends of the Earth International (an environmental NGO [non-governmental organisation]) says, 'We see frantic efforts being made to stop the spill in the US. But in Nigeria, oil companies largely ignore their spills, cover them up and destroy people's livelihood and environments. The Gulf spill can be seen as a metaphor for what is happening daily in the oilfields of Nigeria and other parts of Africa.'

Source: John Vidal, 'Nigeria's agony dwarfs the Gulf oil spill. The US and Europe ignore it' in the Guardian, 30 May 2010.

Measures to increase MNC responsiveness to developing country needs

Nobel Prize-winning economist Joseph E. Stiglitz suggests a 'five-pronged agenda' that would help developing countries gain the potential benefits of MNCs while reducing corporate abuses:

- **Improving corporate social responsibility.** Multinational corporations are highly visible, and are keenly aware of their public image. They can be held in check by the knowledge that practices that do not meet with ethical standards are likely to damage their reputation with the public. A negative image of a corporation held by its customers can lower profits by lowering sales. Therefore, corporations face an incentive to engage in socially beneficial behaviour. Issues of particular concern are the environment and workers' rights.

- **Limiting the power of corporations.** MNCs are usually large oligopolies that try to increase their market power by limiting competition between them. Governments in the home countries should try to discourage the growth of excessive market power by preventing anti-competitive behaviour and promoting competition between them.

- **Improving corporate governance.** Laws should be enacted that would make corporations behave in ways that are consistent with the broader public interest. For example, just as cheating stockholders is a crime, so new laws could be passed that would consider causing environmental damage to be a crime.

- **Global laws for a global economy.** The establishment of an international legal framework would allow parties across national boundaries who have been injured by a particular activity to band together and file a single suit against the offender. Moreover, developed countries could (and should) provide legal assistance for the poor in developing countries.

- **Reducing the scope of corruption.** It is well known that MNCs engage in corrupt behaviour, which includes everything from bribing officials to be allowed to bypass laws and regulations, to evading taxes and engaging in transfer pricing. Efforts on an international scale should be made to reduce corruption.

Source: Adapted from Joseph E. Stiglitz (2006) Making Globalization Work, W. W. Norton.

Applying your skills

How can the global community help Nigeria (and other countries) reduce the environmental destruction caused by oil (and other) MNCs?

18.3 Foreign aid

Understanding foreign aid

- Explain that aid is extended to economically less developed countries either by governments of donor countries, in which case it is called official development assistance (ODA), or by non-governmental organisations (NGOs).
- Explain that humanitarian aid consists of food aid, medical aid and emergency relief aid.
- Explain that development aid consists of grants, concessional long-term loans, project aid that includes support for schools and hospitals, and programme aid that includes support for sectors such as the education sector and the financial sector.

Foreign aid is defined as the transfer of funds or goods and services to developing countries with the main objective to bring about improvements in their

economic, social or political conditions. In Figure 18.2, which provides an overview of foreign aid, we see that for such transfers to be considered as foreign aid, they must satisfy two conditions:

- They must be **concessional**, which means that the transfers involve more favourable conditions than could be achieved in the market. In other words, when the aid involves loans, interest rates are lower and repayment periods are longer than borrowers would get in the commercial banking system. Also, the aid may involve **grants**, which are gifts of either money or goods and services that do not need to be repaid.
- They must be *non-commercial*, meaning that they must not involve buying and selling (commerce) or other activities concerned with making a profit.

Figure 18.2 also shows what does *not* account as foreign aid, for example military aid, peacekeeping, refugee assistance, and others. The reason these activities are not 'foreign aid' (though they involve aid of some sort) is that they are not directly concerned with bringing about improvements in the economic, social or political conditions of developing countries.

Under 'Who offers foreign aid' in Figure 18.2, we see there are two sources of aid. The first is *Official Development Assistance (ODA)*, provided by developed country governments, and the second is aid provided by *non-governmental organisations (NGOs)*. All the providers of aid (whether governments or organisations) are referred to as 'donors' of aid; the developing countries that receive the aid are 'recipients' of aid.

Under 'Types of foreign aid' in the figure, we see that there are two main categories of aid: humanitarian and development.

Humanitarian aid
Humanitarian aid involves aid extended in regions where there are emergencies caused by violent conflicts or natural disasters such as floods, earthquakes and tsunamis. They are intended to save lives, to ensure access to basic necessities such as food, water, shelter and health care, and to provide assistance with reconstruction work in order to help displaced people cope.

As shown in Figure 18.2, humanitarian aid is extended by donors through grants (sending money as a gift) or through goods-in-kind (food, medical supplies, blankets, etc.).

Development aid
Development aid is intended to help developing countries achieve their economic growth and development objectives. It may take the following forms:

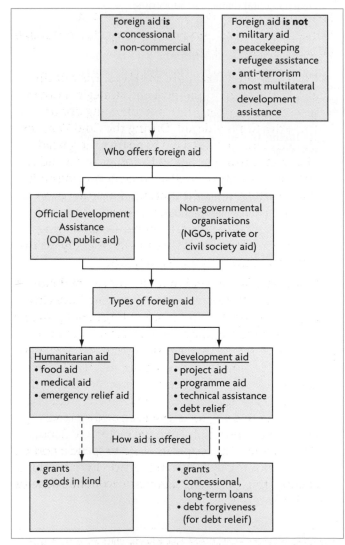

Figure 18.2 Overview of foreign aid

- **Project aid** involves financial support for specific projects, such as building schools, clinics, hospitals, irrigation systems or other agricultural infrastructure.
- **Programme aid** involves financial support to sectors, such as education, health care, agriculture, urban development, the financial sector (credit, banking, insurance), energy, the environment, or others.
- **Technical assistance** involves the provision of technical advice by developed country specialists such as doctors, teachers, agronomists, etc. Technical assistance may sometimes be part of project aid or programme aid.
- **Debt relief.** Very poor countries with high levels of foreign debt sometimes receive aid involving some debt forgiveness (see page 522 below).

As Figure 18.2 indicates, development aid is extended by donors through grants or through concessional long-term loans as well as debt forgiveness.

Humanitarian aid and development aid are offered by both ODA and NGOs. Whatever the kind of aid, whenever it involves financial inflows, these enter as credits in the balance of payments, thus bringing in foreign exchange and helping countries offset possible deficits in their trade balance.

Official Development Assistance (ODA)

♦ Explain the motivations of economically more developed countries giving aid.

Who are the donors of ODA?

Official Development Assistance (ODA), all of which is public in the sense that it comes from government funds, forms the largest part of foreign aid. Most ODA funds (nearly three-quarters) take the form of grants.

ODA funds reach developing countries in three ways:

- through *bilateral aid*, which is the most important way – funds go directly from the donor government to the developing country recipient; examples of bilateral aid agencies are USAID (US Agency for Internal Development) in the United States and DFID (Department for International Development) in the United Kingdom
- through *multilateral aid*, going indirectly from donor governments to international

organisations, which transfer the funds to developing country governments
- through NGOs – donor governments transfer ODA funds to NGOs which spend them in developing countries.

The donor countries include most of the members of the Organisation for Economic Co-operation and Development (OECD), some members of the Organization of the Petroleum Exporting Countries (OPEC), and more recently also some eastern European countries.

International organisations providing ODA include United Nations agencies; single-issue funds like the Global Fund for Aids, Tuberculosis and Malaria; the International Development Association (IDA, which is an organisation of the World Bank[8]), regional development banks (such as the European Bank for Reconstruction and Development (EBRD), the Inter-American Development Bank (IDB); the International Monetary Fund (IMF) assistance for debt relief under debt relief initiatives.

Donor motives for providing ODA

Donor countries are motivated to provide aid through ODA for a variety of reasons:

- **Political and strategic motives.** Historically and to the present, political and strategic motives have played a strong role in motivating donor countries to provide aid. During the Cold War, the United States provided aid to restrict the spread of communism. The Soviet Union provided aid to communist states as well as some non-communist states with communist leanings. European powers provided aid to their former colonies. Often aid has been used to support regimes in developing countries that are considered to be 'friendly' to the interests of the donor governments.
- **Economic motives.** Economic motives of donor countries, historically and to the present, have also played a significant role in prompting donor provision of aid. Developed countries often regard it to be in their interest to assist countries with which they have strong economic ties. For example, much of Japan's aid is directed towards neighbouring countries with which it has strong trade and investment links. The practice of tied aid (to be discussed below), is an important example of economic motives of donors. Tied aid forces the recipients of aid to spend a portion of aid funds to buy goods and services from the donor country, thus providing significant economic benefits to donor countries.

---

[8] The International Development Association (IDA) is part of the World Bank but it offers the poorest of developing countries concessional loans, i.e. soft loans – unlike World Bank loans, which are extended on commercial terms.

- **Humanitarian and moral motives.** Some aid is provided on humanitarian grounds for short-term emergency assistance, such as in the case of famines, wars or natural disasters. Concern about the extent of poverty in developing countries is a motive for allocating aid funds for long-term development purposes. The Millennium Development Goals (MDGs) adopted in 2000 were a global commitment to the alleviation of extreme poverty, hunger, malnutrition, disease, premature deaths and environmental damage (see Chapter 16, pages 450–51), and aid funds are often linked with achieving these goals.

The evidence on the distribution of ODA funds across countries suggests that all these motives play a role in the thinking of donors. This can be seen in Table 18.2, showing ODA *per capita* and GNI *per capita* for developing countries grouped by income level and by geographical regions (GNI is measured in US$ PPP to ensure that GNI figures are comparable across regions; see Chapter 16, page 453). We can see that low-income countries receive more ODA *per capita* than lower middle and upper middle income countries. Similarly, sub-Saharan Africa, with its relatively low GNI *per capita* also receives a large amount of ODA *per capita*.

	ODA $ *per capita* (2007)	GNI $ PPP *per capita* (2007)
Low income	37	1494
Lower middle income	9	4543
Upper middle income	9	11 868

East Asia and Pacific	4	4937
Europe and Central Asia	13	11 115
Latin America and the Caribbean	12	9321
Middle East and North Africa	56	7385
South Asia	7	2537
Sub-Saharan Africa	44	1870

Table 18.2 Official Development Assistance (ODA) by level of development and by region

Source: Data on ODA from The World Bank, *World Development Report, 2010*; data on GNI $ PPP *per capita* from The World Bank, *World Development Report, 2009*.

However, there are major exceptions from the pattern where countries with lower GNI *per capita* receive more ODA *per capita*. For example, upper middle income countries receive the same ODA *per capita* as lower middle income countries, though they have GNI *per capita* levels more than two and a half times greater than the latter. They also receive about one-fourth the ODA *per capita* of lower income countries, though their GNI *per capita* is about eight times greater.

The Middle East and North Africa, with GNI *per capita* about three times *greater* than in South Asia, receive eight times the amount of aid *per capita*, and 14 times the amount of aid given to East Asia and the Pacific, which has a much lower GNI *per capita*. Further, Europe and Central Asia,[9] with a GNI *per capita* more than four times greater than South Asia's, receive nearly double the *per capita* aid.

The reasons for these patterns can be found in the strategic importance that donor countries attach to the Middle East and North Africa, as well as to Europe and Central Asia.

The problem of tied aid

♦ Explain that aid might also come in the form of tied aid.

Tied aid refers to the practice where donors make the recipients of aid spend a portion of borrowed funds to buy goods and services from the donor country. It occurs only in the context of bilateral (not multilateral) aid, and gives rise to several serious disadvantages:

- Recipient countries cannot seek lower price alternatives for the goods and services they are forced to buy from the donor country. It has been estimated that tied aid reduces the value of aid by 11–30%, and in the case of tied food aid the costs to the recipient country are as much as 40% higher than in the market.[10] This means that recipients of tied aid face much higher than necessary import costs.

- Having to buy specific goods and services from the donor country often results in buying inappropriate, capital-intensive technologies.

- Those who benefit from tied aid are usually large firms in developed countries whose goods and services the recipient countries are forced to buy. This is a kind of support for industry

[9] This group includes eastern European countries undergoing a transition from central planning under communism to mixed market economies, as well as the Central Asian states of the former Soviet Union.

[10] United Nations Development Programme, *Human Development Report 2005* (available at http://hdr.undp.org/en/reports/).

of developed countries, occurring at the expense of poor country development objectives.

Approximately one-third to one-half of bilateral aid is tied aid.

Comparing and contrasting ODA to two developing countries

♦ Compare and contrast the extent, nature and sources of ODA to two economically less developed countries.

As our discussion above suggests, aid financed by ODA can vary widely across recipient countries depending on the amount of aid (some countries receive much more than others), the type of aid (humanitarian aid, project aid, programme aid), the form it takes (grants and concessional loans) the sectors that are supported, and the sources of aid (donor countries offering bilateral aid, international organisations offering multilateral aid, or NGOs). In addition, it can vary widely with respect to how effective it is in helping recipient countries achieve their growth and development objectives (this will be discussed below). You will be given the opportunity to compare two developing countries with respect to these factors in a data response question (see CD-ROM 'Exam practice: Paper 2' chapter, page 35).

Private (civil society) aid: non-governmental organisations (NGOs)

♦ Explain that, for the most part, the priority of NGOs is to provide aid on a small scale to achieve development objectives.

Non-governmental organisations (NGOs) are the second type of aid flowing into developing countries (see Figure 18.1, page 500). Like ODA, they involve concessional flows, but they are all grants (there are no loans that must be repaid).

The World Bank defines NGOs as 'private organizations that pursue activities to relieve suffering, promote the interests of the poor, protect the environment, provide basic social services, or undertake community development.'[11] NGOs are 'private' in the sense that they are not part of any governmental structure; they are not private in the sense of being part of the market system. NGOs are an expression of civil society, and as such are often

referred to as comprising a third sector (the first and second being the government and market sectors).

NGOs include a wide variety of organisations, such as charitable organisations, non-profit organisations, nationally based groups with a national or international reach, locally based community groups, or grassroots organisations, and they may operate in developed or developing countries (or both). Among the better known international NGOs (INGOs) are Amnesty International, Greenpeace, Oxfam, Save the Children and World Wide Fund for Nature, also known as the World Wildlife Fund (both abbreviated as WWF).

NGOs in developing countries have grown massively in numbers and in involvement since the 1980s. It is estimated that developing countries now have several tens of thousands of *national* NGOs, and several hundreds of thousands of *community-based* NGOs. A growing number of these now have consultative status with United Nations agencies; from 41 in 1948, the number of NGOs with consultative status today is in the thousands. Most of these are small local groups pursuing development objectives within a relatively small community.

NGOs obtain their funds from private voluntary contributions including private sector corporations and, increasingly, from bilateral and multilateral ODA funds. In other words, more and more of ODA funds are channelled through NGOs, particularly in the case of humanitarian assistance. The reason for this is that NGOs can perform functions that are not performed as effectively by national governments (see page 512 below).

NGOs are involved in a vast range of activities, including provision of humanitarian aid in times of crisis, promotion of sustainable development, promotion of community development, service delivery, poverty alleviation, protection of child health, promotion of women's rights, promotion of small-scale entrepreneurs, support of the poor in the informal sector, provision of technical assistance to small farmers, provision of credit to poor people (micro-credit schemes), research activities, political advocacy, support for people's movements, and more.

Evaluating foreign aid

♦ Evaluate the effectiveness of foreign aid in contributing to economic development.

---

[11] The World Bank, Operational Directive 14.70, 28 August 1989.

Arguments in favour of Official Development Assistance (ODA)

Aid and the poverty cycle

Very poor societies trapped in the poverty cycle face a savings–investment constraint due to very low incomes (see Chapter 16, page 444). To emerge from a poverty cycle, poor people and poor communities need the government to intervene by undertaking the necessary investments in physical, human and natural capital. However, if the government does not have enough tax revenues, the only way the country, or community within a country, can escape the poverty cycle is through foreign aid that makes up for the lack of savings. The United Nations Development Programme (UNDP), providing examples, notes that spending on health in Sub-Saharan Africa is US$3–10 per person, while the cost of providing basic health care is $30 per person. Low-income countries do not have enough funds to provide universal primary education, as well as basic infrastructure services.[12] To be able to finance these services themselves, poor countries would need to achieve economic growth that would provide them with increased economic resources that can be used to invest in health, education and infrastructure. However, economic growth is not possible unless there is first some investment in these areas. Therefore, these countries are caught in a poverty cycle from which they can escape only if foreign aid provides the financing for these investments.

Aid and provision of basic services

Even if a country is not caught in a poverty cycle, aid can make resources available for investments in health, education and infrastructure, which can help poor people improve their employment opportunities and improve their incomes. In a number of Sub-Saharan African countries, foreign aid is an important component of social budgets; in Tanzania, it accounts for more than one-third of social spending. In Zambia, US$5 out of $8 of health spending *per capita* is due to foreign aid. Many of these programmes contribute to significantly limiting the incidence of preventable diseases and reducing infant and child deaths: in Egypt, for example, an aid-funded diarrhoea programme reduced infant deaths by 82% in five years and prevented 300 000 child deaths.

Aid and improved income distribution

By focusing on the most disadvantaged groups in society, aid can help improve the relative income positions of the beneficiaries and contribute to improved income distribution. Highly unequal income distribution can be a barrier to growth and development (see page 473).

Aid and economic growth

There is strong evidence that aid leads to economic growth, because it makes possible increased investment and consumption levels, leading to increased volumes of output. Evidence cited by the UNDP indicates that countries in Sub-Saharan Africa that rely heavily on aid (Mozambique, Tanzania and Uganda) have achieved high growth rates.[13]

Aid and the Millennium Development Goals (MDGs)

The provision of aid is crucially important to the achievement of the Millennium Development Goals (MDGs; see pages 450–51). Much of the aid is closely linked to the achievement of these goals. According to the United Nations Development Programme, it will not be possible for developing countries to achieve the MDGs without enough aid.

Aid, the debt trap and debt relief

Countries that are heavily indebted (have high levels of debt) face serious negative consequences for their growth and development, especially when caught in a 'debt trap', where they must go on borrowing more and more in order to service old debts (see page 521 below). Aid for debt relief helps countries reduce their debt burden and releases resources that can be used for poverty reduction and economic growth and development.

Factors that limit the effectiveness of Official Development Assistance (ODA)

A number of factors limit the effectiveness of aid as a mechanism for achieving economic and human development and poverty alleviation. The most important of these include the following.

Tied aid

One of the most important limitations of the effectiveness of ODA funds is the practice of tied aid, whose disadvantages for developing countries were explained above (page 508).

Conditional aid (conditionality)

Most donors of ODA impose numerous conditions that must be met by the recipients of aid. Donors see these conditions as a mechanism for forcing developing countries to make important policy changes, as well as for ensuring that aid funds are used effectively. The kinds of conditions that

---

[12] United Nations Development Programme, *Human Development Report 2005*.

[13] United Nations Development Programme, *Human Development Report 2005*.

are imposed vary from requiring the recipient to pursue policies intended to achieve a greater market orientation in the economy (such as privatisation, elimination of protective trade barriers, greater reliance on the price mechanism, etc.), to forcing the recipient to accept particular projects that have been decided upon by the donors. Conditional lending has been found to create disadvantages for developing countries. Donors do not pay sufficient attention to the preferences of the government or of the population groups the project is intended to benefit. Policy prescriptions by donors may be incorrect; they may not fit in with the government's development strategy and priorities; and they may weaken the recipient government's authority and accountability to its citizens.

Aid volatility and unpredictability

The flow of aid funds (particularly bilateral flows) into developing countries is volatile (unstable) and unpredictable. This is partly due to changing volumes of aid in donor budgets, and changing donor priorities on how to allocate aid funds. This makes it difficult for recipient governments to implement policies that depend on aid funds, as they cannot be sure if and when funds will be available to undertake necessary investments and activities. In very poor countries that depend heavily on aid for provision of basic services (such as education or health care services), disruptions in aid flows can have very serious effects on the welfare of the population groups affected by the aid cuts.

Unco-ordinated donors

In any recipient country there are usually large numbers of donors (bilateral and multilateral) who finance unco-ordinated activities, giving rise to numerous inefficiencies in the use of aid resources. Sometimes the numbers of aid-funded projects are in the hundreds. Lack of co-ordination of such projects results in overlapping and duplication of some projects, inconsistencies between other projects, and the lack of coherence in the entire aid effort.

Aid may substitute for rather than supplement domestic resources

Aid resources are intended to supplement insufficient domestic resources. A possible danger is that governments in recipient countries may use aid funds to substitute for domestic resources, and not make enough effort to increase domestic revenues through taxation. The evidence on this issue is mixed; whereas some countries have been unable to raise tax rates in spite of growth, others have succeeded in increasing tax revenues even as aid increases rapidly.

Aid may not reach those most in need

Aid resources are not allocated on the basis of the greatest need for poverty alleviation. There are two aspects to this issue: the distribution of aid funds across countries, and the use of aid funds within recipient countries. We have already seen in connection with the first that bilateral donors do not always allocate aid resources according to country needs. The second, involving the use of aid funds within countries, is related to a number of factors: recipient country governments may not be genuinely committed to poverty alleviation; they may lack the necessary expertise to design and implement poverty alleviation policies; tied aid may favour projects that are not appropriate for poverty alleviation; donors may select projects that are not the most effective from the point of view of poverty alleviation.

Aid may be associated with corruption

Corruption involves misuse of aid funds by recipient countries, and is a key problem associated with the provision of aid. Corruption is a reflection of the degree of transparency and accountability in public affairs, and tends to be more prominent the lower the *per capita* income of a country.

The quantity of aid and poverty alleviation

Donors have repeatedly promised to allocate 0.7% of their GNI for ODA. As Table 18.3 indicates, a few countries more than meet this target. However, others do not, and since some of these are among the larger and wealthier donors, it means that overall ODA funds

Country	ODA/GNI (%)	Country	ODA/GNI (%)
Australia	0.29	Luxembourg	1.04
Austria	0.30	Netherlands	0.82
Belgium	0.55	New Zealand	0.28
Canada	0.30	Norway	1.06
Denmark	0.88	Portugal	0.23
Finland	0.54	Spain	0.46
France	0.47	Sweden	1.12
Germany	0.35	Switzerland	0.45
Greece	0.19	United Kingdom	0.52
Ireland	0.54	United States	0.21
Italy	0.16	Total DAC	0.31
Japan	0.18		

Table 18.3   ODA as a proportion of GNI of DAC* donors, 2009

* DAC = Development Assistance Committee, a forum of bilateral donors of the Organisation for Economic Co-operation and Development (OECD).

Source: Data from OECD, Aid statistics – data and databases (www.oecd.org/dac/stats/data)

are far less than the target amount. According to the United Nations Development Programme, if rich countries fail to follow through on their commitments, developing countries will be unable to make the investments in health, education and infrastructure needed to improve welfare and support the economy on the scale required to achieve the MDGs.

Advantages of NGO: why NGOs are growing in importance

More and more bilateral and multilateral donors of ODA are channelling their funds through NGOs because of their ability to perform some functions better than developing country governments. The reasons for better performance include:

Strong anti-poverty orientation of activities

NGO activities are for the most part concerned with reaching poor people and helping them emerge from their poverty. Governments often have difficulties in reaching the very poor; NGOs have an advantage by working very closely with communities of poor people and responding to their particular needs as these arise in their own particular economic, social and environmental conditions.

Working closely with project beneficiaries

One of the strongest advantages of NGOs is that they work closely with their beneficiaries, involving local people in the design and implementation of development projects. Involvement by local people allows them to provide inputs into deciding what problems should be addressed and how they should be solved, and gives them a sense of ownership and commitment to the project, all of which contribute greatly to success. Moreover, this approach contributes to the promotion of self-help and mutual assistance in problems of development.

Contributing to democratisation

Such participatory practices contribute to a process of democratisation, which can be important in countries that do not have democratic institutions.

Offering expertise and advice

International NGOs accumulate experience from a variety of countries and local settings, many of which may be relevant and transferable to similar settings in other countries. They recruit experts in a variety of areas in accordance with need, and the experts are highly motivated out of a strong commitment to the objectives of the NGO with which they are affiliated.

Ability to be innovative

Unlike governments, which often take a uniform approach to problems, NGOs, by working closely with their beneficiaries, can be more creative and innovative in devising solutions to very specific problems that arise in local settings.

Independent assessment of problems and pursuit of solutions

Unlike government programmes, which must conform to general policy guidelines and are subject to following government agendas, NGOs have a greater degree of freedom to use their expertise and technical knowledge to assess problems independently and arrive at suggestions for solutions. In addition, NGOs also enjoy more freedom because their activities are not subject to the conditions often imposed by donors of aid (conditionality); and they are not subject to the restrictions associated with tied aid.

Enjoying the trust of beneficiaries

Poor people are often highly suspicious and mistrusting of government officials and administrators, feeling at best neglected and at worst exploited. NGOs sometimes enjoy greater trust than governments, because of their close relationship with project beneficiaries, and their commitment to solving problems at grassroots level.

Advocacy and raising public awareness and support

Poor people usually lack political voice and representation, and their concerns are not heard at higher government levels. NGOs play an important leadership role in acting as advocates on public policy issues, and ensuring that poor people's concerns are heard.

Criticisms of NGOs

Critics charge that NGOs have a number of weaknesses:

Small size and weakness of many NGOs

NGOs may be too small and weak to be able to play an important role as agents of change and development. They often have limited resources, and may face difficulties in attracting skilled personnel, so that the effectiveness of their projects may be limited.

Possible loss of independence due to growing dependence on governments and aid agencies for funding

One of the potential strengths of NGOs is their ability to act independently, free of constraints imposed by governments, aid agencies and bilateral and multilateral donors. However, as they become more and more dependent on these outside sources for their funding, they may lose their independence if they are forced to conform to the demands of funders.

Food aid for developing countries

Many people believe that food aid consists of handouts of free food. Yet this is only one type of food aid provided by rich countries, falling within the category of humanitarian aid, intended to prevent hunger and malnutrition in countries facing serious food shortages. In addition, there is another type of food aid called 'programme food aid', which is unrelated to hunger and malnutrition, and is not free of charge to the people who receive it.

Programme food aid grew many years ago out of the practice of developed countries to subsidise their agricultural production. The subsidies gave rise to surpluses that governments needed to dispose of. Food aid offered them one way to do this. Programme food aid is now being gradually phased out by most donor countries, but continues to be a part of food aid provided by the United States.

Programme food aid is a type of bilateral aid involving donations of food from a rich country government to a developing country one. The developing country government then sells the food locally at low prices, and uses the revenues to finance economic growth and development. Donor governments sometimes donate the food to non-governmental organisations (NGOs) involved with promoting economic development. These NGOs also sell the donated food locally at low prices and use the proceeds to finance economic development projects.

Programme food aid has some potential advantages. Through sales of food at low prices, it can help prevent sharp food price increases, and can make food more affordable to poor people. It reduces the need for food imports, results in savings of foreign exchange, and can help countries improve their balance of payments. It allows governments and NGOs to raise funds that can be used for economic growth and development.

Yet according to some NGOs, programme food aid also has serious flaws. It is argued that this aid is harmful for recipient countries because it leads to an increase in the supply of food in local markets, resulting in cheap food that has forced millions of small farmers to go out of business, and to lose their sole source of income. Lower prices also mean reduced incentives for local farmers to produce food, and increased dependence on food aid or on food imports. An NGO, CARE, has argued that this type of food aid causes rather than reduces poverty, by harming the people it is intended to help.

Further, programme food aid is tied aid. The US government must buy the food to be used as aid from US agricultural producers, and the food must be transported on US ships. This results in much higher than necessary food costs and transportation costs. A proposal in the United States to 'untie' a portion of the aid would allow the US government to purchase food in local (developing country) markets, and would result in greatly reducing travel distance and transportation costs while supporting local production. However, the proposal was not approved. Supporters of programme food aid in the US government argue that large commercial farming and shipping interests are important allies in the fight to end poverty.

A number of other donor countries have started to provide cash rather than food as food aid. Many NGOs prefer cash donations for food aid because these offer greater flexibility, including the ability to buy food locally and boost demand for locally produced food, as well as to buy the right kind of food according to local needs.

Source: Adapted from: 'Square pegs in round holes: how the Farm Bill squanders chances for a pro-development trade deal', Oxfam Briefing Note, 21 July 2008; Margaret Besheer, 'US food aid groups debate practice of monetization' in *Voice of America*, 2 September 2007; Celia W. Dugger, 'Charity finds that US food aid for Africa hurts instead of helps' in *International Herald Tribune*, 14 August 2007.

Applying your skills

1 Explain the difference between humanitarian aid and programme aid (which is a type of development aid).

2 What is 'tied aid'? What are its disadvantages for developing countries?

3 Explain the advantages and disadvantages of programme food aid.

4 Using a diagram, explain how an increase in the supply of food due to food aid results in lower prices that reduce incentives for local farmers to grow food.

NGOs may attract the best qualified personnel away from government

The growing role of NGOs in development creates a demand for technical experts and personnel that may deprive governments of scarce highly qualified personnel, as NGOs are often in a position to offer higher salaries and benefits than the government.

Challenge to state authority

Whereas governments generally welcome NGOs that complement their activities in poverty alleviation, they often dislike the advocacy role taken on by many NGOs, which may conflict with government policy or question its authority.

The consensus view on NGOs overall is favourable. However, NGOs must act in partnership with the government, and must not be considered to be a replacement of government. Governments have crucial roles to play in the development process, which NGOs, even under the most favourable circumstances, cannot possibly undertake. Governments are essential for establishing an overall policy framework for the economy, including a framework for sustainable development; for providing a legal, institutional and regulatory framework for the economy; for pursuing policies to ensure economic stability; and for correcting market failures.

An example of an NGO, the Grameen Bank, which provides credit to poor people in Bangladesh, is discussed on page 469.

Comparing and contrasting the roles of aid and trade

♦ Compare and contrast the roles of aid and trade in economic development.

There has been an ongoing debate for decades regarding the relative roles of foreign aid and international trade in economic growth and development. We will examine the controversy by considering three popular slogans, each representing a different perspective:

- 'trade, not aid'
- 'trade and aid'
- 'aid for trade'.

Arguments supporting the 'trade, not aid' perspective

Supporters of the 'trade, not aid' perspective argue that development should be based on an expansion of international trade and increasing exports of developing countries, while aid should be limited if not altogether abandoned. The arguments centre on two main points: the failures of aid to effectively address the problem of growth and development; and the ability of trade to make major contributions to growth and development, provided rich countries abandon their protectionist policies.

Regarding the failures of aid, its critics emphasise the dangers of corruption, the idea that aid replaces government funds rather than supplementing them,

and that because of corruption and mishandling, aid does not reach those most in need. The conclusion is that, in spite of several decades of experience during which rich country governments have spent billions of dollars on aid, many countries are still as poor as ever. Aid has therefore failed to contribute to growth and development, and to poverty alleviation.

In contrast to aid, international trade can make important contributions to growth and development and poverty alleviation, as shown by the highly successful growth and development performance of East Asian countries. However, if developing countries are to exploit their trade potential to the benefit of their growth and development, developed countries should eliminate their trade protection policies, as well as protection of their agricultures.

Arguments supporting the 'trade and aid' perspective

Supporters of 'trade and aid' argue that while trade and export growth are very important for growth and development, they are not enough in the case of low-income (very poor) developing countries.

Many of the serious weaknesses of aid are the responsibility of donors. These include tied aid, conditionality of aid, volatility and unpredictability of aid, and lack of donor co-ordination of aid. There is strong pressure on donors by aid organisations to correct these problems, to make aid more effective.

At the same time, there are some situations where international trade may be unable to help, making aid necessary:

- **Rich country agricultural subsidies.** As long as these are in place, developing countries that depend on exports of protected goods cannot rely on trade to grow and develop.
- **Developing country dependence on commodity exports.** Some of the poorest countries in the world depend on production and export of primary commodities and are hurt by price volatility and deteriorating terms of trade. These countries cannot grow and develop by use of trade.
- **The poverty cycle.** Countries trapped in the poverty cycle cannot escape from this by means of trade.
- **Countries may have little to export.** Many poor countries cannot take advantage of trade opportunities because they have difficulties moving into new areas of production of goods that can be exported. Limited access to credit is a major obstacle to opening up a new business that produces for export. For example, in 2001 the European Union opened its markets to imports from the poorest developing countries

by eliminating most tariffs and other trade restrictions, and yet there was hardly any noticeable increase in the exports of these countries. Aid is therefore essential to help such countries develop the necessary institutions that will help them move into production for export.

- **Exclusion of geographically isolated communities and countries.** There are many poor communities, particularly in landlocked countries, which are geographically isolated and have no access to markets, to urban centres or to ports. It is very difficult for the people in these communities to be integrated into the market economy, much less to participate in the benefits of increasing exports. As an example, development economist Jeffrey Sachs uses the extreme case of Mongolia, which is:

> '1500 kilometres away from big population centres and has a few million people. Half of the people live in yurts. Their connectivity is low. They have no viable industry right now. They sell some camel hair but can't process it because they get a higher price by selling it to China, which processes it at much lower costs and gets it out of the ports cheaper than they can do by having a knitting factory in Ulan Bator. The real economic answer is for Mongolians to leave. But that's not the answer for Mongolia.'[14]

Examples abound. In Zambia (which is landlocked), the cost of shipping a tonne of maize to its neighbour Tanzania is greater than sending a tonne of maize from Tanzania to Europe or the United States. Poor roads in Uganda increase transport costs by 80%. Geographical isolation makes countries such as these, or isolated communities within countries, unable to compete in international markets, and therefore unable to take advantage of the potential benefits of trade in the absence of major investments in communications and transportation, which can be greatly facilitated by the provision of aid.

Arguments supporting the 'aid for trade' perspective

More and more economists believe that to be able to benefit from international trade, developing countries must have the institutional capacity to increase their exports. This perspective is an extension of the 'trade and aid' perspective; it asserts that both trade and aid are important to growth and development, and, in addition, aid and trade should be linked together so that a portion of aid is used to support the development of institutions that improve a country's

abilities to export. This view is based on the idea that many poor countries face institutional constraints that prevent them from taking advantage of growing international markets. Even if all rich country trade protection disappeared overnight, countries that do not have the institutions enabling them to increase and diversify their exports will experience limited benefits from trade.

The constraints faced by developing countries include everything from high transport costs due to poor transport networks, limited access to credit, poor power supplies adding to costs of production, high administrative costs related to complicated border procedures, and lack of institutional capacity to meet technical and sanitary standards increasingly required by importing countries.

This approach requires that aid and trade policies be integrated, so that a policy geared toward increasing exports is based on assistance aiming to strengthen the abilities of developing countries to achieve increases in exports. The 'aid for trade' would be in addition to, and not a replacement of Official Development Assistance (ODA) funds. Moreover, efforts to address institutional constraints to trade should not concentrate only on very poor developing countries (which receive ODA funds), but also on middle-income developing countries (which do not qualify for ODA funds).

Test your understanding 18.2

1 Define foreign aid, using the concept of concessional flows.

2 Distinguish between **(a)** ODA and NGOs, **(b)** humanitarian aid and development aid, and **(c)** project aid and programme aid, explaining in each case what these consist of.

3 What factors motivate donor governments to provide foreign aid?

4 **(a)** Explain the meaning of tied aid and the reasons it limits the effectiveness of aid. **(b)** What other factors limit aid's effectiveness?

5 **(a)** What kinds of activities do NGOs support in developing countries? **(b)** Why is more and more ODA channelled through NGOs? **(c)** What are some strengths and weaknesses of NGOs?

6 Explain some arguments **(a)** in favour of foreign aid, and **(b)** against foreign aid.

7 Discuss the roles of aid and trade in economic development.

---

[14] Jeffrey Sachs, 'Why "Trade, Not Aid" isn't enough', interview in *Business Week*, 10 October 2000.

18.4 Multilateral development assistance

♦ Examine the current roles of the IMF and the World Bank in promoting economic development.

Multilateral development assistance involves lending to developing countries on *non-concessional* terms, in other words with rates of interest and repayment periods determined in the market.

There are a number of major multilateral lenders to developing countries such as:

- multilateral development banks, which lend in order to support economic growth and development, including the:
  - World Bank
  - African Development Bank
  - Asian Development Bank
  - Inter-American Development Bank
  - European Bank for Reconstruction and Development
- the International Monetary Fund, which lends in order to alleviate external payments difficulties.

Lending by both multilateral development banks and by the International Monetary Fund differ from commercial bank lending because they are involved with lending for economic development or international financial stability, rather than for commercial or profit reasons.

The World Bank

The **World Bank** is a development assistance organisation that extends long-term loans to developing country governments for the purpose of promoting economic development and structural change. It was established in 1944, at the end of the Second World War, as part of an effort to help reconstruct Europe. Its activities were extended to developing countries from the late 1950s when European reconstruction was completed. It is composed of 187 member states that are its joint owners. It consists of two organisations:

- the International Bank for Reconstruction and Development (IBRD), which lends on non-concessional (i.e. commercial) terms to *middle income* developing countries, therefore its activities and lending do not form part of foreign aid; by far the greatest part of World Bank lending for development purposes (about 75%) is offered by the IBRD, and for this reason the World Bank, for the most part, is not considered to be an aid agency.

- the International Development Association (IDA), established in 1960, which has similar activities to the IBRD but extends loans to *low income countries* on highly concessional terms.

The IBRD and IDA are complemented by three additional organisations, that focus mainly on private investments in developing countries. The International Finance Corporation (IFC), established in 1956, finances private sector investments. The International Centre for Settlement of Investment Disputes (ICSID), established in 1966, provides a forum for the settlement of investment disputes in developing countries. The Multilateral Investment Guarantee Agency (MIGA), established in 1988, provides insurance to multinational corporations against political risk, and helps promote foreign direct investment in developing countries.

The importance of the World Bank as a development assistance organisation lies mainly in its role as a lender of funds to governments, and therefore focuses on the roles of the IBRD and IDA.

Brief history of World Bank activities

The World Bank's activities have changed their focus over the years. In the early years of its involvement with developing countries, the World Bank focused on lending for the development of infrastructure, such as energy, transport, telecommunications and irrigation.

By the early 1970s, the World Bank had turned its attention towards poverty alleviation. At the time, it grew enormously through an expansion of its funding and technical personnel, and greatly stepped up its lending to developing countries. It redirected a portion of its lending towards poverty alleviation, promising to help the poorest 40% of developing country populations through projects focusing on water supplies, sanitation, education, health, employment, and more.

At the end of the 1970s and in the early 1980s, the Bank's focus changed once more to a new type of lending: *structural adjustment loans* (SALs) intended to change the course of policy-making in developing countries by reducing government intervention and promoting competition and the role of markets. The focus of SALs was on dismantling interventionist policies and reorienting them towards the market system. It was believed that a strong market orientation of the economy would help developing countries expand their exports and increase their rates of growth.

Loans were intended to provide assistance in areas like the removal of price controls; interest rate liberalisation (freeing up of interest rates); trade liberalisation (lowering and eliminating tariff and other barriers to trade); eliminating restrictions to new foreign direct investments (by multinational corporations); privatisation (aimed at reducing the size of the public sector); deregulation (aimed at increasing the scope of market forces); cuts in government spending (to reduce budget deficits); and others. Acceptance of the measures included in the loans was a condition that had to be met in order for a country to qualify for a loan.

SALs were a method used by the World Bank in assisting (and forcing) developing countries to adopt economic and trade liberalisation policies (according to the Washington Consensus; see page 485). By the 1990s, SALs had come under very strong and widespread criticism because of their negative consequences on developing country economies.

Current World Bank activities

Since the mid-1990s, the World Bank has again shifted towards a poverty orientation, and has committed itself to helping countries achieve the Millennium Development Goals. It also began to focus on sustainable development. Its poverty-oriented projects are meant to be environmentally sustainable; they must not give rise to environmental destruction, and whenever possible they must also improve upon the quality of the environment.

In addition, the World Bank has changed its views on the appropriate role of government in economic growth and development. According to the new perspective, poverty alleviation requires intervention by governments in many areas: education, health care, public health, infrastructure (water, sanitation, transport, irrigation, and many others); access to credit by the poor; land reforms for a more equitable distribution of agricultural land; policies to reverse environmental degradation; policies to help the poor escape the poverty cycle; policies to promote gender equity. (These issues had been ignored by SALs, with negative consequences for income distribution, poverty and the environment.)

The World Bank is also paying increasing attention to the need for institutional development, based on the idea that markets need institutions that provide education and health services; ensure availability of and access to necessary infrastructure (water, sanitation, transport, etc.); provide an effective and equitable taxation system; ensure access to credit by all who need it; secure property rights; minimise the possibilities for the exercise of corruption; empower women and other disadvantaged groups; promote appropriate technology development and innovation; give a political voice to the economically weak; ensure and promote competition; and more.

Evaluating the role of the World Bank

Some of the more important issues include the following:

- **Social and environmental concerns.** The World Bank has been criticised for implementing socially unsound projects (such as building hydroelectric

dams that displace indigenous people), as well as environmentally unsustainable projects (such as building infrastructure that destroys the natural environment and local ecosystem). In recent years, the World Bank has become far more aware of the social and environmental implications of the projects it funds, and currently makes greater efforts to ensure that project objectives are consistent with social and environmental concerns.

- **World Bank governance dominated by rich countries.** The World Bank is owned by its 185 member states; however, voting power in its governance is determined by the size of financial contributions made by each country to the organisation, which are in proportion to the size of each economy. This clearly gives far greater power to rich countries. Critics argue that decisions are made without due regard for the needs and wishes of developing countries, which, being the poorest, have the least representation in decision-making.

- **Excessive interference in countries' domestic affairs.** Critics argue that the World Bank interferes excessively in the domestic policy affairs of developing countries.

- **Conditional assistance (lending).** Conditional assistance (or conditional lending) refers to the imposition of conditions that must be met by borrowing countries to qualify for a loan. (It is also one of the problems of foreign aid; see page 510.) The World Bank sees the imposition of conditions as a mechanism for inducing desirable policy changes. Conditional lending is problematic because it deprives countries of control over their domestic economic activities.

- **Damaging effect on developing countries.** One of the strongest criticisms involves the negative effects on developing country economies of structural adjustment lending. SALs have been criticised for increasing income inequalities and poverty within developing countries, because of such factors as increasing unemployment, cuts in provision of merit goods by governments, cuts in food subsidies, introduction of payments of fees for health and education, and limited possibilities for the poor and the unskilled to take advantage of opportunities opened up by the freer market environment. Increasing poverty is considered by many to be among the World Bank's greatest failures.

- **Inadequate attention to poverty alleviation.** Although the World Bank has in recent years turned its attention to poverty issues, critics argue that it is not doing enough to meet the challenges of extreme poverty in developing countries by not allocating enough funds for loans intended to meet the needed investments in education, health services, and infrastructure (clean water supplies, sanitation, etc.). In addition, it has been criticised for not doing enough in the area of debt relief through the Heavily Indebted Poor Countries (HIPC) Initiative (see page 522 below); many very poor and highly indebted countries do not qualify for debt relief because, according to requirements for eligibility established by the World Bank, they are not poor enough or indebted enough. The result is that a number of countries do not receive the assistance they require.

The International Monetary Fund

The **International Monetary Fund (IMF)** is a multilateral financial institution that was established jointly with the World Bank in 1944 with the original purpose of lending to countries experiencing balance of payments deficits under the system of fixed exchange rates that existed at the time. Its objectives have changed over the years in accordance with the evolution of the international financial system. At the present time, the IMF is composed of 185 member countries. Its purpose is to oversee the global financial system, follow the macroeconomic policies of its member countries, stabilise exchange rates and help countries that experience difficulties making their international payments by extending them short-term loans on commercial (i.e. non-concessional) terms.

Activities of the International Monetary Fund

In the first two decades of IMF's existence, more than half of its lending was to developed countries. Its role in developing countries grew with the debt crisis beginning in the 1970s and 1980s. This was the time when many poor oil-importing countries developed serious balance of payments difficulties as a result of dramatic increases in oil import expenditures (see page 520 below). During the 1990s, the IMF expanded its lending to transition economies in central and eastern Europe and the former Soviet Union. Since 2008 its lending has increased significantly to countries around the world as a result of international payments difficulties brought on by the global financial crisis, including some developed countries (Greece, Iceland, Ireland, Portugal).

The loans provided by the IMF usually come with a package of policies that the country must adopt as a condition for receiving the loan (another example of conditionality). These policies, known as *stabilisation policies*, vary from country to country, but typically include the following:

- tight monetary policy, through increases in interest rates, intended to lower aggregate demand, reduce the level of economic activity and reduce demand for imports while encouraging inflows of financial capital, thereby helping the balance of payments position

- tight fiscal policy, also intended to lower aggregate demand and reduce the level of economic activity, through cuts in government spending (including cuts in provision of merit goods, such as health services, education, infrastructure, etc.) and cuts in food and other subsidies, as well as increases in taxation, and the imposition of fees for schooling and health care services[15]

- currency devaluation or depreciation, intended to discourage imports and encourage exports and help the balance of payments position

- cuts in real wages (i.e. wages after taking into account the impact of price changes), to reduce aggregate demand and the level of economic activity

- liberalisation policies, such as eliminating or reducing controls on prices, interest rates, imports and foreign exchange, to promote a free market and free trade environment.

Evaluating the role of the International Monetary Fund

The IMF is a far more controversial institution than the World Bank, and is subject to more intense criticism due to the highly negative impact on countries that almost always results from its stabilisation policies. While it shares some of the criticisms against the World Bank, the main criticism focuses on the harshness of the measures that borrowers are forced to adopt. The criticisms may be summarised as follows:

- **IMF governance dominated by rich countries.** As with the World Bank voting power in its governance is in proportion to the size of each economy, giving rich countries far greater power in decision-making.

- **Excessive interference in countries' domestic affairs.** Even more than in the case of the World Bank, critics argue that IMF interference in domestic economies is far too great.

- **Conditional lending (conditionality).** Loans are made available only on condition that

---

[15] Countries with serious balance of payments problems also typically face large government budget deficits (an excess of government spending over government revenues), and so an additional objective of these policies is to reduce government spending and increase revenues in order to reduce the size of the budget deficit.

the borrowing country agrees to implement the stabilisation policies designed by the IMF. Given their vulnerability in times of severe external payments difficulties, countries are forced to accept harsh conditions that run counter to their growth and development objectives.

- **Damaging effects on developing countries.** IMF policies come at an immense human cost. Stabilisation policies have the impact of lowering economic growth, often creating a recession with increasing unemployment and increasing levels of poverty. In developing countries that in any case face high unemployment and underemployment, the effects can be devastating. Cuts in real wages where wages are low to begin with, cuts in government spending on merit goods and food subsidies on which many poor people depend for their physical survival, the imposition of fees for schooling and health care services among people who cannot afford them, along with the increases in poverty that arise from liberalisation policies, are wholly inconsistent with economic growth and development objectives.

- **IMF stabilisation policies based on a flawed concept.** Some economists argue that in addition to the human cost, there may be something fundamentally wrong with the stabilisation concept pursued by the IMF. The reason is that whatever success the IMF stabilisation policies have had

in alleviating external payments problems, the success tends to be short-lived. The fundamental balance of payments problem of many developing countries does not get resolved through IMF loans and restrictive macroeconomic policies. Experience shows that many countries that have tried the IMF programme suffer not only increasing poverty but also low or negative rates of growth, and therefore are unable to 'grow' out of their balance of payments difficulties or external debt problems.

18.5 The role of international debt

Explaining foreign debt and why countries borrow from abroad

- Outline the meaning of foreign debt and explain why countries borrow from foreign creditors.

The meaning of foreign debt

A country's foreign debt refers to its level of *external debt*, meaning the total amount of debt (public and private) incurred by borrowing from foreign creditors (i.e. lenders). The problem of developing country debt involves large volumes of public (i.e. government) debt.

Foreign government debt (see Figure 18.1) arises from three sources: (i) government borrowing from multilateral organisations, (ii) government borrowing from foreign commercial banks, and (iii) government sales of bonds to foreigners.[16]

Borrowing has major costs, which take the form of 'debt servicing'; this involves payment of the principal (the amount of the loan) plus interest. When a country borrows from a foreign creditor, the debt service payments must be made in foreign exchange, which can come from increased exports, reduced imports, or financing from external sources. Under favourable circumstances, debt service payments are made possible by greater economic growth and increased export earnings.

Why countries borrow from foreign sources

Borrowing from foreign sources enters the balance of payments as a credit in the financial account and helps countries pay for deficits (an excess of debits) in the current account. Therefore, a very important reason why countries borrow from abroad is to acquire foreign exchange allowing them to pay for an excess

---

[16] The sale of government bonds as a form of borrowing is explained on page 330, footnote 5. Note that only some, not all, of private lending by commercial banks and foreign portfolio investment involves government borrowing, as some commercial bank lending and some foreign portfolio investments involve private borrowers.

of imports over exports (a trade deficit). A trade deficit allows a country to reach a point outside its production possibilities curve (*PPC*), meaning it enjoys more goods and services than it can produce itself (see page 399), but this means it must have a method of paying for the extra goods and services; borrowing from abroad is one method allowing it to do this. The rationale, over the longer term, is that countries will spend at least a portion of imports made possible by foreign finance on capital goods that are inputs in production, which will accelerate their growth and their exports, so that over the longer term they will be able to pay back their debts plus interest.

Yet the developing countries suffering today from high levels of debt have been victims of an unfortunate set of circumstances: low growth in export earnings, higher import costs, lower than expected (and sometimes negative) rates of economic growth, as well as increasing interest rates (which increase the cost of debt servicing). These circumstances give rise to serious problems in the balance of payments, resulting in an ever-growing need for foreign borrowing.

How some developing countries became heavily indebted

Before the 1970s, borrowing by developing country governments took place on a small scale. Countries borrowed from international organisations like the World Bank and International Monetary Fund as well as foreign governments, mainly in order to supplement insufficient savings and increase domestic resources to pursue growth and development objectives.

The beginnings of the debt problem date back to the oil shock of 1973–74, when the Organization of the Petroleum Exporting Countries (OPEC) suddenly increased the price of oil. Almost overnight, oil-importing developing countries were faced with larger import expenditures due to higher oil prices. In addition, they faced lower export revenues because the oil price increases created recessions (stagflation) in developed countries, resulting in a lower demand for developing country exports. These two events resulted in larger trade and current account deficits in developing countries, creating a need for increased foreign borrowing that would provide the foreign exchange needed to cover their deficits.

A related event made it easier for developing countries to borrow more. After the oil price increases the OPEC nations found themselves with much larger oil revenues, much of which they deposited in commercial banks in developed countries, mainly in the United States, Europe and Japan. The commercial banks, seeing very large increases in their supply of loanable funds, began aggressively competing with each other to lend to developing countries. The developing countries' need for new loans coincided with the international banking system's need to make new loans. This lending pattern came to be known as 'petrodollar recycling', involving commercial banks lending to oil-importing countries the same funds that came from oil exporters, to allow the developing countries to continue to import oil.

As commercial banks competed with each other to lend as much as possible of their petrodollars, they did not take care to lend prudently. There was a belief that if there were losses on their loans (if developing countries could not make loan re-payments), the losses would be covered by the public sector (developed country governments, the World Bank and International Monetary Fund).

In the meantime, developed country governments supported the rapid growth of commercial bank lending to developing countries, because they saw petrodollar recycling as an opportunity to cut back on foreign aid and development assistance. Developing countries, for their part, did not always spend the loan funds wisely. While a portion of the funds was used for investments in infrastructure and debt servicing, in some countries loan funds supported public spending that should have been financed by government tax revenues. This allowed governments to enjoy broad political support by maintaining low tax rates as well as poor and low tax collection. Loan funds were sometimes used to finance the operation of inefficient public enterprises; even worse, they often disappeared into the pockets of corrupt bureaucrats and elites.

A second oil price shock occurred in 1979. Apart from increased import costs and reduced export revenues, developing countries also faced deteriorating terms of trade due to falling commodity prices, developed country trade protection, and higher interest rates on their loans due to tight monetary policies in developed countries. Developing countries were faced with two options: they could pursue restrictive monetary and fiscal policies to create a recession that would cut back on imports, thus saving on the need for foreign exchange (expenditure reducing policies; see page 408); or they could borrow more. As more borrowing was preferable to recession, levels of debt in many countries reached massive proportions.

By the early 1980s, the level of debt had grown massively in some countries, especially in Latin America and Sub-Saharan Africa, and some were on the verge of bankruptcy. Commercial banks and the international community suddenly woke up to the possibility of a banking collapse and a major global financial crisis, should countries default on their loans.

Debt rescheduling and conditional assistance

♦ Explain that in some cases countries have become heavily indebted, requiring rescheduling of the debt payments and/or conditional assistance from international organisations, including the IMF and the World Bank.

Beginning in 1982, the international community, led by the International Monetary Fund, the World Bank and the US government, stepped in with a series of measures to prevent developing country defaults.

Debt rescheduling

One of these measures was debt rescheduling (restructuring), involving new loans by commercial banks to developing country debtors, but on better terms. Debt rescheduling did not include debt forgiveness, as the loan still had to be paid back in full; it involved granting of new loans that were stretched out over longer periods of time and at lower interest rates. The loans were used to pay off some of the old loans, and therefore ease the pain of having to service the debts.

IMF lending and stabilisation policies

A second measure involved turning to the International Monetary Fund (IMF) for loans that would help cover large and growing current account deficits. The role of the IMF in this regard was explained on page 518 above. The loans were *conditional* in that they were made only if the borrowing country government agreed to pursue stabilisation policies prescribed by the IMF (tight fiscal and monetary policies, liberalisation policies, etc.).

World Bank lending and structural adjustment loans

At the same time that countries turned to the IMF, they often also borrowed from the World Bank, which also made *conditional* loans. These were the structural adjustment loans (SALs) explained above on page 516, which forced the borrowing country government to pursue economic and trade liberalisation policies to qualify for receiving a loan.

Other initiatives: debt-for-equity swaps

Another measure involved 'debt-for-equity swaps'. This occurs when a highly indebted country exchanges a portion of its debt for equity, which is taken up by foreign corporations. What this means is that the foreign corporation takes responsibility for a portion of a government's debt, and in exchange the government gives it ownership of some of its assets (such as a telephone company or a steel mill). The indebted country benefits, because it can significantly lower the level of its debt by giving up some of its assets. Much of Latin American privatisation occurred this way. However, a key problem is that foreign corporations can be persuaded to engage in a debt-for-equity swap only if they acquire the state assets at a low price. As a result, governments lose control of some of their major assets to foreign-owned corporations at a price that is far lower than if these assets were sold at market prices.

Consequences of high levels of foreign debt

♦ Explain why the servicing of international debt causes balance of payments problems and has an opportunity cost in terms of foregone spending on development objectives.

High levels of foreign debt have strong negative effects on the economies of debtor countries.

Balance of payments problems

When a country borrows from foreign institutions, whether these are commercial banks or multilateral organisations like the World Bank and IMF, its debt servicing obligations (repayment of loan plus payment of interest) must be paid in foreign exchange. If its export earnings are not enough to cover its foreign exchange needs for debt servicing, it can borrow more from abroad to acquire the needed foreign exchange. However, as it borrows more, its debt servicing obligations increase. This means that there will be continuous pressure on the balance of payments and a constant quest for foreign exchange with which to service the debt.

Possibility of a debt trap

As levels of debt rise, there comes a point where the level of debt cannot be sustained: new debt requires higher debt service payments, which require more foreign borrowing, which leads to more debt servicing payments, and so on, in a self-reinforcing spiral in which the country is trapped. This has been termed the 'debt trap', involving a situation where a country must keep on taking out new loans in order to pay back the old ones. Many countries, particularly in Latin America and Sub-Saharan Africa, were caught in a debt trap during the 1980s.

Opportunity costs

Large debt service payments have major opportunity costs because the government has fewer resources to invest in social services (health, education, etc.) and infrastructure, all necessary for poverty alleviation and economic growth and development.

In addition, since a highly indebted country is forced to use a large portion of its export earnings for debt servicing, it has less foreign exchange to pay for imports of needed capital equipment, other production inputs and goods and services generally. The foregone imports are an additional opportunity cost with negative consequences for economic growth.

Lower private investment

Fears that a government may be unable to service its debts create uncertainty regarding economic conditions and scare away private investors, both domestic and foreign. Even if investment does take place, it is more likely to involve short-term investment projects with quick returns, rather than longer-term ones with greater potentials to support economic growth.

Lower economic growth

The above three factors, lower public investments in merit goods, lower imports of production inputs and lower private investment, work to lower economic growth in highly indebted countries. This in turn translates into a reduced ability to service debts.

Debt cancellation and the HIPC initiative

> ♦ Explain that the burden of debt has led to pressure to cancel the debt of heavily indebted countries.

The difficulties caused by high levels of debt have led to pressure on creditors to cancel debts of highly indebted countries. In 1996, the World Bank and IMF began the Heavily Indebted Poor Countries (HIPC) Initiative, intended to provide debt relief to some highly indebted poor countries by cancelling a portion of their debts. In 2005, this was supplemented by the Multilateral Debt Relief Initiative (MDRI), which provides 100% debt relief for debts by three multilateral organisations (the International Development Association (IDA) of the World Bank, the IMF and the African Development Fund).

To qualify for debt cancellation, countries must have a *per capita* GNI below a particular level; they must have a debt level that cannot be sustained (i.e. they must be in a debt trap); they must show evidence that they are following certain elements of IMF and World Bank policies (such as cutting government expenditures and liberalising their markets); and they must commit themselves to pursuing a poverty reduction strategy. The funds made available through debt relief, in other words the country's savings from debt reduction, must be spent on projects that attack poverty, such as the development of rural infrastructure, providing health services and education, creating new jobs, and providing family planning services.

The HICP Initiative is considered to be a welcome step in the direction of solving the debt problem, but has been criticised for several reasons:

- The level of debt reduction which the programme makes possible (level of debt is to be reduced to 150% of exports) is considered insufficient; if a country's export earnings fall for whatever reason, it risks sliding back towards a debt trap.

- The programme takes effect too slowly, risking that the benefits of debt relief may follow too slowly to be of much use to the countries.

- Some measures that are imposed as conditions for a country to qualify are too severe (for example, charging fees for schools and hospitals, privatising key public enterprises such as electricity and telephone, reductions in government expenditures that reduce the provision of social services and infrastructure).

- There are many other countries that are highly indebted but which have not been included in the HIPC Initiative; these countries, whose debt situation is considered to be more manageable, are still suffering the consequences of high levels of debt, yet are unable to benefit from debt relief.

Test your understanding 18.4

1 **(a)** What is the meaning of foreign debt? **(b)** Why do economically less developed countries borrow from abroad? **(c)** How did many developing countries find themselves with high levels of foreign debt?

2 **(a)** Explain the policies adopted by the IMF and World Bank to help countries with high levels of foreign debt meet their debt obligations. **(b)** Why have these policies been criticised (refer also to pages 516 and 518)?

3 What are the main economic consequences of high levels of foreign debt for developing countries, and how do these affect their growth and development efforts?

4 **(a)** What are some debt relief initiatives? **(b)** What would be some advantages of debt cancellation for heavily indebted countries?

Assessment

The Student's CD-ROM at the back of this book provides practice of examination questions based on the material you have studied in this chapter.

Chapter 19
Consequences of economic growth and the balance between markets and intervention

In this chapter we will consider two final topics, the consequences of economic growth and the balance between markets and government intervention.

19.1 Consequences of economic growth

♦ Discuss the possible consequences of economic growth, including the possible impacts on living standards, unemployment, inflation, the distribution of income, the current account of the balance of payments, and sustainability.

This topic is actually part of Chapter 11 (page 301) but is discussed here because it requires an understanding of topics considered in subsequent chapters.

Economic growth impacts upon many aspects of the economy, and some of its possible consequences are positive while others may be negative. It is important to note that many of these consequences, whether positive or negative, are not inevitable, *but rather follow from the ways that growth is pursued.*

Economic growth and living standards

If the total GDP of a country increases faster than its population, then an increase in GDP *per capita* results.

This indicates that *there is a greater potential for people to increase their consumption of goods and services, and improve their standards of living.*

However, remember that GDP *per capita* or income *per capita* is only an average measure, and does not tell us how the increase in income is distributed or whether there is a broadly distributed improvement in living standards. More appropriate measures of living standards are provided by the Human Development Index (HDI; see Chapter 16, pages 450–51), as well as other indicators of development, such as infant mortality or maternal mortality (see page 456). The interesting question therefore is whether economic growth leads to human and economic development, measured as improvements in a country's HDI or other development indicators. (See also pages 13 and 436–38 on the relationship between growth and development.)

According to studies making cross-country comparisons, economic growth is associated with improvements in indicators measuring economic and human development.[1] This is what we would expect, since growth provides additional resources allowing for improvements in standards of living. However,

[1] International Monetary Fund (2001) *Finance and Development*, Volume 38, Number 2, June.

improvements in development indicators are highly variable, so that for a given rate of growth they are in some cases small and in others much larger. What accounts for differences in the contributions made by economic growth to standard of living improvements?

According to an important study of this topic for developing countries,[2] major factors allowing economic growth to have positive effects on economic and human development include the following:

- **The distribution of income.** The greater the income going to poorer households, the greater the potential for contributing to human development, as the poorer households are those with the greatest deprivations in terms of education and health. If increases in income made possible by economic growth bypass the poorer households, growth has limited effects on human development.

- **Household spending on items that promote human development.** The greater the share of household income spent on goods and services such as food, education and health care, the greater the effect on human development.

- **The share of income controlled by women.** The greater this is, the stronger the impact on human development (see also page 470 on the role of women).

- **Government spending on items that promote human development.** This relates to the share of the government budget allocated to priority areas like education, health care and infrastructure including clean water supplies and sanitation; the larger this is, the greater the effects of growth on human development.

- **Contributions by non-governmental organisations (NGOs).** Because of their poverty orientation and their general effectiveness in reaching poor people, NGOs contribute to increasing the impact of growth on more development and higher standards of living.

- **Effectiveness of spending to promote human development.** Depending on their level of development, different countries have different needs, which determine the effectiveness of spending to achieve human development. For

example, very poor countries need to invest more in primary education to achieve universal literacy (see page 457), rather than in secondary or tertiary education. Some countries may need to invest more in safe drinking water or sanitation rather than in health care services in order to have a greater impact on health. The greater the effectiveness of spending, the greater the impacts on human development.

For example, Nepal showed the fastest increase in its HDI in the period 1980–2007, whereas its rates of economic growth have been low, averaging 1.9% per year over 30 years.[3] Yet India, with much higher growth rates, has made much smaller progress in its HDI. Nepal's progress is attributed to the emphasis placed by the government on education and health.

A major study of data between 1970 and 2005 for 111 countries by the United Nations Development Programme (UNDP)[4] shows that the greatest improvements in literacy and life expectancy (two components of the HDI; see page 459) *are not occurring in the fastest growing economies of the world* (the only two exceptions being China and Korea). Factors contributing to HDI improvements are government expansion of education and health care, together with the international community's contribution of vaccines and antibiotics. According to the head of the report's research team, 'The increase in human development is actually an example of how state intervention works'.

Therefore, *while economic growth offers the potential to achieve improvements in human development and standards of living, these improvements do not occur automatically as a result of economic growth* but require appropriate policies to make effective use of the resources growth makes available.

Economic growth and unemployment

To understand the effects of economic growth on unemployment, we must make a distinction between different types of unemployment, the key distinction being between cyclical and natural (of which structural is the most important). In addition, it is useful to make a distinction between economic growth occurring in the expansionary phase of the business cycle, and long-term economic

[2] Gustav Ranis and Frances Stewart, 'Economic growth and human development in Latin America' in *Cepal Review*, December 2002.
[3] United Nations Development Programme, *Human Development Report 2009*.
[4] United Nations Development Programme, *Human Development Report 2010*.

growth shown by increases in potential output (see Chapter 9, page 256).

Economic growth due to the expansionary phase of the business cycle affects *cyclical unemployment*, which as we know falls in an expansion (and increases in a contraction). If aggregate demand continues to increase beyond the full employment level of real GDP, leading to an inflationary gap, unemployment falls below the natural rate. However, this will only be temporary as government authorities are likely to step in with contractionary policies intended to close the inflationary gap and bring real GDP back toward its potential level with unemployment returning to the natural rate.

Therefore, economic growth due to the short-term fluctuations of the business cycle can mainly reduce (and possibly eliminate) cyclical unemployment, but with only a temporary impact on natural unemployment.

Sustained (not temporary) reductions in natural, and particularly structural, unemployment may result from long-term economic growth, involving increases in potential output, shown by rightward shifts in the *LRAS* or Keynesian *AS* curves (see page 256). Increases in potential output are caused by supply-side factors, such as increases in resource quantities, improvements in resource quality, technological change, etc. However, not all increases in potential output lower natural unemployment. *Depending on the particular factors that cause potential output to increase, natural and therefore structural unemployment may increase, decrease, or remain the same.*

In certain situations, economic growth may itself lead to increases in structural unemployment (a part of natural unemployment). This could occur when growth results from technological changes leading to a fall in the demand for certain labour skills (see page 268). In developing countries, growth could result from the introduction of inappropriate technologies (such as capital intensive technologies), which would cause unemployment to rise.

Economic policies pursued by government can also work both ways, either increasing or reducing unemployment over the longer term. This topic was discussed in Chapter 12, page 344, where our analysis of the effects of supply-side policies on unemployment showed that market-based policies based on labour market reforms, and certain interventionist policies including investments in human capital, can work to reduce the natural rate of unemployment. Other market-based policies, however, such as privatisation, and trade and market liberalisation, may work to increase it.

It follows then, that long-term reductions in unemployment require economic growth, but not all economic growth results in lower unemployment. *While economic growth offers the potential to reduce unemployment, whether or not this will occur depends on the particular factors and policies that lead to growth.*

Economic growth and inflation

As in the case of unemployment, it is useful to make a distinction between economic growth due to the expansionary phase of the business cycle, and long-term economic growth or increases in potential output. In addition, the effects of growth on inflation depend partly on whether we use a monetarist/new classical or Keynesian approach.

In the expansionary phase of the business cycle, as real GDP increases due to increases in aggregate demand, *the price level remains constant* in the Keynesian model because of spare capacity and the presence of unemployed resources in the economy; this involves real GDP increases along the horizontal part of the *AS* curve, as shown in Figure 9.13 (page 254). However, as real GDP approaches the level of potential output, resource bottlenecks begin to cause increases in resource and product prices, and continued aggregate demand increases beyond the level of potential output become highly inflationary.

In the new classical/monetarist model, an increase in aggregate demand always causes an increase in the price level, even if the economy is initially in recession (see Figure 9.4(a), page 245); in the long run an increase in *AD* leads only to price level increases (see Figure 9.13, page 254).

Therefore, while there is disagreement between the two models on what happens to the price level in a recession, *there is agreement between them that growth caused by increases in aggregate demand at about or beyond the level of potential output is inflationary.*

In addition, there is agreement between the two models that long-term economic growth, involving increases in potential output, work to reduce inflationary pressures. This can be seen clearly in Figure 9.15 (page 256), where increases in aggregate demand are matched by increases in the LRAS and AS curves respectively. With increases in the productive capacity of the economy due to economic growth, growth in aggregate demand can be easily met without causing upward pressures on the price level. (See also the discussion on the ability of supply-side policies to reduce inflationary pressures, page 344.)

Economic growth and the distribution of income

A large number of studies have been carried out investigating the relationship between growth in GDP *per capita* and income distribution in developing and developed countries. The results have been inconclusive: while in some countries income distribution worsened in the early periods of growth and then improved, in some others the opposite happened, while in many others, income distribution did not show any clear pattern of change. These results lead to the conclusion that *there is no clear relationship between growth in GDP per capita and income distribution*; instead, what happens to income distribution as a country grows is a reflection of particular conditions in each country and the kinds of growth policies that are pursued.

For example, many countries in Latin America had highly unequal income distributions to begin with; income distribution in these countries has tended to remain highly unequal. A number of countries in East Asia (for example Taiwan and South Korea) had far more equal income distributions when they began their rapid growth, and this remained so even with rapid growth during the 1970s and 1980s. In addition, countries of East Asia placed a strong emphasis on the development of human capital, a policy that played a key role in ensuring broad-based participation in the benefits of growth, with positive effects on the equality of income distribution.

Yet, income inequalities in many countries around the world have been widening over the past three or so decades. They have been growing in China, India, Indonesia, Thailand and other East Asian and South-East Asian countries that had achieved greater income equality and reductions in poverty in their early years of growth. Russia and most other central and eastern European countries have similarly been experiencing sharp rises in income inequalities. A number of countries in Latin America have seen growing inequalities as well. Almost all OECD[5] countries also show worsening income distributions, with the most serious deteriorations appearing in Sweden, the United Kingdom and the United States. Some of these countries have also experienced increases in the number of households below the poverty line.

In both developed and developing countries, a major factor behind increasing income inequalities has been the growing use of market-based supply-side policies (see Chapter 12, page 344). Transition economies (in central and eastern Europe and the former Soviet Union) have additionally been influenced by the switch to market economies and the loss of government protection of vulnerable groups. In developing countries, income inequalities increased due to economic and trade liberalisation, which we have seen gives rise to both winners and losers (Chapter 17, page 486). While those who can take advantage of new opportunities gain, many become worse off, if they are less educated or skilled, cannot get credit, are geographically isolated, have nothing to produce for export, lose their jobs due to privatisations or reductions in the size of the government sector, and so on.

In addition, income distribution in developing countries can worsen as a result of economic growth due to inappropriate government policies, such as:

* the introduction of capital-using (labour-saving) technologies in industry and agriculture, creating rural and urban unemployment
* low levels of government investment in human capital, which negatively affect people on lower incomes and the poor disproportionately more than wealthier people
* allocating most services and infrastructure investments to urban areas and ignoring the rural sector where most of the poor live
* within the urban sector, concentrating infrastructure and services investments within the formal (modern and highly paid) sector and ignoring the urban slums.

You may remember that many of the policy prescriptions of the New Development Consensus emerging in the late 1990s to early 2000s (see Chapter 17, page 487) try to address these kinds of problems. If countries follow these policy prescriptions, they may prevent a further worsening in income distribution and may even see an improvement, even as they continue to experience economic growth.

It can therefore be concluded that *economic growth is neither 'good' nor 'bad' for income distribution; this instead depends very much on the kinds of policies countries adopt in order to achieve growth.*

Economic growth and the current account

Short-term economic growth, occurring over the business cycle, may lead to a larger current account

---

[5] The OECD is the Organisation for Economic Co-operation and Development.

deficit (or a smaller current account surplus). The reason is that increasing incomes lead to an increase in the demand for imports, and therefore a worsening balance of trade (the most important part of the current account balance). This is especially the case if consumers' marginal propensity to import is high, indicating that a large fraction of an increase in incomes leaks out of the spending flow to purchase imports (see Chapter 8, page 217); or when the demand for imports is income elastic, indicating that a given percentage increase in income will lead to a proportionately larger increase in the quantity of imports demanded.

However, when a country experiences long-term economic growth, the trade balance (and the current account balance) are determined by factors that are likely to be unrelated to the rate of economic growth, such as the following:

- **The international competitiveness of domestic industries.** If domestic industries are efficient, low-cost producers, they may have a competitive advantage over other countries, resulting in higher levels of exports, and therefore a smaller trade deficit (or larger trade surplus) even as the economy grows.

- **Exchange rates.** If the country's exchange rate is weak or undervalued (relative to its market value; see page 391) it creates an artificial competitive advantage, resulting in more exports and fewer imports, working to reduce the size of a trade deficit, even as the economy may be growing.

- **The degree of export orientation of the economy.** Economic growth that depends heavily on increases in exports may result in strong trade surpluses even as incomes increase. A good example is China, which has been achieving high rates of growth together with large trade surpluses.

- **Growth of incomes of trading partners.** If incomes abroad are growing rapidly and for extended periods, there will likely result increases in exports, even as the country itself is growing.

- **The degree of protectionist trade policies faced by exports.** If a country's exports do not face trade barriers in other countries, it may be able to increase its exports (assuming it is an efficient producer) even as its economy grows.

Therefore, in examining the relationship between economic growth and the current account balance of a country, we may find *economic growth leading to a larger deficit or smaller surplus in the upward phase of the business cycle, while over the longer term we are likely to find that there is no clear relationship*: as the economy grows, the current account balance may improve, stay the same or worsen, depending on what happens to the factors listed above.

Economic growth and sustainability

Experience shows that growth, especially rapid growth, often leads to unsustainable resource use (particularly in the case of common access resources; see Chapter 5, page 123). For example, very high growth rates in East Asian countries have been associated with serious environmental losses taking the form of very high levels of urban air pollution, soil degradation due to soil erosion, waterlogging and overgrazing, threats to biodiversity, and serious deforestation. The reasons were explored in Chapter 5. Industrialisation based on fossil fuels is a major source of pollution (negative production externalities). Increasing incomes lead to consumption patterns also based on greater fossil fuel consumption (use of cars, air conditioners, etc., creating negative consumption externalities). Other activities, such as commercial logging and agricultural practices based on a lack of pricing mechanism for common access resources result in their unsustainable use. In addition, economic activities due to poverty similarly lead to environmental losses.

Experiences like these have led to the widespread belief that economic growth and environmental sustainability are conflicting objectives: more of one means less of the other. Many governments around the world base their policies on this belief by following the 'grow now, clean up later' way of thinking, which argues that since using resources to preserve the environment reduces growth, it is preferable to pursue growth with all its negative effects on the environment, and postpone the 'clean-up' job of environmental preservation for later when incomes will be higher.[6] This way of thinking is followed not only by rapidly growing economies, but also slow-growth economies, because the evidence shows that even countries that do not experience rapid growth also suffer major environmental losses.

---

[6] For example, the installation of pollution-control equipment involves greater costs for firms, which may mean lower profits, lower investment and lower economic growth. Switching to environmentally sound agricultural practices similarly involves costs that may cut into future economic growth prospects.

Setting limits to deforestation for timber places restrictions on the growth of the timber industry. Therefore, allocating resources for environmental protection arguably translates into smaller increases in output and hence lower economic growth.

The conflict between economic growth and sustainability

The apparent conflict between growth and sustainability arises because of the way *economic growth is defined*. The idea of conflict follows from the conventional measure of economic growth, taken to be the increase in real GDP *per capita*. This in turn depends on the definition of GDP, which is the value of all goods and services produced in a country in the course of a year.

As you may remember from Chapter 8, this measure of aggregate output suffers from a serious limitation because it does not account for environmental and human health losses that arise from environmental degradation. This limitation would be corrected if countries adopted green accounting methods that calculated green GDP (page 225). If economic growth was calculated as rates of increase in *green GDP per capita*, environmental destruction (as well as possible negative health consequences) would be accounted for in the measure of GDP, which would be correspondingly reduced: we would find that in most countries around the world economic growth rates would be far lower than those based on conventional GDP measures, and in many cases would be negative. If a country has positive GDP *per capita* growth but negative green GDP *per capita* growth, this means that its losses due to environmental degradation are greater than its gains due to increased production of goods and services.

If economic growth were defined as increases in green real GDP *per capita*, the only way to achieve high rates of growth would be by increasing the production of goods and services without causing environmental destruction (or causing only small amounts of environmental destruction); alternatively, increases in the production

of goods and services would include improvements in the quality of environmental resources resulting from investments in natural capital.

The problem of the conflict between growth (conventionally defined) and sustainability is related to economists' systematic neglect of the factor of production 'land'. Growth models in mainstream economics show how output increases in relation to labour and capital (in the sense of physical capital), sometimes also considering human capital, while completely ignoring land, that was taken to be an unimportant factor that was permanently fixed in quantity and quality. It is only in recent years that land has been redefined by environmental economists to consist of 'natural capital', which can be destroyed or improved through investments (see page 297).

Thinking points

- How does the way we think of (or define) growth affect its relationship to the environment?
- Do we have a moral obligation to nature and the environment?
- Is our choice of how to measure growth based on economic or moral criteria (or both)?
- If growth were defined as increases in green real GDP *per capita*, would there be a conflict between growth and sustainable resource use?
- If governments began using green accounting methods, would production and consumption patterns necessarily change so as to become more consistent with sustainability?

Yet, there are a number of things seriously wrong with this way of thinking. One is that *some environmental damage is irreversible*; it will not be possible to correct the damage in the future, and some resources will be lost forever. For example, lost biodiversity can never be recovered; lost lives due to pollution-induced illnesses can similarly never be recovered. A second is that *it justifies government inaction on the environment*. Governments and policymakers often wrongly assume that environmental issues will automatically be regained in the future as incomes increase with growth. This is unrealistic, because preservation of the environment requires

policies aiming to limit negative environmental externalities. A third, related reason is that *it is not growth itself that is bad for the environment, but rather the ways that growth is pursued*. If growth were pursued differently, it need not conflict with environmental sustainability. A fourth reason is that *growth based on unsustainable resource use may lead to destruction of natural resources on such a wide scale that the possibility of continued future growth may be threatened*.

Modern growth theory shows that economic growth and environmental sustainability are in fact consistent with each other, and *can be successfully pursued together under certain conditions*, such as the following:

- Governments implement market-based policies that 'internalise the externalities', thus not only correcting them (at least in part) but also providing incentives for sustainable resource use and promotion of green (or 'clean') technologies (see page 105).
- Governments pursue more environmental regulations that encourage pollution-free technological change (green technologies).
- There is an increased emphasis on human capital in production (which is pollution-free) as opposed to physical capital.
- An increased emphasis on 'green' investments, which promote growth while not hurting the environment: building public transportation systems; investing in insulation in homes and buildings; investing in clean technology research and development (R&D) and clean technologies (see page 128).
- There are changes in the structure of the economy toward more services (which tend to be pollution-free), together with more investments in the protection of natural resources.

As incomes increase with economic growth, more resources are made available with which governments can pursue the above kinds of policies, encouraging economic growth at the same time that they encourage sustainability. Therefore, *economic growth and sustainability can be pursued together provided governments take appropriate measures to ensure sustainable resource use*. This is the very meaning behind the concept of 'sustainable development' (see page 122).

However, even under the best possible circumstances where all of the above conditions are fulfilled, modern growth theories show that *there is a maximum rate of growth that is consistent with environmental sustainability*, and that if an economy exceeds this rate, resource use will become unsustainable. The reason is that pursuit of sustainability uses up some resources (for example anti-pollution controls, costs of regulation, etc.), and these resources represent an opportunity cost in terms of lost economic growth. Note, however, that this only applies to a loss of a portion of very high rates of growth.[7]

A concluding note

We have examined the effects of economic growth on a number of factors. Note that all these factors can also impact on economic growth:

- **Living standards.** Economic growth can be expected to impact on living standards, but improved living standards measured as improvements in human development, involving improved human capital or reduced income inequalities, are major factors contributing to economic growth (see pages 463 and 473).
- **Unemployment.** Economic growth may lower cyclical or structural unemployment, but reductions in unemployment can contribute to economic growth by making better use of available resources (movement closer to the economy's production possibilities curve (*PPC*); see page 295).
- **Inflation.** Economic growth may contribute to a higher rate of inflation, but a high rate of inflation may contribute to lower economic growth, by discouraging investment (see page 279).
- **Distribution of income.** Economic growth can make the distribution of income more or less equal (equitable), but a more equal distribution of income has a positive effect on growth (see page 473).
- **Current account of the balance of payments.** Economic growth may worsen the current account, but a serious current account deficit can lower economic growth by increasing the need for foreign borrowing (see page 407).
- **Sustainability.** Economic growth that ignores the effects on the environment leads to environmental unsustainability, but unsustainability also leads to lower economic growth due to destruction of common access resources. On the other hand, economic growth based on the principle of sustainable development leads to environmental preservation, which in turn can be expected to lead to higher economic growth in the future.

The likelihood of a two-way causality, where economic growth impacts upon factors such as the above, and where these factors in turn impact upon economic growth, sometimes makes it difficult in the real world to determine what causes what.

---

[7] You may be wondering what these rates of growth are. It is not possible to attach numerical values to these given the present state of economists' and scientists' knowledge, because not enough is known about the costs and benefits of growth and environmental sustainability.

Explain the possible consequences of economic growth on **(a)** living standards, **(b)** unemployment, **(c)** inflation, **(d)** income distribution, **(e)** the current account, and **(f)** sustainability.

19.2 Balance between markets and intervention

Most countries in the world today are *mixed market economies*, meaning economies strongly based on markets, but with a degree of government intervention. However, countries differ enormously with respect to the degree and types of government intervention. This raises the questions: how much should governments intervene in developing countries, and what are the appropriate roles of markets and intervention? This topic directly addresses one of the four central themes of this course (page 14).

This section brings together many topics examined in previous chapters. You will therefore frequently be referred to the relevant pages for a review of the important issues.

Strengths and weaknesses of market-oriented policies

Market-oriented policies, as the term suggests, are based on the market mechanism introduced in Chapter 2. Market-oriented policies we have studied include:

- market-based supply-side policies, including:
  - policies encouraging competition (deregulation, privatisation and anti-monopoly regulation (page 340)
  - labour market reforms (page 341)
  - incentive-related policies (page 342)
- trade liberalisation (free or freer trade; page 485)
- freely floating exchange rates (page 382)
- liberalised capital flows, or the absence of exchange controls which limit the amount of foreign exchange that can be purchased with the domestic currency (page 495).

Strengths

- Discuss the positive outcomes of market-oriented policies (such as liberalised trade and capital flows, privatisation and deregulation), including a more efficient allocation of resources and economic growth.

Market-oriented policies are based on the idea that free markets, working under competitive conditions, offer a method to answer the *what to produce* and *how to produce* questions of resource allocation in the best possible way. With market-determined prices working as signals and incentives, markets co-ordinate the countless independent decisions of consumers, firms and resource owners, allowing social surplus to be maximised, thus achieving allocative efficiency (see page 43).

At the same time, the pursuit of self-interest by all economic decision-makers (consumers, firms and resource-owners) gives rise to incentives for hard work, risk-taking, innovation and investment, which lead to higher levels of output (economic growth) and possibly higher standards of living. The operation of markets therefore also promotes general welfare by achieving economic growth.

It thus follows that policies encouraging competition, such as deregulation, privatisation and anti-monopoly regulation, which work by freeing market forces and making markets more competitive, are intended to result in greater efficiency in production, lower prices and improved quality, and a better allocation of resources, as well as increased levels of output, or economic growth.

Labour market reforms similarly promote free market forces in labour markets, allowing the allocation of resources to improve. Incentive-related policies, involving adjustments to various types of taxes, are intended to work by improving the incentives to work, innovate and invest, thus making the signalling and incentive functions of the price mechanism more effective, again improving the allocation of resources and also allowing for economic growth.

Trade liberalisation is based on the same ideas, and has the same intended benefits. The elimination of trade barriers and the opening up of countries to free trade has the effect of making markets much larger than they would be with trade barriers. The result of larger free markets is to increase competition, increase efficiency in production, lower prices and improve quality, increase consumer choice, improve the allocation of resources, and allow for greater economic growth.

Freely floating exchange rates are simply another aspect of the price mechanism of free markets. A market-determined exchange rate is one that reflects the forces of supply and demand for a currency, and therefore can effectively carry out the signalling and incentive function of prices (here applied to the 'price' of a currency) for those carrying out international transactions of all kinds. Just as a market-determined price of a good 'clears' the market, so too a freely floating exchange rate automatically adjusts to excess demand or supply of a currency, bringing about a balance in the balance of payments and offering greater flexibility to policy-makers to pursue policies needed domestically (see page 403).

Liberalised capital flows (or absence of exchange controls) allow domestic residents to purchase any amount of foreign exchange without restrictions, whether for imports, or for travel or investment abroad, etc. This is important for attracting multinational corporations (MNCs) because it means the MNC is free to repatriate profits or to purchase inputs from abroad (import them). In addition, free capital flows mean a more efficient global allocation of savings, since savers are free to make financial investments anywhere in the world without restrictions, in accordance with the expected profitability of their investments.

Weaknesses

♦ Discuss the negative outcomes of market-oriented strategies, including market failure, the development of a dual economy and income inequalities.

Market failure

One of the most important weaknesses of market-oriented strategies is that they cannot deal with the issue of market failures, discussed in Chapter 5. While this issue is important for any country, it is of special importance in many developing countries where market failures of all kinds are far more widespread.

Market failures we have studied include:

* negative environmental externalities (of production and consumption) and the problems of common access resources

* insufficient provision of merit goods (goods with positive consumption externalities) including education, health care and infrastructure, such as sanitation, clean water supplies, road and transport systems, irrigation, power supplies, etc.

* failure to provide public goods

* abuse of monopoly power

* information asymmetries

There are two additional failures of concern to developing countries: co-ordination failures and weak or missing market institutions.

Co-ordination failures   Co-ordination failures provide a possible explanation for the failure of firms to be set up and to contribute to growth. Suppose that firms would be able to increase their output if they began producing in a market requiring skilled labour. However, they will not enter this market if the skilled labour is not available; at the same time, workers will not acquire the skills if the firms that could hire them do not exist. As a result, the firms do not enter this market, and the workers do not acquire the skills. Both the firms and the workers get stuck in a position where they are worse off than they would have been if they could co-ordinate their activities and simultaneously enter the new market and acquire the necessary skills.

In another example, farmers could increase their production of agricultural goods for sale in the market, but to do this they need intermediaries, or 'middlemen', who will effectively represent them in distant markets. As long as the middlemen are not available, the farmers will not begin producing for the market; and as long as the agricultural output for the market is not produced, the middlemen will not become available.[8] The farmers get stuck in a position where they are producing less output than they could, and potential middlemen that could have benefited themselves and the economy do not emerge. Everyone is worse off, and the possibilities for expanding output remain unrealised.

Co-ordination failures arise when two or more activities that must begin simultaneously fail to do so, even though decision-makers make economic decisions that are in their best self-interest. The inability of decision-makers to co-ordinate their behaviours results in an outcome where everyone is worse off than they would have been had co-ordination been possible. These failures lead to *underdevelopment traps*, where people are trapped in a situation from which they cannot escape without outside help.

Weak or missing market institutions   To be able to function effectively, markets need an institutional and legal environment that is often missing in less developed countries (and some transition economies). This environment must include enforcement of property rights, enforcement of legal contracts, effective legal recourse, a stable currency, a well-developed banking and insurance system, an effective road and utility infrastructure system, and readily available information on prices, quantities and quality of goods, services and resources to consumers, firms and resource owners. In the absence of these conditions, markets are highly imperfect in their functions and fail to function effectively.

---

[8] See Michael P. Todaro and Stephen C. Smith (2006) *Economic Development,* Pearson Education, where these ideas are explored more fully.

Development of dual economies

A dual economy (or dualism) was explained in Chapter 16, page 444. Dual economies may persist even as a country grows and develops. They are the outcome of market forces that do not work to the benefit of all or most people in a country because of the presence of market failures such as weak market institutions or co-ordination failures, because of the geographical isolation of many groups of people, the persistence or growth of great income inequalities and extreme poverty, or government policies that support one sector of the economy at the expense of another. Like all kinds of market failures that require some government intervention for their correction, so dual economies also require government policies that attempt to eliminate the dualism. The appropriate policy depends on the nature of the dual economy, i.e. whether it involves an advanced agricultural sector together with traditional, subsistence agriculture, or an advanced capital-intensive industrial sector together with a traditional labour-intensive urban informal sector.

Income inequalities

We have studied the effects of market-oriented policies on income distribution in Chapter 12, in connection with market-based supply-side policies, and in Chapter 17 in connection with the effects of trade and market liberalisation. The loss of protection of workers resulting from labour-market reforms, and increases in unemployment resulting from some policies to increase competition, including trade liberalisation which often involves the closure of firms, often result in increases in income inequalities. In addition, the inability of certain groups of people to take advantage of opportunities opened by trade and market liberalisation can also lead to increasing income inequalities (page 486).

Insufficient credit for poor people

As discussed in Chapter 17, page 467, poor people do not have access to credit, as the market working on its own does not allow poor people with no collateral and seeking very small loans to acquire the credit they need. This results in lower investment possibilities, greater poverty and poorer income distribution, as well as the inability to escape the poverty cycle.

Questionable effects on economic growth and development

Contrary to expectations, trade and market liberalisation may not lead to improved export performance and greater economic growth and development in some countries. Experiences have shown performance to be highly variable, with some countries faring better than others. According to the evidence, the countries that are better able to take advantage of opportunities offered by trade and market liberalisation are those that have already developed an industrial base, and are therefore better able to withstand the competition arising from the elimination or reduction of trade barriers. Low-income countries tend to perform the worst, because they can least withstand the competition with larger, more 'mature' foreign firms, and this sometimes leads to a weakening of their industry together with increased unemployment, poverty and growth of the urban informal sector (see page 485).

Capital liberalisation, if undertaken before countries have developed the necessary institutions, may lead to capital flight, reduced ability to conduct monetary policy in accordance with domestic priorities, and even financial crisis (see page 496).

The withdrawal of government from provision of merit goods that often comes with market liberalisation has negative effects on economic and human development.

These processes have the effect of increasing inequalities between rich and poor countries, as well as between higher income and lower income groups within countries.

Strengths and weaknesses of interventionist policies

Strengths

♦ Discuss the strengths of interventionist policies, including the provision of infrastructure, investment in human capital, the provision of a stable macroeconomic economy and the provision of a social safety net.

Interventionist policies are based on government intervention in markets intended to correct market deficiencies and create an environment in which markets can work more effectively. The strengths of interventionist policies include their potential to contribute to the following.

Correcting market failures

Governments have a major role to play in the correction of market failures. This includes policies that try to:

- correct negative environmental externalities of production and consumption and overuse of common access resources (Chapter 5)
- provide public goods as well as merit goods that are underprovided by the market due to positive

consumption externalities – as we know this involves investments in human capital (health and education) and investments in infrastructure (Chapter 5)

- assist in the correction of co-ordination failures (see page 532 above) – government intervention is needed to help people escape underdevelopment traps by allowing the simultaneous occurrence of necessary activities

- contribute to the development of market institutions that enable markets to operate more effectively (see page 532 above).

Investment in human capital

Investment in human capital (education and health) was noted above in connection with government policies to correct market failures. Education and health have significant external benefits, thus calling for government intervention (such as direct provision) that increases the consumption of both. Education and health are major factors behind increases in productivity that contribute to economic growth, and they also directly lead to greater economic and human development. Investment in human capital also forms a part of industrial policies, discussed below. (See also page 463.)

Provision of infrastructure

The provision of infrastructure also forms part of policies to correct market failures (noted above). Infrastructure includes a broad range of goods and services, also with significant positive externalities. As a type of physical capital, it includes water supplies, sanitation and sewerage, power, communication, transportation, roads, irrigation, and many others. All of these play a very important role in encouraging economic growth, as well as making possible economic and human development (see page 475). They increase productivity, and make a direct contribution to improved standards of living. Therefore, there is a strong role for governments in order to ensure the provision of the appropriate kinds of infrastructure, with the appropriate access by the population.

Provision of a stable macroeconomic environment

A stable macroeconomic environment includes price stability (the general price level should rise only gradually); full employment (people willing and able to work should be able to find a job); a reasonable budget deficit; and a reasonable balance of trade (avoidance of large trade or current account deficits). The market mechanism cannot accomplish these tasks on its own,

and requires government intervention through the use of appropriate policies in pursuit of these objectives. We studied these policies in Chapters 12 and 14. A stable macroeconomic environment is important for ensuring that economic decision-makers (consumers, firms and resource owners) can plan their future economic activities (such as consumption investment, imports, exports, etc.). It is a key condition for investment, in particular, leading to the formation of physical and human capital, which are fundamental prerequisites for economic growth.

Provision of a social safety net

In Chapter 11, we saw that the market cannot ensure that everyone in a society can secure enough income to satisfy basic needs (food, shelter, etc.). The government must therefore step in with the provision of a social safety net to ensure that people falling below a minimum income level will be able to secure their basic needs. A social safety net is a system of government transfers of cash or goods to vulnerable groups, undertaken to ensure that these groups do not fall below a socially acceptable minimum standard of living (see page 309 on transfer payments). The provision of a social safety net by the government is very important in a market-based economy, where there are risks of becoming unemployed or falling into poverty.

Redistributing income

Another method to deal with the market's inability to secure everyone a minimum income involves government's policy of income redistribution, discussed in Chapter 11.

Industrial policies

Industrial policies are interventionist supply-side policies that include support for small and medium-sized businesses as well as protection of infant industries (such as through tariffs or subsidies) in order to help developing countries in the early stages of their industrialisation (page 339).

In addition, industrial policies include government support of appropriate technology transfer from developed countries and the establishment of a research and development capability, as well as the investments in human capital.

Industrial policies were a key factor behind the success of the Asian Tigers (page 484). Whereas these policies were discouraged by the Washington Consensus, according to New Development Consensus they can play an important role in helping developing countries develop their industries and higher value-added activities (page 487).

Weaknesses

♦ Discuss the limitations of interventionist policies, including excessive bureaucracy, poor planning and corruption.

Government activities are subject to several weaknesses that limit the effectiveness of their interventions in the market.

Excessive bureaucracy

A bureaucracy is an administrative structure of an organisation involving rules that determine how the organisation functions and carries out its tasks. Governments often run into the problem of excessive bureaucracy, meaning there are too many rules governing procedures, red-tape, unproductive workers, high administrative costs and inefficiency. This is a key argument often used in favour of reducing the size of the government sector through privatisation of government-owned enterprises, contracting-out of government activities, and private financing of public sector projects (see page 340) to reduce bureaucratic procedures and improve efficiency.

Poor planning

Government planning involves making decisions on what and how much of certain goods and services it will produce, how these will be produced (by use of what resources), how much they will cost and what revenues they might be expected to provide. Planning plays a major role in government provision of merit goods and public goods, as well as numerous government policies such as taxes, subsidies, transfer payments as well as virtually all of its economic activities.

Planning may run into difficulties because it requires technical knowledge and expertise on the part of planners, which they may not possess, as well as a tremendous amount of detailed information, much of which is often not available. The result is that planning can become highly bureaucratic and inefficient, resulting in a waste of resources.

Corruption

Corruption is defined by the World Bank as 'the abuse of public office for private gain'. It can take many forms including bribery, construction kickbacks, procurement fraud, extortion, false certification, nepotism, embezzlement, and more. It occurs everywhere in the world, but tends to be more important in countries where the legal system, mass media and the system of public administration are weak. It should be noted that multinational corporations in their dealings with governments play an important role with respect to bribes.

Corruption is often associated with lower growth and poorer development prospects. When it takes the form of a payment for something, it works like a tax that makes private investments more costly, reducing the overall level of investment. If it involves bribes to receive basic services like education or health care it works like a regressive tax, because the bribe is a higher fraction of the income of lower income earners. Unlike taxes paid to the government that become available for use in socially desirable activities, bribes go into the pockets of public servants and politicians, depriving society of resources that could have been used to pay for the provision of important merit goods. Bribes for tax evasion result in further reducing government revenues. Corruption can also result in a misallocation of resources as government officials accept bribes to pursue uneconomic projects (such as dams and power plants) instead of socially necessary services like education, health care, sanitation, etc. Corruption can also weaken sustainable development as government officials may accept bribes to bypass environmental regulations. Finally, corruption damages the people's trust in the state and encourages contempt for the rule of law.

Market with government intervention

Why good governance is important

♦ Explain the importance of good governance in the development process.

According to the World Bank, **governance** is 'the manner in which power is exercised in the management of a country's economic and social resources for development. Good governance ... is synonymous with sound development management.'[9]

Governance is not about *what* is done for economic growth and development, but rather *how* it is done. It is about the effectiveness of government, but also it involves the relations between government and society, and how they interact to make decisions. According to researchers on this topic, *good* governance consists of six principles:[10]

- **Participation** – the extent to which the stakeholders affected by policies are involved in making decisions and in the implementation of decisions.

---

[9] The World Bank (1992) *Governance and Development.*
[10] Goran Hyden, Julius Court and Kenneth Mease (2004) 'Making sense of governance: empirical evidence from 16 developing countries', Overseas Development Institute.

- **Fairness** – the extent to which rules apply to everyone in society equally.
- **Decency** – the extent to which the formation and implementation of rules does not harm or humiliate anyone.
- **Accountability** – the extent to which political figures and decision-makers are responsible to society for the actions and their statements.
- **Transparency** – the extent to which decisions made by government are clear and open.
- **Efficiency** – the extent to which scarce resources are used without waste, delays or corruption.

Good governance is important because according to studies making cross-country comparisons, better governance is related to more investment and greater economic growth. The effectiveness of government, the efficiency of bureaucracy and rule of law are positively related to economic performance and adult literacy, and negatively related to infant mortality.[11]

Achieving a balance between markets and intervention

♦ Discuss the view that economic development may best be achieved through a complementary approach, involving a balance of market-oriented policies and government intervention.

During much of the 20th century, many countries around the world saw significant increases in government intervention. In developing countries, intervention took the form of import-substituting industrialisation during the 1950s and 1960s, followed later by export promotion (pages 482–84). In communist countries there was a very strong government presence that largely replaced the market system and took the form of central planning (government planning of most economic activities).

From the 1980s, there was a shift in most countries in the direction of less government intervention and a stronger emphasis on markets. This shift was influenced by the weaknesses of import-substituting industrialisation policies, as well as by market-based supply-side thinking that emerged in the United Kingdom and the United States at that time. It was also strongly encouraged by the Washington Consensus (page 485), part of which involved World

Bank lending (structural adjustment loans) and lending by the International Monetary Fund (and its stabilisation policies). At the same time, there was a growing recognition of the limitations of central planning in communist states. In China and former communist countries, a deliberate choice was made to move toward a stronger market orientation; these economies are called 'economies in transition'.[12]

By the early 2000s, it had become apparent that neither the extreme of very strong government intervention, nor the extreme of a highly free market orientation, is appropriate for the conditions of developing countries (page 487). Attention of policy-makers therefore turned toward finding an appropriate mix of market-based and interventionist policies.

Based on the experiences of developing countries accumulated over a 60-year period and the evolution of economists' thinking on this subject, we can arrive at the following broad conclusions:

- **Very strong government intervention in the market, such as that pursued during the 1950s and 1960s, has been mostly discredited as a strategy for economic growth and development, and international trade.** It is now well understood that very strong government intervention leads to misallocation of resources and inefficiencies in production, and may result in lower rates of growth. As of the early 2000s, there tends to be a convergence on the idea that market forces should be allowed to play an important role, and that trade, growth and development strategies should be for the most part market-led, though with varying degrees and forms of government intervention.

- **A market-led economic development strategy with a minimum amount of government intervention, such as is represented by the Washington Consensus, does not take into account the special set of circumstances faced by developing countries.** If such a policy is pursued over an extended period, it is likely to lead to only limited progress in economic growth and economic and human development, as a result of persisting and possibly increasing poverty, a likely increase in unemployment and underemployment, persisting and probably increasing inequalities in income distribution, insufficient investments in education and health (human capital) as well as

---

[11] Julius Court (2006) 'Governance, development and aid effectiveness: a quick guide to complex relationships', Overseas Development Institute.

[12] Most economies in transition appeared after the collapse of communist regimes in eastern Europe and the former Soviet Union in 1989–90. The countries in this group include the ones

that emerged after the break-up of the Soviet Union (15) and Yugoslavia (7), plus the countries of eastern Europe that experienced a transition to democratic regimes. China, also a transition economy, has taken a different route by choosing to introduce market reforms gradually under the direction of its Communist Party.

in infrastructure, unsustainable development, the continued use of inappropriate technologies, and limited opportunities to expand exports.

- **The New Development Consensus outlines a number of areas in which governments of developing countries should intervene in order to promote growth and development.** As of the early 2000s, there is broad agreement among development economists that there should be government intervention in areas including: poverty alleviation; reductions in income inequalities and inequalities in economic opportunities; investments in health, education, infrastructure, technology transfer and the establishment of a research and development capability; some support for small and medium-sized businesses; protection of the environment and sustainable development. In addition, many economists support the idea that developing countries, especially the very poor ones, may require some protection for their domestic industries in the initial phases of their industrialisation in the form of industrial policies, including protection of infant industries.

- **It would be a mistake to take a blanket (or uniform) approach to all developing (or any other) countries with regard to proposals for market-led or interventionist strategies (or any other type of strategies for that matter).** Each country is unique, and should be able to tailor its strategies to its own particular needs and conditions, in consultation with aid and development assistance agencies.

- **It is likely that countries at lower levels of economic development can benefit from strategies that are more strongly interventionist; government can gradually withdraw and give greater reign to market forces as the country grows and develops.** Countries at lower levels of development are more likely to be lacking in the necessary institutions and regulatory and legal mechanisms required for markets to work well, thus needing a relatively greater degree of government intervention. With growth and development, and the gradual establishment of more effective institutions, the government can increasingly withdraw, allowing market forces to take a stronger hold.

Test your understanding 19.2

1 Explain some of the main strengths and weaknesses of market-oriented policies.

2 Explain some of the main strengths and weaknesses of interventionist policies.

3 **(a)** Explain the meaning of good governance. **(b)** Why is good governance important in economic development?

4 Why would it be inappropriate to take a uniform approach to making policy recommendations on the roles of the market and government intervention in developing countries?

5 Explain whether you agree with the propositions that **(a)** markets and government intervention should complement each other in developing countries, and **(b)** governments should intervene more strongly in countries that are at a relatively lower level of economic development, and less strongly as countries grow and develop.

Real world focus

Economic growth and development in Peru

During the 1990s, Peru reoriented its economy toward the market to achieve economic growth and development. This involved abandoning its policies of import substitution, including elimination of price controls, lowering trade protection barriers, lowering restrictions on foreign direct investment, and reducing state ownership of firms. Since 2002, it has experienced high rates of growth, and has been the fastest growing economy in Latin America.

Peru's economic performance was not always so favourable. In the late 1970s the economy had suffered a serious collapse, and remained mostly depressed for about two decades. By 2005–6, real GDP *per capita* just managed to reach the same levels of the 1970s.

An important factor behind the collapse involved massive declines in export revenues, due to excessive specialisation in the export of only a few primary commodities: minerals (mining of copper, gold and zinc) and agriculture (coffee, sugar, potatoes). Terms of trade shocks caused by declines in global commodity prices reduced the value of exports by more than 80% in 1979–93, resulting in declining incomes, increasing unemployment and poverty, a balance

(continued over)

Glossary

HL   **abnormal profit**   Refers to positive economic profit, arising when total revenue is greater than total economic costs (implicit plus explicit costs); is also known as 'supernormal profit'. See *economic profit*.

HL   **absolute advantage**   Refers to the ability of a country to produce a good using fewer resources than another country, or, what is the same thing, the ability of a certain amount of resources in a country to produce more than the same resources can produce in another country.

absolute poverty   The inability of an individual or a family to afford a basic standard of goods and services, where this standard is absolute and unchanging over time. Absolute poverty is defined in relation to a nationally or internationally determined 'poverty line', which determines the minimum income that can sustain a family in terms of its basic needs.

actual output   The quantity of output actually produced by an economy. In the context of the production possibilities model, it may be contrasted with production possibilities: actual output occurs somewhere inside an economy's production possibilities curve (*PPC*) because of the presence of unemployed resources and productive inefficiency. In the context of the *AD-AS* model, it may be contrasted with potential output, given by the position of an economy's long-run aggregate supply (*LRAS*) curve: actual output may be higher or lower than potential output (if there is an inflationary or deflationary gap) or it may be equal to potential output (if the economy is in long-run equilibrium).

ad valorem taxes   Taxes calculated as a fixed percentage of the price of the good or service; the amount of tax increases as the price of the good or service increases.

administrative barriers   Trade protection measures taking the form of administrative procedures that countries may use to prevent the free flow of imports into a country; these may include customs procedures involving inspections and valuation, controls on packaging, and others. Often considered to be a kind of 'hidden' trade protection as they don't involve obvious trade protection measures such as tariffs and quotas.

aggregate demand   The total quantity of goods and services that all buyers in an economy (consumers, firms, the government and foreigners) want to buy over a particular time period, at different possible price levels, *ceteris paribus*.

aggregate demand curve   The curve that shows the relationship between total quantity of goods and services that all buyers in an economy want to buy over a particular

time period (aggregate demand), measured on the horizontal axis, plotted against the price level, measured on the vertical axis.

aggregate supply   The total quantity of goods and services produced in an economy over a particular time period, at different price levels, *ceteris paribus*.

aid   See *foreign aid*.

allocation of resources   See *resource allocation*.

allocative efficiency   An allocation of resources that results in producing the combination and quantity of goods and services mostly preferred by consumers. It is achieved when the economy allocates its resources so that no one can become better off in terms of increasing their benefit from consumption without **HL**   someone else becoming worse off. The condition for allocative efficiency is given by $P = MC$ (price is equal to marginal cost).

anti-dumping   An argument that justifies trade protection policies: if a country's trading partner is suspected of practising dumping, then the country should have the right to impose trade protection measures (tariffs or quotas) to limit quantities of the dumped good; see *dumping*.

appreciation (of a currency)   Refers to an increase in the value of a currency in the context of a floating (or flexible) exchange rate system or managed exchange rate system (compare with *revaluation*, which refers to an increase in currency value in the context of a fixed exchange rate system).

appropriate technology   Technologies that are well-suited to a country's particular economic, geographical, ecological and climate conditions. Often used in connection with labour-abundant developing countries that require labour-intensive (as opposed to capita- intensive) technologies.

HL   **asymmetric information**   A type of market failure where buyers and sellers do not have equal access to information, usually resulting in an underallocation of resources to the production of goods and services, as parties to a transaction with less access to information try to protect themselves against the consequences of the information asymmetry.

automatic stabilisers   Factors that automatically, without any action by government authorities, work toward stabilising the economy by reducing the short term fluctuations of the business cycle. Two important automatic stabilisers are progressive income taxes and unemployment benefits.

HL   **average costs**   Costs per unit of output, or the cost of each unit of output on average. They are calculated by dividing total cost by the number of units of output produced.

HL   **average fixed costs**   Fixed cost per unit of output, or the fixed cost of each unit of output on average. They are calculated by dividing fixed cost by the number of units of output produced.

HL   **average product**   The total quantity of output of a firm per unit of variable input (such as labour); shows how much output each unit of the variable input (for example, each worker) produces on average.

HL   **average revenue**   Revenue per unit of output sold, calculated by dividing total revenue by the number of units of output produced.

HL   **average tax rate**   Tax paid divided by total income, expressed as a percentage (i.e. tax paid divided by total income multiplied by 100).

HL   **average total costs**   Total cost per unit of output, or the total cost of each unit of output on average. They are calculated by dividing total costs by the number of units of output; they are also equal to the sum of average fixed costs and average variable costs.

HL   **average variable costs**   Variable cost per unit of output, or the variable cost of each unit of output on average. They are calculated by dividing variable cost by the number of units of output.

balance of payments   A record (usually for a year) of all transactions between the residents of a country and the residents of all other countries, showing all payments received from other countries (credits), and all payments made to other countries (debits). In the course of a year, the sum of all the credits must be equal to the sum of all the debits.

balance of trade in goods   Part of the balance of payments, it is the value of exports of goods minus the value of imports of goods over a specific period of time (usually a year).

balance of trade in services   Part of the balance of payments, it is the value of exports of services minus the value of imports of services over a specific period of time (usually a year)

balance on capital account   The sum of inflows minus outflows of funds in the capital account of the balance of payments. See *capital account*.

balance on current account   The sum of inflows minus outflows of funds in the current account of the balance of payments. See *current account*.

balance on financial account The sum of inflows of funds minus outflows in the financial account of the balance of payments. See *financial account*.

balanced budget Referring usually to the government's budget, it is the situation where government tax revenues are equal to government expenditures over a specific period of time (usually a year).

barriers to entry Anything that can prevent a firm from entering an industry and beginning production, as a result limiting the degree of competition in the industry.

bilateral trade agreement Any trade agreement (or agreement to lower international trade barriers) involving two trading partners, usually two countries. It may also involve a trade agreement between one country and another group of countries when this groups acts as a single unit (such as the European Union). May be contrasted with *regional trade agreement* and *multilateral trade agreement*.

break-even point The point of production of a firm where its total revenue is exactly equal to its total costs (economic costs), and it is therefore earning normal profit, or zero economic (supernormal) profit

break-even price A price at which the firm breaks even, meaning that its total revenues are just equal to its total costs (economic costs); at the break-even price the firm is earning zero economic (supernormal) profit, but it is earning normal profit.

budget deficit Referring usually to the government's budget, it is the situation where government tax revenues are less than government expenditures over a specific period of time (usually a year).

budget surplus Referring usually to the government's budget, it is the situation where government tax revenues are greater than government expenditures over a specific period of time (usually a year).

business confidence A measure of the degree of optimism among firms in an economy about the future performance of firms and the economy; it is measured on the basis of surveys of business managers. Is an important determinant of the investment component of aggregate demand.

business cycle Fluctuations in the growth of real output, or real GDP, consisting of alternating periods of expansion (increasing real output) and contraction (decreasing real output); also known as trade cycles.

cap and trade scheme A scheme in which a government authority (of a single country or a group of countries) sets a limit or 'cap' on the amount of pollutants that can be legally emitted by a firm, set by an amount of pollution permits (known as *tradable permits*) distributed to firms; firms that want to pollute more than their permits allow can buy more permits in a market, while firms that want to pollute less can sell their excess permits.

capital One of the factors of production, which itself has been produced (it does not occur naturally), also known as 'physical capital', including machinery, tools, equipment, buildings, etc. Physical capital is also referred to as a 'capital good' or 'investment good'. Other types of capital include 'human capital', or the skills, abilities, knowledge and levels of good health acquired by people; 'natural capital', or everything that traditionally has been included in the factor of production 'land'; and 'financial capital', or purchases of financial instruments such as stocks and bonds.

capital account In the balance of payments, refers to the inflows minus outflows of funds for (i) capital transfers' (including such things as debt forgiveness and non-life insurance claims), and (ii) the purchase or use of non-produced natural resources (such as mineral rights, forestry rights, fishing rights and airspace); it is a relatively unimportant part of the balance of payments.

capital account balance See *balance on capital account*.

capital expenditures With reference to government expenditures, these include public investments, or the production of physical capital, such as building roads, airports, harbours, school buildings, hospitals, etc.

capital liberalisation Refers to the free movement of financial capital in and out of a country, occurring through the elimination by the government of exchange controls (government restrictions on the quantity of foreign exchange that can be bought by domestic residents of a country).

capital transfers A part of the capital account of the balance of payments, they include inflows minus outflows for such things as debt forgiveness, non-life insurance claims, and investment. See *capital account*.

carbon tax A tax per unit of carbon emissions of fossil fuels, considered by many countries as a policy to deal with the problem of climate change.

cartel A formal agreement between firms in an industry to undertake concerted actions to limit competition; is formed in connection with *collusive oligopoly*. It may involve fixing the quantity to be produced by each firm, or fixing the price at which output can be sold, and other actions. The objective is to increase the monopoly power of the firms in the cartel. Cartels are illegal in many countries.

central bank A financial institution that is responsible for regulating the country's financial system and commercial banks, and carrying out monetary policy.

ceteris paribus A Latin expression that means 'other things being equal'. Another way of saying this is that all other things are assumed to be constant or unchanging. It is used in economics theories and models to isolate changes in only those variables that are being studied.

circular flow of income model A model showing the flow of resources from consumers (households) to firms, and the flow of products from firms to consumers, as well as money flows consisting of consumers' income arising from the sale of their resources and firms' revenues arising from the sale of their products. It illustrates the equivalence of *expenditure flows*, *value of output flows*, and *income flows*.

clean technology Technology that is not polluting, associated with environmental sustainability; includes solar power, wind power, hydropower, recycling, and many more.

closed economy An economy that has no international trade (no imports and exports); usually appears in connection with economic theories and models as virtually no cconomy in the real world is a closed economy. To be contrasted with *open economy*.

collusion An agreement among firms to fix prices, or divide the market between them, so as to limit competition and maximise profit; usually involves firms in oligopoly.

collusive oligopoly Refers to the type of oligopoly where firms agree to restrict output or fix the price, in order to limit competition, increase monopoly power and increase profits. See also *cartel*.

commercial bank A financial institution (which may be private or public) whose main functions are to hold deposits for their customers (consumers and firms), to make loans to their customers, to transfer funds by cheque (check) from one bank to another, and to buy government bonds.

common access resources Resources that are not owned by anyone, do not have a price, and are available for anyone to use without payment (for example, lakes, rivers, fish in the open seas, open grazing land, the ozone layer and many more); their depletion or degradation leads to environmental unsustainability.

common market A type of trading bloc in which countries that have formed a customs union proceed further to eliminate any remaining tariffs in trade between them; they continue to have a common external policy (as in a *customs union*), and in addition agree to eliminate all restrictions on movements of any factors of production within them; factors affected are mainly labour and capital, which are free to cross all borders and move, travel and find employment freely within all member countries. The best-known common market is the European Economic Community (EEC, the precursor of the present European Union).

community surplus See *social surplus*.

comparative advantage Arises when a country has a lower relative cost, or opportunity cost, in the production of a good than another country. Forms the basis of the *theory of comparative advantage*.

competitive market A market composed of many buyers and sellers acting independently, none of whom has any ability to influence the price of the product (i.e. no *market power*).

competitive supply   In the case of two goods, refers to production of one or the other by a firm; in other words the two goods compete with each other for the same resources (for example, if a farmer can produce wheat or corn, producing more of one means producing less of the other).

competition   Occurs when there are many buyers and sellers acting independently, so that no one has the ability to influence the price at which the product is sold in the market.

complements (complementary goods)   Two or more goods that tend to be used together. If two goods are complements, an increase in the price of one will lead to a decrease in the demand of the other.

composite indicator   A summary measure of more than one indicator, often used to measure economic development; for example the *Human Development Index* (*HDI*), that measures income, education and health indicators.

HL   **concentration ratio**   A measure of how much an industry's production is concentrated among the industry's largest firms; it measures the percentage of output produced by the largest firms in an industry, and is used to provide an indication of the degree of competition or degree of monopoly power in an industry. The higher the ratio, the greater the degree of monopoly power.

concessional loan   Loans that are offered as part of *foreign aid*, made on concessional terms, i.e. that they are offered at interest rates that are lower than commercial rates, with longer repayment periods.

conditional assistance   Refers to development assistance provided by bilateral or multilateral development organisations, which is extended to countries on condition that they satisfy certain requirements, usually requiring that they adopt particular policies.

HL   **constant returns to scale**   Refers to the situation where the output of a firm changes in the same proportion as all its inputs; given a percentage increase in all inputs, output increases by the same percentage. May be contrasted with *increasing returns to scale* and *decreasing returns to scale*.

consumer confidence   A measure of the degree of optimism of consumers about their future income and the future of the economy; it is measured on the basis of surveys consumers. Is an important determinant of the consumption component of aggregate demand.

consumer price index   A measure of the cost of living for the typical household; it compares the value of a basket of goods and services in one year with the value of the same basket in a base year. Inflation (and deflation) are measured as a percentage change in the value of the basket from one year to another.

consumer surplus   Refers to the difference between the highest prices consumers are willing to pay for a good and the price actually paid. In a diagram, it is shown by the area under the demand curve and above the price paid by consumers.

consumption   Spending by households (consumers) on goods and services (excludes spending on housing).

contractionary fiscal policy   Refers to fiscal policy usually pursued in an inflation, involving a decrease in government spending or an increase in taxes (or both). May be contrasted with *expansionary fiscal policy*. See also *fiscal policy*.

contractionary monetary policy   Refers to monetary policy usually pursued in an inflation, involving an increase in interest rates, intended to lower investment and consumption spending; also known as 'tight monetary policy'. May be contrasted with *expansionery monetary policy*. See also *monetary policy*.

core rate of inflation   A rate of inflation based on a consumer price index that excludes goods with highly volatile (unstable) prices, notably food and energy prices.

corporate indebtedness   The degree to which corporations have debts (see *indebtedness*).

HL   **corporate social responsibility**   The practice of some corporations to avoid socially undesirable activities, such as polluting activities, employing children, or employing workers under unhealthy conditions; as well as undertaking socially desirable activities, such as support for human rights and donations to charities.

cost-push inflation   A type of inflation caused by a fall in aggregate supply, in turn resulting from increases in costs of production (for example, wages or prices of other inputs), shown in the *AD-AS* model as leftward shifts of the *AS* curve.

HL   **costs of production**   The total opportunity costs incurred by firms in order to acquire resources for use in production; include explicit costs (for purchased resources) and implicit costs (for self-owned resources).

credit items   In the balance of payments, refer to payments received from other countries, entering the balance of payments accounts with a plus sign; they represent an inflow of foreign exchange into a country.

cross-price elasticity of demand   (XED) A measure of the responsiveness of the demand for one good to a change in the price of another good; measured by the percentage change in the quantity of one good demanded divided by the percentage change in the price of another good. If XED > 0 the two goods are substitutes; if XED < 0, the two goods are complements.

crowding-out   Refers to the possible impacts on real GDP of increased government spending (expansionary fiscal policy) financed by borrowing; if increased government borrowing results in a higher rate of interest, this could reduce private investment spending, thus reversing the impacts of the government's expansionary fiscal policy.

current account   In the balance of payments, this includes the balance of trade (recording exports minus imports of goods) plus the balance on services (recording exports of services minus imports of services), plus inflows minus outflows of income and current transfers. The most important part of the current account in most countries is the balance of trade.

current account balance   See *balance on current account*.

current account deficit   Occurs when the current account balance has a negative value, meaning that debits are larger than credits (there is an excess of debits).

current account surplus   Occurs when the current account balance has a positive value, meaning that credits are larger than debits (there is an excess of credits).

current expenditures   In the government budget, refers to government spending on day-to-day items that are recurring (i.e. repeat themselves) and items that are used up or 'consumed' as a good or service is provided. Include wages and salaries (for all government employees); spending for supplies and equipment for the day-to-day operation of government activities (for example, school supplies and medical supplies for public schools and public health care services); provision of subsidies; and interest payments on government loans.

current transfers   An item in the current account of the balance of payments, refers to inflows and outflows of funds for items including gifts, foreign aid, and pensions.

customs union   A type of trading bloc, consisting of a group of countries that fulfil the requirements of a free trade area (elimination of trade barriers between members) and in addition adopt a common policy towards all non-member countries; members of a customs union also act as a group in all trade negotiations and agreements with non-members. It achieves a higher degree of economic integration than a free trade area, but lower than a common market.

cyclical unemployment   A type of unemployment that occurs during the downturns of the business cycle, when the economy is in a recessionary gap; the downturn is seen as arising from declining or low aggregate demand, and therefore is also known as 'demand-deficient' unemployment.

debit items   In the balance of payments, refer to payments made to other countries, entering the balance of payments accounts with a minus sign; they represent an outflow of foreign exchange from a country.

deciles   Division of a population into ten equal groups with respect to the distribution of a variable, such as income; for example, the lowest income decile refers to 10% of the population with the lowest income.

HL **decreasing returns to scale** Refers to the situation where the output of a firm changes less than in proportion to a change in all its inputs; given a percentage increase in all inputs, output increases by a smaller percentage. May be contrasted with *constant returns to scale* and *increasing returns to scale*.

deficit In general, this is the deficiency of something compared with something else. (i) In the balance of payments, a 'deficit' in an account occurs when the credits (inflows of money from abroad) are smaller than the debits (outflows of money to other countries); for example, a deficit in the balance of trade means that the value of exports (credits) is smaller than the value of imports (debits). (ii) In the case of the government budget, a 'deficit' occurs when government revenues are smaller than government expenditures.

deflation A continuing (or sustained) decrease in the general price level.

deflationary gap See *recessionary gap*.

demand Indicates the various quantities of a good that consumers (or a consumer) are willing and able to buy at different possible prices during a particular time period, *ceteris paribus* (all other things being equal).

demand-deficient unemployment See *cyclical unemployment*.

demand curve A curve showing the relationship between the quantities of a good consumers (or a consumer) are willing and able to buy during a particular time period, and their respective prices, *ceteris paribus* (all other things being equal).

demand management Policies that focus on the demand side of the economy, attempting to influence aggregate demand to achieve the goals of price stability, full employment and economic growth.

demand-pull inflation A type of inflation caused by an increase in aggregate demand, shown in the *AD-AS* model as a rightward shift in the *AD* curve.

demand-side policies Policies that attempt to change aggregate demand (shift the aggregate demand curve in the *AD-AS* model) in order to achieve the goals of price stability, full employment and economic growth, and minimise the severity of the business cycle. In the event of an inflationary or recessionary (deflationary) gap, they try to bring aggregate demand to the full employment level of real GDP, or potential GDP. They can also impact on economic growth by contributing to increases in potential GDP. Consists of fiscal and monetary policies. To be contrasted with *supply-side policies*.

demerit goods Goods that are considered to be undesirable for consumers and are overprovided by the market. Reasons for overprovision may be that the goods have negative externalities, or consumer ignorance about the harmful effects.

depreciation (of a currency) Refers to a decrease in the value of a currency in the context of a floating (or flexible) exchange rate system or managed exchange rate

system (to be compared with *devaluation*, which is a decrease in currency value in a fixed exchange rate system). (Note that depreciation also refers to capital goods that become worn out and are discarded.)

deregulation Policies involving the elimination or reduction of government regulation of private sector activities, based on the argument that government regulation stifles competition and increases inefficiency.

HL **deterioration in the terms of trade** A decrease in the value of the terms of trade index. See *terms of trade*.

determinants of aggregate demand Factors that cause shifts of the aggregate demand curve; include factors that influence consumption spending (C), investment spending (I), government spending (G) and net exports (Xn).

determinants of demand See *non-price determinants of demand*.

determinants of supply See *non-price determinants of supply*.

devaluation (of a currency) Refers to a decrease in the value of a currency in the context of a fixed exchange rate system (to be compared with *depreciation*, which is a decrease in currency value in the context of a floating (or flexible) or managed exchange rate system).

development aid Foreign aid intended to help economically less development countries; may involve *project aid*, *programme aid*, technical assistance or debt relief.

direct investment In the balance of payments, refers to inflows or outflows of funds for the purpose of foreign direct investment. See *foreign direct investment*.

direct taxes Taxes paid directly to the government tax authorities by the taxpayer, including personal income taxes, corporate income taxes and wealth taxes.

HL **diseconomies of scale** Increases in the average costs of production that occur as a firm increases its output by varying all its inputs (i.e. in the long run). Diseconomies of scale are responsible for the upward-sloping part of the long-run average total cost curve: as a firm increases its size, costs per unit of output increase.

disinflation Refers to a fall in the rate of inflation; it involves a positive rate of inflation and should be contrasted with *deflation*.

disposable income The income of consumers that is left over after the payment of income taxes.

distribution of income Concerned with how much of an economy's total income different individuals or different groups in the population receive, and involves answering the 'for whom' basic economic question.

diversification Generally refers to change involving greater variety, and is used to refer to increasing the variety of goods and services produced and/or exported by a country; it is the opposite of *specialisation*.

dual economy Arises when there are two different and opposing sets of circumstances that exist simultaneously, often found in economically less developed countries, such as for example, wealthy, highly educated groups co-existing with poor, illiterate groups, a formal and informal urban sector, and a low-productivity agricultural sector and a high-productivity urban industrial sector.

dumping The practice of selling a good in international markets at a price that is below the cost of producing it (usually by providing export subsidies); while it is illegal according to international trade rules, many countries practise it anyway. Forms the basis of the anti-dumping argument in favour of trade protection. See also *anti-dumping*.

easy monetary policy See *expansionary monetary policy*.

HL **economic costs** The sum of explicit costs and implicit costs, or the total opportunity costs incurred by a firm for its use of resources, whether purchased or self-owned. When economists refer to 'costs' they are actually referring to 'economic costs'.

economic development Broad-based rises in the standard of living and well-being of a population, particularly in economically less developed countries. It involves increasing income levels and reducing poverty, reducing income inequalities and unemployment, and increasing provision of and access to basic goods and services such as food and shelter, sanitation, education and health care services.

economic efficiency A condition that arises when allocative efficiency is achieved. See *allocative efficiency*.

economic growth Increases in total real output produced by an economy (real GDP) over time; may also refer to increases in real output (real GDP) *per capita* (or per person).

economic integration Refers to economic interdependence between countries, usually achieved by agreement between countries to reduce or eliminate trade and other barriers between them. There are various degrees of integration, depending on the type of agreement and the degree to which barriers between countries are removed; see *trading bloc*, *free trade area*, *customs union*, *common market*, *monetary union*.

HL **economic profit** Is a firm's total revenue minus total economic costs (explicit plus implicit). If economic profit is positive, the firm is earning supernormal (abnormal) profit; if it is zero, the firm is earning normal profit; if it is negative, the firm is making a loss.

economically less developed countries According to the World Bank's classification system, includes countries that have a per capital GNI below a particular level (which changes from year to year); some common characteristics include low levels of GDP per capita, high levels of poverty, large agricultural sectors and large urban informal sectors (though it is dangerous to generalise about these characteristics).

economically more developed countries According to the World Bank's classification system, includes countries that have a per capital GNI above a particular level (which changes from year to year); they generally have relatively high levels of GDP per capita, relatively low levels of poverty, small agricultural sectors, and large industrial and services sectors (though it is dangerous to generalise about these characteristics).

economics The study of choices leading to the best possible use of scarce resources in order to best satisfy unlimited human needs and wants.

economies of scale Decreases in the average costs of production that occur as a firm increases its output by varying all its inputs (i.e. in the long run). Economies of scale explain the downward-sloping portion of the long-run average total cost curve: as a firm increases its size, the costs per unit of output fall.

elasticity In general, this is a measure of the responsiveness or sensitivity of a variable to changes in any of the variable's determinants. See specific elasticities: *price elasticity of demand, cross-price elasticity of demand, income elasticity of demand, price elasticity of supply*.

empowerment Creation of conditions for equality of opportunities; involves increasing the political, social, and economic power of individuals or groups of individuals.

entrepreneurship One of the factors of production, involving a special human skill that includes the ability to innovate by developing new ways of doing things, to take business risks and to seek new opportunities for opening and running a business. Entrepreneurship organises the other three factors of production (land, labour and capital) and takes on the risks of success or failure of a business.

equilibrium A state of balance such that there is no tendency to change. See also *market equilibrium* and *equilibrium level of output (or of real GDP)*.

equilibrium level of output The level of output (real GDP) where the aggregate demand curve intersects the aggregate supply curve (also known as the 'equilibrium level of income'). Note the distinction between *short-run equilibrium level of output* and *long-run equilibrium level of output*.

equilibrium level of real GDP See *equilibrium level of output*.

equilibrium price The price determined in a market when quantity demanded is equal to quantity supplied, and there is no tendency for the price to change; it is the price that prevails when there is *market equilibrium*.

equilibrium quantity The quantity that is bought and sold when a market is in equilibrium, i.e. when quantity demanded is equal to quantity supplied.

equity The condition of being fair or just; should be contrasted with the term 'equality'. Often used in connection with income distribution, in which case it is usually interpreted to mean income equality (though this is only one possible interpretation of equity).

errors and omissions In the balance of payments, refers to an item that is included to account for possible omissions and errors in items that have been included or excluded, in order to ensure that the balance of payments balances, i.e. that the sum of credits and debits is equal to zero.

excess demand In the context of demand and supply, occurs when the quantity of a good demanded is greater than the quantity supplied, leading to a shortage of the good; see *shortage*.

excess supply In the context of demand and supply, occurs when the quantity of a good demanded is smaller than the quantity supplied, leading to a surplus; see *surplus*.

exchange rate The rate at which one currency can be exchanged for another, or the number of units of foreign currency that correspond to the domestic currency; can be thought of as the 'price' of a currency, which is expressed in terms of another currency.

excise taxes Taxes imposed on spending on particular goods or services (for example, gasoline/petrol); are a type of indirect tax. See *indirect taxes*.

excludable A characteristic of goods according to which it is possible to exclude people from using the good by charging a price for it; if someone is unwilling or unable to pay the price they will be excluded from using it. Most goods are excludable. It is one of the two characteristics of 'private goods'. See also *rivalrous*.

expansionary fiscal policy Refers to fiscal policy usually pursued in a recession, involving an increase in government spending or a decrease in taxes (or both). May be contrasted with contractionary *fiscal policy*. See also *fiscal policy*.

expansionary monetary policy Refers to monetary policy usually pursued in a recession, involving a decrease in interest rates, intended to increase investment and consumption spending; also known as 'easy monetary policy'. May be contrasted with *contractionery monetary policy*. See also *monetary policy*.

expenditure approach A method used to measure the value of aggregate output of an economy, which adds up all spending on final goods and services produced within a country within a given time period. As suggested by the circular flow model, it is equivalent to measurement by the *income approach* and the *output approach*.

expenditure flow In the simple circular flow of income model, it is the flow of spending from households to firms to buy the goods and services produced by the firms; the expenditure flow is equal to the *income flow* and the *value of output flow*.

expenditure-reducing policies Policies that involve reducing expenditures in the domestic economy so as to bring about a decrease in imports in order to correct a current account deficit; they include contractionary fiscal and monetary policies.

expenditure-switching policies Policies that involve switching consumption away from imported goods and towards domestically produced goods, in order to correct a current account deficit; include trade protection policies and depreciation.

explicit costs Costs of production that involve a money payment by a firm to an outsider in order to acquire a factor of production that is not owned by the firm. Is a type of opportunity cost; should be contrasted with *implicit costs*.

export promotion Refers to a growth and trade strategy where a country attempts to achieve economic growth by expanding its exports. As a trade strategy, it looks outward towards foreign markets and is based on stronger links between the domestic and global economies. To be contrasted with *import substitution*.

externality Occurs when the actions of consumers or producers give rise to positive or negative side-effects on other people who are not part of these actions, and whose interests are not taken into consideration. Positive externalities give rise to positive side-effects; negative externalities to negative side-effects.

factor endowments The factors of production that a country is 'endowed with', or possesses. Differing factor endowments among countries suggests that different countries are better suited to the production of certain kinds of goods and services than others, or, to put it differently, they are more efficient in the production of some things rather than others. Differing factor endowments form the basis of the *theory of comparative advantage*. (Also known as 'resource endowments'.)

factors of production All resources, or inputs (land, labour, capital, entrepreneurship) used to produce goods and services.

financial account In the balance of payments, refers to inflows minus outflows of funds due to foreign direct investment, portfolio investment and changes in reserve assets.

financial account balance See *balance on financial account*.

fiscal policy Manipulations by the government of its own expenditures and taxes in order to influence the level of aggregate demand; it is a type of *demand-side policy* or *demand management*.

fixed costs Costs that arise from the use of fixed inputs, which do not change as output increases or decreases (hence they are 'fixed'). Fixed costs arise only in the short run, or the period of time when there is at least one fixed input. Examples include rental payments, property taxes and insurance premiums.

fixed exchange rate Refers to an exchange rate that is fixed by the central bank of a country, and is not permitted to change in response to changes in currency supply and demand. Maintaining the value of a currency at its fixed rate requires constant intervention by the central bank or government.

fixed exchange rate system An exchange rate system where exchange rates are fixed by the central bank of each country. See *fixed exchange rate*.

flexible labour market See *labour market flexibility*.

floating exchange rate See *freely floating exchange rate*.

floating exchange rate system See *freely floating exchange rate system*.

foreign aid Consists of concessional financial flows from the developed world to economically less developed countries, and includes *concessional loans* and grants. See also *concessional loan* and *official development assistance*. To be contrasted with *multilateral development assistance*.

foreign debt Refers to external debt, meaning the total amount of debt (public and private) incurred by borrowing from foreign creditors (i.e. lenders). The global problem of debt involves large volumes of public (i.e. government) debt.

foreign direct investment (FDI) Refers to investment by firms based in one country (the home country) in productive activities in another country (the host country). Firms that undertake FDI are called *multinational corporations*.

foreign exchange Refers to foreign national currencies, i.e. for any country, it refers to currencies other than its own.

formal collusion HL An agreement between firms (usually in oligopoly) to limit output or fix prices, in order to restrict competition; is likely to involve the formation of a *cartel*. Also known as 'open collusion'.

free entry and exit HL The condition in which firms face no barriers to entering or exiting an industry, characteristic of the market structures of *perfect competition* and *monopolistic competition*.

free rider problem Occurs when people can enjoy the use of a good without paying for it, and arises from non-excludability: people cannot be excluded from using the good, because it is not possible to charge a price. Is often associated with public goods, which are a type of market failure: due to the free rider problem, private firms fail to produce these goods.

free trade The absence of government intervention of any kind in international trade, so that trade takes place without any restrictions (or barriers) between individuals or firms in different countries.

free trade area A type of trading bloc, consisting of a group of countries that agree to eliminate trade barriers between themselves; it is the most common type of integration area, and involves a lower degree of economic integration than a customs union or common market. Each member country retains the right to pursue its own trade policy towards non-member countries. An example of a free trade area is NAFTA (North American Free Trade Agreement).

freely floating exchange rate An exchange rate determined entirely by market forces, or the forces of supply and demand. There is no government intervention in the foreign exchange market to influence the value of the exchange rate. Also known as 'floating exchange rate' or 'flexible exchange rate'.

freely floating exchange rate system An exchange rate system where exchange rates are determined entirely by market forces; see *freely floating exchange rate*.

frictional unemployment A type of unemployment that occurs when workers are between jobs; workers may leave their job because they have been fired, or because their employer went out of business, or because they are in search of a better job, or they may be waiting to begin a new job; tends to be short term.

full employment (i) In the context of the production possibilities model, refers to maximum use of all resources in the economy to produce the maximum quantity of goods and services that the economy is capable of producing (production possibilities), implying zero unemployment. (ii) In the context of the *AD–AS* model, refers to the natural rate of unemployment, or unemployment that prevails when the economy is producing potential output, or real GDP, determined by the position of the *LRAS* curve (when the economy is in long equilibrium). See also *natural rate of unemployment*. Note that in this context, 'full employment' refers to employment of labour resources.

full employment level of output (real GDP) The level of output (or real GDP) at which unemployment is equal to the natural rate of unemployment; the level of output (real GDP) where there is no deflationary or recessionary gap. Also known as *potential output (potential GDP)*.

game theory HL A mathematical technique analyzing the behaviour of decision-makers who are dependent on each other, and who use strategic behaviour as they try to anticipate the behaviour of their rivals. Has become an important tool in microeconomics, often used to analyse the behaviour of oligopolistic firms; is based heavily on the work of American mathematician and economist John Nash.

GDP See *gross domestic product*.

GDP deflator HL See *price deflator*.

GDP *per capita* Gross domestic product divided by the number of people in the population; is an indicator of the amount of domestic output per person in the population.

Gini coefficient A summary measure of the information contained in the *Lorenz curve* of an economy, defined as the area between the diagonal and the Lorenz curve, divided by the entire area under the diagonal. The Gini coefficient has a value between 0 and 1; the larger the Gini coefficient, and the closer it is to 1, the greater is the income inequality.

GNI See *gross national income*.

GNI *per capita* Gross national income divided by the number of people in the population; is an indicator of the amount of income in an economy per person in the population.

governance Refers to the way of governing, and the exercise of power in the management of an economy's economic and social resources, in order to achieve particular objectives such as economic growth and development.

government budget A type of plan of a country's tax revenues and government expenditures over a period of time (usually a year).

government debt See *public debt*.

government intervention The practice of government to intervene (interfere) in markets, preventing the free functioning of the market, usually for the purpose of achieving particular economic or social objectives.

government spending Spending undertaken by the government, as part of its fiscal policy or as part of an effort to meet particular economic and social objectives (such as provision of subsidies, provision of public goods, etc.).

grant A type of foreign aid consisting of funds that are in effect gifts (they do not have to be repaid).

green GDP Gross domestic product (GDP) which has been adjusted to take into account environmental destruction and/or health consequences of environmental problems.

gross domestic product (GDP) A measure of the value of aggregate output of an economy, it is the market value of all final goods and services produced within a country during a given time period (usually a year); it is a commonly used measure of the value of aggregate output; to be contrasted with *gross national income (GNI)*.

gross national income (GNI) A measure of the total income received by the residents of a country, equal to the value of all final goods and services produced by the factors of production supplied by the country's residents regardless of where the factors are located; GNI = GDP plus income from abroad minus income sent abroad. Formerly known as gross national product (GNP); may be contrasted with *gross domestic product* (GDP).

gross national product (GNP) See *gross national income*.

growth See *economic growth*.

growth maximisation HL A possible goal of firms, that differs from the goal of profit maximisation assumed by standard microeconomic theory, involving the achievement of the highest possible growth, for various reasons such as achieving economies of scale, diversifying, achieving market power, or others.

hidden unemployment Unemployment that is not counted in official unemployment statistics because of such factors as the exclusion of 'discouraged workers', the practice of considering part-time workers as full-time workers, and others.

homogeneous product A product that is completely standardised and not differentiated; is characteristic of products in perfect competition.

household indebtedness The degree to which households have debts (see *indebtedness*).

human capital The skills, abilities and knowledge acquired by people, as well as good levels of health, all of which make them more productive; considered to be a kind of 'capital' because it provides a stream of future benefits by increasing the amount of output that can be produced in the future.

Human Development Index (HDI) A composite indicator of development which includes indicators that measure three dimensions of development: income per capita, levels of health and educational attainment; is considered to be a better indicator of development than single indicators such as GNI per capita.

humanitarian aid Foreign aid extended in regions where there are emergencies caused by violent conflicts or natural disasters such as floods, earthquakes and tsunamis, intended to save lives, ensure access to basic necessities such as food, water, shelter and health care, and provide assistance with reconstruction.

implicit costs Costs of production involving sacrificed income arising from the use of self-owned resources by a firm; is a type of opportunity cost; should be contrasted with *explicit costs*.

import quota see *quota*.

import substitution Also known as import-substituting industrialisation, refers to a growth and trade strategy where a country begins to manufacture simple consumer goods oriented towards the domestic market (such as shoes, textiles, beverages, electrical appliances) in order to promote its domestic industry; it presupposes the imposition of protective measures (tariffs, quotas, etc.) that will prevent the entry of imports that compete with domestic producers. To be contrasted with *export promotion*.

improvement in the terms of trade An increase in the value of the terms of trade index. See *terms of trade*.

incentive-related policies Policies involving reduction of various types of taxes (such as income taxes and business taxes), in the expectation that the tax cuts will change the incentives faced by tax-payers; for example, cuts in income taxes may encourage the desire to work; cuts in business taxes may encourage investment. Are a type of *supply-side policy*.

incidence of taxes See *tax incidence*.

income In the current account of the balance of payments, refers to inflows of wages, rents, interest and profits earned

abroad minus the same income factors that are sent abroad.

income approach A method used to measure the value of aggregate output of an economy, which adds up all income earned by the factors of production in the course of producing all goods and services within a country in a given time period. As suggested by the circular flow model, it is equivalent to measurement by the *expenditure approach* and the *output approach*.

income distribution See *distribution of income*.

income elastic demand Relatively high responsiveness of demand to changes in income; YED (income elasticity of demand) > 1. See *income elasticity of demand*.

income elasticity of demand A measure of the responsiveness of demand to changes in income; measured by the percentage change in quantity demanded divided by the percentage change in price.

income flow In the simple circular flow of income model, refers to the flow of income of households that they receive by selling their factors of production (resources) to firms; the income flow is equal to the *expenditure flow* and the *value of output flow*.

income inelastic demand Relatively low responsiveness of demand to changes in income; YED (income elasticity of demand) < 1. See *income elasticity of demand*.

income redistribution See *redistribution of income*.

increasing returns to scale Refers to the situation where the output of a firm changes more than in proportion to a change in all its inputs; given a percentage increase in all inputs, output increases by a larger percentage. May be contrasted with *constant returns to scale* and *decreasing returns to scale*.

indebtedness Refers to the level of debt, or the amount of money owed to creditors (lenders); may be on a household, firm, or country level.

indirect taxes Taxes levied on spending to buy goods and services, called indirect because, whereas payment of some or all of the tax by the consumer is involved, they are paid to the government authorities by the suppliers (firms), that is, indirectly.

industrial policies Government policies designed to support the growth of the industrial sector of an economy; may include support for small and medium-sized firms or support for 'infant industries' through tax cuts, grants, low interest loans and other measures, as well as investment in human capital, research and development, or infrastructure development in support of industry.

infant industry A new domestic industry that has not had time to establish itself and achieve efficiencies in production, and may therefore be unable to compete with more 'mature' competitor firms from

abroad. The presence of infant industries is considered to be one of the strongest arguments in favour of trade protection policies in developing countries.

inferior good A good the demand for which varies negatively (or indirectly) with income; this means that as income increases, the demand for the good decreases.

inflation A continuing (or sustained) increase in the general price level.

inflation targeting A type of monetary policy carried out by some central banks that focuses on achieving a particular inflation target, rather than focusing on the goals of low and stable rate of inflation and low unemployment; common inflation targets are between 1.5% and 2.5%.

inflationary gap A situation where real GDP is greater than potential GDP, and unemployment is lower than the natural rate of unemployment; it arises when the *AD* curve intersects the *SRAS* curve at a higher level of real GDP than potential GDP.

informal collusion See *tacit collusion*.

infrastructure Numerous types of physical capital resulting from investments, making major contributions to economic growth and development by lowering costs of production and increasing productivity; include power, telecommunications, piped water supplies, sanitation, roads, major dam and canal works for irrigation and drainage, urban transport, ports and airports.

injections In the circular flow of income model, refer to the entry into income flow of funds corresponding to investment, government spending or exports.

integration See *economic integration*.

interest (i) A payment, per unit of time, for the use of borrowed money (borrowers pay interest, lenders receive interest). (ii) A payment, per unit of time, to owners of capital resources.

interest rate Interest expressed as a percentage; in the case of borrowed money, it is interest as a percentage of the amount borrowed. Changes in interest rates form the basis of *monetary policy*.

International Monetary Fund (IMF) An international financial institution composed of 185 member countries, whose purpose is to make short-term loans to governments on commercial terms (i.e. non-concessional) in order to stabilise exchange rates, alleviate balance of payments difficulties and help countries meet their foreign debt obligations.

interventionist policy Any policy based on government intervention in the market; to be contrasted with *market-oriented policy*. See also *government intervention*.

interventionist supply-side policy Any policy based on government intervention in the market intended to affect the supply-side of the economy, usually to shift the LRAS curve to the right, increase potential output and achieve long term economic growth; see *industrial policy* as an example. May be contrasted with *market-based supply side policy*.

investment   Includes spending by firms or the government on capital goods (i.e. buildings, machinery, equipment, etc.) and all spending on new construction (housing and other buildings).

HL J-curve effect   A curve that plots the balance of trade (exports minus imports) on the vertical axis and time on the horizontal axis, showing that a country with a devaluing/depreciating currency may see a worsening in its trade balance (an increase in a trade deficit) in the period immediately following the devaluation or depreciation, while in a later period the trade deficit will begin to shrink provided the Marshall–Lerner condition holds (see *Marshall–Lerner condition*).

joint supply   Refers to production of two or more goods that are derived from a single product, so that it is not possible to produce more of one without producing more of the other (for example, butter and skimmed milk are both produced from whole milk, and producing more of one means producing more of the other as well).

Keynesian aggregate supply curve   An aggregate supply curve that has a flat (horizontal) section, and upward sloping section and a vertical section.

HL Keynesian multiplier   The ratio of real GDP divided by a change in any of the components of aggregate spending (consumption C, investment I, government spending G, or net exports $X-M$); alternatively it is $1/(1-MPC)$, where MPC is the marginal propensity to consume. The value of this ratio is usually greater than one because of a multiplied effect of an initial change in a component of aggregate spending on the final value of real output.

HL kinked demand curve   A model developed to explain price inflexibility of oligopolistic firms that do not collude (do not agree to collaborate in order to limit competition between them).

labour   A factor of production, which includes the physical and mental effort that people contribute to the production of goods and services.

labour market flexibility   Refers to the operation of market forces (supply and demand) in the labour market; to be contrasted with *labour market rigidities*. May be achieved by reducing or eliminating interference with market forces (for example, reducing or eliminating minimum wages and labour union activities, reducing job security, etc.); see *labour market reforms*.

labour market reforms   Reforms intended to make labour markets more competitive and flexible, to make wages respond to the forces of supply and demand, to lower labour costs and increase employment by lowering the natural rate of unemployment; include

abolishing or reducing minimum wages, reducing job security and reducing unemployment benefits. Are a type of *supply-side policy*.

labour market rigidities   Factors preventing the forces of supply and demand from operating in the labour market, and therefore preventing labour market flexibility; include minimum wage legislation, job security, etc. See *labour market reforms*.

land   A factor of production which includes all natural resources: land and agricultural land, as well as everything that is under or above the land, such as minerals, oil reserves, underground water, forests, rivers and lakes. Natural resources are also called 'gifts of nature' or 'natural capital'.

law of demand   A law stating that there is a negative causal relationship between the price of a good and quantity of the good demanded, over a particular time period, *ceteris paribus*: as the price of the good increases, the quantity of the good demanded falls (and vice versa).

HL law of diminishing returns   A law that states that as more and more units of a variable input (such as labour) are added to one or more fixed inputs (such as land), the marginal product of the variable input at first increases, but there comes a point when the marginal product of the variable input begins to decrease. This relationship presupposes that the fixed input(s) remain fixed, and that the technology of production is also fixed (unchanging).

law of supply   A law stating that there is a positive causal relationship between the price of a good and quantity of the good supplied, over a particular time period, *ceteris paribus*: as the price of the good increases, the quantity of the good supplied also increases (and vice versa).

leakages   In the circular flow of income model, refer to the withdrawal from the income flow of funds corresponding to savings, taxes or imports; also known as 'withdrawals'.

HL long run   (i) In microeconomics, it is a time period in which all inputs can be changed; there are no fixed inputs. (ii) In macroeconomics, it is the period of time when prices of resources (especially wages) change along with changes in the price level.

long-run aggregate supply (LRAS) curve   A curve showing the relationship between real GDP produced and the price level when wages (and other resource prices) change to reflect changes in the price level, *ceteris paribus*. The *LRAS* curve is vertical at the full employment level of GDP, or potential GDP, indicating that in the long run the economy produces potential GDP, which is independent of the price level.

HL long run average total costs   The lowest possible average costs that can be attained by a firm for any level of output when all the firm's inputs are variable, i.e. in the long run.

HL long-run average total cost curve   A curve that shows the lowest possible average cost that can be attained by a firm for any level of output when all of the firm's inputs are variable.

long-run equilibrium level of output   The level of output (real GDP) that results when the economy is in long run equilibrium, occurring when the aggregate demand and short-run aggregate supply curves intersect at a point on the long run aggregate supply curve; occurs where the vertical LRAS curve intersects the horizontal axis, known as *potential output*.

HL long-run Phillips curve   See *Phillips curve*.

long term growth trend   In the business cycle diagram, refers to the line that runs through the business cycle curve, representing average growth over long periods of time; shows how output grows over time when cyclical fluctuations are ironed out. The output represented by the long-term growth trend is known as *potential output*.

Lorenz curve   A curve illustrating the degree of equality (or inequality) of income distribution in an economy. It plots the cumulative percentage of income received by cumulative shares of the population. Perfect income equality would be represented by a straight line. The closer the Lorenz curve is to the straight line, the greater the equality in income distribution.

HL loss   Refers to the difference between economic costs and total revenue of a firm when economic costs are greater than revenues; it is negative economic profit. See *economic profit*.

luxuries   Goods that are not necessary or essential; they have a *price elastic demand* (PED>1) and *income elastic demand* (YED>1). To be contrasted with *necessities*.

macroeconomic objectives   Objectives of policy makers in the macroeconomy; include full employment, low rate of inflation, economic growth, an equitable distribution of income and external balance (balance of trade and avoidance of balance of payments problems).

macroeconomics   The branch of economics that examines the economy as a whole by use of aggregates, which are wholes or collections of many individual units, such as the sum of consumer behaviours and the sum of firm behaviours, total income and output of the entire economy as well as total employment and the general price level.

managed exchange rates   Exchange rates that are for the most part free to float to their market levels (i.e. their equilibrium levels) over long periods of time; however, central banks periodically intervene in order to stabilise them over the short term.

managed exchange rate system   The exchange rate system in use since 1973, also known as the 'managed float'; see *managed exchange rates*.

managed float   See *managed exchange rates*.

marginal benefit The extra or additional benefit received from consuming one more unit of a good.

marginal cost The extra or additional cost of producing one more unit of output.

marginal private benefits (MPB) The extra benefit received by consumers when they consume one more unit of a good.

marginal private costs (MPC) The extra costs to producers of producing one more unit of a good.

HL **marginal product** The extra or additional output that results from one additional unit of a variable input (such as labour).

HL **marginal propensity to consume (MPC)** The fraction of additional income spent on domestically produced goods and services. Determines the size of the Keynesian multiplier; the larger the MPC, the larger the multiplier.

HL **marginal propensity to import (MPI)** The fraction of additional income spent on imports. The larger the MPI, the smaller the Keynesian multiplier.

HL **marginal propensity to save (MPS)** The fraction of additional income that is saved. The larger the MPS, the smaller the Keynesian multiplier.

HL **marginal propensity to tax (MPT)** The fraction of additional income that is paid as taxes. The larger the MPT, the smaller the Keynesian multiplier.

HL **marginal revenue** The additional revenue arising from the sale of an additional unit of output.

marginal social benefits (MSB) The extra benefits to society of consuming one more unit of a good; are equal to marginal private benefits (MPB) when there are no consumption externalities.

marginal social costs (MSC) The extra costs to society of producing one more unit of a good; are equal to marginal private costs (MPC) when there are no production externalities.

HL **marginal tax rate** The tax rate paid on additional income; refers to the tax rate that applies to the highest tax bracket of an individual's personal income.

market Any kind of arrangement where buyers and sellers of a particular good, service or resource are linked together to carry out an exchange.

market demand Refers to the sum of all individual consumer demands for a good or service.

market equilibrium Occurs where quantity demanded is equal to quantity supplied, and there is no tendency for the price or quantity to change.

market failure Occurs when the market fails to allocate resources efficiently, or to provide the quantity and combination of goods and services mostly wanted by society. Market failure results in allocative inefficiency,

where too much or too little of goods or services are produced and consumed from the point of view of what is socially most desirable.

HL **market power** Refers to the control that a seller may have over the price of the product it sells; the greater the market power, the greater is the seller's control over price. Also known as 'monopoly power'.

HL **market structure** The characteristics of a market organisation that determine the behaviour of firms within an industry.

market supply Refers to the sum of all individual firm supplies of a good or service.

market-based supply-side policy Any policy based on promoting well-functioning, competitive markets in order to influence the supply-side of the economy, usually to shift the LRAS curve to the right, increase potential output and achieve long term economic growth; include labour market reforms, competition policies and incentive-related policies. May be contrasted with *interventionist supply side policy*.

market-oriented policy A policy in which government intervention is limited, economic decisions are made mainly by the private decision-makers (firms and consumers) and the market has significant freedom to determine resource allocation; to be contrasted with *interventionist policy*.

HL **Marshall–Lerner condition** A condition stating when depreciation or devaluation of a country's currency will lead to an improvement in that country's balance of trade: the sum of the price elasticities of demand for imports and exports must be greater than 1 for the trade balance to improve (for a trade deficit to become smaller). This usually holds over the longer term, but not in the shorter term (see *J-curve*).

maximum price A legal price set by the government, which is below the market equilibrium price; this does not allow the price to rise to its equilibrium level determined by a free market; also known as a *price ceiling*.

merit goods Goods that are held to be desirable for consumers, but which are underprovided by the market. Reasons for underprovision may be that the good has positive externalities, or consumers with low incomes cannot afford it (and so do not demand it), or consumer ignorance about the benefits of the good.

micro-credit A programme to provide credit (loans) in small amounts to people who do not ordinarily have access to credit. 'Micro' is the Greek word for 'small', and refers to the small amounts of the loans, the very small size of businesses or activities that are financed by the loans (very small businesses are known as 'micro-enterprises') and the short repayment periods involved.

microeconomics The branch of economics that examines the behaviour of individual decision-making units, consumers and firms; is concerned with consumer and firm behaviour and how their interactions in markets determine prices in goods markets and resource markets.

Millennium Development Goals (MDGs) Eight development goals adopted by the Millennium Declaration of 2000, consisting of 18 targets to be achieved by the year 2015; among the eight goals, four include eradicating extreme poverty and hunger, achieving universal primary education, reducing child mortality, promoting gender equality.

minimum price A legal price set by the government which is above the market equilibrium price; this does not allow the price to fall to its equilibrium level determined by a free market; also known as a *price floor*.

minimum wage A minimum price of labour (the 'wage') set by governments in the labour market, in order to ensure that low-skilled workers can earn a wage high enough to secure them with access to basic goods and services. It is a type of *price floor*.

monetarist/new classical model Actually includes two different models of the macroeconomy (the monetarist and the new classical); both are based on the following principles: the importance of the price mechanism in coordinating economic activities, the concept of competitive market equilibrium, and thinking about the economy as a harmonious system that automatically tends toward full employment.

monetary policy Policy carried out by the central bank, aiming to change interest rates in order to influence aggregate demand; it is a type of *demand-side policy*, or *demand management*.

monetary union A high form of economic integration, involving the adoption by a group of countries of a single currency, such as some of the countries of the European Union ('euro zone' countries) that have adopted the euro. Monetary integration in addition involves the adoption of a common monetary policy carried out by a single central bank, which is necessitated by the use of a single currency.

money Anything that is acceptable as payment for goods and services; more precisely, money consists of currency (coins and paper money) and checking accounts.

HL **monopolistic competition** One of the four market structures, with the following characteristics: a large number of firms; substantial control over market price; product differentiation; no barriers to entry. Examples include the shoe, clothing, detergent, computer, publishing, furniture and restaurant industries.

HL **monopoly**   One of the four market structures, with the following characteristics: a single or dominant large firm in the industry; significant control over price; produces and sells a unique product with no close substitutes; high barriers to entry into the industry. Examples include telephone, water and electricity companies in areas where they operate as a single supplier.

HL **monopoly power**   Occurs whenever a firm has the ability to control the price of the product it sells (also known as 'market power').

multilateral development assistance Lending to developing countries for the purpose of assisting their development on non-concessional terms (market rates of interest and repayment periods) by multilateral organisations, i.e. organisations composed of many countries, including development banks such as the World Bank, and the International Monetary Fund; to be contrasted with *foreign aid*.

multilateral trade agreement   A trade agreement (or agreement to lower international trade barriers) between many countries; at the present time these are mainly carried out within the framework of the *World Trade Organization* (WTO), and involve agreements between WTO member countries. May be contrasted with *bilateral trade agreement* and *regional trade agreement*.

multinational corporation (MNC)   A firm involved in foreign direct investment (FDI); it is a firm that is based in one country (the home country) and that undertakes productive investments in another country (the host country).

HL **multiplier**   See *Keynesian multiplier*.

national income   The total income of an economy, often used interchangeably with the value of aggregate output, particularly in the context of macroeconomic models (such as the *AD-AS* model).

national income statistics   Statistical data used to measure an economy's national income and output as well as other measures of economic performance.

HL **nationalisation**   A transfer in ownership of a firm away from the private sector and toward government ownership; a nationalised firm is a government-owned firm.

natural capital   Refers to an expanded meaning of the factor of production *land*, including everything that is included in land plus additional natural resources occurring naturally in the environment such as the air, biodiversity, soil quality, the ozone layer and the global climate. Is considered to be a type of 'capital' because it provides a stream of future benefits as it is necessary for humankind's ability to live, survive and produce in the future.

HL **natural monopoly**   A single firm (a monopoly) that can produce for the entire market at a lower average cost than two or more smaller firms. This happens when the market demand for the monopolist's product is within the range of falling long-run average cost, where there are economies of scale.

HL **natural rate of unemployment** Unemployment that occurs when the economy is producing at its potential or full employment level of output (real GDP), and is equal to the sum of structural, frictional plus seasonal unemployment.

necessities   Goods that are necessary or essential: they have a *price inelastic demand* (PED<1) and *income inelastic demand* (YED<1). To be contrasted with *luxuries*.

negative causal relationship   A relationship between two variables in which an increase in the value of one causes a decrease in the value of the other, i.e. the two variables change in opposite directions; also known as an indirect relationship.

negative externality   A type of externality where the side-effects on third parties are negative or harmful, also known as 'spillover costs'. To be contrasted with *positive externality*; see also *externality*.

negative externality of consumption   A negative externality caused by consumption activities, leading to a situation where marginal social benefits are less than marginal private benefits (MSB<MPB); see also *externality* and *negative externality*.

negative externality of production   A negative externality caused by production activities, leading to a situation where marginal social costs are greater than marginal private costs (MSC>MPC); see also *externality* and *negative externality*.

net exports   Refers to the value of exports minus the value of imports.

nominal GDP   Gross domestic product measured in terms of current (or nominal) prices, which are prices prevailing at the time of measurement. Does not account for changes in the price level; to be distinguished from *real GDP*.

nominal value   Value that is in money terms, measured in terms of prices that prevail at the time of measurement, and that does not account for changes in the price level; to be distinguished from *real* values.

HL **non-collusive oligopoly**   A type of oligopoly where firms do not make agreements among themselves (i.e. do not collude) in order to fix prices or collaborate in some way. See the *kinked demand curve*, one of the better-known models of non-collusive oligopoly.

non-excludable   A characteristic of some goods where it is not possible to exclude someone from using a good, because it is not possible to charge a price; it is one of the two characteristics of public goods (to be contrasted with *excludable*). See also *non-rivalrous*.

non-governmental organisations (NGOs)   Non-profit organisations that provide a very wide range of services and humanitarian functions; in developing countries they provide foreign aid, all of which takes the form of grants (there are no loans involved). They are involved with an enormous range of

activities, including emergency assistance, promotion of sustainable development, poverty alleviation, protection of child health, provision of technical assistance, and many more.

HL **non-price competition**   Occurs when firms compete with each other on the basis of methods other than price (such as product differentiation, advertising and branding). Non-price competition occurs in oligopoly and monopolistic competition.

non-price determinants of demand   The variables (other than price) that can influence demand, and that determine the position of a demand curve; a change in any determinant of demand causes a shift of the demand curve, which is referred to as a 'change in demand'.

non-price determinants of supply   The variables (other than price) that can influence supply, and that determine the position of a supply curve; a change in any determinant of supply causes a shift of the supply curve, which is referred to as a 'change in supply'.

non-price rationing   The apportioning or distributing of goods among interested users/buyers through means other than price, often necessary when there are price ceilings (maximum prices); may include waiting in line (queues) and underground markets; to be contrasted with 'price rationing', which involves distributing goods among users by means of market-determined prices.

non-produced, non-financial assets   A part of the capital account of the balance of payments, which includes a variety of items such as mineral rights, forestry rights, fishing rights and airspace.

non-rivalrous   A characteristic of some goods where the consumption of the good by one person does not reduce consumption by someone else; it is one of the two characteristics of public goods (to be contrasted with *rivalrous*). See also *non-excludable*.

normal good   A good the demand for which varies positively (or directly) with income; this means that as income increases, demand for the good increases.

HL **normal profit**   The minimum amount of revenue that a firm must receive so that it keeps the business running (as opposed to shutting down); also defined as the amount of revenue needed to cover implicit costs, including entrepreneurship. (This presupposes that total revenue is also enough to cover explicit costs.) Normal profit is included among the economic costs of the firm, and is earned when economic profit is zero.

normative economics   The body of economics based on normative statements, which involve beliefs, or value judgements about what ought to be. Normative statements cannot be true or false; they can only be assessed relative to beliefs and value judgements. Normative economics forms the basis of economic policies; to be contrasted with *positive economics*.

Official Development Assistance (ODA) The most important part of foreign aid, referring to foreign aid that is offered by countries or by international organisations composed of a number of countries (it does not include aid offered by non-governmental organisations).

HL oligopoly One of the four market structures, with the following characteristics: small number of large firms in the industry; firms have significant control over price; firms are interdependent; products may be differentiated or homogeneous; there are high barriers to entry. Examples include the car industry, airlines, electrical appliances (differentiated products) and the steel, aluminium, copper, cement industries (homogeneous products).

HL open collusion See *formal collusion*.

open economy An economy that has international trade: (imports and exports) usually appears in connection with economic theories and models as virtually all economies in the real world are open economies (though to varying degrees). To be contrasted with *closed economy*.

opportunity cost The value of the next best alternative that must be given up or sacrificed in order to obtain something else.

output approach A method used to measure the value of aggregate output of an economy, which calculates the value of all final goods and services produced in the country within a given time period. As suggested by the circular flow model, it is equivalent to measurement by the *expenditure approach* and the *income approach*.

overallocation of resources Occurs when too many resources are allocated to the production of a good relative to what is socially most desirable, resulting in its overproduction.

overvalued currency A currency whose value is higher than its free-market value; may occur if the exchange rate is fixed (or pegged), or in a managed exchange rate system, but not in a freely floating exchange rate system. To be contrasted with *undervalued currency*.

parallel market See *underground market*.

per capita Per person, or per head. For example, GDP *per capita* is total GDP divided by the number of people in the population.

HL perfect competition One of the four market structures, with the following characteristics: a large number of small firms; no control over price; all firms sell a homogeneous product; no barriers to entry, perfect information and perfect resource mobility. Examples include agricultural commodity markets and the foreign exchange market.

perfectly elastic demand Refers to a price elasticity of demand value of infinity, and arises in the case of a horizontal demand curve; see *price elasticity of demand*.

perfectly elastic supply Refers to a price elasticity of supply value of infinity, and arises in the case of a horizontal supply curve; see *price elasticity of supply*.

perfectly inelastic demand Refers to a price elasticity of demand value of zero, and arises in the case of a vertical demand curve; see *price elasticity of demand*.

perfectly inelastic supply Refers to a price elasticity of supply value of zero, and arises in the case of a vertical supply curve; see *price elasticity of supply*.

personal income taxes Taxes paid by households or individuals in households on all forms of income, including wages, rental income, interest income, and dividends (income from ownership of shares in a company); is the most important source of government tax revenues in many countries (especially economically more developed countries).

HL Phillips curve A curve showing the relationship between unemployment and inflation. The short-run Phillips curve shows a negative relationship between the rate of inflation and the unemployment rate (as the rate of inflation increases, unemployment falls) suggesting that in the short run policy-makers can choose between the competing alternatives of low inflation or low unemployment by selecting appropriate demand-side policies. The long-run Phillips curve is a vertical line at the natural rate of unemployment, indicating that there is no negative relationship between inflation and unemployment, and suggesting that policy-makers do not have a choice between the two competing alternatives. In the long run, the only impact of an increase in aggregate demand is to increase the rate of inflation, while the level of real output is unaffected and the unemployment rate remains unchanged at the natural rate of unemployment.

physical capital One of the factors of production, which is itself produced (it doesn't occur naturally), used to produce goods and services; includes machinery, tools, factories, buildings, road systems, airports, telephone supply lines, etc. Also referred to as 'capital', or 'capital good' or 'investment good'.

portfolio investment Financial investment, including investment in stocks and bonds. Appears as an item in the financial account of the balance of payments.

positive causal relationship A relationship between two variables in which an increase in the value of one causes an increase in the value of the other, i.e. the two variables change in the same direction; also known as a direct relationship.

positive economics The body of economics based on positive statements, which are about things that are, were or will be. Positive statements may be true or false. They form the basis of theories and models that try to explain economic events. To be contrasted with *normative economics*.

positive externality A type of externality where the side-effects on third parties are positive or beneficial, also known as 'spillover benefits'; to be contrasted with *negative externality*; see also *externality*.

positive externality of consumption A positive externality caused by consumption activities, leading to a situation where marginal social benefits are greater than marginal private benefits (MSB>MPB); see also *externality* and *positive externality*.

positive externality of production A positive externality caused by production activities, leading to a situation where marginal social costs are less than marginal private costs (MSC<MPC); see also *externality* and *positive externality*.

potential output (potential GDP) The level of output (real GDP) that can be produced when there is 'full employment', meaning that unemployment is equal to the natural rate of unemployment; also known as the *full employment level of output*.

poverty The inability of an individual or family to afford an adequate standard of goods and services; this standard may be absolute or relative; see *absolute poverty* and *relative poverty*.

poverty cycle Arises when low incomes result in low (or zero) savings, permitting only low (or zero) investments in physical, human and natural capital, and therefore low productivity of labour and of land, which in turn gives rise to low, if any, growth in income (sometimes growth may be negative), and hence low incomes once again. A poverty cycle may occur in a family, a community, a part of an economy, or in an economy as a whole. An important feature of the poverty cycle is that poverty is transmitted from generation to generation.

poverty trap See *poverty cycle*.

preferential trade agreement An agreement between two or more countries to lower trade barriers between them on particular products, resulting in easier access to the markets of other members for the selected products, compared with the access of countries that are not members.

price ceiling A maximum price set by the government for a particular good, meaning that the price that can be legally charged by the sellers of the good cannot be higher than the legal maximum price. Results in a *shortage* of the product.

HL price competition Occurs when a firm lowers its price to attract customers away from rival firms, thus increasing sales at the expense of other firms. May occur in the case of monopolistic competition or oligopoly, but not in perfect competition (or monopoly).

price control Setting of minimum or maximum prices by the government (or private organisations) so that prices are unable to adjust to their equilibrium level determined by demand and supply. Price controls result in shortages or surpluses.

HL price deflator A price index used to calculate real GDP from nominal GDP; better known as the 'GDP deflator'.

price discrimination The practice of charging a different price for the same product when the price difference is not justified by differences in costs of production.

price elastic demand Relatively high responsiveness of demand to changes in price; PED (price elasticity of demand) > 1. See *price elasticity of demand*.

price elastic supply Relatively high responsiveness of supply to changes in price; PES (price elasticity of supply) > 1. See *price elasticity of supply*.

price elasticity of demand (PED) A measure of the responsiveness of the quantity of a good demanded to changes in its price, given by the percentage change in quantity demanded divided by the percentage change in price. In general, if there is a large responsiveness of quantity demanded (PED > 1), demand is referred to as being elastic; if there is a small responsiveness (PED < 1), demand is inelastic.

price elasticity of supply (PES) A measure of the responsiveness of the quantity of a good supplied to changes in its price, given by the percentage change in quantity supplied divided by the percentage change in price. In general, if there is a large responsiveness of quantity supplied (PES > 1), supply is referred to as being elastic; if there is a small responsiveness (PES < 1), supply is inelastic.

price floor A minimum price set by the government for a particular good, meaning that the price that can be legally charged by the sellers of the good cannot be lower than the legal minimum price. Results in a *surplus* of the product.

price inelastic demand Relatively low responsiveness of demand to changes in price; PED (price elasticity of demand) < 1. See *price elasticity of demand*.

price inelastic supply Relatively low responsiveness of supply to changes in price; PES (price elasticity of supply) < 1. See *price elasticity supply*.

price leadership A type of tacit (or informal) collusion among oligopolistic firms, where a dominant firm in the industry (which may be the largest, or the one with lowest costs) sets a price and also initiates any price changes; the remaining firms in the industry become price-takers, accepting the price that has been established by the leader. Under price leadership price changes tend to be infrequent, and are undertaken by the leader only when major demand or cost changes occur.

price support Minimum prices (or price floors) set by the government for agricultural products; see *minimum price*.

price taker A firm that accepts a price at which it sells its product. Usually refers to firms in perfect competition, which being small and numerous have no control over price, and therefore accept the price determined in the market; may also be used to refer to firms in oligopoly that practice tacit collusion and accept a price set by a price leader (see *price leadership*).

price war Competitive price-cutting by firms; usually in oligopoly. As each one tries to capture market shares from rival firms; results in lower profits for firms.

prices as incentives The ability of prices, and changes in prices, to convey information to consumers and producers that motivates them to respond by offering them incentives to behave in their best-self-interest; compare with *prices as signals*, which together with prices as incentives lead to an efficient allocation of resources (assuming no market failures).

prices as signals The ability of prices, and changes in prices, to communicate information to consumers and producers, on the basis of which they make economic decisions.

primary commodity Any product that is produced in the *primary sector*, which includes agriculture, forestry, fishing and the extractive industries; also known as 'commodity'.

primary products All products produced in the primary sector of an economy; also known as commodities; see *primary sector*.

primary sector A part of an economy that is dominated by agriculture, also including fishing, forestry and all extractive activities (such as mining).

prisoner's dilemma A problem in game theory showing that in some situations, although it is in the best interests of decision-makers to co-operate, when each actor acts in his/her best interests there results an outcome where they are all worse off. Is often used to illustrate the *strategic interdependence* of oligopolistic firms.

private good A good that is both *rivalrous* and *excludable*. To be contrasted with *public good*.

privatisation A transfer of ownership from the public sector (the government) to the private sector, i.e. private owners.

producer price index (PPI) Consists of several indices of prices received by producers of goods at various stages in the production process (such as a PPI for inputs, a PPI for intermediate goods, and a PPI for final goods); considered to be predictors of changes in the consumer price index (CPI) because they measure price changes at an earlier stage in the production process.

producer surplus Refers to the difference between the price received by firms for selling their good and the lowest price they are willing to accept to produce the good. In a diagram, it is shown as the area under the price received by producers and above the supply curve.

product differentiation Occurs when each firm in an industry tries to make its product different from those of its competitors; usually in order to create some monopoly power; products can be differentiated by physical differences, quality differences, location, services, and product image.

production possibilities All possible combinations of the maximum amounts of two goods that can produced by an economy, given fixed and unchanging resources and technology, when there is full employment of resources and productive efficiency.

production possibilities curve (PPC) A curve showing *production possibilities*.

production possibilities frontier (PPF) See *production possibilities curve*.

productive efficiency Occurs when firms produce at the lowest possible cost; is one of the conditions for producing on the production possibilities curve (PPC). The condition for productive efficiency is that production takes place where ATC is minimum.

productivity Refers to the quantity of output produced for each hour of work of the working population; for an economy as a whole it can be measured as real GDP divided by the total number of hours worked. Increases in productivity are a major factor leading to economic growth.

profit A payment, per unit of time, to owners of entrepreneurship/management (a factor of production). See *economic profit* and *normal profit*.

profit maximisation The goal of firms, according to the standard theory of the firm. It involves making profit as large as possible, and is achieved by producing the level of output where the difference between total revenue and total costs is the largest, or where marginal cost is equal to marginal revenue.

programme aid Foreign aid involving financial support to sectors, such as education, health care, agriculture, urban development, the financial sector (credit, banking, insurance), the environment, or others.

progressive taxation Taxation where, as income increases, the fraction of income paid as taxes increases; there is an increasing tax rate.

project aid Foreign aid involving support for specific projects, such as building schools, clinics, hospitals, irrigation systems, other agricultural infrastructure, or others.

proportional taxation Taxation where, as income increases, the fraction of income paid as taxes remains constant; there is a constant tax rate.

protection of trade See *trade protection*.

public debt Refers to the government's accumulation of budget deficits minus budget surpluses; is the total amount owed by the government to all creditors (lenders); also known as 'government debt'.

public good A good that is *non-rivalrous* (its consumption by one person does not reduce consumption by someone else) and *non-excludable* (it is not possible to exclude someone from using the good). Since it is not possible to exclude someone from using the good even though they do not pay for it, firms do not have an incentive to produce it. Public goods are therefore provided by the government. This is a type of market failure.

purchasing power parity (PPP) exchange rates Special exchange rates between currencies that makes the buying power of each currency equal to the buying power of US$1, and therefore equal to each other. The use of PPP exchange rates to convert GDP (or GNI or any other output or income variable) eliminates the influence of price level differences across countries and is very important for making cross-country comparisons.

quintiles Division of a population into five equal groups with respect to the distribution of a variable, such as income; for example, the lowest income quintile refers to 20% of the population with the lowest income.

quota A type of trade protection that involves setting a legal limit to the quantity of a good that can be imported over a particular time period (typically a year). (More generally, a 'quota' is a limited or fixed number of things.)

rate of interest See *interest rate*.

rational economic decision-making The assumption in economics that all economic decision-makers act in their best self-interest, trying to maximise the satisfaction or benefit they receive from their economic decisions; for example consumers try to maximise the satisfaction of consumption, firms maximise profit, workers try to secure the highest wage possible, etc.

real GDP Gross domestic product (GDP) measured in constant prices, i.e. prices that prevail in one particular year, called a 'base year'; this is useful for making comparisons of changes in GDP over time that have taken into account the influence of changing prices.

real value Value that has eliminated the influence of changes in the price level.

reallocation of resources Refers to reassigning resources to particular uses, so that the allocation of resources changes and becomes a new allocation.

recession An economic contraction, where there is falling real GDP (negative growth) and increasing unemployment of resources which last six months or more.

recessionary gap A situation where real GDP is less than potential GDP, and unemployment is greater than the natural rate of unemployment; it arises when the *AD* curve intersects the *SRAS* curve at a lower level of real GDP than potential GDP. Also known as 'deflationary gap'.

redistribution of income Refers to changing the distribution of income, giving rise to a new distribution.

regional trade agreement A trade agreement (or agreement to lower international trade barriers) between several countries that are located within a geographical region (such as NAFTA, or North American Free Trade Agreement). May be contrasted with *bilateral trade agreement and multilateral trade agreement*.

regressive taxation Taxation where, as income increases, the fraction of income paid as taxes decreases; there is a decreasing tax rate.

relative poverty The inability of an individual or a family to afford an adequate standard of goods and services, where the adequate standard is relative and changes over time; this standard is defined as what is 'typical' in a society,

taken to be a particular percentage (often 50%) of society's median income. As incomes increase and the median income rises, the standard also rises.

rent A payment, per unit of time, to owners of land resources who supply their land to the production process.

reserve assets Refers to foreign currency reserves that the central bank maintains and can buy or sell to influence the value of the country's currency exchange rate; in the balance of payments appears as an item in the *financial account*. Also known as 'official reserves'.

resources Factors of production, used by firms as inputs in the production process; see *factors of production*.

resource allocation Assigning available resources, or factors or production, to specific uses chosen among many possible and competing alternatives; involves answering the 'what to produce' and 'how to produce' basic economic questions.

returns to scale Refers to the relationship between inputs and output, and in particular by how much output changes if all inputs change (increase or decrease) by the same proportion; see *constant, increasing* and *decreasing returns to scale*.

revaluation (of a currency) Refers to an increase in the value of a currency in the context of a fixed exchange rate system (compare with appreciation, which is an increase in currency value in the contest of a floating or managed exchange rate system).

revenue maximisation The objective of some firms to maximise revenue (rather than profit, as assumed by the standard theory of the firm). The revenue-maximising firm produces the level of output where its marginal revenue is equal to zero (as that is where total revenue is maximum).

rivalrous A characteristic of a good according to which its consumption by one person reduces its availability for someone else; most goods are rivalrous. It is one of the two characteristics of 'private goods'. See also *excludable*.

satisficing A goal of firms to achieve satisfactory results, rather than pursue a single maximising objective, such as to maximise profits or revenues; based on the argument that large, modern firms have numerous objectives which may partly overlap or conflict, thus forcing them to compromise and reconcile conflicts, rather than pursue optimal results.

scarcity The condition in which available resources (land, labour, capital, entrepreneurship) are limited; they are not enough to produce everything that human beings need and want.

seasonal unemployment A type of unemployment that occurs when the demand for labour in certain industries changes on a seasonal basis because of variations in needs; for example, farm workers are hired during peak harvesting seasons and let off for the rest of the year.

short run (i) In microeconomics, it is a time period during which at least one input is fixed and cannot be changed by the firm. (ii) In macroeconomics, it is the period of time during which the prices of resources, particularly the price of labour (wages) do not change (they are constant).

short-run aggregate supply (SRAS) curve A curve showing the relationship between the price level and the quantity of real GDP produced by firms when resource prices do not change.

short-run equilibrium level of output In the monetarist/new classical model, it is the level of output (real GDP) determined by the intersection of the aggregate demand and short run aggregate supply curves; in the Keynesian model, it is the level of output determined by the intersection of the aggregate demand and Keynesian aggregate supply curves. In both models, equilibrium may occur where there is (i) a recessionary (deflationary) gap, (ii) an inflationary gap, or (iii) full employment output.

short-run Phillips curve See *Phillips curve*.

shortage In the context of demand and supply, is the amount by which quantity demanded is greater than quantity supplied.

shut-down price The price at which a firm that is making losses and will stop producing in the short run. In perfect competition, it is given by price = minimum average variable cost. (If price is greater than average variable cost, the firm will go on producing in the short run even if it is making a loss.)

slope In the case of a straight line, refers to the change in the dependent variable divided by the change in the independent variable between any two points on the line. According to mathematical convention, where the dependent variable is plotted on the vertical axis, the slope is the 'rise over run' (i.e. the vertical change divided by the horizontal change), however in microeconomics where quantity, the dependent variable, is plotted on the horizontal axis, the slope is the 'run over rise' (the horizontal change divided by the vertical change).

social optimum Refers to a situation that is the best from the social point of view, determined by the achievement of allocative efficiency (or economic efficiency); occurs when marginal social benefits are equal to marginal social costs (MSB=MSC).

social safety net A system of government transfers of cash or goods to vulnerable groups, undertaken to ensure that these groups do not fall below a socially acceptable minimum standard of living; see also *transfer payments*.

social sciences Academic disciplines that study human society and social relationships, concerned with discovering general principles describing how societies function and are organised; include anthropology, economics, political science, psychology, sociology and others.

social scientific method The same as the scientific method, it is a method of investigation used in sciences and social sciences allowing the accumulation of scientific and social scientific knowledge; involves making a hypothesis based on observations, testing the hypothesis, and rejecting or accepting the hypothesis based on empirical (real-world) evidence.

social surplus The sum of consumer and producer surplus; it is maximum in a competitive market with no market failures. See *consumer surplus* and *producer surplus*.

social welfare See *welfare*.

spare capacity Refers to physical capital that firms have available but do not use; arises in a recession when there is unemployment of resources.

HL **specialisation** Occurs when a firm or a country concentrates production on one or a few goods and services. In international trade theory, specialisation forms the basis for the gains from trade, arising when countries specialise according to their comparative advantage, and when firms specialise in production of goods and services that offer them economies of scale. Specialisation of labour occurs when workers perform one or a few tasks, and is one factor leading to economies of scale.

specific tax A tax calculated as an absolute amount per unit of the good or service sold.

speculation (currency) Buying and selling of something in the hope of making a profit. 'Currency speculation' involves buying and selling currencies based on expectations of changes in the value of a currency (exchange rates) in order to make a profit in the future.

HL **stagflation** Arising from a combination of the works 'stagnation' and 'inflation', refers to the simultaneous appearance of inflation and recession (and therefore also unemployment).

HL **strategic interdependence** Characteristic of oligopolies, refers to the mutual interdependence of firms and their strategic behaviour (planning their actions based on guesses about what their rivals will do), in view of the expectation that what happens to the profits of one firm depends on the strategies adopted by the other firms.

structural unemployment A type of unemployment that occurs as a result of technological changes and changing patterns of demand (causing changes in demand for labour skills), as well as changes in the geographical location of jobs, and labour market rigidities.

subsidy An amount of money paid by the government to firms for a variety of reasons: to prevent an industry from failing, to support producers' incomes, or as a form of protection against imports (due to the lower costs and lower prices that arise from the subsidy). A subsidy given to a firm results in a higher level of output and lower price for consumers. May also be paid to consumers as financial assistance or for income redistribution.

substitute goods Two or more goods that satisfy a similar need, so that one good can be used in place of another. If two goods are substitutes, an increase in the price of one leads to an increase in the demand for the other.

HL **supernormal profit** Refers to positive economic profit, arising when total revenue is greater than total economic costs (implicit plus explicit costs); is also known as 'abnormal profit'. See *economic profit*.

supply Indicates the various quantities of a good that firms (or a firm) are willing and able to produce and sell at different possible prices during a particular time period, *ceteris paribus* (all other things being equal).

supply curve A curve showing the relationship between the quantities of a good that firms (or a firm) are willing and able to produce and sell during a particular time period and their respective prices, *ceteris paribus* (all other things being equal).

supply of money The amount of money in circulation, determined by the central bank of a country; in combination with the demand for money, the supply of money determines the equilibrium rate of interest. (In practice central banks have difficulties in accurately controlling the supply of money.)

supply shock Events that have a sudden and strong impact on short-run aggregate supply (SRAS), leading to SRAS curve shifts; for example, a war or violent conflict that destroys physical capital and disrupts the economy, favourable or unfavourable weather conditions, etc.

supply-side policies A variety of policies that focus on aggregate supply, namely factors aiming to shift the long-run aggregate supply (LRAS) curve to the right, in order to achieve long-term economic growth. They do not attempt to stabilise the economy (i.e. to reduce the severity of the business cycle). There are two major categories of supply-side policies: market-based and interventionist. To be contrasted with *demand-side policies*.

surplus In general, this is the excess of something over something else to which it is being compared. (i) In the context of demand and supply, it is the extra supply that results when quantity supplied is greater than quantity demanded. (ii) In the case of consumer and producer surplus, it is the extra benefit consumers get by paying less for a good than the amount they are willing to pay, or the extra benefit producers get by receiving a higher price for the good they are selling than the price they are willing to receive. (iii) In the case of the government budget, a surplus occurs when government revenues are greater than government expenditures. (iv) In the balance of payments, a surplus in an account occurs when the credits (inflows of money from abroad) are larger than the debits (outflows of money to other countries).

sustainability Refers to maintaining the ability of the environment and the economy to continue to produce and satisfy needs and wants into the future; depends crucially on the preservation of the environment over time. Related to the concept of sustainable development, meaning 'Development which meets the needs of the present without compromising the ability of future generations to meet their own needs' (according to the Brundtland Commission), which is the idea that the use of natural resources in the present should not leave behind fewer or lower quality resources for use by future generations.

HL **tacit collusion** Refers to cooperation that is implicit or understood between cooperating oligopolistic firms, without a formal agreement, with the objectives to coordinate prices, avoid competitive price-cutting, limit competition, reduce uncertainties and increase profits; may take the form of *price leadership*.

tariffs Taxes on imported goods; they are the most common form of trade restriction. Tariffs may serve two purposes: to protect a domestic industry from foreign competition (a protective tariff); or to raise revenue for the government (a revenue tariff). Whatever the purpose, the impacts on the economy are the same.

HL **tax incidence** Refers to the burden of a tax, or those who are the ultimate payers of the tax.

HL **technical efficiency** See *productive efficiency*.

HL **terms of trade** Relates the prices a country receives for its exports to the prices paid for its imports, and is given by the ratio of index of average export prices to index of average import prices times 100. An increase in the value of this ratio indicates a terms of trade improvement, meaning that a country can now buy more imports for the same amount of exports; a decrease in the value of this ratio indicates a terms of trade deterioration, meaning that a country can now buy fewer imports for the same amount of exports.

HL **theory of absolute advantage** According to this theory, if countries specialise in and export the goods in which they have an absolute advantage (can produce with fewer resources), there results an improvement in resource allocation and increased production and consumption in each country.

HL **theory of comparative advantage** According to this theory (also known as a law), as long as opportunity costs in two (or more) countries differ, it is possible for all countries to gain from specialisation and trade according to their comparative advantage; this results in an improvement in the global allocation of resources, resulting in greater global output and consumption. Is a more powerful explanation of the gains from trade than the theory of absolute advantage.

third degree price discrimination
HL Occurs when a firm price discriminates (i.e. changes different prices that are not justified by difference in costs) among different consumer groups; is based on the principle that different consumer groups have different price elasticities of demand (PED) for a product, so that higher prices are charged to consumers with a lower PED and lower prices to consumers with a higher PED.

tied aid   The practice whereby donors make the recipients of foreign aid spend a portion of the borrowed funds on the purchase of goods and services from the donor country. It occurs only in the context of bilateral (not multilateral) aid.

tight monetary policy   See *contractionary monetary policy*.

HL **total costs**   The sum of fixed and variable costs.

HL **total product**   The total quantity of output produced by a firm.

total revenue   The amount of money received by firms when they sell a good (or service); it is equal to the price (P) of the good times the quantity (Q) of the good sold. Therefore total revenue = $P \times Q$.

tradable permits   Permits that can be issued to firms by a government or an international body, and that can be traded (bought and sold) in a market, the objective being to limit the total amount of pollutants emitted by the firms. If a firm can produce its product by emitting a lower level of pollutants than the level set by its permits, it can sell its extra permits in the market. If a firm needs to emit more pollutants than the level set by its permits, it can buy more permits in the market. Tradable permits are part of *cap-and-trade schemes*.

HL **trade creation**   The replacement of higher cost products (imported or domestically produced) by lower cost imports that results when a trading bloc is formed and trade barriers are removed. (To be contrasted with *trade diversion*.)

HL **trade diversion**   The replacement of lower cost products (imported or domestically produced) by higher cost imports that results when a trading bloc is formed and trade barriers are removed. (To be contrasted with *trade creation*.)

trade liberalisation   The policy of liberalising (freeing up) international trade by eliminating trade protection and barriers to trade (i.e. tariffs, quotas, etc.)

trade protection   Government intervention in international trade through the imposition of trade restrictions (or barriers) to prevent the free entry of imports into a country and protect the domestic economy from foreign competition.

trading bloc   A group of countries that have agreed to reduce tariff and other barriers to trade for the purpose of encouraging the development of free or freer trade and cooperation between them.

See also *free trade area, customs union* and *common market*.

transfer payments   Payments made by the government to individuals specifically for the purpose of redistributing income, thus transferring income from those who work and pay taxes towards those who cannot work and need assistance. Groups receiving transfer payments may include older people, sick people, very poor people, children of poor families, unemployed people and others; in their entirety they are referred to as 'vulnerable groups'.

underallocation of resources   Occurs when too few resources are allocated to the production of a good relative to what is socially most desirable, resulting in its underproduction.

underemployment   The number of underemployed people, defined as all people above a particular age (i.e. not children) who have part-time jobs when they would prefer to have full-time jobs; or have jobs that do not make full use of their skills and education.

underground market   Refers to a market that arises whenever a buying/selling transaction is unrecorded; may involve legal goods and services (such as plumbing done by a plumber who does not report the income) or illegal goods and services (such as drugs). May also arise due to the imposition of price ceilings leading to shortages. Also known as 'parallel market'.

undervalued currency   A currency whose value is lower than its free-market value; may occur if the exchange rate is fixed (or pegged), or in a managed exchange rate system, but not in a freely floating exchange rate system. To be contrasted with *overvalued currency*.

unemployment   The number of unemployed people, defined as all people above a particular age (i.e. not children) who are not working and who are actively looking for a job.

unemployment rate   A measure of the amount of unemployment in an economy, expressed as a percentage, calculated by taking the total number of unemployed people in an economy and dividing by the labour force, and multiplying by 100.

unit elastic demand   Refers to a price elasticity of demand value of one; see *price elasticity of demand*.

unit elastic supply   Refers to a price elasticity of supply value of one; see *price elasticity of supply*.

urban informal sector   That part of an urban economy that lies outside the formal economy, consisting of economic activities that are unregistered and legally unregulated. In developing countries these activities are often a very large part of the urban economy; unlike in developed countries, where they are usually pursued to avoid taxes and labour laws, in developing countries they are a matter of physical survival of substantial portions of the population.

value of output flow   In the circular flow of income model, refers to the value of output that is sold by firms and purchased by consumers, which is equal to the *expenditure flow* and *the income flow*.

HL **variable costs**   Costs that arise from the use of variable inputs, and that vary or change as output increases or decreases (hence they are 'variable'). An example of a variable cost is wages, or the payment for labour resources (a variable input).

wage   A payment, per unit of time, to those who provide labour; this includes all wages and salaries, as well as supplements (such as bonuses and commissions).

HL **weighted price index**   A measure of average prices in one period relative to average prices in a reference period called a base period; a weighted price index is a price index that 'weights' the various goods and services according to their relative importance. In the consumer price index (CPI), goods and services are weighted according to their relative importance in consumer spending.

welfare   In general, refers to the well-being of a population. In microeconomics, it is measured by the amount of social surplus (consumer and producer surplus) that is generated in a market. Welfare is greatest, i.e. social surplus is greatest, in competitive market equilibrium when there are no externalities, and marginal social benefits are equal to marginal social costs (MSB=MSC).

welfare loss   Refers to loss of a portion of social surplus that arises when marginal social benefits are not equal to marginal social costs (MSB≠MSC), due to market failure.

withdrawals   See *leakages*.

World Bank   A development assistance organisation, composed of 185 member countries which are its joint owners, that extends long-term credit (loans) to developing country governments for the purpose of promoting economic development and structural change. It consists of two organisations: the International Bank for Reconstruction and Development (IBRD), which lends to middle income countries on non-concessional (i.e. commercial) terms (therefore its activities and lending do not form part of foreign aid); and the International Development Association (IDA), which has similar activities to the IBRD but extends loans to low income countries on highly concessional terms; these activities form part of foreign aid (see *concessional loans*). About 75% of World Bank lending is through the IBRD.

World Trade Organization (WTO)   An international organisation that provides the institutional and legal framework for the trading system that exists between member nations worldwide, responsible for liberalising trade, operating a system of trade rules and providing a forum for trade negotiations between governments, and for settling trade disputes.

Index

Note: Page numbers in **bold** indicate Higher Level topics

ability-to-pay principle 315
abnormal profit **159**
absolute advantage **356–8**
absolute poverty 305–6, 307–8
actual output 232–5
AD-AS model 253–4, 258
    and economic growth 299–300
    short-run aggregate supply 241–3
    short-run equilibrium 244–7
    and unemployment 272
ad valorem taxes 73–4
administrative barriers 375
adverse selection **134–5**
advertising
    by oligopolies **210**
    to correct negative externalities 110, 111–12, 117, 118
aggregate demand/AD curve 236–8
    determinants of 238–41
    effect of multiplier on **262–3**
    and fiscal policy 322–8
    and monetary policy 333–4
    and possible causes of business cycle 246–7
    and price-level 250, 253–4
    and short-run equilibrium 244–7, 252–3
aggregate output value *see* national income
aggregate supply/AS curve 241–2
    changes in over long term 254–7
    Keynesian model 251–2
    long-run AS curve 248–50
    short-run AS curve 242–7
agricultural sector
    and appropriate technology 465–6
    deteriorating terms of trade **432–4**
    in developing countries 441
    price supports 93–4, 480–1
    see also primary commodities
aid 506–15
'aid for trade' perspective 515
allocation of resources *see* resource allocation
allocative efficiency 15–16, 42, 90, 94, 179, 180, 211
    failure to achieve 101
    and market equilibrium 43–4
    and Pareto optimality 99–100
    social optimum condition 102–3
    and taxation **317–18**
    and transfer payments 318
allocative inefficiency *see* welfare loss
anti-dumping 379
appreciation of currency 383–7

appropriate technologies 465–7
Asian Tigers 497–8
asymmetric information **132–5**
automatic stabilisers 325, **326**
average cost pricing **194**
average costs (AC) **146**
average fixed costs (AFC) **146**
average product (AP) **140, 141–2, 143**
average revenue (AR) **156**
average tax rate **316**
average total costs (ATC) **146**
    long-run ATC curve **151–4**
average variable costs (AVC) **146**

balance on capital account 397
balance on current account 396–7
balance on financial account 398
balance of payments 395–400
    calculating elements of **406**
    and exchange rates 400–5
    J-curve effect **410–11**
    Marshall-Lerner condition **409–10**
    and persistent current account deficits **406–9**
    and persistent current account surpluses **411–12**
balance of trade 395–7
    Marshall-Lerner condition and J-curve **409–11**
    and the terms of trade **427–30**
balanced budget 321
banks/banking 330–3
    access to credit 467–70
barriers to entry **182–3**
benefits-received principle 315
bilateral trade agreements 413, 491–3
birth rates, developing countries 442
brain drain 464–5
branding **182, 197**
break-even point **158**
break-even price **172, 178**
budget deficit 321–2, 323, 344
budget surplus 321, 323
business confidence 239
business cycle 230–5
    and equilibrium states 244–5, 252–3
    monetarist vs Keynesian models 256, 259
    possible causes of 246–7
    stabilisation policies 320
business taxes 239, 243, 323, 342

cap and trade schemes 106, 126, 130
capital 3, 4
    investment in 296–8
    see also human capital; natural capital; physical capital

capital account 397
capital expenditures 321
capital goods *see* physical capital
capital-intensive technologies 466
capital liberalisation 495–7
capital transfers 397
carbon taxes 106, 125–7, 130
cartels **205–7**
cash transfers 310
central banks, role of 330–3
ceteris paribus 10–11
China, and the global economy 404
choice 1–2
circular flow of income model 216–18
clean technologies 128
climate change *see* sustainability
climate differences 447
closed economy 216
collusion **202**
  open/formal **204–5**
  tacit/informal **206–7**
commercial banks 330, 332–3
commodities *see* primary commodities
common access resources 121, 298
  Ostrom's work on managing 131–2
  role of international co-operation 129–30
  and sustainability 121–4
common market 414–15
community surplus 43
comparative advantage **358–62**
competition
  lack of in monopoly **191**
  legislation protecting **192–3**
  supply-side policies 340–1, **409**
competitive markets 20–1
  demand and supply 21–30
  efficiency in 42–5
  market equilibrium 30–9
  and price mechanism 39–41
competitive supply 28–9
complementary goods (complements)
  prices of 24
  and XED 58–9, 60, 61
composite indicators 457–60
concentration ratios **203–4**
conditional aid 511–12
constant returns to scale **151**, **154**
consumer confidence 238
consumer price index (CPI) 275–6, **283–6**
consumer surplus 42–3, **77–9**, **86–7**, 90, 94
consumption patterns 276
consumption spending 219
  and automatic stabilisers 325
  causes of changes in 238–9
  demand-side policies 323, 326, 333–4
  effect of price ceilings on **92**
  versus investment 299
contractionary fiscal policy 323–4
contractionary monetary policy 334
core rate of inflation 276

corporate indebtedness 239
corporate social responsibility (CSR) **165–6**
  multinational corporations 505
corruption 483, 511, 514, 535
cost of living measures 275–6
cost curves **146–50**
  and product curves **149–50**
cost-push inflation 281, 349, 386–7, 405
costs of production **144**, **160**
  in the long run **151–5**
  in the short run **145–50**
credit, access to by poor people 467–70
creditors, effects of inflation 278
credits 395
cross-price elasticity of demand (XED) 58–9
  applications of 60–1
  complements 60, 61
  substitutes 59–60, 61
crowding out 329
currency appreciation 383–7
currency convertibility 496–7
currency demand & supply functions **393–4**
currency depreciation 383–7, 409
currency devaluation/revaluation 389
current account 397
  and economic growth 527–8
  independence from financial account 399
  and terms of trade **427–30**
current account balance
  effects of exchange rate changes 387
current account deficits 395, 396–7, 398–400
  consequences of persistent **406–8**
  and exchange rates 400–2
  methods to correct **408–9**
current account surpluses 398–400
  consequences of persistent **411–12**
  and exchange rate 400–2
current expenditures 321
current transfers 396
customs duties *see* tariffs
customs union 414
cyclical unemployment 271–2, 347, 387

deadweight loss *see* welfare loss
debits 395
debt 239, 321–2, 421–3, 519–22
deciles 303
decision-making, rational 11
decreasing returns to scale **151**
deficit 395
deflation 275, 282–3
deflationary gaps *see* recessionary gaps
demand 21–5
demand curve 22
  downward slope of 22
  linear functions **33–5**
  movement along 25
  shifts of 23–4, 25, 31–2
demand-deficient unemployment 271–2
demand management 320
demand-pull inflation 280, 348–9, 387

demand-side policies 320
fiscal policy 320–30
monetary policy 330–8
demerit goods 109–10
Denmark, 'flexicurity' 346
depreciation of currency 383–4
causes & effects of 385–7
expenditure-switching policy **409**
deregulation 340
devaluation, currency 389
development aid 506–7
development diamond, World Bank 461–2
development economics *see* economic
development
direct investment 397
direct taxes 72, 311–12
discretionary fiscal policy **325–6**
diseconomies of scale **153–4**
disinflation 275
disposable income 238–9
distribution of income 3, 301–2
and allocative efficiency 318
and economic growth 473–5, 527
equality/inequality measures 302–5
equity versus efficiency in **317–18**
and foreign aid 510
methods of promoting equity in 309–11
poverty 305–9
and taxation 311–15
distribution of output 3
diversification 378, 478, 493–4
Doha Development Round 490
domestic assets, sale of **407–8**
dual economies 444, 533
dumping 379

easy monetary policy 333
economic activity 216–18
business cycle 230–5
measures of 219–30
economic costs **144–5**
economic development 13, 436–8, 448
appropriate technologies 465–7
banking and credit 467–70
education & health 463–5
and international trade barriers 477–82
measurement of 449, 452–62
relating to economic growth 439–40
and trade strategies 482–98
versus economic growth 436
economic efficiency *see* allocative efficiency
economic fluctuations *see* business cycle
economic growth 13, 230–5, 293
and AS curve shifts 255
calculating **293–4**
and commodity-type natural resources 439
consequences of 524–30
and the current account 527–8
in economically less developed countries 438–9
effect of exchange rate changes 387
and fiscal policy 326–7

importance of banking and credit 467–70
and income distribution 473–5, 527
and inflation 526
and infrastructure 475–7
and investment in capital 296–8
Keynesian perspective 258, 259
and living standards 524–5
long-term vs short-term 256
and the LRAS curve 299–300
monetarist/new classical perspective 257, 258, 259
possible consequences of 301
and production possibilities model 295–6
productivity as source of 298
relating to economic development 439–40
significance of 294–5
supply-side policies 343–4
and sustainability 528–30
trade strategies for 482–98
and unemployment 525–6
versus economic development 436–8
economic integration 413
monetary union 418–23
preferential trade agreements 413–14
trade creation & diversion **416–18**
trading blocs 414–16
Economic Partnership Agreements (EPAs) 492
economic profit **158–9**
economically less developed (ELD) countries 440
common characteristics 440–4
diversity among 446–8
foreign debt 519–22
foreign finance 499–519
sources of economic growth in 438–9
terms of trade deterioration **432–3**, **434**
trade barriers 477–82
trade strategies 482–98
economically more developed countries 440
economics 2, 7–11
economies of scale **153**, **415**
as a barrier to entry **182**
in a monopoly **187–8**, **192**
economists' political beliefs and ideology 259–60
low unemployment vs low inflation **290–1**
economy
impact of minimum wages 97–8
impact of price ceilings 89–90
impact of price floors on 93–4
education 338–9, 463–5
education indicators 457, 458
efficiency *see* allocative efficiency
efficiency-equity conflict 16, 318
elasticities 47
cross-price elasticity of demand (XED) 58–62
income elasticity of demand (YED) 62–5
price elasticity of supply (PES) 66–71
summary of concepts 71
entrepreneurship 4, 216
and profits **158–9**
environmental sustainability *see* sustainability
equality, income distribution 301–2
equilibrium 31

equilibrium exchange rate 382–3
equilibrium level of output/real GDP 244
equilibrium price 31, **38**
equilibrium quantity 31, **38**
equilibrium states, Keynesian model 244–5, 252–3
equity 16
equity in income distribution 301–2
    policies promoting 309–11
    role of taxation in promoting 311–15
    supply-side policies 344–5
    versus efficiency **317–18**
ethical concerns, firms **165–6**
European Monetary Union (EMU) 418–19
    and Greek debt problem 421–3
    optimum currency areas (OCAs) 420–1
excess demand *see* shortages
excess supply *see* surpluses
exchange rate changes 383–4
    causes of 384–6
    and changes in net exports 240
    effects of 386–7
    and terms of trade **430**
exchange rates 382
    appreciation & depreciation 383–4
    and balance of payments 400–5
    calculations **392–4**
    government intervention in 388–91
    purchasing power parities (PPPs) 453–4
excise taxes *see* indirect taxes
excludabilty, private goods 119
expansionary fiscal policy 322–3
    and crowding out of private investment 329
    and size of multiplier **325–6**
expansionary monetary policy 333
expenditure approach 219–20, 227
expenditure flow 216–17
expenditure-reducing policies **408**
expenditure-switching policies **408–9**
explicit costs **144**
export promotion 484–5
export subsidies 375
exports 217–18, 220
    developing countries 514–15
    effect of inflation on 279
external benefits *see* positive externalities
external costs *see* negative externalities
externalities 101–3
    negative consumption 108–12
    negative production 103–8
    positive consumption 115–18
    positive production 113–15

factor endowments 354–5
factors of production 1, 3–4, 216–17
    and income distribution 302
    role in economic growth 296–8
financial account 397–8
    independence from current account
        399
financial capital 4
financial capital flows 385, 495–7

fiscal policy 320
    and automatic stabilisers 325, **326**
    conflicting objectives 405
    evaluation of 327–9
    government budget 320–2
    and long-term economic growth 326–7
    role of 322–4
fixed costs **145**
fixed exchange rates 388–9, 401–2, 403
'flexicurity', Denmark 346
floating exchange rates 381–7, 402, 403
food aid 513
food price controls 91
foreign aid 506–15
foreign currency reserves 386, 388, 398, 402–3
foreign debt 519–22
foreign direct investment (FDI) 500–4
formal collusion **205**
formal sector 441
free entry and exit **168**
free rider problem 119–20
free trade **356–63**
    moral judgement in favour of 380
    versus trade protection 364–5
free trade agreements (FTAs) 491–3
free trade area (FTA) 414
freely floating exchange rates 381–7
frictional unemployment 270–1, 348
full employment 271
    see also natural rate of unemployment
full employment level of output/real GDP 232, 245
    demand-side policies 322–4
    Keynesian model 252–3, 258, 259
    monetarist/new classical model 248–50, 258

game theory **202–3**
GATT (General Agreement on Tariffs and Trade) 363
GDP deflator **229, 285–6**
GDP *per capita* **294**
    and GNI per capita 452–3
    and human development 459
    in terms of PPPs 453–4
gender inequalities 470–3
geographic isolation 515
Germany, prosperity of 423
Gini coefficient 304
global demand and supply 425–6
global redistribution of income, terms of trade **427**
global warming *see* sustainability
GNI *per capita* 440, 441
    comparing in terms of PPPs 453–4
    and education indicators 457, 458
    and GDP *per capita* 452–3
    and health indicators 455–6
    Human Development Index (HDI) 459
    see also gross national income
goals of firms **161–6**
governance 535–6
government budget 320–2, 344
government debt 321–2
government intervention 14–15, 72, 251–2, 253, 259

and allocative efficiency 318
and efficiency-equity trade-off 16, 318
and income distribution 311
indirect taxes 72–81
inflation policies 281, 348–9
and managed exchange rates 390–1
price controls 88–99
subsidies 81–8
to maintain fixed exchange rates 388–9
unemployment policies 272–3, 347–8
see also interventionist policies
government policy, failure of 137
government regulation
correcting negative externalities 104–5, 107–8, 110, 125
information asymmetry **133**
and monopoly power **136**
of natural monopoly **193–4**
government revenue **77**
government spending 217, 220, 321
causes of changes in 239
on subsidies **86–7**
see also expansionary fiscal policy
grants 506
Greece, debt problem 421–3
green GDP 225–7, 529
gross domestic product (GDP) 220
and the business cycle 230–5
calculations of **227–30**
green GDP 225–7
nominal versus real 221–2, **227–9**
real GDP **228–9**, **262–3**
total versus *per capita* 222
versus GNI/GNP 221
gross investment 222–3
gross national income (GNI) 221
calculating **227**
inaccuracy of measure 223–5
total versus *per capita* 222
versus gross domestic product (GDP) 221
versus nominal value 221–2
see also GNI *per capita*
gross national product (GNP) *see* gross national income
growth maximisation **164–5**

health 338–9, 463–5
health indicators 454–6
hidden unemployment 266
homogeneous products **168, 201**
household indebtedness 239
human capital 4, 296–7
developing countries 446–7
and economic growth 297–8, 438
investment in 338–9, 463–5, 534
human development 437–8
indicators of 457–60
Human Development Index (HDI) 459–60
human rights 463, 477
humanitarian aid 506
hyperinflation 279–80
hypothesis testing 8–9, 17

implicit costs **144–5**
and profit **158–9**
import quotas 368–70
calculating effects of **371**
import substitution 482–4
imports 217–18, 220
changes in spending on 240
tariff barriers 479–80
and trade agreements 413–14, 490–3
trade creation & diversion **416–18**
and trading blocs 414–18
incentive-related policies 342, 343–4, 345
incidence of taxes *see* tax incidence
income approach 220
income, current account 396
income distribution *see* distribution of income
income elasticity of demand (YED) 62
applications of 63–5
interpreting 62–3
long-term impacts on primary commodity prices **65**
income flow 216–17
income inelastic demand 63, 64
income redistribution *see* redistribution of income
increasing returns to scale **151**
indebtedness 239
indicators of development 449–52
composite indicators 457–60
education indicators 457, 458
health indicators 454–6
Millennium Development Goals 448–9, 450–1
single indicators 452–4
indirect taxes 72–3, 312, 313–14
calculating effects of **75–9**
consequences for stakeholders 74–5
equity & efficiency in product markets **317–18**
impact on market outcomes 73–4
and negative consumption externalities 110–12
and price elasticities of demand 57–8
and price elasticities of demand and supply **79–81**
individual demand 21–2
individual supply 26
industrial policies 339–40, 534
industry growth 64
infant industries 377
infant mortality 455, 456
inferior goods 24
inflation 274–5
calculating rate of **284–6**
consequences of 277–80
core rate of 276
and currency depreciation 385
and economic growth 526
and exchange rate changes 386–7
and GDP deflator **285–6**
measuring 275–7
and terms of trade **430**
types and causes of 280–1
and unemployment **287–91**
inflation targeting 335–6, 349
inflationary gaps 244–6
creating and eliminating 249–50

informal collusion **206**, **206–7**
informal sector 441–2, 470, 533
information, asymmetric **132–5**
infrastructure 310–11, 339, 475–7, 534
injections 217–18
   effect of multiplier on **260–2**
insurance services, asymmetric information **133–5**
interest 216
interest rate
   control by central banks 332, 333
   and currency value 385
   determination of 331–2
   micro-credit schemes 470
   role of monetary policy 333–4
interest rate changes
   and aggregate demand 238, 333
   and investment 239, 329, 389, 407, 408
interest rate effect 237, 241
international co-operation 129–30
international debt 519–22
international development goals 448–9, 450–1
International Monetary Fund (IMF) 518–19
international trade 354–5
   barriers to 477–82
   free trade **356–63**
   objectives of 477
   trade protection 364–79
   World Trade Organization 363–4
international trade effect 237
interventionist policies
   balancing with market-oriented 536–7
   strengths & weaknesses of 533–5
   supply-side 338–40, 343, 344–5, 348
investment goods *see* physical capital
investment spending 219–20
   in capital 296–8
   causes of changes in 239
   crowding out 329
   demand-side policies 334
   gross versus net 222–3
   and multiplier effect **261–3**
   versus consumption 299

J-curve effect **410–11**
joint supply 29

Keynesian cross model **264**
Keynesian model 250–2, 258–60, 350
   AS curve 252, 255–6, 258
   equilibrium economic states 252–3
   and fiscal policy in a recession 337
   key features of 253–4
   with the ratchet effect 324
Keynesian multiplier **260–3**
kinked-demand curve **207–8**

labour 3, 297
   and minimum wage 96–9
   see also human capital
labour-intensive technologies 466
labour market flexibility 341

labour market reforms 341–2
labour market rigidities 269–70, 341
land 3, 297
law of demand 22
law of diminishing returns **142–4**, **149**
law of supply 26
leakages 217–18
   and the multiplier **260–2**
   see also taxes
legal barriers to entry, monopoly **182–3**
legislation
   anti-monopoly laws **136**, **192–3**
   and externalities 117, 118, 125
   minimum wage 311, 341
life expectancy at birth 455, 456
linear functions
   and currency **393–4**
   demand curve **33–5**
   indirect (excise) taxes **75–9**
   and market equilibrium **38–9**
   subsidies **84–8**
   supply curve **35–8**
   tax incidence **79–81**
living standards *see* standards of living
loans **278–9**, **330**, **331**, **332–3**
   for current account deficits 406–7
   from the IMF 518–19
   from the World Bank 516–17
   micro-credit schemes 468–70
long-run (in macroeconomics) 241–2
   equilibrium, monetarist model 248
   Keynesian analysis 251–2
long run (in microeconomics) **139**
   costs of production **151–5**
long-run aggregate supply (LRAS) curve 248–50
   and economic growth 299–300
   factors causing shift in 254–7
long-run average total cost curve **151–4**
long-run Phillips curve **288–90**
long-term growth trend 232
Lorenz curve 303–5
loss minimisation *see* profit maximisation
loss (negative economic profit) **159**
luxuries 52, 63

macroeconomics 12, 215
   aggregate demand/supply 236–64
   demand-side policies 320–38
   distribution of income 301–18
   economic activity 216–35
   economic growth 293–301
   inflation & unemployment 274–90
   paradigm shifts 350–1
   supply-side policies 338–49
managed exchange rates 390–1, 401, 403–4, **409**
managerial utility maximisation 165
manufactured products
   relatively high PED 56, 57
   relatively high PES 69–70
   relatively high YED 64
manufacturing sector 63–4

marginal benefit 22, 43–4
marginal cost pricing **193–4**
marginal costs (MC) 43–4, **146**
  cost curves **146–50**
  and profit maximisation **163**
marginal private benefits & costs 102–3
marginal product (MP) **140–3**, **149**
marginal propensities **261–2**
marginal revenue (MR) **156**
  and profit maximisation **163**
marginal social benefits & costs 102–3
marginal tax rates **316**
market 20–1
market-based policies
  supply-side policies 340–5, 348
  to correct negative production externalities 105–7
  to reduce negative consumption
    externalities 110–12
market demand 22–3
market equilibrium 30–1
  and allocative efficiency 43–4
  calculation using linear functions **38–9**
  changes in 31–2
market failure 101
  and abuse of monopoly power **135–7**
  and asymmetric information **132–5**
  due to lack of public goods 119–20
  and environmental sustainability 121–32
  and externalities 101–19
  problem of government failure 137
market-oriented policies
  balancing with interventionist 536–7
  strengths & weaknesses of 531–3
market outcomes
  effects of excise taxes on 73–4, **76–9**
  impact of minimum wages 96–7
  impact of price ceilings on 89
  impact of price floors on 93
  impact of subsidies 82–3, **84–7**
market power **136**
market structure **168**
  monopolistic competition **195–201**
  monopoly **181–95**
  oligopoly **201–11**
  perfect competition **168–81**
market supply 27
market system and income distribution 302
Marshall–Lerner condition **409–10**
maternal mortality 455, 456
maximum price *see* price ceilings
mergers **193**
merit goods 116–17
  direct or subsidised provision of 310–11, 318
  education and health 463–5
micro-credit schemes 468–70
microeconomics 12, 19
  demand and supply 21–45
  elasticities 47–71
  market failure 101–37
  market structures **168–214**
  production, costs, revenues & profit **139–66**

theory of the firm **139–214**
  see also government intervention
Millennium Development Goals (MDGs) 448–9,
  450–1
minimum price *see* price floors
minimum wage 96–9, 341
model building 9–11
monetarist/new classical model 248, 350–1
  comparing with Keynesian model 254, 255, 256,
    258–60
  and fiscal policy in a recession 337
  link between SRAS-LRAS curves 257
  long-run aggregate supply & equilibrium 248–50
monetary policy 320, 333–4
  central bank & interest rates 330–4
  and conflicting objectives in an open economy 405
  evaluation of 336–7
  and inflation targeting 335–6
monetary union 418–19
  advantages & disadvantages 419–20
  optimum currency areas (OCAs) 420–1
money 331
money supply, control of 331–3
monopolistic competition **195–6**
  demand and revenue curves **196–7**
  efficiency in **199**
  profit maximisation **197–9**
  versus other market structures **199–200**
monopoly **181–2**
  advantages & disadvantages of **194–5**
  barriers to entry **182–3**
  demand and revenue curves **183–5**
  efficiency of **189–92**
  natural monopoly **187–8**
  output and PED **185**
  profit maximisation **185–7**
  regulation of **192–4**
  revenue maximisation **187**
monopoly power, abuse of **135–7**
moral hazard **134**
multilateral development assistance 516–19
multilateral trade agreements 413
multinational corporations (MNCs) 500–5
multiplier **260–4**
  and fiscal policy **325–6**

national income 219
  measurement of 219–21
  and shifts in the AD curve 240
  statistics, evaluating 223–5
nationalisation **136**
natural capital/resources 4, 297
  in developing countries 446, 501, 502
  and economic growth 298, 439
  and green GDP 226, 529
  overuse of 13–14, 121–2, 444
natural monopoly **187–8**
natural rate of unemployment 232, 235, 255–6, 271
  and the long-run Phillips curve **288–90**
  and short-run equilibrium 244–5, 252–3
  supply-side policies reducing 344, 347–8

necessities 52, 63
negative economic profit (loss) **159**
negative externalities 102
   of consumption 108–12
   of production 103–8
net exports (exports minus imports) 220
   causes of changes in 240
net investment 222–3
new classical economics *see* monetarist/new classical
   model
New Development Consensus 487
new technology 438
   investment in 297, 339
   and terms of trade **426**
nominal GDP 222
   calculations **227–9**
nominal vs. real values 221–2, 277–8, 279
non-collusive oligopoly **207–8**
non-convertible currency 495–6
non-discretionary fiscal policy **326**
non-excludability, public goods 119
non-governmental organisations (NGOs) 506, 509
   evaluation of 512–14
non-price competition **197, 208–9**
non-price determinants of demand 23–4
non-price determinants of supply 28–9
non-price rationing 89
non-produced, non-financial assets 397
non-renewable resources 124
non-rivalry, public goods 119
normal goods 24
normal profit **158–9**
normative economics 12

Official Development Assistance (ODA) 507–9
   evaluation of 510–12
oligopoly **201–4**
   collusive **204–7**
   evaluating **209–11**
   non-collusive **207–8**
   and non-price competition **208–9**
open access resources 121, 122, 123, 129, 131
open collusion **205**
open economy 218
open market operations 332–3
opportunity cost 4
   economic costs as **144–5, 158–9**
   of large debt service payments 521–2
optimum currency areas (OCAs) 420–1
output approach 220–1
output gap 232–3
overallocation of resources 3
   and asymmetric information **133–5**
   due to subsidies **86–7**
   and price support for farmers 94, 481
   see also welfare loss
overvalued currencies 391

paradigm shifts 350–1
parallel markets 89–90
Pareto optimality 99–100

PED *see* price elasticity of demand
pegged currencies 390–1
per capita measures 222
perfect competition **168–9, 211**
   demand and revenue curves **169–70**
   efficiency of **179–80**
   evaluation of **180–1**
   and profit maximisation **170–7**
   shut-down & break-even price **173**
perfectly elastic demand 49, 50
perfectly elastic supply 67, 68
perfectly inelastic demand 49, 50
perfectly inelastic supply 67, 68
persistent current account deficits **406–9**
persistent current account surpluses **411–12**
personal income taxes 238–9, 311, 342
Peru, economic growth 537–8
PES *see* price elasticity of supply
Phillips curve **287–91**
physical capital 4, 296, 438
   consumption versus investment 299
   depreciation of **409**
   in developing countries 446–7, 465–6
   gross and net investment 222–3
   and technological advances 297
political instability 447–8
pollution 103
   affluence versus poverty 123–4
   attempts to reduce 104–8
population growth 442–3, 446
portfolio investment 397–8
positive economics 11–12
positive externalities 102
   of consumption 115–18
   education & health 464
   of production 113–15
potential output 232–5
   and fiscal policy 326–7
   supply-side policies 343
   see also full employment level of output
poverty 305–8
   and pollution 123–4
   possible causes & consequences 308–9
poverty cycle (trap) 444–6
   and foreign aid 510
preferential trade agreements 413–14, 490–3
price as incentives 40
price ceilings 89–91
   calculating effects of **92**
price competition **196–7**
price controls 88
   price ceilings 89–92
   price floors 92–9
price deflator **229, 285–6**
price discrimination **211–14**
price elasticity of demand (PED) 47–51, 72
   applications of 54–8
   determinants of 51–2
   for exports and imports **428–30**
   and incidence of indirect taxes **80–1**
   and monopolist's output **185**

and the slope **51**
and steepness of demand curve 53–4
price elasticity of supply (PES) 66
    applications of 69–71
    determinants of 68–9
    and incidence of indirect taxes **80–1**
    interpreting 66–8
price fixing 98–9
price floors 92–5
    calculating effects of **96**
    minimum wages 96–9
price index 229
price inelastic demand 49, 52, 56
price inelastic supply 67, 68
price leadership **206**
price level
    differing domestic, GDP & GNI 224
    downward inflexibility of 251–2
    effect of changes in 237
    effect of multiplier on **263**
    and increases in aggregate demand 253–4
    and long run change in AD 250
price mechanism 39–41
price support 93–4, 480–1
price taker **169**
prices as incentives 40
prices as signals 40
primary commodities 56
    dependency on 478
    and economic growth 298, 439
    impact of low YED **65**, **432**
    and low PED 56–7
    and low PES 69–70
    price volatility of 479–80
primary sector 64–5, 478
prisoner's dilemma, game theory **202–3**
private financing initiatives 340–1
private goods 119
privatisation 340
producer price index (PPI) 277
producer surplus 43, **77–9**, **86–7**, 90, 94
product curves **139–43**
    and cost curves **149–50**
product differentiation **195–7**
product markets 21, 26, 40, 216, **317**
production possibilities curves (PPCs) 5–7
    absolute advantage **356–8**
    and comparative advantage **358–61**
production possibilities model 295–6
production subsidies 372–4
    calculating effects of **374–5**
productive efficiency 5, **179–80**, **211**
productive inefficiency **190–1**, **194–5**, **199**
productivity 444
    and economic growth 298
    and terms of trade **426**
profit **158–9**, **160**, 216
profit maximisation **161–3**, **166**
    by the monopolist **185–7**
    monopolistic competition **197–9**
    and perfect competition **170–7**

programme aid 507
progressive taxation 312–14, 318
    calculations **316**
    equity versus efficiency **317**
    stabilising effect of 325
project aid 507
proportional taxation 312–14
public debt 321–2
public goods 119–20
purchasing power 277–8, 279
purchasing power parities (PPPs) 453–4

quasi-public goods 120
quintiles 303
quotas 368–70, **371**

rate of interest *see* interest rate
rational economic decision-making 11
real GDP 222
    calculations **228–30**
    and economic growth 230–4
    effect of multiplier on **262–3**
    and unemployment 232
    see also aggregate demand; aggregate supply
real income, calculating **285**
real vs. nominal values 221–2, 277–8, 279
reallocation of resources 3
recession 231, 233
    and fiscal policy 327–8, 337
    and monetary policy 337–8, 405
recessionary gaps 244, 245
    Keynesian model 252–3, 259
    persistence over long time periods 249–50,
        253
    wage and price inflexibility 251–2
redistribution of income 3
    and deflation 282
    effects of inflation 278–9
    and inflation 278–9
    Lorenz curves illustrating 304–5
    methods used for 309–11
    role of taxation in 311–14
    terms of trade **427**
regional trade agreements 413, 491, 493
regressive taxation 312–13
    indirect taxes 313–14
regulation *see* government regulation
relative poverty 306–8
renewable resources 124
rent 216
rent controls 91
research & development (R&D) **191**, **195**, **197**, **339**
    clean technologies 128
reserve assets 398
resource allocation 2–3, 90, 94, **317–18**
    government intervention 14–15, 16
    and indirect (excise) taxes 72, 73
    role of price mechanism in 39–41
    and subsidies 81, 82
    and sustainability 14
    see also market failure

resource endowments 446–7
resource markets 41, 216, **317**
resources *see* factors of production
returns to scale **151, 154**
revaluation of currency 389
revenue maximisation **164, 187**
revenues **155–8, 160**
rivalry, private goods 119

safety in the workplace **135**
sales taxes 312, 314, 317
satisficing **165**
savings/savers 217, 278
scarcity 1–2, 39
seasonal unemployment 271, 344, 348
self-interested behaviour 131, 165
short run (in macroeconomics) 241–2
    equilibrium in AD-AS model 244–7, 252–3
    Keynesian perspective 251–2, 254
short run (in microeconomics) **139**
    costs of production **145–50**
short-run aggregate supply curve (SRAS) 242–3
    and LRAS curve 257
    and short-run equilibrium 244–7, 252–3
short-run Phillips curve **287–90**
shortages (excess demand) 30–1
    calculating **38–9**
    and price controls 88–92, 98–9
shut-down price **173, 178**
single indicators 452–4
slope **51**
social optimum 102, 104, 109, 113–14, 116
social safety net 534
social sciences 7
social scientific method 7–9, 17
social surplus 43, **77–9, 86**, 90, 94, 98
social welfare *see* welfare
spare capacity 252
specialisation **153**, 354–5
    and trade **356–62**
specific taxes 73
speculation 385–6, 405
stabilisation policies *see* fiscal policy; monetary policy
stagflation 246, 257, **287–8**
stakeholders
    certainty & exchange rates 402
    consequences of minimum wage 98
    consequences of subsidies 83
    impact of indirect taxes on 74–5
    impact of price ceilings on 90–1
    impact of price floors on 95
standards of living
    comparisons over time/between countries 225
    and economic growth 436, 524–5
    GDP/GNI as inaccurate measures of 224–5
    GNI *per capita* as indicator for 452–3
    and poverty 309
strategic interdependence, oligopolies **201–3**
strategic trade policy 377–8
structural unemployment 268–70, 341, 344, 347–8
subsidies 29, 81
    consequences for stakeholders 83
    correcting market failure 114–15, 117–18
    effects on markets & social welfare **84–7**
    environmentally harmful 128–9
    export subsidies 375
    impact on market outcomes 82–3
    production subsidies 372–5
    reasons for 81–2
    and resource allocation 81
substitute goods 24
    cross-price elasticity of demand 60–1
    and degree of substitutability 59–60
    number and closeness of 51–2
supernormal profit **159**
supply of money 331–3
supply shocks 243, 288
supply-side policies 338
    evaluation of 342–5
    interventionist 338–40
    market-based 340–2
    to increase competitiveness **409**
supply & supply curve 26–8
    linear functions **35–8**
    movement along 28, 29
    shifts of 28, 29, 32
    upward slope of 27
    vertical 27–8
surpluses (excess supply) 30–1, 396
    calculating **38–9**
    and price controls 88–9, 93–4, 96
    as result of minimum wage 97–8
    social surplus **77–9, 86**, 90, 94, 98
sustainability 13–14, 121–2
    and common access resources 121–3
    conflict with economic growth 528–30
    economic thinking on 131–2
    government action 125–9
    and international co-operation 129–30
    threats to 123–5
sustainable development 13–14, 122, 124, 517, 530

tacit collusion **206**
tariffs 312, 366–7
    barriers and escalation 479–80, 489
    calculating effects of **367–8**
    as source of government revenue 378–9
tax incidence **79–81**
taxes 217, 311–14
    and allocative efficiency **317–18**
    calculations **316**
    carbon taxes 106, 125–7, 130
    on consumption externalities 110–12
    equity principles 315
    excise (indirect) 72–5, **75–81**
    lowering 342, 343–4, 345
    on production externalities 105–6, 107
technology
    appropriate 465–7
    clean technologies 128
    innovation in monopoly **191**
    investment in new 297, 339